# 2015 EDITION

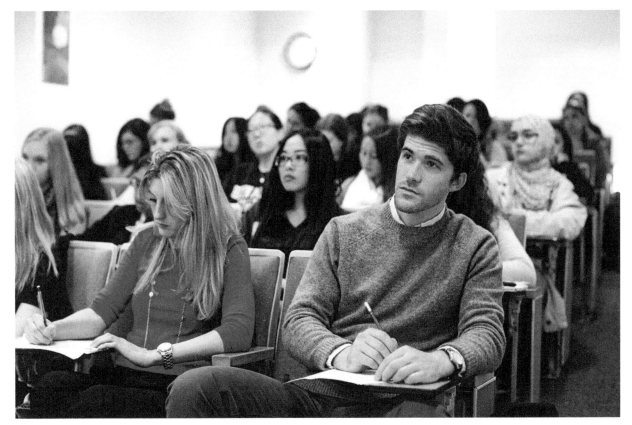

# Best Colleges

**Bryn Mawr College in Pennsylvania**
BRETT ZIEGLER FOR USN&WR

# Contents

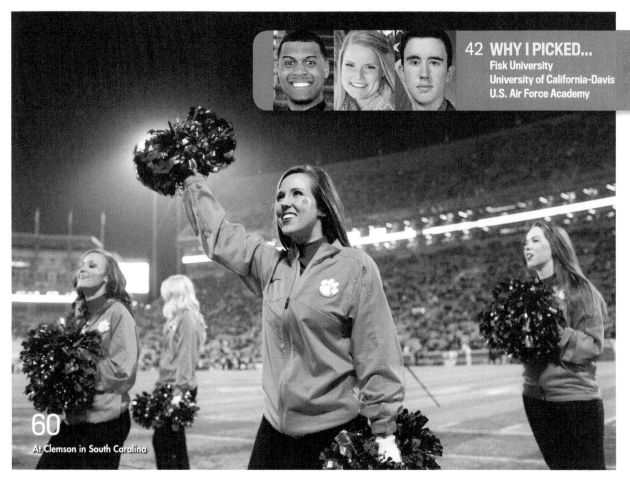

60
At Clemson in South Carolina

# Contents continued...

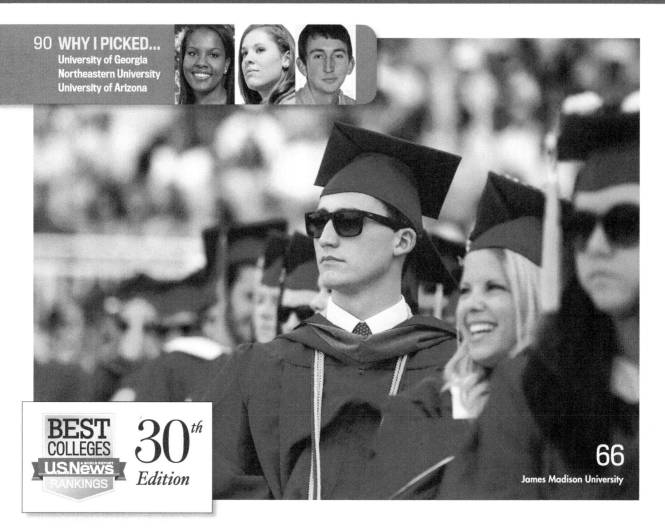

BEST COLLEGES
U.S.News & WORLD REPORT
RANKINGS
**30**th *Edition*

**66**
James Madison University

152

Eric Tims is attending
Bowdoin College
in Maine

## Chapter Four
**NEWS YOU CAN USE**
# Getting In

## Chapter Five
**NEWS YOU CAN USE**
# Finding the Money

BRETT ZIEGLER FOR USN&WR

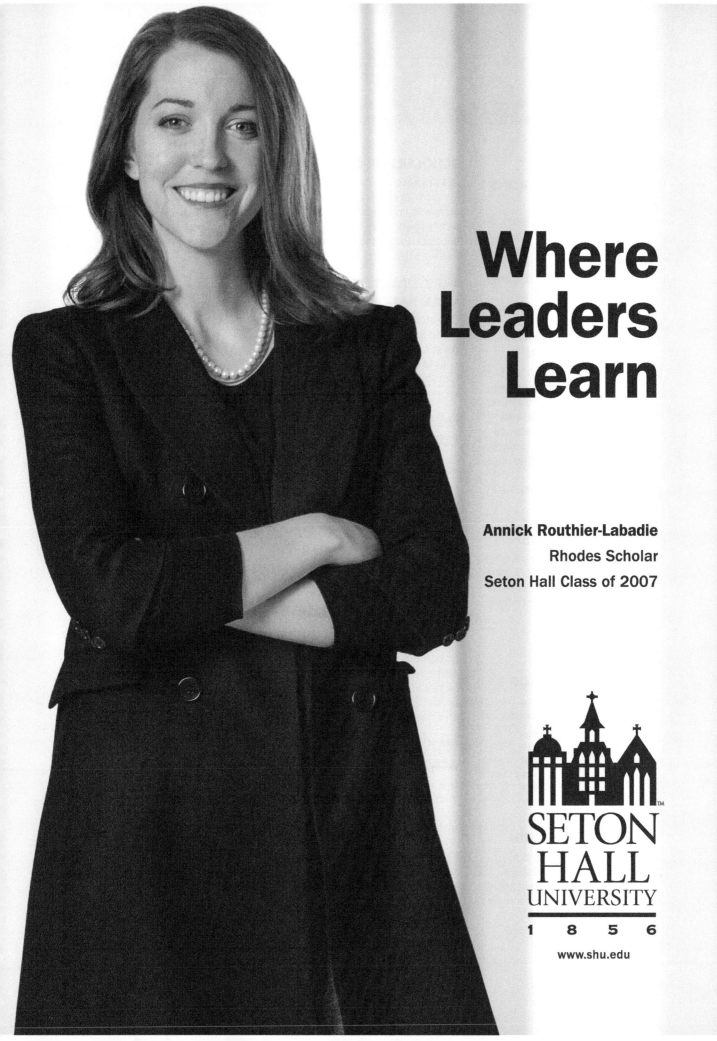

# Where Leaders Learn

Annick Routhier-Labadie
Rhodes Scholar
Seton Hall Class of 2007

SETON HALL
UNIVERSITY
1 8 5 6

www.shu.edu

## GETTING IN

### COLLEGE ADMISSIONS PLAYBOOK

Get tips from Varsity Tutors, an academic tutoring and test prep provider. This blog offers advice on mastering the SAT and ACT as well as the college application process.
usnews.com/collegeplaybook

### STUDENTS ON HOW THEY MADE IT IN

Seniors from high schools across the country – including several that have been ranked as Best High Schools by U.S. News – talk about their admissions experiences and offer advice to students getting ready to apply to college.
usnews.com/studentprofiles

## COLLEGE VISITS

### TAKE A ROAD TRIP

We've gone on numerous trips to visit campuses in case you can't. Check out our compendium of more than 20 different trips to 90-plus schools.
usnews.com/roadtrips

## RANKINGS INSIGHT

### MORSE CODE BLOG

Get the inside scoop on the rankings – and the commentary and controversy surrounding them – from U.S. News' Bob Morse, the mastermind behind our education rankings projects.
usnews.com/morsecode

## PAYING FOR COLLEGE

### RESEARCHING AID

Visit our guide to all your possible sources of college funds. Learn about your savings options and which schools meet students' full need.
usnews.com/payforcollege

### SCHOLARSHIP COACH

Get the latest advice from Scholarship America bloggers on how to find great scholarships, apply for them successfully and more.
usnews.com/scholarshipcoach

### THE STUDENT LOAN RANGER

Don't fall into the trap of taking on too much debt. Bloggers from American Student Assistance provide guidance if you must turn to loans to pay for college.
usnews.com/studentloanranger

## IN-DEPTH DATA

### COLLEGE COMPASS

Gain access to the U.S. News College Compass, which offers comprehensive searchable data and tools for high school students starting down the path to campus. To get a 25 percent discount, subscribe at:
usnews.com/compassoffer

## DISTANCE LEARNING

### ONLINE EDUCATION

Do you need to balance school with work or other obligations? Consult our rankings of the best online degree programs for leads on how to get your diploma without leaving home.
usnews.com/online

## FOR SCHOOLS ONLY

### ACADEMIC INSIGHTS

U.S. News Academic Insights is an analytics dashboard intended for use by institutions that comprises all of the undergraduate and graduate historical rankings data we've collected. The dashboard allows for peer group comparisons and includes easy-to-understand visualizations.
ai.usnews.com

# Paying for college is one of the biggest risks families face – AXA Achievement℠ can help.

## TAB STICKERS

Use these stickers to tab your college choices inside this issue.

# Next steps toward college

## Taking the right small steps today can help eliminate the risk of not being able to afford a college education

Filling out the FAFSA helps you minimize borrowing. It's a misconception that filling out the Free Application for Federal Student Aid (FAFSA) is the fast track to student loan debt. You risk losing need-based grants and scholarships from the university. The reason? The universities you selected on the FAFSA to receive your information use it to evaluate your financial aid eligibility.

*To avoid losing need-based aid for which you are eligible:*

1. Fill out the FAFSA as early as possible. Some need-based aid is limited in numbers and available on a first come first serve basis for those who qualify. For instance, a university could have a limited amount of grant aid. Applying late could cost you that money.

2. Select schools. Always select schools that are being considered on the form. Otherwise, the information won't arrive to the colleges who need it. Amend the FAFSA form online if school choices change.

3. Fill out the special circumstances forms when needed. Whether you're applying for next year or are already in college, you need to fill out a special circumstances form if your income changes due to a number of reasons including a medical situation, a layoff, or a salary reduction.

4. Practice filling out the FAFSA on the FAFSA4caster site from the department of education as early as middle school. It's designed to roughly estimate financial aid years in advance.

5. Teens should follow up with schools to make sure information is received and to check on financial aid availability. Bonus: you may find out about a scholarship you previously didn't know about during the phone call.

Choosing universities with the lowest listed tuition prices sometimes can cost you more money. A private school with a "sticker price" that is four times more than that of a state school may offer scholarships and grants that make it the cheaper alternative. How do you find out which schools offer the best financial aid packages before applying for college? Net price calculators available on most college websites are one way to estimate what you would pay based on individual circumstances.

*To better understand the relative costs of higher education:*

1. Narrow college choices down to ten by factors such as majors, campus size and internship placement. Teens should visit with their high school counselor to start the process of college selection and career exploration.

2. Students should request information from each school on what's important to them. For instance, they can and should call the career center to ask about graduate employment rates.

3. Visit the websites of your top 10 college choices and enter information such as family income and number of children in college. To find the net price calculator on a university website, enter net price calculator into the search box on the school's homepage.

4. Call financial aid offices at the top 5 choices to see if there are any changes in grant awards for the year the student will be attending. Available funds change, so you want to make sure you factor in the most recent information into your family's application decisions.

5. Use the Net price calculator as a baseline. Teens could also qualify for merit-based educational assistance.

## To learn more and apply, visit www.axa-achievement.com

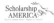

By **BRIAN KELLY** and **ROBERT J. MORSE**

**Brian Kelly**
*Editor and Chief*
*Content Officer*

This college search thing can be a little intimidating, especially if you're going through it for the first time. This is our 30th go-round at U.S. News, so we feel like we've got some experience worth sharing.

We're proud of the fact that the U.S. News Best Colleges rankings have now been published 30 times, starting in 1983. Over the years, we've improved our information and sharpened our focus, with our primary objective being to help students and their parents make one of life's major decisions. There was a big void in that kind of information when we started this project. Colleges, like a lot of institutions, are not always eager to share facts, especially when doing so opens them up to comparisons with their competitors. In the early days, many schools did not want to cooperate with us. Some education experts said we were making the college evaluation process too simple. We disagreed, and the positive response from our readers assured us that we were on the right track. We've played a key role in the years since in making all college information more standard, more reliable, and more useful.

U.S. News started the rankings for the same reason we do them today: A college education is one of the most important – and most costly – investments that people ever make. Prospective students and their parents need objective measures that allow them

**Robert J. Morse**
*Chief Data Strategist*

to evaluate and compare schools; the rankings are one tool to help them make choices. This perspective is more relevant than ever with some private colleges now costing around $250,000 for a bachelor's degree. At the same time, many public high schools have greatly reduced their college counseling resources, leaving students and parents to educate themselves about the admission process.

Of course, we have changed our ranking methodology formula over the years to reflect changes in the world of higher education. We make it clear that we are not doing peer reviewed social science research, though we do maintain very high survey and data standards. We have always been open and transparent. We have always said that the rankings are evolving and not perfect. The first were based solely on schools' academic reputation among leaders at peer institutions; in the late

1980s, we developed a ranking methodology in which reputation accounted for 25 percent of a school's score and important quantitative measures such as graduation and retention rates, average class size and student-faculty ratios, for 75 percent. Over time, we have shifted weight from inputs (indicators of the quality of students and resources) to outputs (success in graduating students). We operate under this guiding principle: The methodology is altered only if a change will better help our readers and web audience compare schools as they're making decisions about where to apply and enroll.

It has helped us a great deal to have these principles to focus on as we have faced the inevitable and continuous criticisms from academia about our rankings and their growing influence. One main critique remains: that it is impossible to reduce the complexities

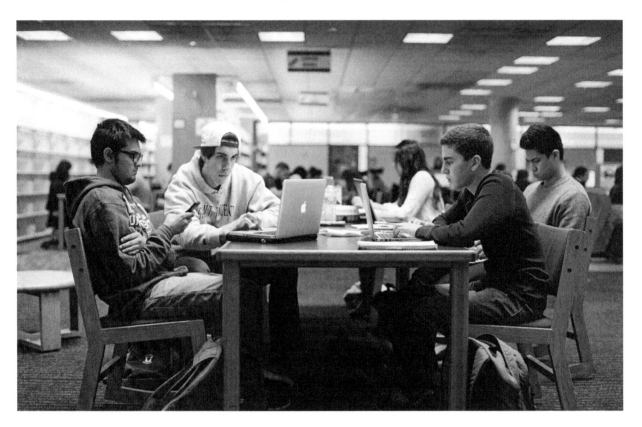

of any given college's offerings and attributes to one rank number. Indeed, it's important to keep in mind that our information is a starting point. The next steps in a college search should include detailed research on a smaller list of choices, campus visits and conversations with students, faculty and alumni wherever you can find them. This feedback from academia has helped improve the rankings over time. We constantly meet with our critics, listen to their points of view, debate them on the merits of what we do and make appropriate changes.

U.S. News is keenly aware that the higher education community is also a major audience for and consumer of our rankings. We understand how seriously academics, college presidents, top administrators, trustees and governing boards take our rankings and data. They study, analyze and use them in various ways, including benchmarking against peers, alumni fundraising and advertising to attract students.

**A trusted source.** What does all of this mean in today's global information marketplace? U.S. News has become a trusted, respected, unbiased source that higher education administrators and policymakers and the collegebound public in the U.S. and worldwide turn to for reliable guidance. In the process of helping consumers, U.S. News provides colleges a great deal of free exposure to potential applicants; our Internet traffic for education nears 10 mil-

*Students hit the books, and their laptops, at Drexel University in Philadelphia.*

lion visitors a month, with more than 10 percent coming from foreign countries. U.S. News is on balance helping, not hurting, colleges. And the Best Colleges rankings are a part of the still-evolving higher education accountability movement. Universities are increasingly being held responsible for their educational policies, how their funds are spent, the level of student engagement and how much graduates have learned. The U.S. News rankings have become the annual public benchmark to measure the academic performance of the country's colleges and universities.

We know our role has limits. The rankings should only be used as one factor in the college search process and not as the sole basis upon which to choose one school over another. We've long said that there is no single "best college." There is only the best college for you or, more likely, a handful of schools that make sense, one of which will turn out to be the right fit. Besides the rankings, we can help collegebound high school students and their parents with a great deal of information on all aspects of the application process, from getting in to getting financial aid. Our website, usnews.com, has thousands of pages of rankings, research, sortable data, photos, videos and a personalized tool called College Compass.

We've been doing this for 30 years, so we know the process is not simple. But our experience tells us the hard work is worth it in the end. ●

# THE CURE FOR CANCER MAY HAVE BEEN IN OUR LAPS THIS WHOLE TIME.

The search to find a cure for cancer has spanned decades in hospitals and research labs all over the globe. But at Texas A&M University, we're looking for a cure in a brand-new place: man's best friend. As one of the leading veterinary schools in the country, we know all too well about treating animals with cancer. And what we have discovered is that dogs experience this disease much like humans do. So as we treat these dogs for cancer, we are working to develop new therapies that could also work on us. Today the world faces countless challenges, but we don't hesitate. At Texas A&M, we step up.

**To see more, visit tamu.edu.**

# Study

# the Schools

Viewing books from the
Italian Renaissance, at the
University of Pennsylvania

BRETT ZIEGLER FOR USN&WR

# YOUR GOAL:
# Four Fabulous Years

## AS YOU SEARCH FOR A GOOD FIT, LOOK FOR PROGRAMS THAT AIM TO ENGAGE AND BOND STUDENTS

*By* **CHRISTOPHER J. GEARON**

Consider this shocking stat as you shop for a college: Fully one-third of freshmen don't return for sophomore year. And only 61 percent of undergraduates get a degree within six years.

So your guidance counselor isn't kidding when she says your job is to find the right college, one that's a great fit for you. Not your parents, not your friends – you. But you also might want to check out what each of your

FREEDOM SCHO

## Service learning

A University of Maryland–Baltimore County summer education practicum includes service experience in a local school. Students also meet to discuss what they're learning; below, they hear from psych major Monique Brewer.

schools of interest is doing to make itself "sticky." The goal "is to get students connected," says Martha McCaughey, a sociology professor and faculty coordinator of the required first-year seminar at Appalachian State University in North Carolina. The semesterlong discussion-based class pairs small groups of freshmen with faculty members teaching a topic they are passionate about.

"It boosted my excitement to learn more," says Eguono Akpoduado, a 2014 graduate in psychology from Raleigh who picked a course that explored the science, psychology and philosophy of consciousness from among 100-plus topics. The seminar format emphasizes communication and writing skills and introduces students to research tools and methods they'll need to be successful scholars. ASU's first-year retention rate is 88 percent.

The reasons students drop out or transfer run the gamut, of course – from family issues and money problems to loneliness and academic struggles. Some can't be overcome. But research has made it pretty clear that creating bonds "both academically and socially" is key to success in college, says Alexander McCormick, director of the annual National Survey

# Fully ONE-THIRD of **freshmen** DON'T RETURN for **sophomore** year.

**Close community**

A dorm room on Elon's living-learning arts floor

of Student Engagement and associate professor in the department of education leadership and policy studies at Indiana University–Bloomington. Schools of all types are adding "high-impact practices" shown to get students pumped up about their studies and help them connect with peers and professors, from service-learning classes that incorporate volunteer work to internships to undergraduate research (Page 26). These practices, along with a move to make advising "intrusive" (read: unavoidable), are worth looking for in your college search.

Last year's NSSE survey of nearly 335,000 freshmen and seniors at 568 schools, designed to find out if students are getting the learning experiences that research shows matter, revealed that freshmen who participated in at least one high-impact practice were more satisfied with their college experience and more likely to say they'd choose the same school again. Better yet, "experience at least two," McCormick says, one when you're a freshman and one in your major.

Retention and graduation rates certainly merit comparison. Columbia University, the University of Chicago and Yale University can

KIM WALKER – ELON UNIVERSITY

all boast that 99 percent of their first-year students come back, and all but a few of them graduate. But the rates at many places run much lower. "More than half our students aren't ready for college and only half our students graduate within six years," says Ken O'Donnell, senior director of student engagement and academic initiatives and partnerships for the California State University System, where retention rates range from 92 percent at California Polytechnic State University–San Luis Obispo to 71 percent at Cal State–Bakersfield. The 23-school system is raising its investment in high-impact practices by 40 percent this school year, to $12 million.

If schools on your shortlist have a low freshman retention or graduation rate, it's smart to ask the admissions office why. And ask for details about programs aimed at bringing the rates up. Many schools can say they've added these practices, but "the quality varies a lot," cautions Debra Humphreys, vice president for policy and public engagement at the Association of American Colleges and Universities.

The homesickness and rocky adjustment to college-level work many freshmen face can be eased by "first-year experiences" like the seminars at ASU and others that regularly mix small groups of students and faculty to engage in critical inquiry, writing and collaborative learning. Some institutions, including Ohio State, Syracuse University in New York, Elon University in North Carolina and Vanderbilt in Tennessee, emphasize "learning communities" for freshmen (older students, too), in which groups of students who share an interest take two or more linked classes together and get to know one another and their professors well. The idea: to keep the discussions going after class ends.

## Living and learning together

Many of these schools stretch the concept into "living-learning communities," so that classmates who study together live together, too, and those conversations can carry over into the dorm. The University of Maryland offers 25 to 30 such residential options, for example, focused around themes ranging from social change to globalization and women in engineering; about half of the 4,000 freshmen join one. Members live on the same floor or in the same dorm for their first two years. The communities provide themed experiences (the global issues community might take a field trip to the World Bank or an embassy in

**INSIDE SCOOP**

**DEBRA SHAVER**
Dean of Admission, Smith College

## WHY CONSIDER A WOMEN'S COLLEGE?

There are incredible role models at women's colleges. At Smith, over half the faculty are women, and every leadership position is filled by a woman. Leadership becomes a habit at a women's college. This is an unbelievable network of women invested in other women and in their success in all sorts of ways. The bonds among graduates, I think, are really strong in terms of making sure that their sisters have every opportunity in career paths or life paths.

nearby Washington, D.C., for example, or hold a session on international internships), and students take a class related to the theme each semester.

"We bonded almost immediately," says Beena Raghavendran, a Maryland Honors College senior from Mason, Ohio, double-majoring in journalism and government and politics. She chose the "Design, Cultures and Creativity" community, an interdisciplinary program focused on exploring the digital world and emerging technologies. Maryland boasts nearly a 95 percent retention rate, while 97 percent of those in the Honors College return.

Building community service into the coursework is another method a whole range of schools, including Brown University in Rhode Island, the University of Michigan and James Madison University in Virginia, are using to engage students. A sociology class might operate a food pantry, for example; an architecture class might design a green community center. By supplementing material covered in class with a team effort to actually solve problems in the community, service-learning courses help make "what's happening in the textbooks come alive," says Richard Guarasci, president of Wagner College in New York City, a liberal arts school considered a leader in the practice.

The class discussion, in turn, adds meaning to the fieldwork. University of Maryland–Baltimore County senior Monique Brewer is a psychology and education major who took a service-learning practicum over the summer that involved assisting at a local elementary school with enrichment activities in reading and other subjects. The meetings of practicum members, she notes, offered them all the chance to "actively reflect on their service" and better "guide their own learning."

Wagner College tees up service learning from the get-go, combining it with first-year learning communities. Students choose a community and take courses that combine two seemingly disparate topics, such as introductory environmental biology and introductory economics, and consider them in an integrated manner – focusing on environmental sustainability, for example. The service component for that class gets students interacting with families and local officials and chemical company representatives in an area impacted by high cancer rates, researching how to improve community health, developing policy papers and taking ideas to members of Congress.

"I fell in love with the community and fell in love with teaching English and Spanish," says Kellie Griffith, a 2014

# World Renowned, Nationally Ranked

## At the University of Memphis, Real-World Experience Is...Real.

Memphis has a way of changing the world. Whether it's the birth of rock 'n' roll, the advent of overnight package delivery at FedEx® or the lifesaving treatments continually being developed at St. Jude Children's Research Hospital, Memphis is a place where innovation thrives.

The University of Memphis is part of that innovation. We offer several programs that are nationally ranked by *U.S. News & World Report*, including one of the nation's most successful internship programs.

Our faculty, students and alumni are known as *Dreamers. Thinkers. Doers.*, and they're changing the world every single day.

**U.S. News & World Report has ranked the University of Memphis nationally for the following:**

- Internship Programs — Ranked Top 10 for percentage of students with internships (Feb. 2013)

- Online MBA Programs for Veterans — #24

- Elementary and Secondary Education: NCTQ Teacher Prep Honor Roll — Ranked #27 and #28 out of 800

- Audiology — #12

- Speech-Language Pathology — #15

- Rehabilitation Counseling — #17

**us.memphis.edu**

*A Tennessee Board of Regents Institution · An Equal Opportunity/Affirmative Action University*

THE UNIVERSITY OF
**MEMPHIS**®
Dreamers. Thinkers. Doers.

Wagner grad from Long Island who spent time working in the Port Richmond community near campus. As part of her first-year learning community combining courses in Spanish and philosophy, she studied contemporary moral ethics and wrestled with immigration issues in class, then saw firsthand how existing policies affect the lives of area immigrants by volunteering at an immigrant advocacy center.

Academic frustration can certainly derail the best-laid plans, so many schools are greatly strengthening their advisory systems and revamping remedial education. It's become common for faculty members teaching first-year seminars to also take on advisory duties for students in the class, for example. At Arizona State, eAdvisor, an online system, maps the route to a degree and sends out an alert if a student loses his or her way. Challenging core classes

times a week instead of three," says Tom Sugar, senior vice president of Complete College America, which advocates corequisite remediation as one way to boost college completion and close attainment gaps. Another innovation: Summer bridge programs that include four to six weeks of intensive coursework and tutoring, and give incoming students the added boost of a comfort level with dorm life and some friendships.

## Beyond the first year

Practices that benefit older students, both because they make the educational experience more interesting and because they burnish the bona fides needed to land a job, include study abroad, the opportunity to conduct undergraduate research, an internship program and a capstone program that asks students to integrate and apply what they've learned in a culminating project. It was "a stressful process at times, but 100 percent worth it," says Zoë Zwegat, a 2014 grad of the College of Wooster in anthropology, of her project: a 100-plus page thesis on historical Japanese woodblock prints and their impact on gender roles and national identity.

The Ohio college requires all students to seal their undergrad careers with Independent Study at Wooster, which carries through all of senior year and includes weekly advising sessions with a faculty mentor. President Grant Cornwell thinks the program has a lot to do with the fact that more than 90 percent of Wooster grads get a job or go on for more education within six months of gradua-

**At Wagner.** Kellie Griffith's first-year experience involved volunteering at an immigrant center.

are required sooner rather than later – an electrical engineering major must take calculus in the first term, for example – to minimize the odds of changing majors too late to finish college on time. Anyone who gets off track for any reason can't enroll for classes before meeting with his or her adviser, who also gets an alert to meet with the student.

Traditional remedial programs, which require noncredit refresher work in the basics before allowing on-level classes, are in some cases being replaced with "corequisite" remediation that provides extra instruction along with the regular coursework. At Austin Peay State University in Tennessee, for example, enhanced sections of college-level algebra have been subbed for two remedial courses. One-time remedial students enroll in a regular course, along with a linked workshop that provides added instruction on key concepts and in areas of weakness flagged by an initial assessment. Students are succeeding at twice the rate of peers in traditional remedial courses. "It can be as simple as math that takes place five

tion. Clemson University in South Carolina, Portland State University in Oregon and Princeton University in New Jersey are a few other schools with capstone programs.

For many students, of course, it's a budget crisis that throws them off track. Cord Speck, who just completed his bachelor's in exercise science at Georgia State, thought last summer that he might not make it, since money was tight. But then the school gave him $2,000, which "helped out big time." Georgia State had been dropping 1,000-plus students for nonpayment each semester, including many seniors. "We realized that in many cases the balances they owed were less than $300," says Vice Provost Timothy Renick. "They just needed a helping hand to cover the gap."

In 2011, officials began calling students minutes after they'd been dropped from a class to let them know that the gap in funding had been covered. Last year, the school awarded 2,600 Panther Retention Grants averaging about $900 each. And some 700 students collected a diploma who otherwise would have missed graduation. ●

# A Focus on Student

Some colleges and universities are much more determined than others to provide freshmen and all undergrads with the best possible educational experience, recognizing that certain enriched offerings, from learning communities and internships to study abroad and senior capstone projects, are linked to student success. Here, U.S. News highlights schools with outstanding examples of eight programs that education experts, including staff members of the Association of American Colleges and Universities, agree are key.

College presidents, chief academic officers and deans of admissions were invited in the spring of 2014 to nominate up to 10 institutions with stellar examples of each, from a list of all bachelor's-granting regionally accredited colleges. Schools that were named the most times in each area are listed in alphabetical order.

(*Public)

## First-Year Experience

Orientation can go only so far in making freshmen feel connected. Many schools now build into the curriculum first-year seminars or other academic programs that bring small groups of students together with faculty or staff on a regular basis.

Alverno College (WI)
Appalachian State University (NC)*
Butler University (IN)
Columbia University (NY)
Elon University (NC)
Evergreen State College (WA)*
Indiana U.-Purdue U.-Indianapolis*
Ohio State University-Columbus*
Stanford University (CA)
Univ. of Maryland–College Park*
University of Michigan-Ann Arbor*
U. of North Carolina–Chapel Hill*
Univ. of South Carolina*
University of Virginia*
Wagner College (NY)

## Internships

Schools nominated in this category require or encourage students to apply what they're learning in the classroom to work in the real world through closely supervised internships or practicums, or through cooperative education, in which one period of study typically alternates with one of work.

Belmont University (TN)
Berea College (KY)

Butler University (IN)
Cornell University (NY)
Drexel University (PA)
Elon University (NC)
Georgia Institute of Technology*
Northeastern University (MA)
Purdue Univ.-West Lafayette (IN)*
Rochester Inst. of Technology (NY)
University of Cincinnati*
Univ. of Southern California
Wagner College (NY)

## Learning Communities

In these communities, students typically take two or more linked courses as a group and get to know one another and their professors well. Some learning communities are also residential.

Elon University (NC)
Evergreen State College (WA)*
Indiana U.-Purdue U.-Indianapolis*
Ohio State University-Columbus*
Syracuse University (NY)
Univ. of Maryland–College Park*
University of Michigan-Ann Arbor*
Univ. of Missouri*
Univ. of South Carolina*
Univ. of Wisconsin-Madison*
Wagner College (NY)
Yale University (CT)

## Senior Capstone

Whether they're called a senior capstone or go by some other name, these culminating experiences ask students nearing the end of their college years to create a project that integrates and synthesizes what they've learned. The project might be a thesis, a performance or an exhibit of artwork.

Brown University (RI)
Carleton College (MN)
College of Wooster (OH)
Elon University (NC)
Kalamazoo College (MI)
Northeastern University (MA)
Portland State University (OR)*
Princeton University (NJ)
Stanford University (CA)
Yale University (CT)

## Service Learning

Required (or for-credit) volunteer work in the community is an instructional strategy in these programs. What's learned in the field bolsters what happens in class, and vice versa.

Berea College (KY)
Brown University (RI)
Butler University (IN)
College of the Ozarks (MO)
Duke University (NC)
Elon University (NC)
Georgetown University (DC)
James Madison University (VA)*
John Carroll University (OH)
Loyola University Maryland
Michigan State University*
Northeastern University (MA)
Portland State University (OR)*
Stanford University (CA)
Tulane University (LA)
University of Michigan-Ann Arbor*
U. of North Carolina–Chapel Hill*
University of Pennsylvania

▶ **More @** usnews.com/bestcolleges

# Success

Wagner College (NY)
Warren Wilson College (NC)

## Study Abroad

Programs at these schools involve substantial academic work abroad for credit – a year, a semester or an intensive experience equal to a course – and considerable interaction with the local culture.

American University (DC)
Arcadia University (PA)
Beloit College (WI)
Boston University
Butler University (IN)
Carleton College (MN)
Centre College (KY)
College of St. Benedict (MN)
Dartmouth College (NH)
Dickinson College (PA)
Elon University (NC)
Goucher College (MD)
Kalamazoo College (MI)
Lee University (TN)
Lewis & Clark College (OR)
Macalester College (MN)
Michigan State University*
Middlebury College (VT)

New York University
Northeastern University (MA)
Oberlin College (OH)
Stanford University (CA)
St. John's University (MN)
St. Olaf College (MN)
Syracuse University (NY)
University of Chicago
University of Evansville (IN)
Univ. of Minnesota-Twin Cities*
University of Texas-Austin*
Webster University (MO)

## Undergraduate Research/Creative Projects

Independently or in small teams, and mentored by a faculty member, students do intensive and self-directed research or creative work that results in an original scholarly paper or product that can be formally presented on or off campus.

Butler University (IN)
California Institute of Technology
Calvin College (MI)
Carleton College (MN)
Carnegie Mellon University (PA)

College of Wooster (OH)
Creighton University (NE)
Dartmouth College (NH)
Duke University (NC)
Elon University (NC)
Furman University (SC)
Grinnell College (IA)
Harvard University (MA)
Hope College (MI)
James Madison University (VA)*
Johns Hopkins University (MD)
Massachusetts Inst. of Technology
Oberlin College (OH)
Ohio State University-Columbus*
Princeton University (NJ)
Rice University (TX)
Stanford University (CA)
Trinity University (TX)
Truman State University (MO)*
University of California-Berkeley*
Univ. of California-Los Angeles*
Univ. of Maryland-Baltimore County*
University of Michigan-Ann Arbor*
U. of North Carolina-Chapel Hill*
University of Washington*
Williams College (MA)
Yale University (CT)

## Writing in the Disciplines

These colleges typically make writing a priority at all levels of instruction and across the curriculum. Students are encouraged to produce and refine various forms of writing for a range of audiences in different disciplines.

Brown University (RI)
Carleton College (MN)
Clemson University (SC)*
Cornell University (NY)
Duke University (NC)
George Mason University (VA)*
Hamilton College (NY)
Harvard University (MA)
Princeton University (NJ)
University of California-Davis*
Washington State University*

# Companies Come to Class

## EMPLOYERS IN NEED OF SKILLED HIGH-TECH HIRES ARE TEAMING UP WITH COLLEGES TO TRAIN THEM

*By* **CATHIE GANDEL**

Tom Hubschman adjusts his safety glasses as sparks fly from the computer-controlled plasma torch slicing through a piece of metal. This spring day, the Boston University mechanical engineering major from Andover, Massachusetts, is working on his senior design project in the school's high-tech Engineering Product Innovation Center. At his disposal are hardware and software for computer-assisted design and 3D prototyping, a machine shop, an automated robotic manufacturing line, a metals foundry and a carpentry shop. These riches are the result of a collaboration with four big partners – General Electric Aviation, Schlumberger, Procter & Gamble and technology company PTC – plus a substantial investment by the university.

Any BU student interested in taking a product from design to manufacturing is welcome at 9-month-old EPIC, although the chief beneficiaries are the future engineers. These days, having access to cutting-edge technologies while in college can lower the odds of making costly and time-consuming mistakes later – when the task is to design parts for a jet engine, for example – and thus be a big advantage in the job search. For engineers in training, "EPIC is a savior," Hubschman says. "They can say, 'Oh yes, I know that machine, and not from a book. I've worked with it. I've had my hands on it.'"

Businesses expect to reap the rewards in the form of experienced hires. Employers are struggling to find talent in engineering, data analytics, cybersecurity, health care and environmental sciences; a recent Gallup poll reported that only about 1 in 10 business leaders "strongly agree" that American higher education is graduating students with the competencies necessary in their workforce. "Industry is not getting either the quality or quantity of employees they need," says Anthony P. Carnevale, director of Georgetown University's Center on Education and the Workforce. "So they are having to get involved. It's a new era."

What does this new era look like? Besides EPIC's four principal partners, companies like Stanley Black and Decker and GibbsCAM have donated money, equipment or software as well as expertise in the form of seminars, curriculum development and mentoring. Parsons, an engineering management firm in Pasadena, California, is providing scholarships to undergrads in a cybersecurity honors program at the University of Maryland–College Park. At schools like North Carolina State University in Raleigh and New York's Fordham University, IBM provides access to case study projects and analytics software to give business and computer science students experience with data mining, predictive analytics and interactive marketing. IBM data scientists also visit campus as guest lecturers.

## A payoff in real-world practice

The hoped-for result: "What's going to come out of EPIC is that perfect mesh of highly motivated, very talented engineers who have had hands-on experience," predicts Greg Morris, head of the additive technologies group at GE Aviation in Cincinnati and a member of EPIC's Industrial Advisory Board. "And those students will be very attractive to companies like GE." Among them is Tom Hubschman, who upon graduation is joining the Lynn, Massachusetts, office of GE Aviation in an entry-level program that will rotate him through departments such as design, systems engineering and aircraft electrical systems.

For students, the payoff is in practical experience and contacts. Hubschman's design problem at the moment, for

Tom Hubschman's senior project is a task for an energy company.

example, is hardly theoretical. He's working on a project for electronics firm Schneider Electric. "We're pretesting a new generation of HVAC controllers and will report back to Schneider where the failures are and how to improve the design," he says.

Many Fridays at the University of Tennessee-Knoxville, an executive from FedEx, JPMorgan Chase or the Kroger Co., among other companies, sits down with undergrads in the business analytics program. "The students have an opportunity to get up close and personal with someone who is using data analytics every day," says Frank Guess, a professor in the department. At industry partner Pershing, Yoakley & Associates Analytics in Knoxville, students hired as interns "work directly with clients at all levels of the analytics lifecycle," from project planning to selection of appropriate mathematical models to imple-

> STUDENTS CAN SAY, "OH, YES, I KNOW THAT MACHINE, AND NOT FROM A BOOK. I'VE WORKED WITH IT."

mentation and delivery, says Blair Christian, a data scientist at the firm who spends 30 percent of his time at the university teaching business analytics.

Students also benefit from one-on-one interaction with executives by acting as hosts when they come to speak on campus. "He became my mentor," says Camille Crumpton, a 2013 grad now getting her master's in business analytics at UT, of her pairing with an executive from American Express. She still talks to him when she needs advice.

Some of these developing partnerships take an especially local focus, which has long been the particular province of

## COMMUNITY COLLEGES

# Tricks of the Transfer

When a community college is the economical first step toward a bachelor's degree, an articulation agreement is often the key to getting to Step 2. These agreements, which spell out what it takes to transfer to four-year institutions in the same area, are often complicated and murky. Some states, including Florida, California, Massachusetts, Pennsylvania and Virginia, guarantee that anyone who earns an associate degree in the state will also earn admission as a junior to a state university. Many students are on their own, however. And they all too often find that courses do not transfer or will not apply toward a major, slowing down the march toward a degree and adding to its cost. The National Center for Education Statistics reported in 2011 that 37 percent of community college students plan to complete a bachelor's, but only 12 percent actually do.

"The ladder between two-year and four-year schools is often very weak," says Anthony P. Carnevale, director of Georgetown University's Center on Education

and the Workforce. He advises anyone who plans to use community college as a steppingstone to a particular university to first find out from the four-year college which schools it has articulation agreements with. Ask, too, if other students have climbed that particular ladder. If the answer is "two in the last 10 years," go find another community college, Carnevale says.

**The fine print.** It's also vital to read any agreement carefully, says Anthony Ervin, an academic advisor in the Biomanufacturing Research Institute and Technology Enterprise program at North Carolina Central University in Durham. His advice: Don't assume anything – ask upfront. What classes will transfer for full credit? The content of the coursework needs to measure up. It's entirely possible, says Ervin, to take general chemistry in community college only to find that the class does not fulfill the general chemistry requirement at your chosen four-year school. And most public universities require a minimum grade of "C" to transfer credits. In 2012,

the College Board's Initiative on Transfer Policy and Practice recommended that four-year colleges create more transparent transfer policies and establish a presence on the community college campus to help guide transfers.

Meantime, FinAid.org, a website that offers comprehensive information about financial aid, also lists articulation agreements by state. And many states have created their own websites that provide background on articulation agreements and the transfer process.

Some universities also publicize the information. At Central Michigan University's site, for example, you can see which courses meet its requirements both by community college and by degree program. Someone attending Henry Ford Community College in the biomedical sciences who wants to transfer to CMU later, for example, can see that Bio 251, a microbiology course, will count as CMU's Bio 208. If community college is a moneysaving move, such research upfront on a planned transfer is apt to be a worthwhile investment. –C.G.

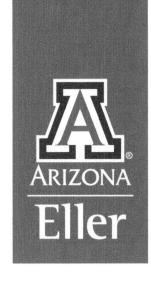

# MCGUIRE CENTER
## FOR ENTREPRENEURSHIP
*30 Years of Excellence in Entrepreneurship Education*

**One of the first**

# UNIVERSITY ENTREPRENEURSHIP CENTERS

in the world and still one of the best.

entrepreneurship.eller.arizona.edu          mcguireexperience.com community colleges. While more than one-third of community college students intend to transfer on for a bachelor's degree (box, Page 30), many are using these tailored programs to slip directly into their area's technical workforce. Since 2008, for example, Pacific Gas & Electric has worked closely with California community colleges to train workers for PG&E and other utility companies. Des Moines Area Community College in Iowa has teamed up with Accumold, a manufacturer of micromolded parts for cell phones and medical devices. Students learn everything from tool- and die-making to robotics and automation.

Scaling up these sorts of local programs is a major goal

Sydnee Shannon (center) lives and studies with her peers in Maryland's cybersecurity honors program.

of the Business-Higher Education Forum, which last year launched a six-year effort to work with business leaders in various regions "to identify their specific needs, and then get them together with local universities to align education with those needs," says Brian Fitzgerald, the group's CEO. A number of projects are in various stages of development, with additional collaborations expected in the future.

Northeast Natural Energy of Charleston, West Virginia, is working with West Virginia University in Morgantown to create a curriculum in the emerging field of shale energy research. Case Western Reserve University in Cleveland has partnered with Sherwin Williams and power management company Eaton to develop a program on materials and polymer science. The Milwaukee region, home to over 150 water technology companies like Badger Meter, A. O. Smith Corp. and Kohler Co., has become a "global water technology center," says Dean Amhaus, president of the area Water Council, comprised of schools, local governments, nongovernmental organizations and corporations. "We have students coming here for an undergraduate degree because they want to be in the water network we have," he says. The University of Wisconsin–

Milwaukee, the University of Wisconsin–Whitewater, Marquette University and Gateway Technical College all offer courses that explore the scientific, legal, social, economic and ecological facets of water.

If cybersecurity is your thing, chances are you might head to Baltimore or Washington. Last year, Northrop Grumman Corp., a leading global security company, joined the University of Maryland–College Park in launching the Advanced Cybersecurity Experience for Students, a pioneering undergraduate cybersecurity honors program. Participants, who might be majoring in math, engineering, computer science, business or criminology, live and study together. Technical skills are part of the curriculum, but "they will be out of date in five, six, 10 years," says Michel Cukier, director of ACES. "It's much more important to learn to identify the right problem to solve." To do that, students study cybersecurity policy, economics, ethics, history and psychology along with the technology. Northrop Grumman is providing feedback on the curriculum, internship opportunities and advisers who will help students with professional development.

Sydnee Shannon, a sophomore from Ellicott City, Maryland, says the ACES program is "a perfect way to connect my math major with cryptography," and that she is particularly enjoying seeing "how students with different backgrounds approach the same problem." She applied for and landed a summer internship at Northrop Grumman as a software engineer.

## Softer skills, too

Beyond honing their technical chops in the real world, the aim is that students gain exposure to the soft skills they're going to need, too: the ability to work on a team, to think critically, to synthesize data, to ask the right question and to communicate with others about problems and challenges. Knowing how to make sense of data, and also how to translate it for nontechnical audiences, is a characteristic of "the real gems" his company is looking for in hiring, says Sean Groer, managing director of customer analytics at consulting firm KPMG in Atlanta, which has a partnership with the University of Tennessee.

The advantages work the other way, too, says GE Aviation's Morris. Management and marketing students, say, can take advantage of EPIC to get a background in manufacturing, adding the ability to talk technology with customers and suppliers. That added ease, he says, makes them "just that much more valuable" to potential employers. ●

# THIS IS A SMART CHOICE.

## THIS IS AUBURN.

Whether you've known about Auburn all your life or are just learning about this university, we invite you to discover the real Auburn.

This is a university whose alumni include the CEO of Apple, the founders of Habitat for Humanity and Wikipedia, an Oscar-winning actor, sports legends, and astronauts. Graduates are recruited by top companies around the globe.

This is a university where you will make friends for a lifetime with a 250,000-strong, worldwide network of alumni who will think of you as family.

This is a university that will surprise you, impress you, and propel you to success as it has for generations before you. **auburn.edu**

# Gee-Whiz

# GYMS

*By* **COURTNEY RUBIN**

There are eight basketball courts, a 1/3-mile corkscrew track suspended high above the ground floor, a 20-foot climbing wall rising out of an outdoor pool, a PGA golf simulator and a hot tub that seats 50 people. Atop the "fitness tower," five stories of cardio equipment and exercise rooms, sits a yoga studio whose enormous windows open up to the sky like garage doors.

A five-star spa? A billionaire's vacation home? Actually, this is the new student recreation center at Auburn University in Alabama, $72 million worth of exercise opportunities.

Auburn is hardly alone in offering up fitness facilities "that you can't match once you leave," says Patricia Ketcham, president of the American College Health Association. Eastern Washington University boasts an indoor climbing wall with 33 routes, including one that simulates ice-climbing. Virginia Commonwealth University has a water slide, 18,000 square feet of fitness and weight lifting equipment, and a gym with artificial turf for indoor soccer games. The University of Missouri–Columbia's website describes a "resort quality" beach club, complete with waterfalls, whirlpools and a "lazy river" for floating. "It's always Spring Break in the Tiger Grotto," adds the website.

The University of North Carolina–Greensboro has broken ground on a $91 million recreation center; a $78 million expansion at Louisiana State University will include a suspended track and an indoor rock climbing wall. James Madison University in Virginia is spending $57 million to double its recreation facilities, adding, among other things, a batting cage, a water volleyball court and an additional indoor running track. According to a survey released in 2013 by NIRSA: Leaders in Collegiate Recreation, 92 institutions reported plans for construction or renovation, for a total of more than $1.7 billion in capital projects.

What's driving the boom? "Students are a lot more in-

One highlight of Auburn University's new rec center is a "corkscrew" track suspended above ground level.

The University of Missouri's swimming facilities include a lazy river, waterfalls and whirlpools.

terested in health and wellness these days," says Brad Cardinal, a professor of exercise and sports science at Oregon State University who has studied student fitness. Cardinal recently surveyed international students within their first five years in America and found that "they all noticed how prominent student health is relative to the culture they'd come from," he says.

Often, in fact, the push to build comes directly from students, who vote to tax themselves to pay for facilities that won't even be open until nearly all have graduated. Auburn University's project, for example, got its start in 2008, when the student government president ran on a platform to overhaul student recreation. During her term, more than 70 percent of students voted in favor of gradually raising their activity fee from $7.50 to $200 to help fund the building.

## And the move toward bigger, shinier rec centers is coinciding

with society's growing focus on preventing disease, as well as accumulating evidence that physical activity and academic success appear to go hand in hand. As Donna Shalala, former Health and Human Services secretary and current president of the University of Miami noted in March during a discussion about the role of colleges at a Partnership for a Healthier America summit, "We have a captive audience, and campuses are good places to learn healthy habits."

Many schools are wasting no time. Stanford University recently launched a Student Wellness Passport Program, which awards students stamps for 12 health-related "trips" such as attending a group fitness class, getting a physical and wearing a bike helmet. Students who complete nine of the 12 are entered in a drawing to win a prize. At the University of Miami, students are encouraged to take classes on meditation, healthy cooking and smoking cessation, as well as to attend play sessions that include finger painting, board games and hula hooping. "It takes more than daily physical activity to maintain good health," notes the wellness center's website. Indeed, many of these new gyms – actually, they're more apt to be called "recreation and wellness centers" – are designed with sofas, meeting rooms and courtyards as places to de-stress, socialize and study as well as sweat.

"It's easy to criticize these amenities as overdone, and say it's just administrators saying, 'We need to have the best and the biggest,'" says Don Stenta, director of student life's recreational sports department at Ohio State University. "We need to help students be successful academically and then successful after graduation, and there's a lot of research about how important a positive recreation experience is."

Maybe it's just that overachievers are more likely to hit the gym: A 2009 study published in the journal Medicine & Science in Sports & Exercise found that the more hours a student spent studying, the more likely he or she was to also show up for some exercise. On the other hand, a 2010 study at Saginaw Valley State University in Michigan found that even controlling for study time, students who regularly participated in vigorous exercise had higher GPAs. Whatever the explanation, a Purdue University analysis of student behavior has linked gym time and GPA, too. Students who worked out 16 times a month earned a GPA of 3.1 or higher, while students who used the gym at least seven times had an average GPA of 3.06. Students

# WHO SAYS YOU CAN'T

FIGHT FOR THE MOST VULNERABLE  HEAL THE PLANET  LEAD THE WAY IN A NEW ECONOMY  UNLOCK THE MIND OF A STUDENT

CHANGE

*Will you join us?*

## CLARK UNIVERSITY
1887

clarku.edu

CHALLENGE CONVENTION. CHANGE OUR WORLD.

who didn't use the gym at all: 2.82. Purdue's fitness facilities recently underwent a $98 million makeover.

The ever-increasing range of activities available isn't just for show – it's to draw students in for one thing, and intrigue them enough to come back for others. It gets much harder to form an exercise habit, Ketcham notes, once students graduate and land a job. At Ohio State University, for example, a Hogwarts Express spin class invited participants to wear Harry Potter costumes. Stenta says the class drew people who'd never been inside the rec center or tried a cycling class – his goal.

Auburn University's old facility drew about 900 students a day. The new one generally draws 3,500 and has even topped 5,000 on occasion. Colorado State University in 2011 spent $32 million renovating its recreation center. An additional $3.3 million was spent on converting a virtually unused lap pool into a leisure pool, complete with a climbing wall, lights and speakers for a grotto effect. There was a 77 percent jump in aquatic facility traffic from fall 2011 to fall 2013.

The increasingly luxe facilities can be potent recruiting tools, some observers say. "I can't tell you how many tours I start with prospective students where I say, 'Hey, are you thinking of coming here?' And the kid is like, 'Eh, I don't know,'" says David Frock, Clemson University's director of student recreation. "But by the time you leave the rec center, they're like, 'Oh, I want to come here.'" A 2013 study released by the National Bureau of Economic Research suggests that fancy amenities matter less at elite colleges and universities, where prospective students tend to be more focused on the quality of instruction.

Growing up in a working-class neighborhood of Portland, Oregon, Tram Hoang, the first member of her family to get a four-year degree, had never worked out at a gym – and in fact had only seen cardio equipment on TV. Hoang, who graduated from Oregon State University in the spring, was drawn to the rec center first to play volleyball, and gradually got up the nerve to ask for help using the machines. By senior year, she practically lived there, she says. "During a weekend where it snowed, the campus was closed for three days, but the rec facilities were open. Everyone was there, renting snowshoes, working out and studying," she says. "I don't think people realize how important recreation is until they get here." ●

# Good News on Gluten

**N**ever mind the beer and pizza. From salad dressings to French fries, most processed foods are a no-go for students who suffer from celiac disease and sensitivity to gluten. Until recently, the limited options available for gluten-free students left them little choice but to eat in their rooms, convince a cafeteria worker to make them a plain chicken breast on a grill not used for buns, or throw caution to the wind, sometimes ending up too sick for class.

"We had students with celiac disease who were having to drop out, or were selecting colleges and universities based on where they can eat," says Beckee Moreland, director of a gluten-free kitchens education program at the National Foundation for Celiac Awareness. The advocacy group a couple years ago began offering university dining services workers a two-hour online or onsite seminar on gluten-free meal prep. So far, about 700 have taken the course, Moreland says.

**The spur to action.** One reason dining halls are rapidly changing their practices: A 2013 Justice Department settlement with Lesley University in Massachusetts, requiring the school to "continually provide" gluten-free options, after a complaint that the school was in violation of the Americans With Disabilities Act by requiring students to live on campus and buy meal plans, but not accommodating the gluten-free diners. Lesley now labels meals "made without gluten" and stores and prepares them in a separate area in the kitchen. There are separate toaster ovens and microwaves for students heating meals.

At Boston College, those who head for the dining hall's "Plain & Simple" line also get food made in an isolated preparation station. And a campus deli offers sandwiches on gluten-free bread, prepared on dedicated cutting boards. North Carolina State University has set up a "worry-free" station with a dedicated toaster and gluten-free breads, bagels and muffins. "Secret shoppers" occasionally go to the dining halls to watch preparation and buy menu items – and write up reports highlighting any problems.

"Now when there's Mexican food I can get corn tortillas instead of flour," says Matthew Schneider, a senior at Michigan State who was diagnosed with celiac disease in sixth grade. "And sometimes they even have gluten-free dessert." There's also a locked refrigerator – students must ask for a key – stocked with safe options for the taking. –C.R.

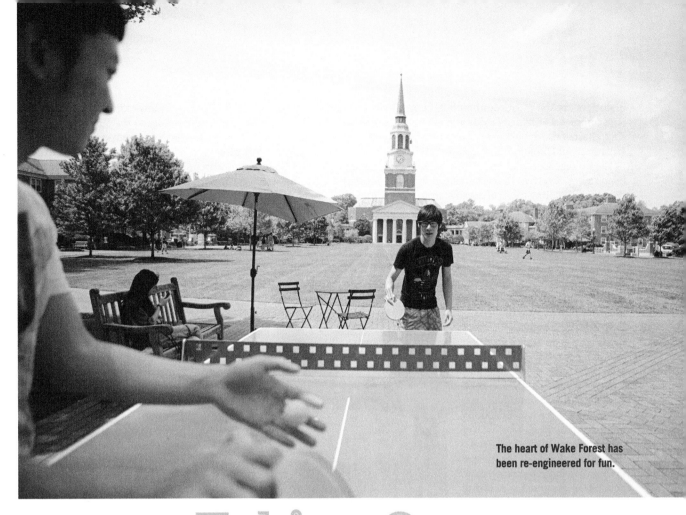

The heart of Wake Forest has been re-engineered for fun.

# Taking On
# STRESS

## COLLEGES ARE FINDING NEW WAYS TO PROMOTE
## STUDENTS' SOCIAL AND EMOTIONAL WELLBEING

*By* **BETH HOWARD**

The quad at Wake Forest University in North Carolina once existed to showcase the handsome brick Georgian buildings; the broad lawns were even cordoned off to student traffic. Now, students gather here at café tables, sit and play the outdoor piano, grab a Frisbee or a football from a pile of equipment for some impromptu play, and read magazines from an al fresco library while sipping coffee from a nearby cart.

Engineered by Dan Biederman, the man who revitalized New York City's once drug-ridden Bryant Park, the campus redo was executed expressly to help harried students take some down time and mingle – and breathe. "You used to see students checking emails on their smartphones when they walked from one part of campus to another," says Elizabeth Law, a May grad in communications. "This encourages you to unplug a little bit. More people are making eye contact and stopping to actually talk to each other."

The Wake Forest project is one example of the myriad ways colleges and universities are working to relieve student stress and to prevent or tackle anxiety and depression, lately at record highs. According to the 2013 National College Health Assessment, almost a third of college students said they felt so depressed during the previous year that it was difficult to function, and more than half had experienced overwhelming anxiety. Almost 8 percent seriously considered suicide. "Mental health disorders are the most common health problems on college campuses outside of colds and allergies," says Jerald Kay, chair of the department of psychiatry at Wright State University in Ohio and co-author of "Mental Health Care in the College Community." While suicide rates have not been rising, Kay says, that is small comfort: Suicide is still the second-leading cause of death among college students, after vehicle accidents. The University of Pennsylvania, shaken by three suicides in four months this past year, has convened a task force to confront the vexing problem.

To nip stress before it leads to bigger problems, a growing number of schools, including New York University, Harvard, and the University of Missouri, are offering training in meditation and mindfulness to quiet the tendency to worry about all sorts of potential catastrophes; after students at Santa Clara University in California took an eight-week meditation class, they reported greater reductions in stress than those who did not take the class. During finals, staff, faculty and alumni of Macalester College in Minnesota bring their pooches to campus for cuddling breaks and camaraderie. Says senior Kenzie Ellis, a Russian studies major: "There's that look you get from other students that says, 'Hey, we're both freaking out about finals right now, but at least we're petting dogs, isn't this great?'" Kent State University in Ohio has a similar program.

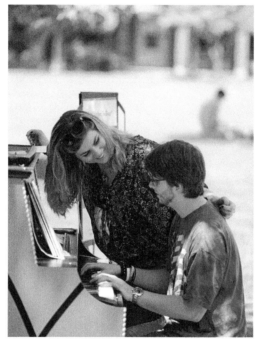

**Wake Forest students stop to play a solar-powered piano.**

Besides the prevention efforts, counseling departments are trying innovative approaches to meet the growing demand for their services. "More schools have walk-in hours so that students don't get wait-listed," says Josh Gunn, director of counseling and psychological services at Kennesaw State University near Atlanta and president of the American College Counseling Association. With budgets stretched thin, he notes, students at some colleges have to wait days or weeks to see a counselor. Many schools, including Kennesaw and Wake Forest, have added the option of group therapy to that of private sessions. The University of Florida offers a seven-week anxiety education class to give students tools for taming their tension. Schools are also experimenting with technology, using web-based resources to teach students how to cope, for instance.

Going to college has always involved the stress of making new friends and learning to regulate one's sleeping, eating, studying and partying. Yet today's students face a unique set of emotional challenges in the still-sputtering economy. "There's tremendous pressure to succeed," says Victor Schwartz, medical director of The JED Foundation, a nonprofit that promotes emotional health on campus

founded by Phil and Donna Satow after their son took his own life in 1999 as a sophomore at the University of Arizona. "Students anticipate stiff competition when it comes to getting a job after graduation, and, with soaring tuitions, there's more financial pressure on them."

The result, he says: A need to "work the résumé and do well at every endeavor." And when you compare yourself "to everyone else's highlight reels," it's easy to feel "like you're not measuring up," says Kaitlin Gladney, a recent Duke University grad who has experienced anxiety and depression and received counseling on campus. The Duke Endowment is funding a four-year Student Resiliency Project at Duke and several other schools that will investigate ways colleges can foster an ability to bounce back from reversals.

Ironically, hovering "helicopter" parents seeking only to help their college kids, by mediating disputes between roommates and calling professors about grades, say, may be making matters worse. A new study in the Journal of Child and Family Studies shows that children with overinvolved parents were more prone to depressive symptoms. Helicopter parenting undermines students' sense of competence, explains study author Holly Schiffrin, a psychology professor at the University of Mary Washington in Virginia. "It tells students that parents don't think they're capable of handling problems, and it prevents students from practicing the very skills they need to feel confident."

Other relatively new factors colleges face include the growing population of students with conditions such as schizophrenia and bipolar disorder who can attend school thanks to improved therapies, and an expected wave of veterans, many of whom will be bringing issues to campus that colleges are not accustomed to seeing, such as post-traumatic stress disorder and traumatic brain injury. More than a million vets have tapped the GI bill to attend college since 2009. Being older, soldiers are less likely to find social support on campus. "The vet population is one of our biggest challenges now," Kay says.

**Families have a big role to play in safeguarding their** students' mental health. At the college research stage, it's possible to find out what resources are offered by talking to admissions officers and checking out school websites. "School programs vary tremendously, from comprehensive and robust to having next-to-nothing," Schwartz says. One measure: participation in the JED Campus Seal program,

which signifies comprehensive mental health and suicide prevention programming.

So far, 30 schools, including Cornell, Columbia and Alfred University in New York; Pennsylvania State University in Altoona and Emory University in Georgia have the JED Seal. Anyone who has struggled or is taking a psychiatric medication can let the school know without repercussions once accepted – and should, experts say. Work out a plan if you decide to transition care to campus, and at the very least make sure someone there is keeping the student "on the school's radar," Schwartz advises.

## Starting well before college, parents should be conscious of

promoting their child's independence and autonomy, experts advise. Instead of jumping in to take care of everyday issues, Schiffrin says, offer support by, for example, role-playing tricky conversations a student might need to have with a high school teacher, professor or peer: "'What would you say when X?' and 'And how would you respond if Y?'"

But do keep the lines of communication to campus open, experts advise. "No one knows a child better than a parent," says Penny Rue, vice president for campus life at Wake Forest. "Look for a change in their energy levels and listen for changes in vocal modulation. Probe a little about their sleep and nutrition habits. Both too much and too little sleep are signs of depression."

Students can inoculate themselves in a couple of ways. One good step is to seek out a niche from the start where you feel you fit in, perhaps by choosing to live in a learning community (story, Page 18) or by joining an organization that suits your interests. Another healthful measure: Get some exercise. Charlie Shuford, a sophomore studying music and art at Appalachian State University in North Carolina who has battled depression, keeps symptoms at bay by competing on the cycling team. A 2013 University of Minnesota study showed that students who engaged in vigorous exercise for 20 minutes at least three times a week were less likely to report poor mental health and stress. Shuford is cautious about loading his schedule, too: "I'm thinking of going to college for five years instead of four so I don't allow myself to get too stressed out."

Beyond the anti-anxiety and meditation workshops, many students who feel vulnerable swear by support groups such as those sponsored by Active Minds, an advocacy group on 453 college campuses. At Duke, Gladney started a chapter of the national nonprofit To Write Love on Her Arms, aimed at supporting people coping with depression, addiction and self-injury. It's not therapy. But "students have told me that it's created a safe space where they're comfortable discussing the topic, free from fear of rejection or stigma," Gladney says.

When a student experiences a bout of depression or another issue, it's important to reach out for counseling services. There are people on most campuses whose sincere wish it is "to make sure you are emotionally well and socially adjusted," says Gunn. Don't wait, he cautions, until you feel hopeless. ●

NASHVILLE, TENNESSEE

# ...Fisk University

## Lamar Allen, '16

I wanted to attend a historically black institution that would culturally nurture and academically challenge me. Fisk pulled me in with its rich history, family-oriented environment and its reputation for academic achievement.

As a business administration major concentrating in accounting, I have been able to develop my quantitative and financial skills with the help of the small class sizes and my professors, who have given me the personal attention I desired. Fisk's Exceptional Confidence In Emerging Leaders program has further en-

abled me to refine my professional skills, build my "brand," and strategically set goals as I pursue a career in corporate America. As part of the EXCEL program, Fisk has given me the opportunity to interact and build relationships with associates of top investing firms such as Goldman Sachs and Morgan Stanley.

Fisk is located in Nashville, and one can find plenty to do in the Music City, whether it's grabbing a bite to eat on the West End or enjoying a great day at Centennial Park. I have been enriched by the legacy and history of this institution and am truly thankful for the support of my Fisk family. ●

DAVIS

# ...University of California-Davis
## Carly Sandstrom, '14

The first time I visited Davis I fell in love with this university – the trees, arboretum, a picturesque downtown that seems straight out of a movie, and the smiles of people as you pass by. There was an instant comfort here that I hadn't felt at other universities. UC-Davis gave me a chance to attend a school that's both strong academically and encourages service. As a double major in international relations and economics, I worked, for example, with the provost's staff to oversee the Education Abroad Center (which coordinates international study opportunities), and I had an eye-opening internship with Gov. Jerry Brown's Let's Get Healthy California task force that devised a comprehensive plan to make residents healthier by encouraging everything from increased immunizations to better eating habits.

A favorite memory: One day freshman year, I was biking through campus with the student body president (a position I took over my third year) and another student. The president saw members of the student ministry doing some landscaping in their front yard. He got off his bike and urged us to pitch in and help. That is UC Davis – spontaneous and giving. ●

# I Picked...

COLORADO

# ...U.S. Air Force Academy
## Michael Gallagher, '14

Since I was 6 years old, I've wanted to be an Air Force pilot, so the academy was the obvious choice for me after high school. The experience has been both rigorous and rewarding. During the week, cadets study everything from the military strategy of Operation Iraqi Freedom to the rocket propulsion needed to transfer from low Earth to high Earth orbit. Training continues on weekends, when we learn skills like land navigation and marksmanship. Instructors are constantly available, even on weekends, for cadets needing help with class work or coping with the stresses of training. I have participated in specialized training like the Unmanned Aerial Systems program, while also studying cyberwarfare and space operations to expose myself to the many different career paths in the Air Force. The academy demands mastery and will ensure you get extra instruction, if necessary, till you achieve it. Though we work hard, cadets still manage to have fun doing everything from seeing movies to applying woodland tactics with the Airsoft Club to learning blues dancing. Beyond just preparing me well for my future in the Air Force, the academy has enabled me to form close friendships with fellow cadets. They are my brothers and sisters in arms whom I would trust with my car – or my life. ●

Cheering on the
Clemson Tigers

# TAKE A

# Road Trip

# Missouri

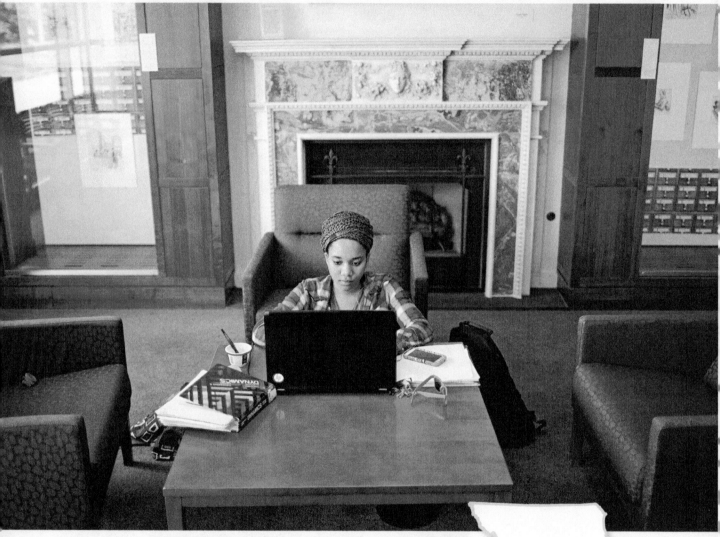

A student at work in the Olin Library at Washington University in St. Louis

University of Missouri

Washington University in St. Louis

Missouri University of Science and Technology

College of the Ozarks

## By **DELECE SMITH-BARROW**

Take a break and enjoy the ride as U.S. News hits the road for you through the college towns of Missouri. The trip begins in St. Louis, at Wash U, then heads to Rolla and the Missouri University of Science & Technology, drops down to the College of the Ozarks in Point Lookout, and ends up in Columbia at Mizzou.

   Photography by **MATT SLABY** – Luceo for USN&WR

# Washington University in St. Louis

Rohan Puthanangady, a Wash U sophomore from Massachusetts, was drawn to the medium-sized university at the heart of the country by the school's academic strength; compared to his high school curriculum, says the business major, "the workload is way more here." He's come to love just about everything about the place: the food (from locally grown vegetarian to Indian and kosher fare), the faculty (even deans invite students over for dinner), the residence halls (which come with peer and faculty mentors) and a collegial atmosphere that makes it easier to get through long nights of studying. "The people here are incredibly down to earth and friendly," observes Puthanangady. "There's no sense of competitiveness."

That feeling of support and togetherness is a common theme on the sprawling green campus located west of downtown St. Louis, about 10 miles from the iconic Gateway Arch and adjacent to Forest Park's acres of bike and running trails; golf and tennis facilities; and art, history and science museums and zoo. Two upperclass "student associates" are assigned to each freshman floor to help newcomers make a happy transition to college; peer mentors who live in the residential colleges are available for

group or one-on-one academic assistance. You can study, sleep and still have a social life, says Vera Schulte, a sophomore from Seattle who likes to do some of her work curled up by the fireplace in Danforth University Center, near all the hubbub of the adjacent dining area. Schulte, who is majoring in philosophy,

**UNDERGRADUATES**
Full-time: 6,587

**TOTAL COST***
$60,844

**U.S. NEWS RANKING**
National Universities
**#14**

*Tuition, fees and room & board

one of the 10 residential colleges specially designed to foster community. In gardens and other gathering spaces, undergrads and faculty fellows can continue conversations started in class or simply

people together on campus for several days of fun and fundraising for charity; in the fall, a widely attended event inspired by the Hindu Festival of Lights known as Diwali is hosted by Ashoka, the South Asian student association, as a way to celebrate those cultures. Students can join any of several hundred interest groups, from one dedicated to collegiate jugglers to a society for people who like to churn butter the "olde-fashioned way." They can also join a Greek organization or play one of 33 club sports.

If campus activities

The university's architecture was inspired by that of Oxford and Cambridge.

neuroscience and psychology – that's one major – as a premed student, relies on a team of advisers to keep her on track academically: a four-year adviser, a major adviser, a residential adviser and her premed adviser.

Outside of class hours, freshmen and sophomores might well be found hanging out in the South 40, in

socialize. Students often play Frisbee on the large field affectionately known as The Swamp, grab a bite at Bear's Den, or stop in at the fitness center or several student-run businesses, such as Bears Bikes or Wash-U-Wash.

In the spring, Thurtene, a popular student-run carnival complete with rides, brings students and towns-

don't offer enough excitement, St. Louis serves up plenty, too, from Cardinals games at Busch Stadium to the nightlife of the Delmar Loop. In this popular section of the city, students can dine at Blueberry Hill, catch a show at Tivoli Theatre, browse through the art galleries and check out some live music. ●

In the design center, future engineers can work on projects around the clock.

# Missouri University of Science and Technology

*Rolla*

A message painted outside of the library at Missouri University of Science and Technology one day last fall read "121 daze" – a countdown to the much-anticipated 10-day extravaganza every March that sweeps campus and the city of Rolla in honor of St. Patrick's Day. S&T, as the school is commonly known, does not have a religious affiliation, but St. Patrick is the patron saint of engineers, and there are plenty of those here. "It's pretty much like Rolla's homecoming," says

**UNDERGRADUATES**
Full-time: 5,472

**TOTAL COST***
In-state: $19,077
Out-of-state: $34,944

**U.S. NEWS RANKING**
National Universities
**#138**

*Tuition, fees and room & board

Steve Ludwig, a senior mechanical engineering major from St. Louis and a member of the board of the festivities, which include parties, a parade and a leprechaun look-alike

contest. Even the mayor has been known to attend. As early as November, the booth selling green S&T sweatshirts is set up and in business.

Engineering is indeed one of the university's strongest departments; undergraduates interested in the field can select from 15 majors, from aerospace and ceramic to metallurgical and nuclear. All told, more than 90 percent of the student body majors in a science, technology, engineering or math – STEM – discipline. The rest choose from among the select few other pathways, which include business, economics, psychology, English and history.

The engineering bent is evident on a stroll around campus. There's the windmill that contributes to wind turbine research, and

the student-built "smart" bridge spanning a creekbed that is made of material often used in advanced aircraft; sensors feed instrumentation that measures strain on the bridge. You'll pass Solar Village, where four solar homes students built over the years provide housing and a self-sustaining electrical power grid. S&T is the kind of school where students spend their free time in the advanced computer labs of the 24/7 design center, working in teams to develop everything from solar cars and hydrogen fuel cells to concrete canoes and off-road vehicles.

When they aren't studying, many students are active in the vibrant 28-chapter Greek system. To fight the common association of Greek life with partying, anyone

# *DUCKS HAPPEN HERE*

Deep in the woods of the Pacific Northwest there is a premier public research university
—a place where innovators gather, and green is a way of life. There, nestled in a valley
between the blue Pacific and the mighty Cascade Range, you'll find a curious sort ... those
that boldly advance the pursuit of excellence, and do the deeds that change the world.
They flock together in a proud space that is inclusive, supportive, and reminds you of home.
This is the Rubicon of the new frontier, out West—where you'll find the Ducks ... in flight.

UNIVERSITY OF
**OREGON**

1-800-BE-A-DUCK
uoregon.edu

# College of the Ozarks
## *Point Lookout*

who wants to participate is strongly encouraged to get involved in other aspects of campus life as well; some fraternities and sororities even require three other extracurricular activities. It forces you to "structure your day," says Pi Kappa Alpha member Raheel Hassan, a senior majoring in biology who has also been active in the Industrial Designers Society of America and the spring break community service program.

**Life lessons.** Women say they learn some valuable life lessons, like how to make your voice heard when you're one of only a few women in the room. (The student body is about 75 percent male.) Shelby McNeil, a senior applied mathematics major from Republic, Missouri, says that she sometimes has felt not taken seriously – when, for example, students needing help in math class bypass her, a math major, to ask a guy who is not a major for assistance.

Victoria Willcut, a junior environmental engineering student from Puxico, Missouri, has noticed that women may have to [...] to make sure they [...] sirable roles in [...] jects. But male [...] generally treat [...] says, and she [...] the campus [...] ants her to [...]

[...] ribe [...] hard- [...] coming. [...] er- [...] ri [...] tor of [...] ural [...] e

A 1973 Wall Street Journal article dubbed College of the Ozarks "Hard Work U." More than 40 years later, students and faculty at this unique Christian college still embrace the name. Banners shout it out from every corner of campus. You can even see it inscribed on the white coats of nursing students.

The moniker is more than a catchy slogan. From freshman year on, full-time students are assigned to some 15 hours a week (plus two 40-hour work-weeks) at one of more than 75 job stations, as part of the college's required work education program. Some butcher or milk cows on one of the campus's three farms, while others pre-

**UNDERGRADUATES**
Full-time: 1,498

**TOTAL COST\***
$6,630

**U.S. NEWS RANKING**
Regional Colleges,
Midwest
**#4**

\*Fees, room & board. Tuition ($18,100) is covered by work and aid.

pare food in the cafeteria or write press releases in the public relations office.

"Our students are crucial to the operation of this place," says Chris Larsen, the dean of work education. Students learn initiative, responsibility, communication and other skills through their campus jobs, he says.

While figuring out how

to balance work with study and other activities can be challenging for incoming students, there's a big payoff: no out-of-pocket tuition. The work education program (which some students participate in during the summer, too), federal grants and College of the Ozarks scholarships cover tuition for all full-time students; very few students graduate with debt. Fees and room and board run a bit over $6,500 a year.

"I have a lot of friends at home that are up to their eyeballs in debt," says Kelsea Inson, a senior from Warrenton, Virginia. College of the Ozarks is the only four-year institution she applied to after attending community college. She's majoring in graphic design, one of 44 majors

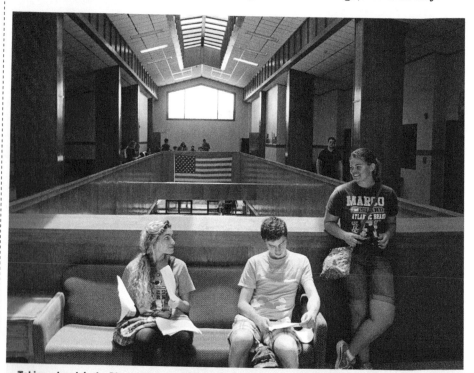

Taking a break in the Plaster Business Building, also home to criminal justice and computer science

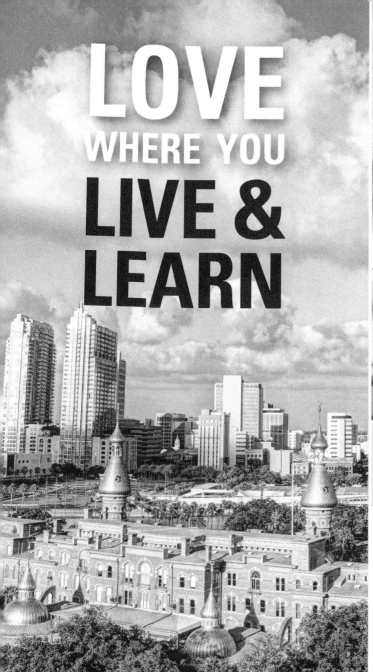

# LOVE
## WHERE YOU
# LIVE &
# LEARN

**THE UNIVERSITY OF TAMPA** offers students the best of it all: academic excellence, abundant internships, big-city living and beautiful weather. With more than 160 areas of study, UT is committed to preparing students for success through experiential learning. Ranked as one of the top universities in the south by *U.S. News & World Report*, UT produces outstanding graduates who are ready to compete in the global marketplace.

**www.ut.edu/explore**

THE UNIVERSITY OF TAMPA

offered; the others, along with general liberal arts options, include business, nursing and education.

Inson is one of the fraction of students – some 20 percent of the 1,500 population – who hail from outside the Ozarks region; most slots go to students within the area, which encompasses parts of Missouri, Arkansas, Illinois, Oklahoma and Kansas. The hilly landscape provides a bucolic backdrop for the manicured grounds, some 1,000 acres of lawns and flower beds. Besides the farms, students heading to class might pass the farmer's market during the fall months and Edwards Mill, a grist mill where they can grind whole grain into flour and weave textiles.

**For fun.** Ozarks students have a sizable menu of activities to choose from for the hours when they're not studying or working, from the College Republicans club and student government to the basketball, baseball and volleyball teams to jazz band and the Ozarks Fisheries and Wildlife Club. Popular campuswide yearly events include the bluegrass-

heavy Sadie Hawkins dance and Mudfest, which involves a fiercely fought tug-of-war contest over a pit of mud.

There's a strong interest in spirituality here. "I wanted to go somewhere where I would enhance my faith," says Michaela Moore, a sophomore nursing major from Waynesville, Missouri. Moore is a Southern Baptist who participates in the Fellowship of Christian Athletes and plans to get involved with the Nurses Christian Fellowship. At noon, activity in the dining hall pauses for a moment of prayer, and students are required to attend at least five chapel services each semester.

Everyone is encouraged to pursue an experience abroad, although the school doesn't offer any semesterlong options; past opportunities have included study trips to China and Belize. Through the Patriotic Education Travel program, students travel with veterans to battlegrounds where they have served to get an understanding of the history and an appreciation for what it was like to be on the front lines. ●

Among the college's 75 work stations are three farms.

# University of Missouri
## *Columbia*

One landmark you're sure to notice as you walk around the University of Missouri is the set of six pillars called The Columns that symbolize the beginning and the end of a student's time at the school. Before fall classes begin, freshmen run through the columns toward the heart of campus as part of "Tiger Walk," an event that marks the start of their college careers. Graduating students pass through in the opposite direction during "Senior Sendoff."

In between, the 27,000 undergraduates at Mizzou, which prides itself in being both a land-grant institu-

tion with a public service mission and a research university, find plenty to do. More than 280 degree programs are offered through 13 colleges and schools. Many undergrads participate in research projects, investigating everything from how plants defend themselves against bacterial infections to highway safety, either independently or with faculty mentors. The university emphasizes experiential learning in other ways as well; about 18 percent of undergraduates each year receive credit through courses that intersperse classwork with community service.

And budding reporters and editors in the univerwould at any paper.

"The journalism school was a huge draw for me," says Madalyne Bird, a senior from Kansas City who is focusing on multiplatform design. "It's so rewarding, but it's also a huge time commitment."

In general, the 1,262-acre campus – which also happens to be a registered botanic garden, a "living museum" of some 42,000 plants and trees – has the

**UNDERGRADUATES**
Full-time: 25,258

**TOTAL COST***
In-state: $18,819
Out-of-state: $33,846

**U.S. NEWS RANKING**
National Universities
**#99**

*Tuition, fees and room & board

students may find a tight community within the Honors College, which offers small classes and a book club, among other activities. Much of the bonding happens within the 750-plus student organizations, which range from UNICEF Mizzou to the chess club to the Quarter Scale Tractor Pulling Team.

Anyone who is into playing sports has more than 45 club options to choose from. Fans can also cheer on some 20 teams that compete for the university in the Southeastern Conference; the football team recently added 2014 AT&T Cotton Bowl champions to its list of accolades. The women's volleyball team also celebrated a big victory last November when it won the Southeastern Conference championship.

The tiger spirit is on full display during the week-long Homecoming spectacular, one of the most unifying campus events. Homecoming is also an opportunity each year to embrace the university's multicultural identity – its varied student body, alumni, faculty and staff – by hosting events such as the Black Family Reunion.

Columbia is a college "town" of just over 113,000 residents that welcomes and caters to the school community, and students regularly head off campus to its coffee shops, music venues and many restaurants. Shakespeare's Pizza and Lakota Coffee on South 9th Street are some of the more popular dining spots, while The Blue Note and Missouri Theatre are a safe bet for finding some live entertainment. ●

Practicing at Mizzou's pool (top), and studying and socializing at the university center

sity's renowned School of Journalism are trained using the hands-on Missouri Method; to complement their classwork, they get intensive practice at one of several publications, radio stations or advertising agencies. Stu-

dents guided by faculty put out the local Columbia Missourian newspaper, for example, which publishes five days a week and is updated online 24/7. Students discuss how stories are told during budget meetings, as they

feel of a "big small place," says Nick Droege, a 2014 grad from St. Louis and former president of the Missouri Students Association. "There are so many opportunities here to make it smaller."

For example, some

# Pennsylvania

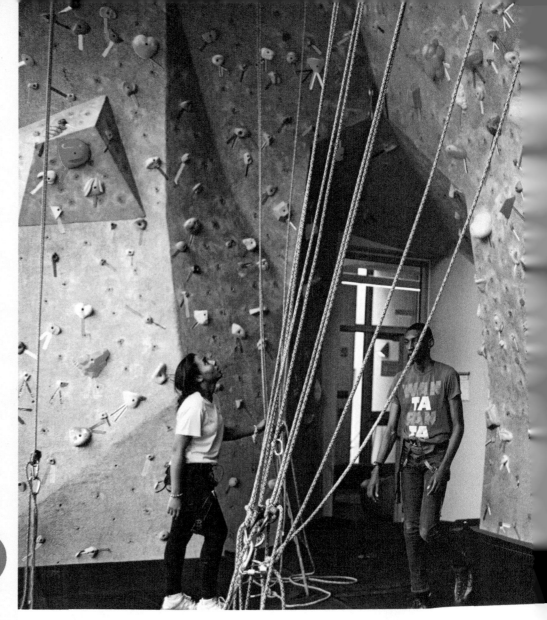

By **MICHAEL MORELLA**

The Keystone State is home to about 100 colleges and universities, and the Philadelphia metro area alone claims several hundred thousand college students. U.S. News spent a few days in and around the City of Brotherly Love, touring Drexel and the University of Pennsylvania downtown before stopping by the suburban liberal arts enclaves of Haverford and Bryn Mawr.

PA

Bryn Mawr College
Haverford College
Drexel University
University of Pennsylvania
PHILADELPHIA

*Photography by* **BRETT ZIEGLER** *for USN&WR*

# Drexel University
## Philadelphia

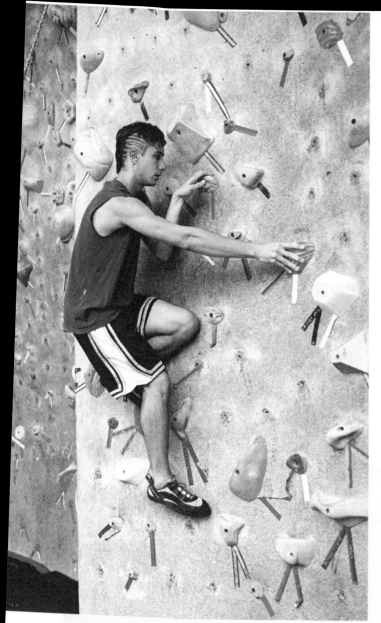

Almost a century ago, engineering students at what was then the Drexel Institute of Art, Science and Industry near Center City Philadelphia began alternating periods of classroom instruction with hands-on work experience. Today, more than 75 majors offer such co-operative education programs; by the time they graduate, some 90 percent of Drexel undergrads will have had at least one (full-time) six-month co-op job at one of 1,600-plus employers, including the Children's Hospital of Philadelphia, Merck, the Philadelphia Housing Authority and the Philadelphia Museum of Art.

"They throw you right in when you get here," says international business major Sandra Petri, class of 2016. Petri, from Mount Royal, New Jersey, has completed co-ops at Comcast and the nonprofit World Trade Center of Greater Philadelphia. The average six-month salary is a little more than $16,000, though some positions are not paid. And roughly half of each graduating class is offered a job with a co-op employer, notes Peter Franks, vice provost for career education.

The career development center helps facilitate the co-op process, but students must be proactive in securing their positions. Most complete their degrees in five years with up to three co-ops, though some choose a four-year, single-placement program. Classes are arranged in 10-week quarters, which students say tend to be fast-paced and require careful time management. "Drexel has this kind of motif of initiative," says senior Christopher Gray, a business administration and entrepreneurship major from Birmingham, Alabama, who has had a co-op at Fannie Mae and a self-guided one with other students that involved designing a mobile app for finding college scholarships.

The co-op program attracted Ethan Collik, a

**UNDERGRADUATES**
Full-time: 11,480

**TOTAL COST***
$61,418

**U.S. NEWS RANKING**
National Universities
**#95**

*Tuition, fees and room & board

Scaling the rec center climbing wall (above). A draping class in Drexel's fashion design program recent accounting and legal studies grad from Cherry Hill, New Jersey, "but there were so many other things keeping me here," he says. Undergrads can choose from among 300 organizations, including the Campus Activities Board, The Triangle campus newspaper, and the Drexel football team, an improv comedy group. (The university doesn't have an athletic football team, though the Dragons do compete in 18 Division I sports.) About 10 percent of students join fraternities and sororities.

**Urban vibe.** Drexel's 126 acres in the University City neighborhood have an "urban college town" feel, notes recent mechanical engineering grad Graham Donaldson of Woodcliff Lake, New Jersey. The campus can feel crowded, students say, though most welcome the chance to explore the nearby music, art, sports, culture and other attractions. Popular hangouts on campus include the Creese Student Center with lounges, a theater and Drexel's underground main dining center; the recreation center; and Buckley field and green, home to frequent pickup sports games.

Classes average about 18 undergraduates, and the student-faculty ratio is 9-to-1. First-year students live in one of several mostly high-rise dorms clustered around the north end of campus, and they may apply to live in learning communities based on field of study. (Engineering, business and health professions are popular.) Some upperclassmen reside on campus, but most find places around Philly. ●

# University of Pennsylvania
## Philadelphia

Upon founding what would become the University of Pennsylvania, Benjamin Franklin stressed the importance of students learning all that is "most useful and most ornamental." Today, cultivating "Renaissance students" remains a major part of Penn's DNA, says Chicago native and recent communication grad Ernest Owens. More than 9,000 undergraduates attend the Ivy League school, situated on about 300 acres in the heart of Philadelphia, just west of downtown and the Schuylkill River.

One of the oldest and most selective institutions in the country, Penn accepted around 12 percent of its 31,200-plus applicants for fall 2013; 94 percent of those admitted came from the top 10 percent of their high school classes. "People are competitive," notes Yadavan Mahendraraj, a spring grad in management and marketing from Allendale, New Jersey, but "it's not cutthroat."

Undergrads can select from 91 different majors – or create their own – at the schools of arts and sciences, engineering, nursing and the storied Wharton business school. (The 11,000 graduate students can enroll at eight additional schools.) Students often

Members of the Onda Latina dance club practice between classes (top). In a forensic anthropology lab class (above), students examine skulls.

undergrads live on campus, which spans about eight blocks and includes several museums and galleries, La Casa Latina and five other cultural resource centers and no shortage of green spaces.

Students can keep busy with more than 400 activities, and about a third join fraternities and sororities. The Netter Center for Community Partnerships coordinates volunteer and civic engagement programs, as well as a range of service-learning courses that, for example, examine urban education in underserved West Philadelphia schools. Penn also boasts 11 undergraduate research journals and more than 100 research centers through which student scholars can earn grants for their own projects or join faculty efforts. And at least 4 out of 5 undergrads participate in internships.

"I can barely wrap my head around how there's so much to do," notes senior Jacob Meiner, of New Rochelle, New York, who is studying Near Eastern languages and civilizations and marketing and operations management.

Some undergrads say the university can feel decentralized and that school spirit can be lacking at Quaker athletic events. But Penn pride shows at gatherings like Spring Fling, billed as one of the biggest college festivals on the East Coast, and Hey Day, when juniors don straw hats and red shirts and march around campus with canes to celebrate their soon-to-be seniority. ●

**UNDERGRADUATES**
Full-time: 9,407

**TOTAL COST\***
$61,132

**U.S. NEWS RANKING**
National Universities
**#8**

*\*Tuition, fees and room & board*

marvel at "how much individual attention you can get at such a large school," says sophomore nursing major Maci McCravy, from Tulsa, Oklahoma. A low 6-to-1 student-faculty ratio helps, as do opportunities like Wharton's Lunch & Learn program, through which the university pays for undergrads to take faculty members out for meals.

The small-school-within-a-large-university feel owes much to the system of College Houses. All freshmen reside in these 11 living-learning communities, along with a number of faculty members (and sometimes their families) and have access to in-house advising and tutoring, house-based social and educational events and research opportunities, as well as more than 40 themed programs focused on music and social change, for instance, or international studies and business. Over half of

# Haverford College
## *Haverford*

'There are no closed doors" at Haverford, says junior Alana Thurston, a Boston-area native majoring in chemistry, of the academic, social and other opportunities available to undergraduates. Many students attribute that pervasive feeling of openness to a highly influential honor code, rooted in the Quaker traditions of the college's founders, that

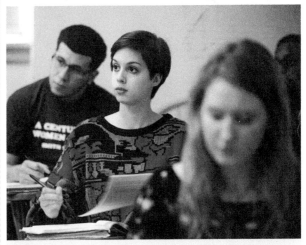

**Students in class at Quaker-founded Haverford**

aims to promote integrity and mutual respect. Set along Philadelphia's historic Main Line, about 8 miles from the city center, the liberal arts college's campus is an arboretum

(where trees outnumber students), complete with a duck pond and bounded by a 2 ¼-mile nature trail. Virtually everybody lives on campus, as do 60 percent of professors (most in faculty housing), so the Haverford community is close-knit. Classes average 15 students, and – count on it – "the professor will know your name," says Chloe Wang, a sophomore interested

in chemistry from Dobbs Ferry, New York.

There's widespread agreement that the honor code really works. No resident assistants are needed to police the dorms (though students have access to upperclassmen and administrative support), and it's standard practice to take exams without proctors and to leave laptops unattended and bikes unlocked around campus. Haverfordians come together each semester for Plenary to discuss issues on campus and to make changes to policies as needed. "Really,

**UNDERGRADUATES**
Full-time: 1,187

**TOTAL COST\***
$61,564

**U.S. NEWS RANKING**
National Liberal Arts
Colleges
**#8**

*\*Tuition, fees and room & board*

at its core, every student is invested in making this a healthy community that's inclusive," says Dylan Reichman, a junior majoring in political science from Maplewood, New Jersey.

In keeping with Haverford's liberal arts mission, at least 19 of the 32 courses required to complete a degree must be outside one's major. Nearly all undergrads complete a thesis in their chosen field. About half study abroad.

In their residence halls, first-year students join a

Hard at work in a cell and molecular biology "super lab"

"customs group," a community of peers and upperclass students who can offer advice on academics, programs on campus, and other topics. Older students can opt to live in housing built around a theme, in which residents often host events for all students. Examples: Nerd House, a community where residents have regular board game nights and murder mystery parties, and Culinary House, where they hold dinners and cooking classes.

While some students acknowledge the school can seem a bit insular, "it doesn't feel small if you

make the effort to get off campus," notes Rosalie Samide, a spring psychology grad from Latrobe, Pennsylvania. One option is to take classes or eat at sister school Bryn Mawr (story, at right), with whom many activities are shared. Haverfordians can also take classes at the University of Pennsylvania and local rival Swarthmore College.

Moreover, given the proximity to Philadelphia, Haverford isn't "kind of stuck in the woods like

a lot of similarly sized schools," says Phil Drexler, a recent grad in physics from Wilmington, Delaware. Many students take advantage of the city's museums, shows, dining and sports teams. Especially popular are events organized by the student-run group Fords Against Boredom, such as Ben & Jerry's bingo and midnight cheesesteak runs. On campus, students cheer on the Division III Fords, hang out in the Coop or the student-run Lunt Café, and enjoy frequent a capella concerts and events like the winter SnowBall and spring festival. ●

# Bryn Mawr College
*Bryn Mawr*

Ivy Gray-Klein was working on her thesis and venting her stress on her blog when she received a surprise in the mail: a care package of snacks and study-break reading material from a 2001 Bryn Mawr alumna, a loyal reader she had never met. "We all kind of have each other's backs," says Gray-Klein, a Chicago native who graduated in May with a degree in art history.

Surrounded by trees, elegant lawns and castle-like Gothic architecture, some 1,300 women attend the suburban Philadelphia institution, the smallest of the Northeast's elite women's colleges once collectively known as the Seven Sisters. Students credit much of the family atmosphere to the honor code, under which they can safely leave belongings around campus, schedule their own exams (and take them without proctors) and typically avoid discussing grades. They also value the school's self-governance system, within which students decide policies.

**Close partner.** Bryn Mawr enjoys a partnership with neighboring Haverford College (Page 57); students at each have access to the other's facilities, organizations, social activities and classes, and even can complete majors at the other institution. Bryn Mawr offers majors in archaeology and geology, for instance, while Haverford has religion, music and fine arts.

Whatever their intended major, all first-year students must complete the Emily Balch Seminar, an intensive writing course centered on a broad subject like humanity and technology. Popular among older students are 360-degree course clusters, interdisciplinary cohorts of classes that often involve off-campus experiences and are taught by faculty

**UNDERGRADUATES**
Full-time: 1,315

**TOTAL COST\***
$59,890

**U.S. NEWS RANKING**
National Liberal Arts
Colleges
**#27**

*Tuition, fees and room & board

from a range of fields; the eco-literacy cluster, for example, blends economics, education and literature.

Campus dining earns rave reviews – it's not uncommon to see Haverford students in line – as do the residence halls, where many rooms contain comfy touches like fireplaces and window seats. Most Mawrters share the view that attending a women's college is empowering, and praise the school's diversity; undergraduates hail from 43 states and 62 countries, and more than half are from abroad or students of color. "There is no one set Bryn Mawr woman," says senior economics major Mfon-ido Akpan, who is from Nigeria. Classes are typically small, and the student-faculty ratio is just 8-to-1. Professors "care about your well-being," says Lindsey Crowe, a 2014 grad in English from Los Angeles.

On the other hand, students say that the college can feel small. But town is just a short walk away, and downtown Philly is about a 20-minute train ride. There are 100-plus organizations and clubs (Ultimate Frisbee with Haverford is especially popular), and social activities include teas hosted by campus clubs or academic departments, and performances at the cathedral-like Goodhart Hall. Cherished traditions include Lantern Night, when sophomores present freshmen with lanterns in a gesture of passing on "the light of knowledge," and leaving food and other tokens at the statue of Athena, the college's patron goddess, for luck. "It's not a typical college experience," says recent math and computer science grad Natalie Kato of Los Angeles. "But that doesn't mean it's not wonderful." ●

# South

Furman University
Clemson University
• University of South Carolina
College of Charleston

## By MARGARET LOFTUS

Come along with U.S. News on a tour of South Carolina, as we check out a range of college options for you. The trip begins in the historic heart of Charleston, then heads north to the home of the Carolina Gamecocks and on to Tigers country, and ends in Greenville, at Furman University.

# College of Charleston

Ask College of Charleston students what it was about their campus visit that drew them to the school, and you might hear something like, "They had me at the Cistern." Hollywood couldn't conjure a more storybook backdrop for a southern college than this grand grassy yard (named for the oval cistern at its center), shaded by majestic oaks draped with Spanish moss and fronted by 19th-century Randall Hall, a national historic landmark and one of the oldest academic buildings still in use in the country.

Outside the yard's stone walls, campus is concentrated in 20-odd blocks of historic downtown Charleston, its buildings ranging from the sleek and corporate-looking Beatty Center, which houses the business school, to rehabbed "singles," the narrow, deep homes characteristic of the city that house some academic departments. Students consider the city their turf, says Jimmie Foster, assistant vice president for admissions and enrollment management. "King Street is an extension of campus," he says of the historic main thoroughfare and shopping district. Some 30

**UNDERGRADUATES**
Full-time: 9,708

**TOTAL COST\***
In-state: $22,145
Out-of-state: $39,135

**U.S. NEWS RANKING**
Regional Universities, South
**#13**
\*Tuition, fees and room & board

percent of the college population (and 90 percent of freshmen) live on campus, which, like the city itself, is easily negotiated on foot or by using the school's bike share program. Students who want to explore more widely can hop on the city's CARTA bus system for free.

Of 57 majors, the most popular coincide with the region's strong suits. Those pursuing the health sciences conduct undergraduate research at the Medical University of South Carolina a few blocks away; tourism and hospitality students feed into the city's booming hotel industry. Marine biology students benefit from the coastal location and from the recent purchase of Dixie Plantation along the nearby Stono River, whose wetlands, pine forest and tidal marshes will be used for

*Photography by* **BRETT ZIEGLER** *for USN&WR*

# Carolina

research. The college also boasts strong programs in studio art, dance and theater. And the School of Languages, Culture and World Affairs offers one of the most extensive foreign language programs in the region, ranging from ancient Greek to Japanese.

The Honors College enrolls some 700 students, who take 30 percent of their courses – small seminars – through the program and have special opportunities like a semester in Washington and priority access to funds for undergraduate research. They also have the option of living with other honors students in a living-learning community.

**Student stats.** Two-thirds of Charleston undergrads come from the Palmetto State, and the rest are largely from the East Coast. There are more women (64 percent) than men, and minorities now stand at 15 percent of the total population, a figure the school's new president has pledged to increase.

Students rally around Cougars basketball, and enjoy the nearby beaches in warm weather and a thriving nightlife scene on King Street. Many stick around after graduation, says Justin Lyons (class of 2014), a Spanish major from Fort Mill, South Carolina, who plans to find work and stay on for at least a year. "Why," he wonders, "would you want to leave?" ●

Art students tackle welding at the College of Charleston. Below, the choir rehearses.

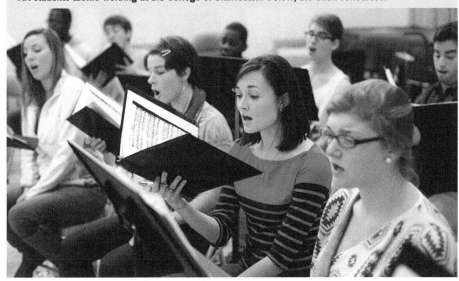

# University of South Carolina
## Columbia

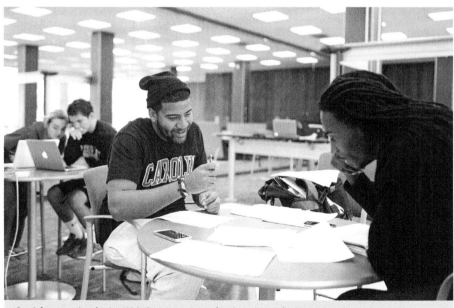

The change of classes at the University of South Carolina is a sea of garnet sweatshirts and baseball caps, moving in waves along the brick paths that crisscross campus. USC students are fanatics about their sports teams, which are named after the Carolina Gamecock, a moniker the British gave to South Carolina planter and revolutionary war hero Thomas Sumter for his fierce fighting tactics. "Sports are a huge part of the culture," says Katy Hallman, a junior public health major from Greenville, South Carolina. So much so that the fight song is played every morning at 9:00. "It puts some pep in your step to make those early classes," she says.

The school was founded in 1801 as part of a movement spurred by Thomas Jefferson to establish public colleges in the South. During the Civil War, its gracious federal-style buildings served as hospitals for both sides, and thus were spared when General William Tecumseh Sherman torched much of Columbia. Today, the university is anchored by the oak-lined lawn known as the horseshoe, flanked by the original buildings that now house honors student apartments, the president's quarters and

**UNDERGRADUATES**
Full-time: **22,533**

**TOTAL COST***
In-state: **$19,725**
Out-of-state: **$37,437**

**U.S. NEWS RANKING**
National Universities
**#113**

*Tuition, fees and room & board

the country's oldest freestanding college library.

While the campus spans some 480 acres, its historic heart feels more like a leafy liberal arts college than the center of a large public university in a city of 132,000. Yes, there's sometimes too much bureaucracy, students say, and occasional lectures with 100-plus attendees. But they also remark on how small the school can seem. "It doesn't feel like 30,000 people are here until you're in the stadium," says Erik Telford of Columbia, who recently graduated with a manage-

ment major. Some 400 student organizations, from the Clarinet Association to the skydiving club, provide newcomers access to others with similar interests.

**Family feel.** "If you find the right place, [it's] going to feel like a family," says Lauren Harper, a sophomore public relations major from Fort Mill, South Carolina. More than a fifth of students belong to a fraternity or sorority, but "if you're not Greek, you're not going to feel left out," says senior broadcast journalism major Sydney Patterson, from Lancaster, an hour or so from campus.

Like a lot of universities, USC boasts multiple living-learning communities – niche housing designed to bring like-minded students together, both in class and socially. Administrators also tout the University 101 class, a semesterlong course to help smooth the transition to college by introducing resources and teaching study skills. "The whole focus is to take a large group and make it a small group," says Jerry Brewer, associate vice president for student life and development. An honors college gives students the opportunity to design their own course of study, take small

**Studying together in the USC library, and pausing for a break in the lounge (at top)**

# Clemson University
## *Clemson*

**UNDERGRADUATES**
Full-time: 16,050

**TOTAL COST***
In-state: $21,524
Out-of-state: $38,958

**U.S. NEWS RANKING**
National Universities
**#62**

*Tuition, fees and room & board

Lest visitors lose their way to Clemson University, a trail of tiger paw prints painted on the highway leads to campus – advance notice of the fervent school spirit at this institution in the foothills of the Blue Ridge. Once you're here, the tiger paw logo and the color orange are ubiquitous. As mechanical engineering senior Chris Hapstack puts it, "our blood runs orange."

Clemson stands on what was once the estate of 19th-century politician John Calhoun, whose son-in-law, Thomas Green Clemson, willed the land and the bulk of his fortune to the state to establish a college. Opened in 1893 as an all-male military college, the school went coed and civilian in 1955; the old family home, Fort Hill, still anchors Clemson's 17,000 acres, which are bordered on the west by Hartwell Lake, a hub of

discussion-based classes and live in a tight-knit community while enjoying access to the facilities of a large university. Roughly 65 percent of the population hails from South Carolina, with most of the out-of-staters coming from the East Coast.

A city that often is defined in terms of its proximity to the beach and mountains (both two hours away), Columbia is becoming a destination in its own right, with a revitalized downtown, a world-class art museum, Riverbanks Zoo and year-round festivals. Nonetheless, the action comes to a halt on the fall Saturdays when the Gamecocks play at home. ●

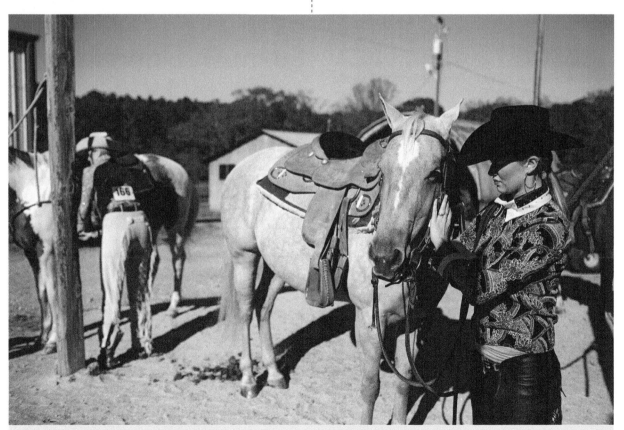

At Clemson University's equine center, members of the equestrian team prepare to head out for a ride.

student recreation.

Despite the size, the main part of campus is walkable, with residential halls encircling the library and academic buildings. The tiny town of Clemson is also within walking distance, and nearby Greenville and Anderson are reachable by a free bus service. While approximately 60 percent of the some 20,000 students are from South Carolina, Director of Admission Robert Barkley says the school has seen an uptick in popularity outside the region. "Thirty years ago we were this sleepy little university in the hills. [Now] it's big-time opportunities with a small-school feel."

**Strong in science.** As a land grant university, the school is particularly strong in the sciences. Engineering is by far the most popular major, pursued by a full third of the freshman class, with business coming in second. The university also boasts a nursing program and the only architectural school in the state.

With faculty members engaged in ongoing studies of everything from computational modeling to the behavior of wild Brazilian monkeys or people using social media, Clemson offers undergraduates ample opportunities to assist professors in their research projects. Two cutting-edge social media "listening centers" feature arrays of large screens that display streams of data from online communities and social media sources and feed research on sentiment and trending topics, for instance. Students can also conduct their own studies through the Creative

Inquiry program, in a team effort that can span up to four semesters.

The Calhoun Honors College offers qualified students smaller, more intimate classes, from a 15-person section of Chemistry 101 to a course on "Harry Potter," as well as the chance to reside together in a living-learning community. Each year, the honors college awards travel grants to support the pursuit of internships, volunteer work and study elsewhere during winter and summer breaks.

Several years ago, Clemson launched a transfer program that invites a select group of students whose applications aren't quite strong enough for admission to come to town and attend community college freshman year. The program provides housing off campus, academic advising and access to university facilities and activities to participating students, three-quarters of whom make the transfer to Clemson for sophomore year.

With few distractions outside of campus besides a handful of bars in town and the Smokin' Pig for an occasional barbecue fix, social activities revolve around football, Greek life (23 percent of students are in sororities or frats) and intramural sports. More than 400 clubs are active, too, from the Fellowship of Christian Athletes and the Darfur Awareness Club to the Model Railroaders. ●

# Furman University
## *Greenville*

With a spring-fed lake, golf course and miles of paved woodland trails, Furman University has a peaceful gated-community feel – conducive, administrators hope, to what they and students both describe as a rigorous academic experience. "It's hard. Get ready to work. But it's worth it," says student body president Brian Boda, a senior from Marietta, Georgia, majoring in political science.

A student-faculty ratio of 11-to-1 keeps average class size to 19 and fosters close relationships between students and professors, students say. "There's no handholding," says Boda, but professors are supportive. He was especially impressed that one of his political science professors spent hours helping him hone a personal statement for a grad school application last semester. Health sci-

**UNDERGRADUATES**
Full-time: 2,675

**TOTAL COST\***
$55,872

**U.S. NEWS RANKING**
National Liberal Arts Colleges
#51

\*Tuition, fees and room & board

portunities with faculty abound. Undergrads are "the primary collaborators," says Brad Pochard, associate vice president for admission. "When they leave here, they have grad-level research experience." Six years ago, the school launched an annual "engage day," during which students present research across campus, with topics ranging from population control policies of China and India to the significance of the millennial vote. Internships are strongly encouraged: Some 68 percent of students now complete at least one at partnering institutions such as Greenville Hospital System, the accounting

**A lakeside study session outside Furman's student center, and hanging out over lunch (below)**

students are from South Carolina; two-thirds are from the Southeast. Pochard says that 15 to 18 percent of the population is considered "nonwhite," including international students; but to some, at least, the campus seems too homogenous and affluent. "I wish it was more diverse," says health sciences major Melanie Brannon, a junior from Roswell, Georgia. A taste of the wider world is provided by the location on the edge of Greenville, a city of 61,000 noted for its lively downtown and arts and music scene. Thanks to the nearby North American headquarters of French tire manufacturer Michelin and German carmaker BMW, the former textile hub has a thriving international community.

**Outdoor action.** Furman fields 20 NCAA Division I teams, and club teams in rugby and cycling are known for being extremely competitive. The region is rich in outdoor recreation, including kayaking, skiing, rock climbing and biking (as the home of former professional cyclist George Hincapie, Greenville is a cycling hub). More than 150 organizations offer the possibility to get active, the most popular of which is the Heller Service Corps, a volunteer organization that involves some 1,800 students a year with 50 partners; they do everything from host a Valentine's dance for adults with special needs to volunteer at animal shelters. A big attraction, says programming director Deanna Heine, a senior from Carrollton, Georgia, is that volunteering gets students "out of the Furman bubble." ●

ences, political science and business administration are the most popular of 45 majors, and the music program is particularly well-regarded; among its alumni is Boston Pops conductor Keith Lockhart.

Though Furman has only two graduate programs, in education and chemistry, research op- firm KPMG in Atlanta, and the U.S. Trade and Development Agency in Washington, D.C. The goal is 100 percent.

About a quarter of

# The
# U.S. NEW
# RANKI

# RANKINGS

# A Close Look at the Methodology

## HOW COLLEGEBOUND STUDENTS CAN MAKE THE MOST OF OUR STATISTICS

*By* **ROBERT J. MORSE AND SAMUEL FLANIGAN**

The host of intangibles that make up the college experience can't be measured by a series of data points. But for families concerned with finding the best academic value for their money, the U.S. News Best Colleges rankings, now in their 30th year, provide an excellent starting point for the search. They allow you to compare at a glance the relative quality of institutions based on such widely accepted indicators of excellence as freshman reten-

tion and graduation rates and the strength of the faculty. And as you check out the data for colleges already on your short list, you may discover unfamiliar schools with similar metrics, and thus broaden your options.

Yes, many factors other than those spotlighted here will figure in your decision, including location and the feel of campus life; the range of academic offerings, activities and sports; and the cost and availability of financial aid. But

BRETT ZIEGLER FOR USN&WR

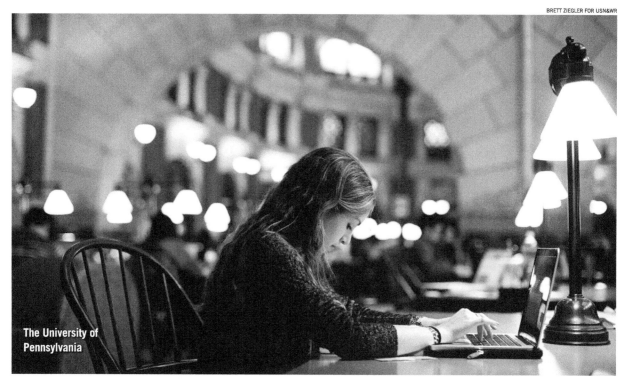

The University of Pennsylvania

**More @** usnews.com/bestcolleges

if you combine the information in this book with campus visits, interviews and your own intuition, our rankings can be a powerful tool in your quest for the right college.

How does the methodology work? The U.S. News ranking system rests on two pillars. The formula uses quantitative measures that education experts have proposed as reliable indicators of academic quality, and it's based on our researched view of what matters in education. First, schools are categorized by their mission, which is derived from the breakdown of types of higher education institutions developed by the Carnegie Foundation for the Advancement of Teaching. The Carnegie classification has been the basis of the Best Colleges ranking category system since our first ranking was published three decades ago, given that it is used extensively by higher education researchers. The U.S. Department of Education and many higher education associations use the system to organize their data and to determine colleges' eligibility for grant money, for example.

In short, the Carnegie categories are the accepted standard. The category names we use are our own – National Universities, National Liberal Arts Colleges, Regional Universities and Regional Colleges – but the definitions of each rely on the Carnegie principles.

The national universities (Page 72) offer a full range of undergraduate majors, plus master's and Ph.D. programs, and emphasize faculty research. The national liberal arts colleges (Page 82) focus almost exclusively on undergraduate education. They award at least 50 percent of their degrees in the arts and sciences.

The regional universities (Page 92) offer a broad scope of undergraduate degrees and some master's degree programs but few, if any, doctoral programs. The regional colleges (Page 108) focus on undergraduate education but grant fewer than 50 percent of their degrees in liberal arts disciplines; this category also includes schools that have small bachelor's degree programs but primarily grant two-year associate degrees. The regional universities and regional colleges are further divided and ranked in four geographical groups: North, South, Midwest and West.

Next, we gather data from each college on up to 16 indicators of academic excellence. Each factor is assigned a weight that reflects our judgment about how much a measure matters. Finally, the colleges and universities in

each category are ranked against their peers, based on their composite weighted score.

Some schools are not ranked and thus do not appear in the tables. The main reason a school falls into this group is that SAT or ACT test scores are not used in admissions decisions for first-time, first-year, degree-seeking applicants. In a few cases, colleges were ineligible because they received too few ratings in the peer assessment survey to be reliably ranked or had a total enrollment of fewer than 200 students, a large proportion of nontraditional students, or no first-year students (as is the situation at so-called upper-division schools).

As a result of these eligibility standards, many of the for-profit institutions are not ranked; their bachelor's degree candidates are largely nontraditional students in degree completion programs, for example, or they don't use test scores in making admissions decisions. We also did not rank a number of highly specialized schools in the arts, business and engineering.

Most of the data come from the colleges themselves, via the U.S. News statistical survey. This year, 91.5 percent of the 1,365 ranked colleges and universities returned their statistical information during our spring and summer data collection period.

For colleges that were eligible to be ranked but declined to fill out our survey, we made extensive use of the data those institutions reported to the U.S. Department of Education's National Center for Education Statistics and other organizations. We obtained missing data on faculty salaries from the American Association of University Professors, for example, information on graduation rates from the National Collegiate Athletic Association and data on alumni giving from the Council for Aid to Education. The National Center for Education Statistics is a rich source on SAT and ACT scores, acceptance rates, retention and graduation rates, student-faculty ratios, and information on financial resources and faculty.

Data that did not come from this year's survey are footnoted, and schools are identified as nonresponders. Estimates may be used in the calculations when schools fail to report data points that are not available from other sources, but estimates are not displayed in the tables. Missing data are reported as N/A.

The indicators we use to capture academic quality fall into a number of categories: assessment by administrators at peer institutions (and, for national universities and

## Measuring What's Important

The U.S. News rankings are based on several key measures of quality, listed below. Scores for each measure are weighted as shown to arrive at a final overall score. In the case of the national universities and national liberal arts colleges, the assessment figure represents input from both academic peers (15 percent) and high school guidance counselors (7.5 percent); for regional universities and colleges, it reflects peer opinion only.

### The Scoring Breakdown

Graduation and retention rates ..............**22.5%**
Assessment of excellence......................**22.5%**
Faculty resources .....................................**20%**
Student selectivity ................................ **12.5%**
Financial resources.................................. **10%**
Graduation rate performance* ................**7.5%**
Alumni giving ..............................................**5%**

*The difference between actual and predicted graduation rates.

liberal arts colleges, by high school guidance counselors as well), how well schools perform at retaining and graduating students, the quality of and investment in the faculty, student selectivity, financial resources and the state of alumni giving. The indicators include input measures that reflect a school's student body, its faculty and its resources, along with outcome measures that signal how well the institution does its job of educating students.

An explanation of the measures and their weightings in the ranking formula follows; more detail on the methodology can be found at usnews.com/collegemeth.

### Assessment by peers and counselors

(22.5 percent). The ranking formula gives significant weight to the opinions of those in a position to judge a school's undergraduate academic excellence. The academic peer assessment survey allows presidents, provosts and deans of admissions to account for intangibles at peer institutions such as faculty dedication to teaching. For their views on the

are judged based on the peer assessment only.

In order to reduce the impact of strategic voting by respondents, we eliminated the two highest and two lowest scores each school received before calculating the average score. Ipsos Public Affairs collected the data in the spring of 2014; of the 4,533 academics who were sent questionnaires, 42 percent responded. The counselors' response rate this past spring was 9 percent.

### Retention (22.5 percent). The higher the proportion of freshmen who return to campus for sophomore year and eventually graduate, the better a school most likely is at offering the classes and services that students need to succeed. This measure has two components: six-year graduation rate (80 percent of the retention score) and freshman retention rate (20 percent).

The graduation rate indicates the average proportion of a graduating class earning a degree in six years or less. We consider freshman classes that started from fall 2004 through fall

## THE RANKINGS provide a launching pad for more research – not an easy answer.

national universities and the national liberal arts colleges, we also surveyed 2,152 counselors at public high schools that appeared in the 2013 U.S. News ranking of Best High Schools and 400 college counselors at the largest independent schools.

Each person surveyed was asked to rate schools' academic programs on a 5-point scale from 1 (marginal) to 5 (distinguished). Those who didn't know enough about a school to evaluate it fairly were asked to mark "don't know." The score used in the rankings is the average of these scores; "don't knows" are not counted.

In the case of the national universities and national liberal arts colleges, the academic peer assessment accounts for 15 percentage points of the weighting, and 7.5 percentage points go to the counselors' ratings. The two most recent years' results were averaged to compute the high school counselor score, a way of reducing year-to-year volatility in the average. The academic peer assessment score continues to be based only on the most recent year's results. (For the full results of the high school counselors' ratings of the colleges, visit usnews.com/counselors.) The regional universities and the regional colleges

2007. Freshman retention indicates the average proportion of freshmen who entered the school in the fall of 2009 through fall 2012 and returned the following fall.

### Faculty resources (20 percent). Research shows that the more satisfied students are about their contact with professors, the more they will learn and the more likely they are to graduate. We use six factors from the 2013-2014 academic year to assess a school's commitment to instruction.

Class size has two components, the proportion of classes with fewer than 20 students (30 percent of the faculty resources score) and the proportion with 50 or more students (10 percent of the score). Faculty salary (35 percent) is the average faculty pay, plus benefits, during the 2012-13 and 2013-14 academic years, adjusted for regional differences in the cost of living using indexes from the consulting firm Runzheimer International.

We also weigh the proportion of professors with the highest degree in their field (15 percent), the student-faculty ratio (5 percent) and the proportion of faculty who are full time (5 percent).

**Student selectivity** (12.5 percent). A school's academic atmosphere is determined in part by the abilities and ambitions of the students. We factor in the admissions test scores for all enrollees who took the critical reading and math portions of the SAT and the composite ACT score (65 percent of the selectivity score); the proportion of enrolled freshmen at national universities and national liberal arts colleges who graduated in the top 10 percent of their high school classes or in the top quarter at regional universities and regional colleges (25 percent); and the acceptance rate, or the ratio of students admitted to applicants (10 percent). The data are all for the fall

Haverford College

2013 entering class. While the ranking calculation takes account of both the SAT and ACT scores of all entering students, the table displays the score range for whichever test was taken by most students.

For the second year, we're using footnotes to more clearly indicate schools that did not report fall 2013 SAT and ACT test scores for all new students for whom they had scores (including athletes, international students, minority students, legacies, those admitted by special arrangement, and those who started in the summer of 2013) or schools that declined to tell us whether all students with scores were represented. We have long discounted the value of such schools' reported scores in the ranking model since the effect of leaving students out could be that lower scores are omitted.

**Financial resources** (10 percent). Generous per-student spending indicates that a college can offer a wide variety of programs and services. U.S. News measures financial resources by using the average spending per student on instruction, research, student services and related educational expenditures in the 2012 and 2013 fiscal years. Spending on sports, dorms and hospitals doesn't count.

**Graduation rate performance** (7.5 percent). For the second year, the graduation rate performance indicator has been applied in all of the Best Colleges ranking categories. This indicator shows the effect of programs and policies on the graduation rate after controlling for spending and student characteristics such as test scores and the proportion receiving Pell grants.

We measure the difference between a school's six-year graduation rate for the class that entered in 2007 and the rate we predicted for the class. If the actual graduation rate is higher than the predicted rate, then the college is enhancing achievement.

**Alumni giving rate** (5 percent). This reflects the average percentage of living alumni with bachelor's degrees who gave to their school during 2011-12 and 2012-13, an indirect measure of student satisfaction.

To arrive at a school's rank, we calculated the weighted sum of its scores. The final scores were rescaled so that the top college or university in each category received a value of 100, and the other schools' weighted scores were calculated as a proportion of that top score. Final scores were rounded to the nearest whole number and ranked in descending order. Schools that are tied appear in alphabetical order.

Be sure to check out usnews.com regularly over the coming year, since we may add content to the Best Colleges pages as we obtain additional information. And as you mine the tables that follow for insights (a sense of which schools might be impressed enough by your SAT or ACT scores to offer some merit aid, for example, or where you will be apt to get the most attention from professors), keep in mind that the rankings provide a launching pad for more research – not an easy answer. ●

| Rank School (State) (*Public) | Overall score | Peer assessment score (5.0=highest) | High school counselor assessment score | Graduation and retention rank | Average freshman retention rate | 2013 graduation rate | | | Faculty resources rank |
|---|---|---|---|---|---|---|---|---|---|
| | | | | | | Predicted | Actual | Over-performance(+) Under-performance(-) | |
| 1. Princeton University (NJ) | 100 | 4.8 | 4.9 | 2 | 98% | 94% | 97% | +3 | 5 |
| 2. Harvard University (MA) | 99 | 4.9 | 4.9 | 2 | 97% | 95% | 97% | +2 | 3 |
| 3. Yale University (CT) | 98 | 4.8 | 4.9 | 1 | 99% | 95% | 98% | +3 | 8 |
| 4. Columbia University (NY) | 95 | 4.6 | 4.9 | 5 | 99% | 94% | 96% | +2 | 4 |
| 4. Stanford University (CA) | 95 | 4.9 | 4.9 | 5 | 98% | 94% | 96% | +2 | 10 |
| 4. University of Chicago | 95 | 4.6 | 4.7 | 10 | 99% | 93% | 93% | None | 1 |
| 7. Massachusetts Inst. of Technology | 93 | 4.9 | 4.9 | 15 | 98% | 95% | 93% | -2 | 12 |
| 8. Duke University (NC) | 92 | 4.4 | 4.8 | 10 | 97% | 94% | 94% | None | 1 |
| 8. University of Pennsylvania | 92 | 4.4 | 4.8 | 2 | 98% | 94% | 96% | +2 | 6 |
| 10. California Institute of Technology | 91 | 4.6 | 4.8 | 22 | 97% | 95% | 93% | -2 | 11 |
| 11. Dartmouth College (NH) | 90 | 4.2 | 4.8 | 5 | 98% | 93% | 95% | +2 | 15 |
| 12. Johns Hopkins University (MD) | 89 | 4.6 | 4.8 | 18 | 97% | 93% | 93% | None | 18 |
| 13. Northwestern University (IL) | 88 | 4.3 | 4.7 | 10 | 97% | 94% | 94% | None | 6 |
| 14. Washington University in St. Louis | 86 | 4.0 | 4.6 | 10 | 97% | 95% | 94% | -1 | 12 |
| 15. Cornell University (NY) | 85 | 4.5 | 4.8 | 15 | 97% | 92% | 93% | +1 | 20 |
| 16. Brown University (RI) | 84 | 4.4 | 4.8 | 5 | 98% | 93% | 94% | +1 | 17 |
| 16. University of Notre Dame (IN) | 84 | 3.9 | 4.7 | 5 | 98% | 92% | 95% | +3 | 16 |
| 16. Vanderbilt University (TN) | 84 | 4.1 | 4.6 | 18 | 97% | 92% | 93% | +1 | 12 |
| 19. Rice University (TX) | 82 | 4.0 | 4.5 | 18 | 97% | 92% | 91% | -1 | 9 |
| 20. University of California–Berkeley* | 79 | 4.7 | 4.7 | 22 | 97% | 87% | 91% | +4 | 32 |
| 21. Emory University (GA) | 77 | 4.0 | 4.5 | 29 | 95% | 92% | 91% | -1 | 24 |
| 21. Georgetown University (DC) | 77 | 4.0 | 4.8 | 15 | 96% | 92% | 92% | None | 44 |
| 23. Univ. of California–Los Angeles* | 76 | 4.2 | 4.5 | 22 | 97% | 86% | 90% | +4 | 32 |
| 23. University of Virginia* | 76 | 4.3 | 4.5 | 10 | 97% | 88% | 93% | +5 | 32 |
| 25. Carnegie Mellon University (PA) | 75 | 4.2 | 4.7 | 32 | 95% | 91% | 88% | -3 | 20 |
| 25. Univ. of Southern California | 75 | 3.9 | 4.3 | 27 | 97% | 91% | 91% | None | 38 |
| 27. Tufts University (MA) | 73 | 3.6 | 4.5 | 18 | 97% | 92% | 92% | None | 31 |
| 27. Wake Forest University (NC) | 73 | 3.5 | 4.4 | 33 | 94% | 89% | 86% | -3 | 28 |
| 29. University of Michigan–Ann Arbor* | 72 | 4.4 | 4.4 | 22 | 97% | 89% | 90% | +1 | 68 |
| 30. U. of North Carolina–Chapel Hill* | 71 | 4.1 | 4.5 | 29 | 97% | 87% | 90% | +3 | 68 |
| 31. Boston College | 69 | 3.6 | 4.4 | 22 | 95% | 90% | 91% | +1 | 53 |
| 32. New York University | 68 | 3.8 | 4.5 | 40 | 92% | 89% | 84% | -5 | 20 |
| 33. College of William and Mary (VA)* | 67 | 3.7 | 4.4 | 27 | 96% | 89% | 90% | +1 | 55 |
| 33. University of Rochester (NY) | 67 | 3.4 | 4.1 | 37 | 96% | 90% | 85% | -5 | 23 |
| 35. Brandeis University (MA) | 66 | 3.5 | 4.1 | 29 | 93% | 91% | 90% | -1 | 49 |
| 35. Georgia Institute of Technology* | 66 | 4.2 | 4.4 | 50 | 95% | 87% | 82% | -5 | 110 |
| 37. Univ. of California–San Diego* | 65 | 3.8 | 4.1 | 35 | 95% | 84% | 86% | +2 | 99 |
| 38. Case Western Reserve Univ. (OH) | 64 | 3.5 | 4.3 | 62 | 93% | 88% | 80% | -8 | 32 |
| 38. University of California–Davis* | 64 | 3.8 | 4.2 | 48 | 93% | 80% | 84% | +4 | 55 |
| 40. Lehigh University (PA) | 63 | 3.3 | 4.1 | 33 | 94% | 91% | 86% | -5 | 41 |
| 40. Univ. of California–Santa Barbara* | 63 | 3.5 | 3.9 | 50 | 92% | 81% | 86% | +5 | 28 |
| 42. Boston University | 62 | 3.5 | 4.2 | 40 | 92% | 84% | 84% | None | 32 |
| 42. Northeastern University (MA) | 62 | 3.2 | 4.2 | 56 | 95% | 79% | 83% | +4 | 24 |
| 42. Rensselaer Polytechnic Inst. (NY) | 62 | 3.4 | 4.2 | 45 | 93% | 89% | 85% | -4 | 41 |
| 42. University of California–Irvine* | 62 | 3.6 | 4.0 | 37 | 94% | 82% | 86% | +4 | 38 |
| 42. U. of Illinois–Urbana-Champaign* | 62 | 3.9 | 4.1 | 40 | 94% | 83% | 84% | +1 | 55 |
| 47. Univ. of Wisconsin–Madison* | 61 | 4.1 | 4.1 | 40 | 95% | 85% | 84% | -1 | 91 |
| 48. Pennsylvania State U.–Univ. Park* | 60 | 3.6 | 4.1 | 37 | 92% | 76% | 85% | +9 | 90 |
| 48. University of Florida* | 60 | 3.6 | 3.8 | 35 | 96% | 83% | 87% | +4 | 99 |
| 48. University of Miami (FL) | 60 | 3.2 | 4.0 | 62 | 91% | 86% | 82% | -4 | 44 |
| 48. University of Washington* | 60 | 3.8 | 4.0 | 56 | 93% | 80% | 82% | +2 | 144 |
| 48. Yeshiva University (NY) | 60 | 2.8 | 3.4 | 40 | 91% | 83% | 89% | +6 | 24 |

**Note:** Key to footnotes, Page 80.

# sities

| % of classes under 20 ('13) | % of classes of 50 or more ('13) | Student/faculty ratio ('13) | Selectivity rank | SAT/ACT 25th-75th percentile ('13) | Freshmen in top 10% of HS class ('13) | Acceptance rate ('13) | Financial resources rank | Alumni giving rank | Average alumni giving rate |
|---|---|---|---|---|---|---|---|---|---|
| 71% | 11% | 6/1 | 5 | 1410-1600 | 95%[5] | 7% | 10 | 1 | 63% |
| 76% | 10% | 7/1 | 5 | 1410-1600 | 95%[5] | 6% | 5 | 10 | 35% |
| 77% | 7% | 6/1 | 3 | 1420-1590 | 95%[5] | 7% | 1 | 7 | 36% |
| 82% | 9% | 6/1 | 5 | 1400-1570 | 93%[5] | 7% | 11 | 13 | 34% |
| 69% | 12% | 5/1 | 5 | 1380-1570 | 96%[5] | 6% | 8 | 7 | 36% |
| 76% | 5% | 6/1 | 3 | 1440-1590 | 98% | 9% | 6 | 4 | 40% |
| 69% | 12% | 8/1 | 1 | 1430-1570 | 99%[5] | 8% | 7 | 6 | 37% |
| 71% | 6% | 7/1 | 14 | 1360-1550 | 90%[5] | 12% | 14 | 10 | 35% |
| 68% | 10% | 6/1 | 10 | 1360-1540 | 94%[5] | 12% | 11 | 15 | 34% |
| 63% | 10% | 3/1 | 1 | 1490-1600 | 99%[5] | 11% | 1 | 30 | 23% |
| 62% | 9% | 8/1 | 10 | 1360-1560 | 90%[5] | 10% | 16 | 2 | 48% |
| 72% | 10% | 10/1 | 18 | 1340-1520 | 84%[5] | 17% | 3 | 12 | 34% |
| 75% | 7% | 7/1 | 10 | 1390-1550 | 91%[5] | 14% | 11 | 24 | 26% |
| 65% | 12% | 8/1 | 5 | 32-34 | 95%[5] | 16% | 4 | 19 | 27% |
| 56% | 18% | 9/1 | 20 | 1320-1520 | 87%[5] | 16% | 17 | 16 | 30% |
| 69% | 10% | 8/1 | 39 | 1330-1540[3] | 94%[5] | 9% | 24 | 5 | 38% |
| 60% | 9% | 10/1 | 15 | 32-34 | 90%[5] | 22% | 29 | 3 | 42% |
| 65% | 9% | 8/1 | 10 | 32-34 | 88%[5] | 13% | 15 | 27 | 26% |
| 68% | 10% | 6/1 | 15 | 1370-1550 | 87% | 17% | 23 | 17 | 29% |
| 60% | 16% | 17/1 | 20 | 1250-1500 | 98% | 18% | 38 | 98 | 13% |
| 59% | 8% | 8/1 | 29 | 1260-1470 | 76%[5] | 27% | 18 | 18 | 28% |
| 60% | 7% | 11/1 | 18 | 1320-1500 | 92%[5] | 17% | 29 | 19 | 26% |
| 50% | 22% | 17/1 | 25 | 1190-1450 | 97% | 20% | 20 | 104 | 12% |
| 55% | 16% | 16/1 | 24 | 1250-1460 | 92%[5] | 30% | 59 | 32 | 22% |
| 67% | 11% | 13/1 | 22 | 1340-1530 | 80%[5] | 25% | 29 | 54 | 17% |
| 57% | 13% | 9/1 | 22 | 1280-1480 | 88%[5] | 20% | 26 | 13 | 34% |
| 68% | 8% | 9/1 | 15 | 1370-1520 | 91%[5] | 19% | 29 | 37 | 20% |
| 57% | 1% | 11/1 | 32 | 1230-1420[2] | 76%[5] | 35% | 9 | 24 | 26% |
| 47% | 18% | 15/1 | 39 | 28-32 | 65%[4] | 33% | 41 | 46 | 19% |
| 39% | 13% | 13/1 | 32 | 1200-1410 | 78% | 27% | 34 | 42 | 20% |
| 51% | 7% | 13/1 | 25 | 1270-1450 | 81%[5] | 32% | 71 | 24 | 26% |
| 62% | 9% | 10/1 | 45 | 1260-1460 | 63%[5] | 32% | 34 | 147 | 9% |
| 48% | 8% | 12/1 | 25 | 1270-1460 | 80%[5] | 33% | 110 | 29 | 24% |
| 70% | 13% | 10/1 | 30 | 1250-1450[2] | 75%[5] | 36% | 21 | 52 | 18% |
| 60% | 10% | 10/1 | 42 | 1230-1470 | 65%[5] | 37% | 52 | 19 | 27% |
| 39% | 25% | 18/1 | 28 | 1290-1480 | 81%[5] | 41% | 43 | 19 | 27% |
| 40% | 35% | 19/1 | 30 | 1180-1400 | 100% | 37% | 21 | 166 | 8% |
| 64% | 11% | 10/1 | 32 | 1270-1480 | 67%[5] | 42% | 26 | 42 | 20% |
| 40% | 23% | 17/1 | 50 | 1080-1340 | 100% | 41% | 28 | 156 | 8% |
| 48% | 11% | 10/1 | 43 | 1220-1410 | 60%[5] | 31% | 55 | 30 | 23% |
| 49% | 18% | 17/1 | 39 | 1130-1370 | 100% | 40% | 69 | 60 | 16% |
| 62% | 12% | 13/1 | 50 | 1190-1390 | 58%[5] | 37% | 47 | 132 | 9% |
| 66% | 7% | 13/1 | 32 | 1300-1480 | 64%[5] | 32% | 82 | 104 | 12% |
| 51% | 13% | 15/1 | 36 | 1290-1488 | 72%[5] | 41% | 43 | 98 | 12% |
| 50% | 20% | 19/1 | 64 | 1040-1290 | 96% | 41% | 46 | 196 | 6% |
| 42% | 20% | 18/1 | 50 | 26-31 | 55%[5] | 62% | 64 | 127 | 10% |
| 46% | 19% | 17/1 | 54 | 26-30 | 51% | 51% | 59 | 132 | 9% |
| 42% | 13% | 17/1 | 107 | 1070-1280 | 36%[5] | 55% | 52 | 65 | 15% |
| 47% | 16% | 21/1 | 45 | 1170-1360 | 77% | 47% | 47 | 72 | 15% |
| 50% | 8% | 12/1 | 36 | 1230-1420 | 72%[5] | 40% | 25 | 65 | 15% |
| 34% | 22% | 11/1 | 54 | 1100-1360 | 92%[5] | 55% | 34 | 75 | 14% |
| 64% | 1% | 6/1 | 88 | 1100-1370 | 45% | 82% | 18 | 48 | 18% |

## What Is a National University?

•••••

To assess nearly 1,600 of the country's four-year colleges and universities, U.S. News first assigns each to a group of its peers, based on the categories of higher education institutions developed in 2010 by the Carnegie Foundation for the Advancement of Teaching. The National Universities category consists of the 280 institutions (173 public, 100 private and seven for-profit) that offer a wide range of undergraduate majors as well as master's and doctoral degrees; some emphasize research. A list of the top 30 public national universities appears on Page 80.

Data on up to 16 indicators of academic quality are gathered from each institution and tabulated. Schools are ranked by their total weighted score; those receiving the same rank are tied and listed in alphabetical order. For a description of the methodology, see Page 68, and for more on a college, turn to the directory at the back of the book.

| Rank | School (State) (*Public) | Overall score | Peer assessment score (5.0=highest) | High school counselor assessment score | Average freshman retention rate | 2013 graduation rate Predicted | 2013 graduation rate Actual | % of classes under 20 ('13) | % of classes of 50 or more ('13) | SAT/ACT 25th-75th percentile ('13) | Freshmen in top 10% of HS class ('13) | Acceptance rate ('13) | Average alumni giving rate |
|---|---|---|---|---|---|---|---|---|---|---|---|---|---|
| 53. | University of Texas–Austin* | 59 | 4.0 | 4.2 | 93% | 82% | 79% | 35% | 26% | 1140-1380 | 75% | 40% | 12% |
| 54. | George Washington University (DC) | 58 | 3.5 | 4.3 | 93% | 87% | 81% | 56% | 9% | 1200-1390 | 50%[5] | 34% | 9% |
| 54. | Ohio State University–Columbus* | 58 | 3.7 | 4.1 | 93% | 80% | 83% | 30% | 23% | 27-31 | 58% | 56% | 14% |
| 54. | Pepperdine University (CA) | 58 | 3.2 | 4.3 | 91% | 78% | 80% | 68% | 3% | 1130-1340 | 47%[5] | 37% | 9% |
| 54. | Tulane University (LA) | 58 | 3.4 | 4.2 | 90% | 82% | 76% | 64% | 6% | 29-32[3] | 58%[5] | 26% | 18% |
| 58. | Fordham University (NY) | 57 | 3.2 | 4.1 | 89% | 78% | 80% | 51% | 1% | 1160-1350 | 47%[5] | 47% | 20% |
| 58. | Southern Methodist University (TX) | 57 | 3.0 | 3.9 | 90% | 77% | 79% | 59% | 7% | 27-31 | 48%[5] | 51% | 21% |
| 58. | Syracuse University (NY) | 57 | 3.3 | 4.0 | 92% | 75% | 81% | 63% | 9% | 1040-1270 | 39%[5] | 49% | 16% |
| 58. | University of Connecticut* | 57 | 3.1 | 4.0 | 93% | 76% | 83% | 47% | 17% | 1130-1330 | 45%[5] | 54% | 17% |
| 62. | Brigham Young Univ.–Provo (UT) | 56 | 3.0 | 4.0 | 87% | 78% | 77% | 57% | 14% | 26-31 | 54% | 49% | 14% |
| 62. | Clemson University (SC)* | 56 | 3.1 | 4.0 | 91% | 77% | 82% | 51% | 14% | 1150-1340 | 56% | 57% | 24% |
| 62. | Purdue Univ.–West Lafayette (IN)* | 56 | 3.6 | 4.2 | 90% | 68% | 71% | 38% | 18% | 1080-1320 | 47%[5] | 60% | 20% |
| 62. | University of Georgia* | 56 | 3.4 | 4.0 | 94% | 81% | 83% | 40% | 11% | 1150-1330 | 53% | 55% | 11% |
| 62. | Univ. of Maryland–College Park* | 56 | 3.6 | 4.0 | 95% | 84% | 84% | 44% | 17% | 1200-1420 | 71% | 47% | 8% |
| 62. | University of Pittsburgh* | 56 | 3.4 | 3.9 | 92% | 78% | 80% | 41% | 19% | 1180-1360 | 53% | 54% | 11% |
| 68. | Texas A&M Univ.–College Station* | 55 | 3.6 | 4.1 | 92% | 75% | 81% | 21% | 25% | 1070-1290 | 53% | 69% | 22% |
| 68. | Worcester Polytechnic Inst. (MA) | 55 | 2.9 | 4.0 | 96% | 84% | 81% | 65% | 11% | 1220-1410[2] | 64% | 52% | 14% |
| 70. | Rutgers, St. U. of N.J.–New Brunswick* | 53 | 3.4 | 4.0 | 92% | 75% | 79% | 35% | 21% | 1090-1330 | 38%[5] | 60% | 8% |
| 71. | American University (DC) | 52 | 3.1 | 4.0 | 90% | 83% | 80% | 47% | 2% | 1160-1350[2] | 47%[5] | 43% | 9% |
| 71. | Baylor University (TX) | 52 | 3.2 | 4.1 | 86% | 77% | 75% | 51% | 10% | 24-29 | 42% | 57% | 15% |
| 71. | University of Iowa* | 52 | 3.5 | 3.8 | 86% | 65% | 70% | 55% | 12% | 23-28 | 24% | 80% | 9% |
| 71. | Univ. of Minnesota–Twin Cities* | 52 | 3.6 | 3.9 | 90% | 78% | 75% | 39% | 20% | 26-30 | 45% | 44% | 10% |
| 71. | Virginia Tech* | 52 | 3.4 | 4.0 | 92%[8] | 78% | 83% | 27% | 20% | 1120-1320 | 41% | 70% | 13% |
| 76. | Clark University (MA) | 50 | 2.8 | 3.8 | 90% | 76% | 81% | 58% | 5% | 1110-1320[2] | 38%[5] | 62% | 16% |
| 76. | Indiana University–Bloomington* | 50 | 3.6 | 4.0 | 89% | 70% | 77% | 36% | 17% | 1060-1290 | 35%[5] | 72% | 14% |
| 76. | Marquette University (WI) | 50 | 3.0 | 3.9 | 89% | 73% | 78% | 41% | 13% | 25-29 | 36%[5] | 57% | 15% |
| 76. | Miami University–Oxford (OH)* | 50 | 3.1 | 3.9 | 89% | 73% | 81% | 30% | 12% | 25-30 | 39%[5] | 67% | 19% |
| 76. | Stevens Institute of Technology (NJ) | 50 | 2.7 | 3.8 | 94% | 82% | 79% | 38% | 9% | 1210-1390 | 68%[5] | 38% | 15% |
| 76. | SUNY Col. of Envir. Sci. and Forestry* | 50 | 2.8 | 3.7 | 86% | 63% | 72% | 66% | 9% | 1080-1260 | 27% | 51% | 22% |
| 76. | Texas Christian University | 50 | 2.8 | 3.9 | 88% | 71% | 76% | 41% | 7% | 25-29 | 42%[5] | 47% | 22% |
| 76. | University of Delaware* | 50 | 3.1 | 3.8 | 92% | 77% | 82% | 33% | 16% | 1090-1300 | 37%[5] | 63% | 10% |
| 76. | Univ. of Massachusetts–Amherst* | 50 | 3.2 | 4.0 | 89% | 65% | 73% | 44% | 19% | 1110-1310 | 28%[5] | 63% | 10% |
| 85. | Michigan State University* | 49 | 3.5 | 3.9 | 91% | 70% | 78% | 25% | 22% | 23-28[3] | 28%[5] | 69% | 12% |
| 85. | Univ. of California–Santa Cruz* | 49 | 3.0 | 3.8 | 90% | 78% | 76% | 46% | 25% | 1000-1280 | 96% | 52% | 6% |
| 85. | University of Vermont* | 49 | 2.9 | 3.7 | 86% | 68% | 76% | 52% | 14% | 1080-1290 | 33%[5] | 78% | 11% |
| 88. | Binghamton University–SUNY* | 48 | 2.9 | 3.8 | 91% | 79% | 81% | 45% | 14% | 1203-1385 | 52%[5] | 42% | 7% |
| 88. | Colorado School of Mines* | 48 | 3.3 | 4.1 | 90% | 80% | 70% | 24% | 17% | 28-32 | 66% | 36% | 18% |
| 88. | Stony Brook–SUNY* | 48 | 3.2 | 3.6 | 90% | 70% | 66% | 43% | 21% | 1150-1350 | 47%[5] | 39% | 9% |
| 88. | University of Alabama* | 48 | 3.0 | 3.7 | 86% | 65% | 67% | 43% | 18% | 22-30 | 41% | 57% | 36% |
| 88. | University of Colorado–Boulder* | 48 | 3.5 | 3.8 | 85% | 68% | 70% | 47% | 16% | 24-29 | 27% | 88% | 8% |
| 88. | University of Denver | 48 | 2.8 | 3.6 | 87% | 73% | 78% | 50% | 6% | 25-30 | 45%[5] | 77% | 9% |
| 88. | University of Tulsa (OK) | 48 | 2.6 | 3.6 | 88% | 81% | 69% | 62% | 2% | 25-32 | 74%[5] | 41% | 21% |
| 95. | Drexel University (PA) | 47 | 3.0 | 4.0 | 85% | 73% | 70% | 57% | 7% | 1070-1310 | 33%[5] | 82% | 9% |
| 95. | Florida State University* | 47 | 3.0 | 3.6 | 92% | 69% | 77% | 34% | 15% | 25-29 | 42% | 57% | 18% |
| 95. | North Carolina State U.–Raleigh* | 47 | 3.1 | 3.8 | 92% | 74% | 74% | 28% | 17% | 1150-1320 | 50% | 47% | 13% |
| 95. | University of San Diego | 47 | 2.8 | 3.9 | 89% | 76% | 75% | 39% | 0.3% | 1110-1320 | 45% | 49% | 12% |
| 99. | St. Louis University | 46 | 2.9 | 3.9 | 86% | 74% | 70% | 54% | 8% | 25-30 | 41%[5] | 64% | 13% |
| 99. | Univ. of Missouri* | 46 | 3.3 | 3.7 | 84% | 66% | 70% | 42% | 16% | 23-28 | 27% | 79% | 16% |
| 99. | Univ. of Nebraska–Lincoln* | 46 | 3.1 | 3.8 | 84% | 64% | 67% | 41% | 15% | 22-28 | 26% | 64% | 21% |
| 99. | University of New Hampshire* | 46 | 2.8 | 3.7 | 87% | 65% | 80% | 44% | 16% | 1000-1210 | 20% | 78% | 8% |
| 103. | Auburn University (AL)* | 45 | 3.1 | 3.9 | 89% | 67% | 68% | 30% | 16% | 24-30 | 29% | 83% | 11% |
| 103. | University at Buffalo–SUNY* | 45 | 3.0 | 3.7 | 88% | 65% | 72% | 33% | 21% | 1050-1260 | 28%[5] | 57% | 8% |
| 103. | University of Dayton (OH) | 45 | 2.6 | 3.5 | 88% | 67% | 77% | 35% | 4% | 24-29 | 24%[5] | 52% | 15% |
| 106. | Iowa State University* | 44 | 3.2 | 3.8 | 87% | 66% | 68% | 30% | 23% | 22-28 | 25% | 85% | 14% |
| 106. | Loyola University Chicago | 44 | 2.9 | 4.0 | 86% | 73% | 71% | 38% | 7% | 24-29 | 37%[5] | 91% | 11% |
| 106. | University of Kansas* | 44 | 3.3 | 3.8 | 80% | 67% | 62% | 45% | 12% | 22-28 | 26% | 88% | 16% |
| 106. | University of Oklahoma* | 44 | 3.0 | 3.8 | 84% | 69% | 66% | 41% | 11% | 23-29 | 33% | 80% | 19% |
| 106. | University of Oregon* | 44 | 3.3 | 3.9 | 86% | 62% | 67% | 38% | 21% | 990-1240 | 25%[5] | 74% | 10% |
| 106. | University of San Francisco | 44 | 2.8 | 3.8 | 86% | 64% | 69% | 52% | 3% | 1070-1270 | 33%[5] | 61% | 9% |
| 106. | University of Tennessee* | 44 | 3.1 | 3.8 | 86% | 72% | 68% | 29% | 15% | 24-29 | 52%[5] | 72% | 10% |
| 113. | Univ. of California–Riverside* | 43 | 3.1 | 3.8 | 88% | 70% | 69% | 28% | 30% | 990-1210 | 94% | 60% | 4% |
| 113. | Univ. of South Carolina* | 43 | 2.9 | 3.8 | 87% | 70% | 73% | 33% | 16% | 1110-1300 | 30% | 64% | 18% |
| 113. | University of St. Thomas (MN) | 43 | 2.5 | 3.6 | 88% | 66% | 75% | 41% | 2% | 23-28[3] | 22% | 86% | 18% |
| 116. | Catholic University of America (DC) | 42 | 2.7 | 3.7 | 82% | 62% | 69% | 61% | 5% | 1010-1220 | N/A | 60% | 8% |

**Note:** Key to footnotes, Page 80.

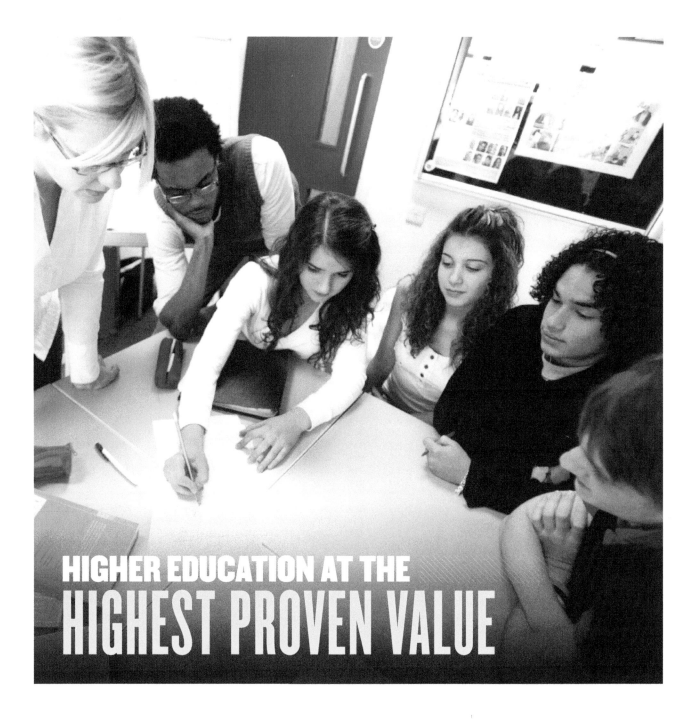

# HIGHER EDUCATION AT THE
# HIGHEST PROVEN VALUE

## TOP 40 BEST VALUE
### IN PUBLIC COLLEGES
KIPLINGER

We get it — higher education is an expensive investment. So we're increasing scholarships. Managing costs. And doing everything we can to increase the long-term value of a Purdue degree. Because when we say that big ideas are at the core of higher education — we mean it. Which is why we're forging the way in STEM leadership by investing in our students. And changing the world as a result.

## PURDUE
### UNIVERSITY

purdue.edu/purduemoves

**WE ARE PURDUE. WHAT WE MAKE MOVES THE WORLD FORWARD.**

EA/EOU

| Rank School (State) (*Public) | Overall score | Peer assessment score (5.0=highest) | High school counselor assessment score | Average freshman retention rate | 2013 graduation rate Predicted | 2013 graduation rate Actual | % of classes under 20 ('13) | % of classes of 50 or more ('13) | SAT/ACT 25th-75th percentile ('13) | Freshmen in top 10% of HS class ('13) | Accept-ance rate ('13) | Average alumni giving rate |
|---|---|---|---|---|---|---|---|---|---|---|---|---|
| 116. Duquesne University (PA) | 42 | 2.6 | 3.7 | 87% | 65% | 76% | 44% | 8% | 1050-1220² | 27% | 74% | 8% |
| 116. Illinois Institute of Technology | 42 | 2.7 | 3.7 | 93% | 80% | 63% | 59% | 7% | 25-30 | 45%⁵ | 57% | 9% |
| 116. Michigan Technological University* | 42 | 2.7 | 3.9 | 82% | 69% | 66% | 47% | 13% | 24-29 | 30% | 78% | 13% |
| 116. University of the Pacific (CA) | 42 | 2.6 | 3.7 | 86% | 73% | 63% | 52% | 5% | 1030-1320 | 36% | 73% | 11% |
| 121. Clarkson University (NY) | 41 | 2.7 | 3.6 | 87% | 73% | 75% | 35% | 24% | 1090-1290 | 40% | 64% | 14% |
| 121. Colorado State University* | 41 | 2.9 | 3.6 | 85% | 60% | 64% | 37% | 19% | 22-27 | 22% | 77% | 9% |
| 121. DePaul University (IL) | 41 | 2.8 | 3.7 | 86% | 61% | 70% | 41% | 1% | 23-28² | 25%⁵ | 60% | 6% |
| 121. Temple University (PA)* | 41 | 2.9 | 3.8 | 88% | 58% | 66% | 38% | 7% | 1010-1230² | 20% | 64% | 7% |
| 121. University of Arizona* | 41 | 3.5 | 3.7 | 79% | 65% | 61% | 37% | 16% | 970-1220² | 31% | 78% | 6% |
| 126. Rutgers, The State U. of N.J.–Newark* | 40 | 2.7 | 3.8 | 85% | 55% | 67% | 29% | 18% | 960-1158 | 22% | 54% | 5% |
| 126. Seton Hall University (NJ) | 40 | 2.7 | 3.8 | 82% | 59% | 64% | 47% | 3% | 1020-1220 | 35% | 79% | 7% |
| 126. University at Albany–SUNY* | 40 | 2.8 | 3.6 | 84% | 58% | 66% | 23% | 20% | 1010-1180 | 19% | 56% | 7% |
| 129. Arizona State University–Tempe* | 39 | 3.2 | 3.6 | 83% | 56% | 59% | 43% | 18% | 1020-1270² | 31% | 80% | 8% |
| 129. Louisiana State Univ.–Baton Rouge* | 39 | 2.8 | 3.5 | 84% | 65% | 69% | 36% | 20% | 23-28 | 25% | 75% | 11% |
| 129. Ohio University* | 39 | 2.9 | 3.7 | 80% | 52% | 67% | 35% | 16% | 22-26 | 17% | 73% | 7% |
| 129. University of Cincinnati* | 39 | 2.7 | 3.5 | 85% | 58% | 64% | 42% | 13% | 22-28 | 22% | 73% | 13% |
| 129. University of Kentucky* | 39 | 2.9 | 3.7 | 82% | 61% | 60% | 30% | 17% | 22-28 | 31% | 69% | 17% |
| 129. University of Utah* | 39 | 3.0 | 3.5 | 87% | 60% | 60% | 35% | 22% | 21-27 | 21%⁵ | 82% | 11% |
| 135. Hofstra University (NY) | 38 | 2.8 | 3.7 | 78% | 68% | 62% | 50% | 4% | 1050-1230² | 24%⁵ | 59% | 10% |
| 135. New School (NY) | 38 | 2.7 | 3.9 | 82% | 64% | 65% | 89% | 1% | 990-1240² | 15%⁴ | 67% | 3% |
| 135. University of Arkansas* | 38 | 2.8 | 3.4 | 82% | 68% | 60% | 44% | 18% | 23-28 | 28% | 59% | 27% |
| 138. George Mason University (VA)* | 37 | 3.0 | 3.9 | 87% | 62% | 67% | 29% | 15% | 1050-1250² | 20%⁵ | 62% | 5% |
| 138. Missouri Univ. of Science & Tech.* | 37 | 2.7 | 3.6 | 84% | 72% | 63% | 30% | 20% | 25-31 | 41% | 82% | 16% |
| 138. Oregon State University* | 37 | 2.9 | 3.7 | 83% | 53% | 61% | 28% | 23% | 970-1220 | 25% | 79% | 12% |
| 138. Washington State University* | 37 | 3.0 | 3.5 | 82% | 62% | 65% | 37% | 20% | 910-1150 | 30% | 82% | 14% |
| 142. Illinois State University* | 36 | 2.4 | 3.5 | 84% | 55% | 72% | 34% | 11% | 22-26³ | N/A | 69% | 7% |
| 142. Kansas State University* | 36 | 2.9 | 3.7 | 81% | 64% | 60% | 41% | 13% | 21-27² | 22% | 96% | 22% |
| 142. St. John Fisher College (NY) | 36 | 2.2 | 3.2 | 83% | 60% | 73% | 45% | 0.3% | 990-1170 | 26% | 63% | 15% |
| 145. Howard University (DC) | 35 | 2.8 | 3.9 | 82% | 57% | 61% | 42% | 10% | 980-1190³ | 23% | 57% | 5% |
| 145. Oklahoma State University* | 35 | 2.7 | 3.5 | 79% | 64% | 61% | 36% | 12% | 22-28 | 28% | 76% | 14% |
| 145. St. John's University (NY) | 35 | 2.7 | 3.8 | 78% | 52% | 55% | 38% | 6% | 990-1210 | 17%⁴ | 53% | 5% |
| 145. University of Texas–Dallas* | 35 | 2.7 | 3.8 | 86% | 74% | 63% | 25% | 27% | 1150-1370 | 38% | 59% | 3% |
| 149. Adelphi University (NY) | 34 | 2.2 | 3.3 | 82% | 58% | 63% | 52% | 2% | 1020-1220⁹ | 26%⁵ | 68% | 7% |
| 149. New Jersey Inst. of Technology* | 34 | 2.6 | 3.5 | 83% | 64% | 58% | 28% | 8% | 1030-1250 | 27%⁵ | 65% | 9% |
| 149. San Diego State University* | 34 | 2.8 | 3.6 | 88% | 52% | 67% | 26% | 26% | 1000-1200 | 27% | 37% | 5% |
| 149. University of Alabama–Birmingham* | 34 | 2.7 | 3.4 | 80% | 62% | 53% | 42% | 15% | 22-28 | 30% | 87% | 12% |
| 149. University of Illinois–Chicago* | 34 | 3.0 | 3.7 | 80% | 63% | 57% | 38% | 19% | 22-26³ | 24% | 71% | 4% |
| 149. Univ. of Maryland–Baltimore County* | 34 | 2.8 | 3.6 | 86% | 68% | 65% | 39% | 12% | 1110-1310 | 25% | 63% | 4% |
| 149. University of Mississippi* | 34 | 2.7 | 3.5 | 83% | 55% | 58% | 42% | 17% | 21-27² | 24% | 59% | 14% |
| 156. Maryville Univ. of St. Louis | 32 | 1.9 | 3.3 | 85% | 63% | 67% | 69% | 0.2% | 23-27 | 27% | 76% | 7% |
| 156. Mississippi State University* | 32 | 2.5 | 3.4 | 81% | 60% | 59%⁶ | 37% | 14% | 20-28 | 28% | 71% | 16% |
| 156. Texas Tech University* | 32 | 2.8 | 3.6 | 82% | 58% | 59% | 24% | 20% | 1010-1210 | 22% | 66% | 13% |
| 156. Univ. of Massachusetts–Lowell* | 32 | 2.4 | 3.6 | 81% | 55% | 54% | 50% | 5% | 1030-1230 | 22%⁵ | 64% | 11% |
| 156. Virginia Commonwealth University* | 32 | 2.8 | 3.7 | 86% | 54% | 57% | 31% | 17% | 1000-1210 | 20% | 64% | 5% |
| 161. Biola University (CA) | 31 | 1.9 | 3.5 | 86% | 62% | 69% | 47% | 6% | 1000-1240 | 33%⁵ | 75% | 11% |
| 161. University of Louisville (KY)* | 31 | 2.7 | 3.6 | 78% | 60% | 53% | 31% | 10% | 22-28³ | 20%⁴ | 71% | 14% |
| 161. University of Rhode Island* | 31 | 2.7 | 3.5 | 81% | 60% | 60% | 34% | 11% | 1000-1210³ | 19% | 76% | 6% |
| 161. University of South Florida* | 31 | 2.7 | 3.3 | 89% | 65% | 63% | 28% | 14% | 1080-1260 | 36% | 45% | 13% |
| 161. University of Wyoming* | 31 | 2.6 | 3.4 | 74% | 60% | 54% | 43% | 10% | 22-27 | 23% | 96% | 9%⁴ |
| 166. University of Idaho* | 30 | 2.6 | 3.5 | 79% | 54% | 54% | 49% | 11% | 910-1170 | 16% | 65% | 9% |
| 166. University of La Verne (CA) | 30 | 1.9 | 3.2 | 85% | 52% | 59% | 62% | 1% | 950-1130 | 23% | 34% | 6% |
| 168. Andrews University (MI) | 29 | 1.7 | 3.3 | 79% | 54% | 60% | 67% | 8% | 20-27 | 22%⁵ | 39% | 6% |
| 168. University of Hawaii–Manoa* | 29 | 2.7 | 3.1 | 78% | 63% | 57% | 50% | 13% | 970-1200³ | 27% | 80% | 7% |
| 168. University of North Dakota* | 29 | 2.5 | 3.6 | 76% | 54% | 55% | 41% | 9% | 21-26³ | 15% | 71% | 12% |
| 168. University of South Dakota* | 29 | 2.4 | 3.6 | 76% | 51% | 56% | 50% | 6% | 21-26 | 15% | 88% | 8% |
| 168. West Virginia University* | 29 | 2.6 | 3.2 | 78% | 55% | 57% | 36% | 19% | 21-26 | 20%⁵ | 85% | 13% |
| 173. Azusa Pacific University (CA) | 28 | 1.9 | 3.4 | 85% | 62% | 65% | 59% | 3% | 980-1190 | 27% | 82% | 7%⁴ |
| 173. Ball State University (IN)* | 28 | 2.5 | 3.4 | 79% | 53% | 60% | 33% | 9% | 980-1170² | 19% | 61% | 11% |
| 173. Bowling Green State University (OH)* | 28 | 2.5 | 3.4 | 72% | 47% | 54% | 46% | 8% | 20-25 | 12% | 72% | 7% |
| 173. Florida Institute of Technology | 28 | 2.2 | 3.3 | 79% | 66% | 54% | 53% | 5% | 1030-1260³ | 28%⁵ | 60% | 20% |
| 173. Pace University (NY) | 28 | 2.3 | 3.6 | 77% | 56% | 51% | 51% | 2% | 940-1150 | 13%⁵ | 81% | 5% |
| 173. University of Central Florida* | 28 | 2.6 | 3.1 | 87% | 71% | 67% | 29% | 24% | 1090-1270 | 30% | 49% | 10% |
| 173. University of Maine* | 28 | 2.5 | 3.5 | 79% | 58% | 56% | 45% | 15% | 950-1190 | 19% | 83% | 7%⁴ |
| 173. Western Michigan University* | 28 | 2.3 | 3.3 | 74% | 47% | 55% | 39% | 10% | 19-25 | 12% | 83% | 6% |

**Note:** Key to footnotes, Page 80.

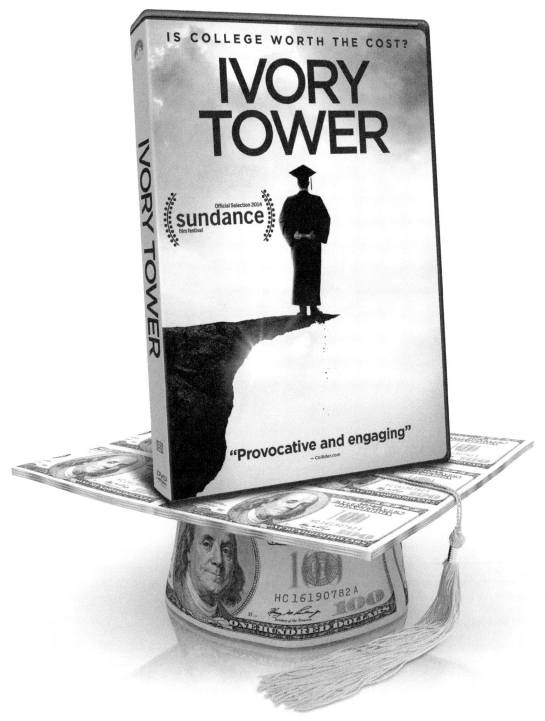

# "I urge anyone dealing with the insanity of financing a college education to see this movie..."

— Robin Abcarian, *LOS ANGELES TIMES*

**OWN IT NOW ON DIGITAL HD**
**ON DVD SEPTEMBER 30**

| Rank | School (State) (*Public) | Overall score | Peer assessment score (5.0=highest) | High school counselor assessment score | Average freshman retention rate | 2013 graduation rate | | % of classes under 20 ('13) | % of classes of 50 or more ('13) | SAT/ACT 25th-75th percentile ('13) | Freshmen in top 10% of HS class ('13) | Acceptance rate ('13) | Average alumni giving rate |
|---|---|---|---|---|---|---|---|---|---|---|---|---|---|
| | | | | | | Predicted | Actual | | | | | | |
| 181. | Edgewood College (WI) | 27 | 1.7 | 3.1 | 80% | 50% | 57% | 78% | 0% | 20-25 | 15% | 77% | 11% |
| 181. | Immaculata University (PA) | 27 | 1.9 | 3.0 | 82% | 42% | 48% | 86% | 0.2% | 830-1060 | N/A | 82% | 12% |
| 181. | North Dakota State University* | 27 | 2.4 | 3.7 | 78% | 53% | 53% | 30% | 20% | 21-26[3] | 16% | 84% | 11% |
| 181. | South Dakota State University* | 27 | 2.3 | 3.6 | 75% | 52% | 57% | 32% | 15% | 20-25 | 13% | 92% | 14% |
| 181. | Spalding University[1] (KY) | 27 | 1.7 | 3.4 | 73%[8] | 29% | 42%[6] | 79%[4] | 1%[4] | 18-22[4] | N/A | 29%[4] | 4%[4] |
| 181. | St. Mary's Univ. of Minnesota | 27 | 2.0 | 3.5 | 77% | 55% | 55% | 72% | 0% | 20-26 | 18%[5] | 75% | 13% |
| 181. | University of Alabama–Huntsville* | 27 | 2.4 | 3.6 | 79% | 61% | 48% | 41% | 11% | 23-29 | 28%[5] | 81% | 2% |
| 181. | U. of North Carolina–Greensboro* | 27 | 2.5 | 3.5 | 76% | 52% | 55% | 45% | 13% | 950-1120 | 22% | 58% | 5%[7] |
| 189. | Southern Illinois U.–Carbondale* | 26 | 2.5 | 3.2 | 65% | 46% | 44% | 56% | 5% | 19-25 | 11% | 79% | 6% |
| 189. | University of Houston* | 26 | 2.5 | 3.4 | 83% | 55% | 48% | 31% | 22% | 1030-1250 | 34% | 58% | 13% |
| 189. | Univ. of Missouri–Kansas City* | 26 | 2.5 | 3.3 | 73% | 63% | 51% | 57% | 10% | 21-27 | 26% | 65% | 8% |
| 189. | University of New Mexico* | 26 | 2.7 | 3.6 | 77% | 54% | 48% | 39% | 15% | 19-25 | N/A | 57% | 4% |
| 189. | Widener University (PA) | 26 | 2.0 | 3.2 | 73% | 50% | 56% | 58% | 2% | 920-1130[3] | 15% | 67% | 3% |
| 194. | Central Michigan University* | 25 | 2.2 | 3.3 | 77% | 50% | 59% | 33% | 8% | 20-24 | 15% | 63% | 6% |
| 194. | Indiana U.–Purdue U.–Indianapolis* | 25 | 2.8 | 3.9 | 72% | 48% | 42% | 37% | 10% | 890-1120 | 15% | 70% | 9% |
| 194. | Kent State University (OH)* | 25 | 2.4 | 3.3 | 77% | 45% | 51% | 52% | 8% | 20-25 | 14% | 83% | 4% |
| 194. | Northern Illinois University* | 25 | 2.3 | 3.2 | 70% | 48% | 51% | 48% | 11% | 19-24 | 12% | 52% | 5% |
| 194. | University of Montana* | 25 | 2.6 | 3.4 | 73% | 49% | 48% | 47% | 11% | 21-26 | 18% | 96% | 7% |
| 194. | University of Nevada–Reno* | 25 | 2.4 | 3.2 | 79% | 56% | 51% | 35% | 19% | 960-1150 | 23% | 84% | 9% |
| 194. | Utah State University* | 25 | 2.5 | 3.4 | 70% | 56% | 51% | 41% | 16% | 20-26 | 19% | 98% | 6% |
| 201. | Louisiana Tech University* | 24 | 2.3 | 3.3 | 77% | 54% | 50% | 49% | 8% | 21-26 | 24% | 67% | 12% |
| 201. | U. of North Carolina–Charlotte* | 24 | 2.6 | 3.6 | 78% | 54% | 54% | 25% | 23% | 1000-1170 | 19% | 63% | 4% |

| School (State) (*Public) | Peer assessment score (5.0=highest) | High school counselor assessment score | Average freshman retention rate | 2013 graduation rate | | % of classes under 20 ('13) | % of classes of 50 or more ('13) | SAT/ACT 25th-75th percentile ('13) | Freshmen in top 10% of HS class ('13) | Acceptance rate ('13) | Average alumni giving rate |
|---|---|---|---|---|---|---|---|---|---|---|---|
| | | | | Predicted | Actual | | | | | | |
| SECOND TIER (SCHOOLS RANKED 203 THROUGH 268 ARE LISTED HERE ALPHABETICALLY) | | | | | | | | | | | |
| Ashland University (OH) | 1.8 | 3.2 | 72% | 58% | 56% | 68% | 0.1% | 20-25 | 19% | 72% | 5% |
| Barry University (FL) | 1.9 | 3.1 | 60%[8] | 43% | 37% | 68% | 1% | 833-1040 | N/A | 47% | 4% |
| Benedictine University (IL) | 2.0 | 3.5 | 77%[8] | 56% | 52% | 72% | 0.3% | 20-26[3] | 21% | 70% | 5% |
| Bowie State University (MD)* | 1.8 | 3.2 | 72% | 30% | 38%[6] | 45% | 1% | 810-960[3] | N/A | 52% | 6% |
| Cardinal Stritch University[1] (WI) | 1.7 | 3.2 | 69%[8] | 48% | 50%[6] | 93%[4] | 0%[4] | 1067-1084[4] | 9%[4] | 42%[4] | 3%[4] |
| Clark Atlanta University | 2.2 | 3.4 | 64% | 34% | 39% | 45% | 3% | 770-940[3] | 9%[4] | 57% | 3%[7] |
| Cleveland State University* | 2.1 | 3.0 | 66% | 38% | 32% | 36% | 11% | 19-25[3] | 14% | 63% | 3% |
| East Carolina University (NC)* | 2.2 | 3.3 | 80% | 53% | 57% | 31% | 14% | 960-1130 | 15% | 73% | 4% |
| East Tennessee State University[1]* | 2.0 | 3.2 | 69%[8] | 50% | 41%[8] | 42%[4] | 7%[4] | 19-25[4] | 19%[4] | 89%[4] | 4%[4] |
| Florida A&M University* | 2.1 | 3.3 | 81% | 43% | 41% | 32% | 12% | 18-22 | 16%[5] | 45% | 6% |
| Florida Atlantic University* | 2.2 | 3.0 | 78% | 48% | 41% | 24% | 16% | 960-1130 | 11% | 48% | 3% |
| Florida International University* | 2.2 | 3.3 | 83% | 62% | 52% | 21% | 22% | 1070-1230 | 23%[5] | 43% | 7% |
| Georgia Southern University* | 2.2 | 3.2 | 79% | 53% | 50% | 25% | 10% | 1040-1180 | 19%[5] | 57% | 8% |
| Georgia State University* | 2.6 | 3.5 | 83% | 57% | 53% | 19% | 15% | 960-1170 | N/A | 54% | 6% |
| Indiana State University* | 2.4 | 3.4 | 62% | 39% | 42% | 29% | 11% | 800-1020 | 8% | 83% | 6% |
| Indiana Univ. of Pennsylvania* | 2.0 | 3.1 | 75% | 41% | 51% | 29% | 14% | 880-1070[3] | 8% | 90% | 7% |
| Jackson State University[1] (MS)* | 1.8 | 2.9 | 73%[8] | 33% | 42%[6] | N/A | N/A | 17-21[9] | N/A | 65% | 4%[7] |
| Lamar University (TX)* | 2.0 | 3.0 | 59% | 39% | 34% | 48% | 6% | 870-1080 | 15% | 77% | 2% |
| Lynn University (FL) | 1.8 | 2.8 | 65% | 32% | 41% | 38% | 0.3% | 820-1050 | 1%[5] | 78% | 8% |
| Middle Tennessee State Univ.* | 2.1 | 3.2 | 71% | 48% | 47% | 40% | 8% | 19-24[3] | 16% | 70% | 5% |
| Montana State University* | 2.5 | 3.5 | 75% | 55% | 49% | 40% | 16% | 21-27[3] | 19% | 85% | 8% |
| Morgan State University (MD)* | 1.9 | 3.1 | 72% | 36% | 35% | 42% | 0.1% | 820-980[2] | 3% | 56% | 14% |
| National-Louis University (IL) | 1.7 | 2.8 | 72%[8] | 47% | 30%[6] | N/A | N/A | N/A[2] | N/A | N/A | N/A |
| New Mexico State University* | 2.4 | 3.4 | 72% | 44% | 43% | 48% | 10% | 18-24 | 21% | 85% | 7% |
| North Carolina A&T State Univ.* | 2.0 | 3.2 | 73%[8] | 32% | 42% | 34% | 7% | 830-990 | 10% | 57% | 8% |
| Northern Arizona University* | 2.4 | 3.3 | 73% | 52% | 49% | 33% | 12% | 940-1160[2] | 21% | 91% | 4% |
| Nova Southeastern University (FL) | 1.8 | 2.6 | 71% | 55% | 41% | 81% | 0.1% | 950-1190 | 24% | 57% | 2% |
| Oakland University (MI)* | 2.1 | 3.2 | 74% | 54% | 43% | 37% | 14% | 20-26 | 17% | 66% | 4% |
| Old Dominion University (VA)* | 2.6 | 3.6 | 80% | 53% | 51% | 34% | 11% | 930-1130 | 10% | 77% | 6% |
| Our Lady of the Lake University (TX) | 1.6 | 3.4 | 62% | 43% | 32% | 68% | 0% | 870-960 | 12% | 23% | 14% |
| Portland State University[1] (OR)* | 2.5 | 3.6 | 72%[8] | 51% | 39%[6] | N/A | N/A | 19-26[4] | N/A | N/A | 3%[4] |
| Regent University (VA) | 1.8 | 3.4 | 74% | 56% | 54% | 49% | 0% | 940-1170 | 14% | 85% | 4% |
| Sam Houston State University (TX)* | 2.0 | 3.3 | 75% | 48% | 51% | 24% | 13% | 880-1090[3] | 14% | 74% | 9% |
| South Carolina State University* | 2.1 | 3.3 | 63% | 24% | 36% | 53% | 3% | 720-870 | 2% | 92% | N/A |
| Tennessee State University* | 2.0 | 3.2 | 62%[8] | 31% | 29% | 54% | 1% | 16-20[3] | N/A | 53% | 4%[4] |

**Note:** Key to footnotes, Page 80.

| School (State) (*Public) | Peer assessment score (5.0=highest) | High school counselor assessment score | Average freshman retention rate | 2013 graduation rate | | % of classes under 20 ('13) | % of classes of 50 or more ('13) | SAT/ACT 25th-75th percentile ('13) | Freshmen in top 10% of HS class ('13) | Accept-ance rate ('13) | Average alumni giving rate |
|---|---|---|---|---|---|---|---|---|---|---|---|
| | | | | Predicted | Actual | | | | | | |
| SECOND TIER (SCHOOLS RANKED 203 THROUGH 268 ARE LISTED HERE ALPHABETICALLY) | | | | | | | | | | | |
| Texas A&M University–Commerce* | 2.1 | 3.8 | 68%[8] | 42% | 45% | 46% | 4% | 880-1090 | 16% | 68% | 3% |
| Texas A&M Univ.–Corpus Christi* | 2.1 | 3.8 | 61% | 38% | 35% | 18% | 19% | 870-1060[3] | 10% | 87% | 2%[4] |
| Texas A&M Univ.–Kingsville* | 2.0 | 3.7 | 60% | 30% | 34% | 37% | 5% | 16-21 | 9% | 88% | N/A |
| Texas Southern University* | 2.0 | 3.3 | 60% | 14% | 16% | 38% | 11% | 750-920 | 5% | 45% | 2% |
| Texas Woman's University* | 2.2 | 3.4 | 69% | 47% | 42% | 44% | 13% | 840-1070[2] | 16% | 86% | 1% |
| Trevecca Nazarene University (TN) | 1.6 | 3.4 | 74% | 55% | 47% | 75% | 2% | 21-26[3] | N/A | 68% | 7% |
| Trinity International Univ. (IL) | 1.7 | 3.2 | 71%[8] | 56% | 45% | 71% | 0.4% | 25-29 | 17% | 94% | 7% |
| University of Akron (OH)* | 2.3 | 3.2 | 69% | 40% | 40% | 38% | 7% | 18-25 | 13% | 96% | 14% |
| University of Alaska–Fairbanks* | 2.4 | 3.2 | 76% | 56% | 38% | 65% | 4% | 18-25 | 18% | 80% | 5% |
| Univ. of Arkansas–Little Rock* | 2.1 | 3.1 | 70%[8] | 38% | 24% | 60% | 3% | 22 | N/A | 69% | 2% |
| University of Colorado–Denver* | 2.7 | 3.6 | 74% | 55% | 41% | 35% | 11% | 20-25[3] | 21% | 69% | 3% |
| University of Louisiana–Lafayette* | 2.2 | 3.2 | 74% | 49% | 45% | 33% | 8% | 21-25 | 17% | 59% | 7% |
| Univ. of Massachusetts–Boston* | 2.5 | 3.6 | 77% | 55% | 44% | 32% | 6% | 950-1160[3] | N/A | 70% | 5% |
| University of Memphis* | 2.4 | 3.3 | 77% | 50% | 44% | 44% | 11% | 20-26 | 16% | 73% | 6% |
| Univ. of Missouri–St. Louis* | 2.4 | 3.3 | 76% | 53% | 46% | 47% | 9% | 21-26 | 30% | 74% | 6% |
| University of Nebraska–Omaha* | 2.5 | 3.5 | 73% | 50% | 42% | 35% | 11% | 20-26 | 15% | 71% | 5% |
| University of Nevada–Las Vegas* | 2.4 | 3.2 | 77% | 54% | 43% | 26% | 18% | 890-1110 | 21% | 85% | 5% |
| University of New Orleans* | 2.0 | 3.3 | 66% | 46% | 32% | 31%[4] | 16%[4] | 21-25 | 16% | 50% | 1% |
| University of Northern Colorado* | 2.2 | 3.3 | 69%[8] | 48% | 46% | 25% | 13% | 20-24[2] | 12% | 70% | 5%[7] |
| University of North Texas* | 2.4 | 3.3 | 77% | 56% | 46% | 26% | 24% | 1000-1210[3] | 20% | 61% | 3% |
| University of South Alabama* | 2.0 | 2.8 | 66% | 53% | 33% | 46% | 9% | 20-26[2] | N/A | 86% | 2%[7] |
| Univ. of Southern Mississippi* | 2.2 | 3.3 | 74% | 51% | 45% | 45% | 9% | 19-25 | 6%[5] | 66% | 9% |
| University of Texas–Arlington* | 2.5 | 3.6 | 74% | 58% | 44% | 28% | 26% | 960-1200 | 28% | 60% | 3% |
| University of Texas–El Paso* | 2.2 | 3.3 | 73%[8] | 36% | 37%[8] | 33%[4] | 12%[4] | 17-22[4] | 17%[4] | 100%[4] | 5%[7] |
| University of Texas–San Antonio* | 2.3 | 3.5 | 62% | 42% | 30% | 20% | 26% | 950-1180 | 19% | 62% | 5% |
| University of Toledo (OH)* | 2.3 | 3.2 | 65% | 49% | 46% | 27% | 16% | 19-25 | 17% | 91% | 5% |
| University of West Florida* | 2.0 | 3.0 | 72% | 54% | 42% | 32% | 11% | 21-25[3] | 12% | 48% | 15% |
| Univ. of Wisconsin–Milwaukee* | 2.7 | 3.6 | 71% | 43% | 41% | 43% | 10% | 19-24[3] | 9% | 88% | 3% |
| Wayne State University (MI)* | 2.5 | 3.4 | 77% | 49% | 32% | 49% | 9% | 19-26 | 23% | 76% | 5% |
| Wichita State University (KS)* | 2.4 | 3.2 | 72% | 53% | 46% | 41% | 11% | 21-26[2] | 23% | 96% | 7% |
| Wright State University (OH)* | 2.3 | 3.2 | 63% | 43% | 41% | 44% | 13% | 19-25 | 15% | 96% | 4% |

# ▶ The Top 30 Public National Universities

### Rank School (State)

1. University of California–Berkeley
2. Univ. of California–Los Angeles
2. University of Virginia
4. University of Michigan–Ann Arbor
5. U. of North Carolina–Chapel Hill
6. College of William and Mary (VA)
7. Georgia Institute of Technology
8. Univ. of California–San Diego
9. University of California–Davis

### Rank School (State)

10. Univ. of California–Santa Barbara
11. University of California–Irvine
11. U. of Illinois–Urbana-Champaign
13. Univ. of Wisconsin–Madison
14. Pennsylvania State U.–Univ. Park
14. University of Florida
14. University of Washington
17. University of Texas–Austin
18. Ohio State University–Columbus

### Rank School (State)

19. University of Connecticut
20. Clemson University (SC)
20. Purdue Univ.–West Lafayette (IN)
20. University of Georgia
20. Univ. of Maryland–College Park
20. University of Pittsburgh
25. Texas A&M Univ.–College Station
26. Rutgers, St. U. of N.J.–New Brunswick

### Rank School (State)

27. University of Iowa
27. Univ. of Minnesota–Twin Cities
27. Virginia Tech
30. Indiana University–Bloomington
30. Miami University–Oxford (OH)
30. SUNY Col. of Envir. Sci. and Forestry
30. University of Delaware
30. Univ. of Massachusetts–Amherst

**Footnotes:**
**1.** School refused to fill out U.S. News statistical survey. Data that appear are from school in previous years or from another source such as the National Center for Education Statistics.
**2.** SAT and/or ACT not required by school for some or all applicants.
**3.** In reporting SAT/ACT scores, the school did not include all students for whom it had scores or refused to tell U.S. News whether all students with scores had been included.
**4.** Data reported to U.S. News in previous years.
**5.** Data based on fewer than 51 percent of enrolled freshmen.
**6.** Some or all data reported to the NCAA and/or the National Center for Education Statistics.
**7.** Data reported to the Council for Aid to Education.

**8.** Average graduation or freshman retention rates, normally based on four years of data, are given here for less than four years because school didn't report rates for the most recent year or years to U.S. News.
**9.** SAT and/or ACT may not be required by school for some or all applicants, and in reporting SAT/ACT scores, the school did not include all students for whom it had scores, or refused to tell U.S. News whether all students with scores had been included.

N/A means not available.

# Best National Liberal

| Rank School (State) (*Public) | Overall score | Peer assessment score (5.0=highest) | High school counselor assessment score | Graduation and retention rank | Average freshman retention rate | 2013 graduation rate | | | Faculty resources rank |
|---|---|---|---|---|---|---|---|---|---|
| | | | | | | Predicted | Actual | Over-performance(+) Under-performance(-) | |
| 1. Williams College (MA) | 100 | 4.7 | 4.7 | 3 | 97% | 94% | 95% | +1 | 3 |
| 2. Amherst College (MA) | 96 | 4.6 | 4.6 | 1 | 98% | 93% | 96% | +3 | 16 |
| 3. Swarthmore College (PA) | 94 | 4.5 | 4.5 | 4 | 96% | 95% | 93% | -2 | 10 |
| 4. Wellesley College (MA) | 93 | 4.4 | 4.6 | 12 | 96% | 91% | 91% | None | 9 |
| 5. Bowdoin College (ME) | 92 | 4.3 | 4.5 | 4 | 96% | 93% | 93% | None | 14 |
| 5. Pomona College (CA) | 92 | 4.3 | 4.5 | 1 | 98% | 94% | 96% | +2 | 25 |
| 7. Middlebury College (VT) | 91 | 4.3 | 4.4 | 4 | 96% | 93% | 94% | +1 | 33 |
| 8. Carleton College (MN) | 90 | 4.3 | 4.4 | 4 | 97% | 91% | 92% | +1 | 16 |
| 8. Claremont McKenna College (CA) | 90 | 4.1 | 4.5 | 12 | 96% | 93% | 93% | None | 5 |
| 8. Haverford College (PA) | 90 | 4.0 | 4.3 | 4 | 97% | 94% | 93% | -1 | 5 |
| 11. Davidson College (NC) | 88 | 4.2 | 4.3 | 9 | 96% | 93% | 92% | -1 | 4 |
| 11. Vassar College (NY) | 88 | 4.2 | 4.6 | 9 | 96% | 90% | 94% | +4 | 22 |
| 13. United States Naval Academy (MD)* | 87 | 4.1 | 4.8 | 20 | 97% | 79% | 88% | +9 | 52 |
| 14. Washington and Lee University (VA) | 86 | 3.7 | 4.2 | 15 | 95% | 93% | 90% | -3 | 2 |
| 15. Colby College (ME) | 85 | 4.0 | 4.3 | 15 | 94% | 87% | 93% | +6 | 20 |
| 15. Hamilton College (NY) | 85 | 3.8 | 4.3 | 15 | 95% | 90% | 93% | +3 | 10 |
| 15. Harvey Mudd College (CA) | 85 | 4.3 | 4.6 | 23 | 98% | 95% | 91% | -4 | 57 |
| 15. Wesleyan University (CT) | 85 | 4.1 | 4.5 | 9 | 96% | 90% | 92% | +2 | 40 |
| 19. Bates College (ME) | 84 | 4.0 | 4.3 | 20 | 93% | 86% | 93% | +7 | 45 |
| 19. Grinnell College (IA) | 84 | 4.2 | 4.3 | 28 | 94% | 88% | 86% | -2 | 20 |
| 19. Smith College (MA) | 84 | 4.2 | 4.5 | 35 | 93% | 82% | 86% | +4 | 29 |
| 22. Colgate University (NY) | 83 | 3.9 | 4.3 | 20 | 94% | 87% | 91% | +4 | 22 |
| 23. Oberlin College (OH) | 82 | 4.1 | 4.3 | 31 | 93% | 88% | 88% | None | 22 |
| 24. Macalester College (MN) | 81 | 4.0 | 4.3 | 28 | 95% | 88% | 87% | -1 | 29 |
| 24. Scripps College (CA) | 81 | 3.7 | 4.4 | 33 | 93% | 89% | 84% | -5 | 19 |
| 24. United States Military Academy (NY)* | 81 | 4.1 | 4.8 | 41 | 95% | 78% | 84% | +6 | 81 |
| 27. Bryn Mawr College (PA) | 80 | 4.0 | 4.3 | 50 | 91% | 85% | 84% | -1 | 25 |
| 27. Colorado College | 80 | 3.8 | 4.1 | 23 | 96% | 85% | 87% | +2 | 10 |
| 27. United States Air Force Acad. (CO)* | 80 | 4.0 | 4.7 | 50 | 90% | 80% | 85% | +5 | 57 |
| 30. Kenyon College (OH) | 79 | 3.8 | 4.2 | 28 | 94% | 90% | 89% | -1 | 33 |
| 30. University of Richmond (VA) | 79 | 3.7 | 4.1 | 41 | 94% | 86% | 85% | -1 | 7 |
| 32. Barnard College (NY) | 78 | 3.9 | 4.4 | 15 | 96% | 87% | 90% | +3 | 91 |
| 32. Bucknell University (PA) | 78 | 3.8 | 4.3 | 15 | 94% | 88% | 91% | +3 | 76 |
| 34. College of the Holy Cross (MA) | 76 | 3.5 | 4.0 | 12 | 95% | 86% | 91% | +5 | 52 |
| 35. Lafayette College (PA) | 75 | 3.4 | 4.0 | 23 | 94% | 87% | 88% | +1 | 45 |
| 35. Pitzer College (CA) | 75 | 3.5 | 4.3 | 48 | 92% | 76% | 82% | +6 | 33 |
| 37. Dickinson College (PA) | 74 | 3.6 | 4.1 | 48 | 90% | 81% | 85% | +4 | 25 |
| 37. Franklin and Marshall College (PA) | 74 | 3.6 | 4.0 | 35 | 93% | 85% | 87% | +2 | 49 |
| 37. Skidmore College (NY) | 74 | 3.5 | 4.2 | 35 | 94% | 78% | 86% | +8 | 40 |
| 37. Whitman College (WA) | 74 | 3.4 | 4.1 | 31 | 94% | 85% | 88% | +3 | 40 |
| 41. Mount Holyoke College (MA) | 73 | 4.0 | 4.2 | 50 | 91% | 83% | 82% | -1 | 76 |
| 41. Soka University of America (CA) | 73 | 2.3 | 3.0 | 23 | 96% | 76% | 84% | +8 | 1 |
| 41. Union College (NY) | 73 | 3.2 | 4.0 | 35 | 93% | 83% | 88% | +5 | 16 |
| 44. Occidental College (CA) | 72 | 3.7 | 4.0 | 35 | 93% | 83% | 88% | +5 | 81 |
| 45. Bard College (NY) | 71 | 3.4 | 4.0 | 77 | 88% | 88% | 74% | -14 | 15 |
| 45. Centre College (KY) | 71 | 3.4 | 4.1 | 44 | 91% | 81% | 82% | +1 | 84 |
| 45. Connecticut College | 71 | 3.5 | 4.1 | 44 | 90% | 84% | 84% | None | 73 |
| 45. Sewanee–University of the South (TN) | 71 | 3.5 | 4.1 | 61 | 88% | 80% | 78% | -2 | 36 |
| 45. Trinity College (CT) | 71 | 3.5 | 4.1 | 41 | 91% | 81% | 86% | +5 | 91 |
| 50. Gettysburg College (PA) | 70 | 3.4 | 3.9 | 44 | 90% | 86% | 84% | -2 | 52 |

**Note:** Key to footnotes, Page 89.

# Arts Colleges

| % of classes under 20 ('13) | % of classes of 50 or more ('13) | Student/faculty ratio ('13) | Selectivity rank | SAT/ACT 25th-75th percentile ('13) | Freshmen in top 10% of HS class ('13) | Acceptance rate ('13) | Financial resources rank | Alumni giving rank | Average alumni giving rate |
|---|---|---|---|---|---|---|---|---|---|
| 75% | 3% | 7/1 | 5 | 1330-1540 | 88%[5] | 18% | 4 | 2 | 58% |
| 71% | 3% | 8/1 | 5 | 1350-1530 | 86%[5] | 14% | 10 | 6 | 53% |
| 75% | 2% | 8/1 | 3 | 1350-1530 | 89%[5] | 14% | 8 | 16 | 43% |
| 73% | 0.4% | 7/1 | 8 | 1310-1510 | 83%[5] | 29% | 8 | 11 | 47% |
| 71% | 2% | 9/1 | 5 | 1360-1510[2] | 83%[5] | 15% | 13 | 5 | 53% |
| 68% | 2% | 8/1 | 2 | 1380-1540 | 92%[5] | 14% | 7 | 25 | 38% |
| 62% | 3% | 9/1 | 12 | 1280-1490 | 74%[5] | 18% | 3 | 6 | 53% |
| 66% | 1% | 9/1 | 8 | 1340-1520 | 79%[5] | 21% | 25 | 4 | 54% |
| 85% | 1% | 9/1 | 11 | 1320-1500 | 74%[5] | 12% | 13 | 16 | 43% |
| 82% | 0.3% | 9/1 | 3 | 1310-1490 | 95%[5] | 23% | 12 | 13 | 45% |
| 72% | 0% | 10/1 | 33 | 1230-1440[3] | 81%[5] | 26% | 27 | 3 | 55% |
| 64% | 1% | 8/1 | 17 | 1310-1480 | 66% | 24% | 13 | 47 | 32% |
| 68% | 0% | 9/1 | 24 | 1180-1380 | 54% | 7% | 2 | 123 | 20% |
| 73% | 0.2% | 8/1 | 8 | 30-33 | 80%[5] | 18% | 25 | 15 | 44% |
| 71% | 2% | 10/1 | 19 | 1260-1430[2] | 64%[5] | 26% | 27 | 22 | 39% |
| 74% | 1% | 9/1 | 14 | 1300-1470 | 72%[5] | 27% | 21 | 18 | 42% |
| 60% | 5% | 9/1 | 1 | 1400-1560 | 97% | 19% | 17 | 59 | 29% |
| 72% | 5% | 9/1 | 14 | 1310-1490 | 67%[5] | 20% | 45 | 13 | 45% |
| 68% | 3% | 10/1 | 24 | 1260-1430[2] | 56%[5] | 24% | 34 | 6 | 53% |
| 68% | 0% | 9/1 | 21 | 28-32 | 63%[5] | 35% | 22 | 31 | 37% |
| 68% | 5% | 9/1 | 31 | 1220-1450[2] | 62%[5] | 43% | 19 | 36 | 35% |
| 66% | 2% | 9/1 | 13 | 1270-1450 | 76%[5] | 27% | 38 | 21 | 40% |
| 77% | 2% | 9/1 | 21 | 1270-1455 | 62%[5] | 30% | 31 | 37 | 34% |
| 71% | 1% | 10/1 | 21 | 1240-1460 | 64%[5] | 34% | 45 | 25 | 38% |
| 84% | 1% | 10/1 | 17 | 1280-1453 | 75%[5] | 36% | 22 | 19 | 41% |
| 92% | 0% | 7/1 | 52 | 1180-1385[3] | 46% | 9% | 4 | 63 | 29% |
| 75% | 3% | 8/1 | 28 | 1210-1470 | 65%[5] | 40% | 19 | 25 | 38% |
| 64% | 0% | 10/1 | 19 | 1220-1430[2] | 66%[5] | 22% | 31 | 131 | 19% |
| 75% | 0% | 8/1 | 24 | 29-32 | 55% | 15% | 4 | 177 | 12% |
| 67% | 0% | 10/1 | 24 | 1230-1410 | 65%[5] | 38% | 34 | 31 | 36% |
| 67% | 0% | 8/1 | 28 | 1210-1410 | 64%[5] | 31% | 22 | 75 | 26% |
| 73% | 10% | 10/1 | 14 | 1240-1440 | 77%[5] | 21% | 56 | 75 | 25% |
| 58% | 3% | 9/1 | 28 | 1200-1400 | 62%[5] | 30% | 42 | 51 | 31% |
| 65% | 2% | 10/1 | 52 | 1220-1390[2] | 57%[5] | 33% | 50 | 9 | 51% |
| 60% | 1% | 10/1 | 33 | 1180-1370 | 62%[5] | 34% | 31 | 40 | 34% |
| 71% | 0% | 10/1 | 47 | 1210-1400[2] | 55%[5] | 15% | 27 | 40 | 33% |
| 76% | 0% | 9/1 | 43 | 1190-1365[2] | 46%[5] | 45% | 59 | 65 | 28% |
| 63% | 0.4% | 9/1 | 33 | 1220-1410[2] | 56%[5] | 36% | 42 | 65 | 27% |
| 73% | 1% | 9/1 | 45 | 1130-1350 | 45%[5] | 35% | 47 | 73 | 26% |
| 66% | 1% | 9/1 | 36 | 1220-1422 | 61% | 57% | 62 | 35 | 36% |
| 66% | 4% | 10/1 | 60 | 1220-1430[2] | 57%[5] | 47% | 38 | 48 | 31% |
| 98% | 0% | 8/1 | 52 | 1080-1340 | 50%[5] | 43% | 1 | 131 | 19% |
| 72% | 0% | 10/1 | 46 | 1220-1400[2] | 64%[5] | 37% | 50 | 43 | 33% |
| 58% | 0.2% | 10/1 | 38 | 1210-1400 | 51%[5] | 42% | 62 | 86 | 25% |
| 77% | 1% | 10/1 | 63 | 1170-1380[2] | 58%[5] | 38% | 13 | 22 | 39% |
| 60% | 0% | 10/1 | 42 | 26-31 | 52% | 69% | 71 | 10 | 50% |
| 67% | 2% | 9/1 | 60 | 1240-1410[2] | 52%[5] | 37% | 42 | 51 | 31% |
| 61% | 1% | 11/1 | 47 | 26-30[2] | 42%[5] | 60% | 56 | 25 | 38% |
| 60% | 2% | 9/1 | 66 | 1150-1330 | 23%[5] | 32% | 27 | 43 | 33% |
| 68% | 0.3% | 10/1 | 32 | 1200-1370[2] | 69%[5] | 42% | 61 | 92 | 24% |

## What Is a National Liberal Arts College?

The country's 249 liberal arts colleges emphasize undergraduate education and award at least half of their degrees in the arts and sciences, which include such disciplines as English, the biological and physical sciences, history, foreign languages and the visual and performing arts but exclude professional disciplines such as business, education and nursing. There are 221 private and 27 public liberal arts colleges; one is for-profit. The top 10 public colleges appear below.

## The Top 10 Public Colleges

Rank School (State)

1. United States Naval Academy (MD)
2. United States Military Academy (NY)
3. United States Air Force Acad. (CO)
4. Virginia Military Institute
5. New College of Florida
6. St. Mary's College of Maryland
7. University of Minnesota–Morris
8. U. of North Carolina–Asheville
9. Massachusetts Col. of Liberal Arts
10. Purchase College–SUNY

| Rank | School (State) (*Public) | Overall score | Peer assessment score (5.0=highest) | High school counselor assessment score | Average freshman retention rate | 2013 graduation rate Predicted | 2013 graduation rate Actual | % of classes under 20 ('13) | % of classes of 50 or more ('13) | SAT/ACT 25th-75th percentile ('13) | Freshmen in top 10% of HS class ('13) | Accept-ance rate ('13) | Average alumni giving rate |
|---|---|---|---|---|---|---|---|---|---|---|---|---|---|
| 51. | Denison University (OH) | 68 | 3.3 | 3.9 | 90% | 82% | 81% | 73% | 0% | 27-31[2] | 45% | 46% | 29% |
| 51. | DePauw University (IN) | 68 | 3.4 | 3.9 | 91% | 79% | 79% | 65% | 0% | 25-29 | 49%[5] | 61% | 30% |
| 51. | Furman University (SC) | 68 | 3.4 | 3.9 | 89% | 84% | 84% | 53% | 0.2% | 1130-1340[2] | 48%[5] | 64% | 26% |
| 54. | Rhodes College (TN) | 67 | 3.4 | 4.1 | 91% | 82% | 79% | 68% | 0% | 27-31 | 50%[5] | 58% | 36% |
| 54. | St. Olaf College (MN) | 67 | 3.6 | 4.0 | 94% | 82% | 87% | 54% | 3% | 26-31 | 54%[5] | 59% | 23% |
| 56. | St. John's College (MD) | 65 | 3.4 | 3.9 | 86% | 75% | 65% | 97% | 1% | 1140-1410[2] | 19%[5] | 87% | 21% |
| 56. | St. Lawrence University (NY) | 65 | 3.2 | 3.7 | 91% | 74% | 80% | 64% | 1% | 1120-1310[2] | 34%[5] | 46% | 27% |
| 56. | Wheaton College (IL) | 65 | 3.3 | 3.9 | 95% | 84% | 87% | 57% | 5% | 27-32 | 58%[5] | 70% | 26% |
| 59. | Lawrence University (WI) | 64 | 3.1 | 3.9 | 89% | 79% | 82% | 76% | 2% | 26-31[2] | 42%[5] | 73% | 33% |
| 59. | Sarah Lawrence College (NY) | 64 | 3.4 | 4.2 | 87% | 76% | 69% | 93% | 1% | 1150-1350[2] | 35%[5] | 77% | 19% |
| 61. | Beloit College (WI) | 63 | 3.2 | 3.8 | 89% | 75% | 78% | 74% | 0% | 24-30[2] | 29% | 68% | 25% |
| 61. | Hobart & William Smith Colleges (NY) | 63 | 3.2 | 3.8 | 88% | 74% | 79% | 65% | 0.4% | 1120-1290[2] | 36%[5] | 50% | 29% |
| 61. | Wabash College (IN) | 63 | 3.3 | 3.8 | 86% | 73% | 69% | 73% | 2% | 1028-1250 | 33% | 70% | 38% |
| 64. | Gustavus Adolphus College (MN) | 62 | 3.2 | 3.7 | 92% | 73% | 82% | 60% | 1% | 24-30[2] | 33% | 63% | 27% |
| 64. | Kalamazoo College (MI) | 62 | 3.3 | 3.9 | 92% | 80% | 77% | 60% | 2% | 25-30 | 38%[5] | 67% | 29% |
| 64. | Muhlenberg College (PA) | 62 | 2.8 | 3.5 | 92% | 79% | 86% | 71% | 1% | 1140-1340[2] | 45%[5] | 46% | 18% |
| 64. | Virginia Military Institute* | 62 | 3.1 | 3.8 | 84% | 60% | 76% | 64% | 0.2% | 1050-1250 | 16% | 48% | 31% |
| 64. | Willamette University (OR) | 62 | 3.2 | 3.8 | 88% | 78% | 78% | 63% | 0% | 1080-1310 | 41% | 58% | 17% |
| 69. | Berea College (KY) | 61 | 3.3 | 3.4 | 80% | 47% | 62% | 70% | 0% | 22-26 | 25% | 34% | 18% |
| 69. | College of Wooster (OH) | 61 | 3.1 | 3.7 | 89% | 74% | 75% | 71% | 1% | 25-30 | 40%[5] | 56% | 26% |
| 69. | Hillsdale College (MI) | 61 | 2.5 | 3.5 | 97% | 80% | 81% | 72% | 1% | 27-31 | 56%[5] | 50% | 21% |
| 69. | Wheaton College (MA) | 61 | 3.4 | 4.0 | 86% | 82% | 76% | 69% | 2% | 1110-1340[2] | 37%[5] | 74% | 25% |
| 73. | Agnes Scott College (GA) | 60 | 3.1 | 3.7 | 82% | 72% | 72% | 71% | 0% | 1010-1310[2] | 40% | 67% | 41% |
| 73. | Earlham College (IN) | 60 | 3.3 | 3.9 | 85% | 73% | 71% | 73% | 3% | 1150-1340[2] | 29%[5] | 64% | 25% |
| 73. | Illinois Wesleyan University | 60 | 3.0 | 3.6 | 90% | 79% | 78% | 66% | 1% | 25-30 | 45% | 58% | 20% |
| 73. | St. John's University (MN) | 60 | 3.2 | 3.7 | 90% | 71% | 79% | 57% | 1% | 23-28 | 22% | 75% | 27% |
| 77. | Lewis & Clark College (OR) | 59 | 3.3 | 3.8 | 86% | 81% | 74% | 69% | 1% | 1180-1370[2] | 39%[5] | 63% | 20% |
| 77. | Reed College[1] (OR) | 59 | 3.7 | 4.4 | 92%[8] | 86% | 78%[6] | N/A | N/A | 1280-1470[9] | N/A | 49% | 26%[7] |

Pomona College in California, tied at No. 5

**Note:** Key to footnotes, Page 89.

**HELPING HERE**

**CAN HELP YOU HERE**

THE UNIVERSITY OF

**HELP YOUR NEIGHBORS**

**ATTEND COLLEGE FULL-TIME**

**SERVE PART-TIME**

**EXTRA PAYCHECK**

**GI BILL**

**OTHER BENEFITS**

**CAREER TRAINING**

**BE PART OF A TEAM**

College doesn't have to mean debt. Earn the money you need to pay your way by serving part-time in your community and state. Check out the Guard online. Help is on the way.

**NATIONAL GUARD**
NATIONALGUARD.com

| Rank School (State) (*Public) | Overall score | Peer assessment score (5.0=highest) | High school counselor assessment score | Average freshman retention rate | 2013 graduation rate Predicted | 2013 graduation rate Actual | % of classes under 20 ('13) | % of classes of 50 or more ('13) | SAT/ACT 25th-75th percentile ('13) | Freshmen in top 10% of HS class ('13) | Acceptance rate ('13) | Average alumni giving rate |
|---|---|---|---|---|---|---|---|---|---|---|---|---|
| 77. **Thomas Aquinas College** (CA) | 59 | 2.7 | 3.0 | 87% | 80% | 80% | 100% | 0% | 1160-1340 | 29%[5] | 81% | 61% |
| 77. **Wofford College** (SC) | 59 | 2.9 | 3.6 | 89% | 80% | 82% | 58% | 0.2% | 1080-1260 | 42% | 69% | 32% |
| 81. **Allegheny College** (PA) | 58 | 3.0 | 3.5 | 87% | 76% | 79% | 64% | 1% | 1070-1290 | 41% | 65% | 24% |
| 81. **Hendrix College** (AR) | 58 | 3.3 | 3.9 | 85% | 77% | 68% | 66% | 0.3% | 26-32 | 46% | 80% | 25% |
| 81. **Knox College** (IL) | 58 | 3.0 | 3.5 | 88% | 77% | 79% | 75% | 1% | 25-30[2] | 26% | 75% | 33% |
| 81. **Spelman College** (GA) | 58 | 3.4 | 3.8 | 89% | 64% | 68% | 63% | 3% | 850-1215 | 31% | 41% | 34% |
| 81. **Transylvania University** (KY) | 58 | 2.8 | 3.3 | 87% | 75% | 72% | 74% | 0% | 24-30 | 39% | 83% | 37% |
| 81. **University of Puget Sound** (WA) | 58 | 3.2 | 3.7 | 87%[8] | 77% | 78% | 57% | 0.3% | 1120-1330[3] | 26%[5] | 85% | 16% |
| 87. **New College of Florida*** | 57 | 3.0 | 3.9 | 83% | 74% | 66% | 77% | 1% | 1190-1380 | 41% | 69% | 21% |
| 87. **Southwestern University** (TX) | 57 | 3.1 | 3.6 | 86% | 79% | 70% | 71% | 1% | 1055-1280 | 37% | 52% | 21% |
| 89. **Austin College** (TX) | 56 | 3.1 | 3.7 | 82% | 74% | 72% | 66% | 1% | 1100-1330[3] | 35% | 59% | 12%[7] |
| 89. **Bennington College** (VT) | 56 | 2.8 | 3.7 | 85% | 72% | 67% | 89% | 0.4% | 1180-1380[2] | 44%[5] | 65% | 25% |
| 89. **College of St. Benedict** (MN) | 56 | 3.1 | 3.4 | 89% | 75% | 82% | 57% | 1% | 23-28 | 33% | 76% | 19% |
| 89. **Luther College** (IA) | 56 | 3.1 | 3.5 | 87% | 69% | 76% | 56% | 1% | 23-29 | 32% | 72% | 25% |
| 89. **Millsaps College** (MS) | 56 | 3.0 | 3.6 | 80% | 74% | 64% | 84% | 0% | 23-28 | 31% | 47% | 20% |
| 89. **St. John's College** (NM)‡ | 56 | 3.1 | 4.1 | 74% | 74% | 57% | 95% | 0% | 1160-1450[2] | 25%[5] | 93% | 14% |
| 89. **St. Mary's College of Maryland*** | 56 | 2.9 | 3.6 | 88% | 70% | 79% | 65% | 1% | 1070-1310[3] | 28%[5] | 73% | 11% |
| 96. **St. Mary's College** (IN) | 55 | 3.0 | 3.9 | 87% | 71% | 71% | 57% | 1% | 23-28[3] | 27%[5] | 86% | 30% |
| 96. **Washington and Jefferson Col.** (PA) | 55 | 2.8 | 3.5 | 83%[8] | 71% | 77% | 65% | 0% | 1050-1230[2] | 37% | 40% | 17% |
| 96. **Westmont College** (CA) | 55 | 2.9 | 3.2 | 87% | 77% | 76% | 59% | 3% | 1060-1310 | 29% | 70% | 24% |
| 99. **Albion College** (MI) | 54 | 2.8 | 3.4 | 79% | 70% | 74% | 70% | 1% | 22-28 | 21% | 56% | 23% |
| 99. **College of the Atlantic** (ME) | 54 | 2.7 | 3.3 | 85% | 70% | 69% | 93% | 0% | 1110-1330[2] | 10% | 73% | 39% |
| 99. **Drew University** (NJ) | 54 | 2.9 | 3.4 | 79% | 71% | 69% | 73% | 0.3% | 990-1220 | 31%[5] | 77% | 21% |
| 99. **Hope College** (MI) | 54 | 3.1 | 3.6 | 89% | 73% | 78% | 54% | 2% | 24-29 | 34% | 70% | 23% |
| 99. **Ohio Wesleyan University** | 54 | 3.0 | 3.7 | 83% | 71% | 69% | 68% | 0% | 22-27[2] | 32%[5] | 75% | 23% |
| 99. **St. Michael's College** (VT) | 54 | 2.8 | 3.4 | 89% | 68% | 75% | 56% | 1% | 1060-1290[2] | 26% | 75% | 17% |
| 105. **Augustana College** (IL) | 53 | 2.9 | 3.4 | 86% | 71% | 78% | 64% | 1% | 22-27[9] | 24% | 59% | 27% |
| 105. **Cornell College** (IA) | 53 | 2.9 | 3.8 | 82% | 69% | 68% | 71% | 0% | 23-29 | 39% | 59% | 23% |
| 105. **Goucher College** (MD) | 53 | 3.1 | 3.7 | 84% | 70% | 68% | 77% | 1% | 1010-1280[2] | 31%[5] | 72% | 18% |
| 105. **Hampden-Sydney College** (VA) | 53 | 2.8 | 3.3 | 79% | 66% | 62% | 73% | 0% | 1005-1215 | 13% | 55% | 32% |
| 105. **Juniata College** (PA) | 53 | 2.7 | 3.5 | 87% | 71% | 75% | 69% | 2% | 1040-1260[9] | 34% | 74% | 28% |
| 105. **Stonehill College** (MA) | 53 | 2.8 | 3.5 | 88% | 77% | 85% | 55% | 1% | 1030-1230[2] | 31% | 71% | 15% |
| 105. **Washington College** (MD) | 53 | 2.8 | 3.7 | 83% | 72% | 68% | 62% | 1% | 1050-1280[2] | 33%[5] | 66% | 21% |
| 112. **Hollins University** (VA) | 52 | 2.6 | 3.5 | 70% | 63% | 60% | 90% | 0% | 970-1220 | 24% | 69% | 31% |
| 113. **Hanover College** (IN) | 51 | 2.7 | 3.4 | 81% | 73% | 72% | 74% | 0% | 1000-1200 | 32% | 67% | 22% |
| 113. **Ripon College** (WI) | 51 | 2.6 | 3.2 | 85% | 64% | 74% | 73% | 2% | 21-28 | 23% | 75% | 31% |
| 113. **Siena College** (NY) | 51 | 2.8 | 3.3 | 87% | 65% | 80% | 44% | 0% | 1000-1200[3] | 24% | 58% | 17% |
| 116. **Calvin College** (MI) | 50 | 2.9 | 3.4 | 87% | 71% | 73% | 35% | 2% | 23-29[2] | 30% | 70% | 25% |
| 116. **Susquehanna University** (PA) | 50 | 2.8 | 3.1 | 84% | 70% | 75% | 55% | 0% | 1020-1230[2] | 26% | 72% | 15% |
| 116. **Sweet Briar College** (VA) | 50 | 2.6 | 3.4 | 74% | 68% | 57% | 88% | 0% | 938-1210 | 30% | 84% | 33% |
| 116. **Westminster College** (PA) | 50 | 2.6 | 3.2 | 86% | 61% | 77% | 70% | 1% | 920-1150 | 17% | 73% | 20% |
| 120. **Coe College** (IA) | 49 | 2.8 | 3.3 | 80% | 69% | 67% | 72% | 1% | 23-28 | 31% | 62% | 21% |
| 120. **Lake Forest College** (IL) | 49 | 2.9 | 3.6 | 84% | 72% | 64% | 60% | 1% | 23-28[2] | 27%[5] | 57% | 24% |
| 120. **St. Anselm College** (NH) | 49 | 2.7 | 3.1 | 86% | 68% | 74% | 60% | 3% | 1060-1230[2] | 22% | 74% | 20% |
| 123. **St. Norbert College** (WI) | 48 | 2.7 | 3.4 | 83% | 67% | 74% | 45% | 1% | 22-27 | 27% | 82% | 18% |
| 124. **Birmingham-Southern Col.** (AL) | 47 | 2.8 | 3.3 | 81%[8] | 72% | 62% | 62% | 1% | 23-27 | 24% | 64% | 28% |
| 124. **Eckerd College** (FL) | 47 | 2.9 | 3.6 | 81% | 64% | 66% | 45% | 1% | 1030-1220 | N/A | 72% | N/A |
| 124. **Linfield College** (OR) | 47 | 2.7 | 3.4 | 83% | 67% | 68% | 64% | 1% | 980-1200 | 34%[4] | 92% | 15% |
| 124. **Presbyterian College** (SC) | 47 | 2.6 | 3.4 | 82% | 70% | 68% | 62% | 0% | 1000-1210[2] | 35% | 66% | 16% |
| 124. **Randolph-Macon College** (VA) | 47 | 2.7 | 3.4 | 78% | 64% | 61% | 72% | 0% | 970-1180 | 14% | 64% | 36% |
| 129. **Berry College** (GA) | 46 | 2.8 | 3.5 | 78% | 71% | 60% | 50% | 0.2% | 24-29 | 32% | 60% | 20% |
| 129. **Concordia College–Moorhead** (MN) | 46 | 2.8 | 3.4 | 84% | 69% | 71% | 50% | 1% | 22-28 | 30% | 78% | 19% |
| 129. **Goshen College** (IN) | 46 | 2.6 | 3.3 | 79% | 67% | 70% | 68% | 1% | 950-1250 | 25% | 55% | 25% |
| 129. **McDaniel College** (MD) | 46 | 2.7 | 3.4 | 83% | 69% | 72% | 63% | 0% | 1000-1210[3] | 26% | 76% | 16% |
| 133. **Moravian College** (PA) | 45 | 2.4 | 3.0 | 78% | 67% | 74% | 67% | 1% | 940-1170[2] | 19% | 80% | 16% |
| 133. **Morehouse College** (GA) | 45 | 3.2 | 3.8 | 82% | 55% | 54% | 48% | 2% | 900-1110 | 21% | 67% | 23% |
| 133. **Randolph College** (VA) | 45 | 2.5 | 3.2 | 77% | 67% | 52% | 84% | 0% | 970-1200 | 17% | 83% | 21% |
| 133. **Roanoke College** (VA) | 45 | 2.8 | 3.3 | 80% | 65% | 64% | 57% | 1% | 980-1190 | 18% | 73% | 20% |
| 133. **Wesleyan College** (GA) | 45 | 2.7 | 3.5 | 79% | 62% | 64% | 85% | 0.3% | 880-1130 | N/A | 43% | 27% |
| 133. **Whittier College** (CA) | 45 | 3.0 | 3.4 | 83% | 67% | 66% | 55% | 1% | 930-1150[3] | 23% | 63% | 21% |
| 139. **Alma College** (MI) | 44 | 2.6 | 3.2 | 80% | 65% | 61% | 71% | 2% | 22-27[3] | 27% | 69% | 22% |
| 139. **Central College** (IA) | 44 | 2.6 | 3.2 | 81% | 65% | 65% | 60% | 0.3% | 21-26 | 21% | 66% | 18% |
| 139. **Gordon College** (MA) | 44 | 2.6 | 3.3 | 82% | 71% | 72% | 67% | 3% | 1015-1292[3] | 34%[5] | 43% | 8% |
| 139. **Grove City College** (PA) | 44 | 2.4 | 3.0 | 90% | 81% | 82% | 46% | 5% | 1079-1334 | 41% | 81% | 21% |

**Note:** Key to footnotes, Page 89.

| Rank | School (State) (*Public) | Overall score | Peer assessment score (5.0=highest) | High school counselor assessment score | Average freshman retention rate | 2013 graduation rate | | % of classes under 20 ('13) | % of classes of 50 or more ('13) | SAT/ACT 25th-75th percentile ('13) | Freshmen in top 10% of HS class ('13) | Accept-ance rate ('13) | Average alumni giving rate |
|---|---|---|---|---|---|---|---|---|---|---|---|---|---|
| | | | | | | Predicted | Actual | | | | | | |
| 139. | Houghton College (NY) | 44 | 2.4 | 3.0 | 87% | 67% | 73% | 73% | 2% | 980-1235 | 35% | 91% | 18% |
| 139. | Principia College (IL) | 44 | 2.2 | 2.9 | 80%[8] | 76% | 82% | N/A | N/A | 918-1223 | 26%[5] | 84% | N/A |
| 139. | Simpson College (IA) | 44 | 2.6 | 3.2 | 80% | 63% | 65% | 72% | 1% | 21-27 | 29% | 88% | 16% |
| 139. | University of Minnesota–Morris* | 44 | 2.8 | 3.6 | 82% | 59% | 63% | 55% | 4% | 23-28[3] | 31% | 58% | 13% |
| 139. | Wittenberg University (OH) | 44 | 2.5 | 3.7 | 77% | 67% | 63% | 54% | 1% | 23-28[2] | 22% | 89% | 12% |
| 148. | Centenary College of Louisiana | 43 | 2.3 | 3.2 | 71% | 70% | 59% | 83% | 0.4% | 22-28 | 25% | 66% | 13% |
| 148. | Hiram College (OH) | 43 | 2.4 | 3.4 | 76% | 60% | 66% | 78% | 0% | 19-25 | 12% | 57% | 14% |
| 148. | Nebraska Wesleyan University | 43 | 2.6 | 3.4 | 79% | 63% | 68% | 65% | 2% | 22-26 | 23% | 77% | 15% |
| 148. | Oglethorpe University (GA) | 43 | 2.7 | 3.4 | 78% | 63% | 62% | 84% | 0% | 1030-1240 | 20% | 56% | 14% |
| 148. | Salem College (NC) | 43 | 2.4 | 3.1 | 77% | 63% | 64% | 90% | 0% | 1000-1200 | 39% | 58% | 23% |
| 148. | St. Vincent College (PA) | 43 | 2.4 | 2.9 | 83% | 64% | 70% | 55% | 0% | 910-1150 | 20% | 69% | 20% |
| 148. | Wells College (NY) | 43 | 2.7 | 3.6 | 73%[8] | 63% | 58% | 89% | 0% | 930-1070[2] | 32% | 60% | 23% |
| 155. | Carthage College (WI) | 42 | 2.5 | 3.4 | 76% | 63% | 65% | 64% | 0.1% | 21-27 | 21% | 70% | 14% |
| 155. | Georgetown College (KY) | 42 | 2.5 | 3.6 | 75% | 67% | 57% | 79% | 0% | 20-25 | 20% | 86% | 14% |
| 155. | Illinois College | 42 | 2.5 | 2.8 | 81% | 62% | 64% | 70% | 1% | 19-25[2] | 22% | 61% | 25% |
| 155. | William Jewell College (MO) | 42 | 2.5 | 3.4 | 75% | 69% | 59% | 72% | 0% | 22-28[2] | 23% | 58% | 11% |
| 159. | College of Idaho | 41 | 2.6 | 3.1 | 85% | 67% | 67% | 60% | 1% | 21-27 | 26% | 68% | 34% |
| 159. | Lycoming College (PA) | 41 | 2.5 | 3.2 | 81% | 60% | 64% | 62% | 1% | 930-1150[2] | 19% | 72% | 19% |
| 159. | U. of North Carolina–Asheville* | 41 | 2.9 | 3.4 | 80% | 58% | 60% | 50% | 2% | 1100-1290 | 22% | 69% | 8% |
| 159. | Wartburg College (IA) | 41 | 2.6 | 3.4 | 79% | 66% | 63% | 50% | 2% | 21-26[3] | 26% | 78% | 23% |
| 159. | Westminster College (MO) | 41 | 2.5 | 3.2 | 79% | 65% | 68% | 65% | 0% | 21-27 | 28% | 69% | 16% |
| 164. | Doane College (NE) | 40 | 2.2 | 3.1 | 76% | 53% | 61% | 74% | 1% | 21-26[3] | 20% | 72% | 21% |
| 165. | Fisk University (TN) | 39 | 2.6 | 3.4 | N/A | 54% | 52% | 68% | 1% | 17-23 | N/A | 21% | 24% |
| 165. | Hartwick College (NY) | 39 | 2.6 | 3.4 | 74% | 63% | 58% | 62% | 0.2% | 1010-1230[2] | 20% | 84% | 16% |
| 165. | Lyon College (AR) | 39 | 2.6 | 3.1 | 67% | 65% | 50% | 68% | 1% | 23-28 | 29% | 59% | 17% |
| 165. | Massachusetts Col. of Liberal Arts* | 39 | 2.5 | 3.3 | 75% | 49% | 57% | 72% | 0.2% | 910-1150[3] | 25%[5] | 67% | 10% |

| Rank | School (State) (*Public) | Overall score | Peer assessment score (5.0=highest) | High school counselor assessment score | Average freshman retention rate | 2013 graduation rate | | % of classes under 20 ('13) | % of classes of 50 or more ('13) | SAT/ACT 25th-75th percentile ('13) | Freshmen in top 10% of HS class ('13) | Accept-ance rate ('13) | Average alumni giving rate |
|------|--------------------------|---------------|--------------------------------------|------------------------------------------|----------------------------------|-----------|--------|------------------------------|------------------------------------|-------------------------------------|----------------------------------------|------------------------|------------------------------|
| | | | | | | Predicted | Actual | | | | | | |
| 165. | Monmouth College (IL) | 39 | 2.6 | 2.9 | 75% | 58% | 59% | 67% | 0.3% | 20-25 | 15% | 64% | 20% |
| 165. | Warren Wilson College (NC) | 39 | 2.6 | 3.3 | 68% | 68% | 51% | 84% | 0% | 1010-1250 | 22% | 70% | 11% |
| 171. | Purchase College–SUNY* | 38 | 2.4 | 3.3 | 82% | 48% | 60% | 77% | 1% | 980-1180[3] | 13%[5] | 33% | 4% |
| 172. | Eastern Mennonite University (VA) | 37 | 2.4 | 3.0 | 78% | 62% | 63% | 69% | 2% | 863-1128 | 16% | 65% | 23% |
| 172. | Emory and Henry College (VA) | 37 | 2.5 | 3.1 | 73% | 55% | 48% | 74% | 0% | 880-1120[3] | 26%[4] | 66% | 30%[4] |
| 172. | Guilford College (NC) | 37 | 2.8 | 3.2 | 74% | 58% | 57% | 55% | 0% | 970-1220[2] | 11% | 68% | 13% |
| 172. | Northland College (WI) | 37 | 2.3 | 3.0 | 71% | 61% | 58% | 70% | 0% | 21-27 | 18% | 59% | 11% |
| 176. | Ouachita Baptist University (AR) | 36 | 2.2 | 3.2 | 79% | 65% | 60% | 54% | 1% | 21-27 | 29% | 70% | 18% |
| 177. | Albright College (PA) | 34 | 2.5 | 3.1 | 74% | 58% | 54% | 63% | 1% | 930-1130[2] | 20% | 62% | 11% |
| 178. | Bridgewater College (VA) | 33 | 2.4 | 3.0 | 75% | 57% | 60% | 43% | 0% | 930-1130 | 20% | 55% | 18% |
| 178. | Erskine College (SC) | 33 | 2.3 | 3.3 | 68%[8] | 65% | 58% | 79% | 0.3% | 910-1110 | N/A | 70% | 16% |
| 178. | Wisconsin Lutheran College | 33 | 2.1 | 2.7 | 78% | 66% | 64% | 68% | 1% | 21-27 | 19% | 64% | 16% |
| 178. | Xavier University of Louisiana | 33 | 2.7 | 3.4 | 68% | 51% | 46% | 51% | 6% | 20-26 | 28% | 54% | 12% |

| School (State) (*Public) | Peer assessment score (5.0=highest) | High school counselor assessment score | Average freshman retention rate | 2013 graduation rate | | % of classes under 20 ('13) | % of classes of 50 or more ('13) | SAT/ACT 25th-75th percentile ('13) | Freshmen in top 10% of HS class ('13) | Accept-ance rate ('13) | Average alumni giving rate |
|--------------------------|--------------------------------------|------------------------------------------|----------------------------------|-----------|--------|------------------------------|------------------------------------|-------------------------------------|----------------------------------------|------------------------|------------------------------|
| | | | | Predicted | Actual | | | | | | |
| **SECOND TIER (SCHOOLS RANKED 182 THROUGH 236 ARE LISTED HERE ALPHABETICALLY)** | | | | | | | | | | | |
| Allen University (SC) | 1.7 | 2.2 | 46% | 35% | 23% | N/A | N/A | 16[2] | N/A | 50% | N/A |
| American Jewish University (CA) | 2.2 | 2.8 | 70% | 69% | 53%[6] | N/A | N/A | 780-1240[9] | N/A | 42% | N/A |
| Amridge University (AL) | 1.4 | 2.0 | N/A | 46% | 23%[6] | N/A | N/A | N/A[2] | N/A | N/A | N/A |
| Ave Maria University[1] (FL) | 2.1 | 2.6 | 70%[8] | 68% | 43%[6] | N/A | N/A | 20-27[4] | N/A | 61%[4] | N/A |
| Bay Path University (MA) | 2.2 | 2.4 | 74% | 50% | 55% | 78% | 0% | 840-1090[2] | 14% | 58% | 5% |

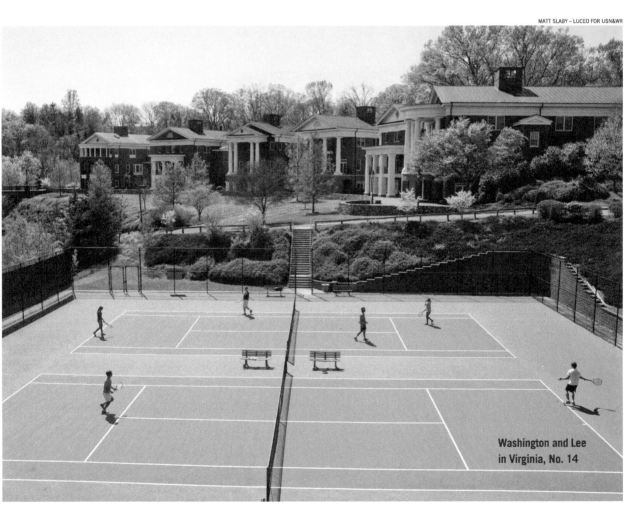

Washington and Lee
in Virginia, No. 14

| School (State) (*Public) | Peer assessment score (5.0=highest) | High school counselor assessment score | Average freshman retention rate | 2013 graduation rate | | % of classes under 20 ('13) | % of classes of 50 or more ('13) | SAT/ACT 25th-75th percentile ('13) | Freshmen in top 10% of HS class ('13) | Accept- ance rate ('13) | Average alumni giving rate |
|---|---|---|---|---|---|---|---|---|---|---|---|
| | | | | Predicted | Actual | | | | | | |
| SECOND TIER (SCHOOLS RANKED 182 THROUGH 236 ARE LISTED HERE ALPHABETICALLY) | | | | | | | | | | | |
| Bennett College[1] (NC) | 2.2 | 2.1 | 68%[8] | 32% | 41%[6] | 74%[4] | 0.4%[4] | 15-20[4] | 5%[4] | 69%[4] | N/A |
| Bethany College (WV) | 2.4 | 3.0 | 60% | 53% | 48% | 80% | 0% | 770-1040 | 12% | 49% | 18% |
| Bethany Lutheran College (MN) | 2.1 | 2.7 | 72% | 59% | 49% | 75% | 0.4% | 20-26 | 14% | 75% | 15% |
| Bloomfield College (NJ) | 2.0 | 2.5 | 67% | 31% | 37% | 71% | 1% | 770-930 | 6% | 59% | 4% |
| Brevard College (NC) | 2.3 | 3.0 | 58% | 49% | 43% | 74% | 0% | 850-1050 | 5% | 45% | 6% |
| Bryn Athyn Col. of New Church (PA) | 1.8 | 2.5 | 64% | 62% | 50% | 81%[4] | 0%[4] | 920-1130[3] | N/A | 52% | N/A |
| Burlington College (VT) | 2.3 | 3.2 | 62%[8] | 39% | 17% | 97%[4] | 0%[4] | 820-1130[9] | 5%[5] | 83% | 9% |
| Castleton State College (VT)* | 2.0 | 2.4 | 71% | 41% | 51% | 73% | 2% | 850-1060[3] | 8%[5] | 79% | 9% |
| Claflin University (SC) | 2.1 | 2.4 | 73% | 38% | 44% | 63% | 1% | 710-960 | 13% | 61% | 47% |
| Clearwater Christian College (FL) | 1.8 | 2.4 | 66% | 53% | 54% | 75% | 2% | 19-25 | 10%[5] | 70% | 3% |
| Col. of Sts. John Fisher & Thomas More[1] (TX) | 2.3 | 2.4 | N/A | 65% | 33%[6] | N/A | N/A | N/A[2] | N/A | N/A | N/A |
| Colorado Mesa University* | 2.0 | 2.9 | 65% | 37% | 33% | 50% | 7% | 18-23 | 10% | 82% | 2% |
| Dillard University (LA) | 2.1 | 3.0 | 64%[8] | 34% | 48% | 63% | 1% | 17-20 | 14%[5] | 35% | 4% |
| Eastern Nazarene College (MA) | 2.2 | 2.5 | 68% | 55% | 58% | 80% | 5% | 820-1090[3] | 9% | 51% | N/A |
| Fort Lewis College (CO)* | 2.5 | 2.9 | 64% | 44% | 37% | 46% | 3% | 20-25[3] | 10% | 88% | 2% |
| Green Mountain College (VT) | 2.1 | 2.8 | 70%[8] | 55% | 40% | 61% | 0% | 920-1200[9] | N/A | 76% | 7% |
| Harrisburg Univ. of Science and Tech. (PA) | 1.9 | 3.0 | 62%[8] | N/A | 24% | 76% | 0% | 830-1050[9] | N/A | 47%[4] | N/A |
| Holy Cross College[1] (IN) | 2.6 | 3.6 | 55%[8] | 45% | 21%[6] | 66%[4] | 1%[4] | 19-24[4] | N/A | 81%[4] | 5%[4] |
| Huston-Tillotson University[1] (TX) | 2.0 | 2.7 | 57%[8] | 25% | 23%[6] | N/A | N/A | 700-900[9] | N/A | 46% | N/A |
| Johnson C. Smith University (NC) | 2.1 | 2.5 | 68% | 36% | 44% | 75% | 0.2% | 733-920 | 8% | 37% | 15% |
| Judson College[1] (AL) | 2.2 | 2.8 | 71%[8] | 53% | 38%[6] | N/A | N/A | 19-24[9] | N/A | 74% | 20%[7] |
| Kentucky State University* | 2.0 | 3.3 | 51% | 28% | 18% | 53% | 0.2% | 16-20 | N/A | 38% | 4% |
| The King's College (NY) | 2.2 | 2.7 | 64% | 58% | 61% | 35% | 0% | 1050-1230 | 15%[5] | 71% | 14% |
| Lane College[1] (TN) | 1.9 | 2.1 | 55%[8] | 18% | 33%[6] | 50%[4] | 0%[4] | 14-17[4] | 3%[4] | 33%[4] | N/A |
| Life University (GA) | 1.6 | 2.6 | 70% | 50% | 22% | 68% | 1% | 19[3] | N/A | 41% | 1% |
| Louisiana State University–Alexandria* | 2.0 | 3.1 | 57% | 22% | 20% | 50% | 4% | 18-22 | 13% | 61% | 3% |
| Marymount Manhattan College (NY) | 2.2 | 3.2 | 66% | 60% | 44% | 57% | 1% | 930-1153 | N/A | 75% | 7% |
| Maryville College (TN) | 2.4 | 2.6 | 72% | 64% | 56% | 45% | 0.4% | 21-26 | 14%[5] | 73% | 25% |
| Pacific Union College (CA) | 2.4 | 3.1 | 76% | 55% | 37% | 60% | 5% | 890-1150 | N/A | 51% | 7% |
| Pine Manor College (MA) | 2.0 | 2.5 | 59% | 29% | 36% | 88% | 0% | 660-860[3] | N/A | 64% | 6% |
| Rust College (MS) | 2.1 | 2.6 | 60% | 19% | 20% | N/A | N/A | 13-14 | N/A | 14% | 5% |
| San Diego Christian College[1] | 1.9 | 2.9 | 59%[8] | 47% | 44%[8] | 80%[4] | 1%[4] | 18-22[4] | 5%[4] | 43%[4] | N/A |
| Savannah State University (GA)* | 2.0 | 2.8 | 70%[8] | 23% | 29% | 30% | 1% | 770-910 | N/A | 83% | N/A |
| Shawnee State University (OH)* | 2.0 | 2.5 | 52% | 35% | 24% | 44% | 3% | 17-23[2] | 12% | 83% | 1% |
| Shorter University[1] (GA) | 2.0 | 2.7 | 54%[8] | 51% | 49%[6] | N/A | N/A | 820-1060[9] | N/A | 68% | N/A |
| Simpson University (CA) | 2.4 | 3.2 | 71% | 50% | 49% | 71% | 5% | 910-1150 | 23% | 56% | 4% |
| Stillman College[1] (AL) | 2.4 | 3.1 | 60%[8] | 32% | 28%[8] | 65%[4] | 1%[4] | 16-19[4] | 5%[4] | 41%[4] | 5%[4] |
| SUNY College–Old Westbury* | 2.4 | 3.0 | 77% | 32% | 37% | 38% | 1% | 920-1080[3] | N/A | 58% | 1% |
| Tougaloo College (MS) | 2.1 | 2.1 | 74% | 46% | 50% | 70% | 0.3% | 15-21 | 19% | 34% | 13% |
| University of Hawaii–Hilo* | 2.5 | 3.2 | 70%[8] | 44% | 36% | 47% | 4% | 823-1050[3] | 18% | 75% | N/A |
| University of Maine–Machias* | 2.2 | 2.8 | 66% | 38% | 31% | 77% | 0% | 820-1050 | N/A | 85% | 0.1% |
| University of Pikeville (KY) | 1.7 | 3.3 | 52% | 45% | 29% | 48% | 3% | 17-22 | 15% | 100% | 5% |
| Univ. of Science and Arts of Okla.* | 2.5 | 3.2 | 67% | 43% | 37%[6] | 75% | 2% | 19-24 | 29% | 62% | 7% |
| University of Virginia–Wise* | 2.5 | 3.4 | 69% | 40% | 42% | 67% | 1% | 860-1050[3] | 15% | 75% | 10% |
| Univ. of Wisconsin–Parkside* | 2.1 | 2.9 | 65% | 41% | 31% | 45% | 9% | 19-23[2] | 10% | 69% | 1% |
| Virginia Intermont College[1] | 1.5 | 2.7 | 63%[8] | 44% | 25%[6] | 95%[4] | 0.3%[4] | 18-23[4] | 9%[4] | 99%[4] | 4%[4] |
| Virginia Wesleyan College | 2.5 | 3.0 | 65% | 53% | 44% | 81% | 0% | 907-1142[9] | 14% | 93% | 8% |
| Western State Colorado University* | 2.1 | 3.1 | 64% | 45% | 42% | 56% | 0.4% | 19-24 | 6% | 92% | N/A |
| West Virginia State University* | 2.1 | 3.1 | 53% | 29% | 17% | 53% | 2% | 18-22 | N/A | 45% | 2% |
| William Peace University[1] (NC) | 2.0 | 2.7 | 68%[8] | 46% | 38%[6] | 55%[4] | 1%[4] | 16-24[4] | 6%[4] | 61%[4] | 2%[4] |

**Footnotes:**
**1.** School refused to fill out U.S. News statistical survey. Data that appear are from school in previous years or from another source such as the National Center for Education Statistics.
**2.** SAT and/or ACT not required by school for some or all applicants.
**3.** In reporting SAT/ACT scores, the school did not include all students for whom it had scores, or refused to tell U.S. News whether all students with scores had been included.
**4.** Data reported to U.S. News in previous years.
**5.** Data based on fewer than 51 percent of enrolled freshmen.
**6.** Some or all data reported to the NCAA and/or the National Center for Education Statistics.
**7.** Data reported to the Council for Aid to Education.

**8.** Average graduation or freshman retention rates, normally based on four years of data, are given here for less than four years because school didn't report rates for the most recent year or years to U.S. News.
**9.** SAT and/or ACT may not be required by school for some or all applicants, and in reporting SAT/ACT scores, the school did not include all students for whom it had scores, or refused to tell U.S. News whether all students with scores had been included.
**‡** School appeared in a different U.S. News ranking category last year.

N/A means not available.

ATHENS

# ...University of Georgia
## Tia Samrawit Ayele, '14

I chose UGA because of its affordability, excellent academic reputation and strong sense of community. After completing my first year, I realized that it was the best decision I had ever made. As an Honors student, I have the best of both worlds: I attend a large land-grant university but still get a tightknit community feel from the Honors college. As an international affairs major, I've been able to pursue undergraduate research

# Why I

TUCSON

# ...University of Arizona
## Daniel Fried, '14

I chose UA for its rich, research-driven academic environment and opportunities for student involvement. As a computer science, information science and mathematics major, I took advantage of research opportunities in artificial intelligence and data visualization beginning my freshman year. I was impressed by the freedom and support that the school gives students to pursue their

passions. My interests have led me outside the campus borders: UA's study abroad program allowed me to spend a summer in Germany doing machine learning research, and I also had the opportunity to do a semesterlong research internship in Japan working in computational linguistics.

UA students have strikingly diverse backgrounds and extracurricular interests. They help guide NASA rov-

ers on Mars, launch award-winning businesses, and participate in over 600 student organizations on campus. Tucson's idyllic weather and nearby mountains allow year-round hiking, cycling and rock climbing, and the city has a thriving art and cultural scene. My time at UA has shaped my personal development and opened doors for my future that I never anticipated. ●

90   USN&WR • BEST COLLEGES

with renowned experts on Middle Eastern Studies, intern at a leading economic policy think tank, and develop other areas of interest – from women's issues to the Arabic language. UGA really encourages students to gain experience outside the classroom. With the enthusiastic support of school administrators, I received a prestigious 11-month grant to intern abroad in Ethiopia. And through UGA's School of

Public and International Affairs, I received a public policy fellowship that afforded me another internship opportunity, this time in the Washington, D.C., office of Georgia Sen. Johnny Isakson. My entire experience at UGA has given me outstanding contacts and policy exposure, which will be invaluable as I pursue a career in foreign affairs. ●

# Picked...

## BOSTON

## ...Northeastern University

### Rachael Tompa, '14

When I originally applied to Northeastern, I was excited because it was located in a vibrant city – Boston – and because it put such a strong emphasis on practical learning. I knew I wanted a career in aerospace and defense, so when I visited campus, I was happy not only to be shown the usual sights like dorms, classrooms and the beautiful rec center, but also to be taken on faculty-led tours of the university's state-of-the art electrical, mechanical and civil engineering labs. I was impressed, too, by Northeastern's outstanding co-op program, which enables students to rotate classroom work with on-the-job experience at major companies. Over the last few years, this has al-

lowed me to work on real-world projects in the fields I am particularly interested in. I got tremendous experience as I spent six-month rotations working in operations at Raytheon Company, flight testing at Sikorsky Aircraft, and in thermal engineering at NASA's Jet Propulsion Laboratory. These rotations, along with relationships I formed with professors, have helped me grow and have made it possible for me to be accepted to graduate school, where I will be studying aeronautics and astronautics. ●

# Best
# Regional Universities

## What Is a Regional University?

Like the national universities, the institutions that appear here provide a full range of undergraduate majors and master's programs; the difference is that they offer few, if any, doctoral programs. The 620 universities in this category are not ranked nationally but rather against their peer group in one of four regions – North, South, Midwest and West – because, in general, they tend to draw students most heavily from surrounding states.

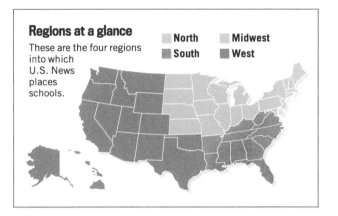

**Regions at a glance**
These are the four regions into which U.S. News places schools.

- North
- Midwest
- South
- West

## NORTH ▶

| Rank School (State) (*Public) | Overall score | Peer assessment score (5.0=highest) | Average freshman retention rate | 2013 graduation rate Predicted | 2013 graduation rate Actual | % of classes under 20 ('13) | % of classes of 50 or more ('13) | Student/ faculty ratio ('13) | SAT/ACT 25th-75th percentile ('13) | Freshmen in top 25% of HS class ('13) | Accept- ance rate ('13) | Average alumni giving rate |
|---|---|---|---|---|---|---|---|---|---|---|---|---|
| 1. Villanova University (PA) | 100 | 4.3 | 94% | 89% | 90% | 48% | 2% | 12/1 | 1210-1400 | 88%[5] | 49% | 23% |
| 2. Providence College (RI) | 83 | 3.7 | 91% | 78% | 85% | 48% | 3% | 12/1 | 1050-1260[2] | 67%[5] | 60% | 19% |
| 3. College of New Jersey* | 80 | 3.5 | 94% | 81% | 85% | 39% | 0.2% | 13/1 | 1130-1340 | 89% | 43% | 6% |
| 3. Fairfield University (CT) | 80 | 3.5 | 88% | 79% | 82% | 53% | 0.4% | 11/1 | 1090-1250[2] | 64%[4] | 70% | 16% |
| 3. Loyola University Maryland | 80 | 3.6 | 88% | 81% | 84% | 38% | 1% | 12/1 | 1100-1268[2] | 67%[5] | 58% | 14% |
| 6. Bentley University (MA) | 78 | 3.4 | 94% | 82% | 87% | 29% | 0.3% | 14/1 | 1140-1310[3] | 75%[5] | 44% | 7% |
| 7. University of Scranton (PA) | 76 | 3.4 | 89% | 68% | 82% | 49% | 0.1% | 11/1 | 1030-1210 | 59%[5] | 75% | 15% |
| 8. Rochester Inst. of Technology (NY) | 74 | 4.0 | 88% | 72% | 66% | 43% | 5% | 14/1 | 1110-1320 | 64% | 60% | 7% |
| 9. Ithaca College (NY) | 72 | 3.5 | 84%[8] | 73% | 76% | 59% | 4% | 11/1 | 1080-1270[2] | 63%[5] | 67% | 9% |
| 9. Quinnipiac University (CT) | 72 | 3.4 | 87% | 73% | 76% | 47% | 1% | 11/1 | 1000-1190 | 66% | 67% | 10% |
| 11. Bryant University (RI) | 70 | 3.0 | 88% | 72% | 82% | 25% | 0% | 16/1 | 1050-1220[2] | 50%[5] | 77% | 8% |
| 11. Marist College (NY) | 70 | 3.3 | 90% | 73% | 80% | 48% | 0% | 16/1 | 1090-1260[9] | 64%[5] | 37% | 15% |
| 11. St. Joseph's University (PA) | 70 | 3.3 | 89% | 73% | 79% | 34% | 1% | 14/1 | 1020-1200[2] | 52%[5] | 79% | 11% |
| 14. Emerson College (MA) | 69 | 3.2 | 88% | 82% | 81% | 63% | 2% | 13/1 | 1140-1320 | 68%[5] | 48% | 7% |
| 14. SUNY–Geneseo* | 69 | 3.6 | 91% | 80% | 78% | 33% | 9% | 19/1 | 1178-1360 | 84%[5] | 53% | 10% |
| 16. Simmons College (MA) | 66 | 3.1 | 85% | 69% | 71% | 69% | 4% | 10/1 | 1040-1250[3] | 61%[5] | 49% | 17% |
| 17. Gallaudet University (DC) | 64 | 3.2 | 72% | 47% | 48% | 94% | 0% | 8/1 | 15-20 | N/A | 65% | N/A |
| 18. Manhattan College (NY) | 63 | 3.0 | 85% | 66% | 74% | 47% | 0% | 12/1 | 970-1190 | 52%[5] | 66% | 15% |
| 19. Le Moyne College (NY) | 61 | 3.0 | 85% | 59% | 74% | 40% | 2% | 13/1 | 980-1170[3] | 51% | 62% | 16% |
| 19. Mount St. Mary's University (MD) | 61 | 3.1 | 80% | 63% | 66% | 46% | 1% | 13/1 | 990-1180 | 35% | 67% | 23% |
| 19. Pratt Institute (NY) | 61 | 3.3 | 83% | 67% | 62% | 71% | 1% | 10/1 | 1070-1300 | N/A | 67% | N/A |
| 19. Rowan University (NJ)* | 61 | 3.1 | 86% | 58% | 70% | 45% | 1% | 13/1 | 1000-1230 | 63%[4] | 60% | 4% |
| 23. Rider University (NJ) | 60 | 2.9 | 80% | 55% | 65% | 51% | 1% | 12/1 | 930-1150 | 38% | 69% | 10% |
| 24. St. Bonaventure University (NY) | 59 | 3.0 | 81% | 57% | 67% | 62% | 0% | 11/1 | 930-1180 | 45%[5] | 80% | 20% |
| 25. CUNY–Baruch College* | 58 | 3.1 | 90% | 54% | 67% | 20% | 15% | 16/1 | 1130-1330 | 70% | 27% | 6% |
| 25. SUNY–New Paltz* | 58 | 3.0 | 88% | 56% | 70% | 40% | 3% | 15/1 | 1030-1220 | 70%[5] | 44% | 7% |
| 27. Canisius College (NY) | 57 | 2.8 | 83% | 64% | 67% | 49% | 0.3% | 12/1 | 980-1200 | 53% | 73% | 12% |
| 28. Ramapo College of New Jersey* | 56 | 2.8 | 88% | 69% | 73% | 37% | 0% | 17/1 | 990-1200 | 52%[5] | 55% | 13% |
| 28. Rutgers, The State U. of N.J.–Camden* | 56 | 3.1 | 82% | 50% | 55% | 37% | 8% | 11/1 | 930-1140[3] | 43% | 59% | 3% |
| 28. Wagner College (NY) | 56 | 3.0 | 82% | 71% | 62% | 63% | 1% | 14/1 | 1050-1270[2] | 73% | 70% | 11% |
| 31. Assumption College (MA) | 55 | 2.7 | 83% | 59% | 73% | 40% | 0% | 12/1 | 1020-1215[2] | 40% | 74% | 13% |
| 31. CUNY–Queens College* | 55 | 2.8 | 87% | 42% | 56% | 41% | 5% | 14/1 | 1030-1220 | 65% | 37% | 20% |
| 31. Hood College (MD) | 55 | 2.9 | 77% | 62% | 66% | 72% | 0.3% | 12/1 | 910-1160[2] | 45%[5] | 81% | 19% |
| 31. La Salle University (PA) | 55 | 3.1 | 81% | 59% | 65% | 44% | 2% | 13/1 | 880-1100 | 38% | 80% | 11% |
| 31. Nazareth College (NY) | 55 | 2.6 | 81% | 70% | 68% | 62% | 0% | 10/1 | 1020-1180[2] | 65% | 68% | 12% |
| 31. Springfield College (MA) | 55 | 2.8 | 85% | 51% | 69% | 52% | 2% | 13/1 | 920-1130 | 35% | 70% | 12% |
| 37. Monmouth University (NJ) | 54 | 2.9 | 80% | 59% | 61% | 44% | 0% | 14/1 | 970-1150 | 49%[5] | 78% | 5% |
| 38. Alfred University (NY) | 53 | 2.9 | 74% | 60% | 62% | 59% | 3% | 12/1 | 1000-1200 | 43% | 70% | 15% |

**Note:** Key to footnotes, Page 106.

# Best Regional Universities

## NORTH ▶

| Rank | School (State) (*Public) | Overall score | Peer assessment score (5.0=highest) | Average freshman retention rate | 2013 graduation rate Predicted | Actual | % of classes under 20 ('13) | % of classes of 50 or more ('13) | Student/ faculty ratio ('13) | SAT/ACT 25th-75th percentile ('13) | Freshmen in top 25% of HS class ('13) | Accept- ance rate ('13) | Average alumni giving rate |
|---|---|---|---|---|---|---|---|---|---|---|---|---|---|
| 38. | Marywood University (PA) | 53 | 2.6 | 83% | 56% | 65% | 62% | 1% | 11/1 | 950-1150 | 47% | 70% | 16% |
| 38. | Sacred Heart University (CT) | 53 | 2.9 | 79% | 63% | 70% | 42% | 1% | 14/1 | 1020-1170[2] | 39%[5] | 61% | 7% |
| 41. | Arcadia University (PA) | 52 | 2.8 | 80% | 64% | 61% | 75% | 4% | 12/1 | 1000-1178 | 62% | 60% | 14% |
| 41. | College of St. Rose (NY) | 52 | 2.6 | 79% | 59% | 66% | 65% | 0.1% | 13/1 | 940-1150[9] | 44% | 78% | 19% |
| 41. | King's College (PA) | 52 | 2.6 | 78% | 54% | 66% | 59% | 0% | 13/1 | 940-1150[2] | 38% | 72% | 13% |
| 41. | Misericordia University (PA) | 52 | 2.6 | 84% | 55% | 69% | 48% | 0% | 13/1 | 970-1140[3] | 56% | 65% | 21% |
| 41. | Molloy College (NY) | 52 | 2.3 | 89% | 54% | 66% | 69% | 0% | 10/1 | 970-1140 | 56%[5] | 73% | 10% |
| 41. | Richard Stockton Col. of N.J.* | 52 | 2.8 | 86% | 55% | 65% | 24% | 2% | 17/1 | 980-1170 | 60% | 62% | 3% |
| 41. | Roger Williams University (RI) | 52 | 2.9 | 80% | 63% | 62% | 46% | 1% | 14/1 | 1020-1200[9] | 37%[5] | 81% | 7% |
| 41. | SUNY College–Oneonta* | 52 | 2.9 | 85% | 59% | 68% | 38% | 4% | 18/1 | 1020-1180 | 58%[5] | 43% | 7% |
| 41. | SUNY–Fredonia* | 52 | 2.8 | 81% | 52% | 65% | 62% | 5% | 15/1 | 950-1140 | 39% | 52% | 6% |
| 50. | CUNY–Hunter College* | 51 | 3.2 | 86% | 49% | 50% | 38% | 7% | 14/1 | 1070-1270 | 56% | 31% | 11% |
| 50. | Montclair State University (NJ)* | 51 | 3.0 | 83% | 52% | 63% | 34% | 2% | 17/1 | 880-1060 | 35% | 65% | 4% |
| 50. | New York Inst. of Technology | 51 | 2.8 | 75% | 60% | 47% | 62% | 1% | 11/1 | 1020-1220 | 52%[5] | 74% | 14% |
| 50. | Niagara University (NY) | 51 | 2.8 | 80% | 54% | 65% | 51% | 1% | 12/1 | 930-1120[3] | 41% | 66% | 12% |
| 50. | Notre Dame of Maryland University | 51 | 2.8 | 73% | 56% | 53% | 88% | 0% | 12/1 | 930-1150 | 61% | 50% | 11% |
| 50. | Salve Regina University (RI) | 51 | 2.7 | 81% | 65% | 64% | 39% | 0% | 13/1 | 1020-1190[2] | 45% | 67% | 16% |
| 56. | Chatham University (PA) | 50 | 2.6 | 74% | 61% | 50% | 83% | 0% | 10/1 | 950-1190[2] | 65% | 61% | 22% |
| 56. | Mercyhurst University (PA) | 50 | 2.6 | 80% | 54% | 61% | 52% | 1% | 14/1 | 940-1160 | 29% | 75% | 15% |
| 56. | St. Francis University (PA) | 50 | 2.5 | 82% | 59% | 70% | 55% | 2% | 14/1 | 930-1160 | 42% | 76% | 15% |
| 56. | SUNY–Oswego* | 50 | 3.0 | 80% | 51% | 58% | 56% | 6% | 18/1 | 1040-1180[3] | 55% | 49% | 8% |
| 60. | College at Brockport–SUNY* | 49 | 2.7 | 83% | 51% | 67% | 36% | 6% | 19/1 | 960-1150 | 39% | 48% | 5% |
| 60. | Emmanuel College (MA) | 49 | 2.6 | 82% | 56% | 58% | 44% | 0% | 14/1 | 1000-1180[2] | 54%[5] | 60% | 18% |
| 60. | Gannon University (PA) | 49 | 2.7 | 79% | 58% | 64% | 54% | 1% | 14/1 | 930-1150 | 54% | 80% | 10% |
| 60. | Suffolk University (MA) | 49 | 2.9 | 75% | 57% | 55% | 37% | 1% | 11/1 | 890-1130 | 42%[5] | 83% | 5% |
| 60. | Towson University (MD)* | 49 | 3.1 | 85% | 57% | 65% | 30% | 2% | 17/1 | 990-1170 | 49% | 60% | 4% |
| 65. | CUNY–City College* | 48 | 3.0 | 84% | 55% | 42% | 44% | 0.4% | 14/1 | 970-1090[3] | 44%[5] | 34% | 23% |
| 65. | Johnson & Wales University (RI) | 48 | 2.9 | 76% | 37% | 54% | 44% | 0.1% | 24/1 | N/A[2] | N/A | 76% | N/A |
| 65. | Salisbury University (MD)* | 48 | 2.9 | 82% | 62% | 67% | 34% | 4% | 16/1 | 1080-1230[9] | 59%[5] | 55% | 13% |
| 65. | West Chester Univ. of Pennsylvania* | 48 | 2.8 | 86% | 55% | 69% | 22% | 7% | 20/1 | 1020-1190 | 45% | 52% | 6% |
| 65. | Western New England Univ. (MA) | 48 | 2.6 | 75% | 59% | 59% | 51% | 0% | 13/1 | 960-1180 | 44%[5] | 82% | 6% |
| 70. | CUNY–Brooklyn College* | 47 | 3.0 | 84% | 45% | 51% | 33% | 3% | 16/1 | 980-1170 | 50%[5] | 34% | 6% |
| 70. | DeSales University (PA) | 47 | 2.5 | 83% | 60% | 70% | 44% | 2% | 14/1 | 930-1190 | 47%[5] | 76% | 9% |
| 70. | St. Joseph's College New York | 47 | 2.5 | 85% | 56% | 72% | 66% | 0% | 14/1 | 950-1150 | N/A | 75% | 5% |
| 70. | SUNY College–Cortland* | 47 | 2.7 | 83% | 52% | 70% | 25% | 8% | 17/1 | 980-1130[2] | 61%[4] | 47% | 7% |
| 74. | Endicott College (MA) | 46 | 2.5 | 83% | 59% | 70% | 51% | 0% | 14/1 | 980-1160 | 39%[5] | 72% | 16% |
| 74. | Iona College (NY) | 46 | 2.8 | 82% | 62% | 63% | 38% | 0.1% | 15/1 | 900-1110 | 31%[5] | 92% | 9% |
| 74. | Keene State College (NH)* | 46 | 2.8 | 77% | 48% | 63% | 55% | 1% | 16/1 | 860-1080[3] | 19% | 82% | 7% |
| 74. | Norwich University (VT) | 46 | 2.7 | 79% | 59% | 57% | 57% | 1% | 13/1 | 950-1160[3] | 33% | 63% | 14% |
| 74. | SUNY–Plattsburgh* | 46 | 2.7 | 81% | 50% | 60% | 45% | 5% | 16/1 | 930-1120[3] | 45% | 46% | 7% |
| 79. | Fairleigh Dickinson Univ. (NJ) | 45 | 3.0 | 73% | 55% | 51% | 67% | 1% | 14/1 | 900-1100 | 43% | 53% | 4% |
| 79. | Philadelphia University | 45 | 2.6 | 76% | 61% | 58% | 61% | 1% | 12/1 | 960-1160 | 45% | 63% | 7% |
| 79. | University of New England (ME) | 45 | 2.8 | 76% | 62% | 58% | 50% | 6% | 13/1 | 950-1150 | 58%[4] | 86% | 10% |
| 79. | Wheelock College (MA) | 45 | 2.6 | 71% | 53% | 54% | 60% | 0% | 12/1 | 890-1090 | 38%[5] | 73% | 15% |
| 83. | Manhattanville College (NY) | 44 | 2.6 | 73% | 63% | 58% | 71% | 0% | 12/1 | 970-1180[2] | N/A | 77% | 13% |
| 83. | Slippery Rock U. of Pennsylvania* | 44 | 2.7 | 82% | 47% | 63% | 17% | 8% | 20/1 | 910-1090 | 36% | 67% | 9% |
| 83. | University of Hartford (CT) | 44 | 2.8 | 72% | 60% | 58% | 62% | 1% | 10/1 | 950-1150[3] | N/A | 65% | 4% |
| 83. | Wilkes University (PA) | 44 | 2.5 | 80% | 59% | 58% | 52% | 6% | 14/1 | 930-1150 | 53% | 80% | 14% |
| 87. | College of St. Elizabeth (NJ) | 43 | 2.3 | 69% | 47% | 56% | 87% | 0% | 10/1 | 748-960 | 10% | 48% | 15% |
| 87. | Millersville U. of Pennsylvania* | 43 | 2.7 | 81% | 54% | 61% | 23% | 7% | 22/1 | 920-1110 | 34% | 65% | 6% |
| 87. | Roberts Wesleyan College (NY) | 43 | 2.5 | 81% | 56% | 61% | 64% | 2% | 12/1 | 920-1170 | 52% | 73% | 12% |
| 87. | The Sage Colleges (NY) | 43 | 2.4 | 76% | 40% | 58% | 59% | 0% | 11/1 | 840-1090[2] | 43% | 57% | 11% |
| 87. | Shippensburg U. of Pennsylvania* | 43 | 2.8 | 71% | 48% | 55% | 26% | 3% | 19/1 | 890-1080 | 26% | 83% | 13% |
| 87. | SUNY College–Potsdam* | 43 | 2.7 | 76% | 46% | 51% | 68% | 2% | 13/1 | 930-1170[2] | 23%[5] | 68% | 9% |
| 87. | Univ. of Massachusetts–Dartmouth* | 43 | 3.0 | 73% | 55% | 49% | 38% | 12% | 18/1 | 980-1180 | 46% | 75% | 6% |
| 87. | University of St. Joseph (CT) | 43 | 2.6 | 77%[8] | 55% | 52% | 73% | 1% | 10/1 | 880-1040 | 41% | 64% | 14% |
| 87. | York College of Pennsylvania | 43 | 2.5 | 76% | 55% | 58% | 44% | 0.3% | 16/1 | 950-1138 | 40% | 74% | 8% |
| 96. | Robert Morris University (PA) | 42 | 2.6 | 78% | 51% | 56% | 43% | 5% | 15/1 | 940-1140 | 42% | 80% | 5% |
| 96. | Rosemont College (PA) | 42 | 2.2 | 71% | 51% | 68% | 85% | 0% | 10/1 | 800-1040 | 49%[5] | 58% | 14% |
| 98. | Bloomsburg U. of Pennsylvania* | 41 | 2.7 | 80% | 49% | 62% | 19% | 7% | 21/1 | 890-1070 | 26% | 89% | 8% |
| 98. | Eastern University (PA) | 41 | 2.3 | 79% | 56% | 55% | 85% | 0.2% | 13/1 | 920-1160 | 51% | 75% | 11% |

**Note:** Key to footnotes, Page 106.

# Go beyond.

Florida Southern College's programs are infused with experiences that take you beyond the classroom to immerse you fully in your field. Science students conduct collaborative research with faculty and publish in national journals. Performance majors take the stage alongside world-renowned artists. Business students intern at international Fortune 500 companies. Small classes and a commitment to engaged learning that includes guaranteed internships and study-abroad experiences ensure that *your program* is tailored to *your goals*. Go beyond the ordinary.

FLORIDA SOUTHERN COLLEGE®
FLSOUTHERN.EDU • LAKELAND, FLORIDA

## NORTH ▶

| Rank | School (State) (*Public) | Overall score | Peer assessment score (5.0=highest) | Average freshman retention rate | 2013 graduation rate Predicted | 2013 graduation rate Actual | % of classes under 20 ('13) | % of classes of 50 or more ('13) | Student/ faculty ratio ('13) | SAT/ACT 25th-75th percentile ('13) | Freshmen in top 25% of HS class ('13) | Accept-ance rate ('13) | Average alumni giving rate |
|---|---|---|---|---|---|---|---|---|---|---|---|---|---|
| 98. | Stevenson University (MD) | 41 | 2.7 | 74% | 55% | 56% | 65% | 0% | 13/1 | 890-1100[3] | 31% | 60% | 4% |
| 98. | St. Peter's University (NJ) | 41 | 2.5 | 74% | 46% | 53% | 67% | 0% | 13/1 | 830-1000 | 38% | 54% | 13% |
| 98. | University of New Haven (CT) | 41 | 2.6 | 75% | 55% | 55% | 38% | 3% | 16/1 | 930-1130 | 41%[5] | 74% | 9% |
| 103. | Eastern Connecticut State Univ.* | 40 | 2.6 | 77% | 50% | 51% | 37% | 1% | 16/1 | 930-1100 | 31% | 65% | 8% |
| 103. | Plymouth State University (NH)* | 40 | 2.7 | 74% | 45% | 56% | 53% | 2% | 16/1 | 860-1070 | 20% | 78% | 6% |
| 103. | William Paterson Univ. of N.J.* | 40 | 2.6 | 77% | 47% | 49% | 52% | 0.4% | 15/1 | 920-1100 | N/A | 68% | 5% |
| 106. | SUNY Buffalo State* | 39 | 2.7 | 75% | 42% | 50% | 46% | 7% | 15/1 | 890-1060 | 32%[5] | 49% | 4%[4] |
| 106. | SUNY Institute of Tech.–Utica/Rome* | 39 | 2.4 | 75% | 52% | 48% | 64% | 1% | 18/1 | 1010-1160 | 45% | 48% | 4% |
| 106. | Waynesburg University (PA) | 39 | 2.4 | 80% | 51% | 54% | 68% | 1% | 14/1 | 890-1110 | 47% | 83% | 7% |
| 109. | Gwynedd Mercy University (PA) | 38 | 2.4 | 80% | 49% | 67% | 70% | 3% | 14/1 | 850-1050 | 21% | 66% | 6% |
| 109. | Mount St. Mary College (NY) | 38 | 2.4 | 70% | 48% | 52% | 48% | 0.2% | 14/1 | 910-1093 | 38% | 86% | 11% |
| 111. | Alvernia University (PA) | 37 | 2.5 | 73% | 44% | 51% | 64% | 1% | 12/1 | 890-1070[3] | 33% | 78% | 9% |
| 111. | Cairn University | 37 | 2.1 | 76%[8] | 52% | 60%[6] | 68% | 1% | 13/1 | 900-1170[3] | 49%[5] | 68% | 14% |
| 111. | Central Connecticut State Univ.* | 37 | 2.6 | 78% | 50% | 52% | 42% | 2% | 16/1 | 910-1100 | 21% | 64% | 5% |
| 111. | Lesley University (MA) | 37 | 2.5 | 76%[8] | 57% | 48%[6] | 73%[4] | 0%[4] | 28/1[4] | 970-1180[4] | 40%[4] | 64%[4] | N/A |
| 115. | Albertus Magnus College (CT) | 36 | 2.4 | 80%[8] | 42% | 43% | 98% | 0% | 14/1 | 820-930 | 26%[5] | 71% | 18% |
| 115. | Caldwell University (NJ) | 36 | 2.2 | 75% | 46% | 55% | 70% | 0% | 11/1 | 830-1070 | 25%[5] | 66% | 14% |
| 115. | CUNY–College of Staten Island* | 36 | 2.7 | 83% | 38% | 50% | 30% | 3% | 15/1 | 920-1100 | N/A | 100% | 2% |
| 115. | University of Baltimore[1] (MD)* | 36 | 2.7 | 77%[8] | N/A | N/A | 30%[4] | 0%[4] | 19/1[4] | 17-21[4] | N/A | 64%[4] | 8%[4] |
| 115. | Westfield State University (MA)* | 36 | 2.5 | 80% | 49% | 59% | 35% | 1% | 17/1 | 910-1090 | 22% | 75% | 6% |
| 120. | College of Mount St. Vincent (NY) | 35 | 2.3 | 71% | 47% | 52% | 53% | 0% | 13/1 | 810-990[4] | 26% | 91% | 16% |
| 120. | Utica College (NY) | 35 | 2.5 | 66% | 46% | 47% | 66% | 0% | 11/1 | 830-1050[9] | 28% | 85% | 9% |
| 122. | CUNY–John Jay Col. of Crim. Justice* | 34 | 3.0 | 78% | 42% | 43% | 31% | 1% | 18/1[4] | 840-1030 | N/A | 53% | 1% |
| 122. | Point Park University (PA) | 34 | 2.3 | 76% | 46% | 50% | 75% | 1% | 13/1 | 870-1100 | 31%[5] | 74% | 3% |
| 122. | Rhode Island College* | 34 | 2.8 | 76% | 47% | 43% | 50% | 1% | 14/1 | 820-1030[3] | 40% | 72% | 6% |
| 125. | CUNY–Lehman College* | 33 | 2.7 | 80%[8] | 33% | 36% | 46% | 1% | 15/1 | 890-1050 | N/A | 25% | 4%[7] |
| 125. | Frostburg State University (MD)* | 33 | 2.7 | 74% | 46% | 47% | 50% | 2% | 16/1 | 860-1070 | 27% | 59% | 5% |
| 125. | Georgian Court University (NJ) | 33 | 2.1 | 71% | 48% | 51% | 73% | 0% | 12/1 | 790-1010[3] | 30% | 78% | 10% |
| 125. | Holy Family University (PA) | 33 | 2.0 | 77% | 49% | 55% | 63% | 0.2% | 12/1 | 850-1020 | 35% | 78% | 5% |
| 125. | Keuka College (NY) | 33 | 2.4 | 71% | 42% | 48% | 63% | 1% | 14/1 | 860-1050[3] | 27% | 88% | 11% |
| 125. | Kutztown Univ. of Pennsylvania* | 33 | 2.6 | 75% | 47% | 55% | 23% | 12% | 20/1 | 870-1050 | 20% | 75% | 6% |
| 125. | St. Thomas Aquinas College (NY) | 33 | 2.5 | 77%[8] | 46% | 53% | 50% | 13% | 20/1 | 830-1050[3] | 30%[5] | 82% | 14% |
| 125. | Worcester State University (MA)* | 33 | 2.6 | 78% | 50% | 49% | 69% | 0.2% | 18/1 | 920-1110 | N/A | 61% | 7% |
| 133. | Cabrini College (PA) | 32 | 2.3 | 72% | 50% | 46% | 76% | 0% | 12/1 | 780-1000[3] | 21% | 74% | 7% |
| 133. | East Stroudsburg Univ. of Pa.* | 32 | 2.5 | 73%[8] | 47% | 56% | 28% | 11% | 22/1 | 880-1010[3] | 10%[5] | 78% | 5%[7] |
| 135. | Delaware State University* | 31 | 2.5 | 66% | 36% | 37% | 50% | 3% | 16/1 | 820-970 | 26% | 45% | 6% |
| 135. | Edinboro Univ. of Pennsylvania* | 31 | 2.5 | 72% | 38% | 46% | 30% | 9% | 19/1 | 820-1040 | 24% | 87% | 5% |
| 135. | Mansfield Univ. of Pennsylvania* | 31 | 2.3 | 71% | 44% | 50% | 35% | 6% | 17/1 | 850-1070 | 29% | 92% | 8% |
| 135. | Western Connecticut State Univ.* | 31 | 2.5 | 73% | 51% | 44% | 36% | 2% | 15/1 | 890-1080 | 28% | 65% | N/A |

| School (State) (*Public) | Peer assessment score (5.0=highest) | Average freshman retention rate | 2013 graduation rate Predicted | 2013 graduation rate Actual | % of classes under 20 ('13) | % of classes of 50 or more ('13) | Student/ faculty ratio ('13) | SAT/ACT 25th-75th percentile ('13) | Freshmen in top 25% of HS class ('13) | Accept-ance rate ('13) | Average alumni giving rate |
|---|---|---|---|---|---|---|---|---|---|---|---|
| SECOND TIER (SCHOOLS RANKED 139 THROUGH 181 ARE LISTED HERE ALPHABETICALLY) | | | | | | | | | | | |
| American International College (MA) | 2.0 | 64% | 45% | 45% | 54% | 3% | 14/1 | 836-869 | N/A | 68% | 8% |
| Anna Maria College (MA) | 1.9 | 61%[8] | 41% | 47% | 77% | 1% | 10/1 | 765-975[4] | N/A | 78% | 9% |
| Bridgewater State University (MA)* | 2.5 | 81%[8] | 50% | 58% | 44% | 1% | 19/1 | 890-1090[3] | N/A | 79% | 5% |
| California U. of Pennsylvania* | 2.4 | 76% | 46% | 54% | 22% | 15% | 20/1 | 850-1040 | 25% | 90% | 5% |
| Carlow University[1] (PA) | 2.2 | 70%[8] | 46% | 53%[6] | N/A | N/A | 11/1[4] | 855-1035[9] | N/A | 95% | N/A |
| Centenary College (NJ) | 2.1 | 76% | 46% | 57% | 82% | 0% | 17/1 | 820-1090 | 28%[5] | 91% | 6% |
| Chestnut Hill College (PA) | 2.3 | 72% | 48% | 41% | 82% | 0% | 10/1 | 850-1060 | 29% | 57% | 18% |
| Cheyney U. of Pennsylvania* | 1.8 | 55% | 25% | 25% | 47% | 10% | 16/1 | 670-850[3] | 9%[5] | 88% | 4% |
| Clarion U. of Pennsylvania* | 2.3 | 70%[8] | 39% | 53% | 21% | 7% | 20/1 | 840-1030 | 9% | 93% | 6% |
| College of New Rochelle[1] (NY) | 2.2 | 56%[8] | 27% | 29%[6] | N/A | N/A | 14/1[4] | 900-1055[9] | N/A | 57% | N/A |
| College of St. Joseph (VT) | 2.3 | 53% | 35% | 21% | 97% | 0% | 7/1 | 705-985[3] | 20%[4] | 73% | 4% |
| Coppin State University[1] (MD)* | 2.2 | 66%[8] | 29% | 16%[6] | N/A | N/A | 14/1[4] | 810-950[4] | N/A | 36%[4] | 6%[7] |
| Curry College (MA) | 2.1 | 68% | 47% | 45% | 61% | 0% | 11/1 | 840-1030[2] | 20%[5] | 87% | 5% |
| Daemen College (NY) | 2.2 | 78% | 55% | 49% | 57% | 2% | 14/1 | 920-1140[2] | 51% | 49% | 5% |
| Dominican College (NY) | 2.1 | 68% | 43% | 36% | 61% | 1% | 15/1 | 810-1000 | N/A | 72% | N/A |
| Dowling College (NY) | 1.9 | 64% | 43% | 34% | 75% | 1% | 15/1 | N/A[2] | N/A | 74% | N/A |

**Note:** Key to footnotes, Page 106.

# 1

## FLORIDA'S FIRST AND FINEST REGIONAL UNIVERSITY

**NO. 1 IN FLORIDA** *"America's Top Colleges" by Forbes* (2011)

**NO. 1 IN FLORIDA AND NO. 9 IN THE NATION FOR PART-TIME MBA** *Bloomberg Businessweek* (2013)

**NO. 1 MBA IN FLORIDA** *Forbes* 2005–2013

**MOST BEAUTIFUL CAMPUSES** *The Best Colleges* 2011-2013

Winter Park · Orlando, FL  |  rollins.edu

ROLLINS

## NORTH ▶

SECOND TIER CONTINUED (SCHOOLS RANKED 139 THROUGH 181 ARE LISTED HERE ALPHABETICALLY)

| School (State) (*Public) | Peer assessment score (5.0=highest) | Average freshman retention rate | 2013 graduation rate Predicted | 2013 graduation rate Actual | % of classes under 20 ('13) | % of classes of 50 or more ('13) | Student/ faculty ratio ('13) | SAT/ACT 25th-75th percentile ('13) | Freshmen in top 25% of HS class ('13) | Accept- ance rate ('13) | Average alumni giving rate |
|---|---|---|---|---|---|---|---|---|---|---|---|
| D'Youville College (NY) | 2.1 | 74% | 50% | 41% | 63% | 3% | 11/1 | 950-1140 | 47%[5] | 79% | 18% |
| Felician College (NJ) | 2.1 | 70% | 43% | 46% | 85% | 0% | 12/1 | 780-980[3] | 24% | 88% | 5% |
| Fitchburg State University (MA)* | 2.5 | 76% | 50% | 50% | 38% | 1% | 15/1 | 900-1090 | N/A | 74% | 5% |
| Framingham State University (MA)* | 2.5 | 74% | 53% | 51% | 41% | 1% | 16/1 | 930-1100 | 28%[5] | 56% | 5% |
| Franklin Pierce University (NH) | 2.4 | 65% | 50% | 44% | 67% | 2% | 12/1 | 860-1060 | 20% | 93% | 5% |
| Husson University (ME) | 2.2 | 70% | 39% | 44% | 57% | 0.4% | 15/1 | 850-1080 | 59% | 80% | 5% |
| Johnson State College (VT)* | 2.2 | N/A | 38% | 33%[6] | N/A | N/A | N/A | N/A[2] | N/A | N/A | N/A |
| Kean University (NJ)* | 2.4 | 77% | 44% | 46% | 31% | 0% | 17/1 | 810-1000[3] | 26% | 80% | 2% |
| Lincoln University (PA)* | 2.3 | 66% | 33% | 40% | 49% | 1% | 17/1 | 770-960 | 28% | 61% | 8% |
| LIU Post (NY) | 2.4 | 71% | 52% | 39% | 62% | 2% | 11/1 | 880-1060 | N/A | 81% | 2% |
| Lock Haven U. of Pennsylvania* | 2.3 | 70%[8] | 42% | 50% | 30% | 12% | 21/1 | 840-1050 | 30% | 86% | 6% |
| Medaille College (NY) | 1.9 | 67%[8] | 48% | 53%[6] | 52% | 1% | 18/1 | 760-970[3] | N/A | 54% | N/A |
| Monroe College (NY) | 2.0 | 75% | N/A | 71% | 46% | 0% | 15/1 | N/A[2] | N/A | 44% | 1% |
| Neumann University (PA) | 2.3 | 72% | 48% | 50% | 51% | 1% | 14/1 | 770-950 | N/A | 94% | 10% |
| New England College (NH) | 2.4 | 60% | 44% | 40% | 80% | 0% | 14/1 | 810-1020[2] | 12%[5] | 90% | 6% |
| New Jersey City University* | 2.3 | 70% | 39% | 32% | 55% | 0% | 15/1 | 820-1012 | 37%[5] | 41% | 4% |
| Nyack College[1] (NY) | 2.1 | 66%[8] | 44% | 41%[6] | N/A | N/A | 13/1[4] | 770-1055[9] | N/A | 97% | N/A |
| Rivier University (NH) | 2.1 | 77%[8] | 50% | 59% | N/A | N/A | 17/1 | 860-1020[9] | N/A | N/A | N/A |
| Salem State University (MA)* | 2.5 | 77% | 46% | 46% | 47% | 1% | 15/1 | 890-1080[3] | N/A | 72% | 5% |
| Southern Connecticut State Univ.* | 2.6 | 76% | 47% | 49% | 41% | 1% | 14/1 | 820-1020 | 21% | 75% | 3%[7] |
| St. Joseph's College[1] (ME) | 2.5 | 75%[8] | 52% | 55%[6] | N/A | N/A | 15/1[4] | 870-1050[9] | N/A | 78% | N/A |
| Touro College (NY) | 1.9 | 83%[8] | 63% | 50% | 87% | 1% | 16/1 | 1040-1260[2] | N/A | 65% | 1% |
| Trinity University[1] (DC) | 2.7 | 64%[8] | 46% | 37%[6] | N/A | N/A | 12/1[4] | N/A[2] | N/A | 52% | N/A |
| University of Bridgeport (CT) | 2.1 | 58% | 44% | 27% | 62% | 1% | 17/1 | 830-1010 | 30%[5] | 64% | 2% |
| Univ. of Maryland–Eastern Shore* | 2.6 | 68% | 35% | 32% | 57% | 4% | 14/1 | 790-960[3] | N/A | 55% | 3% |
| University of Southern Maine* | 2.7 | 67% | 49% | 32% | 43% | 3% | 14/1 | 870-1100[3] | 34% | 82% | 3%[7] |
| Univ. of the District of Columbia* | 1.9 | 50%[8] | 44% | 14%[6] | N/A | N/A | N/A | N/A[2] | N/A | 43%[4] | N/A |

## SOUTH ▶

| Rank School (State) (*Public) | Overall score | Peer assessment score (5.0=highest) | Average freshman retention rate | 2013 graduation rate Predicted | 2013 graduation rate Actual | % of classes under 20 ('13) | % of classes of 50 or more ('13) | Student/ faculty ratio ('13) | SAT/ACT 25th-75th percentile ('13) | Freshmen in top 25% of HS class ('13) | Accept- ance rate ('13) | Average alumni giving rate |
|---|---|---|---|---|---|---|---|---|---|---|---|---|
| 1. Elon University (NC) | 100 | 4.0 | 90% | 79% | 82% | 49% | 0.2% | 12/1 | 1120-1320 | 63%[5] | 54% | 20% |
| 2. Rollins College (FL) | 98 | 3.8 | 83% | 75% | 68% | 69% | 0% | 10/1 | 1100-1290[2] | 67%[5] | 47% | 15% |
| 3. Samford University (AL) | 89 | 3.8 | 86% | 72% | 69% | 67% | 2% | 12/1 | 23-28 | 59%[5] | 77% | 11% |
| 4. The Citadel (SC)* | 88 | 3.9 | 83% | 59% | 69% | 37% | 3% | 14/1 | 970-1190[3] | 34% | 76% | 27% |
| 5. Belmont University (TN) | 85 | 3.8 | 82% | 71% | 68% | 43% | 0.1% | 13/1 | 24-29 | 61% | 80% | 25% |
| 6. James Madison University (VA)* | 84 | 3.9 | 91% | 69% | 81% | 33% | 13% | 16/1 | 1050-1240 | 45% | 61% | 7% |
| 6. Stetson University (FL) | 84 | 3.5 | 78% | 69% | 64% | 57% | 1% | 12/1 | 1070-1270[2] | 61% | 59% | 11% |
| 8. Mercer University (GA) | 82 | 3.7 | 82% | 72% | 59% | 64% | 2% | 12/1 | 1080-1270 | 72% | 69% | 10% |
| 9. Appalachian State University (NC)* | 78 | 3.6 | 88% | 61% | 68% | 38% | 9% | 16/1 | 1050-1220 | 58% | 66% | 9% |
| 10. Embry-Riddle Aeronautical U. (FL) | 77 | 3.6 | 75% | 61% | 56% | 25% | 1% | 14/1 | 980-1230[2] | 52%[5] | 74% | 2% |
| 11. Loyola University New Orleans | 76 | 3.6 | 78% | 70% | 55% | 50% | 2% | 11/1 | 22-28 | 43%[5] | 87% | 9% |
| 12. Union University (TN) | 74 | 3.2 | 91% | 67% | 64% | 70% | 1% | 11/1 | 22-29[3] | 62% | 74% | 12%[4] |
| 13. Bellarmine University (KY) | 72 | 3.2 | 81% | 64% | 66% | 52% | 1% | 12/1 | 22-27 | 54%[5] | 95% | 16% |
| 13. College of Charleston (SC)* | 72 | 3.6 | 83% | 68% | 64% | 37% | 5% | 16/1 | 1070-1250[3] | 60% | 72% | 7% |
| 13. Univ. of Mary Washington (VA)* | 72 | 3.3 | 83% | 69% | 74% | 50% | 3% | 14/1 | 1010-1210 | 50% | 81% | 16% |
| 16. Univ. of North Carolina–Wilmington* | 70 | 3.2 | 86% | 65% | 71% | 34% | 7% | 17/1 | 1110-1270 | 64% | 57% | 6% |
| 17. Christopher Newport Univ. (VA)* | 69 | 3.2 | 84% | 66% | 66% | 47% | 4% | 16/1 | 1070-1250[2] | 53% | 59% | 13% |
| 18. Hampton University (VA) | 67 | 3.0 | 77% | 53% | 68% | 55% | 4% | 10/1 | 920-1090[2] | 45% | 36% | 12% |
| 18. Lipscomb University (TN) | 67 | 3.0 | 74% | 66% | 64% | 54% | 7% | 12/1 | 22-28 | 55%[5] | 53% | 14% |
| 18. Queens University of Charlotte (NC) | 67 | 3.0 | 70% | 54% | 52% | 68% | 0% | 12/1 | 940-1140 | 42% | 77% | 27% |
| 18. Spring Hill College (AL) | 67 | 3.0 | 76% | 63% | 56% | 56% | 0% | 13/1 | 21-27 | 45% | 44% | 19% |
| 22. Harding University (AR) | 65 | 3.1 | 81% | 60% | 62% | 54% | 7% | 15/1 | 22-28 | 50% | 76% | 11% |
| 23. Converse College (SC) | 64 | 2.7 | 70%[8] | 63% | 62% | 83% | 0% | 11/1 | 960-1160[3] | 43% | 52% | 23%[4] |
| 24. University of Tampa (FL) | 63 | 3.1 | 73% | 58% | 60% | 41% | 1% | 17/1 | 980-1150 | 46%[5] | 52% | 18% |
| 25. Winthrop University (SC)* | 61 | 3.2 | 72% | 51% | 56% | 49% | 2% | 14/1 | 920-1140 | 51% | 72% | 6% |
| 26. Christian Brothers University (TN) | 60 | 2.8 | 76% | 58% | 55% | 76% | 0% | 10/1 | 21-27 | 60% | 51% | 12% |
| 26. Murray State University (KY)* | 60 | 3.0 | 71% | 56% | 53% | 55% | 5% | 16/1 | 20-26 | 43% | 82% | 22% |
| 28. Georgia College & State Univ.* | 58 | 3.0 | 85% | 60% | 61% | 39% | 6% | 17/1 | 1050-1230 | N/A | 68% | 5% |

**Note:** Key to footnotes, Page 106.

| Rank | School (State) (*Public) | Overall score | Peer assessment score (5.0=highest) | Average freshman retention rate | 2013 graduation rate Predicted | 2013 graduation rate Actual | % of classes under 20 ('13) | % of classes of 50 or more ('13) | Student/ faculty ratio ('13) | SAT/ACT 25th-75th percentile ('13) | Freshmen in top 25% of HS class ('13) | Accept-ance rate ('13) | Average alumni giving rate |
|---|---|---|---|---|---|---|---|---|---|---|---|---|---|
| 29. | Mississippi College (MS) | 57 | 3.1 | 72% | 57% | 53% | 60% | 1% | 15/1 | 21-27 | 42% | 67% | 6% |
| 30. | Longwood University (VA)* | 56 | 2.8 | 79% | 54% | 63% | 48% | 1% | 18/1 | 920-1090 | 33% | 81% | 11% |
| 31. | Campbell University (NC) | 54 | 3.0 | 75% | 67% | 49% | 59% | 7% | 16/1 | 820-1290[3] | 54% | 70% | 12% |
| 31. | Western Kentucky University* | 54 | 2.9 | 73% | 45% | 50% | 49% | 6% | 18/1 | 19-25 | 50%[5] | 92% | 11% |
| 33. | Lynchburg College (VA) | 53 | 2.6 | 74% | 55% | 56% | 60% | 0.1% | 11/1 | 890-1110 | 37%[4] | 64% | 13% |
| 34. | Gardner-Webb University (NC) | 52 | 2.7 | 71% | 50% | 56% | 69% | 0% | 13/1 | 900-1120 | 55% | 48% | 9% |
| 34. | Radford University (VA)* | 52 | 3.0 | 76% | 48% | 59% | 34% | 7% | 18/1 | 900-1080 | 22% | 78% | 5% |
| 34. | Tennessee Technological Univ.* | 52 | 3.0 | 73% | 56% | 51% | 37% | 11% | 20/1 | 20-26 | 55% | 93% | 9% |
| 37. | Columbia College (SC) | 51 | 2.7 | 64% | 49% | 42% | 75% | 0% | 11/1 | 920-1130 | 63% | 64% | 13% |
| 37. | Columbia International Univ. (SC) | 51 | 2.4 | 82% | 59% | 65% | 66% | 7% | 16/1 | 940-1200[3] | 37% | 63% | 6% |
| 37. | Marymount University (VA) | 51 | 2.8 | 70% | 56% | 58% | 49% | 0.2% | 13/1 | 930-1130 | 44%[5] | 83% | 7% |
| 37. | University of Montevallo (AL)* | 51 | 3.0 | 75% | 51% | 45% | 48% | 1% | 16/1 | 20-26 | N/A | 67% | 15% |
| 37. | Western Carolina University (NC)* | 51 | 3.0 | 75% | 50% | 51% | 26% | 6% | 16/1 | 940-1120 | 38% | 39% | 5% |
| 37. | William Carey University (MS) | 51 | 2.5 | 76% | 44% | 62% | 69% | 1% | 14/1 | 21-28[3] | 59% | 50% | 5% |
| 43. | Brenau University (GA) | 50 | 2.8 | 69% | 39% | 46% | 82% | 0.4% | 12/1 | 890-1070 | N/A | 78% | 6% |
| 43. | Freed-Hardeman University (TN) | 50 | 2.5 | 74% | 58% | 52% | 51% | 1% | 13/1 | 21-27 | 55% | 92% | 13% |
| 43. | Wingate University (NC) | 50 | 2.8 | 74% | 54% | 53% | 42% | 1% | 16/1 | 910-1120 | 50% | 79% | 14% |
| 46. | Marshall University (WV)* | 49 | 3.2 | 70% | 49% | 45% | 42% | 4% | 19/1 | 20-24 | N/A | 79% | 6% |
| 47. | Mississippi Univ. for Women* | 48 | 3.0 | 76% | 43% | 39% | 67% | 2% | 13/1 | 18-24 | 59% | 43% | 5% |
| 47. | Shenandoah University (VA) | 48 | 2.7 | 76% | 55% | 45% | 71% | 1% | 10/1 | 850-1090 | 36% | 84% | 7% |
| 49. | Mary Baldwin College (VA) | 47 | 2.9 | 62% | 51% | 39% | 54% | 1% | 10/1 | 830-1060 | 46% | 93% | 18% |
| 49. | Thomas More College (KY) | 47 | 2.6 | 66% | 54% | 57% | 79% | 0% | 13/1 | 20-25 | 27% | 88% | 18% |
| 51. | Palm Beach Atlantic University (FL) | 46 | 2.7 | 69% | 57% | 48% | 64% | 2% | 13/1 | 925-1180 | N/A | 84% | 5% |
| 51. | University of North Florida* | 46 | 2.8 | 83% | 56% | 50% | 25% | 12% | 20/1 | 1080-1230 | 56% | 53% | 8% |
| 53. | Arkansas State University* | 44 | 2.9 | 71% | 40% | 36% | 48% | 5% | 18/1 | 21-26 | 47% | 76% | 9% |
| 53. | Lincoln Memorial University (TN) | 44 | 2.3 | 68% | 45% | 48% | 82% | 1% | 13/1 | 19-27[3] | N/A | 70% | 5% |
| 53. | Morehead State University (KY)* | 44 | 2.7 | 69% | 42% | 45% | 55% | 4% | 18/1 | 19-25 | 46% | 83% | 8% |
| 53. | University of Tennessee–Martin* | 44 | 2.7 | 73% | 50% | 46% | 54% | 7% | 17/1 | 20-25[3] | 59%[5] | 77% | 6% |
| 57. | Coastal Carolina University (SC)* | 43 | 2.8 | 63% | 50% | 46% | 36% | 3% | 17/1 | 910-1090 | 33% | 64% | 5% |
| 57. | Lee University (TN) | 43 | 2.7 | 73% | 53% | 52% | 52% | 7% | 18/1 | 21-27[3] | 49% | 92% | 9% |
| 57. | Univ. of Tennessee–Chattanooga* | 43 | 3.1 | 68% | 51% | 37% | 39% | 9% | 18/1 | 21-25 | 45% | 78% | 5% |
| 60. | University of North Georgia* | 42 | 2.8 | 79% | 57% | 52%[8] | 30% | 3% | 22/1 | 1010-1190 | 70%[5] | 60% | 8% |
| 60. | Winston-Salem State Univ.[1] (NC)* | 42 | 2.5 | 78%[8] | 32% | 39%[6] | 47%[4] | 1%[4] | 13/1[4] | 16-19[4] | 35%[4] | 56%[4] | 7%[4] |
| 62. | Austin Peay State University (TN)* | 40 | 3.0 | 68% | 41% | 38% | 53% | 5% | 19/1[4] | 19-24[9] | 37% | 86% | 5% |
| 62. | Eastern Kentucky University* | 40 | 2.8 | 66% | 43% | 39% | 56% | 4% | 16/1 | 19-25 | N/A | 74% | N/A |
| 62. | Pfeiffer University (NC) | 40 | 2.5 | 68% | 49% | 48% | 75% | 0% | 12/1 | 870-1080 | 35% | 98% | 12% |
| 65. | Belhaven University (MS) | 39 | 2.7 | 67% | 51% | 39% | 77% | 0.3% | 12/1 | 19-25 | 26% | 56% | 9% |
| 65. | North Carolina Central Univ.* | 39 | 2.4 | 71% | 32% | 40% | 40% | 5% | 15/1 | 800-950 | 22% | 39% | 11% |
| 65. | St. Leo University (FL) | 39 | 2.6 | 70% | 45% | 46% | 52% | 0% | 14/1 | 910-1093[2] | 29% | 77% | 5% |
| 65. | St. Thomas University (FL) | 39 | 2.5 | 67% | 45% | 40% | 60% | 0% | 14/1 | 785-990 | 11%[5] | 42% | 1% |
| 65. | University of Central Arkansas* | 39 | 2.7 | 71% | 50% | 42% | 45% | 3% | 17/1 | 20-26 | 43% | 92% | 7% |
| 70. | Kennesaw State University (GA)* | 38 | 3.0 | 77% | 54% | 43% | 25% | 16% | 21/1 | 990-1170 | 53%[5] | 55% | 8% |
| 70. | Northern Kentucky University* | 38 | 2.7 | 67% | 46% | 38% | 34% | 3% | 19/1 | 20-25 | 32% | 59% | 8% |
| 70. | Piedmont College (GA) | 38 | 2.3 | 73% | 53% | 46% | 74% | 0.2% | 14/1 | 920-1150 | 47% | 60% | 5% |
| 73. | Alcorn State University (MS)* | 37 | 2.5 | 68% | 29% | 35% | 51% | 5% | 16/1 | 16-19 | N/A | 83% | 5%[4] |
| 73. | Jacksonville University (FL) | 37 | 2.6 | 63% | 52% | 38% | 67% | 0.3% | 14/1 | 910-1110[3] | N/A | 47% | 5% |
| 75. | Valdosta State University (GA)* | 36 | 2.7 | 68% | 44% | 40% | 46% | 4% | 20/1 | 950-1120 | N/A | 55% | 3% |
| 76. | Albany State University (GA)* | 35 | 2.4 | 69% | 30% | 43% | 52% | 1% | 20/1 | 820-950 | 27%[5] | 24% | 4% |
| 76. | Auburn University–Montgomery (AL)* | 35 | 3.0 | 58% | 43% | 33% | 52% | 1% | 16/1 | 18-23 | 38% | 72% | N/A |
| 76. | Francis Marion University (SC)* | 35 | 2.5 | 67% | 43% | 41% | 44% | 6% | 15/1 | 830-1060 | 42% | 57% | 3% |
| 76. | Troy University (AL)* | 35 | 2.8 | 68% | 41% | 34% | 45% | 4% | 19/1 | 18-25 | 52%[5] | 67% | 9% |
| 80. | Liberty University (VA) | 34 | 2.5 | 77% | 46% | 50% | 42% | 5% | 18/1 | 900-1150 | 38% | 21% | 2% |
| 81. | Campbellsville University (KY) | 33 | 2.5 | 69%[8] | 46% | 41% | 59% | 0.2% | 13/1 | 18-24 | N/A | 68% | 10% |
| 81. | Union College (KY) | 33 | 2.3 | 56% | 38% | 34% | 78% | 0% | 13/1 | 19-24 | N/A | 75% | 17% |
| 81. | University of Louisiana–Monroe* | 33 | 2.7 | 71% | 44% | 40% | 38% | 14% | 21/1 | 20-25 | 50% | 77% | 5% |
| 81. | University of North Alabama* | 33 | 2.8 | 69% | 48% | 32% | 45% | 3% | 21/1 | 19-25 | N/A | 73% | 7% |
| 85. | King University (TN) | 32 | 2.3 | 70% | 53% | 47% | 71% | 0.2% | 12/1 | 20-25[3] | 40% | 64% | 12% |
| 85. | Southern Polytechnic State U. (GA)* | 32 | 2.7 | 75%[8] | 55% | 38% | 42%[4] | 3%[4] | 19/1[4] | 21-26[4] | 42%[4] | 79%[4] | 2%[4] |
| 87. | Florida Gulf Coast University* | 31 | 2.7 | 75%[8] | 54% | 44% | 19% | 16% | 23/1 | 940-1100[3] | 36% | 66% | N/A |
| 87. | McNeese State University (LA)* | 31 | 2.6 | 69% | 39% | 37% | 36% | 9% | 22/1 | 20-24 | 41% | 60% | 7% |
| 87. | Nicholls State University (LA)* | 31 | 2.5 | 70%[8] | 43% | 42% | 40% | 11% | 20/1 | 20-24 | 40% | 87% | 7% |

# BEST REGIONAL UNIVERSITIES

## SOUTH ▶

| Rank | School (State) (*Public) | Overall score | Peer assessment score (5.0=highest) | Average freshman retention rate | 2013 graduation rate Predicted | 2013 graduation rate Actual | % of classes under 20 ('13) | % of classes of 50 or more ('13) | Student/ faculty ratio ('13) | SAT/ACT 25th-75th percentile ('13) | Freshmen in top 25% of HS class ('13) | Accept- ance rate ('13) | Average alumni giving rate |
|---|---|---|---|---|---|---|---|---|---|---|---|---|---|
| 87. | Northwestern State U. of La.* | 31 | 2.4 | 70% | 38% | 42% | 45% | 10% | 19/1 | 19-24 | 44% | 58% | 3% |
| 87. | U. of North Carolina–Pembroke* | 31 | 2.5 | 67% | 36% | 33% | 44% | 2% | 15/1 | 840-1010 | 35% | 71% | 3% |
| 92. | Arkansas Tech University* | 30 | 2.6 | 69% | 42% | 41% | 42% | 6% | 20/1 | 18-25 | 33% | 85% | 4% |
| 92. | Delta State University (MS)* | 30 | 2.5 | 63% | 43% | 35% | 68% | 1% | 19/1 | 18-22 | 40% | 89% | N/A |
| 92. | U. of South Florida–St. Petersburg[1]* | 30 | 2.7 | 67%[8] | N/A | 31%[6] | 21%[4] | 14%[4] | 21/1[4] | 21-24[4] | 56%[4] | 46%[4] | 6%[4] |
| 92. | University of the Cumberlands (KY) | 30 | 2.3 | 58% | 50% | 43% | 59% | 2% | 14/1 | 19-25 | 38% | 71% | 17% |
| 92. | University of West Georgia* | 30 | 2.8 | 72% | 44% | 42% | 28% | 10% | 19/1 | 870-1030[3] | N/A | 54% | 4% |
| 92. | Virginia State University* | 30 | 2.5 | 65%[8] | 32% | 42%[6] | N/A | N/A | 16/1 | 730-910[3] | 17% | 54% | N/A |

| School (State) (*Public)` | Peer assessment score (5.0=highest) | Average freshman retention rate | 2013 graduation rate Predicted | 2013 graduation rate Actual | % of classes under 20 ('13) | % of classes of 50 or more ('13) | Student/ faculty ratio ('13) | SAT/ACT 25th-75th percentile ('13) | Freshmen in top 25% of HS class ('13) | Accept- ance rate ('13) | Average alumni giving rate |
|---|---|---|---|---|---|---|---|---|---|---|---|
| **SECOND TIER (SCHOOLS RANKED 98 THROUGH 126 ARE LISTED HERE ALPHABETICALLY)** | | | | | | | | | | | |
| Alabama A&M University* | 2.3 | 69% | 31% | 29% | 48% | 4% | 18/1 | 15-19 | N/A | 90% | 6% |
| Alabama State University* | 2.5 | 61% | 24% | 26% | N/A | N/A | 17/1 | 15-20[3] | 1% | 54% | N/A |
| Armstrong State University (GA)* | 2.3 | 68% | 43% | 34% | 39% | 5% | 19/1 | 920-1090 | N/A | 68% | 5% |
| Bethel University (TN) | 2.2 | 62%[8] | 36% | 34% | 70% | 1% | 13/1 | 17-23[9] | N/A | 62% | 3% |
| Charleston Southern University (SC) | 2.6 | 64%[8] | 46% | 36% | 56% | 4% | 15/1 | 870-1080[3] | 37%[4] | 69% | 4% |
| Columbus State University (GA)* | 2.5 | 68% | 41% | 31% | 42% | 7% | 17/1 | 880-1100 | 38%[5] | 56% | 5% |
| Cumberland University (TN) | 2.5 | 67% | 47% | 37% | 59% | 3% | 14/1 | 19-23 | 29% | 47% | 5% |
| Fairmont State University (WV)* | 2.2 | 65% | 35% | 34% | 46% | 5% | 17/1 | 18-23 | 39% | 66% | 1% |
| Fayetteville State University (NC)* | 2.2 | 72% | 27% | 32% | 38% | 1% | 17/1 | 770-910[3] | 17% | 61% | 2% |
| Florida Memorial University[1] | 1.9 | 70%[8] | 30% | 40%[6] | N/A | N/A | 17/1[4] | N/A[2] | N/A | 42% | N/A |
| Georgia Southwestern State University* | 2.4 | 65% | 41% | 36% | 52% | 2% | 17/1 | 860-1050 | 36% | 68% | 1% |
| Grambling State University (LA)* | 2.4 | N/A | 25% | 31% | 40% | 10% | 23/1 | 16-20[3] | 22% | 44% | 2%[7] |
| Henderson State University (AR)* | 2.6 | 60% | 43% | 29% | 59% | 2% | 15/1 | 19-24 | 26% | 62% | 3% |
| Jacksonville State University (AL)* | 2.7 | 69% | 40% | 31% | 38% | 6% | 17/1 | 19-26[3] | 39% | 83% | 7% |
| Lindsey Wilson College (KY) | 2.4 | 56% | 34% | 29% | 61% | 0% | 14/1 | 19-24[2] | 33% | 72% | 12% |
| Louisiana State U.–Shreveport* | 2.7 | 67% | 44% | 31% | 56% | 6% | 21/1[4] | 20-24[3] | N/A | 89% | N/A |
| Mississippi Valley State Univ.[1]* | 2.2 | 61%[8] | 21% | 24%[6] | N/A | N/A | 13/1[4] | 15-19[9] | N/A | 23% | N/A |
| Montreat College[1] (NC) | 2.1 | 51%[8] | 46% | 39%[6] | N/A | N/A | 13/1[4] | 820-1080[9] | N/A | 54% | N/A |
| Norfolk State University (VA)* | 2.4 | N/A | 34% | 33% | 51%[4] | 4%[4] | 18/1 | 770-948[3] | 26%[4] | 65% | 3%[4] |
| Our Lady of Holy Cross College[1] (LA) | 2.7 | 77%[8] | 36% | 24%[6] | N/A | N/A | 12/1[4] | N/A[2] | N/A | 48% | N/A |
| Shepherd University (WV)* | 2.5 | 67%[8] | 46% | 38% | 53% | 1% | 17/1 | 900-1080[3] | N/A | 94% | 7% |
| Southeastern Louisiana University* | 2.4 | 67% | 39% | 36% | 31% | 8% | 22/1 | 20-24 | 30% | 89% | 4% |
| Southern Arkansas University* | 2.2 | 62% | 36% | 31% | 47% | 3% | 15/1 | 18-24 | 42% | 61% | 4% |
| Southern Univ. and A&M College (LA)* | 2.3 | 69% | 30% | 32% | N/A | N/A | 25/1 | 17-20[3] | 23% | N/A | N/A |
| Southern University–New Orleans[1]* | 2.3 | 61%[8] | 26% | 11%[6] | N/A | N/A | 19/1[4] | 840-1290[4] | N/A | 49%[4] | N/A |
| Southern Wesleyan University[1] (SC) | 2.3 | 63%[8] | 42% | 47%[6] | N/A | N/A | 21/1[4] | 810-1050[9] | N/A | 94% | N/A |
| South University[1] (GA) | 1.9 | 30%[8] | N/A | 18%[6] | N/A | N/A | 10/1[4] | N/A[2] | N/A | 52% | N/A |
| Tusculum College[1] (TN) | 2.4 | 57%[8] | 45% | 34%[6] | N/A | N/A | 17/1[4] | 840-1040[4] | N/A | 72%[4] | 5%[7] |
| University of West Alabama* | 2.4 | 56%[8] | 36% | 31% | 57% | 3% | 15/1 | 18-22 | N/A | 61% | 4% |
| Warner University[1] (FL) | 2.3 | 59%[8] | 36% | 38%[6] | 58%[4] | 1%[4] | 17/1[4] | 16-21[4] | 21%[4] | 50%[4] | 1%[4] |

## MIDWEST ▶

| Rank | School (State) (*Public) | Overall score | Peer assessment score (5.0=highest) | Average freshman retention rate | 2013 graduation rate Predicted | 2013 graduation rate Actual | % of classes under 20 ('13) | % of classes of 50 or more ('13) | Student/ faculty ratio ('13) | SAT/ACT 25th-75th percentile ('13) | Freshmen in top 25% of HS class ('13) | Accept- ance rate ('13) | Average alumni giving rate |
|---|---|---|---|---|---|---|---|---|---|---|---|---|---|
| 1. | Creighton University (NE) | 100 | 4.0 | 89% | 82% | 76% | 49% | 4% | 11/1 | 24-30 | 68% | 77% | 16% |
| 2. | Butler University (IN) | 96 | 3.9 | 90% | 79% | 74% | 55% | 4% | 11/1 | 25-30 | 81% | 66% | 23% |
| 3. | Drake University (IA) | 92 | 3.8 | 87% | 75% | 73% | 52% | 6% | 11/1 | 25-30 | 73% | 66% | 12% |
| 4. | Bradley University (IL) | 90 | 3.6 | 87% | 69% | 76% | 55% | 3% | 12/1 | 23-28 | 64% | 67% | 12% |
| 5. | Valparaiso University (IN) | 89 | 3.8 | 84% | 69% | 70% | 52% | 4% | 14/1 | 23-29 | 68% | 80% | 15% |
| 5. | Xavier University (OH) | 89 | 3.6 | 83% | 73% | 76% | 43% | 2% | 12/1 | 23-27 | 54%[5] | 70% | 17% |
| 7. | John Carroll University (OH) | 83 | 3.4 | 88% | 64% | 75% | 44% | 0.1% | 13/1 | 22-27 | 51%[5] | 83% | 15% |
| 8. | Drury University (MO) | 80 | 3.0 | 83% | 44% | 64% | 71% | 1% | 11/1 | 22-28 | 59% | 73% | 15% |
| 9. | Truman State University (MO)* | 77 | 3.6 | 87% | 76% | 72% | 45% | 2% | 17/1 | 25-30 | 80% | 72% | 9% |
| 9. | University of Evansville (IN) | 77 | 3.3 | 84% | 69% | 63% | 64% | 1% | 13/1 | 23-29 | 66% | 84% | 15% |
| 11. | Elmhurst College (IL) | 75 | 3.2 | 78% | 63% | 74% | 64% | 0.3% | 13/1 | 21-26 | 47% | 72% | 9% |
| 12. | Hamline University (MN) | 71 | 3.2 | 81% | 65% | 66% | 52% | 5% | 13/1 | 21-27 | 47% | 66% | 15% |

**Note:** Key to footnotes, Page 106.

## MIDWEST ▶

| Rank | School (State) (*Public) | Overall score | Peer assessment score (5.0=highest) | Average freshman retention rate | 2013 graduation rate Predicted | 2013 graduation rate Actual | % of classes under 20 ('13) | % of classes of 50 or more ('13) | Student/ faculty ratio ('13) | SAT/ACT 25th-75th percentile ('13) | Freshmen in top 25% of HS class ('13) | Accept-ance rate ('13) | Average alumni giving rate |
|---|---|---|---|---|---|---|---|---|---|---|---|---|---|
| 13. | St. Catherine University (MN) | 69 | 3.1 | 83% | 57% | 61% | 65% | 2% | 12/1 | 22-26 | 52% | 59% | 15% |
| 14. | Baldwin Wallace University (OH) | 68 | 2.9 | 81% | 64% | 71% | 60% | 1% | 13/1 | 21-27[2] | 50% | 64% | 12% |
| 14. | Milwaukee School of Engineering | 68 | 3.4 | 80% | 69% | 56% | 40% | 0% | 14/1 | 25-30 | N/A | 68% | 9% |
| 14. | North Central College (IL) | 68 | 3.0 | 80% | 67% | 64% | 36% | 0% | 16/1 | 22-27 | 57% | 64% | 20% |
| 14. | Rockhurst University (MO) | 68 | 3.0 | 84% | 67% | 69% | 41% | 1% | 11/1 | 23-28 | 53% | 75% | 15% |
| 18. | University of Northern Iowa* | 67 | 3.1 | 82% | 57% | 66% | 47% | 6% | 16/1 | 20-24[3] | 45% | 83% | 10% |
| 19. | Dominican University (IL) | 65 | 2.8 | 82% | 60% | 63% | 61% | 0.2% | 11/1 | 20-24 | 48% | 60% | 19% |
| 20. | Bethel University (MN) | 64 | 2.6 | 85% | 67% | 71% | 52% | 2% | 12/1 | 22-28 | 60% | 95% | 12% |
| 20. | Kettering University (MI) | 64 | 2.6 | 91% | 74% | 61% | 62% | 1% | 13/1 | 25-30 | 66% | 65% | 7% |
| 20. | Otterbein University (OH) | 64 | 3.0 | 76% | 59% | 59% | 70% | 0.3% | 12/1 | 22-27[3] | 54% | 74% | 15% |
| 23. | Augsburg College (MN) | 63 | 3.0 | 81% | 54% | 64% | 67% | 0.2% | 13/1 | 20-24[3] | 43% | 74% | 11% |
| 23. | College of St. Scholastica (MN) | 63 | 2.8 | 82% | 59% | 68% | 60% | 2% | 15/1 | 21-26 | 55% | 73% | 11% |
| 23. | Lewis University (IL) | 63 | 2.7 | 81% | 54% | 63% | 66% | 0.2% | 13/1 | 21-26 | 47% | 56% | 7% |
| 26. | Grand Valley State University (MI)* | 62 | 3.1 | 83%[8] | 60% | 66% | 25% | 7% | 17/1 | 21-26 | 50% | 83% | 5% |
| 26. | Indiana Wesleyan University | 62 | 2.5 | 75% | 55% | 71% | 63% | 2% | 14/1 | 21-27 | 57% | 97% | 9% |
| 26. | University of Indianapolis | 62 | 3.2 | 74% | 57% | 57% | 62% | 0.2% | 12/1 | 910-1120 | 56% | 81% | 13% |
| 26. | Webster University (MO) | 62 | 2.7 | 80% | 66% | 59% | 85% | 0% | 9/1 | 20-27 | 42% | 57% | 5% |
| 30. | Franciscan Univ. of Steubenville (OH) | 61 | 2.3 | 86% | 65% | 71% | 50% | 2% | 14/1 | 23-28 | 52%[5] | 76% | 14% |
| 31. | Eastern Illinois University* | 59 | 2.7 | 79% | 48% | 60% | 45% | 3% | 14/1 | 19-24 | 32% | 62% | 5% |
| 31. | Univ. of Wisconsin–La Crosse* | 59 | 3.0 | 86% | 69% | 69% | 28% | 10% | 20/1 | 23-27 | 69% | 77% | 5% |
| 33. | Univ. of Wisconsin–Eau Claire* | 58 | 3.0 | 83% | 63% | 68% | 29% | 11% | 21/1 | 22-26 | 51% | 80% | 9% |
| 34. | St. Ambrose University (IA) | 57 | 2.7 | 79% | 54% | 61% | 65% | 0.1% | 10/1 | 20-25 | 36% | 71% | 8% |
| 35. | University of Michigan–Dearborn* | 56 | 2.8 | 83% | 56% | 52% | 34% | 6% | 14/1 | 22-27 | 57% | 63% | 8% |
| 36. | Capital University (OH) | 55 | 2.5 | 75% | 59% | 58% | 59% | 2% | 12/1 | 21-27[3] | 45% | 76% | 8% |
| 36. | Univ. of Illinois–Springfield* | 55 | 2.7 | 74% | 55% | 43% | 54% | 2% | 13/1 | 20-27 | 44% | 60% | 5% |
| 36. | University of Minnesota–Duluth* | 55 | 2.9 | 76% | 53% | 59% | 37% | 13% | 19/1 | 22-26 | 44% | 78% | 9% |
| 39. | University of St. Francis (IL) | 53 | 2.4 | 80% | 57% | 57% | 65% | 0% | 12/1 | 21-25 | 46% | 51% | 6% |
| 39. | Western Illinois University* | 53 | 2.7 | 69% | 46% | 56% | 49% | 4% | 15/1 | 18-23 | 28% | 59% | 5% |
| 41. | Anderson University (IN) | 52 | 2.5 | 74% | 57% | 57% | 69% | 2% | 13/1 | 940-1140 | 52% | 55% | 8% |
| 41. | Carroll University (WI) | 52 | 2.7 | 77% | 58% | 57% | 58% | 3% | 16/1 | 21-26 | 58% | 81% | 11% |
| 41. | University of Detroit Mercy | 52 | 2.5 | 81% | 63% | 57% | 59% | 3% | 13/1 | 21-26[3] | 55% | 62% | 10% |
| 44. | Aquinas College (MI) | 51 | 2.6 | 76% | 57% | 58% | 60% | 1% | 13/1 | 21-26 | 45% | 71% | 12% |
| 44. | Baker University (KS) | 51 | 2.4 | 78% | 60% | 52% | 69% | 1% | 12/1 | 21-26 | 42% | 88% | 16% |
| 44. | Concordia University (NE) | 51 | 2.4 | 77% | 60% | 64% | 51% | 1% | 14/1 | 21-27 | 43% | 72% | 22% |
| 47. | Southern Illinois U.–Edwardsville* | 50 | 2.8 | 71% | 56% | 50% | 37% | 11% | 18/1 | 20-25 | 39% | 84% | 5% |
| 48. | Univ. of Wisconsin–Whitewater* | 49 | 2.8 | 78% | 50% | 55% | 34% | 6% | 21/1 | 20-24 | 30% | 70% | 10% |
| 49. | Heidelberg University (OH) | 48 | 2.6 | 62% | 52% | 51% | 61% | 1% | 15/1 | 19-25 | 33%[4] | 74% | 20% |
| 49. | Olivet Nazarene University (IL) | 48 | 2.6 | 75% | 60% | 57% | 42% | 8% | 17/1 | 20-26 | 48% | 79% | 16% |
| 49. | Spring Arbor University (MI) | 48 | 2.4 | 74% | 51% | 57% | 69% | 1% | 15/1 | 20-26 | 48% | 65% | 12% |
| 49. | St. Xavier University (IL) | 48 | 2.7 | 72% | 52% | 47% | 38% | 2% | 13/1 | 19-24[3] | 54% | 79% | 8% |
| 49. | University of Findlay (OH) | 48 | 2.6 | 77% | 60% | 56% | 57% | 3% | 14/1 | 20-25[3] | 44% | 66% | 8% |
| 54. | Ferris State University (MI)* | 47 | 2.8 | 73% | 47% | 54% | 34% | 7% | 16/1 | 19-24[3] | N/A | 76% | 3% |
| 54. | Lawrence Technological Univ. (MI) | 47 | 2.6 | 78% | 61% | 44% | 72% | 0.3% | 11/1 | 22-29 | 52% | 58% | 4% |
| 54. | Malone University (OH) | 47 | 2.2 | 69% | 54% | 59% | 59% | 1% | 13/1 | 19-26 | 42% | 72% | 12% |
| 54. | North Park University (IL) | 47 | 2.6 | 74% | 56% | 56% | 57% | 3% | 11/1 | 19-25 | N/A | 52% | 10% |
| 54. | Univ. of Nebraska–Kearney* | 47 | 2.7 | 79% | 47% | 53% | 44% | 4% | 16/1 | 20-25 | 41% | 85% | 9% |
| 54. | Univ. of Wisconsin–Stevens Point* | 47 | 2.7 | 81% | 55% | 58% | 26% | 12% | 20/1 | 21-25 | 45% | 80% | 5% |
| 54. | Ursuline College (OH) | 47 | 2.2 | 68% | 45% | 50% | 84% | 0% | 9/1 | 19-24 | 38% | 58% | 17% |
| 61. | Concordia University Wisconsin | 46 | 2.5 | 75% | 50% | 56% | 53% | 2% | 12/1 | 20-25[3] | 43% | 70% | 5% |
| 61. | Mount St. Joseph University (OH) | 46 | 2.3 | 71% | 48% | 57% | 56% | 0.3% | 11/1 | 19-24 | 29% | 88% | 12% |
| 61. | Muskingum University (OH) | 46 | 2.4 | 69% | 54% | 48% | 68% | 1% | 14/1 | 18-24 | 43% | 76% | 18% |
| 61. | Winona State University (MN)* | 46 | 2.9 | 78% | 53% | 56% | 28% | 11% | 20/1 | 21-25 | 31% | 61% | 8% |
| 65. | University of Wisconsin–Stout* | 45 | 2.7 | 72% | 47% | 54% | 36% | 2% | 18/1 | 20-24 | 28% | 82% | 5% |
| 65. | Walsh University (OH) | 45 | 2.2 | 75% | 51% | 55% | 66% | 0.3% | 13/1 | 20-25[3] | 46% | 77% | 12% |
| 67. | Missouri State Univ.* | 44 | 2.7 | 75% | 55% | 53% | 27% | 10% | 20/1 | 21-26 | 53% | 85% | 7% |
| 67. | Mount Vernon Nazarene U. (OH) | 44 | 2.1 | 74% | 54% | 60% | 71% | 1% | 13/1 | 20-26 | 49% | 64% | 7% |
| 69. | Alverno College (WI) | 43 | 2.8 | 71% | 40% | 39% | 69% | 0% | 10/1 | 17-23 | 35% | 79% | 13% |
| 69. | College of St. Mary (NE) | 43 | 2.3 | 68% | 38% | 42% | 74% | 0% | 8/1 | 20-26 | 51% | 54% | 27% |
| 69. | McKendree University (IL) | 43 | 2.4 | 78% | 58% | 48% | 71% | 0% | 14/1 | 20-25 | 43% | 63% | 8% |
| 69. | Minnesota State Univ.–Mankato* | 43 | 2.8 | 74% | 48% | 49% | 35% | 8% | 25/1 | 20-24 | 23% | 66% | 6% |
| 69. | Quincy University (IL) | 43 | 2.5 | 71% | 51% | 50% | 70% | 0.3% | 14/1 | 20-25 | 40% | 89% | 13% |

| Rank | School (State) (*Public) | Overall score | Peer assessment score (5.0=highest) | Average freshman retention rate | 2013 graduation rate Predicted | 2013 graduation rate Actual | % of classes under 20 ('13) | % of classes of 50 or more ('13) | Student/ faculty ratio ('13) | SAT/ACT 25th-75th percentile ('13) | Freshmen in top 25% of HS class ('13) | Accept- ance rate ('13) | Average alumni giving rate |
|---|---|---|---|---|---|---|---|---|---|---|---|---|---|
| 69. | University of St. Francis (IN) | 43 | 2.5 | 71% | 46% | 57% | 54% | 1% | 12/1 | 890-1060 | 38% | 97% | 7% |
| 69. | Univ. of Wisconsin–Oshkosh* | 43 | 2.8 | 76% | 51% | 54% | 38% | 9% | 22/1 | 20-24[3] | 33% | 67% | 5% |
| 69. | Univ. of Wisconsin–River Falls* | 43 | 2.7 | 72% | 51% | 52% | 46% | 4% | 21/1 | 20-24 | 32% | 73% | 7%[7] |
| 77. | Concordia University Chicago | 41 | 2.4 | 66% | 60% | 53% | 66% | 0.2% | 12/1 | 20-24 | 18%[4] | 54% | 9% |
| 77. | Eastern Michigan University* | 41 | 2.7 | 75% | 47% | 38% | 41% | 4% | 18/1 | 19-25 | 40% | 61% | 3% |
| 77. | Univ. of Wisconsin–Green Bay* | 41 | 2.8 | 73% | 53% | 46% | 35% | 10% | 21/1 | 21-25 | N/A | 66% | 5% |
| 80. | Dakota State University (SD)* | 40 | 2.4 | 65% | 46% | 49% | 61% | 1% | 18/1 | 19-24 | 23% | 83% | 12% |
| 80. | Northwest Missouri State Univ.* | 40 | 2.7 | 67%[8] | 50% | 48% | 45% | 7% | 22/1 | 20-25 | 40% | 73% | 4% |
| 80. | Robert Morris University (IL) | 40 | 2.3 | 49% | 27% | 46%[8] | 63% | 0.4% | 18/1 | 15-21[3] | 14% | 21% | 2% |
| 80. | Univ. of Wisconsin–Platteville* | 40 | 2.8 | 76%[8] | 50% | 52% | 29% | 7% | 23/1 | 21-26[3] | 36% | 79% | N/A |
| 84. | Madonna University (MI) | 39 | 2.2 | 82% | 50% | 56% | 70% | 4% | 12/1 | 19-25 | 40% | 62% | 3% |
| 84. | Ohio Dominican University | 39 | 2.5 | 65%[8] | 41% | 42% | 59% | 0% | 14/1 | 20-24 | 46% | 49% | 8% |
| 84. | Pittsburg State University (KS)* | 39 | 2.5 | 72% | 46% | 46% | 37% | 10% | 19/1 | 19-24 | 38% | 79% | 9% |
| 84. | Rockford University (IL) | 39 | 2.3 | 64%[8] | 50% | 50% | 79% | 0% | 10/1 | 19-25 | N/A | 41% | 9% |
| 84. | Southwestern College (KS) | 39 | 1.9 | 63% | 50% | 53% | 81% | 1% | 10/1 | 20-25 | 49% | 90% | 7% |
| 84. | University of Central Missouri* | 39 | 2.6 | 68%[8] | 49% | 53% | 41% | 5% | 16/1 | 19-24[3] | 32% | 81% | 3%[7] |
| 84. | Wayne State College (NE)* | 39 | 2.4 | 67% | 43% | 46% | 48% | 1% | 20/1 | 19-24[2] | 29% | 100% | 13% |
| 91. | Mount Mary University (WI) | 38 | 2.2 | 67% | 42% | 41% | 89% | 0% | 10/1 | 17-23 | 53% | 54% | 15% |
| 91. | Northern Michigan University[1]* | 38 | 2.8 | 72%[8] | 50% | 49%[6] | 31%[4] | 11%[4] | 22/1[4] | 19-24[4] | 35%[4] | 68%[4] | 6%[4] |
| 91. | Roosevelt University (IL) | 38 | 2.4 | 60%[8] | 48% | 42% | 60% | 1% | 11/1 | 19-25 | 11% | 79% | 5%[4] |
| 91. | Washburn University (KS)* | 38 | 2.6 | 65% | 46% | 37% | 45% | 2% | 14/1 | 19-25 | 38% | 98% | 9% |
| 95. | Lindenwood University (MO) | 37 | 1.9 | 72% | 40% | 45% | 62% | 0.1% | 15/1 | 20-25 | 33% | 66% | 38% |
| 95. | Marian University (WI) | 37 | 2.1 | 68% | 45% | 49% | 73% | 1% | 11/1 | 18-22 | 32% | 76% | 8% |
| 95. | Southeast Missouri State Univ.* | 37 | 2.4 | 72% | 48% | 49% | 36% | 3% | 21/1 | 20-25 | 43% | 88% | 6% |
| 95. | William Woods University (MO) | 37 | 2.2 | 73% | 53% | 56% | 82% | 1% | 10/1 | 19-25 | 37% | 78% | 10% |
| 99. | Bemidji State University (MN)* | 36 | 2.5 | 69% | 46% | 48% | 45% | 6% | 26/1 | 19-23 | 23% | 67% | 5% |
| 99. | St. Cloud State University (MN)* | 36 | 2.7 | 71%[8] | 45% | 47% | 38% | 4% | 19/1 | 18-24 | 24% | 82% | 3% |
| 99. | University of Michigan–Flint* | 36 | 2.7 | 74% | 47% | 38% | 44% | 5% | 16/1 | 18-24 | 42% | 78% | N/A |
| 99. | Univ. of Wisconsin–Superior* | 36 | 2.5 | 69% | 48% | 41% | 58% | 2% | 13/1 | 19-24 | 17% | 66% | 3% |
| 103. | Emporia State University (KS)* | 35 | 2.5 | 71% | 48% | 41% | 48% | 4% | 18/1 | 19-25[3] | 36% | 61% | 8% |
| 103. | Graceland University (IA) | 35 | 2.0 | 68% | 46% | 47% | 63% | 3% | 15/1 | 18-24 | 34% | 50% | 17% |
| 105. | Oakland City University (IN) | 34 | 1.9 | 75% | 46% | 52% | 84%[4] | 0%[4] | 15/1 | 870-1070[9] | N/A | 73% | N/A |
| 106. | Concordia University–St. Paul (MN) | 33 | 2.5 | 69% | 49% | 46% | 60% | 0% | 16/1 | 18-24[3] | 22% | 53% | 3% |
| 106. | Minnesota State Univ.–Moorhead* | 33 | 2.6 | 67% | 46% | 46% | 40% | 6% | 17/1 | 20-25 | 30% | 89% | 2%[7] |
| 106. | Minot State University (ND)* | 33 | 2.4 | 67% | 42% | 37% | 65% | 1% | 13/1 | 19-24 | 22% | 57% | 4% |
| 109. | Fontbonne University (MO) | 32 | 2.4 | 71%[8] | 45% | 41% | N/A | N/A | 10/1 | 21-25 | N/A | 65% | N/A |
| 109. | Upper Iowa University | 32 | 2.1 | 64% | 35% | 40% | 82% | 0.1% | 17/1 | 19-25 | 32% | 58% | 4% |
| 109. | Viterbo University[1] (WI) | 32 | 2.5 | 76%[8] | 53% | 51%[6] | N/A | N/A | 12/1[4] | 21-26[9] | N/A | 71% | N/A |

| School (State) (*Public) | Peer assessment score (5.0=highest) | Average freshman retention rate | 2013 graduation rate Predicted | 2013 graduation rate Actual | % of classes under 20 ('13) | % of classes of 50 or more ('13) | Student/ faculty ratio ('13) | SAT/ACT 25th-75th percentile ('13) | Freshmen in top 25% of HS class ('13) | Accept- ance rate ('13) | Average alumni giving rate |
|---|---|---|---|---|---|---|---|---|---|---|---|
| SECOND TIER (SCHOOLS RANKED 112 THROUGH 146 ARE LISTED HERE ALPHABETICALLY) | | | | | | | | | | | |
| Aurora University[1] (IL) | 2.2 | 70%[8] | 52% | 50%[6] | N/A | N/A | 17/1[4] | 19-24[9] | N/A | 76% | 3%[7] |
| Avila University[1] (MO) | 2.2 | 66%[8] | 54% | 45%[6] | N/A | N/A | 15/1[4] | 20-24[9] | N/A | 61% | N/A |
| Black Hills State University[1] (SD)* | 2.5 | 61%[8] | 43% | 32%[6] | N/A | N/A | 19/1[4] | 19-23[9] | N/A | 89% | N/A |
| Calumet College of St. Joseph (IN) | 2.0 | 57% | 36% | 34% | 72% | 2% | 12/1 | 780-940[9] | 14% | 40% | 2% |
| Chicago State University* | 1.8 | 55% | 29% | 21% | 60% | 0.1% | 12/1 | 17-20 | N/A | 29% | N/A |
| Columbia College Chicago[1] (IL) | 2.6 | 63%[8] | 54% | 41%[6] | N/A | N/A | 10/1[4] | N/A[2] | N/A | 91% | N/A |
| Cornerstone University (MI) | 2.0 | 76% | 54% | 43% | 52% | 3% | 24/1 | 21-26[3] | 49% | 68% | 8% |
| Davenport University (MI) | 1.8 | 79%[8] | 30% | 42% | 72% | 0.1% | 14/1[4] | N/A[2] | N/A | 92% | N/A |
| DeVry University (IL) | 1.7 | N/A | N/A | 31% | N/A | N/A | 19/1 | N/A[2] | N/A | N/A | N/A |
| Fort Hays State University (KS)* | 2.3 | 68%[8] | 45% | 40%[6] | 43% | 3% | 18/1 | 740-1230[4] | 31% | 89% | N/A |
| Friends University[1] (KS) | 2.1 | 60%[8] | 46% | 29%[6] | N/A | N/A | 9/1[4] | 18-24[9] | N/A | 59% | N/A |
| Indiana University Northwest* | 2.1 | 67% | 33% | 24% | 32% | 8% | 17/1 | 780-1020 | 32% | 76% | 7% |
| Indiana U.–Purdue U.–Fort Wayne* | 2.6 | 62% | 41% | 25% | 48% | 4% | 17/1 | 890-1090 | 38% | 83% | 4% |
| Indiana University–South Bend* | 2.3 | 64% | 37% | 26% | 47% | 2% | 13/1 | 860-1060 | 29% | 70% | 8% |
| Indiana University Southeast* | 2.2 | 62% | 39% | 30% | 38% | 1% | 15/1 | 850-1050 | 34% | 79% | 9% |
| Lake Erie College (OH) | 1.8 | 67% | 46% | 46% | 66% | 0% | 14/1 | 19-23[3] | 28% | 56% | 8% |
| Lakeland College[1] (WI) | 2.0 | 71%[8] | 44% | 44%[6] | N/A | N/A | 15/1[4] | 19-24[3] | N/A | 66% | N/A |

**Note:** Key to footnotes, Page 106.

SECOND TIER (SCHOOLS RANKED 112 THROUGH 146 ARE LISTED HERE ALPHABETICALLY)

| School (State) (*Public) | Peer assessment score (5.0=highest) | Average freshman retention rate | 2013 graduation rate | | % of classes under 20 ('13) | % of classes of 50 or more ('13) | Student/faculty ratio ('13) | SAT/ACT 25th-75th percentile ('13) | Freshmen in top 25% of HS class ('13) | Acceptance rate ('13) | Average alumni giving rate |
|---|---|---|---|---|---|---|---|---|---|---|---|
| | | | Predicted | Actual | | | | | | | |
| Marygrove College (MI) | 2.0 | 67%[8] | 40% | 29% | N/A | N/A | 11/1 | 14-18[9] | N/A | 94% | N/A |
| Metropolitan State University[1] (MN)* | 2.4 | 69%[8] | 42% | 30%[6] | N/A | N/A | 16/1[4] | N/A[2] | N/A | 100% | 3%[7] |
| MidAmerica Nazarene University[1] (KS) | 2.1 | 74%[8] | 54% | 48%[6] | N/A | N/A | 7/1[4] | 19-21[9] | N/A | 72% | 4%[7] |
| Missouri Baptist University[1] | 2.0 | 65%[8] | 46% | 34%[6] | N/A | N/A | 19/1[4] | 830-1120[4] | N/A | 58%[4] | N/A |
| Newman University (KS) | 2.1 | 71% | 53% | 52% | 66% | 1% | 15/1 | 20-27[2] | 51% | 44% | 6% |
| Northeastern Illinois University* | 2.3 | 64% | 36% | 20% | 38% | 2% | 16/1 | 16-21[3] | 16% | 60% | 2% |
| Park University[1] (MO) | 2.1 | 67%[8] | 41% | 39%[8] | 80%[4] | 0%[4] | 11/1[4] | 17-23[4] | 37%[4] | 69%[4] | 1%[4] |
| Purdue University–Calumet (IN)* | 2.5 | 69% | 36% | 30% | 26% | 7% | 19/1 | 870-1080 | 36% | 76% | 5% |
| Saginaw Valley State Univ. (MI)* | 2.4 | 69%[8] | 46% | 42% | 33% | 3% | 20/1 | 19-24 | 39% | 79% | N/A |
| Siena Heights University (MI) | 2.2 | 64% | 43% | 43% | 79% | 0.2% | 12/1 | 19-23 | 33% | 68% | 5% |
| Southwest Baptist University[1] (MO) | 2.2 | 67%[8] | 50% | 48%[6] | N/A | N/A | 16/1[4] | 20-26[9] | N/A | 90% | N/A |
| Southwest Minnesota State University* | 2.3 | 68% | 43% | 43% | 43% | 3% | 16/1 | 19-24[3] | 27% | 65% | 11% |
| Tiffin University (OH) | 2.3 | 66% | 39% | 43% | 61% | 0% | 18/1 | 18-23[9] | N/A | 59% | 12% |
| University of Dubuque (IA) | 2.5 | 69%[8] | 45% | 40%[6] | 65%[4] | 1%[4] | 13/1[4] | 17-22[3] | 17%[4] | 77% | 9%[4] |
| University of Mary[1] (ND) | 2.4 | 71%[8] | 51% | 48%[6] | N/A | N/A | 17/1[4] | 20-25[9] | N/A | 83% | N/A |
| University of Southern Indiana* | 2.4 | 68% | 42% | 37% | 44% | 4% | 16/1 | 890-1110 | 36% | 69% | 4% |
| University of St. Mary (KS) | 2.1 | 60% | 53% | 53% | 72% | 0% | 10/1 | 19-24[3] | 3% | 47% | N/A |
| Youngstown State University (OH)* | 2.1 | 68% | 37% | 33% | 39% | 7% | 17/1 | 17-23 | 17% | 86% | 4% |

| Rank | School (State) (*Public) | Overall score | Peer assessment score (5.0=highest) | Average freshman retention rate | 2013 graduation rate | | % of classes under 20 ('13) | % of classes of 50 or more ('13) | Student/faculty ratio ('13) | SAT/ACT 25th-75th percentile ('13) | Freshmen in top 25% of HS class ('13) | Acceptance rate ('13) | Average alumni giving rate |
|---|---|---|---|---|---|---|---|---|---|---|---|---|---|
| | | | | | Predicted | Actual | | | | | | | |
| 1. | Trinity University (TX) | 100 | 4.1 | 89% | 92% | 82% | 64% | 1% | 9/1 | 1150-1370 | 73% | 64% | 14% |
| 2. | Santa Clara University (CA) | 98 | 3.9 | 94% | 82% | 84% | 40% | 2% | 12/1 | 1190-1380 | 80%[5] | 50% | 22% |
| 3. | Gonzaga University (WA) | 89 | 3.9 | 93% | 76% | 82% | 41% | 2% | 12/1 | 1100-1290 | 68% | 68% | 18% |
| 3. | Loyola Marymount University (CA) | 89 | 3.8 | 90% | 74% | 76% | 47% | 2% | 11/1 | 1090-1300 | 57%[5] | 54% | 20% |
| 5. | Seattle University | 82 | 3.6 | 87% | 71% | 77% | 58% | 1% | 12/1 | 1050-1260 | 62%[5] | 73% | 10% |
| 6. | Mills College (CA) | 81 | 3.5 | 79% | 71% | 62% | 75% | 0.3% | 10/1 | 1040-1250 | 71% | 68% | 21% |

JIM LO SCALZO FOR USN&WR

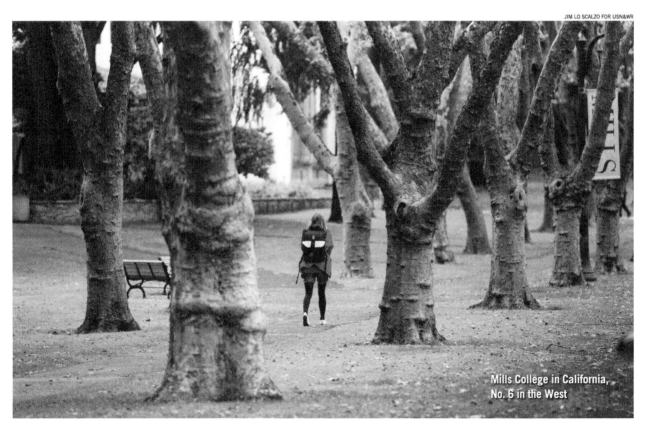

Mills College in California, No. 6 in the West

## WEST ▶

| Rank | School (State) (*Public) | Overall score | Peer assessment score (5.0=highest) | Average freshman retention rate | 2013 graduation rate Predicted | 2013 graduation rate Actual | % of classes under 20 ('13) | % of classes of 50 or more ('13) | Student/ faculty ratio ('13) | SAT/ACT 25th-75th percentile ('13) | Freshmen in top 25% of HS class ('13) | Accept-ance rate ('13) | Average alumni giving rate |
|---|---|---|---|---|---|---|---|---|---|---|---|---|---|
| 7. | Chapman University (CA) | 79 | 3.5 | 92% | 80% | 76% | 42% | 2% | 14/1 | 1120-1300 | 93%[5] | 45% | 9% |
| 8. | University of Portland (OR) | 75 | 3.6 | 90% | 75% | 75% | 35% | 1% | 13/1 | 1090-1300 | 70% | 67% | 11% |
| 9. | Whitworth University (WA) | 74 | 3.5 | 86% | 75% | 74% | 58% | 2% | 11/1 | 1090-1290[2] | N/A | 78% | 18% |
| 10. | Cal. Poly. State U.–San Luis Obispo* | 73 | 3.9 | 93% | 72% | 72% | 16% | 13% | 19/1 | 1130-1320[3] | 83%[5] | 35% | 5% |
| 11. | St. Mary's College of California | 72 | 3.4 | 88% | 62% | 60% | 50% | 0.2% | 12/1 | 1010-1210 | 64%[5] | 69% | 12% |
| 12. | University of Redlands (CA) | 71 | 3.2 | 88% | 70% | 73% | 58% | 1% | 14/1 | 1030-1230 | 65% | 67% | 13% |
| 13. | St. Edward's University (TX) | 67 | 3.3 | 82% | 60% | 69% | 55% | 0.1% | 13/1 | 1020-1220 | 54% | 79% | 7% |
| 13. | University of Dallas | 67 | 3.2 | 80% | 74% | 66% | 63% | 3% | 11/1 | 1090-1330 | 68%[5] | 90% | 21% |
| 15. | California Lutheran University | 66 | 3.3 | 84% | 68% | 70% | 55% | 1% | 15/1 | 1010-1203 | 68%[5] | 48% | 15% |
| 16. | Point Loma Nazarene University (CA) | 65 | 3.1 | 85% | 71% | 72% | 45% | 4% | 14/1 | 1040-1260 | 67% | 67% | 9% |
| 17. | Abilene Christian University (TX) | 64 | 3.4 | 75% | 59% | 57% | 48% | 8% | 14/1 | 21-27 | 57% | 49% | 10% |
| 17. | Pacific Lutheran University (WA) | 64 | 3.2 | 82% | 66% | 70% | 46% | 3% | 14/1 | 980-1220[3] | 70%[5] | 77% | 11% |
| 19. | Seattle Pacific University | 63 | 3.2 | 86% | 69% | 69% | 44% | 5% | 15/1 | 1030-1250 | 57% | 83% | 6%[7] |
| 20. | Westminster College (UT) | 61 | 3.0 | 78% | 64% | 60% | 67% | 0% | 9/1 | 22-28 | 55% | 75% | 15% |
| 21. | St. Mary's Univ. of San Antonio (TX) | 57 | 3.0 | 73% | 60% | 56% | 53% | 0% | 12/1 | 950-1150 | 57% | 58% | 7% |
| 21. | Western Washington University* | 57 | 3.2 | 84% | 61% | 69% | 36% | 16% | 20/1 | 990-1220 | 50% | 84% | 5% |
| 23. | Mount St. Mary's College (CA) | 56 | 3.1 | 82% | 42% | 66% | 54% | 1% | 12/1 | 830-1020 | 46%[5] | 91% | 12% |
| 23. | N.M. Inst. of Mining and Tech.* | 56 | 3.3 | 74% | 78% | 44% | 56% | 6% | 13/1 | 23-29 | 67% | 32% | N/A |
| 25. | Oklahoma City University | 54 | 3.1 | 77%[8] | 70% | 59% | 72% | 1% | 11/1 | 23-29 | 61% | 70% | 5% |
| 25. | Pacific University (OR) | 54 | 3.0 | 79% | 71% | 62% | 67% | 3% | 10/1 | 990-1210 | N/A | 86% | 9% |
| 27. | LeTourneau University (TX) | 52 | 2.8 | 76% | 59% | 52% | 63% | 2% | 13/1 | 1030-1300[2] | 67% | 41% | 8% |
| 27. | University of St. Thomas (TX) | 52 | 3.1 | 78% | 62% | 51% | 70% | 0% | 10/1 | 1000-1210 | 54% | 77% | 8% |
| 29. | Regis University (CO) | 51 | 3.1 | 84% | 61% | 58% | 71% | 1% | 14/1 | 22-27[3] | 56% | 92% | 6% |
| 30. | George Fox University (OR) | 50 | 2.9 | 82% | 61% | 62% | 55% | 4% | 14/1 | 940-1200 | 57% | 75% | 5% |
| 31. | Calif. State Poly. Univ.–Pomona* | 49 | 3.5 | 90% | 43% | 53% | 16% | 12% | 28/1 | 930-1190[3] | N/A | 53% | 3% |
| 31. | Evergreen State College (WA)* | 49 | 3.2 | 73% | 50% | 57% | 38% | 8% | 23/1 | 950-1210 | 23%[5] | 97% | 6% |
| 33. | California State U.–Long Beach* | 48 | 3.2 | 88% | 58% | 60% | 22% | 11% | 22/1 | 940-1160 | 84%[4] | 35% | 5% |
| 33. | Dominican University of California | 48 | 2.8 | 84% | 54% | 53% | 60%[4] | 1%[4] | 10/1 | 960-1160[3] | 54%[4] | 78% | 7%[4] |
| 35. | California State Univ.–Chico* | 45 | 2.9 | 86% | 55% | 56% | 28% | 13% | 24/1 | 910-1110 | 76%[5] | 67% | 5% |
| 35. | Dallas Baptist University | 45 | 2.8 | 73% | 55% | 55% | 68% | 2% | 14/1 | 18-27 | 46% | 42% | 1% |
| 35. | Hardin-Simmons University (TX) | 45 | 2.7 | 65% | 52% | 51% | 71% | 0.2% | 12/1 | 20-25 | 56% | 38% | 7% |
| 38. | California Baptist University | 44 | 2.9 | 77% | 55% | 58% | 55% | 5% | 18/1 | 850-1110 | 43% | 79% | 3% |
| 38. | San Jose State University (CA)* | 44 | 3.1 | 86% | 45% | 48% | 20% | 15% | 29/1 | 880-1160 | N/A | 64% | 2% |
| 40. | California State U.–Fullerton* | 43 | 3.1 | 87% | 47% | 53% | 22% | 10% | 26/1 | 920-1120 | 61% | 48% | 2% |
| 40. | Fresno Pacific University (CA) | 43 | 2.9 | 78% | 51% | 54% | 68% | 3% | 13/1 | 880-1100 | 66% | 78% | N/A |
| 40. | Oklahoma Christian U. | 43 | 3.0 | 75% | 57% | 46% | 56% | 5% | 16/1 | 22-28 | 58% | 63% | 11% |
| 43. | Northwest Nazarene University (ID) | 42 | 2.7 | 74%[8] | 58% | 53%[6] | 63% | 4% | 17/1 | 920-1160 | 57% | 29% | 14%[4] |
| 43. | Sonoma State University (CA)* | 42 | 3.0 | 81% | 51% | 54% | 40% | 9% | 25/1 | 880-1090[3] | N/A | 90% | 1% |
| 43. | Univ. of Mary Hardin-Baylor (TX) | 42 | 3.0 | 64% | 50% | 47% | 49% | 2% | 16/1 | 940-1140 | 51% | 85% | 6% |
| 46. | California State Univ.–Fresno* | 41 | 2.9 | 85% | 36% | 49% | 17% | 11% | 22/1 | 800-1020 | 80% | 60% | 4% |
| 46. | Oral Roberts University (OK) | 41 | 2.6 | 81% | 53% | 53% | 61% | 5% | 15/1 | 20-25[3] | 46%[4] | 44% | 8% |
| 46. | St. Martin's University (WA) | 41 | 2.8 | 76% | 51% | 48% | 64% | 4% | 12/1 | 950-1190[3] | 52% | 88% | 7% |
| 49. | Texas Wesleyan University | 40 | 2.8 | 65% | 48% | 42% | 75% | 0.2% | 15/1 | 940-1090 | 30% | 46% | 5% |
| 50. | Texas State University* | 39 | 2.8 | 78% | 54% | 57% | 26% | 17% | 20/1 | 940-1130 | 49% | 74% | 4% |
| 51. | Central Washington University* | 38 | 2.8 | 76% | 44% | 51% | 45% | 5% | 17/1 | 880-1100[3] | N/A | 82% | 2% |
| 51. | Concordia University (CA) | 38 | 2.8 | 75% | 59% | 63% | 50% | 1% | 20/1 | 903-1110 | 40%[5] | 67% | 5% |
| 51. | Notre Dame de Namur University[1] (CA) | 38 | 2.8 | 77%[8] | 51% | 49%[6] | 65%[4] | 0%[4] | 12/1[4] | 18-22[4] | 29%[4] | 75%[4] | 7%[4] |
| 51. | Univ. of Colo.–Colorado Springs* | 38 | 3.1 | 69% | 52% | 46% | 37% | 7% | 17/1 | 21-25 | 36% | 91% | 3% |
| 55. | California State U.–Stanislaus* | 37 | 2.7 | 86% | 41% | 53% | 19% | 11% | 21/1 | 810-1020[2] | N/A | 74% | 1% |
| 56. | La Sierra University (CA) | 36 | 2.4 | 76% | 50% | 59% | 67% | 4% | 14/1 | 810-1040[3] | 41% | 47% | 5% |
| 56. | Woodbury University (CA) | 36 | 2.5 | 77% | 43% | 45% | 80% | 0% | 10/1 | 880-1110 | N/A | 57% | 3% |
| 58. | California State U.–Sacramento* | 35 | 3.1 | 81% | 41% | 42% | 20% | 17% | 28/1 | 830-1060[2] | N/A | 71% | 2%[7] |
| 58. | Humboldt State University (CA)* | 35 | 2.8 | 75% | 48% | 42% | 31% | 14% | 23/1 | 870-1110[2] | 39% | 76% | 7% |
| 58. | San Francisco State University* | 35 | 3.1 | 80% | 46% | 45% | 25% | 20% | 22/1 | 880-1110 | N/A | 60% | 2% |
| 58. | Southern Utah University* | 35 | 2.8 | 65% | 47% | 41% | 43% | 7% | 20/1 | 20-26 | 42% | 57% | 3% |
| 58. | Walla Walla University (WA) | 35 | 2.7 | 79% | 53% | 44% | N/A | N/A | 13/1 | 930-1190[9] | N/A | 94% | 15%[4] |
| 63. | Boise State University (ID)* | 34 | 3.1 | 70% | 45% | 38% | 35% | 11% | 20/1 | 920-1150 | 38% | 78% | 8% |
| 63. | Texas A&M International University* | 34 | 2.6 | 72% | 36% | 44% | 33% | 14% | 22/1 | 800-1010 | 53% | 49% | 10% |
| 63. | Univ. of the Incarnate Word (TX) | 34 | 2.7 | 74% | 43% | 40% | 56% | 1% | 14/1 | 870-1060 | 43% | 93% | 6% |
| 66. | Calif. State U.–San Bernardino* | 33 | 2.7 | 88% | 36% | 44% | 21% | 20% | 27/1 | 790-990[2] | N/A | 55% | 2% |

**Note:** Key to footnotes, Page 106.

## WEST ▶

| Rank | School (State) (*Public) | Overall score | Peer assessment score (5.0=highest) | Average freshman retention rate | 2013 graduation rate | | % of classes under 20 ('13) | % of classes of 50 or more ('13) | Student/ faculty ratio ('13) | SAT/ACT 25th-75th percentile ('13) | Freshmen in top 25% of HS class ('13) | Accept-ance rate ('13) | Average alumni giving rate |
|---|---|---|---|---|---|---|---|---|---|---|---|---|---|
| | | | | | Predicted | Actual | | | | | | | |
| 66. | Eastern Washington University* | 33 | 2.7 | 75% | 42% | 45% | 37% | 12% | 21/1 | 870-1090 | N/A | 78% | 4% |
| 68. | California State U.–Monterey Bay* | 32 | 2.8 | 79% | 46% | 38% | 17% | 6% | 28/1 | 870-1090 | 46% | 45% | 2% |
| 68. | California State U.–Northridge* | 32 | 3.1 | 76% | 37% | 46% | 11% | 18% | 27/1 | 800-1040[3] | N/A | 61% | 1%[7] |
| 68. | Holy Names University (CA) | 32 | 2.6 | 72% | 51% | 35% | 76% | 0% | 10/1 | 820-1000 | N/A | 57% | 11% |
| 68. | Houston Baptist University | 32 | 2.6 | 65% | 54% | 43% | 60% | 2% | 16/1 | 960-1170 | 53% | 36% | 4% |
| 68. | University of Alaska–Anchorage* | 32 | 3.0 | 71% | 42% | 28% | 53% | 4% | 12/1 | 880-1080[2] | 31% | 80% | 5% |
| 68. | University of Texas–Tyler* | 32 | 2.8 | 65% | 49% | 44% | 31% | 13% | 17/1 | 960-1158 | 44%[5] | 82% | 1%[7] |
| 68. | Weber State University (UT)* | 32 | 2.9 | 72% | 44% | 43% | 45% | 7% | 21/1 | 18-24[2] | N/A | 100% | 2% |
| 75. | Alaska Pacific University | 31 | 2.5 | 69%[8] | 62% | 39% | 96% | 0% | 8/1 | 915-1085[3] | 35%[4] | 37% | N/A |
| 75. | California State U.–Channel Islands[1]* | 31 | 2.7 | 84%[8] | N/A | 53%[6] | N/A | N/A | 21/1[4] | 850-1060[4] | N/A | 64%[4] | 1%[7] |
| 75. | Prescott College (AZ) | 31 | 2.6 | 67% | 52% | 37% | 99% | 1% | 9/1 | 910-1260 | 28%[4] | 73% | 3%[4] |
| 75. | University of Central Oklahoma* | 31 | 3.1 | 66% | 42% | 36% | 32% | 2% | 21/1 | 20-24 | 37% | 80% | 1% |
| 79. | Southern Oregon University* | 29 | 2.8 | 69% | 48% | 38% | 46% | 4% | 19/1 | 890-1120 | N/A | 93% | 2% |
| 80. | California State Univ.–Bakersfield[1]* | 28 | 2.7 | 72%[8] | 36% | 41%[6] | N/A | N/A | 28/1[4] | 790-1020[4] | N/A | 66%[4] | 1%[7] |
| 80. | Concordia University[1] (OR) | 28 | 2.6 | 70%[8] | 49% | 47%[6] | 58%[4] | 1%[4] | 23/1[4] | 880-1120[4] | 44%[4] | 54%[4] | 1%[4] |
| 80. | Hawaii Pacific University | 28 | 2.7 | 69% | 53% | 41% | 46% | 1% | 15/1 | 870-1110 | 53% | 64% | 2% |
| 80. | West Texas A&M University* | 28 | 2.7 | 64% | 48% | 43% | 42% | 8% | 19/1 | 19-24 | 42% | 74% | 3% |
| 84. | California State U.–Los Angeles* | 27 | 2.9 | 82% | 33% | 36% | 27% | 8% | 27/1 | 770-990[2] | 3% | 63% | 2% |
| 84. | California State Univ.–San Marcos* | 27 | 2.6 | 80%[8] | 45% | 48% | 15% | 10% | 25/1[4] | 850-1050[9] | N/A | 67% | 1%[7] |
| 84. | Lubbock Christian University (TX) | 27 | 2.5 | 64% | 43% | 41% | 67% | 3% | 12/1 | 19-24[3] | 39% | 95% | 5% |
| 84. | Northeastern State University (OK)* | 27 | 2.7 | 65% | 34% | 30% | 58% | 4% | 19/1 | 18-23 | 43% | 73% | 3% |
| 84. | Southern Nazarene University (OK) | 27 | 2.6 | 57%[8] | 51% | 46% | 70% | 2% | 15/1 | 19-24[4] | 49%[5] | N/A | 4%[7] |
| 84. | Stephen F. Austin State Univ. (TX)* | 27 | 2.7 | 65% | 45% | 43% | 30% | 11% | 19/1 | 890-1090 | 41% | 57% | 3% |
| 84. | Western Oregon University* | 27 | 2.7 | 70%[8] | 46% | 44% | 55% | 3% | 16/1 | 840-1070 | 32% | 91% | N/A |

# B EST REGIONAL UNIVERSITIES

## WEST ▶

| School (State) (*Public) | Peer assessment score (5.0=highest) | Average freshman retention rate | 2013 graduation rate Predicted | 2013 graduation rate Actual | % of classes under 20 ('13) | % of classes of 50 or more ('13) | Student/ faculty ratio ('13) | SAT/ACT 25th-75th percentile ('13) | Freshmen in top 25% of HS class ('13) | Accept- ance rate ('13) | Average alumni giving rate |
|---|---|---|---|---|---|---|---|---|---|---|---|
| SECOND TIER (SCHOOLS RANKED 91 THROUGH 120 ARE LISTED HERE ALPHABETICALLY) | | | | | | | | | | | |
| Adams State University[1] (CO)* | 2.6 | 59%[8] | 31% | 25%[6] | N/A | N/A | 16/1[4] | 17-22[9] | N/A | 53% | N/A |
| Angelo State University (TX)* | 2.4 | 60% | 41% | 28% | 31% | 9% | 18/1 | 18-23[3] | 35% | 80% | 2% |
| California State U.–Dominguez Hills* | 2.4 | 76% | 30% | 29% | 18% | 12% | 27/1 | 760-940[2] | N/A | 80% | 2% |
| California State Univ.–East Bay* | 2.5 | 76% | 41% | 38% | 17% | 19% | 27/1 | 800-1010[9] | N/A | 68% | 1%[7] |
| Cameron University (OK)* | 2.4 | 56% | 36% | 20% | 45% | 1% | 20/1 | 16-21[2] | 15% | 100% | 3% |
| Chaminade Univ. of Honolulu | 2.6 | 70% | 46% | 38% | 59% | 0% | 11/1 | 870-1060 | 6% | 84% | 5% |
| Colorado Christian University[1] | 2.5 | 69%[8] | 51% | 42%[6] | N/A | N/A | 13/1[4] | N/A[2] | N/A | 98%[4] | N/A |
| Colorado State University–Pueblo* | 2.7 | 63% | 33% | 33% | 45% | 7% | 15/1 | 18-23[3] | 34% | 95% | 2% |
| Concordia University Texas[1] | 2.6 | 56%[8] | 50% | 34%[6] | 63%[4] | 0%[4] | 10/1[4] | 900-1130[4] | 45%[4] | 95%[4] | N/A |
| East Central University[1] (OK)* | 2.4 | 59%[8] | 39% | 33%[6] | N/A | N/A | 19/1[4] | 18-23[9] | N/A | 98% | N/A |
| Eastern New Mexico University[1]* | 2.4 | 63%[8] | 42% | 26%[6] | N/A | N/A | 19/1[4] | 17-22[9] | N/A | 63% | N/A |
| Eastern Oregon University[1]* | 2.4 | 68%[8] | 38% | 32%[6] | 64%[4] | 3%[4] | 23/1[4] | 820-1050[4] | 36%[4] | 67%[4] | 2%[4] |
| Grand Canyon University[1] (AZ) | 2.0 | 42%[8] | N/A | 30%[6] | 34%[4] | 19%[4] | 16/1[4] | 20[4] | N/A | 41%[4] | N/A |
| Midwestern State University (TX)* | 2.4 | 70% | 44% | 44% | 37% | 12% | 17/1 | 900-1090[3] | 36% | 72% | 5% |
| Montana State Univ.–Billings* | 2.9 | 57% | 42% | 27% | 51% | 3% | 18/1 | 18-23 | 31% | 99% | 6% |
| Northwestern Oklahoma State U.* | 2.4 | 62% | 40% | 35% | 47% | 4% | 17/1 | 18-22 | 28% | 66% | 3% |
| Prairie View A&M University (TX)* | 2.2 | 67% | 34% | 34%[6] | 22% | 10% | 18/1 | 750-940 | 14% | 85% | N/A |
| Sierra Nevada College (NV) | 2.1 | 68% | 56% | 45% | 81% | 0% | 11/1 | 870-1070[3] | 20% | 87% | 4% |
| Southeastern Oklahoma State U.* | 2.4 | 56% | 42% | 31% | 56% | 4% | 17/1 | 18-22 | 38% | 80% | 11% |
| Southwestern Assemblies of God University (TX) | 2.4 | 66% | 35% | 38%[6] | N/A | N/A | 18/1 | 19-24[4] | N/A | 30% | 1% |
| Southwestern Oklahoma State U.* | 2.4 | 65% | 42% | 30% | 45% | 7% | 18/1 | 18-24 | 43% | 90% | 1% |
| Sul Ross State University (TX)* | 2.2 | N/A | 29% | 30% | 60% | 4% | 16/1 | 14-19[3] | 16% | N/A | N/A |
| Tarleton State University (TX)* | 2.4 | 67% | 42% | 43% | 28% | 9% | 19/1 | 870-1060[3] | 24% | 77% | 2%[7] |
| Texas A&M University–Texarkana* | 2.5 | 44%[8] | N/A | N/A | N/A | N/A | N/A | 19-24[3] | 39% | 36% | N/A |
| University of Houston–Clear Lake* | 2.7 | N/A | N/A | N/A | 30% | 5% | 16/1 | N/A | N/A | N/A | 3% |
| University of Houston–Victoria* | 2.5 | N/A | N/A | N/A | 30% | 2% | 19/1 | 810-1005[9] | 23% | 52% | 1%[7] |
| University of Texas–Brownsville* | 2.4 | 58% | 22% | 26% | 38% | 10% | 19/1 | 810-1000 | 43% | 87% | 0.4%[7] |
| U. of Texas of the Permian Basin* | 2.5 | 63% | 43% | 27% | 41% | 9% | 20/1 | 910-1122 | 60% | 82% | 6% |
| University of Texas–Pan American* | 2.6 | 75% | 33% | 39% | 16% | 24% | 22/1 | 18-22 | 53% | 69% | 5%[4] |
| Wayland Baptist University (TX) | 2.1 | 52% | 30% | 33% | 86% | 0.1% | 10/1 | 17-23 | 28% | 99% | 1% |

# The Top Public Regional Universities ▶

## NORTH
Rank School (State)
1. College of New Jersey
2. SUNY–Geneseo
3. Rowan University (NJ)
4. CUNY–Baruch College
4. SUNY–New Paltz
6. Ramapo College of New Jersey
6. Rutgers, The State U. of New Jersey–Camden
8. CUNY–Queens College
9. Richard Stockton Col. of N.J.
9. SUNY College–Oneonta
9. SUNY–Fredonia
12. CUNY–Hunter College
12. Montclair State University (NJ)
14. SUNY–Oswego
15. College at Brockport–SUNY
15. Towson University (MD)

## SOUTH
Rank School (State)
1. The Citadel (SC)
2. James Madison University (VA)
3. Appalachian State University (NC)
4. College of Charleston (SC)
4. Univ. of Mary Washington (VA)
6. Univ. of North Carolina–Wilmington
7. Christopher Newport Univ. (VA)
8. Winthrop University (SC)
9. Murray State University (KY)
10. Georgia College & State Univ.
11. Longwood University (VA)
12. Western Kentucky University
13. Radford University (VA)
13. Tennessee Technological Univ.
15. University of Montevallo (AL)
15. Western Carolina University (NC)

## MIDWEST
Rank School (State)
1. Truman State University (MO)
2. University of Northern Iowa
3. Grand Valley State University (MI)
4. Eastern Illinois University
4. Univ. of Wisconsin–La Crosse
6. Univ. of Wisconsin–Eau Claire
7. University of Michigan–Dearborn
8. Univ. of Illinois–Springfield
8. University of Minnesota–Duluth
10. Western Illinois University
11. Southern Illinois U.–Edwardsville
12. Univ. of Wisconsin–Whitewater
13. Ferris State University (MI)
13. Univ. of Nebraska–Kearney
13. Univ. of Wisconsin–Stevens Point

## WEST
Rank School (State)
1. Cal. Poly. State U.–San Luis Obispo
2. Western Washington University
3. N.M. Inst. of Mining and Tech.
4. Calif. State Poly. Univ.–Pomona
4. Evergreen State College (WA)
6. California State U.–Long Beach
7. California State Univ.–Chico
8. San Jose State University (CA)
9. California State U.–Fullerton
10. Sonoma State University (CA)
11. California State Univ.–Fresno
12. Texas State University
13. Central Washington University
13. Univ. of Colo.–Colorado Springs
15. California State U.–Stanislaus

Footnotes:
**1.** School refused to fill out U.S. News statistical survey. Data that appear are from school in previous years or from another source such as the National Center for Education Statistics. **2.** SAT and/or ACT not required by school for some or all applicants. **3.** In reporting SAT/ACT scores, the school did not include all students for whom it had scores, or refused to tell U.S. News whether all students with scores had been included. **4.** Data reported to U.S. News in previous years. **5.** Data based on fewer than 51 percent of enrolled freshmen. **6.** Some or all data reported to the NCAA and/or the National Center for Education Statistics.

**7.** Data reported to the Council for Aid to Education. **8.** Average graduation or freshman retention rates, normally based on four years of data, are given here for less than four years because school didn't report rates for the most recent year or years to U.S. News. **9.** SAT and/or ACT may not be required by school for some or all applicants, and in reporting SAT/ACT scores, the school did not include all students for whom it had scores, or refused to tell U.S. News whether all students with scores had been included.

N/A means not available.

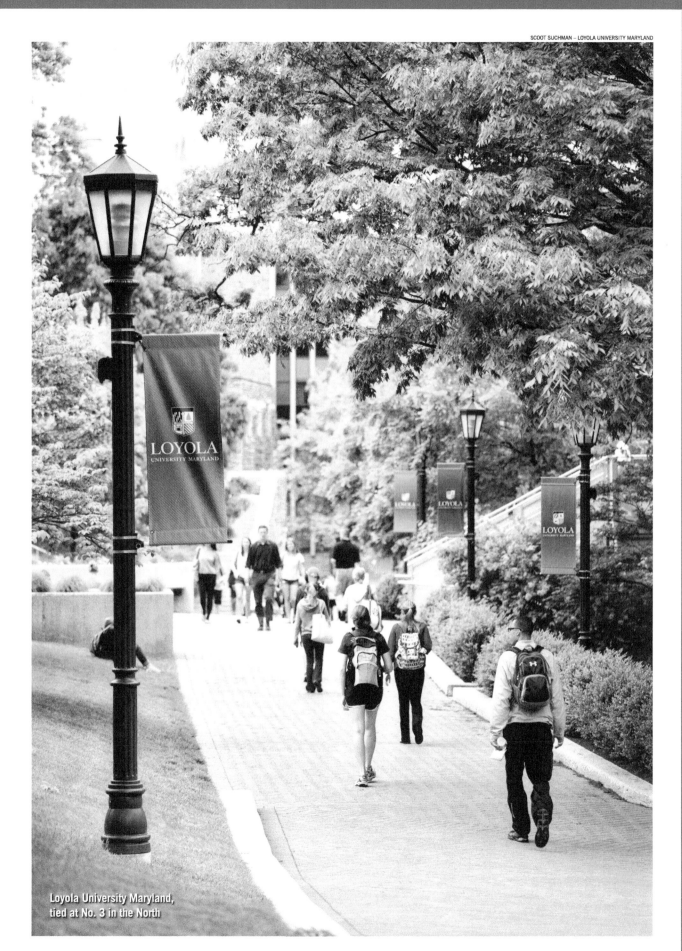

Loyola University Maryland,
tied at No. 3 in the North

# Best Regional Colleges

## What Is a Regional College?

According to the Carnegie Classification of Institutions of Higher Education, these schools focus almost entirely on the undergraduate experience and offer a broad range of programs in the liberal arts (which account for fewer than half of all bachelor's degrees granted) and in fields such as business, nursing and education. They grant few graduate degrees. Because most of the 364 colleges in the category draw heavily from nearby states, they are ranked by region.

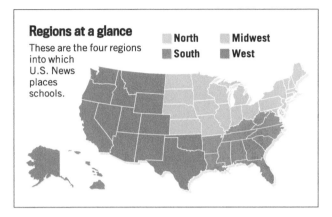

**Regions at a glance**
These are the four regions into which U.S. News places schools.
■ North ■ Midwest ■ South ■ West

## NORTH ▶

| Rank | School (State) (*Public) | Overall score | Peer assessment score (5.0=highest) | Average freshman retention rate | 2013 graduation rate Predicted | 2013 graduation rate Actual | % of classes under 20 ('13) | % of classes of 50 or more ('13) | Student/ faculty ratio ('13) | SAT/ACT 25th-75th percentile ('13) | Freshmen in top 25% of HS class ('13) | Accept-ance rate ('13) | Average alumni giving rate |
|---|---|---|---|---|---|---|---|---|---|---|---|---|---|
| 1. | U. S. Coast Guard Acad. (CT)* | 100 | 4.1 | 91% | 83% | 91% | 71% | 0.3% | 7/1 | 1190-1360[3] | 80% | 16% | 31% |
| 2. | Cooper Union (NY) | 96 | 4.1 | 94% | 83% | 82% | 64% | 2% | 7/1 | 1220-1490 | 95%[5] | 8% | 25% |
| 3. | U.S. Merchant Marine Acad. (NY)* | 76 | 3.7 | 86%[8] | 73% | 74% | 70% | 3% | 13/1 | 1183-1351 | 57% | 18% | N/A |
| 4. | Elizabethtown College (PA) | 71 | 3.4 | 85% | 65% | 77% | 65% | 1% | 12/1 | 1000-1230 | 65% | 70% | 23% |
| 5. | Messiah College (PA) | 68 | 3.5 | 86% | 67% | 76% | 46% | 3% | 13/1 | 1030-1260 | 68% | 66% | 15% |
| 6. | Lebanon Valley College (PA) | 63 | 3.2 | 85% | 64% | 73% | 57% | 1% | 12/1 | 1000-1220[2] | 74% | 67% | 18% |
| 7. | Massachusetts Maritime Academy* | 60 | 3.4 | 88% | 56% | 67% | 50% | 0% | 15/1 | 980-1170 | N/A | 59% | 9% |
| 8. | Maine Maritime Academy* | 59 | 3.3 | 80%[8] | 49% | 65% | 50% | 1% | 11/1 | 920-1130 | 32% | 65% | 15% |
| 9. | Elmira College (NY) | 54 | 3.1 | 73% | 63% | 62% | 63% | 0% | 10/1 | 940-1160 | 58% | 80% | 21% |
| 9. | Merrimack College (MA) | 54 | 3.4 | 82% | 61% | 60% | 42% | 0% | 13/1 | 920-1130[2] | 34% | 79% | 13% |
| 11. | Seton Hill University (PA) | 52 | 3.2 | 76%[8] | 54% | 62% | 59% | 0% | 14/1 | 900-1150[2] | 47% | 65% | 18% |
| 12. | Bard College at Simon's Rock (MA) | 50 | 3.3 | 75% | 76% | 28% | 99% | 0% | 6/1 | 1290-1460[2] | 67%[5] | 92% | 14% |
| 12. | Wentworth Inst. of Technology (MA) | 50 | 3.3 | 80% | 54% | 61% | 36% | 1% | 17/1 | 1010-1210 | 40% | 57% | 5% |
| 14. | Champlain College (VT) | 48 | 3.0 | 78% | 54% | 57% | 61% | 0% | 14/1 | 990-1240[3] | 39%[5] | 71% | 6% |
| 14. | Geneva College (PA) | 48 | 2.8 | 77% | 53% | 67% | 63% | 4% | 14/1 | 950-1190 | 45% | 69% | 11% |
| 16. | Cedar Crest College (PA) | 46 | 2.7 | 71% | 54% | 60% | 79% | 2% | 9/1 | 840-1050 | 43% | 59% | 11% |
| 17. | Wilson College (PA) | 45 | 2.4 | 61% | 49% | 56% | 88% | 0% | 8/1 | 860-1120[2] | 53% | 53% | 24% |
| 18. | University of Maine–Farmington* | 44 | 2.8 | 73% | 43% | 55% | 62% | 1% | 13/1 | 880-1150[2] | 43% | 84% | 4% |
| 19. | Delaware Valley College (PA) | 43 | 2.9 | 72% | 55% | 57% | 57% | 3% | 13/1 | 880-1123 | 41% | 68% | 8% |
| 20. | St. Francis College (NY) | 42 | 2.9 | 79% | 40% | 52% | 47% | 1% | 18/1 | 850-1030 | N/A | 64% | 10% |
| 20. | SUNY Maritime College* | 42 | 3.0 | 79% | 53% | 50% | 37% | 3% | 15/1 | 930-1170 | 30%[5] | 64% | 5% |
| 22. | SUNY College of Technology–Alfred* | 41 | 2.8 | 82%[8] | 34% | 52% | 56% | 5% | 18/1 | 840-1070[2] | N/A | 55% | 6%[4] |
| 22. | Vaughn Col. of Aeron. and Tech. (NY) | 41 | 2.6 | 80% | 38% | 56% | 64% | 0% | 15/1 | 885-1093 | N/A | 77% | 2% |
| 24. | Cazenovia College (NY) | 40 | 2.6 | 67% | 48% | 59% | 70% | 0% | 12/1 | 860-1070[2] | 40% | 78% | 14% |
| 24. | College of Our Lady of the Elms (MA) | 40 | 2.3 | 81% | 44% | 68% | 67% | 1% | 13/1 | 820-1040[3] | 35%[4] | 75% | 17% |
| 26. | Dean College (MA) | 36 | 2.7 | 69%[8] | 42% | 62% | 63% | 0% | 16/1 | 750-950 | 11%[5] | 68% | N/A |
| 27. | Lasell College (MA) | 35 | 2.6 | 70% | 47% | 53% | 64% | 0% | 14/1 | 880-1070 | N/A | 76% | 12% |
| 28. | Farmingdale State College–SUNY* | 33 | 2.6 | 82% | 38% | 43% | 24% | 1% | 19/1 | 950-1110 | 36%[5] | 51% | 2% |
| 28. | Pennsylvania College of Technology* | 33 | 2.9 | 67% | 44% | 55% | 62% | 0% | 17/1 | N/A[2] | N/A | 90% | N/A |
| 28. | SUNY College of A&T–Cobleskill* | 33 | 2.7 | 75% | 32% | 44% | 33% | 6% | 18/1 | 760-1000[2] | 22% | 73% | 5% |
| 31. | Concordia College[1] (NY) | 32 | 2.7 | 69%[8] | 47% | 48%[6] | 60%[4] | 0%[4] | 13/1[4] | 18-24[4] | 25%[4] | 72%[4] | 8%[4] |
| 31. | Unity College (ME) | 32 | 2.5 | 75% | 50% | 51% | 66% | 0% | 11/1 | 910-1110[2] | 29% | 89% | 3% |
| 33. | La Roche College (PA) | 30 | 2.4 | 71% | 44% | 46% | 70% | 0% | 13/1 | 800-1040 | 26%[5] | 56% | 4% |
| 33. | SUNY College of Technology–Delhi* | 30 | 2.7 | 70% | 30% | 35% | 48% | 4% | 18/1 | 808-983[2] | 14%[5] | 59% | 4% |
| 33. | Thiel College (PA) | 30 | 2.6 | 63% | 45% | 34% | 62% | 2% | 14/1 | 870-1060[3] | 34% | 66% | 18% |
| 36. | Vermont Technical College* | 29 | 2.3 | 70% | 47% | 40%[6] | 74% | 0.2% | 10/1 | 810-1040[9] | 27%[5] | 67% | N/A |

**Note:** Key to footnotes, Page 114.

| Rank | School (State) (*Public) | Overall score | Peer assessment score (5.0=highest) | Average freshman retention rate | 2013 graduation rate | | % of classes under 20 ('13) | % of classes of 50 or more ('13) | Student/ faculty ratio ('13) | SAT/ACT 25th-75th percentile ('13) | Freshmen in top 25% of HS class ('13) | Accept- ance rate ('13) | Average alumni giving rate |
|---|---|---|---|---|---|---|---|---|---|---|---|---|---|
| | | | | | Predicted | Actual | | | | | | | |
| 37. | University of Maine–Fort Kent* | 27 | 2.4 | 62% | 37% | 44% | 71% | 1% | 14/1 | 818-1000[2] | 10% | 63% | 7% |
| 38. | Keystone College (PA) | 26 | 2.4 | 67% | 35% | 39% | 80% | 0% | 11/1 | 800-1000 | N/A | 72% | 7%[4] |
| 38. | Mount Aloysius College (PA) | 26 | 2.8 | 63%[8] | 36% | 35%[8] | 66% | 0% | 13/1 | 830-1030[3] | N/A | 71% | N/A |
| 40. | Mount Ida College (MA) | 25 | 2.3 | 61% | 41% | 39% | 79% | 0% | 14/1 | 790-980 | N/A | 68% | 2% |
| 40. | Nichols College (MA) | 25 | 2.5 | 63% | 45% | 46% | 34% | 0% | 17/1 | 840-1030[2] | 16%[5] | 82% | 10% |
| 40. | Paul Smith's College[1] (NY) | 25 | 2.7 | 76%[8] | 49% | 42%[6] | N/A | N/A | 15/1[4] | 880-1060[9] | N/A | 75% | N/A |
| 43. | Morrisville State College (NY)* | 24 | 2.5 | 60% | N/A | 29% | 47% | 3% | 16/1 | 840-1030[2] | 16% | 59% | 4% |
| 44. | Thomas College (ME) | 22 | 2.3 | 65%[8] | 37% | 45% | 53% | 0% | 22/1 | 790-1010 | 34% | 73% | 5% |
| 44. | Valley Forge Christian College[1] (PA) | 22 | 2.2 | 75%[8] | 46% | 52%[6] | N/A | N/A | 17/1[4] | 890-1040[9] | N/A | 66% | N/A |
| 46. | Univ. of Maine–Presque Isle* | 21 | 2.4 | 63% | 36% | 30% | 71% | 0% | 14/1 | N/A[2] | 25%[5] | 78% | 2% |
| 46. | Washington Adventist Univ. (MD) | 21 | 2.2 | 70% | 41% | 34% | 78% | 0% | 10/1 | 720-960 | N/A | 53% | 3% |

| School (State) (*Public) | Peer assessment score (5.0=highest) | Average freshman retention rate | 2013 graduation rate | | % of classes under 20 ('13) | % of classes of 50 or more ('13) | Student/ faculty ratio ('13) | SAT/ACT 25th-75th percentile ('13) | Freshmen in top 25% of HS class ('13) | Accept- ance rate ('13) | Average alumni giving rate |
|---|---|---|---|---|---|---|---|---|---|---|---|
| | | | Predicted | Actual | | | | | | | |
| SECOND TIER (SCHOOLS RANKED 48 THROUGH 61 ARE LISTED HERE ALPHABETICALLY) | | | | | | | | | | | |
| Bay State College (MA) | 2.1 | N/A | N/A | 17%[6] | N/A | N/A | 18/1 | N/A[2] | N/A | 59% | N/A |
| Becker College (MA) | 2.5 | 64%[8] | 38% | 24% | 59% | 1% | 17/1 | 890-1120 | 26%[5] | 63% | N/A |
| CUNY–Medgar Evers College* | 2.2 | 53%[8] | 39% | 13% | 25% | 0.1% | 18/1 | 690-860[9] | N/A | 100% | N/A |
| CUNY–New York City Col. of Tech.* | 2.7 | 76% | 33% | 25% | 29% | 0% | 19/1 | N/A[2] | N/A | 71% | 1%[4] |
| CUNY–York College* | 2.4 | 76% | 24% | 24% | 20% | 43% | 21/1 | 871[4] | N/A | 65% | N/A |
| Daniel Webster College[1] (NH) | 2.4 | 61%[8] | 52% | 42%[6] | N/A | N/A | 13/1[4] | 830-1100[3] | N/A | 60% | N/A |
| Fisher College (MA) | 2.4 | 63% | 26% | 35% | 26%[4] | 0%[4] | 16/1 | 730-920[2] | N/A | 65% | N/A |
| Five Towns College (NY) | 2.2 | N/A | N/A | 38%[6] | 51% | 1% | 15/1 | 770-1000 | 36%[5] | 55% | N/A |
| Lyndon State College[1] (VT)* | 2.5 | 65%[8] | 37% | 34%[6] | N/A | N/A | 14/1[4] | 810-1050[9] | N/A | 99% | N/A |
| Post University (CT) | 2.4 | 47% | 37% | 35% | 59% | 0% | 19/1 | 760-960 | 20%[5] | 64% | N/A |
| Southern Vermont College | 2.4 | 63%[8] | 39% | 31%[6] | N/A | N/A | N/A | N/A[2] | N/A | N/A | N/A |
| SUNY College of Technology–Canton* | 2.5 | 73%[8] | 35% | 29% | 44% | 3% | 19/1 | 820-1020[2] | 15% | 78% | 3% |
| University of Maine–Augusta* | 2.6 | 53% | 11% | 12% | 72% | 0.3% | 17/1 | 760-1010[9] | 9% | 95% | 0.2% |
| Wesley College (DE) | 2.7 | 46% | 45% | 22% | 78%[4] | 0%[4] | 16/1 | 750-940[3] | 23% | 63%[4] | 8%[4] |

| Rank | School (State) (*Public) | Overall score | Peer assessment score (5.0=highest) | Average freshman retention rate | 2013 graduation rate | | % of classes under 20 ('13) | % of classes of 50 or more ('13) | Student/ faculty ratio ('13) | SAT/ACT 25th-75th percentile ('13) | Freshmen in top 25% of HS class ('13) | Accept- ance rate ('13) | Average alumni giving rate |
|---|---|---|---|---|---|---|---|---|---|---|---|---|---|
| | | | | | Predicted | Actual | | | | | | | |
| 1. | Asbury University (KY) | 100 | 3.3 | 80% | 63% | 64% | 62% | 0% | 13/1 | 21-27 | 54% | 66% | 18% |
| 1. | High Point University (NC) | 100 | 3.5 | 77% | 50% | 62% | 57% | 1% | 14/1 | 980-1170 | 51%[5] | 84% | 7% |
| 1. | John Brown University (AR) | 100 | 3.2 | 80% | 62% | 65% | 50% | 0% | 15/1 | 23-29 | 65% | 70% | 18% |
| 4. | University of the Ozarks (AR) | 94 | 3.3 | 63%[8] | 56% | 48% | 84% | 0% | 10/1 | 20-26 | 44% | 61% | 15% |
| 5. | Florida Southern College | 92 | 3.2 | 76% | 55% | 58% | 58% | 0% | 13/1 | 1010-1180 | 56%[4] | 50% | 14% |
| 6. | Covenant College (GA) | 91 | 3.0 | 83% | 59% | 58% | 54% | 1% | 14/1 | 1060-1280 | 55%[5] | 57% | 15% |
| 6. | Meredith College (NC) | 91 | 3.1 | 76%[8] | 57% | 62% | N/A | N/A | 12/1 | 930-1140[2] | 52% | 62% | 19% |
| 8. | Flagler College (FL) | 88 | 3.3 | 72% | 54% | 63% | 42% | 0% | 17/1 | 930-1130[3] | 31% | 50% | 20% |
| 9. | Milligan College (TN) | 86 | 2.9 | 82% | 61% | 52% | 70%[4] | 1%[4] | 12/1 | 22-26 | 65%[4] | 68% | 23% |
| 9. | Tuskegee University (AL) | 86 | 3.1 | 76% | 48% | 42% | 56% | 9% | 12/1 | 18-23[3] | 60% | 41% | 24% |
| 11. | Wheeling Jesuit University (WV) | 85 | 3.0 | 74% | 58% | 54% | 61% | 0% | 12/1 | 20-24 | 43% | 67% | 15% |
| 12. | West Virginia Wesleyan College | 83 | 3.0 | 67% | 56% | 60% | 59% | 0.3% | 13/1 | 20-25 | 56% | 77% | 17% |
| 13. | LaGrange College (GA) | 82 | 3.0 | 62% | 50% | 38% | 75% | 2% | 11/1 | 910-1090 | 36% | 58% | 13% |
| 14. | Aquinas College (TN) | 80 | 2.8 | 75% | 44% | 67% | 85% | 8% | 9/1 | 23-27 | 43%[5] | 52% | N/A |
| 15. | Carson-Newman University (TN) | 79 | 3.1 | 65% | 42% | 50% | 63% | 0% | 12/1 | 20-26[3] | 47%[4] | 67% | 9% |
| 16. | Catawba College (NC) | 77 | 2.9 | 69% | 54% | 52% | 68% | 0% | 14/1 | 850-1090[2] | 22% | 41% | 17% |
| 16. | Coker College (SC) | 77 | 2.8 | 74%[8] | 34% | 43% | 72% | 0% | 12/1 | 870-1050 | 21% | 53% | 12% |
| 18. | Univ. of South Carolina–Aiken* | 75 | 3.3 | 69% | 43% | 42% | 52% | 1% | 15/1 | 860-1070 | 36% | 70% | 7% |
| 19. | University of Charleston (WV) | 74 | 3.2 | 67% | 56% | 46% | 59% | 2% | 14/1 | 19-24 | 70%[4] | 69% | 7% |
| 20. | Lenoir-Rhyne University (NC) | 73 | 3.0 | 65% | 54% | 49% | 46% | 1% | 13/1 | 880-1080[3] | 44% | 68% | 20% |
| 21. | Anderson University (SC) | 72 | 3.2 | 73% | 48% | 41% | 47% | 3% | 16/1 | 960-1180 | 64% | 65% | 8% |
| 22. | Bryan College (TN) | 71 | 2.8 | 71% | 54% | 62% | 68% | 1% | 15/1 | 20-25 | 51%[4] | 38% | 11% |

## SOUTH ▶

| Rank | School (State) (*Public) | Overall score | Peer assessment score (5.0=highest) | Average freshman retention rate | 2013 graduation rate Predicted | 2013 graduation rate Actual | % of classes under 20 ('13) | % of classes of 50 or more ('13) | Student/ faculty ratio ('13) | SAT/ACT 25th-75th percentile ('13) | Freshmen in top 25% of HS class ('13) | Accept- ance rate ('13) | Average alumni giving rate |
|---|---|---|---|---|---|---|---|---|---|---|---|---|---|
| 23. | Blue Mountain College (MS) | 70 | 2.7 | 77% | 46% | 51% | 71% | 0% | 13/1 | 18-23 | 38% | 51% | 7% |
| 23. | Huntingdon College (AL) | 70 | 2.8 | 59% | 52% | 43% | 63% | 0% | 14/1 | 19-24 | 40% | 63% | 24% |
| 25. | Averett University (VA) | 69 | 2.9 | 59% | 35% | 33% | 76% | 0% | 12/1 | 840-1030 | 30% | 88% | 5% |
| 25. | Barton College (NC) | 69 | 2.7 | 68% | 42% | 48% | 65% | 0% | 11/1 | 840-1020 | 38% | 42% | 9% |
| 25. | North Greenville University (SC) | 69 | 2.8 | 71% | 43% | 55% | 71% | 0% | 14/1 | 920-1340 | 39% | 58% | 5% |
| 25. | University of Mobile (AL) | 69 | 3.1 | 74% | 49% | 49% | 59% | 1% | 12/1 | 20-25 | 50% | 71% | 1% |
| 29. | Alice Lloyd College (KY) | 67 | 3.0 | 58% | 43% | 32% | 51% | 2% | 17/1 | 18-23 | 51% | 9% | 42% |
| 29. | Elizabeth City State Univ. (NC)* | 67 | 2.5 | 75% | 28% | 42% | 66% | 1% | 16/1 | 780-945[3] | 5% | 52% | 10% |
| 31. | Kentucky Wesleyan College | 66 | 2.7 | 60% | 45% | 38% | 84% | 0.4% | 11/1 | 19-25 | 39% | 67% | 15% |
| 32. | U. of South Carolina–Upstate* | 64 | 3.1 | 67% | 41% | 40% | 53% | 1% | 16/1 | 870-1038[3] | 40% | 57% | 2% |
| 33. | Newberry College (SC) | 63 | 2.7 | 66% | 46% | 44% | 64% | 0% | 12/1 | 830-1060 | 16% | 59% | 14% |
| 34. | Southern Adventist University[1] (TN) | 62 | 2.8 | 74%[8] | 52% | 44% | 57%[4] | 7%[4] | 14/1[4] | 20-25[3] | N/A | 45%[4] | 7%[7] |
| 35. | Bethune-Cookman University (FL) | 61 | 2.8 | 66% | 26% | 55% | 44% | 2% | 18/1 | 15-18 | 12% | 67% | 4% |
| 35. | Toccoa Falls College (GA) | 61 | 2.6 | 69% | 46% | 46% | 61% | 1% | 14/1 | 880-1130[2] | 44% | 54% | 3% |
| 37. | Alderson Broaddus University (WV) | 60 | 2.6 | 64% | 48% | 45% | 70% | 5% | 15/1 | 19-24 | 36% | 43% | 14% |
| 37. | Belmont Abbey College (NC) | 60 | 2.9 | 65% | 49% | 38% | 63% | 0% | 17/1 | 868-1070[2] | 26% | 68% | 9% |
| 37. | Mars Hill University (NC) | 60 | 2.9 | 57% | 41% | 38% | 72% | 0% | 12/1 | 830-1040 | 26% | 64% | 10% |
| 40. | Keiser University (FL) | 59 | 2.2 | 76% | N/A | 68% | 81% | 0% | 12/1 | N/A[2] | N/A | N/A | N/A |
| 41. | Southeastern University (FL) | 58 | 2.8 | 66% | 44% | 39% | 64% | 5% | 20/1 | 850-1080[3] | N/A | 59% | 3% |
| 41. | Tennessee Wesleyan College | 58 | 2.6 | 63% | 48% | 44% | 71% | 4% | 12/1 | 19-24 | 20%[5] | 71% | 12% |
| 43. | Brescia University (KY) | 57 | 2.8 | 58% | 47% | 30% | 88% | 0% | 13/1 | 19-24 | N/A | 45% | 14% |
| 43. | Philander Smith College (AR) | 57 | 2.2 | 63% | 27% | 44% | 83% | 0% | 10/1 | 16-22 | 44% | 42% | 13% |
| 43. | Univ. of Arkansas–Pine Bluff* | 57 | 2.8 | 56% | 23% | 26% | 55% | 4% | 15/1 | 15-20 | 27% | 28% | 11% |
| 46. | Oakwood University[1] (AL) | 56 | 2.9 | 71%[8] | 40% | 38%[6] | N/A | N/A | N/A | 17-22[4] | N/A | 34%[4] | N/A |
| 47. | Emmanuel College (GA) | 55 | 2.4 | 62% | 33% | 46% | 68% | 0% | 13/1 | 830-1030 | N/A | 48% | 8% |
| 47. | Faulkner University[1] (AL) | 55 | 2.7 | 53%[8] | 36% | 34%[6] | 72%[4] | 2%[4] | 15/1[4] | 18-23[4] | 22%[4] | 60%[4] | 3%[4] |
| 47. | Ferrum College (VA) | 55 | 3.0 | 54% | 38% | 32% | 56% | 0% | 16/1 | 780-990 | 15%[5] | 74% | 9% |
| 50. | Concord University (WV)* | 53 | 2.8 | 63% | 37% | 35% | 57% | 2% | 17/1 | 18-24[3] | 44% | 45% | 4% |
| 50. | Davis and Elkins College[1] (WV) | 53 | 2.7 | 55%[8] | 44% | 51%[6] | N/A | N/A | 14/1[4] | 17-23[9] | N/A | 57% | N/A |
| 52. | Welch College (TN) | 52 | 2.3 | 65% | 42% | 37% | 84% | 3% | 10/1 | 18-25 | 42% | 52% | 14% |
| 52. | West Liberty University (WV)* | 52 | 2.6 | 70% | 36% | 41% | 67% | 0.4% | 14/1 | 18-24[3] | 37% | 71% | N/A |
| 54. | Bluefield College (VA) | 51 | 2.5 | 53% | 41% | 45% | 77% | 0% | 14/1 | 800-1010 | 27% | 57% | 8% |
| 54. | Lees-McRae College (NC) | 51 | 2.7 | 60% | 47% | 38% | 72% | 0% | 15/1 | 840-1080[2] | 29% | 66% | 9% |
| 56. | Kentucky Christian University | 50 | 2.5 | 61% | 39% | 39% | 67% | 1% | 12/1 | 18-23 | 32% | 51% | 3% |
| 56. | Ohio Valley University (WV) | 50 | 2.2 | 59% | 46% | 40% | 86% | 0% | 10/1 | 19-23 | 29% | 38% | 5% |
| 56. | University of Mount Olive (NC) | 50 | 2.4 | 64% | 34% | 37% | 70%[4] | 0%[4] | 14/1 | 833-1060[9] | N/A | 48% | 4%[7] |
| 59. | Univ. of South Carolina–Beaufort* | 49 | 2.9 | 53% | 40% | 27% | 59% | 1% | 17/1 | 830-1010 | 24% | 68% | 4% |
| 59. | Williams Baptist College (AR) | 49 | 2.6 | N/A | 43% | 39% | 58% | 0% | 13/1 | 20-25[3] | N/A | 68% | 4% |
| 61. | Midway College[1] (KY) | 48 | 2.4 | 72%[8] | 37% | 48%[6] | N/A | N/A | 14/1[4] | 19-25[9] | N/A | 54% | N/A |
| 62. | Clayton State University (GA)* | 47 | 2.8 | 67% | 35% | 29% | 44% | 4% | 18/1 | 860-1030 | 40%[4] | 46% | 4% |
| 62. | Methodist University[1] (NC) | 47 | 2.9 | 55%[8] | 47% | 40%[6] | N/A | N/A | 12/1[4] | 860-1060[4] | N/A | 61%[4] | N/A |
| 64. | Indian River State College (FL)* | 45 | 2.9 | 60%[8] | N/A | N/A | 39% | 2% | 23/1 | N/A[2] | N/A | 100% | 1%[7] |
| 64. | Lander University[1] (SC)* | 45 | 2.6 | 61%[8] | 42% | 40%[6] | N/A | N/A | 16/1[4] | 833-1050[4] | N/A | 42%[4] | N/A |
| 64. | Limestone College (SC) | 45 | 2.4 | 59% | 44% | 37% | 63% | 0% | 13/1 | 930-1090[3] | 19% | 54% | 5% |
| 64. | Reinhardt University (GA) | 45 | 2.6 | 64%[8] | 46% | 28% | 79% | 0% | 14/1 | 860-1120[3] | 30% | 60% | 5% |
| 68. | Virginia Union University | 43 | 2.7 | 54%[8] | 27% | 35% | 48% | 1% | 14/1 | 670-840 | 18% | 83% | 9% |
| 69. | Central Baptist College (AR) | 42 | 2.2 | 59% | 34% | 38% | 85% | 0% | 12/1 | 19-23[3] | 38% | 55% | 9% |
| 70. | Everglades University[1] (FL) | 41 | 2.2 | 66%[8] | N/A | 62%[6] | N/A | N/A | 8/1[4] | N/A[2] | N/A | 91%[4] | N/A |
| 71. | Fort Valley State University (GA)* | 40 | 2.4 | 61% | 36% | 28% | 47% | 5% | 19/1 | 15-18 | 23%[5] | 31% | 16% |
| 71. | Glenville State College (WV)* | 40 | 2.4 | 64% | 30% | 30% | 65% | 0.4% | 16/1 | 16-21 | 20% | 67% | 6% |
| 71. | North Carolina Wesleyan College | 40 | 2.5 | 55% | 36% | 33% | 74% | 0% | 13/1 | 760-970[2] | 14% | 47% | 3% |
| 74. | Louisiana College[1] | 38 | 2.5 | 64%[8] | 51% | 39%[6] | N/A | N/A | 16/1[4] | 18-23[9] | N/A | 74% | N/A |
| 74. | Point University (GA) | 38 | 2.2 | 59% | 40% | 48% | N/A | N/A | 19/1 | 18-22 | 34%[5] | 54% | 6%[4] |

**Note:** Key to footnotes, Page 114.

# SOUTH ▶

| School (State) (*Public) | Peer assessment score (5.0=highest) | Average freshman retention rate | 2013 graduation rate | | % of classes under 20 ('13) | % of classes of 50 or more ('13) | Student/ faculty ratio ('13) | SAT/ACT 25th-75th percentile ('13) | Freshmen in top 25% of HS class ('13) | Accept- ance rate ('13) | Average alumni giving rate |
|---|---|---|---|---|---|---|---|---|---|---|---|
| | | | Predicted | Actual | | | | | | | |
| SECOND TIER (SCHOOLS RANKED 76 THROUGH 98 ARE LISTED HERE ALPHABETICALLY) | | | | | | | | | | | |
| Abraham Baldwin Agricultural College (GA)* | 2.7 | 59%[8] | N/A | N/A | N/A | N/A | 22/1 | 810-990[3] | N/A | 71% | N/A |
| Bluefield State College (WV)* | 2.4 | 57% | 28% | 22% | 75% | 0.3% | 15/1 | 16-21 | N/A | 41% | 4% |
| Brewton-Parker College[1] (GA) | 2.3 | 42%[8] | 31% | 21%[6] | N/A | N/A | 15/1[4] | 810-990[9] | N/A | 51% | N/A |
| Chipola College[1] (FL)* | 2.6 | N/A | N/A | N/A | N/A | N/A | 19/1[4] | N/A[2] | N/A | N/A | N/A |
| Chowan University (NC) | 2.3 | 44% | 33% | 24% | 34% | 2% | 17/1 | 700-870 | 11% | 62% | 10% |
| Edward Waters College[1] (FL) | 1.9 | 54%[8] | 30% | 19%[6] | N/A | N/A | 17/1[4] | 15-18[9] | N/A | 27% | N/A |
| Florida College | 2.6 | N/A | 55% | 11%[6] | 67% | 6% | 11/1 | 20-26[3] | N/A | 74% | 65% |
| Georgia Gwinnett College* | 2.7 | 67%[8] | N/A | 27% | 24% | 0% | 19/1 | 820-1055[2] | 15% | 90% | 9% |
| Gordon State College[1] (GA)* | 2.5 | N/A | N/A | N/A | N/A | N/A | 21/1[4] | 750-950[9] | N/A | 45% | N/A |
| Greensboro College[1] (NC) | 2.6 | 47%[8] | 45% | 40%[6] | N/A | N/A | 11/1[4] | 790-1020[9] | N/A | 78% | N/A |
| LeMoyne-Owen College (TN) | 2.6 | 54%[8] | 25% | 15%[6] | 95% | 0% | 13/1 | N/A | N/A | 27% | N/A |
| Livingstone College (NC) | 2.0 | 52% | 17% | 20% | 46% | 1% | 15/1 | 11-16[3] | 6% | 72% | 36% |
| Mid-Continent University[1] (KY) | 1.6 | 65%[8] | 31% | 23%[6] | 88%[4] | 0%[4] | 21/1[4] | N/A[2] | 26%[4] | 87%[4] | N/A |
| Middle Georgia State College[1]* | 2.7 | 68%[8] | 15% | 20%[6] | N/A | N/A | 19/1[4] | 810-1020[4] | N/A | 47%[4] | N/A |
| Paine College (GA) | 2.3 | 61% | 26% | 21% | 65% | 0% | 13/1 | 14-18 | 15%[5] | 44% | 13% |
| Shaw University[1] (NC) | 2.2 | 52%[8] | 20% | 27%[8] | 66%[4] | 1%[4] | 15/1[4] | 13-16[4] | 5%[4] | 54%[4] | N/A |
| St. Augustine's University (NC) | 2.1 | 52% | 25% | 38% | N/A | N/A | 13/1 | 665-858[3] | N/A | 67% | 5% |
| Thomas University (GA) | 2.2 | 47%[8] | 29% | 27% | N/A | N/A | 10/1 | 810-1060[2] | N/A | 69% | N/A |
| Truett McConnell College (GA) | 2.5 | 65% | 40% | 16% | 62% | 4% | 16/1 | 840-1050 | 32% | 81% | 9% |
| University of Arkansas–Fort Smith[1]* | 2.8 | 63%[8] | 35% | 23%[6] | N/A | N/A | 18/1[4] | 19-25[9] | N/A | 57% | N/A |
| Victory University[1] (TN) | 1.8 | 64%[8] | 31% | 13%[6] | N/A | N/A | 24/1[4] | N/A[2] | N/A | 95%[4] | N/A |
| Voorhees College[1] (SC) | 2.1 | 46%[8] | 26% | 30%[6] | N/A | N/A | 13/1[4] | N/A[2] | N/A | 51% | N/A |
| Webber International University (FL) | 2.4 | 48% | 36% | 32% | 42% | 0% | 24/1 | 17-21 | 22% | 64% | 0.3%[4] |

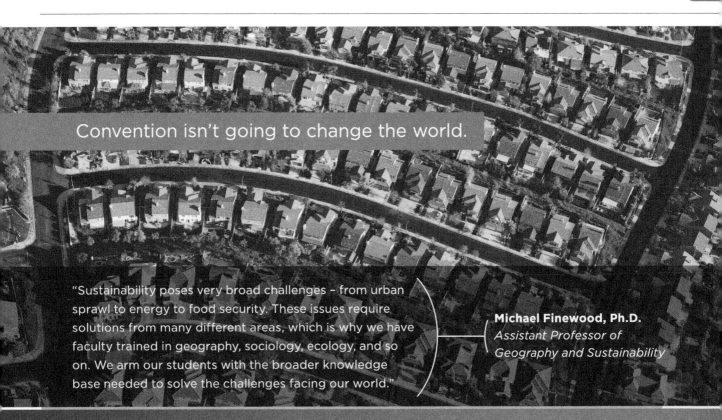

## MIDWEST ▶

| Rank | School (State) (*Public) | Overall score | Peer assessment score (5.0=highest) | Average freshman retention rate | 2013 graduation rate Predicted | 2013 graduation rate Actual | % of classes under 20 ('13) | % of classes of 50 or more ('13) | Student/ faculty ratio ('13) | SAT/ACT 25th-75th percentile ('13) | Freshmen in top 25% of HS class ('13) | Accept-ance rate ('13) | Average alumni giving rate |
|---|---|---|---|---|---|---|---|---|---|---|---|---|---|
| 1. | Taylor University (IN) | 100 | 3.8 | 88% | 67% | 74% | 63% | 5% | 13/1 | 24-31 | 67%[5] | 88% | 22% |
| 2. | Ohio Northern University | 93 | 3.5 | 86% | 67% | 69% | 64% | 1% | 12/1 | 23-29 | 69% | 68% | 15% |
| 3. | Augustana College (SD) | 87 | 3.5 | 83% | 62% | 66% | 53% | 1% | 12/1 | 23-28 | 63% | 68% | 18% |
| 4. | College of the Ozarks (MO) | 83 | 3.6 | 87% | 51% | 65% | 50% | 2% | 15/1 | 20-25[3] | 50% | 12% | 19% |
| 5. | Dordt College (IA) | 80 | 3.4 | 79% | 59% | 62% | 59% | 5% | 12/1 | 21-28 | 44% | 76% | 26% |
| 6. | Cedarville University (OH) | 79 | 3.2 | 85% | 67% | 73% | 65% | 6% | 13/1 | 24-29 | 61% | 74% | 11% |
| 6. | Franklin College[1] (IN) | 79 | 3.2 | 77%[8] | 55% | 59%[6] | 79%[4] | 0%[4] | 12/1[4] | 19-24[4] | 46%[4] | 65%[4] | 27%[4] |
| 6. | Marietta College (OH) | 79 | 3.2 | 78%[8] | 58% | 55% | 78% | 0% | 11/1 | 21-27[3] | 59% | 64% | 20% |
| 6. | Northwestern College (IA) | 79 | 3.3 | 78% | 60% | 63% | 68% | 0.3% | 11/1 | 22-27 | 49% | 76% | 22% |
| 10. | Univ. of Northwestern–St. Paul (MN) | 75 | 3.0 | 78%[8] | 58% | 66%[6] | 61%[4] | 3%[4] | 14/1[4] | 22-27[4] | 50% | 59%[4] | 17%[4] |
| 11. | Buena Vista University (IA) | 74 | 3.1 | 73% | 53% | 53% | 75% | 1% | 9/1 | 20-25 | 42% | 70% | 7% |
| 11. | Loras College (IA) | 74 | 3.2 | 79% | 55% | 61% | 55% | 1% | 12/1 | 21-26 | 39%[5] | 69% | 20% |
| 11. | University of Mount Union (OH) | 74 | 3.1 | 74% | 52% | 63% | 53% | 0.4% | 13/1 | 20-25[3] | 34% | 71% | 21% |
| 14. | Huntington University (IN) | 73 | 3.1 | 77% | 59% | 62% | 71% | 1% | 13/1 | 880-1130 | 53% | 97% | 18% |
| 14. | Millikin University (IL) | 73 | 3.4 | 77% | 55% | 60% | 60% | 1% | 11/1 | 21-26 | 41% | 55% | 13% |
| 16. | St. Mary-of-the-Woods College (IN) | 72 | 3.0 | 73% | 43% | 60% | 92% | 0% | 8/1 | 780-1020 | 41% | 98% | 24% |
| 17. | Clarke University (IA) | 71 | 2.8 | 78% | 51% | 70% | 75% | 2% | 10/1 | 20-25[3] | 46% | 78% | 19% |
| 18. | Hastings College (NE) | 70 | 3.0 | 71% | 56% | 61% | 67% | 0% | 13/1 | 21-26 | 40% | 74% | 22% |
| 19. | Bethel College (IN) | 68 | 3.0 | 80% | 50% | 62% | 77% | 1% | 13/1 | 900-1130 | 51% | 72% | 8% |
| 20. | Benedictine College (KS) | 67 | 3.3 | 79% | 48% | 59% | 55% | 2% | 14/1 | 22-28[3] | 46% | 97% | 24% |
| 21. | Mount Mercy University (IA) | 66 | 2.7 | 79% | 51% | 73% | 60% | 1% | 14/1 | 20-24 | 41% | 68% | 14% |
| 22. | Adrian College (MI) | 64 | 3.2 | 66% | 55% | 54% | 72% | 1% | 13/1 | 19-24 | 41%[4] | 56% | 16% |
| 23. | Morningside College (IA) | 63 | 3.0 | 72% | 53% | 58% | 53% | 0.4% | 13/1 | 20-25 | 46% | 53% | 23% |
| 23. | Stephens College (MO) | 63 | 2.8 | 68% | 53% | 57% | 79% | 0% | 10/1 | 19-26 | 39%[5] | 68% | 12% |
| 25. | Bethel College (KS) | 62 | 3.0 | 73% | 55% | 53% | 68% | 2% | 10/1 | 19-26 | 21% | 64% | 23% |
| 25. | Marian University (IN) | 62 | 3.0 | 71% | 47% | 53% | 63% | 5% | 12/1 | 19-25 | 43% | 58% | 15% |
| 27. | Manchester University (IN) | 60 | 3.2 | 69% | 55% | 48% | 54% | 1% | 15/1 | 890-1130 | 48% | 71% | 18% |
| 28. | Bluffton University (OH) | 59 | 2.8 | 65% | 54% | 60% | 64% | 0.4% | 14/1 | 19-25 | 36% | 53% | 16% |
| 28. | St. Joseph's College (IN) | 59 | 3.0 | 68% | 50% | 45% | 79% | 2% | 14/1 | 890-1080 | 35% | 64% | 20% |
| 28. | Trinity Christian College (IL) | 59 | 2.8 | 78% | 53% | 58% | 56% | 0.4% | 11/1 | 20-25 | 27% | 79% | 13% |
| 31. | Eureka College (IL) | 58 | 2.6 | 65% | 55% | 61% | 73% | 0% | 12/1 | 19-25 | 39% | 66% | 20% |
| 32. | Trine University (IN) | 55 | 2.9 | 73% | 52% | 51% | 61% | 0% | 15/1 | 980-1190[3] | 57% | 75% | 10% |
| 33. | Greenville College (IL) | 53 | 2.7 | 72%[8] | 50% | 50% | 66% | 4% | 15/1 | 18-25 | 40% | 61% | 17% |
| 34. | Culver-Stockton College (MO) | 52 | 3.0 | 68% | 48% | 45% | 64% | 0% | 13/1 | 18-23 | 25% | 59% | 18% |
| 35. | Blackburn College (IL) | 51 | 2.6 | 67% | 47% | 45% | 80% | 0% | 11/1 | 19-26 | 41% | 68% | 18% |
| 36. | Judson University (IL) | 50 | 2.7 | 71% | 55% | 50% | 63% | 2% | 10/1 | 19-25[3] | 29% | 93% | 7% |
| 37. | University of Jamestown (ND) | 49 | 2.8 | 67% | 49% | 52% | 62% | 2% | 12/1 | 21-24[3] | 36% | 57% | 22% |
| 38. | Briar Cliff University (IA) | 48 | 2.6 | 65% | 44% | 45% | 66% | 0.4% | 12/1 | 19-25 | 32% | 54% | 16% |
| 38. | University of Sioux Falls (SD) | 48 | 2.8 | 69% | 50% | 47% | 60% | 1% | 14/1 | 20-26 | 46% | 97% | 5% |
| 40. | Central Methodist University (MO) | 45 | 2.7 | 65% | 42% | 43% | 66% | 1% | 13/1 | 19-24[3] | 43% | 65% | 10% |
| 40. | Defiance College (OH) | 45 | 2.6 | 60% | 48% | 46% | 79% | 0% | 11/1 | 18-23 | 25% | 72% | 10% |
| 40. | Martin Luther College[1] (MN) | 45 | 2.2 | 84%[8] | 61% | 72%[6] | N/A | N/A | 13/1[4] | 22-27[9] | N/A | 96% | N/A |
| 40. | University of Minnesota–Crookston* | 45 | 2.6 | 71% | 43% | 44% | 65% | 1% | 18/1 | 19-24 | 28% | 69% | 7% |
| 44. | Valley City State University (ND)* | 44 | 2.5 | 60% | 43% | 46% | 71% | 0.3% | 11/1 | 18-23 | 21% | 83% | 12% |
| 45. | Mount Marty College (SD) | 43 | 2.3 | 68% | 45% | 52% | 80% | 0% | 10/1 | 19-24[4] | 44% | 72% | 5% |
| 46. | Grace College and Seminary (IN) | 42 | 2.5 | 80% | 57% | 60% | 51% | 5% | 25/1 | 910-1150[3] | 47% | 78% | 15% |
| 47. | Northern State University (SD)* | 40 | 2.5 | 69% | 45% | 53% | 64% | 3% | 19/1 | 19-25 | 26% | 93% | 13% |
| 47. | Olivet College (MI) | 40 | 2.7 | 67% | 37% | 43% | 63% | 1% | 18/1 | 17-22 | N/A | 51% | 11% |
| 49. | Evangel University (MO) | 39 | 2.5 | 73%[8] | 51% | 49%[6] | 65%[4] | 3%[4] | 16/1 | 19-26[3] | 40%[4] | 67%[4] | N/A |
| 49. | Tabor College (KS) | 39 | 2.4 | 63% | 50% | 54% | 64% | 2% | 15/1 | 19-25 | 20% | 74% | 13% |
| 49. | Union College (NE) | 39 | 2.2 | 70% | 51% | 35% | 72% | 3% | 11/1 | 19-26 | 28%[5] | 52% | 24% |
| 52. | MacMurray College (IL) | 37 | 2.4 | 60% | 38% | 38% | 75% | 0% | 12/1 | 19-22 | 33% | 75% | 20% |
| 52. | McPherson College (KS) | 37 | 2.2 | 60% | 51% | 49% | 70% | 0% | 14/1 | 19-24[3] | N/A | 63% | N/A |
| 54. | Crown College[1] (MN) | 36 | 2.4 | 71%[8] | 45% | 52%[6] | N/A | N/A | N/A | 863-1098[4] | N/A | 56%[4] | N/A |
| 54. | Dakota Wesleyan University (SD) | 36 | 2.6 | 67%[8] | 45% | 38% | 70% | 0% | 11/1 | 19-27 | 26% | 73%[4] | N/A |
| 54. | Grand View University[1] (IA) | 36 | 2.6 | 69%[8] | 46% | 45%[8] | 65%[4] | 0.2%[4] | 14/1[4] | 810-1060[4] | 40%[4] | 92%[4] | 5%[4] |
| 54. | Kansas Wesleyan University | 36 | 2.4 | 57% | 46% | 43% | 72% | 1% | 12/1 | 20-24 | 43% | 54% | 12% |
| 58. | Wilmington College (OH) | 34 | 2.8 | N/A | 46% | 46%[6] | N/A | N/A | 15/1 | N/A[2] | N/A | N/A | 9%[7] |
| 59. | Notre Dame College of Ohio[1] | 32 | 2.7 | 66%[8] | 40% | 42%[8] | 55%[4] | 0%[4] | 14/1[4] | 18-22[4] | 15%[4] | 88%[4] | 12%[4] |
| 59. | Ottawa University (KS) | 32 | 2.3 | 58% | 48% | 34% | 70% | 0% | 16/1 | 19-25 | 38% | 99% | 6% |
| 61. | Rochester College (MI) | 31 | 2.4 | 60% | 46% | 44% | 85% | 0.3% | 11/1 | 18-24[9] | N/A | 66% | N/A |
| 62. | Dickinson State University (ND)* | 30 | 2.3 | 55%[8] | 38% | 38% | 80% | 0.2% | 11/1 | 18-23[3] | N/A | 49% | N/A |
| 62. | Maranatha Baptist University (WI) | 30 | 1.5 | 75%[8] | 44% | 57% | 75% | 4% | 16/1 | 20-26 | N/A | 64% | N/A |
| 64. | Dunwoody College of Tech. (MN) | 29 | 2.3 | N/A | N/A | N/A | 92% | 0% | 9/1 | N/A[2] | 1% | 76% | 5% |

**Note:** Key to footnotes, Page 114.

| Rank | School (State) (*Public) | Overall score | Peer assessment score (5.0=highest) | Average freshman retention rate | 2013 graduation rate | | % of classes under 20 ('13) | % of classes of 50 or more ('13) | Student/ faculty ratio ('13) | SAT/ACT 25th-75th percentile ('13) | Freshmen in top 25% of HS class ('13) | Accept- ance rate ('13) | Average alumni giving rate |
|---|---|---|---|---|---|---|---|---|---|---|---|---|---|
| | | | | | Predicted | Actual | | | | | | | |
| 64. | Kuyper College[1] (MI) | 29 | 2.5 | 76%[8] | 51% | 48%[6] | N/A | N/A | 13/1[4] | 18-25[9] | N/A | 68% | N/A |
| 66. | North Central University (MN) | 28 | 2.6 | 68% | 45% | 41% | N/A | N/A | 16/1[4] | 19-26 | 40% | 79% | 4% |
| 67. | Sterling College (KS) | 27 | 2.2 | 63% | 44% | 42% | 70% | 1% | 13/1 | 19-25 | 29% | 44% | N/A |
| 68. | Bethany College (KS) | 26 | 2.3 | 64%[8] | 50% | 39% | 75% | 1% | 12/1 | 18-23 | 20% | 59% | 13% |
| 69. | Bismarck State College (ND)* | 24 | 2.4 | N/A | N/A | N/A | 66% | 0.3% | 15/1 | 17-23[2] | N/A | 100% | N/A |
| 69. | Lake Superior State University (MI)* | 24 | 2.6 | 69%[8] | 42% | 40% | 53% | 7% | 15/1 | 20-25[4] | 40% | 90% | 3%[4] |
| 69. | Midland University[1] (NE) | 24 | 2.1 | 63%[8] | 45% | 48%[6] | 44%[4] | 5%[4] | 10/1[4] | 19-24[4] | 28%[4] | 98%[4] | 11%[4] |

| School (State) (*Public) | Peer assessment score (5.0=highest) | Average freshman retention rate | 2013 graduation rate | | % of classes under 20 ('13) | % of classes of 50 or more ('13) | Student/ faculty ratio ('13) | SAT/ACT 25th-75th percentile ('13) | Freshmen in top 25% of HS class ('13) | Accept- ance rate ('13) | Average alumni giving rate |
|---|---|---|---|---|---|---|---|---|---|---|---|
| | | | Predicted | Actual | | | | | | | |
| **SECOND TIER (SCHOOLS RANKED 72 THROUGH 95 ARE LISTED HERE ALPHABETICALLY)** | | | | | | | | | | | |
| Central Christian College[1] (KS) | 1.7 | 60%[8] | 39% | 36%[6] | N/A | N/A | 12/1[4] | 18-24[9] | N/A | 50% | N/A |
| Central State University (OH)* | 1.9 | 49% | 26% | 25% | 53% | 0.4% | 13/1 | 15-19 | 18% | 33% | 15% |
| Finlandia University[1] (MI) | 2.3 | 49%[8] | 38% | 41%[6] | N/A | N/A | 10/1[4] | 17-22[9] | N/A | 59% | N/A |
| Grace Bible College[1] (MI) | 1.9 | 62%[8] | 47% | 30%[6] | N/A | N/A | 12/1[4] | N/A[2] | N/A | 75% | N/A |
| Grace University[1] (NE) | 2.0 | 79%[8] | 49% | 36%[6] | N/A | N/A | 8/1[4] | 19-24[9] | N/A | 58% | N/A |
| Hannibal-LaGrange University (MO) | 2.0 | 60% | 48% | 48%[6] | 76% | 1% | 13/1[4] | 19-25[3] | N/A | 68% | 5% |
| Herzing University[1] (WI) | 1.6 | 35%[8] | N/A | 38%[6] | N/A | N/A | 14/1[4] | N/A[2] | N/A | 81%[4] | N/A |
| Indiana University East* | 2.5 | 66% | 31% | 24% | 63% | 3% | 15/1 | 820-1030 | 29% | 54% | 8% |
| Indiana University–Kokomo* | 2.4 | 62% | 36% | 28% | 45% | 2% | 16/1 | 850-1040 | 29% | 74% | 9% |
| Iowa Wesleyan College[1] | 2.0 | 43%[8] | 36% | 31%[6] | N/A | N/A | 9/1[4] | 19-24[9] | N/A | 60% | 5%[7] |
| Kendall College[1] (IL) | 2.3 | 55%[8] | 49% | 39%[8] | 60%[4] | 1%[4] | 15/1[4] | N/A[2] | N/A | 99%[4] | N/A |
| Lincoln College[1] (IL) | 2.0 | 53%[8] | N/A | N/A | N/A | N/A | N/A | 15-19[4] | N/A | N/A | 1%[7] |
| Mayville State University (ND)* | 2.0 | 53% | 40% | 36% | 72% | 1% | 14/1 | 17-21 | 34% | 51% | 9% |
| Missouri Southern State University* | 2.4 | 62% | 42% | 36% | 49% | 0.2% | 19/1 | 18-24[3] | 33% | 97% | 4% |
| Missouri Valley College[1] | 1.9 | 49%[8] | 33% | 28%[6] | N/A | N/A | 14/1[4] | 18-21[9] | N/A | 22% | N/A |
| Missouri Western State University* | 2.1 | 61% | 33% | 33% | 50% | 6% | 18/1 | 17-23[2] | 28% | 100% | 7% |
| Ohio Christian University[1] | 2.1 | 53%[8] | 32% | 40%[6] | N/A | N/A | 8/1[4] | 17-23[9] | N/A | 97% | N/A |
| Presentation College[1] (SD) | 2.1 | 50%[8] | 36% | 45%[6] | N/A | N/A | 10/1[4] | 18-22[9] | N/A | 66% | N/A |
| Purdue Univ.–North Central (IN)* | 3.0 | 57%[8] | 32% | 22% | 52% | 3% | 17/1 | 860-1050[2] | 25% | 73% | N/A |
| Silver Lake College[1] (WI) | 2.0 | 74%[8] | 45% | 40%[6] | N/A | N/A | 5/1[4] | 17-23[9] | N/A | 60% | N/A |
| Waldorf College[1] (IA) | 1.9 | 48%[8] | 51% | 41%[6] | N/A | N/A | 21/1[4] | 19-23[9] | N/A | 51% | N/A |
| Wilberforce University[1] (OH) | 2.1 | 78%[8] | 36% | 30%[6] | N/A | N/A | 12/1[4] | N/A[2] | N/A | 58% | N/A |
| William Penn University[1] (IA) | 2.0 | 57%[8] | 29% | 28%[6] | N/A | N/A | 17/1[4] | 17-22[9] | N/A | 58% | N/A |
| York College (NE) | 2.0 | 66%[8] | 50% | 36% | 80% | 0% | 13/1 | 17-22 | 24% | 49% | 13%[4] |

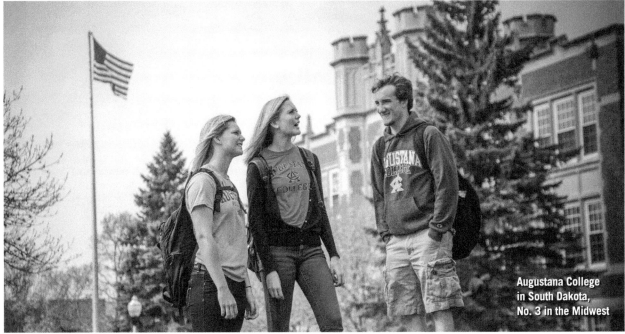

Augustana College in South Dakota, No. 3 in the Midwest

MATT ADDINGTON – AUGUSTANA COLLEGE

## WEST ▶

| Rank School (State) (*Public) | Overall score | Peer assessment score (5.0=highest) | Average freshman retention rate | 2013 graduation rate | | % of classes under 20 ('13) | % of classes of 50 or more ('13) | Student/ faculty ratio ('13) | SAT/ACT 25th-75th percentile ('13) | Freshmen in top 25% of HS class ('13) | Accept- ance rate ('13) | Average alumni giving rate |
|---|---|---|---|---|---|---|---|---|---|---|---|---|
| | | | | Predicted | Actual | | | | | | | |
| 1. Carroll College (MT) | 100 | 3.7 | 82% | 57% | 67% | 66% | 2% | 12/1 | 22-27 | 61% | 53% | 15% |
| 2. Texas Lutheran University | 95 | 3.8 | 70% | 54% | 52% | 65% | 0% | 14/1 | 930-1140 | 53% | 51% | 15% |
| 3. California Maritime Academy* | 92 | 3.5 | 81% | 56% | 60% | N/A | N/A | 14/1 | 990-1200[3] | N/A | 63% | 7%[4] |
| 4. Oklahoma Baptist University | 84 | 3.6 | 75% | 57% | 55% | 70% | 2% | 16/1 | 21-27 | 58% | 56% | 7% |
| 5. Master's Col. and Seminary (CA) | 83 | 3.4 | 81% | 62% | 54% | 74% | 6% | 10/1 | 940-1200 | 55%[5] | 78% | 7% |
| 6. Oklahoma Wesleyan University | 81 | 3.7 | 59% | 45% | 56% | 77% | 1% | 15/1 | 18-24 | N/A | 24% | 7%[4] |
| 7. Corban University (OR) | 80 | 3.4 | 75% | 55% | 54% | 53% | 2% | 13/1 | 950-1180[3] | 63% | 34% | 13% |
| 8. Menlo College (CA) | 75 | 3.2 | 75% | 50% | 60% | 53% | 0% | 14/1 | 882-1097[3] | N/A | 40% | 5% |
| 8. Oregon Inst. of Technology* | 75 | 3.7 | 73% | 44% | 43% | 57% | 3% | 13/1 | 880-1140[3] | 59% | 71% | 2% |
| 8. Warner Pacific College (OR) | 75 | 3.4 | 69% | 44% | 32% | 73% | 1% | 11/1 | 830-1100 | 25% | 53% | 5% |
| 11. Brigham Young Univ.–Idaho[1] | 71 | 4.0 | 72%[8] | 46% | 53%[6] | N/A | N/A | 24/1[4] | 20-25[9] | N/A | 100% | N/A |
| 12. Vanguard Univ. of Southern California | 67 | 3.0 | 74% | 49% | 52% | 62% | 4% | 15/1 | 850-1073 | 41% | 70% | 6% |
| 13. East Texas Baptist University | 65 | 3.5 | 58% | 44% | 33% | 62% | 0.3% | 13/1 | 18-22 | 40% | 74% | 7% |
| 13. Rocky Mountain College (MT) | 65 | 3.0 | 68% | 51% | 40% | 68% | 1% | 12/1 | 19-25 | 35% | 67% | 8% |
| 15. Howard Payne University (TX) | 64 | 3.2 | 62% | 44% | 40% | 71% | 0.3% | 10/1 | 860-1050 | 24% | 54% | 6% |
| 16. Brigham Young University–Hawaii[1] | 63 | 3.7 | 61%[8] | 58% | 52%[6] | N/A | N/A | 16/1[4] | 21-26[9] | N/A | 36% | N/A |
| 16. Northwest University (WA) | 63 | 3.2 | 77% | 48% | 43% | 68% | 4% | 11/1 | 950-1170[3] | N/A | 86% | N/A |
| 18. McMurry University (TX) | 62 | 3.1 | 58% | 42% | 38% | 71% | 1% | 12/1 | 860-1090 | 37% | 59% | 6% |
| 19. Hope International University (CA) | 58 | 3.3 | 69% | 50% | 44% | 70% | 0% | 10/1 | 860-1090 | 13%[5] | 47% | 7% |
| 20. Northwest Christian University (OR) | 52 | 2.8 | 68%[8] | 46% | 45% | 82% | 1% | 12/1 | 885-1065 | N/A | 70% | N/A |
| 21. Lewis-Clark State College (ID)* | 49 | 3.6 | 54%[8] | 36% | 29% | 63% | 1% | 16/1[4] | 820-1030[9] | 12% | 100% | N/A |
| 22. University of Great Falls (MT) | 43 | 3.1 | 62% | 37% | 24%[6] | 67% | 0% | 14/1 | 840-1090[4] | N/A | 84%[4] | N/A |
| 23. Southwestern Christian Univ.[1] (OK) | 37 | 3.1 | 64%[8] | 30% | 21%[6] | 82%[4] | 0%[4] | 20/1[4] | 860-1180[4] | N/A | 88%[4] | 3%[4] |
| 24. Okla. State U. Inst. of Tech.–Okmulgee* | 36 | 3.3 | 55% | 34% | 26% | 81% | 0% | 19/1 | 16-21[3] | 18% | 54% | 2% |
| 25. St. Gregory's University (OK) | 35 | 3.1 | N/A | 38% | 28% | N/A | N/A | N/A | N/A[2] | N/A | 57% | N/A |

| School (State) (*Public) | Peer assessment score (5.0=highest) | Average freshman retention rate | 2013 graduation rate | | % of classes under 20 ('13) | % of classes of 50 or more ('13) | Student/ faculty ratio ('13) | SAT/ACT 25th-75th percentile ('13) | Freshmen in top 25% of HS class ('13) | Accept- ance rate ('13) | Average alumni giving rate |
|---|---|---|---|---|---|---|---|---|---|---|---|
| | | | Predicted | Actual | | | | | | | |
| **SECOND TIER (SCHOOLS RANKED 26 THROUGH 33 ARE LISTED HERE ALPHABETICALLY)** | | | | | | | | | | | |
| Bacone College[1] (OK) | 2.0 | 47%[8] | 22% | 11%[6] | N/A | N/A | 15/1[4] | 15-19[9] | N/A | 72% | N/A |
| Jarvis Christian College (TX) | 2.5 | 52% | 27% | 9% | 58% | 7% | 18/1 | 13-18 | 8% | 100% | 5% |
| Metropolitan State Univ. of Denver[1]* | 3.2 | 65%[8] | 30% | 22%[8] | 34%[4] | 1%[4] | 20/1[4] | 18-23[4] | 22%[4] | 71%[4] | N/A |
| Nevada State College[1]* | 2.4 | 63%[8] | N/A | 18%[6] | N/A | N/A | 19/1[4] | N/A[2] | N/A | 50% | N/A |
| Oklahoma Panhandle State Univ.[1]* | 2.7 | 55%[8] | 33% | 32%[8] | N/A | N/A | N/A | 710-950[4] | N/A | 61%[4] | N/A |
| Patten University[1] (CA) | 2.2 | N/A | 42% | 27%[6] | N/A | N/A | N/A | N/A[2] | N/A | N/A | N/A |
| Rogers State University (OK)* | 2.8 | 58% | 30% | 20% | 50% | 1% | 19/1 | 17-23[3] | 20% | 54% | 3%[4] |
| Wiley College (TX) | 2.8 | 52% | 22% | 19% | 58% | 2% | 17/1 | 14-18[2] | 8% | 94% | 4% |

# The Top Public Regional Colleges ▶

### NORTH

**Rank School (State)**

1. U. S. Coast Guard Acad. (CT)
2. U.S. Merchant Marine Acad. (NY)
3. Massachusetts Maritime Academy
4. Maine Maritime Academy
5. University of Maine–Farmington

### SOUTH

**Rank School (State)**

1. Univ. of South Carolina–Aiken
2. Elizabeth City State Univ. (NC)
3. U. of South Carolina–Upstate
4. Univ. of Arkansas–Pine Bluff
5. Concord University (WV)

### MIDWEST

**Rank School (State)**

1. University of Minnesota–Crookston
2. Valley City State University (ND)
3. Northern State University (SD)
4. Dickinson State University (ND)
5. Bismarck State College (ND)
5. Lake Superior State University (MI)

### WEST

**Rank School (State)**

1. California Maritime Academy
2. Oregon Inst. of Technology
3. Lewis-Clark State College (ID)
4. Oklahoma State University Institute of Technology–Okmulgee

**Footnotes:**
**1.** School refused to fill out U.S. News statistical survey. Data that appear are from school in previous years or from another source such as the National Center for Education Statistics.
**2.** SAT and/or ACT not required by school for some or all applicants.
**3.** In reporting SAT/ACT scores, the school did not include all students for whom it had scores or refused to tell U.S. News whether all students with scores had been included.
**4.** Data reported to U.S. News in previous years.
**5.** Data based on fewer than 51 percent of enrolled freshmen.
**6.** Some or all data reported to the NCAA and/or the National Center for Education Statistics.
**7.** Data reported to the Council for Aid to Education.

**8.** Average graduation or freshman retention rates, normally based on four years of data, are given here for less than four years because school didn't report rates for the most recent year or years to U.S. News.
**9.** SAT and/or ACT may not be required by school for some or all applicants, and in reporting SAT/ACT scores, the school did not include all students for whom it had scores, or refused to tell U.S. News whether all students with scores had been included.

N/A means not available.

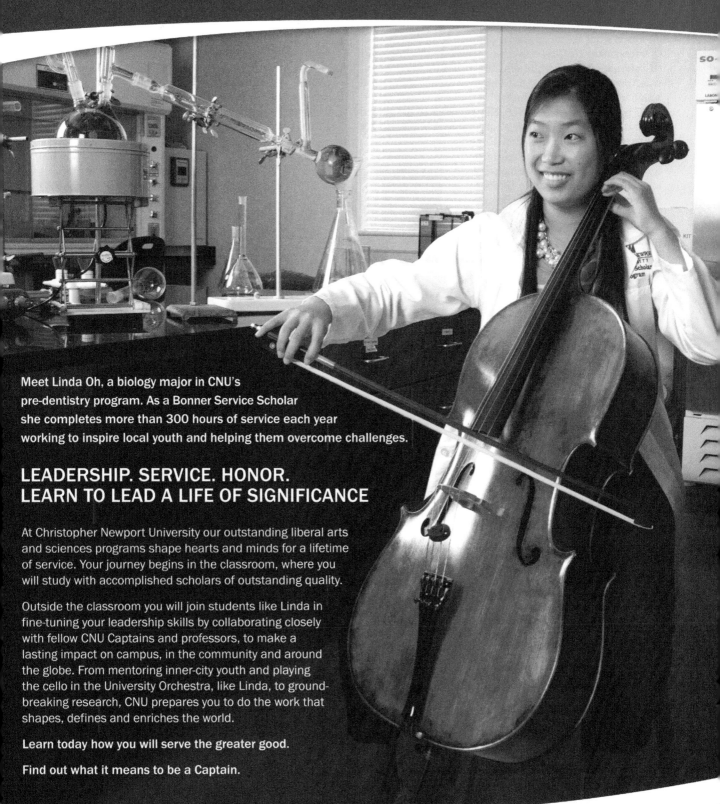

# Best

# Historically Black Colleges

ncreasingly, the nation's top historically black colleges and universities are an appealing option for applicants of all races; many HBCUs, in fact, now actively recruit Hispanic, international and white students in addition to the African-American high school grads heading to college in record numbers. Which schools offer the best undergraduate education? In the spring of 2014, U.S. News conducted the annual separate peer survey of administrators at the HBCUs, asking the president, provost and admissions dean at each to rate the academic quality of all other HBCUs with which they are familiar. In addition to the peer survey results, the rankings below are based on nearly all the same ranking indicators (although weighted slightly differently) as those used in ranking the regional universities (box, right). These include retention and gradua-

tion rates, high school class standing, admission test scores and the strength of the faculty, among others.

To be part of the universe, a school has to be designated by the Department of Education as an HBCU. The college must also be a baccalaureate-granting institution that enrolls primarily first-year, first-time students and have been part of this year's Best Colleges survey and ranking process. If an HBCU is unranked in the 2015 Best Colleges rankings, it is also unranked here; reasons that schools are not ranked vary, but include a school's policy not to use SAT or ACT test scores in admissions decisions. There are 80 HBCUs; 69 were ranked. HBCUs in the top three-quarters are numerically ranked, and those in the bottom quarter are listed alphabetically. For more detail on the HBCU rankings and methodology, visit usnews.com/hbcu.

| Graduation and retention rates | 27.5% |
| Peer assessment | 25% |
| Faculty resources | 20% |
| Student selectivity | 12.5% |
| Financial resources | 10% |
| Alumni giving | 5% |

| Rank | School (State) (*Public) | Overall score | Peer assessment score (5.0=highest) | Average freshman retention rate | Average graduation rate | % of classes under 20 ('13) | % of classes of 50 or more ('13) | Student/ faculty ratio ('13) | % of faculty who are full time ('13) | SAT/ACT 25th-75th percentile ('13) | Freshmen in top 25% of HS class ('13) | Acceptance rate ('13) | Average alumni giving rate |
|---|---|---|---|---|---|---|---|---|---|---|---|---|---|
| 1. | Spelman College (GA) | 100 | 4.7 | 89% | 73% | 63% | 3% | 10/1 | 88% | 850-1215 | 66% | 41% | 34% |
| 2. | Howard University (DC) | 80 | 4.3 | 82% | 64%[6] | 42% | 10% | 8/1 | 90% | 980-1190[3] | 54% | 57% | 5% |
| 3. | Morehouse College (GA) | 78 | 4.4 | 82% | 56%[6] | 48% | 2% | 12/1 | 91% | 900-1110 | 41% | 67% | 23% |
| 4. | Hampton University (VA) | 75 | 4.4 | 77% | 59%[6] | 55% | 4% | 10/1 | 91% | 920-1090[2] | 45% | 36% | 12% |
| 5. | Tuskegee University (AL) | 68 | 4.1 | 76% | 44%[6] | 56% | 9% | 12/1 | 95% | 18-23[3] | 60% | 41% | 24% |
| 6. | Xavier University of Louisiana | 64 | 4.1 | 68% | 46%[6] | 51% | 6% | 13/1 | 96% | 20-26 | 56% | 54% | 12% |
| 7. | Fisk University (TN) | 61 | 3.5 | N/A | 53%[6] | 68% | 1% | 11/1 | 83% | 17-23 | N/A | 21% | 24% |
| 8. | Florida A&M University* | 55 | 3.9 | 81% | 41% | 32% | 12% | 17/1 | 90% | 18-22 | 46%[5] | 45% | 6% |
| 9. | Claflin University (SC) | 54 | 3.5 | 73% | 44% | 63% | 1% | 14/1 | 87% | 710-960 | 35% | 61% | 47% |
| 10. | North Carolina A&T State Univ.* | 52 | 4.0 | 73%[8] | 41%[6] | 34% | 7% | 16/1 | 89% | 830-990 | 31% | 57% | 8% |
| 11. | North Carolina Central Univ.* | 47 | 3.7 | 71% | 40% | 40% | 5% | 15/1 | 89% | 800-950 | 22% | 39% | 11% |
| 12. | Tougaloo College (MS) | 46 | 3.0 | 74% | 47%[6] | 70% | 0.3% | 10/1 | 94% | 15-21 | 25% | 34% | 13% |
| 13. | Delaware State University* | 45 | 3.5 | 66% | 36% | 50% | 3% | 16/1 | 84% | 820-970 | 26% | 45% | 6% |
| 13. | Dillard University (LA) | 45 | 3.5 | 64%[8] | 33%[6] | 63% | 1% | 14/1 | 69% | 17-20 | 31%[5] | 35% | 4% |
| 15. | Morgan State University (MD)* | 44 | 3.7 | 72% | 31%[6] | 42% | 0.1% | 17/1 | 94% | 820-980[2] | 9% | 56% | 14% |
| 15. | Winston-Salem State Univ.[1] (NC)* | 44 | 3.4 | 78%[8] | 39%[6] | 47%[4] | 1%[4] | 13/1[4] | 90%[4] | 16-19[4] | 35%[4] | 56%[4] | 7%[4] |
| 17. | Johnson C. Smith University (NC) | 43 | 3.1 | 68% | 41% | 75% | 0.2% | 11/1 | 85% | 733-920 | 25% | 37% | 15% |
| 18. | Clark Atlanta University | 42 | 3.6 | 64% | 40%[6] | 45% | 3% | 16/1 | 81% | 770-940[3] | 31%[4] | 57% | 3%[7] |
| 19. | Jackson State University[1] (MS)* | 41 | 3.7 | 73%[8] | 42%[6] | N/A | N/A | 18/1[4] | 89%[4] | 17-21[9] | N/A | 65% | 4%[7] |
| 20. | Elizabeth City State Univ. (NC)* | 40 | 2.9 | 75% | 40%[6] | 66% | 1% | 16/1 | 86% | 780-945[3] | 5% | 52% | 10% |
| 21. | Lincoln University (PA)* | 39 | 3.1 | 66% | 38%[6] | 49% | 1% | 17/1 | 79% | 770-960 | 28% | 61% | 8% |
| 21. | Tennessee State University* | 39 | 3.5 | 62%[8] | 32%[6] | 54% | 1% | 15/1 | 86% | 16-20[3] | N/A | 53% | 4%[4] |
| 23. | Alabama A&M University* | 38 | 3.5 | 69% | 32%[6] | 48% | 4% | 18/1 | 91% | 15-19 | N/A | 90% | 6% |
| 23. | Univ. of Maryland–Eastern Shore* | 38 | 3.5 | 68% | 32%[6] | 57% | 4% | 14/1 | 81% | 790-960[3] | N/A | 55% | 3% |
| 25. | Bennett College[1] (NC) | 35 | 3.2 | 68%[8] | 41%[6] | 74%[4] | 0.4%[4] | 10/1[4] | 87%[4] | 15-20[4] | 21%[4] | 69%[4] | N/A |
| 25. | Bowie State University (MD)* | 35 | 3.3 | 72% | 38%[6] | 45% | 1% | 16/1 | 77% | 810-960[3] | N/A | 52% | 6% |
| 27. | Alcorn State University (MS)* | 34 | 3.1 | 68% | 35%[6] | 51% | 5% | 16/1 | 91% | 16-19 | N/A | 83% | 5%[4] |
| 28. | Albany State University (GA)* | 33 | 3.1 | 69% | 42% | 52% | 1% | 20/1 | 84% | 820-950 | 27%[5] | 24% | 4% |
| 28. | Fayetteville State University (NC)* | 33 | 3.2 | 72% | 33%[6] | 38% | 1% | 17/1 | 93% | 770-910[3] | 17% | 61% | 2% |
| 30. | South Carolina State University* | 32 | 2.7 | 63% | 38%[6] | 53% | 3% | 14/1 | 90% | 720-870 | 30% | 92% | N/A |
| 31. | Bethune-Cookman University (FL) | 31 | 3.4 | 66% | 42%[6] | 44% | 2% | 18/1 | 88% | 15-18 | 12% | 67% | 4% |
| 32. | Virginia State University* | 30 | 3.1 | 65%[8] | 42%[6] | N/A | N/A | 16/1 | 86% | 730-910[3] | 17% | 54% | N/A |
| 33. | Oakwood University (AL) | 29 | 3.1 | 71%[8] | 38%[6] | N/A | N/A | N/A | 100%[4] | 17-22[4] | N/A | 34%[4] | N/A |
| 34. | Norfolk State University (VA)* | 28 | 3.3 | N/A | 35%[6] | 51%[4] | 4%[4] | 18/1 | N/A | 770-948[3] | 26%[4] | 65% | 3%[4] |
| 35. | Philander Smith College (AR) | 27 | 2.7 | 63% | 31% | 83% | 0% | 10/1 | 91% | 16-22 | 44% | 42% | 13% |
| 35. | Univ. of Arkansas–Pine Bluff* | 27 | 2.9 | 56% | 25% | 55% | 4% | 15/1 | 93% | 15-20 | 27% | 28% | 11% |
| 37. | Prairie View A&M University (TX)* | 26 | 3.2 | 67% | 34%[6] | 22% | 10% | 18/1 | 93% | 750-940 | 14% | 85% | N/A |
| 38. | Fort Valley State University (GA)* | 25 | 2.9 | 61% | 32%[6] | 47% | 5% | 19/1 | 89% | 15-18 | 23%[5] | 31% | 16% |

**Note:** Key to footnotes, Page 106.

| Rank | School (State) (*Public) | Overall score | Peer assessment score (5.0=highest) | Average freshman retention rate | Average graduation rate | % of classes under 20 ('13) | % of classes of 50 or more ('13) | Student/ faculty ratio ('13) | % of faculty who are full time ('13) | SAT/ACT 25th-75th percentile ('13) | Freshmen in top 25% of HS class ('13) | Accept-ance rate ('13) | Average alumni giving rate |
|---|---|---|---|---|---|---|---|---|---|---|---|---|---|
| 38. | Kentucky State University* | 25 | 3.1 | 51% | 20%[6] | 53% | 0.2% | 14/1 | 91% | 16-20 | N/A | 38% | 4% |
| 40. | Stillman College[1] (AL) | 24 | 2.7 | 60%[8] | 28%[8] | 65%[4] | 1%[4] | 16/1[4] | 95%[4] | 16-19[4] | 25%[4] | 41%[4] | 5%[4] |
| 41. | Alabama State University* | 23 | 3.1 | 61% | 26% | N/A | N/A | 17/1 | 86% | 15-20[3] | 1% | 54% | N/A |
| 41. | Central State University (OH)* | 23 | 2.8 | 49% | 24%[6] | 53% | 0.4% | 13/1 | 74% | 15-19 | 18% | 33% | 15% |
| 41. | West Virginia State University* | 23 | 3.0 | 53% | 22%[6] | 53% | 2% | 15/1 | 84% | 18-22 | N/A | 45% | 2% |
| 44. | Cheyney U. of Pennsylvania* | 22 | 2.9 | 55% | 25%[6] | 47% | 10% | 16/1 | 90% | 670-850[3] | 9%[5] | 88% | 4% |
| 45. | Paine College (GA) | 20 | 2.8 | 61% | 24% | 65% | 0% | 13/1 | 86% | 14-18 | 15%[5] | 44% | 13% |
| 45. | Southern U. and A&M College (LA)* | 20 | 3.1 | 69% | 27%[6] | N/A | N/A | 25/1 | 83% | 17-20[3] | 23% | N/A | N/A |
| 47. | Savannah State University (GA)* | 19 | 3.1 | 70%[8] | 32%[6] | 30% | 1% | 23/1 | 92% | 770-910 | N/A | 83% | N/A |
| 48. | Livingstone College (NC) | 18 | 2.6 | 52% | 27% | 46% | 1% | 15/1 | 98% | 11-16[3] | 6% | 72% | 36% |
| 49. | Texas Southern University* | 17 | 3.0 | 60% | 13%[6] | 38% | 11% | 19/1 | 80% | 750-920 | 20% | 45% | 2% |
| 50. | Bluefield State College (WV)* | 16 | 2.7 | 57% | 26%[6] | 75% | 0.3% | 15/1 | 77% | 16-21 | N/A | 41% | 4% |
| 50. | Florida Memorial University[1] | 16 | 2.7 | 70%[8] | 40%[6] | N/A | N/A | 17/1[4] | 84%[4] | N/A[2] | N/A | 42% | N/A |
| 50. | Grambling State University (LA)* | 16 | 2.9 | N/A | 29%[6] | 40% | 10% | 23/1 | 96% | 16-20[3] | 22% | 44% | 2%[7] |
| 50. | Mississippi Valley State Univ.[1]* | 16 | 2.8 | 61%[8] | 24%[6] | N/A | N/A | 13/1[4] | 93%[4] | 15-19[9] | N/A | 23% | N/A |

| School (State) (*Public) | Peer assessment score (5.0=highest) | Average freshman retention rate | Average graduation rate | % of classes under 20 ('13) | % of classes of 50 or more ('13) | Student/ faculty ratio ('13) | % of faculty who are full time ('13) | SAT/ACT 25th-75th percentile ('13) | Freshmen in top 25% of HS class ('13) | Accept-ance rate ('13) | Average alumni giving rate |
|---|---|---|---|---|---|---|---|---|---|---|---|
| **SECOND TIER (SCHOOLS RANKED 54 THROUGH 69 ARE LISTED HERE ALPHABETICALLY)** | | | | | | | | | | | |
| Allen University (SC) | 2.5 | 46% | 15%[6] | N/A | N/A | 15/1 | 98% | 16[9] | N/A | 50% | N/A |
| Coppin State University (MD)* | 2.8 | 66%[8] | 16%[6] | N/A | N/A | 14/1[4] | 75%[4] | 810-950[4] | N/A | 36%[4] | 6%[7] |
| Edward Waters College (FL) | 2.2 | 54%[8] | 19%[6] | N/A | N/A | 17/1[4] | 100%[4] | 15-18[9] | N/A | 27% | N/A |
| Huston-Tillotson University[1] (TX) | 2.9 | 57%[8] | 23%[6] | N/A | N/A | 13/1[4] | 84%[4] | 700-900[9] | N/A | 46% | N/A |
| Jarvis Christian College (TX) | 2.4 | 52% | 16%[6] | 58% | 7% | 18/1 | 81% | 13-18 | 8% | 100% | 5% |
| Lane College[1] (TN) | 2.7 | 55%[8] | 33%[6] | 50%[4] | 0%[4] | 16/1[4] | 98%[4] | 14-17[4] | 12%[4] | 33%[4] | N/A |
| LeMoyne-Owen College (TN) | 2.4 | 54%[8] | 15%[6] | 95% | 0% | 13/1 | N/A | N/A | N/A | 27% | N/A |
| Rust College (MS) | 2.7 | 60% | 27%[6] | N/A | N/A | 18/1 | 97% | 13-14 | N/A | 14% | N/A |
| Shaw University (NC) | 2.7 | 52%[8] | 27%[8] | 66%[4] | 1%[4] | 15/1[4] | 81%[4] | 13-16[4] | 5%[4] | 54%[4] | N/A |
| Southern University–New Orleans[1]* | 2.7 | 61%[8] | 11%[6] | N/A | N/A | 19/1[4] | 100%[4] | 840-1290[4] | N/A | 49%[4] | N/A |
| St. Augustine's University (NC) | 2.5 | 52% | 25%[6] | N/A | N/A | 13/1 | 80% | 665-858[3] | N/A | 67% | 5% |
| Univ. of the District of Columbia* | 2.4 | 50%[8] | 14%[6] | N/A | N/A | N/A | N/A[4] | N/A[2] | N/A | 43%[4] | N/A |
| Virginia Union University | 2.8 | 54%[8] | 32% | 48% | 1% | 14/1 | 84% | 670-840 | 18% | 83% | 9% |
| Voorhees College (SC) | 2.5 | 46%[8] | 30%[6] | N/A | N/A | 13/1[4] | 80%[4] | N/A[2] | N/A | 51% | N/A |
| Wilberforce University (OH) | 2.7 | 78%[8] | 30%[6] | N/A | N/A | 12/1[4] | 64%[4] | N/A[2] | N/A | 58% | N/A |
| Wiley College (TX) | 2.8 | 52% | 18%[6] | 58% | 2% | 17/1 | 83% | 14-18[9] | 8% | 94% | 4% |

**Sources:** Statistical data from the schools. Peer assessment data collected by Ipsos Public Affairs.

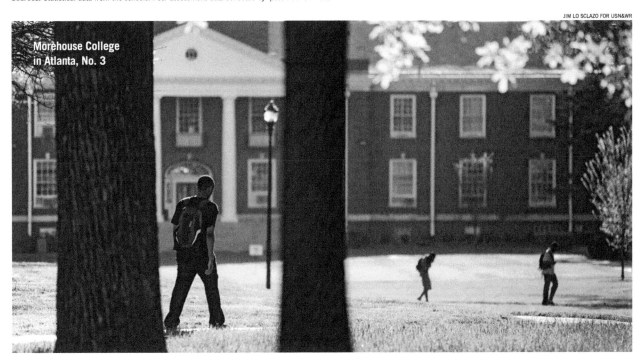

Morehouse College in Atlanta, No. 3

# Best Business Programs

I n the spring of 2014, U.S. News surveyed deans and senior faculty at all undergraduate business programs accredited by the Association to Advance Collegiate Schools of Business. Participants were asked to rate the quality of programs with which they're familiar on a scale of 1 (marginal) to 5 (distinguished); 38 percent of those surveyed responded. The undergrad business rankings are based solely on this peer survey. Deans and faculty, two per school, also were asked to nominate the 10 best programs in a number of specialty areas; the five schools receiving the most mentions in each appear.

## Top Programs ▷

| Rank School (State) (*Public) | Peer assessment score (5.0=highest) | Rank School (State) (*Public) | Peer assessment score (5.0=highest) | Rank School (State) (*Public) | Peer assessment score (5.0=highest) |
|---|---|---|---|---|---|
| 1. University of Pennsylvania (Wharton) | 4.8 | 45. George Washington University (DC) | 3.3 | 79. University of Delaware* | 3.0 |
| 2. Massachusetts Inst. of Technology (Sloan) | 4.6 | 45. Georgia State University (Robinson)* | 3.3 | 79. University of Denver (Daniels) | 3.0 |
| 2. University of California–Berkeley (Haas)* | 4.6 | 45. Southern Methodist University (Cox) (TX) | 3.3 | 79. University of Illinois–Chicago* | 3.0 |
| 4. University of Michigan–Ann Arbor (Ross)* | 4.5 | 45. Syracuse University (Whitman) (NY) | 3.3 | 79. University of Louisville (KY)* | 3.0 |
| 5. New York University (Stern) | 4.4 | 45. Tulane University (Freeman) (LA) | 3.3 | 93. Brandeis University (MA) | 2.9 |
| 6. U. of N. Carolina–Chapel Hill (Kenan-Flagler)* | 4.3 | 45. University of Arkansas (Walton)* | 3.3 | 93. Colorado State University* | 2.9 |
| 6. University of Virginia (McIntire)* | 4.3 | 51. Auburn University (AL)* | 3.2 | 93. Creighton University (NE) | 2.9 |
| 8. Carnegie Mellon University (Tepper) (PA) | 4.2 | 51. Bentley University (MA) | 3.2 | 93. DePaul University (IL) | 2.9 |
| 8. Indiana University–Bloomington (Kelley)* | 4.2 | 51. Pepperdine University (Graziadio) (CA) | 3.2 | 93. Drexel University (LeBow) (PA) | 2.9 |
| 8. University of Texas–Austin (McCombs)* | 4.2 | 51. University of Connecticut* | 3.2 | 93. Lehigh University (PA) | 2.9 |
| 11. Cornell University (Dyson) (NY) | 4.1 | 51. University of Kansas* | 3.2 | 93. Loyola Marymount University (CA) | 2.9 |
| 11. University of Notre Dame (IN) | 4.1 | 51. Univ. of Massachusetts–Amherst (Isenberg)* | 3.2 | 93. Marquette University (WI) | 2.9 |
| 11. Univ. of Southern California (Marshall) | 4.1 | 51. Univ. of Missouri (Trulaske)* | 3.2 | 93. North Carolina State U.–Raleigh* | 2.9 |
| 14. Washington University in St. Louis (Olin) | 4.0 | 51. Univ. of Nebraska–Lincoln* | 3.2 | 93. Oklahoma State University* | 2.9 |
| 15. Emory University (Goizueta) (GA) | 3.9 | 51. University of Oregon (Lundquist)* | 3.2 | 93. Rochester Inst. of Technology (NY) | 2.9 |
| 15. Georgetown University (McDonough) (DC) | 3.9 | 51. University of Tennessee* | 3.2 | 93. Rutgers, St. U. of N.J.–New Brunswick* | 2.9 |
| 15. U. of Illinois–Urbana-Champaign* | 3.9 | 51. University of Utah (Eccles)* | 3.2 | 93. San Diego State University* | 2.9 |
| 15. Univ. of Minnesota–Twin Cities (Carlson)* | 3.9 | 62. Baylor University (Hankamer) (TX) | 3.1 | 93. Seattle University (Albers) | 2.9 |
| 15. Univ. of Wisconsin–Madison* | 3.9 | 62. CUNY–Baruch College (Zicklin)* | 3.1 | 93. Texas Tech University (Rawls)* | 2.9 |
| 20. Ohio State University–Columbus (Fisher)* | 3.8 | 62. Florida State University* | 3.1 | 93. University of Colorado–Denver* | 2.9 |
| 21. Boston College (Carroll) | 3.7 | 62. George Mason University (VA)* | 3.1 | 93. University of Houston (Bauer)* | 2.9 |
| 21. Michigan State University (Broad)* | 3.7 | 62. Miami University–Oxford (Farmer) (OH)* | 3.1 | 93. University of Mississippi* | 2.9 |
| 21. Pennsylvania State U.–Univ. Park (Smeal)* | 3.7 | 62. Northeastern University (MA) | 3.1 | 93. University of Texas–Dallas* | 2.9 |
| 21. Purdue U.–West Lafayette (Krannert) (IN)* | 3.7 | 62. Rensselaer Polytechnic Inst. (Lally) (NY) | 3.1 | 93. Washington State University* | 2.9 |
| 21. University of Arizona (Eller)* | 3.7 | 62. Santa Clara University (Leavey) (CA) | 3.1 | 113. Binghamton University–SUNY* | 2.8 |
| 21. University of Georgia (Terry)* | 3.7 | 62. Temple University (Fox) (PA)* | 3.1 | 113. Gonzaga University (WA) | 2.8 |
| 21. Univ. of Maryland–College Park (Smith)* | 3.7 | 62. United States Air Force Acad. (CO)* | 3.1 | 113. James Madison University (VA)* | 2.8 |
| 21. University of Washington* | 3.7 | 62. University of Alabama (Culverhouse)* | 3.1 | 113. Kansas State University* | 2.8 |
| 29. Arizona State University–Tempe (Carey)* | 3.6 | 62. Univ. of California–San Diego* | 3.1 | 113. Ohio University* | 2.8 |
| 29. Babson College (MA) | 3.6 | 62. University of Kentucky (Gatton)* | 3.1 | 113. Oregon State University* | 2.8 |
| 29. Georgia Institute of Technology* | 3.6 | 62. University of Miami (FL) | 3.1 | 113. Rollins College (FL) | 2.8 |
| 29. Texas A&M Univ.–College Station (Mays)* | 3.6 | 62. University of Oklahoma (Price)* | 3.1 | 113. Rutgers, The State U. of N.J.–Newark* | 2.8 |
| 29. University of Florida (Warrington)* | 3.6 | 62. University of Richmond (Robins) (VA) | 3.1 | 113. Seton Hall University (Stillman) (NJ) | 2.8 |
| 34. Brigham Young Univ.–Provo (Marriott) (UT) | 3.5 | 62. Villanova University (PA) | 3.1 | 113. St. Joseph's University (Haub) (PA) | 2.8 |
| 34. Case Western Reserve U. (Weatherhead) (OH) | 3.5 | 79. American University (Kogod) (DC) | 3.0 | 113. University at Albany–SUNY* | 2.8 |
| 34. University of Colorado–Boulder* | 3.5 | 79. Clemson University (SC)* | 3.0 | 113. University of Alabama–Birmingham* | 2.8 |
| 34. University of Iowa (Tippie)* | 3.5 | 79. Fordham University (NY) | 3.0 | 113. University of Cincinnati* | 2.8 |
| 34. Wake Forest University (Calloway) (NC) | 3.5 | 79. Iowa State University* | 3.0 | 113. Univ. of Colo.–Colorado Springs* | 2.8 |
| 39. Boston University | 3.4 | 79. Louisiana State Univ.–Baton Rouge (Ourso)* | 3.0 | 113. University of Memphis (Fogelman)* | 2.8 |
| 39. College of William and Mary (VA)* | 3.4 | 79. Loyola University Chicago | 3.0 | 113. Univ. of Missouri–St. Louis* | 2.8 |
| 39. University of California–Irvine*† | 3.4 | 79. St. Louis University | 3.0 | 113. U. of North Carolina–Charlotte (Belk)* | 2.8 |
| 39. University of Pittsburgh* | 3.4 | 79. Texas Christian University (Neeley) | 3.0 | 113. University of San Francisco (McLaren) | 2.8 |
| 39. Univ. of South Carolina (Moore)* | 3.4 | 79. University at Buffalo–SUNY* | 3.0 | 113. Univ. of Wisconsin–Milwaukee* | 2.8 |
| 39. Virginia Tech (Pamplin)* | 3.4 | 79. Univ. of California–Riverside* | 3.0 | 113. Virginia Commonwealth University* | 2.8 |

**Note:** Peer assessment survey conducted by Ipsos Public Affairs. To be ranked in a specialty, an undergraduate business school may have either a program or course offerings in that subject area. Extended undergraduate business rankings can be found at usnews.com/bestcolleges. †University of California–Irvine was inadvertently omitted from the ranking originally published in this guidebook.

# BEST BUSINESS PROGRAMS

## Best in the Specialties ▷

(*Public)

**ACCOUNTING\*\***
1. **University of Texas–Austin** (McCombs)*
2. **U. of Illinois–Urbana-Champaign**\*
3. **Brigham Young Univ.–Provo** (Marriott) (UT)
4. **University of Notre Dame** (IN)
5. **University of Pennsylvania** (Wharton)
5. **Univ. of Southern California** (Marshall)

**ENTREPRENEURSHIP\*\***
1. **Babson College** (MA)
2. **Massachusetts Inst. of Technology** (Sloan)
3. **Univ. of Southern California** (Marshall)
4. **Indiana University–Bloomington** (Kelley)*
4. **University of Pennsylvania** (Wharton)

**FINANCE\*\***
1. **University of Pennsylvania** (Wharton)
2. **New York University** (Stern)
3. **University of Michigan–Ann Arbor** (Ross)*
4. **Massachusetts Inst. of Technology** (Sloan)
5. **University of California–Berkeley** (Haas)*
5. **University of Texas–Austin** (McCombs)*

**INSURANCE/RISK MANAGEMENT**
1. **University of Georgia** (Terry)*
2. **University of Pennsylvania** (Wharton)
3. **Univ. of Wisconsin–Madison**\*
4. **Temple University** (Fox) (PA)*
5. **Georgia State University** (Robinson)*

**INTERNATIONAL BUSINESS**
1. **Univ. of South Carolina** (Moore)*
2. **New York University** (Stern)
3. **University of Pennsylvania** (Wharton)
4. **Univ. of Southern California** (Marshall)
5. **University of Michigan–Ann Arbor** (Ross)*

**MANAGEMENT**
1. **University of Michigan–Ann Arbor** (Ross)*
1. **University of Pennsylvania** (Wharton)
3. **University of Virginia** (McIntire)*
4. **University of California–Berkeley** (Haas)*
5. **U. of North Carolina–Chapel Hill** (Kenan-Flagler)*

**MANAGEMENT INFORMATION SYSTEMS**
1. **Massachusetts Inst. of Technology** (Sloan)
2. **Carnegie Mellon University** (Tepper) (PA)
3. **Univ. of Minnesota–Twin Cities** (Carlson)*
4. **University of Texas–Austin** (McCombs)*
5. **University of Arizona** (Eller)*

**MARKETING**
1. **University of Michigan–Ann Arbor** (Ross)*
1. **University of Pennsylvania** (Wharton)
3. **University of Texas–Austin** (McCombs)*
4. **Indiana University–Bloomington** (Kelley)*
5. **University of California–Berkeley** (Haas)*

**PRODUCTION/OPERATIONS MANAGEMENT**
1. **Massachusetts Inst. of Technology** (Sloan)
2. **Carnegie Mellon University** (Tepper) (PA)
3. **Purdue Univ.–West Lafayette** (Krannert) (IN)*
4. **University of Pennsylvania** (Wharton)
5. **University of Michigan–Ann Arbor** (Ross)*

**QUANTITATIVE ANALYSIS/METHODS**
1. **Massachusetts Inst. of Technology** (Sloan)
2. **Carnegie Mellon University** (Tepper) (PA)
3. **University of Pennsylvania** (Wharton)
4. **Purdue Univ.–West Lafayette** (Krannert) (IN)*
5. **Georgia Institute of Technology**\*
5. **University of California–Berkeley** (Haas)*

**REAL ESTATE**
1. **University of Pennsylvania** (Wharton)
2. **Univ. of Wisconsin–Madison**\*
3. **University of California–Berkeley** (Haas)*
4. **University of Georgia** (Terry)*
5. **Univ. of Southern California** (Marshall)

**SUPPLY CHAIN MANAGEMENT/LOGISTICS**
1. **Michigan State University** (Broad)*
2. **Massachusetts Inst. of Technology** (Sloan)
3. **Arizona State University–Tempe** (Carey)*
4. **University of Tennessee**\*
5. **Ohio State University–Columbus** (Fisher)*
5. **Pennsylvania State U.–Univ. Park** (Smeal)*

\*\*The ranking originally published in this guidebook was incorrect and has been revised here.

# Best Engineering Programs

On these pages, U.S. News ranks undergraduate engineering programs accredited by ABET (formerly the Accreditation Board for Engineering and Technology). The rankings are based solely on a survey of engineering deans and senior faculty at accredited programs, conducted during the spring of 2014. Surveys sent to the dean and a faculty member at each program asked them to rate programs with which they're familiar on a scale from 1 (marginal) to 5 (distinguished). Students who prefer an engineering program that focuses on its undergrads can use the list below of top institutions whose terminal engineering degree is a bachelor's or master's; universities that grant doctorates in engineering, whose programs are ranked separately on the next page, may boast a wider range of offerings at the undergraduate level. Thirty-four percent of those surveyed returned ratings of the group below; 52 percent did so for the doctorate group. Respondents were also asked to name 10 top programs in specialty areas; those mentioned most often appear here.

## Top Programs ▷ AT ENGINEERING SCHOOLS WHOSE HIGHEST DEGREE IS A BACHELOR'S OR MASTER'S

| Rank | School (State) (*Public) | Peer assessment score (5.0=highest) |
|---|---|---|
| 1. | Harvey Mudd College (CA) | 4.4 |
| 1. | Rose-Hulman Inst. of Tech. (IN) | 4.4 |
| 3. | Franklin W. Olin Col. of Engineering (MA) | 4.1 |
| 3. | United States Military Academy (NY)* | 4.1 |
| 5. | United States Air Force Acad. (CO)* | 4.0 |
| 6. | United States Naval Academy (MD)* | 3.9 |
| 7. | Cal. Poly. State U.–San Luis Obispo* | 3.8 |
| 8. | Bucknell University (PA) | 3.7 |
| 8. | Cooper Union (NY) | 3.7 |
| 8. | Embry-Riddle Aeronautical U. (FL) | 3.7 |
| 11. | Villanova University (PA) | 3.5 |
| 12. | Baylor University (TX) | 3.4 |
| 12. | U. S. Coast Guard Acad. (CT)* | 3.4 |
| 14. | Embry-Riddle Aeronautical U.–Prescott (AZ) | 3.3 |
| 14. | Kettering University (MI) | 3.3 |
| 14. | Lafayette College (PA) | 3.3 |
| 14. | Milwaukee School of Engineering | 3.3 |
| 14. | Santa Clara University (CA) | 3.3 |
| 14. | Swarthmore College (PA) | 3.3 |
| 14. | Union College (NY) | 3.3 |
| 14. | Univ. of Colo.–Colorado Springs* | 3.3 |

| Rank | School (State) (*Public) | Peer assessment score (5.0=highest) |
|---|---|---|
| 14. | University of San Diego | 3.3 |
| 23. | Calif. State Poly. Univ.–Pomona* | 3.2 |
| 23. | The Citadel (SC)* | 3.2 |
| 23. | Lawrence Technological Univ. (MI) | 3.2 |
| 23. | San Jose State University (CA)* | 3.2 |
| 23. | Trinity University (TX) | 3.2 |
| 23. | Virginia Military Institute* | 3.2 |
| 29. | Gonzaga University (WA) | 3.1 |
| 29. | Miami University–Oxford (OH)* | 3.1 |
| 29. | Smith College (MA) | 3.1 |
| 29. | U.S. Merchant Marine Acad. (NY)* | 3.1 |
| 29. | Valparaiso University (IN) | 3.1 |
| 34. | Bradley University (IL) | 3.0 |
| 34. | Loyola Marymount University (CA) | 3.0 |
| 34. | Mercer University (GA) | 3.0 |
| 34. | Rowan University (NJ)* | 3.0 |
| 34. | Seattle University | 3.0 |
| 34. | University of Michigan–Dearborn* | 3.0 |
| 34. | University of St. Thomas (MN) | 3.0 |
| 41. | Boise State University (ID)* | 2.9 |
| 41. | California State U.–Los Angeles* | 2.9 |

| Rank | School (State) (*Public) | Peer assessment score (5.0=highest) |
|---|---|---|
| 41. | LeTourneau University (TX) | 2.9 |
| 41. | Northern Illinois University* | 2.9 |
| 41. | Ohio Northern University | 2.9 |
| 41. | Univ. of Arkansas–Little Rock* | 2.9 |
| 47. | Brigham Young University–Idaho | 2.8 |
| 47. | California State U.–Long Beach* | 2.8 |
| 47. | California State U.–Northridge* | 2.8 |
| 47. | Grand Valley State University (MI)* | 2.8 |
| 47. | Hofstra University (NY) | 2.8 |
| 47. | Loyola University Maryland | 2.8 |
| 47. | Maine Maritime Academy* | 2.8 |
| 47. | Manhattan College (NY) | 2.8 |
| 47. | Penn State Univ.–Erie, Behrend Col.* | 2.8 |
| 47. | Texas Christian University | 2.8 |
| 47. | Trinity College (CT) | 2.8 |
| 47. | Univ. of Massachusetts–Dartmouth* | 2.8 |
| 47. | University of Minnesota–Duluth* | 2.8 |
| 47. | University of North Texas* | 2.8 |
| 47. | University of Portland (OR) | 2.8 |
| 47. | Univ. of Wisconsin–Platteville* | 2.8 |

## Best in the Specialties ▷

(*Public)

**AEROSPACE/AERONAUTICAL/ASTRONAUTICAL**
1. Embry-Riddle Aeronautical U. (FL)
2. United States Air Force Acad. (CO)*
3. Embry-Riddle Aeronautical U.–Prescott (AZ)
4. Cal. Poly. State U.–San Luis Obispo*

**CHEMICAL**
1. Rose-Hulman Inst. of Tech. (IN)
2. Bucknell University (PA)

**CIVIL**
1. Rose-Hulman Inst. of Tech. (IN)
2. United States Military Academy (NY)*
3. Cal. Poly. State U.–San Luis Obispo*

4. Bucknell University (PA)
5. Harvey Mudd College (CA)

**COMPUTER ENGINEERING**
1. Rose-Hulman Inst. of Tech. (IN)
2. San Jose State University (CA)*
2. United States Air Force Acad. (CO)*
4. Cal. Poly. State U.–San Luis Obispo*
4. Harvey Mudd College (CA)

**ELECTRICAL/ELECTRONIC/COMMUNICATIONS**
1. Rose-Hulman Inst. of Tech. (IN)
2. Cal. Poly. State U.–San Luis Obispo*

3. United States Air Force Acad. (CO)*
4. Harvey Mudd College (CA)
5. Bucknell University (PA)
5. Cooper Union (NY)

**INDUSTRIAL/MANUFACTURING**
1. Cal. Poly. State U.–San Luis Obispo*

**MECHANICAL**
1. Rose-Hulman Inst. of Tech. (IN)
2. Cal. Poly. State U.–San Luis Obispo*
3. United States Military Academy (NY)*
4. Harvey Mudd College (CA)
4. Kettering University (MI)

**Note:** Peer assessment survey conducted by Ipsos Public Affairs. To be ranked in a specialty, a school may have either a program or course offerings in that subject area; ABET accreditation of that program is not needed. Based on a recommendation by the American Society for Engineering Education, a few schools with small doctoral programs are part of the bachelor's and master's category. Extended rankings can be found at usnews.com/bestcolleges.

# BEST ENGINEERING PROGRAMS

## Top Programs ► AT ENGINEERING SCHOOLS WHOSE HIGHEST DEGREE IS A DOCTORATE

| Rank | School (State) (*Public) | Peer assessment score (5.0=highest) |
|---|---|---|
| 1. | Massachusetts Inst. of Technology | 4.8 |
| 2. | Stanford University (CA) | 4.7 |
| 3. | University of California–Berkeley* | 4.6 |
| 4. | California Institute of Technology | 4.5 |
| 4. | Georgia Institute of Technology* | 4.5 |
| 6. | U. of Illinois–Urbana-Champaign* | 4.4 |
| 7. | Carnegie Mellon University (PA) | 4.3 |
| 7. | University of Michigan–Ann Arbor* | 4.3 |
| 9. | Purdue Univ.–West Lafayette (IN)* | 4.2 |
| 10. | Cornell University (NY) | 4.1 |
| 10. | Princeton University (NJ) | 4.1 |
| 10. | University of Texas–Austin* | 4.1 |
| 13. | Northwestern University (IL) | 4.0 |
| 14. | Univ. of Wisconsin–Madison* | 3.9 |
| 15. | Johns Hopkins University (MD) | 3.8 |
| 15. | Texas A&M Univ.–College Station* | 3.8 |
| 15. | Virginia Tech* | 3.8 |
| 18. | Duke University (NC) | 3.7 |
| 18. | Pennsylvania State U.–Univ. Park* | 3.7 |
| 18. | Rice University (TX) | 3.7 |
| 18. | Univ. of California–Los Angeles* | 3.7 |
| 22. | Columbia University (NY) | 3.6 |
| 22. | Univ. of Maryland–College Park* | 3.6 |
| 22. | Univ. of Minnesota–Twin Cities* | 3.6 |
| 22. | University of Washington* | 3.6 |
| 26. | Harvard University (MA) | 3.5 |
| 26. | Ohio State University–Columbus* | 3.5 |
| 26. | Univ. of California–San Diego* | 3.5 |
| 26. | University of Pennsylvania | 3.5 |
| 26. | Univ. of Southern California | 3.5 |
| 31. | North Carolina State U.–Raleigh* | 3.4 |
| 31. | Rensselaer Polytechnic Inst. (NY) | 3.4 |
| 31. | University of California–Davis* | 3.4 |
| 31. | University of Virginia* | 3.4 |
| 31. | Vanderbilt University (TN) | 3.4 |
| 36. | Univ. of California–Santa Barbara* | 3.3 |
| 36. | University of Colorado–Boulder* | 3.3 |
| 36. | University of Florida* | 3.3 |
| 36. | University of Notre Dame (IN) | 3.3 |
| 36. | Yale University (CT) | 3.3 |
| 41. | Arizona State University–Tempe* | 3.2 |
| 41. | Brown University (RI) | 3.2 |
| 41. | Case Western Reserve Univ. (OH) | 3.2 |
| 41. | Colorado School of Mines* | 3.2 |
| 41. | Iowa State University* | 3.2 |
| 41. | Lehigh University (PA) | 3.2 |
| 41. | Washington University in St. Louis | 3.2 |
| 48. | Dartmouth College (NH) | 3.1 |
| 48. | Michigan State University* | 3.1 |
| 48. | University of California–Irvine* | 3.1 |
| 51. | Auburn University (AL)* | 3.0 |
| 51. | Boston University | 3.0 |
| 51. | Northeastern University (MA) | 3.0 |
| 51. | Rutgers, St. U. of N.J.–New Brunswick* | 3.0 |
| 51. | University of Arizona* | 3.0 |
| 51. | University of Pittsburgh* | 3.0 |
| 57. | Clemson University (SC)* | 2.9 |
| 57. | Drexel University (PA) | 2.9 |
| 57. | Tufts University (MA) | 2.9 |
| 57. | University of Delaware* | 2.9 |
| 57. | University of Iowa* | 2.9 |
| 57. | Univ. of Massachusetts–Amherst* | 2.9 |
| 57. | University of Tennessee* | 2.9 |
| 57. | University of Utah* | 2.9 |
| 65. | Illinois Institute of Technology | 2.8 |
| 65. | Missouri Univ. of Science & Tech.* | 2.8 |
| 65. | New York University | 2.8 |
| 65. | Rochester Inst. of Technology (NY) | 2.8 |
| 65. | University at Buffalo–SUNY* | 2.8 |
| 65. | University of Rochester (NY) | 2.8 |
| 65. | Washington State University* | 2.8 |
| 65. | Worcester Polytechnic Inst. (MA) | 2.8 |

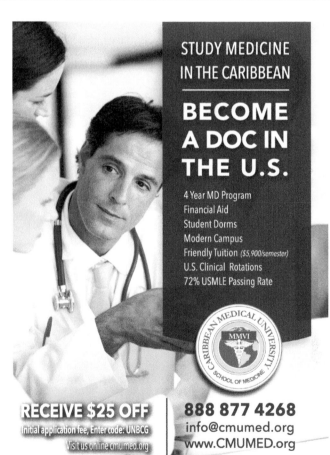

# Best in the Specialties ▶ AT ENGINEERING SCHOOLS WHOSE HIGHEST DEGREE IS A DOCTORATE

(*Public)

## AEROSPACE/AERONAUTICAL/ASTRONAUTICAL
1. Massachusetts Inst. of Technology
2. University of Michigan–Ann Arbor*
3. Georgia Institute of Technology*
4. California Institute of Technology
5. Purdue Univ.–West Lafayette (IN)*

## BIOLOGICAL/AGRICULTURAL
1. Purdue Univ.–West Lafayette (IN)*
1. U. of Illinois–Urbana-Champaign*
3. Texas A&M Univ.–College Station*
4. Iowa State University*
5. University of Florida*

## BIOMEDICAL/BIOMEDICAL ENGINEERING
1. Johns Hopkins University (MD)
2. Duke University (NC)
3. Massachusetts Inst. of Technology
4. Georgia Institute of Technology*
5. Rice University (TX)

## CHEMICAL
1. Massachusetts Inst. of Technology
2. University of California–Berkeley*
3. Univ. of Minnesota–Twin Cities*
4. Stanford University (CA)
5. Univ. of Wisconsin–Madison*

## CIVIL
1. U. of Illinois–Urbana-Champaign*
2. Georgia Institute of Technology*
3. University of California–Berkeley*
4. Purdue Univ.–West Lafayette (IN)*
5. Stanford University (CA)

## COMPUTER ENGINEERING
1. Massachusetts Inst. of Technology
2. Stanford University (CA)
3. Carnegie Mellon University (PA)
4. University of California–Berkeley*
5. U. of Illinois–Urbana-Champaign*

## ELECTRICAL/ELECTRONIC/COMMUNICATIONS
1. Massachusetts Inst. of Technology
2. Stanford University (CA)
3. University of California–Berkeley*
4. U. of Illinois–Urbana-Champaign*
5. University of Michigan–Ann Arbor*

## ENGINEERING SCIENCE/ENGINEERING PHYSICS
1. U. of Illinois–Urbana-Champaign*
2. Massachusetts Inst. of Technology
2. Stanford University (CA)
2. University of California–Berkeley*
5. Harvard University (MA)
5. Virginia Tech*

## ENVIRONMENTAL/ENVIRONMENTAL HEALTH
1. Stanford University (CA)
1. University of California–Berkeley*
3. Georgia Institute of Technology*
4. University of Michigan–Ann Arbor*
5. U. of Illinois–Urbana-Champaign*

## INDUSTRIAL/MANUFACTURING
1. Georgia Institute of Technology*
2. University of Michigan–Ann Arbor*
3. University of California–Berkeley*
4. Purdue Univ.–West Lafayette (IN)*
5. Northwestern University (IL)

## MATERIALS
1. Massachusetts Inst. of Technology
2. U. of Illinois–Urbana-Champaign*
3. University of California–Berkeley*
4. Stanford University (CA)
4. University of Michigan–Ann Arbor*

## MECHANICAL
1. Massachusetts Inst. of Technology
2. Stanford University (CA)
3. University of Michigan–Ann Arbor*
4. University of California–Berkeley*
5. Georgia Institute of Technology*

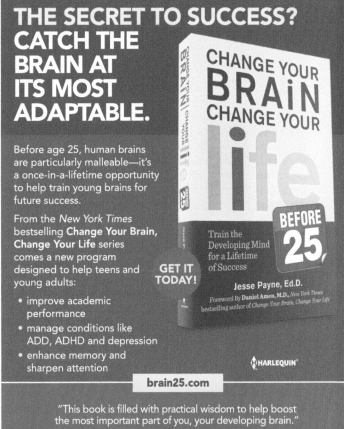

# The Virtual Path

## GETTING YOUR DEGREE FROM A DISTANCE

By **ARLENE WEINTRAUB**

Cynthia Stebbins loved her first two years at Colorado State University in Fort Collins, but after she got married in May of 2013, she found herself in a bind. Her husband, Cody, who is in the Air Force, was transferred to Scott Air Force Base in Illinois. Stebbins, 21, didn't want to have a long-distance marriage, so she decided to finish her bachelor's the 21st-century way: online. She'll graduate next spring from CSU with a degree in psychology.

Although Stebbins sometimes misses the campus social life, she's confident she's getting just as rich an academic experience as when she was trekking from one classroom to another. All of the lectures she "attends" are prerecorded, so the work can be handled on her own time. But she still has to meet strict deadlines and must participate in online discussions with her classmates. One-on-one help from professors is easily available by phone or Skype conference. "The experience is similar to what it is on campus, and I appreciate that," she says. "I don't want my education to be different just because I've chosen this program."

Whether you're an undergrad like Stebbins who faces logistical challenges or a working student who wants a degree without giving up

that salary, attending class virtually is an increasingly viable and popular option. Some universities allow students to earn their degrees entirely online (ranking, Page 128); a growing number are dabbling by letting students earn a handful of credits virtually. Nearly 460 schools offered online bachelor's courses in 2013, according to the latest annual survey by Babson College in Massachusetts, which has been tracking the spread of online education for 11 years. And the proportion of all students, undergraduate and graduate, taking at least one online course hit a high of 33.5 percent in 2013, Babson reports.

**A few bumps.** Moving the lecture hall onto the Web isn't always a smooth process. In April, the high-profile pilot program Semester Online was discontinued; a consortium of 10 universities (Boston College, Northwestern University and Washington University in St. Louis among them) had tried offering for-credit virtual classes to their own students and to attendees of other colleges interested in transferring the credits. The organizer, Landover, Maryland-based 2U, declined to comment but said in a written statement that it found "significant challenges related to the complexities of a consortium structure." The firm contin-

ues to provide software solutions to individual schools developing online offerings, and in October will be working on its first online undergraduate degree program with Simmons College School of Nursing and Health Sciences in Boston.

But the end of Semester Online shouldn't be viewed as a sign that digitally enhanced learning is a bad idea, argues Elliott Visconsi, an English and law professor and chief academic digital officer at consortium member University of Notre Dame, which offered four undergrad courses online during the pilot. Instructors found the teaching "to be exciting and interesting, but new and unfamiliar," he says. While there were problems associated with students moving in and out of classes and seeking credits from other participating schools, he says, Notre Dame is now pursuing a variety of digital initiatives."Our primary goal is to give our students a world-class undergraduate experience," he says, "and certainly digital tools and strategies are part of that puzzle."

The best online courses are organized much like their offline counterparts, with video lectures and group projects accomplished via videoconference and shared documents, exams and opportunities to huddle with professors. When shopping for the best place to complete your bachelor's, check to make sure programs you're considering are fully accredited. You should also consider whether it's important to be able to do all your coursework on your own time – meaning the classes are "asynchronous" – or if you would enjoy synchronous classes that allow you to interact with professors and other students in real time.

And weigh your level of motivation. Most online learners agree that this mode of study is far from easy. You certainly have to be disciplined, particularly if you have a full-time day job. "It's not like going to class a couple of times a week and then doing your homework," says Bettina Smith, 42, a financial services professional in Oakland, California, who entered Pace's online program in computer forensics in 2013 with the goal of finishing her bachelor's.

Arizona State University associate professor Dawn Gilpin, who teaches an online course in social media, says Web-based teaching platforms have become so sophisticated that students can easily be as engaged as they are in physical classes, if not more so.

"We have software that allows them to do a final presentation that's highly visual," with slides and narration, Gilpin says. They also are able to give and receive feedback from other students. And even though Gilpin typically has 200 students in each online class, she finds that she interacts individually with a larger percentage of those students than ones on campus, via Twitter chats and other social media platforms as well as email. Traditional class members often are just not inclined to reach out to professors outside of class hours.

Some of Gilpin's students these days are military servicemen deployed to Afghanistan; indeed, online education is fast becoming a popular route to advancement for both active duty folks and veterans (Page 133). Some programs give veterans credit for time spent serving the country. "More often than not, veterans have had training and experience that could be equivalent to some of our introductory-level courses," says Christine Shakespeare, assistant vice president of continuing and professional education at Pace University. Those who apply to the Pace program submit information outlining their work and any courses they took in the military, which is then evaluated by faculty to determine how many credits they should receive.

**A blend.** The popularity of online study is starting to influence the in-class experience, inspiring a move to "blended learning," says Robert Lue, a professor and director of life sciences education at Harvard. Several professors there have adopted tools that were developed by HarvardX, the university's online-learning initiative that includes a collaboration with the Massachusetts Institute of Technology to offer non-credit massive open online courses, or MOOCs, from more than 30 colleges and universities, at no charge, to anyone interested.

These materials – a video that draws upon cooking techniques to teach basic physics concepts, for instance – are adapted to create what Lue calls the equivalent of "textbooks on steroids." Web-based videos might be interspersed with, say, quizzes or discussion questions that help students assess how well they're absorbing the material. What is becoming clear, says Lue, who is also the faculty director of HarvardX, is that "students find the digital media far more engaging. Time spent on tasks is greater. And the likelihood they'll actually do the preclass work is significantly greater."

Lately, interest has trickled down to collegebound high-schoolers, who are earning credits and even using free MOOCs to check out schools. ●

# The Measure of What You Know

## A COMPETENCY-BASED PROGRAM LETS YOU ADVANCE WHEN YOU'RE READY

*By* **CATHIE GANDEL**

raig Kilgo, 29, has a job as a project manager for the Department of Defense and a 6-month-old son. What he doesn't yet have is an undergrad degree. The obstacles: time and money. His solution? Sign up for a new breed of online bachelor's program that doesn't require regular class time and lets him move rapidly through material he already knows.

Kilgo, who lives in Arlington, Virginia, started out as a student at Cornell University after high school but found an Ivy League degree too costly. Now he's pursuing a bachelor's degree in Information Science and Technology in the "competency-based" Flexible Option offered by the University of Wisconsin–Milwaukee. A traditional college program requires the student to "sit in the classroom and go through the material in lock step with everybody else," says Aaron Brower, interim chancellor at the University of Wisconsin Extension, who is overseeing the Flexible Option. A regular online program allows you to go at your own pace, "but you still have to do A, B and C in sequence," he says.

In a competency-based program such as UW's, "you can skip A and B and go right to C, providing you can pass the assessments that show you have mastered the content of A and B," says Brower. And the assessments are not a matter of passing or failing. Instead, "You pass, or you haven't yet passed," he says. Students are assigned an academic success coach who, if they don't succeed the first time, can provide extra guidance and supplemental materials.

President Obama has encouraged innovation in competency-based education, arguing for the need to award credits based not on "seat time" but on mastering information. "If you're learning the material faster, you can finish faster," he said in a speech last year. Kilgo's experience on the job allowed him to breeze through a required Basics of Web Design course in just three weeks, for example, instead of the typical 16 weeks. The program is "perfect for me," he says. "I can leverage everything I've learned in my career while earning a degree from an accredited university."

And at less cost. At UW, students can take one course for $900 or choose the "all you can learn" option: as many courses as you care to squeeze in over a three-month "subscription" period for $2,250. Kilgo came into the program with about 63 credits from several schools under his belt. He completed five UW courses in each of his first two subscription periods and hopes to finish after two more three-month periods. Total cost: $9,000.

Besides the information science and technology bachelor's, UW offers Flexible Option degrees in diagnostic imaging and nursing, a certificate in professional and technical communication, and an associate degree in arts and sciences. Other competency-based online degree programs include those at Western Governors University (business, teaching, information technology and health) and at Northern Arizona University (small business administration, computer information technology and liberal arts).

## On campus, Purdue University in

West Lafayette, Indiana, is launching a competency-oriented grand experiment this fall known as the Purdue Polytechnic Institute, a collaboration between the colleges of technology, liberal arts, education and science. "Students will be immersed in project-based environments," says Jeffrey Evans, a professor and Purdue Poly-

technic faculty fellow. They will work on mastering a skill set or course material at their own pace, guided by a team of faculty mentors. Competencies will be demonstrated as they are acquired, rather than in a final exam, and will be documented by digital badges or certificates. "These can be stored and viewed by anyone given access, such as a potential employer," notes Evans, who says the belief at Purdue is that this model has the potential to be a game-changer in higher education.

Industry seems to be enthusiastic about the idea. At Southern New Hampshire University, for example,

employers such as McDonald's, Anthem BlueCross BlueShield and the city of Memphis have collaborated in creating the College for America, a program in which employees can learn marketable skills or a bachelor's degree in communications or healthcare management at their own pace for $2,500 per year. Some employers will reimburse the tuition. In the UW program, nurses who have families, are busy in the community and are working full-time can "seamlessly move forward in their careers while bringing new ideas to their workplace," says Mary Beth Kingston, executive vice president and chief nursing officer of Milwaukee-based Aurora Health Care. "It's win-win."

Demand for the UW Flexible Option has certainly been impressive, says Brower. While the university is getting it fully up to speed, nearly 300 students are participating in the program. But almost 10,000 people have so far shown interest. ●

# Best
# Online Degree Programs

hen we surveyed colleges in 2013 about their online options, 283 schools reported having bachelor's programs that can be completed without showing up in person for class (though attendance may be required for testing, orientations or support services). These offerings, typically degree-completion programs aimed at working adults and community college grads, were evaluated on their success at engaging students, the credentials of their faculty and the services and technologies made available remotely. The table below features some of the most significant ranking factors, such as the prevalence of faculty holding a Ph.D., class size, the percentages of new entrants who stayed enrolled and later graduated, and the debt load of recent graduates. The top half of programs are listed here. Ranks are determined by the institutions' overall unrounded scores, which have been rounded below for display purposes. To see the rest of the ranked online bachelor's programs and to read the full methodology, visit usnews.com/online. You'll also find detail-rich profile pages for each of the schools and (in case you want to plan ahead) rankings of online graduate degree programs in business, engineering, nursing and more.

(*Public, **For profit)

| Rank | School | Overall program score | Average peer assessment score (5.0=highest) | '13 total program enrollment | '13 - '14 tuition[1] | '13 full-time faculty with Ph.D. | '13 average class size | '13 retention rate | '13 graduation rate[2] | % graduates with debt ('13) | Average debt of graduates ('13) |
|---|---|---|---|---|---|---|---|---|---|---|---|
| 1. | Central Michigan University* | 100 | 3.0 | 1,346 | $370 | 73% | 19 | 80% | 94% | 47% | $9,757 |
| 1. | SUNY College of Technology–Delhi* | 100 | 3.1 | 700 | $245 | 45% | 16 | 68% | 49% | N/A | N/A |
| 3. | Pace University (NY) | 96 | 3.1 | 250 | $570 | 82% | 10 | 70% | 45% | 15% | $49,113 |
| 3. | Pennsylvania State University–World Campus* | 96 | 4.0 | 3,845 | $518 | 58% | 26 | 70% | 36% | N/A | N/A |
| 5. | Embry-Riddle Aeronautical University (FL) | 93 | 3.5 | 16,222 | $325 | 45% | 22 | 74% | 21% | 2% | $3,763 |
| 5. | University of Florida* | 93 | 3.6 | 785 | $812 | 89% | 530 | 91% | 63% | 60% | $18,159 |
| 7. | Daytona State College (FL)* | 92 | 2.8 | 1,560 | $560 | 79% | 18 | 79% | 62% | 33% | $25,500 |
| 7. | University of Alabama–Huntsville* | 92 | 3.0 | 47 | $427 | 100% | 32 | 87% | 89% | N/A | N/A |
| 9. | Arizona State University* | 91 | 3.7 | 7,437 | $460 | 73% | 46 | 80% | 54% | 72% | $22,087 |
| 9. | Indiana Univ.-Purdue Univ.–Fort Wayne* | 91 | 3.5 | 359 | $328 | 69% | N/A | 60% | N/A | N/A | N/A |
| 9. | University of Illinois–Chicago* | 91 | 3.3 | 139 | $572 | 36% | 18 | 95% | 84% | 57% | $12,524 |
| 9. | University of Wisconsin–Superior* | 91 | 3.8 | 484 | $305 | 33% | 10 | 62% | 21% | N/A | N/A |
| 13. | St. John's University (NY) | 90 | 3.3 | 35 | $1,215 | 88% | 18 | 64% | 15% | 86% | $37,354 |
| 13. | University of Denver | 90 | 3.2 | 50 | $529 | 100% | 11 | 91% | 62% | 33% | N/A |
| 13. | University of La Verne (CA) | 90 | 2.4 | 236 | $570 | 94% | 15 | 76% | 53% | 77% | $23,775 |
| 16. | Colorado State University–Global Campus* | 89 | 3.1 | 5,776 | $350 | N/A | 15 | 84% | 46% | 67% | $21,560 |
| 16. | Fort Hays State University (KS)* | 89 | 2.9 | 7,165 | $182 | 51% | 23 | 73%[3] | 65% | 15% | $23,568 |
| 18. | Bellevue University (NE) | 88 | 2.3 | 6,387 | $375 | 44% | 17 | 87% | 58% | 62% | $17,472 |
| 18. | Marist College (NY) | 88 | 3.4 | 254 | $600 | 77% | 19 | 83% | 71% | 77% | $21,600 |
| 20. | University of Nebraska–Omaha* | 86 | 3.4 | 2,529 | $464 | 87% | 20 | 57% | 32% | 59% | $31,152 |
| 21. | Palm Beach Atlantic University (FL) | 85 | 2.8 | 80 | $430 | 55% | 10 | 82% | 44% | 75% | $27,654 |
| 21. | Regent University (VA) | 85 | 3.0 | 2,612 | $395 | 94% | 16 | 60% | 30% | 72% | $35,435 |
| 21. | Washington State University* | 85 | 3.3 | 2,114 | $1,223 | 73% | 22 | 62% | 45% | 73% | $25,441 |
| 21. | Wayne State University (MI)* | 85 | 3.5 | 60 | $884 | 100% | 23 | 100% | N/A | N/A | N/A |
| 25. | Savannah College of Art and Design (GA) | 84 | 3.3 | 748 | $732 | 32% | 15 | 68%[3] | 42% | 90% | $51,044 |
| 25. | University of Wisconsin–Milwaukee* | 84 | 3.7 | 285 | $337 | 97% | 23 | 65% | N/A | 74% | $21,457 |
| 25. | University of Wisconsin–Platteville* | 84 | 3.8 | 608 | $370 | 71% | 18 | N/A | N/A | 25% | N/A |
| 28. | Loyola University Chicago | 83 | 3.2 | 161 | $615 | 56% | 23 | 93% | N/A | 55% | $17,168 |
| 29. | Ball State University (IN)* | 82 | 3.7 | 284 | $488 | 72% | N/A | 41% | 32% | 70% | $29,679 |
| 29. | University of Bridgeport (CT) | 82 | 2.2 | 127 | $490 | 17% | 14 | 81% | 63% | N/A | N/A |
| 31. | University of Illinois–Springfield* | 81 | 3.6 | 920 | $353 | 77% | N/A | 68% | 36% | N/A | N/A |
| 32. | Loyola University New Orleans | 80 | 1.9 | 43 | $506 | 100% | 16 | 90%[3] | 78% | N/A | N/A |
| 32. | Westfield State University (MA)* | 80 | 1.9 | 176 | $260 | 85% | 20 | 88% | 60% | 75% | $14,500 |
| 34. | American Public University System (WV)** | 79 | 3.1 | 61,776 | $250 | 43% | 16 | 52% | N/A | N/A | $6,267 |
| 34. | University of Missouri–St. Louis* | 79 | 3.4 | 109 | $445 | 50% | 22 | 91% | 68% | 45% | $4,621 |
| 34. | Western Carolina University (NC)* | 79 | 1.9 | 1,367 | $468 | 76% | N/A | 84% | 58% | 36% | $9,075 |
| 37. | California Baptist University | 78 | 2.7 | 1,665 | $495 | 72% | 15 | 75% | N/A | 72% | $35,211 |
| 37. | Drexel University (PA) | 78 | 3.6 | 2,370 | $707 | 59% | 19 | 76% | 26% | 68% | $33,207 |
| 37. | McKendree University (IL) | 78 | 1.9 | 81 | $340 | 87% | 11 | N/A | N/A | 60% | $2,500 |
| 37. | Norwich University (VT) | 78 | 2.8 | 264 | $350 | 100% | 9 | 67% | 17%[4] | 0% | $0 |
| 41. | Brandman University (CA) | 76 | 1.7 | 1,097 | $500 | 100% | 18 | 85% | 52% | 76% | $25,980 |
| 41. | California State University–Chico* | 76 | 3.2 | 206 | $619 | 73% | 28 | 77%[3] | 57% | N/A | N/A |

Note: Key to footnotes, Page 133.

# Discover where AP® can take you.

The Advanced Placement Program® helps students stand out in college admissions, earn college credit and placement, explore interests and discover new passions, and build the skills and knowledge they need to be successful in college.

## Visit **exploreap.org**

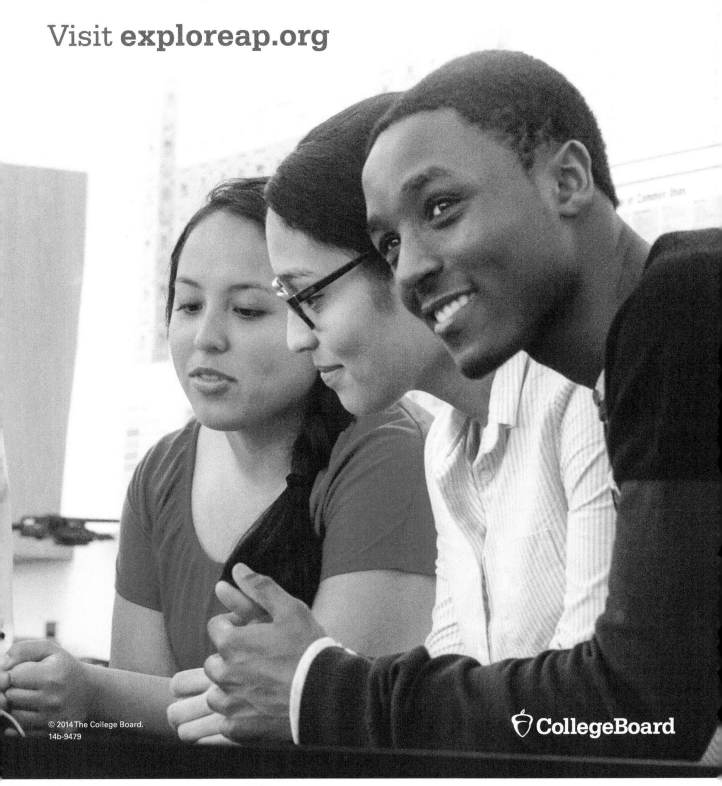

CollegeBoard

(*Public, **For profit)

| Rank | School | Overall program score | Average peer assessment score (5.0=highest) | '13 total program enrollment | '13-'14 tuition[1] | '13 full-time faculty with Ph.D. | '13 average class size | '13 retention rate | '13 graduation rate[2] | % graduates with debt ('13) | Average debt of graduates ('13) |
|---|---|---|---|---|---|---|---|---|---|---|---|
| 41. | Sam Houston State University (TX)* | 76 | 3.1 | 596 | $195 | 94% | 29 | 82% | N/A | 60% | $27,028 |
| 41. | University of South Carolina–Aiken* | 76 | 2.2 | 31 | $768 | 44% | 13 | 92% | 67% | 92% | $14,278 |
| 41. | Wright State University (OH)* | 76 | 1.9 | 120 | N/A | 80% | 25 | 75% | 30%[4] | 5% | $2,500 |
| 46. | City University of Seattle | 75 | 2.2 | 766 | $402 | 55% | 12 | 81%[3] | 33% | N/A | N/A |
| 46. | Oregon State University* | 75 | 1.9 | 2,492 | $191 | 61% | 25 | 72% | 33% | 75% | $26,584 |
| 48. | Charter Oak State College (CT)* | 74 | 1.7 | 1,873 | $339 | N/A | 11 | 85% | 54% | N/A | N/A |
| 48. | DePaul University (IL) | 74 | 3.7 | 235 | $550 | 87% | 18 | N/A | N/A | N/A | N/A |
| 48. | Florida Institute of Technology | 74 | 3.1 | 3,299 | $495 | 71% | 19 | 66% | 10% | 66% | $44,422 |
| 48. | Granite State College (NH)* | 74 | 1.5 | 1,832 | $305 | 33% | 14 | 76% | 47% | 80% | $24,157 |
| 48. | University of Missouri* | 74 | 3.4 | 811 | $274 | 64% | 15 | N/A | N/A | N/A | N/A |
| 48. | University of Northern Colorado* | 74 | 2.9 | 314 | $370 | 19% | 17 | 100% | 67% | N/A | N/A |
| 48. | Utah State University* | 74 | 3.7 | 1,584 | $275 | 64% | 60 | N/A | N/A | 32% | $23,439 |
| 48. | Wilmington University (DE) | 74 | 1.9 | 4,380 | $330 | 62% | 15 | 74% | 53% | 52% | N/A |
| 56. | Charleston Southern University (SC) | 72 | 2.0 | 297 | $490 | 47% | 10 | 77% | 46%[4] | N/A | $30,417 |
| 56. | Concordia University–St. Paul (MN) | 72 | 2.6 | 722 | $420 | 38% | N/A | 80%[3] | 63% | 82% | $23,517 |
| 56. | George Washington University (DC) | 72 | 3.6 | 233 | $552 | N/A | 17 | 67% | 55% | 13% | $29,888 |
| 56. | Kaplan University (IA)** | 72 | 2.0 | 35,372 | $371 | 49% | 20 | 65% | 16% | 88% | $31,915 |
| 56. | University of Arkansas* | 72 | 1.9 | 202 | $212 | 80% | 12 | N/A | 61% | N/A | N/A |
| 61. | St. Joseph's University (PA) | 71 | 2.0 | 76 | $500 | 90% | 12 | 80%[3] | N/A | N/A | N/A |
| 61. | University of Maine–Augusta* | 71 | 2.0 | 3,253 | $525 | 38% | 20 | 78% | 16% | 76% | $23,339 |
| 61. | Upper Iowa University | 71 | 2.6 | 1,424 | $378 | 63% | 13 | 56% | 29% | N/A | N/A |
| 61. | Western Illinois University* | 71 | 2.3 | 754 | $280 | 74% | 35 | 61%[3] | 47% | 48% | $22,980 |
| 65. | Graceland University (IA) | 70 | 1.4 | 143 | $495 | 50% | 15 | 78% | 77% | 65% | $29,864 |
| 65. | Lamar University (TX)* | 70 | 2.1 | 1,151 | $208 | 87% | 30 | 75% | N/A | 9% | $30,303 |
| 65. | Regis University (CO) | 70 | 2.6 | 1,671 | $460 | 6% | 8 | 91% | 34% | N/A | N/A |
| 65. | Southeast Missouri State University* | 70 | 2.7 | 565 | $375 | 73% | 24 | 76% | 47% | N/A | N/A |
| 69. | Columbia College (MO) | 69 | 2.4 | 21,295 | $245 | 67% | 20 | 75% | 45% | 65% | $28,385 |
| 69. | Old Dominion University (VA)* | 69 | 3.1 | 3,542 | $285 | 83% | 36 | 82% | 50% | N/A | N/A |
| 69. | University of Massachusetts–Dartmouth* | 69 | 3.7 | 110 | $304 | N/A | 13 | 73% | N/A | N/A | N/A |
| 69. | University of Minnesota–Crookston* | 69 | 2.8 | 1,048 | $385 | 32% | 24 | 72% | 38% | 72% | $21,682 |
| 69. | University of West Georgia* | 69 | 1.6 | 419 | $256 | 56% | 35 | 90% | N/A | 90% | $19,313 |
| 74. | Belhaven University (MS) | 68 | 1.7 | 380 | $375 | 54% | 12 | 80% | 42% | 72% | $7,619 |
| 74. | Troy University (AL)* | 68 | 3.1 | 6,900 | $308 | 60% | 28 | 62% | 12% | N/A | N/A |
| 74. | University of Nebraska–Lincoln* | 68 | 3.6 | 34 | $501 | 98% | 40 | N/A | N/A | 50% | $32,500 |
| 77. | Eastern Kentucky University* | 67 | 1.9 | 1,207 | $395 | 67% | 22 | 70% | 9% | 74% | $21,859 |
| 77. | Georgia College & State University* | 67 | 2.7 | 22 | $227 | 67% | 15 | N/A | N/A | N/A | N/A |

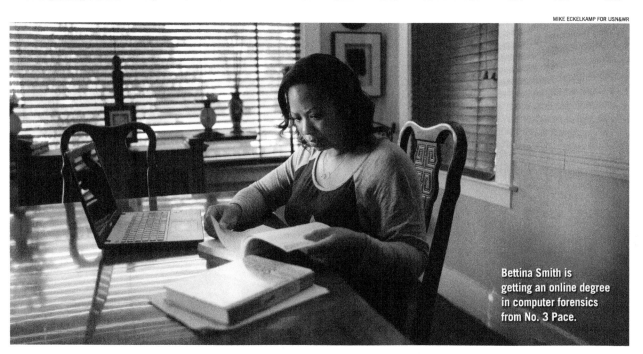

Bettina Smith is getting an online degree in computer forensics from No. 3 Pace.

**Note:** Key to footnotes, Page 133.

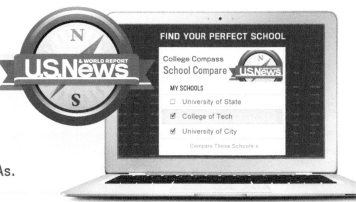

# BEST ONLINE DEGREE PROGRAMS

(*Public, **For profit)

| Rank | School | Overall program score | Average peer assessment score (5.0=highest) | '13 total program enrollment | '13 - '14 tuition[1] | '13 full-time faculty with Ph.D. | '13 average class size | '13 retention rate | '13 graduation rate[2] | % graduates with debt ('13) | Average debt of graduates ('13) |
|---|---|---|---|---|---|---|---|---|---|---|---|
| 77. | John Brown University (AR) | 67 | 1.6 | 99 | $460 | 57% | 14 | 68% | N/A | 80% | $12,566 |
| 77. | Wheeling Jesuit University (WV) | 67 | 1.9 | 106 | $330 | 55% | 20 | 81% | 21%[4] | 63% | $23,797 |
| 81. | Holy Apostles College and Seminary (CT) | 66 | 1.9 | N/A | $430 | 100% | 10 | N/A | N/A | N/A | N/A |
| 81. | Lawrence Technological University (MI) | 66 | 1.5 | 62 | $944 | N/A | 12 | 90% | 29% | N/A | N/A |
| 81. | Malone University (OH) | 66 | 1.4 | 114 | $485 | 71% | 16 | N/A | 61% | 94% | $20,527 |
| 81. | North Carolina State University–Raleigh* | 66 | 3.6 | 82 | $408 | 100% | 25 | N/A | N/A | N/A | N/A |
| 81. | Peirce College (PA) | 66 | 1.1 | 1,343 | $533 | 63% | 17 | 68% | 38% | 85% | $22,784 |
| 81. | University of St. Francis (IL) | 66 | 1.5 | 508 | $585 | 50% | 14 | 82% | 45% | 58% | $25,028 |
| 87. | California State University–Dominguez Hills* | 65 | 2.8 | 814 | N/A | 90% | 18 | 81% | 29% | N/A | N/A |
| 87. | Huntington University (IN) | 65 | 1.5 | 30 | $398 | 58% | 6 | N/A | 100% | 100% | $21,400 |
| 87. | National University (CA) | 65 | 1.9 | N/A | $336 | 64% | 20 | 60% | 37% | 75% | $29,474 |
| 87. | University of Alabama–Birmingham* | 65 | 3.1 | 146 | $666 | 50% | 34 | N/A | N/A | N/A | N/A |
| 87. | University of Cincinnati* | 65 | 3.4 | 1,658 | $396 | N/A | N/A | 70% | 51% | 72% | $29,521 |
| 87. | Western Kentucky University* | 65 | 3.1 | 2,502 | $445 | N/A | 22 | N/A | N/A | 67% | $17,613 |
| 93. | DeVry University (IL)** | 64 | 2.2 | 27,263 | $609 | 31% | 27 | 81% | 14% | 81% | $42,576 |
| 93. | Duquesne University (PA) | 64 | 3.3 | N/A | $661 | 91% | 16 | N/A | N/A | N/A | N/A |
| 93. | Limestone College (SC) | 64 | 1.0 | 1,275 | $376 | 66% | 16 | 68% | 35% | 97% | $34,513 |
| 93. | St. Louis University | 64 | 3.1 | 490 | $610 | 65% | 15 | N/A | N/A | 69% | $39,594 |
| 97. | Champlain College (VT) | 63 | 1.7 | 1,052 | $590 | N/A | 20 | 77%[3] | 33% | N/A | N/A |
| 97. | Concordia University Chicago | 63 | 1.9 | 65 | $475 | 67% | 9 | N/A | N/A | N/A | N/A |
| 97. | Lee University (TN) | 63 | 1.5 | 716 | $175 | 100% | N/A | 83% | N/A | 71% | $2,614 |
| 97. | Linfield College (OR) | 63 | 1.9 | 805 | $435 | 60% | 19 | 85% | 61% | N/A | N/A |
| 97. | Northern Arizona University* | 63 | 3.5 | 3,100 | $755 | N/A | 29 | 67%[3] | 28% | 67% | $22,208 |
| 102. | Benedictine University (IL) | 62 | 1.9 | 56 | $546 | N/A | 11 | 83% | 36%[4] | 82% | $30,045 |
| 102. | Florida State University* | 62 | 3.5 | 494 | $686 | N/A | 25 | N/A | N/A | 62% | $25,055 |
| 102. | Herzing University (WI)** | 62 | 1.2 | 1,979 | $500 | 29% | 18 | N/A | N/A | 87% | $25,665 |
| 102. | Minot State University (ND)* | 62 | 2.4 | N/A | $201 | 57% | 18 | N/A | N/A | N/A | N/A |
| 102. | University of Maine–Fort Kent* | 62 | 1.8 | 198 | $552 | 54% | 20 | 71% | 47% | 48% | $13,948 |
| 102. | University of West Florida* | 62 | 3.2 | 416 | $552 | N/A | 23 | 67%[3] | 12% | N/A | N/A |
| 108. | Neumann University (PA) | 61 | 1.9 | N/A | $547 | 100% | N/A | 83% | 48% | N/A | N/A |
| 108. | Northwestern State University of Louisiana* | 61 | 1.2 | 3,890 | $1,217 | 55% | 29 | 67% | N/A | 65% | $19,181 |
| 108. | Post University (CT)** | 61 | 1.2 | 9,776 | $550 | 50% | 12 | 100% | 30% | N/A | N/A |
| 108. | University of Toledo (OH)* | 61 | 1.9 | 1,324 | $327 | 43% | 15 | 56%[3] | 36% | 86% | $37,692 |
| 112. | Chatham University (PA) | 60 | 1.9 | 122 | $759 | 67% | 14 | 30% | 100% | 73% | $16,163 |
| 112. | Madonna University (MI) | 60 | 1.0 | 108 | N/A | 67% | N/A | 97% | 75% | N/A | N/A |
| 112. | Monroe College (NY)** | 60 | 1.9 | 498 | $514 | N/A | 19 | 54% | 45% | 86% | $23,294 |
| 112. | Southwestern College (KS) | 60 | 1.0 | 1,875 | $411 | 55% | 12 | 73% | 45% | N/A | N/A |
| 112. | University of Southern Indiana* | 60 | 1.4 | 440 | $318 | 67% | N/A | 56% | 51% | N/A | N/A |

University of Florida, tied at No. 5

| Rank. School | Overall program score | Average peer assessment score (5.0=highest) | '13 total program enrollment | '13-'14 tuition[1] | '13 full-time faculty with Ph.D. | '13 average class size | '13 retention rate | '13 graduation rate[2] | % graduates with debt ('13) | Average debt of graduates ('13) |
|---|---|---|---|---|---|---|---|---|---|---|
| 117. Bay State College (MA) | 59 | 1.0 | 42 | $375 | 40% | 18 | 80% | N/A | N/A | N/A |
| 117. Rogers State University (OK)* | 59 | 1.6 | 445 | $333 | 70% | 23 | 67% | 28% | 75% | N/A |
| 117. Toccoa Falls College (GA) | 59 | 1.2 | N/A | $285 | 59% | 15 | 68%[3] | N/A | 45% | $10,935 |
| 120. Fitchburg State University (MA)* | 58 | 1.9 | 86 | N/A | 67% | 14 | N/A | 50%[4] | N/A | N/A |
| 120. Lynn University (FL) | 58 | 1.6 | 183 | $345 | N/A | 11 | 58% | 49% | N/A | N/A |
| 120. New Mexico State University* | 58 | 3.2 | N/A | $764 | 81% | 29 | N/A | N/A | N/A | N/A |
| 120. University of West Alabama* | 58 | 2.4 | N/A | N/A | 73% | 20 | N/A | N/A | N/A | N/A |
| 124. Florida International University* | 57 | 3.0 | N/A | $333 | N/A | 10 | N/A | N/A | N/A | N/A |
| 124. Lindenwood University (MO) | 57 | 1.7 | N/A | $471 | 44% | 15 | N/A | N/A | N/A | N/A |
| 124. University of Tennessee–Martin* | 57 | 3.3 | 605 | N/A | 74% | 18 | N/A | N/A | N/A | N/A |
| 127. Arkansas Tech University* | 56 | 1.7 | N/A | $398 | 61% | 21 | N/A | N/A | N/A | N/A |
| 127. Eastern University (PA) | 56 | 1.9 | N/A | $495 | 100% | 8 | N/A | 50% | 85% | $23,632 |
| 127. Ohio State University–Columbus* | 56 | 1.9 | 177 | $387 | 27% | 150 | 74% | 99% | N/A | N/A |
| 127. Sacred Heart University (CT) | 56 | 1.9 | 349 | $515 | N/A | 12 | N/A | N/A | 36% | $10,371 |
| 131. Baldwin Wallace University (OH) | 55 | 1.2 | 13 | $615 | 63% | N/A | N/A | N/A | N/A | N/A |
| 131. Bismarck State College (ND)* | 55 | 1.2 | 321 | $232 | N/A | 24 | N/A | N/A | N/A | N/A |
| 131. Ferris State University (MI)* | 55 | 2.0 | 811 | $365 | 61% | 20 | N/A | N/A | N/A | N/A |
| 131. Montreat College (NC) | 55 | 1.9 | 26 | $395 | 100% | 10 | N/A | N/A | N/A | N/A |
| 131. Siena Heights University (MI) | 55 | 1.2 | 1,059 | $440 | 67% | 19 | N/A | 84% | 73% | $19,064 |
| 131. University of Houston–Victoria* | 55 | 1.7 | N/A | $518 | 100% | 48 | N/A | N/A | N/A | N/A |
| 131. University of North Dakota* | 55 | 3.5 | N/A | $257 | N/A | 22 | N/A | N/A | N/A | N/A |
| 138. Berkeley College (NY)** | 54 | 1.6 | 1,383 | $487 | 95% | 22 | 79% | 23% | 92% | $33,131 |
| 138. University of Texas of the Permian Basin* | 54 | 1.8 | 484 | $519 | 70% | 22 | N/A | N/A | N/A | N/A |
| 138. Valley City State University (ND)* | 54 | 1.9 | N/A | $430 | 24% | 11 | N/A | N/A | N/A | N/A |
| 141. Davenport University (MI) | 53 | 1.8 | 1,796 | $574 | 29% | 18 | N/A | N/A | N/A | N/A |
| 141. East Carolina University (NC)* | 53 | 3.3 | N/A | $611 | N/A | 17 | N/A | N/A | N/A | N/A |
| 141. Liberty University (VA) | 53 | 2.6 | 39,319 | $340 | N/A | 21 | 60% | 11% | 74% | $27,300 |
| 141. Nicholls State University (LA)* | 53 | 1.9 | 122 | $250 | 69% | N/A | N/A | N/A | N/A | N/A |
| 141. Our Lady of the Lake University (TX) | 53 | 1.7 | N/A | $290 | 100% | N/A | N/A | N/A | N/A | N/A |
| 141. Sullivan University (KY)** | 53 | 1.2 | 268 | $292 | 44% | 19 | N/A | N/A | 76% | $22,508 |
| 141. William Woods University (MO) | 53 | 1.9 | 10 | $200 | 50% | N/A | N/A | N/A | N/A | N/A |

# ▶ Best Online Bachelor's Programs For Veterans

Which programs offer military veterans and active-duty service members the best distance education? To ensure academic quality, all schools included in this ranking had to first qualify for a spot in the overall online ranking, above. They had to be housed in a regionally accredited institution and were judged on a multitude of factors, including program reputation, faculty credentials, high student graduation rate and low graduate debt load. Secondly, because veterans and active-duty members often wish to take full advantage of federal benefits designed to make their course credits more portable and less expensive, programs included in the veterans-focused rankings also had to offer at least one credit-granting course listed in the Defense Activity for Non-Traditional Education Support (DANTES) Nationally Accredited Distance Learning Programs Catalog. They had to belong to an institution that is a member of the Servicemembers Opportunity Colleges (SOC) Consortium, is certified for the GI Bill, and participates in the Yellow Ribbon Program or charges in-state tuition – that can be fully covered by the GI Bill – to all veterans applying from out of state. Programs that met all criteria were then numerically ranked in descending order based on their ranking in Best Online Bachelor's Programs.

| Rank School (State) | Rank School (State) | Rank School (State) | Rank School (State) |
|---|---|---|---|
| 1. Central Michigan University* | 8. Regent University (VA) | 17. City University of Seattle | 27. Belhaven University (MS) |
| 2. Embry-Riddle Aeronautical University–Worldwide (FL) | 8. Washington State University* | 18. Charter Oak State College (CT)* | 27. Troy University (AL)* |
| 3. Arizona State University* | 10. University of Wisconsin–Platteville* | 18. University of Missouri* | 27. University of Nebraska–Lincoln* |
| 3. Indiana University-Purdue University–Fort Wayne* | 11. Ball State University (IN)* | 20. Kaplan University (IA)** | 30. Eastern Kentucky University* |
| 5. Fort Hays State University (KS)* | 12. Western Carolina University (NC)* | 21. University of Maine–Augusta* | 31. Peirce College (PA) |
| 6. Bellevue University (NE) | 13. California Baptist University | 21. Upper Iowa University | 32. National University (CA) |
| 7. University of Nebraska–Omaha* | 13. Drexel University (PA) | 21. Western Illinois University* | 32. University of Alabama–Birmingham* |
| | 15. Brandman University (CA) | 24. Regis University (CO) | 32. University of Cincinnati* |
| | 15. Sam Houston State University (TX)* | 25. Columbia College (MO) | 32. Western Kentucky University* |
| | | 25. Old Dominion University (VA)* | |

N/A=Data were not provided by the school. **1.** Tuition is reported on a per-credit-hour basis. Out-of-state tuition is listed for public institutions. **2.** Displayed here for standardization are four-year graduation rates. **3.** 2012 retention rate is published in place of a 2013 rate when the latter was not reported by school. **4.** Three-year graduation rate is published when a four-year rate was not reported by school. Ranked online degree programs may be less than four years old.

# Getting In

Haverford College in Pennsylvania

BRETT ZIEGLER FOR USN&WR

# 9 WAYS
## *to Convince Admissions You're a* WINNER!

*By* **KATHERINE HOBSON**

**NEWS YOU CAN USE**

Clara Perez knew she wanted to study architecture by freshman year of high school, when she spent hours building virtual houses for the characters in the computer game The Sims. Her college search was equally focused; she worked with her family and an independent counselor to come up with a short list of schools with strong architecture programs. When she decided after a campus visit that Syracuse University was the place, she made frequent contact with the recruiter for SU's architecture school as she worked on a portfolio. She scheduled an interview to show off her ability to speak on her feet. "I wasn't the girl with the strongest grades in high school, but I put myself out there," she says. This fall she'll be a sophomore at Syracuse.

An academic passion, initiative and a proven interest in a school are key to getting your foot in the door – and they're only some of the attributes admissions officers are looking for in their ever more competitive applicant pools. Sixty-four percent of colleges and universities surveyed by the National Association for College Admission Counseling saw a jump in the number of applications for entry in the fall of 2012, the most recent stats available, as students continued to apply to a greater number of schools and interest increased from abroad. There are 40 percent more international students in the U.S. now than a decade ago, according to the Institute of International Education.

The same forces are persisting this year, particularly at the top of the heap. Stanford University accepted just over 5 percent of the 42,167 applications it received for the class of 2018; Yale's acceptance rate was 6.3 percent.

Scary as those statistics may be, it's important to re-member that, on average, colleges are still accepting almost two-thirds of their applicants, according to NACAC. "For most kids, it's not that hard to get into college as long as you're doing the right thing," says Mark Montgomery, an educational consultant in Denver. U.S. News talked with admissions officers, independent college counselors and high school guidance counselors to find out what the right thing is.

## 1. Get a head start

Plenty of kids enter high school figuring they've got lots of time to perfect their act. But freshman year is not a dress rehearsal. "We do start really paying attention to students' grades in the ninth grade year," says Rick Clark, director of admission at Georgia Institute of Technology. "Selective schools will take the whole high school career into account."

Beyond attending to your grades, that means making sure you're on track from the outset to fit in all the courses you might need for admission, advises Thyra Briggs, vice president for admission and financial aid at Harvey Mudd College in Claremont, California. That might mean making sure you have advanced algebra under your belt by the end of sophomore year if a college wants to see a year of calculus, or that you're taking Spanish as a freshman if schools strongly prefer four years of a foreign language.

## 2. Consider your curriculum

Some things haven't changed. Grades in college prep courses still carry the most weight in admissions decisions. People who can show they've successfully challenged themselves in high school are "better prepared to handle college work," says Paul Marthers, vice president for enrollment at Rensselaer Polytechnic Institute in Troy, New York. At the same time, no one expects students to take every AP class offered. Better to do the best you can in the highest level classes that make sense given your interests and aptitudes, while getting eight to nine hours of sleep a night, advises Katy Murphy, director of college counseling at Bellarmine College Preparatory in San Jose, California, and president of NACAC. "We see too many kids taking advanced courses across the curriculum who crash and burn because they've taken on too much."

To repeat: It's most important to take AP classes in your areas of strength. And because your guidance counselor will send colleges a detailed profile of your school and its curriculum, the people vetting applications will know if you've taken wise advantage or gone after easy A's. "We don't need to see the student who intends to pursue magazine journalism in AP biology, chemistry, physics and calculus," says Laura Linn, director of admission at Drake University in Des Moines, Iowa. That person is probably better off with two advanced English courses; someone planning on ma-

*Clara Perez showed Syracuse her passion for architecture and a sincere interest in the school.*

joring in engineering, on the other hand, can prioritize AP math and science.

### 3. Hone your extracurriculars

Have you been joining a laundry list of clubs in order to look impressive? Stop, says Murphy. "Colleges are looking for two or three things done in depth," she says. The goal is to select a well-rounded class of freshmen who are passionate about their particular interests, and admissions wants to get a sense from your application of who you really are. It's even better if your activities show off your different facets – that you're an athlete also doing community service, or an actor performing research.

Even if you need to focus on making money during the summer, those months can often be used strategically to develop your story. Far from expecting you to treat July and August as vacation, "we want to see you doing something generally meaningful," says Georgia Tech's Clark. That doesn't imply an expensive enrichment or study abroad program, he says. Those are no more impressive than a summer job or volunteer activity close to home, and time spent sharpening your skills in a sport or artistic pursuit.

The key is to follow up on academic or extracurricular interests rather than just fill time between trips to the beach.

But best not to repeat the same experience over and over again, cautions Judy Muir, an independent college counselor in Houston. A dedicated baseball player who spends much of one summer practicing and playing, for example, might the next summer volunteer to help coach Little League.

### 4. Develop a smart short list

Picking colleges requires a long look inward as well as study of all those websites. "Pause and assess who you are, what you're good at," advises Muir. Then consider how your learning style and other preferences (large lectures? discussion-intensive seminars? a tight college community? Big Ten sports?) fit with each college's strengths.

Ted Spencer, director of undergraduate admissions at the University of Michigan in Ann Arbor, says you should be able to come up with five reasons for applying to every school on your list. Then run the list by your guidance counselor to be sure you're being realistic about the chances for admission. Some high schools have software that can tell you where you'd stack up against past applicants to a college. Make sure to include a few safe bets, suggests Caroline Brokaw Tucker, an independent college consultant at New Canaan, Connecticut-based Dunbar Educational Consultants – and that they are places where you'll be happy. Just in case.

### 5. Consider early options

Some 47 percent of colleges reported an increase in the number of applicants accepted through binding early decision for the fall of 2012 (meaning the students promised to attend if accepted), and 68 percent saw a jump in non-binding early-action acceptances (students get word early, without an obligation), according to NACAC. Montgomery always advises students to apply early decision if they absolutely know where they want to go and won't need to weigh financial aid offers, since colleges like to admit students who are a sure thing, and the odds of clearing the bar are often better. "We have kids whose applications we're reading in the regular decision round who go on the waitlist, when they would have been admitted early," says Mike Sexton, vice president for enrollment management at Santa Clara University in California.

But early decision has its disadvantages. You have to know your first choice very early senior year. And you have less bargaining power when it comes to financial aid, says Teresa Lloyd, founder of Grosse Pointe College Admissions Counseling in Grosse Pointe Park, Michigan.

### INSIDE SCOOP

**JASON LOCKE**
Associate Vice Provost for
Enrollment, Cornell University

## WHAT IF YOU'RE WAIT-LISTED?

If you agree to join the waiting list, always follow the instructions provided by the admissions office. Most institutions will ask you to reaffirm your interest and provide updated grade reports, new honors and any new activities. If you have questions, always contact the admissions office directly. And do not show up unannounced to press your case. This may actually hurt your chances. Finally, it is very important that you secure your place at another college by the deadline.

### 6. Show sincere interest

As it becomes easier for students to apply to multiple schools electronically and by using the Common Application, admissions officers are alert for "stealth candidates" who do nothing but fill out the forms. If you want to be taken seriously, "you've got to show them some love," says Tucker.

Visiting, the best way to get a feel for schools, is also the best way to show you're interested. Take the tour, but also meet with admissions officers. Ask questions. With a little notice, you can arrange to attend classes and meet with a professor whose area of research intrigues you. If you can't visit, take advantage of local college fairs and every other option for contact. "Write to the admissions office, sign up on their Facebook page – anything to let them know you think they're the bee's knees," says Montgomery.

"I made sure I stood out," says Abigail Fleming of Evansville, Indiana, who applied to 10 small liberal arts colleges and, after visiting a few, zeroed in on Beloit College in Wisconsin. She stayed in touch with the admissions office when she had questions, and even drove three hours to a college fair to connect with the school again. She's now a freshman at Beloit.

### 7. Ace the essay

The goal in choosing an essay topic is to give a sense of your personality to go with the grades and test scores – not to deliver a Big Think piece on world affairs, a common mistake. Often the best inspiration is a routine experience that can be mined for a larger theme saying something about how you tick. That's the approach taken by Max Farbman, an avid percussionist from Arlington Heights, Illinois. After several revisions, he sent off an essay about how he's happiest when he's part of the bigger picture of the orchestra, enjoying the moment as he waits for his parts. One college liked the essay so much it will be included in a packet for next year's applicants. Farbman is now at Yale.

The essay (or an optional personal statement) also provides a great opportunity to address apparent flaws in your application – poor grades during that long bout with mono sophomore year, for example. "Don't let us interpret that blindly," says Linn. If you simply screwed up, tell us the specifics of how you bounced back, suggests Kasey Urquidez, dean of undergraduate admissions at the University of Arizona.

### 8. Pay attention to details

Optional essays? Write them. A chance to elaborate on your extracurricular activities? Take it. For students on the bubble, that bit of extra effort can make the difference in whether or not you're admitted. Briggs, of Harvey Mudd College, advises putting serious thought into the teachers you ask for recommendations. "Don't always choose teachers who gave you a straight A," she says. A recommendation from a teacher who watched you struggle can "show how you respond to challenge." Finally, keep careful track of deadlines. And meet them.

### 9. Take the lead

Throughout the process, it's really crucial to remember that you, not your parents, are running the show. Take charge of creating your list, of arranging visits and interviews (and then do the talking), and of reaching out to the admissions office with questions on your own, rather than having your mom do it on her lunch hour. "It's refreshing when a student does that," says Clark, "because it's so rare." ●

Yale freshman Max Farbman wrote about his pleasure in being part of the big picture, the orchestra.

## The Pros' Pet Peeves

Here are a few moves *not* to make. Don't:

● **Use inappropriate email addresses.** "Like hotlady@gmail.com," says Laura Linn, director of admission at Drake University.

● **Ignore directions.** "Give us what we ask for," says Thyra Briggs, vice president for admission and financial aid at Harvey Mudd College. "We require one recommendation from a math or science teacher and one from a humanities or social science teacher." Students who bother only with the math or science suggest that "they're not going to embrace that [other] important part of the curriculum."

● **Neglect email.** "You may prefer texting and Twitter, but check your email," says Mike Sexton, vice president for enrollment management at Santa Clara University. "That's how we send out midcourse corrections and information."

● **Get sloppy.** "Don't use the wrong school name in your statement!" says Kasey Urquidez, dean of undergraduate admissions at the University of Arizona. Adds Ted Spencer, Michigan's director of undergraduate admissions: "We had a student who wrote how much time he'd spent after school torturing – not tutoring – students. Give it to an outside reader. And proofread." –*K.H.*

# A-Plus Schools for B Students

So you're a scholar with lots to offer and the GPA of a B student, and your heart is set on a great college. No problem. U.S. News has screened the universe of colleges and universities to identify those where nonsuperstars have a decent shot at being accepted and thriving – where spirit and hard work could make all the difference to admissions.

To make this list, which is presented alphabetically, schools had to admit a meaningful proportion of applicants whose test scores and class standing put them in non-A territory (methodology, Page 145). Since many truly seek a broad and engaged student body, be sure to display your individuality and seriousness of purpose as you apply.

## National Universities ▶

| School (State) (*Public) | SAT/ACT 25th-75th percentile ('13) | Average high school GPA ('13) | Freshmen in top 25% of class ('13) | School (State) (*Public) | SAT/ACT 25th-75th percentile ('13) | Average high school GPA ('13) | Freshmen in top 25% of class ('13) |
|---|---|---|---|---|---|---|---|
| Adelphi University (NY) | 1020-1220[9] | 3.4 | 64%[5] | St. John Fisher College (NY) | 990-1170 | 3.5 | 60% |
| American University (DC) | 1160-1350[2] | 3.7 | 78%[5] | St. John's University (NY) | 990-1210 | 3.4 | 42%[4] |
| Andrews University (MI) | 20-27 | 3.5 | 46%[5] | St. Louis University | 25-30 | 3.8 | 74%[5] |
| Arizona State University–Tempe* | 1020-1270[2] | 3.5 | 63% | Stony Brook University–SUNY* | 1150-1350 | 3.8 | 78%[5] |
| Auburn University (AL)* | 24-30 | 3.7 | 60% | Syracuse University (NY) | 1040-1270 | 3.6 | 71%[5] |
| Azusa Pacific University (CA) | 980-1190 | 3.6 | 62% | Temple University (PA)* | 1010-1230[2] | 3.4 | 52% |
| Ball State University (IN)* | 980-1170[2] | 3.4 | 52% | Texas Christian University | 25-29 | N/A | 75%[5] |
| Baylor University (TX) | 24-29 | N/A | 75% | Texas Tech University* | 1010-1210 | 3.5 | 55% |
| Biola University (CA) | 1000-1240 | 3.5 | 63%[5] | University at Albany–SUNY* | 1010-1180 | 3.6 | 53% |
| Clark University (MA) | 1110-1320[2] | 3.5 | 73%[5] | University at Buffalo–SUNY* | 1050-1260 | 3.2 | 63%[5] |
| Clarkson University (NY) | 1090-1290 | 3.6 | 76% | University of Alabama* | 22-30 | 3.6 | 60% |
| Colorado State University* | 22-27 | 3.6 | 52% | University of Alabama–Birmingham* | 22-28 | 3.6 | 56% |
| DePaul University (IL) | 23-28[2] | 3.6 | 57%[5] | University of Alabama–Huntsville* | 23-29 | 3.6 | 50%[5] |
| Drexel University (PA) | 1070-1310 | 3.4 | 61%[5] | University of Arkansas* | 23-28 | 3.6 | 57% |
| Duquesne University (PA) | 1050-1220[2] | 3.7 | 60% | University of Central Florida* | 1090-1270 | 3.8 | 71% |
| Florida Institute of Technology | 1030-1260[3] | 3.6 | 55%[5] | University of Cincinnati* | 22-28 | 3.4 | 50% |
| Florida State University* | 25-29 | 3.9 | 77% | University of Colorado–Boulder* | 24-29 | 3.6 | 56% |
| George Mason University (VA)* | 1050-1250[2] | 3.7 | 56%[5] | University of Dayton (OH) | 24-29 | 3.6 | 54%[5] |
| Hofstra University (NY) | 1050-1230[2] | 3.5 | 56%[5] | University of Delaware* | 1090-1300 | 3.5 | 72%[5] |
| Howard University (DC) | 980-1190[3] | 3.3 | 54% | University of Denver | 25-30 | 3.7 | 76%[5] |
| Illinois Institute of Technology | 25-30 | 3.6 | 74%[5] | University of Houston* | 1030-1250 | N/A | 69% |
| Indiana University–Bloomington* | 1060-1290 | 3.6 | 70%[5] | University of Illinois–Chicago* | 22-26[3] | 3.3 | 63% |
| Iowa State University* | 22-28 | 3.6 | 56% | University of Iowa* | 23-28 | 3.6 | 57% |
| Kansas State University* | 21-27[2] | 3.5 | 48% | University of Kansas* | 22-28 | 3.5 | 59% |
| Kent State University (OH)* | 20-25 | 3.3 | 40% | University of Kentucky* | 22-28 | 3.5 | 58% |
| Louisiana State Univ.–Baton Rouge* | 23-28 | 3.5 | 53% | Univ. of Maryland–Baltimore County* | 1110-1310 | 3.7 | 57% |
| Louisiana Tech University* | 21-26 | 3.4 | 51% | University of Massachusetts–Amherst* | 1110-1310 | 3.7 | 69%[5] |
| Loyola University Chicago | 24-29 | 3.7 | 68%[5] | University of Massachusetts–Lowell* | 1030-1230 | 3.3 | 51%[5] |
| Marquette University (WI) | 25-29 | N/A | 69%[5] | University of Mississippi* | 21-27[2] | 3.5 | 48% |
| Maryville University of St. Louis | 23-27 | 3.7 | 61% | University of Missouri* | 23-28 | N/A | 58% |
| Miami University–Oxford (OH)* | 25-30 | 3.7 | 71%[5] | University of Nebraska–Lincoln* | 22-28 | N/A | 52% |
| Michigan State University* | 23-28[3] | 3.6 | 66%[5] | University of New Hampshire* | 1000-1210 | N/A | 50% |
| Michigan Technological University* | 24-29 | 3.7 | 65% | University of North Carolina–Charlotte* | 1000-1170 | 3.8 | 55% |
| Mississippi State University* | 20-28 | 3.3 | 53% | University of Oklahoma* | 23-29 | 3.6 | 64% |
| New Jersey Institute of Technology* | 1030-1250 | N/A | 54%[5] | University of Oregon* | 990-1240 | 3.6 | 64%[5] |
| New School (NY) | 990-1240[2] | 3.2 | 42%[4] | University of Rhode Island* | 1000-1210[3] | 3.4 | 47% |
| North Carolina State Univ.–Raleigh* | 1150-1320 | 3.6 | 80% | University of San Francisco | 1070-1270 | 3.6 | 71%[5] |
| North Dakota State University* | 21-26[3] | 3.4 | 40% | University of South Carolina* | 1110-1300 | 4.0 | 66% |
| Ohio University* | 22-26 | 3.4 | 42% | University of South Florida* | 1080-1260 | 3.9 | 65% |
| Oklahoma State University* | 22-28 | 3.5 | 56% | University of St. Thomas (MN) | 23-28[3] | 3.5 | 50% |
| Pennsylvania State Univ.–Univ. Park* | 1070-1280 | 3.6 | 78%[5] | University of Utah* | 21-27 | 3.5 | 48%[5] |
| Purdue University–West Lafayette (IN)* | 1080-1320 | 3.7 | 80%[5] | University of Vermont* | 1080-1290 | 3.5 | 68%[5] |
| Rutgers, St. U. of N.J.–New Brunswick* | 1090-1330 | N/A | 74%[5] | University of the Pacific (CA) | 1030-1320 | 3.5 | 68% |
| San Diego State University* | 1000-1200 | 3.6 | 71% | Virginia Commonwealth University* | 1000-1210 | 3.6 | 50% |
| Seton Hall University (NJ) | 1020-1220 | 3.5 | 62% | West Virginia University* | 21-26 | 3.4 | 45%[5] |
| SUNY Col. of Envir. Sci. and Forestry* | 1080-1260 | 3.8 | 66% | | | | |

**Note:** Key to footnotes, Page 80.

Education with purpose. An incredible array of academic choices. Small, engaging classes that provide real-world skills. Experiential opportunities to put those skills into practice. A campus life enriched by arts and athletics. A beautiful suburban campus just minutes from Boston. A close-knit community. **That's Merrimack College.**

# Merrimack

**North Andover, MA** | **www.merrimack.edu**

# A-PLUS SCHOOLS FOR B STUDENTS

## National Liberal Arts Colleges ▶

| School (State) (*Public) | SAT/ACT 25th-75th percentile ('13) | Average high school GPA ('13) | Freshmen in top 25% of class ('13) |
|---|---|---|---|
| Agnes Scott College (GA) | 1010-1310[2] | 3.6 | 67% |
| Albion College (MI) | 22-28 | 3.5 | 52% |
| Allegheny College (PA) | 1070-1290 | 3.7 | 70% |
| Alma College (MI) | 22-27[3] | 3.5 | 53% |
| Augustana College (IL) | 22-27[9] | 3.2 | 51% |
| Austin College (TX) | 1100-1330[3] | 3.5 | 74% |
| Beloit College (WI) | 24-30[2] | 3.4 | 61% |
| Berea College (KY) | 22-26 | 3.4 | 73% |
| Berry College (GA) | 24-29 | 3.7 | 65% |
| Birmingham-Southern College (AL) | 23-27 | 3.5 | 56% |
| Calvin College (MI) | 23-29[2] | 3.7 | 55% |
| Carthage College (WI) | 21-27 | 3.3 | 44% |
| Central College (IA) | 21-26 | 3.5 | 53% |
| Coe College (IA) | 23-28 | 3.6 | 61% |
| College of Idaho | 21-27 | 3.6 | 55% |
| College of St. Benedict (MN) | 23-28 | 3.7 | 70% |
| College of Wooster (OH) | 25-30 | 3.7 | 73%[5] |
| College of the Atlantic (ME) | 1110-1330[2] | 3.6 | 69% |
| Concordia College–Moorhead (MN) | 22-28 | 3.6 | 62% |
| Cornell College (IA) | 23-29 | 3.5 | 69% |
| DePauw University (IN) | 25-29 | 3.8 | 78%[5] |
| Doane College (NE) | 21-26[3] | 3.5 | 46% |
| Drew University (NJ) | 990-1220 | 3.4 | 62%[5] |
| Earlham College (IN) | 1150-1340[2] | 3.5 | 60%[5] |
| Furman University (SC) | 1130-1340[2] | N/A | 76%[5] |
| Georgetown College (KY) | 20-25 | 3.3 | 48% |
| Gordon College (MA) | 1015-1292[3] | 3.6 | 55%[5] |
| Goucher College (MD) | 1010-1280[2] | 3.2 | 58%[5] |
| Grove City College (PA) | 1079-1334 | 3.7 | 65% |
| Gustavus Adolphus College (MN) | 24-30[2] | 3.6 | 67% |
| Hanover College (IN) | 1000-1200 | 3.7 | 66% |
| Hobart and William Smith Colleges (NY) | 1120-1290[2] | 3.4 | 63%[5] |
| Hope College (MI) | 24-29 | 3.7 | 64% |
| Houghton College (NY) | 980-1235 | 3.5 | 61% |
| Illinois Wesleyan University | 25-30 | 3.7 | 77% |
| Juniata College (PA) | 1040-1260[9] | 3.7 | 73% |
| Kalamazoo College (MI) | 25-30 | 3.6 | 80%[5] |
| Knox College (IL) | 25-30[2] | N/A | 59% |
| Lake Forest College (IL) | 23-28[2] | 3.6 | 59%[5] |
| Linfield College (OR) | 980-1200 | 3.7 | 72%[4] |
| Luther College (IA) | 23-29 | 3.7 | 56% |
| McDaniel College (MD) | 1000-1210[3] | 3.5 | 52% |
| Millsaps College (MS) | 23-28 | 3.6 | 59% |
| Muhlenberg College (PA) | 1140-1340[2] | 3.3 | 73%[5] |
| Nebraska Wesleyan University | 22-26 | 3.7 | 50% |
| Oglethorpe University (GA) | 1030-1240 | 3.5 | 55% |
| Ohio Wesleyan University | 22-27[2] | 3.4 | 55%[5] |
| Ouachita Baptist University (AR) | 21-27 | 3.5 | 53% |
| Presbyterian College (SC) | 1000-1210[2] | 3.5 | 61% |
| Ripon College (WI) | 21-28 | 3.4 | 53% |
| Roanoke College (VA) | 980-1190 | 3.4 | 42% |
| Salem College (NC) | 1000-1200 | 3.8 | 75% |
| Sarah Lawrence College (NY) | 1150-1350[2] | 3.6 | 66%[5] |
| Sewanee–University of the South (TN) | 26-30[2] | 3.6 | 72%[5] |
| Siena College (NY) | 1000-1200[3] | 3.4 | 58% |
| Simpson College (IA) | 21-27 | N/A | 58% |
| Soka University of America (CA) | 1080-1340 | 3.8 | 79%[5] |
| Southwestern University (TX) | 1055-1280 | N/A | 72% |
| St. Anselm College (NH) | 1060-1230[2] | 3.2 | 58% |

| School (State) (*Public) | SAT/ACT 25th-75th percentile ('13) | Average high school GPA ('13) | Freshmen in top 25% of class ('13) |
|---|---|---|---|
| St. John's University (MN) | 23-28 | 3.5 | 52% |
| St. Lawrence University (NY) | 1120-1310[2] | 3.5 | 71%[5] |
| St. Mary's College (IN) | 23-28[3] | 3.6 | 57%[5] |
| St. Mary's College of Maryland* | 1070-1310[3] | N/A | 64%[5] |
| St. Michael's College (VT) | 1060-1290[2] | 3.4 | 54% |
| St. Norbert College (WI) | 22-27 | 3.5 | 56% |
| Stonehill College (MA) | 1030-1230[2] | 3.3 | 69% |
| Susquehanna University (PA) | 1020-1230[2] | 3.3 | 52% |
| Thomas Aquinas College (CA) | 1160-1340 | 3.8 | 50%[5] |
| Transylvania University (KY) | 24-30 | 3.7 | 75% |
| Trinity College (CT) | 1150-1330 | N/A | 59%[5] |
| University of Minnesota–Morris* | 23-28[3] | 3.6 | 59% |
| University of North Carolina–Asheville* | 1100-1290 | 3.4 | 54% |
| University of Puget Sound (WA) | 1120-1330[3] | N/A | 51%[5] |
| Virginia Military Institute* | 1050-1250 | 3.6 | 48% |
| Wabash College (IN) | 1028-1250 | 3.7 | 72% |
| Wartburg College (IA) | 21-26[3] | 3.5 | 55% |
| Washington College (MD) | 1050-1280[2] | 3.5 | 62%[5] |
| Washington and Jefferson College (PA) | 1050-1230[2] | 3.3 | 70% |
| Westminster College (MO) | 21-27 | 3.4 | 50% |
| Westmont College (CA) | 1060-1310 | 3.8 | 66% |
| Wheaton College (MA) | 1110-1340[2] | 3.3 | 70%[5] |
| Willamette University (OR) | 1080-1310 | 3.7 | 75% |
| William Jewell College (MO) | 22-28[2] | 3.7 | 58% |
| Wisconsin Lutheran College | 21-27 | 3.4 | 44% |
| Wittenberg University (OH) | 23-28[2] | 3.4 | 49% |
| Wofford College (SC) | 1080-1260 | 3.5 | 77% |

## Regional Universities ▶

| School (State) (*Public) | SAT/ACT 25th-75th percentile ('13) | Average high school GPA ('13) | Freshmen in top 25% of class ('13) |
|---|---|---|---|
| **NORTH** | | | |
| Arcadia University (PA) | 1000-1178 | 3.6 | 62% |
| Assumption College (MA) | 1020-1215[2] | 3.3 | 40% |
| Bentley University (MA) | 1140-1310[3] | N/A | 75%[5] |
| Bryant University (RI) | 1050-1220[2] | 3.3 | 50%[5] |
| Canisius College (NY) | 980-1200 | 3.5 | 53% |
| CUNY–Baruch College* | 1130-1330 | 3.2 | 70% |
| CUNY–Brooklyn College* | 980-1170 | 3.3 | 50%[5] |
| CUNY–Hunter College* | 1070-1270 | 3.3 | 56% |
| CUNY–Queens College* | 1030-1220 | N/A | 65% |
| Emerson College (MA) | 1140-1320 | 3.6 | 68%[5] |
| Emmanuel College (MA) | 1000-1180[2] | 3.6 | 54%[5] |
| Ithaca College (NY) | 1080-1270[2] | N/A | 63%[5] |
| Le Moyne College (NY) | 980-1170[3] | 3.4 | 51% |
| Loyola University Maryland | 1100-1268[2] | 3.4 | 67%[5] |
| Marist College (NY) | 1090-1260[9] | 3.3 | 64%[5] |
| Nazareth College (NY) | 1020-1180[2] | 3.3 | 65% |
| New York Institute of Technology | 1020-1220 | 3.5 | 52%[5] |
| Providence College (RI) | 1050-1260[2] | 3.4 | 67%[5] |
| Quinnipiac University (CT) | 1000-1190 | 3.4 | 66% |
| Ramapo College of New Jersey* | 990-1200 | 3.2 | 52%[5] |
| Richard Stockton Col. of New Jersey* | 980-1170 | N/A | 60% |
| Rochester Institute of Technology (NY) | 1110-1320 | N/A | 64% |
| Rowan University (NJ)* | 1000-1230 | 3.5 | 63%[4] |
| Salisbury University (MD)* | 1080-1230[9] | 3.7 | 59%[5] |
| Salve Regina University (RI) | 1020-1190[2] | 3.0 | 45% |
| Simmons College (MA) | 1040-1250[3] | 3.4 | 61%[5] |
| St. Joseph's University (PA) | 1020-1200[2] | 3.5 | 52%[5] |

**Note:** Key to footnotes, Page 80.

## Regional Universities (continued)

| School (State) (*Public) | SAT/ACT 25th-75th percentile ('13) | Average high school GPA ('13) | Freshmen in top 25% of class ('13) |
|---|---|---|---|
| SUNY College–Oneonta* | 1020-1180 | 3.6 | 58%[5] |
| SUNY Institute of Tech.–Utica/Rome* | 1010-1160 | 3.4 | 45% |
| SUNY–New Paltz* | 1030-1220 | 3.6 | 70%[5] |
| SUNY–Oswego* | 1040-1180[3] | 3.5 | 55% |
| Towson University (MD)* | 990-1170 | 3.6 | 49% |
| University of Scranton (PA) | 1030-1210 | 3.4 | 59%[5] |
| Wagner College (NY) | 1050-1270[2] | 3.6 | 73% |
| West Chester Univ. of Pennsylvania* | 1020-1190 | 3.5 | 45% |
| **SOUTH** | | | |
| Appalachian State University (NC)* | 1050-1220 | 4.0 | 58% |
| Bellarmine University (KY) | 22-27 | 3.5 | 54%[5] |
| Belmont University (TN) | 24-29 | 3.6 | 61% |
| Christian Brothers University (TN) | 21-27 | 3.7 | 60% |

| School (State) (*Public) | SAT/ACT 25th-75th percentile ('13) | Average high school GPA ('13) | Freshmen in top 25% of class ('13) |
|---|---|---|---|
| Christopher Newport University (VA)* | 1070-1250[2] | 3.7 | 53% |
| College of Charleston (SC)* | 1070-1250[3] | 3.9 | 60% |
| Elon University (NC) | 1120-1320 | 3.9 | 63%[5] |
| Embry-Riddle Aeronautical Univ. (FL) | 980-1230[2] | 3.5 | 52%[5] |
| Harding University (AR) | 22-28 | 3.6 | 50% |
| James Madison University (VA)* | 1050-1240 | N/A | 45% |
| Kennesaw State University (GA)* | 990-1170 | 3.2 | 53%[5] |
| Loyola University New Orleans | 22-28 | 3.5 | 43%[5] |
| Mercer University (GA) | 1080-1270 | 3.7 | 72% |
| Rollins College (FL) | 1100-1290[2] | 3.2 | 67%[5] |
| Samford University (AL) | 23-28 | 3.7 | 59%[5] |
| Spring Hill College (AL) | 21-27 | 3.4 | 45% |
| Stetson University (FL) | 1070-1270[2] | 3.9 | 61% |
| Union University (TN) | 22-29[3] | 3.7 | 62% |
| University of Mary Washington (VA)* | 1010-1210 | 3.5 | 50% |

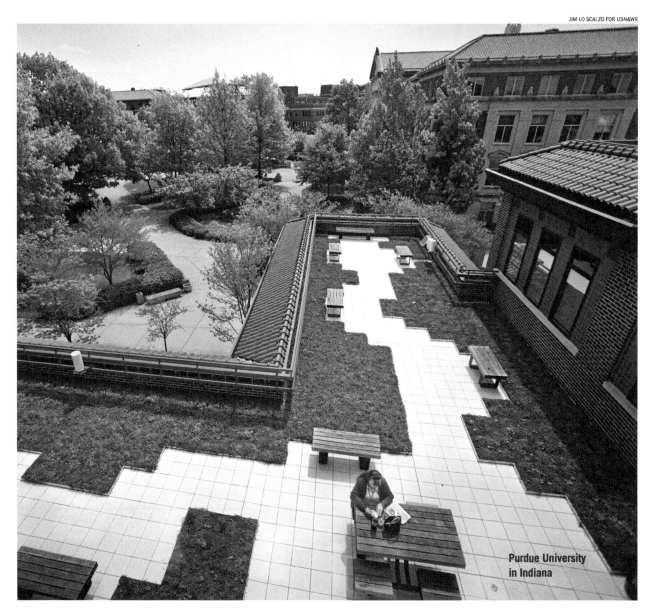

JIM LO SCALZO FOR USN&WR

Purdue University in Indiana

| School (State) (*Public) | SAT/ACT 25th–75th percentile ('13) | Average high school GPA ('13) | Freshmen in top 25% of class ('13) |
|---|---|---|---|
| Univ. of North Carolina–Wilmington* | 1110-1270 | 4.0 | 64% |
| University of North Florida* | 1080-1230 | 3.7 | 56% |
| University of North Georgia* | 1010-1190 | 3.5 | 70%[5] |
| William Carey University (MS) | 21-28[3] | N/A | 59% |
| **MIDWEST** | | | |
| Aquinas College (MI) | 21-26 | 3.5 | 45% |
| Augsburg College (MN) | 20-24[3] | 3.1 | 43% |
| Baker University (KS) | 21-26 | 3.5 | 42% |
| Baldwin Wallace University (OH) | 21-27[2] | 3.5 | 50% |
| Bethel University (MN) | 22-28 | 3.5 | 60% |
| Bradley University (IL) | 23-28 | 3.7 | 64% |
| Capital University (OH) | 21-27[3] | 3.4 | 45% |
| Carroll University (WI) | 21-26 | N/A | 58% |
| College of St. Scholastica (MN) | 21-26 | 3.5 | 55% |
| Concordia University (NE) | 21-27 | 3.6 | 43% |
| Concordia University Wisconsin | 20-25[3] | N/A | 43% |
| Creighton University (NE) | 24-30 | 3.8 | 68% |
| Dominican University (IL) | 20-24 | 3.6 | 48% |
| Drake University (IA) | 25-30 | 3.7 | 73% |
| Drury University (MO) | 22-28 | 3.7 | 59% |
| Elmhurst College (IL) | 21-26 | 3.3 | 47% |
| Franciscan Univ. of Steubenville (OH) | 23-28 | 3.7 | 52%[5] |
| Grand Valley State University (MI)* | 21-26 | 3.5 | 50% |
| Hamline University (MN) | 21-27 | 3.5 | 47% |
| Indiana Wesleyan University | 21-27 | 3.6 | 57% |
| John Carroll University (OH) | 22-27 | 3.5 | 51%[5] |
| Kettering University (MI) | 25-30 | 3.7 | 66% |
| Lawrence Technological Univ. (MI) | 22-29 | 3.4 | 52% |
| Lewis University (IL) | 21-26 | 3.4 | 47% |
| McKendree University (IL) | 20-25 | 3.4 | 43% |
| Missouri State University* | 21-26 | 3.6 | 53% |
| North Central College (IL) | 22-27 | 3.6 | 57% |
| Olivet Nazarene University (IL) | 20-26 | 3.5 | 48% |
| Otterbein University (OH) | 22-27[3] | 3.5 | 54% |
| Rockhurst University (MO) | 23-28 | 3.7 | 53% |
| St. Catherine University (MN) | 22-26 | 3.6 | 52% |
| Truman State University (MO)* | 25-30 | 3.8 | 80% |
| University of Detroit Mercy | 21-26[3] | 3.5 | 55% |
| University of Evansville (IN) | 23-29 | 3.7 | 66% |
| University of Findlay (OH) | 20-25[3] | 3.3 | 44% |
| University of Michigan–Dearborn* | 22-27 | N/A | 57% |
| University of Minnesota–Duluth* | 22-26 | 3.4 | 44% |
| University of Nebraska–Kearney* | 20-25 | 3.4 | 41% |
| University of Northern Iowa* | 20-24[3] | 3.4 | 45% |
| University of St. Francis (IL) | 21-25 | 3.4 | 46% |
| University of Wisconsin–Eau Claire* | 22-26 | N/A | 51% |
| University of Wisconsin–La Crosse* | 23-27 | N/A | 69% |
| Univ. of Wisconsin–Stevens Point* | 21-25 | 3.5 | 45% |
| Valparaiso University (IN) | 23-29 | 3.7 | 68% |
| Walsh University (OH) | 20-25[3] | 3.3 | 46% |
| Webster University (MO) | 20-27 | 3.4 | 42% |
| Xavier University (OH) | 23-27 | 3.6 | 54%[5] |
| **WEST** | | | |
| Abilene Christian University (TX) | 21-27 | 3.6 | 57% |
| California Lutheran University | 1010-1203 | 3.7 | 68%[5] |
| Gonzaga University (WA) | 1100-1290 | 3.7 | 68% |
| LeTourneau University (TX) | 1030-1300[2] | 3.6 | 67% |
| Loyola Marymount University (CA) | 1090-1300 | 3.7 | 57%[5] |
| Mills College (CA) | 1040-1250 | 3.6 | 71% |
| Oklahoma Christian University | 22-28 | 3.5 | 58% |
| Oklahoma City University | 23-29 | 3.6 | 61% |

| School (State) (*Public) | SAT/ACT 25th–75th percentile ('13) | Average high school GPA ('13) | Freshmen in top 25% of class ('13) |
|---|---|---|---|
| Pacific Lutheran University (WA) | 980-1220[3] | 3.7 | 70%[5] |
| Point Loma Nazarene University (CA) | 1040-1260 | 3.8 | 67% |
| Regis University (CO) | 22-27[3] | 3.5 | 56% |
| Seattle Pacific University | 1030-1250 | 3.5 | 57% |
| Seattle University | 1050-1260 | 3.6 | 62%[5] |
| St. Edward's University (TX) | 1020-1220 | N/A | 54% |
| St. Mary's College of California | 1010-1210 | 3.6 | 64%[5] |
| University of Dallas | 1090-1330 | N/A | 68%[5] |
| University of Portland (OR) | 1090-1300 | 3.6 | 70% |
| University of Redlands (CA) | 1030-1230 | 3.7 | 65% |
| University of St. Thomas (TX) | 1000-1210 | 3.6 | 54% |
| Western Washington University* | 990-1220 | 3.4 | 50% |
| Westminster College (UT) | 22-28 | 3.5 | 55% |

## Regional Colleges ▷

| School (State) (*Public) | SAT/ACT 25th–75th percentile ('13) | Average high school GPA ('13) | Freshmen in top 25% of class ('13) |
|---|---|---|---|
| **NORTH** | | | |
| Elizabethtown College (PA) | 1000-1230 | N/A | 65% |
| Lebanon Valley College (PA) | 1000-1220[2] | N/A | 74% |
| Messiah College (PA) | 1030-1260 | 3.7 | 68% |
| Wentworth Institute of Tech. (MA) | 1010-1210 | 3.1 | 40% |
| **SOUTH** | | | |
| Aquinas College (TN) | 23-27 | 3.5 | 43%[5] |
| Asbury University (KY) | 21-27 | N/A | 54% |
| Covenant College (GA) | 1060-1280 | 3.6 | 55%[5] |
| Florida Southern College | 1010-1180 | 3.6 | 56%[4] |
| High Point University (NC) | 980-1170 | 3.1 | 51%[5] |
| John Brown University (AR) | 23-29 | 3.7 | 65% |
| **MIDWEST** | | | |
| Augustana College (SD) | 23-28 | 3.7 | 63% |
| Benedictine College (KS) | 22-28[3] | 3.5 | 46% |
| Cedarville University (OH) | 24-29 | 3.6 | 61% |
| Clarke University (IA) | 20-25[3] | 3.5 | 46% |
| College of the Ozarks (MO) | 20-25[3] | 3.6 | 50% |
| Dordt College (IA) | 21-28 | 3.5 | 44% |
| Marietta College (OH) | 21-27[3] | N/A | 59% |
| Millikin University (IL) | 21-26 | 3.3 | 41% |
| Mount Mercy University (IA) | 20-24 | 3.3 | 41% |
| Northwestern College (IA) | 22-27 | 3.5 | 49% |
| Ohio Northern University | 23-29 | 3.7 | 69% |
| **WEST** | | | |
| Carroll College (MT) | 22-27 | 3.6 | 61% |
| Oklahoma Baptist University | 21-27 | 3.6 | 58% |

**Methodology:** To be eligible, national universities, liberal arts colleges, regional universities and regional colleges all had to be listed among the top three-quarters of their peer groups in the 2015 Best Colleges rankings. They had to admit a meaningful proportion of non-A students, as indicated by fall 2013 admissions data on SAT Critical Reading and Math or Composite ACT scores and high school class standing. The cutoffs were: The 75th percentile for the SAT had to be less than or equal to 1,350; the 25th percentile, greater than or equal to 980. The ACT composite range: less than or equal to 30 and greater than or equal to 20. The proportion of freshmen from the top 10 percent of their high school class had to be less than or equal to 50 percent (for national universities and liberal arts colleges only); for all schools, the proportion of freshmen from the top 25 percent of their high school class had to be less than or equal to 80 percent, and greater than or equal to 40 percent. Average freshman retention rates for all schools had to be greater than or equal to 75 percent. Average high school GPA itself was not used in the calculations identifying the A-plus schools. N/A means not available.

# The Value of a Gap Year

## TAKING TIME OFF AND PUTTING IT TO GOOD USE CAN MAKE YOU A BETTER STUDENT

By **MARGARET LOFTUS**

While most of her high school friends were cracking the books and tailgating at college football games last year, Macon Bianucci of Charleston, South Carolina, was deep in the African bush, rescuing injured and snared wildlife and learning how to track game. College was in her plans – just not quite yet. After being accepted at several top-tier schools the previous fall, the graduate of Ashley Hall, a private all-girls school, decided to defer her admission to Northwestern University in Evanston, Illinois. "I wanted a break from studying," she says. She also wanted to try living in Africa and decided this "was a good time to do it."

Long a rite of passage for affluent Brits, the so-called gap year – time spent traveling, volunteering or working between high school and college – is now really catching on among U.S. students. A survey by the American Gap Association, a nonprofit that accredits companies that coordinate these stints, found that enrollment in respondents' programs climbed 27 percent from 2012 to 2013. "We had 50 percent more participants than we anticipated. It's exceeded our wildest expectations," says Jim Zambrano, the CEO of First Abroad, a Boston-based gap-year company launched in 2013 after a sister company in the U.K. noticed a surge in interest from Americans. And colleges say they're seeing more requests for deferments. At Tufts University, for instance, the number of incoming students asking to take a gap year doubled over the last year.

Many students, like Bianucci, handle their own planning and logistics. But these days,

Macon Bianucci (above right) helps sedate an elephant at the Victoria Wildlife Trust in Zimbabwe. At Northwestern, right.

there's a whole industry bidding for gap-year business, from the Pioneer Project, through which students learn sustainable living skills like beekeeping and blacksmithing on a North Carolina farm to Art History Abroad, which offers six-week courses in Italy. Even colleges, including Tufts, Princeton and the University of North Carolina, have developed their own service-based gap-year offerings. "We aren't creating demand," says Alan Solomont, dean of Tufts' Tisch College of Citizenship and Public Service. "We're responding to appetite."

Burnout is one of the top reasons students take a break, according to an independent study of 280 gap-year participants by education policy experts Karl Haigler and Rae Nelson, authors of "Gap Year, American Style: Journeys Toward Learning, Serving, and Self-Discovery." That was true for Kenneth Hubbell, now a Princeton junior from Anchorage, Alaska, who pushed himself to excel in high school, was active on the debate team and volunteered regularly. "I poured so much energy into it. At the end of four years, I was tired of being that person," he says. He hadn't considered a year off until he received a brochure about Princeton's Bridge Year Program with his acceptance materials. He spent the next year living with a host family in Peru, taking Spanish lessons and working on service projects, including building a community park and assembling and distributing basic water filters, which reinforced his ambition to become a chemical engineer.

**Time to explore.** Subjects in the Haigler and Nelson study also cited a desire to find out more about themselves, a luxury in today's hypercompetitive culture, says Kim Oppelt, a former school counselor, now community relations manager at education solutions provider Hobsons in Arlington, Virginia. High school students used to have the time to sample a variety of electives, she notes, but they're "now under pressure to take advanced courses in every subject for all four years of high school. This gives them little time to explore their true interests."

That a trend in stepping off the

academic treadmill emerges in the wake of the Great Recession is no coincidence. Students and their families increasingly "are looking for value. They're thinking, 'if I'm spending this much on college, I want every year to count,'" says AGA Executive Director Ethan Knight.

Recent Cornell University grad Wes Cornell says his self-designed gap year doing scientific research around the world certainly matured him and shaped his academic focus. In Costa Rica, he researched the health care of workers at coffee farms through Duke University's Organization for Tropical Studies and did a program on sustainable development and tropical ecology with the environmental study abroad organization the School for Field Stud-

He cites Haigler and Nelson data showing that roughly 90 percent of those who opt for a gap year are back in school within a year of completing it. One of the goals of AGA, he says, is to figure out how to make federal financial aid available to students to use for gap years so the experience isn't available only to the affluent.

**For the masses.** Gap years don't have to cost a fortune, Zambrano says. First Abroad offers everything from bare-bones bus tours of Cambodia (starting at $879) to volunteering at a monkey rehab center in South Africa (from $1,059). While many high-end programs offer "a lot of hand-holding," he says, First Abroad's "give you the tools to head out there." For instance, the "Absolute Oz Jobs" package, which

tionately self-paying," says Solomont. "We want to make sure students who need financial assistance aren't precluded, so we'll provide aid."

Inspired by the Franklin Project, an initiative of the Aspen Institute that promotes national service for all Americans, the program will place participants in service organizations domestically and internationally. After the service year, they'll continue to interact with each other on campus through meetings, workshops and other events.

Counselors typically encourage students weighing a year off to apply to college anyway, while resources are easily accessible, and defer acceptance if they decide to go for it. On the other hand, students who are unsure of their college plans (or readiness) may benefit from putting off applying.

"It may be the case that waiting to apply during the gap year could improve your chances of getting in the school of your choice," says Haigler, who once worked as a college counselor. "You might also find a school that is more suited to your evolving interest, the skills and knowledge you develop and what you learn about yourself." One student he and Nelson heard from in researching their book said that when she compared college application essays she wrote after a gap year to those she'd written in high school, "she didn't recognize herself" in the earlier essays.

Oppelt recommends that students who are serious about a year off talk to college counselors and teachers, as well as someone who works in the field they may be interested in, to develop a plan. Bianucci had a very clear idea of her goals and intended path from the outset. She arranged her gap year (funded by her parents) by combining three stints in Africa: a field guide course outside of Kruger National Park in South Africa, where she lived and trained to become a professional safari guide; an internship at a safari company in Arusha, Tanzania; and an internship at Victoria Falls Wildlife Trust in Zimbabwe. Her experiences, she says, strengthened her desire to major in environmental science and return to Africa one day. Meantime, she's really looking forward to school. ●

RESEARCH shows that "GAPPERS" do better in school than **their peers.**

ies. He interned with the Colombia Nature Conservancy in Cartagena, and did research on viral pathways at a summer camp program at the Weizmann Institute of Science in Israel. Once he got to Cornell, where he studied ecology and agriculture policy, he noticed a lot of classmates struggling to find themselves. "Having had time off, I was able to figure out what really interested me," he says.

Indeed, research has shown that "gappers" perform better in school than their peers. A 2011 study at Middlebury College conducted by its former dean of admissions Robert Clagett, now director of college counseling at a high school in Austin, Texas, found that students who had taken a year off had consistently higher GPAs than those who didn't. "A lot of our students say when they enter as freshman that they have a greater sense of purpose in their studies," says Princeton Bridge Year Director John Luria.

Still, parents often take some convincing. Many are "afraid of kids getting off the college path," says Knight.

costs around $1,000 (not including airfare or visa fees), features a weeklong orientation as a prelude to launching young people with a one-year visa into jobs in Australia.

Programs for pre-freshmen sponsored by colleges typically cover part or most of the expense. At UNC, participants in the Global Gap Year Fellowship are granted $7,500 to develop their own six-month service experience. Past fellows have taught English to high school students in China and worked in a medical clinic in Madagascar. Princeton's Bridge Year is a nine-month tuition-free program that places small groups at sites in five countries – Brazil, China, India, Peru and Senegal – to do service projects. "We give them a challenge that's going to push them outside their comfort zone but provides support," says Luria.

Kicking off in the fall of 2015, Tufts' 1+4 program is aimed at democratizing the gap experience. "When we looked at our own data in terms of students who have deferred admission to take a gap year on their own, they are dispropor-

# Meet the
# New SAT

## HERE'S WHAT TO EXPECT FROM BOTH THE CURRENT VERSION
## AND THE OVERHAUL – ASSUMING YOU TAKE THE TEST

### By **DARCY LEWIS**

f you're reading this book as a junior or senior, you're preparing to sit – or have already sat – for the familiar 2400-point SAT, complete with its fancy vocabulary words and mandatory essay. But members of the class of 2017 will begin prepping next year for a completely overhauled test. Last March, College Board President David Coleman announced major revisions to the fall 2015 PSAT and the 2016 SAT, saying the SAT had "become disconnected from the work of high schools."

The changes, which include going back to the old 1600-point composite score based on 800-point math and "evidence-based reading and writing" sections, and making the essay optional, are intended to better reflect the material

*Jessa Stein (left), now a sophomore at Pitzer, opted to be judged on her other merits and held back her scores.*

students are, or should be, learning in high school, as well as to improve the SAT's reliability as an indicator of how prepared applicants are to tackle college work. The current test is designed more to get at innate abilities; hence the "scholastic aptitude" of the SAT's original name. The new test "aligns with the Common Core curriculum standards," says Kasey Urquidez, dean of undergraduate admissions at the University of Arizona, who believes that the changes will be beneficial. Defenders of the current test think the change could weaken what they see as an effective tool to identify smart, capable students at academically weaker schools.

One big innovation is the way vocabulary will be handled; rather than test students' knowledge of obscure words out of context (like "cruciverbalist," "mellifluous," or "prestidigitation"), the focus will be on so-called high-utility words that appear in many disciplines, and they'll be used in a passage.

For example, after reading a selection about population density that uses the word "intense," test-takers might be asked which word has the closest meaning: "emotional," "concentrated," "brilliant" or "determined." Angel Perez, vice president and dean of admission at Pitzer College in Claremont, California, thinks this shift will let students from all backgrounds show what they really know, not just what they've memorized in prepping. Gary Gruber, who has written more than 40 test prep books, remains a fan of the way the current test gets students to tap their critical thinking skills and knowledge of Greek and Latin roots.

## The new SAT will also require students to draw conclusions by

taking account of evidence, to revise and edit text, to analyze data and interpret graphs, and to solve the types of math problems most commonly seen in college courses and the workplace. It's no coincidence, observers say, that the new test will more closely resemble the ACT, which has been growing ever more popular. (The format of the ACT isn't changing, but the company plans to make the optional essay a more analytical exercise next year and break out new scores measuring job skills and proficiency in science, technology, engineering and math.) The redesigned SAT will last three hours, with an extra 50 minutes allotted for an optional essay in which students will analyze a passage and how the author builds an argument.

Another popular change is the elimination of the guessing penalty, the practice of subtracting points for wrong answers. "Being able to guess benefits those students who have some background knowledge," argues Rafael Figueroa, dean of college guidance at Albuquerque Academy in New Mexico.

Juniors and seniors, too, can take advantage of one much-heralded development that takes effect right away: the College Board's new partnership with the nonprofit Khan Academy to provide free online test prep materials. The idea is to start by taking a practice SAT, then master the material by watching in-depth explanatory videos and answering as many practice questions as you want. Starting with the 2015 PSAT, a personalized dashboard will allow students to track their progress.

Admissions deans and college counselors alike welcome the partnership as a possible step toward taming the over-

> THE CHANGES ARE MEANT TO BETTER REFLECT WHAT STUDENTS ARE, OR SHOULD BE, LEARNING IN HIGH SCHOOL.

wrought test prep culture that excludes many less savvy kids and those who are less affluent. "We want to assist students from all backgrounds – suburban, rural, inner city – so that they all have equal access to quality test prep materials, and now we can," says Mike Drish, director of admissions, recruitment and outreach at the University of Illinois at Urbana-Champaign.

Whichever test you take, devoting time to practice should increase your comfort level. But some experts advise against sitting for the real thing several times in an attempt to raise your score; some colleges may ask to see all your results – and they certainly want to see you engaged in more activities than test prep. Try to keep the testing in perspective, urges Stuart Schmill, dean of admissions at Massachusetts Institute of Technology. "There is some predictive value in SAT scores, but they are not determinative," he says. "Certainly there are students who get lower SAT scores who perform well here. And factors like persistence, resilience and organizational skills, which aren't measured on tests, also predict future academic success."

In fact, many fine colleges have concluded that they don't need test scores to make admissions decisions. Two that just joined the group this summer: Temple and Bryn Mawr in Pennsylvania. The National Center for Fair & Open Testing (fairtest.org) maintains a database of some 815 schools that are "test-optional" (applicants choose whether to submit scores) or that de-emphasize the tests. "I think taking standardized tests well is innate and doesn't necessarily show how well one will do in college or in life," says Jessa Stein of Denver, who chose not to send her SAT results of around 1800 to Pitzer College in California, her first choice. She wanted to be judged on her other strengths – teacher recommendations, essays and community service – and is now a sophomore at Pitzer.

Some test-optional schools later request scores for placement, merit aid consideration or internal research. "Many scores are extremely high and come accompanied by a note saying, 'I wanted you to judge me on what matters to me,'" says Martha Allman, dean of admissions at Wake Forest University, which asks freshmen to submit scores for research purposes only. That's "exactly what we like to hear." ●

---

### The Rollout

● **Classes of 2015 and 2016:** Take current SAT; free Khan Academy prep materials available now at khanacademy.org/sat.

● **Class of 2017:** Take redesigned PSAT in October 2015 and redesigned SAT beginning in spring 2016; free Khan Academy prep materials available beginning in spring 2015.

# Explore the U.S. News
# Community College Directory

Search among nearly 950 schools across the U.S.

**U.S.News** & WORLD REPORT

Visit: **usnews.com/education/community-colleges**

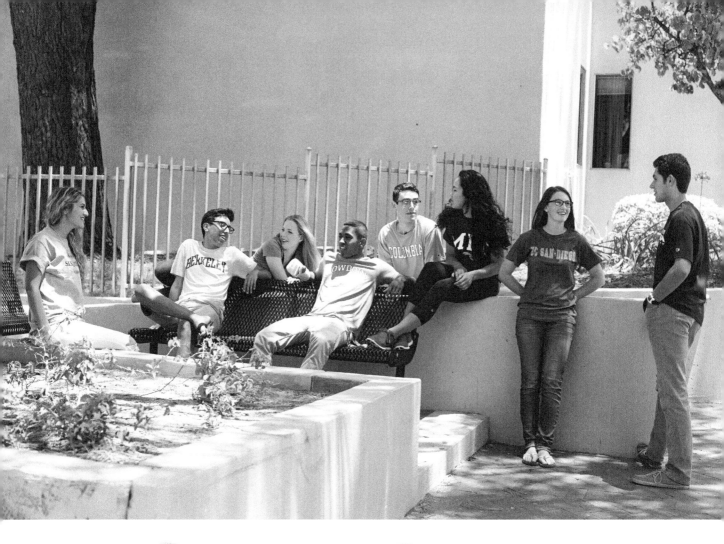

# We Did It!

## HOW EIGHT HIGH SCHOOL SENIORS MADE IT TO COLLEGE

### By CHRISTOPHER J. GEARON

**W**ant to know what the path to college acceptance will really be like? This past spring, U.S. News visited La Jolla High School in the San Diego Unified School District to ask several seniors who had recently gone through the process and were then weighing their options for lessons learned along the way – and their best tips for high school students just getting started.

Set in a postcard-perfect seaside community, La Jolla High is a comprehensive high school serving about 1,650 students. Because of the district's emphasis on school choice, students from an array of San Diego neighborhoods attend La Jolla. The school provides Advanced Placement courses in 21 curricular areas; 98 percent of students graduate, on average, and 70 percent go on to four-year colleges (about 22 percent go to a two-year school). White students comprise 56 percent of the student body, with Hispanics, Asians and African-Americans accounting for most of the rest.

Check out the varied routes that eight members of the class of 2014, now settling in for freshman year at a range of colleges nationwide, took to get there.

*Photography by* **BRETT ZEIGLER** *for USN&WR*

# Eric Tims

▶ After applying to three dozen schools, Tims is attending Bowdoin College in Maine – and it wasn't even one of his original 35. A high school running back, Tims started with a list of 18 possibilities, a combination of Division I and III schools that included places where he would want to play football (Harvard, Brown, Dartmouth and Yale) and places he wouldn't (the University of Colorado-Boulder and the University of Oregon). But the calls just kept coming in from football coaches.

Tims got into half of the colleges he applied to (including Colorado, Oregon, George Fox University in Oregon, and the University of Redlands and the University of the Pacific in California), but no Ivies. Harvard's coach referred him to Bowdoin, and "after doing a lot of research, Bowdoin was a no-doubter," he says. He could see that it was a strong school academically and liked the sense of community: "It was like a big family." In addition to suiting up for the Polar Bears, Tims plans to major in computer science.
**GPA:** 3.3 unweighted
**SAT/ACT scores:** 620 math; 500 critical reading; 530 writing
**Extracurrics:** Football and working in customer service at an auto detailing firm
**Essay:** How he grew personally and as a student and focused on schoolwork while aiming for a possible college football career.
**Big decision:** He had an option to do a fifth-year program at a boarding school for another shot at the Ivies but wasn't interested.
**Parental aid:** "My parents helped me a lot." Mom kept him organized, and Dad talked to coaches.
**Visits:** He toured just three schools: Bowdoin,

> **ESTABLISH RELATIONSHIPS WITH FACULTY OR COACHES.**
> –Eric Tims

Redlands and Pomona. "Bowdoin looks classy," he says.
**Do-over:** After finding out that he was close to qualifying for an Ivy, he says he "would have worked harder" freshman and sophomore years.
**Clincher:** Some $46,000 of Bowdoin's annual $58,000 price tag is covered by grants and other financial aid.
**Advice:** Do research to find schools of interest, then reach out to faculty or coaches to establish relationships that can help you get in.

# Josephine Camacho

▶ Camacho grew up in "the projects of San Diego," she says, a 40-minute bus ride and a world away from La Jolla. A part of the history she shared with colleges was that she'd grown up in a community no stranger to "drugs,

> **I PUT MY STORY OUT THERE ABOUT BEING FROM A TOUGH NEIGHBORHOOD.**
> –Josephine Camacho

gangs and violence." Camacho wants to combine her love of working with older people and an interest in business. Determined to take advantage of all La Jolla had to offer, she pushed herself academically, concentrating on mastering English, Spanish and French and striving for good grades. And she resisted the temptation to transfer to a less rigorous school closer to home, as some kids who are bussed in from afar opt to do after a year or so.

For financial reasons, she applied to only California publics – eight Cal State campuses and the University of California schools at Berkeley, Santa Barbara and Santa Cruz. She got into seven and chose UC-Santa Cruz.
**GPA:** 3.4 unweighted

**SAT scores:** 450 math; 400 critical reading; 410 writing
**Extracurrics:** Cheerleading; hostess and cashier at two restaurants, volunteer as a companion with the elderly, youth group leader and member of her church choir
**Essay:** "I put my story out there" about growing up in a tough neighborhood.
**Incentive:** She wants to finish what her mother, a Mexican university-trained accountant, had hoped to do – move out of the barrio and "achieve the American Dream."
**Regret:** Not studying for the SAT. "My classmates all had tutors and paid consultants." She didn't have the money or time.
**The finances:** The $34,000 in total costs will be covered by her father's unused GI Bill benefits and grants, some help from her parents and private scholarships.
**Advice:** It helped to keep separate folders on her laptop for each application, plus one quick-reference folder for PINs, passwords and usernames.

## Luis Galvan

▶ Galvan is a first generation college student, headed to UC-Berkeley to study biochemistry in hopes of becoming a doctor. With money tight and his mother supporting seven, Galvan was greatly aided by a program called Reality Changers, a San Diego nonprofit that provides youth from disadvantaged backgrounds with academic support, leadership training and assistance with application costs. Galvan credits the program – which

also helped arrange an internship with a UC-San Diego researcher working on fortifying proteins against viruses – for his landing at Berkeley and becoming a Gates Millennium Scholar. The Gates program will cover tuition and living expenses for his undergrad degree and for graduate degrees in certain disciplines.

Galvan got into several California state schools but was turned down by Harvard, Yale, Princeton and the University of Pennsylvania.
**GPA:** 3.9 unweighted
**SAT/ACT scores:** 630 math; 570 critical reading; 510 writing/26 composite
**Extracurrics:** Fight Against Cancer Club; Reality Changers ambassador in the community, volunteer on community landscaping projects and at a soup kitchen
**Essay:** He drew an analogy between his internship and his performance as a student.
**Big push:** He figures he

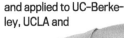

WORK A LITTLE – ONE HOUR – EACH DAY ON YOUR ESSAYS.
*–Luis Galvan*

logged 350 hours applying to colleges and for the Gates program. With the help of Reality Changers, he reworked his Gates essay 20 times.
**Regret:** Putting the college essays off. Would have been better to "do a little – one hour – each day."
**Heads-up:** Found the College Scholarship Service Profile more challenging than the FAFSA.
**Advice:** Get involved in clubs freshman year so you can become an officer as a senior.

## Emily Young

▶ An ACL injury led Young to become "fascinated" with biomedical engineering and biomechanics, she says. That interest led to an internship at a UC-San Diego biomechanics lab, where Young processed data and MRIs for research on rotator cuff problems. Young's interest,

internship and an early action application helped her get into the Massachusetts Institute of Technology, where she will study mechanical engineering with a concentration in biology and will also be playing lacrosse. She also got into Northeastern in Boston, and applied to UC-Berkeley, UCLA and

Georgetown but withdrew those applications once she heard from MIT. Young figures she put a solid month of work into the MIT application, including reading four years' worth of the university's admissions blogs, which offer advice and highlight accepted students.
**GPA:** 3.9 unweighted
**ACT score:** 33 composite
**Extracurrics:** Captain of field hockey and lacrosse teams, anti-bullying club; Girl Scouts, elementary-school lacrosse coach, internships in a biomechanics lab and as a pastry chef (which she suspects got admissions "to look at my application for a second longer")
**Essay:** She described the world she comes from, a family of "engineers, psychologists and doctors" who "inspire me to set high expectations for myself."
**Smart start:** Began considering schools at the end of her freshman year to improve her chances of being recruited for lacrosse.
**Realization:** "Coaches can't pull you through admissions" at schools like MIT.
**Lesson:** Her father, who hires fellows in his medical practice, showed her how little time it takes to screen an application (about 45 seconds).
**Advice:** It's better to focus on a couple of schools than to spread yourself thin by applying to 20. Also: "The first sentence of your essay needs to be incredible," and you need a strong finish.

## Trevor Menders

▶ Menders got into his top choice, Columbia University, to major in dance (and perhaps in chemistry or math as well). He had great grades

THE FIRST SENTENCE OF YOUR ESSAY NEEDS TO BE INCREDIBLE.
—Emily Young

DOUBLE-CHECK AND TRIPLE-CHECK YOUR APPLICATION.
—Trevor Menders

FIND SCHOOLS THAT ARE A GOOD FIT INSTEAD OF FOCUSING ON REACHES.
—Hallie Bodenstab

**SAT/ACT scores:** 720 math; 730 critical reading; 720 writing
**Extracurrics:** Editor and writer on the school newspaper; city ballet preprofessional division and junior company, took classical voice lessons
**Essay:** Making good decisions after seeing friends making not-great ones
**Noteworthy:** He scored 2100 on the SAT after prepping with a $2 used study guide. The next time he worked math problems over a weekend before prom and scored 2170 the morning after it. "The prom helped me to relax."
**Biggest surprise:** Admissions officers are willing to work with you. "Reaching out to these people is scary, but it's really helpful."
**Worked for him:** Doing one application at a time, rather than completing a number simultaneously.
**Campus visits:** Showing up paid off. On the tours, he ruled out applying to Johns Hopkins University and Amherst College because he didn't get the right "vibes."
**Advice:** "Double- and triple-check your application." He had to amend his Columbia app after submitting it because he put links in the wrong place and one of seven essays under the wrong prompt.

# Hallie Bodenstab

▶ Bodenstab's family hired an "expensive college counselor" to help guide the ap-

and SAT scores, but "did very little community service, did not attend a multiweek overpriced SAT prep course, and did not destroy my junior year with all AP courses," he says. "Instead, I pursued what I wanted to do, took the courses I wanted to take at the appropriate level – and it all worked out."

He does have a clear passion for dance, though: He was a trainee with the City Ballet of San Diego for the season ending in May. Menders also got into Tulane University in New Orleans; Pomona College, UC–Berkeley and UC–Santa Barbara in California; and Vassar College and Skidmore College in New York, but not Harvard and Princeton. He was wait-listed at Duke and Vanderbilt.
**GPA:** 4.0 unweighted

plication process, leaving the budding engineer, who wants to go into sales, with mixed feelings. The counselor "kept me on track," which avoided fights with Mom and Dad, and helped her land a spot at her top choice – Lehigh University in Pennsylvania, where she is a third-generation legacy – by advising her to apply early decision.

But a downside, she feels, was that she ended up taking chemistry and AP English – a struggle – rather than regular senior English and an arts class; she loves and is active in the performing arts. She made sure she had applications ready to send to several other schools, including Lafayette College in Pennsylvania, the University of Puget Sound in Washington, and Carleton College in Minnesota, in case Lehigh said no.

In her application, she highlighted being a strong student with an interest in science balanced by a deep résumé in theater, music and art. She also pointed to a summer computer science internship at a local firm (an experience that dissuaded her from majoring in the subject).
**GPA:** 3.9 unweighted
**ACT score:** 32 composite
**Extracurrics:** Drama club; singing, kickboxing, working as a singing princess at kids' birthday parties ("It pays well, and I'm never bored.")
**Essay:** In response to a Lehigh prompt asking her to describe what her 1 million-hit YouTube video is about: "Using my voice against authority, and doing the right thing"
**Helpful resource:** "The Hidden Ivies" book. "A lot of good schools don't get enough credit."
**Major selling point:** She was attracted to Lehigh's "real engineering" program and

undergraduate research opportunities in the field.
**Eye-opener:** While several liberal arts schools tout their 3-2 programs – three years to get one bachelor's degree are followed by two years at a partner engineering school for a second bachelor's – it seemed too big a risk. Only

TRY LISTENING TO YOURSELF MORE THAN OTHERS.
*–Kurt Rustin*

the top students are likely to make the leap.
**Stressor:** Applying to one school while everybody else seems to be applying to 20.
**Advice:** Find schools that are a good fit instead of focusing your energy on reach schools.

# Kurt Rustin

▶ Rustin is going to Northern Arizona University for mechanical engineering, hoping "to one day be an inventor" and hold his own patents. The track-and-field star and kayaker chose NAU for "its many labs that are about using your building skills, not just classroom smarts" because he considers himself to be more of a learn-by-doing kind of guy. "Learning on the job is definitely something I'm better at," he says.

Rustin didn't let ADHD and dyslexia hold him back, getting tutoring and extra help to succeed in AP and other challenging courses. He pursued his engineering interests by working as a hydroplane boat mechanical crew trainee and helping the Maritime Museum of San Diego build a full-scale replica of the Spanish galleon San Salvador. He also built La Jolla High's Latin de-

partment website. Rustin applied to 12 schools and got into almost all, including California Polytechnic State University, Purdue University in Indiana, Colorado School of Mines and the University of Colorado-Boulder; Bucknell University in Pennsylvania turned him down. He seriously considered CalPoly and Purdue, but had the impression they were

more classroom-based than "hands-on" NAU.
**GPA:** 3.8 unweighted
**ACT score:** 31 composite
**Extracurrics:** Track team captain, robotics team, La Jolla High garden club; flat water and ocean kayaking
**Essay:** Most of his schools didn't require an essay. Responding to one prompt asking what three items he would want with him if stranded in a foreign land, he explained why he would pick a machete, the American flag and a family photo album.
**Research tip:** On family road trips to areas he liked, he'd look up nearby colleges. "I'm a location guy" who thinks Flagstaff is beautiful.
**Key realization:** Learning shouldn't be a contest, so he didn't want to go to a school with "too much competition."
**Great perk:** While Rustin is an out-of-stater, he will pay tuition and fees of $14,000, about the halfway point between what in-state and out-of-state residents pay, thanks to being in one of the states in the Western Interstate Commission for Higher Education's Western Undergraduate Exchange.
**Biggest surprise:** "I only had to write two essays to apply to 12 colleges."
**Advice:** "Try to listen to yourself more than others."

# Colleen Mellinger

▶ In hopes of becoming a university physics professor, Mellinger will study chemical physics at the University of California-San Diego. Although UCSD is close to home, Mellinger is still getting used to Southern California, having moved to La Jolla from Missouri before her senior year. She applied to schools where she would be able to do "a lot" of undergraduate research, beginning freshman year. "I also wanted to play college tennis," she says.

With interests ranging from sports to science competitions and community service, she highlighted herself as well-rounded in her applications. Mellinger also got into UC-Berkeley, Case Western Reserve in Cleveland and the University of Tulsa, and was wait-listed by Washington University in St. Louis, the University of Chicago and Johns Hopkins in Baltimore. She visited several colleges and "fell in love" with UCSD.

**GPA:** 3.9 unweighted
**SAT/ACT scores:** 760 math; 600 critical reading; 700 writing/30 composite
**Extracurrics:** Tennis team captain, archery team captain, Science Olympiad, technology club, academic team; volunteer with the Red Cross.
**Essay:** On being an inquisitive knowledge junkie: "Why? That's the question I always ask myself. Why do people do what they do? Why do magnets stick together? Why does 'knife' start with a 'k'?"
**Stressor:** Applying to college at the same time she was getting adjusted to a new school and new part of the country.
**Off the list:** Stanford. After visiting, "I didn't think it would be a good fit for me. I wanted more balance between academics and social."
**Do-over:** Would have started earlier. "It all came so fast."
**Need for structure:** Applying to colleges is a lesson in organization. "I'm very much of a list person."
**Notable step:** She took the SAT four times and the ACT three times. Overkill? Her overall scores didn't rise by a lot, but she was pleased by her improvement in various sections.
**Advice:** Anything you do, write it down so you can remember later to reference it on applications. She had volunteered to help clean up in Joplin, Missouri, after a tornado hit, but nearly forgot to say so. ●

> **ANYTHING YOU DO, WRITE IT DOWN, SO YOU REMEMBER LATER.**
> *—Colleen Mellinger*

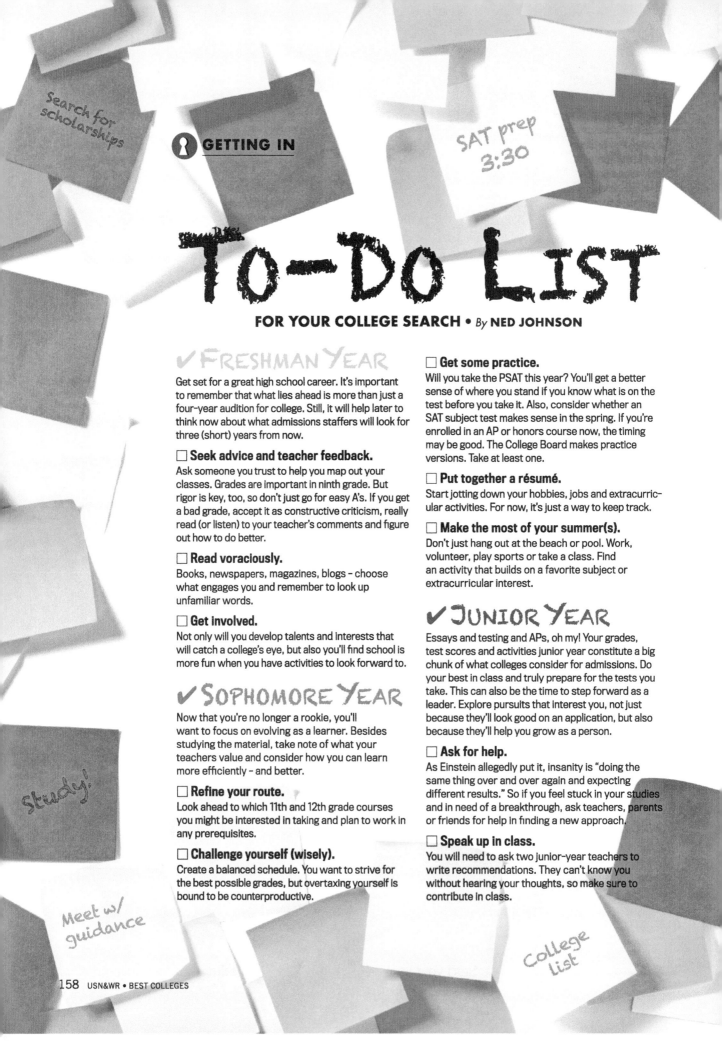

🔑 **GETTING IN**

# TO-DO LIST

## FOR YOUR COLLEGE SEARCH • *By* NED JOHNSON

### ✔ FRESHMAN YEAR

Get set for a great high school career. It's important to remember that what lies ahead is more than just a four-year audition for college. Still, it will help later to think now about what admissions staffers will look for three (short) years from now.

#### ☐ Seek advice and teacher feedback.
Ask someone you trust to help you map out your classes. Grades are important in ninth grade. But rigor is key, too, so don't just go for easy A's. If you get a bad grade, accept it as constructive criticism, really read (or listen) to your teacher's comments and figure out how to do better.

#### ☐ Read voraciously.
Books, newspapers, magazines, blogs – choose what engages you and remember to look up unfamiliar words.

#### ☐ Get involved.
Not only will you develop talents and interests that will catch a college's eye, but also you'll find school is more fun when you have activities to look forward to.

### ✔ SOPHOMORE YEAR

Now that you're no longer a rookie, you'll want to focus on evolving as a learner. Besides studying the material, take note of what your teachers value and consider how you can learn more efficiently – and better.

#### ☐ Refine your route.
Look ahead to which 11th and 12th grade courses you might be interested in taking and plan to work in any prerequisites.

#### ☐ Challenge yourself (wisely).
Create a balanced schedule. You want to strive for the best possible grades, but overtaxing yourself is bound to be counterproductive.

#### ☐ Get some practice.
Will you take the PSAT this year? You'll get a better sense of where you stand if you know what is on the test before you take it. Also, consider whether an SAT subject test makes sense in the spring. If you're enrolled in an AP or honors course now, the timing may be good. The College Board makes practice versions. Take at least one.

#### ☐ Put together a résumé.
Start jotting down your hobbies, jobs and extracurricular activities. For now, it's just a way to keep track.

#### ☐ Make the most of your summer(s).
Don't just hang out at the beach or pool. Work, volunteer, play sports or take a class. Find an activity that builds on a favorite subject or extracurricular interest.

### ✔ JUNIOR YEAR

Essays and testing and APs, oh my! Your grades, test scores and activities junior year constitute a big chunk of what colleges consider for admissions. Do your best in class and truly prepare for the tests you take. This can also be the time to step forward as a leader. Explore pursuits that interest you, not just because they'll look good on an application, but also because they'll help you grow as a person.

#### ☐ Ask for help.
As Einstein allegedly put it, insanity is "doing the same thing over and over again and expecting different results." So if you feel stuck in your studies and in need of a breakthrough, ask teachers, parents or friends for help in finding a new approach.

#### ☐ Speak up in class.
You will need to ask two junior-year teachers to write recommendations. They can't know you without hearing your thoughts, so make sure to contribute in class.

*[note: find a calc. tutor]*

*[note: Practice some test questions]*

*[note: Ask Mr. S for a rec.]*

*[note: Work w/ Dad on FAFSA]*

# TO-DO LIST CONTINUED

☐ **Sleep.**
The average 16-year-old brain needs over nine hours of sleep to function at 100 percent, and that's exactly where you want to be.

☐ **Plan your testing calendar.**
Test scores matter (along with grades), so talk with your parents and guidance counselor about which ones to take and when, and how to prepare for them. First up, the PSAT. If your 10th-grade scores put you in reach of a national merit scholarship, it might be wise to spend concentrated time prepping. Then take the SAT or ACT in winter or early spring. Don't worry if you don't get your ideal score; you can try again. The SAT subject tests are also an option for May or June in areas where you shine or in subjects you covered junior year.

☐ **Get involved.**
It's great to show you've worked hard, are dedicated to an activity, play well with others - and can lead them. Start an arts discussion group that goes to museum openings, say, or be voted team captain.

☐ **Begin building your college list.**
Once you have gotten your test scores, talk to a counselor and start putting together a list of target schools, reaches and safeties. Make use of new technology and apps to aid your research. Explore college websites and resources like ed.gov/finaid and usnews.com/bestcolleges. (While you're online, be sure to clean up your Facebook act. It might get a look.)

☐ **Make some campus visits.**
Spring break and summer vacation are ideal times to check out a few campuses. Attend college fairs and talk with the folks behind the tables. They can give you a feel for their school and some good future contacts.

☐ **Write.**
Procrastination doesn't make for a good college essay. Aim to have first drafts done by Labor Day. Share them with an English teacher or counselor.

## ✔ SENIOR YEAR

You made it. Let's party! Well, not quite yet. This will also be a year of hard work and continued preparation. Colleges do consider senior-year transcripts. They can and will rescind offers to students who slack off, so stay focused.

☐ **Finish testing and check the boxes.**
You're in the final stretch. If necessary, retake the SAT, ACT or subject tests. The early fall test dates will give you time to apply early. Also, make sure you're completing all graduation requirements as well as course requirements for your target colleges.

☐ **Ask for recommendations.**
Early in the school year, ask two teachers if they are willing to write a letter of recommendation for you. Choose teachers with whom you have a good relationship and who will effectively communicate your academic and personal qualities. You will want people who can offer different perspectives on your performance. Be sure to update and polish your résumé, too; it will come in handy when you're filling out applications and preparing for admissions interviews.

☐ **Apply.**
Fill out each application carefully and ask someone to look over your essays critically. Check that your colleges have received records and recs from your high school, and have your SAT or ACT scores officially sent in. A month from the date you submit your application, call the college and confirm that it is complete.

☐ **Follow the money.**
Many colleges require that all of your financial aid application forms be turned in by February. But the earlier the better.

☐ **Make a choice.**
Try to visit the colleges where you've been accepted again. Talk with alumni, attend an accepted-student reception. Then confidently make your college choice official by sending in your deposit. Done!

**Ned Johnson** is founder of and tutor-geek at PrepMatters (prepmatters.com) where, along with colleagues, he torments teens with test prep, educational counseling and general attempts to help them thrive. He also is co-author of "Conquering the SAT: How Parents Can Help Teens Overcome the Pressure and Succeed."

*[note: begin writing essay-]*

ISTOCKPHOTO

# Build Your Plan Online

Start Now at USNewsUniversityDirectory.com/Build

### Connect
with more than
1,900 top colleges
and universities

### Target
your search to the
schools that best
meet your needs

### Access
the latest education
news from *U.S. News
& World Report*

### Discover
how to get more
financial aid with our
free, expert guide

Get Free Assistance
With Your School Search:

# 855-237-2180

The #1 Authority on the Nation's Best Colleges

## GRINNELL, IOWA
## ...Grinnell College
### Jeremy Sanchez, '14

Grinnell fosters a sense of community among students and a desire to serve the "common good," which was obvious from my first visit to the school. A first-year student showed me around and, when I asked about the science facilities and professors, he found

## NEW YORK CITY
## ...Barnard College
### Gabrielle Davenport, '15

I first learned about Barnard when my older sister attended. Visiting campus, I was struck by how excited and confident the students seemed. When I applied, I felt this historic women's college would allow me to explore my varied interests and not press me to specialize too quickly, as I worried might happen at other schools. The campus community itself feels small and personal. I've been able to pursue my interests in hip-hop, wellness and African diasporas.

Barnard encourages students to take initiative, and one of my most rewarding experiences was performing in – and helping organize – a conference celebrating the work of the noted black author Ntozake Shange, a Barnard alumna. The college's partnership with Columbia University gives us access to the resources of an Ivy League institution, while the incomparable New York City lies just outside our gates, offering me the chance to apply what I've learned to real-world situations. Over my years at Barnard, I have built warm relationships with faculty members and know that they will continue to be resources and mentors for me after I graduate. ●

friends who could answer my questions firsthand. The college offers many opportunities to apply what you learn in the classroom. For example, I performed enzyme kinetics research with a dedicated adviser in a biochemical lab and took advantage of the college's many service-learning and volunteer opportunities. For example, over several vacations I joined the student service organization, Alternative Break, on different trips, including one I led that involved working in a self-sustaining farming community that doubles as a home and workplace for people with special needs. Because of Grinnell's active study abroad program, I spent a semester in Marseille, France, where I became fluent in French. The college supported my successful application for a Fulbright scholarship, and after teaching for a year in Korea, I hope to go on to medical school. Grinnell opened doors for me that once seemed unimaginable to a first-generation Latino student. ●

# Picked...

GAMBIER, OHIO

## ...Kenyon College

### Rebecca Katzman, '14

Kenyon had the academic prestige of all of those East Coast liberal arts colleges I visited, but was the only school where I wrote down observations such as "comfortable feeling" and "happy people." It attracts students from all over the world, yet this beautiful middle-of-nowhere hilltop campus in the Midwest has a protective boarding school feel (earning it the name Kamp Kenyon), that is at once immersive and all-encompassing. Yet not far from campus, you'll find a rich agricultural landscape and people of vastly different political and socioeconomic backgrounds. As a sociology major and as the manager of Kenyon's Rural Life Center, I've met some of these people on projects ranging from an oral history of an Amish-run produce auction to a photo shoot involving local gun enthusiasts. I appreciate that Kenyon emphasizes writing throughout the curriculum and, as an English minor, I've been able to take classes with amazing professors like David Lynn, editor of the famous "Kenyon Review." I feel the college has prepared me for the future as I head off now to New York on a fellowship with a new media group. ●

Washington University in St. Louis

# Finding the Money

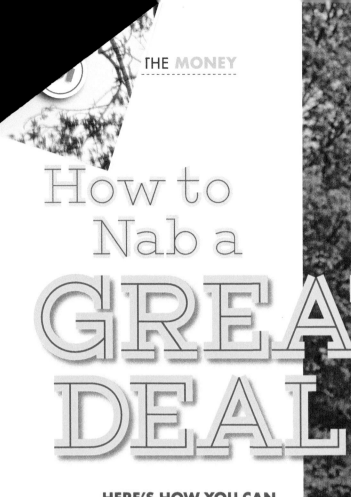

# How to Nab a GREAT DEAL

## HERE'S HOW YOU CAN NEGOTIATE THE FATTEST POSSIBLE AID PACKAGE

*By* **ARLENE WEINTRAUB**

**NEWS YOU CAN USE**

Heather McDonnell, associate dean of financial aid and admission at Sarah Lawrence College in Bronxville, New York, was shopping at the grocery story a few years ago when a man came up to her and appealed for mercy. It was a father who recognized McDonnell from a high school presentation she had given, who wanted to sweet-talk her into handing over a little more cash to cover the college's tuition (now $49,680 a year).

McDonnell prefers that parents email their appeals, but she can sympathize with that dad's desperation. "We've been witnessing an erosion of state and federal funding for years," McDonnell says. Ten years ago, for example, Sarah Lawrence got about $250,000 in Federal Supplemental Education Opportunity Grants for low-income students. By 2014, that figure had dropped to $137,728.

Sarah Lawrence is far from the only school feeling the financial-aid squeeze. The lingering effects of the recession and sputtering

University of Illinois students Nick and Alex Fregeau both snagged a scholarship for descendants of World War I veterans.

economy have exacerbated family need even as they have hurt endowments, and last year, budget cuts hit federal financial-aid programs hard. The situation has improved only slightly this year.

Still, resourceful parents and students will find there's plenty of money out there for those who know where to look – and how to speak up when that fat welcome package announces a scrawnier-than-expected award.

## Before you try to knock down the price

tag of your child's dream school, it's vital to understand the elements of the typical aid package. The first is federal need-based aid, which includes grants, funding for work-study jobs and subsidized Stafford loans (meaning the government pays the interest for you while you're in school). This aid is determined by your family's financial information on the Free Application for Federal Student Aid, or FAFSA. Families with exceptional need may also qualify for a federal Perkins loan. Then there are merit scholarships offered by the institutions themselves for academic achievements or talents.

Finally, there are federal loans that aren't subsidized, for people who don't qualify for that perk or who need more, and parent PLUS loans for Mom and Dad. An incoming freshman can borrow up to $5,500 in Stafford loans, of which no more than $3,500 can be subsidized. (The limits rise in later years and for students who are independent of their parents.) The interest rate on Staffords is now 4.66 percent.

Retired pharmaceutical executive David Goldman, of Flemington, New Jersey, learned the art of negotiating when the oldest of his four children got into two schools she liked. "We went to both colleges and showed each one the other college's offer," says Goldman. "We actually found they were very responsive. They might not like the word 'negotiation,' but clearly this was a negotiation." Using that tactic and others, such as nudging his kids toward well-funded private colleges likely to reward their academic achievements, Goldman estimates he has obtained over $200,000 in merit

### INSIDE SCOOP

**MARK KANTROWITZ**
**Senior vice president and publisher, Edvisors Network; financial aid expert**

## BEWARE, IF YOU BORROW

The idea is to minimize debt. Live like a student while you're in school so you don't have to live like a student after you graduate. A good rule of thumb: Your total student loan debt should be less than your starting salary. Borrow federal first because federal loans are cheaper; they're more available, and they have better repayment terms. Federal loans have fixed rates; most private student loans have variable rates. Parents shouldn't borrow more – for all their children – than their current annual income, and their goal should be to pay off the loans in 10 years or by retirement, whichever comes first.

aid unrelated to need for his kids, including his youngest, Michael, now a senior at Worcester Polytechnic Institute in Massachusetts. (His oldest ended up at Muhlenberg College in Pennsylvania, a choice that Goldman estimates saved $13,000 a year.)

It's important to know, too, that colleges that give you the same bottom line can get there different ways. Schools have plenty of leeway in how they give grants and loans; a much-desired viola player with perfect SAT scores might get 75 percent grants and 25 percent loans, say, while you're offered just the

opposite. You're clearly better off with the biggest possible handout.

But you can't assume you'll save by limiting your choices to public schools, warns Beth Walker, a financial planner at Strategic Wealth Associates in Colorado Springs. "The majority of what state schools have to offer is loans," she says. Well-endowed private colleges often "can give away more free money."

According to a survey released in 2013 by the National Association of College and University Business Officers, 65 percent of private colleges increased the amount by which they "discount" tuition via grants and scholarships for the 2011-2012 year. The average discount rate reached 45 percent in the fall of 2011.

Even if your child isn't a sought-after scholar, you may be able to successfully appeal for more funding after you receive your award letters. Linda Parker, director of financial aid at Union College in Schenectady, New York, says she often reconsiders aid packages when family circumstances have changed since the application arrived – a parent has lost a job or become ill, say. "If they document that," she says, "often students receive increased awards."

Or perhaps you face a challenge not accounted for on the FAFSA form. When Elizabeth Avery's daughter, Charlotte, was accepted by Union a year ago, she was thrilled, but there was a problem: Her father's take-home pay was going to fluctuate over the next few years because of an arrangement with a new employer. "We may look good on paper, but what we can afford is very different from what the government determined we can afford," says Avery, a relocation specialist in Pittsfield, Massachusetts. She sent an email to the aid office spelling out the family's circumstances. Charlotte received a $10,000 merit scholarship that renews every year.

It also can be worth your time to seek scholarships off the beaten path. By searching sites like Fastweb.com, Susan Fregeau, a certified public accountant in Westmont, Illinois, discovered the Laverne Noyes Foundation Scholarship, offered to descendants of people who served overseas in World War I. "I do genealogy, so I knew where Grandpa fought at that time," Fregeau

# Choose the Student Loan with No Origination Fees

Every family is different when it comes to saving, planning, and paying for higher education. When scholarships, grants, and federal student loans aren't enough to cover college expenses, consider a private student loan from Sallie Mae®.

**Choose the Smart Option Student Loan® with:**

• **Choice of interest rates,** variable or fixed

• **No fees** for origination

• **Flexible options** for repayment

• **Money-saving** benefits

• **Ability to apply for cosigner release** after graduation. For additional cosigner release eligibility criteria go to SallieMae.com/cosignerrelease

**The Sallie Mae Smart Option Student Loan**

Learn more at **SallieMae.com/USNews** Or call **1-866-425-2952**

**Encouraging Responsible Borrowing**

Sallie Mae has helped more than 30 million Americans pay for college since 1972. We encourage students and families to supplement their savings by exploring grants, scholarships, federal and state student loans, and to consider the anticipated monthly payments on their total student loan debt and their expected future earnings before considering a private education loan.

This information is for degree-granting institutions only. Credit criteria and eligibility requirements apply.

WE RESERVE THE RIGHT TO MODIFY OR DISCONTINUE PRODUCTS, SERVICES, AND BENEFITS AT ANY TIME WITHOUT NOTICE. CHECK SALLIEMAE.COM FOR THE MOST UP-TO-DATE PRODUCT INFORMATION.

Smart Option Student Loans are made by Sallie Mae Bank or a lender partner. The Sallie Mae logo, Sallie Mae, and Smart Option Student Loan are service marks or registered service marks of Sallie Mae Bank or its subsidiaries. SLM Corporation and its subsidiaries, including Sallie Mae Bank, are not sponsored by or agencies of the United States of America. ©2014 Sallie Mae Bank. All rights reserved. SMSCH MKT9805 0814 says. Her oldest son, Nick, got $5,000 to help pay his four years of tuition at the University of Illinois. He graduated last spring and is starting law school there this fall. Younger brother Alex, now a junior at U of I, received $2,000 from Laverne Noyes for the 2013-2014 academic year.

To help families figure out what college is really going to cost, the Department of Education requires all schools to post "net price calculators" on their websites. The calculators use a family's financial information to estimate the final bill, accounting for the federal and state aid the student is likely to receive. College advisors warn parents not to take an estimate as gospel, though. The quality of the tool varies by school, and it may not collect all the information it needs to spit out a truly accurate figure.

"It's a great thing to examine, but all you're going to get is a ballpark," says William Wozniak, director of marketing at ISM College Planning, an Indianapolis nonprofit that counsels high school students on the application process. What's more, he says, many schools aren't diligent about updates. "Sometimes the calculator is really from the year before and doesn't include the new cost of attendance," he says.

### If you've snatched up all the free money

you can find and need to fill in the gaps with loans, be aware of the long-term ramifications. Subsidized loans cost less over the long run because the government pays the interest while the student is in school. The government also covers it during the six months after graduation before repayment starts, and during any period of deferment for grad school or a period of unemployment, say. Congress in 2012 extended low student-loan interest rates but temporarily did away with the grace period after graduation, so students who received direct subsidized loans between July 1, 2012 and July 1, 2014, must either pay interest that accrues then or it will be added to their principal balance.

Patricia Seaman, a senior director at the National Endowment for Financial Education in Denver, suggests that families look at entry-level sala-

## 6

There's **plenty of** MONEY out there if you know **where to look** – and how to SPEAK UP when that fat welcome package announces a **SCRAWNY** award.'

ries in the fields the student is considering, then calculate just how much of a burden repayment will be. "There's a huge difference between petroleum engineering, where salaries are really high, and social work, which is really low," Seaman says. "That social worker won't be able to buy a car off the bat and will be eating mac and cheese and ramen until she advances a bit."

And as you weigh whether to grab that parent PLUS loan the acceptance letter is offering, you may want to look into cheaper options. The interest rate on PLUS loans is currently fixed at 7.21 percent. Home equity loans are now being offered at an average interest rate of 6.1 percent, according to Bankrate.com, and the interest is deductible.

Seaman recommends knocking off some easy credits, such as electives, at lower-priced colleges, provided the credits will transfer. Her daughter, Katharine Rowan, took five courses one summer at a community college to fulfill elective requirements at the University of Wisconsin, where she's a senior studying electrical engineering. Seaman estimates she saved $6,000 in tuition and fees.

Guido Castellani III, who received about $200,000 in grants and scholarships to cover his four years at Sarah Lawrence, applied during the early decision round and was accepted, but knew there was "no way" he could afford it. So he scoured the Internet and discovered that as the son of a former marine officer, a Vietnam vet who passed away in 2003, he was eligible for certain scholarships and other funding. Castellani, who is originally from Scranton, Pennsylvania, was awarded $10,000 a year from the Marine Corps Scholarship Foundation plus about $950 a month in educational benefits from the U.S. Department of Veterans Affairs.

"I had to be persistent," says Castellani, who graduated in May. He negotiated with Sarah Lawrence's financial aid office to get additional aid junior year, and right before he graduated, he applied for – and won – a scholarship from the Children of Fallen Patriots Foundation to cover the $12,000 he'd accumulated in subsidized loans. His advice for incoming freshmen: "Do your research. The money is there." ●

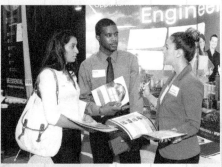

# How Work-Study Works

## IF A JOB IS PART OF YOUR AID AWARD, IT CAN PAY OFF IN SEVERAL WAYS

By **MICHAEL MORELLA**

Amber Bunnell had always wanted to work in a library. So when the option of holding down a work-study job was offered as part of her financial aid package from Macalester College in St. Paul, Minnesota, she stated that preference "in all capital letters" on her application for a position. Working about 10 hours per week at $7.25 an hour, the Savage, Minnesota, native started as a circulation aide, manning the front desk and sorting and shelving. The next year, she was promoted to help manage the staff of about 50 undergraduate employees, with a bump in pay. She added skills "that I can transfer into any career I choose," says Bunnell, who graduated in May with a degree in English and international studies and landed a job at another academic library in St. Paul.

Amber Bunnell's library job confirmed her desire to enter the field.

**The basics.** Hundreds of thousands of college students participate in the federal government's work-study program, part of its financial-aid superstructure for those who demonstrate need. The first step: Opt in when you're asked if you'd like to be considered for the program in question 31 of the Free Application for Federal Student Aid, or FAFSA. If you're eligible, and if you follow through by actually finding a position once you get to college, then you can expect to earn at least federal minimum wage – currently $7.25 an hour – or the state or local baseline, if higher. Most jobs are on campus, in the dining hall, bookstore or athletic department, say, though some might be with local employers. The government awarded a yearly average of nearly $1,700 per student at about 3,300 colleges in 2012-13, according to the latest Department of Education data.

Schools are required to kick in 25 percent of every student's funding, which means that annual awards often run around $2,000 or $2,500. You'll coordinate your own work schedule and may work as much as you like up to the ceiling imposed by the size of your award. (An award of slightly more than $1,000 per 14-week semester would work out to 10 hours a week at $7.25 per hour, for example.)

There are "a lot of different models out there" for actually securing a job, says Joe Weglarz, executive director of student financial services at Marist College in Poughkeepsie, New York. Marist holds a work-study job fair to introduce new students to prospective employers, and the student financial services office helps facilitate the job search. At Iowa State, students have access to a jobs portal of available positions, which they apply for on their own. Other schools, like Macalester, place students in positions based on their skills and academic interests.

Besides providing some tuition or spending money, work-study jobs can help you build a résumé, establish a network of mentors and potential references and learn useful skills. "If you want to be a physician or a pediatrician, it might not be a bad idea to work in a daycare center," suggests Cynthia Meekins, manager for student employment at Rutgers in New Brunswick, New Jersey. And research shows that students who work about 10 to 15 hours a week tend to perform better academically, adds Desiree Noah, who coordinates student employment at La Sierra University in Riverside, California, and is president-elect of the National Student Employment Association. One great perk of a work-study job is that your employer will probably give you a break when you're swamped at exam time and pulling all-nighters. ●

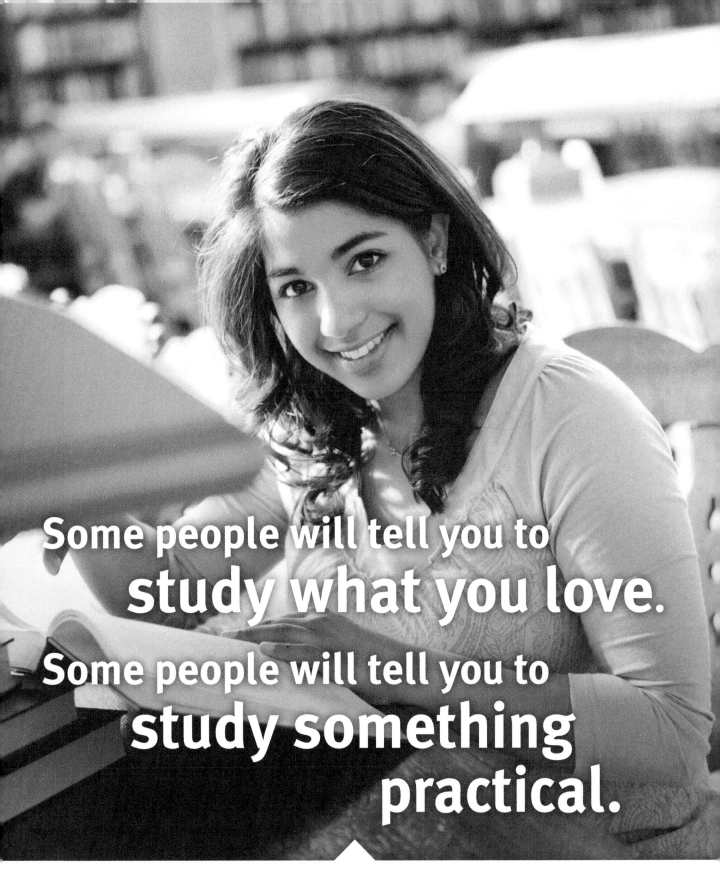

Some people will tell you to
**study what you love.**

Some people will tell you to
**study something
practical.**

No matter what you study, AfterCollege will help
you find scholarships, internships, and jobs
based on your field of study.

**It's never too early to start thinking about AfterCollege.**

AfterCollege®
where your career begins

**aftercollege.com**

# Great Campus Jobs That Will Turbocharge

# YOUR CAREER

**THE SKILLS AND EXPERIENCE YOU GAIN CAN BE WORTH AS MUCH AS THE PAYCHECK**

*By* **COURTNEY RUBIN**

ant to boost your job prospects after graduation? Any part-time work during college can give you an edge, including a stint at Mc-Donald's. "Balancing work and school shows you can manage your time," says Nicole van den Heuvel, director of the Center for Career Development at Rice University in Houston. "And jobs that aren't glamorous show that you're not a prima donna." But with a little strategizing, you can land a position that will really enhance your résumé.

First step: Go to the campus employment office during orientation. "You'll be on campus

Florida A&M student Charles Garner (center) attends a planning meeting for homecoming.

before the upperclassmen. Take advantage of that," suggests Michael Sciola, associate vice president for advancement and director of career services at Colgate University in New York. Here are some job ideas:

## 1. Social media coordinator

This job, which involves using Facebook, Twitter, YouTube and similar platforms to spread the college's or another employer's message, will enhance your communication skills and is likely to make you savvy about the latest technologies. Experience could also include data analysis, looking at various metrics that measure viewer engagement, and strategizing how to improve those metrics.

Another perk is that you practice networking. "Twitter makes the world a lot smaller," says Charles Garner, who worked 11 hours a week as social media coordinator for the Office of Student Activities at Florida Agricultural & Mechanical University before graduating in the spring and being commissioned as a naval officer. In promoting events like homecoming and Women's Week, he says, he used Twitter "to get in contact with celebrities, and to meet a lot of influential legislators and even the governor." Adds Garner, who wanted to burnish his credentials for an eventual career in public affairs: "Your network is your net worth."

## 2. Campus brand ambassador

The race to grab college students' attention and dollars has all sorts of companies, including General Mills, Google and Coca-Cola, hiring on-campus ambassadors to do everything from wear the brand's logo to tweet about the products.

Besides learning sales, marketing and strategy, you'll get a grounding in the products – and perhaps the inside track on a job after graduation. To stand out, you'll need creativity, but if you've got it, work as a brand ambassador often leads to sales and marketing trainee programs.

## 3. Help desk staffer or bookstore computer pro

You'll obviously pick up tech skills manning your school's help desk, but chances are you'll learn them working in the electronics section of the campus store, too. With many schools requiring laptops, this is typically where the machines are issued. You'll often install software and do minor troubleshooting, plus gain product knowledge.

After four years in the campus store at the University of North Carolina–Chapel Hill, Sam Hudson, who graduated in 2012, approached a representative at a job fair looking to fill positions at Lenovo. "I said, 'I've been giving out your computers for a couple of years,'" says Hudson. He's now an account coordinator for the company in North Carolina.

## 4. Assistant in the office of institutional research

This is the office that surveys students, alumni, professors and parents, which could involve quizzing the freshman class about the first-year experience, asking parents about their education financing plans, and gathering alumni perceptions of the school. So any job in this office will offer an opportunity to learn about collecting and analyzing data.

"I think that's one of the best tools any kid can have," says van den Heuvel. "To go into consulting, to go into investment banking, to do so many things."

## 5. Career center staffer

Any job in the career center teaches customer service and how to interact in a professional environment. "You'll learn how to greet people and how to make small talk," says Sciola. "All these little things are so important in getting a job."

Problem-solving and computer skills also will come into play as you help students and employers who are having trouble logging in to the career center's system or who want to

## INSIDE SCOOP

**JOHN ULZHEIMER**
President, The Ulzheimer Group;
expert for CreditSesame.com

## PARENTS, HERE'S A CREDIT CARD MOVE

No one under 21 can get a credit card without a job or a co-signer. If you want your kid to have a card, I suggest adding him or her as an authorized user on one of your accounts. If you fear wild spending sprees, most cards now offer text messages alerting you of transactions within seconds – and you can shut off your kid's access almost as quickly. Or request a low limit. Just because a card offers a $10,000 limit doesn't mean you have to take it. A debit card will keep your kid to a budget, but will do nothing to help him or her build a credit rating.

post a job. Plus, think of the job-search wisdom you'll soak up and the facetime you'll get with potential employers.

## 6. Child care provider

Many schools have an onsite daycare center, and it is probably looking for help. Besides teaching patience and responsibility, the position should allow you to get to know faculty and administrators outside the classroom. No matter how prominent, "they will always want to talk about their child," observes Mark Smith, associate vice chancellor and director of the career center at Washington University in St. Louis, who worked at the Harvard Yard child care center during his four years at Harvard – and then as an au pair while at Washington University School of Law. "These folks can help guide you," he says. As a bonus, you get "great training for possibly one of your most important future jobs, parent."

## 7. Student athletic trainer

You don't have to be interested in a health-related career for this job to be a résumé-enhancer. Assisting with treatments (learning to tape ankles or shoulders, say), helping set up for practices, and preparing for games teaches responsibility and teamwork, says van den Heuvel. And potential future employers will appreciate that you worked nights and weekends, in often stressful or high-pressure environments. Most of these jobs will lead to a certification in CPR, too.

## 8. Chief executive of your own startup

As a freshman at Syracuse University in New York, Courtnee Futch remembers working 20 hours a week at two different jobs and still having just $6.14 socked away in her bank account. "I thought, 'There has to be a better way to make money,'" says Futch, now a senior. She'd always loved to bake, so she whipped up a batch of bacon Rice Krispie treats with white chocolate and caramel drizzle, created a Facebook page for the business, which she named "ThunderCakes," and sold out in two hours. Currently, she has 15 unpaid interns, and this fall, as she prepares to ship her creations (bacon cheesecake brownies, vanilla chiffon cakes) all over New York state, she'll hire five employees.

"Running my own business has really taught me to focus, something I was never able to do before," she says. "I've learned a ton about bootstrapping, accountability and determination." ●

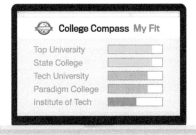

# Great Schools, Great Prices

**W**hich colleges and universities offer students the best value? The calculation used here takes into account a school's academic quality, based on its U.S. News Best Colleges ranking, and the 2013-14 net cost of attendance for a student who received the average level of need-based financial aid. The higher the quality of the program and the lower the cost, the better the deal. Only schools in or near the top half of their U.S. News ranking categories are included because U.S. News considers the most significant values to be among colleges that perform well academically.

## National Universities ▶

| Rank  School (State) (*Public) | % receiving grants based on need ('13) | Average cost after receiving grants based on need ('13) | Average discount from total cost ('13) |
|---|---|---|---|
| 1. Harvard University (MA) | 58% | $15,169 | 75% |
| 2. Princeton University (NJ) | 59% | $17,994 | 68% |
| 3. Yale University (CT) | 52% | $17,352 | 72% |
| 4. Stanford University (CA) | 48% | $19,361 | 68% |
| 5. Massachusetts Inst. of Technology | 57% | $21,363 | 64% |
| 6. Columbia University (NY) | 48% | $21,906 | 66% |
| 7. Dartmouth College (NH) | 49% | $22,503 | 65% |
| 8. California Institute of Technology | 51% | $23,281 | 60% |
| 9. Rice University (TX) | 41% | $19,976 | 63% |
| 10. University of Pennsylvania | 47% | $23,542 | 62% |
| 11. Vanderbilt University (TN) | 45% | $21,731 | 64% |
| 12. Brown University (RI) | 44% | $22,162 | 64% |
| 13. Duke University (NC) | 39% | $23,403 | 63% |
| 14. Brigham Young Univ.–Provo (UT) | 37% | $12,798 | 27% |
| 15. Cornell University (NY) | 48% | $23,936 | 61% |
| 16. University of Chicago | 47% | $27,313 | 57% |
| 17. U. of North Carolina–Chapel Hill* | 42% | $19,614 | 57% |
| 18. Emory University (GA) | 44% | $23,604 | 61% |
| 19. Johns Hopkins University (MD) | 43% | $27,666 | 56% |
| 20. Northwestern University (IL) | 46% | $28,161 | 56% |
| 21. Univ. of California–Santa Cruz* | 60% | $20,855 | 63% |
| 22. University of Notre Dame (IN) | 47% | $29,428 | 51% |
| 23. Georgetown University (DC) | 34% | $25,806 | 59% |
| 24. Pepperdine University (CA) | 55% | $24,090 | 61% |
| 25. Clark University (MA) | 62% | $22,395 | 54% |
| 26. University of California–Berkeley* | 22% | $23,747 | 48% |
| 27. University of Virginia* | 28% | $24,819 | 54% |
| 28. Tufts University (MA) | 36% | $26,347 | 57% |
| 29. University of Rochester (NY) | 52% | $28,024 | 54% |
| 30. Washington University in St. Louis | 35% | $30,344 | 52% |
| 31. Texas A&M Univ.–College Station* | 40% | $20,003 | 47% |
| 32. Brandeis University (MA) | 51% | $28,248 | 54% |
| 33. Case Western Reserve Univ. (OH) | 61% | $30,348 | 48% |
| 34. Lehigh University (PA) | 41% | $25,285 | 56% |
| 35. Wake Forest University (NC) | 37% | $28,126 | 53% |
| 36. Clarkson University (NY) | 84% | $29,774 | 48% |
| 37. Boston College | 37% | $28,248 | 53% |
| 38. Carnegie Mellon University (PA) | 47% | $33,264 | 46% |
| 39. University of California–Irvine* | 22% | $22,773 | 57% |
| 40. Rensselaer Polytechnic Inst. (NY) | 65% | $35,187 | 43% |
| 41. Univ. of Southern California | 37% | $31,530 | 49% |
| 42. Illinois Institute of Technology | 63% | $26,134 | 52% |
| 43. Duquesne University (PA) | 69% | $26,649 | 40% |
| 44. Yeshiva University (NY) | 50% | $31,190 | 45% |
| 45. SUNY Col. of Envir. Sci. and Forestry* | 64% | $26,312 | 20% |
| 46. North Carolina State U.–Raleigh* | 43% | $21,769 | 39% |
| 47. Syracuse University (NY) | 53% | $31,780 | 45% |
| 48. Univ. of California–Riverside* | 45% | $23,743 | 57% |
| 49. Univ. of California–San Diego* | 18% | $26,000 | 51% |
| 50. University of California–Davis* | 27% | $28,040 | 50% |

## National Liberal Arts Colleges ▶

| Rank  School (State) (*Public) | % receiving grants based on need ('13) | Average cost after receiving grants based on need ('13) | Average discount from total cost ('13) |
|---|---|---|---|
| 1. Amherst College (MA) | 56% | $16,590 | 73% |
| 2. Williams College (MA) | 52% | $18,977 | 69% |
| 3. Pomona College (CA) | 56% | $19,040 | 68% |
| 4. Wellesley College (MA) | 59% | $19,717 | 67% |
| 5. Soka University of America (CA) | 90% | $18,602 | 56% |
| 6. Vassar College (NY) | 58% | $20,211 | 67% |
| 7. Grinnell College (IA) | 71% | $20,653 | 63% |
| 8. Bowdoin College (ME) | 45% | $19,875 | 67% |
| 9. Washington and Lee University (VA) | 41% | $18,725 | 68% |
| 10. Haverford College (PA) | 49% | $20,977 | 66% |
| 11. Swarthmore College (PA) | 50% | $21,969 | 64% |
| 12. Middlebury College (VT) | 39% | $21,286 | 64% |
| 13. College of the Atlantic (ME) | 86% | $18,149 | 64% |
| 14. Colby College (ME) | 42% | $21,269 | 64% |
| 15. Macalester College (MN) | 69% | $24,315 | 58% |
| 16. Colgate University (NY) | 35% | $20,517 | 66% |
| 17. Claremont McKenna College (CA) | 40% | $22,911 | 63% |
| 18. Smith College (MA) | 59% | $24,306 | 60% |
| 19. Davidson College (NC) | 45% | $23,741 | 59% |
| 20. Hamilton College (NY) | 47% | $23,663 | 61% |
| 21. Agnes Scott College (GA) | 77% | $20,733 | 56% |
| 22. Bates College (ME) | 45% | $23,545 | 61% |
| 23. University of Richmond (VA) | 39% | $21,438 | 63% |
| 24. Wesleyan University (CT) | 44% | $24,358 | 62% |
| 25. Carleton College (MN) | 55% | $27,084 | 55% |
| 26. Thomas Aquinas College (CA) | 75% | $19,783 | 45% |
| 27. Bryn Mawr College (PA) | 54% | $25,197 | 58% |
| 28. Mount Holyoke College (MA) | 67% | $25,781 | 54% |
| 29. Cornell College (IA) | 77% | $21,408 | 56% |
| 30. Ripon College (WI) | 84% | $21,526 | 50% |
| 31. Centre College (KY) | 59% | $23,722 | 51% |
| 32. Franklin and Marshall College (PA) | 46% | $23,850 | 61% |
| 33. St. Olaf College (MN) | 65% | $24,357 | 53% |
| 34. Trinity College (CT) | 39% | $22,460 | 64% |
| 35. Transylvania University (KY) | 68% | $21,493 | 51% |
| 36. Beloit College (WI) | 69% | $24,005 | 52% |
| 37. Skidmore College (NY) | 43% | $23,750 | 61% |
| 38. Wofford College (SC) | 54% | $20,698 | 58% |
| 39. Knox College (IL) | 75% | $23,894 | 52% |
| 40. Barnard College (NY) | 39% | $24,376 | 60% |

**Methodology:** The rankings were based on the following three variables: **1.** Ratio of quality to price: a school's overall score in the latest Best Colleges rankings divided by the net cost to a student receiving the average need-based scholarship or grant. The higher the ratio of rank to the discounted cost (tuition, fees, room and board and other expenses less average scholarship or grant), the better the value. **2.** Percentage of all undergrads receiving need-based scholarships or grants during the 2013-14 year. **3.** Average discount: percentage of a school's 2013-14 total costs covered by the average need-based scholarship or grant to undergrads. For public institutions, 2013-14 out-of-state tuition and percentage of out-of-state students receiving need-based scholarships or grants were used. Only those schools ranked in or near the top half of their U.S. News ranking categories were considered. Ranks were determined by standardizing scores achieved by every school in each of the three variables and weighting those scores. Ratio of quality to price accounted for 60 percent of the overall score; percentage of undergrads receiving need-based grants, for 25 percent; and average discount, for 15 percent. The school with the most total weighted points became No. 1 in its category.

# ACADEMIC INSIGHTS
## YOUR SCHOOL BY THE NUMBERS

Designed for schools, U.S. News Academic Insights provides instant access to a rich historical archive of undergraduate and graduate school rankings data.

### Advanced Visualizations
Take complex data and turn it into six easily understandable and exportable views.

### Download Center
Export large data sets from the new Download Center to create custom reports.

### Dedicated Account Management
Have access to full analyst support for training, troubleshooting and advanced reporting.

### Peer-Group Analysis
Flexibility to create your own peer groups to compare your intstitution on more than 350 metrics.

### Historical Trending
Find out how institutions have performed over time based on more than 350 metrics.

To request a demo visit **AI.USNEWS.COM**      or call **202.955.2181**

## Regional Universities ▶

| Rank School (State) (*Public) | % receiving grants based on need ('13) | Average cost after receiving grants based on need ('13) | Average discount from total cost ('13) |
|---|---|---|---|
| **NORTH** | | | |
| 1. Villanova University (PA) | 43% | $30,946 | 47% |
| 2. Bentley University (MA) | 44% | $27,905 | 51% |
| 3. St. Bonaventure University (NY) | 76% | $23,511 | 44% |
| 4. Alfred University (NY) | 87% | $22,315 | 48% |
| 5. Rochester Inst. of Technology (NY) | 70% | $29,127 | 39% |
| 6. Le Moyne College (NY) | 83% | $26,332 | 41% |
| 7. Providence College (RI) | 56% | $33,646 | 40% |
| 8. Canisius College (NY) | 77% | $26,359 | 45% |
| 9. Gannon University (PA) | 80% | $22,949 | 45% |
| 10. Niagara University (NY) | 75% | $23,513 | 44% |
| 11. Simmons College (MA) | 77% | $30,372 | 42% |
| 12. University of Scranton (PA) | 71% | $34,826 | 37% |
| 13. Ithaca College (NY) | 66% | $33,131 | 40% |
| 14. Hood College (MD) | 85% | $27,266 | 44% |
| 15. Loyola University Maryland | 50% | $34,970 | 38% |
| **SOUTH** | | | |
| 1. Mercer University (GA) | 73% | $24,314 | 50% |
| 2. Harding University (AR) | 56% | $17,827 | 33% |
| 3. William Carey University (MS) | 91% | $16,500 | 35% |
| 4. Mississippi College | 54% | $16,864 | 37% |
| 5. Converse College (SC) | 89% | $22,624 | 46% |
| 6. Stetson University (FL) | 75% | $28,529 | 47% |
| 7. Christian Brothers University (TN) | 82% | $21,156 | 44% |
| 8. Rollins College (FL) | 52% | $31,693 | 47% |
| 9. Coastal Carolina University (SC)* | 21% | $13,405 | 63% |
| 10. Wingate University (NC) | 72% | $18,370 | 51% |
| 11. Elon University (NC) | 31% | $29,959 | 31% |
| 12. Samford University (AL) | 42% | $27,649 | 32% |
| 13. Columbia International Univ. (SC) | 80% | $18,816 | 40% |
| 14. Appalachian State University (NC)* | 25% | $22,828 | 27% |
| 15. The Citadel (SC)* | 40% | $28,730 | 41% |
| **MIDWEST** | | | |
| 1. Drury University (MO) | 65% | $20,354 | 41% |
| 2. Valparaiso University (IN) | 72% | $24,509 | 47% |
| 3. Creighton University (NE) | 56% | $26,950 | 44% |
| 4. University of Evansville (IN) | 68% | $22,109 | 50% |
| 5. Truman State University (MO)* | 38% | $19,560 | 25% |
| 6. John Carroll University (OH) | 73% | $25,784 | 47% |
| 7. Indiana Wesleyan University | 78% | $19,610 | 43% |
| 8. Dominican University (IL) | 87% | $21,538 | 46% |
| 9. Bradley University (IL) | 72% | $27,024 | 36% |
| 10. Elmhurst College (IL) | 73% | $24,065 | 48% |
| 11. Baldwin Wallace University (OH) | 78% | $22,870 | 43% |
| 12. Hamline University (MN) | 84% | $25,350 | 46% |
| 13. Drake University (IA) | 59% | $28,575 | 36% |
| 14. Butler University (IN) | 64% | $30,932 | 37% |
| 15. Aquinas College (MI) | 85% | $19,548 | 47% |
| **WEST** | | | |
| 1. Trinity University (TX) | 47% | $24,820 | 49% |
| 2. Gonzaga University (WA) | 57% | $29,209 | 40% |
| 3. Whitworth University (WA) | 70% | $26,920 | 44% |
| 4. Seattle Pacific University | 73% | $23,960 | 50% |
| 5. University of Redlands (CA) | 78% | $29,779 | 49% |
| 6. Abilene Christian University (TX) | 67% | $25,084 | 40% |
| 7. Seattle University | 60% | $31,698 | 40% |
| 8. University of Dallas | 63% | $27,462 | 44% |

| Rank School (State) (*Public) | % receiving grants based on need ('13) | Average cost after receiving grants based on need ('13) | Average discount from total cost ('13) |
|---|---|---|---|
| 9. Westminster College (UT) | 58% | $24,509 | 42% |
| 10. Pacific Lutheran University (WA) | 75% | $28,452 | 41% |
| 11. Mills College (CA) | 82% | $37,381 | 35% |
| 12. University of Portland (OR) | 54% | $32,045 | 39% |
| 13. LeTourneau University (TX) | 72% | $24,031 | 38% |
| 14. Santa Clara University (CA) | 35% | $38,610 | 35% |
| 15. Point Loma Nazarene University (CA) | 66% | $29,348 | 34% |

## Regional Colleges ▶

| Rank School (State) (*Public) | % receiving grants based on need ('13) | Average cost after receiving grants based on need ('13) | Average discount from total cost ('13) |
|---|---|---|---|
| **NORTH** | | | |
| 1. Cooper Union (NY) | 27% | $12,066 | 78% |
| 2. Elizabethtown College (PA) | 78% | $27,625 | 44% |
| 3. Lebanon Valley College (PA) | 83% | $26,515 | 45% |
| 4. Elmira College (NY) | 84% | $25,114 | 51% |
| 5. Cedar Crest College (PA) | 93% | $23,971 | 46% |
| 6. Geneva College (PA) | 81% | $21,212 | 42% |
| 7. Seton Hill University (PA) | 86% | $25,087 | 43% |
| 8. Messiah College (PA) | 72% | $27,114 | 37% |
| 9. Bard College at Simon's Rock (MA) | 72% | $24,528 | 59% |
| 10. Wilson College (PA) | 78% | $24,393 | 42% |
| **SOUTH** | | | |
| 1. Alice Lloyd College (KY) | 91% | $13,217 | 40% |
| 2. Blue Mountain College (MS) | 79% | $13,300 | 24% |
| 3. John Brown University (AR) | 66% | $20,844 | 40% |
| 4. Milligan College (TN) | 81% | $19,980 | 47% |
| 5. University of the Ozarks (AR) | 69% | $22,367 | 39% |
| 6. Carson-Newman University (TN) | 81% | $20,123 | 44% |
| 7. Bryan College (TN) | 74% | $17,920 | 42% |
| 8. West Virginia Wesleyan College | 80% | $21,952 | 46% |
| 9. Meredith College (NC) | 76% | $23,657 | 44% |
| 10. Covenant College (GA) | 61% | $22,560 | 44% |
| **MIDWEST** | | | |
| 1. College of the Ozarks (MO) | 94% | $13,292 | 52% |
| 2. Augustana College (SD) | 62% | $19,444 | 49% |
| 3. Buena Vista University (IA) | 85% | $21,145 | 48% |
| 4. Manchester University (IN) | 87% | $19,362 | 51% |
| 5. Huntington University (IN) | 76% | $20,503 | 42% |
| 6. Loras College (IA) | 73% | $21,112 | 47% |
| 7. St. Joseph's College (IN) | 83% | $18,892 | 50% |
| 8. Taylor University (IN) | 61% | $24,832 | 38% |
| 9. Clarke University (IA) | 87% | $23,027 | 44% |
| 10. Culver-Stockton College (MO) | 90% | $18,053 | 48% |
| **WEST** | | | |
| 1. Texas Lutheran University | 81% | $21,505 | 44% |
| 2. Carroll College (MT) | 63% | $25,560 | 37% |
| 3. Corban University (OR) | 83% | $23,974 | 40% |
| 4. Howard Payne University (TX) | 73% | $19,788 | 42% |
| 5. Rocky Mountain College (MT) | 75% | $20,447 | 42% |
| 6. Northwest University (WA) | 83% | $20,631 | 43% |
| 7. Oklahoma Wesleyan University | 70% | $24,238 | 29% |
| 8. Master's Col. and Seminary (CA) | 85% | $27,175 | 37% |
| 9. Warner Pacific College (OR) | 79% | $23,543 | 19% |
| 10. Oklahoma Baptist University | 63% | $26,493 | 21% |

# Two worlds.
## One dream.

Singers and Scientists share more than might be expected. Whether it's a breakout melody or a breakthrough in research. When it comes together, everything fits. It can change lives forever. Stand Up To Cancer supports the collaboration, innovation and research that are turning discoveries into viable treatments and possibly, one day, a cure.

Stand up with us. Let your voice make a difference because when we work together, nothing is impossible.

**STAND UP TO CANCER**®

**Genentech**
*A Member of the Roche Group*

Like, share and join SU2C.
Find out more at standup2cancer.org

Jennifer Hudson, Stand Up To Cancer Ambassador

Shiva Malek, Ph.D.

# The Payback Picture

**W**ith tuition rising and financial aid budgets shrinking, many undergrads have to borrow their way to a degree. U.S. News has compiled a list of the schools whose class of 2013 graduated with the heaviest and lightest debt loads. The data include loans taken out by students from their colleges, from private financial institutions and from federal, state and local governments. Loans to parents are not included. The first data column indicates what percentage of the class graduated owing money and, by extrapolation, what percentage graduated debt free. "Average amount of debt" refers to the cumulative amount borrowed by students who incurred debt; it's not an average for all students.

## MOST DEBT

### National Universities ▷

| School (State) (*Public) | % of grads with debt | Average amount of debt |
|---|---|---|
| Florida Institute of Technology | 53% | $41,060 |
| Rensselaer Polytechnic Inst. (NY) | 67% | $40,584 |
| Andrews University (MI) | 65% | $39,010 |
| Clarkson University (NY) | 83% | $38,390 |
| Texas Christian University | 43% | $38,317 |
| Texas Southern University* | 84% | $37,915 |
| Boston University | 58% | $37,694 |
| University of Dayton (OH) | 63% | $37,551 |
| University of St. Thomas (MN) | 65% | $36,955 |
| St. Louis University | 63% | $36,808 |
| Pace University (NY) | 75% | $36,558 |
| Southern Illinois U.–Carbondale* | 70% | $36,172 |
| University of New Hampshire* | 77% | $36,064 |
| Ashland University (OH) | 87% | $36,058 |
| Wake Forest University (NC) | 47% | $35,902 |

### National Liberal Arts Colleges ▷

| School (State) (*Public) | % of grads with debt | Average amount of debt |
|---|---|---|
| St. Anselm College (NH) | 80% | $42,196 |
| Pacific Union College (CA) | 64% | $42,153 |
| Virginia Wesleyan College | 81% | $40,804 |
| College of St. Benedict (MN) | 68% | $40,034 |
| Wells College (NY) | 78% | $39,965 |
| Morehouse College (GA) | 78% | $38,136 |
| Gordon College (MA) | 82% | $37,410 |
| Albion College (MI) | 67% | $37,191 |
| Wartburg College (IA) | 83% | $36,542 |
| Siena College (NY) | 79% | $35,569 |
| Spelman College (GA) | 60% | $35,516 |
| Washington College (MD) | 65% | $35,510 |
| Johnson C. Smith University (NC) | 99% | $35,505 |
| St. John's University (MN) | 66% | $35,349 |
| St. Vincent College (PA) | 84% | $35,200 |

### Regional Universities ▷

| School (State) (*Public) | % of grads with debt | Average amount of debt |
|---|---|---|
| **NORTH** | | |
| St. Francis University (PA) | 88% | $50,275 |
| Anna Maria College (MA) | 92% | $48,750 |
| Quinnipiac University (CT) | 71% | $44,552 |
| Centenary College (NJ) | 79% | $43,200 |
| Alvernia University (PA) | 85% | $42,552 |
| **SOUTH** | | |
| Florida Gulf Coast University* | 49% | $56,208 |
| The Citadel (SC)* | 60% | $48,862 |
| Freed-Hardeman University (TN) | 75% | $36,434 |
| Belmont University (TN) | 58% | $36,003 |
| Lynchburg College (VA) | 79% | $35,330 |
| **MIDWEST** | | |
| Rockford University (IL) | 89% | $45,577 |
| College of St. Scholastica (MN) | 76% | $43,113 |
| College of St. Mary (NE) | 79% | $40,026 |
| St. Catherine University (MN) | 88% | $39,312 |
| Lawrence Technological Univ. (MI) | 69% | $38,790 |
| **WEST** | | |
| LeTourneau University (TX) | 77% | $44,584 |
| Abilene Christian University (TX) | 66% | $42,585 |
| Trinity University (TX) | 44% | $38,540 |
| Walla Walla University (WA) | 67% | $38,174 |
| Hardin-Simmons University (TX) | 72% | $38,032 |

### Regional Colleges ▷

| School (State) (*Public) | % of grads with debt | Average amount of debt |
|---|---|---|
| **NORTH** | | |
| Mount Ida College (MA) | 85% | $43,860 |
| Maine Maritime Academy* | 97% | $41,630 |
| Delaware Valley College (PA) | 77% | $41,036 |
| Lasell College (MA) | 86% | $40,709 |
| Cedar Crest College (PA) | 91% | $39,198 |
| **SOUTH** | | |
| Chowan University (NC) | 91% | $40,839 |
| Tuskegee University (AL) | 62% | $39,250 |
| Kentucky Christian University | 79% | $37,413 |
| Meredith College (NC) | 64% | $35,425 |
| Ferrum College (VA) | 82% | $33,777 |
| **MIDWEST** | | |
| Adrian College (MI) | 75% | $41,763 |
| Buena Vista University (IA) | 89% | $40,384 |
| Mount Marty College (SD) | 87% | $38,571 |
| University of Jamestown (ND) | 70% | $37,942 |
| Marian University (IN) | 84% | $37,865 |
| **WEST** | | |
| McMurry University (TX) | 82% | $39,704 |
| Texas Lutheran University | 77% | $33,405 |
| Menlo College (CA) | 81% | $30,134 |
| Oregon Inst. of Technology* | 72% | $29,526 |
| Hope International University (CA) | 73% | $28,990 |

**Note:** Student debt load data are as of July 25, 2014.

# LEAST DEBT

## National Universities ▷

| School (State) (*Public) | % of grads with debt | Average amount of debt |
|---|---|---|
| Princeton University (NJ) | 24% | $5,558 |
| Harvard University (MA) | 26% | $12,560 |
| Yale University (CT) | 16% | $13,009 |
| California Institute of Technology | 40% | $15,010 |
| Dartmouth College (NH) | 56% | $15,660 |
| Brigham Young Univ.–Provo (UT) | 30% | $15,769 |
| Stanford University (CA) | 23% | $16,640 |
| University at Buffalo–SUNY* | 45% | $17,455 |
| University of California–Berkeley* | 43% | $17,468 |
| U. of North Carolina–Chapel Hill* | 39% | $17,602 |
| Rice University (TX) | 30% | $17,856 |
| Massachusetts Inst. of Technology | 41% | $17,891 |
| Florida International University* | 49% | $17,893 |
| University of Nevada–Las Vegas* | 44% | $17,930 |
| San Diego State University* | 48% | $18,100 |
| University of Houston* | 49% | $18,244 |
| Duke University (NC) | 37% | $18,456 |
| Utah State University* | 49% | $19,100 |
| University of West Florida* | 54% | $19,239 |
| North Carolina State U.–Raleigh* | 57% | $19,530 |
| University of Pennsylvania | 36% | $19,798 |
| Florida Atlantic University* | 48% | $19,898 |
| University of New Orleans* | 19% | $19,957 |
| University of California–Davis* | 58% | $19,970 |
| SUNY Col. of Envir. Sci. and Forestry* | 67% | $19,989 |

## National Liberal Arts Colleges ▷

| School (State) (*Public) | % of grads with debt | Average amount of debt |
|---|---|---|
| Berea College (KY) | 67% | $6,652 |
| Williams College (MA) | 29% | $12,474 |
| Louisiana State University–Alexandria* | 58% | $12,547 |
| University of Virginia–Wise* | 62% | $12,772 |
| Pomona College (CA) | 33% | $13,441 |
| Wellesley College (MA) | 49% | $14,030 |
| Haverford College (PA) | 29% | $14,110 |
| Amherst College (MA) | 29% | $15,466 |
| Thomas Aquinas College (CA) | 89% | $15,521 |
| Vassar College (NY) | 51% | $16,365 |
| Grinnell College (IA) | 57% | $16,570 |
| SUNY College–Old Westbury* | 56% | $16,653 |
| Whitman College (WA) | 49% | $17,114 |
| Soka University of America (CA) | 71% | $17,439 |
| Middlebury College (VT) | 46% | $17,715 |
| New College of Florida* | 39% | $17,927 |
| Carleton College (MN) | 45% | $18,000 |
| Pitzer College (CA) | 44% | $18,030 |
| Colgate University (NY) | 34% | $18,719 |
| Barnard College (NY) | 45% | $18,815 |
| Kenyon College (OH) | 50% | $18,902 |
| College of the Atlantic (ME) | 61% | $19,285 |
| Swarthmore College (PA) | 36% | $19,338 |
| Hamilton College (NY) | 38% | $19,426 |
| American Jewish University (CA) | 61% | $20,000 |
| Scripps College (CA) | 48% | $20,125 |

## Regional Universities ▷

| School (State) (*Public) | % of grads with debt | Average amount of debt |
|---|---|---|
| **NORTH** | | |
| CUNY–Brooklyn College* | 46% | $11,000 |
| CUNY–John Jay Col. of Crim. Justice* | 20% | $11,246 |
| CUNY–Hunter College* | 72% | $13,000 |
| CUNY–Lehman College* | 24% | $15,075 |
| SUNY College–Oneonta* | 69% | $15,598 |
| **SOUTH** | | |
| Hampton University (VA) | 80% | $9,878 |
| University of North Georgia* | 49% | $12,072 |
| Lincoln Memorial University (TN) | 60% | $12,187 |
| William Carey University (MS) | 87% | $16,500 |
| Tennessee Technological Univ.* | 53% | $17,023 |
| **MIDWEST** | | |
| Northeastern Illinois University* | 18% | $13,213 |
| William Woods University (MO) | 63% | $15,581 |
| Rockhurst University (MO) | 73% | $16,817 |
| Missouri State Univ.* | 85% | $19,521 |
| Univ. of Wisconsin–Eau Claire* | 76% | $22,658 |
| **WEST** | | |
| California State U.–Fullerton* | 42% | $12,962 |
| California State U.–Long Beach* | 43% | $13,386 |
| California State U.–Channel Islands* | 66% | $13,791 |
| Southeastern Oklahoma State U.* | 68% | $14,936 |
| University of Texas–Pan American* | 64% | $15,200 |

## Regional Colleges ▷

| School (State) (*Public) | % of grads with debt | Average amount of debt |
|---|---|---|
| **NORTH** | | |
| U.S. Merchant Marine Acad. (NY)* | 30% | $5,500 |
| Dean College (MA) | 70% | $11,678 |
| Cooper Union (NY) | 27% | $16,640 |
| Fisher College (MA) | 71% | $18,213 |
| Farmingdale State College–SUNY* | 46% | $18,515 |
| **SOUTH** | | |
| Alice Lloyd College (KY) | 52% | $8,314 |
| North Greenville University (SC) | 70% | $15,000 |
| Bryan College (TN) | 88% | $16,494 |
| High Point University (NC) | 57% | $18,244 |
| Newberry College (SC) | 74% | $19,368 |
| **MIDWEST** | | |
| College of the Ozarks (MO) | 13% | $6,424 |
| Maranatha Baptist University (WI) | 67% | $11,162 |
| Bismarck State College (ND)* | 61% | $12,377 |
| Bethany College (KS) | 82% | $16,300 |
| Dunwoody College of Tech. (MN) | 88% | $17,559 |
| **WEST** | | |
| Oklahoma State Univ. Institute of Tech.–Okmulgee* | 75% | $8,675 |
| Rogers State University (OK)* | 58% | $17,153 |
| Master's Col. and Seminary (CA) | 71% | $18,961 |
| Lewis-Clark State College (ID)* | 64% | $20,021 |
| California Maritime Academy* | 65% | $20,665 |

**20**
**15**

SCHOOLS
OF THE **North**

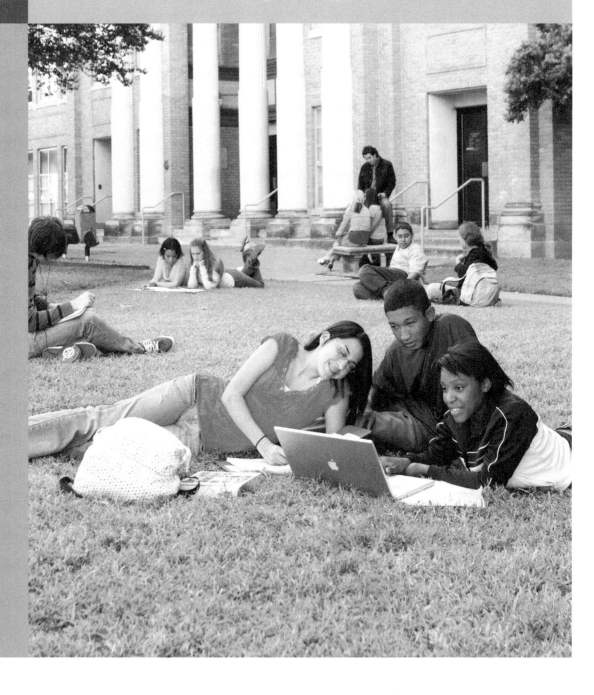

# THE PROMISE OF
# MANHATTAN COLLEGE

The promise of Manhattan College is rooted in Lasallian Catholic traditions of excellence in teaching, respect for human dignity and a commitment to social justice. For more than 160 years, Manhattan College has been delivering on this promise while educating tomorrow's leaders in arts, business, education and health, engineering and the sciences, all on a 22-acre residential campus only a subway ride on the 1 train away from midtown Manhattan.

Visit us at manhattan.edu to learn more about our inspiring academic offerings.

MANHATTAN
COLLEGE

# 20 15 SCHOOLS OF THE South

2015 EDITION

# DIRECTORY OF COLLEGES AND UNIVERSITIES

## INSIDE

The latest facts and figures on nearly
1,600 American colleges and universities,
including schools' U.S. News rankings

New data on tuition, admissions, the
makeup of the undergraduate student body,
popular majors and financial aid

Statistical profiles of freshman classes, including
entrance exam scores and high school class ranks

# Using the Directory

How to interpret the statistics in the following entries on nearly 1,600 American colleges and universities – and how to get the most out of them

The snapshots of colleges and universities presented here, alphabetized by state, contain a wealth of helpful information on everything from the most popular majors offered to the stats on the freshman class that arrived in the fall of 2013. The statistics were collected in the spring and summer of 2014 and are as of Aug. 11, 2014; they are explained in detail below. A school whose name has been footnoted did not return the U.S. News statistical questionnaire, so limited data appear. If a college did not reply to a particular question, you'll see N/A, for "not available." By tapping our online directory at usnews.com/collegesearch, you can experiment with a customized search of our database that allows you to pick schools based on major, location and other criteria. To find a school of interest in the rankings tables, consult the index at the back of the book.

## EXAMPLE

### Fairfield University

Fairfield CT
1 — (203) 254-4100
2 — **U.S. News ranking:** Reg. U. (N), No. 3
3 — **Website:** www.fairfield.edu
4 — **Admissions email:** admis@fairfield.edu
5 — **Private;** founded 1942
**Affiliation:** Roman Catholic (Jesuit)
6 — **Freshman admissions:** more selective; 2013-2014: 9,582 applied, 6,742 accepted. Neither SAT nor ACT required. SAT 25/75 percentile: 1090-1250. High school rank: N/A
7 — **Early decision deadline:** 11/15, notification date: 1/1
**Early action deadline:** 11/1, notification date: 1/1
8 — **Application deadline (fall):** 1/15
9 — **Undergraduate student body:** 3,546 full time, 327 part time; 40% male, 60% female; 0% American Indian, 2% Asian, 3% black, 8% Hispanic, 1% multiracial, 0% Pacific Islander, 72% white, 2% international; 31% from in state; 80% live on campus; 0% of students in fraternities, 0% in sororities
10 — **Most popular majors:** 26% Business, Management, Marketing and Related Support Services, 10% Communication, Journalism and Related Programs, 13% Health Professions and Related Programs, 7% Psychology, 13% Social Sciences
11 — **Expenses:** 2014-2015: $43,770; room/board: $13,190
12 — **Financial aid:** (203) 254-4125; 51% of undergrads determined to have financial need; average aid package $29,726

### 1. TELEPHONE NUMBER
This number reaches the admissions office.

### 2. U.S. NEWS RANKING
The abbreviation indicates which category of institution the school falls into: National University (Nat. U.), National Liberal Arts College (Nat. Lib. Arts), Regional Universities (Reg. U.), or Regional Colleges (Reg. Coll.). The regional universities and regional colleges are further divided by region: North (N), South (S), Midwest (MidW), and West (W). "Business" refers to business specialty schools, and "Engineering" refers to engineering specialty schools. "Arts" refers to schools devoted to the fine and performing arts.

Next, you'll find the school's 2015 rank within its category. Colleges and universities falling in the top three-fourths of their categories are ranked numerically. Those ranked in the bottom 25 percent of their respective category are placed in the second tier, listed alphabetically. But remember: You cannot compare school ranks in different categories; U.S. News ranks schools only against their peers. Specialty schools that focus on business, engineering and the arts aren't ranked and are listed as unranked. Also unranked are schools with fewer than 200 students, a high percentage of older or part-time students, that don't use SAT or ACT test scores for admission decisions or that have received a very small number of peer assessment votes in a survey conducted in Spring 2014.

### 3. WEBSITE
Visit the school's website to research programs, take a virtual tour or submit an application. You can also find a link to each site at usnews.com.

### 4. ADMISSIONS EMAIL
You can use this email address to request information or to submit an application.

### 5. TYPE/AFFILIATION
Is the school public, private or for-profit? Affiliated with a religious denomination?

### 6. FRESHMAN ADMISSIONS
How competitive is the admissions process at this institution? Schools are designated "most selective," "more selective," "selective," "less selective" or "least selective." The more selective a school, the harder it will probably be to get in. All of the admissions statistics reported are for the class that entered in the fall of 2013. The 25/75 percentiles for the SAT Math and Critical Reading or ACT Composite show the range in which half the students scored: 25 percent of students scored at or below the lower end, and 75 percent scored at or below the upper end. If a school reported the averages and not the 25/75 percentiles, the average score is listed. The test score that is published represents the test that the greatest percentage of the entering students took.

### 7. EARLY DECISION/ EARLY ACTION DEADLINES
Applicants who plan to take the early decision route to fall 2015 enrollment will have to meet the deadline listed for the school. If the school offers an early action option, the application deadline and notification date are shown also.

### 8. APPLICATION DEADLINE
The date shown is the regular admission deadline for the academic year starting in the fall of 2015. "Rolling" means the school makes admissions decisions as applications come in until the class is filled.

### 9. UNDERGRADUATE STUDENT BODY
This section gives you the breakdown of full-time vs. part-time students, male and female enrollment, the ethnic makeup of the student body, in-state and out-of-state populations, the percentage of students living on campus, and the percentage in fraternities and sororities. All figures are for the 2013-14 academic year.

### 10. MOST POPULAR MAJORS
The five most popular majors appear, along with the percentage majoring in each among 2013 graduates with a bachelor's degree.

### 11. EXPENSES
The first figure represents tuition (including required fees); next is total room and board. Figures are for the 2014-15 academic year; if data are not available, we use figures for the 2013-14 academic year. For public schools, we list both in-state and out-of-state tuition.

### 12. FINANCIAL AID
The percentage of undergrads determined to have financial need and the amount of the average package (grants, loans and jobs) in 2013-14. We also provide the phone number of the financial aid office.

D-2  USN&WR • BEST COLLEGES

## ALABAMA

### Alabama Agricultural and Mechanical University

Normal AL
(256) 372-5245
**U.S. News ranking:** Reg. U. (S), second tier
**Website:** www.aamu.edu
**Admissions email:** admissions@aamu.edu
**Public;** founded 1875
**Freshman admissions:** less selective; 2013-2014: 6,142 applied, 5,521 accepted. ACT required. ACT 25/75 percentile: 15-19. High school rank: N/A
**Early decision deadline:** N/A, notification date: N/A
**Early action deadline:** N/A, notification date: N/A
**Application deadline (fall):** 7/15
**Undergraduate student body:** 3,802 full time, 253 part time; 49% male, 51% female; 0% American Indian, 1% Asian, 92% black, 1% Hispanic, 0% multiracial, 0% Pacific Islander, 5% white, 0% international; 76% from in state; 56% live on campus; 22% of students in fraternities, 25% in sororities
**Most popular majors:** Information not available
**Expenses:** 2014-2015: $8,298 in state, $15,798 out of state; room/board: $5,440
**Financial aid:** (256) 372-5400; 91% of undergrads determined to have financial need; average aid package $10,250

### Alabama State University

Montgomery AL
(334) 229-4291
**U.S. News ranking:** Reg. U. (S), second tier
**Website:** www.alasu.edu
**Admissions email:** mpettway@alasu.edu
**Public**
**Freshman admissions:** least selective; 2013-2014: 7,446 applied, 4,036 accepted. Either SAT or ACT required. ACT 25/75 percentile: 15-20. High school rank: 1% in top tenth, 1% in top quarter, 42% in top half
**Early decision deadline:** N/A, notification date: N/A
**Early action deadline:** N/A, notification date: N/A
**Undergraduate student body:** 4,872 full time, 484 part time; 41% male, 59% female; 0% American Indian, 0% Asian, 93% black, 1% Hispanic, 1% multiracial, 0% Pacific Islander, 2% white, 2% international
**Most popular majors:** Information not available
**Expenses:** 2014-2015: $8,720 in state, $15,656 out of state; room/board: $5,422
**Financial aid:** (334) 229-4323; 96% of undergrads determined to have financial need; average aid package $18,859

### Amridge University

Montgomery AL
(800) 351-4040
**U.S. News ranking:** Nat. Lib. Arts, second tier
**Website:** www.amridgeuniversity.edu/

**Admissions email:** admissions@amridgeuniversity.edu
**Private;** founded 1967
**Affiliation:** Church of Christ
**Freshman admissions:** selective; 2013-2014: N/A applied, N/A accepted. Neither SAT nor ACT required. ACT 25/75 percentile: N/A. High school rank: N/A
**Early decision deadline:** N/A, notification date: N/A
**Early action deadline:** N/A, notification date: N/A
**Application deadline (fall):** rolling
**Undergraduate student body:** 201 full time, 121 part time; 39% male, 61% female; 1% American Indian, 0% Asian, 42% black, 1% Hispanic, 0% multiracial, 0% Pacific Islander, 29% white, 0% international
**Most popular majors:** 3% Business, Management, Marketing, and Related Support Services, 1% Computer and Information Sciences and Support Services, 72% Liberal Arts and Sciences, General Studies and Humanities, 21% Theology and Religious Vocations
**Expenses:** 2014-2015: $10,305; room/board: N/A
**Financial aid:** (800) 351-4040

### Athens State University

Athens AL
(256) 233-8217
**U.S. News ranking:** Reg. Coll. (S), unranked
**Website:** www.athens.edu/
**Admissions email:** N/A
**Public;** founded 1822
**Freshman admissions:** N/A; 2013-2014: N/A applied, N/A accepted. Neither SAT nor ACT required. ACT 25/75 percentile: N/A. High school rank: N/A
**Early decision deadline:** N/A, notification date: N/A
**Early action deadline:** N/A, notification date: N/A
**Application deadline (fall):** N/A
**Undergraduate student body:** 1,343 full time, 1,819 part time; 35% male, 65% female; 2% American Indian, 0% Asian, 11% black, 2% Hispanic, 1% multiracial, 0% Pacific Islander, 75% white, 0% international
**Most popular majors:** 12% Accounting, 14% Business Administration and Management, General, 14% Elementary Education and Teaching, 4% English Language and Literature, General, 5% Liberal Arts and Sciences/Liberal Studies
**Expenses:** 2014-2015: $6,120 in state, $11,490 out of state; room/board: N/A
**Financial aid:** (256) 233-8122; 69% of undergrads determined to have financial need; average aid package $7,820

### Auburn University

Auburn University AL
(334) 844-6425
**U.S. News ranking:** Nat. U., No. 103
**Website:** www.auburn.edu
**Admissions email:** admissions@auburn.edu
**Public;** founded 1856
**Freshman admissions:** more selective; 2013-2014: 15,745 applied, 13,027 accepted. Either SAT or ACT required. ACT 25/75 percentile: 24-30. High school

rank: 29% in top tenth, 60% in top quarter, 86% in top half
**Early decision deadline:** N/A, notification date: N/A
**Early action deadline:** 2/1, notification date: 10/15
**Application deadline (fall):** 6/1
**Undergraduate student body:** 18,011 full time, 1,788 part time; 51% male, 49% female; 1% American Indian, 2% Asian, 7% black, 3% Hispanic, 0% multiracial, 0% Pacific Islander, 85% white, 1% international; 63% from in state; 21% live on campus; 24% of students in fraternities, 38% in sororities
**Most popular majors:** 8% Biological and Biomedical Sciences, 19% Business, Management, Marketing, and Related Support Services, 6% Communication, Journalism, and Related Programs, 11% Education, 15% Engineering
**Expenses:** 2014-2015: $10,200 in state, $27,384 out of state; room/board: $12,178
**Financial aid:** (334) 844-4634; 38% of undergrads determined to have financial need; average aid package $10,820

### Auburn University–Montgomery

Montgomery AL
(334) 244-3611
**U.S. News ranking:** Reg. U. (S), No. 76
**Website:** www.aum.edu
**Admissions email:** vsamuel@aum.edu
**Public;** founded 1967
**Freshman admissions:** selective; 2013-2014: 2,386 applied, 1,723 accepted. ACT required. ACT 25/75 percentile: 18-23. High school rank: 16% in top tenth, 38% in top quarter, 68% in top half
**Early decision deadline:** N/A, notification date: N/A
**Early action deadline:** N/A, notification date: N/A
**Application deadline (fall):** 8/1
**Undergraduate student body:** 2,997 full time, 1,337 part time; 38% male, 62% female; 0% American Indian, 5% Asian, 31% black, 1% Hispanic, 2% multiracial, 0% Pacific Islander, 55% white, 0% international; 92% from in state; 12% live on campus; 4% of students in fraternities, 9% in sororities
**Most popular majors:** 10% Biological and Biomedical Sciences, 24% Business, Management, Marketing, and Related Support Services, 14% Education, 18% Health Professions and Related Programs, 7% Homeland Security, Law Enforcement, Firefighting and Related Protective Services
**Expenses:** 2014-2015: $9,080 in state, $19,640 out of state; room/board: $5,390
**Financial aid:** (334) 244-3571; 66% of undergrads determined to have financial need; average aid package $10,944

### Birmingham-Southern College

Birmingham AL
(205) 226-4696
**U.S. News ranking:** Nat. Lib. Arts, No. 124
**Website:** www.bsc.edu

**Admissions email:** admission@bsc.edu
**Private;** founded 1856
**Affiliation:** United Methodist
**Freshman admissions:** more selective; 2013-2014: 1,931 applied, 1,240 accepted. Either SAT or ACT required. ACT 25/75 percentile: 23-27. High school rank: 24% in top tenth, 56% in top quarter, 85% in top half
**Early decision deadline:** N/A, notification date: N/A
**Early action deadline:** 11/15, notification date: 12/15
**Application deadline (fall):** 7/15
**Undergraduate student body:** 1,167 full time, 21 part time; 54% male, 46% female; 1% American Indian, 4% Asian, 9% black, 3% Hispanic, 1% multiracial, 0% Pacific Islander, 81% white, 0% international; 45% from in state; 86% live on campus; 39% of students in fraternities, 54% in sororities
**Most popular majors:** 11% Biology/Biological Sciences, General, 22% Business Administration and Management, General, 7% English Language and Literature, General, 6% Psychology, General, 6% Teacher Education, Multiple Levels
**Expenses:** 2014-2015: $31,888; room/board: $10,990
**Financial aid:** (205) 226-4688; 56% of undergrads determined to have financial need; average aid package $26,237

### Concordia College[1]

Selma AL
(334) 874-5700
**U.S. News ranking:** Reg. Coll. (S), unranked
**Website:** www.ccal.edu/
**Admissions email:** admission@ccal.edu
**Private;** founded 1922
**Affiliation:** Lutheran
**Application deadline (fall):** rolling
**Undergraduate student body:** N/A full time, N/A part time
**Expenses:** 2013-2014: $8,190; room/board: $4,340
**Financial aid:** (334) 874-5700

### Faulkner University[1]

Montgomery AL
(334) 386-7200
**U.S. News ranking:** Reg. Coll. (S), No. 47
**Website:** www.faulkner.edu
**Admissions email:** admissions@faulkner.edu
**Private;** founded 1942
**Affiliation:** Church of Christ
**Application deadline (fall):** rolling
**Undergraduate student body:** N/A full time, N/A part time
**Expenses:** 2013-2014: $18,230; room/board: $6,780
**Financial aid:** (334) 386-7195

### Huntingdon College

Montgomery AL
(334) 833-4497
**U.S. News ranking:** Reg. Coll. (S), No. 23
**Website:** www.huntingdon.edu
**Admissions email:** admiss@huntingdon.edu
**Private;** founded 1854
**Affiliation:** Methodist
**Freshman admissions:** selective; 2013-2014: 1,470 applied, 923 accepted. Either SAT or ACT required. ACT 25/75 percentile:

19-24. High school rank: 15% in top tenth, 40% in top quarter, 72% in top half
**Early decision deadline:** N/A, notification date: N/A
**Early action deadline:** N/A, notification date: N/A
**Application deadline (fall):** rolling
**Undergraduate student body:** 902 full time, 208 part time; 50% male, 50% female; 1% American Indian, 1% Asian, 19% black, 2% Hispanic, 3% multiracial, 0% Pacific Islander, 58% white, 0% international; 81% from in state; 59% live on campus; 22% of students in fraternities, 40% in sororities
**Most popular majors:** 9% Biological and Biomedical Sciences, 49% Business, Management, Marketing, and Related Support Services, 4% Communication, Journalism, and Related Programs, 5% Education, 6% Parks, Recreation, Leisure, and Fitness Studies
**Expenses:** 2014-2015: $24,550; room/board: $8,550
**Financial aid:** (334) 833-4519; 76% of undergrads determined to have financial need; average aid package $16,201

### Jacksonville State University

Jacksonville AL
(256) 782-5268
**U.S. News ranking:** Reg. U. (S), second tier
**Website:** www.jsu.edu
**Admissions email:** info@jsu.edu
**Public;** founded 1883
**Freshman admissions:** selective; 2013-2014: 3,083 applied, 2,570 accepted. Either SAT or ACT required. ACT 25/75 percentile: 19-26. High school rank: 18% in top tenth, 39% in top quarter, 70% in top half
**Early decision deadline:** N/A, notification date: N/A
**Early action deadline:** N/A, notification date: N/A
**Application deadline (fall):** rolling
**Undergraduate student body:** 5,779 full time, 1,809 part time; 42% male, 58% female; 0% American Indian, 1% Asian, 28% black, 1% Hispanic, 0% multiracial, 0% Pacific Islander, 65% white, 2% international; 82% from in state; 25% live on campus; 14% of students in fraternities, 15% in sororities
**Most popular majors:** 13% Business Administration and Management, General, 5% Criminal Justice/Safety Studies, 7% Public Administration, 26% Registered Nursing/Registered Nurse, 13% Secondary Education and Teaching
**Expenses:** 2014-2015: $8,790 in state, $17,280 out of state; room/board: $6,985
**Financial aid:** (256) 782-5006; 86% of undergrads determined to have financial need; average aid package $9,094

### Judson College[1]

Marion AL
(800) 447-9472
**U.S. News ranking:** Nat. Lib. Arts, second tier
**Website:** www.judson.edu/
**Admissions email:** admissions@judson.edu
**Private**

**Application deadline (fall):** N/A
**Undergraduate student body:** N/A
full time, N/A part time
**Expenses:** 2013-2014: $15,630;
room/board: $9,060
**Financial aid:** (334) 683-5170

## Miles College[1]

Birmingham AL
(800) 445-0708
**U.S. News ranking:** Reg. Coll. (S),
unranked
**Website:** www.miles.edu
**Admissions email:** admissions@
mail.miles.edu
**Private**
**Application deadline (fall):** N/A
**Undergraduate student body:** N/A
full time, N/A part time
**Expenses:** 2013-2014: $11,454;
room/board: $6,896
**Financial aid:** (205) 929-1665

## Oakwood University[1]

Huntsville AL
(256) 726-7356
**U.S. News ranking:** Reg. Coll. (S),
No. 46
**Website:** www.oakwood.edu
**Admissions email:** admissions@
oakwood.edu
**Private;** founded 1896
**Affiliation:** Seventh-day Adventist
**Application deadline (fall):** rolling
**Undergraduate student body:** N/A
full time, N/A part time
**Expenses:** 2013-2014: $16,234;
room/board: $9,700
**Financial aid:** (256) 726-7210

## Samford University

Birmingham AL
(800) 888-7218
**U.S. News ranking:** Reg. U. (S),
No. 3
**Website:** www.samford.edu
**Admissions email:** admission@
samford.edu
**Private;** founded 1841
**Affiliation:** Baptist
**Freshman admissions:** more
selective; 2013-2014: 3,447
applied, 2,653 accepted. Either
SAT or ACT required. ACT 25/75
percentile: 23-28. High school
rank: 35% in top tenth, 59% in
top quarter, 82% in top half
**Early decision deadline:** N/A,
notification date: N/A
**Early action deadline:** N/A,
notification date: N/A
**Application deadline (fall):** 7/1
**Undergraduate student body:** 2,850
full time, 163 part time; 35%
male, 65% female; 0% American
Indian, 1% Asian, 7% black, 7%
Hispanic, 1% multiracial, 0%
Pacific Islander, 81% white, 3%
international; 37% from in state;
72% live on campus; 10% of
students in fraternities, 32% in
sororities
**Most popular majors:** 19%
Business, Management,
Marketing, and Related Support
Services, 9% Communication,
Journalism, and Related Programs,
7% Education, 15% Health
Professions and Related Programs,
7% Visual and Performing Arts
**Expenses:** 2014-2015: $27,324;
room/board: $9,736
**Financial aid:** (205) 726-2905;
44% of undergrads determined to
have financial need; average aid
package $17,036

## Spring Hill College

Mobile AL
(251) 380-3030
**U.S. News ranking:** Reg. U. (S),
No. 18
**Website:** www.shc.edu
**Admissions email:** admit@shc.edu
**Private;** founded 1830
**Affiliation:** Catholic
**Freshman admissions:** more
selective; 2013-2014: 6,956
applied, 3,052 accepted. Either
SAT or ACT required. ACT 25/75
percentile: 21-27. High school
rank: 20% in top tenth, 45% in
top quarter, 75% in top half
**Early decision deadline:** N/A,
notification date: N/A
**Early action deadline:** N/A,
notification date: N/A
**Application deadline (fall):** 7/15
**Undergraduate student body:** 1,226
full time, 93 part time; 40%
male, 60% female; 1% American
Indian, 1% Asian, 16% black,
9% Hispanic, 2% multiracial,
0% Pacific Islander, 66% white,
1% international; 40% from in
state; 78% live on campus; N/A
of students in fraternities, N/A in
sororities
**Most popular majors:** 8% Biological
and Biomedical Sciences,
23% Business, Management,
Marketing, and Related Support
Services, 12% Education, 8%
Health Professions and Related
Programs, 10% Psychology
**Expenses:** 2014-2015: $32,468;
room/board: $11,696
**Financial aid:** (251) 380-3460;
70% of undergrads determined to
have financial need; average aid
package $30,311

## Stillman College[1]

Tuscaloosa AL
(205) 366-8837
**U.S. News ranking:** Nat. Lib. Arts,
second tier
**Website:** www.stillman.edu
**Admissions email:** admissions@
stillman.edu
**Private;** founded 1876
**Affiliation:** Presbyterian Church
(USA)
**Application deadline (fall):** rolling
**Undergraduate student body:** N/A
full time, N/A part time
**Expenses:** 2013-2014: $14,910;
room/board: $7,056
**Financial aid:** (205) 366-8817

## Talladega College[1]

Talladega AL
(256) 761-6235
**U.S. News ranking:** Nat. Lib. Arts,
unranked
**Website:** www.talladega.edu
**Admissions email:** admissions@
talladega.edu
**Private**
**Application deadline (fall):** N/A
**Undergraduate student body:** N/A
full time, N/A part time
**Expenses:** 2013-2014: $11,492;
room/board: $6,504
**Financial aid:** (256) 761-6341

## Troy University

Troy AL
(334) 670-3179
**U.S. News ranking:** Reg. U. (S),
No. 76
**Website:** www.troy.edu/
**Admissions email:** admit@troy.edu
**Public;** founded 1887

**Freshman admissions:** selective;
2013-2014: 6,538 applied,
4,392 accepted. Either SAT
or ACT required. ACT 25/75
percentile: 18-25. High school
rank: N/A in top tenth, 52% in top
quarter, 84% in top half
**Early decision deadline:** N/A,
notification date: N/A
**Early action deadline:** N/A,
notification date: N/A
**Application deadline (fall):** rolling
**Undergraduate student body:** 9,141
full time, 7,175 part time; 38%
male, 62% female; 1% American
Indian, 1% Asian, 37% black,
3% Hispanic, 2% multiracial,
0% Pacific Islander, 49% white,
2% international; 66% from in
state; 35% live on campus; 13%
of students in fraternities, 15%
in sororities
**Most popular majors:** 46%
Business, Management,
Marketing, and Related Support
Services, 12% Foreign Languages,
Literatures, and Linguistics,
7% Homeland Security, Law
Enforcement, Firefighting and
Related Protective Services,
11% Psychology, 5% Public
Administration and Social Service
Professions
**Expenses:** 2013-2014: $9,416 in
state, $17,336 out of state; room/
board: $7,144
**Financial aid:** (334) 670-3186;
71% of undergrads determined to
have financial need; average aid
package $4,531

## Tuskegee University

Tuskegee AL
(334) 727-8500
**U.S. News ranking:** Reg. Coll. (S),
No. 9
**Website:** www.tuskegee.edu
**Admissions email:**
admiweb@tusk.edu
**Private;** founded 1881
**Freshman admissions:** selective;
2013-2014: 8,894 applied,
3,679 accepted. Either SAT
or ACT required. ACT 25/75
percentile: 18-23. High school
rank: 20% in top tenth, 60% in
top quarter, 100% in top half
**Early decision deadline:** N/A,
notification date: N/A
**Early action deadline:** N/A,
notification date: N/A
**Application deadline (fall):** 3/15
**Undergraduate student body:** 2,468
full time, 116 part time; 42%
male, 58% female; 0% American
Indian, 0% Asian, 80% black,
0% Hispanic, 0% multiracial,
0% Pacific Islander, 0% white,
0% international; 37% from in
state; 74% live on campus; 1%
of students in fraternities, 2% in
sororities
**Most popular majors:** 11%
Agriculture, Agriculture
Operations, and Related Sciences,
7% Biology/Biological Sciences,
General, 20% Engineering,
10% Psychology, General, 5%
Registered Nursing, Nursing
Administration, Nursing Research
and Clinical Nursing
**Expenses:** 2014-2015: $20,025;
room/board: $9,104
**Financial aid:** (334) 727-8201;
87% of undergrads determined to
have financial need; average aid
package $17,250

## University of Alabama

Tuscaloosa AL
(205) 348-5666
**U.S. News ranking:** Nat. U., No. 88
**Website:** www.ua.edu
**Admissions email:**
admissions@ua.edu
**Public;** founded 1831
**Freshman admissions:** more
selective; 2013-2014: 30,975
applied, 17,515 accepted. Either
SAT or ACT required. ACT 25/75
percentile: 22-30. High school
rank: 41% in top tenth, 60% in
top quarter, 83% in top half
**Early decision deadline:** N/A,
notification date: N/A
**Early action deadline:** N/A,
notification date: N/A
**Application deadline (fall):** rolling
**Undergraduate student body:**
26,548 full time, 2,892 part
time; 46% male, 54% female;
0% American Indian, 1% Asian,
11% black, 3% Hispanic, 2%
multiracial, 0% Pacific Islander,
79% white, 3% international;
55% from in state; 26% live
on campus; 24% of students in
fraternities, 35% in sororities
**Most popular majors:** 29%
Business, Management,
Marketing, and Related Support
Services, 10% Communication,
Journalism, and Related Programs,
8% Education, 7% Family and
Consumer Sciences/Human
Sciences, 9% Health Professions
and Related Programs
**Expenses:** 2014-2015: $9,826 in
state, $24,950 out of state; room/
board: $8,866
**Financial aid:** (205) 348-2976;
43% of undergrads determined to
have financial need; average aid
package $11,666

## University of
## Alabama–Birmingham

Birmingham AL
(205) 934-8221
**U.S. News ranking:** Nat. U.,
No. 149
**Website:** www.uab.edu
**Admissions email:**
undergradadmit@uab.edu
**Public;** founded 1969
**Freshman admissions:** more
selective; 2013-2014: 5,689
applied, 4,934 accepted. Either
SAT or ACT required. ACT 25/75
percentile: 22-28. High school
rank: 30% in top tenth, 56% in
top quarter, 83% in top half
**Early decision deadline:** N/A,
notification date: N/A
**Early action deadline:** N/A,
notification date: N/A
**Application deadline (fall):** rolling
**Undergraduate student body:** 8,357
full time, 3,145 part time; 42%
male, 58% female; 0% American
Indian, 5% Asian, 26% black,
3% Hispanic, 3% multiracial,
0% Pacific Islander, 60% white,
1% international; 92% from in
state; 22% live on campus; 4%
of students in fraternities, 4% in
sororities
**Most popular majors:** 17%
Business, Management,
Marketing, and Related Support
Services, 9% Education, 6%
Engineering, 20% Health
Professions and Related Programs,
8% Psychology
**Expenses:** 2014-2015: $9,280 in
state, $21,220 out of state; room/
board: $10,112

**Financial aid:** (205) 934-8223;
61% of undergrads determined to
have financial need; average aid
package $8,941

## University of
## Alabama–Huntsville

Huntsville AL
(256) 824-6070
**U.S. News ranking:** Nat. U.,
No. 181
**Website:** www.uah.edu
**Admissions email:**
admitme@uah.edu
**Public;** founded 1950
**Freshman admissions:** more
selective; 2013-2014: 2,054
applied, 1,656 accepted. Either
SAT or ACT required. ACT 25/75
percentile: 23-29. High school
rank: 28% in top tenth, 50% in
top quarter, 83% in top half
**Early decision deadline:** N/A,
notification date: N/A
**Early action deadline:** N/A,
notification date: N/A
**Application deadline (fall):** 8/20
**Undergraduate student body:** 4,237
full time, 1,459 part time; 56%
male, 44% female; 1% American
Indian, 4% Asian, 13% black,
3% Hispanic, 2% multiracial,
0% Pacific Islander, 70% white,
3% international; 90% from in
state; 20% live on campus; 6%
of students in fraternities, 7% in
sororities
**Most popular majors:** 8% Biological
and Biomedical Sciences,
22% Business, Management,
Marketing, and Related Support
Services, 25% Engineering,
17% Health Professions and
Related Programs, 3% Visual and
Performing Arts
**Expenses:** 2014-2015: $9,158 in
state, $21,232 out of state; room/
board: $8,433
**Financial aid:** (256) 824-6241;
54% of undergrads determined to
have financial need; average aid
package $9,419

## University of Mobile

Mobile AL
(251) 442-2273
**U.S. News ranking:** Reg. Coll. (S),
No. 25
**Website:** www.umobile.edu
**Admissions email:** umadminfo@
umobile.edu
**Private;** founded 1961
**Affiliation:** Southern Baptist
**Freshman admissions:** selective;
2013-2014: 866 applied, 617
accepted. Either SAT or ACT
required. ACT 25/75 percentile:
20-25. High school rank: 18%
in top tenth, 50% in top quarter,
84% in top half
**Early decision deadline:** N/A,
notification date: N/A
**Early action deadline:** N/A,
notification date: N/A
**Application deadline (fall):** 8/1
**Undergraduate student body:** 1,257
full time, 224 part time; 33%
male, 67% female; 2% American
Indian, 1% Asian, 22% black,
1% Hispanic, 2% multiracial,
0% Pacific Islander, 65% white,
3% international; 78% from in
state; 44% live on campus; N/A
of students in fraternities, N/A in
sororities
**Most popular majors:** 19%
Business, Management,
Marketing, and Related Support
Services, 21% Education, 16%
Health Professions and Related

Programs, 10% Liberal Arts and Sciences, General Studies and Humanities, 5% Philosophy and Religious Studies
**Expenses:** 2014-2015: $19,700; room/board: $9,550
**Financial aid:** (251) 442-2385; 72% of undergrads determined to have financial need; average aid package $16,521

## University of Montevallo

Montevallo AL
(205) 665-6030
**U.S. News ranking:** Reg. U. (S), No. 37
**Website:** www.montevallo.edu
**Admissions email:** admissions@um.montevallo.edu
**Public;** founded 1896
**Freshman admissions:** selective; 2013-2014: 1,545 applied, 1,032 accepted. Either SAT or ACT required. ACT 25/75 percentile: 20-26. High school rank: N/A
**Early decision deadline:** N/A, notification date: N/A
**Early action deadline:** N/A, notification date: N/A
**Application deadline (fall):** 8/1
**Undergraduate student body:** 2,350 full time, 270 part time; 34% male, 66% female; 1% American Indian, 1% Asian, 14% black, 2% Hispanic, 2% multiracial, 0% Pacific Islander, 74% white, 1% international; 95% from in state; 47% live on campus; 12% of students in fraternities, 17% in sororities
**Most popular majors:** 12% Business, Management, Marketing, and Related Support Services, 11% Education, 11% English Language and Literature/Letters, 8% Family and Consumer Sciences/Human Sciences, 15% Visual and Performing Arts
**Expenses:** 2014-2015: $10,660 in state, $21,220 out of state; room/board: $6,400
**Financial aid:** (205) 665-6050; 63% of undergrads determined to have financial need; average aid package $9,384

## University of North Alabama

Florence AL
(256) 765-4608
**U.S. News ranking:** Reg. U. (S), No. 81
**Website:** www.una.edu
**Admissions email:** admissions@una.edu
**Public;** founded 1830
**Freshman admissions:** selective; 2013-2014: 2,816 applied, 2,057 accepted. Either SAT or ACT required. ACT 25/75 percentile: 19-25. High school rank: N/A
**Early decision deadline:** N/A, notification date: N/A
**Early action deadline:** N/A, notification date: N/A
**Application deadline (fall):** rolling
**Undergraduate student body:** 4,852 full time, 1,141 part time; 42% male, 58% female; 1% American Indian, 0% Asian, 14% black, 2% Hispanic, 2% multiracial, 0% Pacific Islander, 72% white, 5% international; 84% from in state; 23% live on campus; 11% of students in fraternities, 11% in sororities

**Most popular majors:** 16% Business, Management, Marketing, and Related Support Services, 7% Communication, Journalism, and Related Programs, 12% Education, 17% Health Professions and Related Programs, 8% Social Sciences
**Expenses:** 2014-2015: $9,073 in state, $16,393 out of state; room/board: $6,327
**Financial aid:** (256) 765-4278; 81% of undergrads determined to have financial need; average aid package $7,104

## University of South Alabama

Mobile AL
(251) 460-6141
**U.S. News ranking:** Nat. U., second tier
**Website:** www.southalabama.edu
**Admissions email:** admiss@usouthal.edu
**Public;** founded 1963
**Freshman admissions:** selective; 2013-2014: 4,814 applied, 4,142 accepted. Neither SAT nor ACT required. ACT 25/75 percentile: 20-26. High school rank: N/A
**Early decision deadline:** N/A, notification date: N/A
**Early action deadline:** N/A, notification date: N/A
**Application deadline (fall):** 7/15
**Undergraduate student body:** 8,767 full time, 2,540 part time; 43% male, 57% female; 1% American Indian, 3% Asian, 23% black, 2% Hispanic, 2% multiracial, 0% Pacific Islander, 64% white, 3% international; 81% from in state; 27% live on campus; N/A of students in fraternities, N/A in sororities
**Most popular majors:** 4% Biomedical Sciences, General, 5% Elementary Education and Teaching, 5% Multi-/Interdisciplinary Studies, General, 18% Registered Nursing/Registered Nurse, 5% Speech Communication and Rhetoric
**Expenses:** 2013-2014: $6,948 in state, $13,596 out of state; room/board: $7,260
**Financial aid:** (251) 460-6231

## University of West Alabama

Livingston AL
(205) 652-3578
**U.S. News ranking:** Reg. U. (S), second tier
**Website:** www.uwa.edu
**Admissions email:** admissions@uwa.edu
**Public;** founded 1835
**Freshman admissions:** selective; 2013-2014: 1,363 applied, 831 accepted. Either SAT or ACT required. ACT 25/75 percentile: 18-22. High school rank: N/A
**Early decision deadline:** N/A, notification date: N/A
**Early action deadline:** N/A, notification date: N/A
**Application deadline (fall):** rolling
**Undergraduate student body:** 1,696 full time, 303 part time; 43% male, 57% female; 0% American Indian, 1% Asian, 42% black, 2% Hispanic, 1% multiracial, 0% Pacific Islander, 43% white, 5% international; 80% from in state; 45% live on campus; 5% of students in fraternities, 6% in sororities

**Most popular majors:** 10% Accounting, 10% Finance, General, 13% Physical Education Teaching and Coaching, 6% Sociology, 12% Teacher Education, Multiple Levels
**Expenses:** 2013-2014: $7,660 in state, $14,170 out of state; room/board: $6,618
**Financial aid:** (205) 652-3576

## Alaska Pacific University

Anchorage AK
(800) 252-7528
**U.S. News ranking:** Reg. U. (W), No. 75
**Website:** www.alaskapacific.edu
**Admissions email:** admissions@alaskapacific.edu
**Private;** founded 1957
**Affiliation:** United Methodist
**Freshman admissions:** selective; 2013-2014: 494 applied, 184 accepted. Either SAT or ACT required. SAT 25/75 percentile: 915-1085. High school rank: N/A
**Early decision deadline:** N/A, notification date: N/A
**Early action deadline:** N/A, notification date: N/A
**Application deadline (fall):** rolling
**Undergraduate student body:** 245 full time, 142 part time; 34% male, 66% female; 18% American Indian, 2% Asian, 3% black, 3% Hispanic, 9% multiracial, 0% Pacific Islander, 55% white, 0% international
**Most popular majors:** 19% Business Administration and Management, General, 10% Counseling Psychology, 14% Education, General, 9% Human Services, General, 19% Marine Biology and Biological Oceanography
**Expenses:** 2014-2015: $19,680; room/board: $7,000
**Financial aid:** (907) 564-8341; 72% of undergrads determined to have financial need; average aid package $10,310

## University of Alaska–Anchorage

Anchorage AK
(907) 786-1480
**U.S. News ranking:** Reg. U. (W), No. 68
**Website:** www.uaa.alaska.edu
**Admissions email:** enroll@uaa.alaska.edu
**Public;** founded 1954
**Freshman admissions:** selective; 2013-2014: 3,913 applied, 3,117 accepted. Neither SAT nor ACT required. SAT 25/75 percentile: 880-1080. High school rank: 11% in top tenth, 31% in top quarter, 62% in top half
**Early decision deadline:** N/A, notification date: N/A
**Early action deadline:** N/A, notification date: N/A
**Application deadline (fall):** 7/1
**Undergraduate student body:** 7,683 full time, 8,894 part time; 41% male, 59% female; 7% American Indian, 7% Asian, 4% black, 7% Hispanic, 10% multiracial, 1% Pacific Islander, 58% white, 2% international; 91% from in state; N/A live on campus; N/A of students in fraternities, N/A in sororities

**Most popular majors:** 20% Business, Management, Marketing, and Related Support Services, 8% Engineering, 16% Health Professions and Related Programs, 8% Psychology, 5% Social Sciences
**Expenses:** 2014-2015: $6,002 in state, $19,322 out of state; room/board: $8,680
**Financial aid:** (907) 786-1586; 53% of undergrads determined to have financial need; average aid package $8,933

## University of Alaska–Fairbanks

Fairbanks AK
(800) 478-1823
**U.S. News ranking:** Nat. U., second tier
**Website:** www.uaf.edu
**Admissions email:** fyapply@uaf.edu
**Public;** founded 1917
**Freshman admissions:** selective; 2013-2014: 1,529 applied, 1,221 accepted. Either SAT or ACT required. ACT 25/75 percentile: 18-25. High school rank: 18% in top tenth, 39% in top quarter, 67% in top half
**Early decision deadline:** N/A, notification date: N/A
**Early action deadline:** N/A, notification date: N/A
**Application deadline (fall):** 6/15
**Undergraduate student body:** 3,654 full time, 4,424 part time; 43% male, 57% female; 14% American Indian, 1% Asian, 2% black, 5% Hispanic, 4% multiracial, 0% Pacific Islander, 45% white, 1% international; 87% from in state; 27% live on campus; N/A of students in fraternities, N/A in sororities
**Most popular majors:** 8% Biological and Biomedical Sciences, 9% Business, Management, Marketing, and Related Support Services, 13% Engineering, 8% Social Sciences, 6% Visual and Performing Arts
**Expenses:** 2014-2015: $6,752 in state, $20,072 out of state; room/board: $7,450
**Financial aid:** (907) 474-7256; 54% of undergrads determined to have financial need; average aid package $10,058

## University of Alaska–Southeast[1]

Juneau AK
(907) 465-6350
**U.S. News ranking:** Reg. U. (W), unranked
**Website:** www.uas.alaska.edu
**Admissions email:** admissions@uas.alaska.edu
**Public**
**Application deadline (fall):** N/A
**Undergraduate student body:** N/A full time, N/A part time
**Expenses:** 2013-2014: $5,693 in state, $16,269 out of state; room/board: $9,829
**Financial aid:** (907) 796-6255

## American Indian College of the Assemblies of God[1]

Phoenix AZ
(800) 933-3828
**U.S. News ranking:** Reg. Coll. (W), unranked
**Website:** www.aicag.edu
**Admissions email:** aicadm@aicag.edu
**Private**
**Application deadline (fall):** N/A
**Undergraduate student body:** N/A full time, N/A part time
**Expenses:** 2013-2014: $12,000; room/board: $6,202
**Financial aid:** (800) 933-3828

## Arizona State University–Tempe

Tempe AZ
(480) 965-7788
**U.S. News ranking:** Nat. U., No. 129
**Website:** www.asu.edu
**Admissions email:** admissions@asu.edu
**Public;** founded 1885
**Freshman admissions:** more selective; 2013-2014: 21,770 applied, 17,465 accepted. Neither SAT nor ACT required. SAT 25/75 percentile: 1020-1270. High school rank: 31% in top tenth, 63% in top quarter, 90% in top half
**Early decision deadline:** N/A, notification date: N/A
**Early action deadline:** N/A, notification date: N/A
**Undergraduate student body:** 34,989 full time, 3,746 part time; 56% male, 44% female; 1% American Indian, 7% Asian, 4% black, 19% Hispanic, 4% multiracial, 0% Pacific Islander, 58% white, 7% international; 77% from in state; 23% live on campus; 8% of students in fraternities, 13% in sororities
**Most popular majors:** 8% Biological and Biomedical Sciences, 20% Business, Management, Marketing, and Related Support Services, 7% Engineering, 10% Social Sciences, 8% Visual and Performing Arts
**Expenses:** 2014-2015: $9,811 in state, $23,312 out of state; room/board: $9,440
**Financial aid:** (480) 965-3355; 58% of undergrads determined to have financial need; average aid package $13,786

## Everest College–Phoenix[1]

Phoenix AZ
(888) 523-3117
**U.S. News ranking:** Reg. Coll. (W), unranked
**Website:** www.everestcollegephoenix.edu
**Admissions email:** N/A
**For-profit**
**Application deadline (fall):** N/A
**Undergraduate student body:** N/A full time, N/A part time
**Expenses:** 2013-2014: $12,960; room/board: N/A
**Financial aid:** N/A

## Frank Lloyd Wright School of Architecture

Scottsdale AZ
(608) 588-4770
**U.S. News ranking:** Arts, unranked
**Website:** www.taliesin.edu/
**Admissions email:** N/A
**Private**
**Freshman admissions:** N/A; 2013-2014: N/A applied, N/A accepted. Neither SAT nor ACT required. SAT 25/75 percentile: N/A. High school rank: N/A
**Early decision deadline:** N/A, notification date: N/A
**Early action deadline:** N/A, notification date: N/A
**Application deadline (fall):** 4/1
**Undergraduate student body:** 2 full time, N/A part time; 100% male, 0% female; N/A American Indian, N/A Asian, N/A black, N/A Hispanic, N/A multiracial, N/A Pacific Islander, N/A white, N/A international
**Most popular majors:** Information not available
**Expenses:** 2014-2015 tuition/fees/room/board: $30,300
**Financial aid:** N/A; 0% of undergrads determined to have financial need; average aid package $4,500

## Grand Canyon University[1]

Phoenix AZ
(800) 800-9776
**U.S. News ranking:** Reg. U. (W), second tier
**Website:** apply.gcu.edu
**Admissions email:** golopes@gcu.edu
**For-profit;** founded 1949
**Application deadline (fall):** rolling
**Undergraduate student body:** N/A full time, N/A part time
**Expenses:** 2013-2014: $18,600; room/board: $7,400
**Financial aid:** (602) 639-6600

## Northcentral University

Prescott Valley AZ
(888) 327-2877
**U.S. News ranking:** Nat. U., unranked
**Website:** www.ncu.edu
**Admissions email:** admissions@ncu.edu
**For-profit;** founded 1996
**Freshman admissions:** N/A; 2013-2014: N/A applied, N/A accepted. Neither SAT nor ACT required. ACT 25/75 percentile: N/A. High school rank: N/A
**Early decision deadline:** N/A, notification date: N/A
**Early action deadline:** N/A, notification date: N/A
**Application deadline (fall):** rolling
**Undergraduate student body:** 195 full time, 241 part time; 35% male, 65% female; 0% American Indian, 1% Asian, 11% black, 5% Hispanic, 1% multiracial, 0% Pacific Islander, 33% white, 0% international
**Most popular majors:** 10% Accounting and Business/Management, 59% Business Administration and Management, General, 8% Computer Science, 10% Criminal Justice/Law Enforcement Administration, 6% Homeland Security
**Expenses:** N/A
**Financial aid:** (928) 541-7777

## Northern Arizona University

Flagstaff AZ
(928) 523-5511
**U.S. News ranking:** Nat. U., second tier
**Website:** www.nau.edu
**Admissions email:** undergraduate.admissions@nau.edu
**Public;** founded 1899
**Freshman admissions:** selective; 2013-2014: 33,989 applied, 31,057 accepted. Neither SAT nor ACT required. SAT 25/75 percentile: 940-1160. High school rank: 21% in top tenth, 47% in top quarter, 80% in top half
**Early decision deadline:** N/A, notification date: N/A
**Early action deadline:** N/A, notification date: N/A
**Application deadline (fall):** rolling
**Undergraduate student body:** 18,769 full time, 3,901 part time; 42% male, 58% female; 3% American Indian, 2% Asian, 3% black, 19% Hispanic, 5% multiracial, 0% Pacific Islander, 63% white, 4% international; 72% from in state; 32% live on campus; N/A of students in fraternities, N/A in sororities
**Most popular majors:** 18% Business, Management, Marketing, and Related Support Services, 13% Education, 8% Health Professions and Related Programs, 11% Liberal Arts and Sciences, General Studies and Humanities, 8% Social Sciences
**Expenses:** 2014-2015: $10,030 in state, $22,510 out of state; room/board: N/A
**Financial aid:** (928) 523-4951

## Prescott College

Prescott AZ
(877) 350-2100
**U.S. News ranking:** Reg. U. (W), No. 75
**Website:** www.prescott.edu/
**Admissions email:** admissions@prescott.edu
**Private;** founded 1966
**Freshman admissions:** selective; 2013-2014: 399 applied, 291 accepted. Either SAT or ACT required. SAT 25/75 percentile: 910-1260. High school rank: N/A
**Early decision deadline:** 12/1, notification date: 12/15
**Early action deadline:** N/A, notification date: N/A
**Application deadline (fall):** 8/15
**Undergraduate student body:** 444 full time, 101 part time; 45% male, 55% female; 2% American Indian, 1% Asian, 1% black, 6% Hispanic, 4% multiracial, 0% Pacific Islander, 73% white, 1% international; 11% from in state; 16% live on campus; 0% of students in fraternities, 0% in sororities
**Most popular majors:** 18% Education, 9% Multi/Interdisciplinary Studies, 9% Natural Resources and Conservation, 9% Parks, Recreation, Leisure, and Fitness Studies, 20% Psychology
**Expenses:** 2014-2015: $25,640; room/board: $8,266
**Financial aid:** (928) 350-1111; 67% of undergrads determined to have financial need; average aid package $19,706

## Southwest University of Visual Arts[1]

Tucson AZ
(800) 825-8753
**U.S. News ranking:** Arts, unranked
**Website:** suva.edu/
**Admissions email:** N/A
**For-profit**
**Application deadline (fall):** N/A
**Undergraduate student body:** N/A full time, N/A part time
**Expenses:** 2013-2014: $34,541; room/board: N/A
**Financial aid:** N/A

## University of Advancing Technology[1]

Tempe AZ
(602) 383-8228
**U.S. News ranking:** Reg. Coll. (W), unranked
**Website:** www.uat.edu
**Admissions email:** admissions@uat.edu
**For-profit**
**Application deadline (fall):** N/A
**Undergraduate student body:** N/A full time, N/A part time
**Expenses:** 2013-2014: $19,700; room/board: $10,568
**Financial aid:** (800) 658-5744

## University of Arizona

Tucson AZ
(520) 621-3237
**U.S. News ranking:** Nat. U., No. 121
**Website:** www.arizona.edu
**Admissions email:** admissions@arizona.edu
**Public;** founded 1885
**Freshman admissions:** selective; 2013-2014: 26,481 applied, 20,546 accepted. Neither SAT nor ACT required. SAT 25/75 percentile: 970-1220. High school rank: 31% in top tenth, 60% in top quarter, 88% in top half
**Early decision deadline:** N/A, notification date: N/A
**Early action deadline:** N/A, notification date: N/A
**Application deadline (fall):** 5/1
**Undergraduate student body:** 28,401 full time, 3,269 part time; 48% male, 52% female; 1% American Indian, 6% Asian, 3% black, 24% Hispanic, 4% multiracial, 0% Pacific Islander, 55% white, 6% international; 74% from in state; 20% live on campus; N/A of students in fraternities, N/A in sororities
**Most popular majors:** 10% Biological and Biomedical Sciences, 17% Business, Management, Marketing, and Related Support Services, 5% Multi/Interdisciplinary Studies, 8% Psychology, 9% Social Sciences
**Expenses:** 2014-2015: $10,581 in state, $28,379 out of state; room/board: $9,700
**Financial aid:** (520) 621-5200; 55% of undergrads determined to have financial need; average aid package $12,495

## University of Phoenix[1]

Phoenix AZ
(866) 766-0766
**U.S. News ranking:** Nat. U., unranked
**Website:** www.phoenix.edu
**Admissions email:** N/A
**For-profit**
**Application deadline (fall):** N/A
**Undergraduate student body:** N/A full time, N/A part time
**Expenses:** N/A
**Financial aid:** N/A

## Western International University

Tempe AZ
(602) 943-2311
**U.S. News ranking:** Reg. U. (W), unranked
**Website:** www.west.edu/
**Admissions email:** N/A
**For-profit;** founded 1978
**Freshman admissions:** N/A; 2013-2014: 2 applied, 2 accepted. Neither SAT nor ACT required. ACT 25/75 percentile: N/A. High school rank: N/A
**Early decision deadline:** N/A, notification date: N/A
**Early action deadline:** N/A, notification date: N/A
**Application deadline (fall):** rolling
**Undergraduate student body:** 1,495 full time, 0 part time; 35% male, 65% female; 2% American Indian, 0% Asian, 15% black, 15% Hispanic, 4% multiracial, 1% Pacific Islander, 49% white, 1% international
**Most popular majors:** 11% Accounting, 15% Behavioral Sciences, 10% Business Administration and Management, General, 43% Business/Commerce, General, 4% Information Technology
**Expenses:** 2013-2014: $6,000; room/board: N/A
**Financial aid:** (602) 943-2311

## ARKANSAS

## Arkansas Baptist College[1]

Little Rock AR
(501) 244-5104
**U.S. News ranking:** Reg. Coll. (S), unranked
**Website:** www.arkansasbaptist.edu
**Admissions email:** jocelyn.spriggs@arkansasbaptist.edu
**Private**
**Application deadline (fall):** N/A
**Undergraduate student body:** N/A full time, N/A part time
**Expenses:** 2013-2014: $8,040; room/board: $8,040
**Financial aid:** (501) 374-0804

## Arkansas State University

State University AR
(870) 972-3024
**U.S. News ranking:** Reg. U. (S), No. 53
**Website:** www.astate.edu
**Admissions email:** admissions@astate.edu
**Public;** founded 1909
**Freshman admissions:** selective; 2013-2014: 4,838 applied, 3,653 accepted. Either SAT or ACT required. ACT 25/75 percentile: 21-26. High school rank: 25% in top tenth, 47% in top quarter, 72% in top half
**Early decision deadline:** N/A, notification date: N/A
**Early action deadline:** N/A, notification date: N/A
**Application deadline (fall):** 8/18
**Undergraduate student body:** 7,645 full time, 2,453 part time; 42% male, 58% female; 0% American Indian, 1% Asian, 15% black, 2% Hispanic, 2% multiracial, 0% Pacific Islander, 73% white, 6% international; 90% from in state; 31% live on campus; 12% of students in fraternities, 10% in sororities
**Most popular majors:** 14% Business, Management, Marketing, and Related Support Services, 17% Education, 13% Health Professions and Related Programs, 10% Liberal Arts and Sciences, General Studies and Humanities, 8% Social Sciences
**Expenses:** 2014-2015: $7,720 in state, $13,480 out of state; room/board: $7,750
**Financial aid:** (870) 972-2310; 83% of undergrads determined to have financial need; average aid package $10,500

## Arkansas Tech University

Russellville AR
(479) 968-0343
**U.S. News ranking:** Reg. U. (S), No. 92
**Website:** www.atu.edu
**Admissions email:** tech.enroll@atu.edu
**Public;** founded 1909
**Freshman admissions:** selective; 2013-2014: 3,849 applied, 3,272 accepted. Either SAT or ACT required. ACT 25/75 percentile: 18-25. High school rank: 13% in top tenth, 33% in top quarter, 62% in top half
**Early decision deadline:** N/A, notification date: N/A
**Early action deadline:** N/A, notification date: N/A
**Application deadline (fall):** rolling
**Undergraduate student body:** 7,063 full time, 3,419 part time; 46% male, 54% female; 1% American Indian, 1% Asian, 8% black, 5% Hispanic, 2% multiracial, 0% Pacific Islander, 79% white, 3% international; 96% from in state; 30% live on campus; 5% of students in fraternities, 7% in sororities
**Most popular majors:** 6% Business Administration and Management, General, 8% Early Childhood Education and Teaching, 18% Multi-/Interdisciplinary Studies, Other, 5% Psychology, General, 9% Registered Nursing/Registered Nurse
**Expenses:** 2014-2015: $7,248 in state, $13,518 out of state; room/board: $6,734
**Financial aid:** (479) 968-0399; 69% of undergrads determined to have financial need; average aid package $9,028

## Central Baptist College

Conway AR
(501) 329-6873
**U.S. News ranking:** Reg. Coll. (S), No. 69
**Website:** www.cbc.edu
**Admissions email:** admissions@cbc.edu
**Private;** founded 1952
**Affiliation:** Baptist Missionary Association of America
**Freshman admissions:** selective; 2013-2014: 386 applied, 212 accepted. Either SAT or ACT required. ACT 25/75 percentile: 19-23. High school rank: 18% in top tenth, 38% in top quarter, 64% in top half

Early decision deadline: N/A, notification date: N/A
Early action deadline: N/A, notification date: N/A
Application deadline (fall): rolling
Undergraduate student body: 650 full time, 177 part time; 51% male, 49% female; 1% American Indian, 0% Asian, 22% black, 2% Hispanic, 1% multiracial, 0% Pacific Islander, 70% white, 3% international; 90% from in state; 18% live on campus; 0% of students in fraternities, 0% in sororities
Most popular majors: 21% Bible/Biblical Studies, 5% Business, Management, Marketing, and Related Support Services, Other, 11% General Studies, 6% Management Information Systems, General, 21% Organizational Behavior Studies
Expenses: 2014-2015: $13,800; room/board: $7,500
Financial aid: (501) 329-6872; 76% of undergrads determined to have financial need; average aid package $11,885

## Harding University
Searcy AR
(800) 477-4407
U.S. News ranking: Reg. U. (S), No. 22
Website: www.harding.edu
Admissions email: admissions@harding.edu
Private; founded 1924
Affiliation: Church of Christ
Freshman admissions: more selective; 2013-2014: 2,180 applied, 1,663 accepted. Either SAT or ACT required. ACT 25/75 percentile: 22-28. High school rank: 27% in top tenth, 50% in top quarter, 77% in top half
Early decision deadline: N/A, notification date: N/A
Early action deadline: 11/15, notification date: N/A
Application deadline (fall): rolling
Undergraduate student body: 4,105 full time, 323 part time; 46% male, 54% female; 1% American Indian, 1% Asian, 4% black, 3% Hispanic, 1% multiracial, 0% Pacific Islander, 83% white, 7% international; 28% from in state; 69% live on campus; 55% of students in fraternities, 54% in sororities
Most popular majors: 17% Business, Management, Marketing, and Related Support Services, 14% Education, 12% Health Professions and Related Programs, 8% Liberal Arts and Sciences, General Studies and Humanities, 6% Parks, Recreation, Leisure, and Fitness Studies
Expenses: 2014-2015: $17,040; room/board: $6,516
Financial aid: (501) 279-5278; 61% of undergrads determined to have financial need; average aid package $16,825

## Henderson State University
Arkadelphia AR
(870) 230-5028
U.S. News ranking: Reg. U. (S), second tier
Website: www.hsu.edu/admissions
Admissions email: admissions@hsu.edu
Public; founded 1890
Freshman admissions: selective;

2013-2014: 3,388 applied, 2,106 accepted. Either SAT or ACT required. ACT 25/75 percentile: 19-24. High school rank: 12% in top tenth, 26% in top quarter, 52% in top half
Early decision deadline: N/A, notification date: N/A
Early action deadline: N/A, notification date: N/A
Application deadline (fall): rolling
Undergraduate student body: 2,878 full time, 321 part time; 44% male, 56% female; 0% American Indian, 1% Asian, 24% black, 3% Hispanic, 5% multiracial, 0% Pacific Islander, 66% white, 1% international; 85% from in state; 42% live on campus; 16% of students in fraternities, 13% in sororities
Most popular majors: 14% Business, Management, Marketing, and Related Support Services, 22% Education, 6% Health Professions and Related Programs, 13% Liberal Arts and Sciences, General Studies and Humanities, 8% Psychology
Expenses: 2014-2015: $7,561 in state, $13,921 out of state; room/board: $6,500
Financial aid: (870) 230-5148; 82% of undergrads determined to have financial need; average aid package $12,619

## Hendrix College
Conway AR
(800) 277-9017
U.S. News ranking: Nat. Lib. Arts, No. 81
Website: www.hendrix.edu
Admissions email: adm@hendrix.edu
Private; founded 1876
Affiliation: United Methodist
Freshman admissions: more selective; 2013-2014: 1,926 applied, 1,548 accepted. Either SAT or ACT required. ACT 25/75 percentile: 26-32. High school rank: 46% in top tenth, 74% in top quarter, 95% in top half
Early decision deadline: N/A, notification date: N/A
Early action deadline: 11/15, notification date: 12/15
Application deadline (fall): 6/1
Undergraduate student body: 1,409 full time, 7 part time; 45% male, 55% female; 2% American Indian, 5% Asian, 5% black, 5% Hispanic, 2% multiracial, 0% Pacific Islander, 71% white, 4% international; 49% from in state; 92% live on campus; 0% of students in fraternities, 0% in sororities
Most popular majors: 17% Biology/Biological Sciences, General, 5% Drama and Dramatics/Theatre Arts, General, 4% Multi-/Interdisciplinary Studies, Other, 16% Psychology, General, 17% Sociology
Expenses: 2014-2015: $39,290; room/board: $10,912
Financial aid: (501) 450-1368; 63% of undergrads determined to have financial need; average aid package $29,590

## John Brown University
Siloam Springs AR
(877) 528-4636
U.S. News ranking: Reg. Coll. (S), No. 1
Website: www.jbu.edu
Admissions email: jbuinfo@jbu.edu
Private; founded 1919
Affiliation: Interdenominational
Freshman admissions: more selective; 2013-2014: 1,143 applied, 798 accepted. Either SAT or ACT required. ACT 25/75 percentile: 23-29. High school rank: 30% in top tenth, 65% in top quarter, 86% in top half
Early decision deadline: N/A, notification date: N/A
Early action deadline: N/A, notification date: N/A
Application deadline (fall): rolling
Undergraduate student body: 1,571 full time, 510 part time; 44% male, 56% female; 1% American Indian, 1% Asian, 2% black, 5% Hispanic, 3% multiracial, 0% Pacific Islander, 80% white, 7% international; 40% from in state; 69% live on campus; 0% of students in fraternities, 0% in sororities
Most popular majors: 46% Business, Management, Marketing, and Related Support Services, 6% Communication, Journalism, and Related Programs, 10% Education, 6% Family and Consumer Sciences/Human Sciences, 7% Visual and Performing Arts
Expenses: 2014-2015: $23,588; room/board: $8,468
Financial aid: (479) 524-7115; 72% of undergrads determined to have financial need; average aid package $18,422

## Lyon College
Batesville AR
(800) 423-2542
U.S. News ranking: Nat. Lib. Arts, No. 165
Website: www.lyon.edu
Admissions email: admissions@lyon.edu
Private; founded 1872
Affiliation: Presbyterian
Freshman admissions: more selective; 2013-2014: 1,308 applied, 769 accepted. Either SAT or ACT required. ACT 25/75 percentile: 23-28. High school rank: 29% in top tenth, 55% in top quarter, 87% in top half
Early decision deadline: N/A, notification date: N/A
Early action deadline: 10/31, notification date: 11/15
Application deadline (fall): rolling
Undergraduate student body: 562 full time, 30 part time; 46% male, 54% female; 2% American Indian, 1% Asian, 4% black, 4% Hispanic, 0% multiracial, 0% Pacific Islander, 78% white, 3% international; 80% from in state; 72% live on campus; 39% of students in fraternities, 29% in sororities
Most popular majors: 19% Biology/Biological Sciences, General, 8% Business Administration and Management, General, 12% English Language and Literature, General, 8% Mathematics, General, 18% Psychology, General
Expenses: 2014-2015: $24,300; room/board: $7,790
Financial aid: (870) 698-4257; 78% of undergrads determined to have financial need; average aid package $21,772

## Ouachita Baptist University
Arkadelphia AR
(870) 245-5110
U.S. News ranking: Nat. Lib. Arts, No. 176
Website: www.obu.edu
Admissions email: admissions@obu.edu
Private; founded 1886
Affiliation: Arkansas Baptist State Convention
Freshman admissions: more selective; 2013-2014: 1,740 applied, 1,220 accepted. Either SAT or ACT required. ACT 25/75 percentile: 21-27. High school rank: 29% in top tenth, 53% in top quarter, 80% in top half
Early decision deadline: N/A, notification date: N/A
Early action deadline: N/A, notification date: N/A
Application deadline (fall): rolling
Undergraduate student body: 1,507 full time, 36 part time; 47% male, 53% female; 1% American Indian, 1% Asian, 8% black, 4% Hispanic, 0% multiracial, 0% Pacific Islander, 84% white, 2% international; 61% from in state; 95% live on campus; 20% of students in fraternities, 30% in sororities
Most popular majors: 12% Biological and Biomedical Sciences, 15% Business, Management, Marketing, and Related Support Services, 9% Communication, Journalism, and Related Programs, 11% Theology and Religious Vocations, 13% Visual and Performing Arts
Expenses: 2014-2015: $23,320; room/board: $6,900
Financial aid: (870) 245-5570; 60% of undergrads determined to have financial need; average aid package $22,141

## Philander Smith College
Little Rock AR
(501) 370-5221
U.S. News ranking: Reg. Coll. (S), No. 43
Website: www.philander.edu
Admissions email: admissions@philander.edu
Private; founded 1877
Affiliation: United Methodist
Freshman admissions: selective; 2013-2014: 5,181 applied, 2,151 accepted. Either SAT or ACT required. ACT 25/75 percentile: 16-22. High school rank: 16% in top tenth, 44% in top quarter, 64% in top half
Early decision deadline: N/A, notification date: N/A
Early action deadline: N/A, notification date: N/A
Application deadline (fall): 7/1
Undergraduate student body: 523 full time, 33 part time; 34% male, 66% female; 0% American Indian, 0% Asian, 90% black, 0% Hispanic, 1% multiracial, 0% Pacific Islander, 1% white, 8% international; 50% from in state; 40% live on campus; 4% of students in fraternities, 2% in sororities
Most popular majors: 10% Biological and Biomedical Sciences, 30% Business, Management, Marketing, and Related Support Services, 9% Parks, Recreation, Leisure, and Fitness Studies, 9% Public

Administration and Social Service Professions, 19% Social Sciences
Expenses: 2014-2015: $10,490; room/board: $8,104
Financial aid: (501) 370-5350

## Southern Arkansas University
Magnolia AR
(870) 235-4040
U.S. News ranking: Reg. U. (S), second tier
Website: www.saumag.edu
Admissions email: muleriders@saumag.edu
Public; founded 1909
Freshman admissions: selective; 2013-2014: 2,720 applied, 1,654 accepted. Either SAT or ACT required. ACT 25/75 percentile: 18-24. High school rank: 20% in top tenth, 42% in top quarter, 74% in top half
Early decision deadline: N/A, notification date: N/A
Early action deadline: N/A, notification date: N/A
Application deadline (fall): 8/27
Undergraduate student body: 2,497 full time, 463 part time; 42% male, 58% female; 1% American Indian, 1% Asian, 28% black, 2% Hispanic, 0% multiracial, 1% Pacific Islander, 65% white, 3% international; 77% from in state; 45% live on campus; 2% of students in fraternities, 9% in sororities
Most popular majors: 22% Business, Management, Marketing, and Related Support Services, 13% Education, 8% Health Professions and Related Programs, 7% Homeland Security, Law Enforcement, Firefighting and Related Protective Services, 10% Liberal Arts and Sciences, General Studies and Humanities
Expenses: 2013-2014: $7,466 in state, $10,616 out of state; room/board: $5,740
Financial aid: (870) 235-4023

## University of Arkansas
Fayetteville AR
(800) 377-8632
U.S. News ranking: Nat. U., No. 135
Website: www.uark.edu
Admissions email: uofa@uark.edu
Public; founded 1871
Freshman admissions: more selective; 2013-2014: 18,908 applied, 11,076 accepted. Either SAT or ACT required. ACT 25/75 percentile: 23-28. High school rank: 28% in top tenth, 57% in top quarter, 88% in top half
Early decision deadline: N/A, notification date: N/A
Early action deadline: 11/1, notification date: 12/15
Application deadline (fall): 8/1
Undergraduate student body: 18,565 full time, 2,444 part time; 49% male, 51% female; 1% American Indian, 2% Asian, 5% black, 6% Hispanic, 3% multiracial, 0% Pacific Islander, 79% white, 3% international; 63% from in state; 29% live on campus; 22% of students in fraternities, 36% in sororities
Most popular majors: 22% Business, Management, Marketing, and Related Support Services, 9% Engineering, 6% Health Professions and Related Programs, 6% Parks, Recreation,

Leisure, and Fitness Studies, 9% Social Sciences
**Expenses:** 2014-2015: $8,210 in state, $20,300 out of state; room/board: $9,454
**Financial aid:** (479) 575-3806; 46% of undergrads determined to have financial need; average aid package $9,386

## University of Arkansas–Fort Smith[1]
Fort Smith AR
(479) 788-7120
**U.S. News ranking:** Reg. Coll. (S), second tier
**Website:** www.uafortsmith.edu/Home/Index
**Admissions email:** N/A
**Public**
**Application deadline (fall):** N/A
**Undergraduate student body:** N/A full time, N/A part time
**Expenses:** 2013-2014: $4,528 in state, $10,072 out of state; room/board: $7,920
**Financial aid:** (479) 788-7090

## University of Arkansas–Little Rock
Little Rock AR
(501) 569-3127
**U.S. News ranking:** Nat. U., second tier
**Website:** www.ualr.edu/
**Admissions email:** admissions@ualr.edu
**Public;** founded 1927
**Freshman admissions:** selective; 2013-2014: 997 applied, 685 accepted. Either SAT or ACT required. Average composite ACT score: 22. High school rank: N/A
**Early decision deadline:** N/A, notification date: N/A
**Early action deadline:** N/A, notification date: N/A
**Application deadline (fall):** 8/1
**Undergraduate student body:** 5,552 full time, 4,418 part time; 41% male, 59% female; 0% American Indian, 2% Asian, 26% black, 6% Hispanic, 6% multiracial, 0% Pacific Islander, 55% white, 3% international; 97% from in state; 10% live on campus; 3% of students in fraternities, 2% in sororities
**Most popular majors:** 18% Business, Management, Marketing, and Related Support Services, 16% Health Professions and Related Programs, 9% Homeland Security, Law Enforcement, Firefighting and Related Protective Services, 6% Liberal Arts and Sciences, General Studies and Humanities, 7% Psychology
**Expenses:** 2014-2015: $7,909 in state, $18,979 out of state; room/board: $8,540
**Financial aid:** (501) 569-3035; 73% of undergrads determined to have financial need; average aid package $11,080

## University of Arkansas–Monticello[1]
Monticello AR
(870) 460-1026
**U.S. News ranking:** Reg. U. (S), unranked
**Website:** www.uamont.edu
**Admissions email:** admissions@uamont.edu
**Public**
**Application deadline (fall):** N/A

**Undergraduate student body:** N/A full time, N/A part time
**Expenses:** 2013-2014: $5,793 in state, $11,590 out of state; room/board: $5,834
**Financial aid:** (870) 460-1050

## University of Arkansas–Pine Bluff
Pine Bluff AR
(870) 575-8492
**U.S. News ranking:** Reg. Coll. (S), No. 43
**Website:** www.uapb.edu/
**Admissions email:** jonesm@uapb.edu
**Public;** founded 1873
**Freshman admissions:** less selective; 2013-2014: 4,094 applied, 1,134 accepted. Either SAT or ACT required. ACT 25/75 percentile: 15-20. High school rank: 11% in top tenth, 27% in top quarter, 55% in top half
**Early decision deadline:** N/A, notification date: N/A
**Early action deadline:** N/A, notification date: N/A
**Application deadline (fall):** rolling
**Undergraduate student body:** 2,300 full time, 221 part time; 46% male, 54% female; 0% American Indian, 0% Asian, 93% black, 1% Hispanic, 0% multiracial, 0% Pacific Islander, 4% white, 1% international; 63% from in state; 43% live on campus; 4% of students in fraternities, 5% in sororities
**Most popular majors:** 8% Biology/Biological Sciences, General, 10% Business Administration and Management, General, 11% Criminal Justice/Safety Studies, 8% Family and Consumer Sciences/Human Sciences, General, 10% General Studies
**Expenses:** 2014-2015: $5,956 in state, $11,626 out of state; room/board: $7,400
**Financial aid:** (870) 575-8302; 90% of undergrads determined to have financial need; average aid package $10,960

## University of Central Arkansas
Conway AR
(501) 450-3128
**U.S. News ranking:** Reg. U. (S), No. 65
**Website:** www.uca.edu
**Admissions email:** admissions@uca.edu
**Public;** founded 1907
**Freshman admissions:** selective; 2013-2014: 4,060 applied, 3,738 accepted. Either SAT or ACT required. ACT 25/75 percentile: 20-26. High school rank: 19% in top tenth, 43% in top quarter, 73% in top half
**Early decision deadline:** N/A, notification date: N/A
**Early action deadline:** N/A, notification date: N/A
**Application deadline (fall):** rolling
**Undergraduate student body:** 8,285 full time, 1,469 part time; 42% male, 58% female; 1% American Indian, 1% Asian, 19% black, 4% Hispanic, 3% multiracial, 0% Pacific Islander, 67% white, 3% international; 88% from in state; 36% live on campus; 23% of students in fraternities, 23% in sororities
**Most popular majors:** 5% Biology/Biological Sciences, General, 9% Health Professions and Related

Clinical Sciences, Other, 4% Kindergarten/Preschool Education and Teaching, 4% Psychology, General, 4% Registered Nursing/Registered Nurse
**Expenses:** 2014-2015: $7,889 in state, $13,806 out of state; room/board: $5,778
**Financial aid:** (501) 450-3140

## University of the Ozarks
Clarksville AR
(479) 979-1227
**U.S. News ranking:** Reg. Coll. (S), No. 4
**Website:** www.ozarks.edu
**Admissions email:** admiss@ozarks.edu
**Private;** founded 1834
**Affiliation:** Presbyterian
**Freshman admissions:** selective; 2013-2014: 1,061 applied, 651 accepted. Either SAT or ACT required. ACT 25/75 percentile: 20-26. High school rank: 21% in top tenth, 44% in top quarter, 78% in top half
**Early decision deadline:** N/A, notification date: N/A
**Early action deadline:** N/A, notification date: N/A
**Application deadline (fall):** rolling
**Undergraduate student body:** 571 full time, 14 part time; 48% male, 52% female; 2% American Indian, 0% Asian, 8% black, 2% Hispanic, 0% multiracial, 0% Pacific Islander, 76% white, 12% international; 65% from in state; 76% live on campus; 0% of students in fraternities, 0% in sororities
**Most popular majors:** Information not available
**Expenses:** 2014-2015: $24,350; room/board: $7,000
**Financial aid:** (479) 979-1221; 72% of undergrads determined to have financial need; average aid package $29,788

## Williams Baptist College
Walnut Ridge AR
(800) 722-4434
**U.S. News ranking:** Reg. Coll. (S), No. 59
**Website:** www.williamsbaptistcollege.com
**Admissions email:** admissions@wbcoll.edu
**Private;** founded 1941
**Affiliation:** Southern Baptist Convention
**Freshman admissions:** selective; 2013-2014: 531 applied, 361 accepted. Either SAT or ACT required. ACT 25/75 percentile: 20-25. High school rank: N/A
**Early decision deadline:** N/A, notification date: N/A
**Early action deadline:** N/A, notification date: N/A
**Application deadline (fall):** rolling
**Undergraduate student body:** 474 full time, 98 part time; 38% male, 62% female; 1% American Indian, 0% Asian, 7% black, 3% Hispanic, 0% multiracial, 0% Pacific Islander, 87% white, 3% international
**Most popular majors:** 9% Bible/Biblical Studies, 15% Elementary Education and Teaching, 14% Liberal Arts and Sciences/Liberal Studies, 9% Physical Education Teaching and Coaching, 21% Psychology, General

**Expenses:** 2014-2015: $14,360; room/board: $6,800
**Financial aid:** (870) 759-4112; 73% of undergrads determined to have financial need; average aid package $14,768

CALIFORNIA

## Academy of Art University
San Francisco CA
(800) 544-2787
**U.S. News ranking:** Arts, unranked
**Website:** www.academyart.edu/
**Admissions email:** admissions@academyart.edu
**For-profit;** founded 1929
**Freshman admissions:** N/A; 2013-2014: 2,914 applied, 2,914 accepted. Neither SAT nor ACT required. SAT 25/75 percentile: N/A. High school rank: N/A
**Early decision deadline:** N/A, notification date: N/A
**Early action deadline:** N/A, notification date: N/A
**Application deadline (fall):** rolling
**Undergraduate student body:** 5,727 full time, 4,781 part time; 44% male, 56% female; 1% American Indian, 8% Asian, 7% black, 10% Hispanic, 3% multiracial, 0% Pacific Islander, 26% white, 22% international; 60% from in state; 13% live on campus; N/A of students in fraternities, N/A in sororities
**Most popular majors:** 15% Animation, Interactive Technology, Video Graphics and Special Effects, 11% Cinematography and Film/Video Production, 16% Fashion/Apparel Design, 8% Graphic Design, 11% Illustration
**Expenses:** 2014-2015: $24,600; room/board: $14,160
**Financial aid:** (415) 274-2223; 47% of undergrads determined to have financial need; average aid package $10,242

## Alliant International University
San Diego CA
(858) 635-4772
**U.S. News ranking:** Nat. U., unranked
**Website:** www.alliant.edu
**Admissions email:** admissions@alliant.edu
**Private;** founded 1969
**Freshman admissions:** N/A; 2013-2014: N/A applied, N/A accepted. Neither SAT nor ACT required. ACT 25/75 percentile: N/A. High school rank: N/A
**Early decision deadline:** N/A, notification date: N/A
**Early action deadline:** N/A, notification date: N/A
**Application deadline (fall):** rolling
**Undergraduate student body:** 186 full time, 1,179 part time; 45% male, 55% female; 0% American Indian, 1% Asian, 4% black, 10% Hispanic, 1% multiracial, 0% Pacific Islander, 12% white, 69% international
**Most popular majors:** 76% Business Administration and Management, General, 24% Psychology, General
**Expenses:** 2014-2015: $19,930; room/board: $7,790
**Financial aid:** (858) 635-4700

## American Jewish University
Bel-Air CA
(310) 440-1247
**U.S. News ranking:** Nat. Lib. Arts, second tier
**Website:** www.aju.edu
**Admissions email:** admissions@aju.edu
**Private**
**Affiliation:** Jewish
**Freshman admissions:** selective; 2013-2014: 98 applied, 41 accepted. Neither SAT nor ACT required. SAT 25/75 percentile: 780-1240. High school rank: N/A
**Early decision deadline:** N/A, notification date: N/A
**Early action deadline:** 11/15, notification date: 12/15
**Application deadline (fall):** rolling
**Undergraduate student body:** 108 full time, 4 part time; 50% male, 50% female; N/A American Indian, N/A Asian, N/A black, N/A Hispanic, N/A multiracial, N/A Pacific Islander, N/A white, N/A international
**Most popular majors:** Information not available
**Expenses:** 2014-2015: $29,132; room/board: $15,102
**Financial aid:** (310) 476-9777; 98% of undergrads determined to have financial need; average aid package $42,000

## Argosy University[1]
Orange CA
(800) 377-0617
**U.S. News ranking:** Nat. U., unranked
**Website:** www.argosy.edu/
**Admissions email:** N/A
**For-profit**
**Application deadline (fall):** N/A
**Undergraduate student body:** N/A full time, N/A part time
**Expenses:** 2013-2014: $13,663; room/board: N/A
**Financial aid:** (714) 620-3687

## Art Center College of Design
Pasadena CA
(626) 396-2373
**U.S. News ranking:** Arts, unranked
**Website:** www.artcenter.edu
**Admissions email:** admissions@artcenter.edu
**Private;** founded 1930
**Freshman admissions:** N/A; 2013-2014: 480 applied, 392 accepted. Neither SAT nor ACT required. SAT 25/75 percentile: N/A. High school rank: N/A
**Early decision deadline:** N/A, notification date: N/A
**Early action deadline:** N/A, notification date: N/A
**Application deadline (fall):** rolling
**Undergraduate student body:** 1,499 full time, 268 part time; 50% male, 50% female; 0% American Indian, 35% Asian, 1% black, 11% Hispanic, 4% multiracial, 0% Pacific Islander, 22% white, 24% international
**Most popular majors:** 6% Architecture and Related Services, 7% Communication, Journalism, and Related Programs, 2% Communications Technologies/Technicians and Support Services, 85% Visual and Performing Arts
**Expenses:** 2014-2015: $37,830; room/board: N/A
**Financial aid:** (626) 396-2215

## Azusa Pacific University
Azusa CA
(800) 825-5278
**U.S. News ranking:** Nat. U., No. 173
**Website:** www.apu.edu
**Admissions email:** admissions@apu.edu
**Private;** founded 1899
**Affiliation:** Christian interdenominational
**Freshman admissions:** selective; 2013-2014: 5,105 applied, 4,201 accepted. Either SAT or ACT required. SAT 25/75 percentile: 980-1190. High school rank: 27% in top tenth, 62% in top quarter, 89% in top half
**Early decision deadline:** N/A, notification date: N/A
**Early action deadline:** 11/15, notification date: 1/15
**Application deadline (fall):** 6/1
**Undergraduate student body:** 5,683 full time, 860 part time; 36% male, 64% female; 0% American Indian, 8% Asian, 5% black, 23% Hispanic, 6% multiracial, 1% Pacific Islander, 50% white, 2% international; 83% from in state; 55% live on campus; 0% of students in fraternities, 0% in sororities
**Most popular majors:** 17% Business, Management, Marketing, and Related Support Services, 5% Communication, Journalism, and Related Programs, 14% Health Professions and Related Programs, 12% Liberal Arts and Sciences, General Studies and Humanities, 11% Psychology
**Expenses:** 2014-2015: $33,096; room/board: $8,990
**Financial aid:** (626) 815-6000

## Biola University
La Mirada CA
(562) 903-4752
**U.S. News ranking:** Nat. U., No. 161
**Website:** www.biola.edu
**Admissions email:** admissions@biola.edu
**Private;** founded 1908
**Affiliation:** Christian, Interdenominational
**Freshman admissions:** selective; 2013-2014: 3,615 applied, 2,699 accepted. Either SAT or ACT required. SAT 25/75 percentile: 1000-1240. High school rank: 33% in top tenth, 63% in top quarter, 89% in top half
**Early decision deadline:** N/A, notification date: N/A
**Early action deadline:** 11/15, notification date: 12/15
**Application deadline (fall):** rolling
**Undergraduate student body:** 4,203 full time, 150 part time; 38% male, 62% female; 0% American Indian, 16% Asian, 2% black, 17% Hispanic, 6% multiracial, 0% Pacific Islander, 54% white, 2% international; 78% from in state; 42% live on campus; 0% of students in fraternities, 0% in sororities
**Most popular majors:** 15% Business, Management, Marketing, and Related Support Services, 9% Communication, Journalism, and Related Programs, 10% Psychology, 9% Theology and Religious Vocations, 14% Visual and Performing Arts

**Expenses:** 2014-2015: $33,322; room/board: $9,910
**Financial aid:** (562) 903-4742; 69% of undergrads determined to have financial need; average aid package $18,453

## Brandman University
Irvine CA
(877) 516-4501
**U.S. News ranking:** Reg. U. (W), unranked
**Website:** www.brandman.edu
**Admissions email:** apply@brandman.edu
**Private;** founded 1958
**Freshman admissions:** N/A; 2013-2014: 74 applied, 55 accepted. Neither SAT nor ACT required. ACT 25/75 percentile: N/A. High school rank: N/A
**Early decision deadline:** N/A, notification date: N/A
**Early action deadline:** N/A, notification date: N/A
**Application deadline (fall):** rolling
**Undergraduate student body:** 1,552 full time, 2,333 part time; 38% male, 62% female; 1% American Indian, 3% Asian, 10% black, 27% Hispanic, 4% multiracial, 1% Pacific Islander, 46% white, 0% international; 83% from in state; 0% live on campus; 0% of students in fraternities, 0% in sororities
**Most popular majors:** 9% Business Administration and Management, General, 9% Developmental and Child Psychology, 14% Liberal Arts and Sciences/Liberal Studies, 16% Organizational Behavior Studies, 18% Psychology, General
**Expenses:** 2014-2015: $12,200; room/board: N/A
**Financial aid:** (415) 575-6122; 73% of undergrads determined to have financial need; average aid package $26,614

## California Baptist University
Riverside CA
(877) 228-8866
**U.S. News ranking:** Reg. U. (W), No. 38
**Website:** www.calbaptist.edu
**Admissions email:** admissions@calbaptist.edu
**Private;** founded 1950
**Affiliation:** California Southern Baptist Convention
**Freshman admissions:** selective; 2013-2014: 3,853 applied, 3,036 accepted. Either SAT or ACT required. SAT 25/75 percentile: 850-1110. High school rank: 17% in top tenth, 43% in top quarter, 78% in top half
**Early decision deadline:** N/A, notification date: N/A
**Early action deadline:** 12/15, notification date: 1/31
**Application deadline (fall):** rolling
**Undergraduate student body:** 5,086 full time, 711 part time; 36% male, 64% female; 1% American Indian, 5% Asian, 8% black, 30% Hispanic, 3% multiracial, 1% Pacific Islander, 45% white, 2% international; 95% from in state; 40% live on campus; 0% of students in fraternities, 0% in sororities
**Most popular majors:** 10% Business/Commerce, General, 8% Kinesiology and Exercise Science, 6% Liberal Arts and Sciences/

Liberal Studies, 11% Psychology, General, 9% Registered Nursing/Registered Nurse
**Expenses:** 2014-2015: $29,422; room/board: $7,890
**Financial aid:** (951) 343-4236; 92% of undergrads determined to have financial need; average aid package $16,025

## California College of the Arts
San Francisco CA
(800) 447-1278
**U.S. News ranking:** Arts, unranked
**Website:** www.cca.edu
**Admissions email:** enroll@cca.edu
**Private;** founded 1907
**Freshman admissions:** N/A; 2013-2014: 1,402 applied, 1,144 accepted. Neither SAT nor ACT required. SAT 25/75 percentile: N/A. High school rank: N/A
**Early decision deadline:** N/A, notification date: N/A
**Early action deadline:** N/A, notification date: N/A
**Application deadline (fall):** rolling
**Undergraduate student body:** 1,410 full time, 92 part time; 38% male, 62% female; 0% American Indian, 16% Asian, 4% black, 14% Hispanic, 0% multiracial, 1% Pacific Islander, 33% white, 22% international; 68% from in state; 20% live on campus; 1% of students in fraternities, 0% in sororities
**Most popular majors:** 15% Animation, Interactive Technology, Video Graphics and Special Effects, 16% Architecture, 27% Graphic Design, 17% Illustration, 13% Industrial and Product Design
**Expenses:** 2014-2015: $41,942; room/board: $8,200
**Financial aid:** (415) 703-9573; 61% of undergrads determined to have financial need; average aid package $27,449

## California Institute of Integral Studies
San Francisco CA
(415) 575-6100
**U.S. News ranking:** Nat. U., unranked
**Website:** www.ciis.edu
**Admissions email:** N/A
**Private**
**Freshman admissions:** N/A; 2013-2014: 0 applied, 0 accepted. Neither SAT nor ACT required. ACT 25/75 percentile: N/A. High school rank: N/A
**Early decision deadline:** N/A, notification date: N/A
**Early action deadline:** N/A, notification date: N/A
**Application deadline (fall):** N/A
**Undergraduate student body:** 68 full time, 7 part time; 27% male, 73% female; 0% American Indian, 5% Asian, 8% black, 16% Hispanic, 5% multiracial, 1% Pacific Islander, 55% white, 4% international
**Most popular majors:** Information not available
**Expenses:** 2013-2014: $25,713; room/board: N/A
**Financial aid:** N/A

## California Institute of Technology
Pasadena CA
(626) 395-6341
**U.S. News ranking:** Nat. U., No. 10
**Website:** www.caltech.edu
**Admissions email:** ugadmissions@caltech.edu
**Private;** founded 1891
**Freshman admissions:** most selective; 2013-2014: 5,535 applied, 584 accepted. Either SAT or ACT required. SAT 25/75 percentile: 1490-1600. High school rank: 99% in top tenth, 100% in top quarter, 100% in top half
**Early decision deadline:** N/A, notification date: N/A
**Early action deadline:** 11/1, notification date: 12/15
**Application deadline (fall):** 1/3
**Undergraduate student body:** 977 full time, 0 part time; 63% male, 37% female; 0% American Indian, 42% Asian, 2% black, 10% Hispanic, 6% multiracial, 0% Pacific Islander, 30% white, 9% international; 37% from in state; 84% live on campus; 0% of students in fraternities, 0% in sororities
**Most popular majors:** 12% Biological and Biomedical Sciences, 14% Computer and Information Sciences and Support Services, 43% Engineering, 13% Mathematics and Statistics, 18% Physical Sciences
**Expenses:** 2014-2015: $43,362; room/board: $12,918
**Financial aid:** (626) 395-6280; 51% of undergrads determined to have financial need; average aid package $39,813

## California Institute of the Arts
Valencia CA
(661) 255-1050
**U.S. News ranking:** Arts, unranked
**Website:** www.calarts.edu
**Admissions email:** admiss@calarts.edu
**Private;** founded 1961
**Freshman admissions:** N/A; 2013-2014: N/A applied, N/A accepted. Neither SAT nor ACT required. SAT 25/75 percentile: N/A. High school rank: N/A
**Early decision deadline:** N/A, notification date: N/A
**Early action deadline:** N/A, notification date: N/A
**Application deadline (fall):** 1/5
**Undergraduate student body:** 973 full time, 13 part time; 47% male, 53% female; 1% American Indian, 11% Asian, 6% black, 11% Hispanic, 11% multiracial, 1% Pacific Islander, 44% white, 13% international
**Most popular majors:** 8% Acting, 6% Fine/Studio Arts, General, 8% Fine/Studio Arts, General, 8% Photography, 8% Technical Theatre/Theatre Design and Technology
**Expenses:** 2014-2015: $42,276; room/board: $13,000
**Financial aid:** (661) 253-7869; 74% of undergrads determined to have financial need; average aid package $35,705

## California Lutheran University
Thousand Oaks CA
(877) 258-3678
**U.S. News ranking:** Reg. U. (W), No. 15
**Website:** www.callutheran.edu
**Admissions email:** admissions@callutheran.edu
**Private;** founded 1959
**Affiliation:** Lutheran
**Freshman admissions:** more selective; 2013-2014: 6,920 applied, 3,323 accepted. Either SAT or ACT required. SAT 25/75 percentile: 1010-1203. High school rank: 33% in top tenth, 68% in top quarter, 94% in top half
**Early decision deadline:** N/A, notification date: N/A
**Early action deadline:** 11/1, notification date: 1/15
**Application deadline (fall):** 3/15
**Undergraduate student body:** 2,717 full time, 171 part time; 45% male, 55% female; 1% American Indian, 6% Asian, 4% black, 25% Hispanic, 2% multiracial, 1% Pacific Islander, 52% white, 4% international; 88% from in state; 53% live on campus; 0% of students in fraternities, 0% in sororities
**Most popular majors:** 7% Biological and Biomedical Sciences, 25% Business, Management, Marketing, and Related Support Services, 13% Communication, Journalism, and Related Programs, 12% Psychology, 8% Social Sciences
**Expenses:** 2014-2015: $37,140; room/board: $12,400
**Financial aid:** (805) 493-3115; 68% of undergrads determined to have financial need; average aid package $24,570

## California Maritime Academy
Vallejo CA
(707) 654-1330
**U.S. News ranking:** Reg. Coll. (W), No. 3
**Website:** www.csum.edu
**Admissions email:** admission@csum.edu
**Public;** founded 1929
**Freshman admissions:** selective; 2013-2014: 1,291 applied, 819 accepted. Either SAT or ACT required. SAT 25/75 percentile: 990-1200. High school rank: N/A
**Early decision deadline:** N/A, notification date: N/A
**Early action deadline:** N/A, notification date: N/A
**Application deadline (fall):** rolling
**Undergraduate student body:** 1,001 full time, 43 part time; 86% male, 14% female; 1% American Indian, 9% Asian, 4% black, 11% Hispanic, 8% multiracial, 2% Pacific Islander, 62% white, 0% international
**Most popular majors:** Information not available
**Expenses:** 2014-2015: $6,598 in state, $17,758 out of state; room/board: $11,610
**Financial aid:** (707) 654-1275; 60% of undergrads determined to have financial need; average aid package $17,560

## California Polytechnic State University–San Luis Obispo

San Luis Obispo CA
(805) 756-2311
**U.S. News ranking:** Reg. U. (W), No. 10
**Website:** www.calpoly.edu
**Admissions email:** admissions@calpoly.edu
**Public;** founded 1901
**Freshman admissions:** more selective; 2013-2014: 40,402 applied, 13,953 accepted. Either SAT or ACT required. SAT 25/75 percentile: 1130-1320. High school rank: 49% in top tenth, 83% in top quarter, 98% in top half
**Early decision deadline:** 10/31, notification date: 12/15
**Early action deadline:** N/A, notification date: N/A
**Application deadline (fall):** 11/30
**Undergraduate student body:** 18,058 full time, 681 part time; 55% male, 45% female; 0% American Indian, 11% Asian, 1% black, 15% Hispanic, 7% multiracial, 0% Pacific Islander, 60% white, 1% international; 90% from in state; 38% live on campus; N/A of students in fraternities, N/A in sororities
**Most popular majors:** 12% Agriculture, Agriculture Operations, and Related Sciences, 6% Architecture and Related Services, 13% Business, Management, Marketing, and Related Support Services, 27% Engineering, 6% Social Sciences
**Expenses:** 2014-2015: $8,919 in state, $20,079 out of state; room/board: $11,447
**Financial aid:** (805) 756-2927; 43% of undergrads determined to have financial need; average aid package $10,129

## California State Polytechnic University–Pomona

Pomona CA
(909) 869-3210
**U.S. News ranking:** Reg. U. (W), No. 31
**Website:** www.csupomona.edu
**Admissions email:** admissions@csupomona.edu
**Public;** founded 1938
**Freshman admissions:** less selective; 2013-2014: 31,465 applied, 16,636 accepted. Either SAT or ACT required. SAT 25/75 percentile: 930-1190. High school rank: N/A
**Early decision deadline:** N/A, notification date: N/A
**Early action deadline:** N/A, notification date: N/A
**Application deadline (fall):** 11/30
**Undergraduate student body:** 18,413 full time, 2,539 part time; 57% male, 43% female; 0% American Indian, 25% Asian, 3% black, 37% Hispanic, 4% multiracial, 0% Pacific Islander, 22% white, 4% international; 99% from in state; 12% live on campus; 2% of students in fraternities, 1% in sororities
**Most popular majors:** 24% Business Administration and Management, General, 6% Civil Engineering, General, 7% Hospitality Administration/Management, General, 4% Mechanical Engineering, 5% Psychology, General

**Expenses:** 2014-2015: $6,350 in state, $17,510 out of state; room/board: $12,111
**Financial aid:** (909) 869-3700; 67% of undergrads determined to have financial need; average aid package $11,558

## California State University–Bakersfield[1]

Bakersfield CA
(661) 654-3036
**U.S. News ranking:** Reg. U. (W), No. 80
**Website:** www.csub.edu
**Admissions email:** admissions@csub.edu
**Public**
**Application deadline (fall):** N/A
**Undergraduate student body:** N/A full time, N/A part time
**Expenses:** 2013-2014: $6,775 in state, $17,935 out of state; room/board: $9,894
**Financial aid:** (661) 654-3016

## California State University–Channel Islands[1]

Camarillo CA
(805) 437-8500
**U.S. News ranking:** Reg. U. (W), No. 75
**Website:** www.csuci.edu
**Admissions email:** N/A
**Public**
**Application deadline (fall):** N/A
**Undergraduate student body:** N/A full time, N/A part time
**Expenses:** 2013-2014: $6,471 in state, $17,631 out of state; room/board: $14,020
**Financial aid:** (805) 437-8530; 41% of undergrads determined to have financial need; average aid package $5,702

## California State University–Chico

Chico CA
(800) 542-4426
**U.S. News ranking:** Reg. U. (W), No. 35
**Website:** www.csuchico.edu
**Admissions email:** info@csuchico.edu
**Public;** founded 1887
**Freshman admissions:** selective; 2013-2014: 19,217 applied, 12,905 accepted. Either SAT or ACT required. SAT 25/75 percentile: 910-1110. High school rank: 35% in top tenth, 76% in top quarter, 100% in top half
**Early decision deadline:** N/A, notification date: N/A
**Early action deadline:** N/A, notification date: N/A
**Application deadline (fall):** 11/30
**Undergraduate student body:** 14,209 full time, 1,083 part time; 48% male, 52% female; 1% American Indian, 6% Asian, 2% black, 23% Hispanic, 5% multiracial, 0% Pacific Islander, 52% white, 4% international; 99% from in state; 1% live on campus; 1% of students in fraternities, 1% in sororities
**Most popular majors:** 16% Business, Management, Marketing, and Related Support Services, 9% Health Professions and Related Programs, 8% Parks, Recreation, Leisure, and Fitness

Studies, 9% Social Sciences, 7% Visual and Performing Arts
**Expenses:** 2014-2015: $8,472 in state, $19,632 out of state; room/board: $10,480
**Financial aid:** (530) 898-6451; 58% of undergrads determined to have financial need; average aid package $15,927

## California State University–Dominguez Hills

Carson CA
(310) 243-3300
**U.S. News ranking:** Reg. U. (W), second tier
**Website:** www.csudh.edu
**Admissions email:** info@csudh.edu
**Public;** founded 1960
**Freshman admissions:** less selective; 2013-2014: 9,719 applied, 7,766 accepted. SAT nor ACT required. SAT 25/75 percentile: 760-940. High school rank: N/A
**Early decision deadline:** N/A, notification date: N/A
**Early action deadline:** N/A, notification date: N/A
**Application deadline (fall):** rolling
**Undergraduate student body:** 8,565 full time, 3,858 part time; 36% male, 64% female; 0% American Indian, 9% Asian, 17% black, 54% Hispanic, 3% multiracial, 0% Pacific Islander, 9% white, 2% international; 100% from in state; 5% live on campus; 1% of students in fraternities, 1% in sororities
**Most popular majors:** 20% Business, Management, Marketing, and Related Support Services, 12% Health Professions and Related Programs, 8% Liberal Arts and Sciences, General Studies and Humanities, 10% Psychology, 10% Social Sciences
**Expenses:** 2014-2015: $6,099 in state, $15,027 out of state; room/board: $12,358
**Financial aid:** (310) 243-3691; 73% of undergrads determined to have financial need; average aid package $6,328

## California State University–East Bay

Hayward CA
(510) 885-2784
**U.S. News ranking:** Reg. U. (W), second tier
**Website:** www.csueastbay.edu
**Admissions email:** admissions@csueastbay.edu
**Public;** founded 1957
**Freshman admissions:** less selective; 2013-2014: 14,128 applied, 9,637 accepted. Neither SAT nor ACT required. SAT 25/75 percentile: 800-1010. High school rank: N/A
**Early decision deadline:** N/A, notification date: N/A
**Early action deadline:** N/A, notification date: N/A
**Application deadline (fall):** 11/30
**Undergraduate student body:** 10,505 full time, 1,555 part time; 39% male, 61% female; 0% American Indian, 24% Asian, 11% black, 26% Hispanic, 6% multiracial, 1% Pacific Islander, 21% white, 6% international; 99% from in state; N/A live on campus; N/A of students in fraternities, N/A in sororities

**Most popular majors:** 27% Business Administration and Management, General, 14% Health Services/Allied Health/Health Sciences, General, 7% Psychology, General, 6% Public Administration, 9% Social Sciences, General
**Expenses:** 2013-2014: $6,550 in state, $17,710 out of state; room/board: $11,742
**Financial aid:** (510) 885-2784; average aid package $11,366

## California State University–Fresno

Fresno CA
(559) 278-2191
**U.S. News ranking:** Reg. U. (W), No. 46
**Website:** www.csufresno.edu
**Admissions email:** tinab@csufresno.edu
**Public;** founded 1911
**Freshman admissions:** selective; 2013-2014: 17,578 applied, 10,523 accepted. Either SAT or ACT required. SAT 25/75 percentile: 800-1020. High school rank: 15% in top tenth, 80% in top quarter, 100% in top half
**Early decision deadline:** N/A, notification date: N/A
**Early action deadline:** N/A, notification date: N/A
**Application deadline (fall):** 11/30
**Undergraduate student body:** 17,571 full time, 2,724 part time; 43% male, 57% female; 0% American Indian, 16% Asian, 4% black, 43% Hispanic, 3% multiracial, 0% Pacific Islander, 25% white, 3% international; 99% from in state; 5% live on campus; 6% of students in fraternities, 6% in sororities
**Most popular majors:** 14% Business, Management, Marketing, and Related Support Services, 13% Health Professions and Related Programs, 7% Homeland Security, Law Enforcement, Firefighting and Related Protective Services, 8% Liberal Arts and Sciences, General Studies and Humanities, 7% Psychology
**Expenses:** 2014-2015: $6,298 in state, $17,458 out of state; room/board: $10,604
**Financial aid:** (559) 278-2182; 74% of undergrads determined to have financial need; average aid package $10,717

## California State University–Fullerton

Fullerton CA
(657) 278-7788
**U.S. News ranking:** Reg. U. (W), No. 40
**Website:** www.fullerton.edu
**Admissions email:** admissions@fullerton.edu
**Public;** founded 1957
**Freshman admissions:** selective; 2013-2014: 41,013 applied, 19,668 accepted. SAT required. SAT 25/75 percentile: 920-1120. High school rank: 20% in top tenth, 61% in top quarter, 95% in top half
**Early decision deadline:** N/A, notification date: N/A
**Early action deadline:** N/A, notification date: N/A
**Application deadline (fall):** 11/30
**Undergraduate student body:** 26,682 full time, 6,434 part time; 45% male, 55% female;

0% American Indian, 22% Asian, 2% black, 38% Hispanic, 4% multiracial, 0% Pacific Islander, 26% white, 4% international; 99% from in state; 6% live on campus; 2% of students in fraternities, 2% in sororities
**Most popular majors:** 24% Business, Management, Marketing, and Related Support Services, 13% Communication, Journalism, and Related Programs, 8% Health Professions and Related Programs, 7% Psychology, 6% Social Sciences
**Expenses:** 2014-2015: $6,316 in state, $17,476 out of state; room/board: $13,510
**Financial aid:** (714) 278-3128; 59% of undergrads determined to have financial need; average aid package $12,298

## California State University–Long Beach

Long Beach CA
(562) 985-5471
**U.S. News ranking:** Reg. U. (W), No. 33
**Website:** www.csulb.edu
**Admissions email:** N/A
**Public;** founded 1949
**Freshman admissions:** selective; 2013-2014: 55,896 applied, 19,681 accepted. Either SAT or ACT required. SAT 25/75 percentile: 940-1160. High school rank: N/A
**Early decision deadline:** N/A, notification date: N/A
**Early action deadline:** N/A, notification date: N/A
**Application deadline (fall):** 11/30
**Undergraduate student body:** 25,756 full time, 4,718 part time; 43% male, 57% female; 1% American Indian, 22% Asian, 4% black, 37% Hispanic, 4% multiracial, 1% Pacific Islander, 21% white, 6% international; 99% from in state; 9% live on campus; 2% of students in fraternities, 2% in sororities
**Most popular majors:** 15% Business, Management, Marketing, and Related Support Services, 10% Communication, Journalism, and Related Programs, 10% Health Professions and Related Programs, 10% Social Sciences, 10% Visual and Performing Arts
**Expenses:** 2014-2015: $6,420 in state, $12,108 out of state; room/board: $11,300
**Financial aid:** (562) 985-8403; 70% of undergrads determined to have financial need; average aid package $13,877

## California State University–Los Angeles

Los Angeles CA
(323) 343-3901
**U.S. News ranking:** Reg. U. (W), No. 84
**Website:** www.calstatela.edu
**Admissions email:** admission@calstatela.edu
**Public;** founded 1947
**Freshman admissions:** least selective; 2013-2014: 28,506 applied, 17,816 accepted. Neither SAT nor ACT required. SAT 25/75 percentile: 770-990. High school rank: N/A in top tenth, 3% in top quarter, 100% in top half

**Early decision deadline:** N/A, notification date: N/A
**Early action deadline:** N/A, notification date: N/A
**Application deadline (fall):** 11/30
**Undergraduate student body:** 16,276 full time, 3,298 part time; 41% male, 59% female; 0% American Indian, 16% Asian, 5% black, 59% Hispanic, 2% multiracial, 0% Pacific Islander, 8% white, 5% international; 99% from in state; 5% live on campus; 1% of students in fraternities, 1% in sororities
**Most popular majors:** 21% Business, Management, Marketing, and Related Support Services, 9% Health Professions and Related Programs, 7% Homeland Security, Law Enforcement, Firefighting and Related Protective Services, 7% Psychology, 9% Social Sciences
**Expenses:** 2013-2014: $6,335 in state, $15,263 out of state; room/board: $10,851
**Financial aid:** (323) 343-1784; 81% of undergrads determined to have financial need; average aid package $12,724

## California State University–Monterey Bay
Seaside CA
(831) 582-3738
**U.S. News ranking:** Reg. U. (W), No. 68
**Website:** www.csumb.edu
**Admissions email:** admissions@csumb.edu
**Public;** founded 1994
**Freshman admissions:** selective; 2013-2014: 13,803 applied, 6,161 accepted. Either SAT or ACT required. SAT 25/75 percentile: 870-1090. High school rank: 12% in top tenth, 46% in top quarter, 87% in top half
**Early decision deadline:** N/A, notification date: N/A
**Early action deadline:** N/A, notification date: N/A
**Application deadline (fall):** 11/30
**Undergraduate student body:** 4,954 full time, 354 part time; 38% male, 62% female; 1% American Indian, 5% Asian, 7% black, 34% Hispanic, 7% multiracial, 1% Pacific Islander, 38% white, 2% international; 98% from in state; 44% live on campus; 6% of students in fraternities, 4% in sororities
**Most popular majors:** 17% Business, Management, Marketing, and Related Support Services, 17% Liberal Arts and Sciences, General Studies and Humanities, 9% Parks, Recreation, Leisure, and Fitness Studies, 12% Psychology, 9% Social Sciences
**Expenses:** 2013-2014: $5,963 in state, $17,123 out of state; room/board: $9,748
**Financial aid:** (831) 582-5100

## California State University–Northridge
Northridge CA
(818) 677-3700
**U.S. News ranking:** Reg. U. (W), No. 68
**Website:** www.csun.edu
**Admissions email:** admissions.records@csun.edu
**Public;** founded 1958

**Freshman admissions:** less selective; 2013-2014: 30,903 applied, 18,947 accepted. Either SAT or ACT required. SAT 25/75 percentile: 800-1040. High school rank: N/A
**Early decision deadline:** N/A, notification date: N/A
**Early action deadline:** N/A, notification date: N/A
**Application deadline (fall):** 11/30
**Undergraduate student body:** 27,993 full time, 5,405 part time; 45% male, 55% female; 0% American Indian, 11% Asian, 6% black, 40% Hispanic, 3% multiracial, 0% Pacific Islander, 26% white, 7% international; 97% from in state; N/A live on campus; N/A of students in fraternities, N/A in sororities
**Most popular majors:** 20% Business, Management, Marketing, and Related Support Services, 8% Communication, Journalism, and Related Programs, 7% English Language and Literature/Letters, 6% Liberal Arts and Sciences, General Studies and Humanities, 14% Social Sciences
**Expenses:** 2014-2015: $6,296 in state, $17,716 out of state; room/board: $12,404
**Financial aid:** (818) 677-4085

## California State University–Sacramento
Sacramento CA
(916) 278-3901
**U.S. News ranking:** Reg. U. (W), No. 58
**Website:** www.csus.edu
**Admissions email:** admissions@csus.edu
**Public;** founded 1947
**Freshman admissions:** less selective; 2013-2014: 20,803 applied, 14,696 accepted. Neither SAT nor ACT required. SAT 25/75 percentile: 830-1060. High school rank: N/A
**Early decision deadline:** N/A, notification date: N/A
**Early action deadline:** 11/30, notification date: N/A
**Application deadline (fall):** 11/30
**Undergraduate student body:** 21,034 full time, 4,978 part time; 44% male, 56% female; 1% American Indian, 22% Asian, 6% black, 21% Hispanic, 5% multiracial, 1% Pacific Islander, 37% white, 1% international; 99% from in state; 4% live on campus; 7% of students in fraternities, 5% in sororities
**Most popular majors:** 20% Business, Management, Marketing, and Related Support Services, 7% Communication, Journalism, and Related Programs, 8% Homeland Security, Law Enforcement, Firefighting and Related Protective Services, 6% Psychology, 9% Social Sciences
**Expenses:** 2014-2015: $6,648 in state, $17,808 out of state; room/board: N/A
**Financial aid:** (916) 278-6554; 75% of undergrads determined to have financial need; average aid package $10,690

## California State University–San Bernardino
San Bernardino CA
(909) 537-5188
**U.S. News ranking:** Reg. U. (W), No. 66
**Website:** www.csusb.edu
**Admissions email:** moreinfo@csusb.edu
**Public;** founded 1962
**Freshman admissions:** less selective; 2013-2014: 13,062 applied, 7,147 accepted. Neither SAT nor ACT required. SAT 25/75 percentile: 790-990. High school rank: N/A
**Early decision deadline:** N/A, notification date: N/A
**Early action deadline:** N/A, notification date: 5/1
**Application deadline (fall):** rolling
**Undergraduate student body:** 14,246 full time, 1,837 part time; 39% male, 61% female; 0% American Indian, 6% Asian, 7% black, 55% Hispanic, 3% multiracial, 0% Pacific Islander, 17% white, 6% international; 99% from in state; 8% live on campus; 4% of students in fraternities, 4% in sororities
**Most popular majors:** 21% Business Administration and Management, General, 8% Criminal Justice/Law Enforcement Administration, 8% Liberal Arts and Sciences/Liberal Studies, 13% Psychology, General, 5% Sociology
**Expenses:** 2014-2015: $6,549 in state, $17,709 out of state; room/board: $9,933
**Financial aid:** (909) 537-7800; 82% of undergrads determined to have financial need; average aid package $8,834

## California State University–San Marcos
San Marcos CA
(760) 750-4848
**U.S. News ranking:** Reg. U. (W), No. 84
**Website:** www.csusm.edu
**Admissions email:** apply@csusm.edu
**Public;** founded 1989
**Freshman admissions:** less selective; 2013-2014: 11,402 applied, 7,604 accepted. Neither SAT nor ACT required. SAT 25/75 percentile: 850-1050. High school rank: N/A
**Early decision deadline:** N/A, notification date: N/A
**Early action deadline:** N/A, notification date: N/A
**Undergraduate student body:** 8,819 full time, 1,856 part time; 40% male, 60% female; 0% American Indian, 10% Asian, 3% black, 34% Hispanic, 5% multiracial, 0% Pacific Islander, 37% white, 2% international; 98% from in state; N/A live on campus; N/A of students in fraternities, N/A in sororities
**Most popular majors:** Information not available
**Expenses:** 2014-2015: $7,704 in state, $24,336 out of state; room/board: N/A
**Financial aid:** (760) 750-4850

## California State University–Stanislaus
Turlock CA
(209) 667-3152
**U.S. News ranking:** Reg. U. (W), No. 55
**Website:** www.csustan.edu
**Admissions email:** Outreach_Help_Desk@csustan.edu
**Public;** founded 1957
**Freshman admissions:** less selective; 2013-2014: 5,804 applied, 4,280 accepted. Neither SAT nor ACT required. SAT 25/75 percentile: 810-1020. High school rank: N/A
**Early decision deadline:** N/A, notification date: N/A
**Early action deadline:** N/A, notification date: N/A
**Application deadline (fall):** 11/30
**Undergraduate student body:** 6,547 full time, 1,207 part time; 36% male, 64% female; 0% American Indian, 11% Asian, 3% black, 45% Hispanic, 4% multiracial, 1% Pacific Islander, 28% white, 2% international; 100% from in state; 7% live on campus; 7% of students in fraternities, 6% in sororities
**Most popular majors:** 19% Business Administration and Management, General, 9% Liberal Arts and Sciences/Liberal Studies, 11% Psychology, General, 12% Social Sciences, General
**Expenses:** 2014-2015: $6,491 in state, $17,651 out of state; room/board: $8,546
**Financial aid:** (209) 667-3336; 68% of undergrads determined to have financial need; average aid package $10,840

## Chapman University
Orange CA
(888) 282-7759
**U.S. News ranking:** Reg. U. (W), No. 7
**Website:** www.chapman.edu
**Admissions email:** admit@chapman.edu
**Private;** founded 1861
**Affiliation:** Christian Church (Disciples of Christ)
**Freshman admissions:** more selective; 2013-2014: 11,750 applied, 5,253 accepted. Either SAT or ACT required. SAT 25/75 percentile: 1120-1300. High school rank: 48% in top tenth, 93% in top quarter, 98% in top half
**Early decision deadline:** N/A, notification date: N/A
**Early action deadline:** 11/1, notification date: 1/10
**Application deadline (fall):** 1/15
**Undergraduate student body:** 5,753 full time, 252 part time; 41% male, 59% female; 0% American Indian, 10% Asian, 2% black, 14% Hispanic, 6% multiracial, 0% Pacific Islander, 60% white, 4% international; 74% from in state; 32% live on campus; 28% of students in fraternities, 38% in sororities
**Most popular majors:** 15% Business Administration and Management, General, 14% Cinematography and Film/Video Production, 6% Psychology, General, 6% Public Relations/Image Management, 9% Speech Communication and Rhetoric
**Expenses:** 2014-2015: $45,393; room/board: $12,954

**Financial aid:** (714) 997-6741; 60% of undergrads determined to have financial need; average aid package $31,182

## Claremont McKenna College
Claremont CA
(909) 621-8088
**U.S. News ranking:** Nat. Lib. Arts, No. 8
**Website:** www.claremontmckenna.edu
**Admissions email:** admission@cmc.edu
**Private;** founded 1946
**Freshman admissions:** most selective; 2013-2014: 5,518 applied, 647 accepted. Either SAT or ACT required. SAT 25/75 percentile: 1320-1500. High school rank: 74% in top tenth, 96% in top quarter, 100% in top half
**Early decision deadline:** 11/1, notification date: 12/15
**Early action deadline:** N/A, notification date: N/A
**Application deadline (fall):** 1/1
**Undergraduate student body:** 1,312 full time, 4 part time; 52% male, 48% female; 0% American Indian, 11% Asian, 4% black, 11% Hispanic, 8% multiracial, 0% Pacific Islander, 44% white, 14% international; 46% from in state; 94% live on campus; 0% of students in fraternities, 0% in sororities
**Most popular majors:** 14% Accounting, 25% Economics, General, 12% International Relations and Affairs, 21% Political Science and Government, General, 8% Psychology, General
**Expenses:** 2014-2015: $47,395; room/board: $14,820
**Financial aid:** (909) 621-8356; 40% of undergrads determined to have financial need; average aid package $40,677

## Cogswell Polytechnical College
Sunnyvale CA
(408) 541-0100
**U.S. News ranking:** Reg. Coll. (W), unranked
**Website:** www.cogswell.edu
**Admissions email:** info@cogswell.edu
**Private;** founded 1887
**Freshman admissions:** N/A; 2013-2014: 194 applied, 151 accepted. Neither SAT nor ACT required. SAT 25/75 percentile: 1000-1360. High school rank: N/A
**Early decision deadline:** N/A, notification date: N/A
**Early action deadline:** N/A, notification date: N/A
**Application deadline (fall):** rolling
**Undergraduate student body:** 315 full time, 147 part time; 76% male, 24% female; 0% American Indian, 12% Asian, 4% black, 15% Hispanic, 12% multiracial, 3% Pacific Islander, 42% white, 1% international; 89% from in state; N/A live on campus; N/A of students in fraternities, N/A in sororities
**Most popular majors:** 44% Animation, Interactive Technology, Video Graphics and Special Effects

**Expenses:** 2014-2015: $16,160; room/board: $7,200
**Financial aid:** (408) 541-0100

## Concordia University
Irvine CA
(949) 214-3010
**U.S. News ranking:** Reg. U. (W), No. 51
**Website:** www.cui.edu
**Admissions email:** admission@cui.edu
**Private;** founded 1972
**Affiliation:** Lutheran Church-Missouri Synod
**Freshman admissions:** selective; 2013-2014: 2,768 applied, 1,850 accepted. Either SAT or ACT required. SAT 25/75 percentile: 903-1110. High school rank: 20% in top tenth, 40% in top quarter, 79% in top half
**Early decision deadline:** N/A, notification date: N/A
**Early action deadline:** 12/1, notification date: 12/15
**Application deadline (fall):** rolling
**Undergraduate student body:** 1,746 full time, 198 part time; 38% male, 62% female; 0% American Indian, 6% Asian, 3% black, 18% Hispanic, 4% multiracial, 0% Pacific Islander, 49% white, 3% international; 88% from in state; 47% live on campus; N/A of students in fraternities, N/A in sororities
**Most popular majors:** 23% Business Administration and Management, General, 7% Communication, General, 11% Liberal Arts and Sciences/Liberal Studies, 8% Psychology, General, 16% Registered Nursing/Registered Nurse
**Expenses:** 2014-2015: $30,640; room/board: $9,270
**Financial aid:** (949) 854-8002; 72% of undergrads determined to have financial need; average aid package $18,553

## Dominican University of California
San Rafael CA
(415) 485-3204
**U.S. News ranking:** Reg. U. (W), No. 33
**Website:** www.dominican.edu
**Admissions email:** enroll@dominican.edu
**Private;** founded 1890
**Freshman admissions:** selective; 2013-2014: 2,322 applied, 1,800 accepted. Either SAT or ACT required. SAT 25/75 percentile: 960-1160. High school rank: N/A
**Early decision deadline:** N/A, notification date: N/A
**Early action deadline:** N/A, notification date: N/A
**Application deadline (fall):** rolling
**Undergraduate student body:** 1,298 full time, 305 part time; 26% male, 74% female; 1% American Indian, 17% Asian, 4% black, 23% Hispanic, 3% multiracial, 1% Pacific Islander, 33% white, 2% international
**Most popular majors:** Information not available
**Expenses:** 2014-2015: $41,730; room/board: $13,940
**Financial aid:** (415) 257-1321; 80% of undergrads determined to have financial need; average aid package $27,587

## Fashion Institute of Design & Merchandising
Los Angeles CA
(800) 624-1200
**U.S. News ranking:** Arts, unranked
**Website:** fidm.edu/
**Admissions email:** admissions@fidm.edu
**Private**
**Freshman admissions:** N/A; 2013-2014: 2,431 applied, 1,278 accepted. Neither SAT nor ACT required. SAT 25/75 percentile: N/A. High school rank: N/A
**Early decision deadline:** N/A, notification date: N/A
**Early action deadline:** N/A, notification date: N/A
**Application deadline (fall):** rolling
**Undergraduate student body:** 4,008 full time, 471 part time; 10% male, 90% female; 1% American Indian, 13% Asian, 6% black, 23% Hispanic, 3% multiracial, 1% Pacific Islander, 36% white, 11% international
**Most popular majors:** Information not available
**Expenses:** 2013-2014: $28,920; room/board: N/A
**Financial aid:** N/A

## Fresno Pacific University
Fresno CA
(559) 453-2039
**U.S. News ranking:** Reg. U. (W), No. 40
**Website:** www.fresno.edu
**Admissions email:** ugadmis@fresno.edu
**Private;** founded 1944
**Affiliation:** Mennonite Brethren
**Freshman admissions:** selective; 2013-2014: 705 applied, 553 accepted. Either SAT or ACT required. SAT 25/75 percentile: 880-1100. High school rank: 31% in top tenth, 66% in top quarter, 94% in top half
**Early decision deadline:** N/A, notification date: N/A
**Early action deadline:** N/A, notification date: N/A
**Application deadline (fall):** 7/31
**Undergraduate student body:** 2,158 full time, 254 part time; 31% male, 69% female; 1% American Indian, 4% Asian, 6% black, 41% Hispanic, 2% multiracial, 0% Pacific Islander, 38% white, 2% international; 95% from in state; 26% live on campus; 0% of students in fraternities, 0% in sororities
**Most popular majors:** 25% Business, Management, Marketing, and Related Support Services, 25% Education, 5% Health Professions and Related Programs, 16% Liberal Arts and Sciences, General Studies and Humanities, 6% Social Sciences
**Expenses:** 2014-2015: $26,638; room/board: $7,360
**Financial aid:** (559) 453-2027; 86% of undergrads determined to have financial need; average aid package $19,359

## Golden Gate University
San Francisco CA
(415) 442-7800
**U.S. News ranking:** Reg. U. (W), unranked
**Website:** www.ggu.edu
**Admissions email:** info@ggu.edu
**Private;** founded 1901
**Freshman admissions:** N/A; 2013-2014: N/A applied, N/A accepted. Neither SAT nor ACT required. ACT 25/75 percentile: N/A. High school rank: N/A
**Early decision deadline:** N/A, notification date: N/A
**Early action deadline:** N/A, notification date: N/A
**Application deadline (fall):** rolling
**Undergraduate student body:** 104 full time, 371 part time; 46% male, 54% female; 0% American Indian, 18% Asian, 11% black, 17% Hispanic, 4% multiracial, 2% Pacific Islander, 29% white, 2% international
**Most popular majors:** Information not available
**Expenses:** 2013-2014: $14,400; room/board: N/A
**Financial aid:** (415) 442-7270

## Harvey Mudd College
Claremont CA
(909) 621-8011
**U.S. News ranking:** Nat. Lib. Arts, No. 15
**Website:** www.hmc.edu
**Admissions email:** admission@hmc.edu
**Private;** founded 1955
**Freshman admissions:** most selective; 2013-2014: 3,375 applied, 643 accepted. Either SAT or ACT required. SAT 25/75 percentile: 1400-1560. High school rank: 97% in top tenth, 100% in top quarter, 100% in top half
**Early decision deadline:** 11/15, notification date: 12/15
**Early action deadline:** N/A, notification date: N/A
**Application deadline (fall):** 1/2
**Undergraduate student body:** 805 full time, 2 part time; 54% male, 46% female; 0% American Indian, 22% Asian, 1% black, 9% Hispanic, 4% multiracial, 0% Pacific Islander, 47% white, 11% international; 42% from in state; 99% live on campus; 0% of students in fraternities, 0% in sororities
**Most popular majors:** 1% Biological and Biomedical Sciences, 27% Computer and Information Sciences and Support Services, 33% Engineering, 14% Mathematics and Statistics, 19% Physical Sciences
**Expenses:** 2014-2015: $48,594; room/board: $15,833
**Financial aid:** (909) 621-8055; 50% of undergrads determined to have financial need; average aid package $39,799

## Holy Names University
Oakland CA
(510) 436-1351
**U.S. News ranking:** Reg. U. (W), No. 68
**Website:** www.hnu.edu
**Admissions email:** admissions@hnu.edu
**Private;** founded 1868

**Affiliation:** Roman Catholic
**Freshman admissions:** less selective; 2013-2014: 561 applied, 318 accepted. Either SAT or ACT required. SAT 25/75 percentile: 820-1000. High school rank: N/A
**Early decision deadline:** N/A, notification date: N/A
**Early action deadline:** N/A, notification date: N/A
**Application deadline (fall):** rolling
**Undergraduate student body:** 677 full time, 211 part time; 31% male, 69% female; 1% American Indian, 17% Asian, 21% black, 28% Hispanic, 4% multiracial, 4% Pacific Islander, 18% white, 2% international; 92% from in state; 44% live on campus; N/A of students in fraternities, N/A in sororities
**Most popular majors:** 30% Business, Management, Marketing, and Related Support Services, 14% Health Professions and Related Programs, 9% Liberal Arts and Sciences, General Studies and Humanities, 18% Psychology, 12% Social Sciences
**Expenses:** 2014-2015: $34,488; room/board: $11,608
**Financial aid:** (510) 436-1327; 89% of undergrads determined to have financial need; average aid package $25,551

## Hope International University
Fullerton CA
(714) 879-3901
**U.S. News ranking:** Reg. Coll. (W), No. 19
**Website:** www.hiu.edu
**Admissions email:** admissions@hiu.edu
**Private;** founded 1928
**Affiliation:** Christian Churches/Churches of Christ
**Freshman admissions:** less selective; 2013-2014: 376 applied, 178 accepted. Either SAT or ACT required. SAT 25/75 percentile: 860-1090. High school rank: 2% in top tenth, 13% in top quarter, 40% in top half
**Early decision deadline:** N/A, notification date: N/A
**Early action deadline:** N/A, notification date: N/A
**Application deadline (fall):** rolling
**Undergraduate student body:** 672 full time, 249 part time; 45% male, 55% female; 0% American Indian, 3% Asian, 8% black, 17% Hispanic, 14% multiracial, 1% Pacific Islander, 44% white, 1% international; 76% from in state; 60% live on campus; N/A of students in fraternities, N/A in sororities
**Most popular majors:** 18% Business Administration and Management, General, 16% Human Development and Family Studies, General, 16% Psychology, General, 9% Social Sciences, General, 27% Theological and Ministerial Studies, Other
**Expenses:** 2014-2015: $27,130; room/board: $8,750
**Financial aid:** (714) 879-3901; 78% of undergrads determined to have financial need; average aid package $15,152

## Humboldt State University
Arcata CA
(707) 826-4402
**U.S. News ranking:** Reg. U. (W), No. 58
**Website:** www.humboldt.edu
**Admissions email:** hsuinfo@humboldt.edu
**Public;** founded 1913
**Freshman admissions:** selective; 2013-2014: 11,261 applied, 8,514 accepted. Neither SAT nor ACT required. SAT 25/75 percentile: 870-1110. High school rank: 9% in top tenth, 39% in top quarter, 76% in top half
**Early decision deadline:** N/A, notification date: N/A
**Early action deadline:** N/A, notification date: N/A
**Application deadline (fall):** 11/30
**Undergraduate student body:** 7,255 full time, 498 part time; 47% male, 53% female; 1% American Indian, 3% Asian, 4% black, 27% Hispanic, 6% multiracial, 0% Pacific Islander, 50% white, 1% international; 93% from in state; 25% live on campus; 1% of students in fraternities, 1% in sororities
**Most popular majors:** 10% Biological and Biomedical Sciences, 8% Liberal Arts and Sciences, General Studies and Humanities, 14% Natural Resources and Conservation, 11% Social Sciences, 10% Visual and Performing Arts
**Expenses:** 2014-2015: $7,154 in state, $18,314 out of state; room/board: $11,678
**Financial aid:** (707) 826-4321; 76% of undergrads determined to have financial need; average aid package $13,368

## Humphreys College[1]
Stockton CA
(209) 478-0800
**U.S. News ranking:** Reg. Coll. (W), unranked
**Website:** www.humphreys.edu
**Admissions email:** ugadmission@humphreys.edu
**Private**
**Application deadline (fall):** N/A
**Undergraduate student body:** N/A full time, N/A part time
**Expenses:** 2013-2014: $11,277; room/board: N/A
**Financial aid:** (209) 478-0800

## John F. Kennedy University[1]
Pleasant Hill CA
(925) 969-3330
**U.S. News ranking:** Reg. U. (W), unranked
**Website:** www.jfku.edu
**Admissions email:** proginfo@jfku.edu
**Private**
**Application deadline (fall):** N/A
**Undergraduate student body:** N/A full time, N/A part time
**Expenses:** N/A
**Financial aid:** (925) 969-3385

## Laguna College of Art and Design
Laguna Beach CA
(949) 376-6000
**U.S. News ranking:** Arts, unranked
**Website:** www.lcad.edu/
**Admissions email:** admissions@lcad.edu

**Private**
**Freshman admissions:** N/A;
2013-2014: 818 applied, 346
accepted. Neither SAT nor ACT
required. SAT 25/75 percentile:
N/A. High school rank: N/A
**Early decision deadline:** N/A,
notification date: N/A
**Early action deadline:** N/A,
notification date: N/A
**Application deadline (fall):** 8/1
**Undergraduate student body:** 466
full time, 48 part time; 40%
male, 60% female; 2% American
Indian, 15% Asian, 2% black,
16% Hispanic, 0% multiracial,
1% Pacific Islander, 48% white,
4% international
**Most popular majors:** Information
not available
**Expenses:** 2014-2015: $27,300;
room/board: N/A
**Financial aid:** (949) 376-6000

## La Sierra University
Riverside CA
(951) 785-2176
**U.S. News ranking:** Reg. U. (W),
No. 56
**Website:** www.lasierra.edu
**Admissions email:**
admissions@lasierra.edu
**Private;** founded 1922
**Affiliation:** Seventh-day Adventist
**Freshman admissions:** less
selective; 2013-2014: 3,479
applied, 1,627 accepted. Either
SAT or ACT required. SAT 25/75
percentile: 810-1040. High school
rank: 10% in top tenth, 41% in
top quarter, 63% in top half
**Early decision deadline:** N/A,
notification date: N/A
**Early action deadline:** N/A,
notification date: N/A
**Application deadline (fall):** 7/1
**Undergraduate student body:** 1,912
full time, 193 part time; 42%
male, 58% female; 0% American
Indian, 15% Asian, 7% black,
41% Hispanic, 4% multiracial,
2% Pacific Islander, 16% white,
13% international; 93% from in
state; 35% live on campus; 0%
of students in fraternities, 0% in
sororities
**Most popular majors:** 11% Biology/
Biological Sciences, General,
25% Business Administration and
Management, General, 9% Health
and Physical Education/Fitness,
General, 7% History, General, 8%
Psychology, General
**Expenses:** 2014-2015: $29,895;
room/board: $7,650
**Financial aid:** (909) 785-2175;
78% of undergrads determined to
have financial need; average aid
package $22,673

## Loyola Marymount University
Los Angeles CA
(310) 338-2750
**U.S. News ranking:** Reg. U. (W),
No. 3
**Website:** www.lmu.edu
**Admissions email:**
admissions@lmu.edu
**Private;** founded 1911
**Affiliation:** Roman Catholic
**Freshman admissions:** more
selective; 2013-2014: 11,472
applied, 6,209 accepted. Either
SAT or ACT required. SAT 25/75
percentile: 1090-1300. High
school rank: 29% in top tenth,
57% in top quarter, 89% in
top half

**Early decision deadline:** N/A,
notification date: N/A
**Early action deadline:** 11/1,
notification date: 12/20
**Application deadline (fall):** 1/15
**Undergraduate student body:** 5,935
full time, 270 part time; 43%
male, 57% female; 0% American
Indian, 10% Asian, 6% black,
22% Hispanic, 7% multiracial,
0% Pacific Islander, 49% white,
5% international; 78% from in
state; 52% live on campus; 19%
of students in fraternities, 34%
in sororities
**Most popular majors:** 23%
Business/Commerce, General,
6% English Language and
Literature, General, 12% Social
Sciences, General, 11% Speech
Communication and Rhetoric,
15% Visual and Performing Arts,
General
**Expenses:** 2014-2015: $41,372;
room/board: $14,395
**Financial aid:** (310) 338-2753;
59% of undergrads determined to
have financial need; average aid
package $27,339

## Master's College and Seminary
Santa Clarita CA
(800) 568-6248
**U.S. News ranking:** Reg. Coll. (W),
No. 5
**Website:** www.masters.edu
**Admissions email:**
admissions@masters.edu
**Private;** founded 1927
**Affiliation:** Evangelical
**Freshman admissions:** selective;
2013-2014: 556 applied, 433
accepted. Either SAT or ACT
required. SAT 25/75 percentile:
940-1200. High school rank:
28% in top tenth, 55% in top
quarter, 82% in top half
**Early decision deadline:** N/A,
notification date: N/A
**Early action deadline:** 11/15,
notification date: 12/22
**Application deadline (fall):** rolling
**Undergraduate student body:** 967
full time, 131 part time; 52%
male, 48% female; 1% American
Indian, 6% Asian, 3% black,
9% Hispanic, 6% multiracial,
1% Pacific Islander, 66% white,
5% international; 73% from in
state; 82% live on campus; N/A
of students in fraternities, N/A in
sororities
**Most popular majors:** 29% Bible/
Biblical Studies, 8% Biology/
Biological Sciences, General,
13% Business, Management,
Marketing, and Related Support
Services, 9% Communication,
Journalism, and Related Programs,
11% Liberal Arts and Sciences,
General Studies and Humanities
**Expenses:** 2014-2015: $29,860;
room/board: $9,720
**Financial aid:** (661) 259-3540;
88% of undergrads determined to
have financial need; average aid
package $19,982

## Menlo College
Atherton CA
(800) 556-3656
**U.S. News ranking:** Reg. Coll. (W),
No. 8
**Website:** www.menlo.edu
**Admissions email:** admissions@
menlo.edu
**Private;** founded 1927

**Freshman admissions:** less
selective; 2013-2014: 3,752
applied, 1,519 accepted. Either
SAT or ACT required. SAT 25/75
percentile: 882-1097. High
school rank: N/A
**Early decision deadline:** N/A,
notification date: N/A
**Early action deadline:** 11/15,
notification date: 1/15
**Application deadline (fall):** 4/1
**Undergraduate student body:**
704 full time, 9 part time; 62%
male, 38% female; 0% American
Indian, 7% Asian, 5% black,
21% Hispanic, 8% multiracial,
2% Pacific Islander, 35% white,
13% international; 83% from in
state; 61% live on campus; 0%
of students in fraternities, 0% in
sororities
**Most popular majors:** 8%
Accounting, 9% Finance, General,
20% Marketing/Marketing
Management, General, 8%
Psychology, General
**Expenses:** 2014-2015: $37,520;
room/board: $12,260
**Financial aid:** (650) 543-3880;
64% of undergrads determined to
have financial need; average aid
package $28,231

## Mills College
Oakland CA
(510) 430-2135
**U.S. News ranking:** Reg. U. (W),
No. 6
**Website:** www.mills.edu
**Admissions email:** admission@
mills.edu
**Private;** founded 1852
**Freshman admissions:** more
selective; 2013-2014: 1,827
applied, 1,242 accepted. Either
SAT or ACT required. SAT 25/75
percentile: 1040-1250. High
school rank: 41% in top tenth,
71% in top quarter, 97% in
top half
**Early decision deadline:** N/A,
notification date: N/A
**Early action deadline:** 11/15,
notification date: 12/15
**Application deadline (fall):** 3/1
**Undergraduate student body:** 922
full time, 63 part time; 0% male,
100% female; 1% American
Indian, 12% Asian, 6% black,
22% Hispanic, 9% multiracial,
1% Pacific Islander, 47% white,
1% international; 82% from in
state; 58% live on campus; 0%
of students in fraternities, 0% in
sororities
**Most popular majors:** 10%
Biological and Biomedical
Sciences, 16% English Language
and Literature/Letters, 10%
Psychology, 24% Social Sciences,
13% Visual and Performing Arts
**Expenses:** 2014-2015: $42,918;
room/board: $12,914
**Financial aid:** (510) 430-2000;
85% of undergrads determined to
have financial need; average aid
package $37,766

## Mount St. Mary's College
Los Angeles CA
(310) 954-4250
**U.S. News ranking:** Reg. U. (W),
No. 23
**Website:** www.msmc.la.edu
**Admissions email:** admissions@
msmc.la.edu
**Private;** founded 1925
**Affiliation:** Roman Catholic

**Freshman admissions:** less
selective; 2013-2014: 1,886
applied, 1,716 accepted. Either
SAT or ACT required. SAT 25/75
percentile: 830-1020. High school
rank: 17% in top tenth, 46% in
top quarter, 91% in top half
**Early decision deadline:** N/A,
notification date: N/A
**Early action deadline:** 12/1,
notification date: 1/30
**Application deadline (fall):** 8/1
**Undergraduate student body:** 2,092
full time, 533 part time; 6%
male, 94% female; 0% American
Indian, 16% Asian, 7% black,
58% Hispanic, 2% multiracial,
1% Pacific Islander, 10% white,
1% international; 99% from in
state; 20% live on campus; 0%
of students in fraternities, 2% in
sororities
**Most popular majors:** 5% Biological
and Biomedical Sciences,
12% Business, Management,
Marketing, and Related Support
Services, 37% Health Professions
and Related Programs, 9%
Psychology, 11% Social Sciences
**Expenses:** 2014-2015: $34,826;
room/board: $10,793
**Financial aid:** (310) 954-4191;
91% of undergrads determined to
have financial need; average aid
package $28,423

## National Hispanic University[1]
San Jose CA
(408) 254-2772
**U.S. News ranking:** Nat. Lib. Arts,
unranked
**Website:** www.nhu.edu
**Admissions email:**
university@nhu.edu
**For-profit**
**Application deadline (fall):** N/A
**Undergraduate student body:** N/A
full time, N/A part time
**Expenses:** 2013-2014: $8,196;
room/board: N/A
**Financial aid:** (408) 254-2708

## National University[1]
La Jolla CA
(800) 628-8648
**U.S. News ranking:** Reg. U. (W),
unranked
**Website:** www.nu.edu
**Admissions email:** advisor@nu.edu
**Private;** founded 1971
**Application deadline (fall):** rolling
**Undergraduate student body:** N/A
full time, N/A part time
**Expenses:** 2013-2014: $11,796;
room/board: N/A
**Financial aid:** (858) 642-8500

## NewSchool of Architecture and Design[1]
San Diego CA
(800) 490-7081
**U.S. News ranking:** Arts, unranked
**Website:** newschoolarch.edu/
**Admissions email:** N/A
**For-profit**
**Application deadline (fall):** N/A
**Undergraduate student body:** N/A
full time, N/A part time
**Expenses:** 2013-2014: $24,536;
room/board: N/A
**Financial aid:** N/A

## Notre Dame de Namur University[1]
Belmont CA
(650) 508-3600
**U.S. News ranking:** Reg. U. (W),
No. 51
**Website:** www.ndnu.edu
**Admissions email:** admissions@
ndnu.edu
**Private;** founded 1851
**Affiliation:** Catholic
**Application deadline (fall):** rolling
**Undergraduate student body:** N/A
full time, N/A part time
**Expenses:** 2013-2014: $31,206;
room/board: $12,152
**Financial aid:** (650) 508-3600

## Occidental College
Los Angeles CA
(800) 825-5262
**U.S. News ranking:** Nat. Lib. Arts,
No. 44
**Website:** www.oxy.edu
**Admissions email:**
admission@oxy.edu
**Private;** founded 1887
**Freshman admissions:** more
selective; 2013-2014: 6,072
applied, 2,574 accepted. Either
SAT or ACT required. SAT 25/75
percentile: 1210-1400. High
school rank: 51% in top tenth,
83% in top quarter, 100% in
top half
**Early decision deadline:** 11/15,
notification date: 12/15
**Early action deadline:** N/A,
notification date: N/A
**Application deadline (fall):** 1/10
**Undergraduate student body:** 2,113
full time, 15 part time; 44%
male, 56% female; 0% American
Indian, 13% Asian, 4% black,
16% Hispanic, 9% multiracial,
0% Pacific Islander, 51% white,
4% international; 51% from in
state; 80% live on campus; 9%
of students in fraternities, 14%
in sororities
**Most popular majors:** 10% Biology/
Biological Sciences, General,
14% Economics, General, 6%
English Language and Literature/
Letters, Other, 11% International
Relations and Affairs, 8%
Psychology, General
**Expenses:** 2014-2015: $47,522;
room/board: $13,450
**Financial aid:** (323) 259-2548;
58% of undergrads determined to
have financial need; average aid
package $41,535

## Otis College of Art and Design
Los Angeles CA
(310) 665-6820
**U.S. News ranking:** Arts, unranked
**Website:** www.otis.edu
**Admissions email:**
admissions@otis.edu
**Private;** founded 1918
**Freshman admissions:** N/A;
2013-2014: 1,584 applied, 733
accepted. Either SAT or ACT
required. SAT 25/75 percentile:
N/A. High school rank: N/A
**Early decision deadline:** N/A,
notification date: N/A
**Early action deadline:** N/A,
notification date: N/A
**Application deadline (fall):** rolling
**Undergraduate student body:** 1,018
full time, 14 part time; 35%
male, 65% female; 1% American
Indian, 32% Asian, 3% black,

13% Hispanic, 6% multiracial, 0% Pacific Islander, 22% white, 18% international
**Most popular majors:** Information not available
**Expenses:** 2014-2015: $40,490; room/board: $11,800
**Financial aid:** (310) 665-6880; 69% of undergrads determined to have financial need; average aid package $24,527

## Pacific Union College
Angwin CA
(707) 965-6425
**U.S. News ranking:** Nat. Lib. Arts, second tier
**Website:** www.puc.edu
**Admissions email:** enroll@puc.edu
**Private;** founded 1882
**Affiliation:** Seventh-day Adventist
**Freshman admissions:** selective; 2013-2014: 2,103 applied, 1,063 accepted. Either SAT or ACT required. SAT 25/75 percentile: 890-1150. High school rank: N/A
**Early decision deadline:** N/A, notification date: N/A
**Early action deadline:** N/A, notification date: N/A
**Application deadline (fall):** rolling
**Undergraduate student body:** 1,454 full time, 191 part time; 44% male, 56% female; 0% American Indian, 18% Asian, 8% black, 27% Hispanic, 7% multiracial, 2% Pacific Islander, 27% white, 2% international
**Most popular majors:** 19% Biological and Biomedical Sciences, 13% Business, Management, Marketing, and Related Support Services, 7% Education, 23% Health Professions and Related Programs, 7% Visual and Performing Arts
**Expenses:** 2014-2015: $28,131; room/board: $7,485
**Financial aid:** (707) 965-7200; 79% of undergrads determined to have financial need; average aid package $22,489

## Patten University[1]
Oakland CA
(877) 472-8836
**U.S. News ranking:** Reg. Coll. (W), second tier
**Website:** www.patten.edu/
**Admissions email:** Admissions@patten.edu
**Private**
**Application deadline (fall):** N/A
**Undergraduate student body:** N/A full time, N/A part time
**Expenses:** N/A
**Financial aid:** (510) 261-8500

## Pepperdine University
Malibu CA
(310) 506-4392
**U.S. News ranking:** Nat. U., No. 54
**Website:** www.pepperdine.edu
**Admissions email:** admission-seaver@pepperdine.edu
**Private;** founded 1937
**Affiliation:** Church of Christ
**Freshman admissions:** more selective; 2013-2014: 9,721 applied, 3,630 accepted. Either SAT or ACT required. SAT 25/75 percentile: 1130-1340. High school rank: 47% in top tenth, 83% in top quarter, 96% in top half
**Early decision deadline:** N/A, notification date: N/A

**Early action deadline:** N/A, notification date: N/A
**Application deadline (fall):** 1/5
**Undergraduate student body:** 3,172 full time, 366 part time; 41% male, 59% female; 0% American Indian, 14% Asian, 7% black, 16% Hispanic, 6% multiracial, 0% Pacific Islander, 42% white, 9% international; 85% from in state; 58% live on campus; 18% of students in fraternities, 31% in sororities
**Most popular majors:** 29% Business, Management, Marketing, and Related Support Services, 18% Communication, Journalism, and Related Programs, 6% Multi/Interdisciplinary Studies, 8% Psychology, 11% Social Sciences
**Expenses:** 2014-2015: $46,692; room/board: $13,390
**Financial aid:** (310) 506-4301; 57% of undergrads determined to have financial need; average aid package $40,616

## Pitzer College
Claremont CA
(909) 621-8129
**U.S. News ranking:** Nat. Lib. Arts, No. 35
**Website:** www.pitzer.edu
**Admissions email:** admission@pitzer.edu
**Private;** founded 1963
**Freshman admissions:** most selective; 2013-2014: 4,115 applied, 597 accepted. Neither SAT nor ACT required. SAT 25/75 percentile: 1210-1400. High school rank: 55% in top tenth, 96% in top quarter, 100% in top half
**Early decision deadline:** 11/15, notification date: 12/22
**Early action deadline:** N/A, notification date: N/A
**Application deadline (fall):** 1/1
**Undergraduate student body:** 1,044 full time, 37 part time; 40% male, 60% female; 0% American Indian, 6% Asian, 5% black, 15% Hispanic, 8% multiracial, 0% Pacific Islander, 49% white, 5% international; 48% from in state; 75% live on campus; 0% of students in fraternities, 0% in sororities
**Most popular majors:** 7% English Language and Literature, General, 10% Environmental Studies, 14% Multi-/Interdisciplinary Studies, Other, 7% Political Science and Government, General, 14% Psychology, General
**Expenses:** 2014-2015: $46,992; room/board: $14,758
**Financial aid:** (909) 621-8208; 33% of undergrads determined to have financial need; average aid package $40,635

## Point Loma Nazarene University
San Diego CA
(619) 849-2273
**U.S. News ranking:** Reg. U. (W), No. 16
**Website:** www.pointloma.edu
**Admissions email:** admissions@pointloma.edu
**Private;** founded 1902
**Affiliation:** Church of the Nazarene
**Freshman admissions:** more selective; 2013-2014: 3,138 applied, 2,088 accepted. Either SAT or ACT required. SAT 25/75 percentile: 1040-1260. High

school rank: 30% in top tenth, 67% in top quarter, 89% in top half
**Early decision deadline:** N/A, notification date: N/A
**Early action deadline:** 11/15, notification date: 12/21
**Application deadline (fall):** 2/15
**Undergraduate student body:** 2,483 full time, 73 part time; 37% male, 63% female; 1% American Indian, 6% Asian, 3% black, 19% Hispanic, 5% multiracial, 1% Pacific Islander, 64% white, 0% international; 82% from in state; 67% live on campus; N/A of students in fraternities, N/A in sororities
**Most popular majors:** 7% Biological and Biomedical Sciences, 20% Business, Management, Marketing, and Related Support Services, 14% Health Professions and Related Programs, 7% Parks, Recreation, Leisure, and Fitness Studies, 10% Psychology
**Expenses:** 2014-2015: $31,406; room/board: $9,600
**Financial aid:** (619) 849-2538; 71% of undergrads determined to have financial need; average aid package $20,816

## Pomona College
Claremont CA
(909) 621-8134
**U.S. News ranking:** Nat. Lib. Arts, No. 5
**Website:** www.pomona.edu
**Admissions email:** admissions@pomona.edu
**Private;** founded 1887
**Freshman admissions:** most selective; 2013-2014: 7,153 applied, 996 accepted. Either SAT or ACT required. SAT 25/75 percentile: 1380-1540. High school rank: 92% in top tenth, 99% in top quarter, 100% in top half
**Early decision deadline:** 11/1, notification date: 12/15
**Early action deadline:** N/A, notification date: N/A
**Application deadline (fall):** 1/1
**Undergraduate student body:** 1,596 full time, 16 part time; 48% male, 52% female; 0% American Indian, 12% Asian, 6% black, 15% Hispanic, 7% multiracial, 0% Pacific Islander, 45% white, 7% international; 33% from in state; 98% live on campus; 5% of students in fraternities, 0% in sororities
**Most popular majors:** 11% Economics, General, 9% Mathematics, General, 5% Molecular Biology, 8% Neuroscience, 5% Political Science and Government, General
**Expenses:** 2014-2015: $45,832; room/board: $14,700
**Financial aid:** (909) 621-8205; 56% of undergrads determined to have financial need; average aid package $43,665

## San Diego Christian College[1]
El Cajon CA
(619) 588-7747
**U.S. News ranking:** Nat. Lib. Arts, second tier
**Website:** www.sdcc.edu/
**Admissions email:** admissions@sdcc.edu
**Private;** founded 1970
**Application deadline (fall):** rolling

**Undergraduate student body:** N/A full time, N/A part time
**Expenses:** 2013-2014: $25,888; room/board: $9,278
**Financial aid:** (619) 590-1786

## San Diego State University
San Diego CA
(619) 594-6336
**U.S. News ranking:** Nat. U., No. 149
**Website:** www.sdsu.edu
**Admissions email:** admissions@sdsu.edu
**Public;** founded 1897
**Freshman admissions:** more selective; 2013-2014: 54,509 applied, 20,292 accepted. Either SAT or ACT required. SAT 25/75 percentile: 1000-1200. High school rank: 27% in top tenth, 71% in top quarter, 96% in top half
**Early decision deadline:** N/A, notification date: N/A
**Early action deadline:** N/A, notification date: N/A
**Application deadline (fall):** 11/30
**Undergraduate student body:** 24,431 full time, 3,378 part time; 45% male, 55% female; 0% American Indian, 7% Asian, 4% black, 31% Hispanic, 6% multiracial, 7% Pacific Islander, 36% white, 5% international; 93% from in state; 16% live on campus; 7% of students in fraternities, 8% in sororities
**Most popular majors:** 18% Business, Management, Marketing, and Related Support Services, 6% Health Professions and Related Programs, 6% Homeland Security, Law Enforcement, Firefighting and Related Protective Services, 9% Psychology, 13% Social Sciences
**Expenses:** 2014-2015: $6,866 in state, $18,026 out of state; room/board: $14,745
**Financial aid:** (619) 594-6323; 57% of undergrads determined to have financial need; average aid package $11,100

## San Francisco Art Institute
San Francisco CA
(800) 345-7324
**U.S. News ranking:** Arts, unranked
**Website:** www.sfai.edu
**Admissions email:** admissions@sfai.edu
**Private;** founded 1871
**Freshman admissions:** N/A; 2013-2014: 415 applied, 344 accepted. Neither SAT nor ACT required. SAT 25/75 percentile: N/A. High school rank: N/A
**Early decision deadline:** N/A, notification date: N/A
**Early action deadline:** N/A, notification date: N/A
**Application deadline (fall):** rolling
**Undergraduate student body:** 444 full time, 34 part time; 43% male, 57% female; 1% American Indian, 4% Asian, 2% black, 16% Hispanic, 9% multiracial, 0% Pacific Islander, 48% white, 13% international; 61% from in state; 28% live on campus; 0% of students in fraternities, 0% in sororities

**Most popular majors:** 9% Cinematography and Film/Video Production, 7% Design and Visual Communications, General, 44% Painting, 17% Photography, 8% Printmaking
**Expenses:** 2014-2015: $40,096; room/board: $11,500
**Financial aid:** (415) 749-4520; 61% of undergrads determined to have financial need; average aid package $17,165

## San Francisco Conservatory of Music
San Francisco CA
(800) 899-7326
**U.S. News ranking:** Arts, unranked
**Website:** www.sfcm.edu
**Admissions email:** admit@sfcm.edu
**Private;** founded 1917
**Freshman admissions:** N/A; 2013-2014: 296 applied, 118 accepted. Neither SAT nor ACT required. SAT 25/75 percentile: N/A. High school rank: N/A
**Early decision deadline:** N/A, notification date: N/A
**Early action deadline:** N/A, notification date: N/A
**Application deadline (fall):** 12/1
**Undergraduate student body:** 171 full time, 3 part time; 51% male, 49% female; 1% American Indian, 7% Asian, 3% black, 3% Hispanic, 15% multiracial, 0% Pacific Islander, 38% white, 26% international; 61% from in state; 13% live on campus; 0% of students in fraternities, 0% in sororities
**Most popular majors:** 7% Brass Instruments, 16% Keyboard Instruments, 11% Music Theory and Composition, 36% Stringed Instruments, 27% Voice and Opera
**Expenses:** 2014-2015: $40,992; room/board: N/A
**Financial aid:** (415) 759-3414; 88% of undergrads determined to have financial need; average aid package $24,016

## San Francisco State University
San Francisco CA
(415) 338-6486
**U.S. News ranking:** Reg. U. (W), No. 58
**Website:** www.sfsu.edu
**Admissions email:** ugadmit@sfsu.edu
**Public;** founded 1899
**Freshman admissions:** selective; 2013-2014: 34,930 applied, 20,889 accepted. Either SAT or ACT required. SAT 25/75 percentile: 880-1110. High school rank: N/A
**Early decision deadline:** N/A, notification date: N/A
**Early action deadline:** N/A, notification date: N/A
**Application deadline (fall):** 11/30
**Undergraduate student body:** 22,111 full time, 4,045 part time; 43% male, 57% female; 0% American Indian, 29% Asian, 5% black, 24% Hispanic, 6% multiracial, 1% Pacific Islander, 24% white, 7% international; 99% from in state; 12% live on campus; 2% of students in fraternities, 5% in sororities
**Most popular majors:** 24% Business, Management, Marketing, and Related Support Services, 9% Communication, Journalism, and Related

Programs, 6% Health Professions and Related Programs, 10% Social Sciences, 9% Visual and Performing Arts
**Expenses:** 2014-2015: $6,468 in state, $17,628 out of state; room/board: $13,052
**Financial aid:** (415) 338-7000; 66% of undergrads determined to have financial need; average aid package $11,643

## San Jose State University
San Jose CA
(408) 283-7500
**U.S. News ranking:** Reg. U. (W), No. 38
**Website:** www.sjsu.edu
**Admissions email:** admissions@sjsu.edu
**Public;** founded 1857
**Freshman admissions:** selective; 2013-2014: 27,679 applied, 17,733 accepted. Either SAT or ACT required. SAT 25/75 percentile: 880-1160. High school rank: N/A
**Early decision deadline:** N/A, notification date: N/A
**Early action deadline:** N/A, notification date: N/A
**Application deadline (fall):** 11/29
**Undergraduate student body:** 20,852 full time, 5,010 part time; 51% male, 49% female; 0% American Indian, 35% Asian, 3% black, 24% Hispanic, 5% multiracial, 1% Pacific Islander, 22% white, 5% international; 100% from in state; 14% live on campus; N/A of students in fraternities, N/A in sororities
**Most popular majors:** 26% Business, Management, Marketing, and Related Support Services, 8% Engineering, 9% Health Professions and Related Programs, 7% Psychology, 9% Visual and Performing Arts
**Expenses:** 2014-2015: $9,496 in state, $13,172 out of state; room/board: $13,350
**Financial aid:** (408) 283-7500; 71% of undergrads determined to have financial need; average aid package $14,956

## Santa Clara University
Santa Clara CA
(408) 554-4700
**U.S. News ranking:** Reg. U. (W), No. 2
**Website:** www.scu.edu
**Admissions email:** Admission@scu.edu
**Private;** founded 1851
**Affiliation:** Catholic
**Freshman admissions:** more selective; 2013-2014: 14,980 applied, 7,456 accepted. Either SAT or ACT required. SAT 25/75 percentile: 1190-1380. High school rank: 50% in top tenth, 80% in top quarter, 97% in top half
**Early decision deadline:** 11/1, notification date: 12/23
**Early action deadline:** 11/1, notification date: 12/23
**Application deadline (fall):** 1/7
**Undergraduate student body:** 5,338 full time, 97 part time; 50% male, 50% female; 0% American Indian, 14% Asian, 3% black, 17% Hispanic, 7% multiracial, 0% Pacific Islander, 48% white, 3% international; 73% from in

state; 52% live on campus; N/A of students in fraternities, N/A in sororities
**Most popular majors:** 29% Business, Management, Marketing, and Related Support Services, 9% Communication, Journalism, and Related Programs, 11% Engineering, 7% Psychology, 13% Social Sciences
**Expenses:** 2014-2015: $43,812; room/board: $12,921
**Financial aid:** (408) 554-4505; 52% of undergrads determined to have financial need; average aid package $27,559

## Scripps College
Claremont CA
(909) 621-8149
**U.S. News ranking:** Nat. Lib. Arts, No. 24
**Website:** www.scrippscollege.edu/
**Admissions email:** admission@scrippscollege.edu
**Private;** founded 1926
**Freshman admissions:** most selective; 2013-2014: 2,378 applied, 849 accepted. Either SAT or ACT required. SAT 25/75 percentile: 1280-1453. High school rank: 75% in top tenth, 99% in top quarter, 100% in top half
**Early decision deadline:** 11/15, notification date: 12/15
**Early action deadline:** N/A, notification date: N/A
**Application deadline (fall):** 1/1
**Undergraduate student body:** 979 full time, 11 part time; 0% male, 100% female; 0% American Indian, 17% Asian, 3% black, 8% Hispanic, 7% multiracial, 0% Pacific Islander, 51% white, 4% international; 51% from in state; 96% live on campus; 0% of students in fraternities, 0% in sororities
**Most popular majors:** 14% Area, Ethnic, Cultural, Gender, and Group Studies, 13% Biological and Biomedical Sciences, 8% Psychology, General, 19% Social Sciences, 9% Visual and Performing Arts
**Expenses:** 2014-2015: $47,378; room/board: $14,562
**Financial aid:** (909) 621-8275; 43% of undergrads determined to have financial need; average aid package $40,258

## Simpson University
Redding CA
(530) 226-4606
**U.S. News ranking:** Nat. Lib. Arts, second tier
**Website:** www.simpsonu.edu
**Admissions email:** admissions@simpsonu.edu
**Private;** founded 1921
**Affiliation:** Christian and Missionary Alliance
**Freshman admissions:** selective; 2013-2014: 573 applied, 318 accepted. Either SAT or ACT required. SAT 25/75 percentile: 910-1150. High school rank: 23% in top tenth, 50% in top quarter, 88% in top half
**Early decision deadline:** N/A, notification date: N/A
**Early action deadline:** 8/31, notification date: N/A
**Application deadline (fall):** rolling
**Undergraduate student body:** 993 full time, 31 part time; 34% male, 66% female; 4% American Indian, 6% Asian, 3% black, 14% Hispanic, 0% multiracial,

0% Pacific Islander, 62% white, 0% international; 85% from in state; 61% live on campus; 0% of students in fraternities, 0% in sororities
**Most popular majors:** 29% Business/Commerce, General, 6% Communication and Media Studies, 23% Psychology, General, 12% Registered Nursing, Nursing Administration, Nursing Research and Clinical Nursing, 9% Theology and Religious Vocations, Other
**Expenses:** 2014-2015: $24,300; room/board: $7,700
**Financial aid:** (530) 226-4111; 89% of undergrads determined to have financial need; average aid package $20,435

## Soka University of America
Aliso Viejo CA
(888) 600-Soka
**U.S. News ranking:** Nat. Lib. Arts, No. 41
**Website:** www.soka.edu
**Admissions email:** admission@soka.edu
**Private;** founded 1987
**Freshman admissions:** more selective; 2013-2014: 422 applied, 183 accepted. Either SAT or ACT required. SAT 25/75 percentile: 1080-1340. High school rank: 50% in top tenth, 79% in top quarter, 98% in top half
**Early decision deadline:** N/A, notification date: N/A
**Early action deadline:** 10/15, notification date: 12/1
**Application deadline (fall):** 1/15
**Undergraduate student body:** 412 full time, 0 part time; 36% male, 64% female; 1% American Indian, 19% Asian, 5% black, 8% Hispanic, 1% multiracial, 0% Pacific Islander, 20% white, 39% international; 60% from in state; 100% live on campus; 0% of students in fraternities, 0% in sororities
**Most popular majors:** 100% Liberal Arts and Sciences/Liberal Studies
**Expenses:** 2014-2015: $30,214; room/board: $11,134
**Financial aid:** N/A; 92% of undergrads determined to have financial need; average aid package $30,691

## Sonoma State University
Rohnert Park CA
(707) 664-2778
**U.S. News ranking:** Reg. U. (W), No. 43
**Website:** www.sonoma.edu
**Admissions email:** student.outreach@sonoma.edu
**Public;** founded 1960
**Freshman admissions:** less selective; 2013-2014: 14,272 applied, 12,870 accepted. Either SAT or ACT required. SAT 25/75 percentile: 880-1090. High school rank: N/A
**Early decision deadline:** N/A, notification date: N/A
**Early action deadline:** N/A, notification date: N/A
**Application deadline (fall):** 11/30
**Undergraduate student body:** 7,652 full time, 699 part time; 39% male, 61% female; 1% American Indian, 5% Asian, 3% black, 19% Hispanic, 8% multiracial, 1% Pacific Islander, 60% white,

2% international; 99% from in state; 37% live on campus; 20% of students in fraternities, 13% in sororities
**Most popular majors:** 20% Business Administration and Management, General, 5% Health and Physical Education/Fitness, General, 6% Liberal Arts and Sciences/Liberal Studies, 8% Psychology, General, 7% Sociology
**Expenses:** 2014-2015: $7,276 in state, $18,436 out of state; room/board: $11,799
**Financial aid:** (707) 664-2287; 49% of undergrads determined to have financial need; average aid package $10,209

## Southern California Institute of Architecture[1]
Los Angeles CA
(800) 774-7242
**U.S. News ranking:** Arts, unranked
**Website:** www.sciarc.edu
**Admissions email:** admissions@sciarc.edu
**Private**
**Application deadline (fall):** 1/15
**Undergraduate student body:** N/A full time, N/A part time
**Expenses:** 2013-2014: $37,300; room/board: N/A
**Financial aid:** (213) 613-2200

## Stanford University
Stanford CA
(650) 723-2091
**U.S. News ranking:** Nat. U., No. 4
**Website:** www.stanford.edu
**Admissions email:** admission@stanford.edu
**Private;** founded 1885
**Freshman admissions:** most selective; 2013-2014: 38,828 applied, 2,208 accepted. Either SAT or ACT required. SAT 25/75 percentile: 1380-1570. High school rank: 96% in top tenth, 100% in top quarter, 100% in top half
**Early decision deadline:** N/A, notification date: N/A
**Early action deadline:** 11/1, notification date: 12/15
**Application deadline (fall):** 1/1
**Undergraduate student body:** 6,980 full time, 81 part time; 53% male, 47% female; 1% American Indian, 19% Asian, 6% black, 17% Hispanic, 11% multiracial, 0% Pacific Islander, 37% white, 8% international; 43% from in state; 91% live on campus; 24% of students in fraternities, 28% in sororities
**Most popular majors:** 6% Biological and Biomedical Sciences, 8% Computer and Information Sciences and Support Services, 15% Engineering, 16% Multi/Interdisciplinary Studies, 18% Social Sciences
**Expenses:** 2014-2015: $44,757; room/board: $13,631
**Financial aid:** (650) 723-3058; 50% of undergrads determined to have financial need; average aid package $43,900

## St. Mary's College of California
Moraga CA
(925) 631-4224
**U.S. News ranking:** Reg. U. (W), No. 11
**Website:** www.stmarys-ca.edu
**Admissions email:** smcadmit@stmarys-ca.edu
**Private;** founded 1863
**Affiliation:** Roman Catholic
**Freshman admissions:** selective; 2013-2014: 4,864 applied, 3,379 accepted. Either SAT or ACT required. SAT 25/75 percentile: 1010-1210. High school rank: 31% in top tenth, 64% in top quarter, 92% in top half
**Early decision deadline:** N/A, notification date: N/A
**Early action deadline:** 11/15, notification date: 12/15
**Application deadline (fall):** 2/1
**Undergraduate student body:** 2,823 full time, 232 part time; 41% male, 59% female; 0% American Indian, 11% Asian, 4% black, 25% Hispanic, 6% multiracial, 1% Pacific Islander, 46% white, 2% international; 91% from in state; 55% live on campus; N/A of students in fraternities, N/A in sororities
**Most popular majors:** 23% Business, Management, Marketing, and Related Support Services, 11% Communication, Journalism, and Related Programs, 9% Liberal Arts and Sciences, General Studies and Humanities, 10% Psychology, 12% Social Sciences
**Expenses:** 2014-2015: $41,380; room/board: $14,400
**Financial aid:** (925) 631-4370; 75% of undergrads determined to have financial need; average aid package $26,434

## Thomas Aquinas College
Santa Paula CA
(800) 634-9797
**U.S. News ranking:** Nat. Lib. Arts, No. 77
**Website:** www.thomasaquinas.edu
**Admissions email:** admissions@thomasaquinas.edu
**Private;** founded 1971
**Affiliation:** Catholic
**Freshman admissions:** selective; 2013-2014: 189 applied, 154 accepted. Either SAT or ACT required. SAT 25/75 percentile: 1160-1340. High school rank: 29% in top tenth, 50% in top quarter, 93% in top half
**Early decision deadline:** N/A, notification date: N/A
**Early action deadline:** N/A, notification date: N/A
**Application deadline (fall):** rolling
**Undergraduate student body:** 366 full time, 0 part time; 51% male, 49% female; 0% American Indian, 1% Asian, 0% black, 15% Hispanic, 5% multiracial, 0% Pacific Islander, 72% white, 4% international; 40% from in state; 99% live on campus; 0% of students in fraternities, 0% in sororities
**Most popular majors:** 100% Liberal Arts and Sciences, General Studies and Humanities
**Expenses:** 2014-2015: $24,500; room/board: $7,950

Financial aid: (805) 525-4417; 80% of undergrads determined to have financial need; average aid package $22,092

## Trident University International[1]
Cypress CA
(800) 579-3170
U.S. News ranking: Nat. U., unranked
Website: www.trident.edu
Admissions email: N/A
For-profit
Application deadline (fall): rolling
Undergraduate student body: N/A full time, N/A part time
Expenses: 2013-2014: $6,600; room/board: N/A
Financial aid: (877) 835-9818

## University of California–Berkeley
Berkeley CA
(510) 642-3175
U.S. News ranking: Nat. U., No. 20
Website: students.berkeley.edu/admissions/
Admissions email: N/A
Public; founded 1868
Freshman admissions: most selective; 2013-2014: 66,794 applied, 11,828 accepted. Either SAT or ACT required. SAT 25/75 percentile: 1250-1500. High school rank: 98% in top tenth, 100% in top quarter, 100% in top half
Early decision deadline: N/A, notification date: N/A
Early action deadline: N/A, notification date: N/A
Application deadline (fall): 11/30
Undergraduate student body: 25,220 full time, 731 part time; 48% male, 52% female; 0% American Indian, 35% Asian, 2% black, 13% Hispanic, 5% multiracial, 0% Pacific Islander, 29% white, 13% international
Most popular majors: Information not available
Expenses: 2014-2015: $13,844 in state, $25,064 out of state; room/board: $15,438
Financial aid: (510) 642-6442; 47% of undergrads determined to have financial need; average aid package $23,517

## University of California–Davis
Davis CA
(530) 752-2971
U.S. News ranking: Nat. U., No. 38
Website: www.ucdavis.edu
Admissions email: undergraduateadmissions@ucdavis.edu
Public; founded 1905
Freshman admissions: most selective; 2013-2014: 55,833 applied, 23,049 accepted. Either SAT or ACT required. SAT 25/75 percentile: 1080-1340. High school rank: 100% in top tenth, 100% in top quarter, 100% in top half
Early decision deadline: N/A, notification date: N/A
Early action deadline: N/A, notification date: N/A
Application deadline (fall): 11/30
Undergraduate student body: 26,305 full time, 358 part time; 44% male, 56% female; 0% American Indian, 35% Asian, 2% black, 17% Hispanic, 5%

multiracial, 0% Pacific Islander, 31% white, 6% international; 97% from in state; 25% live on campus; N/A of students in fraternities, N/A in sororities
Most popular majors: 5% Biology/Biological Sciences, General, 4% Business/Managerial Economics, 6% Economics, General, 4% Political Science and Government, General, 10% Research and Experimental Psychology, Other
Expenses: 2014-2015: $13,896 in state, $36,774 out of state; room/board: $14,218
Financial aid: (530) 752-2396; 66% of undergrads determined to have financial need; average aid package $19,685

## University of California–Irvine
Irvine CA
(949) 824-6703
U.S. News ranking: Nat. U., No. 42
Website: www.uci.edu
Admissions email: admissions@uci.edu
Public; founded 1965
Freshman admissions: more selective; 2013-2014: 60,690 applied, 24,931 accepted. Either SAT or ACT required. SAT 25/75 percentile: 1040-1290. High school rank: 96% in top tenth, 100% in top quarter, 100% in top half
Early decision deadline: N/A, notification date: N/A
Early action deadline: N/A, notification date: N/A
Application deadline (fall): 11/30
Undergraduate student body: 23,117 full time, 413 part time; 46% male, 54% female; 0% American Indian, 44% Asian, 2% black, 22% Hispanic, 4% multiracial, 0% Pacific Islander, 17% white, 9% international; 98% from in state; 43% live on campus; 9% of students in fraternities, 10% in sororities
Most popular majors: 13% Biology/Biological Sciences, General, 6% Business/Managerial Economics, 6% Political Science and Government, General, 5% Public Health, Other, 7% Social Psychology
Expenses: 2014-2015: $14,757 in state, $37,635 out of state; room/board: $12,638
Financial aid: (949) 824-5337; 69% of undergrads determined to have financial need; average aid package $21,592

## University of California–Los Angeles
Los Angeles CA
(310) 825-3101
U.S. News ranking: Nat. U., No. 23
Website: www.ucla.edu/
Admissions email: ugadm@saonet.ucla.edu
Public; founded 1919
Freshman admissions: most selective; 2013-2014: 80,522 applied, 16,448 accepted. Either SAT or ACT required. SAT 25/75 percentile: 1190-1450. High school rank: 97% in top tenth, 100% in top quarter, 100% in top half
Early decision deadline: N/A, notification date: N/A
Early action deadline: N/A, notification date: N/A

Application deadline (fall): 11/30
Undergraduate student body: 28,084 full time, 590 part time; 45% male, 55% female; 0% American Indian, 31% Asian, 3% black, 18% Hispanic, 5% multiracial, 0% Pacific Islander, 29% white, 12% international; 92% from in state; 39% live on campus; 15% of students in fraternities, 15% in sororities
Most popular majors: Information not available
Expenses: 2014-2015: $12,702 in state, $35,580 out of state; room/board: $14,511
Financial aid: (310) 206-0400; 55% of undergrads determined to have financial need; average aid package $21,984

## University of California–Riverside
Riverside CA
(951) 827-3411
U.S. News ranking: Nat. U., No. 113
Website: www.ucr.edu
Admissions email: admit@ucr.edu
Public; founded 1954
Freshman admissions: more selective; 2013-2014: 34,816 applied, 20,973 accepted. Either SAT or ACT required. SAT 25/75 percentile: 990-1210. High school rank: 94% in top tenth, 100% in top quarter, 100% in top half
Early decision deadline: N/A, notification date: N/A
Early action deadline: N/A, notification date: N/A
Application deadline (fall): 11/30
Undergraduate student body: 18,205 full time, 416 part time; 49% male, 51% female; 0% American Indian, 36% Asian, 5% black, 36% Hispanic, 4% multiracial, 0% Pacific Islander, 14% white, 3% international; 100% from in state; 31% live on campus; 5% of students in fraternities, 8% in sororities
Most popular majors: 13% Biological and Biomedical Sciences, 15% Business, Management, Marketing, and Related Support Services, 10% Psychology, 22% Social Sciences, 6% Visual and Performing Arts
Expenses: 2014-2015: $13,408 in state, $36,286 out of state; room/board: N/A
Financial aid: (951) 827-3878; 79% of undergrads determined to have financial need; average aid package $20,947

## University of California–San Diego
La Jolla CA
(858) 534-4831
U.S. News ranking: Nat. U., No. 37
Website: www.ucsd.edu/
Admissions email: admissionsinfo@ucsd.edu
Public; founded 1960
Freshman admissions: most selective; 2013-2014: 67,400 applied, 24,832 accepted. Either SAT or ACT required. SAT 25/75 percentile: 1180-1400. High school rank: 100% in top tenth, 100% in top quarter, 100% in top half
Early decision deadline: N/A, notification date: N/A
Early action deadline: N/A, notification date: N/A
Application deadline (fall): 11/30

Undergraduate student body: 23,397 full time, 408 part time; 52% male, 48% female; 0% American Indian, 41% Asian, 2% black, 15% Hispanic, 0% multiracial, 0% Pacific Islander, 21% white, 17% international; 95% from in state; 45% live on campus; 10% of students in fraternities, 10% in sororities
Most popular majors: 20% Biology, General, 5% Communication and Media Studies, 13% Economics, 7% Political Science and Government, General, 8% Psychology, General
Expenses: 2013-2014: $13,302 in state, $36,180 out of state; room/board: $11,978
Financial aid: (858) 534-4480; 63% of undergrads determined to have financial need; average aid package $22,347

## University of California–Santa Barbara
Santa Barbara CA
(805) 893-2485
U.S. News ranking: Nat. U., No. 40
Website: www.ucsb.edu
Admissions email: admissions@sa.ucsb.edu
Public; founded 1909
Freshman admissions: most selective; 2013-2014: 62,427 applied, 24,813 accepted. Either SAT or ACT required. SAT 25/75 percentile: 1130-1370. High school rank: 100% in top tenth, 100% in top quarter, 100% in top half
Early decision deadline: N/A, notification date: N/A
Early action deadline: N/A, notification date: N/A
Application deadline (fall): 11/30
Undergraduate student body: 19,076 full time, 286 part time; 48% male, 52% female; 1% American Indian, 24% Asian, 4% black, 24% Hispanic, 0% multiracial, 0% Pacific Islander, 40% white, 3% international; 96% from in state; 38% live on campus; 8% of students in fraternities, 12% in sororities
Most popular majors: 8% Biological and Biomedical Sciences, 6% Communication, Journalism, and Related Programs, 4% Physical Sciences, 10% Psychology, 23% Social Sciences
Expenses: 2014-2015: $13,746 in state, $36,624 out of state; room/board: $13,805
Financial aid: (805) 893-2432; 62% of undergrads determined to have financial need; average aid package $22,609

## University of California–Santa Cruz
Santa Cruz CA
(831) 459-4008
U.S. News ranking: Nat. U., No. 85
Website: www.ucsc.edu
Admissions email: admissions@ucsc.edu
Public; founded 1965
Freshman admissions: more selective; 2013-2014: 38,640 applied, 20,039 accepted. Either SAT or ACT required. SAT 25/75 percentile: 1000-1280. High school rank: 96% in top tenth, 100% in top quarter, 100% in top half

Early decision deadline: N/A, notification date: N/A
Early action deadline: N/A, notification date: N/A
Application deadline (fall): 11/30
Undergraduate student body: 15,450 full time, 245 part time; 47% male, 53% female; 0% American Indian, 20% Asian, 2% black, 30% Hispanic, 7% multiracial, 0% Pacific Islander, 37% white, 1% international; 96% from in state; 48% live on campus; 1% of students in fraternities, 0% in sororities
Most popular majors: 6% Business/Managerial Economics, 5% English Language and Literature/Letters, Other, 5% Environmental Studies, 10% Psychology, General, 4% Sociology
Expenses: 2014-2015: $13,398 in state, $36,276 out of state; room/board: $14,730
Financial aid: (831) 459-2963; 71% of undergrads determined to have financial need; average aid package $22,938

## University of La Verne
La Verne CA
(800) 876-4858
U.S. News ranking: Nat. U., No. 166
Website: www.laverne.edu
Admissions email: admission@laverne.edu
Private; founded 1891
Freshman admissions: selective; 2013-2014: 8,264 applied, 2,843 accepted. Either SAT or ACT required. SAT 25/75 percentile: 950-1130. High school rank: 23% in top tenth, 60% in top quarter, 89% in top half
Early decision deadline: N/A, notification date: N/A
Early action deadline: N/A, notification date: N/A
Application deadline (fall): rolling
Undergraduate student body: 2,595 full time, 87 part time; 41% male, 59% female; 0% American Indian, 7% Asian, 5% black, 51% Hispanic, 4% multiracial, 0% Pacific Islander, 26% white, 5% international; 96% from in state; 31% live on campus; 7% of students in fraternities, 16% in sororities
Most popular majors: 19% Business, Management, Marketing, and Related Support Services, 11% Education, 11% Liberal Arts and Sciences, General Studies and Humanities, 10% Psychology, 15% Social Sciences
Expenses: 2014-2015: $36,744; room/board: $12,200
Financial aid: (800) 649-0160; 83% of undergrads determined to have financial need; average aid package $28,603

## University of Redlands
Redlands CA
(800) 455-5064
U.S. News ranking: Reg. U. (W), No. 12
Website: www.redlands.edu
Admissions email: admissions@redlands.edu
Private; founded 1907
Freshman admissions: more selective; 2013-2014: 4,668 applied, 3,137 accepted. Either SAT or ACT required. SAT 25/75 percentile: 1030-1230. High

school rank: 35% in top tenth, 65% in top quarter, 96% in top half
**Early decision deadline:** N/A, notification date: N/A
**Early action deadline:** 11/15, notification date: 12/31
**Application deadline (fall):** rolling
**Undergraduate student body:** 2,702 full time, 907 part time; 45% male, 55% female; 1% American Indian, 5% Asian, 5% black, 26% Hispanic, 4% multiracial, 1% Pacific Islander, 51% white, 1% international; 81% from in state; 59% live on campus; 13% of students in fraternities, 20% in sororities
**Most popular majors:** 42% Business, Management, Marketing, and Related Support Services, 6% Liberal Arts and Sciences, General Studies and Humanities, 6% Natural Resources and Conservation, 7% Psychology, 9% Social Sciences
**Expenses:** 2014-2015: $43,186; room/board: $12,710
**Financial aid:** (909) 335-4047; 78% of undergrads determined to have financial need; average aid package $34,707

## University of San Diego
San Diego CA
(619) 260-4506
**U.S. News ranking:** Nat. U., No. 95
**Website:** www.SanDiego.edu
**Admissions email:** admissions@SanDiego.edu
**Private;** founded 1949
**Affiliation:** Roman Catholic
**Freshman admissions:** more selective; 2013-2014: 14,693 applied, 7,178 accepted. Either SAT or ACT required. SAT 25/75 percentile: 1110-1320. High school rank: 45% in top tenth, 91% in top quarter, 95% in top half
**Early decision deadline:** N/A, notification date: N/A
**Early action deadline:** N/A, notification date: N/A
**Application deadline (fall):** 12/15
**Undergraduate student body:** 5,486 full time, 179 part time; 45% male, 55% female; 0% American Indian, 6% Asian, 3% black, 19% Hispanic, 6% multiracial, 0% Pacific Islander, 55% white, 6% international; 62% from in state; 44% live on campus; 21% of students in fraternities, 36% in sororities
**Most popular majors:** 6% Biological and Biomedical Sciences, 42% Business, Management, Marketing, and Related Support Services, 9% Communication, Journalism, and Related Programs, 7% Psychology, 13% Social Sciences
**Expenses:** 2014-2015: $42,908; room/board: $11,910
**Financial aid:** (619) 260-4514; 55% of undergrads determined to have financial need; average aid package $31,193

## University of San Francisco
San Francisco CA
(415) 422-6563
**U.S. News ranking:** Nat. U., No. 106
**Website:** www.usfca.edu
**Admissions email:** admission@usfca.edu

**Private;** founded 1855
**Affiliation:** Jesuit Catholic
**Freshman admissions:** more selective; 2013-2014: 14,844 applied, 9,076 accepted. Either SAT or ACT required. SAT 25/75 percentile: 1070-1270. High school rank: 33% in top tenth, 71% in top quarter, 94% in top half
**Early decision deadline:** 11/15, notification date: 1/1
**Early action deadline:** 11/15, notification date: 1/1
**Application deadline (fall):** rolling
**Undergraduate student body:** 6,111 full time, 281 part time; 38% male, 62% female; 0% American Indian, 19% Asian, 3% black, 19% Hispanic, 7% multiracial, 0% Pacific Islander, 31% white, 18% international; 79% from in state; 34% live on campus; 1% of students in fraternities, 1% in sororities
**Most popular majors:** 6% Business Administration and Management, General, 6% Finance, General, 5% Hematology Technology/Technician, 9% Psychology, General, 10% Registered Nursing/Registered Nurse
**Expenses:** 2014-2015: $41,450; room/board: $13,320
**Financial aid:** (415) 422-2620; 56% of undergrads determined to have financial need; average aid package $28,727

## University of Southern California
Los Angeles CA
(213) 740-1111
**U.S. News ranking:** Nat. U., No. 25
**Website:** www.usc.edu/
**Admissions email:** admitusc@usc.edu
**Private;** founded 1880
**Freshman admissions:** most selective; 2013-2014: 47,358 applied, 9,395 accepted. Either SAT or ACT required. SAT 25/75 percentile: 1280-1480. High school rank: 88% in top tenth, 97% in top quarter, 100% in top half
**Early decision deadline:** N/A, notification date: N/A
**Early action deadline:** N/A, notification date: N/A
**Application deadline (fall):** 1/10
**Undergraduate student body:** 17,729 full time, 716 part time; 50% male, 50% female; 0% American Indian, 23% Asian, 4% black, 14% Hispanic, 5% multiracial, 0% Pacific Islander, 38% white, 12% international; 69% from in state; 33% live on campus; 25% of students in fraternities, 19% in sororities
**Most popular majors:** 25% Business, Management, Marketing, and Related Support Services, 10% Communication, Journalism, and Related Programs, 10% Engineering, 13% Social Sciences, 12% Visual and Performing Arts
**Expenses:** 2014-2015: $48,280; room/board: $13,334
**Financial aid:** (213) 740-1111; 41% of undergrads determined to have financial need; average aid package $42,978

## University of the Pacific
Stockton CA
(209) 946-2285
**U.S. News ranking:** Nat. U., No. 116
**Website:** www.pacific.edu
**Admissions email:** admissions@pacific.edu
**Private;** founded 1851
**Freshman admissions:** more selective; 2013-2014: 14,222 applied, 10,332 accepted. Either SAT or ACT required. SAT 25/75 percentile: 1030-1320. High school rank: 36% in top tenth, 68% in top quarter, 90% in top half
**Early decision deadline:** N/A, notification date: N/A
**Early action deadline:** 11/15, notification date: 1/15
**Application deadline (fall):** 1/15
**Undergraduate student body:** 3,780 full time, 97 part time; 48% male, 52% female; 1% American Indian, 32% Asian, 3% black, 19% Hispanic, 4% multiracial, 0% Pacific Islander, 32% white, 5% international; 93% from in state; 46% live on campus; 15% of students in fraternities, 16% in sororities
**Most popular majors:** 14% Biology/Biological Sciences, General, 15% Business Administration and Management, General, 7% Curriculum and Instruction, 8% Engineering, General, 7% Health and Physical Education/Fitness, General
**Expenses:** 2014-2015: $41,342; room/board: $12,582
**Financial aid:** (209) 946-2421; 73% of undergrads determined to have financial need; average aid package $29,290

## University of the West[1]
Rosemead CA
(855) 469-3378
**U.S. News ranking:** Reg. Coll. (W), unranked
**Website:** www.uwest.edu
**Admissions email:** N/A
**Private**
**Application deadline (fall):** N/A
**Undergraduate student body:** N/A full time, N/A part time
**Expenses:** 2013-2014: $9,486; room/board: $6,070
**Financial aid:** (626) 571-8811

## Vanguard University of Southern California
Costa Mesa CA
(800) 722-6279
**U.S. News ranking:** Reg. Coll. (W), No. 12
**Website:** www.vanguard.edu
**Admissions email:** admissions@vanguard.edu
**Private;** founded 1920
**Affiliation:** Assemblies of God
**Freshman admissions:** selective; 2013-2014: 1,497 applied, 1,043 accepted. Either SAT or ACT required. SAT 25/75 percentile: 850-1073. High school rank: 16% in top tenth, 41% in top quarter, 76% in top half
**Early decision deadline:** N/A, notification date: N/A
**Early action deadline:** 12/1, notification date: 1/15
**Application deadline (fall):** rolling
**Undergraduate student body:** 1,576 full time, 559 part time; 32%

male, 68% female; 1% American Indian, 4% Asian, 4% black, 35% Hispanic, 5% multiracial, 1% Pacific Islander, 46% white, 1% international; 91% from in state; 46% live on campus; 0% of students in fraternities, 0% in sororities
**Most popular majors:** 20% Business, Management, Marketing, and Related Support Services, 9% Communication, Journalism, and Related Programs, 9% Health Professions and Related Programs, 20% Psychology, 9% Social Sciences
**Expenses:** 2014-2015: $30,050; room/board: $8,870
**Financial aid:** (714) 556-3610; 81% of undergrads determined to have financial need; average aid package $14,137

## Westmont College
Santa Barbara CA
(800) 777-9011
**U.S. News ranking:** Nat. Lib. Arts, No. 96
**Website:** www.westmont.edu
**Admissions email:** admissions@westmont.edu
**Private;** founded 1937
**Affiliation:** Christian nondenominational
**Freshman admissions:** more selective; 2013-2014: 2,145 applied, 1,505 accepted. Either SAT or ACT required. SAT 25/75 percentile: 1060-1310. High school rank: 29% in top tenth, 66% in top quarter, 94% in top half
**Early decision deadline:** N/A, notification date: N/A
**Early action deadline:** 11/15, notification date: 1/5
**Application deadline (fall):** 8/15
**Undergraduate student body:** 1,291 full time, 14 part time; 39% male, 61% female; 0% American Indian, 7% Asian, 1% black, 13% Hispanic, 7% multiracial, 0% Pacific Islander, 66% white, 1% international; 75% from in state; 84% live on campus; 0% of students in fraternities, 0% in sororities
**Most popular majors:** 9% Biology/Biological Sciences, General, 14% Business/Managerial Economics, 9% English Language and Literature, General, 12% Kinesiology and Exercise Science, 11% Speech Communication and Rhetoric
**Expenses:** 2014-2015: $39,990; room/board: $12,580
**Financial aid:** (805) 565-6063; 65% of undergrads determined to have financial need; average aid package $28,681

## Whittier College
Whittier CA
(562) 907-4238
**U.S. News ranking:** Nat. Lib. Arts, No. 133
**Website:** www.whittier.edu
**Admissions email:** admission@whittier.edu
**Private;** founded 1887
**Freshman admissions:** selective; 2013-2014: 4,380 applied, 2,771 accepted. Either SAT or ACT required. SAT 25/75 percentile: 930-1150. High school rank: 23% in top tenth, 39% in top quarter, 89% in top half
**Early decision deadline:** N/A, notification date: N/A

**Early action deadline:** 12/1, notification date: 12/30
**Application deadline (fall):** rolling
**Undergraduate student body:** 1,668 full time, 27 part time; 44% male, 56% female; 1% American Indian, 11% Asian, 6% black, 38% Hispanic, 0% multiracial, 0% Pacific Islander, 36% white, 3% international; 81% from in state; 51% live on campus; 9% of students in fraternities, 13% in sororities
**Most popular majors:** 6% Biological and Biomedical Sciences, 14% Business, Management, Marketing, and Related Support Services, 9% Parks, Recreation, Leisure, and Fitness Studies, 10% Psychology, 19% Social Sciences
**Expenses:** 2014-2015: $41,711; room/board: $12,046
**Financial aid:** (562) 907-4285; 79% of undergrads determined to have financial need; average aid package $31,328

## Woodbury University
Burbank CA
(818) 767-0888
**U.S. News ranking:** Reg. U. (W), No. 56
**Website:** www.woodbury.edu
**Admissions email:** info@woodbury.edu
**Private;** founded 1884
**Freshman admissions:** selective; 2013-2014: 858 applied, 486 accepted. Either SAT or ACT required. SAT 25/75 percentile: 880-1110. High school rank: N/A
**Early decision deadline:** N/A, notification date: N/A
**Early action deadline:** N/A, notification date: N/A
**Application deadline (fall):** rolling
**Undergraduate student body:** 1,172 full time, 185 part time; 49% male, 51% female; 0% American Indian, 10% Asian, 5% black, 29% Hispanic, 0% multiracial, 0% Pacific Islander, 38% white, 18% international; 97% from in state; 14% live on campus; 5% of students in fraternities, 7% in sororities
**Most popular majors:** 12% Accounting, 35% Architecture, 12% Business Administration and Management, General, 5% Film/Video and Photographic Arts, Other, 5% Psychology, General
**Expenses:** 2014-2015: $35,048; room/board: $10,522
**Financial aid:** (818) 767-0888; 87% of undergrads determined to have financial need; average aid package $21,758

## Adams State University[1]
Alamosa CO
(800) 824-6494
**U.S. News ranking:** Reg. U. (W), second tier
**Website:** www.adams.edu
**Admissions email:** ascadmit@adams.edu
**Public**
**Application deadline (fall):** N/A
**Undergraduate student body:** N/A full time, N/A part time
**Expenses:** 2013-2014: $7,449 in state, $18,081 out of state; room/board: $8,282
**Financial aid:** (719) 587-7306

## Art Institute of Colorado[1]

Denver CO
(800) 275-2420
**U.S. News ranking:** Arts, unranked
**Website:** www.artinstitutes.edu/denver/
**Admissions email:** N/A
**For-profit**
**Application deadline (fall):** N/A
**Undergraduate student body:** N/A full time, N/A part time
**Expenses:** 2013-2014: $17,632; room/board: $10,287
**Financial aid:** (800) 275-2420

## Colorado Christian University[1]

Lakewood CO
(303) 963-3200
**U.S. News ranking:** Reg. U. (W), second tier
**Website:** www.ccu.edu
**Admissions email:** admission@ccu.edu
**Private**
**Application deadline (fall):** N/A
**Undergraduate student body:** N/A full time, N/A part time
**Expenses:** 2013-2014: $25,046; room/board: $9,640
**Financial aid:** (303) 963-3230

## Colorado College

Colorado Springs CO
(719) 389-6344
**U.S. News ranking:** Nat. Lib. Arts, No. 27
**Website:** www.ColoradoCollege.edu
**Admissions email:** admission@ColoradoCollege.edu
**Private;** founded 1874
**Freshman admissions:** most selective; 2013-2014: 5,780 applied, 1,288 accepted. Neither SAT nor ACT required. SAT 25/75 percentile: 1220-1430. High school rank: 66% in top tenth, 94% in top quarter, 99% in top half
**Early decision deadline:** 11/15, notification date: 12/15
**Early action deadline:** 11/15, notification date: 12/20
**Application deadline (fall):** 1/15
**Undergraduate student body:** 2,025 full time, 15 part time; 45% male, 55% female; 0% American Indian, 4% Asian, 2% black, 9% Hispanic, 8% multiracial, 0% Pacific Islander, 70% white, 6% international; 19% from in state; 76% live on campus; 9% of students in fraternities, 11% in sororities
**Most popular majors:** 6% Biology/Biological Sciences, General, 6% Economics, General, 6% Environmental Science, 5% Fine/Studio Arts, General, 7% Sociology
**Expenses:** 2014-2015: $46,410; room/board: $10,752
**Financial aid:** (719) 389-6651; 38% of undergrads determined to have financial need; average aid package $39,513

## Colorado Mesa University

Grand Junction CO
(800) 982-6372
**U.S. News ranking:** Nat. Lib. Arts, second tier
**Website:** www.coloradomesa.edu/
**Admissions email:** admissions@coloradomesa.edu
**Public;** founded 1925

**Freshman admissions:** selective; 2013-2014: 6,420 applied, 5,265 accepted. Either SAT or ACT required. ACT 25/75 percentile: 18-23. High school rank: 10% in top tenth, 24% in top quarter, 52% in top half
**Early decision deadline:** N/A, notification date: N/A
**Early action deadline:** N/A, notification date: N/A
**Application deadline (fall):** rolling
**Undergraduate student body:** 7,267 full time, 2,308 part time; 45% male, 55% female; 1% American Indian, 1% Asian, 3% black, 15% Hispanic, 4% multiracial, 1% Pacific Islander, 72% white, 0% international; 88% from in state; 23% live on campus; 0% of students in fraternities, 0% in sororities
**Most popular majors:** 6% Biology/Biological Sciences, General, 26% Business/Commerce, General, 8% Kinesiology and Exercise Science, 7% Psychology, General, 12% Registered Nursing/Registered Nurse
**Expenses:** 2014-2015: $7,625 in state, $18,985 out of state; room/board: $10,065
**Financial aid:** (970) 248-1396; 70% of undergrads determined to have financial need; average aid package $7,859

## Colorado School of Mines

Golden CO
(303) 273-3220
**U.S. News ranking:** Nat. U., No. 88
**Website:** www.mines.edu
**Admissions email:** admit@mines.edu
**Public;** founded 1874
**Freshman admissions:** most selective; 2013-2014: 12,169 applied, 4,434 accepted. Either SAT or ACT required. ACT 25/75 percentile: 28-32. High school rank: 66% in top tenth, 93% in top quarter, 100% in top half
**Early decision deadline:** N/A, notification date: N/A
**Early action deadline:** N/A, notification date: N/A
**Application deadline (fall):** 4/1
**Undergraduate student body:** 4,082 full time, 211 part time; 73% male, 27% female; 0% American Indian, 5% Asian, 1% black, 8% Hispanic, 4% multiracial, 0% Pacific Islander, 75% white, 4% international; 68% from in state; 40% live on campus; 10% of students in fraternities, 16% in sororities
**Most popular majors:** 1% Computer and Information Sciences and Support Services, 88% Engineering, 6% Mathematics and Statistics, 3% Physical Sciences, 2% Social Sciences
**Expenses:** 2014-2015: $16,918 in state, $33,598 out of state; room/board: $10,484
**Financial aid:** (303) 273-3220; 54% of undergrads determined to have financial need; average aid package $11,887

## Colorado State University

Fort Collins CO
(970) 491-6909
**U.S. News ranking:** Nat. U., No. 121
**Website:** www.colostate.edu
**Admissions email:** admissions@colostate.edu
**Public;** founded 1870
**Freshman admissions:** more selective; 2013-2014: 17,970 applied, 13,914 accepted. Either SAT or ACT required. ACT 25/75 percentile: 22-27. High school rank: 22% in top tenth, 52% in top quarter, 88% in top half
**Early decision deadline:** N/A, notification date: N/A
**Early action deadline:** 12/1, notification date: 2/1
**Application deadline (fall):** 2/1
**Undergraduate student body:** 21,283 full time, 2,515 part time; 49% male, 51% female; 0% American Indian, 2% Asian, 2% black, 10% Hispanic, 3% multiracial, 0% Pacific Islander, 74% white, 3% international; 81% from in state; 25% live on campus; 7% of students in fraternities, 9% in sororities
**Most popular majors:** 9% Biological and Biomedical Sciences, 14% Business, Management, Marketing, and Related Support Services, 10% Family and Consumer Sciences/Human Sciences, 7% Parks, Recreation, Leisure, and Fitness Studies, 10% Social Sciences
**Expenses:** 2014-2015: $9,897 in state, $26,077 out of state; room/board: $10,488
**Financial aid:** (970) 491-6321; 57% of undergrads determined to have financial need; average aid package $11,806

## Colorado State University–Pueblo

Pueblo CO
(719) 549-2461
**U.S. News ranking:** Reg. U. (W), second tier
**Website:** www.colostate-pueblo.edu
**Admissions email:** info@colostate-pueblo.edu
**Public;** founded 1933
**Freshman admissions:** less selective; 2013-2014: 3,038 applied, 2,897 accepted. Either SAT or ACT required. ACT 25/75 percentile: 18-23. High school rank: 11% in top tenth, 34% in top quarter, 67% in top half
**Early decision deadline:** N/A, notification date: N/A
**Early action deadline:** N/A, notification date: N/A
**Application deadline (fall):** 8/1
**Undergraduate student body:** 3,742 full time, 1,465 part time; 44% male, 56% female; 1% American Indian, 2% Asian, 8% black, 31% Hispanic, 3% multiracial, 0% Pacific Islander, 51% white, 1% international; 93% from in state; 19% live on campus; 2% of students in fraternities, 2% in sororities
**Most popular majors:** 12% Business/Commerce, General, 9% Kinesiology and Exercise Science, 7% Mass Communication/Media Studies, 10% Registered Nursing/Registered Nurse, 13% Sociology
**Expenses:** 2013-2014: $7,327 in state, $17,649 out of state; room/board: $8,856

**Financial aid:** (719) 549-2753; 77% of undergrads determined to have financial need; average aid package $9,424

## Colorado Technical University[1]

Colorado Springs CO
(888) 897-6555
**U.S. News ranking:** Nat. U., unranked
**Website:** www.coloradotech.edu
**Admissions email:** info@ctuonline.edu
**For-profit**
**Application deadline (fall):** N/A
**Undergraduate student body:** N/A full time, N/A part time
**Expenses:** 2013-2014: $11,300; room/board: N/A
**Financial aid:** (719) 598-2900

## Fort Lewis College

Durango CO
(970) 247-7184
**U.S. News ranking:** Nat. Lib. Arts, second tier
**Website:** www.fortlewis.edu
**Admissions email:** admission@fortlewis.edu
**Public;** founded 1911
**Freshman admissions:** selective; 2013-2014: 2,560 applied, 2,240 accepted. Either SAT or ACT required. ACT 25/75 percentile: 20-25. High school rank: 10% in top tenth, 32% in top quarter, 65% in top half
**Early decision deadline:** N/A, notification date: N/A
**Early action deadline:** 1/15, notification date: 3/15
**Application deadline (fall):** 8/1
**Undergraduate student body:** 3,698 full time, 330 part time; 51% male, 49% female; 22% American Indian, 1% Asian, 1% black, 10% Hispanic, 6% multiracial, 0% Pacific Islander, 58% white, 1% international; 57% from in state; 38% live on campus; 0% of students in fraternities, 0% in sororities
**Most popular majors:** 21% Business, Management, Marketing, and Related Support Services, 8% Physical Sciences, 8% Psychology, 10% Social Sciences
**Expenses:** 2014-2015: $7,252 in state, $17,780 out of state; room/board: $10,346
**Financial aid:** (970) 247-7142; 70% of undergrads determined to have financial need; average aid package $13,241

## Jones International University

Centennial CO
(800) 811-5663
**U.S. News ranking:** Reg. U. (W), unranked
**Website:** www.jonesinternational.edu/
**Admissions email:** info@jonesinternational.edu
**For-profit;** founded 1995
**Freshman admissions:** N/A; 2013-2014: N/A applied, N/A accepted. Neither SAT nor ACT required. ACT 25/75 percentile: N/A. High school rank: N/A
**Early decision deadline:** N/A, notification date: N/A
**Early action deadline:** N/A, notification date: N/A

**Application deadline (fall):** rolling
**Undergraduate student body:** 758 full time, 833 part time; 33% male, 67% female; 1% American Indian, 1% Asian, 33% black, 3% Hispanic, 10% multiracial, 0% Pacific Islander, 26% white, 0% international
**Most popular majors:** 78% Business Administration and Management, General, 22% Business/Corporate Communications
**Expenses:** 2013-2014: $12,720; room/board: N/A
**Financial aid:** (800) 811-5663

## Metropolitan State University of Denver[1]

Denver CO
(303) 556-3058
**U.S. News ranking:** Reg. Coll. (W), second tier
**Website:** www.mscd.edu
**Admissions email:** askmetro@mscd.edu
**Public;** founded 1963
**Application deadline (fall):** 4/30
**Undergraduate student body:** N/A full time, N/A part time
**Expenses:** 2013-2014: $5,744 in state, $17,837 out of state; room/board: N/A
**Financial aid:** (303) 556-4741

## Naropa University

Boulder CO
(303) 546-3572
**U.S. News ranking:** Reg. U. (W), unranked
**Website:** www.naropa.edu
**Admissions email:** admissions@naropa.edu
**Private;** founded 1974
**Freshman admissions:** N/A; 2013-2014: 79 applied, 63 accepted. Neither SAT nor ACT required. ACT 25/75 percentile: N/A. High school rank: N/A
**Early decision deadline:** N/A, notification date: N/A
**Early action deadline:** N/A, notification date: N/A
**Application deadline (fall):** rolling
**Undergraduate student body:** 359 full time, 24 part time; 36% male, 64% female; 0% American Indian, 1% Asian, 1% black, 8% Hispanic, 8% multiracial, 0% Pacific Islander, 65% white, 3% international; 37% from in state; 19% live on campus; N/A of students in fraternities, N/A in sororities
**Most popular majors:** 9% English Language and Literature, General, 7% Environmental Studies, 9% Health and Physical Education/Fitness, Other, 22% Multi-/Interdisciplinary Studies, Other, 29% Psychology, General
**Expenses:** 2014-2015: $29,970; room/board: $9,072
**Financial aid:** (303) 546-3565; 67% of undergrads determined to have financial need; average aid package $37,824

## Regis University

Denver CO
(303) 458-4900
**U.S. News ranking:** Reg. U. (W), No. 29
**Website:** www.regis.edu
**Admissions email:** regisadm@regis.edu
**Private;** founded 1877
**Affiliation:** Roman Catholic (Jesuit)

**Freshman admissions:** selective; 2013-2014: 2,298 applied, 2,122 accepted. Either SAT or ACT required. ACT 25/75 percentile: 22-27. High school rank: 27% in top tenth, 56% in top quarter, 85% in top half **Early decision deadline:** N/A, notification date: N/A **Early action deadline:** N/A, notification date: N/A **Application deadline (fall):** 8/1 **Undergraduate student body:** 2,508 full time, 2,664 part time; 37% male, 63% female; 1% American Indian, 4% Asian, 5% black, 18% Hispanic, 2% multiracial, 0% Pacific Islander, 62% white, 1% international; 69% from in state; 48% live on campus; 0% of students in fraternities, 0% in sororities **Most popular majors:** 26% Business, Management, Marketing, and Related Support Services, 5% Computer and Information Sciences and Support Services, 35% Health Professions and Related Programs, 7% Liberal Arts and Sciences, General Studies and Humanities, 5% Social Sciences **Expenses:** 2014-2015: $33,060; room/board: $9,500 **Financial aid:** (303) 458-4066; 71% of undergrads determined to have financial need; average aid package $27,538

## Rocky Mountain College of Art and Design

Lakewood CO
(303) 225-8576
**U.S. News ranking:** Arts, unranked
**Website:** www.rmcad.edu/
**Admissions email:** admissions@rmcad.edu
**For-profit;** founded 1963
**Freshman admissions:** N/A; 2013-2014: 279 applied, 190 accepted. Neither SAT nor ACT required. SAT 25/75 percentile: N/A. High school rank: N/A **Early decision deadline:** N/A, notification date: N/A **Early action deadline:** N/A, notification date: N/A **Application deadline (fall):** rolling **Undergraduate student body:** 554 full time, 185 part time; 37% male, 63% female; 4% American Indian, 3% Asian, 6% black, 10% Hispanic, 2% multiracial, 0% Pacific Islander, 62% white, 0% international; 59% from in state; 0% live on campus; 0% of students in fraternities, 0% in sororities **Most popular majors:** 10% Animation, Interactive Technology, Video Graphics and Special Effects, 17% Computer Graphics, 20% Fine/Studio Arts, General, 26% Illustration, 11% Interior Design **Expenses:** 2014-2015: $22,470; room/board: N/A **Financial aid:** (303) 753-6046; 78% of undergrads determined to have financial need; average aid package $19,249

## United States Air Force Academy

USAF Academy CO
(800) 443-9266
**U.S. News ranking:** Nat. Lib. Arts, No. 27
**Website:** academyadmissions.com
**Admissions email:** rr_webmail@usafa.edu
**Public;** founded 1954
**Freshman admissions:** most selective; 2013-2014: 9,634 applied, 1,486 accepted. Either SAT or ACT required. ACT 25/75 percentile: 29-32. High school rank: 55% in top tenth, 85% in top quarter, 97% in top half **Early decision deadline:** N/A, notification date: N/A **Early action deadline:** N/A, notification date: N/A **Application deadline (fall):** 12/31 **Undergraduate student body:** 3,993 full time, 0 part time; 78% male, 22% female; 0% American Indian, 5% Asian, 6% black, 9% Hispanic, 7% multiracial, 1% Pacific Islander, 67% white, 1% international; 8% from in state; 100% live on campus; 0% of students in fraternities, 0% in sororities **Most popular majors:** 7% Biological and Biomedical Sciences, 11% Business, Management, Marketing, and Related Support Services, 40% Engineering, 11% Multi/Interdisciplinary Studies, 15% Social Sciences **Expenses:** N/A **Financial aid:** (719) 333-3160

## University of Colorado–Boulder

Boulder CO
(303) 492-6301
**U.S. News ranking:** Nat. U., No. 88
**Website:** www.colorado.edu
**Admissions email:** apply@colorado.edu
**Public;** founded 1876
**Freshman admissions:** more selective; 2013-2014: 22,473 applied, 19,710 accepted. Either SAT or ACT required. ACT 25/75 percentile: 24-29. High school rank: 27% in top tenth, 56% in top quarter, 88% in top half **Early decision deadline:** N/A, notification date: N/A **Early action deadline:** 11/15, notification date: 2/1 **Application deadline (fall):** 1/15 **Undergraduate student body:** 23,853 full time, 2,128 part time; 55% male, 45% female; 0% American Indian, 5% Asian, 2% black, 10% Hispanic, 4% multiracial, 0% Pacific Islander, 74% white, 4% international; 63% from in state; 28% live on campus; 11% of students in fraternities, 17% in sororities **Most popular majors:** 10% Biological and Biomedical Sciences, 11% Business, Management, Marketing, and Related Support Services, 9% Communication, Journalism, and Related Programs, 10% Psychology, 15% Social Sciences **Expenses:** 2014-2015: $10,789 in state, $33,151 out of state; room/board: $12,810 **Financial aid:** (303) 492-5091; 40% of undergrads determined to have financial need; average aid package $16,054

## University of Colorado– Colorado Springs

Colorado Springs CO
(719) 255-3383
**U.S. News ranking:** Reg. U. (W), No. 51
**Website:** www.uccs.edu
**Admissions email:** admrecor@uccs.edu
**Public;** founded 1965
**Freshman admissions:** selective; 2013-2014: 7,034 applied, 6,401 accepted. Either SAT or ACT required. ACT 25/75 percentile: 21-25. High school rank: 13% in top tenth, 36% in top quarter, 70% in top half **Early decision deadline:** N/A, notification date: N/A **Early action deadline:** N/A, notification date: N/A **Application deadline (fall):** rolling **Undergraduate student body:** 6,940 full time, 2,111 part time; 47% male, 53% female; 1% American Indian, 3% Asian, 4% black, 14% Hispanic, 6% multiracial, 0% Pacific Islander, 69% white, 1% international; 89% from in state; 13% live on campus; 1% of students in fraternities, 3% in sororities **Most popular majors:** 8% Biological and Biomedical Sciences, 21% Business Administration, Management and Operations, 12% Health Professions and Related Programs, 8% Psychology, 11% Social Sciences **Expenses:** 2014-2015: $16,212 in state, $21,522 out of state; room/board: N/A **Financial aid:** (719) 262-3460; 57% of undergrads determined to have financial need; average aid package $6,759

## University of Colorado–Denver

Denver CO
(303) 556-2704
**U.S. News ranking:** Nat. U., second tier
**Website:** www.ucdenver.edu
**Admissions email:** admissions@ucdenver.edu
**Public;** founded 1912
**Freshman admissions:** selective; 2013-2014: 4,370 applied, 3,029 accepted. Either SAT or ACT required. ACT 25/75 percentile: 20-25. High school rank: 21% in top tenth, 50% in top quarter, 81% in top half **Early decision deadline:** N/A, notification date: N/A **Early action deadline:** N/A, notification date: N/A **Application deadline (fall):** rolling **Undergraduate student body:** 7,782 full time, 5,228 part time; 47% male, 53% female; 0% American Indian, 10% Asian, 5% black, 15% Hispanic, 3% multiracial, 0% Pacific Islander, 52% white, 10% international; 93% from in state; 5% live on campus; N/A of students in fraternities, N/A in sororities **Most popular majors:** 9% Biology/Biological Sciences, General, 16% Business Administration and Management, General, 6% Psychology, General, 11% Registered Nursing/Registered Nurse, 6% Speech Communication and Rhetoric

**Expenses:** 2013-2014: $9,625 in state, $26,105 out of state; room/board: $10,790 **Financial aid:** (303) 556-2886; 60% of undergrads determined to have financial need; average aid package $9,061

## University of Denver

Denver CO
(303) 871-2036
**U.S. News ranking:** Nat. U., No. 88
**Website:** www.du.edu
**Admissions email:** admission@du.edu
**Private;** founded 1864
**Freshman admissions:** more selective; 2013-2014: 13,735 applied, 10,539 accepted. Either SAT or ACT required. ACT 25/75 percentile: 25-30. High school rank: 45% in top tenth, 76% in top quarter, 95% in top half **Early decision deadline:** N/A, notification date: N/A **Early action deadline:** 11/1, notification date: 1/15 **Application deadline (fall):** 1/15 **Undergraduate student body:** 5,129 full time, 388 part time; 45% male, 55% female; 1% American Indian, 4% Asian, 3% black, 9% Hispanic, 3% multiracial, 0% Pacific Islander, 68% white, 9% international; 46% from in state; 45% live on campus; 24% of students in fraternities, 28% in sororities **Most popular majors:** 7% Biological and Biomedical Sciences, 35% Business, Management, Marketing, and Related Support Services, 7% Communication, Journalism, and Related Programs, 17% Social Sciences, 8% Visual and Performing Arts **Expenses:** 2014-2015: $42,090; room/board: $11,307 **Financial aid:** (303) 871-4020; 42% of undergrads determined to have financial need; average aid package $32,462

## University of Northern Colorado

Greeley CO
(970) 351-2881
**U.S. News ranking:** Nat. U., second tier
**Website:** www.unco.edu
**Admissions email:** admissions.help@unco.edu
**Public;** founded 1890
**Freshman admissions:** selective; 2013-2014: 7,602 applied, 5,289 accepted. Neither SAT nor ACT required. ACT 25/75 percentile: 20-24. High school rank: 12% in top tenth, 38% in top quarter, 73% in top half **Early decision deadline:** N/A, notification date: N/A **Early action deadline:** N/A, notification date: N/A **Undergraduate student body:** 8,723 full time, 987 part time; 37% male, 63% female; 0% American Indian, 2% Asian, 4% black, 16% Hispanic, 3% multiracial, 0% Pacific Islander, 58% white, 1% international; 87% from in state; 32% live on campus; 3% of students in fraternities, 5% in sororities **Most popular majors:** 9% Business, Management, Marketing, and Related Support Services, Other, 14% Health Professions and Related Clinical Sciences, Other, 17% Multi-/Interdisciplinary

Studies, General, 8% Parks, Recreation, Leisure, and Fitness Studies, Other, 7% Psychology, Other **Expenses:** 2014-2015: $7,573 in state, $18,817 out of state; room/board: $10,360 **Financial aid:** (970) 351-2502; 72% of undergrads determined to have financial need; average aid package $6,416

## Western State Colorado University

Gunnison CO
(800) 876-5309
**U.S. News ranking:** Nat. Lib. Arts, second tier
**Website:** www.western.edu
**Admissions email:** discover@western.edu
**Public;** founded 1901
**Freshman admissions:** selective; 2013-2014: 1,523 applied, 1,406 accepted. Either SAT or ACT required. ACT 25/75 percentile: 19-24. High school rank: 6% in top tenth, 25% in top quarter, 62% in top half **Early decision deadline:** N/A, notification date: N/A **Early action deadline:** N/A, notification date: N/A **Application deadline (fall):** rolling **Undergraduate student body:** 1,869 full time, 323 part time; 58% male, 42% female; 0% American Indian, 1% Asian, 2% black, 9% Hispanic, 3% multiracial, 0% Pacific Islander, 75% white, 1% international; 74% from in state; 45% live on campus; 0% of students in fraternities, 0% in sororities **Most popular majors:** 9% Biological and Biomedical Sciences, 24% Business, Management, Marketing, and Related Support Services, 18% Parks, Recreation, Leisure, and Fitness Studies, 9% Psychology, 9% Social Sciences **Expenses:** 2014-2015: $7,874 in state, $18,319 out of state; room/board: $9,050 **Financial aid:** (970) 943-3085; 60% of undergrads determined to have financial need; average aid package $11,909

## Albertus Magnus College

New Haven CT
(800) 578-9160
**U.S. News ranking:** Reg. U. (N), No. 115
**Website:** www.albertus.edu
**Admissions email:** admissions@albertus.edu
**Private;** founded 1925
**Affiliation:** Roman Catholic
**Freshman admissions:** least selective; 2013-2014: 698 applied, 496 accepted. Either SAT or ACT required. SAT 25/75 percentile: 820-930. High school rank: 5% in top tenth, 26% in top quarter, 69% in top half **Early decision deadline:** N/A, notification date: N/A **Early action deadline:** N/A, notification date: N/A **Application deadline (fall):** 8/15 **Undergraduate student body:** 1,199 full time, 79 part time; 35% male, 65% female; 0% American Indian, 1% Asian, 28% black, 14% Hispanic, 2% multiracial,

0% Pacific Islander, 45% white, 0% international; 93% from in state; N/A live on campus; N/A of students in fraternities, N/A in sororities
**Most popular majors:** Information not available
**Expenses:** 2014-2015: $28,930; room/board: $12,960
**Financial aid:** (203) 773-8508; 83% of undergrads determined to have financial need; average aid package $15,988

## Central Connecticut State University
New Britain CT
(860) 832-2278
**U.S. News ranking:** Reg. U. (N), No. 111
**Website:** www.ccsu.edu
**Admissions email:** admissions@ccsu.edu
**Public;** founded 1849
**Freshman admissions:** selective; 2013-2014: 5,551 applied, 3,560 accepted. Either SAT or ACT required. SAT 25/75 percentile: 910-1100. High school rank: 10% in top tenth, 21% in top quarter, 71% in top half
**Early decision deadline:** N/A, notification date: N/A
**Early action deadline:** N/A, notification date: N/A
**Application deadline (fall):** 5/1
**Undergraduate student body:** 7,624 full time, 2,147 part time; 52% male, 48% female; 0% American Indian, 3% Asian, 11% black, 12% Hispanic, 2% multiracial, 0% Pacific Islander, 68% white, 1% international; 97% from in state; 21% live on campus; 0% of students in fraternities, 0% in sororities
**Most popular majors:** 25% Business, Management, Marketing, and Related Support Services, 7% Communication, Journalism, and Related Programs, 8% Education, 5% Engineering Technologies and Engineering-Related Fields, 16% Social Sciences
**Expenses:** 2014-2015: $8,877 in state, $19,163 out of state; room/board: $10,872
**Financial aid:** (860) 832-2200; 74% of undergrads determined to have financial need; average aid package $8,113

## Charter Oak State College
New Britain CT
(860) 832-3855
**U.S. News ranking:** Nat. Lib. Arts, unranked
**Website:** www.charteroak.edu
**Admissions email:** info@charteroak.edu
**Public**
**Freshman admissions:** N/A; 2013-2014: N/A applied, N/A accepted. Neither SAT nor ACT required. ACT 25/75 percentile: N/A. High school rank: N/A
**Early decision deadline:** N/A, notification date: N/A
**Early action deadline:** N/A, notification date: N/A
**Application deadline (fall):** rolling
**Undergraduate student body:** 301 full time, 1,280 part time; 34% male, 66% female; 0% American Indian, 2% Asian, 17% black, 11% Hispanic, 1% multiracial, 0% Pacific Islander, 64% white, 1% international; 73% from in

state; 0% live on campus; 0% of students in fraternities, 0% in sororities
**Most popular majors:** Information not available
**Expenses:** 2014-2015: $8,592 in state, $11,082 out of state; room/board: N/A
**Financial aid:** N/A; 69% of undergrads determined to have financial need; average aid package $7,618

## Connecticut College
New London CT
(860) 439-2200
**U.S. News ranking:** Nat. Lib. Arts, No. 45
**Website:** www.conncoll.edu
**Admissions email:** admission@conncoll.edu
**Private;** founded 1911
**Freshman admissions:** more selective; 2013-2014: 4,701 applied, 1,726 accepted. Neither SAT nor ACT required. SAT 25/75 percentile: 1240-1410. High school rank: 52% in top tenth, 90% in top quarter, 100% in top half
**Early decision deadline:** 11/15, notification date: 12/15
**Early action deadline:** N/A, notification date: N/A
**Application deadline (fall):** 1/1
**Undergraduate student body:** 1,877 full time, 38 part time; 39% male, 61% female; 0% American Indian, 3% Asian, 4% black, 9% Hispanic, 3% multiracial, 0% Pacific Islander, 70% white, 5% international; 19% from in state; 99% live on campus; 0% of students in fraternities, 0% in sororities
**Most popular majors:** 10% Biology, General, 14% Economics, 7% International Relations and National Security Studies, 7% Political Science and Government, 10% Psychology, General
**Expenses:** 2014-2015: $47,740; room/board: $13,155
**Financial aid:** (860) 439-2058; 52% of undergrads determined to have financial need; average aid package $37,372

## Eastern Connecticut State University
Willimantic CT
(860) 465-5286
**U.S. News ranking:** Reg. U. (N), No. 103
**Website:** www.easternct.edu
**Admissions email:** admissions@easternct.edu
**Public;** founded 1889
**Freshman admissions:** selective; 2013-2014: 5,111 applied, 3,299 accepted. Either SAT or ACT required. SAT 25/75 percentile: 930-1100. High school rank: 9% in top tenth, 31% in top quarter, 72% in top half
**Early decision deadline:** N/A, notification date: N/A
**Early action deadline:** N/A, notification date: N/A
**Application deadline (fall):** rolling
**Undergraduate student body:** 4,395 full time, 784 part time; 46% male, 54% female; 0% American Indian, 2% Asian, 6% black, 9% Hispanic, 2% multiracial, 0% Pacific Islander, 70% white, 1% international; 96% from in state; 53% live on campus; N/A of students in fraternities, N/A in sororities

**Most popular majors:** 15% Business, Management, Marketing, and Related Support Services, 9% Communication, Journalism, and Related Programs, 13% Liberal Arts and Sciences, General Studies and Humanities, 12% Psychology, 12% Social Sciences
**Expenses:** 2014-2015: $9,560 in state, $19,846 out of state; room/board: $11,610
**Financial aid:** (860) 465-5205; 68% of undergrads determined to have financial need; average aid package $8,245

## Fairfield University
Fairfield CT
(203) 254-4100
**U.S. News ranking:** Reg. U. (N), No. 3
**Website:** www.fairfield.edu
**Admissions email:** admis@fairfield.edu
**Private;** founded 1942
**Affiliation:** Roman Catholic (Jesuit)
**Freshman admissions:** more selective; 2013-2014: 9,582 applied, 6,742 accepted. Neither SAT nor ACT required. SAT 25/75 percentile: 1090-1250. High school rank: N/A
**Early decision deadline:** 11/15, notification date: 1/1
**Early action deadline:** 11/1, notification date: 1/1
**Application deadline (fall):** 1/15
**Undergraduate student body:** 3,546 full time, 327 part time; 40% male, 60% female; 0% American Indian, 2% Asian, 3% black, 8% Hispanic, 1% multiracial, 0% Pacific Islander, 72% white, 2% international; 31% from in state; 80% live on campus; 0% of students in fraternities, 0% in sororities
**Most popular majors:** 26% Business, Management, Marketing, and Related Support Services, 10% Communication, Journalism, and Related Programs, 13% Health Professions and Related Programs, 7% Psychology, 13% Social Sciences
**Expenses:** 2014-2015: $43,770; room/board: $13,190
**Financial aid:** (203) 254-4125; 51% of undergrads determined to have financial need; average aid package $29,726

## Lyme Academy College of Fine Arts
Old Lyme CT
(860) 434-5232
**U.S. News ranking:** Arts, unranked
**Website:** www.lymeacademy.edu
**Admissions email:** admissions@lymeacademy.edu
**Private**
**Freshman admissions:** N/A; 2013-2014: N/A applied, N/A accepted. Neither SAT nor ACT required. SAT 25/75 percentile: N/A. High school rank: N/A
**Early decision deadline:** N/A, notification date: N/A
**Early action deadline:** N/A, notification date: N/A
**Application deadline (fall):** N/A
**Undergraduate student body:** N/A full time, N/A part time; N/A male, N/A female; N/A American Indian, N/A Asian, N/A black, N/A Hispanic, N/A multiracial, N/A Pacific Islander, N/A white, N/A international

**Most popular majors:** Information not available
**Expenses:** 2013-2014: $29,616; room/board: N/A
**Financial aid:** (860) 434-5232

## Mitchell College[1]
New London CT
(800) 443-2811
**U.S. News ranking:** Reg. Coll. (N), unranked
**Website:** www.mitchell.edu
**Admissions email:** admissions@mitchell.edu
**Private**
**Application deadline (fall):** N/A
**Undergraduate student body:** N/A full time, N/A part time
**Expenses:** 2013-2014: $29,458; room/board: $12,492
**Financial aid:** (860) 701-5061

## Post University
Waterbury CT
(203) 596-4520
**U.S. News ranking:** Reg. Coll. (N), second tier
**Website:** www.post.edu
**Admissions email:** admissions@post.edu
**For-profit;** founded 1890
**Freshman admissions:** less selective; 2013-2014: 5,923 applied, 3,762 accepted. Either SAT or ACT required. SAT 25/75 percentile: 760-960. High school rank: 5% in top tenth, 20% in top quarter, 50% in top half
**Early decision deadline:** N/A, notification date: N/A
**Early action deadline:** N/A, notification date: N/A
**Application deadline (fall):** rolling
**Undergraduate student body:** 2,903 full time, 4,468 part time; 41% male, 59% female; 0% American Indian, 1% Asian, 16% black, 6% Hispanic, 2% multiracial, 0% Pacific Islander, 30% white, 1% international; 49% from in state; 11% live on campus; 0% of students in fraternities, 0% in sororities
**Most popular majors:** 14% Accounting, 50% Business Administration and Management, General, 5% Child Development, 14% Criminal Justice/Safety Studies, 17% Human Services, General
**Expenses:** 2013-2014: $27,450; room/board: $10,430
**Financial aid:** (203) 596-4526

## Quinnipiac University
Hamden CT
(800) 462-1944
**U.S. News ranking:** Reg. U. (N), No. 9
**Website:** www.quinnipiac.edu
**Admissions email:** admissions@quinnipiac.edu
**Private;** founded 1929
**Freshman admissions:** selective; 2013-2014: 20,693 applied, 13,912 accepted. Either SAT or ACT required. SAT 25/75 percentile: 1000-1190. High school rank: 25% in top tenth, 66% in top quarter, 93% in top half
**Early decision deadline:** 11/1, notification date: 12/1
**Early action deadline:** N/A, notification date: N/A
**Application deadline (fall):** 2/1

**Undergraduate student body:** 6,307 full time, 235 part time; 38% male, 62% female; 0% American Indian, 2% Asian, 4% black, 8% Hispanic, 2% multiracial, 0% Pacific Islander, 78% white, 2% international; 25% from in state; 75% live on campus; 14% of students in fraternities, 15% in sororities
**Most popular majors:** 21% Business, Management, Marketing, and Related Support Services, 19% Communication, Journalism, and Related Programs, 30% Health Professions and Related Programs, 6% Psychology, 6% Social Sciences
**Expenses:** 2014-2015: $40,670; room/board: $14,490
**Financial aid:** (203) 582-8750; 63% of undergrads determined to have financial need; average aid package $24,214

## Sacred Heart University
Fairfield CT
(203) 371-7880
**U.S. News ranking:** Reg. U. (N), No. 38
**Website:** www.sacredheart.edu
**Admissions email:** enroll@sacredheart.edu
**Private;** founded 1963
**Affiliation:** Roman Catholic
**Freshman admissions:** selective; 2013-2014: 7,908 applied, 4,800 accepted. Neither SAT nor ACT required. SAT 25/75 percentile: 1020-1170. High school rank: 14% in top tenth, 39% in top quarter, 80% in top half
**Early decision deadline:** 12/1, notification date: 12/15
**Early action deadline:** N/A, notification date: N/A
**Application deadline (fall):** rolling
**Undergraduate student body:** 3,773 full time, 722 part time; 36% male, 64% female; 0% American Indian, 2% Asian, 3% black, 6% Hispanic, 0% multiracial, 0% Pacific Islander, 66% white, 1% international; 41% from in state; 54% live on campus; 6% of students in fraternities, 14% in sororities
**Most popular majors:** 4% Biological and Biomedical Sciences, 31% Business, Management, Marketing, and Related Support Services, Other, 18% Health Professions and Related Clinical Sciences, Other, 5% Homeland Security, Law Enforcement, Firefighting and Related Protective Services, 10% Psychology
**Expenses:** 2014-2015: $35,750; room/board: $13,514
**Financial aid:** (203) 371-7980; 72% of undergrads determined to have financial need; average aid package $19,511

## Southern Connecticut State University
New Haven CT
(203) 392-5656
**U.S. News ranking:** Reg. U. (N), second tier
**Website:** www.southernct.edu/
**Admissions email:** information@southernct.edu
**Public;** founded 1893
**Freshman admissions:** less selective; 2013-2014: 4,870 applied, 3,673 accepted. Either SAT or ACT required. SAT 25/75

percentile: 820-1020. High school rank: 5% in top tenth, 21% in top quarter, 59% in top half
**Early decision deadline:** N/A, notification date: N/A
**Early action deadline:** N/A, notification date: N/A
**Application deadline (fall):** rolling
**Undergraduate student body:** 7,016 full time, 1,241 part time; 39% male, 61% female; 0% American Indian, 2% Asian, 15% black, 11% Hispanic, 2% multiracial, 0% Pacific Islander, 60% white, 0% international; 96% from in state; 32% live on campus; 1% of students in fraternities, 1% in sororities
**Most popular majors:** 12% Business/Commerce, General, 10% Education, General, 15% Health and Wellness, General, 14% Liberal Arts and Sciences/ Liberal Studies, 10% Psychology, General
**Expenses:** 2014-2015: $9,156 in state, $19,442 out of state; room/board: $11,334
**Financial aid:** (203) 392-5222; 69% of undergrads determined to have financial need; average aid package $13,685

## Trinity College
Hartford CT
(860) 297-2180
**U.S. News ranking:** Nat. Lib. Arts, No. 45
**Website:** www.trincoll.edu
**Admissions email:** admissions.office@trincoll.edu
**Private;** founded 1823
**Freshman admissions:** more selective; 2013-2014: 7,652 applied, 2,432 accepted. Either SAT or ACT required. SAT 25/75 percentile: 1150-1330. High school rank: 23% in top tenth, 59% in top quarter, 99% in top half
**Early decision deadline:** 11/15, notification date: 12/15
**Early action deadline:** N/A, notification date: N/A
**Application deadline (fall):** 1/1
**Undergraduate student body:** 2,214 full time, 117 part time; 52% male, 48% female; 0% American Indian, 5% Asian, 6% black, 7% Hispanic, 3% multiracial, 0% Pacific Islander, 65% white, 8% international; 18% from in state; 89% live on campus; 20% of students in fraternities, 16% in sororities
**Most popular majors:** 19% Economics, General, 5% English Language and Literature, General, 5% History, General, 12% Political Science and Government, General, 5% Psychology, General
**Expenses:** 2014-2015: $49,056; room/board: $12,700
**Financial aid:** (860) 297-2046; 42% of undergrads determined to have financial need; average aid package $42,585

## United States Coast Guard Academy
New London CT
(800) 883-8724
**U.S. News ranking:** Reg. Coll. (N), No. 1
**Website:** www.uscga.edu
**Admissions email:** admissions@uscga.edu
**Public;** founded 1931

**Freshman admissions:** more selective; 2013-2014: 1,992 applied, 328 accepted. Either SAT or ACT required. SAT 25/75 percentile: 1190-1360. High school rank: 47% in top tenth, 80% in top quarter, 94% in top half
**Early decision deadline:** N/A, notification date: N/A
**Early action deadline:** 11/15, notification date: 2/1
**Application deadline (fall):** 2/1
**Undergraduate student body:** 902 full time, N/A part time; 66% male, 34% female; 1% American Indian, 5% Asian, 2% black, 13% Hispanic, 7% multiracial, 1% Pacific Islander, 68% white, 3% international; 6% from in state; 100% live on campus; 0% of students in fraternities, 0% in sororities
**Most popular majors:** 18% Business Administration and Management, General, 31% Engineering, 19% Marine Biology and Biological Oceanography, 14% Mathematics and Statistics, Other, 18% Political Science and Government, General
**Expenses:** N/A
**Financial aid:** N/A; 0% of undergrads determined to have financial need; average aid package $0

## University of Bridgeport
Bridgeport CT
(203) 576-4552
**U.S. News ranking:** Reg. U. (N), second tier
**Website:** www.bridgeport.edu
**Admissions email:** admit@bridgeport.edu
**Private;** founded 1927
**Freshman admissions:** less selective; 2013-2014: 5,248 applied, 3,351 accepted. Either SAT or ACT required. SAT 25/75 percentile: 830-1010. High school rank: 8% in top tenth, 30% in top quarter, 70% in top half
**Early decision deadline:** N/A, notification date: N/A
**Early action deadline:** N/A, notification date: N/A
**Application deadline (fall):** rolling
**Undergraduate student body:** 2,035 full time, 800 part time; 34% male, 66% female; 1% American Indian, 3% Asian, 35% black, 18% Hispanic, 2% multiracial, 0% Pacific Islander, 27% white, 14% international; 62% from in state; 44% live on campus; 5% of students in fraternities, 5% in sororities
**Most popular majors:** 6% Business/Commerce, General, 11% Dental Hygiene/Hygienist, 15% General Studies, 12% Human Services, General, 28% Psychology, General
**Expenses:** 2014-2015: $29,910; room/board: $12,710
**Financial aid:** (203) 576-4568; 81% of undergrads determined to have financial need; average aid package $24,745

## University of Connecticut
Storrs CT
(860) 486-3137
**U.S. News ranking:** Nat. U., No. 58
**Website:** www.uconn.edu
**Admissions email:** beahusky@uconn.edu
**Public;** founded 1881

**Freshman admissions:** more selective; 2013-2014: 27,479 applied, 14,745 accepted. Either SAT or ACT required. SAT 25/75 percentile: 1130-1330. High school rank: 45% in top tenth, 82% in top quarter, 97% in top half
**Early decision deadline:** N/A, notification date: N/A
**Early action deadline:** N/A, notification date: N/A
**Application deadline (fall):** 1/15
**Undergraduate student body:** 17,219 full time, 813 part time; 51% male, 49% female; 0% American Indian, 9% Asian, 5% black, 8% Hispanic, 3% multiracial, 0% Pacific Islander, 63% white, 3% international; 79% from in state; 72% live on campus; 11% of students in fraternities, 15% in sororities
**Most popular majors:** 12% Business, Management, Marketing, and Related Support Services, 9% Engineering, 13% Health Professions and Related Programs, 8% Psychology, 12% Social Sciences
**Expenses:** 2014-2015: $12,700 in state, $32,880 out of state; room/board: $12,074
**Financial aid:** (860) 486-2819; 58% of undergrads determined to have financial need; average aid package $12,917

## University of Hartford
West Hartford CT
(860) 768-4296
**U.S. News ranking:** Reg. U. (N), No. 83
**Website:** www.hartford.edu
**Admissions email:** admission@hartford.edu
**Private;** founded 1877
**Freshman admissions:** less selective; 2013-2014: 16,481 applied, 10,750 accepted. Either SAT or ACT required. SAT 25/75 percentile: 950-1150. High school rank: N/A
**Early decision deadline:** N/A, notification date: N/A
**Early action deadline:** 11/15, notification date: 12/1
**Application deadline (fall):** rolling
**Undergraduate student body:** 4,495 full time, 692 part time; 50% male, 50% female; 1% American Indian, 3% Asian, 15% black, 9% Hispanic, 2% multiracial, 0% Pacific Islander, 60% white, 5% international; 44% from in state; 68% live on campus; 5% of students in fraternities, 5% in sororities
**Most popular majors:** 14% Business, Management, Marketing, and Related Support Services, Other, 7% Education, Other, 8% Engineering, Other, 15% Health Professions and Related Clinical Sciences, Other, 15% Visual and Performing Arts, Other
**Expenses:** 2014-2015: $35,444; room/board: $11,518
**Financial aid:** (860) 768-4296; 75% of undergrads determined to have financial need; average aid package $23,729

## University of New Haven
West Haven CT
(203) 932-7319
**U.S. News ranking:** Reg. U. (N), No. 98
**Website:** www.newhaven.edu
**Admissions email:** adminfo@newhaven.edu
**Private;** founded 1920
**Freshman admissions:** selective; 2013-2014: 10,169 applied, 7,567 accepted. Either SAT or ACT required. SAT 25/75 percentile: 930-1130. High school rank: 14% in top tenth, 41% in top quarter, 76% in top half
**Early decision deadline:** N/A, notification date: N/A
**Early action deadline:** 12/1, notification date: 1/15
**Application deadline (fall):** rolling
**Undergraduate student body:** 4,407 full time, 457 part time; 51% male, 49% female; 0% American Indian, 2% Asian, 8% black, 8% Hispanic, 1% multiracial, 0% Pacific Islander, 53% white, 8% international; 43% from in state; 52% live on campus; N/A of students in fraternities, N/A in sororities
**Most popular majors:** 7% Biological and Biomedical Sciences, 12% Business, Management, Marketing, and Related Support Services, 6% Engineering, 43% Homeland Security, Law Enforcement, Firefighting and Related Protective Services, 7% Visual and Performing Arts
**Expenses:** 2014-2015: $34,630; room/board: $14,410
**Financial aid:** (203) 932-7315; 78% of undergrads determined to have financial need; average aid package $20,633

## University of St. Joseph
West Hartford CT
(860) 231-5216
**U.S. News ranking:** Reg. U. (N), No. 87
**Website:** www.usj.edu
**Admissions email:** admissions@usj.edu
**Private;** founded 1932
**Affiliation:** Roman Catholic
**Freshman admissions:** less selective; 2013-2014: 1,153 applied, 737 accepted. Either SAT or ACT required. SAT 25/75 percentile: 880-1040. High school rank: 1% in top tenth, 41% in top quarter, 83% in top half
**Early decision deadline:** N/A, notification date: N/A
**Early action deadline:** N/A, notification date: N/A
**Application deadline (fall):** rolling
**Undergraduate student body:** 794 full time, 255 part time; 2% male, 98% female; 0% American Indian, 3% Asian, 13% black, 13% Hispanic, 2% multiracial, 0% Pacific Islander, 57% white, 0% international; 93% from in state; 41% live on campus; N/A of students in fraternities, N/A in sororities
**Most popular majors:** 9% Business, Management, Marketing, and Related Support Services, 10% Family and Consumer Sciences/ Human Sciences, 28% Health Professions and Related Programs, 13% Psychology, 13% Public Administration and Social Service Professions

**Expenses:** 2014-2015: $34,755; room/board: $14,426
**Financial aid:** (860) 231-5223; 89% of undergrads determined to have financial need; average aid package $22,299

## Wesleyan University
Middletown CT
(860) 685-3000
**U.S. News ranking:** Nat. Lib. Arts, No. 15
**Website:** www.wesleyan.edu
**Admissions email:** admissions@wesleyan.edu
**Private;** founded 1831
**Freshman admissions:** most selective; 2013-2014: 10,690 applied, 2,181 accepted. Either SAT or ACT required. SAT 25/75 percentile: 1310-1490. High school rank: 67% in top tenth, 91% in top quarter, 99% in top half
**Early decision deadline:** 11/15, notification date: 12/15
**Early action deadline:** N/A, notification date: N/A
**Application deadline (fall):** 1/1
**Undergraduate student body:** 2,899 full time, 7 part time; 48% male, 52% female; 0% American Indian, 8% Asian, 7% black, 10% Hispanic, 6% multiracial, 0% Pacific Islander, 53% white, 8% international; 8% from in state; 99% live on campus; 4% of students in fraternities, 1% in sororities
**Most popular majors:** 6% Economics, General, 7% English Language and Literature, General, 6% Physiological Psychology/ Psychobiology, 6% Political Science and Government, General, 9% Psychology, General
**Expenses:** 2014-2015: $47,972; room/board: $13,226
**Financial aid:** (860) 685-2800; 47% of undergrads determined to have financial need; average aid package $43,670

## Western Connecticut State University
Danbury CT
(203) 837-9000
**U.S. News ranking:** Reg. U. (N), No. 135
**Website:** www.wcsu.edu
**Admissions email:** admissions@wcsu.edu
**Public;** founded 1903
**Freshman admissions:** selective; 2013-2014: 3,613 applied, 2,366 accepted. Either SAT or ACT required. SAT 25/75 percentile: 890-1080. High school rank: 10% in top tenth, 28% in top quarter, 69% in top half
**Early decision deadline:** N/A, notification date: N/A
**Early action deadline:** N/A, notification date: N/A
**Application deadline (fall):** rolling
**Undergraduate student body:** 4,394 full time, 1,098 part time; 47% male, 53% female; 0% American Indian, 3% Asian, 11% black, 15% Hispanic, 1% multiracial, 0% Pacific Islander, 68% white, 0% international; 93% from in state; 26% live on campus; N/A of students in fraternities, N/A in sororities
**Most popular majors:** 31% Business, Management, Marketing, and Related Support Services, 10% Education, 11% Health Professions and Related

Programs, 10% Homeland Security, Law Enforcement, Firefighting and Related Protective Services, 8% Psychology
**Expenses:** 2014-2015: $9,077 in state, $19,363 out of state; room/board: $11,311
**Financial aid:** (203) 837-8580; 70% of undergrads determined to have financial need; average aid package $8,566

## Yale University
New Haven CT
(203) 432-9300
**U.S. News ranking:** Nat. U., No. 3
**Website:** www.yale.edu/
**Admissions email:** student.questions@yale.edu
**Private;** founded 1701
**Freshman admissions:** most selective; 2013-2014: 29,610 applied, 2,031 accepted. Either SAT or ACT required. SAT 25/75 percentile: 1420-1590. High school rank: 95% in top tenth, 99% in top quarter, 100% in top half
**Early decision deadline:** N/A, notification date: N/A
**Early action deadline:** 11/1, notification date: 12/15
**Application deadline (fall):** 1/1
**Undergraduate student body:** 5,424 full time, 6 part time; 51% male, 49% female; 1% American Indian, 16% Asian, 7% black, 10% Hispanic, 6% multiracial, 0% Pacific Islander, 47% white, 11% international; 6% from in state; 87% live on campus; N/A of students in fraternities, N/A in sororities
**Most popular majors:** 7% Biology/Biological Sciences, General, 11% Economics, General, 7% History, General, 10% Political Science and Government, General, 7% Psychology, General
**Expenses:** 2014-2015: $45,800; room/board: $14,000
**Financial aid:** (203) 432-2700; 52% of undergrads determined to have financial need; average aid package $46,844

## DELAWARE

## Delaware State University
Dover DE
(302) 857-6353
**U.S. News ranking:** Reg. U. (N), No. 135
**Website:** www.desu.edu
**Admissions email:** admissions@desu.edu
**Public;** founded 1891
**Freshman admissions:** less selective; 2013-2014: 7,700 applied, 3,428 accepted. Either SAT or ACT required. SAT 25/75 percentile: 820-970. High school rank: 10% in top tenth, 26% in top quarter, 62% in top half
**Early decision deadline:** N/A, notification date: N/A
**Early action deadline:** N/A, notification date: N/A
**Application deadline (fall):** rolling
**Undergraduate student body:** 3,579 full time, 313 part time; 38% male, 62% female; 0% American Indian, 1% Asian, 75% black, 6% Hispanic, 4% multiracial, 0% Pacific Islander, 11% white, 2% international; 46% from in state;

59% live on campus; 4% of students in fraternities, 7% in sororities
**Most popular majors:** 12% Business, Management, Marketing, and Related Support Services, 11% Communication, Journalism, and Related Programs, 11% Health Professions and Related Programs, 10% Psychology, 9% Social Sciences
**Expenses:** 2014-2015: $7,336 in state, $15,692 out of state; room/board: $10,708
**Financial aid:** (302) 857-6250; 82% of undergrads determined to have financial need; average aid package $11,479

## Goldey-Beacom College[1]
Wilmington DE
(302) 225-6248
**U.S. News ranking:** Business, unranked
**Website:** gbc.edu
**Admissions email:** admissions@gbc.edu
**Private;** founded 1886
**Application deadline (fall):** rolling
**Undergraduate student body:** N/A full time, N/A part time
**Expenses:** 2013-2014: $22,140; room/board: $5,353
**Financial aid:** (302) 225-6265

## University of Delaware
Newark DE
(302) 831-8123
**U.S. News ranking:** Nat. U., No. 76
**Website:** www.udel.edu/
**Admissions email:** admissions@udel.edu
**Public;** founded 1743
**Freshman admissions:** more selective; 2013-2014: 24,657 applied, 15,621 accepted. Either SAT or ACT required. SAT 25/75 percentile: 1090-1300. High school rank: 37% in top tenth, 72% in top quarter, 96% in top half
**Early decision deadline:** N/A, notification date: N/A
**Early action deadline:** N/A, notification date: N/A
**Application deadline (fall):** 1/15
**Undergraduate student body:** 16,037 full time, 1,592 part time; 43% male, 57% female; 0% American Indian, 4% Asian, 5% black, 7% Hispanic, 3% multiracial, 0% Pacific Islander, 76% white, 4% international; 40% from in state; 44% live on campus; 17% of students in fraternities, 19% in sororities
**Most popular majors:** 20% Business, Management, Marketing, and Related Support Services, 8% Education, 8% Engineering, 9% Health Professions and Related Programs, 12% Social Sciences
**Expenses:** 2014-2015: $12,342 in state, $30,692 out of state; room/board: $11,868
**Financial aid:** (302) 831-8761; 51% of undergrads determined to have financial need; average aid package $15,357

## Wesley College
Dover DE
(302) 736-2400
**U.S. News ranking:** Reg. Coll. (N), second tier
**Website:** www.wesley.edu
**Admissions email:** admissions@wesley.edu
**Private;** founded 1873
**Affiliation:** United Methodist
**Freshman admissions:** least selective; 2013-2014: N/A applied, N/A accepted. SAT required. SAT 25/75 percentile: 750-940. High school rank: 5% in top tenth, 23% in top quarter, 58% in top half
**Early decision deadline:** 11/1, notification date: 11/15
**Early action deadline:** N/A, notification date: N/A
**Application deadline (fall):** 4/30
**Undergraduate student body:** 1,416 full time, 184 part time; 48% male, 52% female; 0% American Indian, 1% Asian, 42% black, 5% Hispanic, 3% multiracial, 0% Pacific Islander, 45% white, 0% international
**Most popular majors:** Information not available
**Expenses:** 2014-2015: $24,100; room/board: $10,890
**Financial aid:** (302) 736-2321

## Wilmington University
New Castle DE
(302) 328-9407
**U.S. News ranking:** Nat. U., unranked
**Website:** www.wilmu.edu
**Admissions email:** undergradadmissions@wilmu.edu
**Private;** founded 1967
**Freshman admissions:** N/A; 2013-2014: 1,075 applied, 1,070 accepted. Neither SAT or ACT required. ACT 25/75 percentile: N/A. High school rank: N/A
**Early decision deadline:** N/A, notification date: N/A
**Early action deadline:** N/A, notification date: N/A
**Application deadline (fall):** rolling
**Undergraduate student body:** 3,509 full time, 5,102 part time; 35% male, 65% female; 1% American Indian, 2% Asian, 23% black, 3% Hispanic, 1% multiracial, 0% Pacific Islander, 48% white, 3% international
**Most popular majors:** Information not available
**Expenses:** 2014-2015: $10,190; room/board: N/A
**Financial aid:** (302) 328-9437

## DISTRICT OF COLUMBIA

## American University
Washington DC
(202) 885-6000
**U.S. News ranking:** Nat. U., No. 71
**Website:** www.american.edu
**Admissions email:** admissions@american.edu
**Private;** founded 1893
**Affiliation:** United Methodist
**Freshman admissions:** more selective; 2013-2014: 17,545 applied, 7,565 accepted. Neither SAT nor ACT required. SAT 25/75 percentile: 1160-1350. High school rank: 47% in top tenth, 78% in top quarter, 96% in top half
**Early decision deadline:** 11/15, notification date: 12/31
**Early action deadline:** N/A, notification date: N/A

**Application deadline (fall):** 1/15
**Undergraduate student body:** 6,986 full time, 355 part time; 39% male, 61% female; 0% American Indian, 6% Asian, 6% black, 10% Hispanic, 5% multiracial, 0% Pacific Islander, 57% white, 7% international; 19% from in state; N/A live on campus; 21% of students in fraternities, 19% in sororities
**Most popular majors:** 14% Business Administration and Management, General, 5% Criminal Justice/Safety Studies, 25% International Relations and Affairs, 6% Mass Communication/Media Studies, 9% Political Science and Government, General
**Expenses:** 2014-2015: $41,833; room/board: $14,408
**Financial aid:** (202) 885-6100; 54% of undergrads determined to have financial need; average aid package $27,414

## The Catholic University of America
Washington DC
(800) 673-2772
**U.S. News ranking:** Nat. U., No. 116
**Website:** www.cua.edu
**Admissions email:** cua-admissions@cua.edu
**Private;** founded 1887
**Affiliation:** Roman Catholic
**Freshman admissions:** selective; 2013-2014: 6,298 applied, 3,783 accepted. Either SAT or ACT required. SAT 25/75 percentile: 1010-1220. High school rank: N/A
**Early decision deadline:** N/A, notification date: N/A
**Early action deadline:** 11/15, notification date: 12/15
**Application deadline (fall):** 2/15
**Undergraduate student body:** 3,456 full time, 257 part time; 46% male, 54% female; 0% American Indian, 3% Asian, 5% black, 11% Hispanic, 3% multiracial, 0% Pacific Islander, 63% white, 5% international; 4% from in state; 59% live on campus; 1% of students in fraternities, 1% in sororities
**Most popular majors:** 11% Architecture, 5% Mass Communication/Media Studies, 12% Political Science and Government, General, 8% Psychology, General, 11% Registered Nursing/Registered Nurse
**Expenses:** 2014-2015: $39,726; room/board: $14,518
**Financial aid:** (202) 319-5307; 60% of undergrads determined to have financial need; average aid package $24,381

## Corcoran College of Art and Design[1]
Washington DC
(202) 639-1814
**U.S. News ranking:** Arts, unranked
**Website:** www.corcoran.edu
**Admissions email:** admissions@corcoran.org
**Private;** founded 1890
**Application deadline (fall):** rolling
**Undergraduate student body:** N/A full time, N/A part time
**Expenses:** 2013-2014: $31,130; room/board: N/A
**Financial aid:** (202) 639-1818

## Gallaudet University
Washington DC
(202) 651-5750
**U.S. News ranking:** Reg. U. (N), No. 17
**Website:** www.gallaudet.edu
**Admissions email:** admissions.office@gallaudet.edu
**Private;** founded 1864
**Freshman admissions:** less selective; 2013-2014: 521 applied, 341 accepted. Either SAT or ACT required. ACT 25/75 percentile: 15-20. High school rank: N/A
**Early decision deadline:** N/A, notification date: N/A
**Early action deadline:** N/A, notification date: N/A
**Application deadline (fall):** rolling
**Undergraduate student body:** 1,006 full time, 71 part time; 46% male, 54% female; 0% American Indian, 4% Asian, 11% black, 14% Hispanic, 3% multiracial, 0% Pacific Islander, 60% white, 7% international; 3% from in state; 75% live on campus; 18% of students in fraternities, 10% in sororities
**Most popular majors:** 9% Business, Management, Marketing, and Related Support Services, 8% Communication, Journalism, and Related Programs, 8% Parks, Recreation, Leisure, and Fitness Studies, 8% Psychology, 9% Visual and Performing Arts
**Expenses:** 2013-2014: $13,800; room/board: $11,580
**Financial aid:** (202) 651-5290

## Georgetown University
Washington DC
(202) 687-3600
**U.S. News ranking:** Nat. U., No. 21
**Website:** www.georgetown.edu
**Admissions email:** guadmiss@georgetown.edu
**Private;** founded 1789
**Affiliation:** Roman Catholic (Jesuit)
**Freshman admissions:** most selective; 2013-2014: 19,885 applied, 3,397 accepted. Either SAT or ACT required. SAT 25/75 percentile: 1320-1500. High school rank: 92% in top tenth, 98% in top quarter, 100% in top half
**Early decision deadline:** N/A, notification date: N/A
**Early action deadline:** 11/1, notification date: 12/15
**Application deadline (fall):** 1/10
**Undergraduate student body:** 7,300 full time, 336 part time; 45% male, 55% female; 0% American Indian, 9% Asian, 6% black, 8% Hispanic, 4% multiracial, 0% Pacific Islander, 59% white, 11% international; 3% from in state; 64% live on campus; 0% of students in fraternities, 0% in sororities
**Most popular majors:** 22% Business, Management, Marketing, and Related Support Services, 7% English Language and Literature/Letters, 6% Foreign Languages, Literatures, and Linguistics, 7% Health Professions and Related Programs, 33% Social Sciences
**Expenses:** 2014-2015: $46,744; room/board: $14,348
**Financial aid:** (202) 687-4547; 37% of undergrads determined to have financial need; average aid package $39,305

## George Washington University
Washington DC
(202) 994-6040
**U.S. News ranking:** Nat. U., No. 54
**Website:** www.gwu.edu
**Admissions email:** gwadm@gwu.edu
**Private;** founded 1821
**Freshman admissions:** more selective; 2013-2014: 21,789 applied, 7,493 accepted. Either SAT or ACT required. SAT 25/75 percentile: 1200-1390. High school rank: 50% in top tenth, 84% in top quarter, 98% in top half
**Early decision deadline:** 11/1, notification date: 12/15
**Early action deadline:** N/A, notification date: N/A
**Application deadline (fall):** 1/15
**Undergraduate student body:** 9,609 full time, 748 part time; 45% male, 55% female; 0% American Indian, 9% Asian, 7% black, 7% Hispanic, 3% multiracial, 0% Pacific Islander, 60% white, 9% international; 2% from in state; 66% live on campus; 23% of students in fraternities, 23% in sororities
**Most popular majors:** 17% Business, Management, Marketing, and Related Support Services, 5% Communication, Journalism, and Related Programs, 6% Health Professions and Related Programs, 6% Psychology, 37% Social Sciences
**Expenses:** 2014-2015: $48,760; room/board: $11,700
**Financial aid:** (202) 994-6620; 47% of undergrads determined to have financial need; average aid package $42,335

## Howard University
Washington DC
(202) 806-2700
**U.S. News ranking:** Nat. U., No. 145
**Website:** www.howard.edu
**Admissions email:** admission@howard.edu
**Private;** founded 1867
**Freshman admissions:** selective; 2013-2014: 11,599 applied, 6,612 accepted. Either SAT or ACT required. SAT 25/75 percentile: 980-1190. High school rank: 23% in top tenth, 54% in top quarter, 85% in top half
**Early decision deadline:** N/A, notification date: N/A
**Early action deadline:** 11/1, notification date: 12/20
**Application deadline (fall):** 2/15
**Undergraduate student body:** 6,495 full time, 479 part time; 33% male, 67% female; 2% American Indian, 1% Asian, 91% black, 0% Hispanic, 0% multiracial, 0% Pacific Islander, 1% white, 3% international; 5% from in state; 56% live on campus; 3% of students in fraternities, 5% in sororities
**Most popular majors:** 7% Biological and Biomedical Sciences, 18% Business, Management, Marketing, and Related Support Services, 16% Communication, Journalism, and Related Programs, 22% Health Professions and Related Programs, 6% Social Sciences
**Expenses:** 2014-2015: $23,970; room/board: $13,646

## Strayer University[1]
Washington DC
(202) 408-2400
**U.S. News ranking:** Reg. U. (N), unranked
**Website:** www.strayer.edu
**Admissions email:** mzm@strayer.edu
**For-profit**
**Application deadline (fall):** N/A
**Undergraduate student body:** N/A full time, N/A part time
**Expenses:** 2013-2014: $15,495; room/board: N/A
**Financial aid:** (888) 311-0355

## Trinity University[1]
Washington DC
(202) 884-9400
**U.S. News ranking:** Reg. U. (N), second tier
**Website:** www.trinitydc.edu
**Admissions email:** admissions@trinitydc.edu
**Private**
**Application deadline (fall):** N/A
**Undergraduate student body:** N/A full time, N/A part time
**Expenses:** 2013-2014: $21,630; room/board: $9,660
**Financial aid:** (202) 884-9530

## University of the District of Columbia
Washington DC
(202) 274-5010
**U.S. News ranking:** Reg. U. (N), second tier
**Website:** www.udc.edu/
**Admissions email:** N/A
**Public;** founded 1976
**Freshman admissions:** less selective; 2013-2014: N/A applied, N/A accepted. Neither SAT nor ACT required. ACT 25/75 percentile: N/A. High school rank: N/A
**Early decision deadline:** N/A, notification date: N/A
**Early action deadline:** N/A, notification date: N/A
**Application deadline (fall):** 6/15
**Undergraduate student body:** 1,986 full time, 2,726 part time; 37% male, 63% female; N/A American Indian, N/A Asian, N/A black, N/A Hispanic, N/A multiracial, N/A Pacific Islander, N/A white, N/A international
**Most popular majors:** Information not available
**Expenses:** 2014-2015: $7,255 in state, $14,535 out of state; room/board: N/A
**Financial aid:** (202) 274-5060; 70% of undergrads determined to have financial need; average aid package $8,990

## University of the Potomac
Washington DC
(202) 686-0876
**U.S. News ranking:** Business, unranked
**Website:** www.potomac.edu
**Admissions email:** admissions@potomac.edu
**For-profit;** founded 1989
**Freshman admissions:** least selective; 2013-2014: N/A applied, N/A accepted. Neither

**Financial aid:** (202) 806-2762; 85% of undergrads determined to have financial need; average aid package $17,178

SAT nor ACT required. ACT 25/75 percentile: N/A. High school rank: N/A
**Early decision deadline:** N/A, notification date: N/A
**Early action deadline:** N/A, notification date: N/A
**Application deadline (fall):** rolling
**Undergraduate student body:** 277 full time, 24 part time; 52% male, 48% female; 1% American Indian, 2% Asian, 58% black, 6% Hispanic, 3% multiracial, 0% Pacific Islander, 23% white, 0% international
**Most popular majors:** Information not available
**Expenses:** 2013-2014: $13,434; room/board: N/A
**Financial aid:** (888) 635-1121

## Ave Maria University[1]
Ave Maria FL
(877) 283-8648
**U.S. News ranking:** Nat. Lib. Arts, second tier
**Website:** www.avemaria.edu
**Admissions email:** N/A
**Private;** founded 2003
**Affiliation:** Catholic
**Application deadline (fall):** rolling
**Undergraduate student body:** N/A full time, N/A part time
**Expenses:** 2013-2014: $23,000; room/board: $9,286
**Financial aid:** N/A

## Barry University
Miami Shores FL
(305) 899-3100
**U.S. News ranking:** Nat. U., second tier
**Website:** www.barry.edu
**Admissions email:** admissions@mail.barry.edu
**Private;** founded 1940
**Affiliation:** Roman Catholic
**Freshman admissions:** selective; 2013-2014: 7,845 applied, 3,670 accepted. Either SAT or ACT required. SAT 25/75 percentile: 833-1040. High school rank: N/A
**Early decision deadline:** N/A, notification date: N/A
**Early action deadline:** N/A, notification date: N/A
**Application deadline (fall):** rolling
**Undergraduate student body:** 3,619 full time, 722 part time; 38% male, 62% female; 0% American Indian, 1% Asian, 32% black, 29% Hispanic, 1% multiracial, 0% Pacific Islander, 20% white, 7% international
**Most popular majors:** Information not available
**Expenses:** 2014-2015: $28,160; room/board: $10,200
**Financial aid:** (800) 899-3673; 82% of undergrads determined to have financial need; average aid package $19,214

## Beacon College
Leesburg FL
(706) 323-5364
**U.S. News ranking:** Nat. Lib. Arts, unranked
**Website:** www.beaconcollege.edu/
**Admissions email:** admissions@beaconcollege.edu
**Private;** founded 1989
**Freshman admissions:** N/A; 2013-2014: 139 applied, 90 accepted.

Neither SAT nor ACT required. ACT 25/75 percentile: N/A. High school rank: N/A
**Early decision deadline:** N/A, notification date: N/A
**Early action deadline:** N/A, notification date: N/A
**Application deadline (fall):** rolling
**Undergraduate student body:** 188 full time, 2 part time; 69% male, 31% female; 1% American Indian, 4% Asian, 15% black, 5% Hispanic, 3% multiracial, 0% Pacific Islander, 70% white, 3% international
**Most popular majors:** 54% Human Services, General, 31% Information Science/Studies, 15% Liberal Arts and Sciences, General Studies and Humanities
**Expenses:** 2013-2014: $31,496; room/board: $8,862
**Financial aid:** (352) 787-7660

## Bethune-Cookman University
Daytona Beach FL
(800) 448-0228
**U.S. News ranking:** Reg. Coll. (S), No. 35
**Website:** www.bethune.cookman.edu
**Admissions email:** admissions@cookman.edu
**Private;** founded 1904
**Affiliation:** Methodist
**Freshman admissions:** least selective; 2013-2014: 7,420 applied, 4,943 accepted. Either SAT or ACT required. ACT 25/75 percentile: 15-18. High school rank: 4% in top tenth, 12% in top quarter, 47% in top half
**Early decision deadline:** N/A, notification date: N/A
**Early action deadline:** N/A, notification date: N/A
**Application deadline (fall):** rolling
**Undergraduate student body:** 3,608 full time, 116 part time; 41% male, 59% female; 0% American Indian, 0% Asian, 90% black, 3% Hispanic, 2% multiracial, 0% Pacific Islander, 2% white, 2% international; 67% from in state; 49% live on campus; 3% of students in fraternities, 5% in sororities
**Most popular majors:** 9% Business Administration and Management, General, 14% Corrections and Criminal Justice, Other, 9% Mass Communication/Media Studies, 10% Psychology, General, 12% Registered Nursing/Registered Nurse
**Expenses:** 2013-2014: $14,410; room/board: $8,548
**Financial aid:** (386) 481-2620

## Chipola College[1]
Marianna FL
(850) 718-2211
**U.S. News ranking:** Reg. Coll. (S), second tier
**Website:** www.chipola.edu
**Admissions email:** N/A
**Public**
**Application deadline (fall):** N/A
**Undergraduate student body:** N/A full time, N/A part time
**Expenses:** 2013-2014: $3,120 in state, $8,950 out of state; room/board: $4,560
**Financial aid:** (800) 433-3243

## Clearwater Christian College
Clearwater FL
(800) 348-4463
**U.S. News ranking:** Nat. Lib. Arts, second tier
**Website:** www.clearwater.edu
**Admissions email:** admissions@clearwater.edu
**Private;** founded 1966
**Affiliation:** Christian nondenominational
**Freshman admissions:** selective; 2013-2014: 468 applied, 328 accepted. Either SAT or ACT required. ACT 25/75 percentile: 19-25. High school rank: 10% in top tenth, 32% in top quarter, 65% in top half
**Early decision deadline:** N/A, notification date: N/A
**Early action deadline:** N/A, notification date: N/A
**Application deadline (fall):** rolling
**Undergraduate student body:** 475 full time, 20 part time; 52% male, 48% female; 0% American Indian, 2% Asian, 4% black, 12% Hispanic, 1% multiracial, 0% Pacific Islander, 79% white, 1% international; 43% from in state; 68% live on campus; 0% of students in fraternities, 0% in sororities
**Most popular majors:** 13% Biological and Biomedical Sciences, 15% Business, Management, Marketing, and Related Support Services, 19% Education, 12% Liberal Arts and Sciences, General Studies and Humanities
**Expenses:** 2014-2015: $17,765; room/board: $8,300
**Financial aid:** (727) 726-1153; 80% of undergrads determined to have financial need; average aid package $13,050

## Daytona State College[1]
Daytona Beach FL
(386) 506-3059
**U.S. News ranking:** Reg. Coll. (S), unranked
**Website:** www.daytonastate.edu
**Admissions email:** N/A
**Public;** founded 1957
**Application deadline (fall):** rolling
**Undergraduate student body:** N/A full time, N/A part time
**Expenses:** 2013-2014: $3,134 in state, $12,421 out of state; room/board: N/A
**Financial aid:** (386) 506-3015

## Eckerd College
St. Petersburg FL
(727) 864-8331
**U.S. News ranking:** Nat. Lib. Arts, No. 124
**Website:** www.eckerd.edu
**Admissions email:** admissions@eckerd.edu
**Private;** founded 1958
**Affiliation:** Presbyterian
**Freshman admissions:** selective; 2013-2014: 3,509 applied, 2,534 accepted. Either SAT or ACT required. SAT 25/75 percentile: 1030-1220. High school rank: N/A
**Early decision deadline:** N/A, notification date: N/A
**Early action deadline:** 11/15, notification date: 12/15
**Application deadline (fall):** rolling

Undergraduate student body: 1,780 full time, 41 part time; 40% male, 60% female; 1% American Indian, 1% Asian, 2% black, 8% Hispanic, 3% multiracial, 0% Pacific Islander, 79% white, 5% international; 21% from in state; 85% live on campus; N/A of students in fraternities, N/A in sororities
Most popular majors: 9% Biology, General, 8% Communication and Media Studies, 14% Environmental Studies, 13% Marine Sciences, 10% Psychology, General
Expenses: 2014-2015: $38,668; room/board: $10,550
Financial aid: (727) 864-8334; 59% of undergrads determined to have financial need; average aid package $30,880

## Edison State College

Fort Myers FL
(800) 749-2322
U.S. News ranking: Reg. Coll. (S), unranked
Website: www.edison.edu
Admissions email: N/A
Public
Freshman admissions: N/A; 2013-2014: 4,759 applied, 3,768 accepted. Neither SAT nor ACT required. SAT 25/75 percentile: 850-1030. High school rank: N/A
Early decision deadline: N/A, notification date: N/A
Early action deadline: N/A, notification date: N/A
Application deadline (fall): 8/20
Undergraduate student body: 5,354 full time, 10,446 part time; 40% male, 60% female; 0% American Indian, 2% Asian, 11% black, 25% Hispanic, 1% multiracial, 0% Pacific Islander, 55% white, 2% international
Most popular majors: 34% Business, Management, Marketing, and Related Support Services, 29% Education, 25% Health Professions and Related Programs
Expenses: 2013-2014: $3,281 in state, $12,979 out of state; room/board: $7,626
Financial aid: (239) 489-9127

## Edward Waters College[1]

Jacksonville FL
(904) 470-8200
U.S. News ranking: Reg. Coll. (S), second tier
Website: www.ewc.edu
Admissions email: admissions@ewc.edu
Private
Application deadline (fall): N/A
Undergraduate student body: N/A full time, N/A part time
Expenses: 2013-2014: $11,525; room/board: $7,156
Financial aid: (904) 470-8192

## Embry-Riddle Aeronautical University

Daytona Beach FL
(800) 862-2416
U.S. News ranking: Reg. U. (S), No. 10
Website: www.embryriddle.edu
Admissions email: dbadmit@erau.edu
Private; founded 1926

Freshman admissions: selective; 2013-2014: 4,074 applied, 3,017 accepted. Neither SAT nor ACT required. SAT 25/75 percentile: 980-1230. High school rank: 23% in top tenth, 52% in top quarter, 80% in top half
Early decision deadline: N/A, notification date: N/A
Early action deadline: N/A, notification date: N/A
Application deadline (fall): rolling
Undergraduate student body: 4,359 full time, 320 part time; 83% male, 17% female; 0% American Indian, 5% Asian, 6% black, 7% Hispanic, 4% multiracial, 0% Pacific Islander, 53% white, 16% international; 35% from in state; 36% live on campus; N/A of students in fraternities, N/A in sororities
Most popular majors: 33% Aeronautics/Aviation/Aerospace Science and Technology, General, 24% Aerospace, Aeronautical and Astronautical/Space Engineering, 10% Air Traffic Controller, 6% Business Administration, Management and Operations, Other, 5% Homeland Security
Expenses: 2014-2015: $31,948; room/board: $9,850
Financial aid: (800) 943-6279; 66% of undergrads determined to have financial need; average aid package $14,099

## Everglades University[1]

Boca Raton FL
(888) 772-6077
U.S. News ranking: Reg. Coll. (S), No. 70
Website: www.evergladesuniversity.edu
Admissions email: N/A
Private
Application deadline (fall): N/A
Undergraduate student body: N/A full time, N/A part time
Expenses: 2013-2014: $15,400; room/board: N/A
Financial aid: (888) 772-6077

## Flagler College

St. Augustine FL
(800) 304-4208
U.S. News ranking: Reg. Coll. (S), No. 8
Website: www.flagler.edu
Admissions email: admiss@flagler.edu
Private; founded 1968
Freshman admissions: selective; 2013-2014: 5,396 applied, 2,691 accepted. Either SAT or ACT required. SAT 25/75 percentile: 930-1130. High school rank: 9% in top tenth, 31% in top quarter, 67% in top half
Early decision deadline: 12/1, notification date: 12/15
Early action deadline: N/A, notification date: N/A
Application deadline (fall): 3/1
Undergraduate student body: 2,746 full time, 93 part time; 41% male, 59% female; 0% American Indian, 1% Asian, 4% black, 8% Hispanic, 3% multiracial, 0% Pacific Islander, 76% white, 3% international; 62% from in state; 34% live on campus; N/A of students in fraternities, N/A in sororities
Most popular majors: 15% Business, Management, Marketing, and Related Support Services, 13% Communication,

Journalism, and Related Programs, 11% Psychology, 12% Visual and Performing Arts
Expenses: 2014-2015: $16,180; room/board: $9,000
Financial aid: (904) 819-6225; 64% of undergrads determined to have financial need; average aid package $11,619

## Florida A&M University

Tallahassee FL
(850) 599-3796
U.S. News ranking: Nat. U., second tier
Website: www.famu.edu
Admissions email: ugradmissions@famu.edu
Public; founded 1887
Freshman admissions: selective; 2013-2014: 5,029 applied, 2,263 accepted. Either SAT or ACT required. ACT 25/75 percentile: 18-22. High school rank: 16% in top tenth, 46% in top quarter, 84% in top half
Early decision deadline: N/A, notification date: N/A
Early action deadline: N/A, notification date: N/A
Application deadline (fall): 5/15
Undergraduate student body: 8,024 full time, 906 part time; 39% male, 61% female; 0% American Indian, 1% Asian, 94% black, 1% Hispanic, 0% multiracial, 0% Pacific Islander, 3% white, 1% international; 84% from in state; 27% live on campus; 2% of students in fraternities, 2% in sororities
Most popular majors: 12% Business, Management, Marketing, and Related Support Services, 6% Communication, Journalism, and Related Programs, 20% Health Professions and Related Programs, 7% Psychology, 8% Social Sciences
Expenses: 2013-2014: $5,785 in state, $17,725 out of state; room/board: $9,356
Financial aid: (850) 412-7927; 85% of undergrads determined to have financial need; average aid package $13,039

## Florida Atlantic University

Boca Raton FL
(561) 297-3040
U.S. News ranking: Nat. U., second tier
Website: www.fau.edu
Admissions email: Admissions@fau.edu
Public; founded 1961
Freshman admissions: selective; 2013-2014: 24,889 applied, 11,880 accepted. Either SAT or ACT required. SAT 25/75 percentile: 960-1130. High school rank: 11% in top tenth, 37% in top quarter, 77% in top half
Early decision deadline: N/A, notification date: N/A
Early action deadline: N/A, notification date: N/A
Application deadline (fall): 5/1
Undergraduate student body: 15,891 full time, 9,899 part time; 44% male, 56% female; 0% American Indian, 4% Asian, 17% black, 24% Hispanic, 3% multiracial, 0% Pacific Islander, 48% white, 2% international; 96% from in state; 6% live on campus; 2% of students in fraternities, 3% in sororities

Most popular majors: Information not available
Expenses: 2014-2015: $6,039 in state, $21,575 out of state; room/board: $11,847
Financial aid: (561) 297-3530; 66% of undergrads determined to have financial need; average aid package $10,405

## Florida College

Temple Terrace FL
(800) 326-7655
U.S. News ranking: Reg. Coll. (S), second tier
Website: www.floridacollege.edu/
Admissions email: N/A
Private
Freshman admissions: selective; 2013-2014: 344 applied, 255 accepted. Either SAT or ACT required. ACT 25/75 percentile: 20-26. High school rank: N/A
Early decision deadline: N/A, notification date: N/A
Early action deadline: N/A, notification date: N/A
Application deadline (fall): 8/1
Undergraduate student body: 533 full time, 25 part time; 50% male, 50% female; 1% American Indian, 1% Asian, 6% black, 5% Hispanic, 5% multiracial, 0% Pacific Islander, 81% white, 1% international
Most popular majors: Information not available
Expenses: 2013-2014: $14,490; room/board: $7,760
Financial aid: N/A

## Florida Gulf Coast University

Fort Myers FL
(239) 590-7878
U.S. News ranking: Reg. U. (S), No. 87
Website: www.fgcu.edu
Admissions email: admissions@fgcu.edu
Public; founded 1991
Freshman admissions: selective; 2013-2014: 10,804 applied, 7,108 accepted. Either SAT or ACT required. SAT 25/75 percentile: 940-1100. High school rank: 11% in top tenth, 36% in top quarter, 77% in top half
Early decision deadline: N/A, notification date: N/A
Early action deadline: N/A, notification date: N/A
Application deadline (fall): rolling
Undergraduate student body: 10,138 full time, 2,723 part time; 44% male, 56% female; 0% American Indian, 2% Asian, 7% black, 19% Hispanic, 2% multiracial, 0% Pacific Islander, 67% white, 2% international; 93% from in state; 33% live on campus; N/A of students in fraternities, N/A in sororities
Most popular majors: 27% Business, Management, Marketing, and Related Support Services, 10% Communication, Journalism, and Related Programs, 10% Education, 9% Health Professions and Related Programs
Expenses: 2013-2014: $6,118 in state, $24,255 out of state; room/board: $8,359
Financial aid: (239) 590-7920; 54% of undergrads determined to have financial need; average aid package $9,083

## Florida Institute of Technology

Melbourne FL
(800) 888-4348
U.S. News ranking: Nat. U., No. 173
Website: www.fit.edu
Admissions email: admission@fit.edu
Private; founded 1958
Freshman admissions: selective; 2013-2014: 7,820 applied, 4,727 accepted. Either SAT or ACT required. SAT 25/75 percentile: 1030-1260. High school rank: 28% in top tenth, 55% in top quarter, 89% in top half
Early decision deadline: N/A, notification date: N/A
Early action deadline: N/A, notification date: N/A
Application deadline (fall): rolling
Undergraduate student body: 3,068 full time, 190 part time; 73% male, 27% female; 0% American Indian, 2% Asian, 5% black, 6% Hispanic, 2% multiracial, 0% Pacific Islander, 43% white, 30% international; 55% from in state; 50% live on campus; 14% of students in fraternities, 16% in sororities
Most popular majors: 8% Aerospace, Aeronautical and Astronautical/Space Engineering, 5% Aviation/Airway Management and Operations, 7% Electrical and Electronics Engineering, 5% Marine Biology and Biological Oceanography, 9% Mechanical Engineering
Expenses: 2014-2015: $37,990; room/board: $13,110
Financial aid: (321) 674-8070; 54% of undergrads determined to have financial need; average aid package $32,854

## Florida International University

Miami FL
(305) 348-2363
U.S. News ranking: Nat. U., second tier
Website: www.fiu.edu
Admissions email: admiss@fiu.edu
Public; founded 1972
Freshman admissions: more selective; 2013-2014: 16,549 applied, 7,122 accepted. Either SAT or ACT required. SAT 25/75 percentile: 1070-1230. High school rank: 23% in top tenth, 51% in top quarter, 79% in top half
Early decision deadline: N/A, notification date: N/A
Early action deadline: N/A, notification date: N/A
Application deadline (fall): 5/1
Undergraduate student body: 25,938 full time, 13,107 part time; 45% male, 55% female; 0% American Indian, 3% Asian, 12% black, 67% Hispanic, 2% multiracial, 0% Pacific Islander, 10% white, 5% international; 97% from in state; 8% live on campus; N/A of students in fraternities, N/A in sororities
Most popular majors: 5% Biological and Biomedical Sciences, 35% Business, Management, Marketing, and Related Support Services, 6% Homeland Security, Law Enforcement, Firefighting and Related Protective Services, 10% Psychology, 9% Social Sciences

**Expenses:** 2014-2015: $6,496 in state, $18,895 out of state; room/board: $10,702
**Financial aid:** (305) 348-2431; 74% of undergrads determined to have financial need; average aid package $7,964

## Florida Memorial University[1]

Miami FL
(305) 626-3750
**U.S. News ranking:** Reg. U. (S), second tier
**Website:** www.fmuniv.edu/
**Admissions email:** admit@fmuniv.edu
**Private**
**Application deadline (fall):** N/A
**Undergraduate student body:** N/A full time, N/A part time
**Expenses:** 2013-2014: $14,776; room/board: $6,112
**Financial aid:** (305) 626-3745

## Florida Southern College

Lakeland FL
(863) 680-4131
**U.S. News ranking:** Reg. Coll. (S), No. 5
**Website:** www.flsouthern.edu
**Admissions email:** fscadm@flsouthern.edu
**Private;** founded 1883
**Affiliation:** United Methodist
**Freshman admissions:** selective; 2013-2014: 4,963 applied, 2,476 accepted. Either SAT or ACT required. SAT 25/75 percentile: 1010-1180. High school rank: 20% in top tenth, 56% in top quarter, 81% in top half
**Early decision deadline:** 12/1, notification date: 12/15
**Early action deadline:** N/A, notification date: N/A
**Application deadline (fall):** rolling
**Undergraduate student body:** 2,120 full time, 72 part time; 41% male, 59% female; 0% American Indian, 2% Asian, 6% black, 9% Hispanic, 4% multiracial, 0% Pacific Islander, 73% white, 6% international; 64% from in state; 79% live on campus; 37% of students in fraternities, 32% in sororities
**Most popular majors:** 26% Business, Management, Marketing, and Related Support Services, 8% Communication, Journalism, and Related Programs, 10% Education, 11% Health Professions and Related Programs, 9% Visual and Performing Arts
**Expenses:** 2014-2015: $29,990; room/board: $10,000
**Financial aid:** (863) 680-4140; 73% of undergrads determined to have financial need; average aid package $23,599

## Florida State College–Jacksonville[1]

Jacksonville FL
(877) 633-5950
**U.S. News ranking:** Reg. Coll. (S), unranked
**Website:** www.fscj.edu
**Admissions email:** N/A
**Public**
**Application deadline (fall):** N/A
**Undergraduate student body:** N/A full time, N/A part time

**Expenses:** 2013-2014: $2,830 in state, $9,944 out of state; room/board: N/A
**Financial aid:** (904) 359-5433

## Florida State University

Tallahassee FL
(850) 644-6200
**U.S. News ranking:** Nat. U., No. 95
**Website:** www.fsu.edu
**Admissions email:** admissions@admin.fsu.edu
**Public;** founded 1851
**Freshman admissions:** more selective; 2013-2014: 29,579 applied, 16,803 accepted. Either SAT or ACT required. ACT 25/75 percentile: 25-29. High school rank: 42% in top tenth, 77% in top quarter, 97% in top half
**Early decision deadline:** N/A, notification date: N/A
**Early action deadline:** N/A, notification date: N/A
**Application deadline (fall):** 1/15
**Undergraduate student body:** 28,910 full time, 3,618 part time; 45% male, 55% female; 0% American Indian, 3% Asian, 8% black, 17% Hispanic, 2% multiracial, 0% Pacific Islander, 67% white, 1% international; 90% from in state; 20% live on campus; 16% of students in fraternities, 22% in sororities
**Most popular majors:** 5% Criminal Justice/Safety Studies, 6% English Language and Literature, General, 5% Finance, General, 5% International Relations and Affairs, 6% Psychology, General
**Expenses:** 2014-2015: $6,507 in state, $21,673 out of state; room/board: $10,208
**Financial aid:** (850) 644-1993; 56% of undergrads determined to have financial need; average aid package $9,033

## Hodges University

Naples FL
(239) 513-1122
**U.S. News ranking:** Reg. U. (S), unranked
**Website:** www.hodges.edu
**Admissions email:** admit@hodges.edu
**Private;** founded 1990
**Freshman admissions:** N/A; 2013-2014: 204 applied, 195 accepted. Neither SAT nor ACT required. ACT 25/75 percentile: N/A. High school rank: N/A
**Early decision deadline:** N/A, notification date: N/A
**Early action deadline:** N/A, notification date: N/A
**Application deadline (fall):** rolling
**Undergraduate student body:** 1,303 full time, 576 part time; 36% male, 64% female; 1% American Indian, 2% Asian, 16% black, 35% Hispanic, 1% multiracial, 0% Pacific Islander, 44% white, 0% international
**Most popular majors:** Information not available
**Expenses:** 2013-2014: $12,740; room/board: N/A
**Financial aid:** (239) 513-1122

## Indian River State College

Fort Pierce FL
(772) 462-7460
**U.S. News ranking:** Reg. Coll. (S), No. 64
**Website:** www.irsc.edu
**Admissions email:** N/A
**Public**
**Freshman admissions:** least selective; 2013-2014: 1,725 applied, 1,725 accepted. Neither SAT nor ACT required. ACT 25/75 percentile: N/A. High school rank: N/A
**Early decision deadline:** N/A, notification date: N/A
**Early action deadline:** N/A, notification date: N/A
**Application deadline (fall):** rolling
**Undergraduate student body:** 5,939 full time, 11,308 part time; 40% male, 60% female; 0% American Indian, 1% Asian, 18% black, 17% Hispanic, 2% multiracial, 0% Pacific Islander, 57% white, 1% international
**Most popular majors:** Information not available
**Expenses:** 2013-2014: $2,764 in state, $10,201 out of state; room/board: N/A
**Financial aid:** (772) 462-7450

## Jacksonville University

Jacksonville FL
(800) 225-2027
**U.S. News ranking:** Reg. U. (S), No. 73
**Website:** www.jacksonville.edu
**Admissions email:** admissions@ju.edu
**Private;** founded 1934
**Freshman admissions:** selective; 2013-2014: 3,498 applied, 1,657 accepted. Either SAT or ACT required. SAT 25/75 percentile: 910-1110. High school rank: N/A
**Early decision deadline:** N/A, notification date: N/A
**Early action deadline:** N/A, notification date: N/A
**Application deadline (fall):** rolling
**Undergraduate student body:** 2,201 full time, 1,224 part time; 38% male, 62% female; 1% American Indian, 3% Asian, 16% black, 7% Hispanic, 0% multiracial, 0% Pacific Islander, 49% white, 3% international; 61% from in state; 29% live on campus; 8% of students in fraternities, 7% in sororities
**Most popular majors:** 13% Business, Management, Marketing, and Related Support Services and Related Programs, 4% Parks, Recreation, Leisure, and Fitness Studies, 5% Social Sciences, 5% Visual and Performing Arts
**Expenses:** 2014-2015: $31,370; room/board: $10,820
**Financial aid:** (904) 256-7060; 72% of undergrads determined to have financial need; average aid package $22,702

## Keiser University

Ft. Lauderdale FL
(954) 776-4456
**U.S. News ranking:** Reg. Coll. (S), No. 40
**Website:** www.keiseruniversity.edu
**Admissions email:** N/A
**Private;** founded 1977

**Freshman admissions:** less selective; 2013-2014: N/A applied, N/A accepted. Neither SAT nor ACT required. ACT 25/75 percentile: N/A. High school rank: N/A
**Early decision deadline:** N/A, notification date: N/A
**Early action deadline:** N/A, notification date: N/A
**Application deadline (fall):** rolling
**Undergraduate student body:** 12,007 full time, 4,032 part time; 32% male, 68% female; 0% American Indian, 2% Asian, 20% black, 31% Hispanic, 4% multiracial, 0% Pacific Islander, 40% white, 0% international; 89% from in state; 0% live on campus; N/A of students in fraternities, N/A in sororities
**Most popular majors:** 21% Business Administration and Management, General, 20% Criminal Justice/Safety Studies, 13% Health Services Administration, 10% Health Services/Allied Health/Health Sciences, General, 10% Multi-/Interdisciplinary Studies, General
**Expenses:** 2013-2014: $16,284; room/board: N/A
**Financial aid:** (954) 351-4456

## Lynn University

Boca Raton FL
(800) 888-5966
**U.S. News ranking:** Nat. U., second tier
**Website:** www.lynn.edu
**Admissions email:** admission@lynn.edu
**Private;** founded 1962
**Freshman admissions:** less selective; 2013-2014: 2,698 applied, 2,094 accepted. Either SAT or ACT required. SAT 25/75 percentile: 820-1050. High school rank: 1% in top tenth, 9% in top quarter, 41% in top half
**Early decision deadline:** N/A, notification date: N/A
**Early action deadline:** 11/15, notification date: 12/15
**Application deadline (fall):** rolling
**Undergraduate student body:** 1,634 full time, 151 part time; 53% male, 47% female; 1% American Indian, 2% Asian, 10% black, 13% Hispanic, 0% multiracial, 0% Pacific Islander, 39% white, 24% international; 44% from in state; 50% live on campus; 5% of students in fraternities, 8% in sororities
**Most popular majors:** 48% Business, Management, Marketing, and Related Support Services, 10% Communication, Journalism, and Related Programs, 6% Homeland Security, Law Enforcement, Firefighting and Related Protective Services, 9% Psychology, 8% Visual and Performing Arts
**Expenses:** 2014-2015: $34,550; room/board: $10,900
**Financial aid:** (561) 237-7186; 43% of undergrads determined to have financial need; average aid package $20,042

## Miami Dade College[1]

Miami FL
(305) 237-8888
**U.S. News ranking:** Reg. Coll. (S), unranked
**Website:** www.mdc.edu/
**Admissions email:** mdcinfo@mdc.edu
**Public**

**Application deadline (fall):** N/A
**Undergraduate student body:** N/A full time, N/A part time
**Expenses:** 2013-2014: $3,426 in state, $11,955 out of state; room/board: N/A
**Financial aid:** (305) 237-6040

## Miami International University of Art & Design[1]

Miami FL
(305) 428-5700
**U.S. News ranking:** Arts, unranked
**Website:** www.aimiu.aii.edu/
**Admissions email:** N/A
**For-profit**
**Application deadline (fall):** N/A
**Undergraduate student body:** N/A full time, N/A part time
**Expenses:** 2013-2014: $17,704; room/board: $10,350
**Financial aid:** N/A

## New College of Florida

Sarasota FL
(941) 487-5000
**U.S. News ranking:** Nat. Lib. Arts, No. 87
**Website:** www.ncf.edu
**Admissions email:** admissions@ncf.edu
**Public;** founded 2001
**Freshman admissions:** more selective; 2013-2014: 1,205 applied, 834 accepted. Either SAT or ACT required. SAT 25/75 percentile: 1190-1380. High school rank: 41% in top tenth, 75% in top quarter, 94% in top half
**Early decision deadline:** N/A, notification date: N/A
**Early action deadline:** N/A, notification date: N/A
**Application deadline (fall):** 4/15
**Undergraduate student body:** 793 full time, 0 part time; 43% male, 57% female; 0% American Indian, 3% Asian, 3% black, 14% Hispanic, 4% multiracial, 0% Pacific Islander, 74% white, 1% international; 82% from in state; 80% live on campus; 0% of students in fraternities, 0% in sororities
**Most popular majors:** 100% Liberal Arts and Sciences, General Studies and Humanities, Other
**Expenses:** 2014-2015: $6,872 in state, $29,900 out of state; room/board: $8,856
**Financial aid:** (941) 359-4255; 57% of undergrads determined to have financial need; average aid package $13,005

## Northwest Florida State College[1]

Niceville FL
(850) 729-6922
**U.S. News ranking:** Reg. Coll. (S), unranked
**Website:** www.owcc.cc.fl.us/
**Admissions email:** N/A
**Public**
**Application deadline (fall):** N/A
**Undergraduate student body:** N/A full time, N/A part time
**Expenses:** 2013-2014: $3,064 in state, $11,373 out of state; room/board: N/A
**Financial aid:** (850) 729-5370

## Nova Southeastern University

Ft. Lauderdale FL
(954) 262-8000
**U.S. News ranking:** Nat. U., second tier
**Website:** www.nova.edu
**Admissions email:** admissions@nova.edu
**Private;** founded 1964
**Freshman admissions:** selective; 2013-2014: 4,328 applied, 2,487 accepted. Either SAT or ACT required. SAT 25/75 percentile: 950-1190. High school rank: 24% in top tenth, 53% in top quarter, 85% in top half
**Early decision deadline:** N/A, notification date: N/A
**Early action deadline:** N/A, notification date: N/A
**Application deadline (fall):** rolling
**Undergraduate student body:** 3,452 full time, 1,704 part time; 29% male, 71% female; 0% American Indian, 7% Asian, 21% black, 31% Hispanic, 2% multiracial, 0% Pacific Islander, 31% white, 5% international; 83% from in state; 18% live on campus; 2% of students in fraternities, 4% in sororities
**Most popular majors:** 21% Biological and Biomedical Sciences, 20% Business, Management, Marketing, and Related Support Services, 5% Education, 31% Health Professions and Related Programs, 8% Psychology
**Expenses:** 2014-2015: $26,700; room/board: $10,580
**Financial aid:** (954) 262-3380; 77% of undergrads determined to have financial need; average aid package $25,035

## Palm Beach Atlantic University

West Palm Beach FL
(888) 468-6722
**U.S. News ranking:** Reg. U. (S), No. 51
**Website:** www.pba.edu
**Admissions email:** admit@pba.edu
**Private;** founded 1968
**Affiliation:** Christian Interdenominational
**Freshman admissions:** selective; 2013-2014: 1,618 applied, 1,361 accepted. Either SAT or ACT required. SAT 25/75 percentile: 925-1180. High school rank: N/A
**Early decision deadline:** N/A, notification date: N/A
**Early action deadline:** 3/31, notification date: 4/15
**Application deadline (fall):** rolling
**Undergraduate student body:** 2,358 full time, 529 part time; 37% male, 63% female; 0% American Indian, 1% Asian, 14% black, 13% Hispanic, 2% multiracial, 0% Pacific Islander, 61% white, 4% international; 68% from in state; 47% live on campus; N/A of students in fraternities, N/A in sororities
**Most popular majors:** 30% Business, Management, Marketing, and Related Support Services, 11% Health Professions and Related Programs, 11% Psychology, 11% Theology and Religious Vocations, 11% Visual and Performing Arts
**Expenses:** 2014-2015: $26,274; room/board: $8,600

**Financial aid:** (561) 803-2000; 76% of undergrads determined to have financial need; average aid package $17,424

## Ringling College of Art and Design

Sarasota FL
(800) 255-7695
**U.S. News ranking:** Arts, unranked
**Website:** www.ringling.edu
**Admissions email:** admissions@ringling.edu
**Private;** founded 1931
**Freshman admissions:** N/A; 2013-2014: 1,225 applied, 898 accepted. Neither SAT nor ACT required. SAT 25/75 percentile: N/A. High school rank: N/A
**Early decision deadline:** N/A, notification date: N/A
**Early action deadline:** N/A, notification date: N/A
**Application deadline (fall):** rolling
**Undergraduate student body:** 1,212 full time, 41 part time; 39% male, 61% female; 1% American Indian, 8% Asian, 3% black, 16% Hispanic, 2% multiracial, 0% Pacific Islander, 58% white, 13% international; 59% from in state; 63% live on campus; 0% of students in fraternities, 0% in sororities
**Most popular majors:** 22% Animation, Interactive Technology, Video Graphics and Special Effects, 7% Game and Interactive Media Design, 11% Graphic Design, 31% Illustration, 7% Photography
**Expenses:** 2014-2015: $40,040; room/board: $13,580
**Financial aid:** (941) 351-5100; 81% of undergrads determined to have financial need; average aid package $18,218

## Rollins College

Winter Park FL
(407) 646-2161
**U.S. News ranking:** Reg. U. (S), No. 2
**Website:** www.rollins.edu
**Admissions email:** admission@rollins.edu
**Private;** founded 1885
**Freshman admissions:** more selective; 2013-2014: 4,729 applied, 2,233 accepted. Neither SAT nor ACT required. SAT 25/75 percentile: 1100-1290. High school rank: 34% in top tenth, 67% in top quarter, 90% in top half
**Early decision deadline:** 11/15, notification date: 12/15
**Early action deadline:** N/A, notification date: N/A
**Application deadline (fall):** 2/15
**Undergraduate student body:** 1,890 full time, N/A part time; 42% male, 58% female; 0% American Indian, 3% Asian, 3% black, 13% Hispanic, 3% multiracial, 0% Pacific Islander, 68% white, 7% international; 51% from in state; 62% live on campus; 24% in sororities
**Most popular majors:** 11% Business, Management, Marketing, and Related Support Services, 11% Communication, Journalism, and Related Programs, 10% Psychology, 27% Social Sciences, 12% Visual and Performing Arts
**Expenses:** 2014-2015: $43,080; room/board: $13,470

**Financial aid:** (407) 646-2395; 54% of undergrads determined to have financial need; average aid package $34,014

## Southeastern University

Lakeland FL
(800) 500-8760
**U.S. News ranking:** Reg. Coll. (S), No. 41
**Website:** www.seu.edu
**Admissions email:** admission@seu.edu
**Private;** founded 1935
**Affiliation:** Assemblies of God
**Freshman admissions:** less selective; 2013-2014: 2,124 applied, 1,260 accepted. Either SAT or ACT required. SAT 25/75 percentile: 850-1080. High school rank: N/A
**Early decision deadline:** N/A, notification date: N/A
**Early action deadline:** N/A, notification date: N/A
**Application deadline (fall):** 5/1
**Undergraduate student body:** 2,473 full time, 610 part time; 45% male, 55% female; 0% American Indian, 1% Asian, 14% black, 16% Hispanic, 1% multiracial, 0% Pacific Islander, 62% white, 1% international; 69% from in state; 47% live on campus; N/A in sororities
**Most popular majors:** 16% Business, Management, Marketing, and Related Support Services, 10% Communication, Journalism, and Related Programs, 11% Education, 12% Public Administration and Social Service Professions, 23% Theology and Religious Vocations
**Expenses:** 2014-2015: $22,202; room/board: $9,298
**Financial aid:** (863) 667-5026; 84% of undergrads determined to have financial need; average aid package $12,967

## Stetson University

DeLand FL
(800) 688-0101
**U.S. News ranking:** Reg. U. (S), No. 6
**Website:** www.stetson.edu
**Admissions email:** admissions@stetson.edu
**Private;** founded 1883
**Freshman admissions:** more selective; 2013-2014: 10,509 applied, 6,227 accepted. Neither SAT nor ACT required. SAT 25/75 percentile: 1070-1270. High school rank: 26% in top tenth, 61% in top quarter, 89% in top half
**Early decision deadline:** N/A, notification date: N/A
**Early action deadline:** N/A, notification date: N/A
**Application deadline (fall):** rolling
**Undergraduate student body:** 2,692 full time, 37 part time; 43% male, 57% female; 0% American Indian, 2% Asian, 8% black, 14% Hispanic, 4% multiracial, 0% Pacific Islander, 66% white, 4% international; 74% from in state; 68% live on campus; 28% of students in fraternities, 27% in sororities
**Most popular majors:** 6% Biological and Biomedical Sciences, 25% Business, Management, and Related Support

Services, 9% Psychology, 9% Social Sciences, 11% Visual and Performing Arts
**Expenses:** 2014-2015: $40,040; room/board: $11,476
**Financial aid:** (386) 822-7120; 75% of undergrads determined to have financial need; average aid package $31,980

## St. Leo University

Saint Leo FL
(800) 334-5532
**U.S. News ranking:** Reg. U. (S), No. 65
**Website:** www.saintleo.edu
**Admissions email:** admission@saintleo.edu
**Private;** founded 1889
**Affiliation:** Roman Catholic
**Freshman admissions:** less selective; 2013-2014: 3,178 applied, 2,435 accepted. Neither SAT nor ACT required. SAT 25/75 percentile: 910-1093. High school rank: 9% in top tenth, 29% in top quarter, 66% in top half
**Early decision deadline:** N/A, notification date: N/A
**Early action deadline:** N/A, notification date: N/A
**Application deadline (fall):** rolling
**Undergraduate student body:** 2,163 full time, 71 part time; 48% male, 52% female; 0% American Indian, 1% Asian, 11% black, 17% Hispanic, 3% multiracial, 0% Pacific Islander, 47% white, 13% international; 71% from in state; 61% live on campus; 20% of students in fraternities, 23% in sororities
**Most popular majors:** 32% Business, Management, Marketing, and Related Support Services, 7% Education, 11% Homeland Security, Law Enforcement, Firefighting and Related Protective Services, 9% Parks, Recreation, Leisure, and Fitness Studies, 10% Psychology
**Expenses:** 2014-2015: $20,110; room/board: $9,920
**Financial aid:** (352) 588-8270; 72% of undergrads determined to have financial need; average aid package $19,072

## St. Petersburg College[1]

St. Petersburg FL
(727) 341-4772
**U.S. News ranking:** Reg. Coll. (S), unranked
**Website:** www.spcollege.edu/
**Admissions email:** information@spcollege.edu
**Public**
**Application deadline (fall):** N/A
**Undergraduate student body:** N/A full time, N/A part time
**Expenses:** 2013-2014: $3,232 in state, $11,477 out of state; room/board: N/A
**Financial aid:** (727) 791-2442

## St. Thomas University

Miami Gardens FL
(305) 628-6546
**U.S. News ranking:** Reg. U. (S), No. 65
**Website:** www.stu.edu
**Admissions email:** signup@stu.edu
**Private;** founded 1961
**Affiliation:** Roman Catholic
**Freshman admissions:** less selective; 2013-2014: 817 applied, 347 accepted. Either SAT or ACT required. SAT 25/75

percentile: 785-990. High school rank: 6% in top tenth, 11% in top quarter, 46% in top half
**Early decision deadline:** N/A, notification date: N/A
**Early action deadline:** N/A, notification date: N/A
**Application deadline (fall):** rolling
**Undergraduate student body:** 963 full time, 72 part time; 45% male, 55% female; 0% American Indian, 0% Asian, 24% black, 43% Hispanic, 1% multiracial, 0% Pacific Islander, 8% white, 19% international; 89% from in state; 30% live on campus; N/A of students in fraternities, N/A in sororities
**Most popular majors:** 52% Business, Management, Marketing, and Related Support Services, 4% Education, 13% Homeland Security, Law Enforcement, Firefighting and Related Protective Services, 10% Psychology, 5% Social Sciences
**Expenses:** 2014-2015: $27,150; room/board: $7,720
**Financial aid:** (305) 474-6960; 72% of undergrads determined to have financial need

## University of Central Florida

Orlando FL
(407) 823-3000
**U.S. News ranking:** Nat. U., No. 173
**Website:** www.ucf.edu
**Admissions email:** admission@ucf.edu
**Public;** founded 1963
**Freshman admissions:** more selective; 2013-2014: 31,820 applied, 15,572 accepted. Either SAT or ACT required. SAT 25/75 percentile: 1090-1270. High school rank: 30% in top tenth, 71% in top quarter, 97% in top half
**Early decision deadline:** N/A, notification date: N/A
**Early action deadline:** N/A, notification date: N/A
**Application deadline (fall):** 5/1
**Undergraduate student body:** 36,160 full time, 15,109 part time; 45% male, 55% female; 0% American Indian, 6% Asian, 11% black, 22% Hispanic, 3% multiracial, 0% Pacific Islander, 57% white, 1% international; 95% from in state; 18% live on campus; 6% of students in fraternities, 7% in sororities
**Most popular majors:** 22% Business, Management, Marketing, and Related Support Services, 8% Education, 6% Engineering, 14% Health Professions and Related Programs, 10% Psychology
**Expenses:** 2014-2015: $6,368 in state, $22,467 out of state; room/board: $9,300
**Financial aid:** (407) 823-2827; 66% of undergrads determined to have financial need; average aid package $7,998

## University of Florida

Gainesville FL
(352) 392-1365
**U.S. News ranking:** Nat. U., No. 48
**Website:** www.ufl.edu
**Admissions email:** N/A
**Public;** founded 1853

**Freshman admissions:** more selective; 2013-2014: 27,107 applied, 12,618 accepted. Either SAT or ACT required. SAT 25/75 percentile: 1170-1360. High school rank: 77% in top tenth, 97% in top quarter, 100% in top half
**Early decision deadline:** N/A, notification date: N/A
**Early action deadline:** N/A, notification date: N/A
**Application deadline (fall):** 11/1
**Undergraduate student body:** 30,314 full time, 2,854 part time; 45% male, 55% female; 0% American Indian, 8% Asian, 7% black, 19% Hispanic, 3% multiracial, 1% Pacific Islander, 58% white, 1% international; 97% from in state; 23% live on campus; 20% of students in fraternities, 21% in sororities
**Most popular majors:** 10% Biological and Biomedical Sciences, 10% Business, Management, Marketing, and Related Support Services, 8% Communication, Journalism, and Related Programs, 13% Engineering, 13% Social Sciences
**Expenses:** 2014-2015: $6,313 in state, $28,591 out of state; room/board: $9,630
**Financial aid:** (352) 392-1271; 56% of undergrads determined to have financial need; average aid package $11,745

## University of Miami
Coral Gables FL
(305) 284-4323
**U.S. News ranking:** Nat. U., No. 48
**Website:** www.miami.edu
**Admissions email:** admission@miami.edu
**Private;** founded 1925
**Freshman admissions:** most selective; 2013-2014: 28,902 applied, 11,691 accepted. Either SAT or ACT required. SAT 25/75 percentile: 1230-1420. High school rank: 72% in top tenth, 92% in top quarter, 98% in top half
**Early decision deadline:** 11/1, notification date: 12/20
**Early action deadline:** 11/1, notification date: 2/1
**Application deadline (fall):** 1/1
**Undergraduate student body:** 10,637 full time, 743 part time; 49% male, 51% female; 0% American Indian, 5% Asian, 7% black, 22% Hispanic, 3% multiracial, 0% Pacific Islander, 43% white, 14% international; 46% from in state; 38% live on campus; 14% of students in fraternities, 17% in sororities
**Most popular majors:** 14% Biological and Biomedical Sciences, 16% Business, Management, Marketing, and Related Support Services, 9% Communication, Journalism, and Related Programs, 11% Health Professions and Related Programs, 12% Social Sciences
**Expenses:** 2014-2015: $44,350; room/board: $12,684
**Financial aid:** (305) 284-5212; 46% of undergrads determined to have financial need; average aid package $32,813

## University of North Florida
Jacksonville FL
(904) 620-2624
**U.S. News ranking:** Reg. U. (S), No. 51
**Website:** www.unf.edu
**Admissions email:** admissions@unf.edu
**Public;** founded 1965
**Freshman admissions:** more selective; 2013-2014: 10,635 applied, 5,682 accepted. Either SAT or ACT required. SAT 25/75 percentile: 1080-1230. High school rank: 24% in top tenth, 56% in top quarter, 87% in top half
**Early decision deadline:** N/A, notification date: N/A
**Early action deadline:** N/A, notification date: N/A
**Application deadline (fall):** rolling
**Undergraduate student body:** 10,088 full time, 4,175 part time; 45% male, 55% female; 0% American Indian, 4% Asian, 10% black, 9% Hispanic, 5% multiracial, 0% Pacific Islander, 70% white, 1% international; 97% from in state; 21% live on campus; N/A of students in fraternities, N/A in sororities
**Most popular majors:** 20% Business, Management, Marketing, and Related Support Services, 9% Communication, Journalism, and Related Programs, 8% Education, 15% Health Professions and Related Programs, 10% Psychology
**Expenses:** 2014-2015: $6,385 in state, $20,103 out of state; room/board: $9,484
**Financial aid:** (904) 620-2604; 59% of undergrads determined to have financial need; average aid package $8,042

## University of South Florida
Tampa FL
(813) 974-3350
**U.S. News ranking:** Nat. U., No. 161
**Website:** www.usf.edu
**Admissions email:** admission@admin.usf.edu
**Public;** founded 1956
**Freshman admissions:** more selective; 2013-2014: 28,512 applied, 12,900 accepted. Either SAT or ACT required. SAT 25/75 percentile: 1080-1260. High school rank: 36% in top tenth, 65% in top quarter, 76% in top half
**Early decision deadline:** N/A, notification date: N/A
**Early action deadline:** N/A, notification date: N/A
**Application deadline (fall):** 3/1
**Undergraduate student body:** 23,734 full time, 7,366 part time; 45% male, 55% female; 0% American Indian, 6% Asian, 11% black, 20% Hispanic, 3% multiracial, 0% Pacific Islander, 55% white, 3% international; 93% from in state; 24% live on campus; 7% of students in fraternities, 8% in sororities
**Most popular majors:** 15% Criminology, 17% Finance, General, 9% Medical Microbiology and Bacteriology, 9% Psychology, General, 10% Registered Nursing/Registered Nurse
**Expenses:** 2014-2015: $6,410 in state, $17,325 out of state; room/board: $9,400

**Financial aid:** (813) 974-4700; 74% of undergrads determined to have financial need; average aid package $9,376

## University of South Florida–St. Petersburg[1]
St. Petersburg FL
(727) 873-4142
**U.S. News ranking:** Reg. U. (S), No. 92
**Website:** www.usfsp.edu
**Admissions email:** admissions@usfsp.edu
**Public;** founded 1965
**Application deadline (fall):** 4/15
**Undergraduate student body:** N/A full time, N/A part time
**Expenses:** 2013-2014: $5,716 in state, $15,638 out of state; room/board: $9,190
**Financial aid:** (727) 873-4128

## University of Tampa
Tampa FL
(888) 646-2738
**U.S. News ranking:** Reg. U. (S), No. 24
**Website:** www.ut.edu
**Admissions email:** admissions@ut.edu
**Private;** founded 1931
**Freshman admissions:** selective; 2013-2014: 15,345 applied, 8,011 accepted. Either SAT or ACT required. SAT 25/75 percentile: 980-1150. High school rank: 18% in top tenth, 46% in top quarter, 84% in top half
**Early decision deadline:** N/A, notification date: N/A
**Early action deadline:** 11/15, notification date: 12/15
**Application deadline (fall):** rolling
**Undergraduate student body:** 6,188 full time, 311 part time; 45% male, 55% female; 0% American Indian, 1% Asian, 6% black, 12% Hispanic, 2% multiracial, 0% Pacific Islander, 59% white, 10% international; 40% from in state; 63% live on campus; 10% of students in fraternities, 23% in sororities
**Most popular majors:** 7% Biological and Biomedical Sciences, 26% Business, Management, Marketing, and Related Support Services, 12% Communication, Journalism, and Related Programs, 10% Parks, Recreation, Leisure, and Fitness Studies, 12% Social Sciences
**Expenses:** 2014-2015: $26,330; room/board: $9,624
**Financial aid:** (813) 253-6219; 60% of undergrads determined to have financial need; average aid package $16,113

## University of West Florida
Pensacola FL
(850) 474-2230
**U.S. News ranking:** Nat. U., second tier
**Website:** uwf.edu
**Admissions email:** admissions@uwf.edu
**Public;** founded 1963
**Freshman admissions:** selective; 2013-2014: 12,347 applied, 5,937 accepted. Either SAT or ACT required. ACT 25/75 percentile: 21-25. High school rank: 12% in top tenth, 36% in top quarter, 75% in top half

## Early decision deadline: N/A,
notification date: N/A
**Early action deadline:** N/A, notification date: N/A
**Application deadline (fall):** 6/30
**Undergraduate student body:** 7,581 full time, 2,577 part time; 43% male, 57% female; 1% American Indian, 3% Asian, 13% black, 9% Hispanic, 4% multiracial, 0% Pacific Islander, 67% white, 2% international; 90% from in state; 19% live on campus; N/A of students in fraternities, N/A in sororities
**Most popular majors:** 15% Business Administration and Management, General, 13% Health Services/Allied Health/Health Sciences, General, 7% Mass Communication/Media Studies, 7% Social Sciences, General, 8% Special Education and Teaching, General
**Expenses:** 2014-2015: $8,942 in state, $21,824 out of state; room/board: $9,323
**Financial aid:** (850) 474-3127; 67% of undergrads determined to have financial need; average aid package $8,412

## Warner University[1]
Lake Wales FL
(800) 309-9563
**U.S. News ranking:** Reg. U. (S), second tier
**Website:** www.warner.edu
**Admissions email:** admissions@warner.edu
**Private**
**Affiliation:** Church of God, Anderson IN
**Application deadline (fall):** rolling
**Undergraduate student body:** N/A full time, N/A part time
**Expenses:** 2013-2014: $18,430; room/board: $7,649
**Financial aid:** (863) 638-7202

## Webber International University
Babson Park FL
(800) 741-1844
**U.S. News ranking:** Reg. Coll. (S), second tier
**Website:** www.webber.edu
**Admissions email:** admissions@webber.edu
**Private;** founded 1927
**Freshman admissions:** less selective; 2013-2014: 944 applied, 602 accepted. Either SAT or ACT required. ACT 25/75 percentile: 17-21. High school rank: 6% in top tenth, 22% in top quarter, 53% in top half
**Early decision deadline:** N/A, notification date: N/A
**Early action deadline:** N/A, notification date: N/A
**Application deadline (fall):** 8/1
**Undergraduate student body:** 633 full time, 34 part time; 69% male, 31% female; 0% American Indian, 2% Asian, 22% black, 16% Hispanic, 3% multiracial, 0% Pacific Islander, 48% white, 8% international; 90% from in state; 52% live on campus; N/A of students in fraternities, N/A in sororities
**Most popular majors:** 67% Business, Management, Marketing, and Related Support Services, 5% Computer and Information Sciences and Support Services, 4% Homeland Security, Law Enforcement, Firefighting and

Related Protective Services, 4% Legal Professions and Studies, 17% Parks, Recreation, Leisure, and Fitness Studies
**Expenses:** 2014-2015: $24,034; room/board: $8,462
**Financial aid:** (863) 638-2930; 69% of undergrads determined to have financial need; average aid package $19,481

## Abraham Baldwin Agricultural College
Tifton GA
(800) 733-3653
**U.S. News ranking:** Reg. Coll. (S), second tier
**Website:** www.abac.edu/
**Admissions email:** N/A
**Public;** founded 1908
**Freshman admissions:** least selective; 2013-2014: 1,567 applied, 1,111 accepted. Either SAT or ACT required. SAT 25/75 percentile: 810-990. High school rank: N/A
**Early decision deadline:** N/A, notification date: N/A
**Early action deadline:** N/A, notification date: N/A
**Application deadline (fall):** 8/1
**Undergraduate student body:** 2,350 full time, 1,044 part time; 46% male, 54% female; 0% American Indian, 1% Asian, 12% black, 6% Hispanic, 1% multiracial, 0% Pacific Islander, 78% white, 2% international
**Most popular majors:** Information not available
**Expenses:** 2013-2014: $4,281 in state, $10,415 out of state; room/board: N/A
**Financial aid:** (229) 391-4910

## Agnes Scott College
Decatur GA
(800) 868-8602
**U.S. News ranking:** Nat. Lib. Arts, No. 73
**Website:** www.agnesscott.edu
**Admissions email:** admission@agnesscott.edu
**Private;** founded 1889
**Affiliation:** Presbyterian Church (USA)
**Freshman admissions:** more selective; 2013-2014: 1,340 applied, 896 accepted. Neither SAT nor ACT required. SAT 25/75 percentile: 1010-1310. High school rank: 40% in top tenth, 67% in top quarter, 91% in top half
**Early decision deadline:** N/A, notification date: N/A
**Early action deadline:** N/A, notification date: N/A
**Application deadline (fall):** 5/1
**Undergraduate student body:** 897 full time, 18 part time; 1% male, 99% female; 0% American Indian, 5% Asian, 35% black, 9% Hispanic, 6% multiracial, 0% Pacific Islander, 31% white, 10% international; 63% from in state; 82% live on campus; N/A of students in fraternities, N/A in sororities
**Most popular majors:** 13% Biological and Biomedical Sciences, 11% English Language and Literature/Letters, 17% Psychology, 20% Social Sciences, 8% Visual and Performing Arts

**Expenses:** 2014-2015: $35,982; room/board: $10,850
**Financial aid:** (404) 471-6395; 77% of undergrads determined to have financial need; average aid package $32,875

## Albany State University
Albany GA
(229) 430-4646
**U.S. News ranking:** Reg. U. (S), No. 76
**Website:** www.asurams.edu/
**Admissions email:** admissions@asurams.edu
**Public;** founded 1903
**Freshman admissions:** less selective; 2013-2014: 6,393 applied, 1,537 accepted. Either SAT or ACT required. SAT 25/75 percentile: 820-950. High school rank: 7% in top tenth, 27% in top quarter, 66% in top half
**Early decision deadline:** N/A, notification date: N/A
**Early action deadline:** N/A, notification date: N/A
**Application deadline (fall):** 6/1
**Undergraduate student body:** 3,019 full time, 641 part time; 34% male, 66% female; 0% American Indian, 0% Asian, 92% black, 1% Hispanic, 0% multiracial, 0% Pacific Islander, 4% white, 0% international; 98% from in state; 42% live on campus; 6% of students in fraternities, 10% in sororities
**Most popular majors:** 8% Biology/Biological Sciences, General, 11% Business Administration and Management, General, 11% Criminal Justice/Safety Studies, 8% Early Childhood Education and Teaching, 9% Psychology, General
**Expenses:** 2014-2015: $6,024 in state, $18,226 out of state; room/board: $7,646
**Financial aid:** (229) 430-4650; 94% of undergrads determined to have financial need; average aid package $4,977

## Armstrong State University
Savannah GA
(912) 344-2503
**U.S. News ranking:** Reg. U. (S), second tier
**Website:** www.armstrong.edu
**Admissions email:** adm-info@mail.armstrong.edu
**Public;** founded 1935
**Freshman admissions:** selective; 2013-2014: 2,497 applied, 1,692 accepted. Either SAT or ACT required. SAT 25/75 percentile: 920-1090. High school rank: N/A
**Early decision deadline:** N/A, notification date: N/A
**Early action deadline:** N/A, notification date: N/A
**Application deadline (fall):** 7/15
**Undergraduate student body:** 4,699 full time, 1,678 part time; 33% male, 67% female; 0% American Indian, 4% Asian, 24% black, 7% Hispanic, 4% multiracial, 0% Pacific Islander, 60% white, 2% international; 93% from in state; 49% live on campus; N/A of students in fraternities, N/A in sororities
**Most popular majors:** 42% Health Services/Allied Health/Health Sciences, General

**Expenses:** 2014-2015: $5,934 in state, $17,700 out of state; room/board: $8,946
**Financial aid:** (912) 921-5990; 66% of undergrads determined to have financial need; average aid package $9,145

## Art Institute of Atlanta[1]
Atlanta GA
(770) 394-8300
**U.S. News ranking:** Arts, unranked
**Website:** www.artinstitutes.edu/atlanta/
**Admissions email:** aiaadm@aii.edu
**For-profit**
**Application deadline (fall):** N/A
**Undergraduate student body:** N/A full time, N/A part time
**Expenses:** 2013-2014: $17,596; room/board: $11,268
**Financial aid:** (770) 394-8300

## Bauder College[1]
Atlanta GA
(800) 241-3797
**U.S. News ranking:** Reg. Coll. (S), unranked
**Website:** www.bauder.edu
**Admissions email:** N/A
**For-profit**
**Application deadline (fall):** N/A
**Undergraduate student body:** N/A full time, N/A part time
**Expenses:** 2013-2014: $13,089; room/board: N/A
**Financial aid:** N/A

## Berry College
Mount Berry GA
(706) 236-2215
**U.S. News ranking:** Nat. Lib. Arts, No. 129
**Website:** www.berry.edu
**Admissions email:** admissions@berry.edu
**Private;** founded 1902
**Freshman admissions:** more selective; 2013-2014: 3,901 applied, 2,353 accepted. Either SAT or ACT required. ACT 25/75 percentile: 24-29. High school rank: 32% in top tenth, 65% in top quarter, 92% in top half
**Early decision deadline:** N/A, notification date: N/A
**Early action deadline:** N/A, notification date: N/A
**Application deadline (fall):** 7/25
**Undergraduate student body:** 2,107 full time, 34 part time; 38% male, 62% female; 0% American Indian, 1% Asian, 4% black, 6% Hispanic, 3% multiracial, 0% Pacific Islander, 84% white, 1% international; 69% from in state; 86% live on campus; N/A of students in fraternities, N/A in sororities
**Most popular majors:** 10% Agriculture, Agriculture Operations, and Related Sciences, 13% Biological and Biomedical Sciences, 13% Business, Management, Marketing, and Related Support Services, 10% Psychology, 9% Social Sciences
**Expenses:** 2014-2015: $30,530; room/board: $10,660
**Financial aid:** (706) 236-1714; 74% of undergrads determined to have financial need; average aid package $24,002

## Brenau University
Gainesville GA
(770) 534-6100
**U.S. News ranking:** Reg. U. (S), No. 43
**Website:** www.brenau.edu
**Admissions email:** admissions@brenau.edu
**Private;** founded 1878
**Freshman admissions:** less selective; 2013-2014: 2,160 applied, 1,691 accepted. Either SAT or ACT required. SAT 25/75 percentile: 890-1070. High school rank: N/A
**Early decision deadline:** N/A, notification date: N/A
**Early action deadline:** N/A, notification date: N/A
**Application deadline (fall):** rolling
**Undergraduate student body:** 1,074 full time, 626 part time; 11% male, 89% female; 0% American Indian, 2% Asian, 31% black, 6% Hispanic, 3% multiracial, 0% Pacific Islander, 51% white, 3% international; 95% from in state; 23% live on campus; 0% of students in fraternities, 24% in sororities
**Most popular majors:** 31% Business, Management, Marketing, and Related Support Services, 10% Education, 32% Health Professions and Related Programs, 6% Liberal Arts and Sciences, General Studies and Humanities, 8% Visual and Performing Arts
**Expenses:** 2014-2015: $24,780; room/board: $11,998
**Financial aid:** (770) 534-6176; 84% of undergrads determined to have financial need; average aid package $16,844

## Brewton-Parker College[1]
Mount Vernon GA
(912) 583-3265
**U.S. News ranking:** Reg. Coll. (S), second tier
**Website:** www.bpc.edu
**Admissions email:** admissions@bpc.edu
**Private**
**Application deadline (fall):** N/A
**Undergraduate student body:** N/A full time, N/A part time
**Expenses:** 2013-2014: $13,560; room/board: $6,926
**Financial aid:** (912) 583-3215

## Clark Atlanta University
Atlanta GA
(800) 688-3228
**U.S. News ranking:** Nat. U., second tier
**Website:** www.cau.edu
**Admissions email:** cauadmissions@cau.edu
**Private;** founded 1988
**Affiliation:** Methodist
**Freshman admissions:** less selective; 2013-2014: 5,873 applied, 3,336 accepted. Either SAT or ACT required. SAT 25/75 percentile: 770-940. High school rank: 9% in top tenth, 31% in top quarter, 65% in top half
**Early decision deadline:** N/A, notification date: N/A
**Early action deadline:** N/A, notification date: N/A
**Application deadline (fall):** 6/1

**Undergraduate student body:** 2,514 full time, 115 part time; 25% male, 75% female; 0% American Indian, 0% Asian, 87% black, 1% Hispanic, 0% multiracial, 0% Pacific Islander, 0% white, 1% international; 36% from in state; 62% live on campus; 2% of students in fraternities, 3% in sororities
**Most popular majors:** 7% Biological and Biomedical Sciences, 23% Business, Management, Marketing, and Related Support Services, 23% Communication, Journalism, and Related Programs, 12% Psychology, 10% Visual and Performing Arts
**Expenses:** 2014-2015: $21,334; room/board: $10,262
**Financial aid:** (404) 880-8111; 95% of undergrads determined to have financial need; average aid package $7,879

## Clayton State University
Morrow GA
(678) 466-4115
**U.S. News ranking:** Reg. Coll. (S), No. 62
**Website:** www.clayton.edu
**Admissions email:** ccsu-info@mail.clayton.edu
**Public;** founded 1969
**Freshman admissions:** selective; 2013-2014: 2,048 applied, 949 accepted. Either SAT or ACT required. SAT 25/75 percentile: 860-1030. High school rank: N/A
**Early decision deadline:** N/A, notification date: N/A
**Early action deadline:** N/A, notification date: N/A
**Application deadline (fall):** 7/1
**Undergraduate student body:** 3,939 full time, 2,954 part time; 30% male, 70% female; 0% American Indian, 4% Asian, 65% black, 1% Hispanic, 0% multiracial, 3% Pacific Islander, 21% white, 1% international; 88% from in state; 5% live on campus; 8% of students in fraternities, 8% in sororities
**Most popular majors:** 5% Business Administration and Management, General, 13% Community Psychology, 11% Hospital and Health Care Facilities Administration/Management, 12% Liberal Arts and Sciences/Liberal Studies, 13% Registered Nursing/Registered Nurse
**Expenses:** 2014-2015: $6,194 in state, $18,700 out of state; room/board: $9,692
**Financial aid:** (678) 466-4185; 87% of undergrads determined to have financial need; average aid package $8,842

## Columbus State University
Columbus GA
(706) 507-8800
**U.S. News ranking:** Reg. U. (S), second tier
**Website:** www.columbusstate.edu
**Admissions email:** admissions@columbusstate.edu
**Public;** founded 1958
**Freshman admissions:** selective; 2013-2014: 3,172 applied, 1,775 accepted. Either SAT or ACT required. SAT 25/75 percentile: 880-1100. High school rank: 17% in top tenth, 38% in top quarter, 67% in top half

**Early decision deadline:** N/A, notification date: N/A
**Early action deadline:** N/A, notification date: N/A
**Application deadline (fall):** 6/30
**Undergraduate student body:** 4,979 full time, 2,042 part time; 40% male, 60% female; 1% American Indian, 2% Asian, 36% black, 5% Hispanic, 3% multiracial, 0% Pacific Islander, 52% white, 1% international; 83% from in state; 19% live on campus; 4% of students in fraternities, 4% in sororities
**Most popular majors:** Information not available
**Expenses:** 2014-2015: $6,898 in state, $19,794 out of state; room/board: $9,684
**Financial aid:** (706) 568-2036; 72% of undergrads determined to have financial need; average aid package $9,124

## Covenant College
Lookout Mountain GA
(706) 820-2398
**U.S. News ranking:** Reg. Coll. (S), No. 6
**Website:** www.covenant.edu
**Admissions email:** admissions@covenant.edu
**Private;** founded 1955
**Affiliation:** Presbyterian Church in America
**Freshman admissions:** more selective; 2013-2014: 1,109 applied, 629 accepted. Either SAT or ACT required. SAT 25/75 percentile: 1060-1280. High school rank: 24% in top tenth, 55% in top quarter, 88% in top half
**Early decision deadline:** N/A, notification date: N/A
**Early action deadline:** N/A, notification date: N/A
**Application deadline (fall):** rolling
**Undergraduate student body:** 1,050 full time, 54 part time; 44% male, 56% female; 1% American Indian, 2% Asian, 3% black, 2% Hispanic, 2% multiracial, 0% Pacific Islander, 88% white, 2% international; 24% from in state; 83% live on campus; 0% of students in fraternities, 0% in sororities
**Most popular majors:** 12% Business, Management, Marketing, and Related Support Services, 20% Education, 10% English Language and Literature/Letters, 10% Psychology, 11% Social Sciences
**Expenses:** 2014-2015: $30,160; room/board: $8,830
**Financial aid:** (706) 419-1126; 62% of undergrads determined to have financial need; average aid package $24,354

## Dalton State College[1]
Dalton GA
(706) 272-4436
**U.S. News ranking:** Reg. Coll. (S), unranked
**Website:** www.daltonstate.edu/
**Admissions email:** N/A
**Public**
**Application deadline (fall):** N/A
**Undergraduate student body:** N/A full time, N/A part time
**Expenses:** 2013-2014: $3,910 in state, $11,768 out of state; room/board: $6,590
**Financial aid:** (706) 272-4545

## Emmanuel College

Franklin Springs GA
(800) 860-8800
**U.S. News ranking:** Reg. Coll. (S),
No. 47
**Website:** www.ec.edu
**Admissions email:** admissions@
ec.edu
**Private;** founded 1919
**Affiliation:** International
Pentecostal Holiness
**Freshman admissions:** less
selective; 2013-2014: 876
applied, 419 accepted. Either
SAT or ACT required. SAT 25/75
percentile: 830-1030. High
school rank: N/A
**Early decision deadline:** N/A,
notification date: N/A
**Early action deadline:** N/A,
notification date: N/A
**Application deadline (fall):** 8/1
**Undergraduate student body:** 702
full time, 104 part time; 49%
male, 51% female; 0% American
Indian, 1% Asian, 19% black,
4% Hispanic, 2% multiracial,
0% Pacific Islander, 68% white,
5% international; 76% from in
state; 59% live on campus; 0%
of students in fraternities, 0% in
sororities
**Most popular majors:** 8% Biological
and Biomedical Sciences, 18%
Health and Physical Education/
Fitness, 19% Teacher Education
and Professional Development,
Specific Levels and Methods, 17%
Theology and Religious Vocations
**Expenses:** 2014-2015: $18,170;
room/board: $7,200
**Financial aid:** (706) 245-2843;
80% of undergrads determined to
have financial need; average aid
package $15,077

## Emory University

Atlanta GA
(404) 727-6036
**U.S. News ranking:** Nat. U., No. 21
**Website:** www.emory.edu
**Admissions email:** admission@
emory.edu
**Private;** founded 1836
**Affiliation:** Methodist
**Freshman admissions:** most
selective; 2013-2014: 17,681
applied, 4,685 accepted. SAT
or ACT required. SAT 25/75
percentile: 1260-1470. High
school rank: 76% in top tenth,
95% in top quarter, 99% in
top half
**Early decision deadline:** 11/1,
notification date: 12/15
**Early action deadline:** N/A,
notification date: N/A
**Application deadline (fall):** 1/15
**Undergraduate student body:** 7,676
full time, 160 part time; 43%
male, 57% female; 0% American
Indian, 22% Asian, 9% black,
6% Hispanic, 3% multiracial,
0% Pacific Islander, 40% white,
15% international; 27% from in
state; 67% live on campus; 30%
of students in fraternities, 31%
in sororities
**Most popular majors:** 9% Biology/
Biological Sciences, General,
14% Business Administration
and Management, General,
9% Economics, General, 6%
Psychology, General, 6%
Registered Nursing/Registered
Nurse
**Expenses:** 2014-2015: $45,008;
room/board: $12,760

**Financial aid:** (404) 727-6039;
48% of undergrads determined to
have financial need; average aid
package $38,978

## Fort Valley State University

Fort Valley GA
(478) 825-6307
**U.S. News ranking:** Reg. Coll. (S),
No. 71
**Website:** www.fvsu.edu
**Admissions email:** admissap@
mail.fvsu.edu
**Public;** founded 1895
**Freshman admissions:** less
selective; 2013-2014: 3,465
applied, 1,069 accepted. Either
SAT or ACT required. ACT 25/75
percentile: 15-18. High school
rank: 5% in top tenth, 23% in top
quarter, 47% in top half
**Early decision deadline:** N/A,
notification date: N/A
**Early action deadline:** N/A,
notification date: N/A
**Application deadline (fall):** 7/19
**Undergraduate student body:** 2,570
full time, 288 part time; 43%
male, 57% female; 0% American
Indian, 0% Asian, 97% black,
0% Hispanic, 0% multiracial,
0% Pacific Islander, 2% white,
0% international; 98% from in
state; 43% live on campus; N/A
of students in fraternities, N/A in
sororities
**Most popular majors:** 19%
Biology, General, 14% Business
Administration, Management and
Operations, 14% Criminal Justice
and Corrections, 9% Human
Development, Family Studies,
and Related Services, 19%
Psychology, General
**Expenses:** 2014-2015: $6,448 in
state, $19,364 out of state; room/
board: $7,920
**Financial aid:** (478) 825-6351;
93% of undergrads determined to
have financial need; average aid
package $14,962

## Georgia College & State University

Milledgeville GA
(478) 445-1283
**U.S. News ranking:** Reg. U. (S),
No. 28
**Website:** www.gcsu.edu
**Admissions email:** info@gcsu.edu
**Public;** founded 1889
**Freshman admissions:** selective;
2013-2014: 4,051 applied,
2,754 accepted. Either SAT
or ACT required. SAT 25/75
percentile: 1050-1230. High
school rank: N/A
**Early decision deadline:** N/A,
notification date: N/A
**Early action deadline:** 11/1,
notification date: 12/15
**Application deadline (fall):** 4/1
**Undergraduate student body:** 5,264
full time, 465 part time; 40%
male, 60% female; 0% American
Indian, 1% Asian, 5% black,
5% Hispanic, 2% multiracial,
0% Pacific Islander, 85% white,
1% international; 99% from in
state; 35% live on campus; 3%
of students in fraternities, 15%
in sororities
**Most popular majors:** 11%
Business Administration and
Management, General, 7%
Community Health and Preventive

Medicine, 6% Marketing/
Marketing Management, General,
9% Psychology, General, 10%
Registered Nursing/Registered
Nurse
**Expenses:** 2014-2015: $8,960 in
state, $27,308 out of state; room/
board: $9,940
**Financial aid:** (478) 445-5149;
56% of undergrads determined to
have financial need; average aid
package $9,398

## Georgia Gwinnett College

Lawrenceville GA
(877) 704-4422
**U.S. News ranking:** Reg. Coll. (S),
second tier
**Website:** www.ggc.edu
**Admissions email:** N/A
**Public;** founded 2005
**Freshman admissions:** less
selective; 2013-2014: 3,454
applied, 3,111 accepted. Neither
SAT nor ACT required. SAT 25/75
percentile: 820-1055. High
school rank: 4% in top tenth, 15%
in top quarter, 42% in top half
**Early decision deadline:** N/A,
notification date: N/A
**Early action deadline:** N/A,
notification date: N/A
**Application deadline (fall):** 6/1
**Undergraduate student body:** 6,832
full time, 2,887 part time; 46%
male, 54% female; 0% American
Indian, 8% Asian, 38% black,
17% Hispanic, 4% multiracial,
0% Pacific Islander, 33% white,
1% international; 99% from in
state; 7% live on campus; N/A
of students in fraternities, N/A in
sororities
**Most popular majors:** 14%
Biological and Biomedical
Sciences, 38% Business,
Management, Marketing, and
Related Support Services, 6%
Computer and Information
Sciences and Support Services,
14% Education, 10% Psychology
**Expenses:** 2014-2015: $5,352 in
state, $15,048 out of state; room/
board: $11,890
**Financial aid:** N/A; 78% of
undergrads determined to have
financial need; average aid
package $7,613

## Georgia Institute of Technology

Atlanta GA
(404) 894-4154
**U.S. News ranking:** Nat. U.,
No. 35
**Website:** admission.gatech.edu/
information/
**Admissions email:** admission@
gatech.edu
**Public;** founded 1885
**Freshman admissions:** most
selective; 2013-2014: 17,669
applied, 7,265 accepted. Either
SAT or ACT required. SAT 25/75
percentile: 1290-1480. High
school rank: 81% in top tenth,
95% in top quarter, 99% in
top half
**Early decision deadline:** N/A,
notification date: N/A
**Early action deadline:** 10/21,
notification date: 1/4
**Application deadline (fall):** 1/10
**Undergraduate student body:**
13,291 full time, 1,267 part
time; 67% male, 33% female; 0%
American Indian, 17% Asian,

6% black, 7% Hispanic, 3%
multiracial, 0% Pacific Islander,
55% white, 10% international;
71% from in state; 52% live
on campus; 23% of students in
fraternities, 29% in sororities
**Most popular majors:** 6% Biological
and Biomedical Sciences,
14% Business, Management,
Marketing, and Related Support
Services, 7% Computer and
Information Sciences and Support
Services, 58% Engineering, 3%
Multi/Interdisciplinary Studies
**Expenses:** 2014-2015: $11,394
in state, $30,698 out of state;
room/board: $12,840
**Financial aid:** (404) 894-4582;
45% of undergrads determined to
have financial need; average aid
package $11,347

## Georgia Southern University

Statesboro GA
(912) 478-5391
**U.S. News ranking:** Nat. U.,
second tier
**Website:**
www.georgiasouthern.edu/
**Admissions email:** admissions@
georgiasouthern.edu
**Public;** founded 1906
**Freshman admissions:** selective;
2013-2014: 10,134 applied,
5,759 accepted. Either SAT
or ACT required. SAT 25/75
percentile: 1040-1180. High
school rank: 19% in top tenth,
45% in top quarter, 76% in
top half
**Early decision deadline:** N/A,
notification date: N/A
**Early action deadline:** N/A,
notification date: N/A
**Application deadline (fall):** 5/1
**Undergraduate student body:**
15,762 full time, 2,142 part
time; 50% male, 50% female;
0% American Indian, 1% Asian,
26% black, 4% Hispanic, 2%
multiracial, 0% Pacific Islander,
63% white, 1% international;
96% from in state; 29% live
on campus; 12% of students in
fraternities, 15% in sororities
**Most popular majors:** 20%
Business, Management,
Marketing, and Related Support
Services, 8% Education, 7%
Health Professions and Related
Programs, 8% Liberal Arts
and Sciences, General Studies
and Humanities, 7% Parks,
Recreation, Leisure, and Fitness
Studies
**Expenses:** 2014-2015: $7,190 in
state, $20,086 out of state; room/
board: $9,752
**Financial aid:** (912) 681-5413;
69% of undergrads determined to
have financial need; average aid
package $9,393

## Georgia Southwestern State University

Americus GA
(229) 928-1273
**U.S. News ranking:** Reg. U. (S),
second tier
**Website:** www.gsw.edu
**Admissions email:** admissions@
gsw.edu
**Public;** founded 1906
**Freshman admissions:** selective;
2013-2014: 1,245 applied, 847
accepted. Either SAT or ACT
required. SAT 25/75 percentile:

860-1050. High school rank:
16% in top tenth, 36% in top
quarter, 68% in top half
**Early decision deadline:** 12/15,
notification date: 1/15
**Early action deadline:** N/A,
notification date: N/A
**Application deadline (fall):** 7/21
**Undergraduate student body:** 1,870
full time, 797 part time; 36%
male, 64% female; 0% American
Indian, 1% Asian, 30% black,
3% Hispanic, 1% multiracial,
0% Pacific Islander, 61% white,
2% international; 99% from in
state; 28% live on campus; 8%
of students in fraternities, 8% in
sororities
**Most popular majors:** 14%
Accounting, 20% Business
Administration and Management,
General, 9% Elementary
Education and Teaching, 8%
Psychology, General, 18%
Registered Nursing/Registered
Nurse
**Expenses:** 2014-2015: $6,106 in
state, $18,612 out of state; room/
board: $7,140
**Financial aid:** (229) 928-1378;
77% of undergrads determined to
have financial need; average aid
package $8,929

## Georgia State University

Atlanta GA
(404) 413-2500
**U.S. News ranking:** Nat. U.,
second tier
**Website:** www.gsu.edu
**Admissions email:** admissions@
gsu.edu
**Public;** founded 1913
**Freshman admissions:** selective;
2013-2014: 13,489 applied,
7,269 accepted. Either SAT
or ACT required. SAT 25/75
percentile: 960-1170. High
school rank: N/A
**Early decision deadline:** N/A,
notification date: N/A
**Early action deadline:** 11/15,
notification date: 1/30
**Application deadline (fall):** 3/1
**Undergraduate student body:**
18,429 full time, 6,436 part
time; 42% male, 58% female;
0% American Indian, 11% Asian,
40% black, 9% Hispanic, 4%
multiracial, 0% Pacific Islander,
31% white, 2% international;
97% from in state; 17% live
on campus; N/A of students in
fraternities, N/A in sororities
**Most popular majors:** 27%
Business, Management,
Marketing, and Related Support
Services, 8% Education, 9%
Psychology, 12% Social Sciences,
7% Visual and Performing Arts
**Expenses:** 2014-2015: $10,240
in state, $28,450 out of state;
room/board: $13,342
**Financial aid:** (404) 651-2227;
78% of undergrads determined to
have financial need; average aid
package $9,292

## Gordon State College[1]

Barnesville GA
(678) 359-5021
**U.S. News ranking:** Reg. Coll. (S),
second tier
**Website:** www.gordonstate.edu/
**Admissions email:** N/A
**Public**
**Application deadline (fall):** N/A

**Undergraduate student body:** N/A full time, N/A part time
**Expenses:** 2013-2014: $3,408 in state, $9,695 out of state; room/board: $6,357
**Financial aid:** N/A

## Kennesaw State University

Kennesaw GA
(770) 423-6300
**U.S. News ranking:** Reg. U. (S), No. 70
**Website:** www.kennesaw.edu
**Admissions email:** ksuadmit@kennesaw.edu
**Public;** founded 1963
**Freshman admissions:** selective; 2013-2014: 10,058 applied, 5,572 accepted. Either SAT or ACT required. SAT 25/75 percentile: 990-1170. High school rank: 21% in top tenth, 53% in top quarter, 81% in top half
**Early decision deadline:** N/A, notification date: N/A
**Early action deadline:** N/A, notification date: N/A
**Application deadline (fall):** 5/9
**Undergraduate student body:** 16,869 full time, 5,752 part time; 42% male, 58% female; 0% American Indian, 3% Asian, 17% black, 7% Hispanic, 4% multiracial, 0% Pacific Islander, 62% white, 2% international; 94% from in state; 14% live on campus; 4% of students in fraternities, 5% in sororities
**Most popular majors:** 23% Business, Management, Marketing, and Related Support Services, 8% Communication, Journalism, and Related Programs, 15% Education, 5% Health Professions and Related Programs, 8% Social Sciences
**Expenses:** 2014-2015: $6,932 in state, $19,828 out of state; room/board: $6,014
**Financial aid:** (770) 423-6074; 70% of undergrads determined to have financial need; average aid package $7,590

## LaGrange College

LaGrange GA
(706) 880-8005
**U.S. News ranking:** Reg. Coll. (S), No. 13
**Website:** www.lagrange.edu
**Admissions email:** admission@lagrange.edu
**Private;** founded 1831
**Affiliation:** United Methodist
**Freshman admissions:** selective; 2013-2014: 1,664 applied, 966 accepted. Either SAT or ACT required. SAT 25/75 percentile: 910-1090. High school rank: 16% in top tenth, 36% in top quarter, 69% in top half
**Early decision deadline:** N/A, notification date: N/A
**Early action deadline:** N/A, notification date: N/A
**Application deadline (fall):** rolling
**Undergraduate student body:** 786 full time, 70 part time; 46% male, 54% female; 1% American Indian, 1% Asian, 23% black, 2% Hispanic, 2% multiracial, 0% Pacific Islander, 70% white, 1% international; 85% from in state; 56% live on campus; 22% of students in fraternities, 28% in sororities

**Most popular majors:** 10% Biology/Biological Sciences, General, 8% Business Administration and Management, General, 9% Psychology, General, 19% Registered Nursing/Registered Nurse, 8% Visual and Performing Arts, General
**Expenses:** 2014-2015: $26,590; room/board: $11,050
**Financial aid:** (706) 880-8229; 87% of undergrads determined to have financial need; average aid package $23,456

## Life University

Marietta GA
(770) 426-2884
**U.S. News ranking:** Nat. Lib. Arts, second tier
**Website:** www.life.edu
**Admissions email:** admissions@life.edu
**Private;** founded 1974
**Freshman admissions:** selective; 2013-2014: 269 applied, 110 accepted. Either SAT or ACT required. Average composite ACT score: 19. High school rank: N/A
**Early decision deadline:** N/A, notification date: N/A
**Early action deadline:** N/A, notification date: N/A
**Application deadline (fall):** 9/1
**Undergraduate student body:** 556 full time, 255 part time; 52% male, 48% female; 1% American Indian, 2% Asian, 25% black, 8% Hispanic, 0% multiracial, 0% Pacific Islander, 33% white, 3% international
**Most popular majors:** 28% Biology/Biological Sciences, General, 11% Business Administration and Management, General, 9% Dietetics/Dietitian, 19% Kinesiology and Exercise Science, 11% Psychology, General
**Expenses:** 2013-2014: $9,747; room/board: N/A
**Financial aid:** (770) 426-2901; 82% of undergrads determined to have financial need; average aid package $10,600

## Mercer University

Macon GA
(478) 301-2650
**U.S. News ranking:** Reg. U. (S), No. 8
**Website:** www.mercer.edu
**Admissions email:** admissions@mercer.edu
**Private;** founded 1833
**Freshman admissions:** more selective; 2013-2014: 3,864 applied, 2,666 accepted. Either SAT or ACT required. SAT 25/75 percentile: 1080-1270. High school rank: 41% in top tenth, 72% in top quarter, 92% in top half
**Early decision deadline:** N/A, notification date: N/A
**Early action deadline:** 11/1, notification date: 11/15
**Application deadline (fall):** 7/1
**Undergraduate student body:** 3,659 full time, 760 part time; 37% male, 63% female; 0% American Indian, 5% Asian, 33% black, 4% Hispanic, 2% multiracial, 0% Pacific Islander, 47% white, 3% international; 83% from in state; 72% live on campus; 22% of students in fraternities, 24% in sororities

**Most popular majors:** 12% Biological and Biomedical Sciences, 18% Business, Management, Marketing, and Related Support Services, 10% Engineering, 10% Psychology, 9% Social Sciences
**Expenses:** 2014-2015: $33,780; room/board: $11,271
**Financial aid:** (478) 301-2670; 73% of undergrads determined to have financial need; average aid package $32,951

## Middle Georgia State College[1]

Macon GA
(800) 272-7619
**U.S. News ranking:** Reg. Coll. (S), second tier
**Website:** www.mga.edu/
**Admissions email:** N/A
**Public**
**Application deadline (fall):** rolling
**Undergraduate student body:** N/A full time, N/A part time
**Expenses:** 2013-2014: $3,326 in state, $9,613 out of state; room/board: $8,270
**Financial aid:** (800) 272-7619

## Morehouse College

Atlanta GA
(404) 215-2632
**U.S. News ranking:** Nat. Lib. Arts, No. 133
**Website:** www.morehouse.edu
**Admissions email:** admissions@morehouse.edu
**Private;** founded 1867
**Freshman admissions:** selective; 2013-2014: 2,689 applied, 1,797 accepted. Either SAT or ACT required. SAT 25/75 percentile: 900-1110. High school rank: 21% in top tenth, 41% in top quarter, 73% in top half
**Early decision deadline:** 11/1, notification date: 12/15
**Early action deadline:** 11/1, notification date: 12/15
**Application deadline (fall):** 2/15
**Undergraduate student body:** 2,017 full time, 172 part time; 100% male, 0% female; 0% American Indian, 0% Asian, 95% black, 0% Hispanic, 0% multiracial, 0% Pacific Islander, 0% white, 2% international; 32% from in state; 66% live on campus; 19% of students in fraternities, N/A in sororities
**Most popular majors:** 9% Biology/Biological Sciences, General, 23% Business Administration and Management, General, 8% Kinesiology and Exercise Science, 11% Political Science and Government, General, 7% Psychology, General
**Expenses:** 2014-2015: $26,090; room/board: $13,322
**Financial aid:** (404) 681-2800; 84% of undergrads determined to have financial need; average aid package $19,258

## Oglethorpe University

Atlanta GA
(404) 364-8307
**U.S. News ranking:** Nat. Lib. Arts, No. 148
**Website:** www.oglethorpe.edu
**Admissions email:** admission@oglethorpe.edu
**Private;** founded 1835

**Freshman admissions:** selective; 2013-2014: 4,403 applied, 2,455 accepted. Either SAT or ACT required. SAT 25/75 percentile: 1030-1240. High school rank: 20% in top tenth, 55% in top quarter, 86% in top half
**Early decision deadline:** N/A, notification date: N/A
**Early action deadline:** 11/15, notification date: 12/5
**Application deadline (fall):** rolling
**Undergraduate student body:** 992 full time, 81 part time; 43% male, 57% female; 0% American Indian, 4% Asian, 18% black, 10% Hispanic, 2% multiracial, 0% Pacific Islander, 35% white, 5% international; 69% from in state; 58% live on campus; 12% of students in fraternities, 13% in sororities
**Most popular majors:** 18% Business, Management, Marketing, and Related Support Services, 26% English Language and Literature/Letters, 14% Social Sciences, 11% Visual and Performing Arts
**Expenses:** 2014-2015: $32,500; room/board: $11,700
**Financial aid:** (404) 364-8356; 71% of undergrads determined to have financial need; average aid package $25,722

## Paine College

Augusta GA
(706) 821-8320
**U.S. News ranking:** Reg. Coll. (S), second tier
**Website:** www.paine.edu
**Admissions email:** admissions@paine.edu
**Private;** founded 1882
**Affiliation:** Christian Methodist Episcopal and United Methodist Churches
**Freshman admissions:** less selective; 2013-2014: 2,771 applied, 1,213 accepted. Either SAT or ACT required. ACT 25/75 percentile: 14-18. High school rank: 5% in top tenth, 15% in top quarter, 42% in top half
**Early decision deadline:** N/A, notification date: N/A
**Early action deadline:** N/A, notification date: N/A
**Application deadline (fall):** 7/15
**Undergraduate student body:** 838 full time, 86 part time; 51% male, 49% female; 0% American Indian, 0% Asian, 91% black, 2% Hispanic, 1% multiracial, 0% Pacific Islander, 2% white, 1% international; 71% from in state; 53% live on campus; 9% of students in fraternities, 3% in sororities
**Most popular majors:** 23% Business Administration and Management, General, 10% Communication, General, 8% History, General, 11% Psychology, General, 18% Sociology
**Expenses:** 2013-2014: $13,332; room/board: $6,494
**Financial aid:** (706) 821-8262

## Piedmont College

Demorest GA
(800) 277-7020
**U.S. News ranking:** Reg. U. (S), No. 70
**Website:** www.piedmont.edu
**Admissions email:** ugrad@piedmont.edu
**Private;** founded 1897

**Affiliation:** Nat. Assoc. of Congreg. Christ. Churches & United Church of Christ
**Freshman admissions:** selective; 2013-2014: 920 applied, 553 accepted. Either SAT or ACT required. SAT 25/75 percentile: 920-1150. High school rank: 22% in top tenth, 47% in top quarter, 83% in top half
**Early decision deadline:** N/A, notification date: N/A
**Early action deadline:** N/A, notification date: N/A
**Application deadline (fall):** 7/1
**Undergraduate student body:** 1,131 full time, 150 part time; 35% male, 65% female; 1% American Indian, 1% Asian, 9% black, 3% Hispanic, 2% multiracial, 0% Pacific Islander, 78% white, 0% international; 92% from in state; 45% live on campus; 0% of students in fraternities, 0% in sororities
**Most popular majors:** 21% Business, Management, Marketing, and Related Support Services, 24% Education, General, 15% Health Professions and Related Programs, 22% Social Sciences, 7% Visual and Performing Arts
**Expenses:** 2014-2015: $21,350; room/board: $8,786
**Financial aid:** (706) 776-0114; 84% of undergrads determined to have financial need; average aid package $17,457

## Point University

West Point GA
(706) 385-1202
**U.S. News ranking:** Reg. Coll. (S), No. 74
**Website:** www.point.edu
**Admissions email:** admissions@point.edu
**Private;** founded 1937
**Affiliation:** Christian Churches/Churches of Christ
**Freshman admissions:** selective; 2013-2014: 934 applied, 500 accepted. Either SAT or ACT required. ACT 25/75 percentile: 18-22. High school rank: 12% in top tenth, 34% in top quarter, 66% in top half
**Early decision deadline:** N/A, notification date: N/A
**Early action deadline:** N/A, notification date: N/A
**Application deadline (fall):** 8/5
**Undergraduate student body:** 1,293 full time, 146 part time; 44% male, 56% female; 0% American Indian, 0% Asian, 41% black, 4% Hispanic, 3% multiracial, 0% Pacific Islander, 36% white, 1% international; 74% from in state; 77% live on campus; N/A of students in fraternities, N/A in sororities
**Most popular majors:** 5% Biological and Biomedical Sciences, 15% Business, Management, Marketing, and Related Support Services, 10% Education, 25% Philosophy and Religious Studies, 35% Social Sciences
**Expenses:** 2014-2015: $17,650; room/board: $6,350
**Financial aid:** (800) 766-1222; 79% of undergrads determined to have financial need; average aid package $20,000

## Reinhardt University

Waleska GA
(770) 720-5526
**U.S. News ranking:** Reg. Coll. (S),
No. 64
**Website:** www.reinhardt.edu/
**Admissions email:** admissions@
reinhardt.edu
**Private**
**Affiliation:** United Methodist
**Freshman admissions:** less
selective; 2013-2014: 1,731
applied, 1,032 accepted. Either
SAT or ACT required. SAT 25/75
percentile: 860-1120. High
school rank: 8% in top tenth, 30%
in top quarter, 61% in top half
**Early decision deadline:** N/A,
notification date: N/A
**Early action deadline:** N/A,
notification date: N/A
**Application deadline (fall):** 8/15
**Undergraduate student body:** 1,148
full time, 76 part time; 50%
male, 50% female; N/A American
Indian, N/A Asian, N/A black, N/A
Hispanic, N/A multiracial, N/A
Pacific Islander, N/A white, N/A
international
**Most popular majors:** 11%
Business/Commerce, General,
18% Elementary Education and
Teaching, 8% Music Teacher
Education, 8% Music, General,
19% Organizational Leadership
**Expenses:** 2014-2015: $19,166;
room/board: $7,276
**Financial aid:** (770) 720-5667;
80% of undergrads determined to
have financial need; average aid
package $13,546

## Savannah College of Art and Design

Savannah GA
(912) 525-5100
**U.S. News ranking:** Arts, unranked
**Website:** www.scad.edu
**Admissions email:** admission@
scad.edu
**Private;** founded 1978
**Freshman admissions:** N/A; 2013-
2014: 8,626 applied, 5,611
accepted. Either SAT or ACT
required. SAT 25/75 percentile:
N/A. High school rank: 16% in top
tenth, 42% in top quarter, 76%
in top half
**Early decision deadline:** N/A,
notification date: N/A
**Early action deadline:** N/A,
notification date: N/A
**Application deadline (fall):** rolling
**Undergraduate student body:** 7,739
full time, 1,593 part time; 36%
male, 64% female; 1% American
Indian, 7% Asian, 10% black,
8% Hispanic, 0% multiracial,
0% Pacific Islander, 54% white,
12% international; 23% from in
state; 41% live on campus; N/A
of students in fraternities, N/A in
sororities
**Most popular majors:** 10%
Animation, Interactive Technology,
Video Graphics and Special
Effects, 7% Cinematography
and Film/Video Production, 6%
Fashion/Apparel Design, 9%
Graphic Design, 12% Illustration
**Expenses:** 2014-2015: $34,295;
room/board: $13,710
**Financial aid:** (912) 525-6104;
56% of undergrads determined to
have financial need; average aid
package $26,987

## Savannah State University

Savannah GA
(912) 356-2181
**U.S. News ranking:** Nat. Lib. Arts,
second tier
**Website:** www.savannahstate.edu
**Admissions email:** admissions@
savannahstate.edu
**Public;** founded 1890
**Freshman admissions:** less
selective; 2013-2014: 2,786
applied, 2,309 accepted. Either
SAT or ACT required. SAT 25/75
percentile: 770-910. High school
rank: N/A
**Early decision deadline:** N/A,
notification date: N/A
**Early action deadline:** N/A,
notification date: N/A
**Application deadline (fall):** 8/1
**Undergraduate student body:** 4,098
full time, 504 part time; 45%
male, 55% female; 0% American
Indian, 0% Asian, 89% black,
2% Hispanic, 3% multiracial,
0% Pacific Islander, 4% white,
0% international; 92% from in
state; 55% live on campus; N/A
of students in fraternities, N/A in
sororities
**Most popular majors:** 7% Biological
and Biomedical Sciences,
9% Business, Management,
Marketing, and Related Support
Services, 7% Homeland Security,
Law Enforcement, Firefighting
and Related Protective Services,
6% Psychology, 7% Public
Administration and Social Service
Professions
**Expenses:** 2013-2014: $5,415 in
state, $15,176 out of state; room/
board: $7,154
**Financial aid:** (912) 356-2253

## Shorter University[1]

Rome GA
(800) 868-6980
**U.S. News ranking:** Nat. Lib. Arts,
second tier
**Website:** www.shorter.edu
**Admissions email:** admissions@
shorter.edu
**Private**
**Application deadline (fall):** N/A
**Undergraduate student body:** N/A
full time, N/A part time
**Expenses:** 2013-2014: $19,670;
room/board: $10,200
**Financial aid:** (706) 233-7227

## Southern Polytechnic State University

Marietta GA
(678) 915-4188
**U.S. News ranking:** Reg. U. (S),
No. 85
**Website:** www.spsu.edu/
**Admissions email:**
admiss@spsu.edu
**Public;** founded 1948
**Freshman admissions:** selective;
2013-2014: N/A applied, N/A
accepted. Either SAT or ACT
required. ACT 25/75 percentile:
21-26. High school rank: N/A
**Early decision deadline:** N/A,
notification date: N/A
**Early action deadline:** N/A,
notification date: N/A
**Application deadline (fall):** 7/1
**Undergraduate student body:** 4,142
full time, 1,590 part time; 81%
male, 19% female; 0% American
Indian, 7% Asian, 18% black,
8% Hispanic, 4% multiracial, 0%
Pacific Islander, 57% white, 3%
international

**Most popular majors:** Information
not available
**Expenses:** 2013-2014: $6,810 in
state, $20,594 out of state; room/
board: $7,650
**Financial aid:** (678) 915-7290

## South University[1]

Savannah GA
(912) 201-8000
**U.S. News ranking:** Reg. U. (S),
second tier
**Website:** www.southuniversity.edu
**Admissions email:** cshall@
southuniversity.edu
**Private**
**Application deadline (fall):** N/A
**Undergraduate student body:** N/A
full time, N/A part time
**Expenses:** 2013-2014: $16,360;
room/board: $9,105
**Financial aid:** (912) 201-8000

## Spelman College

Atlanta GA
(800) 982-2411
**U.S. News ranking:** Nat. Lib. Arts,
No. 81
**Website:** www.spelman.edu
**Admissions email:** admiss@
spelman.edu
**Private;** founded 1881
**Freshman admissions:** selective;
2013-2014: 5,701 applied,
2,325 accepted. Either SAT
or ACT required. SAT 25/75
percentile: 850-1215. High school
rank: 31% in top tenth, 66% in
top quarter, 90% in top half
**Early decision deadline:** 11/1,
notification date: 12/15
**Early action deadline:** 11/15,
notification date: 12/31
**Application deadline (fall):** 2/1
**Undergraduate student body:** 2,061
full time, 68 part time; 0% male,
100% female; 0% American
Indian, 0% Asian, 84% black,
0% Hispanic, 3% multiracial,
0% Pacific Islander, 0% white,
1% international; 27% from in
state; 71% live on campus; 0%
of students in fraternities, 10%
in sororities
**Most popular majors:** 13% Biology/
Biological Sciences, General,
6% Economics, General, 9%
English Language and Literature,
General, 12% Political Science
and Government, General, 24%
Psychology, General
**Expenses:** 2014-2015: $25,496;
room/board: $11,945
**Financial aid:** (404) 270-5212;
84% of undergrads determined to
have financial need; average aid
package $18,184

## Thomas University

Thomasville GA
(229) 227-6934
**U.S. News ranking:** Reg. Coll. (S),
second tier
**Website:** www.thomasu.edu
**Admissions email:** rgagliano@
thomasu.edu
**Private;** founded 1950
**Freshman admissions:** less
selective; 2013-2014: 153
applied, 105 accepted. Neither
SAT nor ACT required. SAT 25/75
percentile: 810-1060. High
school rank: N/A
**Early decision deadline:** N/A,
notification date: N/A
**Early action deadline:** N/A,
notification date: N/A
**Application deadline (fall):** rolling

**Undergraduate student body:** 506
full time, 380 part time; 46%
male, 54% female; 0% American
Indian, 1% Asian, 25% black,
5% Hispanic, 0% multiracial, 0%
Pacific Islander, 52% white, 4%
international
**Most popular majors:** 14%
Business Administration and
Management, General, 15%
Criminal Justice/Law Enforcement
Administration, 21% Registered
Nursing, Nursing Administration,
Nursing Research and Clinical
Nursing, Other, 10% Social Work,
12% Vocational Rehabilitation
Counseling/Counselor
**Expenses:** 2014-2015: $15,750;
room/board: $5,050
**Financial aid:** (229) 227-6925

## Toccoa Falls College

Toccoa Falls GA
(888) 785-5624
**U.S. News ranking:** Reg. Coll. (S),
No. 35
**Website:** www.tfc.edu
**Admissions email:** admissions@
tfc.edu
**Private;** founded 1907
**Affiliation:** Christian and
Missionary Alliance
**Freshman admissions:** selective;
2013-2014: 1,128 applied, 609
accepted. Neither SAT nor ACT
required. SAT 25/75 percentile:
880-1130. High school rank:
18% in top tenth, 44% in top
quarter, 75% in top half
**Early decision deadline:** N/A,
notification date: N/A
**Early action deadline:** N/A,
notification date: N/A
**Application deadline (fall):** rolling
**Undergraduate student body:** 777
full time, 93 part time; 47%
male, 53% female; 1% American
Indian, 8% Asian, 6% black,
2% Hispanic, 0% multiracial,
0% Pacific Islander, 81% white,
1% international; 61% from in
state; 69% live on campus; 0%
of students in fraternities, 0% in
sororities
**Most popular majors:** 7% Bible/
Biblical Studies, 6% Business
Administration and Management,
General, 21% Counseling
Psychology, 14% Missions/
Missionary Studies and Missiology,
6% Youth Ministry
**Expenses:** 2014-2015: $19,700;
room/board: $7,020
**Financial aid:** (706) 886-6831;
88% of undergrads determined to
have financial need; average aid
package $15,725

## Truett McConnell College

Cleveland GA
(706) 865-2134
**U.S. News ranking:** Reg. Coll. (S),
second tier
**Website:** www.truett.edu
**Admissions email:** admissions@
truett.edu
**Private;** founded 1946
**Affiliation:** Southern Baptist
**Freshman admissions:** less
selective; 2013-2014: 470
applied, 379 accepted. Either
SAT or ACT required. SAT 25/75
percentile: 840-1050. High school
rank: 11% in top tenth, 32% in
top quarter, 62% in top half
**Early decision deadline:** N/A,
notification date: N/A

**Early action deadline:** N/A,
notification date: N/A
**Application deadline (fall):** 8/1
**Undergraduate student body:** 691
full time, 915 part time; 43%
male, 57% female; 0% American
Indian, 0% Asian, 7% black,
4% Hispanic, 0% multiracial,
0% Pacific Islander, 82% white,
3% international; 93% from in
state; 68% live on campus; N/A
of students in fraternities, N/A in
sororities
**Most popular majors:** 17%
Business, Management,
Marketing, and Related Support
Services, 16% Education, 29%
Philosophy and Religious Studies,
9% Psychology, 7% Visual and
Performing Arts
**Expenses:** 2014-2015: $17,300;
room/board: $6,820
**Financial aid:** (800) 226-8621;
84% of undergrads determined to
have financial need; average aid
package $13,444

## University of Georgia

Athens GA
(706) 542-8776
**U.S. News ranking:** Nat. U.,
No. 62
**Website:** www.admissions.uga.edu
**Admissions email:** adm-info@
uga.edu
**Public;** founded 1785
**Freshman admissions:** more
selective; 2013-2014: 20,045
applied, 10,962 accepted. Either
SAT or ACT required. SAT 25/75
percentile: 1150-1330. High
school rank: 53% in top tenth,
91% in top quarter, 99% in
top half
**Early decision deadline:** N/A,
notification date: N/A
**Early action deadline:** 10/15,
notification date: 12/1
**Application deadline (fall):** 1/15
**Undergraduate student body:**
24,746 full time, 1,532 part
time; 43% male, 57% female;
0% American Indian, 9% Asian,
7% black, 5% Hispanic, 3%
multiracial, 0% Pacific Islander,
73% white, 1% international;
92% from in state; 28% live
on campus; 22% of students in
fraternities, 29% in sororities
**Most popular majors:** 6% Biology/
Biological Sciences, General,
5% Finance, General, 3%
International Relations and
Affairs, 4% Marketing/Marketing
Management, General, 7%
Psychology, General
**Expenses:** 2014-2015: $10,836
in state, $29,046 out of state;
room/board: $9,246
**Financial aid:** (706) 542-6147;
40% of undergrads determined to
have financial need; average aid
package $11,169

## University of North Georgia

Dahlonega GA
(706) 864-1800
**U.S. News ranking:** Reg. U. (S),
No. 60
**Website:** ung.edu/
**Admissions email:**
bacheloradmissions@ung.edu
**Public;** founded 1873
**Freshman admissions:** more
selective; 2013-2014: 3,711
applied, 2,236 accepted. Either

SAT or ACT required. SAT 25/75 percentile: 1010-1190. High school rank: 28% in top tenth, 70% in top quarter, 97% in top half
**Early decision deadline:** N/A, notification date: N/A
**Early action deadline:** N/A, notification date: N/A
**Application deadline (fall):** 7/1
**Undergraduate student body:** 10,022 full time, 4,829 part time; 44% male, 56% female; 0% American Indian, 3% Asian, 4% black, 9% Hispanic, 1% multiracial, 0% Pacific Islander, 62% white, 1% international; 97% from in state; 17% live on campus; 2% of students in fraternities, 3% in sororities
**Most popular majors:** 7% Business Administration and Management, General, 7% Criminal Justice/Safety Studies, 8% Early Childhood Education and Teaching, 6% Elementary Education and Teaching, 7% Special Education and Teaching, General
**Expenses:** 2014-2015: $6,816 in state, $19,712 out of state; room/board: $9,162
**Financial aid:** (706) 864-1412; 61% of undergrads determined to have financial need; average aid package $12,752

## University of West Georgia
Carrollton GA
(678) 839-5600
**U.S. News ranking:** Reg. U. (S), No. 92
**Website:** www.westga.edu
**Admissions email:** admiss@westga.edu
**Public;** founded 1906
**Freshman admissions:** less selective; 2013-2014: 7,266 applied, 3,913 accepted. Either SAT or ACT required. SAT 25/75 percentile: 870-1030. High school rank: N/A
**Early decision deadline:** N/A, notification date: N/A
**Early action deadline:** N/A, notification date: N/A
**Application deadline (fall):** 6/1
**Undergraduate student body:** 8,369 full time, 1,590 part time; 37% male, 63% female; 0% American Indian, 1% Asian, 34% black, 4% Hispanic, 3% multiracial, 0% Pacific Islander, 53% white, 1% international; 97% from in state; 31% live on campus; 3% of students in fraternities, 4% in sororities
**Most popular majors:** 21% Business, Management, Marketing, and Related Support Services, 16% Education, 15% Health Professions and Related Programs, 6% Psychology, 14% Social Sciences
**Expenses:** 2014-2015: $6,956 in state, $19,852 out of state; room/board: $8,532
**Financial aid:** (678) 839-6421; 77% of undergrads determined to have financial need; average aid package $7,209

## Valdosta State University
Valdosta GA
(229) 333-5791
**U.S. News ranking:** Reg. U. (S), No. 75
**Website:** www.valdosta.edu
**Admissions email:** admissions@valdosta.edu
**Public;** founded 1906
**Freshman admissions:** selective; 2013-2014: 5,701 applied, 3,148 accepted. Either SAT or ACT required. SAT 25/75 percentile: 950-1120. High school rank: N/A
**Early decision deadline:** N/A, notification date: N/A
**Early action deadline:** N/A, notification date: N/A
**Application deadline (fall):** 6/15
**Undergraduate student body:** 8,277 full time, 1,441 part time; 41% male, 59% female; 0% American Indian, 1% Asian, 36% black, 4% Hispanic, 3% multiracial, 0% Pacific Islander, 52% white, 2% international; 95% from in state; 33% live on campus; 4% of students in fraternities, 3% in sororities
**Most popular majors:** 21% Business, Management, Marketing, and Related Support Services, 15% Education, 8% English Language and Literature/Letters, 10% Health Professions and Related Programs, 6% Homeland Security, Law Enforcement, Firefighting and Related Protective Services
**Expenses:** 2014-2015: $7,162 in state, $20,058 out of state; room/board: $7,992
**Financial aid:** (229) 333-5935; 78% of undergrads determined to have financial need; average aid package $13,406

## Wesleyan College
Macon GA
(800) 447-6610
**U.S. News ranking:** Nat. Lib. Arts, No. 133
**Website:** www.wesleyancollege.edu
**Admissions email:** admissions@wesleyancollege.edu
**Private;** founded 1836
**Affiliation:** United Methodist
**Freshman admissions:** selective; 2013-2014: 779 applied, 338 accepted. Either SAT or ACT required. SAT 25/75 percentile: 880-1130. High school rank: N/A
**Early decision deadline:** 11/15, notification date: 12/15
**Early action deadline:** 1/15, notification date: 3/15
**Application deadline (fall):** rolling
**Undergraduate student body:** 469 full time, 179 part time; 0% male, 100% female; 0% American Indian, 1% Asian, 29% black, 4% Hispanic, 3% multiracial, 0% Pacific Islander, 41% white, 21% international; 92% from in state; 85% live on campus; N/A of students in fraternities, N/A in sororities
**Most popular majors:** 9% Biology/Biological Sciences, General, 24% Business Administration, Management and Operations, Other, 8% Communication and Media Studies, 9% Psychology, General, 8% Social Sciences, General
**Expenses:** 2014-2015: $19,900; room/board: $8,800

## Brigham Young University–Hawaii[1]
Laie Oahu HI
(808) 293-3738
**U.S. News ranking:** Reg. Coll. (W), No. 16
**Website:** www.byuh.edu
**Admissions email:** admissions@byuh.edu
**Private**
**Application deadline (fall):** N/A
**Undergraduate student body:** N/A full time, N/A part time
**Expenses:** 2013-2014: $4,770; room/board: $5,240
**Financial aid:** (808) 293-3530

## Chaminade University of Honolulu
Honolulu HI
(808) 735-4735
**U.S. News ranking:** Reg. U. (W), second tier
**Website:** www.chaminade.edu
**Admissions email:** admissions@chaminade.edu
**Private;** founded 1955
**Affiliation:** Roman Catholic
**Freshman admissions:** less selective; 2013-2014: 914 applied, 764 accepted. Either SAT or ACT required. SAT 25/75 percentile: 870-1060. High school rank: 3% in top tenth, 6% in top quarter, 23% in top half
**Early decision deadline:** N/A, notification date: N/A
**Early action deadline:** N/A, notification date: N/A
**Application deadline (fall):** rolling
**Undergraduate student body:** 1,286 full time, 40 part time; 32% male, 68% female; 0% American Indian, 38% Asian, 3% black, 5% Hispanic, 18% multiracial, 15% Pacific Islander, 16% white, 2% international; 76% from in state; 27% live on campus; 0% of students in fraternities, 0% in sororities
**Most popular majors:** 11% Business Administration and Management, General, 21% Criminal Justice/Safety Studies, 6% Elementary Education and Teaching, 10% History, Other, 16% Psychology, General
**Expenses:** 2014-2015: $21,084; room/board: $11,640
**Financial aid:** (808) 735-4780; 71% of undergrads determined to have financial need; average aid package $17,742

## Hawaii Pacific University
Honolulu HI
(808) 544-0238
**U.S. News ranking:** Reg. U. (W), No. 80
**Website:** www.hpu.edu
**Admissions email:** admissions@hpu.edu
**Private;** founded 1965
**Freshman admissions:** selective; 2013-2014: 4,206 applied, 2,697 accepted. Either SAT or ACT required. SAT 25/75

percentile: 870-1110. High school rank: 25% in top tenth, 53% in top quarter, 85% in top half
**Early decision deadline:** N/A, notification date: N/A
**Early action deadline:** N/A, notification date: N/A
**Application deadline (fall):** rolling
**Undergraduate student body:** 3,719 full time, 1,863 part time; 44% male, 56% female; 0% American Indian, 18% Asian, 5% black, 14% Hispanic, 19% multiracial, 3% Pacific Islander, 30% white, 7% international; 68% from in state; 4% live on campus; N/A of students in fraternities, N/A in sororities
**Most popular majors:** 23% Business, Management, Marketing, and Related Support Services, 8% Communication, Journalism, and Related Programs, 6% Computer and Information Sciences and Support Services, 23% Health Professions and Related Programs, 7% Psychology
**Expenses:** 2014-2015: $21,130; room/board: $13,330
**Financial aid:** (808) 544-0253; 53% of undergrads determined to have financial need; average aid package $16,906

## University of Hawaii–Hilo
Hilo HI
(800) 897-4456
**U.S. News ranking:** Nat. Lib. Arts, second tier
**Website:** www.uhh.hawaii.edu
**Admissions email:** uhhadm@hawaii.edu
**Public**
**Freshman admissions:** less selective; 2013-2014: 1,676 applied, 1,257 accepted. Either SAT or ACT required. SAT 25/75 percentile: 823-1050. High school rank: 18% in top tenth, 53% in top quarter, 85% in top half
**Early decision deadline:** N/A, notification date: N/A
**Early action deadline:** N/A, notification date: N/A
**Application deadline (fall):** 7/1
**Undergraduate student body:** 2,766 full time, 691 part time; 41% male, 59% female; 1% American Indian, 19% Asian, 1% black, 2% Hispanic, 14% multiracial, 32% Pacific Islander, 26% white, 5% international; 69% from in state; N/A live on campus; N/A of students in fraternities, N/A in sororities
**Most popular majors:** 10% Biological and Biomedical Sciences, 9% Business, Management, Marketing, and Related Support Services, 11% Health Professions and Related Programs, 12% Psychology, 15% Social Sciences
**Expenses:** 2014-2015: $7,036 in state, $19,036 out of state; room/board: $9,382
**Financial aid:** (808) 974-7323; 65% of undergrads determined to have financial need; average aid package $12,761

## University of Hawaii–Manoa
Honolulu HI
(808) 956-8975
**U.S. News ranking:** Nat. U., No. 168
**Website:** www.manoa.hawaii.edu/
**Admissions email:** ar-info@hawaii.edu
**Public;** founded 1907
**Freshman admissions:** selective; 2013-2014: 7,361 applied, 5,869 accepted. Either SAT or ACT required. SAT 25/75 percentile: 970-1200. High school rank: 27% in top tenth, 58% in top quarter, 89% in top half
**Early decision deadline:** N/A, notification date: N/A
**Early action deadline:** N/A, notification date: N/A
**Application deadline (fall):** 3/1
**Undergraduate student body:** 12,064 full time, 2,435 part time; 45% male, 55% female; 0% American Indian, 41% Asian, 1% black, 2% Hispanic, 15% multiracial, 20% white, 2% international; 73% from in state; 23% live on campus; 2% of students in fraternities, 1% in sororities
**Most popular majors:** 19% Business, Management, Marketing, and Related Support Services, 7% Education, 6% Engineering, 6% Psychology, 12% Social Sciences
**Expenses:** 2014-2015: $10,620 in state, $29,412 out of state; room/board: $13,284
**Financial aid:** (808) 956-7251; 55% of undergrads determined to have financial need; average aid package $11,649

## University of Hawaii–Maui College[1]
Kahului HI
(808) 479-6692
**U.S. News ranking:** Reg. Coll. (W), unranked
**Website:** maui.hawaii.edu/
**Admissions email:** N/A
**Public**
**Application deadline (fall):** N/A
**Undergraduate student body:** N/A full time, N/A part time
**Expenses:** 2013-2014: $2,670 in state, $7,422 out of state; room/board: N/A
**Financial aid:** (808) 984-3277

## University of Hawaii–West Oahu[1]
Kapolei HI
(808) 689-2900
**U.S. News ranking:** Reg. Coll. (W), unranked
**Website:** www.uhwo.hawaii.edu
**Admissions email:** uhwo.admissions@hawaii.edu
**Public;** founded 1976
**Application deadline (fall):** 8/1
**Undergraduate student body:** N/A full time, N/A part time
**Expenses:** 2013-2014: $6,296 in state, $17,816 out of state; room/board: N/A
**Financial aid:** (808) 689-2900

## IDAHO

### Boise State University
Boise ID
(208) 426-1156
**U.S. News ranking:** Reg. U. (W), No. 63
**Website:** www.BoiseState.edu
**Admissions email:** bsuinfo@boisestate.edu
**Public;** founded 1932
**Freshman admissions:** selective; 2013-2014: 7,822 applied, 6,078 accepted. Either SAT or ACT required. SAT 25/75 percentile: 920-1150. High school rank: 14% in top tenth, 38% in top quarter, 74% in top half
**Early decision deadline:** N/A, notification date: N/A
**Early action deadline:** N/A, notification date: N/A
**Application deadline (fall):** 5/15
**Undergraduate student body:** 12,452 full time, 6,574 part time; 46% male, 54% female; 1% American Indian, 2% Asian, 2% black, 9% Hispanic, 3% multiracial, 0% Pacific Islander, 76% white, 4% international; 80% from in state; 6% live on campus; 2% of students in fraternities, 2% in sororities
**Most popular majors:** 5% Accounting, 5% Business/Commerce, General, 5% Psychology, General, 9% Registered Nursing/Registered Nurse, 7% Speech Communication and Rhetoric
**Expenses:** 2014-2015: $6,292 in state, $18,892 out of state; room/board: $7,540
**Financial aid:** (208) 426-1540; 59% of undergrads determined to have financial need; average aid package $10,072

### Brigham Young University–Idaho[1]
Rexburg ID
(208) 496-1036
**U.S. News ranking:** Reg. Coll. (W), No. 11
**Website:** www.byui.edu
**Admissions email:** admissions@byui.edu
**Private**
**Application deadline (fall):** N/A
**Undergraduate student body:** N/A full time, N/A part time
**Expenses:** 2013-2014: $3,850; room/board: $4,000
**Financial aid:** (208) 496-1600

### College of Idaho
Caldwell ID
(800) 224-3246
**U.S. News ranking:** Nat. Lib. Arts, No. 159
**Website:** www.collegeofidaho.edu
**Admissions email:** admission@collegeofidaho.edu
**Private;** founded 1891
**Freshman admissions:** more selective; 2013-2014: 1,302 applied, 889 accepted. Either SAT or ACT required. ACT 25/75 percentile: 21-27. High school rank: 26% in top tenth, 55% in top quarter, 87% in top half
**Early decision deadline:** N/A, notification date: N/A
**Early action deadline:** 11/15, notification date: 12/15
**Application deadline (fall):** 7/15

**Undergraduate student body:** 1,055 full time, 40 part time; 45% male, 55% female; 1% American Indian, 3% Asian, 1% black, 15% Hispanic, 1% multiracial, 0% Pacific Islander, 62% white, 8% international; 83% from in state; 65% live on campus; 18% of students in fraternities, 17% in sororities
**Most popular majors:** 9% Biological and Biomedical Sciences, 13% Business, Management, Marketing, and Related Support Services, 12% Psychology, 9% Social Sciences, 9% Visual and Performing Arts
**Expenses:** 2014-2015: $24,625; room/board: $8,764
**Financial aid:** (208) 459-5307; 73% of undergrads determined to have financial need; average aid package $24,550

### Idaho State University[1]
Pocatello ID
(208) 282-2475
**U.S. News ranking:** Nat. U., unranked
**Website:** www.isu.edu
**Admissions email:** info@isu.edu
**Public**
**Application deadline (fall):** N/A
**Undergraduate student body:** N/A full time, N/A part time
**Expenses:** 2013-2014: $6,344 in state, $18,676 out of state; room/board: $8,280
**Financial aid:** (208) 282-2756

### Lewis-Clark State College
Lewiston ID
(208) 792-2210
**U.S. News ranking:** Reg. Coll. (W), No. 21
**Website:** www.lcsc.edu
**Admissions email:** admissions@lcsc.edu
**Public;** founded 1893
**Freshman admissions:** least selective; 2013-2014: 861 applied, 859 accepted. Neither SAT nor ACT required. SAT 25/75 percentile: 820-1030. High school rank: 3% in top tenth, 12% in top quarter, 44% in top half
**Early decision deadline:** N/A, notification date: N/A
**Early action deadline:** N/A, notification date: N/A
**Application deadline (fall):** 8/8
**Undergraduate student body:** 2,443 full time, 1,861 part time; 39% male, 61% female; 2% American Indian, 1% Asian, 1% black, 5% Hispanic, 3% multiracial, 0% Pacific Islander, 83% white, 3% international; 80% from in state; N/A live on campus; 0% of students in fraternities, 0% in sororities
**Most popular majors:** 29% Business, Management, Marketing, and Related Support Services, 10% Education, 18% Health Professions and Related Programs, 6% Parks, Recreation, Leisure, and Fitness Studies, 8% Public Administration and Social Service Professions
**Expenses:** 2014-2015: $5,900 in state, $16,418 out of state; room/board: $6,570
**Financial aid:** (208) 792-2224; 78% of undergrads determined to have financial need; average aid package $8,160

### Northwest Nazarene University
Nampa ID
(208) 467-8000
**U.S. News ranking:** Reg. U. (W), No. 43
**Website:** www.nnu.edu
**Admissions email:** Admissions@nnu.edu
**Private;** founded 1913
**Affiliation:** Church of the Nazarene
**Freshman admissions:** selective; 2013-2014: 1,227 applied, 357 accepted. Either SAT or ACT required. SAT 25/75 percentile: 920-1160. High school rank: 27% in top tenth, 57% in top quarter, 82% in top half
**Early decision deadline:** N/A, notification date: N/A
**Early action deadline:** 12/15, notification date: 1/15
**Application deadline (fall):** 8/15
**Undergraduate student body:** 1,136 full time, 352 part time; 44% male, 56% female; 0% American Indian, 2% Asian, 2% black, 8% Hispanic, 2% multiracial, 0% Pacific Islander, 73% white, 2% international; 57% from in state; 70% live on campus; N/A of students in fraternities, N/A in sororities
**Most popular majors:** 7% Biological and Biomedical Sciences, 21% Business, Management, Marketing, and Related Support Services, 13% Education, 15% Health Professions and Related Programs, 6% Liberal Arts and Sciences, General Studies and Humanities
**Expenses:** 2014-2015: $27,340; room/board: $6,400
**Financial aid:** (208) 467-8347; 83% of undergrads determined to have financial need; average aid package $18,967

### University of Idaho
Moscow ID
(888) 884-3246
**U.S. News ranking:** Nat. U., No. 166
**Website:** www.uidaho.edu/admissions
**Admissions email:** admissions@uidaho.edu
**Public;** founded 1889
**Freshman admissions:** selective; 2013-2014: 7,994 applied, 5,173 accepted. Either SAT or ACT required. SAT 25/75 percentile: 910-1170. High school rank: 16% in top tenth, 42% in top quarter, 73% in top half
**Early decision deadline:** N/A, notification date: N/A
**Early action deadline:** N/A, notification date: N/A
**Application deadline (fall):** 8/1
**Undergraduate student body:** 7,927 full time, 1,529 part time; 53% male, 47% female; 1% American Indian, 1% Asian, 1% black, 8% Hispanic, 3% multiracial, 0% Pacific Islander, 80% white, 3% international; 76% from in state; 19% live on campus; 20% of students in fraternities, 20% in sororities
**Most popular majors:** 3% Elementary Education and Teaching, 5% General Studies, 3% Human Resources Management/Personnel Administration, General, 9% Psychology, General, 3% Sociology

## ILLINOIS

### American Academy of Art[1]
Chicago IL
(312) 461-0600
**U.S. News ranking:** Arts, unranked
**Website:** www.aaart.edu
**Admissions email:** N/A
**For-profit**
**Application deadline (fall):** N/A
**Undergraduate student body:** N/A full time, N/A part time
**Expenses:** 2013-2014: $29,020; room/board: N/A
**Financial aid:** N/A

### American InterContinental University[1]
Hoffman Estates IL
(855) 377-1888
**U.S. News ranking:** Reg. U. (Mid. W), unranked
**Website:** www.aiuniv.edu
**Admissions email:** N/A
**For-profit**
**Application deadline (fall):** N/A
**Undergraduate student body:** N/A full time, N/A part time
**Expenses:** N/A
**Financial aid:** N/A

### Augustana College
Rock Island IL
(800) 798-8100
**U.S. News ranking:** Nat. Lib. Arts, No. 105
**Website:** www.augustana.edu
**Admissions email:** admissions@augustana.edu
**Private;** founded 1860
**Affiliation:** Evangelical Lutheran Church in America
**Freshman admissions:** selective; 2013-2014: 5,831 applied, 3,421 accepted. Neither SAT nor ACT required. ACT 25/75 percentile: 22-27. High school rank: 24% in top tenth, 51% in top quarter, 84% in top half
**Early decision deadline:** N/A, notification date: N/A
**Early action deadline:** N/A, notification date: N/A
**Application deadline (fall):** rolling
**Undergraduate student body:** 2,509 full time, 15 part time; 43% male, 57% female; 0% American Indian, 2% Asian, 4% black, 9% Hispanic, 3% multiracial, 0% Pacific Islander, 78% white, 2% international; 85% from in state; 68% live on campus; 23% of students in fraternities, 37% in sororities
**Most popular majors:** 20% Biological and Biomedical Sciences, 18% Business, Management, Marketing, and Related Support Services, 7% Education, 9% Psychology, 9% Social Sciences
**Expenses:** 2014-2015: $37,236; room/board: $9,435
**Financial aid:** (309) 794-7207; 78% of undergrads determined to have financial need; average aid package $26,018

**Expenses:** 2014-2015: $6,784 in state, $20,314 out of state; room/board: $8,022
**Financial aid:** (208) 885-6312; 66% of undergrads determined to have financial need; average aid package $13,202

### Aurora University[1]
Aurora IL
(800) 742-5281
**U.S. News ranking:** Reg. U. (Mid. W), second tier
**Website:** www.aurora.edu
**Admissions email:** admission@aurora.edu
**Private**
**Application deadline (fall):** N/A
**Undergraduate student body:** N/A full time, N/A part time
**Expenses:** 2013-2014: $20,720; room/board: $8,636
**Financial aid:** (630) 844-5533

### Benedictine University
Lisle IL
(630) 829-6300
**U.S. News ranking:** Nat. U., second tier
**Website:** www.ben.edu
**Admissions email:** admissions@ben.edu
**Private;** founded 1887
**Affiliation:** Roman Catholic
**Freshman admissions:** selective; 2013-2014: 2,108 applied, 1,465 accepted. Either SAT or ACT required. ACT 25/75 percentile: 20-26. High school rank: 21% in top tenth, 48% in top quarter, 79% in top half
**Early decision deadline:** N/A, notification date: N/A
**Early action deadline:** N/A, notification date: N/A
**Application deadline (fall):** rolling
**Undergraduate student body:** 2,431 full time, 529 part time; 42% male, 58% female; 0% American Indian, 18% Asian, 8% black, 10% Hispanic, 0% multiracial, 0% Pacific Islander, 44% white, 1% international; 92% from in state; 22% live on campus; N/A of students in fraternities, N/A in sororities
**Most popular majors:** 10% Biology/Biological Sciences, General, 7% Educational Leadership and Administration, General, 19% Health Services/Allied Health/Health Sciences, General, 39% Marketing/Marketing Management, General, 8% Psychology, General
**Expenses:** 2014-2015: $26,950; room/board: $8,280
**Financial aid:** (630) 829-6108; 78% of undergrads determined to have financial need; average aid package $18,064

### Blackburn College
Carlinville IL
(800) 233-3550
**U.S. News ranking:** Reg. Coll. (Mid. W), No. 35
**Website:** www.blackburn.edu
**Admissions email:** admit@mail.blackburn.edu
**Private;** founded 1837
**Affiliation:** Presbyterian
**Freshman admissions:** selective; 2013-2014: 528 applied, 359 accepted. Either SAT or ACT required. ACT 25/75 percentile: 19-26. High school rank: 15% in top tenth, 41% in top quarter, 72% in top half
**Early decision deadline:** N/A, notification date: N/A
**Early action deadline:** N/A, notification date: N/A
**Application deadline (fall):** rolling

**Undergraduate student body:** 523 full time, 20 part time; 42% male, 58% female; 1% American Indian, 0% Asian, 9% black, 1% Hispanic, 1% multiracial, 0% Pacific Islander, 87% white, 0% international; 89% from in state; 71% live on campus; 0% of students in fraternities, 0% in sororities
**Most popular majors:** 11% Biology/Biological Sciences, General, 9% Business Administration, Management and Operations, Other, 9% Criminal Justice/Safety Studies, 13% Psychology, General, 9% Sport and Fitness Administration/Management
**Expenses:** 2014-2015: $19,560; room/board: $6,750
**Financial aid:** (800) 233-3550; 82% of undergrads determined to have financial need; average aid package $16,445

## Bradley University
Peoria IL
(800) 447-6460
**U.S. News ranking:** Reg. U. (Mid. W), No. 4
**Website:** www.bradley.edu
**Admissions email:** admissions@bradley.edu
**Private;** founded 1897
**Freshman admissions:** more selective; 2013-2014: 8,969 applied, 6,004 accepted. Either SAT or ACT required. ACT 25/75 percentile: 23-28. High school rank: 30% in top tenth, 64% in top quarter, 91% in top half
**Early decision deadline:** N/A, notification date: N/A
**Early action deadline:** N/A, notification date: N/A
**Application deadline (fall):** rolling
**Undergraduate student body:** 4,620 full time, 235 part time; 48% male, 52% female; 1% American Indian, 4% Asian, 7% black, 6% Hispanic, 0% multiracial, 0% Pacific Islander, 74% white, 1% international; 87% from in state; 68% live on campus; 31% of students in fraternities, 31% in sororities
**Most popular majors:** 4% Civil Engineering, General, 5% Elementary Education and Teaching, 6% Mechanical Engineering, 6% Psychology, General, 6% Registered Nursing/Registered Nurse
**Expenses:** 2014-2015: $30,844; room/board: $9,420
**Financial aid:** (309) 677-3089; 75% of undergrads determined to have financial need; average aid package $19,802

## Chicago State University
Chicago IL
(773) 995-2513
**U.S. News ranking:** Reg. U. (Mid. W), second tier
**Website:** www.csu.edu
**Admissions email:** ug-admissions@csu.edu
**Public;** founded 1867
**Freshman admissions:** less selective; 2013-2014: 5,219 applied, 1,495 accepted. ACT required. ACT 25/75 percentile: 17-20. High school rank: N/A
**Early decision deadline:** N/A, notification date: N/A
**Early action deadline:** N/A, notification date: N/A

**Application deadline (fall):** rolling
**Undergraduate student body:** 2,852 full time, 1,488 part time; 29% male, 71% female; 0% American Indian, 1% Asian, 78% black, 6% Hispanic, 0% multiracial, 0% Pacific Islander, 2% white, 0% international
**Most popular majors:** 12% Business Administration and Management, General, 8% Criminal Justice/Safety Studies, 11% General Studies, 18% Liberal Arts and Sciences/Liberal Studies, 13% Psychology, General
**Expenses:** 2014-2015: $11,396 in state, $20,096 out of state; room/board: $8,724
**Financial aid:** (773) 995-2304; 97% of undergrads determined to have financial need; average aid package $11,693

## Columbia College Chicago[1]
Chicago IL
(312) 344-7130
**U.S. News ranking:** Reg. U. (Mid. W), second tier
**Website:** www.colum.edu
**Admissions email:** admissions@colum.edu
**Private**
**Application deadline (fall):** N/A
**Undergraduate student body:** N/A full time, N/A part time
**Expenses:** 2013-2014: $22,792; room/board: $12,375
**Financial aid:** (312) 344-7054

## Concordia University Chicago
River Forest IL
(877) 282-4422
**U.S. News ranking:** Reg. U. (Mid. W), No. 77
**Website:** www.cuchicago.edu/
**Admissions email:** admission@cuchicago.edu
**Private;** founded 1864
**Affiliation:** Lutheran
**Freshman admissions:** selective; 2013-2014: 3,692 applied, 2,009 accepted. Either SAT or ACT required. ACT 25/75 percentile: 20-24. High school rank: 9% in top tenth, 18% in top quarter, 82% in top half
**Early decision deadline:** N/A, notification date: N/A
**Early action deadline:** N/A, notification date: N/A
**Application deadline (fall):** rolling
**Undergraduate student body:** 1,489 full time, 115 part time; 40% male, 60% female; 0% American Indian, 2% Asian, 14% black, 23% Hispanic, 3% multiracial, 0% Pacific Islander, 56% white, 1% international; 74% from in state; 41% live on campus; 0% of students in fraternities, 0% in sororities
**Most popular majors:** 21% Business, Management, Marketing, and Related Support Services, 24% Education, 8% Parks, Recreation, Leisure, and Fitness Studies, 10% Psychology, 7% Social Sciences
**Expenses:** 2014-2015: $28,908; room/board: $8,992
**Financial aid:** (708) 209-3113; 86% of undergrads determined to have financial need; average aid package $19,291

## DePaul University
Chicago IL
(312) 362-8300
**U.S. News ranking:** Nat. U., No. 121
**Website:** www.depaul.edu
**Admissions email:** admission@depaul.edu
**Private;** founded 1898
**Affiliation:** Roman Catholic
**Freshman admissions:** more selective; 2013-2014: 19,957 applied, 11,948 accepted. Neither SAT nor ACT required. ACT 25/75 percentile: 23-28. High school rank: 25% in top tenth, 57% in top quarter, 89% in top half
**Early decision deadline:** N/A, notification date: N/A
**Early action deadline:** 11/15, notification date: 1/15
**Application deadline (fall):** 2/1
**Undergraduate student body:** 13,594 full time, 2,826 part time; 46% male, 54% female; 0% American Indian, 7% Asian, 8% black, 17% Hispanic, 4% multiracial, 0% Pacific Islander, 56% white, 3% international; 80% from in state; 16% live on campus; 6% of students in fraternities, 9% in sororities
**Most popular majors:** 28% Business/Commerce, General, 11% Liberal Arts and Sciences/Liberal Studies, 7% Psychology, General, 9% Social Sciences, General, 13% Speech Communication and Rhetoric
**Expenses:** 2014-2015: $35,071; room/board: $12,552
**Financial aid:** (312) 362-8091; 70% of undergrads determined to have financial need; average aid package $20,634

## DeVry University
Downers Grove IL
(866) 338-7940
**U.S. News ranking:** Reg. U. (Mid. W), second tier
**Website:** www.devry.edu
**Admissions email:** N/A
**For-profit;** founded 1931
**Freshman admissions:** less selective; 2013-2014: N/A applied, N/A accepted. Neither SAT nor ACT required. ACT 25/75 percentile: N/A. High school rank: N/A
**Early decision deadline:** N/A, notification date: N/A
**Early action deadline:** N/A, notification date: N/A
**Application deadline (fall):** rolling
**Undergraduate student body:** 19,414 full time, 29,368 part time; 55% male, 45% female; 1% American Indian, 4% Asian, 21% black, 16% Hispanic, 1% multiracial, 1% Pacific Islander, 39% white, 1% international
**Most popular majors:** 21% Business Administration and Management, General, 46% Business Administration, Management and Operations, Other, 10% Computer Systems Analysis/Analyst, 8% Computer Systems Networking and Telecommunications, 4% Electrical, Electronic and Communications Engineering Technology/Technician
**Expenses:** 2014-2015: $17,132; room/board: N/A
**Financial aid:** N/A

## Dominican University
River Forest IL
(708) 524-6800
**U.S. News ranking:** Reg. U. (Mid. W), No. 19
**Website:** public.dom.edu/
**Admissions email:** domadmis@dom.edu
**Private;** founded 1901
**Affiliation:** Roman Catholic
**Freshman admissions:** selective; 2013-2014: 3,502 applied, 2,100 accepted. Either SAT or ACT required. ACT 25/75 percentile: 20-24. High school rank: 22% in top tenth, 48% in top quarter, 85% in top half
**Early decision deadline:** N/A, notification date: N/A
**Early action deadline:** N/A, notification date: N/A
**Application deadline (fall):** 7/1
**Undergraduate student body:** 1,907 full time, 162 part time; 34% male, 66% female; 0% American Indian, 3% Asian, 7% black, 40% Hispanic, 1% multiracial, 0% Pacific Islander, 44% white, 3% international; 91% from in state; 29% live on campus; 0% of students in fraternities, 0% in sororities
**Most popular majors:** 23% Business, Management, Marketing, and Related Support Services, 14% Health Professions and Related Programs, 8% Multi/Interdisciplinary Studies, 12% Social Sciences, 8% Visual and Performing Arts
**Expenses:** 2014-2015: $29,770; room/board: $9,100
**Financial aid:** (708) 524-6809; 91% of undergrads determined to have financial need; average aid package $21,837

## Eastern Illinois University
Charleston IL
(877) 581-2348
**U.S. News ranking:** Reg. U. (Mid. W), No. 31
**Website:** www.eiu.edu
**Admissions email:** admissions@eiu.edu
**Public;** founded 1895
**Freshman admissions:** selective; 2013-2014: 7,881 applied, 4,879 accepted. Either SAT or ACT required. ACT 25/75 percentile: 19-24. High school rank: 10% in top tenth, 32% in top quarter, 67% in top half
**Early decision deadline:** N/A, notification date: N/A
**Early action deadline:** N/A, notification date: N/A
**Application deadline (fall):** 8/15
**Undergraduate student body:** 7,327 full time, 1,020 part time; 40% male, 60% female; 0% American Indian, 1% Asian, 18% black, 5% Hispanic, 2% multiracial, 0% Pacific Islander, 71% white, 1% international; 97% from in state; 37% live on campus; 21% of students in fraternities, 18% in sororities
**Most popular majors:** 12% Business, Management, Marketing, and Related Support Services, 23% Education, 8% Liberal Arts and Sciences, General Studies and Humanities, 9% Parks, Recreation, Leisure, and Fitness Studies, 6% Social Sciences

**Expenses:** 2014-2015: $11,108 in state, $28,088 out of state; room/board: $9,358
**Financial aid:** (217) 581-3713; 68% of undergrads determined to have financial need; average aid package $10,588

## East-West University[1]
Chicago IL
(312) 939-0111
**U.S. News ranking:** Nat. Lib. Arts, unranked
**Website:** www.eastwest.edu
**Admissions email:** seeyou@eastwest.edu
**Private;** founded 1980
**Application deadline (fall):** rolling
**Undergraduate student body:** N/A full time, N/A part time
**Expenses:** 2013-2014: $18,795; room/board: $8,541
**Financial aid:** (312) 939-0111

## Elmhurst College
Elmhurst IL
(630) 617-3400
**U.S. News ranking:** Reg. U. (Mid. W), No. 11
**Website:** www.elmhurst.edu
**Admissions email:** admit@elmhurst.edu
**Private;** founded 1871
**Affiliation:** United Church of Christ
**Freshman admissions:** selective; 2013-2014: 2,702 applied, 1,940 accepted. Either SAT or ACT required. ACT 25/75 percentile: 21-26. High school rank: 20% in top tenth, 47% in top quarter, 78% in top half
**Early decision deadline:** N/A, notification date: N/A
**Early action deadline:** N/A, notification date: N/A
**Application deadline (fall):** 7/15
**Undergraduate student body:** 2,736 full time, 164 part time; 40% male, 60% female; 0% American Indian, 5% Asian, 5% black, 13% Hispanic, 3% multiracial, 0% Pacific Islander, 73% white, 0% international; 90% from in state; 37% live on campus; 10% of students in fraternities, 16% in sororities
**Most popular majors:** 20% Business, Management, Marketing, and Related Support Services, 12% Education, 13% Health Professions and Related Programs, 9% Psychology, 9% Social Sciences
**Expenses:** 2014-2015: $33,950; room/board: $9,386
**Financial aid:** (630) 617-3075; 73% of undergrads determined to have financial need; average aid package $26,127

## Eureka College
Eureka IL
(309) 467-6350
**U.S. News ranking:** Reg. Coll. (Mid. W), No. 31
**Website:** www.eureka.edu
**Admissions email:** admissions@eureka.edu
**Private;** founded 1855
**Affiliation:** Christian Church (Disciples of Christ)
**Freshman admissions:** selective; 2013-2014: 884 applied, 586 accepted. Either SAT or ACT required. ACT 25/75 percentile: 19-25. High school rank: 17% in top tenth, 39% in top quarter, 68% in top half

Early decision deadline: N/A, notification date: N/A
Early action deadline: N/A, notification date: N/A
Application deadline (fall): 8/1
Undergraduate student body: 641 full time, 51 part time; 41% male, 59% female; 0% American Indian, 1% Asian, 4% black, 3% Hispanic, 2% multiracial, 0% Pacific Islander, 86% white, 0% international; 95% from in state; 52% live on campus; 23% of students in fraternities, 19% in sororities
Most popular majors: 19% Business Administration and Management, General, 7% Corrections and Criminal Justice, Other, 14% Elementary Education and Teaching, 8% History, Other, 9% Speech Communication and Rhetoric
Expenses: 2014-2015: $20,060; room/board: $8,500
Financial aid: (309) 467-6311; 79% of undergrads determined to have financial need; average aid package $13,993

## Governors State University[1]
University Park IL
(708) 534-4490
U.S. News ranking: Reg. U. (Mid. W), unranked
Website: www.govst.edu/
Admissions email: N/A
Public
Application deadline (fall): N/A
Undergraduate student body: N/A full time, N/A part time
Expenses: N/A
Financial aid: (708) 534-4480

## Greenville College
Greenville IL
(618) 664-7100
U.S. News ranking: Reg. Coll. (Mid. W), No. 33
Website: www.greenville.edu
Admissions email: admissions@greenville.edu
Private; founded 1892
Affiliation: Free Methodist
Freshman admissions: selective; 2013-2014: 1,851 applied, 1,132 accepted. Either SAT or ACT required. ACT 25/75 percentile: 18-25. High school rank: 14% in top tenth, 40% in top quarter, 79% in top half
Early decision deadline: N/A, notification date: N/A
Early action deadline: N/A, notification date: N/A
Application deadline (fall): rolling
Undergraduate student body: 1,090 full time, 39 part time; 52% male, 48% female; 0% American Indian, 1% Asian, 8% black, 4% Hispanic, 2% multiracial, 0% Pacific Islander, 76% white, 3% international; 64% from in state; 81% live on campus; 0% of students in fraternities, 0% in sororities
Most popular majors: 6% Biological and Biomedical Sciences, 26% Business, Management, Marketing, and Related Support Services, 5% Communication, Journalism, and Related Programs, 19% Education, 12% Visual and Performing Arts
Expenses: 2014-2015: $24,360; room/board: $8,044

Financial aid: (618) 664-7110; 86% of undergrads determined to have financial need; average aid package $19,350

## Harrington College of Design[1]
Chicago IL
(866) 590-4423
U.S. News ranking: Arts, unranked
Website: www.harrington.edu/
Admissions email: N/A
For-profit
Application deadline (fall): N/A
Undergraduate student body: N/A full time, N/A part time
Expenses: 2013-2014: $19,305; room/board: N/A
Financial aid: N/A

## Illinois College
Jacksonville IL
(217) 245-3030
U.S. News ranking: Nat. Lib. Arts, No. 155
Website: www.ic.edu
Admissions email: admissions@ic.edu
Private; founded 1829
Affiliation: Presbyterian Church (USA) and United Church of Christ
Freshman admissions: selective; 2013-2014: 2,560 applied, 1,569 accepted. Neither SAT nor ACT required. ACT 25/75 percentile: 19-25. High school rank: 22% in top tenth, 56% in top quarter, 88% in top half
Early decision deadline: N/A, notification date: N/A
Early action deadline: 12/15, notification date: 12/23
Application deadline (fall): rolling
Undergraduate student body: 981 full time, 29 part time; 50% male, 50% female; 0% American Indian, 1% Asian, 12% black, 7% Hispanic, 3% multiracial, 0% Pacific Islander, 73% white, 3% international; 87% from in state; 81% live on campus; 0% of students in fraternities, 0% in sororities
Most popular majors: 25% Biological and Biomedical Sciences, 10% English Language and Literature/Letters, 13% Multi/Interdisciplinary Studies, 9% Psychology
Expenses: 2014-2015: $29,210; room/board: $9,190
Financial aid: (217) 245-3035; 84% of undergrads determined to have financial need; average aid package $25,220

## Illinois Institute of Art at Chicago[1]
Chicago IL
(800) 351-3450
U.S. News ranking: Arts, unranked
Website: www.artinstitutes.edu/chicago/
Admissions email: N/A
For-profit
Application deadline (fall): N/A
Undergraduate student body: N/A full time, N/A part time
Expenses: 2013-2014: $17,488; room/board: $12,897
Financial aid: N/A

## Illinois Institute of Technology
Chicago IL
(800) 448-2329
U.S. News ranking: Nat. U., No. 116
Website: iit.edu/undergrad_admission/
Admissions email: admission@iit.edu
Private; founded 1890
Freshman admissions: more selective; 2013-2014: 2,840 applied, 1,618 accepted. Either SAT or ACT required. ACT 25/75 percentile: 25-30. High school rank: 45% in top tenth, 74% in top quarter, 96% in top half
Early decision deadline: N/A, notification date: N/A
Early action deadline: 12/1, notification date: N/A
Application deadline (fall): 8/1
Undergraduate student body: 2,712 full time, 214 part time; 70% male, 30% female; 0% American Indian, 11% Asian, 7% black, 15% Hispanic, 0% multiracial, 0% Pacific Islander, 37% white, 25% international; 86% from in state; 59% live on campus; 10% of students in fraternities, 14% in sororities
Most popular majors: 20% Architecture and Related Services, 4% Business, Management, Marketing, and Related Support Services, 12% Computer and Information Sciences and Support Services, 45% Engineering, 3% Mathematics and Statistics
Expenses: 2014-2015: $41,335; room/board: $10,900
Financial aid: (312) 567-7219; 63% of undergrads determined to have financial need; average aid package $33,658

## Illinois State University
Normal IL
(309) 438-2181
U.S. News ranking: Nat. U., No. 142
Website: www.ilstu.edu
Admissions email: admissions@ilstu.edu
Public; founded 1857
Freshman admissions: selective; 2013-2014: 15,354 applied, 10,582 accepted. Either SAT or ACT required. ACT 25/75 percentile: 22-26. High school rank: N/A
Early decision deadline: N/A, notification date: N/A
Early action deadline: N/A, notification date: N/A
Application deadline (fall): 5/1
Undergraduate student body: 16,683 full time, 1,066 part time; 45% male, 55% female; 0% American Indian, 2% Asian, 7% black, 8% Hispanic, 2% multiracial, 0% Pacific Islander, 80% white, 0% international; 97% from in state; 33% live on campus; 8% of students in fraternities, 11% in sororities
Most popular majors: 22% Business, Management, Marketing, and Related Support Services, 6% Communication, Journalism, and Related Programs, 17% Education, 6% Social Sciences, 6% Visual and Performing Arts
Expenses: 2014-2015: $12,830 in state, $20,420 out of state; room/board: $9,970

Financial aid: (309) 438-2231; 65% of undergrads determined to have financial need; average aid package $10,074

## Illinois Wesleyan University
Bloomington IL
(800) 332-2498
U.S. News ranking: Nat. Lib. Arts, No. 73
Website: www.iwu.edu
Admissions email: iwuadmit@iwu.edu
Private; founded 1850
Freshman admissions: more selective; 2013-2014: 3,556 applied, 2,076 accepted. Either SAT or ACT required. ACT 25/75 percentile: 25-30. High school rank: 45% in top tenth, 77% in top quarter, 96% in top half
Early decision deadline: N/A, notification date: N/A
Early action deadline: 11/15, notification date: 1/15
Application deadline (fall): rolling
Undergraduate student body: 2,001 full time, 8 part time; 44% male, 56% female; 0% American Indian, 5% Asian, 5% black, 6% Hispanic, 1% multiracial, 0% Pacific Islander, 74% white, 5% international; 88% from in state; 71% live on campus; 31% of students in fraternities, 33% in sororities
Most popular majors: 7% Accounting, 8% Biological and Biomedical Sciences, 14% Business/Commerce, General, 8% Psychology, General, 7% Registered Nursing/Registered Nurse
Expenses: 2014-2015: $40,844; room/board: $9,446
Financial aid: (309) 556-3096; 63% of undergrads determined to have financial need; average aid package $28,729

## Judson University
Elgin IL
(800) 879-5376
U.S. News ranking: Reg. Coll. (Mid. W), No. 36
Website: www.judsonu.edu
Admissions email: admissions@judsonu.edu
Private; founded 1913
Affiliation: American Baptist
Freshman admissions: selective; 2013-2014: 556 applied, 519 accepted. Either SAT or ACT required. ACT 25/75 percentile: 19-25. High school rank: 8% in top tenth, 29% in top quarter, 76% in top half
Early decision deadline: N/A, notification date: N/A
Early action deadline: N/A, notification date: N/A
Application deadline (fall): rolling
Undergraduate student body: 783 full time, 283 part time; 44% male, 56% female; 0% American Indian, 2% Asian, 6% black, 9% Hispanic, 2% multiracial, 0% Pacific Islander, 60% white, 4% international; 74% from in state; 65% live on campus; 0% of students in fraternities, 0% in sororities
Most popular majors: 13% Architecture and Related Services, 36% Business, Management, Marketing, and Related Support Services, 7% Communication,

Journalism, and Related Programs, 7% Education, 10% Public Administration and Social Service Professions
Expenses: 2013-2014: $27,530; room/board: $8,990
Financial aid: (847) 628-2532

## Kendall College[1]
Chicago IL
(877) 588-8860
U.S. News ranking: Reg. Coll. (Mid. W), second tier
Website: www.kendall.edu
Admissions email: admissions@kendall.edu
For-profit; founded 1934
Application deadline (fall): rolling
Undergraduate student body: N/A full time, N/A part time
Expenses: 2013-2014: $24,396; room/board: $11,700
Financial aid: (312) 752-2028

## Knox College
Galesburg IL
(800) 678-5669
U.S. News ranking: Nat. Lib. Arts, No. 81
Website: www.knox.edu
Admissions email: admission@knox.edu
Private; founded 1837
Freshman admissions: more selective; 2013-2014: 2,660 applied, 1,994 accepted. Neither SAT nor ACT required. ACT 25/75 percentile: 25-30. High school rank: 26% in top tenth, 59% in top quarter, 91% in top half
Early decision deadline: N/A, notification date: N/A
Early action deadline: 12/1, notification date: 12/31
Application deadline (fall): 2/1
Undergraduate student body: 1,399 full time, 25 part time; 43% male, 57% female; 0% American Indian, 5% Asian, 7% black, 10% Hispanic, 4% multiracial, 0% Pacific Islander, 58% white, 12% international; 58% from in state; 86% live on campus; 26% of students in fraternities, 16% in sororities
Most popular majors: 5% Biology/Biological Sciences, General, 10% Creative Writing, 6% Economics, General, 6% Psychology, General, 5% Social Sciences, Other
Expenses: 2014-2015: $40,497; room/board: $8,724
Financial aid: (309) 341-7130; 77% of undergrads determined to have financial need; average aid package $31,441

## Lake Forest College
Lake Forest IL
(847) 735-5000
U.S. News ranking: Nat. Lib. Arts, No. 120
Website: www.lakeforest.edu
Admissions email: admissions@lakeforest.edu
Private; founded 1857
Freshman admissions: more selective; 2013-2014: 3,684 applied, 2,110 accepted. Neither SAT nor ACT required. ACT 25/75 percentile: 23-28. High school rank: 27% in top tenth, 59% in top quarter, 90% in top half
Early decision deadline: 11/15, notification date: 12/13
Early action deadline: 11/15, notification date: 12/13

**Application deadline (fall):** 2/15
**Undergraduate student body:** 1,575 full time, 19 part time; 42% male, 58% female; 0% American Indian, 5% Asian, 6% black, 15% Hispanic, 3% multiracial, 0% Pacific Islander, 58% white, 10% international; 66% from in state; 75% live on campus; 11% of students in fraternities, 17% in sororities
**Most popular majors:** 7% Biology, General, 12% Communication and Media Studies, 6% Economics, 7% English Language and Literature, General, 8% Psychology, General
**Expenses:** 2013-2014: $39,842; room/board: $9,292
**Financial aid:** (847) 735-5104

## Lewis University

Romeoville IL
(800) 897-9000
**U.S. News ranking:** Reg. U. (Mid. W), No. 23
**Website:** www.lewisu.edu
**Admissions email:** admissions@lewisu.edu
**Private;** founded 1932
**Affiliation:** Roman Catholic
**Freshman admissions:** selective; 2013-2014: 5,432 applied, 3,035 accepted. Either SAT or ACT required. ACT 25/75 percentile: 21-26. High school rank: 18% in top tenth, 47% in top quarter, 81% in top half
**Early decision deadline:** N/A, notification date: N/A
**Early action deadline:** N/A, notification date: N/A
**Application deadline (fall):** rolling
**Undergraduate student body:** 3,723 full time, 890 part time; 44% male, 56% female; 0% American Indian, 3% Asian, 8% black, 17% Hispanic, 2% multiracial, 0% Pacific Islander, 65% white, 1% international; 94% from in state; 26% live on campus; 3% of students in fraternities, 3% in sororities
**Most popular majors:** 4% Aviation/Airway Management and Operations, 8% Business Administration and Management, General, 10% Criminal Justice/Safety Studies, 8% Psychology, General, 18% Registered Nursing/Registered Nurse
**Expenses:** 2014-2015: $27,830; room/board: $9,750
**Financial aid:** (815) 836-5263; 77% of undergrads determined to have financial need; average aid package $19,415

## Lexington College

Chicago IL
(312) 226-6294
**U.S. News ranking:** Business, unranked
**Website:** www.lexingtoncollege.edu
**Admissions email:** admissions@lexingtoncollege.edu
**Private**
**Affiliation:** Roman Catholic
**Freshman admissions:** least selective; 2013-2014: N/A applied, N/A accepted. Neither SAT nor ACT required. ACT 25/75 percentile: N/A. High school rank: N/A
**Early decision deadline:** N/A, notification date: N/A
**Early action deadline:** N/A, notification date: N/A
**Application deadline (fall):** N/A

**Undergraduate student body:** 46 full time, 13 part time; 0% male, 100% female; N/A American Indian, N/A Asian, N/A black, N/A Hispanic, N/A multiracial, N/A Pacific Islander, N/A white, N/A international
**Most popular majors:** Information not available
**Expenses:** 2013-2014: $25,800; room/board: N/A
**Financial aid:** (312) 226-6294

## Lincoln College[1]

Lincoln IL
(800) 569-0556
**U.S. News ranking:** Reg. Coll. (Mid. W), second tier
**Website:** www.lincolncollege.edu
**Admissions email:** admission@lincolncollege.edu
**Private;** founded 1865
**Application deadline (fall):** rolling
**Undergraduate student body:** N/A full time, N/A part time
**Expenses:** 2013-2014: $17,500; room/board: $7,000
**Financial aid:** (309) 452-0500

## Loyola University Chicago

Chicago IL
(312) 915-6500
**U.S. News ranking:** Nat. U., No. 106
**Website:** www.luc.edu
**Admissions email:** admission@luc.edu
**Private;** founded 1870
**Affiliation:** Roman Catholic
**Freshman admissions:** more selective; 2013-2014: 14,355 applied, 13,121 accepted. Either SAT or ACT required. ACT 25/75 percentile: 24-29. High school rank: 37% in top tenth, 68% in top quarter, 92% in top half
**Early decision deadline:** N/A, notification date: N/A
**Early action deadline:** N/A, notification date: N/A
**Application deadline (fall):** rolling
**Undergraduate student body:** 9,339 full time, 829 part time; 36% male, 64% female; 0% American Indian, 11% Asian, 4% black, 13% Hispanic, 6% multiracial, 0% Pacific Islander, 61% white, 3% international; 67% from in state; 44% live on campus; 9% of students in fraternities, 12% in sororities
**Most popular majors:** 12% Biological and Biomedical Sciences, 21% Business, Management, Marketing, and Related Support Services, 10% Health Professions and Related Programs, 11% Psychology, 11% Social Sciences
**Expenses:** 2014-2015: $37,412; room/board: $13,110
**Financial aid:** (773) 508-3155; 71% of undergrads determined to have financial need; average aid package $30,280

## MacMurray College

Jacksonville IL
(217) 479-7056
**U.S. News ranking:** Reg. Coll. (Mid. W), No. 52
**Website:** www.mac.edu
**Admissions email:** admissions@mac.edu
**Private;** founded 1846
**Affiliation:** United Methodist

**Freshman admissions:** selective; 2013-2014: 1,027 applied, 769 accepted. Either SAT or ACT required. ACT 25/75 percentile: 19-22. High school rank: 7% in top tenth, 33% in top quarter, 74% in top half
**Early decision deadline:** N/A, notification date: N/A
**Early action deadline:** N/A, notification date: N/A
**Application deadline (fall):** 8/25
**Undergraduate student body:** 517 full time, 54 part time; 44% male, 56% female; 1% American Indian, 1% Asian, 13% black, 5% Hispanic, 2% multiracial, 0% Pacific Islander, 75% white, 0% international; 83% from in state; 49% live on campus; N/A of students in fraternities, N/A in sororities
**Most popular majors:** Information not available
**Expenses:** 2014-2015: $23,600; room/board: $8,000
**Financial aid:** (217) 479-7041; 90% of undergrads determined to have financial need; average aid package $20,237

## McKendree University

Lebanon IL
(618) 537-6831
**U.S. News ranking:** Reg. U. (Mid. W), No. 69
**Website:** www.mckendree.edu
**Admissions email:** inquiry@mckendree.edu
**Private;** founded 1828
**Affiliation:** Methodist
**Freshman admissions:** selective; 2013-2014: 1,617 applied, 1,017 accepted. Either SAT or ACT required. ACT 25/75 percentile: 20-25. High school rank: 13% in top tenth, 43% in top quarter, 75% in top half
**Early decision deadline:** N/A, notification date: N/A
**Early action deadline:** N/A, notification date: N/A
**Application deadline (fall):** rolling
**Undergraduate student body:** 1,777 full time, 581 part time; 44% male, 56% female; 1% American Indian, 1% Asian, 15% black, 4% Hispanic, 1% multiracial, 0% Pacific Islander, 70% white, 1% international; 85% from in state; 63% live on campus; 1% of students in fraternities, 14% in sororities
**Most popular majors:** 15% Business Administration and Management, 6% Elementary Education and Teaching, 8% Human Resources Management/Personnel Administration, General, 7% Psychology, General, 19% Registered Nursing/Registered Nurse
**Expenses:** 2014-2015: $26,900; room/board: $8,920
**Financial aid:** (618) 537-6828; 87% of undergrads determined to have financial need; average aid package $19,908

## Midstate College[1]

Peoria IL
(309) 692-4092
**U.S. News ranking:** Reg. Coll. (Mid. W), unranked
**Website:** www.midstate.edu/
**Admissions email:** jauer@midstate.edu
**For-profit**
**Application deadline (fall):** rolling

**Undergraduate student body:** N/A full time, N/A part time
**Expenses:** 2013-2014: $16,230; room/board: N/A
**Financial aid:** (309) 692-4092

## Millikin University

Decatur IL
(217) 424-6210
**U.S. News ranking:** Reg. Coll. (Mid. W), No. 14
**Website:** www.millikin.edu
**Admissions email:** admis@millikin.edu
**Private;** founded 1901
**Affiliation:** Presbyterian
**Freshman admissions:** selective; 2013-2014: 3,906 applied, 2,153 accepted. Either SAT or ACT required. ACT 25/75 percentile: 21-26. High school rank: 19% in top tenth, 41% in top quarter, 71% in top half
**Early decision deadline:** N/A, notification date: N/A
**Early action deadline:** N/A, notification date: N/A
**Application deadline (fall):** rolling
**Undergraduate student body:** 2,044 full time, 110 part time; 41% male, 59% female; 0% American Indian, 1% Asian, 12% black, 6% Hispanic, 4% multiracial, 0% Pacific Islander, 76% white, 1% international; 89% from in state; 64% live on campus; 16% of students in fraternities, 18% in sororities
**Most popular majors:** 18% Business, Management, Marketing, and Related Support Services, 6% Communication, Journalism, and Related Programs, 14% Education, 12% Health Professions and Related Programs, 22% Visual and Performing Arts
**Expenses:** 2014-2015: $29,620; room/board: $9,240
**Financial aid:** (217) 424-6343; 82% of undergrads determined to have financial need; average aid package $22,862

## Monmouth College

Monmouth IL
(800) 747-2687
**U.S. News ranking:** Nat. Lib. Arts, No. 165
**Website:** www.monmouthcollege.edu/admissions
**Admissions email:** admissions@monmouthcollege.edu
**Private;** founded 1853
**Affiliation:** Presbyterian USA
**Freshman admissions:** selective; 2013-2014: 2,973 applied, 1,912 accepted. Either SAT or ACT required. ACT 25/75 percentile: 20-25. High school rank: 15% in top tenth, 37% in top quarter, 72% in top half
**Early decision deadline:** N/A, notification date: N/A
**Early action deadline:** N/A, notification date: N/A
**Application deadline (fall):** rolling
**Undergraduate student body:** 1,243 full time, 13 part time; 45% male, 55% female; 1% American Indian, 1% Asian, 13% black, 9% Hispanic, 1% multiracial, 0% Pacific Islander, 68% white, 2% international; 92% from in state; 92% live on campus; 26% of students in fraternities, 23% in sororities
**Most popular majors:** 6% Business Administration and Management, General, 6% Elementary Education and Teaching, 4%

**Most popular majors:** 20% Business, Management, Marketing, and Related Support Services, 14% Communication, Journalism, and Related Programs, 15% Education, 6% History, 7% Psychology
**Expenses:** 2014-2015: $33,200; room/board: $7,650
**Financial aid:** (309) 457-2129; 86% of undergrads determined to have financial need; average aid package $28,809

## National-Louis University

Chicago IL
(888) 658-8632
**U.S. News ranking:** Nat. U., second tier
**Website:** www.nl.edu
**Admissions email:** nluinfo@nl.edu
**Private**
**Freshman admissions:** selective; 2013-2014: N/A applied, N/A accepted. Neither SAT nor ACT required. ACT 25/75 percentile: N/A. High school rank: N/A
**Early decision deadline:** N/A, notification date: N/A
**Early action deadline:** N/A, notification date: N/A
**Application deadline (fall):** rolling
**Undergraduate student body:** 784 full time, 643 part time; 23% male, 77% female; 0% American Indian, 2% Asian, 41% black, 25% Hispanic, 1% multiracial, 1% Pacific Islander, 24% white, 1% international
**Most popular majors:** 9% Elementary Education and Teaching, 6% Management Information Systems, General, 31% Management Science, 30% Multi-/Interdisciplinary Studies, Other, 5% Public Administration and Social Service Professions, Other
**Expenses:** 2013-2014: $15,915; room/board: N/A
**Financial aid:** (847) 465-5350

## North Central College

Naperville IL
(630) 637-5800
**U.S. News ranking:** Reg. U. (Mid. W), No. 14
**Website:** www.noctrl.edu
**Admissions email:** ncadm@noctrl.edu
**Private;** founded 1861
**Affiliation:** United Methodist
**Freshman admissions:** more selective; 2013-2014: 4,082 applied, 2,598 accepted. Either SAT or ACT required. ACT 25/75 percentile: 22-27. High school rank: 20% in top tenth, 57% in top quarter, 86% in top half
**Early decision deadline:** N/A, notification date: N/A
**Early action deadline:** N/A, notification date: N/A
**Application deadline (fall):** rolling
**Undergraduate student body:** 2,592 full time, 205 part time; 45% male, 55% female; 0% American Indian, 2% Asian, 3% black, 8% Hispanic, 3% multiracial, 0% Pacific Islander, 78% white, 1% international; 94% from in state; 55% live on campus; N/A of students in fraternities, N/A in sororities
**Most popular majors:** 6% Business Administration and Management, General, 6% Elementary Education and Teaching, 4%

Graphic Design, 5% Marketing/ Marketing Management, General, 8% Psychology, General
**Expenses:** 2014-2015: $34,230; room/board: $9,795
**Financial aid:** (630) 637-5600; 76% of undergrads determined to have financial need; average aid package $23,286

## Northeastern Illinois University
Chicago IL
(773) 442-4000
**U.S. News ranking:** Reg. U. (Mid. W), second tier
**Website:** www.neiu.edu
**Admissions email:** admrec@neiu.edu
**Public;** founded 1867
**Freshman admissions:** less selective; 2013-2014: 5,291 applied, 3,181 accepted. Either SAT or ACT required. ACT 25/75 percentile: 16-21. High school rank: 3% in top tenth, 16% in top quarter, 61% in top half
**Early decision deadline:** N/A, notification date: N/A
**Early action deadline:** N/A, notification date: N/A
**Application deadline (fall):** 7/1
**Undergraduate student body:** 5,068 full time, 3,882 part time; 45% male, 55% female; 0% American Indian, 9% Asian, 10% black, 35% Hispanic, 2% multiracial, 0% Pacific Islander, 37% white, 4% international; 99% from in state; 0% live on campus; 1% of students in fraternities, 1% in sororities
**Most popular majors:** 16% Business, Management, Marketing, and Related Support Services, 12% Education, 10% Liberal Arts and Sciences, General Studies and Humanities, 9% Public Administration and Social Service Professions, 9% Social Sciences
**Expenses:** 2014-2015: $10,764 in state, $19,884 out of state; room/board: N/A
**Financial aid:** (773) 442-5000; 71% of undergrads determined to have financial need; average aid package $8,085

## Northern Illinois University
DeKalb IL
(815) 753-0446
**U.S. News ranking:** Nat. U., No. 194
**Website:** www.niu.edu/
**Admissions email:** admission@niu.edu
**Public;** founded 1895
**Freshman admissions:** selective; 2013-2014: 19,763 applied, 10,278 accepted. Either SAT or ACT required. ACT 25/75 percentile: 19-24. High school rank: 12% in top tenth, 34% in top quarter, 70% in top half
**Early decision deadline:** N/A, notification date: N/A
**Early action deadline:** N/A, notification date: N/A
**Application deadline (fall):** 8/1
**Undergraduate student body:** 13,821 full time, 1,993 part time; 50% male, 50% female; 0% American Indian, 5% Asian, 17% black, 13% Hispanic, 3% multiracial, 0% Pacific Islander, 59% white, 1% international;

98% from in state; 28% live on campus; 9% of students in fraternities, 7% in sororities
**Most popular majors:** 4% Accounting, 4% Health/Medical Preparatory Programs, Other, 6% Psychology, General, 6% Registered Nursing/ Registered Nurse, 6% Speech Communication and Rhetoric
**Expenses:** 2014-2015: $13,636 in state, $22,914 out of state; room/board: $10,756
**Financial aid:** (815) 753-1300; 74% of undergrads determined to have financial need; average aid package $12,919

## North Park University
Chicago IL
(773) 244-5500
**U.S. News ranking:** Reg. U. (Mid. W), No. 54
**Website:** www.northpark.edu
**Admissions email:** admissions@northpark.edu
**Private;** founded 1891
**Affiliation:** Evangelical Covenant Church
**Freshman admissions:** selective; 2013-2014: 3,961 applied, 2,073 accepted. Either SAT or ACT required. ACT 25/75 percentile: 19-25. High school rank: N/A
**Early decision deadline:** N/A, notification date: N/A
**Early action deadline:** N/A, notification date: N/A
**Application deadline (fall):** 7/1
**Undergraduate student body:** 1,861 full time, 343 part time; 37% male, 63% female; 0% American Indian, 5% Asian, 9% black, 18% Hispanic, 3% multiracial, 0% Pacific Islander, 52% white, 4% international; 73% from in state; 46% live on campus; 0% of students in fraternities, 0% in sororities
**Most popular majors:** 7% Biology/ Biological Sciences, General, 18% Business Administration and Management, General, 6% Criminal Justice/Safety Studies, 5% Elementary Education and Teaching, 19% Registered Nursing/Registered Nurse
**Expenses:** 2014-2015: $24,540; room/board: $8,660
**Financial aid:** (773) 244-5526

## Northwestern University
Evanston IL
(847) 491-7271
**U.S. News ranking:** Nat. U., No. 13
**Website:** www.northwestern.edu
**Admissions email:** ug-admission@northwestern.edu
**Private;** founded 1851
**Freshman admissions:** most selective; 2013-2014: 32,796 applied, 4,598 accepted. Either SAT or ACT required. SAT 25/75 percentile: 1390-1550. High school rank: 91% in top tenth, 99% in top quarter, 99% in top half
**Early decision deadline:** 11/1, notification date: 12/15
**Early action deadline:** N/A, notification date: N/A
**Application deadline (fall):** 1/1
**Undergraduate student body:** 8,423 full time, 265 part time; 49% male, 51% female; 0% American

Indian, 17% Asian, 5% black, 10% Hispanic, 5% multiracial, 0% Pacific Islander, 54% white, 7% international; 28% from in state; 65% live on campus; 38% of students in fraternities, 42% in sororities
**Most popular majors:** 6% Biology/Biological Sciences, General, 12% Economics, General, 8% Journalism, 7% Psychology, General, 6% Speech Communication and Rhetoric
**Expenses:** 2014-2015: $47,251; room/board: $14,389
**Financial aid:** (847) 491-7400; 47% of undergrads determined to have financial need; average aid package $38,798

## Olivet Nazarene University
Bourbonnais IL
(815) 939-5011
**U.S. News ranking:** Reg. U. (Mid. W), No. 49
**Website:** www.olivet.edu
**Admissions email:** admissions@olivet.edu
**Private;** founded 1907
**Affiliation:** Church of the Nazarene
**Freshman admissions:** selective; 2013-2014: 3,775 applied, 2,975 accepted. Either SAT or ACT required. ACT 25/75 percentile: 20-26. High school rank: 21% in top tenth, 48% in top quarter, 79% in top half
**Early decision deadline:** N/A, notification date: N/A
**Early action deadline:** N/A, notification date: N/A
**Application deadline (fall):** 8/1
**Undergraduate student body:** 2,905 full time, 430 part time; 37% male, 63% female; 0% American Indian, 2% Asian, 10% black, 5% Hispanic, 1% multiracial, 0% Pacific Islander, 80% white, 1% international; 67% from in state; 82% live on campus; 0% of students in fraternities, 0% in sororities
**Most popular majors:** 4% Biology/ Biological Sciences, General, 4% Business Administration and Management, General, 9% Elementary Education and Teaching, 24% Registered Nursing/Registered Nurse, 4% Social Work
**Expenses:** 2014-2015: $31,390; room/board: $7,900
**Financial aid:** (815) 939-5249; 81% of undergrads determined to have financial need; average aid package $23,598

## Principia College
Elsah IL
(618) 374-5181
**U.S. News ranking:** Nat. Lib. Arts, No. 139
**Website:** www.principiacollege.edu
**Admissions email:** collegeadmissions@principia.edu
**Private;** founded 1910
**Affiliation:** Christian Science
**Freshman admissions:** selective; 2013-2014: 189 applied, 159 accepted. Either SAT or ACT required. SAT 25/75 percentile: 918-1223. High school rank: 26% in top tenth, 50% in top quarter, 83% in top half
**Early decision deadline:** N/A, notification date: N/A
**Early action deadline:** N/A, notification date: N/A

**Application deadline (fall):** rolling
**Undergraduate student body:** 480 full time, N/A part time; 46% male, 54% female; 0% American Indian, 0% Asian, 1% black, 3% Hispanic, 3% multiracial, 0% Pacific Islander, 69% white, 18% international; 12% from in state; 99% live on campus; 0% of students in fraternities, 0% in sororities
**Most popular majors:** Information not available
**Expenses:** 2014-2015: $26,850; room/board: $10,650
**Financial aid:** (618) 374-5186; 68% of undergrads determined to have financial need; average aid package $28,291

## Quincy University
Quincy IL
(217) 228-5210
**U.S. News ranking:** Reg. U. (Mid. W), No. 69
**Website:** www.quincy.edu
**Admissions email:** admissions@quincy.edu
**Private;** founded 1860
**Affiliation:** Catholic
**Freshman admissions:** selective; 2013-2014: 1,078 applied, 955 accepted. Either SAT or ACT required. ACT 25/75 percentile: 20-25. High school rank: 16% in top tenth, 40% in top quarter, 71% in top half
**Early decision deadline:** N/A, notification date: N/A
**Early action deadline:** N/A, notification date: N/A
**Application deadline (fall):** rolling
**Undergraduate student body:** 1,082 full time, 114 part time; 44% male, 56% female; 1% American Indian, 1% Asian, 11% black, 4% Hispanic, 2% multiracial, 0% Pacific Islander, 71% white, 0% international; 72% from in state; 57% live on campus; 6% of students in fraternities, 8% in sororities
**Most popular majors:** 11% Biological and Biomedical Sciences, 23% Business, Management, Marketing, and Related Support Services, 10% Education, 10% Health Professions and Related Programs, 9% Liberal Arts and Sciences, General Studies and Humanities
**Expenses:** 2014-2015: $26,572; room/board: $9,968
**Financial aid:** (217) 228-5260; 87% of undergrads determined to have financial need; average aid package $23,232

## Robert Morris University
Chicago IL
(312) 935-4400
**U.S. News ranking:** Reg. U. (Mid. W), No. 80
**Website:** www.robertmorris.edu/
**Admissions email:** enroll@robertmorris.edu
**Private;** founded 1913
**Freshman admissions:** less selective; 2013-2014: 4,080 applied, 857 accepted. Either SAT or ACT required. ACT 25/75 percentile: 15-21. High school rank: 3% in top tenth, 14% in top quarter, 38% in top half
**Early decision deadline:** N/A, notification date: N/A
**Early action deadline:** N/A, notification date: N/A

**Application deadline (fall):** rolling
**Undergraduate student body:** 2,649 full time, 132 part time; 49% male, 51% female; 0% American Indian, 3% Asian, 28% black, 27% Hispanic, 1% multiracial, 0% Pacific Islander, 38% white, 1% international; 92% from in state; 8% live on campus; N/A of students in fraternities, N/A in sororities
**Most popular majors:** 64% Business, Management, Marketing, and Related Support Services, 10% Computer and Information Sciences and Support Services, 19% Multi/ Interdisciplinary Studies, 7% Visual and Performing Arts
**Expenses:** 2014-2015: $23,700; room/board: $11,649
**Financial aid:** (312) 935-4408; 93% of undergrads determined to have financial need; average aid package $15,243

## Rockford University
Rockford IL
(815) 226-4050
**U.S. News ranking:** Reg. U. (Mid. W), No. 84
**Website:** www.rockford.edu
**Admissions email:** rcadmissions@rockford.edu
**Private;** founded 1847
**Freshman admissions:** selective; 2013-2014: 1,074 applied, 440 accepted. Either SAT or ACT required. ACT 25/75 percentile: 19-25. High school rank: N/A
**Early decision deadline:** N/A, notification date: N/A
**Early action deadline:** N/A, notification date: N/A
**Application deadline (fall):** rolling
**Undergraduate student body:** 838 full time, 143 part time; 36% male, 64% female; 0% American Indian, 2% Asian, 7% black, 5% Hispanic, 9% multiracial, 0% Pacific Islander, 67% white, 1% international; 87% from in state; 32% live on campus; 0% of students in fraternities, N/A in sororities
**Most popular majors:** Information not available
**Expenses:** 2014-2015: $27,500; room/board: $7,710
**Financial aid:** (815) 226-3396; 92% of undergrads determined to have financial need; average aid package $19,056

## Roosevelt University
Chicago IL
(877) 277-5978
**U.S. News ranking:** Reg. U. (Mid. W), No. 91
**Website:** www.roosevelt.edu
**Admissions email:** admission@roosevelt.edu
**Private;** founded 1945
**Freshman admissions:** selective; 2013-2014: 3,370 applied, 2,655 accepted. Either SAT or ACT required. ACT 25/75 percentile: 19-25. High school rank: 2% in top tenth, 11% in top quarter, 39% in top half
**Early decision deadline:** N/A, notification date: N/A
**Early action deadline:** N/A, notification date: N/A
**Application deadline (fall):** rolling
**Undergraduate student body:** 2,731 full time, 927 part time; 38% male, 62% female; 0% American Indian, 5% Asian, 20% black,

19% Hispanic, 3% multiracial, 0% Pacific Islander, 47% white, 3% international; 85% from in state; 25% live on campus; 0% of students in fraternities, 2% in sororities
**Most popular majors:** 29% Business, Management, Marketing, and Related Support Services, 7% Education, 16% Psychology, 7% Social Sciences, 7% Visual and Performing Arts
**Expenses:** 2014-2015: $26,900; room/board: $12,532
**Financial aid:** (312) 341-3565; 82% of undergrads determined to have financial need; average aid package $23,001

## School of the Art Institute of Chicago
Chicago IL
(312) 629-6100
**U.S. News ranking:** Arts, unranked
**Website:** www.saic.edu
**Admissions email:** admiss@saic.edu
**Private;** founded 1866
**Freshman admissions:** N/A; 2013-2014: 3,704 applied, 2,655 accepted. Either SAT or ACT required. SAT 25/75 percentile: N/A. High school rank: N/A
**Early decision deadline:** N/A, notification date: N/A
**Early action deadline:** 1/3, notification date: 9/1
**Application deadline (fall):** 6/1
**Undergraduate student body:** 2,469 full time, 245 part time; 30% male, 70% female; 0% American Indian, 13% Asian, 3% black, 6% Hispanic, 3% multiracial, 0% Pacific Islander, 45% white, 27% international; 30% from in state; 17% live on campus; 0% of students in fraternities, 0% in sororities
**Most popular majors:** 5% Art History, Criticism and Conservation, 3% Art Teacher Education, 3% Art Therapy/Therapist, 4% Creative Writing, 72% Fine/Studio Arts, General
**Expenses:** 2014-2015: $42,230; room/board: $15,230
**Financial aid:** (312) 629-6600; 50% of undergrads determined to have financial need; average aid package $31,525

## Shimer College[1]
Chicago IL
(312) 235-3500
**U.S. News ranking:** Nat. Lib. Arts, unranked
**Website:** www.shimer.edu
**Admissions email:** admission@shimer.edu
**Private**
**Application deadline (fall):** N/A
**Undergraduate student body:** N/A full time, N/A part time
**Expenses:** 2013-2014: $31,527; room/board: N/A
**Financial aid:** (847) 249-7180

## Southern Illinois University–Carbondale
Carbondale IL
(618) 536-4405
**U.S. News ranking:** Nat. U., No. 189
**Website:** www.siu.edu
**Admissions email:** admissions@siu.edu

**Public;** founded 1869
**Freshman admissions:** selective; 2013-2014: 11,573 applied, 9,176 accepted. Either SAT or ACT required. ACT 25/75 percentile: 19-25. High school rank: 11% in top tenth, 31% in top quarter, 61% in top half
**Early decision deadline:** N/A, notification date: N/A
**Early action deadline:** N/A, notification date: N/A
**Application deadline (fall):** 5/1
**Undergraduate student body:** 11,844 full time, 1,507 part time; 55% male, 45% female; 0% American Indian, 2% Asian, 20% black, 7% Hispanic, 3% multiracial, 0% Pacific Islander, 64% white, 3% international; 87% from in state; 31% live on campus; 4% of students in fraternities, 2% in sororities
**Most popular majors:** 9% Business, Management, Marketing, and Related Support Services, 17% Education, 7% Engineering Technologies and Engineering-Related Fields, 8% Health Professions and Related Programs, 6% Social Sciences
**Expenses:** 2014-2015: $12,251 in state, $24,874 out of state; room/board: $9,694
**Financial aid:** (618) 453-4334; 71% of undergrads determined to have financial need; average aid package $13,707

## Southern Illinois University–Edwardsville
Edwardsville IL
(618) 650-3705
**U.S. News ranking:** Reg. U. (Mid. W), No. 47
**Website:** www.siue.edu
**Admissions email:** admissions@siue.edu
**Public;** founded 1957
**Freshman admissions:** selective; 2013-2014: 7,646 applied, 6,437 accepted. Either SAT or ACT required. ACT 25/75 percentile: 20-25. High school rank: 16% in top tenth, 39% in top quarter, 73% in top half
**Early decision deadline:** N/A, notification date: N/A
**Early action deadline:** N/A, notification date: N/A
**Application deadline (fall):** 5/1
**Undergraduate student body:** 9,556 full time, 1,673 part time; 47% male, 53% female; 0% American Indian, 2% Asian, 15% black, 4% Hispanic, 3% multiracial, 0% Pacific Islander, 75% white, 1% international; N/A from in state; N/A live on campus; 8% of students in fraternities, 9% in sororities
**Most popular majors:** 9% Biology/Biological Sciences, General, 9% Business Administration and Management, General, 4% Elementary Education and Teaching, 7% Psychology, General, 10% Registered Nursing/Registered Nurse
**Expenses:** 2014-2015: $9,738 in state, $20,682 out of state; room/board: $8,750
**Financial aid:** (618) 650-3839; 70% of undergrads determined to have financial need; average aid package $11,179

## St. Augustine College[1]
Chicago IL
(773) 878-3656
**U.S. News ranking:** Reg. Coll. (Mid. W), unranked
**Website:** www.staugustinecollege.edu/index.asp
**Admissions email:** info@staugustine.edu
**Private**
**Application deadline (fall):** N/A
**Undergraduate student body:** N/A full time, N/A part time
**Expenses:** 2013-2014: $9,120; room/board: N/A
**Financial aid:** (773) 878-3813

## St. Xavier University
Chicago IL
(773) 298-3050
**U.S. News ranking:** Reg. U. (Mid. W), No. 49
**Website:** www.sxu.edu
**Admissions email:** admission@sxu.edu
**Private;** founded 1846
**Affiliation:** Roman Catholic
**Freshman admissions:** selective; 2013-2014: 6,693 applied, 5,307 accepted. Either SAT or ACT required. ACT 25/75 percentile: 19-24. High school rank: 25% in top tenth, 54% in top quarter, 84% in top half
**Early decision deadline:** N/A, notification date: N/A
**Early action deadline:** N/A, notification date: N/A
**Application deadline (fall):** rolling
**Undergraduate student body:** 2,452 full time, 468 part time; 33% male, 67% female; 0% American Indian, 3% Asian, 16% black, 23% Hispanic, 2% multiracial, 0% Pacific Islander, 50% white, 0% international; 95% from in state; 22% live on campus; 0% of students in fraternities, 0% in sororities
**Most popular majors:** 16% Business, Management, Marketing, and Related Support Services, 12% Education, 24% Health Professions and Related Programs, 11% Liberal Arts and Sciences, General Studies and Humanities, 12% Psychology
**Expenses:** 2014-2015: $30,100; room/board: $10,320
**Financial aid:** (773) 298-3070; 89% of undergrads determined to have financial need; average aid package $23,096

## Trinity Christian College
Palos Heights IL
(800) 748-0085
**U.S. News ranking:** Reg. Coll. (Mid. W), No. 28
**Website:** www.trnty.edu
**Admissions email:** admissions@trnty.edu
**Private;** founded 1959
**Affiliation:** Reformed
**Freshman admissions:** selective; 2013-2014: 670 applied, 526 accepted. Either SAT or ACT required. ACT 25/75 percentile: 20-25. High school rank: 13% in top tenth, 27% in top quarter, 56% in top half
**Early decision deadline:** N/A, notification date: N/A
**Early action deadline:** N/A, notification date: N/A
**Application deadline (fall):** rolling

**Undergraduate student body:** 1,106 full time, 227 part time; 35% male, 65% female; 1% American Indian, 2% Asian, 9% black, 11% Hispanic, 2% multiracial, 0% Pacific Islander, 72% white, 3% international; 71% from in state; 45% live on campus; N/A of students in fraternities, N/A in sororities
**Most popular majors:** 18% Business, Management, Marketing, and Related Support Services, 33% Education, 13% Health Professions and Related Programs, 6% Psychology, 6% Public Administration and Social Service Professions
**Expenses:** 2014-2015: $25,290; room/board: $9,390
**Financial aid:** (708) 239-4706; 80% of undergrads determined to have financial need; average aid package $16,080

## Trinity International University
Deerfield IL
(800) 822-3225
**U.S. News ranking:** Nat. U., second tier
**Website:** www.tiu.edu
**Admissions email:** tcadmissions@tiu.edu
**Private;** founded 1897
**Affiliation:** Evangelical Free Church of America
**Freshman admissions:** selective; 2013-2014: 439 applied, 412 accepted. Either SAT or ACT required. ACT 25/75 percentile: 25-29. High school rank: 17% in top tenth, 34% in top quarter, 74% in top half
**Early decision deadline:** N/A, notification date: N/A
**Early action deadline:** N/A, notification date: N/A
**Application deadline (fall):** rolling
**Undergraduate student body:** 850 full time, 313 part time; 47% male, 53% female; 0% American Indian, 2% Asian, 20% black, 20% Hispanic, 2% multiracial, 1% Pacific Islander, 45% white, 1% international
**Most popular majors:** Information not available
**Expenses:** 2014-2015: $27,360; room/board: $8,710
**Financial aid:** (847) 317-8060; 82% of undergrads determined to have financial need; average aid package $22,707

## University of Chicago
Chicago IL
(773) 702-8650
**U.S. News ranking:** Nat. U., No. 4
**Website:** www.uchicago.edu
**Admissions email:** collegeadmissions@uchicago.edu
**Private;** founded 1890
**Freshman admissions:** most selective; 2013-2014: 30,271 applied, 2,670 accepted. Either SAT or ACT required. SAT 25/75 percentile: 1440-1590. High school rank: 98% in top tenth, 100% in top quarter, 100% in top half
**Early decision deadline:** N/A, notification date: N/A
**Early action deadline:** 11/8, notification date: 12/16
**Application deadline (fall):** 1/1

**Undergraduate student body:** 5,585 full time, 74 part time; 53% male, 47% female; 0% American Indian, 18% Asian, 5% black, 9% Hispanic, 4% multiracial, 0% Pacific Islander, 45% white, 9% international; 18% from in state; 53% live on campus; N/A of students in fraternities, N/A in sororities
**Most popular majors:** 10% Biological and Biomedical Sciences, 5% English Language and Literature/Letters, 8% Mathematics and Statistics, 5% Public Administration and Social Service Professions, 26% Social Sciences
**Expenses:** 2014-2015: $48,253; room/board: $14,205
**Financial aid:** (773) 702-8666; 48% of undergrads determined to have financial need; average aid package $38,808

## University of Illinois–Chicago
Chicago IL
(312) 996-4350
**U.S. News ranking:** Nat. U., No. 149
**Website:** www.uic.edu
**Admissions email:** uicadmit@uic.edu
**Public;** founded 1965
**Freshman admissions:** selective; 2013-2014: 14,653 applied, 10,427 accepted. Either SAT or ACT required. ACT 25/75 percentile: 22-26. High school rank: 24% in top tenth, 63% in top quarter, 92% in top half
**Early decision deadline:** N/A, notification date: N/A
**Early action deadline:** N/A, notification date: N/A
**Application deadline (fall):** 1/15
**Undergraduate student body:** 15,402 full time, 1,258 part time; 50% male, 50% female; 0% American Indian, 23% Asian, 8% black, 25% Hispanic, 2% multiracial, 0% Pacific Islander, 38% white, 2% international; 98% from in state; 17% live on campus; 1% of students in fraternities, 1% in sororities
**Most popular majors:** 5% Accounting, 12% Biology/Biological Sciences, General, 5% Finance, General, 15% Psychology, General, 5% Registered Nursing/Registered Nurse
**Expenses:** 2014-2015: $13,640 in state, $26,030 out of state; room/board: $10,882
**Financial aid:** (312) 996-3126; 76% of undergrads determined to have financial need; average aid package $14,130

## University of Illinois–Springfield
Springfield IL
(217) 206-4847
**U.S. News ranking:** Reg. U. (Mid. W), No. 36
**Website:** www.uis.edu
**Admissions email:** admissions@uis.edu
**Public;** founded 1969
**Freshman admissions:** selective; 2013-2014: 1,469 applied, 878 accepted. Either SAT or ACT required. ACT 25/75 percentile: 20-27. High school rank: 21% in top tenth, 44% in top quarter, 80% in top half

Early decision deadline: N/A, notification date: N/A
Early action deadline: N/A, notification date: N/A
Application deadline (fall): rolling
Undergraduate student body: 1,969 full time, 1,070 part time; 49% male, 51% female; 0% American Indian, 4% Asian, 13% black, 6% Hispanic, 2% multiracial, 0% Pacific Islander, 68% white, 3% international; 87% from in state; 30% live on campus; 0% of students in fraternities, 0% in sororities
Most popular majors: 16% Business Administration and Management, General, 7% Communication, General, 8% Computer Science, 7% Criminal Justice/Safety Studies, 10% Psychology, General
Expenses: 2014-2015: $11,367 in state, $20,517 out of state; room/board: $9,600
Financial aid: (217) 206-6724; 70% of undergrads determined to have financial need; average aid package $12,257

## University of Illinois–Urbana-Champaign
Champaign IL
(217) 333-0302
U.S. News ranking: Nat. U., No. 42
Website: www.illinois.edu
Admissions email: ugradadmissions@illinois.edu
Public; founded 1867
Freshman admissions: more selective; 2013-2014: 33,203 applied, 20,716 accepted. Either SAT or ACT required. ACT 25/75 percentile: 26-31. High school rank: 55% in top tenth, 87% in top quarter, 99% in top half
Early decision deadline: N/A, notification date: N/A
Early action deadline: N/A, notification date: N/A
Application deadline (fall): 1/2
Undergraduate student body: 31,516 full time, 1,179 part time; 56% male, 44% female; 0% American Indian, 15% Asian, 6% black, 8% Hispanic, 3% multiracial, 0% Pacific Islander, 53% white, 15% international; 89% from in state; 50% live on campus; 21% of students in fraternities, 21% in sororities
Most popular majors: 8% Biological and Biomedical Sciences, 14% Business, Management, Marketing, and Related Support Services, 9% Communication, Journalism, and Related Programs, 17% Engineering, 9% Social Sciences
Expenses: 2014-2015: $15,602 in state, $30,228 out of state; room/board: $10,848
Financial aid: (217) 333-0100; 46% of undergrads determined to have financial need; average aid package $15,312

## University of St. Francis
Joliet IL
(800) 735-7500
U.S. News ranking: Reg. U. (Mid. W), No. 39
Website: www.stfrancis.edu
Admissions email: admissions@stfrancis.edu
Private; founded 1920
Affiliation: Roman Catholic

Freshman admissions: selective; 2013-2014: 1,706 applied, 877 accepted. Either SAT or ACT required. ACT 25/75 percentile: 21-25. High school rank: 20% in top tenth, 46% in top quarter, 84% in top half
Early decision deadline: N/A, notification date: N/A
Early action deadline: N/A, notification date: N/A
Application deadline (fall): 8/1
Undergraduate student body: 1,364 full time, 58 part time; 35% male, 65% female; 0% American Indian, 2% Asian, 7% black, 15% Hispanic, 2% multiracial, 0% Pacific Islander, 71% white, 1% international; 95% from in state; 26% live on campus; 0% of students in fraternities, 0% in sororities
Most popular majors: 6% Biology/Biological Sciences, General, 14% Business, Management, Marketing, and Related Support Services, 11% Education, 6% Homeland Security, Law Enforcement, Firefighting and Related Protective Services, 31% Registered Nursing/Registered Nurse
Expenses: 2014-2015: $28,790; room/board: $8,770
Financial aid: (815) 740-3403; 86% of undergrads determined to have financial need; average aid package $22,137

## VanderCook College of Music
Chicago IL
(800) 448-2655
U.S. News ranking: Arts, unranked
Website: www.vandercook.edu
Admissions email: admissions@vandercook.edu
Private; founded 1909
Freshman admissions: N/A; 2013-2014: 123 applied, 46 accepted. Neither SAT nor ACT required. SAT 25/75 percentile: 0% in top tenth, 77% in top quarter, 92% in top half
Early decision deadline: N/A, notification date: N/A
Early action deadline: N/A, notification date: N/A
Application deadline (fall): rolling
Undergraduate student body: 99 full time, 34 part time; 52% male, 48% female; 0% American Indian, 1% Asian, 6% black, 21% Hispanic, 3% multiracial, 0% Pacific Islander, 66% white, 3% international; 77% from in state; 8% live on campus; N/A of students in fraternities, N/A in sororities
Most popular majors: 100% Music Teacher Education
Expenses: 2014-2015: $25,690; room/board: $10,888
Financial aid: (312) 225-6288; 89% of undergrads determined to have financial need; average aid package $16,599

## Western Illinois University
Macomb IL
(309) 298-3157
U.S. News ranking: Reg. U. (Mid. W), No. 39
Website: www.wiu.edu
Admissions email: admissions@wiu.edu
Public; founded 1899

Freshman admissions: selective; 2013-2014: 10,554 applied, 6,260 accepted. Either SAT or ACT required. ACT 25/75 percentile: 18-23. High school rank: 9% in top tenth, 28% in top quarter, 61% in top half
Early decision deadline: N/A, notification date: N/A
Early action deadline: N/A, notification date: N/A
Application deadline (fall): 5/15
Undergraduate student body: 8,805 full time, 1,068 part time; 51% male, 49% female; 0% American Indian, 1% Asian, 17% black, 8% Hispanic, 2% multiracial, 0% Pacific Islander, 67% white, 2% international; 89% from in state; 42% live on campus; 5% of students in fraternities, 6% in sororities
Most popular majors: 12% Business Administration and Management, General, 16% Criminal Justice/Law Enforcement Administration, 8% Elementary Education and Teaching, 13% General Studies, 7% Parks, Recreation and Leisure Facilities Management, General
Expenses: 2014-2015: $11,283 in state, $15,599 out of state; room/board: $9,450
Financial aid: (309) 298-2446; 74% of undergrads determined to have financial need; average aid package $10,450

## Wheaton College
Wheaton IL
(630) 752-5005
U.S. News ranking: Nat. Lib. Arts, No. 56
Website: www.wheaton.edu
Admissions email: admissions@wheaton.edu
Private; founded 1860
Affiliation: Christian nondenominational
Freshman admissions: more selective; 2013-2014: 1,941 applied, 1,364 accepted. Either SAT or ACT required. ACT 25/75 percentile: 27-32. High school rank: 58% in top tenth, 82% in top quarter, 97% in top half
Early decision deadline: N/A, notification date: N/A
Early action deadline: 11/1, notification date: 12/31
Application deadline (fall): 1/10
Undergraduate student body: 2,378 full time, 66 part time; 49% male, 51% female; 0% American Indian, 8% Asian, 2% black, 5% Hispanic, 5% multiracial, 0% Pacific Islander, 78% white, 2% international; 26% from in state; 90% live on campus; N/A of students in fraternities, N/A in sororities
Most popular majors: 8% Business, Management, Marketing, and Related Support Services, 8% English Language and Literature/Letters, 14% Social Sciences, 8% Theology and Religious Vocations, 8% Visual and Performing Arts
Expenses: 2014-2015: $31,900; room/board: $8,820
Financial aid: (630) 752-5021; 52% of undergrads determined to have financial need; average aid package $23,691

## Anderson University
Anderson IN
(765) 641-4080
U.S. News ranking: Reg. U. (Mid. W), No. 41
Website: www.anderson.edu
Admissions email: info@anderson.edu
Private; founded 1917
Affiliation: Church of God
Freshman admissions: selective; 2013-2014: 2,734 applied, 1,516 accepted. Either SAT or ACT required. SAT 25/75 percentile: 940-1140. High school rank: 20% in top tenth, 52% in top quarter, 82% in top half
Early decision deadline: N/A, notification date: N/A
Early action deadline: N/A, notification date: N/A
Application deadline (fall): rolling
Undergraduate student body: 1,737 full time, 279 part time; 40% male, 60% female; 0% American Indian, 1% Asian, 6% black, 3% Hispanic, 0% multiracial, 0% Pacific Islander, 81% white, 3% international; 74% from in state; 64% live on campus; N/A of students in fraternities, N/A in sororities
Most popular majors: 24% Business, Management, Marketing, and Related Support Services, 15% Education, 10% Health Professions and Related Programs, 6% Psychology, 10% Visual and Performing Arts
Expenses: 2014-2015: $26,850; room/board: $9,250
Financial aid: (765) 641-4180; 84% of undergrads determined to have financial need; average aid package $21,552

## Ball State University
Muncie IN
(765) 285-8300
U.S. News ranking: Nat. U., No. 173
Website: www.bsu.edu
Admissions email: askus@bsu.edu
Public; founded 1918
Freshman admissions: selective; 2013-2014: 17,118 applied, 10,367 accepted. Neither SAT nor ACT required. SAT 25/75 percentile: 980-1170. High school rank: 19% in top tenth, 52% in top quarter, 90% in top half
Early decision deadline: N/A, notification date: N/A
Early action deadline: N/A, notification date: N/A
Application deadline (fall): 8/15
Undergraduate student body: 15,128 full time, 1,172 part time; 42% male, 58% female; 0% American Indian, 1% Asian, 7% black, 3% Hispanic, 2% multiracial, 0% Pacific Islander, 82% white, 3% international; 88% from in state; 41% live on campus; 10% of students in fraternities, 13% in sororities
Most popular majors: 13% Business, Management, Marketing, and Related Support Services, 13% Communication, Journalism, and Related Programs, 13% Education, 10% Health Professions and Related Programs, 7% Liberal Arts and Sciences, General Studies and Humanities
Expenses: 2014-2015: $9,344 in state, $24,610 out of state; room/board: $9,246

Financial aid: (765) 285-5600; 67% of undergrads determined to have financial need; average aid package $11,277

## Bethel College
Mishawaka IN
(800) 422-4101
U.S. News ranking: Reg. Coll. (Mid. W), No. 19
Website: www.bethelcollege.edu
Admissions email: admissions@bethelcollege.edu
Private; founded 1947
Affiliation: Missionary Church
Freshman admissions: selective; 2013-2014: 1,241 applied, 889 accepted. Either SAT or ACT required. SAT 25/75 percentile: 900-1130. High school rank: 24% in top tenth, 51% in top quarter, 87% in top half
Early decision deadline: N/A, notification date: N/A
Early action deadline: N/A, notification date: N/A
Application deadline (fall): rolling
Undergraduate student body: 1,304 full time, 351 part time; 34% male, 66% female; 0% American Indian, 0% Asian, 12% black, 5% Hispanic, 2% multiracial, 0% Pacific Islander, 77% white, 2% international; 74% from in state; 47% live on campus; 0% of students in fraternities, 0% in sororities
Most popular majors: 31% Business, Management, Marketing, and Related Support Services, 11% Education, 11% Health Professions and Related Programs, 6% Public Administration and Social Service Professions, 7% Theology and Religious Vocations
Expenses: 2014-2015: $25,830; room/board: $7,780
Financial aid: (574) 257-3316; 86% of undergrads determined to have financial need; average aid package $17,321

## Butler University
Indianapolis IN
(888) 940-8100
U.S. News ranking: Reg. U. (Mid. W), No. 2
Website: www.butler.edu
Admissions email: admission@butler.edu
Private; founded 1855
Freshman admissions: more selective; 2013-2014: 9,357 applied, 6,185 accepted. Either SAT or ACT required. ACT 25/75 percentile: 25-30. High school rank: 49% in top tenth, 81% in top quarter, 97% in top half
Early decision deadline: N/A, notification date: N/A
Early action deadline: 11/1, notification date: 12/15
Application deadline (fall): 2/1
Undergraduate student body: 4,049 full time, 77 part time; 39% male, 61% female; 0% American Indian, 3% Asian, 3% black, 3% Hispanic, 1% multiracial, 0% Pacific Islander, 83% white, 2% international; 48% from in state; 67% live on campus; 29% of students in fraternities, 33% in sororities
Most popular majors: 21% Business, Management, Marketing, and Related Support Services, 9% Communication, Journalism, and Related Programs, 14% Education, 8%

Social Sciences, 12% Visual and Performing Arts
**Expenses:** 2014-2015: $35,652; room/board: $11,920
**Financial aid:** (317) 940-8200; 66% of undergrads determined to have financial need; average aid package $22,443

## Calumet College of St. Joseph
Whiting IN
(219) 473-4295
**U.S. News ranking:** Reg. U. (Mid. W), second tier
**Website:** www.ccsj.edu
**Admissions email:** admissions@ccsj.edu
**Private;** founded 1951
**Affiliation:** Roman Catholic
**Freshman admissions:** least selective; 2013-2014: 545 applied, 218 accepted. Neither SAT nor ACT required. SAT 25/75 percentile: 780-940. High school rank: 5% in top tenth, 14% in top quarter, 44% in top half
**Early decision deadline:** N/A, notification date: N/A
**Early action deadline:** N/A, notification date: N/A
**Application deadline (fall):** rolling
**Undergraduate student body:** 580 full time, 408 part time; 56% male, 44% female; 1% American Indian, 0% Asian, 27% black, 31% Hispanic, 1% multiracial, 0% Pacific Islander, 40% white, 0% international; 57% from in state; 0% live on campus; N/A of students in fraternities, N/A in sororities
**Most popular majors:** 6% Business Administration and Management, General, 12% Business Administration, Management and Operations, Other, 55% Criminal Justice/Safety Studies, 5% Elementary Education and Teaching, 3% Psychology, General
**Expenses:** 2014-2015: $16,440; room/board: N/A
**Financial aid:** (219) 473-4213; 83% of undergrads determined to have financial need; average aid package $12,356

## DePauw University
Greencastle IN
(765) 658-4006
**U.S. News ranking:** Nat. Lib. Arts, No. 51
**Website:** www.depauw.edu
**Admissions email:** admission@depauw.edu
**Private;** founded 1837
**Affiliation:** United Methodist
**Freshman admissions:** more selective; 2013-2014: 5,086 applied, 3,113 accepted. Either SAT or ACT required. ACT 25/75 percentile: 25-29. High school rank: 49% in top tenth, 78% in top quarter, 100% in top half
**Early decision deadline:** 11/1, notification date: 1/1
**Early action deadline:** 12/1, notification date: 1/31
**Application deadline (fall):** 2/1
**Undergraduate student body:** 2,280 full time, 24 part time; 45% male, 55% female; 0% American Indian, 3% Asian, 6% black, 3% Hispanic, 6% multiracial, 0% Pacific Islander, 68% white, 10% international; 40% from in state; 96% live on campus; 78% of students in fraternities, 64% in sororities

## Goshen College
Goshen IN
(574) 535-7535
**U.S. News ranking:** Nat. Lib. Arts, No. 129
**Website:** www.goshen.edu
**Admissions email:** admissions@goshen.edu
**Private;** founded 1894
**Affiliation:** Mennonite Church USA

**Most popular majors:** 13% Biological and Biomedical Sciences, 10% Communication, Journalism, and Related Programs, 10% English Language and Literature/Letters, 7% Foreign Languages, Literatures, and Linguistics, 23% Social Sciences
**Expenses:** 2014-2015: $42,746; room/board: $11,200
**Financial aid:** (765) 658-4030; 53% of undergrads determined to have financial need; average aid package $34,151

## Earlham College
Richmond IN
(765) 983-1600
**U.S. News ranking:** Nat. Lib. Arts, No. 73
**Website:** www.earlham.edu/admissions
**Admissions email:** admission@earlham.edu
**Private;** founded 1847
**Affiliation:** Quaker
**Freshman admissions:** more selective; 2013-2014: 1,890 applied, 1,204 accepted. Neither SAT nor ACT required. SAT 25/75 percentile: 1150-1340. High school rank: 29% in top tenth, 60% in top quarter, 92% in top half
**Early decision deadline:** 11/1, notification date: 12/1
**Early action deadline:** 12/1, notification date: 2/1
**Application deadline (fall):** 2/15
**Undergraduate student body:** 1,031 full time, 33 part time; 45% male, 55% female; 1% American Indian, 4% Asian, 14% black, 6% Hispanic, 0% multiracial, 0% Pacific Islander, 54% white, 18% international; 33% from in state; 96% live on campus; 0% of students in fraternities, 0% in sororities
**Most popular majors:** 16% Biology, General, 9% Fine and Studio Arts, 15% Multi-/Interdisciplinary Studies, Other, 9% Psychology, General, 11% Sociology
**Expenses:** 2014-2015: $42,870; room/board: $8,600
**Financial aid:** (765) 983-1217; 66% of undergrads determined to have financial need; average aid package $37,334

## Franklin College[1]
Franklin IN
(317) 738-8062
**U.S. News ranking:** Reg. Coll. (Mid. W), No. 6
**Website:** www.franklincollege.edu
**Admissions email:** admissions@franklincollege.edu
**Private;** founded 1834
**Affiliation:** American Baptist
**Application deadline (fall):** rolling
**Undergraduate student body:** N/A full time, N/A part time
**Expenses:** 2013-2014: $27,695; room/board: $8,190
**Financial aid:** (317) 738-8075

**Freshman admissions:** selective; 2013-2014: 770 applied, 424 accepted. Either SAT or ACT required. SAT 25/75 percentile: 950-1250. High school rank: 25% in top tenth, 33% in top quarter, 89% in top half
**Early decision deadline:** N/A, notification date: N/A
**Early action deadline:** N/A, notification date: N/A
**Application deadline (fall):** 8/1
**Undergraduate student body:** 745 full time, 83 part time; 43% male, 57% female; 0% American Indian, 1% Asian, 4% black, 12% Hispanic, 3% multiracial, 0% Pacific Islander, 72% white, 8% international; 50% from in state; 66% live on campus; N/A of students in fraternities, N/A in sororities
**Most popular majors:** 10% Biological and Biomedical Sciences, 15% Business, Management, Marketing, and Related Support Services, 7% Education, 19% Health Professions and Related Programs, 10% Visual and Performing Arts
**Expenses:** 2014-2015: $29,700; room/board: $9,700
**Financial aid:** (574) 535-7583; 74% of undergrads determined to have financial need; average aid package $23,539

## Grace College and Seminary
Winona Lake IN
(574) 372-5100
**U.S. News ranking:** Reg. Coll. (Mid. W), No. 46
**Website:** www.grace.edu
**Admissions email:** enroll@grace.edu
**Private;** founded 1948
**Affiliation:** Fellowship of Grace Brethren Churches
**Freshman admissions:** selective; 2013-2014: 3,572 applied, 2,789 accepted. Either SAT or ACT required. SAT 25/75 percentile: 910-1150. High school rank: 21% in top tenth, 47% in top quarter, 79% in top half
**Early decision deadline:** N/A, notification date: N/A
**Early action deadline:** 12/1, notification date: 12/20
**Application deadline (fall):** 3/1
**Undergraduate student body:** 1,275 full time, 340 part time; 41% male, 59% female; 0% American Indian, 1% Asian, 4% black, 3% Hispanic, 3% multiracial, 0% Pacific Islander, 82% white, 0% international; 62% from in state; 70% live on campus; 0% of students in fraternities, 0% in sororities
**Most popular majors:** 19% Business Administration, Management and Operations, Other, 7% Counseling Psychology, 13% Elementary Education and Teaching, 5% Graphic Design, 5% Psychology, General
**Expenses:** 2014-2015: $24,670; room/board: $7,930
**Financial aid:** (574) 372-5100; 52% of undergrads determined to have financial need; average aid package $15,916

## Hanover College
Hanover IN
(812) 866-7021
**U.S. News ranking:** Nat. Lib. Arts, No. 113
**Website:** www.hanover.edu
**Admissions email:** admission@hanover.edu
**Private;** founded 1827
**Affiliation:** Presbyterian
**Freshman admissions:** selective; 2013-2014: 3,174 applied, 2,118 accepted. Either SAT or ACT required. SAT 25/75 percentile: 1000-1200. High school rank: 32% in top tenth, 66% in top quarter, 95% in top half
**Early decision deadline:** N/A, notification date: N/A
**Early action deadline:** 12/1, notification date: 12/20
**Application deadline (fall):** 3/1
**Undergraduate student body:** 1,158 full time, 5 part time; 43% male, 57% female; 0% American Indian, 1% Asian, 4% black, 2% Hispanic, 2% multiracial, 0% Pacific Islander, 82% white, 5% international; 95% live on campus; 44% of students in fraternities, 29% in sororities
**Most popular majors:** 8% Biology/Biological Sciences, General, 7% Economics, General, 9% Elementary Education and Teaching, 8% Kinesiology and Exercise Science, 10% Psychology, General
**Expenses:** 2014-2015: $33,023; room/board: $10,050
**Financial aid:** (800) 213-2178; 77% of undergrads determined to have financial need; average aid package $26,398

## Holy Cross College[1]
Notre Dame IN
(574) 239-8400
**U.S. News ranking:** Nat. Lib. Arts, second tier
**Website:** www.hcc-nd.edu/home
**Admissions email:** admissions@hcc-nd.edu
**Private;** founded 1966
**Affiliation:** Roman Catholic
**Application deadline (fall):** rolling
**Undergraduate student body:** N/A full time, N/A part time
**Expenses:** 2014-2015: $27,150; room/board: $9,500
**Financial aid:** (574) 239-8408

## Huntington University
Huntington IN
(800) 642-6493
**U.S. News ranking:** Reg. Coll. (Mid. W), No. 14
**Website:** www.huntington.edu
**Admissions email:** admissions@huntington.edu
**Private;** founded 1897
**Affiliation:** United Brethren in Christ
**Freshman admissions:** selective; 2013-2014: 780 applied, 759 accepted. Either SAT or ACT required. SAT 25/75 percentile: 880-1130. High school rank: 26% in top tenth, 53% in top quarter, 80% in top half
**Early decision deadline:** N/A, notification date: N/A
**Early action deadline:** N/A, notification date: N/A
**Application deadline (fall):** 8/1

**Undergraduate student body:** 961 full time, 92 part time; 43% male, 57% female; 0% American Indian, 0% Asian, 2% black, 3% Hispanic, 1% multiracial, 0% Pacific Islander, 88% white, 4% international; 65% from in state; 76% live on campus; 0% of students in fraternities, 0% in sororities
**Most popular majors:** 19% Business, Management, Marketing, and Related Support Services, 15% Education, 9% Health Professions and Related Programs, 13% Theology and Religious Vocations, 9% Visual and Performing Arts
**Expenses:** 2014-2015: $24,771; room/board: $8,306
**Financial aid:** (260) 359-4015; 81% of undergrads determined to have financial need; average aid package $18,334

## Indiana Institute of Technology
Fort Wayne IN
(800) 937-2448
**U.S. News ranking:** Business, unranked
**Website:** www.indianatech.edu
**Admissions email:** admissions@indianatech.edu
**Private;** founded 1930
**Freshman admissions:** selective; 2013-2014: 2,324 applied, 1,679 accepted. Either SAT or ACT required. ACT 25/75 percentile: 17-23. High school rank: 8% in top tenth, 28% in top quarter, 59% in top half
**Early decision deadline:** N/A, notification date: N/A
**Early action deadline:** N/A, notification date: N/A
**Application deadline (fall):** rolling
**Undergraduate student body:** 3,710 full time, 2,007 part time; 38% male, 62% female; 0% American Indian, 0% Asian, 39% black, 4% Hispanic, 2% multiracial, 0% Pacific Islander, 48% white, 1% international; 83% from in state; N/A live on campus; 2% of students in fraternities, 1% in sororities
**Most popular majors:** 9% Accounting, 41% Business Administration and Management, General, 11% Business/Commerce, General, 4% General Studies, 10% Organizational Leadership
**Expenses:** 2014-2015: $24,860; room/board: $11,150
**Financial aid:** (260) 422-5561; 91% of undergrads determined to have financial need; average aid package $15,351

## Indiana State University
Terre Haute IN
(812) 237-2121
**U.S. News ranking:** Nat. U., second tier
**Website:** web.indstate.edu/
**Admissions email:** admissions@indstate.edu
**Public;** founded 1865
**Freshman admissions:** less selective; 2013-2014: 11,016 applied, 9,150 accepted. Either SAT or ACT required. SAT 25/75 percentile: 800-1020. High school rank: 8% in top tenth, 28% in top quarter, 67% in top half

Early decision deadline: N/A, notification date: N/A
Early action deadline: N/A, notification date: N/A
Application deadline (fall): 8/15
Undergraduate student body: 9,131 full time, 1,137 part time; 46% male, 54% female; 0% American Indian, 1% Asian, 18% black, 3% Hispanic, 3% multiracial, 0% Pacific Islander, 67% white, 6% international; 84% from in state; 40% live on campus; 2% of students in fraternities, 2% in sororities
Most popular majors: 17% Business, Management, Marketing, and Related Support Services, 9% Education, 6% Engineering Technologies and Engineering-Related Fields, 18% Health Professions and Related Programs, 12% Social Sciences
Expenses: 2014-2015: $8,416 in state, $18,346 out of state; room/board: $9,182
Financial aid: (812) 237-2215; 74% of undergrads determined to have financial need; average aid package $10,252

## Indiana University–Bloomington
Bloomington IN
(812) 855-0661
U.S. News ranking: Nat. U., No. 76
Website: www.iub.edu
Admissions email: iuadmit@indiana.edu
Public; founded 1820
Freshman admissions: more selective; 2013-2014: 37,826 applied, 27,300 accepted. Either SAT or ACT required. SAT 25/75 percentile: 1060-1290. High school rank: 35% in top tenth, 70% in top quarter, 95% in top half
Early decision deadline: N/A, notification date: N/A
Early action deadline: N/A, notification date: N/A
Application deadline (fall): rolling
Undergraduate student body: 31,050 full time, 5,812 part time; 49% male, 51% female; 0% American Indian, 4% Asian, 4% black, 4% Hispanic, 3% multiracial, 0% Pacific Islander, 73% white, 11% international; 71% from in state; 28% live on campus; 21% of students in fraternities, 23% in sororities
Most popular majors: 5% Biological and Biomedical Sciences, 18% Business, Management, Marketing, and Related Support Services, 6% Parks, Recreation, Leisure, and Fitness Studies, 5% Psychology, 7% Public Administration and Social Service Professions
Expenses: 2014-2015: $10,388 in state, $33,241 out of state; room/board: $9,493
Financial aid: (812) 855-0321; 44% of undergrads determined to have financial need; average aid package $11,991

## Indiana University East
Richmond IN
(765) 973-8208
U.S. News ranking: Reg. Coll. (Mid. W), second tier
Website: www.iue.edu
Admissions email: eaadmit@indiana.edu

Public; founded 1971
Freshman admissions: less selective; 2013-2014: 1,219 applied, 656 accepted. Either SAT or ACT required. SAT 25/75 percentile: 820-1030. High school rank: 8% in top tenth, 29% in top quarter, 68% in top half
Early decision deadline: N/A, notification date: N/A
Early action deadline: N/A, notification date: N/A
Application deadline (fall): rolling
Undergraduate student body: 1,948 full time, 2,378 part time; 35% male, 65% female; 0% American Indian, 1% Asian, 4% black, 2% Hispanic, 2% multiracial, 0% Pacific Islander, 89% white, 0% international; 78% from in state; 0% live on campus; N/A of students in fraternities, N/A in sororities
Most popular majors: 29% Business, Management, Marketing, and Related Support Services, 9% Education, 18% Health Professions and Related Programs, 13% Liberal Arts and Sciences, General Studies and Humanities, 6% Public Administration and Social Service Professions
Expenses: 2014-2015: $6,787 in state, $18,081 out of state; room/board: N/A
Financial aid: (765) 973-8206; 83% of undergrads determined to have financial need; average aid package $8,814

## Indiana University–Kokomo
Kokomo IN
(765) 455-9217
U.S. News ranking: Reg. Coll. (Mid. W), second tier
Website: www.iuk.edu
Admissions email: Iuadmiss@iuk.edu
Public; founded 1945
Freshman admissions: less selective; 2013-2014: 1,066 applied, 784 accepted. Either SAT or ACT required. SAT 25/75 percentile: 850-1040. High school rank: 9% in top tenth, 29% in top quarter, 68% in top half
Early decision deadline: N/A, notification date: N/A
Early action deadline: N/A, notification date: N/A
Application deadline (fall): 8/6
Undergraduate student body: 2,012 full time, 1,969 part time; 36% male, 64% female; 0% American Indian, 1% Asian, 4% black, 4% Hispanic, 3% multiracial, 0% Pacific Islander, 84% white, 0% international; 99% from in state; 0% live on campus; 0% of students in fraternities, 0% in sororities
Most popular majors: 10% Business, Management, Marketing, and Related Support Services, 9% Education, 33% Health Professions and Related Programs, 13% Liberal Arts and Sciences, General Studies and Humanities, 6% Psychology
Expenses: 2014-2015: $6,811 in state, $18,081 out of state; room/board: N/A
Financial aid: (765) 455-9216; 75% of undergrads determined to have financial need; average aid package $8,303

## Indiana University Northwest
Gary IN
(219) 980-6991
U.S. News ranking: Reg. U. (Mid. W), second tier
Website: www.iun.edu
Admissions email: admit@iun.edu
Public; founded 1948
Freshman admissions: less selective; 2013-2014: 1,773 applied, 1,352 accepted. Either SAT or ACT required. SAT 25/75 percentile: 780-1020. High school rank: 10% in top tenth, 32% in top quarter, 62% in top half
Early decision deadline: N/A, notification date: N/A
Early action deadline: N/A, notification date: N/A
Application deadline (fall): rolling
Undergraduate student body: 3,221 full time, 2,683 part time; 34% male, 66% female; 0% American Indian, 2% Asian, 20% black, 17% Hispanic, 2% multiracial, 0% Pacific Islander, 56% white, 0% international; 98% from in state; 0% live on campus; 0% of students in fraternities, 0% in sororities
Most popular majors: 12% Business, Management, Marketing, and Related Support Services, 14% Health Professions and Related Programs, 10% Homeland Security, Law Enforcement, Firefighting and Related Protective Services, 14% Liberal Arts and Sciences, General Studies and Humanities, 11% Psychology
Expenses: 2014-2015: $6,854 in state, $18,081 out of state; room/board: N/A
Financial aid: (877) 280-4593; 73% of undergrads determined to have financial need; average aid package $8,206

## Indiana University-Purdue University–Fort Wayne
Fort Wayne IN
(260) 481-6812
U.S. News ranking: Reg. U. (Mid. W), second tier
Website: www.ipfw.edu
Admissions email: ask@ipfw.edu
Public; founded 1964
Freshman admissions: selective; 2013-2014: 3,702 applied, 3,076 accepted. Either SAT or ACT required. SAT 25/75 percentile: 890-1090. High school rank: 13% in top tenth, 38% in top quarter, 77% in top half
Early decision deadline: N/A, notification date: N/A
Early action deadline: N/A, notification date: N/A
Application deadline (fall): 8/1
Undergraduate student body: 7,418 full time, 5,510 part time; 45% male, 55% female; 0% American Indian, 2% Asian, 5% black, 5% Hispanic, 3% multiracial, 0% Pacific Islander, 82% white, 2% international; 97% from in state; 7% live on campus; 1% of students in fraternities, 0% in sororities
Most popular majors: 18% Business Administration and Management, General, 11% Education, General, 14% General Studies, 11% Health Services/Allied Health/Health Sciences, General, 7% Visual and Performing Arts, General

Expenses: 2014-2015: $8,040 in state, $19,183 out of state; room/board: $9,242
Financial aid: (260) 481-6820; 78% of undergrads determined to have financial need; average aid package $9,274

## Indiana University-Purdue University–Indianapolis
Indianapolis IN
(317) 274-4591
U.S. News ranking: Nat. U., No. 194
Website: www.iupui.edu
Admissions email: apply@iupui.edu
Public; founded 1969
Freshman admissions: selective; 2013-2014: 12,230 applied, 8,510 accepted. Either SAT or ACT required. SAT 25/75 percentile: 890-1120. High school rank: 15% in top tenth, 45% in top quarter, 86% in top half
Early decision deadline: N/A, notification date: N/A
Early action deadline: N/A, notification date: N/A
Application deadline (fall): 5/1
Undergraduate student body: 16,760 full time, 5,649 part time; 43% male, 57% female; 0% American Indian, 4% Asian, 10% black, 5% Hispanic, 3% multiracial, 0% Pacific Islander, 72% white, 3% international; 98% from in state; 10% live on campus; 3% of students in fraternities, 4% in sororities
Most popular majors: 13% Business, Management, Marketing, and Related Support Services, 5% Education, 11% Health Professions and Related Programs, 12% Liberal Arts and Sciences, General Studies and Humanities, 5% Psychology
Expenses: 2014-2015: $8,909 in state, $30,089 out of state; room/board: $7,981
Financial aid: (317) 274-4162; 71% of undergrads determined to have financial need; average aid package $9,848

## Indiana University–South Bend
South Bend IN
(574) 520-4839
U.S. News ranking: Reg. U. (Mid. W), second tier
Website: www.iusb.edu
Admissions email: admissions@iusb.edu
Public; founded 1922
Freshman admissions: less selective; 2013-2014: 2,456 applied, 1,720 accepted. Either SAT or ACT required. SAT 25/75 percentile: 860-1060. High school rank: 9% in top tenth, 29% in top quarter, 65% in top half
Early decision deadline: N/A, notification date: N/A
Early action deadline: N/A, notification date: N/A
Application deadline (fall): rolling
Undergraduate student body: 3,984 full time, 3,528 part time; 39% male, 61% female; 0% American Indian, 1% Asian, 7% black, 7% Hispanic, 3% multiracial, 0% Pacific Islander, 77% white, 2% international; 97% from in state; 6% live on campus; N/A of students in fraternities, N/A in sororities

Most popular majors: 18% Business, Management, Marketing, and Related Support Services, 7% Education, 11% Health Professions and Related Programs, 15% Liberal Arts and Sciences, General Studies and Humanities, 5% Psychology
Expenses: 2014-2015: $6,905 in state, $18,081 out of state; room/board: N/A
Financial aid: (574) 237-4357; 78% of undergrads determined to have financial need; average aid package $8,655

## Indiana University Southeast
New Albany IN
(812) 941-2212
U.S. News ranking: Reg. U. (Mid. W), second tier
Website: www.ius.edu
Admissions email: admissions@ius.edu
Public; founded 1941
Freshman admissions: less selective; 2013-2014: 2,097 applied, 1,666 accepted. Either SAT or ACT required. SAT 25/75 percentile: 850-1050. High school rank: 10% in top tenth, 34% in top quarter, 71% in top half
Early decision deadline: N/A, notification date: N/A
Early action deadline: N/A, notification date: N/A
Application deadline (fall): rolling
Undergraduate student body: 3,665 full time, 2,483 part time; 42% male, 58% female; 0% American Indian, 1% Asian, 6% black, 3% Hispanic, 2% multiracial, 0% Pacific Islander, 86% white, 0% international; 70% from in state; 6% live on campus; N/A of students in fraternities, N/A in sororities
Most popular majors: 18% Business, Management, Marketing, and Related Support Services, 10% Education, 10% Health Professions and Related Programs, 16% Liberal Arts and Sciences, General Studies and Humanities, 7% Psychology
Expenses: 2014-2015: $6,827 in state, $18,081 out of state; room/board: N/A
Financial aid: (812) 941-2246; 69% of undergrads determined to have financial need; average aid package $7,669

## Indiana Wesleyan University
Marion IN
(866) 468-6498
U.S. News ranking: Reg. U. (Mid. W), No. 26
Website: www.indwes.edu
Admissions email: admissions@indwes.edu
Private; founded 1920
Affiliation: Wesleyan Church
Freshman admissions: selective; 2013-2014: 2,606 applied, 2,521 accepted. Either SAT or ACT required. ACT 25/75 percentile: 21-27. High school rank: 28% in top tenth, 57% in top quarter, 85% in top half
Early decision deadline: N/A, notification date: N/A
Early action deadline: N/A, notification date: N/A
Application deadline (fall): rolling

**Undergraduate student body:** 2,761 full time, 172 part time; 35% male, 65% female; 0% American Indian, 1% Asian, 2% black, 3% Hispanic, 2% multiracial, 0% Pacific Islander, 90% white, 0% international; 55% from in state; 80% live on campus; 0% of students in fraternities, 0% in sororities
**Most popular majors:** 3% Business Administration and Management, General, 8% Elementary Education and Teaching, 5% Psychology, General, 19% Registered Nursing/Registered Nurse, 3% Social Work
**Expenses:** 2014-2015: $24,102; room/board: $7,712
**Financial aid:** (765) 677-2116; 79% of undergrads determined to have financial need; average aid package $21,892

## Manchester University
North Manchester IN
(800) 852-3648
**U.S. News ranking:** Reg. Coll. (Mid. W), No. 27
**Website:** www.manchester.edu
**Admissions email:** admitinfo@manchester.edu
**Private;** founded 1889
**Affiliation:** Church of the Brethren
**Freshman admissions:** selective; 2013-2014: 2,195 applied, 1,562 accepted. Either SAT or ACT required. SAT 25/75 percentile: 890-1130. High school rank: 20% in top tenth, 48% in top quarter, 83% in top half
**Early decision deadline:** N/A, notification date: N/A
**Early action deadline:** N/A, notification date: N/A
**Application deadline (fall):** rolling
**Undergraduate student body:** 1,177 full time, 22 part time; 47% male, 53% female; 0% American Indian, 1% Asian, 4% black, 5% Hispanic, 3% multiracial, 0% Pacific Islander, 84% white, 2% international; 89% from in state; 72% live on campus; N/A of students in fraternities, N/A in sororities
**Most popular majors:** 21% Business, Management, Marketing, and Related Support Services, 16% Education, 11% Health Professions and Related Programs, 10% Parks, Recreation, Leisure, and Fitness Studies, 7% Psychology
**Expenses:** 2014-2015: $29,040; room/board: $9,300
**Financial aid:** (260) 982-5066; 87% of undergrads determined to have financial need; average aid package $25,180

## Marian University
Indianapolis IN
(317) 955-6300
**U.S. News ranking:** Reg. Coll. (Mid. W), No. 25
**Website:** www.marian.edu
**Admissions email:** admissions@marian.edu
**Private;** founded 1851
**Affiliation:** Roman Catholic
**Freshman admissions:** selective; 2013-2014: 2,064 applied, 1,196 accepted. Either SAT or ACT required. ACT 25/75 percentile: 19-25. High school rank: 11% in top tenth, 43% in top quarter, 82% in top half

**Early decision deadline:** N/A, notification date: N/A
**Early action deadline:** N/A, notification date: N/A
**Application deadline (fall):** 8/1
**Undergraduate student body:** 1,679 full time, 525 part time; 36% male, 64% female; 0% American Indian, 1% Asian, 14% black, 4% Hispanic, 2% multiracial, 0% Pacific Islander, 75% white, 0% international; 91% from in state; 34% live on campus; 0% of students in fraternities, 0% in sororities
**Most popular majors:** 3% Accounting, 10% Business Administration and Management, General, 3% Kinesiology and Exercise Science, 8% Marketing/Marketing Management, General, 38% Registered Nursing/Registered Nurse
**Expenses:** 2014-2015: $29,400; room/board: $9,140
**Financial aid:** (317) 955-6040; 85% of undergrads determined to have financial need; average aid package $22,292

## Martin University[1]
Indianapolis IN
(317) 543-3243
**U.S. News ranking:** Nat. Lib. Arts, unranked
**Website:** www.martin.edu
**Admissions email:** bshaheed@martin.edu
**Private**
**Application deadline (fall):** N/A
**Undergraduate student body:** N/A full time, N/A part time
**Expenses:** 2013-2014: $11,960; room/board: N/A
**Financial aid:** (317) 543-3258

## Oakland City University
Oakland City IN
(800) 737-5125
**U.S. News ranking:** Reg. U. (Mid. W), No. 105
**Website:** www.oak.edu
**Admissions email:** admission@oak.edu
**Private;** founded 1885
**Affiliation:** General Association of General Baptist
**Freshman admissions:** less selective; 2013-2014: 652 applied, 475 accepted. Neither SAT nor ACT required. SAT 25/75 percentile: 870-1070. High school rank: N/A
**Early decision deadline:** N/A, notification date: N/A
**Early action deadline:** N/A, notification date: N/A
**Application deadline (fall):** 9/8
**Undergraduate student body:** 461 full time, 1,850 part time; 39% male, 61% female; 0% American Indian, 1% Asian, 6% black, 2% Hispanic, 1% multiracial, 0% Pacific Islander, 77% white, 6% international; 85% from in state; 50% live on campus; N/A of students in fraternities, N/A in sororities
**Most popular majors:** 8% Biological and Biomedical Sciences, 35% Business, Management, Marketing, and Related Support Services, 29% Education, 7% Homeland Security, Law Enforcement, Firefighting and Related Protective Services, 5% Psychology

**Expenses:** 2013-2014: $19,200; room/board: $8,300
**Financial aid:** (812) 749-1224

## Purdue University–Calumet
Hammond IN
(219) 989-2213
**U.S. News ranking:** Reg. U. (Mid. W), second tier
**Website:** www.purduecal.edu/purduecal.edu
**Admissions email:** adms@purduecal.edu
**Public;** founded 1946
**Freshman admissions:** selective; 2013-2014: 1,945 applied, 1,470 accepted. Either SAT or ACT required. SAT 25/75 percentile: 870-1080. High school rank: 12% in top tenth, 36% in top quarter, 71% in top half
**Early decision deadline:** N/A, notification date: N/A
**Early action deadline:** N/A, notification date: N/A
**Application deadline (fall):** 8/1
**Undergraduate student body:** 4,836 full time, 3,554 part time; 43% male, 57% female; 0% American Indian, 2% Asian, 14% black, 17% Hispanic, 2% multiracial, 0% Pacific Islander, 57% white, 6% international; 78% from in state; 6% live on campus; 1% of students in fraternities, 1% in sororities
**Most popular majors:** 20% Business, Management, Marketing, and Related Support Services, 6% Communication, Journalism, and Related Programs, 5% Engineering, 6% Engineering Technologies and Engineering-Related Fields, 33% Health Professions and Related Programs
**Expenses:** 2014-2015: $7,241 in state, $16,356 out of state; room/board: $8,075
**Financial aid:** (219) 989-2301; 64% of undergrads determined to have financial need; average aid package $4,522

## Purdue University–North Central
Westville IN
(219) 785-5505
**U.S. News ranking:** Reg. Coll. (Mid. W), second tier
**Website:** www.pnc.edu/admissions
**Admissions email:** admissions@pnc.edu
**Public;** founded 1946
**Freshman admissions:** less selective; 2013-2014: 1,567 applied, 1,143 accepted. Neither SAT nor ACT required. SAT 25/75 percentile: 860-1050. High school rank: 7% in top tenth, 25% in top quarter, 63% in top half
**Early decision deadline:** N/A, notification date: N/A
**Early action deadline:** N/A, notification date: N/A
**Application deadline (fall):** rolling
**Undergraduate student body:** 2,732 full time, 3,322 part time; 40% male, 60% female; 1% American Indian, 1% Asian, 5% black, 8% Hispanic, 2% multiracial, 0% Pacific Islander, 82% white, 1% international; 98% from in state; N/A live on campus; N/A of students in fraternities, N/A in sororities
**Most popular majors:** Information not available
**Expenses:** 2014-2015: $7,329 in state, $17,445 out of state; room/board: N/A

**Financial aid:** (219) 785-5653; 74% of undergrads determined to have financial need; average aid package $7,608

## Purdue University–West Lafayette
West Lafayette IN
(765) 494-1776
**U.S. News ranking:** Nat. U., No. 62
**Website:** www.purdue.edu
**Admissions email:** admissions@purdue.edu
**Public;** founded 1869
**Freshman admissions:** more selective; 2013-2014: 30,955 applied, 18,684 accepted. Either SAT or ACT required. SAT 25/75 percentile: 1080-1320. High school rank: 47% in top tenth, 80% in top quarter, 98% in top half
**Early decision deadline:** N/A, notification date: N/A
**Early action deadline:** 11/1, notification date: 12/13
**Application deadline (fall):** rolling
**Undergraduate student body:** 28,142 full time, 1,298 part time; 57% male, 43% female; 0% American Indian, 5% Asian, 3% black, 4% Hispanic, 2% multiracial, 0% Pacific Islander, 67% white, 17% international; 68% from in state; 36% live on campus; 10% of students in fraternities, 8% in sororities
**Most popular majors:** 8% Agriculture, Agriculture Operations, and Related Sciences, 17% Business, Management, Marketing, and Related Support Services, 6% Education, 20% Engineering, 15% Liberal Arts and Sciences, General Studies and Humanities
**Expenses:** 2014-2015: $10,002 in state, $28,804 out of state; room/board: $10,030
**Financial aid:** (765) 494-5090; 46% of undergrads determined to have financial need; average aid package $13,081

## Rose-Hulman Institute of Technology
Terre Haute IN
(812) 877-8213
**U.S. News ranking:** Engineering, unranked
**Website:** www.rose-hulman.edu
**Admissions email:** admissions@rose-hulman.edu
**Private;** founded 1874
**Freshman admissions:** more selective; 2013-2014: 5,046 applied, 2,837 accepted. Either SAT or ACT required. ACT 25/75 percentile: 27-32. High school rank: 66% in top tenth, 92% in top quarter, 100% in top half
**Early decision deadline:** N/A, notification date: N/A
**Early action deadline:** 11/1, notification date: 12/15
**Application deadline (fall):** 3/1
**Undergraduate student body:** 2,186 full time, 19 part time; 78% male, 22% female; 0% American Indian, 4% Asian, 2% black, 3% Hispanic, 3% multiracial, 0% Pacific Islander, 78% white, 9% international; 37% from in state; 60% live on campus; 36% of students in fraternities, 33% in sororities

**Most popular majors:** 10% Bioengineering and Biomedical Engineering, 11% Chemical Engineering, 9% Civil Engineering, General, 13% Electrical and Electronics Engineering, 28% Mechanical Engineering
**Expenses:** 2014-2015: $41,283; room/board: $12,057
**Financial aid:** (812) 877-8259; 65% of undergrads determined to have financial need; average aid package $28,577

## St. Joseph's College
Rensselaer IN
(219) 866-6170
**U.S. News ranking:** Reg. Coll. (Mid. W), No. 28
**Website:** www.saintjoe.edu
**Admissions email:** admissions@saintjoe.edu
**Private;** founded 1889
**Affiliation:** Roman Catholic
**Freshman admissions:** selective; 2013-2014: 1,639 applied, 1,052 accepted. Either SAT or ACT required. SAT 25/75 percentile: 890-1080. High school rank: 12% in top tenth, 35% in top quarter, 73% in top half
**Early decision deadline:** N/A, notification date: N/A
**Early action deadline:** N/A, notification date: N/A
**Application deadline (fall):** rolling
**Undergraduate student body:** 1,036 full time, 112 part time; 41% male, 59% female; 1% American Indian, 0% Asian, 9% black, 5% Hispanic, 2% multiracial, 0% Pacific Islander, 80% white, 1% international; 77% from in state; 61% live on campus; N/A of students in fraternities, N/A in sororities
**Most popular majors:** 12% Biology/Biological Sciences, General, 15% Business/Commerce, General, 5% Criminal Justice/Safety Studies, 6% Elementary Education and Teaching, 35% Registered Nursing/Registered Nurse
**Expenses:** 2014-2015: $27,890; room/board: $8,610
**Financial aid:** (219) 866-6163; 85% of undergrads determined to have financial need; average aid package $27,592

## St. Mary-of-the-Woods College
St. Mary-of-the-Woods IN
(800) 926-7692
**U.S. News ranking:** Reg. Coll. (Mid. W), No. 16
**Website:** www.smwc.edu
**Admissions email:** smwcadms@smwc.edu
**Private;** founded 1840
**Affiliation:** Roman Catholic
**Freshman admissions:** less selective; 2013-2014: 325 applied, 317 accepted. Either SAT or ACT required. SAT 25/75 percentile: 780-1020. High school rank: 14% in top tenth, 41% in top quarter, 70% in top half
**Early decision deadline:** N/A, notification date: N/A
**Early action deadline:** N/A, notification date: N/A
**Application deadline (fall):** rolling
**Undergraduate student body:** 384 full time, 265 part time; 3% male, 97% female; 1% American Indian, 0% Asian, 4% black, 1% Hispanic, 0% multiracial, 0% Pacific Islander, 85% white,

0% international; N/A from in state; 60% live on campus; 0% of students in fraternities, 0% in sororities
**Most popular majors:** 4% Accounting, 10% Business Administration and Management, General, 29% Education, 5% Human Resources Management and Services, 11% Psychology
**Expenses:** 2014-2015: $28,226; room/board: $10,250
**Financial aid:** (812) 535-5109; 90% of undergrads determined to have financial need; average aid package $17,832

## St. Mary's College
Notre Dame IN
(574) 284-4587
**U.S. News ranking:** Nat. Lib. Arts, No. 96
**Website:** www.saintmarys.edu
**Admissions email:** admission@saintmarys.edu
**Private;** founded 1844
**Affiliation:** Roman Catholic
**Freshman admissions:** selective; 2013-2014: 1,529 applied, 1,310 accepted. Either SAT or ACT required. ACT 25/75 percentile: 23-28. High school rank: 27% in top tenth, 57% in top quarter, 90% in top half
**Early decision deadline:** 11/15, notification date: 12/15
**Early action deadline:** N/A, notification date: N/A
**Application deadline (fall):** rolling
**Undergraduate student body:** 1,469 full time, 10 part time; 0% male, 100% female; 0% American Indian, 1% Asian, 1% black, 12% Hispanic, 3% multiracial, 0% Pacific Islander, 77% white, 2% international; 25% from in state; 91% live on campus; 0% of students in fraternities, 0% in sororities
**Most popular majors:** 9% Biology/Biological Sciences, General, 11% Elementary Education and Teaching, 8% Psychology, General, 14% Registered Nursing/Registered Nurse, 8% Speech Communication and Rhetoric
**Expenses:** 2014-2015: $35,970; room/board: $10,930
**Financial aid:** (574) 284-4557; 56% of undergrads determined to have financial need; average aid package $29,077

## Taylor University
Upland IN
(765) 998-5134
**U.S. News ranking:** Reg. Coll. (Mid. W), No. 1
**Website:** www.taylor.edu
**Admissions email:** admissions_u@taylor.edu
**Private;** founded 1846
**Affiliation:** Christian interdenominational
**Freshman admissions:** more selective; 2013-2014: 1,637 applied, 1,434 accepted. Either SAT or ACT required. ACT 25/75 percentile: 24-31. High school rank: 37% in top tenth, 67% in top quarter, 89% in top half
**Early decision deadline:** N/A, notification date: N/A
**Early action deadline:** N/A, notification date: N/A
**Application deadline (fall):** rolling
**Undergraduate student body:** 1,852 full time, 294 part time; 45% male, 55% female; 0% American Indian, 3% Asian, 2% black, 3% Hispanic, 1% multiracial,

0% Pacific Islander, 87% white, 4% international; 36% from in state; 87% live on campus; 0% of students in fraternities, 0% in sororities
**Most popular majors:** 14% Business, Management, Marketing, and Related Support Services, 7% Communication, Journalism, and Related Programs, 18% Education, 7% Psychology, 10% Visual and Performing Arts
**Expenses:** 2014-2015: $29,538; room/board: $8,283
**Financial aid:** (765) 998-5358; 61% of undergrads determined to have financial need; average aid package $19,190

## Trine University
Angola IN
(260) 665-4100
**U.S. News ranking:** Reg. Coll. (Mid. W), No. 32
**Website:** www.trine.edu
**Admissions email:** admit@trine.edu
**Private;** founded 1884
**Freshman admissions:** selective; 2013-2014: 2,711 applied, 2,036 accepted. Either SAT or ACT required. SAT 25/75 percentile: 980-1190. High school rank: 25% in top tenth, 57% in top quarter, 87% in top half
**Early decision deadline:** N/A, notification date: N/A
**Early action deadline:** N/A, notification date: N/A
**Application deadline (fall):** 8/1
**Undergraduate student body:** 1,430 full time, 445 part time; 65% male, 35% female; 0% American Indian, 0% Asian, 2% black, 3% Hispanic, 2% multiracial, 0% Pacific Islander, 84% white, 4% international; 61% from in state; 69% live on campus; 26% of students in fraternities, 19% in sororities
**Most popular majors:** 19% Business/Commerce, General, 8% Criminal Justice/Law Enforcement Administration, 9% Education, General, 33% Engineering, General, 7% Psychology, General
**Expenses:** 2014-2015: $29,600; room/board: $9,800
**Financial aid:** (260) 665-4175; 84% of undergrads determined to have financial need; average aid package $24,095

## University of Evansville
Evansville IN
(812) 488-2468
**U.S. News ranking:** Reg. U. (Mid. W), No. 9
**Website:** www.evansville.edu
**Admissions email:** admission@evansville.edu
**Private;** founded 1854
**Affiliation:** Methodist
**Freshman admissions:** more selective; 2013-2014: 2,935 applied, 2,468 accepted. Either SAT or ACT required. ACT 25/75 percentile: 23-29. High school rank: 33% in top tenth, 66% in top quarter, 91% in top half
**Early decision deadline:** N/A, notification date: N/A
**Early action deadline:** 12/1, notification date: 12/15
**Application deadline (fall):** rolling
**Undergraduate student body:** 2,290 full time, 187 part time; 42% male, 58% female; 0% American Indian, 1% Asian, 3% black, 3% Hispanic, 2% multiracial, 0%

Pacific Islander, 78% white, 9% international; 55% from in state; 65% live on campus; 30% of students in fraternities, 28% in sororities
**Most popular majors:** 12% Business, Management, Marketing, and Related Support Services, 9% Engineering, 10% Health Professions and Related Programs, 9% Parks, Recreation, Leisure, and Fitness Studies, 12% Visual and Performing Arts
**Expenses:** 2014-2015: $31,776; room/board: $10,880
**Financial aid:** (812) 488-2364; 69% of undergrads determined to have financial need; average aid package $25,721

## University of Indianapolis
Indianapolis IN
(317) 788-3216
**U.S. News ranking:** Reg. U. (Mid. W), No. 26
**Website:** www.uindy.edu
**Admissions email:** admissions@uindy.edu
**Private;** founded 1902
**Affiliation:** United Methodist
**Freshman admissions:** selective; 2013-2014: 5,530 applied, 4,504 accepted. Either SAT or ACT required. SAT 25/75 percentile: 910-1120. High school rank: 23% in top tenth, 56% in top quarter, 88% in top half
**Early decision deadline:** N/A, notification date: N/A
**Early action deadline:** N/A, notification date: N/A
**Application deadline (fall):** 8/20
**Undergraduate student body:** 3,169 full time, 993 part time; 33% male, 67% female; 0% American Indian, 1% Asian, 11% black, 3% Hispanic, 2% multiracial, 0% Pacific Islander, 69% white, 8% international; 93% from in state; 35% live on campus; 0% of students in fraternities, 0% in sororities
**Most popular majors:** 13% Business Administration and Management, General, 6% Kinesiology and Exercise Science, 7% Liberal Arts and Sciences/Liberal Studies, 10% Psychology, General, 15% Registered Nursing/Registered Nurse
**Expenses:** 2014-2015: $25,414; room/board: $9,550
**Financial aid:** (317) 788-3217; 74% of undergrads determined to have financial need; average aid package $17,356

## University of Notre Dame
Notre Dame IN
(574) 631-7505
**U.S. News ranking:** Nat. U., No. 16
**Website:** www.nd.edu
**Admissions email:** admissions@nd.edu
**Private;** founded 1842
**Affiliation:** Roman Catholic
**Freshman admissions:** most selective; 2013-2014: 17,647 applied, 3,936 accepted. Either SAT or ACT required. ACT 25/75 percentile: 32-34. High school rank: 90% in top tenth, 98% in top quarter, 100% in top half
**Early decision deadline:** N/A, notification date: N/A
**Early action deadline:** 11/1, notification date: 12/21

**Application deadline (fall):** 1/1
**Undergraduate student body:** 8,459 full time, 18 part time; 53% male, 47% female; 0% American Indian, 6% Asian, 4% black, 10% Hispanic, 4% multiracial, 0% Pacific Islander, 71% white, 4% international; 8% from in state; 80% live on campus; N/A of students in fraternities, N/A in sororities
**Most popular majors:** 8% Accounting, 5% Economics, General, 11% Finance, General, 7% Political Science and Government, General, 7% Psychology, General
**Expenses:** 2014-2015: $46,237; room/board: $13,224
**Financial aid:** (574) 631-6436; 49% of undergrads determined to have financial need; average aid package $40,352

## University of Southern Indiana
Evansville IN
(812) 464-1765
**U.S. News ranking:** Reg. U. (Mid. W), second tier
**Website:** www.usi.edu
**Admissions email:** enroll@usi.edu
**Public;** founded 1965
**Freshman admissions:** selective; 2013-2014: 6,204 applied, 4,302 accepted. Either SAT or ACT required. SAT 25/75 percentile: 890-1110. High school rank: 13% in top tenth, 36% in top quarter, 73% in top half
**Early decision deadline:** N/A, notification date: N/A
**Early action deadline:** N/A, notification date: N/A
**Undergraduate student body:** 7,375 full time, 1,538 part time; 41% male, 59% female; 0% American Indian, 1% Asian, 4% black, 1% Hispanic, 2% multiracial, 0% Pacific Islander, 86% white, 3% international; 89% from in state; 27% live on campus; 7% of students in fraternities, 8% in sororities
**Most popular majors:** 15% Business, Management, Marketing, and Related Support Services, 6% Communication, Journalism, and Related Programs, 12% Education, 26% Health Professions and Related Programs, 5% Social Sciences
**Expenses:** 2014-2015: $6,977 in state, $16,317 out of state; room/board: $7,680
**Financial aid:** (812) 464-1767; 66% of undergrads determined to have financial need; average aid package $8,892

## University of St. Francis
Fort Wayne IN
(260) 399-8000
**U.S. News ranking:** Reg. U. (Mid. W), No. 69
**Website:** www.sf.edu
**Admissions email:** admis@sf.edu
**Private;** founded 1890
**Affiliation:** Roman Catholic
**Freshman admissions:** less selective; 2013-2014: 1,057 applied, 1,023 accepted. Either SAT or ACT required. SAT 25/75 percentile: 890-1060. High school rank: 11% in top tenth, 38% in top quarter, 80% in top half
**Early decision deadline:** N/A, notification date: N/A

**Early action deadline:** N/A, notification date: N/A
**Application deadline (fall):** rolling
**Undergraduate student body:** 1,616 full time, 364 part time; 29% male, 71% female; 1% American Indian, 1% Asian, 6% black, 6% Hispanic, 2% multiracial, 0% Pacific Islander, 82% white, 0% international; 90% from in state; 19% live on campus; 0% of students in fraternities, 0% in sororities
**Most popular majors:** 8% Biological and Biomedical Sciences, 10% Business, Management, Marketing, and Related Support Services, 9% Education, 36% Health Professions and Related Programs, 10% Visual and Performing Arts
**Expenses:** 2014-2015: $25,930; room/board: $8,640
**Financial aid:** (260) 434-3283; 87% of undergrads determined to have financial need; average aid package $17,054

## Valparaiso University
Valparaiso IN
(888) 468-2576
**U.S. News ranking:** Reg. U. (Mid. W), No. 5
**Website:** www.valpo.edu
**Admissions email:** undergrad.admission@valpo.edu
**Private;** founded 1859
**Affiliation:** Lutheran
**Freshman admissions:** more selective; 2013-2014: 6,124 applied, 4,880 accepted. Either SAT or ACT required. ACT 25/75 percentile: 23-29. High school rank: 36% in top tenth, 68% in top quarter, 93% in top half
**Early decision deadline:** N/A, notification date: N/A
**Early action deadline:** N/A, notification date: N/A
**Application deadline (fall):** rolling
**Undergraduate student body:** 3,136 full time, 115 part time; 48% male, 52% female; 0% American Indian, 2% Asian, 5% black, 7% Hispanic, 2% multiracial, 0% Pacific Islander, 75% white, 8% international; 40% from in state; 68% live on campus; 21% of students in fraternities, 19% in sororities
**Most popular majors:** 5% Biology/Biological Sciences, General, 4% Civil Engineering, General, 5% English Language and Literature, General, 4% Marketing/Marketing Management, General, 19% Registered Nursing/Registered Nurse
**Expenses:** 2014-2015: $34,760; room/board: $10,180
**Financial aid:** (219) 464-5015; 72% of undergrads determined to have financial need; average aid package $26,875

## Vincennes University
Vincennes IN
(800) 742-9198
**U.S. News ranking:** Reg. Coll. (Mid. W), unranked
**Website:** www.vinu.edu
**Admissions email:** N/A
**Public**
**Freshman admissions:** N/A; 2013-2014: N/A applied, N/A accepted. Neither SAT nor ACT required. ACT 25/75 percentile: N/A. High school rank: N/A
**Early decision deadline:** N/A, notification date: N/A

**Early action deadline:** N/A, notification date: N/A
**Application deadline (fall):** rolling
**Undergraduate student body:** 6,049 full time, 12,334 part time; 56% male, 44% female; 0% American Indian, 1% Asian, 12% black, 3% Hispanic, 2% multiracial, 0% Pacific Islander, 70% white, 0% international; 83% from in state; N/A live on campus; N/A of students in fraternities, N/A in sororities
**Most popular majors:** Information not available
**Expenses:** 2014-2015: $5,174 in state, $12,234 out of state; room/board: $8,732
**Financial aid:** (812) 888-4361

## Wabash College
Crawfordsville IN
(800) 345-5385
**U.S. News ranking:** Nat. Lib. Arts, No. 61
**Website:** www.wabash.edu
**Admissions email:** admissions@wabash.edu
**Private;** founded 1832
**Freshman admissions:** more selective; 2013-2014: 1,129 applied, 786 accepted. Either SAT or ACT required. SAT 25/75 percentile: 1028-1250. High school rank: 33% in top tenth, 72% in top quarter, 93% in top half
**Early decision deadline:** 11/15, notification date: 11/30
**Early action deadline:** 12/1, notification date: 12/19
**Application deadline (fall):** rolling
**Undergraduate student body:** 902 full time, 0 part time; 100% male, 0% female; 0% American Indian, 1% Asian, 6% black, 6% Hispanic, 3% multiracial, 0% Pacific Islander, 76% white, 7% international; 75% from in state; 89% live on campus; 60% of students in fraternities, N/A in sororities
**Most popular majors:** 11% Economics, General, 12% English Language and Literature, General, 12% History, General, 9% Mathematics, General, 9% Political Science and Government, General
**Expenses:** 2014-2015: $37,750; room/board: $9,130
**Financial aid:** (765) 361-6370; 80% of undergrads determined to have financial need; average aid package $34,725

## IOWA

## AIB College of Business
Des Moines IA
(515) 246-5358
**U.S. News ranking:** Business, unranked
**Website:** www.aib.edu
**Admissions email:** admissions@aib.edu
**Private;** founded 1921
**Freshman admissions:** less selective; 2013-2014: 424 applied, 292 accepted. Neither SAT nor ACT required. ACT 25/75 percentile: 17-23. High school rank: 10% in top tenth, 25% in top quarter, 50% in top half
**Early decision deadline:** N/A, notification date: N/A
**Early action deadline:** N/A, notification date: N/A

**Application deadline (fall):** rolling
**Undergraduate student body:** 732 full time, 287 part time; 44% male, 56% female; 1% American Indian, 2% Asian, 5% black, 6% Hispanic, 2% multiracial, 0% Pacific Islander, 63% white, 3% international; 86% from in state; 44% live on campus; 0% of students in fraternities, 0% in sororities
**Most popular majors:** 24% Accounting, 48% Business Administration and Management, General, 3% Sport and Fitness Administration/Management
**Expenses:** 2014-2015: $15,600; room/board: N/A
**Financial aid:** N/A; 78% of undergrads determined to have financial need; average aid package $13,329

## Ashford University[1]
Clinton IA
(563) 242-4153
**U.S. News ranking:** Reg. U. (Mid. W), unranked
**Website:** www.ashford.edu
**Admissions email:** admissions@ashford.edu
**For-profit**
**Application deadline (fall):** N/A
**Undergraduate student body:** N/A full time, N/A part time
**Expenses:** 2013-2014: $10,312; room/board: $6,000
**Financial aid:** (563) 242-4023

## Briar Cliff University
Sioux City IA
(712) 279-5200
**U.S. News ranking:** Reg. Coll. (Mid. W), No. 38
**Website:** www.briarcliff.edu
**Admissions email:** admissions@briarcliff.edu
**Private;** founded 1930
**Affiliation:** Roman Catholic
**Freshman admissions:** selective; 2013-2014: 1,728 applied, 931 accepted. Either SAT or ACT required. ACT 25/75 percentile: 19-25. High school rank: 9% in top tenth, 32% in top quarter, 70% in top half
**Early decision deadline:** N/A, notification date: N/A
**Early action deadline:** N/A, notification date: N/A
**Application deadline (fall):** rolling
**Undergraduate student body:** 848 full time, 194 part time; 43% male, 57% female; 1% American Indian, 2% Asian, 7% black, 9% Hispanic, 2% multiracial, 0% Pacific Islander, 76% white, 4% international; 55% from in state; 46% live on campus; N/A of students in fraternities, N/A in sororities
**Most popular majors:** 6% Biological and Biomedical Sciences, 22% Business, Management, Marketing, and Related Support Services, 12% Education, 23% Health Professions and Related Programs, 8% Visual and Performing Arts
**Expenses:** 2014-2015: $27,102; room/board: $7,888
**Financial aid:** (712) 279-5239; 93% of undergrads determined to have financial need; average aid package $21,148

## Buena Vista University
Storm Lake IA
(800) 383-9600
**U.S. News ranking:** Reg. Coll. (Mid. W), No. 11
**Website:** www.bvu.edu
**Admissions email:** admissions@bvu.edu
**Private;** founded 1891
**Affiliation:** Presbyterian
**Freshman admissions:** selective; 2013-2014: 1,409 applied, 980 accepted. Either SAT or ACT required. ACT 25/75 percentile: 20-25. High school rank: 14% in top tenth, 42% in top quarter, 74% in top half
**Early decision deadline:** N/A, notification date: N/A
**Early action deadline:** N/A, notification date: N/A
**Application deadline (fall):** rolling
**Undergraduate student body:** 899 full time, 21 part time; 49% male, 51% female; 0% American Indian, 2% Asian, 3% black, 8% Hispanic, 2% multiracial, 0% Pacific Islander, 77% white, 4% international; 80% from in state; 87% live on campus; 0% of students in fraternities, 0% in sororities
**Most popular majors:** 14% Biological and Biomedical Sciences, 17% Business, Management, Marketing, and Related Support Services, 9% Education, 6% Homeland Security, Law Enforcement, Firefighting and Related Protective Services, 7% Parks, Recreation, Leisure, and Fitness Studies
**Expenses:** 2014-2015: $30,406; room/board: $8,782
**Financial aid:** (712) 749-2164; 85% of undergrads determined to have financial need; average aid package $32,113

## Central College
Pella IA
(641) 628-5286
**U.S. News ranking:** Nat. Lib. Arts, No. 139
**Website:** www.central.edu
**Admissions email:** admission@central.edu
**Private;** founded 1853
**Affiliation:** Reformed Church in America
**Freshman admissions:** selective; 2013-2014: 2,842 applied, 1,870 accepted. Either SAT or ACT required. ACT 25/75 percentile: 21-26. High school rank: 21% in top tenth, 53% in top quarter, 85% in top half
**Early decision deadline:** N/A, notification date: N/A
**Early action deadline:** N/A, notification date: N/A
**Application deadline (fall):** 8/15
**Undergraduate student body:** 1,340 full time, 46 part time; 47% male, 53% female; 0% American Indian, 1% Asian, 2% black, 3% Hispanic, 1% multiracial, 0% Pacific Islander, 90% white, 0% international; 81% from in state; 94% live on campus; 4% of students in fraternities, 3% in sororities
**Most popular majors:** 13% Business, Management, Marketing, and Related Support Services, 9% Education, 9% Foreign Languages, Literatures, and Linguistics, 11% Parks,

Recreation, Leisure, and Fitness Studies, 11% Social Sciences
**Expenses:** 2014-2015: $32,124; room/board: $9,980
**Financial aid:** (641) 628-5187; 80% of undergrads determined to have financial need; average aid package $24,341

## Clarke University
Dubuque IA
(563) 588-6316
**U.S. News ranking:** Reg. Coll. (Mid. W), No. 17
**Website:** www.clarke.edu
**Admissions email:** admissions@clarke.edu
**Private;** founded 1843
**Affiliation:** Roman Catholic
**Freshman admissions:** selective; 2013-2014: 1,250 applied, 969 accepted. Either SAT or ACT required. ACT 25/75 percentile: 20-25. High school rank: 18% in top tenth, 46% in top quarter, 83% in top half
**Early decision deadline:** N/A, notification date: N/A
**Early action deadline:** N/A, notification date: N/A
**Application deadline (fall):** rolling
**Undergraduate student body:** 877 full time, 134 part time; 34% male, 66% female; 1% American Indian, 1% Asian, 3% black, 3% Hispanic, 0% multiracial, 0% Pacific Islander, 88% white, 1% international; 59% from in state; 56% live on campus; 0% of students in fraternities, 0% in sororities
**Most popular majors:** 15% Business Administration and Management, General, 10% Education, General, 9% Psychology, General, 29% Registered Nursing/Registered Nurse
**Expenses:** 2014-2015: $28,900; room/board: $8,700
**Financial aid:** (563) 588-6327; 87% of undergrads determined to have financial need; average aid package $22,591

## Coe College
Cedar Rapids IA
(319) 399-8500
**U.S. News ranking:** Nat. Lib. Arts, No. 120
**Website:** www.coe.edu
**Admissions email:** admission@coe.edu
**Private;** founded 1851
**Affiliation:** Presbyterian
**Freshman admissions:** more selective; 2013-2014: 2,972 applied, 1,834 accepted. Either SAT or ACT required. ACT 25/75 percentile: 23-28. High school rank: 31% in top tenth, 61% in top quarter, 91% in top half
**Early decision deadline:** N/A, notification date: N/A
**Early action deadline:** 12/10, notification date: 1/20
**Application deadline (fall):** 3/1
**Undergraduate student body:** 1,351 full time, 69 part time; 46% male, 54% female; 0% American Indian, 2% Asian, 4% black, 5% Hispanic, 3% multiracial, 0% Pacific Islander, 79% white, 2% international; 51% from in state; 86% live on campus; 12% of students in fraternities, 13% in sororities
**Most popular majors:** 13% Business, Management, Marketing, and Related Support Services, 9% Education, 9%

**Most popular majors:** 22% Business, Management, Marketing, and Related Support Services, 8% Communication, Journalism, and Related Programs, 9% Health Professions and Related Programs, 12% Psychology, 7% Social Sciences
**Expenses:** 2014-2015: $37,230; room/board: $8,230
**Financial aid:** (319) 399-8540; 82% of undergrads determined to have financial need; average aid package $28,412

## Cornell College
Mount Vernon IA
(800) 747-1112
**U.S. News ranking:** Nat. Lib. Arts, No. 105
**Website:** www.cornellcollege.edu
**Admissions email:** admissions@cornellcollege.edu
**Private;** founded 1853
**Affiliation:** United Methodist
**Freshman admissions:** more selective; 2013-2014: 2,498 applied, 1,471 accepted. Either SAT or ACT required. ACT 25/75 percentile: 23-29. High school rank: 39% in top tenth, 69% in top quarter, 90% in top half
**Early decision deadline:** 11/1, notification date: 12/15
**Early action deadline:** 12/1, notification date: 2/1
**Application deadline (fall):** 2/1
**Undergraduate student body:** 1,117 full time, 8 part time; 45% male, 55% female; 1% American Indian, 3% Asian, 5% black, 13% Hispanic, 3% multiracial, 0% Pacific Islander, 65% white, 6% international; 18% from in state; 92% live on campus; 16% of students in fraternities, 22% in sororities
**Most popular majors:** 12% Biological and Biomedical Sciences, 8% English Language and Literature/Letters, 13% Psychology, 8% Social Sciences, 9% Visual and Performing Arts
**Expenses:** 2014-2015: $37,500; room/board: $8,500
**Financial aid:** (319) 895-4216; 77% of undergrads determined to have financial need; average aid package $28,332

## Dordt College
Sioux Center IA
(800) 343-6738
**U.S. News ranking:** Reg. Coll. (Mid. W), No. 5
**Website:** www.dordt.edu
**Admissions email:** admissions@dordt.edu
**Private;** founded 1955
**Affiliation:** Christian Reformed
**Freshman admissions:** selective; 2013-2014: 1,344 applied, 1,016 accepted. Either SAT or ACT required. ACT 25/75 percentile: 21-28. High school rank: 21% in top tenth, 44% in top quarter, 73% in top half
**Early decision deadline:** N/A, notification date: N/A
**Early action deadline:** N/A, notification date: N/A
**Application deadline (fall):** 8/1
**Undergraduate student body:** 1,345 full time, 31 part time; 54% male, 46% female; 0% American Indian, 1% Asian, 1% black, 1% Hispanic, 3% multiracial, 0% Pacific Islander, 85% white, 8% international; 46% from in

state; 89% live on campus; 0% of students in fraternities, 0% in sororities
**Most popular majors:** 8% Agricultural Business and Management, General, 8% Business/Commerce, General, 22% Elementary Education and Teaching, 8% Health and Wellness, General, 7% Parks, Recreation and Leisure Studies
**Expenses:** 2014-2015: $27,460; room/board: $8,000
**Financial aid:** (712) 722-6087; 71% of undergrads determined to have financial need; average aid package $21,345

## Drake University
Des Moines IA
(800) 443-7253
**U.S. News ranking:** Reg. U. (Mid. W), No. 3
**Website:** www.drake.edu
**Admissions email:** admission@drake.edu
**Private;** founded 1881
**Freshman admissions:** more selective; 2013-2014: 5,930 applied, 3,911 accepted. Either SAT or ACT required. ACT 25/75 percentile: 25-30. High school rank: 44% in top tenth, 73% in top quarter, 95% in top half
**Early decision deadline:** N/A, notification date: N/A
**Early action deadline:** N/A, notification date: N/A
**Application deadline (fall):** rolling
**Undergraduate student body:** 3,185 full time, 198 part time; 44% male, 56% female; 0% American Indian, 4% Asian, 3% black, 3% Hispanic, 1% multiracial, 0% Pacific Islander, 79% white, 7% international; 35% from in state; 75% live on campus; 34% of students in fraternities, 28% in sororities
**Most popular majors:** 36% Business, Management, Marketing, and Related Support Services, 12% Communication, Journalism, and Related Programs, 7% Social Sciences, 7% Visual and Performing Arts
**Expenses:** 2014-2015: $32,246; room/board: $9,270
**Financial aid:** (515) 271-2905; 60% of undergrads determined to have financial need; average aid package $23,125

## Graceland University
Lamoni IA
(866) 472-2352
**U.S. News ranking:** Reg. U. (Mid. W), No. 103
**Website:** www.graceland.edu
**Admissions email:** admissions@graceland.edu
**Private;** founded 1895
**Affiliation:** Community of Christ
**Freshman admissions:** selective; 2013-2014: 1,981 applied, 994 accepted. Either SAT or ACT required. ACT 25/75 percentile: 18-24. High school rank: 12% in top tenth, 34% in top quarter, 62% in top half
**Early decision deadline:** N/A, notification date: N/A
**Early action deadline:** N/A, notification date: N/A
**Application deadline (fall):** rolling
**Undergraduate student body:** 1,293 full time, 266 part time; 43% male, 57% female; 1% American Indian, 1% Asian, 9% black,

7% Hispanic, 4% multiracial, 1% Pacific Islander, 64% white, 7% international; 25% from in state; 68% live on campus; 0% of students in fraternities, 0% in sororities
**Most popular majors:** 4% Biological and Biomedical Sciences, 11% Business, Management, Marketing, and Related Support Services, 29% Education, 30% Health Professions and Related Programs, 4% Parks, Recreation, Leisure, and Fitness Studies
**Expenses:** 2014-2015: $24,920; room/board: $8,060
**Financial aid:** (641) 784-5136; 76% of undergrads determined to have financial need; average aid package $20,935

## Grand View University[1]
Des Moines IA
(515) 263-2810
**U.S. News ranking:** Reg. Coll. (Mid. W), No. 54
**Website:** www.grandview.edu/
**Admissions email:** admissions@grandview.edu
**Private;** founded 1896
**Affiliation:** Evangelical Lutheran Church in America
**Application deadline (fall):** 8/15
**Undergraduate student body:** N/A full time, N/A part time
**Expenses:** 2014-2015: $23,516; room/board: $7,554
**Financial aid:** (515) 263-2820; 82% of undergrads determined to have financial need; average aid package $15,640

## Grinnell College
Grinnell IA
(800) 247-0113
**U.S. News ranking:** Nat. Lib. Arts, No. 19
**Website:** www.grinnell.edu
**Admissions email:** askgrin@grinnell.edu
**Private;** founded 1846
**Freshman admissions:** most selective; 2013-2014: 3,979 applied, 1,395 accepted. Either SAT or ACT required. ACT 25/75 percentile: 28-32. High school rank: 63% in top tenth, 88% in top quarter, 98% in top half
**Early decision deadline:** 11/15, notification date: 12/15
**Early action deadline:** N/A, notification date: N/A
**Application deadline (fall):** 1/15
**Undergraduate student body:** 1,664 full time, 57 part time; 46% male, 54% female; 0% American Indian, 8% Asian, 6% black, 8% Hispanic, 4% multiracial, 0% Pacific Islander, 58% white, 13% international; 12% from in state; 88% live on campus; 0% of students in fraternities, 0% in sororities
**Most popular majors:** 13% Biology/Biological Sciences, General, 10% Foreign Languages and Literatures, General, 8% History, General, 26% Social Sciences, General, 7% Visual and Performing Arts, General
**Expenses:** 2014-2015: $45,620; room/board: $10,997
**Financial aid:** (641) 269-3250; 72% of undergrads determined to have financial need; average aid package $41,315

## Iowa State University
Ames IA
(800) 262-3810
**U.S. News ranking:** Nat. U., No. 106
**Website:** www.iastate.edu
**Admissions email:** admissions@iastate.edu
**Public;** founded 1858
**Freshman admissions:** more selective; 2013-2014: 17,525 applied, 14,975 accepted. Either SAT or ACT required. ACT 25/75 percentile: 22-28. High school rank: 25% in top tenth, 56% in top quarter, 89% in top half
**Early decision deadline:** N/A, notification date: N/A
**Early action deadline:** N/A, notification date: N/A
**Application deadline (fall):** 7/1
**Undergraduate student body:** 26,171 full time, 1,488 part time; 57% male, 43% female; 0% American Indian, 3% Asian, 3% black, 4% Hispanic, 2% multiracial, 0% Pacific Islander, 77% white, 7% international; 71% from in state; 34% live on campus; 11% of students in fraternities, 16% in sororities
**Most popular majors:** 10% Agriculture, Agriculture Operations, and Related Sciences, 6% Biological and Biomedical Sciences, 18% Business, Management, Marketing, and Related Support Services, 19% Engineering, 6% Visual and Performing Arts
**Expenses:** 2014-2015: $7,731 in state, $20,617 out of state; room/board: $7,830
**Financial aid:** (515) 294-2223; 55% of undergrads determined to have financial need; average aid package $11,841

## Iowa Wesleyan College[1]
Mount Pleasant IA
(319) 385-6231
**U.S. News ranking:** Reg. Coll. (Mid. W), second tier
**Website:** www.iwc.edu
**Admissions email:** admit@iwc.edu
**Private**
**Application deadline (fall):** N/A
**Undergraduate student body:** N/A full time, N/A part time
**Expenses:** 2013-2014: $25,550; room/board: $8,800
**Financial aid:** (319) 385-6242

## Kaplan University[1]
Davenport IA
(800) 987-7734
**U.S. News ranking:** Reg. U. (Mid. W), unranked
**Website:** www.kaplan.edu
**Admissions email:** N/A
**For-profit**
**Application deadline (fall):** N/A
**Undergraduate student body:** N/A full time, N/A part time
**Expenses:** N/A
**Financial aid:** (866) 428-2008

## Loras College
Dubuque IA
(800) 245-6727
**U.S. News ranking:** Reg. Coll. (Mid. W), No. 11
**Website:** www.loras.edu
**Admissions email:** admissions@loras.edu
**Private;** founded 1839
**Affiliation:** Roman Catholic

**Freshman admissions:** selective; 2013-2014: 1,873 applied, 1,293 accepted. Either SAT or ACT required. ACT 25/75 percentile: 21-26. High school rank: 16% in top tenth, 39% in top quarter, 76% in top half
**Early decision deadline:** N/A, notification date: N/A
**Early action deadline:** N/A, notification date: N/A
**Application deadline (fall):** rolling
**Undergraduate student body:** 1,484 full time, 70 part time; 52% male, 48% female; 0% American Indian, 1% Asian, 2% black, 6% Hispanic, 2% multiracial, 0% Pacific Islander, 83% white, 2% international; 37% from in state; 65% live on campus; 4% of students in fraternities, 4% in sororities
**Most popular majors:** 8% Biological and Biomedical Sciences, 16% Business, Management, Marketing, and Related Support Services, 7% Communication, Journalism, and Related Programs, 18% Education, 9% English Language and Literature/Letters
**Expenses:** 2014-2015: $29,729; room/board: $8,353
**Financial aid:** (563) 588-7136; 73% of undergrads determined to have financial need; average aid package $23,000

## Luther College
Decorah IA
(563) 387-1287
**U.S. News ranking:** Nat. Lib. Arts, No. 89
**Website:** www.luther.edu
**Admissions email:** admissions@luther.edu
**Private;** founded 1861
**Affiliation:** Lutheran
**Freshman admissions:** more selective; 2013-2014: 3,490 applied, 2,517 accepted. Either SAT or ACT required. ACT 25/75 percentile: 23-29. High school rank: 32% in top tenth, 56% in top quarter, 87% in top half
**Early decision deadline:** N/A, notification date: N/A
**Early action deadline:** N/A, notification date: N/A
**Application deadline (fall):** rolling
**Undergraduate student body:** 2,413 full time, 53 part time; 43% male, 57% female; 0% American Indian, 2% Asian, 2% black, 3% Hispanic, 2% multiracial, 0% Pacific Islander, 86% white, 6% international; 32% from in state; 84% live on campus; 1% of students in fraternities, 2% in sororities
**Most popular majors:** 13% Biology/Biological Sciences, General, 8% Business Administration and Management, General, 5% Mathematics, General, 11% Music, General, 7% Psychology, General
**Expenses:** 2014-2015: $38,370; room/board: $7,350
**Financial aid:** (563) 387-1018; 71% of undergrads determined to have financial need; average aid package $28,581

## Maharishi University of Management[1]
Fairfield IA
(641) 472-1110
**U.S. News ranking:** Reg. U. (Mid. W), unranked
**Website:** www.mum.edu
**Admissions email:** admissions@mum.edu
**Private**
**Application deadline (fall):** N/A
**Undergraduate student body:** N/A full time, N/A part time
**Expenses:** 2013-2014: $26,430; room/board: $7,400
**Financial aid:** (641) 472-1156

## Morningside College
Sioux City IA
(712) 274-5111
**U.S. News ranking:** Reg. Coll. (Mid. W), No. 23
**Website:** www.morningside.edu
**Admissions email:** mscadm@morningside.edu
**Private;** founded 1894
**Affiliation:** United Methodist
**Freshman admissions:** selective; 2013-2014: 3,721 applied, 1,986 accepted. Either SAT or ACT required. ACT 25/75 percentile: 20-25. High school rank: 19% in top tenth, 46% in top quarter, 78% in top half
**Early decision deadline:** N/A, notification date: N/A
**Early action deadline:** N/A, notification date: N/A
**Application deadline (fall):** rolling
**Undergraduate student body:** 1,263 full time, 42 part time; 47% male, 53% female; 0% American Indian, 1% Asian, 1% black, 5% Hispanic, 2% multiracial, 0% Pacific Islander, 84% white, 2% international; 64% from in state; 63% live on campus; 5% of students in fraternities, 3% in sororities
**Most popular majors:** 13% Biology/Biological Sciences, General, 22% Business, Management, Marketing, and Related Support Services, 19% Elementary Education and Teaching, 7% Psychology, General, 9% Registered Nursing/Registered Nurse
**Expenses:** 2014-2015: $27,180; room/board: $8,250
**Financial aid:** (712) 274-5159; 87% of undergrads determined to have financial need; average aid package $25,931

## Mount Mercy University
Cedar Rapids IA
(319) 368-6460
**U.S. News ranking:** Reg. Coll. (Mid. W), No. 21
**Website:** www.mtmercy.edu
**Admissions email:** admission@mtmercy.edu
**Private;** founded 1928
**Affiliation:** Roman Catholic
**Freshman admissions:** selective; 2013-2014: 542 applied, 371 accepted. Either SAT or ACT required. ACT 25/75 percentile: 20-24. High school rank: 12% in top tenth, 41% in top quarter, 76% in top half
**Early decision deadline:** N/A, notification date: N/A
**Early action deadline:** N/A, notification date: N/A
**Application deadline (fall):** rolling

Undergraduate student body: 882 full time, 594 part time; 31% male, 69% female; 0% American Indian, 2% Asian, 4% black, 2% Hispanic, 1% multiracial, 0% Pacific Islander, 83% white, 3% international; 95% from in state; 37% live on campus; N/A of students in fraternities, N/A in sororities
Most popular majors: 7% Accounting, 9% Business/Commerce, General, 1% Criminal Justice/Law Enforcement Administration, 5% Elementary Education and Teaching, 22% Registered Nursing/Registered Nurse
Expenses: 2014-2015: $27,010; room/board: $8,310
Financial aid: (319) 368-6467; 77% of undergrads determined to have financial need; average aid package $18,114

## Northwestern College
Orange City IA
(712) 707-7130
U.S. News ranking: Reg. Coll. (Mid. W), No. 6
Website: www.nwciowa.edu
Admissions email: admissions@nwciowa.edu
Private; founded 1882
Affiliation: Reformed Church in America
Freshman admissions: selective; 2013-2014: 1,221 applied, 929 accepted. Either SAT or ACT required. ACT 25/75 percentile: 22-27. High school rank: 19% in top tenth, 49% in top quarter, 81% in top half
Early decision deadline: N/A, notification date: N/A
Early action deadline: N/A, notification date: N/A
Application deadline (fall): rolling
Undergraduate student body: 1,133 full time, 100 part time; 43% male, 57% female; 0% American Indian, 1% Asian, 2% black, 6% Hispanic, 2% multiracial, 0% Pacific Islander, 85% white, 3% international; 52% from in state; 87% live on campus; 0% of students in fraternities, 0% in sororities
Most popular majors: 8% Biology/Biological Sciences, General, 17% Business Administration and Management, General, 17% Elementary Education and Teaching, 6% Psychology, General, 8% Registered Nursing/Registered Nurse
Expenses: 2014-2015: $27,930; room/board: $8,410
Financial aid: (712) 707-7131; 80% of undergrads determined to have financial need; average aid package $22,344

## Simpson College
Indianola IA
(515) 961-1624
U.S. News ranking: Nat. Lib. Arts, No. 139
Website: www.simpson.edu
Admissions email: admiss@simpson.edu
Private; founded 1860
Affiliation: United Methodist
Freshman admissions: more selective; 2013-2014: 1,302 applied, 1,146 accepted. Either SAT or ACT required. ACT 25/75 percentile: 21-27. High school rank: 29% in top tenth, 58% in top quarter, 88% in top half

Early decision deadline: N/A, notification date: N/A
Early action deadline: N/A, notification date: N/A
Application deadline (fall): rolling
Undergraduate student body: 1,486 full time, 226 part time; 44% male, 56% female; 1% American Indian, 1% Asian, 2% black, 2% Hispanic, 2% multiracial, 0% Pacific Islander, 87% white, 1% international; 86% from in state; 86% live on campus; 23% of students in fraternities, 22% in sororities
Most popular majors: 7% Accounting, 5% Biology/Biological Sciences, General, 13% Business/Commerce, General, 7% Elementary Education and Teaching, 5% Mathematics, General
Expenses: 2014-2015: $32,550; room/board: $7,963
Financial aid: (515) 961-1630; 83% of undergrads determined to have financial need; average aid package $28,770

## St. Ambrose University
Davenport IA
(563) 333-6300
U.S. News ranking: Reg. U. (Mid. W), No. 34
Website: www.sau.edu
Admissions email: admit@sau.edu
Private; founded 1882
Affiliation: Roman Catholic
Freshman admissions: selective; 2013-2014: 3,948 applied, 2,803 accepted. Either SAT or ACT required. ACT 25/75 percentile: 20-25. High school rank: 15% in top tenth, 36% in top quarter, 67% in top half
Early decision deadline: N/A, notification date: N/A
Early action deadline: N/A, notification date: N/A
Application deadline (fall): rolling
Undergraduate student body: 2,440 full time, 303 part time; 41% male, 59% female; 0% American Indian, 1% Asian, 4% black, 6% Hispanic, 2% multiracial, 0% Pacific Islander, 82% white, 2% international; 44% from in state; 62% live on campus; 0% of students in fraternities, 0% in sororities
Most popular majors: 21% Business, Management, Marketing, and Related Support Services, 13% Education, 11% Health Professions and Related Programs, 13% Parks, Recreation, Leisure, and Fitness Studies, 11% Psychology
Expenses: 2014-2015: $27,540; room/board: $9,280
Financial aid: (563) 333-6314; 77% of undergrads determined to have financial need; average aid package $18,817

## University of Dubuque
Dubuque IA
(800) 722-5583
U.S. News ranking: Reg. U. (Mid. W), second tier
Website: www.dbq.edu
Admissions email: admssns@univ.dbq.edu
Private; founded 1852
Affiliation: Presbyterian

Freshman admissions: less selective; 2013-2014: 1,457 applied, 1,128 accepted. Either SAT or ACT required. ACT 25/75 percentile: 17-22. High school rank: N/A
Early decision deadline: N/A, notification date: N/A
Early action deadline: N/A, notification date: N/A
Application deadline (fall): rolling
Undergraduate student body: 1,545 full time, 150 part time; 57% male, 43% female; 1% American Indian, 1% Asian, 10% black, 6% Hispanic, 2% multiracial, 0% Pacific Islander, 70% white, 1% international
Most popular majors: Information not available
Expenses: 2013-2014: $25,520; room/board: $8,160
Financial aid: (563) 589-3396

## University of Iowa
Iowa City IA
(319) 335-3847
U.S. News ranking: Nat. U., No. 71
Website: www.uiowa.edu
Admissions email: admissions@uiowa.edu
Public; founded 1847
Freshman admissions: more selective; 2013-2014: 21,644 applied, 17,363 accepted. Either SAT or ACT required. ACT 25/75 percentile: 23-28. High school rank: 24% in top tenth, 57% in top quarter, 90% in top half
Early decision deadline: N/A, notification date: N/A
Early action deadline: N/A, notification date: N/A
Application deadline (fall): 4/1
Undergraduate student body: 19,522 full time, 2,452 part time; 48% male, 52% female; 0% American Indian, 3% Asian, 3% black, 6% Hispanic, 2% multiracial, 0% Pacific Islander, 72% white, 10% international; 66% from in state; 25% live on campus; 12% of students in fraternities, 17% in sororities
Most popular majors: 19% Business, Management, Marketing, and Related Support Services, 8% Communication, Journalism, and Related Programs, 8% Parks, Recreation, Leisure, and Fitness Studies, 9% Social Sciences, 7% Visual and Performing Arts
Expenses: 2014-2015: $8,079 in state, $27,409 out of state; room/board: $9,614
Financial aid: (319) 335-1450; 48% of undergrads determined to have financial need; average aid package $11,805

## University of Northern Iowa
Cedar Falls IA
(800) 772-2037
U.S. News ranking: Reg. U. (Mid. W), No. 18
Website: www.uni.edu/
Admissions email: admissions@uni.edu
Public; founded 1876
Freshman admissions: selective; 2013-2014: 4,081 applied, 3,403 accepted. Either SAT or ACT required. ACT 25/75 percentile: 20-24. High school rank: 17% in top tenth, 45% in top quarter, 81% in top half

Early decision deadline: N/A, notification date: N/A
Early action deadline: N/A, notification date: N/A
Application deadline (fall): 8/15
Undergraduate student body: 9,330 full time, 1,050 part time; 43% male, 57% female; 0% American Indian, 1% Asian, 3% black, 3% Hispanic, 2% multiracial, 0% Pacific Islander, 87% white, 3% international; 94% from in state; 66% live on campus; N/A of students in fraternities, N/A in sororities
Most popular majors: 20% Business, Management, Marketing, and Related Support Services, 6% Communication, Journalism, and Related Programs, 17% Education, 7% Parks, Recreation, Leisure, and Fitness Studies, 7% Social Sciences
Expenses: 2014-2015: $7,749 in state, $17,647 out of state; room/board: $8,046
Financial aid: (319) 273-2700; 64% of undergrads determined to have financial need; average aid package $7,642

## Upper Iowa University
Fayette IA
(563) 425-5281
U.S. News ranking: Reg. U. (Mid. W), No. 109
Website: www.uiu.edu
Admissions email: admission@uiu.edu
Private; founded 1857
Freshman admissions: selective; 2013-2014: 1,229 applied, 715 accepted. SAT required. ACT 25/75 percentile: 19-25. High school rank: 11% in top tenth, 32% in top quarter, 59% in top half
Early decision deadline: N/A, notification date: N/A
Early action deadline: N/A, notification date: N/A
Application deadline (fall): rolling
Undergraduate student body: 2,997 full time, 1,635 part time; 40% male, 60% female; 0% American Indian, 1% Asian, 19% black, 4% Hispanic, 1% multiracial, 0% Pacific Islander, 66% white, 3% international; 40% from in state; 5% live on campus; 10% of students in fraternities, 12% in sororities
Most popular majors: 43% Business, Management, Marketing, and Related Support Services, 7% Health Professions and Related Programs, 11% Psychology, 20% Public Administration and Social Service Professions, 15% Social Sciences
Expenses: 2014-2015: $26,834; room/board: $7,824
Financial aid: (563) 425-5274; 88% of undergrads determined to have financial need; average aid package $7,201

## Waldorf College[1]
Forest City IA
(641) 585-8112
U.S. News ranking: Reg. Coll. (Mid. W), second tier
Website: www.waldorf.edu
Admissions email: admissions@waldorf.edu
For-profit
Application deadline (fall): N/A

Undergraduate student body: N/A full time, N/A part time
Expenses: 2013-2014: $20,316; room/board: $6,856
Financial aid: (641) 585-8120

## Wartburg College
Waverly IA
(319) 352-8264
U.S. News ranking: Nat. Lib. Arts, No. 159
Website: www.wartburg.edu
Admissions email: admissions@wartburg.edu
Private; founded 1852
Affiliation: Lutheran
Freshman admissions: selective; 2013-2014: 2,268 applied, 1,761 accepted. Either SAT or ACT required. ACT 25/75 percentile: 21-26. High school rank: 26% in top tenth, 55% in top quarter, 79% in top half
Early decision deadline: N/A, notification date: N/A
Early action deadline: 12/1, notification date: N/A
Application deadline (fall): rolling
Undergraduate student body: 1,643 full time, 71 part time; 47% male, 53% female; 0% American Indian, 1% Asian, 6% black, 2% Hispanic, 2% multiracial, 0% Pacific Islander, 78% white, 10% international; 74% from in state; 81% live on campus; 0% of students in fraternities, 0% in sororities
Most popular majors: 15% Biology/Biological Sciences, General, 20% Business/Commerce, General, 15% Elementary Education and Teaching, 7% Speech Communication and Rhetoric, 8% Visual and Performing Arts, General
Expenses: 2014-2015: $36,120; room/board: $8,920
Financial aid: (319) 352-8262; 75% of undergrads determined to have financial need; average aid package $25,732

## William Penn University[1]
Oskaloosa IA
(641) 673-1012
U.S. News ranking: Reg. Coll. (Mid. W), second tier
Website: www.wmpenn.edu
Admissions email: admissions@wmpenn.edu
Private
Application deadline (fall): N/A
Undergraduate student body: N/A full time, N/A part time
Expenses: 2013-2014: $23,210; room/board: $5,472
Financial aid: (641) 673-1040

KANSAS

## Baker University
Baldwin City KS
(800) 873-4282
U.S. News ranking: Reg. U. (Mid. W), No. 44
Website: www.bakeru.edu
Admissions email: admission@bakeru.edu
Private; founded 1858
Affiliation: United Methodist
Freshman admissions: selective; 2013-2014: 949 applied, 832 accepted. Either SAT or ACT required. ACT 25/75 percentile: 21-26. High school rank: 15%

in top tenth, 42% in top quarter, 77% in top half
**Early decision deadline:** N/A, notification date: N/A
**Early action deadline:** N/A, notification date: N/A
**Application deadline (fall):** rolling
**Undergraduate student body:** 800 full time, 142 part time; 49% male, 51% female; 3% American Indian, 1% Asian, 10% black, 5% Hispanic, 1% multiracial, 1% Pacific Islander, 74% white, 0% international; 70% from in state; 76% live on campus; 27% of students in fraternities, 42% in sororities
**Most popular majors:** 20% Business, Management, Marketing, and Related Support Services, 7% Communication, Journalism, and Related Programs, 15% Education, 13% Parks, Recreation, Leisure, and Fitness Studies, 8% Social Sciences
**Expenses:** 2014-2015: $26,290; room/board: $8,040
**Financial aid:** (785) 594-4595; 82% of undergrads determined to have financial need; average aid package $20,157

## Benedictine College
Atchison KS
(800) 467-5340
**U.S. News ranking:** Reg. Coll. (Mid. W), No. 20
**Website:** www.benedictine.edu
**Admissions email:** bcadmiss@benedictine.edu
**Private;** founded 1859
**Affiliation:** Roman Catholic
**Freshman admissions:** selective; 2013-2014: 2,195 applied, 2,130 accepted. Either SAT or ACT required. ACT 25/75 percentile: 22-28. High school rank: 25% in top tenth, 46% in top quarter, 74% in top half
**Early decision deadline:** N/A, notification date: N/A
**Early action deadline:** N/A, notification date: N/A
**Application deadline (fall):** rolling
**Undergraduate student body:** 1,750 full time, 363 part time; 48% male, 52% female; 0% American Indian, 1% Asian, 3% black, 6% Hispanic, 3% multiracial, 0% Pacific Islander, 80% white, 3% international; 27% from in state; 85% live on campus; 0% of students in fraternities, 0% in sororities
**Most popular majors:** 14% Business, Management, Marketing, and Related Support Services, 6% Communication, Journalism, and Related Programs, 20% Education, 10% Social Sciences, 9% Theology and Religious Vocations
**Expenses:** 2014-2015: $25,100; room/board: $8,750
**Financial aid:** (913) 360-7484; 72% of undergrads determined to have financial need; average aid package $18,934

## Bethany College
Lindsborg KS
(800) 826-2281
**U.S. News ranking:** Reg. Coll. (Mid. W), No. 68
**Website:** www.bethanylb.edu
**Admissions email:** admissions@bethanylb.edu
**Private**
**Affiliation:** Evangelical Luteran Chuch in America (ELCA)

**Freshman admissions:** selective; 2013-2014: 1,139 applied, 670 accepted. Either SAT or ACT required. ACT 25/75 percentile: 18-23. High school rank: 8% in top tenth, 20% in top quarter, 63% in top half
**Early decision deadline:** N/A, notification date: N/A
**Early action deadline:** N/A, notification date: N/A
**Application deadline (fall):** rolling
**Undergraduate student body:** 603 full time, 62 part time; 60% male, 40% female; 1% American Indian, 1% Asian, 12% black, 12% Hispanic, 4% multiracial, 1% Pacific Islander, 69% white, 0% international; 55% from in state; 67% live on campus; 6% of students in fraternities, 16% in sororities
**Most popular majors:** 14% Biology/Biological Sciences, General, 11% Criminology, 10% Elementary Education and Teaching, 8% Sport and Fitness Administration/Management
**Expenses:** 2014-2015: $24,390; room/board: $7,610
**Financial aid:** (785) 227-3311; 83% of undergrads determined to have financial need; average aid package $24,733

## Bethel College
North Newton KS
(800) 522-1887
**U.S. News ranking:** Reg. Coll. (Mid. W), No. 25
**Website:** www.bethelks.edu
**Admissions email:** admissions@bethelks.edu
**Private;** founded 1887
**Affiliation:** Mennonite Church USA
**Freshman admissions:** selective; 2013-2014: 854 applied, 550 accepted. Either SAT or ACT required. ACT 25/75 percentile: 19-26. High school rank: 17% in top tenth, 21% in top quarter, 70% in top half
**Early decision deadline:** N/A, notification date: N/A
**Early action deadline:** N/A, notification date: N/A
**Application deadline (fall):** rolling
**Undergraduate student body:** 464 full time, 18 part time; 49% male, 51% female; 1% American Indian, 1% Asian, 13% black, 10% Hispanic, 3% multiracial, 0% Pacific Islander, 71% white, 2% international; 66% from in state; 73% live on campus; 0% of students in fraternities, 0% in sororities
**Most popular majors:** 6% Biological and Biomedical Sciences, 11% Business, Management, Marketing, and Related Support Services, 7% Education, 22% Health Professions and Related Programs, 12% Public Administration and Social Service Professions
**Expenses:** 2014-2015: $24,200; room/board: $8,240
**Financial aid:** (316) 284-5232; 85% of undergrads determined to have financial need; average aid package $24,337

## Central Christian College[1]
McPherson KS
(800) 835-0078
**U.S. News ranking:** Reg. Coll. (Mid. W), second tier
**Website:** www.centralchristian.edu/
**Admissions email:** rick.wyatt@centralchristian.edu
**Private**
**Application deadline (fall):** N/A
**Undergraduate student body:** N/A full time, N/A part time
**Expenses:** 2013-2014: $14,800; room/board: $6,500
**Financial aid:** (620) 241-0723

## Donnelly College[1]
Kansas City KS
(913) 621-8700
**U.S. News ranking:** Reg. Coll. (Mid. W), unranked
**Website:** donnelly.edu
**Admissions email:** N/A
**Private**
**Application deadline (fall):** N/A
**Undergraduate student body:** N/A full time, N/A part time
**Expenses:** 2013-2014: $6,579; room/board: $6,224
**Financial aid:** (913) 621-8700

## Emporia State University
Emporia KS
(620) 341-5465
**U.S. News ranking:** Reg. U. (Mid. W), No. 103
**Website:** www.emporia.edu
**Admissions email:** go2esu@emporia.edu
**Public;** founded 1863
**Freshman admissions:** selective; 2013-2014: 2,452 applied, 1,488 accepted. Either SAT or ACT required. ACT 25/75 percentile: 19-25. High school rank: 14% in top tenth, 36% in top quarter, 72% in top half
**Early decision deadline:** N/A, notification date: N/A
**Early action deadline:** N/A, notification date: N/A
**Application deadline (fall):** rolling
**Undergraduate student body:** 3,445 full time, 428 part time; 40% male, 60% female; 0% American Indian, 1% Asian, 6% black, 7% Hispanic, 5% multiracial, 0% Pacific Islander, 72% white, 8% international; 92% from in state; 26% live on campus; 16% of students in fraternities, 12% in sororities
**Most popular majors:** 15% Business, Management, Marketing, and Related Support Services, 22% Education, 10% Health Professions and Related Programs, 10% Social Sciences, 6% Visual and Performing Arts
**Expenses:** 2014-2015: $5,746 in state, $17,896 out of state; room/board: $7,582
**Financial aid:** (620) 341-5457; 66% of undergrads determined to have financial need; average aid package $8,590

## Fort Hays State University
Hays KS
(800) 628-3478
**U.S. News ranking:** Reg. U. (Mid. W), second tier
**Website:** www.fhsu.edu
**Admissions email:** tigers@fhsu.edu

**Public;** founded 1902
**Freshman admissions:** less selective; 2013-2014: 2,511 applied, 2,239 accepted. Either SAT or ACT required. SAT 25/75 percentile: 740-1230. High school rank: 10% in top tenth, 31% in top quarter, 61% in top half
**Early decision deadline:** N/A, notification date: N/A
**Early action deadline:** N/A, notification date: N/A
**Application deadline (fall):** rolling
**Undergraduate student body:** 5,449 full time, 5,984 part time; 41% male, 59% female; 0% American Indian, 1% Asian, 4% black, 5% Hispanic, 2% multiracial, 0% Pacific Islander, 55% white, 31% international
**Most popular majors:** Information not available
**Expenses:** 2013-2014: $5,054 in state, $12,003 out of state; room/board: $7,130
**Financial aid:** (785) 628-4408; 73% of undergrads determined to have financial need; average aid package $6,966

## Friends University[1]
Wichita KS
(316) 295-5100
**U.S. News ranking:** Reg. U. (Mid. W), second tier
**Website:** www.friends.edu
**Admissions email:** learn@friends.edu
**Private**
**Application deadline (fall):** N/A
**Undergraduate student body:** N/A full time, N/A part time
**Expenses:** 2013-2014: $23,430; room/board: $6,800
**Financial aid:** (316) 295-5200

## Kansas State University
Manhattan KS
(785) 532-6250
**U.S. News ranking:** Nat. U., No. 142
**Website:** www.k-state.edu
**Admissions email:** k-state@k-state.edu
**Public;** founded 1863
**Freshman admissions:** selective; 2013-2014: 9,839 applied, 9,437 accepted. Neither SAT nor ACT required. ACT 25/75 percentile: 21-27. High school rank: 22% in top tenth, 48% in top quarter, 77% in top half
**Early decision deadline:** N/A, notification date: N/A
**Early action deadline:** N/A, notification date: N/A
**Application deadline (fall):** rolling
**Undergraduate student body:** 18,110 full time, 2,059 part time; 52% male, 48% female; 0% American Indian, 1% Asian, 4% black, 6% Hispanic, 3% multiracial, 0% Pacific Islander, 78% white, 6% international; 84% from in state; 25% live on campus; 14% of students in fraternities, 20% in sororities
**Most popular majors:** 12% Agriculture, Agriculture Operations, and Related Sciences, 17% Business, Management, Marketing, and Related Support Services, 9% Education, 10% Engineering, 10% Social Sciences
**Expenses:** 2014-2015: $9,034 in state, $22,624 out of state; room/board: $8,060

**Financial aid:** (785) 532-6420; 53% of undergrads determined to have financial need; average aid package $10,873

## Kansas Wesleyan University
Salina KS
(785) 827-5541
**U.S. News ranking:** Reg. Coll. (Mid. W), No. 54
**Website:** www.kwu.edu
**Admissions email:** admissions@kwu.edu
**Private;** founded 1886
**Affiliation:** United Methodist
**Freshman admissions:** selective; 2013-2014: 689 applied, 370 accepted. Either SAT or ACT required. ACT 25/75 percentile: 20-24. High school rank: 11% in top tenth, 43% in top quarter, 81% in top half
**Early decision deadline:** N/A, notification date: N/A
**Early action deadline:** N/A, notification date: N/A
**Application deadline (fall):** rolling
**Undergraduate student body:** 624 full time, 60 part time; 46% male, 54% female; 1% American Indian, 1% Asian, 8% black, 13% Hispanic, 2% multiracial, 0% Pacific Islander, 72% white, 4% international; 59% from in state; 60% live on campus; 0% of students in fraternities, 0% in sororities
**Most popular majors:** 9% Business Administration and Management, General, 8% Criminal Justice/Law Enforcement Administration, 8% Elementary Education and Teaching, 20% Registered Nursing/Registered Nurse, 7% Secondary Education and Teaching
**Expenses:** 2014-2015: $25,200; room/board: $8,000
**Financial aid:** (785) 827-5541; 82% of undergrads determined to have financial need; average aid package $18,643

## McPherson College
McPherson KS
(800) 365-7402
**U.S. News ranking:** Reg. Coll. (Mid. W), No. 52
**Website:** www.mcpherson.edu
**Admissions email:** admissions@mcpherson.edu
**Private;** founded 1887
**Freshman admissions:** selective; 2013-2014: 887 applied, 556 accepted. Either SAT or ACT required. ACT 25/75 percentile: 19-24. High school rank: N/A
**Early decision deadline:** N/A, notification date: N/A
**Early action deadline:** N/A, notification date: N/A
**Application deadline (fall):** 8/1
**Undergraduate student body:** 602 full time, 35 part time; 59% male, 41% female; 0% American Indian, 1% Asian, 14% black, 9% Hispanic, 4% multiracial, 0% Pacific Islander, 70% white, 2% international; 48% from in state; 73% live on campus; 0% of students in fraternities, 0% in sororities
**Most popular majors:** 30% Business, Management, Marketing, and Related Support Services, 6% Education, 23% Engineering Technologies and Engineering-Related Fields, 12% Visual and Performing Arts

**Expenses:** 2014-2015: $24,035; room/board: $8,411
**Financial aid:** (620) 241-0731; 86% of undergrads determined to have financial need; average aid package $25,781

## MidAmerica Nazarene University[1]

Olathe KS
(913) 971-3380
**U.S. News ranking:** Reg. U. (Mid. W), second tier
**Website:** www.mnu.edu
**Admissions email:** admissions@mnu.edu
**Private**
**Application deadline (fall):** N/A
**Undergraduate student body:** N/A full time, N/A part time
**Expenses:** 2013-2014: $22,290; room/board: $7,250
**Financial aid:** (913) 791-3298

## Newman University

Wichita KS
(877) 639-6268
**U.S. News ranking:** Reg. U. (Mid. W), second tier
**Website:** www.newmanu.edu
**Admissions email:** admissions@newmanu.edu
**Private;** founded 1933
**Affiliation:** Roman Catholic
**Freshman admissions:** more selective; 2013-2014: 2,378 applied, 1,050 accepted. Neither SAT nor ACT required. ACT 25/75 percentile: 20-27. High school rank: 19% in top tenth, 51% in top quarter, 77% in top half
**Early decision deadline:** N/A, notification date: N/A
**Early action deadline:** N/A, notification date: N/A
**Application deadline (fall):** rolling
**Undergraduate student body:** 1,121 full time, 1,674 part time; 38% male, 62% female; 1% American Indian, 5% Asian, 6% black, 13% Hispanic, 3% multiracial, 0% Pacific Islander, 66% white, 6% international; 86% from in state; 25% live on campus; 0% of students in fraternities, 0% in sororities
**Most popular majors:** 12% Biology/Biological Sciences, General, 11% Business Administration and Management, General, 17% Elementary Education and Teaching, 7% Multi/Interdisciplinary Studies, 23% Registered Nursing/Registered Nurse
**Expenses:** 2014-2015: $24,800; room/board: $7,060
**Financial aid:** (316) 942-4291; 76% of undergrads determined to have financial need; average aid package $17,256

## Ottawa University

Ottawa KS
(785) 242-5200
**U.S. News ranking:** Reg. Coll. (Mid. W), No. 59
**Website:** www.ottawa.edu
**Admissions email:** admiss@ottawa.edu
**Private;** founded 1865
**Affiliation:** American Baptist
**Freshman admissions:** selective; 2013-2014: 263 applied, 260 accepted. Either SAT or ACT required. ACT 25/75 percentile: 19-25. High school rank: 17% in top tenth, 38% in top quarter, 72% in top half

**Early decision deadline:** N/A, notification date: N/A
**Early action deadline:** N/A, notification date: N/A
**Application deadline (fall):** rolling
**Undergraduate student body:** 515 full time, 24 part time; 56% male, 44% female; 5% American Indian, 1% Asian, 12% black, 7% Hispanic, 0% multiracial, 0% Pacific Islander, 63% white, 1% international; 60% from in state; 72% live on campus; 0% of students in fraternities, 0% in sororities
**Most popular majors:** 10% Biology/Biological Sciences, General, 15% Business Administration and Management, General, 8% Elementary Education and Teaching, 7% Human Services, General, 15% Kinesiology and Exercise Science
**Expenses:** 2014-2015: $25,154; room/board: $8,432
**Financial aid:** (785) 242-5200; 86% of undergrads determined to have financial need; average aid package $12,326

## Pittsburg State University

Pittsburg KS
(800) 854-7488
**U.S. News ranking:** Reg. U. (Mid. W), No. 84
**Website:** www.pittstate.edu
**Admissions email:** psuadmit@pittstate.edu
**Public;** founded 1903
**Freshman admissions:** selective; 2013-2014: 3,073 applied, 2,427 accepted. Either SAT or ACT required. ACT 25/75 percentile: 19-24. High school rank: 20% in top tenth, 38% in top quarter, 70% in top half
**Early decision deadline:** N/A, notification date: N/A
**Early action deadline:** N/A, notification date: N/A
**Application deadline (fall):** rolling
**Undergraduate student body:** 5,625 full time, 611 part time; 52% male, 48% female; 2% American Indian, 1% Asian, 4% black, 5% Hispanic, 4% multiracial, 0% Pacific Islander, 81% white, 3% international; N/A from in state; 19% live on campus; N/A of students in fraternities, N/A in sororities
**Most popular majors:** 5% Biology/Biological Sciences, General, 5% Business/Commerce, General, 7% Multicultural Education, 5% Psychology, General, 8% Registered Nursing/Registered Nurse
**Expenses:** 2014-2015: $6,230 in state, $16,336 out of state; room/board: $6,936
**Financial aid:** (620) 235-4240; average aid package $6,481

## Southwestern College

Winfield KS
(620) 229-6236
**U.S. News ranking:** Reg. U. (Mid. W), No. 84
**Website:** www.sckans.edu
**Admissions email:** scadmit@sckans.edu
**Private;** founded 1885
**Affiliation:** United Methodist
**Freshman admissions:** selective; 2013-2014: 436 applied, 391 accepted. Either SAT or ACT required. ACT 25/75 percentile: 20-25. High school rank: 22%

in top tenth, 49% in top quarter, 77% in top half
**Early decision deadline:** N/A, notification date: N/A
**Early action deadline:** N/A, notification date: N/A
**Application deadline (fall):** 8/25
**Undergraduate student body:** 553 full time, 805 part time; 57% male, 43% female; 2% American Indian, 1% Asian, 10% black, 8% Hispanic, 4% multiracial, 0% Pacific Islander, 61% white, 3% international; 59% from in state; 72% live on campus; N/A of students in fraternities, N/A in sororities
**Most popular majors:** 11% Biological and Biomedical Sciences, 26% Business, Management, Marketing, and Related Support Services, 12% Education, 10% Parks, Recreation, Leisure, and Fitness Studies, 10% Psychology
**Expenses:** 2014-2015: $24,835; room/board: $6,846
**Financial aid:** (620) 229-6215; 80% of undergrads determined to have financial need; average aid package $19,966

## Sterling College

Sterling KS
(800) 346-1017
**U.S. News ranking:** Reg. Coll. (Mid. W), No. 67
**Website:** www.sterling.edu
**Admissions email:** admissions@sterling.edu
**Private;** founded 1887
**Freshman admissions:** selective; 2013-2014: 883 applied, 389 accepted. Either SAT or ACT required. ACT 25/75 percentile: 19-25. High school rank: 12% in top tenth, 29% in top quarter, 63% in top half
**Early decision deadline:** N/A, notification date: N/A
**Early action deadline:** N/A, notification date: N/A
**Application deadline (fall):** rolling
**Undergraduate student body:** 595 full time, 95 part time; 54% male, 46% female; 1% American Indian, 0% Asian, 9% black, 10% Hispanic, 0% multiracial, 1% Pacific Islander, 70% white, 0% international; 52% from in state; 77% live on campus; N/A of students in fraternities, N/A in sororities
**Most popular majors:** 19% Business, Management, Marketing, and Related Support Services, 23% Education, 15% Parks, Recreation, Leisure, and Fitness Studies, 8% Philosophy and Religious Studies, 6% Visual and Performing Arts
**Expenses:** 2014-2015: $22,100; room/board: $6,911
**Financial aid:** (620) 278-4207; 86% of undergrads determined to have financial need; average aid package $21,695

## Tabor College

Hillsboro KS
(620) 947-3121
**U.S. News ranking:** Reg. Coll. (Mid. W), No. 49
**Website:** www.tabor.edu
**Admissions email:** admissions@tabor.edu
**Private;** founded 1908
**Affiliation:** Mennonite Brethren
**Freshman admissions:** selective; 2013-2014: 517 applied, 380 accepted. Either SAT or ACT

required. ACT 25/75 percentile: 19-25. High school rank: 14% in top tenth, 20% in top quarter, 69% in top half
**Early decision deadline:** N/A, notification date: N/A
**Early action deadline:** N/A, notification date: N/A
**Application deadline (fall):** rolling
**Undergraduate student body:** 565 full time, 160 part time; 52% male, 48% female; 1% American Indian, 1% Asian, 7% black, 10% Hispanic, 3% multiracial, 0% Pacific Islander, 60% white, 3% international; 49% from in state; 89% live on campus; 0% of students in fraternities, 0% in sororities
**Most popular majors:** 12% Business Administration and Management, General, 7% Elementary Education and Teaching, 12% Health and Physical Education/Fitness, General, 9% Psychology, General, 20% Registered Nursing, Nursing Administration, Nursing Research and Clinical Nursing, Other
**Expenses:** 2014-2015: $23,900; room/board: $8,620
**Financial aid:** (620) 947-3121; 82% of undergrads determined to have financial need; average aid package $20,544

## University of Kansas

Lawrence KS
(785) 864-3911
**U.S. News ranking:** Nat. U., No. 106
**Website:** www.ku.edu/
**Admissions email:** adm@ku.edu
**Public;** founded 1866
**Freshman admissions:** more selective; 2013-2014: 13,256 applied, 11,715 accepted. Either SAT or ACT required. ACT 25/75 percentile: 22-28. High school rank: 26% in top tenth, 59% in top quarter, 90% in top half
**Early decision deadline:** N/A, notification date: N/A
**Early action deadline:** N/A, notification date: N/A
**Application deadline (fall):** rolling
**Undergraduate student body:** 17,193 full time, 2,024 part time; 50% male, 50% female; 1% American Indian, 4% Asian, 4% black, 6% Hispanic, 4% multiracial, 0% Pacific Islander, 75% white, 5% international; 77% from in state; 25% live on campus; 16% of students in fraternities, 21% in sororities
**Most popular majors:** 13% Business, Management, Marketing, and Related Support Services, 9% Communication, Journalism, and Related Programs, 7% Engineering, 16% Health Professions and Related Programs, 7% Social Sciences
**Expenses:** 2014-2015: $10,448 in state, $25,731 out of state; room/board: $7,896
**Financial aid:** (785) 864-4700; 49% of undergrads determined to have financial need; average aid package $8,799

## University of St. Mary

Leavenworth KS
(913) 758-6118
**U.S. News ranking:** Reg. U. (Mid. W), second tier
**Website:** www.stmary.edu
**Admissions email:** admiss@stmary.edu
**Private;** founded 1923
**Affiliation:** Roman Catholic
**Freshman admissions:** less selective; 2013-2014: 767 applied, 361 accepted. Either SAT or ACT required. ACT 25/75 percentile: 19-24. High school rank: 2% in top tenth, 3% in top quarter, 32% in top half
**Early decision deadline:** N/A, notification date: N/A
**Early action deadline:** N/A, notification date: N/A
**Application deadline (fall):** rolling
**Undergraduate student body:** 566 full time, 324 part time; 35% male, 65% female; 0% American Indian, 1% Asian, 11% black, 6% Hispanic, 2% multiracial, 1% Pacific Islander, 53% white, 1% international; 58% from in state; 30% live on campus; N/A of students in fraternities, N/A in sororities
**Most popular majors:** 7% Business Administration and Management, General, 5% Elementary Education and Teaching, 9% Psychology, General, 45% Registered Nursing/Registered Nurse, 10% Sport and Fitness Administration/Management
**Expenses:** 2013-2014: $23,170; room/board: $7,386
**Financial aid:** (800) 752-7043

## Washburn University

Topeka KS
(785) 670-1030
**U.S. News ranking:** Reg. U. (Mid. W), No. 91
**Website:** www.washburn.edu
**Admissions email:** admissions@washburn.edu
**Public;** founded 1865
**Freshman admissions:** selective; 2013-2014: 2,079 applied, 2,041 accepted. ACT required. ACT 25/75 percentile: 19-25. High school rank: 13% in top tenth, 38% in top quarter, 69% in top half
**Early decision deadline:** N/A, notification date: N/A
**Early action deadline:** N/A, notification date: N/A
**Application deadline (fall):** 8/1
**Undergraduate student body:** 4,072 full time, 2,107 part time; 41% male, 59% female; N/A American Indian, N/A Asian, N/A black, N/A Hispanic, N/A multiracial, N/A Pacific Islander, N/A white, N/A international; 91% from in state; 15% live on campus; 7% of students in fraternities, 7% in sororities
**Most popular majors:** 14% Business, Management, Marketing, and Related Support Services, 6% Communication, Journalism, and Related Programs, 8% Education, 30% Health Professions and Related Programs, 7% Homeland Security, Law Enforcement, Firefighting and Related Protective Services
**Expenses:** 2014-2015: $6,038 in state, $13,526 out of state; room/board: $6,541

Financial aid: (785) 670-1151;
64% of undergrads determined to
have financial need; average aid
package $9,341

## Wichita State University

Wichita KS
(316) 978-3085
U.S. News ranking: Nat. U.,
second tier
Website: www.wichita.edu
Admissions email: admissions@
wichita.edu
Public; founded 1895
Freshman admissions: selective;
2013-2014: 3,492 applied,
3,344 accepted. Neither SAT
nor ACT required. ACT 25/75
percentile: 21-26. High school
rank: 23% in top tenth, 50% in
top quarter, 79% in top half
Early decision deadline: N/A,
notification date: N/A
Early action deadline: N/A,
notification date: N/A
Application deadline (fall): rolling
Undergraduate student body: 8,807
full time, 2,980 part time; 48%
male, 52% female; 1% American
Indian, 7% Asian, 6% black,
9% Hispanic, 2% multiracial,
0% Pacific Islander, 65% white,
6% international; 95% from in
state; 7% live on campus; 4%
of students in fraternities, 4% in
sororities
Most popular majors: 19%
Business, Management,
Marketing, and Related Support
Services, 9% Education, 10%
Engineering, 17% Health
Professions and Related Programs,
6% Homeland Security, Law
Enforcement, Firefighting and
Related Protective Services
Expenses: 2014-2015: $7,267 in
state, $16,697 out of state; room/
board: $8,373
Financial aid: (316) 978-3430

## Alice Lloyd College

Pippa Passes KY
(888) 280-4252
U.S. News ranking: Reg. Coll. (S),
No. 29
Website: www.alc.edu
Admissions email: admissions@
alc.edu
Private; founded 1923
Freshman admissions: selective;
2013-2014: 3,807 applied, 359
accepted. Either SAT or ACT
required. ACT 25/75 percentile:
18-23. High school rank: 18%
in top tenth, 51% in top quarter,
90% in top half
Early decision deadline: N/A,
notification date: N/A
Early action deadline: N/A,
notification date: N/A
Application deadline (fall): 7/1
Undergraduate student body: 606
full time, 25 part time; 46%
male, 54% female; 0% American
Indian, 0% Asian, 1% black,
1% Hispanic, 0% multiracial,
0% Pacific Islander, 96% white,
0% international; 78% from in
state; 85% live on campus; N/A
of students in fraternities, N/A in
sororities
Most popular majors: 33%
Biological and Biomedical
Sciences, 12% Business,
Management, Marketing, and
Related Support Services, 21%

Education, 8% History, 13%
Social Sciences
Expenses: 2014-2015: $10,980;
room/board: $5,660
Financial aid: (606) 368-6059;
91% of undergrads determined to
have financial need; average aid
package $12,581

## Asbury University

Wilmore KY
(800) 888-1818
U.S. News ranking: Reg. Coll. (S),
No. 1
Website: www.asbury.edu
Admissions email: admissions@
asbury.edu
Private; founded 1890
Affiliation: non-denominational
Freshman admissions: more
selective; 2013-2014: 1,211
applied, 796 accepted. Either
SAT or ACT required. ACT 25/75
percentile: 21-27. High school
rank: 27% in top tenth, 54% in
top quarter, 85% in top half
Early decision deadline: N/A,
notification date: N/A
Early action deadline: N/A,
notification date: N/A
Application deadline (fall): rolling
Undergraduate student body: 1,326
full time, 206 part time; 40%
male, 60% female; 0% American
Indian, 1% Asian, 3% black,
2% Hispanic, 5% multiracial,
0% Pacific Islander, 84% white,
2% international; 50% from in
state; 86% live on campus; 0%
of students in fraternities, 0% in
sororities
Most popular majors: 5% Business
Administration and Management,
General, 5% Communication,
General, 9% Elementary
Education and Teaching, 19%
Radio, Television, and Digital
Communication, Other, 4% Social
Work
Expenses: 2013-2014: $26,076;
room/board: $5,962
Financial aid: (800) 888-1818

## Bellarmine University

Louisville KY
(502) 272-8131
U.S. News ranking: Reg. U. (S),
No. 13
Website: www.bellarmine.edu
Admissions email: admissions@
bellarmine.edu
Private; founded 1950
Affiliation: Roman Catholic
Freshman admissions: selective;
2013-2014: 4,160 applied,
3,943 accepted. Either SAT
or ACT required. ACT 25/75
percentile: 22-27. High school
rank: 25% in top tenth, 54% in
top quarter, 82% in top half
Early decision deadline: N/A,
notification date: N/A
Early action deadline: 11/1,
notification date: 11/15
Application deadline (fall): 8/15
Undergraduate student body: 2,378
full time, 215 part time; 36%
male, 64% female; 0% American
Indian, 2% Asian, 4% black,
3% Hispanic, 2% multiracial,
0% Pacific Islander, 84% white,
1% international; 68% from in
state; 43% live on campus; 1%
of students in fraternities, 1% in
sororities
Most popular majors: 6% Biological
and Biomedical Sciences,
14% Business, Management,
Marketing, and Related Support

Services, 6% Education, 31%
Health Professions and Related
Programs, 8% Psychology
Expenses: 2014-2015: $36,290;
room/board: $10,700
Financial aid: (502) 452-8124;
77% of undergrads determined to
have financial need; average aid
package $27,406

## Berea College

Berea KY
(859) 985-3500
U.S. News ranking: Nat. Lib. Arts,
No. 69
Website: www.berea.edu
Admissions email: admissions@
berea.edu
Private; founded 1855
Freshman admissions: more
selective; 2013-2014: 1,620
applied, 551 accepted. Either
SAT or ACT required. ACT 25/75
percentile: 22-26. High school
rank: 25% in top tenth, 73% in
top quarter, 95% in top half
Early decision deadline: N/A,
notification date: N/A
Early action deadline: N/A,
notification date: N/A
Application deadline (fall): 4/30
Undergraduate student body: 1,587
full time, 36 part time; 43%
male, 57% female; 0% American
Indian, 2% Asian, 15% black,
4% Hispanic, 5% multiracial,
0% Pacific Islander, 64% white,
8% international; 46% from in
state; 81% live on campus; N/A
of students in fraternities, N/A in
sororities
Most popular majors: 8%
Education, 8% English Language
and Literature/Letters, 7% Family
and Consumer Sciences/Human
Sciences, 7% Social Sciences,
9% Visual and Performing Arts
Expenses: 2014-2015: $870;
room/board: $6,322
Financial aid: (859) 985-3310;
100% of undergrads determined
to have financial need; average aid
package $29,179

## Brescia University

Owensboro KY
(270) 686-4241
U.S. News ranking: Reg. Coll. (S),
No. 43
Website: www.brescia.edu
Admissions email: admissions@
brescia.edu
Private; founded 1950
Affiliation: Roman Catholic
Freshman admissions: selective;
2013-2014: 3,582 applied,
1,612 accepted. Either SAT
or ACT required. ACT 25/75
percentile: 19-24. High school
rank: N/A
Early decision deadline: N/A,
notification date: N/A
Early action deadline: N/A,
notification date: N/A
Application deadline (fall): rolling
Undergraduate student body: 688
full time, 240 part time; 28%
male, 72% female; 1% American
Indian, 1% Asian, 13% black,
7% Hispanic, 0% multiracial, 0%
Pacific Islander, 67% white, 1%
international
Most popular majors: Information
not available
Expenses: 2014-2015: $19,990;
room/board: $9,500
Financial aid: (270) 686-4253

## Campbellsville University

Campbellsville KY
(270) 789-5220
U.S. News ranking: Reg. U. (S),
No. 81
Website: www.campbellsville.edu
Admissions email: admissions@
campbellsville.edu
Private; founded 1906
Affiliation: Baptist
Freshman admissions: selective;
2013-2014: 2,649 applied,
1,813 accepted. Either SAT
or ACT required. ACT 25/75
percentile: 18-24. High school
rank: N/A
Early decision deadline: N/A,
notification date: N/A
Early action deadline: N/A,
notification date: N/A
Application deadline (fall): 8/1
Undergraduate student body: 1,996
full time, 1,105 part time; 41%
male, 59% female; 0% American
Indian, 0% Asian, 13% black,
2% Hispanic, 2% multiracial,
0% Pacific Islander, 74% white,
8% international; 84% from in
state; 52% live on campus; N/A
of students in fraternities, N/A in
sororities
Most popular majors: 18%
Business, Management,
Marketing, and Related Support
Services, 20% Education,
8% Homeland Security, Law
Enforcement, Firefighting and
Related Protective Services, 10%
Public Administration and Social
Service Professions, 9% Theology
and Religious Vocations
Expenses: 2014-2015: $22,842;
room/board: $7,550
Financial aid: (270) 789-5013;
89% of undergrads determined to
have financial need; average aid
package $18,489

## Centre College

Danville KY
(859) 238-5350
U.S. News ranking: Nat. Lib. Arts,
No. 45
Website: www.centre.edu
Admissions email: admission@
centre.edu
Private; founded 1819
Affiliation: Presbyterian Church
(USA)
Freshman admissions: more
selective; 2013-2014: 2,533
applied, 1,737 accepted. Either
SAT or ACT required. ACT 25/75
percentile: 26-31. High school
rank: 52% in top tenth, 81% in
top quarter, 96% in top half
Early decision deadline: 12/1,
notification date: 12/31
Early action deadline: 12/1,
notification date: 1/15
Application deadline (fall): 1/15
Undergraduate student body:
1,378 full time, 3 part time; 49%
male, 51% female; 0% American
Indian, 2% Asian, 5% black, 2%
Hispanic, 3% multiracial, 0%
Pacific Islander, 83% white, 4%
international; 54% from in state;
98% live on campus; 53% of
students in fraternities, 53% in
sororities
Most popular majors: 10% Biology/
Biological Sciences, General, 14%
Economics, Other, 13% History,
General, 7% International/Global
Studies, 7% Mathematics, General
Expenses: 2014-2015: $37,100;
room/board: $9,520

Financial aid: (859) 238-5365;
59% of undergrads determined to
have financial need; average aid
package $27,581

## Eastern Kentucky University

Richmond KY
(800) 465-9191
U.S. News ranking: Reg. U. (S),
No. 62
Website: www.eku.edu
Admissions email: admissions@
eku.edu
Public; founded 1906
Freshman admissions: selective;
2013-2014: 9,000 applied,
6,642 accepted. Either SAT
or ACT required. ACT 25/75
percentile: 19-25. High school
rank: N/A
Early decision deadline: N/A,
notification date: N/A
Early action deadline: N/A,
notification date: N/A
Application deadline (fall): 8/1
Undergraduate student body:
10,969 full time, 2,922 part
time; 44% male, 56% female;
0% American Indian, 1% Asian,
5% black, 2% Hispanic, 2%
multiracial, 0% Pacific Islander,
85% white, 2% international;
87% from in state; 30% live
on campus; N/A of students in
fraternities, N/A in sororities
Most popular majors: 9% Criminal
Justice/Law Enforcement
Administration, 4% Elementary
Education and Teaching, 10%
General Studies, 5% Psychology,
General, 7% Registered Nursing/
Registered Nurse
Expenses: 2014-2015: $7,920 in
state, $17,448 out of state; room/
board: $7,720
Financial aid: (859) 622-2361;
71% of undergrads determined to
have financial need; average aid
package $10,170

## Georgetown College

Georgetown KY
(502) 863-8009
U.S. News ranking: Nat. Lib. Arts,
No. 155
Website: www.georgetowncollege.
edu/admission/
Admissions email: admissions@
georgetowncollege.edu
Private; founded 1787
Affiliation: Baptist
Freshman admissions: selective;
2013-2014: 1,448 applied,
1,242 accepted. Either SAT
or ACT required. ACT 25/75
percentile: 20-25. High school
rank: 20% in top tenth, 48% in
top quarter, 83% in top half
Early decision deadline: 10/15,
notification date: N/A
Early action deadline: 11/1,
notification date: N/A
Application deadline (fall): 8/1
Undergraduate student body: 1,000
full time, 43 part time; 46%
male, 54% female; 0% American
Indian, 1% Asian, 10% black,
3% Hispanic, 2% multiracial,
0% Pacific Islander, 76% white,
2% international; 77% from in
state; 91% live on campus; 27%
of students in fraternities, 35%
in sororities
Most popular majors: 10%
Biological and Biomedical
Sciences, 12% Business,
Management, Marketing, and
Related Support Services, 9%
Parks, Recreation, Leisure, and

Fitness Studies, 13% Psychology, 11% Social Sciences
**Expenses:** 2014-2015: $32,960; room/board: $8,480
**Financial aid:** (502) 863-8027; 83% of undergrads determined to have financial need; average aid package $32,160

## Kentucky Christian University
Grayson KY
(800) 522-3181
**U.S. News ranking:** Reg. Coll. (S), No. 56
**Website:** www.kcu.edu
**Admissions email:** knights@kcu.edu
**Private;** founded 1919
**Affiliation:** Christian Church/Church of Christ
**Freshman admissions:** selective; 2013-2014: 590 applied, 303 accepted. Either SAT or ACT required. ACT 25/75 percentile: 18-23. High school rank: 10% in top tenth, 32% in top quarter, 64% in top half
**Early decision deadline:** N/A, notification date: N/A
**Early action deadline:** N/A, notification date: N/A
**Application deadline (fall):** 8/1
**Undergraduate student body:** 494 full time, 57 part time; 54% male, 46% female; 0% American Indian, 0% Asian, 12% black, 1% Hispanic, 1% multiracial, 0% Pacific Islander, 70% white, 1% international; 48% from in state; 81% live on campus; 0% of students in fraternities, 0% in sororities
**Most popular majors:** 8% Business Administration and Management, General, 8% Elementary Education and Teaching, 18% Multi-/Interdisciplinary Studies, Other, 12% Registered Nursing/Registered Nurse, 8% Social Work
**Expenses:** 2014-2015: $16,860; room/board: $7,200
**Financial aid:** (606) 474-3226; 93% of undergrads determined to have financial need; average aid package $15,487

## Kentucky State University
Frankfort KY
(800) 325-1716
**U.S. News ranking:** Nat. Lib. Arts, second tier
**Website:** www.kysu.edu
**Admissions email:** admissions@kysu.edu
**Public;** founded 1886
**Freshman admissions:** less selective; 2013-2014: 6,399 applied, 2,414 accepted. Either SAT or ACT required. ACT 25/75 percentile: 16-20. High school rank: N/A
**Early decision deadline:** N/A, notification date: N/A
**Early action deadline:** N/A, notification date: N/A
**Application deadline (fall):** rolling
**Undergraduate student body:** 1,813 full time, 557 part time; 41% male, 59% female; 0% American Indian, 1% Asian, 62% black, 1% Hispanic, 2% multiracial, 0% Pacific Islander, 20% white, 0% international; 58% from in state; 34% live on campus; 5% of students in fraternities, 4% in sororities

**Most popular majors:** 9% Biology/Biological Sciences, General, 9% Business/Commerce, General, 12% Liberal Arts and Sciences/Liberal Studies, 8% Psychology, General, 16% Registered Nursing/Registered Nurse
**Expenses:** 2014-2015: $7,404 in state, $17,214 out of state; room/board: $6,690
**Financial aid:** (502) 597-5960; 85% of undergrads determined to have financial need; average aid package $11,284

## Kentucky Wesleyan College
Owensboro KY
(800) 999-0592
**U.S. News ranking:** Reg. Coll. (S), No. 31
**Website:** www.kwc.edu/page.php?page=354
**Admissions email:** rsmith@kwc.edu
**Private;** founded 1858
**Affiliation:** United Methodist
**Freshman admissions:** selective; 2013-2014: 1,006 applied, 675 accepted. Either SAT or ACT required. ACT 25/75 percentile: 19-25. High school rank: 13% in top tenth, 39% in top quarter, 69% in top half
**Early decision deadline:** N/A, notification date: N/A
**Early action deadline:** N/A, notification date: N/A
**Application deadline (fall):** rolling
**Undergraduate student body:** 621 full time, 36 part time; 52% male, 48% female; 0% American Indian, 0% Asian, 13% black, 2% Hispanic, 0% multiracial, 0% Pacific Islander, 73% white, 2% international; 71% from in state; 50% live on campus; 16% of students in fraternities, 23% in sororities
**Most popular majors:** 11% Biological and Biomedical Sciences, 12% Business, Management, Marketing, and Related Support Services, 11% Education, 11% Homeland Security, Law Enforcement, Firefighting and Related Protective Services, 11% Visual and Performing Arts
**Expenses:** 2014-2015: $22,030; room/board: $7,800
**Financial aid:** (270) 926-3111; 87% of undergrads determined to have financial need; average aid package $17,166

## Lindsey Wilson College
Columbia KY
(270) 384-8100
**U.S. News ranking:** Reg. U. (S), second tier
**Website:** www.lindsey.edu
**Admissions email:** admissions@lindsey.edu
**Private;** founded 1903
**Affiliation:** United Methodist
**Freshman admissions:** selective; 2013-2014: 2,711 applied, 1,939 accepted. Neither SAT nor ACT required. ACT 25/75 percentile: 19-24. High school rank: 13% in top tenth, 33% in top quarter, 70% in top half
**Early decision deadline:** N/A, notification date: N/A
**Early action deadline:** N/A, notification date: N/A
**Application deadline (fall):** rolling

**Undergraduate student body:** 2,101 full time, 99 part time; 41% male, 59% female; 0% American Indian, 1% Asian, 9% black, 1% Hispanic, 2% multiracial, 0% Pacific Islander, 71% white, 0% international; 81% from in state; 52% live on campus; 0% of students in fraternities, 0% in sororities
**Most popular majors:** 2% Biology/Biological Sciences, General, 7% Business Administration and Management, General, 8% Criminal Justice/Safety Studies, 52% Human Services, General, 4% Registered Nursing/Registered Nurse
**Expenses:** 2014-2015: $22,550; room/board: $8,670
**Financial aid:** (270) 384-8022; 94% of undergrads determined to have financial need; average aid package $15,688

## Mid-Continent University[1]
Mayfield KY
(270) 247-8475
**U.S. News ranking:** Reg. Coll. (S), second tier
**Website:** www.midcontinent.edu
**Admissions email:** advantage@midcontinent.edu
**Private;** founded 1949
**Affiliation:** Southern Baptist Convention
**Application deadline (fall):** rolling
**Undergraduate student body:** N/A full time, N/A part time
**Expenses:** 2013-2014: $13,350; room/board: $6,900
**Financial aid:** (270) 247-8521

## Midway College[1]
Midway KY
(800) 755-0031
**U.S. News ranking:** Reg. Coll. (S), No. 61
**Website:** www.midway.edu
**Admissions email:** admissions@midway.edu
**Private**
**Application deadline (fall):** N/A
**Undergraduate student body:** N/A full time, N/A part time
**Expenses:** 2013-2014: $22,150; room/board: $8,000
**Financial aid:** (859) 846-5745

## Morehead State University
Morehead KY
(606) 783-2000
**U.S. News ranking:** Reg. U. (S), No. 53
**Website:** www.moreheadstate.edu
**Admissions email:** admissions@moreheadstate.edu
**Public;** founded 1922
**Freshman admissions:** selective; 2013-2014: 5,241 applied, 4,364 accepted. Either SAT or ACT required. ACT 25/75 percentile: 19-25. High school rank: 19% in top tenth, 46% in top quarter, 78% in top half
**Early decision deadline:** N/A, notification date: N/A
**Early action deadline:** N/A, notification date: N/A
**Application deadline (fall):** rolling
**Undergraduate student body:** 6,209 full time, 3,867 part time; 39% male, 61% female; 0% American Indian, 0% Asian, 4% black, 1% Hispanic, 1% multiracial,

0% Pacific Islander, 91% white, 1% international; 87% from in state; 39% live on campus; 10% of students in fraternities, 9% in sororities
**Most popular majors:** 5% Agriculture, Agriculture Operations, and Related Sciences, 6% Elementary Education and Teaching, 13% General Studies, 5% Registered Nursing/Registered Nurse, 8% Social Work
**Expenses:** 2014-2015: $7,866 in state, $19,666 out of state; room/board: $7,888
**Financial aid:** (606) 783-2011; 78% of undergrads determined to have financial need; average aid package $10,749

## Murray State University
Murray KY
(270) 809-3741
**U.S. News ranking:** Reg. U. (S), No. 26
**Website:** www.murraystate.edu
**Admissions email:** admissions@murraystate.edu
**Public;** founded 1922
**Freshman admissions:** selective; 2013-2014: 4,956 applied, 4,068 accepted. Either SAT or ACT required. ACT 25/75 percentile: 20-26. High school rank: 19% in top tenth, 43% in top quarter, 73% in top half
**Early decision deadline:** N/A, notification date: N/A
**Early action deadline:** N/A, notification date: N/A
**Application deadline (fall):** 8/15
**Undergraduate student body:** 7,153 full time, 2,019 part time; 42% male, 58% female; 0% American Indian, 1% Asian, 7% black, 2% Hispanic, 2% multiracial, 0% Pacific Islander, 83% white, 4% international; 69% from in state; 33% live on campus; 14% of students in fraternities, 15% in sororities
**Most popular majors:** 11% Business, Management, Marketing, and Related Support Services, 13% Education, 7% Engineering Technologies and Engineering-Related Fields, 15% Health Professions and Related Programs, 10% Liberal Arts and Sciences, General Studies and Humanities
**Expenses:** 2014-2015: $7,392 in state, $10,073 out of state; room/board: $7,912
**Financial aid:** (270) 809-2546; 63% of undergrads determined to have financial need; average aid package $10,679

## Northern Kentucky University
Highland Heights KY
(800) 637-9948
**U.S. News ranking:** Reg. U. (S), No. 70
**Website:** www.nku.edu
**Admissions email:** admitnku@nku.edu
**Public;** founded 1968
**Freshman admissions:** selective; 2013-2014: 8,724 applied, 5,105 accepted. Either SAT or ACT required. ACT 25/75 percentile: 20-25. High school rank: 11% in top tenth, 32% in top quarter, 64% in top half
**Early decision deadline:** N/A, notification date: N/A

**Early action deadline:** N/A, notification date: N/A
**Undergraduate student body:** 9,736 full time, 3,058 part time; 45% male, 55% female; 0% American Indian, 1% Asian, 7% black, 2% Hispanic, 2% multiracial, 0% Pacific Islander, 82% white, 4% international; 66% from in state; 14% live on campus; 4% of students in fraternities, 4% in sororities
**Most popular majors:** 12% Health Services/Allied Health/Health Sciences, General
**Expenses:** 2014-2015: $8,856 in state, $17,328 out of state; room/board: $8,610
**Financial aid:** (859) 572-5143; 65% of undergrads determined to have financial need; average aid package $10,384

## Spalding University[1]
Louisville KY
(502) 585-7111
**U.S. News ranking:** Nat. U., No. 181
**Website:** www.spalding.edu
**Admissions email:** admissions@spalding.edu
**Private;** founded 1814
**Affiliation:** Roman Catholic
**Application deadline (fall):** rolling
**Undergraduate student body:** N/A full time, N/A part time
**Expenses:** 2013-2014: $22,425; room/board: $10,400
**Financial aid:** (502) 585-9911

## St. Catharine College[1]
St. Catharine KY
(800) 599-2000
**U.S. News ranking:** Reg. Coll. (S), unranked
**Website:** www.sccky.edu
**Admissions email:** admissions@sccky.edu
**Private**
**Application deadline (fall):** N/A
**Undergraduate student body:** N/A full time, N/A part time
**Expenses:** 2013-2014: $18,026; room/board: $9,031
**Financial aid:** (859) 336-5082

## Sullivan University[1]
Louisville KY
(502) 456-6504
**U.S. News ranking:** Reg. U. (S), unranked
**Website:** www.sullivan.edu
**Admissions email:** admissions@sullivan.edu
**Private**
**Application deadline (fall):** N/A
**Undergraduate student body:** N/A full time, N/A part time
**Expenses:** 2013-2014: $17,970; room/board: $9,120
**Financial aid:** (800) 844-1354

## Thomas More College
Crestview Hills KY
(800) 825-4557
**U.S. News ranking:** Reg. U. (S), No. 49
**Website:** www.thomasmore.edu
**Admissions email:** admissions@thomasmore.edu
**Private;** founded 1921
**Affiliation:** Roman Catholic
**Freshman admissions:** selective; 2013-2014: 1,053 applied, 924 accepted. Either SAT or ACT required. ACT 25/75 percentile:

20-25. High school rank: 11% in top tenth, 27% in top quarter, 64% in top half
**Early decision deadline:** N/A, notification date: N/A
**Early action deadline:** N/A, notification date: N/A
**Application deadline (fall):** 8/1
**Undergraduate student body:** 1,140 full time, 362 part time; 48% male, 52% female; 0% American Indian, 1% Asian, 7% black, 2% Hispanic, 2% multiracial, 0% Pacific Islander, 75% white, 1% international; 47% from in state; 30% live on campus; 2% of students in fraternities, 2% in sororities
**Most popular majors:** 7% Biological and Biomedical Sciences, 44% Business, Management, Marketing, and Related Support Services, 8% Education, 11% Health Professions and Related Programs, 5% Liberal Arts and Sciences, General Studies and Humanities
**Expenses:** 2014-2015: $28,618; room/board: $7,770
**Financial aid:** (859) 344-3319; 58% of undergrads determined to have financial need; average aid package $21,066

## Transylvania University
Lexington KY
(859) 233-8242
**U.S. News ranking:** Nat. Lib. Arts, No. 81
**Website:** www.transy.edu
**Admissions email:** admissions@transy.edu
**Private;** founded 1780
**Affiliation:** Christian Church (Disciples of Christ)
**Freshman admissions:** more selective; 2013-2014: 1,539 applied, 1,275 accepted. Either SAT or ACT required. ACT 25/75 percentile: 24-30. High school rank: 39% in top tenth, 75% in top quarter, 95% in top half
**Early decision deadline:** N/A, notification date: N/A
**Early action deadline:** 12/1, notification date: 1/15
**Application deadline (fall):** 2/1
**Undergraduate student body:** 1,066 full time, 15 part time; 43% male, 57% female; 0% American Indian, 2% Asian, 3% black, 3% Hispanic, 3% multiracial, 0% Pacific Islander, 83% white, 2% international; 77% from in state; 75% live on campus; 44% of students in fraternities, 60% in sororities
**Most popular majors:** 13% Biology/Biological Sciences, General, 17% Business/Commerce, General, 8% English Language and Literature, General, 8% Psychology, General, 15% Social Sciences, General
**Expenses:** 2014-2015: $33,360; room/board: $9,300
**Financial aid:** (859) 233-8239; 68% of undergrads determined to have financial need; average aid package $26,801

## Union College
Barbourville KY
(800) 489-8646
**U.S. News ranking:** Reg. U. (S), No. 81
**Website:** www.unionky.edu
**Admissions email:** enroll@unionky.edu
**Private;** founded 1879

**Affiliation:** United Methodist
**Freshman admissions:** selective; 2013-2014: 1,390 applied, 1,038 accepted. Either SAT or ACT required. ACT 25/75 percentile: 19-24. High school rank: N/A
**Early decision deadline:** N/A, notification date: N/A
**Early action deadline:** N/A, notification date: N/A
**Application deadline (fall):** rolling
**Undergraduate student body:** 729 full time, 89 part time; 51% male, 49% female; 0% American Indian, 0% Asian, 10% black, 2% Hispanic, 2% multiracial, 0% Pacific Islander, 79% white, 6% international; 76% from in state; 48% live on campus; 0% of students in fraternities, 0% in sororities
**Most popular majors:** 9% Athletic Training/Trainer, 8% Business Administration and Management, General, 8% Criminal Justice/Law Enforcement Administration, 10% Psychology, General
**Expenses:** 2014-2015: $22,980; room/board: $6,975
**Financial aid:** (606) 546-1229; 87% of undergrads determined to have financial need; average aid package $20,468

## University of Kentucky
Lexington KY
(859) 257-2000
**U.S. News ranking:** Nat. U., No. 129
**Website:** www.uky.edu
**Admissions email:** admissions@uky.edu
**Public;** founded 1865
**Freshman admissions:** more selective; 2013-2014: 19,810 applied, 13,592 accepted. Either SAT or ACT required. ACT 25/75 percentile: 22-28. High school rank: 31% in top tenth, 58% in top quarter, 85% in top half
**Early decision deadline:** N/A, notification date: N/A
**Early action deadline:** N/A, notification date: N/A
**Application deadline (fall):** rolling
**Undergraduate student body:** 19,884 full time, 1,557 part time; 49% male, 51% female; 0% American Indian, 2% Asian, 8% black, 3% Hispanic, 3% multiracial, 0% Pacific Islander, 78% white, 3% international; 68% from in state; 15% live on campus; 18% of students in fraternities, 28% in sororities
**Most popular majors:** 4% Accounting, 5% Biology/Biological Sciences, General, 4% Finance, General, 5% Psychology, General, 4% Registered Nursing/Registered Nurse
**Expenses:** 2014-2015: $10,616 in state, $22,888 out of state; room/board: $10,506
**Financial aid:** (859) 257-3172; 52% of undergrads determined to have financial need; average aid package $10,872

## University of Louisville
Louisville KY
(502) 852-6531
**U.S. News ranking:** Nat. U., No. 161
**Website:** www.louisville.edu
**Admissions email:** admitme@louisville.edu

**Public;** founded 1798
**Freshman admissions:** selective; 2013-2014: 9,142 applied, 6,496 accepted. Either SAT or ACT required. ACT 25/75 percentile: 22-28. High school rank: 20% in top tenth, 33% in top quarter, 61% in top half
**Early decision deadline:** N/A, notification date: N/A
**Early action deadline:** N/A, notification date: N/A
**Application deadline (fall):** 8/25
**Undergraduate student body:** 12,426 full time, 3,531 part time; 49% male, 51% female; 0% American Indian, 3% Asian, 11% black, 4% Hispanic, 4% multiracial, 0% Pacific Islander, 77% white, 1% international; 85% from in state; 27% live on campus; 18% of students in fraternities, 13% in sororities
**Most popular majors:** 15% Business, Management, Marketing, and Related Support Services, 10% Engineering, 8% Health Professions and Related Programs, 9% Parks, Recreation, Leisure, and Fitness Studies, 8% Social Sciences
**Expenses:** 2014-2015: $10,432 in state, $24,320 out of state; room/board: $7,710
**Financial aid:** (502) 852-5511; 63% of undergrads determined to have financial need; average aid package $10,965

## University of Pikeville
Pikeville KY
(606) 218-5251
**U.S. News ranking:** Nat. Lib. Arts, second tier
**Website:** www.pc.edu/pc.edu
**Admissions email:** wewantyou@pc.edu
**Private;** founded 1889
**Affiliation:** Presbyterian Church (USA)
**Freshman admissions:** selective; 2013-2014: 1,804 applied, 1,804 accepted. Either SAT or ACT required. ACT 25/75 percentile: 17-22. High school rank: 15% in top tenth, 36% in top quarter, 65% in top half
**Early decision deadline:** N/A, notification date: N/A
**Early action deadline:** N/A, notification date: N/A
**Application deadline (fall):** 8/16
**Undergraduate student body:** 1,282 full time, 455 part time; 47% male, 53% female; 0% American Indian, 0% Asian, 13% black, 1% Hispanic, 0% multiracial, 0% Pacific Islander, 82% white, 3% international; 81% from in state; 59% live on campus; N/A of students in fraternities, N/A in sororities
**Most popular majors:** 10% Biological and Biomedical Sciences, 23% Business, Management, Marketing, and Related Support Services, 12% Homeland Security, Law Enforcement, Firefighting and Related Protective Services, 10% Psychology, 12% Social Sciences
**Expenses:** 2014-2015: $18,290; room/board: $7,210
**Financial aid:** (606) 218-5253; 98% of undergrads determined to have financial need; average aid package $18,056

## University of the Cumberlands
Williamsburg KY
(800) 343-1609
**U.S. News ranking:** Reg. U. (S), No. 92
**Website:** www.ucumberlands.edu
**Admissions email:** admiss@ucumberlands.edu
**Private;** founded 1888
**Affiliation:** Baptist
**Freshman admissions:** selective; 2013-2014: 2,529 applied, 1,803 accepted. Either SAT or ACT required. ACT 25/75 percentile: 19-25. High school rank: 15% in top tenth, 38% in top quarter, 71% in top half
**Early decision deadline:** N/A, notification date: N/A
**Early action deadline:** N/A, notification date: N/A
**Application deadline (fall):** 8/15
**Undergraduate student body:** 1,514 full time, 582 part time; 50% male, 50% female; 0% American Indian, 0% Asian, 8% black, 2% Hispanic, 1% multiracial, 0% Pacific Islander, 80% white, 6% international; 69% from in state; 75% live on campus; 0% of students in fraternities, 0% in sororities
**Most popular majors:** 12% Biological and Biomedical Sciences, 16% Business, Management, Marketing, and Related Support Services, 13% Education, 8% Health Professions and Related Programs, 8% Public Administration and Social Service Professions
**Expenses:** 2013-2014: $20,000; room/board: $7,500
**Financial aid:** (800) 532-0828

## Western Kentucky University
Bowling Green KY
(270) 745-2551
**U.S. News ranking:** Reg. U. (S), No. 31
**Website:** www.wku.edu
**Admissions email:** admission@wku.edu
**Public;** founded 1906
**Freshman admissions:** selective; 2013-2014: 8,114 applied, 7,491 accepted. Either SAT or ACT required. ACT 25/75 percentile: 19-25. High school rank: 25% in top tenth, 50% in top quarter, 76% in top half
**Early decision deadline:** N/A, notification date: N/A
**Early action deadline:** N/A, notification date: N/A
**Application deadline (fall):** 8/1
**Undergraduate student body:** 13,382 full time, 4,127 part time; 43% male, 57% female; 0% American Indian, 1% Asian, 11% black, 2% Hispanic, 2% multiracial, 0% Pacific Islander, 77% white, 5% international; 83% from in state; 29% live on campus; 12% of students in fraternities, 13% in sororities
**Most popular majors:** 14% Business, Management, Marketing, and Related Support Services, 12% Education, 9% Health Professions and Related Programs, 9% Liberal Arts and Sciences, General Studies and Humanities, 9% Social Sciences
**Expenses:** 2014-2015: $9,140 in state, $23,352 out of state; room/board: N/A

**Financial aid:** (270) 745-2755; 65% of undergrads determined to have financial need; average aid package $13,809

## Centenary College of Louisiana
Shreveport LA
(800) 234-4448
**U.S. News ranking:** Nat. Lib. Arts, No. 148
**Website:** www.centenary.edu
**Admissions email:** admissions@centenary.edu
**Private;** founded 1825
**Affiliation:** Methodist
**Freshman admissions:** more selective; 2013-2014: 670 applied, 442 accepted. Either SAT or ACT required. ACT 25/75 percentile: 22-28. High school rank: 25% in top tenth, 58% in top quarter, 86% in top half
**Early decision deadline:** N/A, notification date: N/A
**Early action deadline:** 12/15, notification date: N/A
**Application deadline (fall):** 8/1
**Undergraduate student body:** 571 full time, 15 part time; 44% male, 56% female; 1% American Indian, 3% Asian, 15% black, 5% Hispanic, 3% multiracial, 0% Pacific Islander, 69% white, 4% international; 64% from in state; 60% live on campus; 27% of students in fraternities, 38% in sororities
**Most popular majors:** 10% Accounting, 29% Biology/Biological Sciences, General, 17% Communication and Media Studies, 14% Music Performance, General, 24% Psychology, General
**Expenses:** 2014-2015: $32,000; room/board: $10,230
**Financial aid:** (318) 869-5137; 75% of undergrads determined to have financial need; average aid package $24,661

## Dillard University
New Orleans LA
(800) 216-6637
**U.S. News ranking:** Nat. Lib. Arts, second tier
**Website:** www.dillard.edu
**Admissions email:** admissions@dillard.edu
**Private;** founded 1869
**Affiliation:** United Methodist
**Freshman admissions:** selective; 2013-2014: 4,726 applied, 1,675 accepted. Either SAT or ACT required. ACT 25/75 percentile: 17-20. High school rank: 14% in top tenth, 31% in top quarter, 62% in top half
**Early decision deadline:** N/A, notification date: N/A
**Early action deadline:** N/A, notification date: N/A
**Application deadline (fall):** 8/1
**Undergraduate student body:** 1,127 full time, 56 part time; 29% male, 71% female; 0% American Indian, 0% Asian, 90% black, 1% Hispanic, 1% multiracial, 0% Pacific Islander, 0% white, 5% international; 65% from in state; 41% live on campus; 5% of students in fraternities, 5% in sororities

**Most popular majors:** 9% Biology/ Biological Sciences, General, 10% Mass Communication/Media Studies, 10% Public Health, General, 10% Registered Nursing/ Registered Nurse, 9% Sociology
**Expenses:** 2013-2014: $16,191; room/board: $8,878
**Financial aid:** (504) 816-4677

## Grambling State University

Grambling LA
(318) 274-6183
**U.S. News ranking:** Reg. U. (S), second tier
**Website:** www.gram.edu/
**Admissions email:** admissions@ gram.edu
**Public**
**Freshman admissions:** less selective; 2013-2014: 4,248 applied, 1,888 accepted. Either SAT or ACT required. ACT 25/75 percentile: 16-20. High school rank: 8% in top tenth, 22% in top quarter, 52% in top half
**Early decision deadline:** N/A, notification date: N/A
**Early action deadline:** N/A, notification date: N/A
**Application deadline (fall):** 8/15
**Undergraduate student body:** 3,860 full time, 295 part time; 40% male, 60% female; 0% American Indian, 0% Asian, 90% black, 1% Hispanic, 1% multiracial, 0% Pacific Islander, 5% white, 6% international; 65% from in state; N/A live on campus; N/A of students in fraternities, N/A in sororities
**Most popular majors:** 7% Biology/ Biological Sciences, General, 8% Business Administration and Management, General, 21% Criminal Justice/Safety Studies, 7% Mass Communication/Media Studies, 11% Registered Nursing/ Registered Nurse
**Expenses:** 2014-2015: $6,545 in state, $15,744 out of state; room/ board: $8,412
**Financial aid:** (318) 274-6056; 91% of undergrads determined to have financial need; average aid package $3,522

## Louisiana College[1]

Pineville LA
(318) 487-7259
**U.S. News ranking:** Reg. Coll. (S), No. 74
**Website:** www.lacollege.edu
**Admissions email:** admissions@ lacollege.edu
**Private**
**Application deadline (fall):** N/A
**Undergraduate student body:** N/A full time, N/A part time
**Expenses:** 2013-2014: $14,520; room/board: $5,720
**Financial aid:** (318) 487-7386

## Louisiana State University–Alexandria

Alexandria LA
(318) 473-6417
**U.S. News ranking:** Nat. Lib. Arts, second tier
**Website:** www.lsua.edu
**Admissions email:** admissions@ lsua.edu
**Public;** founded 1960
**Freshman admissions:** selective; 2013-2014: 1,080 applied, 656 accepted. ACT required. ACT 25/75 percentile: 18-22.

High school rank: 13% in top tenth, 39% in top quarter, 69% in top half
**Early decision deadline:** N/A, notification date: N/A
**Early action deadline:** N/A, notification date: N/A
**Application deadline (fall):** 8/1
**Undergraduate student body:** 1,257 full time, 954 part time; 30% male, 70% female; 1% American Indian, 1% Asian, 15% black, 4% Hispanic, 2% multiracial, 0% Pacific Islander, 75% white, 0% international; 97% from in state; 11% live on campus; 0% of students in fraternities, 0% in sororities
**Most popular majors:** 20% Business Administration and Management, General, 11% Criminal Justice/Safety Studies, 9% Elementary Education and Teaching, 20% General Studies, 14% Psychology, General
**Expenses:** 2014-2015: $5,315 in state, $12,173 out of state; room/ board: $7,650
**Financial aid:** (318) 473-6423; 64% of undergrads determined to have financial need; average aid package $6,647

## Louisiana State University–Baton Rouge

Baton Rouge LA
(225) 578-1175
**U.S. News ranking:** Nat. U., No. 129
**Website:** www.lsu.edu
**Admissions email:** admissions@ lsu.edu
**Public;** founded 1860
**Freshman admissions:** more selective; 2013-2014: 16,005 applied, 12,002 accepted. Either SAT or ACT required. ACT 25/75 percentile: 23-28. High school rank: 25% in top tenth, 53% in top quarter, 82% in top half
**Early decision deadline:** N/A, notification date: N/A
**Early action deadline:** N/A, notification date: N/A
**Application deadline (fall):** 4/15
**Undergraduate student body:** 22,811 full time, 2,112 part time; 48% male, 52% female; 0% American Indian, 3% Asian, 11% black, 5% Hispanic, 2% multiracial, 0% Pacific Islander, 76% white, 2% international; 81% from in state; 25% live on campus; 17% of students in fraternities, 26% in sororities
**Most popular majors:** 8% Biological and Biomedical Sciences, 18% Business, Management, Marketing, and Related Support Services, 8% Communication, Journalism, and Related Programs, 10% Education, 11% Engineering
**Expenses:** 2014-2015: $8,750 in state, $26,467 out of state; room/ board: $10,804
**Financial aid:** (225) 578-3103; 43% of undergrads determined to have financial need; average aid package $14,693

## Louisiana State University–Shreveport

Shreveport LA
(318) 797-5061
**U.S. News ranking:** Reg. U. (S), second tier
**Website:** www.lsus.edu
**Admissions email:** admissions@ pilot.lsus.edu
**Public;** founded 1967
**Freshman admissions:** selective; 2013-2014: 695 applied, 621 accepted. Either SAT or ACT required. ACT 25/75 percentile: 20-24. High school rank: N/A
**Early decision deadline:** N/A, notification date: N/A
**Early action deadline:** N/A, notification date: N/A
**Application deadline (fall):** rolling
**Undergraduate student body:** 2,097 full time, 1,577 part time; 41% male, 59% female; 1% American Indian, 2% Asian, 22% black, 4% Hispanic, 3% multiracial, 0% Pacific Islander, 61% white, 2% international
**Most popular majors:** 11% Biological and Biomedical Sciences, 23% Business, Management, Marketing, and Related Support Services, 9% Education, 14% Liberal Arts and Sciences, General Studies and Humanities, 11% Psychology
**Expenses:** 2013-2014: $5,606 in state, $5,606 out of state; room/ board: N/A
**Financial aid:** (318) 797-5363

## Louisiana Tech University

Ruston LA
(318) 257-3036
**U.S. News ranking:** Nat. U., No. 201
**Website:** www.latech.edu
**Admissions email:** bulldog@ latech.edu
**Public;** founded 1894
**Freshman admissions:** more selective; 2013-2014: 5,080 applied, 3,424 accepted. Either SAT or ACT required. ACT 25/75 percentile: 21-26. High school rank: 24% in top tenth, 51% in top quarter, 80% in top half
**Early decision deadline:** N/A, notification date: N/A
**Early action deadline:** N/A, notification date: N/A
**Application deadline (fall):** 7/31
**Undergraduate student body:** 6,585 full time, 2,660 part time; 53% male, 47% female; 0% American Indian, 1% Asian, 15% black, 1% Hispanic, 1% multiracial, 0% Pacific Islander, 68% white, 4% international; 90% from in state; 15% live on campus; N/A of students in fraternities, N/A in sororities
**Most popular majors:** 6% Biological and Biomedical Sciences, 16% Business, Management, Marketing, and Related Support Services, 6% Education, 16% Engineering, 5% Social Sciences
**Expenses:** 2014-2015: $8,052 in state, $22,635 out of state; room/ board: $6,495
**Financial aid:** (318) 257-2643; 53% of undergrads determined to have financial need; average aid package $9,932

## Loyola University New Orleans

New Orleans LA
(800) 456-9652
**U.S. News ranking:** Reg. U. (S), No. 11
**Website:** www.loyno.edu
**Admissions email:** admit@loyno.edu
**Private;** founded 1912
**Affiliation:** Roman Catholic (Jesuit)
**Freshman admissions:** selective; 2013-2014: 4,827 applied, 4,203 accepted. Either SAT or ACT required. ACT 25/75 percentile: 22-28. High school rank: 15% in top tenth, 43% in top quarter, 76% in top half
**Early decision deadline:** N/A, notification date: N/A
**Early action deadline:** N/A, notification date: N/A
**Application deadline (fall):** rolling
**Undergraduate student body:** 2,741 full time, 205 part time; 41% male, 59% female; 1% American Indian, 4% Asian, 16% black, 16% Hispanic, 4% multiracial, 0% Pacific Islander, 51% white, 3% international; 46% from in state; 43% live on campus; 3% of students in fraternities, 7% in sororities
**Most popular majors:** 8% English Language and Literature, General, 7% Marketing/ Marketing Management, General, 6% Music Management, 9% Psychology, General, 9% Speech Communication and Rhetoric
**Expenses:** 2014-2015: $36,610; room/board: $12,660
**Financial aid:** (504) 865-3231; 69% of undergrads determined to have financial need; average aid package $27,599

## McNeese State University

Lake Charles LA
(337) 475-5356
**U.S. News ranking:** Reg. U. (S), No. 87
**Website:** www.mcneese.edu
**Admissions email:** admissions@ mcneese.edu
**Public;** founded 1939
**Freshman admissions:** selective; 2013-2014: 3,638 applied, 2,165 accepted. Either SAT or ACT required. ACT 25/75 percentile: 20-24. High school rank: 18% in top tenth, 41% in top quarter, 72% in top half
**Early decision deadline:** N/A, notification date: N/A
**Early action deadline:** N/A, notification date: N/A
**Application deadline (fall):** 8/19
**Undergraduate student body:** 5,959 full time, 1,542 part time; 38% male, 62% female; 1% American Indian, 1% Asian, 19% black, 2% Hispanic, 2% multiracial, 0% Pacific Islander, 71% white, 4% international; 93% from in state; N/A live on campus; 6% of students in fraternities, 6% in sororities
**Most popular majors:** 6% Business Administration and Management, General, 5% Criminal Justice/ Safety Studies, 6% Engineering, General, 15% General Studies, 16% Registered Nursing/ Registered Nurse

**Expenses:** 2013-2014: $5,701 in state, $16,603 out of state; room/ board: $7,230
**Financial aid:** (337) 475-5065

## Nicholls State University

Thibodaux LA
(985) 448-4507
**U.S. News ranking:** Reg. U. (S), No. 87
**Website:** www.nicholls.edu
**Admissions email:** nicholls@ nicholls.edu
**Public;** founded 1948
**Freshman admissions:** selective; 2013-2014: 2,404 applied, 2,090 accepted. Either SAT or ACT required. ACT 25/75 percentile: 20-24. High school rank: 16% in top tenth, 40% in top quarter, 73% in top half
**Early decision deadline:** N/A, notification date: N/A
**Early action deadline:** N/A, notification date: N/A
**Application deadline (fall):** rolling
**Undergraduate student body:** 4,729 full time, 1,163 part time; 38% male, 62% female; 2% American Indian, 1% Asian, 20% black, 3% Hispanic, 3% multiracial, 0% Pacific Islander, 68% white, 2% international; 95% from in state; 25% live on campus; 11% of students in fraternities, 11% in sororities
**Most popular majors:** 22% Business, Management, Marketing, and Related Support Services, 11% Education, 19% Health Professions and Related Programs, 14% Liberal Arts and Sciences, General Studies and Humanities, 5% Personal and Culinary Services
**Expenses:** 2014-2015: $7,234 in state, $17,481 out of state; room/ board: $8,673
**Financial aid:** (985) 448-4048; 64% of undergrads determined to have financial need; average aid package $8,075

## Northwestern State University of Louisiana

Natchitoches LA
(800) 426-3754
**U.S. News ranking:** Reg. U. (S), No. 87
**Website:** www.nsula.edu
**Admissions email:** admissions@ nsula.edu
**Public;** founded 1884
**Freshman admissions:** selective; 2013-2014: 4,088 applied, 2,366 accepted. Either SAT or ACT required. ACT 25/75 percentile: 19-24. High school rank: 19% in top tenth, 44% in top quarter, 75% in top half
**Early decision deadline:** N/A, notification date: N/A
**Early action deadline:** N/A, notification date: N/A
**Application deadline (fall):** 7/6
**Undergraduate student body:** 5,013 full time, 2,823 part time; 32% male, 68% female; 1% American Indian, 1% Asian, 29% black, 5% Hispanic, 3% multiracial, 0% Pacific Islander, 56% white, 1% international; 89% from in state; 19% live on campus; N/A of students in fraternities, N/A in sororities

**Most popular majors:** 12% Business, Management, Marketing, and Related Support Services, 6% Education, 26% Health Professions and Related Programs, 13% Liberal Arts and Sciences, General Studies and Humanities, 8% Psychology
**Expenses:** 2014-2015: $6,807 in state, $17,595 out of state; room/board: $6,846
**Financial aid:** (318) 357-5961; 72% of undergrads determined to have financial need; average aid package $10,556

## Our Lady of Holy Cross College[1]
New Orleans LA
(504) 398-2175
**U.S. News ranking:** Reg. U. (S), second tier
**Website:** www.olhcc.edu
**Admissions email:** admissions@olhcc.edu
**Private**
**Application deadline (fall):** N/A
**Undergraduate student body:** N/A full time, N/A part time
**Expenses:** 2014-2015: $12,620; room/board: N/A
**Financial aid:** (504) 398-2165; 91% of undergrads determined to have financial need; average aid package $7,396

## Southeastern Louisiana University
Hammond LA
(985) 549-5637
**U.S. News ranking:** Reg. U. (S), second tier
**Website:** www.selu.edu
**Admissions email:** admissions@selu.edu
**Public;** founded 1925
**Freshman admissions:** selective; 2013-2014: 3,818 applied, 3,405 accepted. Either SAT or ACT required. ACT 25/75 percentile: 20-24. High school rank: 11% in top tenth, 30% in top quarter, 63% in top half
**Early decision deadline:** N/A, notification date: N/A
**Early action deadline:** N/A, notification date: N/A
**Application deadline (fall):** 8/1
**Undergraduate student body:** 9,999 full time, 3,745 part time; 40% male, 60% female; 0% American Indian, 1% Asian, 16% black, 6% Hispanic, 6% multiracial, 0% Pacific Islander, 69% white, 2% international; 96% from in state; 19% live on campus; 6% of students in fraternities, 6% in sororities
**Most popular majors:** 23% Business, Management, Marketing, and Related Support Services, 15% Education, 12% Health Professions and Related Programs, 13% Liberal Arts and Sciences, General Studies and Humanities, 5% Psychology
**Expenses:** 2013-2014: $5,715 in state, $17,734 out of state; room/board: $6,714
**Financial aid:** (985) 549-2244

## Southern University and A&M College
Baton Rouge LA
(225) 771-2430
**U.S. News ranking:** Reg. U. (S), second tier
**Website:** www.subr.edu/
**Admissions email:** admit@subr.edu
**Public;** founded 1880
**Freshman admissions:** less selective; 2013-2014: N/A applied, N/A accepted. Either SAT or ACT required. ACT 25/75 percentile: 17-20. High school rank: 9% in top tenth, 23% in top quarter, 49% in top half
**Early decision deadline:** N/A, notification date: N/A
**Early action deadline:** N/A, notification date: N/A
**Application deadline (fall):** 7/1
**Undergraduate student body:** 4,631 full time, 967 part time; 37% male, 63% female; 0% American Indian, 0% Asian, 94% black, 1% Hispanic, 1% multiracial, 0% Pacific Islander, 3% white, 0% international
**Most popular majors:** Information not available
**Expenses:** 2013-2014: $6,630 in state, $8,274 out of state; room/board: $8,003
**Financial aid:** (225) 771-2790

## Southern University–New Orleans[1]
New Orleans LA
(504) 286-5314
**U.S. News ranking:** Reg. U. (S), second tier
**Website:** www.suno.edu
**Admissions email:** N/A
**Public**
**Application deadline (fall):** N/A
**Undergraduate student body:** N/A full time, N/A part time
**Expenses:** 2014-2015: $4,911 in state, $4,911 out of state; room/board: $7,080
**Financial aid:** (504) 286-5263

## Tulane University
New Orleans LA
(504) 865-5731
**U.S. News ranking:** Nat. U., No. 54
**Website:** www.tulane.edu
**Admissions email:** undergrad.admission@tulane.edu
**Private;** founded 1834
**Freshman admissions:** more selective; 2013-2014: 30,122 applied, 7,961 accepted. Either SAT or ACT required. ACT 25/75 percentile: 29-32. High school rank: 58% in top tenth, 83% in top quarter, 95% in top half
**Early decision deadline:** N/A, notification date: N/A
**Early action deadline:** 11/15, notification date: 12/15
**Application deadline (fall):** 1/15
**Undergraduate student body:** 6,487 full time, 1,865 part time; 42% male, 58% female; 0% American Indian, 4% Asian, 9% black, 6% Hispanic, 3% multiracial, 0% Pacific Islander, 71% white, 3% international; 27% from in state; 43% live on campus; 26% of students in fraternities, 43% in sororities
**Most popular majors:** 10% Biological and Biomedical Sciences, 22% Business, Management, Marketing, and Related Support Services, 5%

Health Professions and Related Programs, 6% Psychology, 18% Social Sciences
**Expenses:** 2014-2015: $48,305; room/board: $13,102
**Financial aid:** (504) 865-5723; 38% of undergrads determined to have financial need; average aid package $44,160

## University of Louisiana–Lafayette
Lafayette LA
(337) 482-6553
**U.S. News ranking:** Nat. U., second tier
**Website:** www.louisiana.edu
**Admissions email:** enroll@louisiana.edu
**Public;** founded 1898
**Freshman admissions:** selective; 2013-2014: 8,506 applied, 5,044 accepted. Either SAT or ACT required. ACT 25/75 percentile: 21-25. High school rank: 17% in top tenth, 43% in top quarter, 75% in top half
**Early decision deadline:** N/A, notification date: N/A
**Early action deadline:** N/A, notification date: N/A
**Application deadline (fall):** rolling
**Undergraduate student body:** 12,295 full time, 2,758 part time; 45% male, 55% female; 0% American Indian, 2% Asian, 21% black, 3% Hispanic, 2% multiracial, 0% Pacific Islander, 68% white, 2% international; 94% from in state; 18% live on campus; 9% of students in fraternities, 10% in sororities
**Most popular majors:** 20% Business, Management, Marketing, and Related Support Services, 13% Education, 7% Engineering, 9% Health Professions and Related Programs, 14% Liberal Arts and Sciences, General Studies and Humanities
**Expenses:** 2014-2015: $6,948 in state, $19,348 out of state; room/board: $8,566
**Financial aid:** (337) 482-6506; 57% of undergrads determined to have financial need; average aid package $8,339

## University of Louisiana–Monroe
Monroe LA
(318) 342-5430
**U.S. News ranking:** Reg. U. (S), No. 81
**Website:** www.ulm.edu
**Admissions email:** admissions@ulm.edu
**Public;** founded 1931
**Freshman admissions:** selective; 2013-2014: 3,454 applied, 2,668 accepted. Either SAT or ACT required. ACT 25/75 percentile: 20-25. High school rank: 25% in top tenth, 50% in top quarter, 80% in top half
**Early decision deadline:** N/A, notification date: N/A
**Early action deadline:** N/A, notification date: N/A
**Application deadline (fall):** rolling
**Undergraduate student body:** 4,894 full time, 2,382 part time; 37% male, 63% female; 0% American Indian, 2% Asian, 28% black, 2% Hispanic, 2% multiracial, 0% Pacific Islander, 62% white, 2% international; 92% from in state; N/A live on campus; 6% of students in fraternities, N/A in sororities

**Most popular majors:** 6% Business Administration and Management, General, 6% Elementary Education and Teaching, 15% General Studies, 6% Psychology, General, 7% Registered Nursing/Registered Nurse
**Expenses:** 2014-2015: $6,963 in state, $19,121 out of state; room/board: $6,830
**Financial aid:** (318) 342-5320

## University of New Orleans
New Orleans LA
(504) 280-6595
**U.S. News ranking:** Nat. U., second tier
**Website:** www.uno.edu
**Admissions email:** unopec@uno.edu
**Public;** founded 1956
**Freshman admissions:** selective; 2013-2014: 3,197 applied, 1,610 accepted. Either SAT or ACT required. ACT 25/75 percentile: 21-25. High school rank: 16% in top tenth, 41% in top quarter, 66% in top half
**Early decision deadline:** N/A, notification date: N/A
**Early action deadline:** N/A, notification date: N/A
**Application deadline (fall):** 7/25
**Undergraduate student body:** 5,376 full time, 1,768 part time; 50% male, 50% female; 0% American Indian, 8% Asian, 15% black, 10% Hispanic, 3% multiracial, 0% Pacific Islander, 56% white, 3% international; 95% from in state; 10% live on campus; 2% of students in fraternities, 2% in sororities
**Most popular majors:** 8% Biological and Biomedical Sciences, 34% Business, Management, Marketing, and Related Support Services, 11% Engineering, 10% Multi/Interdisciplinary Studies, 11% Visual and Performing Arts
**Expenses:** 2014-2015: $7,482 in state, $21,092 out of state; room/board: $9,274
**Financial aid:** (504) 280-6603; 76% of undergrads determined to have financial need; average aid package $8,762

## Xavier University of Louisiana
New Orleans LA
(504) 520-7388
**U.S. News ranking:** Nat. Lib. Arts, No. 178
**Website:** www.xula.edu
**Admissions email:** apply@xula.edu
**Private;** founded 1915
**Affiliation:** Roman Catholic
**Freshman admissions:** more selective; 2013-2014: 4,703 applied, 2,560 accepted. Either SAT or ACT required. ACT 25/75 percentile: 20-26. High school rank: 28% in top tenth, 56% in top quarter, 81% in top half
**Early decision deadline:** N/A, notification date: N/A
**Early action deadline:** 1/15, notification date: 2/15
**Application deadline (fall):** 7/1
**Undergraduate student body:** 2,380 full time, 124 part time; 28% male, 72% female; 0% American Indian, 10% Asian, 77% black, 2% Hispanic, 3% multiracial, 0% Pacific Islander, 4% white,

2% international; 50% from in state; 47% live on campus; 1% of students in fraternities, 3% in sororities
**Most popular majors:** 23% Biological and Biomedical Sciences, 11% Business, Management, and Related Support Services, 20% Physical Sciences, 17% Psychology, 8% Social Sciences
**Expenses:** 2014-2015: $21,552; room/board: $8,500
**Financial aid:** (504) 520-7517; 84% of undergrads determined to have financial need; average aid package $20,877

## Bates College
Lewiston ME
(855) 228-3755
**U.S. News ranking:** Nat. Lib. Arts, No. 19
**Website:** www.bates.edu
**Admissions email:** admission@bates.edu
**Private;** founded 1855
**Freshman admissions:** more selective; 2013-2014: 5,243 applied, 1,267 accepted. Neither SAT nor ACT required. SAT 25/75 percentile: 1260-1430. High school rank: 56% in top tenth, 87% in top quarter, 98% in top half
**Early decision deadline:** 11/15, notification date: 12/20
**Early action deadline:** N/A, notification date: N/A
**Application deadline (fall):** 1/1
**Undergraduate student body:** 1,791 full time, 0 part time; 50% male, 50% female; 0% American Indian, 5% Asian, 5% black, 6% Hispanic, 4% multiracial, 0% Pacific Islander, 72% white, 6% international; 10% from in state; 93% live on campus; 0% of students in fraternities, 0% in sororities
**Most popular majors:** 14% Biological and Biomedical Sciences, 9% English Language and Literature/Letters, 8% History, 11% Psychology, 21% Social Sciences
**Expenses:** 2014-2015 tuition/fees/room/board: $60,720
**Financial aid:** (207) 786-6096; 48% of undergrads determined to have financial need; average aid package $40,233

## Bowdoin College
Brunswick ME
(207) 725-3100
**U.S. News ranking:** Nat. Lib. Arts, No. 5
**Website:** www.bowdoin.edu
**Admissions email:** admissions@bowdoin.edu
**Private;** founded 1794
**Freshman admissions:** most selective; 2013-2014: 7,052 applied, 1,054 accepted. Neither SAT nor ACT required. SAT 25/75 percentile: 1360-1510. High school rank: 83% in top tenth, 94% in top quarter, 100% in top half
**Early decision deadline:** 11/15, notification date: 12/15
**Early action deadline:** N/A, notification date: N/A
**Application deadline (fall):** 1/1

Undergraduate student body: 1,791 full time, 4 part time; 50% male, 50% female; 0% American Indian, 7% Asian, 5% black, 12% Hispanic, 6% multiracial, 0% Pacific Islander, 64% white, 5% international; 11% from in state; 92% live on campus; N/A of students in fraternities, N/A in sororities
Most popular majors: 17% Economics, General, 8% Environmental Studies, 8% History, General, 9% Mathematics, General, 18% Political Science and Government, General
Expenses: 2014-2015: $46,808; room/board: $12,760
Financial aid: (207) 725-3273; 45% of undergrads determined to have financial need; average aid package $41,712

## Colby College
Waterville ME
(800) 723-3032
U.S. News ranking: Nat. Lib. Arts, No. 15
Website: www.colby.edu
Admissions email: admissions@ colby.edu
Private; founded 1813
Freshman admissions: most selective; 2013-2014: 5,407 applied, 1,408 accepted. Neither SAT nor ACT required. SAT 25/75 percentile: 1260-1430. High school rank: 64% in top tenth, 93% in top quarter, 99% in top half
Early decision deadline: 11/15, notification date: 12/15
Early action deadline: N/A, notification date: N/A
Application deadline (fall): 1/1
Undergraduate student body: 1,820 full time, 0 part time; 48% male, 52% female; 0% American Indian, 5% Asian, 3% black, 6% Hispanic, 5% multiracial, 0% Pacific Islander, 60% white, 9% international; 13% from in state; 95% live on campus; 0% of students in fraternities, 0% in sororities
Most popular majors: 9% Biological and Biomedical Sciences, 7% English Language and Literature/Letters, 13% Multi/ Interdisciplinary Studies, 6% Psychology, 22% Social Sciences
Expenses: 2014-2015: $47,350; room/board: $12,150
Financial aid: (800) 723-3032; 45% of undergrads determined to have financial need; average aid package $40,489

## College of the Atlantic
Bar Harbor ME
(800) 528-0025
U.S. News ranking: Nat. Lib. Arts, No. 99
Website: www.coa.edu/
Admissions email: inquiry@coa.edu
Private; founded 1969
Freshman admissions: more selective; 2013-2014: 455 applied, 333 accepted. Neither SAT nor ACT required. SAT 25/75 percentile: 1110-1330. High school rank: 10% in top tenth, 69% in top quarter, 95% in top half
Early decision deadline: 12/1, notification date: 12/15

Early action deadline: N/A, notification date: N/A
Application deadline (fall): 2/15
Undergraduate student body: 344 full time, 18 part time; 33% male, 67% female; 1% American Indian, 2% Asian, 1% black, 5% Hispanic, 3% multiracial, 0% Pacific Islander, 70% white, 16% international; 17% from in state; 42% live on campus; 0% of students in fraternities, 0% in sororities
Most popular majors: Information not available
Expenses: 2014-2015: $40,491; room/board: $9,300
Financial aid: (800) 528-0025; 89% of undergrads determined to have financial need; average aid package $35,649

## Husson University
Bangor ME
(207) 941-7100
U.S. News ranking: Reg. U. (N), second tier
Website: www.husson.edu
Admissions email: admit@husson.edu
Private; founded 1898
Freshman admissions: selective; 2013-2014: 1,581 applied, 1,263 accepted. Either SAT or ACT required. SAT 25/75 percentile: 850-1080. High school rank: 18% in top tenth, 59% in top quarter, 84% in top half
Early decision deadline: N/A, notification date: N/A
Early action deadline: N/A, notification date: N/A
Application deadline (fall): 8/15
Undergraduate student body: 1,869 full time, 484 part time; 41% male, 59% female; 1% American Indian, 1% Asian, 4% black, 1% Hispanic, 1% multiracial, 0% Pacific Islander, 88% white, 3% international; 84% from in state; 34% live on campus; 3% of students in fraternities, 6% in sororities
Most popular majors: 34% Business, Management, Marketing, and Related Support Services, 5% Computer and Information Sciences and Support Services, 25% Health Professions and Related Programs, 16% Homeland Security, Law Enforcement, Firefighting and Related Protective Services, 10% Psychology
Expenses: 2014-2015: $15,590; room/board: $8,579
Financial aid: (207) 941-7156; 96% of undergrads determined to have financial need; average aid package $10,388

## Maine College of Art
Portland ME
(800) 699-1509
U.S. News ranking: Arts, unranked
Website: www.meca.edu
Admissions email: admissions@ meca.edu
Private; founded 1882
Freshman admissions: N/A; 2013-2014: 527 applied, 357 accepted. Neither SAT nor ACT required. SAT 25/75 percentile: N/A. High school rank: N/A
Early decision deadline: N/A, notification date: N/A
Early action deadline: 12/1, notification date: 12/24
Application deadline (fall): rolling

Undergraduate student body: 361 full time, 17 part time; 29% male, 71% female; 1% American Indian, 2% Asian, 2% black, 5% Hispanic, 4% multiracial, 0% Pacific Islander, 81% white, 1% international; 30% from in state; 18% live on campus; 0% of students in fraternities, 0% in sororities
Most popular majors: 12% Ceramic Arts and Ceramics, 13% Illustration, 17% Painting, 12% Printmaking, 13% Sculpture
Expenses: 2014-2015: $31,620; room/board: $10,660
Financial aid: (207) 775-3052; 84% of undergrads determined to have financial need

## Maine Maritime Academy
Castine ME
(207) 326-2206
U.S. News ranking: Reg. Coll. (N), No. 8
Website: www.mainemaritime.edu
Admissions email: admissions@ mma.edu
Public; founded 1941
Freshman admissions: selective; 2013-2014: 791 applied, 514 accepted. Either SAT or ACT required. SAT 25/75 percentile: 920-1130. High school rank: 8% in top tenth, 32% in top quarter, 76% in top half
Early decision deadline: N/A, notification date: N/A
Early action deadline: 12/31, notification date: 2/15
Application deadline (fall): 3/31
Undergraduate student body: 979 full time, 15 part time; 87% male, 13% female; 0% American Indian, 1% Asian, 1% black, 0% Hispanic, 0% multiracial, 0% Pacific Islander, 96% white, 0% international; 71% from in state; 68% live on campus; 0% of students in fraternities, 0% in sororities
Most popular majors: 6% Biological and Biomedical Sciences, Other, 28% Engineering Technologies and Engineering-Related Fields, Other, 12% International Business/Trade/Commerce, 25% Marine Science/Merchant Marine Officer, 29% Naval Architecture and Marine Engineering
Expenses: 2014-2015: $17,120 in state, $24,040 out of state; room/board: $9,830
Financial aid: (207) 326-2339; 85% of undergrads determined to have financial need; average aid package $9,368

## St. Joseph's College[1]
Standish ME
(207) 893-7746
U.S. News ranking: Reg. U. (N), second tier
Website: www.sjcme.edu
Admissions email: admission@ sjcme.edu
Private
Application deadline (fall): N/A
Undergraduate student body: N/A full time, N/A part time
Expenses: 2013-2014: $29,900; room/board: $11,900
Financial aid: (800) 752-1266

## Thomas College
Waterville ME
(800) 339-7001
U.S. News ranking: Reg. Coll. (N), No. 44
Website: www.thomas.edu
Admissions email: admiss@ thomas.edu
Private; founded 1894
Freshman admissions: less selective; 2013-2014: 1,129 applied, 829 accepted. Either SAT or ACT required. SAT 25/75 percentile: 790-1010. High school rank: 21% in top tenth, 34% in top quarter, 64% in top half
Early decision deadline: N/A, notification date: N/A
Early action deadline: N/A, notification date: N/A
Application deadline (fall): rolling
Undergraduate student body: 780 full time, 559 part time; 48% male, 52% female; 1% American Indian, 0% Asian, 3% black, 3% Hispanic, 9% multiracial, 0% Pacific Islander, 75% white, 3% international; 78% from in state; 65% live on campus; 2% of students in fraternities, 0% in sororities
Most popular majors: 9% Accounting, 14% Business Administration and Management, General, 16% Criminal Justice/ Safety Studies, 10% Elementary Education and Teaching, 10% Psychology, General
Expenses: 2014-2015: $23,460; room/board: $10,100
Financial aid: (207) 859-1112; 87% of undergrads determined to have financial need; average aid package $19,704

## Unity College
Unity ME
(207) 948-3131
U.S. News ranking: Reg. Coll. (N), No. 31
Website: www.unity.edu
Admissions email: admissions@ unity.edu
Private
Freshman admissions: less selective; 2013-2014: 519 applied, 461 accepted. Neither SAT nor ACT required. SAT 25/75 percentile: 910-1110. High school rank: 6% in top tenth, 29% in top quarter, 73% in top half
Early decision deadline: N/A, notification date: N/A
Early action deadline: 12/15, notification date: 12/31
Application deadline (fall): 6/15
Undergraduate student body: 548 full time, 6 part time; 49% male, 51% female; 1% American Indian, 1% Asian, 1% black, 3% Hispanic, 3% multiracial, 0% Pacific Islander, 91% white, 0% international; 23% from in state; 71% live on campus; N/A of students in fraternities, N/A in sororities
Most popular majors: 9% Agroecology and Sustainable Agriculture, 58% Natural Resources Law Enforcement and Protective Services, 4% Outdoor Education, 27% Wildlife Biology
Expenses: 2014-2015: $25,320; room/board: $9,330
Financial aid: (207) 948-3131; 87% of undergrads determined to have financial need; average aid package $18,932

## University of Maine
Orono ME
(877) 486-2364
U.S. News ranking: Nat. U., No. 173
Website: www.umaine.edu
Admissions email: um-admit@ maine.edu
Public; founded 1865
Freshman admissions: selective; 2013-2014: 9,336 applied, 7,789 accepted. Either SAT or ACT required. SAT 25/75 percentile: 950-1190. High school rank: 19% in top tenth, 46% in top quarter, 78% in top half
Early decision deadline: N/A, notification date: N/A
Early action deadline: 12/15, notification date: 1/31
Application deadline (fall): rolling
Undergraduate student body: 7,922 full time, 1,260 part time; 52% male, 48% female; 1% American Indian, 1% Asian, 2% black, 2% Hispanic, 3% multiracial, 0% Pacific Islander, 81% white, 3% international; 80% from in state; 40% live on campus; N/A of students in fraternities, N/A in sororities
Most popular majors: 10% Business, Management, Marketing, and Related Support Services, 12% Education, 12% Engineering, 7% Health Professions and Related Programs, 7% Psychology
Expenses: 2014-2015: $10,604 in state, $28,484 out of state; room/board: $9,296
Financial aid: (207) 581-1324; 71% of undergrads determined to have financial need; average aid package $15,176

## University of Maine–Augusta
Augusta ME
(207) 621-3465
U.S. News ranking: Reg. Coll. (N), second tier
Website: www.uma.edu
Admissions email: umaadm@ maine.edu
Public; founded 1965
Freshman admissions: least selective; 2013-2014: 828 applied, 790 accepted. Neither SAT nor ACT required. SAT 25/75 percentile: 760-1010. High school rank: 2% in top tenth, 9% in top quarter, 34% in top half
Early decision deadline: N/A, notification date: N/A
Early action deadline: N/A, notification date: N/A
Application deadline (fall): 8/15
Undergraduate student body: 1,726 full time, 3,044 part time; 29% male, 71% female; 2% American Indian, 0% Asian, 1% black, 1% Hispanic, 2% multiracial, 0% Pacific Islander, 86% white, 0% international; 97% from in state; 0% live on campus; 0% of students in fraternities, 0% in sororities
Most popular majors: 17% Business, Management, Marketing, and Related Support Services, 31% Health Professions and Related Programs, 5% Homeland Security, Law Enforcement, Firefighting and Related Protective Services, 26% Liberal Arts and Sciences, General Studies and Humanities, 8% Library Science

**Expenses:** 2014-2015: $7,500 in state, $16,740 out of state; room/board: N/A
**Financial aid:** (207) 621-3163; 87% of undergrads determined to have financial need; average aid package $8,873

## University of Maine–Farmington

Farmington ME
(207) 778-7050
**U.S. News ranking:** Reg. Coll. (N), No. 18
**Website:** www.farmington.edu
**Admissions email:** umfadmit@maine.edu
**Public;** founded 1864
**Freshman admissions:** selective; 2013-2014: 1,638 applied, 1,371 accepted. Neither SAT nor ACT required. SAT 25/75 percentile: 880-1150. High school rank: 14% in top tenth, 43% in top quarter, 79% in top half
**Early decision deadline:** N/A, notification date: N/A
**Early action deadline:** 11/15, notification date: 12/15
**Application deadline (fall):** rolling
**Undergraduate student body:** 1,783 full time, 118 part time; 34% male, 66% female; 1% American Indian, 1% Asian, 1% black, 2% Hispanic, 3% multiracial, 0% Pacific Islander, 84% white, 0% international; 85% from in state; 48% live on campus; N/A of students in fraternities, N/A in sororities
**Most popular majors:** 39% Education, 9% English Language and Literature/Letters, 13% Health Professions and Related Programs, 9% Psychology, 5% Social Sciences
**Expenses:** 2014-2015: $9,217 in state, $18,305 out of state; room/board: $8,970
**Financial aid:** (207) 778-7100; 81% of undergrads determined to have financial need; average aid package $13,342

## University of Maine–Fort Kent

Fort Kent ME
(207) 834-7600
**U.S. News ranking:** Reg. Coll. (N), No. 37
**Website:** www.umfk.maine.edu
**Admissions email:** umfkadm@maine.edu
**Public;** founded 1878
**Freshman admissions:** less selective; 2013-2014: 464 applied, 292 accepted. Neither SAT nor ACT required. SAT 25/75 percentile: 818-1000. High school rank: 0% in top tenth, 10% in top quarter, 34% in top half
**Early decision deadline:** N/A, notification date: N/A
**Early action deadline:** N/A, notification date: N/A
**Application deadline (fall):** rolling
**Undergraduate student body:** 594 full time, 615 part time; 29% male, 71% female; 1% American Indian, 0% Asian, 2% black, 1% Hispanic, 2% multiracial, 0% Pacific Islander, 78% white, 11% international; 93% from in state; 24% live on campus; 1% of students in fraternities, 2% in sororities

**Most popular majors:** 14% Business, Management, Marketing, and Related Support Services, 19% Education, 49% Health Professions and Related Programs, 4% Public Administration and Social Service Professions, 7% Social Sciences
**Expenses:** 2014-2015: $7,575 in state, $10,875 out of state; room/board: $7,400
**Financial aid:** (888) 879-8635; 77% of undergrads determined to have financial need; average aid package $11,454

## University of Maine–Machias

Machias ME
(888) 468-6866
**U.S. News ranking:** Nat. Lib. Arts, second tier
**Website:** www.umm.maine.edu
**Admissions email:** ummadmissions@maine.edu
**Public;** founded 1909
**Freshman admissions:** less selective; 2013-2014: 452 applied, 386 accepted. Either SAT or ACT required. SAT 25/75 percentile: 820-1050. High school rank: N/A
**Early decision deadline:** N/A, notification date: N/A
**Early action deadline:** 12/15, notification date: N/A
**Application deadline (fall):** 8/15
**Undergraduate student body:** 439 full time, 453 part time; 30% male, 70% female; 2% American Indian, 0% Asian, 4% black, 4% Hispanic, 3% multiracial, 0% Pacific Islander, 81% white, 1% international; 79% from in state; 37% live on campus; 11% of students in fraternities, 8% in sororities
**Most popular majors:** 20% Biology/Biological Sciences, General, 15% Community Psychology, 7% Entrepreneurial and Small Business Operations, 9% General Studies, 14% Parks, Recreation and Leisure Studies
**Expenses:** 2013-2014: $7,490 in state, $19,370 out of state; room/board: $8,178
**Financial aid:** (207) 255-1203

## University of Maine–Presque Isle

Presque Isle ME
(207) 768-9532
**U.S. News ranking:** Reg. Coll. (N), No. 46
**Website:** www.umpi.edu
**Admissions email:** admissions@umpi.edu
**Public;** founded 1903
**Freshman admissions:** less selective; 2013-2014: 530 applied, 413 accepted. Neither SAT nor ACT required. ACT 25/75 percentile: N/A. High school rank: 13% in top tenth, 25% in top quarter, 49% in top half
**Early decision deadline:** N/A, notification date: N/A
**Early action deadline:** N/A, notification date: N/A
**Application deadline (fall):** rolling
**Undergraduate student body:** 718 full time, 545 part time; 37% male, 63% female; 3% American Indian, 0% Asian, 1% black, 1% Hispanic, 2% multiracial, 0% Pacific Islander, 79% white, 8% international; 98% from in

state; 28% live on campus; N/A of students in fraternities, N/A in sororities
**Most popular majors:** 14% Business, Management, Marketing, and Related Support Services, 16% Education, 17% Liberal Arts and Sciences, General Studies and Humanities, 8% Psychology, 5% Public Administration and Social Service Professions
**Expenses:** 2014-2015: $7,436 in state, $10,736 out of state; room/board: $7,656
**Financial aid:** (207) 768-9511; 78% of undergrads determined to have financial need; average aid package $11,581

## University of New England

Biddeford ME
(207) 283-0171
**U.S. News ranking:** Reg. U. (N), No. 79
**Website:** www.une.edu
**Admissions email:** admissions@une.edu
**Private;** founded 1831
**Freshman admissions:** selective; 2013-2014: 4,231 applied, 3,632 accepted. Either SAT or ACT required. SAT 25/75 percentile: 950-1150. High school rank: N/A
**Early decision deadline:** N/A, notification date: N/A
**Early action deadline:** 12/1, notification date: 12/31
**Application deadline (fall):** 2/15
**Undergraduate student body:** 2,156 full time, 497 part time; 29% male, 71% female; 1% American Indian, 2% Asian, 1% black, 0% Hispanic, 1% multiracial, 0% Pacific Islander, 70% white, 1% international; 34% from in state; 65% live on campus; 0% of students in fraternities, 0% in sororities
**Most popular majors:** 30% Biological and Biomedical Sciences, 5% Business, Management, Marketing, and Related Support Services, 32% Health Professions and Related Programs, 13% Parks, Recreation, Leisure, and Fitness Studies, 5% Psychology
**Expenses:** 2014-2015: $34,080; room/board: $13,390
**Financial aid:** (207) 602-2342

## University of Southern Maine

Gorham ME
(207) 780-5670
**U.S. News ranking:** Reg. U. (N), second tier
**Website:** www.usm.maine.edu
**Admissions email:** usmadm@usm.maine.edu
**Public;** founded 1878
**Freshman admissions:** less selective; 2013-2014: 3,993 applied, 3,284 accepted. Either SAT or ACT required. SAT 25/75 percentile: 870-1100. High school rank: 12% in top tenth, 34% in top quarter, 74% in top half
**Early decision deadline:** N/A, notification date: N/A
**Early action deadline:** N/A, notification date: N/A
**Application deadline (fall):** rolling
**Undergraduate student body:** 4,281 full time, 2,817 part time; 43% male, 57% female; 1% American Indian, 2% Asian, 3% black,

2% Hispanic, 2% multiracial, 0% Pacific Islander, 81% white, 1% international; 90% from in state; 18% live on campus; N/A of students in fraternities, N/A in sororities
**Most popular majors:** 17% Business, Management, Marketing, and Related Support Services, 18% Health Professions and Related Programs, 5% Psychology, 15% Social Sciences, 5% Visual and Performing Arts
**Expenses:** 2013-2014: $8,920 in state, $21,280 out of state; room/board: $9,820
**Financial aid:** (207) 780-5250; 76% of undergrads determined to have financial need; average aid package $13,008

## Bowie State University

Bowie MD
(301) 860-3415
**U.S. News ranking:** Nat. U., second tier
**Website:** www.bowiestate.edu
**Admissions email:** ugradadmissions@bowiestate.edu
**Public;** founded 1865
**Freshman admissions:** less selective; 2013-2014: 3,986 applied, 2,063 accepted. Either SAT or ACT required. SAT 25/75 percentile: 810-960. High school rank: N/A
**Early decision deadline:** N/A, notification date: N/A
**Early action deadline:** N/A, notification date: N/A
**Application deadline (fall):** rolling
**Undergraduate student body:** 3,521 full time, 837 part time; 38% male, 62% female; 0% American Indian, 1% Asian, 83% black, 3% Hispanic, 3% multiracial, 0% Pacific Islander, 2% white, 1% international; 91% from in state; 45% live on campus; 20% of students in fraternities, 15% in sororities
**Most popular majors:** Information not available
**Expenses:** 2013-2014: $6,971 in state, $17,538 out of state; room/board: $9,336
**Financial aid:** (301) 860-3540

## Capitol College[1]

Laurel MD
(800) 950-1992
**U.S. News ranking:** Engineering, unranked
**Website:** www.capitol-college.edu
**Admissions email:** admissions@capitol-college.edu
**Private**
**Application deadline (fall):** N/A
**Undergraduate student body:** N/A full time, N/A part time
**Expenses:** 2013-2014: $22,176; room/board: $5,364
**Financial aid:** (301) 369-2800

## Coppin State University[1]

Baltimore MD
(410) 951-3600
**U.S. News ranking:** Reg. U. (N), second tier
**Website:** www.coppin.edu
**Admissions email:** admissions@coppin.edu
**Public**
**Application deadline (fall):** N/A

**Undergraduate student body:** N/A full time, N/A part time
**Expenses:** 2013-2014: $5,076 in state, $10,010 out of state; room/board: $8,654
**Financial aid:** (410) 951-3636

## Frostburg State University

Frostburg MD
(301) 687-4201
**U.S. News ranking:** Reg. U. (N), No. 125
**Website:** www.frostburg.edu
**Admissions email:** fsuadmissions@frostburg.edu
**Public;** founded 1898
**Freshman admissions:** less selective; 2013-2014: 3,872 applied, 2,302 accepted. Either SAT or ACT required. SAT 25/75 percentile: 860-1070. High school rank: 10% in top tenth, 27% in top quarter, 61% in top half
**Early decision deadline:** 12/15, notification date: N/A
**Early action deadline:** N/A, notification date: N/A
**Application deadline (fall):** rolling
**Undergraduate student body:** 4,189 full time, 515 part time; 51% male, 49% female; 0% American Indian, 1% Asian, 28% black, 5% Hispanic, 4% multiracial, 0% Pacific Islander, 61% white, 1% international; 93% from in state; 32% live on campus; 10% of students in fraternities, 10% in sororities
**Most popular majors:** 11% Business Administration and Management, General, 5% Criminal Justice/Safety Studies, 5% Early Childhood Education and Teaching, 7% Psychology, General, 5% Registered Nursing/Registered Nurse
**Expenses:** 2014-2015: $7,982 in state, $19,274 out of state; room/board: $9,600
**Financial aid:** (301) 687-4301; 64% of undergrads determined to have financial need; average aid package $9,365

## Goucher College

Baltimore MD
(410) 337-6100
**U.S. News ranking:** Nat. Lib. Arts, No. 105
**Website:** www.goucher.edu
**Admissions email:** admissions@goucher.edu
**Private;** founded 1885
**Freshman admissions:** more selective; 2013-2014: 3,466 applied, 2,505 accepted. Neither SAT nor ACT required. SAT 25/75 percentile: 1010-1280. High school rank: 31% in top tenth, 58% in top quarter, 88% in top half
**Early decision deadline:** 11/15, notification date: 12/15
**Early action deadline:** 12/1, notification date: 2/1
**Application deadline (fall):** rolling
**Undergraduate student body:** 1,424 full time, 25 part time; 34% male, 66% female; 0% American Indian, 3% Asian, 9% black, 7% Hispanic, 4% multiracial, 0% Pacific Islander, 68% white, 2% international; 26% from in state; 84% live on campus; 0% of students in fraternities, 0% in sororities

**Most popular majors:** 10% Communication, Journalism, and Related Programs, 7% Foreign Languages, Literatures, and Linguistics, 15% Psychology, 13% Social Sciences, 13% Visual and Performing Arts
**Expenses:** 2014-2015: $40,558; room/board: $11,482
**Financial aid:** (410) 337-6141; 64% of undergrads determined to have financial need; average aid package $29,199

## Hood College
Frederick MD
(800) 922-1599
**U.S. News ranking:** Reg. U. (N), No. 31
**Website:** www.hood.edu
**Admissions email:** admission@hood.edu
**Private;** founded 1893
**Affiliation:** United Church of Christ
**Freshman admissions:** selective; 2013-2014: 1,686 applied, 1,366 accepted. Neither SAT nor ACT required. SAT 25/75 percentile: 910-1160. High school rank: 12% in top tenth, 45% in top quarter, 77% in top half
**Early decision deadline:** N/A, notification date: N/A
**Early action deadline:** N/A, notification date: N/A
**Application deadline (fall):** rolling
**Undergraduate student body:** 1,265 full time, 122 part time; 34% male, 66% female; 0% American Indian, 3% Asian, 12% black, 8% Hispanic, 5% multiracial, 0% Pacific Islander, 66% white, 2% international; 76% from in state; 56% live on campus; 0% of students in fraternities, 0% in sororities
**Most popular majors:** 10% Biological and Biomedical Sciences, 10% Business, Management, Marketing, and Related Support Services, 14% Education, 13% Psychology, 7% Social Sciences
**Expenses:** 2014-2015: $34,120; room/board: $11,610
**Financial aid:** (301) 696-3411; 85% of undergrads determined to have financial need; average aid package $26,534

## Johns Hopkins University
Baltimore MD
(410) 516-8171
**U.S. News ranking:** Nat. U., No. 12
**Website:** www.jhu.edu
**Admissions email:** gotojhu@jhu.edu
**Private;** founded 1876
**Freshman admissions:** most selective; 2013-2014: 20,614 applied, 3,519 accepted. Either SAT or ACT required. SAT 25/75 percentile: 1340-1520. High school rank: 84% in top tenth, 98% in top quarter, 99% in top half
**Early decision deadline:** 11/1, notification date: 12/15
**Early action deadline:** N/A, notification date: N/A
**Application deadline (fall):** 1/1
**Undergraduate student body:** 6,012 full time, 239 part time; 48% male, 52% female; 0% American Indian, 18% Asian, 5% black, 10% Hispanic, 4% multiracial, 0% Pacific Islander, 49% white,

10% international; 13% from in state; 55% live on campus; 27% of students in fraternities, 32% in sororities
**Most popular majors:** 9% Bioengineering and Biomedical Engineering, 7% Cell/Cellular and Molecular Biology, 9% International Relations and Affairs, 8% Neuroscience, 8% Public Health, General
**Expenses:** 2014-2015: $47,060; room/board: $14,246
**Financial aid:** (410) 516-8028; 46% of undergrads determined to have financial need; average aid package $37,345

## Loyola University Maryland
Baltimore MD
(410) 617-5012
**U.S. News ranking:** Reg. U. (N), No. 3
**Website:** www.loyola.edu
**Admissions email:** admissions@loyola.edu
**Private;** founded 1852
**Affiliation:** Roman Catholic
**Freshman admissions:** more selective; 2013-2014: 13,604 applied, 7,891 accepted. Neither SAT nor ACT required. SAT 25/75 percentile: 1100-1268. High school rank: 28% in top tenth, 67% in top quarter, 91% in top half
**Early decision deadline:** N/A, notification date: N/A
**Early action deadline:** 11/1, notification date: 1/15
**Application deadline (fall):** 1/15
**Undergraduate student body:** 3,951 full time, 53 part time; 41% male, 59% female; 0% American Indian, 3% Asian, 5% black, 9% Hispanic, 2% multiracial, 0% Pacific Islander, 79% white, 0% international; 17% from in state; 81% live on campus; 0% of students in fraternities, 0% in sororities
**Most popular majors:** 30% Business/Commerce, General, 7% Psychology, General, 10% Social Sciences, General, 13% Speech Communication and Rhetoric, 7% Speech-Language Pathology/Pathologist
**Expenses:** 2014-2015: $44,255; room/board: $12,790
**Financial aid:** (410) 617-2576; 56% of undergrads determined to have financial need; average aid package $27,655

## Maryland Institute College of Art
Baltimore MD
(410) 225-2222
**U.S. News ranking:** Arts, unranked
**Website:** www.mica.edu
**Admissions email:** admissions@mica.edu
**Private;** founded 1826
**Freshman admissions:** N/A; 2013-2014: 2,914 applied, 1,691 accepted. Either SAT or ACT required. SAT 25/75 percentile: N/A. High school rank: N/A
**Early decision deadline:** 11/15, notification date: 12/13
**Early action deadline:** N/A, notification date: N/A
**Application deadline (fall):** 2/1
**Undergraduate student body:** 1,759 full time, 19 part time; 29% male, 71% female; 0% American Indian, 12% Asian, 5% black, 4% Hispanic, 8% multiracial,

0% Pacific Islander, 55% white, 8% international; N/A from in state; 88% live on campus; N/A of students in fraternities, N/A in sororities
**Most popular majors:** Information not available
**Expenses:** 2014-2015: $42,390; room/board: $11,710
**Financial aid:** (410) 225-2285

## McDaniel College
Westminster MD
(800) 638-5005
**U.S. News ranking:** Nat. Lib. Arts, No. 129
**Website:** www.mcdaniel.edu
**Admissions email:** admissions@mcdaniel.edu
**Private;** founded 1867
**Freshman admissions:** selective; 2013-2014: 2,942 applied, 2,232 accepted. Either SAT or ACT required. SAT 25/75 percentile: 1000-1210. High school rank: 26% in top tenth, 52% in top quarter, 87% in top half
**Early decision deadline:** N/A, notification date: N/A
**Early action deadline:** 12/1, notification date: 12/21
**Application deadline (fall):** 6/1
**Undergraduate student body:** 1,658 full time, 34 part time; 47% male, 53% female; 1% American Indian, 4% Asian, 13% black, 6% Hispanic, 0% multiracial, 0% Pacific Islander, 74% white, 1% international; 64% from in state; 83% live on campus; 17% of students in fraternities, 18% in sororities
**Most popular majors:** 7% English Language and Literature/Letters, 10% Parks, Recreation, Leisure, and Fitness Studies, 9% Psychology, 16% Social Sciences, 7% Visual and Performing Arts
**Expenses:** 2014-2015: $38,350; room/board: $9,100
**Financial aid:** (410) 857-2233; 74% of undergrads determined to have financial need; average aid package $31,352

## Morgan State University
Baltimore MD
(800) 332-6674
**U.S. News ranking:** Nat. U., second tier
**Website:** www.morgan.edu
**Admissions email:** admissions@morgan.edu
**Public;** founded 1867
**Freshman admissions:** less selective; 2013-2014: 4,925 applied, 2,764 accepted. Neither SAT nor ACT required. SAT 25/75 percentile: 820-980. High school rank: 3% in top tenth, 9% in top quarter, 38% in top half
**Early decision deadline:** N/A, notification date: N/A
**Early action deadline:** 11/15, notification date: 2/15
**Application deadline (fall):** rolling
**Undergraduate student body:** 5,504 full time, 748 part time; 45% male, 55% female; 0% American Indian, 1% Asian, 85% black, 3% Hispanic, 3% multiracial, 0% Pacific Islander, 2% white, 4% international; 80% from in state; 32% live on campus; N/A of students in fraternities, N/A in sororities

**Most popular majors:** 20% Business, Management, Marketing, and Related Support Services, 9% Communication, Journalism, and Related Programs, 10% Engineering, 13% Health Professions and Related Programs, 9% Public Administration and Social Service Professions
**Expenses:** 2014-2015: $7,378 in state, $16,862 out of state; room/board: $9,492
**Financial aid:** (443) 885-3170; 82% of undergrads determined to have financial need; average aid package $21,438

## Mount St. Mary's University
Emmitsburg MD
(800) 448-4347
**U.S. News ranking:** Reg. U. (N), No. 19
**Website:** www.msmary.edu
**Admissions email:** admissions@msmary.edu
**Private;** founded 1808
**Affiliation:** Roman Catholic
**Freshman admissions:** selective; 2013-2014: 4,942 applied, 3,332 accepted. Either SAT or ACT required. SAT 25/75 percentile: 990-1180. High school rank: 15% in top tenth, 35% in top quarter, 68% in top half
**Early decision deadline:** N/A, notification date: N/A
**Early action deadline:** 12/1, notification date: 12/25
**Application deadline (fall):** 3/1
**Undergraduate student body:** 1,650 full time, 91 part time; 45% male, 55% female; 0% American Indian, 2% Asian, 10% black, 9% Hispanic, 3% multiracial, 0% Pacific Islander, 73% white, 1% international; 51% from in state; 82% live on campus; 0% of students in fraternities, 0% in sororities
**Most popular majors:** 7% Accounting, 9% Biology/Biological Sciences, 20% Business/Commerce, General, 10% Criminology, 8% Elementary Education and Teaching
**Expenses:** 2014-2015: $36,021; room/board: $11,975
**Financial aid:** (301) 447-5207; 70% of undergrads determined to have financial need; average aid package $23,441

## National Labor College[1]
Silver Spring MD
(301) 431-6400
**U.S. News ranking:** Business, unranked
**Website:** www.nlc.edu/
**Admissions email:** N/A
**Private**
**Application deadline (fall):** N/A
**Undergraduate student body:** N/A full time, N/A part time
**Expenses:** 2013-2014: $9,528; room/board: N/A
**Financial aid:** (301) 628-5592

## Notre Dame of Maryland University
Baltimore MD
(410) 532-5330
**U.S. News ranking:** Reg. U. (N), No. 50
**Website:** www.ndm.edu
**Admissions email:** admiss@ndm.edu

**Private;** founded 1873
**Affiliation:** Roman Catholic
**Freshman admissions:** selective; 2013-2014: 838 applied, 416 accepted. Either SAT or ACT required. SAT 25/75 percentile: 930-1150. High school rank: 33% in top tenth, 61% in top quarter, 88% in top half
**Early decision deadline:** N/A, notification date: N/A
**Early action deadline:** 12/1, notification date: 12/15
**Application deadline (fall):** rolling
**Undergraduate student body:** 525 full time, 709 part time; 5% male, 95% female; 1% American Indian, 5% Asian, 28% black, 5% Hispanic, 0% multiracial, 0% Pacific Islander, 57% white, 1% international; N/A from in state; 47% live on campus; N/A of students in fraternities, N/A in sororities
**Most popular majors:** 4% Biology, General, 9% Business/Commerce, General, 13% Education, General, 11% Liberal Arts and Sciences, General Studies and Humanities, 47% Registered Nursing, Nursing Administration, Nursing Research and Clinical Nursing, Other
**Expenses:** 2014-2015: $33,010; room/board: $10,716
**Financial aid:** (410) 532-5369; 84% of undergrads determined to have financial need; average aid package $23,572

## Salisbury University
Salisbury MD
(410) 543-6161
**U.S. News ranking:** Reg. U. (N), No. 65
**Website:** www.salisbury.edu/
**Admissions email:** admissions@salisbury.edu
**Public;** founded 1925
**Freshman admissions:** selective; 2013-2014: 8,905 applied, 4,895 accepted. Neither SAT nor ACT required. SAT 25/75 percentile: 1080-1230. High school rank: 23% in top tenth, 59% in top quarter, 93% in top half
**Early decision deadline:** 11/15, notification date: 12/15
**Early action deadline:** 12/1, notification date: 1/15
**Application deadline (fall):** 1/15
**Undergraduate student body:** 7,405 full time, 599 part time; 43% male, 57% female; 0% American Indian, 2% Asian, 11% black, 4% Hispanic, 4% multiracial, 0% Pacific Islander, 74% white, 1% international; 86% from in state; 28% live on campus; 6% of students in fraternities, 4% in sororities
**Most popular majors:** 13% Business Administration and Management, General, 12% Elementary Education and Teaching, 9% Psychology, General, 8% Registered Nursing/Registered Nurse, 10% Speech Communication and Rhetoric
**Expenses:** 2014-2015: $8,560 in state, $16,906 out of state; room/board: $10,620
**Financial aid:** (410) 543-6165; 52% of undergrads determined to have financial need; average aid package $7,537

## Sojourner-Douglass College[1]
Baltimore MD
(800) 732-2630
**U.S. News ranking:** Reg. Coll. (N), unranked
**Website:** www.sdc.edu/
**Admissions email:** N/A
**Private**
**Application deadline (fall):** N/A
**Undergraduate student body:** N/A full time, N/A part time
**Expenses:** 2013-2014: $9,830; room/board: N/A
**Financial aid:** (410) 276-0306

## Stevenson University
Stevenson MD
(410) 486-7001
**U.S. News ranking:** Reg. U. (N), No. 98
**Website:** www.stevenson.edu/
**Admissions email:** admissions@stevenson.edu
**Private;** founded 1947
**Freshman admissions:** less selective; 2013-2014: 5,318 applied, 3,169 accepted. Either SAT or ACT required. SAT 25/75 percentile: 890-1100. High school rank: 11% in top tenth, 31% in top quarter, 58% in top half
**Early decision deadline:** N/A, notification date: N/A
**Early action deadline:** N/A, notification date: N/A
**Application deadline (fall):** rolling
**Undergraduate student body:** 3,300 full time, 547 part time; 35% male, 65% female; 0% American Indian, 3% Asian, 29% black, 4% Hispanic, 2% multiracial, 0% Pacific Islander, 57% white, 0% international; 79% from in state; 48% live on campus; 2% of students in fraternities, 2% in sororities
**Most popular majors:** 19% Business, Management, Marketing, and Related Support Services, 6% Computer and Information Sciences and Support Services, 7% Education, 28% Health Professions and Related Programs, 6% Visual and Performing Arts
**Expenses:** 2014-2015: $28,980; room/board: $12,490
**Financial aid:** (443) 334-2559; 76% of undergrads determined to have financial need; average aid package $18,305

## St. John's College
Annapolis MD
(410) 626-2522
**U.S. News ranking:** Nat. Lib. Arts, No. 56
**Website:** sjc.edu
**Admissions email:** annapolis.admissions@sjc.edu
**Private;** founded 1696
**Freshman admissions:** selective; 2013-2014: 318 applied, 277 accepted. Neither SAT nor ACT required. SAT 25/75 percentile: 1140-1410. High school rank: 19% in top tenth, 37% in top quarter, 77% in top half
**Early decision deadline:** N/A, notification date: N/A
**Early action deadline:** 1/15, notification date: 2/15
**Application deadline (fall):** rolling
**Undergraduate student body:** 440 full time, 3 part time; 55% male, 45% female; 0% American Indian, 2% Asian, 2% black, 6% Hispanic, 3% multiracial, 0% Pacific Islander, 70% white,

11% international; 25% from in state; 75% live on campus; 0% of students in fraternities, 0% in sororities
**Most popular majors:** 100% Liberal Arts and Sciences, General Studies and Humanities
**Expenses:** 2014-2015: $47,826; room/board: $11,270
**Financial aid:** (410) 626-2502; 71% of undergrads determined to have financial need; average aid package $35,091

## St. Mary's College of Maryland
St. Mary's City MD
(800) 492-7181
**U.S. News ranking:** Nat. Lib. Arts, No. 89
**Website:** www.smcm.edu
**Admissions email:** admissions@smcm.edu
**Public;** founded 1840
**Freshman admissions:** selective; 2013-2014: 2,321 applied, 1,704 accepted. Either SAT or ACT required. SAT 25/75 percentile: 1070-1310. High school rank: 28% in top tenth, 64% in top quarter, 87% in top half
**Early decision deadline:** 11/1, notification date: 12/15
**Early action deadline:** N/A, notification date: N/A
**Application deadline (fall):** 1/1
**Undergraduate student body:** 1,762 full time, 57 part time; 41% male, 59% female; 0% American Indian, 3% Asian, 8% black, 6% Hispanic, 4% multiracial, 0% Pacific Islander, 75% white, 1% international; 90% from in state; 87% live on campus; 0% of students in fraternities, 0% in sororities
**Most popular majors:** 9% Biology/Biological Sciences, General, 8% Economics, General, 10% English Language and Literature, General, 8% Political Science and Government, General, 14% Psychology, General
**Expenses:** 2014-2015: $14,874 in state, $28,674 out of state; room/board: $11,930
**Financial aid:** (240) 895-3000; 47% of undergrads determined to have financial need; average aid package $14,332

## Towson University
Towson MD
(410) 704-2113
**U.S. News ranking:** Reg. U. (N), No. 60
**Website:** www.towson.edu
**Admissions email:** admissions@towson.edu
**Public;** founded 1866
**Freshman admissions:** selective; 2013-2014: 17,750 applied, 10,710 accepted. Either SAT or ACT required. SAT 25/75 percentile: 990-1170. High school rank: 18% in top tenth, 49% in top quarter, 87% in top half
**Early decision deadline:** N/A, notification date: N/A
**Early action deadline:** N/A, notification date: N/A
**Application deadline (fall):** 2/15
**Undergraduate student body:** 16,588 full time, 2,191 part time; 40% male, 60% female; 0% American Indian, 5% Asian, 15% black, 5% Hispanic, 3% multiracial, 0% Pacific Islander,

65% white, 2% international; 85% from in state; 25% live on campus; 9% of students in fraternities, 7% in sororities
**Most popular majors:** 14% Business, Management, Marketing, and Related Support Services, 12% Education, 11% Health Professions and Related Programs, 8% Psychology, 12% Social Sciences
**Expenses:** 2013-2014: $8,342 in state, $20,020 out of state; room/board: $10,662
**Financial aid:** (410) 704-4236

## United States Naval Academy
Annapolis MD
(410) 293-4361
**U.S. News ranking:** Nat. Lib. Arts, No. 13
**Website:** www.usna.edu
**Admissions email:** webmail@usna.edu
**Public;** founded 1845
**Freshman admissions:** more selective; 2013-2014: 19,146 applied, 1,408 accepted. Either SAT or ACT required. SAT 25/75 percentile: 1180-1380. High school rank: 54% in top tenth, 81% in top quarter, 96% in top half
**Early decision deadline:** N/A, notification date: N/A
**Early action deadline:** N/A, notification date: N/A
**Application deadline (fall):** 1/31
**Undergraduate student body:** 4,526 full time, 0 part time; 78% male, 22% female; 0% American Indian, 6% Asian, 7% black, 11% Hispanic, 7% multiracial, 1% Pacific Islander, 65% white, 1% international; 7% from in state; 100% live on campus; 0% of students in fraternities, 0% in sororities
**Most popular majors:** 9% Economics, General, 9% History, General, 8% Oceanography, Chemical and Physical, 13% Political Science and Government, General, 9% Systems Engineering
**Expenses:** N/A
**Financial aid:** N/A

## University of Baltimore[1]
Baltimore MD
(410) 837-4777
**U.S. News ranking:** Reg. U. (N), No. 115
**Website:** www.ubalt.edu
**Admissions email:** admissions@ubalt.edu
**Public;** founded 1925
**Application deadline (fall):** rolling
**Undergraduate student body:** N/A full time, N/A part time
**Expenses:** 2013-2014: $7,838 in state, $16,288 out of state; room/board: N/A
**Financial aid:** (410) 837-4763

## University of Maryland–Baltimore County
Baltimore MD
(410) 455-2291
**U.S. News ranking:** Nat. U., No. 149
**Website:** www.umbc.edu
**Admissions email:** admissions@umbc.edu
**Public;** founded 1963

**Freshman admissions:** more selective; 2013-2014: 9,755 applied, 6,160 accepted. SAT required. SAT 25/75 percentile: 1110-1310. High school rank: 25% in top tenth, 57% in top quarter, 86% in top half
**Early decision deadline:** N/A, notification date: N/A
**Early action deadline:** 11/1, notification date: 12/15
**Application deadline (fall):** 2/1
**Undergraduate student body:** 9,508 full time, 1,628 part time; 55% male, 45% female; 0% American Indian, 20% Asian, 16% black, 6% Hispanic, 4% multiracial, 0% Pacific Islander, 45% white, 4% international; 94% from in state; 34% live on campus; 4% of students in fraternities, 4% in sororities
**Most popular majors:** 14% Biological and Biomedical Sciences, 14% Computer and Information Sciences and Support Services, 13% Psychology, 16% Social Sciences, 8% Visual and Performing Arts
**Expenses:** 2013-2014: $10,068 in state, $21,642 out of state; room/board: $10,716
**Financial aid:** (410) 455-2387

## University of Maryland–College Park
College Park MD
(301) 314-8385
**U.S. News ranking:** Nat. U., No. 62
**Website:** www.maryland.edu
**Admissions email:** um-admit@umd.edu
**Public;** founded 1856
**Freshman admissions:** more selective; 2013-2014: 26,205 applied, 12,293 accepted. Either SAT or ACT required. SAT 25/75 percentile: 1200-1420. High school rank: 71% in top tenth, 88% in top quarter, 98% in top half
**Early decision deadline:** N/A, notification date: N/A
**Early action deadline:** 11/1, notification date: 1/31
**Application deadline (fall):** 1/20
**Undergraduate student body:** 24,522 full time, 2,136 part time; 53% male, 47% female; 0% American Indian, 16% Asian, 12% black, 9% Hispanic, 4% multiracial, 0% Pacific Islander, 54% white, 3% international; 78% from in state; 44% live on campus; 12% of students in fraternities, 17% in sororities
**Most popular majors:** 8% Biology/Biological Sciences, General, 5% Criminology, 5% Economics, General, 4% Political Science and Government, General, 5% Psychology, General
**Expenses:** 2014-2015: $9,427 in state, $29,720 out of state; room/board: $10,633
**Financial aid:** (301) 314-9000; 43% of undergrads determined to have financial need; average aid package $13,271

## University of Maryland–Eastern Shore
Princess Anne MD
(410) 651-6410
**U.S. News ranking:** Reg. U. (N), second tier
**Website:** www.umes.edu
**Admissions email:** umesadmissions@umes.edu
**Public;** founded 1886
**Freshman admissions:** less selective; 2013-2014: 4,073 applied, 2,241 accepted. Either SAT or ACT required. SAT 25/75 percentile: 790-960. High school rank: N/A
**Early decision deadline:** N/A, notification date: N/A
**Early action deadline:** N/A, notification date: N/A
**Application deadline (fall):** 6/30
**Undergraduate student body:** 3,171 full time, 360 part time; 45% male, 55% female; 0% American Indian, 1% Asian, 74% black, 2% Hispanic, 8% multiracial, 0% Pacific Islander, 11% white, 3% international; 81% from in state; 60% live on campus; N/A of students in fraternities, N/A in sororities
**Most popular majors:** 7% Biology/Biological Sciences, General, 15% Criminal Justice/Police Science, 8% Family and Consumer Sciences/Human Sciences, General, 7% Hotel/Motel Administration/Management, 8% Sociology
**Expenses:** 2014-2015: $7,287 in state, $16,311 out of state; room/board: $8,906
**Financial aid:** (410) 651-6172; 82% of undergrads determined to have financial need; average aid package $10,080

## University of Maryland–University College
Adelphi MD
(800) 888-8682
**U.S. News ranking:** Reg. U. (N), unranked
**Website:** www.umuc.edu/
**Admissions email:** enroll@umuc.edu
**Public;** founded 1947
**Freshman admissions:** N/A; 2013-2014: 2,251 applied, 2,251 accepted. Neither SAT nor ACT required. ACT 25/75 percentile: N/A. High school rank: N/A
**Early decision deadline:** N/A, notification date: N/A
**Early action deadline:** N/A, notification date: N/A
**Application deadline (fall):** rolling
**Undergraduate student body:** 5,917 full time, 20,823 part time; 51% male, 49% female; 0% American Indian, 4% Asian, 29% black, 9% Hispanic, 3% multiracial, 1% Pacific Islander, 42% white, 1% international; 57% from in state; N/A live on campus; N/A of students in fraternities, N/A in sororities
**Most popular majors:** 41% Business, Management, Marketing, and Related Support Services, 23% Computer and Information Sciences and Support Services, 8% Homeland Security, Law Enforcement, Firefighting and Related Protective Services, 8% Psychology

**Expenses:** 2013-2014: $6,552 in state; $12,336 out of state; room/board: N/A
**Financial aid:** (301) 985-7510; 63% of undergrads determined to have financial need; average aid package $7,607

## Washington Adventist University
Takoma Park MD
(301) 891-4080
**U.S. News ranking:** Reg. Coll. (N), No. 46
**Website:** www.wau.edu
**Admissions email:** enroll@wau.edu
**Private;** founded 1904
**Affiliation:** Seventh-day Adventist
**Freshman admissions:** least selective; 2013-2014: 1,116 applied, 596 accepted. Either SAT or ACT required. SAT 25/75 percentile: 720-960. High school rank: N/A
**Early decision deadline:** N/A, notification date: N/A
**Early action deadline:** N/A, notification date: N/A
**Application deadline (fall):** 8/1
**Undergraduate student body:** 806 full time, 205 part time; 35% male, 65% female; 1% American Indian, 7% Asian, 59% black, 11% Hispanic, 1% multiracial, 0% Pacific Islander, 9% white, 2% international; 60% from in state; N/A live on campus; N/A of students in fraternities, N/A in sororities
**Most popular majors:** 9% Business, Management, Marketing, and Related Support Services, 57% Health Professions and Related Programs, 9% Liberal Arts and Sciences, General Studies and Humanities, 8% Psychology, 4% Theology and Religious Vocations
**Expenses:** 2014-2015: $21,395; room/board: $8,300
**Financial aid:** (301) 891-4005; 95% of undergrads determined to have financial need; average aid package $11,026

## Washington College
Chestertown MD
(410) 778-7700
**U.S. News ranking:** Nat. Lib. Arts, No. 105
**Website:** www.washcoll.edu
**Admissions email:** adm.off@washcoll.edu
**Private;** founded 1782
**Freshman admissions:** more selective; 2013-2014: 4,647 applied, 3,088 accepted. Neither SAT nor ACT required. SAT 25/75 percentile: 1050-1280. High school rank: 33% in top tenth, 62% in top quarter, 88% in top half
**Early decision deadline:** 11/1, notification date: 12/1
**Early action deadline:** 12/1, notification date: 12/20
**Application deadline (fall):** 2/15
**Undergraduate student body:** 1,440 full time, 43 part time; 42% male, 58% female; 0% American Indian, 2% Asian, 4% black, 4% Hispanic, 2% multiracial, 0% Pacific Islander, 79% white, 5% international; 52% from in state; 85% live on campus; 8% of students in fraternities, 11% in sororities

**Most popular majors:** 9% Biological and Biomedical Sciences, 14% Business, Management, Marketing, and Related Support Services, 7% English Language and Literature/Letters, 10% Psychology, 25% Social Sciences
**Expenses:** 2014-2015: $42,592; room/board: $10,010
**Financial aid:** (410) 778-7214; 60% of undergrads determined to have financial need; average aid package $31,604

## MASSACHUSETTS

## American International College
Springfield MA
(413) 205-3201
**U.S. News ranking:** Reg. U. (N), second tier
**Website:** www.aic.edu
**Admissions email:** inquiry@aic.edu
**Private;** founded 1885
**Freshman admissions:** least selective; 2013-2014: 1,928 applied, 1,306 accepted. Either SAT or ACT required. SAT 25/75 percentile: 836-869. High school rank: N/A
**Early decision deadline:** N/A, notification date: N/A
**Early action deadline:** N/A, notification date: N/A
**Application deadline (fall):** rolling
**Undergraduate student body:** 1,397 full time, 116 part time; 42% male, 58% female; 0% American Indian, 2% Asian, 25% black, 7% Hispanic, 4% multiracial, 1% Pacific Islander, 44% white, 1% international; 63% from in state; 48% live on campus; 2% of students in fraternities, 2% in sororities
**Most popular majors:** 18% Business, Management, Marketing, and Related Support Services, 30% Health Professions and Related Programs, 12% Homeland Security, Law Enforcement, Firefighting and Related Protective Services, 9% Liberal Arts and Sciences, General Studies and Humanities, 9% Psychology
**Expenses:** 2014-2015: $30,941; room/board: $12,514
**Financial aid:** (413) 205-3259; 95% of undergrads determined to have financial need; average aid package $23,969

## Amherst College
Amherst MA
(413) 542-2328
**U.S. News ranking:** Nat. Lib. Arts, No. 2
**Website:** www.amherst.edu
**Admissions email:** admission@amherst.edu
**Private;** founded 1821
**Freshman admissions:** most selective; 2013-2014: 7,927 applied, 1,132 accepted. Either SAT or ACT required. SAT 25/75 percentile: 1350-1530. High school rank: 86% in top tenth, 98% in top quarter, 100% in top half
**Early decision deadline:** 11/15, notification date: 12/15
**Early action deadline:** N/A, notification date: N/A
**Application deadline (fall):** 1/1
**Undergraduate student body:** 1,785 full time, N/A part time; 50% male, 50% female; 0% American Indian, 13% Asian, 12% black,

13% Hispanic, 6% multiracial, 0% Pacific Islander, 42% white, 10% international; 12% from in state; 98% live on campus; 0% of students in fraternities, 0% in sororities
**Most popular majors:** 15% Economics, General, 9% English Language and Literature, General, 11% History, General, 10% Political Science and Government, General, 8% Psychology, General
**Expenses:** 2014-2015: $48,526; room/board: $12,680
**Financial aid:** (413) 542-2296; 56% of undergrads determined to have financial need; average aid package $46,809

## Anna Maria College
Paxton MA
(508) 849-3360
**U.S. News ranking:** Reg. U. (N), second tier
**Website:** www.annamaria.edu
**Admissions email:** admissions@annamaria.edu
**Private;** founded 1946
**Affiliation:** Roman Catholic
**Freshman admissions:** least selective; 2013-2014: 2,071 applied, 1,607 accepted. Neither SAT nor ACT required. SAT 25/75 percentile: 765-975. High school rank: N/A
**Early decision deadline:** N/A, notification date: N/A
**Early action deadline:** N/A, notification date: N/A
**Application deadline (fall):** rolling
**Undergraduate student body:** 845 full time, 298 part time; 43% male, 57% female; 0% American Indian, 1% Asian, 8% black, 7% Hispanic, 2% multiracial, 0% Pacific Islander, 72% white, 0% international
**Most popular majors:** Information not available
**Expenses:** 2014-2015: $34,330; room/board: $12,730
**Financial aid:** (508) 849-3366; 72% of undergrads determined to have financial need; average aid package $23,637

## Assumption College
Worcester MA
(866) 477-7776
**U.S. News ranking:** Reg. U. (N), No. 31
**Website:** www.assumption.edu
**Admissions email:** admiss@assumption.edu
**Private;** founded 1904
**Affiliation:** Roman Catholic
**Freshman admissions:** selective; 2013-2014: 4,659 applied, 3,458 accepted. Neither SAT nor ACT required. SAT 25/75 percentile: 1020-1215. High school rank: 10% in top tenth, 40% in top quarter, 79% in top half
**Early decision deadline:** N/A, notification date: N/A
**Early action deadline:** 11/1, notification date: 12/15
**Application deadline (fall):** 2/15
**Undergraduate student body:** 2,003 full time, 12 part time; 40% male, 60% female; 0% American Indian, 2% Asian, 4% black, 7% Hispanic, 2% multiracial, 0% Pacific Islander, 74% white, 1% international; 64% from in state; 87% live on campus; N/A of students in fraternities, N/A in sororities

**Most popular majors:** 25% Business, Management, Marketing, and Related Support Services, 11% English Language and Literature/Letters, 9% Health Professions and Related Programs, 10% Psychology, 12% Social Sciences
**Expenses:** 2014-2015: $36,160; room/board: $10,962
**Financial aid:** (508) 767-7158; 78% of undergrads determined to have financial need; average aid package $25,672

## Babson College
Babson Park MA
(781) 239-5522
**U.S. News ranking:** Business, unranked
**Website:** www.babson.edu
**Admissions email:** ugradadmission@babson.edu
**Private;** founded 1919
**Freshman admissions:** more selective; 2013-2014: 6,086 applied, 1,717 accepted. Either SAT or ACT required. SAT 25/75 percentile: 1160-1350. High school rank: N/A
**Early decision deadline:** 11/1, notification date: 12/15
**Early action deadline:** 11/1, notification date: 1/1
**Application deadline (fall):** 1/1
**Undergraduate student body:** 2,106 full time, N/A part time; 55% male, 45% female; 0% American Indian, 12% Asian, 4% black, 10% Hispanic, 2% multiracial, 0% Pacific Islander, 39% white, 26% international; 30% from in state; 81% live on campus; 15% of students in fraternities, 25% in sororities
**Most popular majors:** Information not available
**Expenses:** 2014-2015: $45,120; room/board: $14,494
**Financial aid:** (781) 239-4219; 43% of undergrads determined to have financial need; average aid package $37,060

## Bard College at Simon's Rock
Great Barrington MA
(800) 234-7186
**U.S. News ranking:** Reg. Coll. (N), No. 12
**Website:** www.simons-rock.edu
**Admissions email:** admit@simons-rock.edu
**Private;** founded 1966
**Freshman admissions:** more selective; 2013-2014: 218 applied, 201 accepted. Neither SAT nor ACT required. SAT 25/75 percentile: 1290-1460. High school rank: 46% in top tenth, 67% in top quarter, 89% in top half
**Early decision deadline:** N/A, notification date: N/A
**Early action deadline:** N/A, notification date: N/A
**Application deadline (fall):** 5/1
**Undergraduate student body:** 341 full time, 9 part time; 42% male, 58% female; 0% American Indian, 6% Asian, 7% black, 2% Hispanic, 9% multiracial, 0% Pacific Islander, 57% white, 10% international; N/A from in state; 90% live on campus; N/A of students in fraternities, N/A in sororities

**Most popular majors:** 6% Engineering, 10% English Language and Literature/Letters, 16% Multi/Interdisciplinary Studies, 11% Social Sciences, 18% Visual and Performing Arts
**Expenses:** 2014-2015: $48,551; room/board: $13,198
**Financial aid:** (413) 528-7297; 81% of undergrads determined to have financial need; average aid package $38,911

## Bay Path University
Longmeadow MA
(413) 565-1331
**U.S. News ranking:** Nat. Lib. Arts, second tier
**Website:** www.baypath.edu
**Admissions email:** admiss@baypath.edu
**Private;** founded 1897
**Freshman admissions:** selective; 2013-2014: 908 applied, 523 accepted. Neither SAT nor ACT required. SAT 25/75 percentile: 840-1090. High school rank: 14% in top tenth, 49% in top quarter, 84% in top half
**Early decision deadline:** N/A, notification date: N/A
**Early action deadline:** 12/15, notification date: 1/2
**Application deadline (fall):** rolling
**Undergraduate student body:** 1,179 full time, 279 part time; 0% male, 100% female; 0% American Indian, 1% Asian, 12% black, 15% Hispanic, 2% multiracial, 0% Pacific Islander, 59% white, 0% international; 58% from in state; 53% live on campus; 0% of students in fraternities, 0% in sororities
**Most popular majors:** 26% Business, Management, Marketing, and Related Support Services, 9% Homeland Security, Law Enforcement, Firefighting and Related Protective Services, 8% Legal Professions and Studies, 25% Liberal Arts and Sciences, General Studies and Humanities, 17% Psychology
**Expenses:** 2014-2015: $30,859; room/board: $12,240
**Financial aid:** (413) 565-1261; 97% of undergrads determined to have financial need; average aid package $24,093

## Bay State College
Boston MA
(617) 217-9000
**U.S. News ranking:** Reg. Coll. (N), second tier
**Website:** www.baystate.edu
**Admissions email:** N/A
**For-profit**
**Freshman admissions:** least selective; 2013-2014: 1,669 applied, 985 accepted. Neither SAT nor ACT required. ACT 25/75 percentile: N/A. High school rank: N/A
**Early decision deadline:** N/A, notification date: N/A
**Early action deadline:** N/A, notification date: N/A
**Application deadline (fall):** rolling
**Undergraduate student body:** 769 full time, 427 part time; 28% male, 72% female; 0% American Indian, 5% Asian, 23% black, 18% Hispanic, 8% multiracial, 0% Pacific Islander, 41% white, 2% international
**Most popular majors:** 18% Arts, Entertainment, and Media Management, General, 33% Business Administration and

Management, General, 15% Criminal Justice/Law Enforcement Administration, 14% Fashion Merchandising, 13% Licensed Practical/Vocational Nurse Training
**Expenses:** 2014-2015: $25,280; room/board: $11,800
**Financial aid:** (617) 217-9186

## Becker College
Worcester MA
(877) 523-2537
**U.S. News ranking:** Reg. Coll. (N), second tier
**Website:** www.beckercollege.edu
**Admissions email:** admissions@beckercollege.edu
**Private;** founded 1784
**Freshman admissions:** selective; 2013-2014: 3,936 applied, 2,462 accepted. Either SAT or ACT required. SAT 25/75 percentile: 890-1120. High school rank: 7% in top tenth, 26% in top quarter, 57% in top half
**Early decision deadline:** N/A, notification date: N/A
**Early action deadline:** 11/15, notification date: 12/15
**Application deadline (fall):** rolling
**Undergraduate student body:** 1,449 full time, 453 part time; 43% male, 57% female; 0% American Indian, 1% Asian, 8% black, 10% Hispanic, 3% multiracial, 0% Pacific Islander, 67% white, 1% international; 67% from in state; 41% live on campus; 0% of students in fraternities, 0% in sororities
**Most popular majors:** 27% Business, Management, Marketing, and Related Support Services, 12% Communications Technologies/Technicians and Support Services, 9% Health Professions and Related Programs, 11% Parks, Recreation, Leisure, and Fitness Studies, 17% Psychology
**Expenses:** 2013-2014: $31,500; room/board: $11,500
**Financial aid:** (508) 791-9241

## Benjamin Franklin Institute of Technology[1]
Boston MA
(617) 423-4630
**U.S. News ranking:** Engineering, unranked
**Website:** www.bfit.edu
**Admissions email:** admissions@bfit.edu
**Private**
**Application deadline (fall):** N/A
**Undergraduate student body:** N/A full time, N/A part time
**Expenses:** 2013-2014: $16,950; room/board: $16,900
**Financial aid:** (617) 423-4630

## Bentley University
Waltham MA
(781) 891-2244
**U.S. News ranking:** Reg. U. (N), No. 6
**Website:** www.bentley.edu
**Admissions email:** ugadmission@bentley.edu
**Private;** founded 1917
**Freshman admissions:** more selective; 2013-2014: 7,493 applied, 3,281 accepted. Either SAT or ACT required. SAT 25/75 percentile: 1140-1310. High school rank: 41% in top tenth, 75% in top quarter, 98% in top half

**Early decision deadline:** 11/15, notification date: 12/28
**Early action deadline:** 11/15, notification date: 2/7
**Application deadline (fall):** 1/7
**Undergraduate student body:** 4,142 full time, 105 part time; 60% male, 40% female; 0% American Indian, 8% Asian, 3% black, 7% Hispanic, 2% multiracial, 0% Pacific Islander, 61% white, 15% international; 47% from in state; 78% live on campus; 11% of students in fraternities, 11% in sororities
**Most popular majors:** 14% Accounting, 14% Accounting and Finance, 13% Business, Management, Marketing, and Related Support Services, Other, 14% Finance, General, 15% Marketing/Marketing Management, General
**Expenses:** 2014-2015: $42,511; room/board: $13,949
**Financial aid:** (781) 891-3441; 45% of undergrads determined to have financial need; average aid package $33,956

## Berklee College of Music
Boston MA
(800) 237-5533
**U.S. News ranking:** Arts, unranked
**Website:** www.berklee.edu
**Admissions email:** admissions@berklee.edu
**Private;** founded 1945
**Freshman admissions:** N/A; 2013-2014: 6,412 applied, 2,319 accepted. Neither SAT nor ACT required. SAT 25/75 percentile: N/A. High school rank: N/A
**Early decision deadline:** N/A, notification date: N/A
**Early action deadline:** 11/1, notification date: 1/31
**Application deadline (fall):** 1/15
**Undergraduate student body:** 3,950 full time, 452 part time; 69% male, 31% female; 5% American Indian, 0% Asian, 0% black, 9% Hispanic, 4% multiracial, 39% Pacific Islander, 3% white, 31% international; 16% from in state; 17% live on campus; 0% of students in fraternities, 0% in sororities
**Most popular majors:** 12% Music Management, 16% Music Performance, General, 21% Music Theory and Composition, 20% Music, General, 14% Recording Arts Technology/Technician
**Expenses:** 2014-2015: $38,910; room/board: $17,372
**Financial aid:** (617) 747-2274

## Boston Architectural College
Boston MA
(617) 585-0123
**U.S. News ranking:** Arts, unranked
**Website:** www.the-bac.edu
**Admissions email:** admissions@the-bac.edu
**Private;** founded 1889
**Freshman admissions:** N/A; 2013-2014: 24 applied, 24 accepted. Neither SAT nor ACT required. SAT 25/75 percentile: N/A. High school rank: N/A
**Early decision deadline:** N/A, notification date: N/A
**Early action deadline:** N/A, notification date: N/A
**Application deadline (fall):** rolling

**Undergraduate student body:** 396 full time, 11 part time; 70% male, 30% female; 1% American Indian, 9% Asian, 6% black, 16% Hispanic, 2% multiracial, 0% Pacific Islander, 59% white, 1% international
**Most popular majors:** Information not available
**Expenses:** 2014-2015: $19,706; room/board: N/A
**Financial aid:** (617) 585-0125; 96% of undergrads determined to have financial need; average aid package $9,907

## Boston College
Chestnut Hill MA
(617) 552-3100
**U.S. News ranking:** Nat. U., No. 31
**Website:** www.bc.edu
**Admissions email:** N/A
**Private;** founded 1863
**Affiliation:** Roman Catholic (Jesuit)
**Freshman admissions:** most selective; 2013-2014: 24,538 applied, 7,905 accepted. Either SAT or ACT required. SAT 25/75 percentile: 1270-1450. High school rank: 81% in top tenth, 97% in top quarter, 99% in top half
**Early decision deadline:** N/A, notification date: N/A
**Early action deadline:** 11/1, notification date: 12/25
**Application deadline (fall):** 1/1
**Undergraduate student body:** 9,049 full time, N/A part time; 46% male, 54% female; 0% American Indian, 10% Asian, 4% black, 11% Hispanic, 3% multiracial, 0% Pacific Islander, 60% white, 5% international; 26% from in state; 85% live on campus; 0% of students in fraternities, 0% in sororities
**Most popular majors:** 8% Biology/Biological Sciences, General, 9% Economics, General, 10% Finance, General, 7% Psychology, General, 8% Speech Communication and Rhetoric
**Expenses:** 2014-2015: $47,436; room/board: $13,186
**Financial aid:** (617) 552-3320; 43% of undergrads determined to have financial need; average aid package $36,779

## Boston Conservatory[1]
Boston MA
(617) 912-9153
**U.S. News ranking:** Arts, unranked
**Website:** www.bostonconservatory.edu
**Admissions email:** admissions@bostonconservatory.edu
**Private**
**Application deadline (fall):** N/A
**Undergraduate student body:** N/A full time, N/A part time
**Expenses:** 2013-2014: $40,900; room/board: $17,195
**Financial aid:** (617) 912-9147

## Boston University
Boston MA
(617) 353-2300
**U.S. News ranking:** Nat. U., No. 42
**Website:** www.bu.edu
**Admissions email:** admissions@bu.edu
**Private;** founded 1839
**Freshman admissions:** more selective; 2013-2014: 52,705 applied, 19,420 accepted. Either

SAT or ACT required. SAT 25/75 percentile: 1190-1390. High school rank: 58% in top tenth, 89% in top quarter, 99% in top half
**Early decision deadline:** 11/1, notification date: 12/15
**Early action deadline:** N/A, notification date: N/A
**Application deadline (fall):** 1/1
**Undergraduate student body:** 16,593 full time, 1,572 part time; 40% male, 60% female; 0% American Indian, 13% Asian, 3% black, 9% Hispanic, 4% multiracial, 0% Pacific Islander, 47% white, 16% international; 26% from in state; 75% live on campus; 7% of students in fraternities, 11% in sororities
**Most popular majors:** 8% Biological and Biomedical Sciences, 18% Business, Management, Marketing, and Related Support Services, 15% Communication, Journalism, and Related Programs, 9% Health Professions and Related Programs, 16% Social Sciences
**Expenses:** 2014-2015: $46,664; room/board: $14,030
**Financial aid:** (617) 353-2965; 40% of undergrads determined to have financial need; average aid package $35,633

## Brandeis University
Waltham MA
(781) 736-3500
**U.S. News ranking:** Nat. U., No. 35
**Website:** www.brandeis.edu
**Admissions email:** admissions@brandeis.edu
**Private;** founded 1948
**Freshman admissions:** more selective; 2013-2014: 9,496 applied, 3,517 accepted. Either SAT or ACT required. SAT 25/75 percentile: 1230-1470. High school rank: 65% in top tenth, 89% in top quarter, 99% in top half
**Early decision deadline:** 11/1, notification date: 12/15
**Early action deadline:** N/A, notification date: N/A
**Application deadline (fall):** 1/1
**Undergraduate student body:** 3,599 full time, 15 part time; 43% male, 57% female; 0% American Indian, 12% Asian, 5% black, 7% Hispanic, 3% multiracial, 0% Pacific Islander, 50% white, 15% international; 27% from in state; 79% live on campus; 0% of students in fraternities, 0% in sororities
**Most popular majors:** 10% Biology/Biological Sciences, General, 7% Business Administration, Management and Operations, Other, 9% Economics, General, 6% Health Policy Analysis, 9% Psychology, General
**Expenses:** 2014-2015: $47,833; room/board: $13,192
**Financial aid:** (781) 736-3700; 53% of undergrads determined to have financial need; average aid package $37,333

## Bridgewater State University
Bridgewater MA
(508) 531-1237
**U.S. News ranking:** Reg. U. (N), second tier
**Website:** www.bridgew.edu/admissions

**Admissions email:** admission@bridgew.edu
**Public;** founded 1840
**Freshman admissions:** less selective; 2013-2014: 5,918 applied, 4,651 accepted. Either SAT or ACT required. SAT 25/75 percentile: 890-1090. High school rank: N/A
**Early decision deadline:** N/A, notification date: N/A
**Early action deadline:** 11/15, notification date: 12/15
**Application deadline (fall):** rolling
**Undergraduate student body:** 8,034 full time, 1,581 part time; 42% male, 58% female; 0% American Indian, 2% Asian, 8% black, 5% Hispanic, 3% multiracial, 0% Pacific Islander, 81% white, 0% international; 96% from in state; 39% live on campus; 5% of students in fraternities, 5% in sororities
**Most popular majors:** 16% Business, Management, Marketing, and Related Support Services, 9% Communication, Journalism, and Related Programs, 16% Education, 11% Homeland Security, Law Enforcement, Firefighting and Related Protective Services, 12% Psychology
**Expenses:** 2013-2014: $8,228 in state, $14,368 out of state; room/board: $11,100
**Financial aid:** (508) 531-1341

## Cambridge College[1]
Cambridge MA
(800) 877-4723
**U.S. News ranking:** Reg. U. (N), unranked
**Website:** www.cambridgecollege.edu
**Admissions email:** N/A
**Private;** founded 1971
**Application deadline (fall):** rolling
**Undergraduate student body:** N/A full time, N/A part time
**Expenses:** 2014-2015: $13,392; room/board: N/A
**Financial aid:** (800) 877-4723; average aid package $8,418

## Clark University
Worcester MA
(508) 793-7431
**U.S. News ranking:** Nat. U., No. 76
**Website:** www.clarku.edu
**Admissions email:** admissions@clarku.edu
**Private;** founded 1887
**Freshman admissions:** more selective; 2013-2014: 5,551 applied, 3,416 accepted. Neither SAT nor ACT required. SAT 25/75 percentile: 1110-1320. High school rank: 38% in top tenth, 73% in top quarter, 98% in top half
**Early decision deadline:** N/A, notification date: N/A
**Early action deadline:** 11/15, notification date: 12/23
**Application deadline (fall):** 1/15
**Undergraduate student body:** 2,270 full time, 110 part time; 42% male, 58% female; 0% American Indian, 6% Asian, 4% black, 6% Hispanic, 2% multiracial, 0% Pacific Islander, 62% white, 12% international; 39% from in state; 71% live on campus; 0% of students in fraternities, 0% in sororities
**Most popular majors:** 6% Biology, General, 5% Economics, 6% International Relations and National Security Studies, 9%

Political Science and Government, 17% Psychology
**Expenses:** 2014-2015: $40,730; room/board: $7,800
**Financial aid:** (508) 793-7478; 62% of undergrads determined to have financial need; average aid package $33,320

## College of Our Lady of the Elms
Chicopee MA
(800) 255-3567
**U.S. News ranking:** Reg. Coll. (N), No. 24
**Website:** www.elms.edu
**Admissions email:** admissions@elms.edu
**Private**
**Affiliation:** Roman Catholic, founded by Sisters of Saint Joseph of Springfield
**Freshman admissions:** less selective; 2013-2014: 993 applied, 744 accepted. Either SAT or ACT required. SAT 25/75 percentile: 820-1040. High school rank: N/A
**Early decision deadline:** N/A, notification date: N/A
**Early action deadline:** N/A, notification date: N/A
**Application deadline (fall):** rolling
**Undergraduate student body:** 1,006 full time, 341 part time; 24% male, 76% female; 1% American Indian, 3% Asian, 8% black, 11% Hispanic, 3% multiracial, 0% Pacific Islander, 56% white, 1% international; 82% from in state; 28% live on campus; 0% of students in fraternities, 0% in sororities
**Most popular majors:** 5% Biological and Biomedical Sciences, 16% Business, Management, Marketing, and Related Support Services, 41% Health Professions and Related Programs, 6% Psychology, 11% Public Administration and Social Service Professions
**Expenses:** 2014-2015: $31,188; room/board: $11,312
**Financial aid:** (413) 594-2761; 74% of undergrads determined to have financial need; average aid package $18,695

## College of the Holy Cross
Worcester MA
(508) 793-2443
**U.S. News ranking:** Nat. Lib. Arts, No. 34
**Website:** www.holycross.edu
**Admissions email:** admissions@holycross.edu
**Private;** founded 1843
**Affiliation:** Roman Catholic (Jesuit)
**Freshman admissions:** more selective; 2013-2014: 7,115 applied, 2,346 accepted. Neither SAT nor ACT required. SAT 25/75 percentile: 1220-1390. High school rank: 57% in top tenth, 90% in top quarter, 100% in top half
**Early decision deadline:** 12/15, notification date: 1/15
**Early action deadline:** N/A, notification date: N/A
**Application deadline (fall):** 1/15
**Undergraduate student body:** 2,877 full time, 35 part time; 50% male, 50% female; 0% American Indian, 5% Asian, 4% black, 11% Hispanic, 3% multiracial,

0% Pacific Islander, 68% white, 1% international; 37% from in state; 92% live on campus; 0% of students in fraternities, 0% in sororities
**Most popular majors:** 9% English Language and Literature/ Letters, 7% Foreign Languages, Literatures, and Linguistics, 8% History, 16% Psychology, 31% Social Sciences
**Expenses:** 2014-2015: $45,692; room/board: $12,350
**Financial aid:** (508) 793-2266; 58% of undergrads determined to have financial need; average aid package $31,877

## Curry College
Milton MA
(800) 669-0686
**U.S. News ranking:** Reg. U. (N), second tier
**Website:** www.curry.edu
**Admissions email:** curryadm@curry.edu
**Private;** founded 1879
**Freshman admissions:** less selective; 2013-2014: 5,192 applied, 4,537 accepted. Neither SAT nor ACT required. SAT 25/75 percentile: 840-1030. High school rank: 5% in top tenth, 20% in top quarter, 58% in top half
**Early decision deadline:** N/A, notification date: N/A
**Early action deadline:** 12/1, notification date: 12/15
**Application deadline (fall):** rolling
**Undergraduate student body:** 2,068 full time, 781 part time; 37% male, 63% female; 0% American Indian, 2% Asian, 9% black, 5% Hispanic, 2% multiracial, 0% Pacific Islander, 67% white, 1% international; 78% from in state; 51% live on campus; 0% of students in fraternities, 0% in sororities
**Most popular majors:** 12% Business, Management, Marketing, and Related Support Services, 10% Communication, Journalism, and Related Programs, 44% Health Professions and Related Programs, 12% Homeland Security, Law Enforcement, Firefighting and Related Protective Services, 8% Psychology
**Expenses:** 2014-2015: $35,415; room/board: $13,510
**Financial aid:** (617) 333-2146; 75% of undergrads determined to have financial need; average aid package $21,860

## Dean College
Franklin MA
(508) 541-1508
**U.S. News ranking:** Reg. Coll. (N), No. 26
**Website:** www.dean.edu
**Admissions email:** admission@dean.edu
**Private;** founded 1865
**Freshman admissions:** least selective; 2013-2014: 2,594 applied, 1,773 accepted. Either SAT or ACT required. SAT 25/75 percentile: 750-950. High school rank: 4% in top tenth, 11% in top quarter, 22% in top half
**Early decision deadline:** N/A, notification date: N/A
**Early action deadline:** 12/1, notification date: 1/15
**Application deadline (fall):** rolling
**Undergraduate student body:** 1,076 full time, 224 part time; 53% male, 47% female; 0% American

Indian, 1% Asian, 16% black, 6% Hispanic, 3% multiracial, 0% Pacific Islander, 46% white, 12% international; N/A from in state; 89% live on campus; N/A of students in fraternities, N/A in sororities
**Most popular majors:** Information not available
**Expenses:** 2014-2015: $34,390; room/board: $14,760
**Financial aid:** (508) 541-1519; 74% of undergrads determined to have financial need; average aid package $23,345

## Eastern Nazarene College
Quincy MA
(617) 745-3711
**U.S. News ranking:** Nat. Lib. Arts, second tier
**Website:** www.enc.edu
**Admissions email:** info@enc.edu
**Private;** founded 1918
**Affiliation:** Nazarene
**Freshman admissions:** less selective; 2013-2014: 1,070 applied, 549 accepted. Either SAT or ACT required. SAT 25/75 percentile: 820-1090. High school rank: 9% in top tenth, 25% in top quarter, 59% in top half
**Early decision deadline:** N/A, notification date: N/A
**Early action deadline:** N/A, notification date: N/A
**Application deadline (fall):** rolling
**Undergraduate student body:** 1,302 full time, 19 part time; 27% male, 73% female; 0% American Indian, 2% Asian, 21% black, 11% Hispanic, 3% multiracial, 0% Pacific Islander, 58% white, 2% international; 52% from in state; 72% live on campus; 0% of students in fraternities, 0% in sororities
**Most popular majors:** 5% Biological and Biomedical Sciences, 28% Business, Management, Marketing, and Related Support Services, 30% Education, 11% Psychology
**Expenses:** 2013-2014: $27,922; room/board: $8,700
**Financial aid:** (617) 745-3869

## Emerson College
Boston MA
(617) 824-8600
**U.S. News ranking:** Reg. U. (N), No. 14
**Website:** www.emerson.edu
**Admissions email:** admission@emerson.edu
**Private;** founded 1880
**Freshman admissions:** more selective; 2013-2014: 8,198 applied, 3,933 accepted. Either SAT or ACT required. SAT 25/75 percentile: 1140-1320. High school rank: 29% in top tenth, 68% in top quarter, 95% in top half
**Early decision deadline:** N/A, notification date: N/A
**Early action deadline:** 11/1, notification date: 12/15
**Application deadline (fall):** 1/15
**Undergraduate student body:** 3,668 full time, 63 part time; 38% male, 62% female; 0% American Indian, 4% Asian, 3% black, 10% Hispanic, 5% multiracial, 0% Pacific Islander, 65% white, 5% international; 24% from in state; 58% live on campus; 3% of students in fraternities, 4% in sororities

**Most popular majors:** 6% Broadcast Journalism, 14% Cinematography and Film/Video Production, 16% Creative Writing, 14% Marketing/ Marketing Management, General, 7% Radio and Television
**Expenses:** 2014-2015: $37,350; room/board: $15,096
**Financial aid:** (617) 824-8655; 55% of undergrads determined to have financial need; average aid package $21,243

## Emmanuel College
Boston MA
(617) 735-9715
**U.S. News ranking:** Reg. U. (N), No. 60
**Website:** www.emmanuel.edu
**Admissions email:** enroll@emmanuel.edu
**Private;** founded 1919
**Affiliation:** Roman Catholic
**Freshman admissions:** selective; 2013-2014: 6,623 applied, 4,006 accepted. Neither SAT nor ACT required. SAT 25/75 percentile: 1000-1180. High school rank: 17% in top tenth, 54% in top quarter, 85% in top half
**Early decision deadline:** N/A, notification date: N/A
**Early action deadline:** 11/1, notification date: 12/15
**Application deadline (fall):** 2/15
**Undergraduate student body:** 1,857 full time, 319 part time; 27% male, 73% female; 0% American Indian, 3% Asian, 5% black, 6% Hispanic, 2% multiracial, 0% Pacific Islander, 70% white, 1% international; 58% from in state; 72% live on campus; N/A of students in fraternities, N/A in sororities
**Most popular majors:** 10% Biological and Biomedical Sciences, 21% Business, Management, Marketing, and Related Support Services, 10% Communication, Journalism, and Related Programs, 7% English Language and Literature/Letters, 9% Psychology
**Expenses:** 2014-2015: $35,532; room/board: $13,580
**Financial aid:** (617) 735-9938; 79% of undergrads determined to have financial need; average aid package $27,623

## Endicott College
Beverly MA
(978) 921-1000
**U.S. News ranking:** Reg. U. (N), No. 74
**Website:** www.endicott.edu
**Admissions email:** admission@endicott.edu
**Private;** founded 1939
**Freshman admissions:** selective; 2013-2014: 3,732 applied, 2,682 accepted. Either SAT or ACT required. SAT 25/75 percentile: 980-1160. High school rank: 15% in top tenth, 39% in top quarter, 81% in top half
**Early decision deadline:** N/A, notification date: N/A
**Early action deadline:** N/A, notification date: N/A
**Application deadline (fall):** 2/15
**Undergraduate student body:** 2,531 full time, 321 part time; 41% male, 59% female; 0% American Indian, 1% Asian, 2% black, 4% Hispanic, 2% multiracial, 0% Pacific Islander, 82% white,

2% international; 48% from in state; 82% live on campus; N/A of students in fraternities, N/A in sororities
**Most popular majors:** 26% Business, Management, Marketing, and Related Support Services, 9% Education, 10% Parks, Recreation, Leisure, and Fitness Studies, 10% Psychology, 10% Visual and Performing Arts
**Expenses:** 2014-2015: $29,494; room/board: $13,734
**Financial aid:** (978) 232-2070; 67% of undergrads determined to have financial need; average aid package $20,065

## Fisher College
Boston MA
(617) 236-8818
**U.S. News ranking:** Reg. Coll. (N), second tier
**Website:** www.fisher.edu
**Admissions email:** admissions@fisher.edu
**Private;** founded 1903
**Freshman admissions:** least selective; 2013-2014: 2,281 applied, 1,492 accepted. Neither SAT nor ACT required. SAT 25/75 percentile: 730-920. High school rank: N/A
**Early decision deadline:** N/A, notification date: N/A
**Early action deadline:** N/A, notification date: N/A
**Application deadline (fall):** rolling
**Undergraduate student body:** 1,229 full time, 701 part time; 26% male, 74% female; 0% American Indian, 1% Asian, 10% black, 8% Hispanic, 1% multiracial, 0% Pacific Islander, 32% white, 6% international; 83% from in state; 16% live on campus; N/A of students in fraternities, N/A in sororities
**Most popular majors:** 41% Business Administration and Management, General, 9% Early Childhood Education and Teaching, 21% Health/Health Care Administration/Management, 14% Liberal Arts and Sciences/ Liberal Studies, 5% Public Administration and Social Service Professions, Other
**Expenses:** 2014-2015: $28,260; room/board: $14,714
**Financial aid:** (617) 236-8821; 66% of undergrads determined to have financial need

## Fitchburg State University
Fitchburg MA
(978) 665-3144
**U.S. News ranking:** Reg. U. (N), second tier
**Website:** www.fitchburgstate.edu
**Admissions email:** admissions@fitchburgstate.edu
**Public;** founded 1894
**Freshman admissions:** less selective; 2013-2014: 3,818 applied, 2,834 accepted. Either SAT or ACT required. SAT 25/75 percentile: 900-1090. High school rank: N/A
**Early decision deadline:** N/A, notification date: N/A
**Early action deadline:** N/A, notification date: N/A
**Application deadline (fall):** rolling
**Undergraduate student body:** 3,438 full time, 801 part time; 45% male, 55% female; 0% American Indian, 2% Asian, 6% black, 9% Hispanic, 2% multiracial,

0% Pacific Islander, 77% white, 0% international; 92% from in state; 41% live on campus; 1% of students in fraternities, 3% in sororities
**Most popular majors:** 14% Business, Management, Marketing, and Related Support Services, 9% Education, 8% Health Professions and Related Programs, 10% Multi/Interdisciplinary Studies, 15% Visual and Performing Arts
**Expenses:** 2014-2015: $9,260 in state, $15,340 out of state; room/board: $8,912
**Financial aid:** (978) 665-3156; 67% of undergrads determined to have financial need; average aid package $9,970

## Framingham State University
Framingham MA
(508) 626-4500
**U.S. News ranking:** Reg. U. (N), second tier
**Website:** www.framingham.edu
**Admissions email:** admissions@framingham.edu
**Public;** founded 1839
**Freshman admissions:** selective; 2013-2014: 5,400 applied, 3,020 accepted. Either SAT or ACT required. SAT 25/75 percentile: 930-1100. High school rank: 8% in top tenth, 28% in top quarter, 71% in top half
**Early decision deadline:** N/A, notification date: N/A
**Early action deadline:** 11/15, notification date: 12/15
**Application deadline (fall):** rolling
**Undergraduate student body:** 3,884 full time, 700 part time; 36% male, 64% female; 0% American Indian, 2% Asian, 7% black, 9% Hispanic, 3% multiracial, 0% Pacific Islander, 76% white, 0% international; 96% from in state; 52% live on campus; 0% of students in fraternities, 0% in sororities
**Most popular majors:** 15% Business, Management, Marketing, and Related Support Services, 8% Communications Technologies/Technicians and Support Services, 14% Family and Consumer Sciences/Human Sciences, 10% Psychology, 14% Social Sciences
**Expenses:** 2013-2014: $8,080 in state, $14,160 out of state; room/board: $10,074
**Financial aid:** (508) 626-4534

## Franklin W. Olin College of Engineering
Needham MA
(781) 292-2222
**U.S. News ranking:** Engineering, unranked
**Website:** www.olin.edu/
**Admissions email:** info@olin.edu
**Private;** founded 1997
**Freshman admissions:** most selective; 2013-2014: 782 applied, 131 accepted. Either SAT or ACT required. SAT 25/75 percentile: 1428-1550. High school rank: N/A
**Early decision deadline:** N/A, notification date: N/A
**Early action deadline:** N/A, notification date: N/A
**Application deadline (fall):** 1/1

**Undergraduate student body:** 355 full time, 0 part time; 50% male, 50% female; 0% American Indian, 17% Asian, 1% black, 4% Hispanic, 6% multiracial, 0% Pacific Islander, 53% white, 7% international; 15% from in state; 100% live on campus; 0% of students in fraternities, 0% in sororities
**Most popular majors:** 20% Electrical and Electronics Engineering, 36% Engineering, General, 20% Mechanical Engineering
**Expenses:** 2014-2015: $44,025; room/board: $15,200
**Financial aid:** N/A; 52% of undergrads determined to have financial need; average aid package $37,674

## Gordon College
Wenham MA
(866) 464-6736
**U.S. News ranking:** Nat. Lib. Arts, No. 139
**Website:** www.gordon.edu
**Admissions email:** admissions@gordon.edu
**Private;** founded 1889
**Affiliation:** multi-denominational
**Freshman admissions:** selective; 2013-2014: 3,843 applied, 1,657 accepted. Either SAT or ACT required. SAT 25/75 percentile: 1015-1292. High school rank: 34% in top tenth, 55% in top quarter, 85% in top half
**Early decision deadline:** 11/1, notification date: 12/1
**Early action deadline:** 11/15, notification date: 12/1
**Application deadline (fall):** 8/15
**Undergraduate student body:** 1,669 full time, 38 part time; 38% male, 62% female; 0% American Indian, 3% Asian, 3% black, 7% Hispanic, 3% multiracial, 0% Pacific Islander, 78% white, 5% international; 35% from in state; 89% live on campus; 0% of students in fraternities, 0% in sororities
**Most popular majors:** 8% Biology/Biological Sciences, General, 6% Business Administration and Management, General, 7% English Language and Literature, General, 10% Psychology, General, 8% Speech Communication and Rhetoric
**Expenses:** 2014-2015: $34,390; room/board: $9,930
**Financial aid:** (978) 867-4246; 72% of undergrads determined to have financial need; average aid package $20,999

## Hampshire College
Amherst MA
(413) 559-5471
**U.S. News ranking:** Nat. Lib. Arts, unranked
**Website:** www.hampshire.edu
**Admissions email:** admissions@hampshire.edu
**Private;** founded 1965
**Freshman admissions:** N/A; 2013-2014: 2,827 applied, 1,990 accepted. Neither SAT nor ACT required. ACT 25/75 percentile: N/A. High school rank: N/A
**Early decision deadline:** 11/15, notification date: 12/15
**Early action deadline:** 12/1, notification date: 2/15
**Application deadline (fall):** 1/15

**Undergraduate student body:** 1,492 full time, N/A part time; 43% male, 57% female; 0% American Indian, 2% Asian, 2% black, 9% Hispanic, 5% multiracial, 0% Pacific Islander, 67% white, 6% international
**Most popular majors:** Information not available
**Expenses:** 2013-2014: $46,625; room/board: $12,030
**Financial aid:** (413) 559-5484

## Harvard University
Cambridge MA
(617) 495-1551
**U.S. News ranking:** Nat. U., No. 2
**Website:** www.college.harvard.edu
**Admissions email:** college@fas.harvard.edu
**Private;** founded 1636
**Freshman admissions:** most selective; 2013-2014: 35,023 applied, 2,047 accepted. Either SAT or ACT required. SAT 25/75 percentile: 1410-1600. High school rank: 95% in top tenth, 99% in top quarter, 100% in top half
**Early decision deadline:** N/A, notification date: N/A
**Early action deadline:** 11/1, notification date: 12/16
**Application deadline (fall):** 1/1
**Undergraduate student body:** 6,710 full time, 12 part time; 52% male, 48% female; 0% American Indian, 19% Asian, 7% black, 9% Hispanic, 6% multiracial, 0% Pacific Islander, 45% white, 11% international; 16% from in state; 99% live on campus; N/A of students in fraternities, N/A in sororities
**Most popular majors:** 15% Biology/Biological Sciences, General, 9% History, General, 7% Mathematics, General, 6% Psychology, General, 33% Social Sciences, General
**Expenses:** 2014-2015: $43,938; room/board: $14,669
**Financial aid:** (617) 495-1581; 58% of undergrads determined to have financial need; average aid package $47,759

## Lasell College
Newton MA
(617) 243-2225
**U.S. News ranking:** Reg. Coll. (N), No. 27
**Website:** www.lasell.edu?ctschool=lasell&cttype=referral&ctsource=usnmain
**Admissions email:** info@lasell.edu
**Private;** founded 1851
**Freshman admissions:** less selective; 2013-2014: 3,584 applied, 2,729 accepted. Either SAT or ACT required. SAT 25/75 percentile: 880-1070. High school rank: N/A
**Early decision deadline:** N/A, notification date: N/A
**Early action deadline:** 11/15, notification date: 12/15
**Application deadline (fall):** rolling
**Undergraduate student body:** 1,649 full time, 38 part time; 36% male, 64% female; 0% American Indian, 2% Asian, 7% black, 9% Hispanic, 3% multiracial, 0% Pacific Islander, 71% white, 3% international; 56% from in state; 77% live on campus; 0% of students in fraternities, 0% in sororities

**Most popular majors:** 11% Communication and Media Studies, 14% Fashion Merchandising, 8% Fashion/Apparel Design, 6% Psychology, General, 7% Sport and Fitness Administration/Management
**Expenses:** 2014-2015: $31,000; room/board: $12,750
**Financial aid:** (617) 243-2227; 81% of undergrads determined to have financial need; average aid package $25,070

## Lesley University
Cambridge MA
(617) 349-8800
**U.S. News ranking:** Reg. U. (N), No. 111
**Website:** www.lesley.edu
**Admissions email:** lcadmissions@lesley.edu
**Private;** founded 1909
**Freshman admissions:** selective; 2013-2014: N/A applied, N/A accepted. Either SAT or ACT required. SAT 25/75 percentile: 970-1180. High school rank: N/A
**Early decision deadline:** N/A, notification date: N/A
**Early action deadline:** 12/1, notification date: 12/31
**Application deadline (fall):** rolling
**Undergraduate student body:** N/A full time, N/A part time; N/A male, N/A female; N/A American Indian, N/A Asian, N/A black, N/A Hispanic, N/A multiracial, N/A Pacific Islander, N/A white, N/A international
**Most popular majors:** 8% Business, Management, Marketing, and Related Support Services, 14% Education, 10% English Language and Literature/Letters, 23% Psychology, 24% Visual and Performing Arts
**Expenses:** 2014-2015: $24,560; room/board: $15,000
**Financial aid:** (617) 349-8581; 71% of undergrads determined to have financial need; average aid package $20,133

## Massachusetts College of Art and Design
Boston MA
(617) 879-7222
**U.S. News ranking:** Arts, unranked
**Website:** www.massart.edu
**Admissions email:** admissions@massart.edu
**Public;** founded 1873
**Freshman admissions:** N/A; 2013-2014: 1,403 applied, 980 accepted. Either SAT or ACT required. SAT 25/75 percentile: N/A. High school rank: N/A
**Early decision deadline:** N/A, notification date: N/A
**Early action deadline:** 12/1, notification date: 1/5
**Application deadline (fall):** 2/1
**Undergraduate student body:** 1,677 full time, 443 part time; 30% male, 70% female; 0% American Indian, 6% Asian, 3% black, 7% Hispanic, 2% multiracial, 0% Pacific Islander, 69% white, 2% international; 69% from in state; 38% live on campus; N/A of students in fraternities, N/A in sororities
**Most popular majors:** Information not available
**Expenses:** 2014-2015: $11,225 in state, $29,925 out of state; room/board: $13,000

**Financial aid:** (617) 879-7850; 62% of undergrads determined to have financial need; average aid package $10,452

## Massachusetts College of Liberal Arts
North Adams MA
(413) 662-5410
**U.S. News ranking:** Nat. Lib. Arts, No. 165
**Website:** www.mcla.edu
**Admissions email:** admissions@mcla.edu
**Public;** founded 1894
**Freshman admissions:** selective; 2013-2014: 1,786 applied, 1,200 accepted. Either SAT or ACT required. SAT 25/75 percentile: 910-1150. High school rank: 25% in top tenth, 58% in top quarter, 83% in top half
**Early decision deadline:** N/A, notification date: N/A
**Early action deadline:** 12/1, notification date: 12/15
**Application deadline (fall):** rolling
**Undergraduate student body:** 1,353 full time, 185 part time; 40% male, 60% female; 0% American Indian, 1% Asian, 10% black, 7% Hispanic, 2% multiracial, 0% Pacific Islander, 76% white, 0% international; 76% from in state; 67% live on campus; N/A of students in fraternities, N/A in sororities
**Most popular majors:** 18% Business, Management, Marketing, and Related Support Services, 14% English Language and Literature/Letters, 10% Multi/Interdisciplinary Studies, 9% Psychology, 16% Social Sciences
**Expenses:** 2014-2015: $8,975 in state, $17,920 out of state; room/board: $9,638
**Financial aid:** (413) 662-5219; 76% of undergrads determined to have financial need; average aid package $14,468

## Massachusetts Institute of Technology
Cambridge MA
(617) 253-3400
**U.S. News ranking:** Nat. U., No. 7
**Website:** web.mit.edu/
**Admissions email:** admissions@mit.edu
**Private;** founded 1861
**Freshman admissions:** most selective; 2013-2014: 18,989 applied, 1,548 accepted. Either SAT or ACT required. SAT 25/75 percentile: 1430-1570. High school rank: 99% in top tenth, 100% in top quarter, 100% in top half
**Early decision deadline:** N/A, notification date: N/A
**Early action deadline:** 11/1, notification date: 12/20
**Application deadline (fall):** 1/1
**Undergraduate student body:** 4,499 full time, 29 part time; 55% male, 45% female; 0% American Indian, 24% Asian, 5% black, 16% Hispanic, 5% multiracial, 0% Pacific Islander, 37% white, 10% international; 9% from in state; 88% live on campus; 49% of students in fraternities, 32% in sororities

**Most popular majors:** 9% Biological and Biomedical Sciences, 18% Computer Science, 44% Engineering, 6% Mathematics, General, 10% Physical Sciences **Expenses:** 2014-2015: $45,016; room/board: $13,224 **Financial aid:** (617) 253-4971; 58% of undergrads determined to have financial need; average aid package $41,325

## Massachusetts Maritime Academy

Buzzards Bay MA
(800) 544-3411
**U.S. News ranking:** Reg. Coll. (N), No. 7
**Website:** www.maritime.edu
**Admissions email:** admissions@maritime.edu
**Public;** founded 1891
**Freshman admissions:** selective; 2013-2014: 957 applied, 561 accepted. Either SAT or ACT required. SAT 25/75 percentile: 980-1170. High school rank: N/A
**Early decision deadline:** N/A, notification date: N/A
**Early action deadline:** 11/1, notification date: 12/15
**Application deadline (fall):** rolling
**Undergraduate student body:** 1,333 full time, 43 part time; 88% male, 12% female; 2% American Indian, 3% Asian, 2% black, 1% Hispanic, 0% multiracial, 0% Pacific Islander, 90% white, 1% international; 75% from in state; 95% live on campus; 0% of students in fraternities, 0% in sororities
**Most popular majors:** 10% Environmental Science, 11% Homeland Security, Law Enforcement, Firefighting and Related Protective Services, Other, 16% Marine Science/Merchant Marine Officer, 46% Naval Architecture and Marine Engineering
**Expenses:** 2014-2015: $7,203 in state, $22,109 out of state; room/board: $11,120
**Financial aid:** (508) 830-5087; 56% of undergrads determined to have financial need; average aid package $13,343

## Merrimack College

North Andover MA
(978) 837-5100
**U.S. News ranking:** Reg. Coll. (N), No. 9
**Website:** www.merrimack.edu
**Admissions email:** Admission@Merrimack.edu
**Private;** founded 1947
**Affiliation:** Roman Catholic
**Freshman admissions:** selective; 2013-2014: 6,314 applied, 4,963 accepted. Neither SAT nor ACT required. SAT 25/75 percentile: 920-1130. High school rank: 11% in top tenth, 34% in top quarter, 69% in top half
**Early decision deadline:** 11/15, notification date: 12/1
**Early action deadline:** 11/15, notification date: 12/1
**Application deadline (fall):** 2/15
**Undergraduate student body:** 2,604 full time, 148 part time; 51% male, 49% female; 0% American Indian, 2% Asian, 3% black, 6% Hispanic, 1% multiracial, 0% Pacific Islander, 67% white, 6% international; 73% from in

state; 72% live on campus; 1% of students in fraternities, 4% in sororities
**Most popular majors:** 32% Business, Management, Marketing, and Related Support Services, 6% Communication, Journalism, and Related Programs, 9% Health Professions and Related Programs, 6% Homeland Security, Law Enforcement, Firefighting and Related Protective Services, 8% Social Sciences
**Expenses:** 2014-2015: $36,215; room/board: $13,255
**Financial aid:** (978) 837-5196; 71% of undergrads determined to have financial need; average aid package $21,798

## Montserrat College of Art[1]

Beverly MA
(978) 921-4242
**U.S. News ranking:** Arts, unranked
**Website:** www.montserrat.edu
**Admissions email:** admissions@montserrrat.edu
**Private**
**Application deadline (fall):** N/A
**Undergraduate student body:** N/A full time, N/A part time
**Expenses:** 2013-2014: $27,770; room/board: N/A
**Financial aid:** (978) 921-4242

## Mount Holyoke College

South Hadley MA
(413) 538-2023
**U.S. News ranking:** Nat. Lib. Arts, No. 41
**Website:** www.mtholyoke.edu
**Admissions email:** admission@mtholyoke.edu
**Private;** founded 1837
**Freshman admissions:** more selective; 2013-2014: 3,732 applied, 1,747 accepted. Neither SAT nor ACT required. SAT 25/75 percentile: 1220-1430. High school rank: 57% in top tenth, 84% in top quarter, 97% in top half
**Early decision deadline:** 11/15, notification date: 1/1
**Early action deadline:** N/A, notification date: N/A
**Application deadline (fall):** 1/15
**Undergraduate student body:** 2,151 full time, 32 part time; 0% male, 100% female; 0% American Indian, 9% Asian, 6% black, 8% Hispanic, 3% multiracial, 0% Pacific Islander, 47% white, 25% international; 23% from in state; 95% live on campus; 0% of students in fraternities, 0% in sororities
**Most popular majors:** 9% Biology/Biological Sciences, General, 7% Economics, General, 10% English Language and Literature, General, 7% International Relations and Affairs, 10% Psychology, General
**Expenses:** 2014-2015: $42,656; room/board: $12,490
**Financial aid:** (413) 538-2291; 68% of undergrads determined to have financial need; average aid package $35,454

## Mount Ida College

Newton MA
(617) 928-4535
**U.S. News ranking:** Reg. Coll. (N), No. 40
**Website:** www.mountida.edu

**Admissions email:** admissions@mountida.edu
**Private;** founded 1899
**Freshman admissions:** least selective; 2013-2014: 1,770 applied, 1,201 accepted. Either SAT or ACT required. SAT 25/75 percentile: 790-980. High school rank: N/A
**Early decision deadline:** N/A, notification date: N/A
**Early action deadline:** N/A, notification date: N/A
**Application deadline (fall):** rolling
**Undergraduate student body:** 1,167 full time, 101 part time; 34% male, 66% female; 0% American Indian, 2% Asian, 12% black, 11% Hispanic, 3% multiracial, 0% Pacific Islander, 59% white, 5% international; 37% from in state; 60% live on campus; 0% of students in fraternities, 0% in sororities
**Most popular majors:** 12% Business Administration and Management, General, 12% Dental Hygiene/Hygienist, 7% Fashion Merchandising, 7% Funeral Service and Mortuary Science, General, 18% Veterinary/Animal Health Technology/Technician and Veterinary Assistant
**Expenses:** 2014-2015: $30,447; room/board: $12,500
**Financial aid:** (617) 928-4785; 82% of undergrads determined to have financial need; average aid package $19,475

## National Graduate School of Quality Management[1]

Falmouth MA
(800) 838-2580
**U.S. News ranking:** Business, unranked
**Website:** www.ngs.edu
**Admissions email:** N/A
**Private**
**Application deadline (fall):** N/A
**Undergraduate student body:** N/A full time, N/A part time
**Expenses:** N/A
**Financial aid:** (800) 838-2580

## Newbury College[1]

Brookline MA
(617) 730-7007
**U.S. News ranking:** Reg. Coll. (N), unranked
**Website:** www.newbury.edu/
**Admissions email:** info@newbury.edu
**Private**
**Application deadline (fall):** N/A
**Undergraduate student body:** N/A full time, N/A part time
**Expenses:** 2014-2015: $29,930; room/board: $13,340
**Financial aid:** (617) 730-7100; 91% of undergrads determined to have financial need; average aid package $12,503

## New England Conservatory of Music

Boston MA
(617) 585-1101
**U.S. News ranking:** Arts, unranked
**Website:** www.newenglandconservatory.edu
**Admissions email:** admission@newenglandconservatory.edu
**Private;** founded 1867

**Freshman admissions:** N/A; 2013-2014: 1,253 applied, 348 accepted. Neither SAT nor ACT required. SAT 25/75 percentile: N/A. High school rank: N/A
**Early decision deadline:** N/A, notification date: N/A
**Early action deadline:** N/A, notification date: N/A
**Application deadline (fall):** 12/1
**Undergraduate student body:** 396 full time, 35 part time; 59% male, 41% female; 0% American Indian, 12% Asian, 5% black, 2% Hispanic, 4% multiracial, 0% Pacific Islander, 45% white, 29% international
**Most popular majors:** Information not available
**Expenses:** 2014-2015: $41,405; room/board: $12,850
**Financial aid:** (617) 585-1110; 48% of undergrads determined to have financial need; average aid package $23,718

## New England Institute of Art[1]

Brookline MA
(800) 903-4425
**U.S. News ranking:** Arts, unranked
**Website:** www.artinstitutes.edu/boston/
**Admissions email:** N/A
**For-profit**
**Application deadline (fall):** N/A
**Undergraduate student body:** N/A full time, N/A part time
**Expenses:** 2013-2014: $18,760; room/board: $15,252
**Financial aid:** N/A

## Nichols College

Dudley MA
(800) 470-3379
**U.S. News ranking:** Reg. Coll. (N), No. 40
**Website:** www.nichols.edu/
**Admissions email:** admissions@nichols.edu
**Private;** founded 1815
**Freshman admissions:** less selective; 2013-2014: 2,344 applied, 1,919 accepted. Neither SAT nor ACT required. SAT 25/75 percentile: 840-1030. High school rank: 9% in top tenth, 16% in top quarter, 48% in top half
**Early decision deadline:** N/A, notification date: N/A
**Early action deadline:** 12/1, notification date: N/A
**Application deadline (fall):** rolling
**Undergraduate student body:** 1,100 full time, 181 part time; 59% male, 41% female; 0% American Indian, 1% Asian, 6% black, 7% Hispanic, 3% multiracial, 0% Pacific Islander, 82% white, 1% international; 62% from in state; 80% live on campus; 0% of students in fraternities, 0% in sororities
**Most popular majors:** 12% Accounting, 8% Business Administration and Management, General, 33% Business/Commerce, General, 8% Criminal Justice/Law Enforcement Administration, 12% Sport and Fitness Administration/Management
**Expenses:** 2014-2015: $32,370; room/board: $12,235
**Financial aid:** (508) 213-2278; 86% of undergrads determined to have financial need; average aid package $25,024

## Northeastern University

Boston MA
(617) 373-2200
**U.S. News ranking:** Nat. U., No. 42
**Website:** www.northeastern.edu/
**Admissions email:** admissions@neu.edu
**Private;** founded 1898
**Freshman admissions:** most selective; 2013-2014: 47,364 applied, 15,301 accepted. Either SAT or ACT required. SAT 25/75 percentile: 1300-1480. High school rank: 64% in top tenth, 91% in top quarter, 98% in top half
**Early decision deadline:** 11/1, notification date: 12/15
**Early action deadline:** 11/1, notification date: 12/31
**Application deadline (fall):** 1/1
**Undergraduate student body:** 13,204 full time, N/A part time; 49% male, 51% female; 0% American Indian, 10% Asian, 3% black, 7% Hispanic, 4% multiracial, 0% Pacific Islander, 50% white, 18% international; 33% from in state; N/A live on campus; 8% of students in fraternities, 12% in sororities
**Most popular majors:** 21% Business, Management, Marketing, and Related Support Services, 8% Communication, Journalism, and Related Programs, 12% Engineering, 13% Health Professions and Related Programs, 11% Social Sciences
**Expenses:** 2014-2015: $43,440; room/board: $14,570
**Financial aid:** (617) 373-3190; 39% of undergrads determined to have financial need; average aid package $24,099

## Pine Manor College

Chestnut Hill MA
(617) 731-7104
**U.S. News ranking:** Nat. Lib. Arts, second tier
**Website:** www.pmc.edu
**Admissions email:** admission@pmc.edu
**Private;** founded 1911
**Freshman admissions:** least selective; 2013-2014: 535 applied, 343 accepted. Either SAT or ACT required. SAT 25/75 percentile: 660-860. High school rank: N/A
**Early decision deadline:** N/A, notification date: N/A
**Early action deadline:** N/A, notification date: N/A
**Application deadline (fall):** rolling
**Undergraduate student body:** 305 full time, 8 part time; 15% male, 85% female; 0% American Indian, 5% Asian, 20% black, 15% Hispanic, 12% multiracial, 0% Pacific Islander, 8% white, 29% international
**Most popular majors:** 22% Biology/Biological Sciences, General, 6% Communication and Media Studies, 17% Management Science, 20% Psychology, General, 18% Social Sciences, General
**Expenses:** 2014-2015: $26,180; room/board: $12,820
**Financial aid:** (617) 731-7129; 64% of undergrads determined to have financial need; average aid package $24,014

## Salem State University

Salem MA
(978) 542-6200
**U.S. News ranking:** Reg. U. (N), second tier
**Website:** www.salemstate.edu
**Admissions email:** admissions@ salemstate.edu
**Public;** founded 1854
**Freshman admissions:** less selective; 2013-2014: 5,216 applied, 3,739 accepted. Either SAT or ACT required. SAT 25/75 percentile: 890-1080. High school rank: N/A
**Early decision deadline:** N/A, notification date: N/A
**Early action deadline:** 11/15, notification date: 12/1
**Application deadline (fall):** rolling
**Undergraduate student body:** 5,834 full time, 1,830 part time; 39% male, 61% female; 0% American Indian, 3% Asian, 8% black, 11% Hispanic, 2% multiracial, 0% Pacific Islander, 70% white, 3% international; 97% from in state; 28% live on campus; N/A of students in fraternities, N/A in sororities
**Most popular majors:** 22% Business, Management, Marketing, and Related Support Services, 9% Education, 13% Health Professions and Related Programs, 9% Homeland Security, Law Enforcement, Firefighting and Related Protective Services, 8% Psychology
**Expenses:** 2013-2014: $8,130 in state, $14,270 out of state; room/board: $11,304
**Financial aid:** (978) 542-6139

## Simmons College

Boston MA
(800) 345-8468
**U.S. News ranking:** Reg. U. (N), No. 16
**Website:** www.simmons.edu
**Admissions email:** ugadm@ simmons.edu
**Private;** founded 1899
**Freshman admissions:** selective; 2013-2014: 4,239 applied, 2,076 accepted. Either SAT or ACT required. SAT 25/75 percentile: 1040-1250. High school rank: 26% in top tenth, 61% in top quarter, 90% in top half
**Early decision deadline:** N/A, notification date: N/A
**Early action deadline:** 11/1, notification date: 12/15
**Application deadline (fall):** 2/1
**Undergraduate student body:** 1,577 full time, 155 part time; 0% male, 100% female; 0% American Indian, 9% Asian, 6% black, 6% Hispanic, 3% multiracial, 0% Pacific Islander, 68% white, 3% international; 63% from in state; 58% live on campus; N/A of students in fraternities, 0% in sororities
**Most popular majors:** 9% Business, Management, Marketing, and Related Support Services, 8% Communication, Journalism, and Related Programs, 37% Health Services/Allied Health/Health Sciences, General, 9% Psychology, 9% Social Sciences, General
**Expenses:** 2014-2015: $36,230; room/board: $13,736

**Financial aid:** (617) 521-2001; 77% of undergrads determined to have financial need; average aid package $26,527

## Smith College

Northampton MA
(413) 585-2500
**U.S. News ranking:** Nat. Lib. Arts, No. 19
**Website:** www.smith.edu
**Admissions email:** admission@ smith.edu
**Private;** founded 1871
**Freshman admissions:** more selective; 2013-2014: 4,403 applied, 1,897 accepted. Neither SAT nor ACT required. SAT 25/75 percentile: 1220-1450. High school rank: 62% in top tenth, 89% in top quarter, 99% in top half
**Early decision deadline:** 11/15, notification date: 12/15
**Early action deadline:** N/A, notification date: N/A
**Application deadline (fall):** 1/15
**Undergraduate student body:** 2,585 full time, 21 part time; 0% male, 100% female; 0% American Indian, 13% Asian, 5% black, 10% Hispanic, 5% multiracial, 0% Pacific Islander, 46% white, 13% international; 23% from in state; 95% live on campus; 0% of students in fraternities, 0% in sororities
**Most popular majors:** 9% Area, Ethnic, Cultural, Gender, and Group Studies, 10% Foreign Languages, Literatures, and Linguistics, 10% Psychology, 23% Social Sciences, 10% Visual and Performing Arts
**Expenses:** 2014-2015: $44,724; room/board: $14,950
**Financial aid:** (413) 585-2530; 63% of undergrads determined to have financial need; average aid package $39,958

## Springfield College

Springfield MA
(413) 748-3136
**U.S. News ranking:** Reg. U. (N), No. 31
**Website:** www.springfieldcollege.edu
**Admissions email:** admissions@ springfiledcollege.edu
**Private;** founded 1885
**Freshman admissions:** selective; 2013-2014: 2,231 applied, 1,560 accepted. Either SAT or ACT required. SAT 25/75 percentile: 920-1130. High school rank: 13% in top tenth, 35% in top quarter, 69% in top half
**Early decision deadline:** 12/1, notification date: 2/1
**Early action deadline:** N/A, notification date: N/A
**Application deadline (fall):** 4/1
**Undergraduate student body:** 2,142 full time, 62 part time; 52% male, 48% female; 1% American Indian, 1% Asian, 5% black, 5% Hispanic, 1% multiracial, 0% Pacific Islander, 82% white, 1% international; 40% from in state; 85% live on campus; N/A of students in fraternities, N/A in sororities
**Most popular majors:** 6% Business, Management, Marketing, and Related Support Services, 9% Education, 33% Health Professions and Related Programs, 6% Homeland Security, Law

Enforcement, Firefighting and Related Protective Services, 23% Parks, Recreation, Leisure, and Fitness Studies
**Expenses:** 2014-2015: $33,455; room/board: $11,210
**Financial aid:** (413) 748-3108; 83% of undergrads determined to have financial need; average aid package $23,220

## Stonehill College

Easton MA
(508) 565-1373
**U.S. News ranking:** Nat. Lib. Arts, No. 105
**Website:** www.stonehill.edu
**Admissions email:** admission@ stonehill.edu
**Private;** founded 1948
**Affiliation:** Roman Catholic
**Freshman admissions:** more selective; 2013-2014: 6,547 applied, 4,643 accepted. Neither SAT nor ACT required. SAT 25/75 percentile: 1030-1230. High school rank: 31% in top tenth, 69% in top quarter, 95% in top half
**Early decision deadline:** 12/1, notification date: 12/31
**Early action deadline:** 11/1, notification date: 12/31
**Application deadline (fall):** 1/15
**Undergraduate student body:** 2,458 full time, 23 part time; 38% male, 62% female; 0% American Indian, 2% Asian, 3% black, 4% Hispanic, 2% multiracial, 0% Pacific Islander, 85% white, 1% international; 55% from in state; 90% live on campus; N/A of students in fraternities, N/A in sororities
**Most popular majors:** 10% Biological and Biomedical Sciences, 19% Business, Management, Marketing, and Related Support Services, 7% Communication, Journalism, and Related Programs, 11% Psychology, 19% Social Sciences
**Expenses:** 2014-2015: $37,426; room/board: $14,290
**Financial aid:** (508) 565-1088; 59% of undergrads determined to have financial need; average aid package $27,915

## Suffolk University

Boston MA
(617) 573-8460
**U.S. News ranking:** Reg. U. (N), No. 60
**Website:** www.suffolk.edu
**Admissions email:** admission@ suffolk.edu
**Private;** founded 1906
**Freshman admissions:** selective; 2013-2014: 9,275 applied, 7,652 accepted. Either SAT or ACT required. SAT 25/75 percentile: 890-1130. High school rank: 13% in top tenth, 42% in top quarter, 79% in top half
**Early decision deadline:** N/A, notification date: N/A
**Early action deadline:** 11/15, notification date: 11/20
**Application deadline (fall):** 2/15
**Undergraduate student body:** 5,356 full time, 423 part time; 45% male, 55% female; 0% American Indian, 7% Asian, 5% black, 11% Hispanic, 1% multiracial, 0% Pacific Islander, 41% white, 19% international; 69% from in state; 21% live on campus; N/A of students in fraternities, N/A in sororities

**Most popular majors:** 39% Business, Management, Marketing, and Related Support Services, 16% Communication, Journalism, and Related Programs, 6% Psychology, 15% Social Sciences, 6% Visual and Performing Arts
**Expenses:** 2014-2015: $32,660; room/board: $14,638
**Financial aid:** (617) 573-8470; 64% of undergrads determined to have financial need; average aid package $23,254

## Tufts University

Medford MA
(617) 627-3170
**U.S. News ranking:** Nat. U., No. 27
**Website:** www.tufts.edu
**Admissions email:** admissions. inquiry@ase.tufts.edu
**Private;** founded 1852
**Freshman admissions:** most selective; 2013-2014: 18,406 applied, 3,469 accepted. Either SAT or ACT required. SAT 25/75 percentile: 1370-1520. High school rank: 91% in top tenth, 99% in top quarter, 100% in top half
**Early decision deadline:** 11/1, notification date: 12/15
**Early action deadline:** N/A, notification date: N/A
**Application deadline (fall):** 1/1
**Undergraduate student body:** 5,138 full time, 42 part time; 49% male, 51% female; 0% American Indian, 11% Asian, 4% black, 6% Hispanic, 4% multiracial, 0% Pacific Islander, 56% white, 8% international; 23% from in state; 63% live on campus; 14% of students in fraternities, 19% in sororities
**Most popular majors:** 7% Art/Art Studies, General, 6% Biology/Biological Sciences, General, 9% Economics, General, 6% English Language and Literature, General, 15% International Relations and Affairs
**Expenses:** 2014-2015: $48,643; room/board: $12,634
**Financial aid:** (617) 627-2000; 39% of undergrads determined to have financial need; average aid package $38,008

## University of Massachusetts–Amherst

Amherst MA
(413) 545-0222
**U.S. News ranking:** Nat. U., No. 76
**Website:** www.umass.edu
**Admissions email:** mail@ admissions.umass.edu
**Public;** founded 1863
**Freshman admissions:** more selective; 2013-2014: 35,868 applied, 22,556 accepted. Either SAT or ACT required. SAT 25/75 percentile: 1110-1310. High school rank: 28% in top tenth, 69% in top quarter, 97% in top half
**Early decision deadline:** N/A, notification date: N/A
**Early action deadline:** 11/1, notification date: 12/31
**Application deadline (fall):** 1/15
**Undergraduate student body:** 20,505 full time, 1,629 part time; 51% male, 49% female; 0% American Indian, 8% Asian, 4% black, 5% Hispanic, 2%

multiracial, 0% Pacific Islander, 67% white, 2% international; 78% from in state; 64% live on campus; 7% of students in fraternities, 6% in sororities
**Most popular majors:** 4% Accounting, 4% Biology/Biological Sciences, General, 3% Political Science and Government, General, 8% Psychology, General, 5% Speech Communication and Rhetoric
**Expenses:** 2014-2015: $13,258 in state, $28,813 out of state; room/board: $11,457
**Financial aid:** (413) 545-0801; 60% of undergrads determined to have financial need; average aid package $15,543

## University of Massachusetts–Boston

Boston MA
(617) 287-6000
**U.S. News ranking:** Nat. U., second tier
**Website:** www.umb.edu
**Admissions email:** enrollment.info@umb.edu
**Public;** founded 1964
**Freshman admissions:** selective; 2013-2014: 8,170 applied, 5,709 accepted. SAT required. SAT 25/75 percentile: 950-1160. High school rank: N/A
**Early decision deadline:** N/A, notification date: N/A
**Early action deadline:** N/A, notification date: N/A
**Application deadline (fall):** rolling
**Undergraduate student body:** 8,759 full time, 3,607 part time; 44% male, 56% female; 0% American Indian, 12% Asian, 16% black, 12% Hispanic, 2% multiracial, 0% Pacific Islander, 42% white, 10% international; 95% from in state; N/A live on campus; N/A of students in fraternities, N/A in sororities
**Most popular majors:** 7% Biological and Biomedical Sciences, 20% Business, Management, Marketing, and Related Support Services, 18% Health Professions and Related Programs, 12% Psychology, 12% Social Sciences
**Expenses:** 2014-2015: $13,680 in state, $22,218 out of state; room/board: N/A
**Financial aid:** (617) 287-6300; 68% of undergrads determined to have financial need; average aid package $15,265

## University of Massachusetts–Dartmouth

North Dartmouth MA
(508) 999-8605
**U.S. News ranking:** Reg. U. (N), No. 87
**Website:** www.umassd.edu
**Admissions email:** admissions@ umassd.edu
**Public;** founded 1895
**Freshman admissions:** selective; 2013-2014: 8,119 applied, 6,094 accepted. Either SAT or ACT required. SAT 25/75 percentile: 980-1180. High school rank: 21% in top tenth, 46% in top quarter, 80% in top half
**Early decision deadline:** N/A, notification date: N/A
**Early action deadline:** 11/15, notification date: 12/15
**Application deadline (fall):** rolling

**Undergraduate student body:** 6,373 full time, 1,064 part time; 52% male, 48% female; 0% American Indian, 3% Asian, 12% black, 7% Hispanic, 4% multiracial, 0% Pacific Islander, 69% white, 1% international; 95% from in state; 56% live on campus; 1% of students in fraternities, 1% in sororities
**Most popular majors:** 30% Business, Management, Marketing, and Related Support Services, 10% Engineering, 14% Health Professions and Related Programs, 10% Social Sciences, 8% Visual and Performing Arts
**Expenses:** 2014-2015: $11,681 in state, $18,363 out of state; room/board: $11,069
**Financial aid:** (508) 999-8632; 72% of undergrads determined to have financial need; average aid package $16,048

## University of Massachusetts–Lowell
Lowell MA
(978) 934-3931
**U.S. News ranking:** Nat. U., No. 156
**Website:** www.uml.edu
**Admissions email:** admissions@uml.edu
**Public;** founded 1894
**Freshman admissions:** selective; 2013-2014: 9,110 applied, 5,824 accepted. Either SAT or ACT required. SAT 25/75 percentile: 1030-1230. High school rank: 22% in top tenth, 51% in top quarter, 85% in top half
**Early decision deadline:** N/A, notification date: N/A
**Early action deadline:** 11/15, notification date: 12/20
**Application deadline (fall):** 2/15
**Undergraduate student body:** 9,034 full time, 3,700 part time; 61% male, 39% female; 0% American Indian, 9% Asian, 6% black, 9% Hispanic, 2% multiracial, 0% Pacific Islander, 66% white, 2% international; 91% from in state; 36% live on campus; N/A of students in fraternities, N/A in sororities
**Most popular majors:** 17% Business, Management, Marketing, and Related Support Services, 10% Computer and Information Sciences and Support Services, 14% Engineering, 11% Health Professions and Related Programs, 12% Homeland Security, Law Enforcement, Firefighting and Related Protective Services
**Expenses:** 2014-2015: $12,447 in state, $19,560 out of state; room/board: $11,278
**Financial aid:** (978) 934-4226; 63% of undergrads determined to have financial need; average aid package $14,730

## Wellesley College
Wellesley MA
(781) 283-2270
**U.S. News ranking:** Nat. Lib. Arts, No. 4
**Website:** www.wellesley.edu
**Admissions email:** admission@wellesley.edu
**Private;** founded 1870

**Freshman admissions:** most selective; 2013-2014: 4,765 applied, 1,387 accepted. Either SAT or ACT required. SAT 25/75 percentile: 1310-1510. High school rank: 83% in top tenth, 99% in top quarter, 100% in top half
**Early decision deadline:** 11/1, notification date: 12/15
**Early action deadline:** N/A, notification date: N/A
**Application deadline (fall):** 1/15
**Undergraduate student body:** 2,344 full time, 130 part time; 2% male, 98% female; 0% American Indian, 23% Asian, 6% black, 10% Hispanic, 6% multiracial, 0% Pacific Islander, 43% white, 11% international; 15% from in state; 97% live on campus; N/A of students in fraternities, N/A in sororities
**Most popular majors:** 6% Biology/Biological Sciences, General, 18% Economics, General, 8% English Language and Literature, General, 6% Political Science and Government, General, 10% Psychology, General
**Expenses:** 2014-2015: $45,078; room/board: $13,960
**Financial aid:** (781) 283-2360; 61% of undergrads determined to have financial need; average aid package $41,847

## Wentworth Institute of Technology
Boston MA
(617) 989-4000
**U.S. News ranking:** Reg. Coll. (N), No. 12
**Website:** www.wit.edu
**Admissions email:** admissions@wit.edu
**Private;** founded 1904
**Freshman admissions:** selective; 2013-2014: 6,124 applied, 3,519 accepted. Either SAT or ACT required. SAT 25/75 percentile: 1010-1210. High school rank: 11% in top tenth, 40% in top quarter, 76% in top half
**Early decision deadline:** N/A, notification date: N/A
**Early action deadline:** N/A, notification date: N/A
**Application deadline (fall):** rolling
**Undergraduate student body:** 3,634 full time, 358 part time; 82% male, 18% female; 0% American Indian, 6% Asian, 5% black, 4% Hispanic, 3% multiracial, 0% Pacific Islander, 60% white, 6% international; 63% from in state; 50% live on campus; 0% of students in fraternities, 0% in sororities
**Most popular majors:** 22% Architecture, 27% Business, Management, Marketing, and Related Support Services, 9% Computer and Information Sciences and Support Services, 9% Construction Trades, 32% Engineering Technologies and Engineering-Related Fields
**Expenses:** 2014-2015: $29,320; room/board: $12,840
**Financial aid:** (617) 989-4020; 73% of undergrads determined to have financial need; average aid package $20,610

## Western New England University
Springfield MA
(413) 782-1321
**U.S. News ranking:** Reg. U. (N), No. 65
**Website:** www.wne.edu
**Admissions email:** ugradmis@wne.edu
**Private;** founded 1919
**Freshman admissions:** selective; 2013-2014: 5,988 applied, 4,881 accepted. Either SAT or ACT required. SAT 25/75 percentile: 960-1180. High school rank: 17% in top tenth, 44% in top quarter, 74% in top half
**Early decision deadline:** N/A, notification date: N/A
**Early action deadline:** N/A, notification date: N/A
**Application deadline (fall):** rolling
**Undergraduate student body:** 2,498 full time, 169 part time; 60% male, 40% female; 0% American Indian, 3% Asian, 5% black, 8% Hispanic, 2% multiracial, 0% Pacific Islander, 77% white, 2% international; 47% from in state; 65% live on campus; 0% of students in fraternities, 0% in sororities
**Most popular majors:** 31% Business, Management, Marketing, and Related Support Services, 15% Engineering, 8% Homeland Security, Law Enforcement, Firefighting and Related Protective Services, 8% Psychology, General, 7% Sport and Fitness Administration/Management
**Expenses:** 2014-2015: $33,466; room/board: $12,688
**Financial aid:** (413) 796-2080; 79% of undergrads determined to have financial need; average aid package $23,023

## Westfield State University
Westfield MA
(413) 572-5218
**U.S. News ranking:** Reg. U. (N), No. 115
**Website:** www.westfield.ma.edu
**Admissions email:** admissions@westfield.ma.edu
**Public;** founded 1838
**Freshman admissions:** less selective; 2013-2014: 5,145 applied, 3,853 accepted. Either SAT or ACT required. SAT 25/75 percentile: 910-1090. High school rank: 9% in top tenth, 22% in top quarter, 62% in top half
**Early decision deadline:** N/A, notification date: N/A
**Early action deadline:** N/A, notification date: N/A
**Application deadline (fall):** 3/1
**Undergraduate student body:** 4,999 full time, 692 part time; 48% male, 52% female; 0% American Indian, 1% Asian, 4% black, 7% Hispanic, 4% multiracial, 0% Pacific Islander, 80% white, 0% international; 92% from in state; 55% live on campus; 0% of students in fraternities, 0% in sororities
**Most popular majors:** 12% Business, Management, Marketing, and Related Support Services, 11% Education, 15% Homeland Security, Law Enforcement, Firefighting and Related Protective Services, 15%

Liberal Arts and Sciences, General Studies and Humanities, 7% Psychology
**Expenses:** 2013-2014: $8,697 in state, $14,777 out of state; room/board: $9,795
**Financial aid:** (413) 572-5218

## Wheaton College
Norton MA
(508) 286-8251
**U.S. News ranking:** Nat. Lib. Arts, No. 69
**Website:** www.wheatoncollege.edu
**Admissions email:** admission@wheatoncollege.edu
**Private;** founded 1834
**Freshman admissions:** more selective; 2013-2014: 3,433 applied, 2,537 accepted. Neither SAT nor ACT required. SAT 25/75 percentile: 1110-1340. High school rank: 37% in top tenth, 70% in top quarter, 93% in top half
**Early decision deadline:** 11/15, notification date: 12/15
**Early action deadline:** 11/15, notification date: 1/15
**Application deadline (fall):** 1/15
**Undergraduate student body:** 1,647 full time, 9 part time; 35% male, 65% female; 0% American Indian, 4% Asian, 5% black, 7% Hispanic, 3% multiracial, 0% Pacific Islander, 69% white, 9% international; 40% from in state; 97% live on campus; 0% of students in fraternities, 0% in sororities
**Most popular majors:** 6% Biology/Biological Sciences, General, 8% Economics, General, 8% English Language and Literature, General, 6% Neuroscience, 14% Psychology, General
**Expenses:** 2014-2015: $46,423; room/board: $11,840
**Financial aid:** (508) 286-8232; 69% of undergrads determined to have financial need; average aid package $35,559

## Wheelock College
Boston MA
(617) 879-2206
**U.S. News ranking:** Reg. U. (N), No. 79
**Website:** www.wheelock.edu
**Admissions email:** undergrad@wheelock.edu
**Private;** founded 1888
**Freshman admissions:** selective; 2013-2014: 1,570 applied, 1,149 accepted. Either SAT or ACT required. SAT 25/75 percentile: 890-1090. High school rank: 12% in top tenth, 38% in top quarter, 64% in top half
**Early decision deadline:** N/A, notification date: N/A
**Early action deadline:** 12/1, notification date: 12/20
**Application deadline (fall):** 5/1
**Undergraduate student body:** 809 full time, 71 part time; 12% male, 88% female; 0% American Indian, 3% Asian, 11% black, 12% Hispanic, 3% multiracial, 0% Pacific Islander, 58% white, 2% international; 66% from in state; 63% live on campus; 0% of students in fraternities, 0% in sororities
**Most popular majors:** 38% Education, 21% Family and Consumer Sciences/Human Sciences, 4% Liberal Arts and Sciences, General Studies and

Humanities, 7% Psychology, 19% Public Administration and Social Service Professions
**Expenses:** 2014-2015: $32,830; room/board: $13,600
**Financial aid:** (617) 879-2206; 83% of undergrads determined to have financial need; average aid package $21,783

## Williams College
Williamstown MA
(413) 597-2211
**U.S. News ranking:** Nat. Lib. Arts, No. 1
**Website:** www.williams.edu
**Admissions email:** admission@williams.edu
**Private;** founded 1793
**Freshman admissions:** most selective; 2013-2014: 6,853 applied, 1,200 accepted. Either SAT or ACT required. SAT 25/75 percentile: 1330-1540. High school rank: 88% in top tenth, 98% in top quarter, 100% in top half
**Early decision deadline:** 11/10, notification date: 12/15
**Early action deadline:** N/A, notification date: N/A
**Application deadline (fall):** 1/1
**Undergraduate student body:** 2,045 full time, 32 part time; 49% male, 51% female; 0% American Indian, 11% Asian, 8% black, 12% Hispanic, 6% multiracial, 0% Pacific Islander, 56% white, 7% international; 13% from in state; 93% live on campus; N/A of students in fraternities, N/A in sororities
**Most popular majors:** 12% Economics, General, 13% English Language and Literature, General, 13% History, General, 13% Mathematics, General, 12% Political Science and Government, General
**Expenses:** 2014-2015: $48,310; room/board: $12,760
**Financial aid:** (413) 597-4181; 52% of undergrads determined to have financial need; average aid package $44,933

## Worcester Polytechnic Institute
Worcester MA
(508) 831-5286
**U.S. News ranking:** Nat. U., No. 68
**Website:** admissions.wpi.edu
**Admissions email:** admissions@wpi.edu
**Private;** founded 1865
**Freshman admissions:** more selective; 2013-2014: 8,578 applied, 4,425 accepted. Neither SAT nor ACT required. SAT 25/75 percentile: 1220-1410. High school rank: 64% in top tenth, 91% in top quarter, 99% in top half
**Early decision deadline:** N/A, notification date: N/A
**Early action deadline:** 1/1, notification date: 2/10
**Application deadline (fall):** 2/1
**Undergraduate student body:** 3,959 full time, 175 part time; 67% male, 33% female; 0% American Indian, 5% Asian, 3% black, 7% Hispanic, 3% multiracial, 0% Pacific Islander, 65% white, 13% international; 45% from in state; 49% live on campus; 29% of students in fraternities, 41% in sororities

**Most popular majors:** 10% Bioengineering and Biomedical Engineering, 8% Chemical Engineering, 7% Civil Engineering, General, 9% Electrical and Electronics Engineering, 20% Mechanical Engineering
**Expenses:** 2013-2014: $42,778; room/board: $13,082
**Financial aid:** (508) 831-5469

## Worcester State University
Worcester MA
(508) 929-8040
**U.S. News ranking:** Reg. U. (N), No. 125
**Website:** www.worcester.edu
**Admissions email:** admissions@worcester.edu
**Public;** founded 1874
**Freshman admissions:** selective; 2013-2014: 4,149 applied, 2,515 accepted. Either SAT or ACT required. SAT 25/75 percentile: 920-1110. High school rank: N/A
**Early decision deadline:** N/A, notification date: N/A
**Early action deadline:** N/A, notification date: N/A
**Application deadline (fall):** 5/1
**Undergraduate student body:** 4,115 full time, 1,441 part time; 40% male, 60% female; 1% American Indian, 4% Asian, 6% black, 8% Hispanic, 2% multiracial, 0% Pacific Islander, 74% white, 1% international; 97% from in state; 22% live on campus; 0% of students in fraternities, 0% in sororities
**Most popular majors:** 8% Biological and Biomedical Sciences, 17% Business, Management, Marketing, and Related Support Services, 19% Health Professions and Related Programs, 9% Homeland Security, Law Enforcement, Firefighting and Related Protective Services, 12% Psychology
**Expenses:** 2014-2015: $8,557 in state, $14,637 out of state; room/board: $11,255
**Financial aid:** (508) 929-8056; 60% of undergrads determined to have financial need; average aid package $11,078

## MICHIGAN

## Adrian College
Adrian MI
(800) 877-2246
**U.S. News ranking:** Reg. Coll. (Mid. W), No. 22
**Website:** www.adrian.edu
**Admissions email:** admissions@adrian.edu
**Private;** founded 1859
**Affiliation:** The United Methodist Church
**Freshman admissions:** selective; 2013-2014: 4,675 applied, 2,631 accepted. Either SAT or ACT required. ACT 25/75 percentile: 19-24. High school rank: N/A
**Early decision deadline:** N/A, notification date: N/A
**Early action deadline:** N/A, notification date: N/A
**Application deadline (fall):** rolling
**Undergraduate student body:** 1,582 full time, 67 part time; 51% male, 49% female; 0% American Indian, 0% Asian, 9% black, 2%

Hispanic, 4% multiracial, 0% Pacific Islander, 0% international; 79% from in state; 88% live on campus; 18% of students in fraternities, 19% in sororities
**Most popular majors:** 11% Biological and Biomedical Sciences, 25% Business, Management, Marketing, and Related Support Services, 7% Education, 6% Homeland Security, Law Enforcement, Firefighting and Related Protective Services, 10% Parks, Recreation, Leisure, and Fitness Studies
**Expenses:** 2014-2015: $32,660; room/board: $9,740
**Financial aid:** (517) 264-3107; 87% of undergrads determined to have financial need; average aid package $25,978

## Albion College
Albion MI
(800) 858-6770
**U.S. News ranking:** Nat. Lib. Arts, No. 99
**Website:** albion.edu/
**Admissions email:** admission@albion.edu
**Private;** founded 1835
**Affiliation:** United Methodist
**Freshman admissions:** more selective; 2013-2014: 4,430 applied, 2,498 accepted. Either SAT or ACT required. ACT 25/75 percentile: 22-28. High school rank: 21% in top tenth, 52% in top quarter, 84% in top half
**Early decision deadline:** N/A, notification date: N/A
**Early action deadline:** 12/1, notification date: 1/15
**Application deadline (fall):** rolling
**Undergraduate student body:** 1,272 full time, 35 part time; 51% male, 49% female; 0% American Indian, 2% Asian, 3% black, 3% Hispanic, 3% multiracial, 0% Pacific Islander, 82% white, 3% international; 91% from in state; 89% live on campus; 53% of students in fraternities, 42% in sororities
**Most popular majors:** 11% Biology/Biological Sciences, General, 11% Economics, General, 5% History, General, 5% Kinesiology and Exercise Science, 15% Psychology, General
**Expenses:** 2014-2015: $37,300; room/board: $10,550
**Financial aid:** (517) 629-0440; 71% of undergrads determined to have financial need; average aid package $27,997

## Alma College
Alma MI
(800) 321-2562
**U.S. News ranking:** Nat. Lib. Arts, No. 139
**Website:** www.alma.edu
**Admissions email:** admissions@alma.edu
**Private;** founded 1886
**Affiliation:** Presbyterian
**Freshman admissions:** selective; 2013-2014: 2,554 applied, 1,772 accepted. Either SAT or ACT required. ACT 25/75 percentile: 22-27. High school rank: 27% in top tenth, 53% in top quarter, 84% in top half
**Early decision deadline:** N/A, notification date: N/A
**Early action deadline:** N/A, notification date: N/A

**Application deadline (fall):** rolling
**Undergraduate student body:** 1,378 full time, 41 part time; 45% male, 55% female; 1% American Indian, 2% Asian, 2% black, 3% Hispanic, 2% multiracial, 0% Pacific Islander, 86% white, 0% international; 92% from in state; 90% live on campus; 24% of students in fraternities, 30% in sororities
**Most popular majors:** 9% Biology, General, 19% Business Administration, Management and Operations, 13% Health and Physical Education/Fitness, 8% Psychology, General, 11% Teacher Education and Professional Development, Specific Levels and Methods
**Expenses:** 2014-2015: $34,220; room/board: $9,490
**Financial aid:** (989) 463-7347; 82% of undergrads determined to have financial need; average aid package $24,779

## Andrews University
Berrien Springs MI
(800) 253-2874
**U.S. News ranking:** Nat. U., No. 168
**Website:** www.andrews.edu
**Admissions email:** enroll@andrews.edu
**Private;** founded 1874
**Affiliation:** Seventh-day Adventist
**Freshman admissions:** more selective; 2013-2014: 2,480 applied, 957 accepted. Either SAT or ACT required. ACT 25/75 percentile: 20-27. High school rank: 22% in top tenth, 46% in top quarter, 74% in top half
**Early decision deadline:** N/A, notification date: N/A
**Early action deadline:** N/A, notification date: N/A
**Application deadline (fall):** rolling
**Undergraduate student body:** 1,618 full time, 287 part time; 44% male, 56% female; 0% American Indian, 13% Asian, 22% black, 14% Hispanic, 3% multiracial, 0% Pacific Islander, 29% white, 18% international; 35% from in state; 62% live on campus; 0% of students in fraternities, 0% in sororities
**Most popular majors:** 7% Business, Management, Marketing, and Related Support Services, 8% Communication, Journalism, and Related Programs, 9% Education, 7% Health Professions and Related Programs, 13% Visual and Performing Arts
**Expenses:** 2014-2015: $26,262; room/board: $8,302
**Financial aid:** (269) 471-3334; 65% of undergrads determined to have financial need; average aid package $27,093

## Aquinas College
Grand Rapids MI
(616) 732-4460
**U.S. News ranking:** Reg. U. (Mid. W), No. 44
**Website:** www.aquinas.edu
**Admissions email:** admissions@aquinas.edu
**Private;** founded 1886
**Affiliation:** Roman Catholic
**Freshman admissions:** selective; 2013-2014: 2,602 applied, 1,847 accepted. Either SAT or ACT required. ACT 25/75 percentile: 21-26. High school

rank: 19% in top tenth, 45% in top quarter, 77% in top half
**Early decision deadline:** N/A, notification date: N/A
**Early action deadline:** N/A, notification date: N/A
**Application deadline (fall):** rolling
**Undergraduate student body:** 1,634 full time, 211 part time; 38% male, 62% female; 0% American Indian, 1% Asian, 3% black, 5% Hispanic, 2% multiracial, 0% Pacific Islander, 85% white, 1% international; 94% from in state; 47% live on campus; N/A of students in fraternities, N/A in sororities
**Most popular majors:** 16% Business, Management, Marketing, and Related Support Services, 8% Education, 7% Psychology, 8% Social Sciences, 7% Visual and Performing Arts
**Expenses:** 2014-2015: $27,726; room/board: $8,350
**Financial aid:** (616) 632-2893; 85% of undergrads determined to have financial need; average aid package $20,130

## Baker College of Flint[1]
Flint MI
(810) 766-4000
**U.S. News ranking:** Reg. Coll. (Mid. W), unranked
**Website:** www.baker.edu
**Admissions email:** troy.crowe@baker.edu
**Private**
**Application deadline (fall):** N/A
**Undergraduate student body:** N/A full time, N/A part time
**Expenses:** 2013-2014: $8,100; room/board: $5,400
**Financial aid:** (810) 766-4202

## Calvin College
Grand Rapids MI
(616) 526-6106
**U.S. News ranking:** Nat. Lib. Arts, No. 116
**Website:** www.calvin.edu
**Admissions email:** admissions@calvin.edu
**Private;** founded 1876
**Affiliation:** Christian Reformed
**Freshman admissions:** more selective; 2013-2014: 4,001 applied, 2,792 accepted. Neither SAT nor ACT required. ACT 25/75 percentile: 23-29. High school rank: 30% in top tenth, 55% in top quarter, 82% in top half
**Early decision deadline:** N/A, notification date: N/A
**Early action deadline:** N/A, notification date: N/A
**Application deadline (fall):** 8/15
**Undergraduate student body:** 3,814 full time, 145 part time; 45% male, 55% female; 0% American Indian, 4% Asian, 3% black, 3% Hispanic, 3% multiracial, 0% Pacific Islander, 75% white, 10% international; 56% from in state; 61% live on campus; 0% of students in fraternities, 0% in sororities
**Most popular majors:** 5% Biology/Biological Sciences, General, 10% Business/Commerce, General, 8% Engineering, General, 8% Psychology, General, 8% Registered Nursing/Registered Nurse
**Expenses:** 2014-2015: $29,635; room/board: $9,485

**Financial aid:** (616) 526-6137; 63% of undergrads determined to have financial need; average aid package $20,765

## Central Michigan University
Mount Pleasant MI
(989) 774-3076
**U.S. News ranking:** Nat. U., No. 194
**Website:** www.cmich.edu
**Admissions email:** cmuadmit@cmich.edu
**Public;** founded 1892
**Freshman admissions:** selective; 2013-2014: 19,253 applied, 12,142 accepted. Either SAT or ACT required. ACT 25/75 percentile: 20-24. High school rank: 15% in top tenth, 38% in top quarter, 73% in top half
**Early decision deadline:** N/A, notification date: N/A
**Early action deadline:** N/A, notification date: N/A
**Application deadline (fall):** 7/1
**Undergraduate student body:** 17,880 full time, 2,654 part time; 44% male, 56% female; 1% American Indian, 1% Asian, 7% black, 3% Hispanic, 2% multiracial, 0% Pacific Islander, 80% white, 1% international; 96% from in state; 30% live on campus; 5% of students in fraternities, 7% in sororities
**Most popular majors:** 24% Business, Management, Marketing, and Related Support Services, 7% Communication, Journalism, and Related Programs, 12% Education, 9% Parks, Recreation, Leisure, and Fitness Studies, 7% Psychology
**Expenses:** 2014-2015: $11,550 in state, $23,670 out of state; room/board: $8,780
**Financial aid:** (989) 774-3674; 65% of undergrads determined to have financial need; average aid package $12,569

## Cleary University[1]
Ann Arbor MI
(734) 332-4477
**U.S. News ranking:** Business, unranked
**Website:** www.cleary.edu
**Admissions email:** admissions@cleary.edu
**Private**
**Application deadline (fall):** N/A
**Undergraduate student body:** N/A full time, N/A part time
**Expenses:** 2013-2014: $13,860; room/board: N/A
**Financial aid:** (800) 686-1883

## College for Creative Studies
Detroit MI
(313) 664-7425
**U.S. News ranking:** Arts, unranked
**Website:** www.collegeforcreativestudies.edu
**Admissions email:** admissions@collegeforcreativestudies.edu
**Private;** founded 1906
**Freshman admissions:** N/A; 2013-2014: 1,284 applied, 624 accepted. Either SAT or ACT required. SAT 25/75 percentile: N/A. High school rank: N/A
**Early decision deadline:** N/A, notification date: N/A
**Early action deadline:** 12/1, notification date: N/A

**Application deadline (fall):** rolling
**Undergraduate student body:** 1,082 full time, 281 part time; 51% male, 49% female; 0% American Indian, 5% Asian, 8% black, 4% Hispanic, 3% multiracial, 0% Pacific Islander, 60% white, 6% international; 91% from in state; 32% live on campus; N/A of students in fraternities, N/A in sororities
**Most popular majors:** 100% Visual and Performing Arts
**Expenses:** 2014-2015: $37,092; room/board: $8,250
**Financial aid:** (313) 664-7495

## Cornerstone University

Grand Rapids MI
(616) 222-1426
**U.S. News ranking:** Reg. U. (Mid. W), second tier
**Website:** www.cornerstone.edu
**Admissions email:** admissions@cornerstone.edu
**Private;** founded 1941
**Affiliation:** Evangelical
**Freshman admissions:** selective; 2013-2014: 2,349 applied, 1,599 accepted. Either SAT or ACT required. ACT 25/75 percentile: 21-26. High school rank: 18% in top tenth, 49% in top quarter, 79% in top half
**Early decision deadline:** N/A, notification date: N/A
**Early action deadline:** N/A, notification date: N/A
**Application deadline (fall):** 8/15
**Undergraduate student body:** 1,610 full time, 590 part time; 41% male, 59% female; 1% American Indian, 1% Asian, 11% black, 4% Hispanic, 1% multiracial, 0% Pacific Islander, 81% white, 2% international; 79% from in state; 55% live on campus; N/A of students in fraternities, N/A in sororities
**Most popular majors:** Information not available
**Expenses:** 2014-2015: $25,682; room/board: $8,226
**Financial aid:** (616) 222-1424; 83% of undergrads determined to have financial need; average aid package $19,455

## Davenport University

Grand Rapids MI
(866) 925-3884
**U.S. News ranking:** Reg. U. (Mid. W), second tier
**Website:** www.davenport.edu
**Admissions email:** Davenport.Admissions@davenport.edu
**Private;** founded 1866
**Freshman admissions:** less selective; 2013-2014: 1,385 applied, 1,270 accepted. Neither SAT nor ACT required. ACT 25/75 percentile: N/A. High school rank: N/A
**Early decision deadline:** N/A, notification date: N/A
**Early action deadline:** N/A, notification date: N/A
**Application deadline (fall):** rolling
**Undergraduate student body:** 2,580 full time, 4,776 part time; 38% male, 62% female; 0% American Indian, 2% Asian, 5% black, 0% Pacific Islander, 2% multiracial, 0% Pacific Islander, 70% white, 3% international; N/A from in state; 5% live on campus; N/A of students in fraternities, N/A in sororities

**Most popular majors:** Information not available
**Expenses:** 2014-2015: $14,066; room/board: $8,434
**Financial aid:** (616) 451-3511

## Eastern Michigan University

Ypsilanti MI
(734) 487-3060
**U.S. News ranking:** Reg. U. (Mid. W), No. 77
**Website:** www.emich.edu/
**Admissions email:** undergraduate.admissions@emich.edu
**Public;** founded 1849
**Freshman admissions:** selective; 2013-2014: 12,936 applied, 7,901 accepted. Either SAT or ACT required. ACT 25/75 percentile: 19-25. High school rank: 14% in top tenth, 40% in top quarter, 76% in top half
**Early decision deadline:** N/A, notification date: N/A
**Early action deadline:** N/A, notification date: N/A
**Application deadline (fall):** rolling
**Undergraduate student body:** 13,498 full time, 5,586 part time; 42% male, 58% female; 0% American Indian, 2% Asian, 21% black, 4% Hispanic, 3% multiracial, 0% Pacific Islander, 65% white, 2% international; 91% from in state; 23% live on campus; 4% of students in fraternities, 4% in sororities
**Most popular majors:** 20% Business, Management, Marketing, and Related Support Services, 14% Education, 12% Health Professions and Related Programs, 8% Social Sciences, 6% Visual and Performing Arts
**Expenses:** 2014-2015: $9,604 in state, $25,614 out of state; room/board: $8,940
**Financial aid:** (734) 487-0455; 70% of undergrads determined to have financial need; average aid package $9,187

## Ferris State University

Big Rapids MI
(231) 591-2100
**U.S. News ranking:** Reg. U. (Mid. W), No. 54
**Website:** www.ferris.edu
**Admissions email:** admissions@ferris.edu
**Public;** founded 1884
**Freshman admissions:** selective; 2013-2014: 10,708 applied, 8,128 accepted. Either SAT or ACT required. ACT 25/75 percentile: 19-24. High school rank: N/A
**Early decision deadline:** N/A, notification date: N/A
**Early action deadline:** N/A, notification date: N/A
**Application deadline (fall):** 8/1
**Undergraduate student body:** 9,255 full time, 4,214 part time; 48% male, 52% female; 1% American Indian, 1% Asian, 7% black, 3% Hispanic, 3% multiracial, 0% Pacific Islander, 79% white, 2% international; 95% from in state; 28% live on campus; 4% of students in fraternities, 2% in sororities
**Most popular majors:** 5% Business, Management, Marketing, and Related Support Services, 4% Education, 9% Homeland Security, Law Enforcement, Firefighting and Related Protective Services, 6% Pharmacy, 7%

Registered Nursing/Registered Nurse
**Expenses:** 2014-2015: $10,677 in state, $16,467 out of state; room/board: $9,208
**Financial aid:** (231) 591-2110; 74% of undergrads determined to have financial need; average aid package $10,755

## Finlandia University[1]

Hancock MI
(906) 487-7274
**U.S. News ranking:** Reg. Coll. (Mid. W), second tier
**Website:** www.finlandia.edu
**Admissions email:** N/A
**Private**
**Application deadline (fall):** N/A
**Undergraduate student body:** N/A full time, N/A part time
**Expenses:** 2013-2014: $20,480; room/board: $7,210
**Financial aid:** (906) 487-7240

## Grace Bible College[1]

Grand Rapids MI
(616) 538-2330
**U.S. News ranking:** Reg. Coll. (Mid. W), second tier
**Website:** www.gbcol.edu
**Admissions email:** enrollment@gbcol.edu
**Private**
**Application deadline (fall):** N/A
**Undergraduate student body:** N/A full time, N/A part time
**Expenses:** 2013-2014: $12,235; room/board: $7,150
**Financial aid:** (800) 968-1887

## Grand Valley State University

Allendale MI
(800) 748-0246
**U.S. News ranking:** Reg. U. (Mid. W), No. 26
**Website:** www.gvsu.edu
**Admissions email:** admissions@gvsu.edu
**Public;** founded 1960
**Freshman admissions:** selective; 2013-2014: 18,120 applied, 14,967 accepted. Either SAT or ACT required. ACT 25/75 percentile: 21-26. High school rank: 18% in top tenth, 50% in top quarter, 86% in top half
**Early decision deadline:** N/A, notification date: N/A
**Early action deadline:** N/A, notification date: N/A
**Application deadline (fall):** 5/1
**Undergraduate student body:** 18,686 full time, 2,549 part time; 42% male, 58% female; 0% American Indian, 2% Asian, 5% black, 4% Hispanic, 3% multiracial, 0% Pacific Islander, 84% white, 1% international; 95% from in state; 28% live on campus; N/A of students in fraternities, N/A in sororities
**Most popular majors:** 7% Biological and Biomedical Sciences, 19% Business, Management, Marketing, and Related Support Services, 11% Health Professions and Related Programs, 6% Psychology, 9% Social Sciences
**Expenses:** 2014-2015: $10,752 in state, $15,408 out of state; room/board: $8,200
**Financial aid:** (616) 331-3234; 65% of undergrads determined to have financial need; average aid package $9,280

## Hillsdale College

Hillsdale MI
(517) 607-2327
**U.S. News ranking:** Nat. Lib. Arts, No. 69
**Website:** www.hillsdale.edu
**Admissions email:** admissions@hillsdale.edu
**Private;** founded 1844
**Freshman admissions:** more selective; 2013-2014: 1,902 applied, 942 accepted. Either SAT or ACT required. ACT 25/75 percentile: 27-31. High school rank: 56% in top tenth, 85% in top quarter, 99% in top half
**Early decision deadline:** 11/15, notification date: 12/1
**Early action deadline:** 12/15, notification date: 2/15
**Application deadline (fall):** 2/15
**Undergraduate student body:** 1,462 full time, 24 part time; 47% male, 53% female; N/A American Indian, N/A Asian, N/A black, N/A Hispanic, N/A multiracial, N/A Pacific Islander, N/A white, N/A international; 37% from in state; 80% live on campus; 33% of students in fraternities, 44% in sororities
**Most popular majors:** 10% Biological and Biomedical Sciences, 13% Business, Management, Marketing, and Related Support Services, 14% English Language and Literature/Letters, 10% History, 16% Social Sciences
**Expenses:** 2014-2015: $23,616; room/board: $9,250
**Financial aid:** (517) 607-2350; 43% of undergrads determined to have financial need; average aid package $18,298

## Hope College

Holland MI
(616) 395-7850
**U.S. News ranking:** Nat. Lib. Arts, No. 99
**Website:** www.hope.edu
**Admissions email:** admissions@hope.edu
**Private;** founded 1866
**Affiliation:** Reformed Church in America
**Freshman admissions:** more selective; 2013-2014: 4,158 applied, 2,931 accepted. Either SAT or ACT required. ACT 25/75 percentile: 24-29. High school rank: 34% in top tenth, 64% in top quarter, 92% in top half
**Early decision deadline:** N/A, notification date: N/A
**Early action deadline:** N/A, notification date: N/A
**Application deadline (fall):** rolling
**Undergraduate student body:** 3,235 full time, 153 part time; 40% male, 60% female; 0% American Indian, 2% Asian, 2% black, 7% Hispanic, 2% multiracial, 0% Pacific Islander, 85% white, 2% international; 69% from in state; 81% live on campus; 12% of students in fraternities, 14% in sororities
**Most popular majors:** 6% Biology/Biological Sciences, General, 9% Business Administration and Management, General, 7% Chemistry, General, 7% Kinesiology and Exercise Science, 12% Psychology, General
**Expenses:** 2014-2015: $29,560; room/board: $9,090

**Financial aid:** (616) 395-7765; 60% of undergrads determined to have financial need; average aid package $23,019

## Kalamazoo College

Kalamazoo MI
(800) 253-3602
**U.S. News ranking:** Nat. Lib. Arts, No. 64
**Website:** www.kzoo.edu
**Admissions email:** admission@kzoo.edu
**Private;** founded 1833
**Freshman admissions:** more selective; 2013-2014: 2,528 applied, 1,691 accepted. Either SAT or ACT required. ACT 25/75 percentile: 25-30. High school rank: 38% in top tenth, 80% in top quarter, 98% in top half
**Early decision deadline:** 11/15, notification date: 12/1
**Early action deadline:** 11/15, notification date: 12/20
**Application deadline (fall):** 2/15
**Undergraduate student body:** 1,446 full time, 12 part time; 44% male, 56% female; 0% American Indian, 6% Asian, 4% black, 8% Hispanic, 4% multiracial, 0% Pacific Islander, 63% white, 7% international; 70% from in state; 61% live on campus; 0% of students in fraternities, 0% in sororities
**Most popular majors:** 12% Biological and Biomedical Sciences, 10% English Language and Literature/Letters, 12% Physical Sciences, 10% Psychology, 17% Social Sciences
**Expenses:** 2014-2015: $41,061; room/board: $8,679
**Financial aid:** (269) 337-7192; 67% of undergrads determined to have financial need; average aid package $33,209

## Kettering University

Flint MI
(800) 955-4464
**U.S. News ranking:** Reg. U. (Mid. W), No. 20
**Website:** www.kettering.edu
**Admissions email:** admissions@kettering.edu
**Private;** founded 1919
**Freshman admissions:** more selective; 2013-2014: 2,056 applied, 1,336 accepted. Either SAT or ACT required. ACT 25/75 percentile: 25-30. High school rank: 28% in top tenth, 66% in top quarter, 96% in top half
**Early decision deadline:** N/A, notification date: N/A
**Early action deadline:** N/A, notification date: N/A
**Application deadline (fall):** rolling
**Undergraduate student body:** 1,590 full time, 94 part time; 82% male, 18% female; 0% American Indian, 3% Asian, 3% black, 3% Hispanic, 3% multiracial, 0% Pacific Islander, 78% white, 4% international; 72% from in state; 30% live on campus; 36% of students in fraternities, 31% in sororities
**Most popular majors:** 2% Biological and Biomedical Sciences, 2% Business, Management, Marketing, and Related Support Services, 4% Computer and Information Sciences and Support Services, 91% Engineering, 1% Mathematics and Statistics

**Expenses:** 2013-2014: $35,600; room/board: $6,980
**Financial aid:** (810) 762-7859

## Kuyper College[1]

Grand Rapids MI
(800) 511-3749
**U.S. News ranking:** Reg. Coll. (Mid. W), No. 64
**Website:** www.kuyper.edu
**Admissions email:** admissions@kuyper.edu
**Private**
**Application deadline (fall):** N/A
**Undergraduate student body:** N/A full time, N/A part time
**Expenses:** 2013-2014: $18,454; room/board: $7,050
**Financial aid:** (616) 222-3000

## Lake Superior State University

Sault Ste. Marie MI
(906) 635-2231
**U.S. News ranking:** Reg. Coll. (Mid. W), No. 69
**Website:** www.lssu.edu
**Admissions email:** admissions@lssu.edu
**Public;** founded 1946
**Freshman admissions:** selective; 2013-2014: 1,465 applied, 1,319 accepted. Either SAT or ACT required. ACT 25/75 percentile: 20-25. High school rank: 14% in top tenth, 40% in top quarter, 76% in top half
**Early decision deadline:** N/A, notification date: N/A
**Early action deadline:** N/A, notification date: N/A
**Undergraduate student body:** 1,967 full time, 462 part time; 50% male, 50% female; 8% American Indian, 1% Asian, 1% black, 2% Hispanic, 0% multiracial, 0% Pacific Islander, 79% white, 7% international
**Most popular majors:** 6% Biological and Biomedical Sciences, 14% Business, Management, Marketing, and Related Support Services, 9% Education, 12% Health Professions and Related Programs, 24% Homeland Security, Law Enforcement, Firefighting and Related Protective Services
**Expenses:** 2013-2014: $9,960 in state, $15,000 out of state; room/board: $8,728
**Financial aid:** (906) 635-2678; 69% of undergrads determined to have financial need; average aid package $9,515

## Lawrence Technological University

Southfield MI
(248) 204-3160
**U.S. News ranking:** Reg. U. (Mid. W), No. 54
**Website:** www.ltu.edu
**Admissions email:** admissions@ltu.edu
**Private;** founded 1932
**Freshman admissions:** more selective; 2013-2014: 2,076 applied, 1,196 accepted. Either SAT or ACT required. ACT 25/75 percentile: 22-29. High school rank: 25% in top tenth, 52% in top quarter, 80% in top half
**Early decision deadline:** N/A, notification date: N/A

**Early action deadline:** N/A, notification date: N/A
**Application deadline (fall):** rolling
**Undergraduate student body:** 1,536 full time, 1,497 part time; 76% male, 24% female; 1% American Indian, 6% Asian, 8% black, 3% Hispanic, 0% multiracial, 0% Pacific Islander, 68% white, 8% international; 97% from in state; 20% live on campus; 6% of students in fraternities, 6% in sororities
**Most popular majors:** 34% Architecture, 5% Business Administration and Management, General, 9% Computer Science, 8% Engineering Technology, General, 30% Engineering, General
**Expenses:** 2014-2015: $30,200; room/board: $8,986
**Financial aid:** (248) 204-2280; 61% of undergrads determined to have financial need; average aid package $22,880

## Madonna University

Livonia MI
(734) 432-5339
**U.S. News ranking:** Reg. U. (Mid. W), No. 84
**Website:** www.madonna.edu
**Admissions email:** admissions@madonna.edu
**Private;** founded 1947
**Affiliation:** Roman Catholic
**Freshman admissions:** selective; 2013-2014: 1,071 applied, 665 accepted. Either SAT or ACT required. ACT 25/75 percentile: 19-25. High school rank: 15% in top tenth, 40% in top quarter, 76% in top half
**Early decision deadline:** N/A, notification date: N/A
**Early action deadline:** N/A, notification date: N/A
**Application deadline (fall):** rolling
**Undergraduate student body:** 1,678 full time, 1,674 part time; 33% male, 67% female; 0% American Indian, 1% Asian, 13% black, 2% Hispanic, 2% multiracial, 0% Pacific Islander, 62% white, 17% international; 99% from in state; 8% live on campus; 0% of students in fraternities, 0% in sororities
**Most popular majors:** 4% Biological and Biomedical Sciences, 15% Business, Management, Marketing, and Related Support Services, 5% Family and Consumer Sciences/Human Sciences, 23% Health Professions and Related Programs, 20% Homeland Security, Law Enforcement, Firefighting and Related Protective Services
**Expenses:** 2014-2015: $17,390; room/board: $8,610
**Financial aid:** (734) 432-5662; 73% of undergrads determined to have financial need; average aid package $10,252

## Marygrove College

Detroit MI
(313) 927-1240
**U.S. News ranking:** Reg. U. (Mid. W), second tier
**Website:** www.marygrove.edu
**Admissions email:** info@marygrove.edu
**Private**
**Affiliation:** Roman Catholic

**Freshman admissions:** least selective; 2013-2014: 916 applied, 859 accepted. Neither SAT nor ACT required. ACT 25/75 percentile: 14-18. High school rank: N/A
**Early decision deadline:** N/A, notification date: N/A
**Early action deadline:** N/A, notification date: N/A
**Application deadline (fall):** rolling
**Undergraduate student body:** 801 full time, 240 part time; 25% male, 75% female; 0% American Indian, 0% Asian, 73% black, 3% Hispanic, 3% multiracial, 0% Pacific Islander, 14% white, 1% international
**Most popular majors:** 10% Business, Management, Marketing, and Related Support Services, 11% Health Professions and Related Programs, 34% Public Administration and Social Service Professions, 8% Social Sciences, 6% Visual and Performing Arts
**Expenses:** 2013-2014: $19,850; room/board: $7,600
**Financial aid:** (313) 927-1692

## Michigan State University

East Lansing MI
(517) 355-8332
**U.S. News ranking:** Nat. U., No. 85
**Website:** www.msu.edu/
**Admissions email:** admis@msu.edu
**Public;** founded 1855
**Freshman admissions:** more selective; 2013-2014: 31,479 applied, 21,610 accepted. Either SAT or ACT required. ACT 25/75 percentile: 23-28. High school rank: 28% in top tenth, 66% in top quarter, 94% in top half
**Early decision deadline:** N/A, notification date: N/A
**Early action deadline:** 10/16, notification date: 11/15
**Application deadline (fall):** rolling
**Undergraduate student body:** 34,840 full time, 3,148 part time; 50% male, 50% female; 0% American Indian, 4% Asian, 7% black, 4% Hispanic, 2% multiracial, 0% Pacific Islander, 70% white, 12% international; 90% from in state; 40% live on campus; 8% of students in fraternities, 7% in sororities
**Most popular majors:** 11% Biological and Biomedical Sciences, 17% Business, Management, Marketing, and Related Support Services, 11% Communication, Journalism, and Related Programs, 6% Engineering, 10% Social Sciences
**Expenses:** 2014-2015: $13,200 in state, $34,980 out of state; room/board: $9,154
**Financial aid:** (517) 353-5940; 49% of undergrads determined to have financial need; average aid package $12,041

## Michigan Technological University

Houghton MI
(906) 487-2335
**U.S. News ranking:** Nat. U., No. 116
**Website:** www.mtu.edu
**Admissions email:** mtu4u@mtu.edu
**Public;** founded 1885

**Freshman admissions:** more selective; 2013-2014: 4,905 applied, 3,815 accepted. Either SAT or ACT required. ACT 25/75 percentile: 24-29. High school rank: 30% in top tenth, 65% in top quarter, 91% in top half
**Early decision deadline:** N/A, notification date: N/A
**Early action deadline:** N/A, notification date: N/A
**Application deadline (fall):** rolling
**Undergraduate student body:** 5,198 full time, 423 part time; 75% male, 25% female; 1% American Indian, 1% Asian, 1% black, 2% Hispanic, 2% multiracial, 0% Pacific Islander, 84% white, 6% international; 76% from in state; 48% live on campus; 6% of students in fraternities, 3% in sororities
**Most popular majors:** 5% Biological and Biomedical Sciences, 10% Business, Management, Marketing, and Related Support Services, 6% Computer and Information Sciences and Support Services, 57% Engineering, 3% Natural Resources and Conservation
**Expenses:** 2014-2015: $14,040 in state, $29,520 out of state; room/board: $9,516
**Financial aid:** (906) 487-2622; 65% of undergrads determined to have financial need; average aid package $13,659

## Northern Michigan University[1]

Marquette MI
(906) 227-2650
**U.S. News ranking:** Reg. U. (Mid. W), No. 91
**Website:** www.nmu.edu
**Admissions email:** admiss@nmu.edu
**Public;** founded 1899
**Application deadline (fall):** rolling
**Undergraduate student body:** N/A full time, N/A part time
**Expenses:** 2014-2015: $9,220 in state, $14,400 out of state; room/board: $8,950
**Financial aid:** (906) 227-2327; 70% of undergrads determined to have financial need; average aid package $9,298

## Northwood University

Midland MI
(989) 837-4273
**U.S. News ranking:** Business, unranked
**Website:** www.northwood.edu
**Admissions email:** miadmit@northwood.edu
**Private;** founded 1959
**Freshman admissions:** selective; 2013-2014: 1,447 applied, 946 accepted. Either SAT or ACT required. ACT 25/75 percentile: 20-24. High school rank: 11% in top tenth, 31% in top quarter, 75% in top half
**Early decision deadline:** N/A, notification date: N/A
**Early action deadline:** N/A, notification date: N/A
**Application deadline (fall):** rolling
**Undergraduate student body:** 1,406 full time, 62 part time; 62% male, 38% female; 0% American Indian, 0% Asian, 7% black, 1% Hispanic, 1% multiracial, 1% Pacific Islander, 78% white, 5% international; 85% from in state;

43% live on campus; 13% of students in fraternities, 13% in sororities
**Most popular majors:** 16% Accounting, 20% Business Administration and Management, General, 8% International Business/Trade/Commerce, 15% Marketing/Marketing Management, General, 10% Sport and Fitness Administration/Management
**Expenses:** 2014-2015: $23,132; room/board: $9,310
**Financial aid:** (989) 837-4230; 66% of undergrads determined to have financial need; average aid package $19,950

## Oakland University

Rochester MI
(248) 370-3360
**U.S. News ranking:** Nat. U., second tier
**Website:** www.oakland.edu
**Admissions email:** visit@oakland.edu
**Public;** founded 1957
**Freshman admissions:** selective; 2013-2014: 12,019 applied, 7,933 accepted. Either SAT or ACT required. ACT 25/75 percentile: 20-26. High school rank: 17% in top tenth, 44% in top quarter, 80% in top half
**Early decision deadline:** N/A, notification date: N/A
**Early action deadline:** N/A, notification date: N/A
**Application deadline (fall):** 8/1
**Undergraduate student body:** 12,252 full time, 4,342 part time; 41% male, 59% female; 0% American Indian, 4% Asian, 8% black, 3% Hispanic, 2% multiracial, 0% Pacific Islander, 77% white, 1% international; 99% from in state; 14% live on campus; 2% of students in fraternities, 3% in sororities
**Most popular majors:** 16% Business, Management, Marketing, and Related Support Services, 8% Communication, Journalism, and Related Programs, 7% Education, 25% Health Professions and Related Programs, 7% Psychology
**Expenses:** 2014-2015: $11,460 in state, $24,735 out of state; room/board: $8,894
**Financial aid:** (248) 370-2550; 65% of undergrads determined to have financial need; average aid package $12,636

## Olivet College

Olivet MI
(269) 749-7635
**U.S. News ranking:** Reg. Coll. (Mid. W), No. 47
**Website:** www.olivetcollege.edu
**Admissions email:** admissions@olivetcollege.edu
**Private;** founded 1844
**Affiliation:** United Church of Christ
**Freshman admissions:** selective; 2013-2014: 1,995 applied, 1,027 accepted. Either SAT or ACT required. ACT 25/75 percentile: 17-22. High school rank: N/A
**Early decision deadline:** N/A, notification date: N/A
**Early action deadline:** N/A, notification date: N/A
**Application deadline (fall):** rolling
**Undergraduate student body:** 982 full time, 137 part time; 57% male, 43% female; 1% American Indian, 0% Asian, 10% black,

6% Hispanic, 2% multiracial, 0% Pacific Islander, 80% white, 0% international
**Most popular majors:** 12% Biology/Biological Sciences, General, 15% Criminal Justice/Safety Studies, 11% Insurance, 7% Psychology, General, 8% Sport and Fitness Administration/Management
**Expenses:** 2014-2015: $23,802; room/board: $7,900
**Financial aid:** (269) 749-7102; 92% of undergrads determined to have financial need; average aid package $17,931

## Robert B. Miller College[1]
Battle Creek MI
(269) 660-8021
**U.S. News ranking:** Reg. Coll. (Mid. W), unranked
**Website:** www.millercollege.edu
**Admissions email:** N/A
**Private**
**Application deadline (fall):** N/A
**Undergraduate student body:** N/A full time, N/A part time
**Expenses:** N/A
**Financial aid:** (269) 660-8021

## Rochester College
Rochester Hills MI
(248) 218-2031
**U.S. News ranking:** Reg. Coll. (Mid. W), No. 61
**Website:** www.rc.edu
**Admissions email:** admissions@rc.edu
**Private;** founded 1959
**Affiliation:** Church of Christ
**Freshman admissions:** less selective; 2013-2014: 1,171 applied, 769 accepted. Neither SAT nor ACT required. ACT 25/75 percentile: 18-24. High school rank: N/A
**Early decision deadline:** N/A, notification date: N/A
**Early action deadline:** N/A, notification date: N/A
**Application deadline (fall):** rolling
**Undergraduate student body:** 712 full time, 405 part time; 40% male, 60% female; 0% American Indian, 2% Asian, 16% black, 2% Hispanic, 2% multiracial, 0% Pacific Islander, 52% white, 3% international; 97% from in state; 22% live on campus; N/A of students in fraternities, N/A in sororities
**Most popular majors:** 35% Business, Management, Marketing, and Related Support Services, 12% Communication, Journalism, and Related Programs, 14% Education, 6% Multi/Interdisciplinary Studies, 21% Psychology
**Expenses:** 2014-2015: $21,350; room/board: $6,554
**Financial aid:** (248) 218-2028

## Saginaw Valley State University
University Center MI
(989) 964-4200
**U.S. News ranking:** Reg. U. (Mid. W), second tier
**Website:** www.svsu.edu
**Admissions email:** admissions@svsu.edu
**Public;** founded 1963

**Freshman admissions:** selective; 2013-2014: 6,010 applied, 4,733 accepted. ACT required. ACT 25/75 percentile: 19-24. High school rank: 18% in top tenth, 39% in top quarter, 72% in top half
**Early decision deadline:** N/A, notification date: N/A
**Early action deadline:** N/A, notification date: N/A
**Application deadline (fall):** rolling
**Undergraduate student body:** 7,594 full time, 1,381 part time; 43% male, 57% female; 0% American Indian, 1% Asian, 11% black, 3% Hispanic, 1% multiracial, 0% Pacific Islander, 73% white, 4% international; 99% from in state; 31% live on campus; 3% of students in fraternities, 3% in sororities
**Most popular majors:** 7% Criminal Justice/Safety Studies, 7% Education, 10% Health Professions and Related Programs, 5% Health/Medical Preparatory Programs, Other, 7% Social Work
**Expenses:** 2014-2015: $8,691 in state, $20,409 out of state; room/board: N/A
**Financial aid:** (989) 964-4103; 71% of undergrads determined to have financial need

## Siena Heights University
Adrian MI
(517) 264-7180
**U.S. News ranking:** Reg. U. (Mid. W), second tier
**Website:** www.sienaheights.edu
**Admissions email:** admissions@sienaheights.edu
**Private;** founded 1919
**Affiliation:** Roman Catholic
**Freshman admissions:** selective; 2013-2014: 1,422 applied, 962 accepted. Either SAT or ACT required. ACT 25/75 percentile: 19-23. High school rank: 8% in top tenth, 33% in top quarter, 68% in top half
**Early decision deadline:** N/A, notification date: N/A
**Early action deadline:** N/A, notification date: N/A
**Application deadline (fall):** 8/1
**Undergraduate student body:** 1,237 full time, 1,187 part time; 43% male, 57% female; 1% American Indian, 1% Asian, 13% black, 5% Hispanic, 2% multiracial, 0% Pacific Islander, 76% white, 0% international; 88% from in state; 19% live on campus; 2% of students in fraternities, 2% in sororities
**Most popular majors:** 22% Business, Management, Marketing, and Related Support Services, 24% Health Professions and Related Programs, 11% Homeland Security, Law Enforcement, Firefighting and Related Protective Services, 6% Liberal Arts and Sciences, General Studies and Humanities, 7% Public Administration and Social Service Professions
**Expenses:** 2014-2015: $22,740; room/board: $9,300
**Financial aid:** (517) 264-7130; 80% of undergrads determined to have financial need; average aid package $2,194

## Spring Arbor University
Spring Arbor MI
(800) 968-0011
**U.S. News ranking:** Reg. U. (Mid. W), No. 49
**Website:** www.arbor.edu/
**Admissions email:** admissions@arbor.edu
**Private;** founded 1873
**Affiliation:** Free Methodist
**Freshman admissions:** selective; 2013-2014: 2,698 applied, 1,755 accepted. Either SAT or ACT required. ACT 25/75 percentile: 20-26. High school rank: 22% in top tenth, 48% in top quarter, 77% in top half
**Early decision deadline:** N/A, notification date: N/A
**Early action deadline:** N/A, notification date: N/A
**Application deadline (fall):** 8/1
**Undergraduate student body:** 2,005 full time, 962 part time; 31% male, 69% female; 1% American Indian, 1% Asian, 12% black, 3% Hispanic, 2% multiracial, 0% Pacific Islander, 73% white, 1% international; 88% from in state; 72% live on campus; 0% of students in fraternities, 0% in sororities
**Most popular majors:** 10% Business Administration and Management, General, 9% Christian Studies, 10% Psychology, General, 10% Social Work, 19% Teacher Education and Professional Development, Specific Subject Areas
**Expenses:** 2014-2015: $24,350; room/board: $8,460
**Financial aid:** (517) 750-6463; 87% of undergrads determined to have financial need; average aid package $21,465

## University of Detroit Mercy
Detroit MI
(313) 993-1245
**U.S. News ranking:** Reg. U. (Mid. W), No. 41
**Website:** www.udmercy.edu
**Admissions email:** admissions@udmercy.edu
**Private;** founded 1877
**Affiliation:** Roman Catholic (Jesuit/Sisters of Mercy)
**Freshman admissions:** selective; 2013-2014: 3,959 applied, 2,450 accepted. Either SAT or ACT required. ACT 25/75 percentile: 21-26. High school rank: 26% in top tenth, 55% in top quarter, 90% in top half
**Early decision deadline:** N/A, notification date: N/A
**Early action deadline:** 11/1, notification date: 12/15
**Application deadline (fall):** 3/1
**Undergraduate student body:** 2,196 full time, 687 part time; 35% male, 65% female; 0% American Indian, 3% Asian, 10% black, 3% Hispanic, 3% multiracial, 0% Pacific Islander, 54% white, 6% international
**Most popular majors:** Information not available
**Expenses:** 2014-2015: $37,320; room/board: $8,528
**Financial aid:** (313) 993-3350; 72% of undergrads determined to have financial need; average aid package $28,137

## University of Michigan–Ann Arbor
Ann Arbor MI
(734) 764-7433
**U.S. News ranking:** Nat. U., No. 29
**Website:** www.umich.edu
**Admissions email:** N/A
**Public;** founded 1817
**Freshman admissions:** more selective; 2013-2014: 46,813 applied, 15,570 accepted. Either SAT or ACT required. ACT 25/75 percentile: 28-32. High school rank: N/A
**Early decision deadline:** N/A, notification date: N/A
**Early action deadline:** 11/1, notification date: 12/24
**Application deadline (fall):** 2/1
**Undergraduate student body:** 27,316 full time, 967 part time; 51% male, 49% female; 0% American Indian, 12% Asian, 4% black, 4% Hispanic, 3% multiracial, 0% Pacific Islander, 63% white, 7% international; 66% from in state; 33% live on campus; 17% of students in fraternities, 22% in sororities
**Most popular majors:** 6% Business Administration and Management, General, 7% Economics, General, 4% English Language and Literature, General, 8% Experimental Psychology, 6% Political Science and Government, General
**Expenses:** 2014-2015: $13,977 in state, $41,811 out of state; room/board: $9,996
**Financial aid:** (734) 763-4119; 39% of undergrads determined to have financial need; average aid package $20,188

## University of Michigan–Dearborn
Dearborn MI
(313) 593-5100
**U.S. News ranking:** Reg. U. (Mid. W), No. 35
**Website:** www.umd.umich.edu
**Admissions email:** admissions@umd.umich.edu
**Public;** founded 1959
**Freshman admissions:** more selective; 2013-2014: 4,908 applied, 3,084 accepted. Either SAT or ACT required. ACT 25/75 percentile: 22-27. High school rank: 24% in top tenth, 57% in top quarter, 92% in top half
**Early decision deadline:** N/A, notification date: N/A
**Early action deadline:** N/A, notification date: N/A
**Application deadline (fall):** rolling
**Undergraduate student body:** 4,814 full time, 2,330 part time; 50% male, 50% female; 0% American Indian, 6% Asian, 11% black, 5% Hispanic, 3% multiracial, 0% Pacific Islander, 70% white, 1% international; 95% from in state; 0% live on campus; N/A of students in fraternities, N/A in sororities
**Most popular majors:** 8% Biological and Biomedical Sciences, 18% Business, Management, Marketing, and Related Support Services, 10% Engineering, 10% Psychology, 9% Social Sciences
**Expenses:** 2014-2015: $11,188 in state, $23,386 out of state; room/board: N/A
**Financial aid:** (313) 593-5300; 67% of undergrads determined to have financial need; average aid package $11,298

## University of Michigan–Flint
Flint MI
(810) 762-3300
**U.S. News ranking:** Reg. U. (Mid. W), No. 99
**Website:** www.umflint.edu
**Admissions email:** admissions@umflint.edu
**Public;** founded 1956
**Freshman admissions:** selective; 2013-2014: 3,003 applied, 2,345 accepted. Either SAT or ACT required. ACT 25/75 percentile: 18-24. High school rank: 15% in top tenth, 42% in top quarter, 76% in top half
**Early decision deadline:** N/A, notification date: N/A
**Early action deadline:** N/A, notification date: N/A
**Application deadline (fall):** 8/20
**Undergraduate student body:** 4,490 full time, 2,653 part time; 40% male, 60% female; 1% American Indian, 2% Asian, 12% black, 4% Hispanic, 3% multiracial, 0% Pacific Islander, 68% white, 6% international; 98% from in state; 4% live on campus; 5% of students in fraternities, 4% in sororities
**Most popular majors:** 7% Biological and Biomedical Sciences, 16% Business, Management, Marketing, and Related Support Services, 8% Education, 30% Health Professions and Related Programs, 6% Public Administration and Social Service Professions
**Expenses:** 2014-2015: $10,138 in state, $19,360 out of state; room/board: $7,911
**Financial aid:** (810) 762-3444

## Walsh College of Accountancy and Business Administration[1]
Troy MI
(248) 823-1610
**U.S. News ranking:** Business, unranked
**Website:** www.walshcollege.edu
**Admissions email:** admissions@walshcollege.edu
**Private**
**Application deadline (fall):** N/A
**Undergraduate student body:** N/A full time, N/A part time
**Expenses:** N/A
**Financial aid:** (248) 823-1665

## Wayne State University
Detroit MI
(313) 577-3577
**U.S. News ranking:** Nat. U., second tier
**Website:** www.wayne.edu/
**Admissions email:** admissions@wayne.edu
**Public;** founded 1868
**Freshman admissions:** selective; 2013-2014: 11,524 applied, 8,786 accepted. Either SAT or ACT required. ACT 25/75 percentile: 19-26. High school rank: 23% in top tenth, 46% in top quarter, 77% in top half
**Early decision deadline:** N/A, notification date: N/A
**Early action deadline:** N/A, notification date: N/A
**Application deadline (fall):** rolling

Undergraduate student body: 12,221 full time, 6,381 part time; 44% male, 56% female; 0% American Indian, 8% Asian, 21% black, 4% Hispanic, 3% multiracial, 0% Pacific Islander, 53% white, 2% international; 99% from in state; 10% live on campus; N/A of students in fraternities, N/A in sororities
Most popular majors: 6% Biology/Biological Sciences, General, 4% Criminal Justice/Safety Studies, 4% Organizational Behavior Studies, 12% Psychology, General, 4% Social Work
Expenses: 2014-2015: $12,350 in state, $26,592 out of state; room/board: $9,713
Financial aid: (313) 577-3378; 76% of undergrads determined to have financial need; average aid package $10,248

## Western Michigan University
Kalamazoo MI
(269) 387-2000
U.S. News ranking: Nat. U., No. 173
Website: www.wmich.edu
Admissions email: ask-wmu@wmich.edu
Public; founded 1903
Freshman admissions: selective; 2013-2014: 14,621 applied, 12,113 accepted. Either SAT or ACT required. ACT 25/75 percentile: 19-25. High school rank: 12% in top tenth, 35% in top quarter, 70% in top half
Early decision deadline: N/A, notification date: N/A
Early action deadline: N/A, notification date: N/A
Application deadline (fall): rolling
Undergraduate student body: 15,879 full time, 3,319 part time; 50% male, 50% female; 0% American Indian, 1% Asian, 11% black, 5% Hispanic, 3% multiracial, 0% Pacific Islander, 75% white, 3% international; 93% from in state; 28% live on campus; 5% of students in fraternities, 6% in sororities
Most popular majors: 20% Business, Management, Marketing, and Related Support Services, 6% Communication, Journalism, and Related Programs, 10% Education, 9% Health Professions and Related Programs, 8% Multi/Interdisciplinary Studies
Expenses: 2014-2015: $10,685 in state, $24,917 out of state; room/board: $8,943
Financial aid: (269) 387-6000; 61% of undergrads determined to have financial need; average aid package $14,400

## Augsburg College
Minneapolis MN
(612) 330-1001
U.S. News ranking: Reg. U. (Mid. W), No. 23
Website: www.augsburg.edu
Admissions email: admissions@augsburg.edu
Private; founded 1869
Affiliation: Lutheran
Freshman admissions: selective; 2013-2014: 2,334 applied, 1,718 accepted. Either SAT or ACT required. ACT 25/75

percentile: 20-24. High school rank: 14% in top tenth, 43% in top quarter, 74% in top half
Early decision deadline: N/A, notification date: N/A
Early action deadline: N/A, notification date: N/A
Application deadline (fall): 8/15
Undergraduate student body: 2,038 full time, 678 part time; 45% male, 55% female; 1% American Indian, 8% Asian, 10% black, 6% Hispanic, 4% multiracial, 0% Pacific Islander, 58% white, 2% international
Most popular majors: 38% Business, Management, Marketing, and Related Support Services, 9% Communication, Journalism, and Related Programs, 15% Education, 8% Visual and Performing Arts
Expenses: 2013-2014: $33,209; room/board: $8,556
Financial aid: (612) 330-1046

## Bemidji State University
Bemidji MN
(218) 755-2040
U.S. News ranking: Reg. U. (Mid. W), No. 99
Website: www.bemidjistate.edu
Admissions email: admissions@bemidjistate.edu
Public; founded 1919
Freshman admissions: selective; 2013-2014: 3,606 applied, 2,408 accepted. Either SAT or ACT required. ACT 25/75 percentile: 19-23. High school rank: 7% in top tenth, 23% in top quarter, 57% in top half
Early decision deadline: N/A, notification date: N/A
Early action deadline: N/A, notification date: N/A
Application deadline (fall): rolling
Undergraduate student body: 3,516 full time, 1,213 part time; 44% male, 56% female; 3% American Indian, 1% Asian, 2% black, 2% Hispanic, 3% multiracial, 0% Pacific Islander, 86% white, 2% international; 89% from in state; 28% live on campus; N/A of students in fraternities, N/A in sororities
Most popular majors: 6% Biological and Biomedical Sciences, 20% Business, Management, Marketing, and Related Support Services, 15% Education, 13% Health Professions and Related Programs, 7% Homeland Security, Law Enforcement, Firefighting and Related Protective Services
Expenses: 2014-2015: $8,134 in state, $8,134 out of state; room/board: $7,470
Financial aid: (218) 755-4143; 66% of undergrads determined to have financial need; average aid package $9,060

## Bethany Lutheran College
Mankato MN
(507) 344-7331
U.S. News ranking: Nat. Lib. Arts, second tier
Website: www.blc.edu
Admissions email: admiss@blc.edu
Private; founded 1927
Affiliation: Evangelical Lutheran Synod
Freshman admissions: selective; 2013-2014: 531 applied, 396 accepted. Either SAT or ACT required. ACT 25/75 percentile:

20-26. High school rank: 14% in top tenth, 32% in top quarter, 67% in top half
Early decision deadline: N/A, notification date: N/A
Early action deadline: N/A, notification date: N/A
Application deadline (fall): 7/1
Undergraduate student body: 552 full time, 27 part time; 49% male, 51% female; 1% American Indian, 1% Asian, 1% black, 1% Hispanic, 3% multiracial, 0% Pacific Islander, 88% white, 1% international; 75% from in state; 60% live on campus; 0% of students in fraternities, 0% in sororities
Most popular majors: 11% Biology/Biological Sciences, General, 19% Business Administration and Management, General, 13% Communication, General, 10% Psychology, General, 12% Visual and Performing Arts
Expenses: 2014-2015: $24,450; room/board: $7,710
Financial aid: (507) 344-7307; 88% of undergrads determined to have financial need; average aid package $19,087

## Bethel University
St. Paul MN
(800) 255-8706
U.S. News ranking: Reg. U. (Mid. W), No. 20
Website: www.bethel.edu
Admissions email: BUadmissions-cas@bethel.edu
Private; founded 1871
Affiliation: Converge Worldwide (former Baptist General Conference)
Freshman admissions: more selective; 2013-2014: 2,118 applied, 2,009 accepted. Either SAT or ACT required. ACT 25/75 percentile: 22-28. High school rank: 29% in top tenth, 60% in top quarter, 86% in top half
Early decision deadline: N/A, notification date: N/A
Early action deadline: N/A, notification date: N/A
Application deadline (fall): rolling
Undergraduate student body: 2,617 full time, 663 part time; 37% male, 63% female; 0% American Indian, 3% Asian, 6% black, 2% Hispanic, 2% multiracial, 0% Pacific Islander, 84% white, 0% international; 77% from in state; 69% live on campus; 0% of students in fraternities, 0% in sororities
Most popular majors: 7% Biological and Biomedical Sciences, 15% Business, Management, Marketing, and Related Support Services, 8% Communication, Journalism, and Related Programs, 13% Education, 15% Health Professions and Related Programs
Expenses: 2014-2015: $32,990; room/board: $9,440
Financial aid: (800) 255-8706; 73% of undergrads determined to have financial need; average aid package $23,686

## Capella University[1]
Minneapolis MN
(888) 227-3552
U.S. News ranking: Nat. U., unranked
Website: www.capella.edu
Admissions email: admissionsoffice@capella.edu
For-profit

Application deadline (fall): N/A
Undergraduate student body: N/A full time, N/A part time
Expenses: 2013-2014: $12,348; room/board: N/A
Financial aid: (612) 977-5233

## Carleton College
Northfield MN
(507) 222-4190
U.S. News ranking: Nat. Lib. Arts, No. 8
Website: www.carleton.edu
Admissions email: admissions@carleton.edu
Private; founded 1866
Freshman admissions: most selective; 2013-2014: 7,045 applied, 1,476 accepted. Either SAT or ACT required. SAT 25/75 percentile: 1340-1520. High school rank: 79% in top tenth, 96% in top quarter, 100% in top half
Early decision deadline: 11/15, notification date: 12/15
Early action deadline: N/A, notification date: N/A
Application deadline (fall): 1/15
Undergraduate student body: 2,025 full time, 20 part time; 47% male, 53% female; 0% American Indian, 9% Asian, 4% black, 6% Hispanic, 4% multiracial, 0% Pacific Islander, 66% white, 9% international; 21% from in state; 96% live on campus; 0% of students in fraternities, 0% in sororities
Most popular majors: 11% Biological and Biomedical Sciences, 7% Mathematics and Statistics, 12% Physical Sciences, 20% Social Sciences, 12% Visual and Performing Arts
Expenses: 2014-2015: $47,736; room/board: $12,366
Financial aid: (507) 646-4138; 55% of undergrads determined to have financial need; average aid package $37,888

## College of St. Benedict
St. Joseph MN
(320) 363-5055
U.S. News ranking: Nat. Lib. Arts, No. 89
Website: www.csbsju.edu
Admissions email: admissions@csbsju.edu
Private; founded 1913
Affiliation: Roman Catholic (Benedictine)
Freshman admissions: more selective; 2013-2014: 2,077 applied, 1,569 accepted. Either SAT or ACT required. ACT 25/75 percentile: 23-28. High school rank: 33% in top tenth, 70% in top quarter, 94% in top half
Early decision deadline: N/A, notification date: N/A
Early action deadline: 11/15, notification date: 12/15
Application deadline (fall): 1/15
Undergraduate student body: 2,015 full time, 36 part time; 0% male, 100% female; 0% American Indian, 6% Asian, 2% black, 5% Hispanic, 1% multiracial, 0% Pacific Islander, 80% white, 6% international; 83% from in state; 88% live on campus; 0% of students in fraternities, 0% in sororities
Most popular majors: 11% Biology/Biological Sciences, General, 7% Nutrition Sciences, 10% Psychology, General, 10%

Registered Nursing/Registered Nurse, 9% Rhetoric and Composition
Expenses: 2014-2015: $39,402; room/board: $9,957
Financial aid: (320) 363-5388; 71% of undergrads determined to have financial need; average aid package $30,121

## College of St. Scholastica
Duluth MN
(218) 723-6046
U.S. News ranking: Reg. U. (Mid. W), No. 23
Website: www.css.edu
Admissions email: admissions@css.edu
Private; founded 1912
Affiliation: Roman Catholic
Freshman admissions: selective; 2013-2014: 1,809 applied, 1,315 accepted. Either SAT or ACT required. ACT 25/75 percentile: 21-26. High school rank: 20% in top tenth, 55% in top quarter, 85% in top half
Early decision deadline: N/A, notification date: N/A
Early action deadline: N/A, notification date: N/A
Application deadline (fall): rolling
Undergraduate student body: 2,423 full time, 513 part time; 31% male, 69% female; 2% American Indian, 2% Asian, 3% black, 2% Hispanic, 2% multiracial, 0% Pacific Islander, 80% white, 4% international; 85% from in state; 36% live on campus; 0% of students in fraternities, 0% in sororities
Most popular majors: 13% Biological and Biomedical Sciences, 19% Business, Management, Marketing, and Related Support Services, 39% Health Professions and Related Programs, 7% Psychology, 6% Public Administration and Social Service Professions
Expenses: 2014-2015: $32,842; room/board: $8,598
Financial aid: (218) 723-6047; 80% of undergrads determined to have financial need; average aid package $20,760

## Concordia College–Moorhead
Moorhead MN
(800) 699-9897
U.S. News ranking: Nat. Lib. Arts, No. 129
Website: www.concordiacollege.edu
Admissions email: admissions@cord.edu
Private; founded 1891
Affiliation: Evangelical Lutheran Church in America
Freshman admissions: more selective; 2013-2014: 2,493 applied, 1,944 accepted. Either SAT or ACT required. ACT 25/75 percentile: 22-28. High school rank: 30% in top tenth, 62% in top quarter, 90% in top half
Early decision deadline: N/A, notification date: N/A
Early action deadline: N/A, notification date: N/A
Application deadline (fall): rolling
Undergraduate student body: 2,488 full time, 43 part time; 38% male, 62% female; 1% American Indian, 2% Asian, 2% black, 2% Hispanic, 1% multiracial, 0% Pacific Islander, 84% white,

3% international; 70% from in state; 64% live on campus; 0% of students in fraternities, 0% in sororities
**Most popular majors:** 9% Biology, General, 10% Business Administration, Management and Operations, 13% Education, General, 7% Linguistic, Comparative, and Related Language Studies and Services, 8% Visual and Performing Arts, General
**Expenses:** 2014-2015: $34,114; room/board: $7,370
**Financial aid:** (218) 299-3010; 73% of undergrads determined to have financial need; average aid package $27,251

## Concordia University–St. Paul
St. Paul MN
(651) 641-8230
**U.S. News ranking:** Reg. U. (Mid. W), No. 106
**Website:** www.csp.edu
**Admissions email:** admissions@csp.edu
**Private;** founded 1893
**Affiliation:** Lutheran Church-Missouri Synod
**Freshman admissions:** selective; 2013-2014: 1,349 applied, 720 accepted. ACT required. ACT 25/75 percentile: 18-24. High school rank: 7% in top tenth, 22% in top quarter, 58% in top half
**Early decision deadline:** N/A, notification date: N/A
**Early action deadline:** N/A, notification date: N/A
**Application deadline (fall):** rolling
**Undergraduate student body:** 1,217 full time, 954 part time; 42% male, 58% female; 0% American Indian, 7% Asian, 13% black, 4% Hispanic, 4% multiracial, 0% Pacific Islander, 64% white, 3% international; 79% from in state; 23% live on campus; 0% of students in fraternities, 0% in sororities
**Most popular majors:** 39% Business, Management, Marketing, and Related Support Services, 8% Education, 10% Family and Consumer Sciences/Human Sciences, 7% Homeland Security, Law Enforcement, Firefighting and Related Protective Services, 9% Parks, Recreation, Leisure, and Fitness Studies
**Expenses:** 2014-2015: $20,250; room/board: $8,000
**Financial aid:** (651) 603-6300; 80% of undergrads determined to have financial need; average aid package $14,086

## Crown College[1]
St. Bonifacius MN
(952) 446-4142
**U.S. News ranking:** Reg. Coll. (Mid. W), No. 54
**Website:** www.crown.edu
**Admissions email:** admissions@crown.edu
**Private;** founded 1916
**Affiliation:** Christian and Missionary Alliance
**Application deadline (fall):** 8/20
**Undergraduate student body:** N/A full time, N/A part time
**Expenses:** 2013-2014: $22,430; room/board: $7,480
**Financial aid:** (952) 446-4177

## Dunwoody College of Technology
Minneapolis MN
(800) 292-4625
**U.S. News ranking:** Reg. Coll. (Mid. W), No. 64
**Website:** www.dunwoody.edu
**Admissions email:** admissions@dunwoody.edu
**Private;** founded 1914
**Freshman admissions:** less selective; 2013-2014: 739 applied, 563 accepted. Neither SAT nor ACT required. ACT 25/75 percentile: N/A. High school rank: 1% in top tenth, 1% in top quarter, 21% in top half
**Early decision deadline:** N/A, notification date: N/A
**Early action deadline:** N/A, notification date: N/A
**Application deadline (fall):** rolling
**Undergraduate student body:** 855 full time, 216 part time; 88% male, 12% female; 1% American Indian, 5% Asian, 5% black, 2% Hispanic, 4% multiracial, 0% Pacific Islander, 73% white, 0% international
**Most popular majors:** 55% Business Administration and Management, General, 19% Industrial Technology/Technician, 26% Interior Design
**Expenses:** 2014-2015: $19,454; room/board: N/A
**Financial aid:** N/A; 90% of undergrads determined to have financial need; average aid package $7,851

## Gustavus Adolphus College
St. Peter MN
(507) 933-7676
**U.S. News ranking:** Nat. Lib. Arts, No. 64
**Website:** www.gac.edu
**Admissions email:** admission@gac.edu
**Private;** founded 1862
**Affiliation:** Lutheran–ELCA
**Freshman admissions:** more selective; 2013-2014: 4,804 applied, 3,037 accepted. Neither SAT nor ACT required. ACT 25/75 percentile: 24-30. High school rank: 33% in top tenth, 67% in top quarter, 95% in top half
**Early decision deadline:** N/A, notification date: N/A
**Early action deadline:** 11/1, notification date: 11/20
**Application deadline (fall):** rolling
**Undergraduate student body:** 2,423 full time, 32 part time; 46% male, 54% female; 0% American Indian, 4% Asian, 2% black, 3% Hispanic, 3% multiracial, 0% Pacific Islander, 84% white, 3% international; 81% from in state; 85% live on campus; 17% of students in fraternities, 19% in sororities
**Most popular majors:** 15% Biology/Biological Sciences, General, 11% Business/Commerce, General, 6% Education, General, 10% Psychology, General, 6% Speech Communication and Rhetoric
**Expenses:** 2014-2015: $40,020; room/board: $9,250
**Financial aid:** (507) 933-7527; 72% of undergrads determined to have financial need; average aid package $30,614

## Hamline University
St. Paul MN
(651) 523-2207
**U.S. News ranking:** Reg. U. (Mid. W), No. 12
**Website:** www.hamline.edu
**Admissions email:** admission@hamline.edu
**Private;** founded 1854
**Affiliation:** United Methodist
**Freshman admissions:** selective; 2013-2014: 3,427 applied, 2,247 accepted. Either SAT or ACT required. ACT 25/75 percentile: 21-27. High school rank: 19% in top tenth, 47% in top quarter, 84% in top half
**Early decision deadline:** 11/1, notification date: 11/20
**Early action deadline:** 12/1, notification date: 12/20
**Application deadline (fall):** rolling
**Undergraduate student body:** 2,101 full time, 110 part time; 41% male, 59% female; 0% American Indian, 6% Asian, 6% black, 6% Hispanic, 5% multiracial, 0% Pacific Islander, 72% white, 2% international; 80% from in state; 40% live on campus; 5% of students in fraternities, 5% in sororities
**Most popular majors:** 16% Business, Management, Marketing, and Related Support Services, 7% English Language and Literature/Letters, 7% Legal Professions and Studies, 12% Psychology, 17% Social Sciences
**Expenses:** 2014-2015: $36,260; room/board: $9,392
**Financial aid:** (651) 523-3000; 85% of undergrads determined to have financial need; average aid package $27,515

## Macalester College
St. Paul MN
(651) 696-6357
**U.S. News ranking:** Nat. Lib. Arts, No. 24
**Website:** www.macalester.edu
**Admissions email:** admissions@macalester.edu
**Private;** founded 1874
**Freshman admissions:** most selective; 2013-2014: 6,680 applied, 2,283 accepted. Either SAT or ACT required. SAT 25/75 percentile: 1240-1460. High school rank: 64% in top tenth, 90% in top quarter, 99% in top half
**Early decision deadline:** 11/15, notification date: 12/15
**Early action deadline:** N/A, notification date: N/A
**Application deadline (fall):** 1/15
**Undergraduate student body:** 2,011 full time, 28 part time; 39% male, 61% female; 0% American Indian, 7% Asian, 3% black, 6% Hispanic, 5% multiracial, 0% Pacific Islander, 67% white, 12% international; 18% from in state; 64% live on campus; 0% of students in fraternities, 0% in sororities
**Most popular majors:** 9% Biological and Biomedical Sciences, 7% English Language and Literature/Letters, 9% Foreign Languages, Literatures, and Linguistics, 9% Multi/Interdisciplinary Studies, 26% Social Sciences
**Expenses:** 2014-2015: $47,195; room/board: $10,496
**Financial aid:** (651) 696-6214; 69% of undergrads determined to have financial need; average aid package $39,234

## Martin Luther College[1]
New Ulm MN
(877) 652-1995
**U.S. News ranking:** Reg. Coll. (Mid. W), No. 40
**Website:** www.mlc-wels.edu
**Admissions email:** N/A
**Private**
**Application deadline (fall):** N/A
**Undergraduate student body:** N/A full time, N/A part time
**Expenses:** 2013-2014: $12,300; room/board: $4,860
**Financial aid:** (507) 354-8221

## Metropolitan State University[1]
St. Paul MN
(651) 772-7600
**U.S. News ranking:** Reg. U. (Mid. W), second tier
**Website:** www.metrostate.edu
**Admissions email:** admissions@metrostate.edu
**Public**
**Application deadline (fall):** N/A
**Undergraduate student body:** N/A full time, N/A part time
**Expenses:** 2013-2014: $6,642 in state, $13,227 out of state; room/board: N/A
**Financial aid:** (651) 772-7670

## Minneapolis College of Art and Design
Minneapolis MN
(612) 874-3760
**U.S. News ranking:** Arts, unranked
**Website:** www.mcad.edu
**Admissions email:** admissions@mcad.edu
**Private;** founded 1886
**Freshman admissions:** N/A; 2013-2014: N/A applied, N/A accepted. Either SAT or ACT required. SAT 25/75 percentile: N/A. High school rank: N/A
**Early decision deadline:** N/A, notification date: N/A
**Early action deadline:** 12/1, notification date: 12/15
**Application deadline (fall):** 5/1
**Undergraduate student body:** 665 full time, 23 part time; 36% male, 64% female; N/A American Indian, N/A Asian, N/A black, N/A Hispanic, N/A multiracial, N/A Pacific Islander, N/A white, N/A international; 90% from in state; 25% live on campus; 0% of students in fraternities, 0% in sororities
**Most popular majors:** Information not available
**Expenses:** 2014-2015: $34,146; room/board: N/A
**Financial aid:** (612) 874-3782; 80% of undergrads determined to have financial need; average aid package $21,791

## Minnesota State University–Mankato
Mankato MN
(507) 389-1822
**U.S. News ranking:** Reg. U. (Mid. W), No. 69
**Website:** www.mnsu.edu
**Admissions email:** admissions@mnsu.edu
**Public;** founded 1867
**Freshman admissions:** selective; 2013-2014: 9,938 applied, 6,514 accepted. ACT required. ACT 25/75 percentile: 20-24. High school rank: 6% in top tenth, 23% in top quarter, 64% in top half

## Minnesota State University–Moorhead
Moorhead MN
(800) 593-7246
**U.S. News ranking:** Reg. U. (Mid. W), No. 106
**Website:** www.mnstate.edu
**Admissions email:** admissions@mnstate.edu
**Public;** founded 1887
**Freshman admissions:** selective; 2013-2014: 3,562 applied, 3,174 accepted. Either SAT or ACT required. ACT 25/75 percentile: 20-25. High school rank: 9% in top tenth, 30% in top quarter, 64% in top half
**Early decision deadline:** N/A, notification date: N/A
**Early action deadline:** N/A, notification date: N/A
**Application deadline (fall):** 8/1
**Undergraduate student body:** 5,107 full time, 1,051 part time; 40% male, 60% female; 1% American Indian, 1% Asian, 3% black, 1% Hispanic, 3% multiracial, 0% Pacific Islander, 78% white, 7% international; 65% from in state; 25% live on campus; N/A of students in fraternities, N/A in sororities
**Most popular majors:** 10% Art/Art Studies, General, 15% Business Administration and Management, General, 15% Elementary Education and Teaching, 7% Mass Communication/Media Studies, 11% Registered Nursing/Registered Nurse
**Expenses:** 2014-2015: $7,838 in state, $14,736 out of state; room/board: $7,398
**Financial aid:** (218) 477-2251; 62% of undergrads determined to have financial need

## North Central University
Minneapolis MN
(800) 289-6222
**U.S. News ranking:** Reg. Coll. (Mid. W), No. 66
**Website:** www.northcentral.edu
**Admissions email:** admissions@northcentral.edu
**Private;** founded 1930
**Affiliation:** Assemblies of God
**Freshman admissions:** selective; 2013-2014: 601 applied, 476 accepted. Either SAT or ACT

required. ACT 25/75 percentile: 19-26. High school rank: 15% in top tenth, 40% in top quarter, 67% in top half
**Early decision deadline:** N/A, notification date: N/A
**Early action deadline:** N/A, notification date: N/A
**Application deadline (fall):** 6/1
**Undergraduate student body:** 1,086 full time, 211 part time; 46% male, 54% female; 0% American Indian, 1% Asian, 3% black, 5% Hispanic, 3% multiracial, 0% Pacific Islander, 70% white, 1% international
**Most popular majors:** 7% Business Administration and Management, General, 7% Elementary Education and Teaching, 7% Intercultural/Multicultural and Diversity Studies, 11% Pastoral Studies/Counseling, 9% Youth Ministry
**Expenses:** 2014-2015: $20,776; room/board: $6,360
**Financial aid:** (612) 343-4485; 83% of undergrads determined to have financial need; average aid package $14,026

## Southwest Minnesota State University
Marshall MN
(507) 537-6286
**U.S. News ranking:** Reg. U. (Mid. W), second tier
**Website:** www.smsu.edu
**Admissions email:** N/A
**Public;** founded 1963
**Freshman admissions:** selective; 2013-2014: 2,076 applied, 1,359 accepted. ACT required. ACT 25/75 percentile: 19-24. High school rank: 8% in top tenth, 27% in top quarter, 60% in top half
**Early decision deadline:** N/A, notification date: N/A
**Early action deadline:** N/A, notification date: N/A
**Application deadline (fall):** 9/1
**Undergraduate student body:** 2,108 full time, 4,118 part time; 41% male, 59% female; 1% American Indian, 3% Asian, 5% black, 2% Hispanic, 0% multiracial, 0% Pacific Islander, 85% white, 3% international
**Most popular majors:** 22% Business Administration and Management, General, 6% Early Childhood Education and Teaching, 6% Elementary Education and Teaching, 5% Finance, General, 5% Psychology, General
**Expenses:** 2013-2014: $8,280 in state, $8,280 out of state; room/board: $7,146
**Financial aid:** (507) 537-6281

## St. Catherine University
St. Paul MN
(800) 945-4599
**U.S. News ranking:** Reg. U. (Mid. W), No. 13
**Website:** www.stkate.edu
**Admissions email:** admissions@ stkate.edu
**Private;** founded 1905
**Affiliation:** Roman Catholic
**Freshman admissions:** more selective; 2013-2014: 2,685 applied, 1,571 accepted. Either SAT or ACT required. ACT 25/75 percentile: 22-26. High school rank: 23% in top tenth, 52% in top quarter, 87% in top half

**Early decision deadline:** N/A, notification date: N/A
**Early action deadline:** N/A, notification date: N/A
**Application deadline (fall):** rolling
**Undergraduate student body:** 2,188 full time, 1,371 part time; 3% male, 97% female; 1% American Indian, 11% Asian, 10% black, 5% Hispanic, 2% multiracial, 0% Pacific Islander, 66% white, 1% international; 89% from in state; 44% live on campus; N/A of students in fraternities, N/A in sororities
**Most popular majors:** 5% Business Administration and Management, General, 6% Psychology, General, 6% Public Health Education and Promotion, 23% Registered Nursing/Registered Nurse, 7% Social Work
**Expenses:** 2014-2015: $34,280; room/board: $8,894
**Financial aid:** (651) 690-6540; 88% of undergrads determined to have financial need; average aid package $30,944

## St. Cloud State University
St. Cloud MN
(320) 308-2244
**U.S. News ranking:** Reg. U. (Mid. W), No. 99
**Website:** www.stcloudstate.edu
**Admissions email:** scsu4u@ stcloudstate.edu
**Public;** founded 1869
**Freshman admissions:** selective; 2013-2014: 5,965 applied, 4,905 accepted. Either SAT or ACT required. ACT 25/75 percentile: 18-24. High school rank: 7% in top tenth, 24% in top quarter, 58% in top half
**Early decision deadline:** N/A, notification date: N/A
**Early action deadline:** N/A, notification date: N/A
**Application deadline (fall):** 8/1
**Undergraduate student body:** 9,860 full time, 4,781 part time; 48% male, 52% female; 0% American Indian, 4% Asian, 6% black, 3% Hispanic, 3% multiracial, 0% Pacific Islander, 77% white, 5% international
**Most popular majors:** Information not available
**Expenses:** 2013-2014: $7,514 in state, $15,156 out of state; room/board: $7,236
**Financial aid:** (320) 308-2047

## St. John's University
Collegeville MN
(320) 363-5055
**U.S. News ranking:** Nat. Lib. Arts, No. 73
**Website:** www.csbsju.edu
**Admissions email:** admissions@ csbsju.edu
**Private;** founded 1857
**Affiliation:** Roman Catholic (Benedictine)
**Freshman admissions:** more selective; 2013-2014: 1,747 applied, 1,313 accepted. Either SAT or ACT required. ACT 25/75 percentile: 23-28. High school rank: 22% in top tenth, 52% in top quarter, 83% in top half
**Early decision deadline:** N/A, notification date: N/A
**Early action deadline:** 11/15, notification date: 12/15
**Application deadline (fall):** 1/15

**Undergraduate student body:** 1,850 full time, 21 part time; 100% male, 0% female; 1% American Indian, 3% Asian, 3% black, 4% Hispanic, 1% multiracial, 0% Pacific Islander, 83% white, 5% international; 82% from in state; 85% live on campus; 0% of students in fraternities, 0% in sororities
**Most popular majors:** 9% Accounting, 6% Biology/Biological Sciences, General, 18% Business Administration and Management, General, 5% Political Science and Government, General, 6% Psychology, General
**Expenses:** 2014-2015: $38,704; room/board: $9,280
**Financial aid:** (320) 363-3664; 66% of undergrads determined to have financial need; average aid package $28,897

## St. Mary's University of Minnesota
Winona MN
(507) 457-1700
**U.S. News ranking:** Nat. U., No. 181
**Website:** www.smumn.edu
**Admissions email:** admissions@ smumn.edu
**Private;** founded 1912
**Affiliation:** Roman Catholic
**Freshman admissions:** selective; 2013-2014: 1,551 applied, 1,161 accepted. Either SAT or ACT required. ACT 25/75 percentile: 20-26. High school rank: 18% in top tenth, 35% in top quarter, 73% in top half
**Early decision deadline:** N/A, notification date: N/A
**Early action deadline:** N/A, notification date: N/A
**Application deadline (fall):** 5/1
**Undergraduate student body:** 1,307 full time, 625 part time; 45% male, 55% female; 0% American Indian, 2% Asian, 5% black, 5% Hispanic, 0% multiracial, 0% Pacific Islander, 53% white, 2% international; 60% from in state; 88% live on campus; 3% of students in fraternities, 3% in sororities
**Most popular majors:** 8% Accounting, 17% Business/ Commerce, General, 6% Criminal Justice/Police Science, 5% Human Services, General, 8% Marketing/Marketing Management, General
**Expenses:** 2014-2015: $30,315; room/board: $7,965
**Financial aid:** (507) 457-1438; 77% of undergrads determined to have financial need; average aid package $22,086

## St. Olaf College
Northfield MN
(507) 786-3025
**U.S. News ranking:** Nat. Lib. Arts, No. 54
**Website:** wp.stolaf.edu/
**Admissions email:** admissions@ stolaf.edu
**Private;** founded 1874
**Affiliation:** Lutheran
**Freshman admissions:** more selective; 2013-2014: 4,011 applied, 2,372 accepted. Either SAT or ACT required. ACT 25/75 percentile: 26-31. High school rank: 54% in top tenth, 76% in top quarter, 98% in top half
**Early decision deadline:** 11/15, notification date: 12/17

**Early action deadline:** N/A, notification date: N/A
**Application deadline (fall):** 1/15
**Undergraduate student body:** 3,081 full time, 44 part time; 44% male, 56% female; 0% American Indian, 5% Asian, 1% black, 4% Hispanic, 4% multiracial, 0% Pacific Islander, 78% white, 6% international; 50% from in state; 92% live on campus; 0% of students in fraternities, 0% in sororities
**Most popular majors:** 12% Biological and Biomedical Sciences, 9% Physical Sciences, 8% Psychology, 16% Social Sciences, 11% Visual and Performing Arts
**Expenses:** 2014-2015: $41,700; room/board: $9,500
**Financial aid:** (507) 646-3019; 65% of undergrads determined to have financial need; average aid package $33,317

## University of Minnesota–Crookston
Crookston MN
(800) 232-6466
**U.S. News ranking:** Reg. Coll. (Mid. W), No. 40
**Website:** www.crk.umn.edu
**Admissions email:** UMCinfo@ umn.edu
**Public;** founded 1966
**Freshman admissions:** selective; 2013-2014: 762 applied, 527 accepted. Either SAT or ACT required. ACT 25/75 percentile: 19-24. High school rank: 10% in top tenth, 28% in top quarter, 63% in top half
**Early decision deadline:** N/A, notification date: N/A
**Early action deadline:** N/A, notification date: N/A
**Application deadline (fall):** rolling
**Undergraduate student body:** 1,305 full time, 1,534 part time; 47% male, 53% female; 1% American Indian, 2% Asian, 6% black, 2% Hispanic, 2% multiracial, 0% Pacific Islander, 78% white, 6% international; 72% from in state; 45% live on campus; 1% of students in fraternities, 0% in sororities
**Most popular majors:** 20% Agriculture, Agriculture Operations, and Related Sciences, 31% Business, Management, Marketing, and Related Support Services, 5% Health Professions and Related Programs, 8% Multi/Interdisciplinary Studies, 16% Natural Resources and Conservation
**Expenses:** 2014-2015: $11,468 in state, $11,468 out of state; room/board: $7,350
**Financial aid:** (218) 281-8576; 69% of undergrads determined to have financial need; average aid package $11,543

## University of Minnesota–Duluth
Duluth MN
(218) 726-7171
**U.S. News ranking:** Reg. U. (Mid. W), No. 36
**Website:** www.d.umn.edu
**Admissions email:** umdadmis@d.umn.edu
**Public;** founded 1947
**Freshman admissions:** selective; 2013-2014: 7,074 applied, 5,533 accepted. Either SAT or ACT required. ACT 25/75

percentile: 22-26. High school rank: 16% in top tenth, 44% in top quarter, 84% in top half
**Early decision deadline:** N/A, notification date: N/A
**Early action deadline:** N/A, notification date: N/A
**Application deadline (fall):** 8/1
**Undergraduate student body:** 8,989 full time, 1,090 part time; 53% male, 47% female; 0% American Indian, 3% Asian, 2% black, 2% Hispanic, 2% multiracial, 0% Pacific Islander, 88% white, 2% international; 90% from in state; 31% live on campus; N/A of students in fraternities, N/A in sororities
**Most popular majors:** 11% Biological and Biomedical Sciences, 20% Business, Management, Marketing, and Related Support Services, 8% Education, 10% Engineering, 10% Social Sciences
**Expenses:** 2014-2015: $12,802 in state, $16,467 out of state; room/board: $7,004
**Financial aid:** (218) 726-8000; 60% of undergrads determined to have financial need; average aid package $10,879

## University of Minnesota–Morris
Morris MN
(888) 866-3382
**U.S. News ranking:** Nat. Lib. Arts, No. 139
**Website:** www.morris.umn.edu
**Admissions email:** admissions@ morris.umn.edu
**Public;** founded 1959
**Freshman admissions:** selective; 2013-2014: 2,649 applied, 1,527 accepted. Either SAT or ACT required. ACT 25/75 percentile: 23-28. High school rank: 31% in top tenth, 59% in top quarter, 92% in top half
**Early decision deadline:** N/A, notification date: N/A
**Early action deadline:** N/A, notification date: N/A
**Application deadline (fall):** 3/15
**Undergraduate student body:** 1,815 full time, 131 part time; 45% male, 55% female; 6% American Indian, 3% Asian, 2% black, 3% Hispanic, 11% multiracial, 0% Pacific Islander, 66% white, 9% international; 88% from in state; 51% live on campus; N/A of students in fraternities, N/A in sororities
**Most popular majors:** 10% Biological and Biomedical Sciences, 8% Business, Management, Marketing, and Related Support Services, 6% English Language and Literature/ Letters, 5% History, 10% Psychology
**Expenses:** 2013-2014: $12,584 in state, $12,584 out of state; room/board: $7,482
**Financial aid:** (320) 589-6035

## University of Minnesota– Twin Cities
Minneapolis MN
(800) 752-1000
**U.S. News ranking:** Nat. U., No. 71
**Website:** www.umn.edu
**Admissions email:** N/A
**Public;** founded 1851

Freshman admissions: more selective; 2013-2014: 43,048 applied, 19,121 accepted. Either SAT or ACT required. ACT 25/75 percentile: 26-30. High school rank: 45% in top tenth, 82% in top quarter, 100% in top half
Early decision deadline: N/A, notification date: N/A
Early action deadline: N/A, notification date: N/A
Application deadline (fall): rolling
Undergraduate student body: 28,940 full time, 5,509 part time; 49% male, 51% female; 0% American Indian, 9% Asian, 4% black, 3% Hispanic, 3% multiracial, 0% Pacific Islander, 71% white, 9% international; 74% from in state; 23% live on campus; N/A of students in fraternities, N/A in sororities
Most popular majors: 8% Biological and Biomedical Sciences, 9% Business, Management, Marketing, and Related Support Services, 11% Engineering, 8% Psychology, 12% Social Sciences
Expenses: 2014-2015: $13,626 in state, $20,876 out of state; room/board: $8,920
Financial aid: (612) 624-1111; 51% of undergrads determined to have financial need; average aid package $13,244

## University of Northwestern–St. Paul

St. Paul MN
(800) 827-6827
U.S. News ranking: Reg. Coll. (Mid. W), No. 10
Website: www.unwsp.edu
Admissions email: admissions@ unwsp.edu
Private; founded 1902
Affiliation: Christian nondenominational
Freshman admissions: more selective; 2013-2014: N/A applied, N/A accepted. Either SAT or ACT required. ACT 25/75 percentile: 22-27. High school rank: 28% in top tenth, 50% in top quarter, 83% in top half
Early decision deadline: N/A, notification date: N/A
Early action deadline: N/A, notification date: N/A
Application deadline (fall): 8/1
Undergraduate student body: 1,685 full time, 52 part time; 40% male, 60% female; N/A American Indian, N/A Asian, N/A black, N/A Hispanic, N/A multiracial, N/A Pacific Islander, N/A white, N/A international
Most popular majors: Information not available
Expenses: 2014-2015: $28,676; room/board: $8,780
Financial aid: (651) 631-5212

## University of St. Thomas

St. Paul MN
(651) 962-6150
U.S. News ranking: Nat. U., No. 113
Website: www.stthomas.edu
Admissions email: admissions@ stthomas.edu
Private; founded 1885
Affiliation: Roman Catholic
Freshman admissions: selective; 2013-2014: 5,540 applied, 4,774 accepted. Either SAT or ACT required. ACT 25/75

percentile: 23-28. High school rank: 22% in top tenth, 50% in top quarter, 86% in top half
Early decision deadline: N/A, notification date: N/A
Early action deadline: N/A, notification date: N/A
Application deadline (fall): rolling
Undergraduate student body: 6,094 full time, 256 part time; 53% male, 47% female; 0% American Indian, 4% Asian, 3% black, 4% Hispanic, 3% multiracial, 0% Pacific Islander, 82% white, 3% international; 80% from in state; 39% live on campus; 0% of students in fraternities, 0% in sororities
Most popular majors: 7% Biological and Biomedical Sciences, 38% Business, Management, Marketing, and Related Support Services, 6% Communication, Journalism, and Related Programs, 8% Philosophy and Religious Studies, 9% Social Sciences
Expenses: 2014-2015: $34,442; room/board: $9,166
Financial aid: (651) 962-6550; 58% of undergrads determined to have financial need; average aid package $23,731

## Walden University

Minneapolis MN
(866) 492-5336
U.S. News ranking: Nat. U., unranked
Website: www.waldenu.edu/
Admissions email: N/A
For-profit; founded 1970
Freshman admissions: N/A; 2013-2014: 687 applied, 673 accepted. Neither SAT nor ACT required. ACT 25/75 percentile: N/A. High school rank: N/A
Early decision deadline: N/A, notification date: N/A
Early action deadline: N/A, notification date: N/A
Application deadline (fall): rolling
Undergraduate student body: 815 full time, 7,390 part time; 23% male, 77% female; 0% American Indian, 2% Asian, 35% black, 6% Hispanic, 2% multiracial, 0% Pacific Islander, 42% white, 1% international; 2% from in state; N/A live on campus; N/A of students in fraternities, N/A in sororities
Most popular majors: 19% Business Administration and Management, General, 5% Criminal Justice/Law Enforcement Administration, 6% Human Development and Family Studies, General, 17% Psychology, General, 32% Registered Nursing/ Registered Nurse
Expenses: 2014-2015: $14,300; room/board: N/A
Financial aid: N/A; 77% of undergrads determined to have financial need; average aid package $13,677

## Winona State University

Winona MN
(507) 457-5100
U.S. News ranking: Reg. U. (Mid. W), No. 61
Website: www.winona.edu
Admissions email: admissions@ winona.edu
Public; founded 1858

Freshman admissions: selective; 2013-2014: 7,212 applied, 4,381 accepted. Either SAT or ACT required. ACT 25/75 percentile: 21-25. High school rank: 8% in top tenth, 31% in quarter, 72% in top half
Early decision deadline: N/A, notification date: N/A
Early action deadline: N/A, notification date: N/A
Application deadline (fall): rolling
Undergraduate student body: 7,351 full time, 903 part time; 39% male, 61% female; 0% American Indian, 2% Asian, 2% black, 3% Hispanic, 2% multiracial, 0% Pacific Islander, 88% white, 2% international; 69% from in state; 29% live on campus; N/A of students in fraternities, N/A in sororities
Most popular majors: 17% Business, Management, Marketing, and Related Support Services, 6% Communication, Journalism, and Related Programs, 16% Education, 16% Health Professions and Related Programs, 8% Parks, Recreation, Leisure, and Fitness Studies
Expenses: 2014-2015: $8,750 in state, $14,250 out of state; room/board: $7,890
Financial aid: (507) 457-5090; 61% of undergrads determined to have financial need; average aid package $7,374

## Alcorn State University

Alcorn State MS
(601) 877-6147
U.S. News ranking: Reg. U. (S), No. 73
Website: www.alcorn.edu
Admissions email: ebarnes@alcorn.edu
Public; founded 1871
Freshman admissions: less selective; 2013-2014: 2,265 applied, 1,878 accepted. Either SAT or ACT required. ACT 25/75 percentile: 16-19. High school rank: N/A in top tenth, N/A in top quarter, 68% in top half
Early decision deadline: N/A, notification date: N/A
Early action deadline: N/A, notification date: N/A
Application deadline (fall): rolling
Undergraduate student body: 2,732 full time, 425 part time; 35% male, 65% female; 0% American Indian, 0% Asian, 93% black, 1% Hispanic, 1% multiracial, 0% Pacific Islander, 3% white, 1% international; 87% from in state; 50% live on campus; N/A of students in fraternities, N/A in sororities
Most popular majors: 11% Biological and Biomedical Sciences, 15% Health Professions and Related Programs, 12% Liberal Arts and Sciences, General Studies and Humanities, 8% Military Technologies and Applied Sciences, 6% Social Sciences
Expenses: 2013-2014: $6,096 in state, $15,096 out of state; room/board: $8,430
Financial aid: (601) 877-6190

## Belhaven University

Jackson MS
(601) 968-5940
U.S. News ranking: Reg. U. (S), No. 65
Website: www.belhaven.edu
Admissions email: admission@ belhaven.edu
Private; founded 1883
Affiliation: Presbyterian
Freshman admissions: selective; 2013-2014: 1,980 applied, 1,104 accepted. Either SAT or ACT required. ACT 25/75 percentile: 19-25. High school rank: 8% in top tenth, 26% in top quarter, 56% in top half
Early decision deadline: N/A, notification date: N/A
Early action deadline: N/A, notification date: N/A
Application deadline (fall): rolling
Undergraduate student body: 1,188 full time, 830 part time; 39% male, 61% female; 1% American Indian, 2% Asian, 40% black, 5% Hispanic, 2% multiracial, 0% Pacific Islander, 42% white, 0% international; 33% from in state; 45% live on campus; 0% of students in fraternities, 0% in sororities
Most popular majors: 41% Business, Management, Marketing, and Related Support Services, 8% Health Professions and Related Programs, 7% Parks, Recreation, Leisure, and Fitness Studies, 11% Social Sciences, 13% Visual and Performing Arts
Expenses: 2014-2015: $20,780; room/board: $7,700
Financial aid: (601) 968-5934; 75% of undergrads determined to have financial need; average aid package $15,058

## Blue Mountain College

Blue Mountain MS
(662) 685-4161
U.S. News ranking: Reg. Coll. (S), No. 23
Website: www.bmc.edu
Admissions email: admissions@ bmc.edu
Private; founded 1873
Affiliation: Southern Baptist Convention
Freshman admissions: selective; 2013-2014: 315 applied, 162 accepted. Either SAT or ACT required. ACT 25/75 percentile: 18-23. High school rank: 14% in top tenth, 38% in top quarter, 68% in top half
Early decision deadline: N/A, notification date: N/A
Early action deadline: N/A, notification date: N/A
Application deadline (fall): rolling
Undergraduate student body: 453 full time, 67 part time; 42% male, 58% female; 0% American Indian, 1% Asian, 10% black, 2% Hispanic, 0% multiracial, 0% Pacific Islander, 86% white, 2% international; 81% from in state; 56% live on campus; 0% of students in fraternities, 0% in sororities
Most popular majors: 17% Bible/Biblical Studies, 6% Biology/Biological Sciences, General, 7% Business Administration and Management, General, 48% Education, General, 8% Psychology, General

Expenses: 2014-2015: $10,534; room/board: $4,800
Financial aid: (662) 685-4771; 84% of undergrads determined to have financial need; average aid package $9,738

## Delta State University

Cleveland MS
(662) 846-4018
U.S. News ranking: Reg. U. (S), No. 92
Website: www.deltastate.edu
Admissions email: admissions@ deltastate.edu
Public; founded 1924
Freshman admissions: selective; 2013-2014: 472 applied, 422 accepted. ACT required. ACT 25/75 percentile: 18-22. High school rank: 17% in top tenth, 40% in top quarter, 77% in top half
Early decision deadline: N/A, notification date: N/A
Early action deadline: N/A, notification date: N/A
Application deadline (fall): 8/1
Undergraduate student body: 2,166 full time, 472 part time; 40% male, 60% female; 0% American Indian, 1% Asian, 35% black, 1% Hispanic, 1% multiracial, 0% Pacific Islander, 59% white, 3% international; 88% from in state; 36% live on campus; N/A of students in fraternities, N/A in sororities
Most popular majors: 8% Biology/Biological Sciences, General, 13% Elementary Education and Teaching, 6% Physical Education Teaching and Coaching, 8% Registered Nursing/Registered Nurse, 10% Social Work
Expenses: 2014-2015: $6,187 in state, $6,187 out of state; room/board: $7,045
Financial aid: (662) 846-4670; 67% of undergrads determined to have financial need; average aid package $8,914

## Jackson State University[1]

Jackson MS
(601) 979-2100
U.S. News ranking: Nat. U., second tier
Website: www.jsums.edu
Admissions email: admappl@ jsums.edu
Public
Application deadline (fall): N/A
Undergraduate student body: N/A full time, N/A part time
Expenses: 2013-2014: $6,348 in state, $15,552 out of state; room/board: $7,192
Financial aid: (601) 979-2227

## Millsaps College

Jackson MS
(601) 974-1050
U.S. News ranking: Nat. Lib. Arts, No. 89
Website: www.millsaps.edu
Admissions email: admissions@ millsaps.edu
Private; founded 1890
Affiliation: United Methodist
Freshman admissions: more selective; 2013-2014: 1,901 applied, 902 accepted. Either SAT or ACT required. ACT 25/75 percentile: 23-28. High school rank: 31% in top tenth, 59% in top quarter, 85% in top half

Early decision deadline: N/A, notification date: N/A
Early action deadline: 11/15, notification date: 1/15
Application deadline (fall): 2/1
Undergraduate student body: 730 full time, 14 part time; 52% male, 48% female; 1% American Indian, 5% Asian, 10% black, 3% Hispanic, 0% multiracial, 0% Pacific Islander, 76% white, 3% international; 42% from in state; 88% live on campus; 60% of students in fraternities, 64% in sororities
Most popular majors: 20% Biological and Biomedical Sciences, 24% Business, Management, Marketing, and Related Support Services, 8% Psychology, 10% Social Sciences, 7% Visual and Performing Arts
Expenses: 2014-2015: $33,982; room/board: $11,878
Financial aid: (601) 974-1220; 58% of undergrads determined to have financial need; average aid package $27,915

## Mississippi College
Clinton MS
(601) 925-3800
U.S. News ranking: Reg. U. (S), No. 29
Website: www.mc.edu
Admissions email: enrollment-services@mc.edu
Private; founded 1826
Affiliation: Mississippi Baptist Convention
Freshman admissions: selective; 2013-2014: 1,936 applied, 1,303 accepted. Either SAT or ACT required. ACT 25/75 percentile: 21-27. High school rank: 24% in top tenth, 42% in top quarter, 57% in top half
Early decision deadline: N/A, notification date: N/A
Early action deadline: N/A, notification date: N/A
Application deadline (fall): rolling
Undergraduate student body: 2,589 full time, 316 part time; 41% male, 59% female; 1% American Indian, 2% Asian, 22% black, 2% Hispanic, 1% multiracial, 0% Pacific Islander, 68% white, 3% international; 74% from in state; 59% live on campus; 7% of students in fraternities, 18% in sororities
Most popular majors: 7% Accounting, 7% Biomedical Sciences, General, 8% Business Administration and Management, General, 9% Kinesiology and Exercise Science, 10% Registered Nursing/Registered Nurse
Expenses: 2014-2015: $15,458; room/board: $8,408
Financial aid: (601) 925-3319; 55% of undergrads determined to have financial need; average aid package $13,596

## Mississippi State University
Mississippi State MS
(662) 325-2224
U.S. News ranking: Nat. U., No. 156
Website: www.msstate.edu
Admissions email: admit@admissions.msstate.edu
Public; founded 1878

Freshman admissions: more selective; 2013-2014: 11,117 applied, 7,938 accepted. Either SAT or ACT required. ACT 25/75 percentile: 20-28. High school rank: 28% in top tenth, 53% in top quarter, 83% in top half
Early decision deadline: N/A, notification date: N/A
Early action deadline: N/A, notification date: N/A
Application deadline (fall): rolling
Undergraduate student body: 15,048 full time, 1,351 part time; 52% male, 48% female; 1% American Indian, 1% Asian, 21% black, 2% Hispanic, 1% multiracial, 0% Pacific Islander, 72% white, 1% international; 76% from in state; 28% live on campus; 15% of students in fraternities, 24% in sororities
Most popular majors: 5% Biological and Biomedical Sciences, 18% Business, Management, Marketing, and Related Support Services, 19% Education, 11% Engineering, 5% Psychology
Expenses: 2013-2014: $6,772 in state, $16,960 out of state; room/board: $8,647
Financial aid: (662) 325-2450; 62% of undergrads determined to have financial need; average aid package $12,990

## Mississippi University for Women
Columbus MS
(662) 329-7106
U.S. News ranking: Reg. U. (S), No. 47
Website: www.muw.edu
Admissions email: admissions@muw.edu
Public; founded 1884
Freshman admissions: selective; 2013-2014: 1,274 applied, 554 accepted. Either SAT or ACT required. ACT 25/75 percentile: 18-24. High school rank: 26% in top tenth, 59% in top quarter, 87% in top half
Early decision deadline: N/A, notification date: N/A
Early action deadline: N/A, notification date: N/A
Application deadline (fall): rolling
Undergraduate student body: 1,945 full time, 484 part time; 18% male, 82% female; 0% American Indian, 1% Asian, 39% black, 1% Hispanic, 1% multiracial, 0% Pacific Islander, 56% white, 2% international; 91% from in state; 22% live on campus; 8% of students in fraternities, 12% in sororities
Most popular majors: 6% Business Administration and Management, General, 6% Elementary Education and Teaching, 7% Liberal Arts and Sciences/Liberal Studies, 48% Registered Nursing/Registered Nurse, 4% Speech-Language Pathology/Pathologist
Expenses: 2014-2015: $5,640 in state, $15,360 out of state; room/board: $6,183
Financial aid: (662) 329-7114; 76% of undergrads determined to have financial need; average aid package $8,948

## Mississippi Valley State University[1]
Itta Bena MS
(662) 254-3344
U.S. News ranking: Reg. U. (S), second tier
Website: www.mvsu.edu
Admissions email: admsn@mvsu.edu
Public
Application deadline (fall): N/A
Undergraduate student body: N/A full time, N/A part time
Expenses: 2013-2014: $5,916 in state, $5,916 out of state; room/board: $6,836
Financial aid: (662) 254-3335

## Rust College
Holly Springs MS
(662) 252-8000
U.S. News ranking: Nat. Lib. Arts, second tier
Website: www.rustcollege.edu
Admissions email: admissions@rustcollege.edu
Private; founded 1866
Affiliation: United Methodist
Freshman admissions: less selective; 2013-2014: 3,152 applied, 437 accepted. ACT required. ACT 25/75 percentile: 13-14. High school rank: N/A
Early decision deadline: N/A, notification date: N/A
Early action deadline: N/A, notification date: N/A
Application deadline (fall): rolling
Undergraduate student body: 854 full time, 68 part time; 39% male, 61% female; 0% American Indian, 0% Asian, 95% black, 0% Hispanic, 0% multiracial, 0% Pacific Islander, 0% white, 3% international; 49% from in state; 93% live on campus; 15% of students in fraternities, 15% in sororities
Most popular majors: 34% Biology/Biological Sciences, General, 12% Broadcast Journalism, 9% Computer Science, 8% Education, General, 14% Social Sciences, General
Expenses: 2014-2015: $9,286; room/board: $4,000
Financial aid: (662) 252-8000; 93% of undergrads determined to have financial need; average aid package $11,915

## Tougaloo College
Tougaloo MS
(601) 977-7765
U.S. News ranking: Nat. Lib. Arts, second tier
Website: www.tougaloo.edu
Admissions email: information@mail.tougaloo.edu
Private; founded 1869
Affiliation: United Church Disciples of Christ
Freshman admissions: less selective; 2013-2014: 3,018 applied, 1,028 accepted. Either SAT or ACT required. ACT 25/75 percentile: 15-21. High school rank: 19% in top tenth, 25% in top quarter, 82% in top half
Early decision deadline: N/A, notification date: N/A
Early action deadline: 11/1, notification date: 12/1
Application deadline (fall): 7/1
Undergraduate student body: 848 full time, 30 part time; 35% male, 65% female; 0% American Indian, 0% Asian, 98% black, 0% Hispanic, 0% multiracial,

0% Pacific Islander, 1% white, 1% international; 84% from in state; 65% live on campus; 6% of students in fraternities, 8% in sororities
Most popular majors: 9% Biology/Biological Sciences, General, 7% Chemistry, General, 8% Economics, General, 8% Psychology, General, 27% Sociology
Expenses: 2014-2015: $10,210; room/board: $6,330
Financial aid: (601) 977-7769; 96% of undergrads determined to have financial need; average aid package $13,500

## University of Mississippi
University MS
(662) 915-7226
U.S. News ranking: Nat. U., No. 149
Website: www.olemiss.edu
Admissions email: admissions@olemiss.edu
Public; founded 1844
Freshman admissions: more selective; 2013-2014: 14,258 applied, 8,464 accepted. Neither SAT nor ACT required. ACT 25/75 percentile: 21-27. High school rank: 24% in top tenth, 48% in top quarter, 77% in top half
Early decision deadline: N/A, notification date: N/A
Early action deadline: N/A, notification date: N/A
Application deadline (fall): 7/20
Undergraduate student body: 15,628 full time, 1,049 part time; 45% male, 55% female; 0% American Indian, 2% Asian, 16% black, 3% Hispanic, 2% multiracial, 0% Pacific Islander, 77% white, 1% international; 63% from in state; 32% live on campus; 29% of students in fraternities, 36% in sororities
Most popular majors: 5% Accounting, 5% Business/Managerial Economics, 8% Elementary Education and Teaching, 6% Marketing/Marketing Management, General, 5% Psychology, General
Expenses: 2014-2015: $7,096 in state, $19,144 out of state; room/board: $9,908
Financial aid: (662) 915-7175; 54% of undergrads determined to have financial need; average aid package $7,890

## University of Southern Mississippi
Hattiesburg MS
(601) 266-5000
U.S. News ranking: Nat. U., second tier
Website: www.usm.edu/admissions
Admissions email: admissions@usm.edu
Public; founded 1910
Freshman admissions: selective; 2013-2014: 6,120 applied, 4,058 accepted. Either SAT or ACT required. ACT 25/75 percentile: 19-25. High school rank: 6% in top tenth, 35% in top quarter, 71% in top half
Early decision deadline: N/A, notification date: N/A
Early action deadline: N/A, notification date: N/A
Application deadline (fall): rolling

0% Pacific Islander, 1% white, 1% international; 84% from in state; 65% live on campus; 6% of students in fraternities, 8% in sororities
Most popular majors: 9% Biology/Biological Sciences, General, 7% Chemistry, General, 8% Economics, General, 8% Psychology, General, 27% Sociology
Expenses: 2014-2015: $10,210; room/board: $6,330
Financial aid: (601) 977-7769; 96% of undergrads determined to have financial need; average aid package $13,500

Undergraduate student body: 10,841 full time, 1,634 part time; 36% male, 64% female; 0% American Indian, 1% Asian, 32% black, 3% Hispanic, 2% multiracial, 0% Pacific Islander, 61% white, 1% international; 85% from in state; 27% live on campus; 15% of students in fraternities, 17% in sororities
Most popular majors: 4% Business Administration and Management, General, 8% Elementary Education and Teaching, 5% Multi-/Interdisciplinary Studies, Other, 6% Psychology, General, 8% Registered Nursing/Registered Nurse
Expenses: 2013-2014: $6,744 in state, $15,024 out of state; room/board: $7,206
Financial aid: (601) 266-4774

## William Carey University
Hattiesburg MS
(601) 318-6103
U.S. News ranking: Reg. U. (S), No. 37
Website: www.wmcarey.edu
Admissions email: admissions@wmcarey.edu
Private; founded 1892
Affiliation: Baptist
Freshman admissions: more selective; 2013-2014: 712 applied, 357 accepted. Either SAT or ACT required. ACT 25/75 percentile: 21-28. High school rank: 39% in top tenth, 59% in top quarter, 81% in top half
Early decision deadline: N/A, notification date: N/A
Early action deadline: N/A, notification date: N/A
Application deadline (fall): rolling
Undergraduate student body: 1,886 full time, 371 part time; 36% male, 64% female; 1% American Indian, 1% Asian, 30% black, 2% Hispanic, 0% multiracial, 0% Pacific Islander, 61% white, 4% international; 89% from in state; 31% live on campus; 0% of students in fraternities, 2% in sororities
Most popular majors: 4% Biology/Biological Sciences, General, 11% Business Administration and Management, General, 18% Elementary Education and Teaching, 19% Psychology, General, 23% Registered Nursing/Registered Nurse
Expenses: 2014-2015: $11,400; room/board: $4,140
Financial aid: (601) 318-6153; 91% of undergrads determined to have financial need; average aid package $16,000

## Avila University[1]
Kansas City MO
(816) 501-2400
U.S. News ranking: Reg. U. (Mid. W), second tier
Website: www.Avila.edu
Admissions email: admissions@mail.avila.edu
Private
Application deadline (fall): N/A
Undergraduate student body: N/A full time, N/A part time
Expenses: 2013-2014: $24,950; room/board: $6,908
Financial aid: (816) 501-3600

## Central Methodist University
Fayette MO
(660) 248-6251
**U.S. News ranking:** Reg. Coll.
(Mid. W), No. 40
**Website:**
www.centralmethodist.edu
**Admissions email:** admissions@
centralmethodist.edu
**Private;** founded 1854
**Affiliation:** United Methodist
**Freshman admissions:** selective;
2013-2014: 1,285 applied, 836
accepted. Either SAT or ACT
required. ACT 25/75 percentile:
19-24. High school rank: 18%
in top tenth, 43% in top quarter,
79% in top half
**Early decision deadline:** N/A,
notification date: N/A
**Early action deadline:** N/A,
notification date: N/A
**Application deadline (fall):** rolling
**Undergraduate student body:** 1,024
full time, 83 part time; 49%
male, 51% female; 3% American
Indian, 0% Asian, 0% black, 1%
Hispanic, 0% multiracial, 63%
Pacific Islander, 1% white, 0%
international; 88% from in state;
61% live on campus; 17% of
students in fraternities, 14% in
sororities
**Most popular majors:** 10%
Biological and Biomedical
Sciences, 16% Business,
Management, Marketing, and
Related Support Services,
24% Education, 16% Health
Professions and Related Programs,
8% Multi/Interdisciplinary Studies
**Expenses:** 2014-2015: $21,830;
room/board: $7,130
**Financial aid:** (660) 248-6244;
81% of undergrads determined to
have financial need; average aid
package $19,231

## College of the Ozarks
Point Lookout MO
(800) 222-0525
**U.S. News ranking:** Reg. Coll.
(Mid. W), No. 4
**Website:** www.cofo.edu
**Admissions email:**
admiss4@cofo.edu
**Private;** founded 1906
**Affiliation:** Evangelical Christian
Interdenominational
**Freshman admissions:** selective;
2013-2014: 3,050 applied, 371
accepted. Either SAT or ACT
required. ACT 25/75 percentile:
20-25. High school rank: 19%
in top tenth, 50% in top quarter,
94% in top half
**Early decision deadline:** N/A,
notification date: N/A
**Early action deadline:** N/A,
notification date: N/A
**Application deadline (fall):** rolling
**Undergraduate student body:** 1,498
full time, 33 part time; 47%
male, 53% female; 1% American
Indian, 1% Asian, 1% black,
2% Hispanic, 2% multiracial,
0% Pacific Islander, 92% white,
2% international; 84% from in
state; 81% live on campus; 0%
of students in fraternities, 0% in
sororities
**Most popular majors:** 10%
Agriculture, Agriculture
Operations, and Related Sciences,
12% Business, Management,
Marketing, and Related Support
Services, 17% Education,

General, 9% Homeland Security,
Law Enforcement, Firefighting
and Related Protective Services,
9% Speech Communication and
Rhetoric
**Expenses:** 2014-2015: $18,530;
room/board: $6,200
**Financial aid:** (417) 334-6411;
94% of undergrads determined to
have financial need; average aid
package $17,434

## Columbia College
Columbia MO
(573) 875-7352
**U.S. News ranking:** Reg. U.
(Mid. W), unranked
**Website:** www.ccis.edu
**Admissions email:**
admissions@ccis.edu
**Private;** founded 1851
**Affiliation:** Christian Church
(Disciples of Christ)
**Freshman admissions:** N/A; 2013-
2014: N/A applied, N/A accepted.
Neither SAT nor ACT required.
ACT 25/75 percentile: N/A. High
school rank: N/A
**Early decision deadline:** N/A,
notification date: N/A
**Early action deadline:** N/A,
notification date: N/A
**Application deadline (fall):** rolling
**Undergraduate student body:** N/A
full time, N/A part time; N/A
male, N/A female; N/A American
Indian, N/A Asian, N/A black, N/A
Hispanic, N/A multiracial, N/A
Pacific Islander, N/A white, N/A
international
**Most popular majors:** Information
not available
**Expenses:** 2013-2014: $19,386;
room/board: N/A
**Financial aid:** (573) 875-7390

## Culver-Stockton College
Canton MO
(800) 537-1883
**U.S. News ranking:** Reg. Coll.
(Mid. W), No. 34
**Website:** www.culver.edu
**Admissions email:**
admissions@culver.edu
**Private;** founded 1853
**Affiliation:** Christian Church
(Disciples of Christ)
**Freshman admissions:** selective;
2013-2014: 2,040 applied,
1,209 accepted. Either SAT
or ACT required. ACT 25/75
percentile: 18-23. High school
rank: 11% in top tenth, 25% in
top quarter, 59% in top half
**Early decision deadline:** N/A,
notification date: N/A
**Early action deadline:** N/A,
notification date: N/A
**Application deadline (fall):** rolling
**Undergraduate student body:** 772
full time, 58 part time; 50%
male, 50% female; 0% American
Indian, 0% Asian, 12% black,
4% Hispanic, 2% multiracial,
1% Pacific Islander, 79% white,
2% international; 65% from in
state; 74% live on campus; 36%
of students in fraternities, 39%
in sororities
**Most popular majors:** 12%
Business Administration and
Management, General, 6%
Criminal Justice/Law Enforcement
Administration, 9% Psychology,
General, 8% Registered Nursing/
Registered Nurse, 10% Sport
and Fitness Administration/
Management

**Expenses:** 2014-2015: $24,050;
room/board: $7,780
**Financial aid:** (573) 288-6307;
90% of undergrads determined to
have financial need; average aid
package $20,649

## Drury University
Springfield MO
(417) 873-7205
**U.S. News ranking:** Reg. U.
(Mid. W), No. 8
**Website:** www.drury.edu
**Admissions email:** druryad@
drury.edu
**Private;** founded 1873
**Affiliation:** Christian Church
(Disciples of Christ)
**Freshman admissions:** more
selective; 2013-2014: 1,244
applied, 909 accepted. Either
SAT or ACT required. ACT 25/75
percentile: 22-28. High school
rank: 30% in top tenth, 59% in
top quarter, 87% in top half
**Early decision deadline:** N/A,
notification date: N/A
**Early action deadline:** N/A,
notification date: N/A
**Application deadline (fall):** rolling
**Undergraduate student body:** 1,549
full time, 26 part time; 47%
male, 53% female; 1% American
Indian, 2% Asian, 3% black, 3%
Hispanic, 1% multiracial, 0%
Pacific Islander, 81% white, 10%
international; 85% from in state;
52% live on campus; 25% of
students in fraternities, 26% in
sororities
**Most popular majors:** 11%
Biological and Biomedical
Sciences, 12% Business,
Management, Marketing, and
Related Support Services, 11%
Education, 14% Psychology, 9%
Social Sciences
**Expenses:** 2014-2015: $23,885;
room/board: $7,394
**Financial aid:** (417) 873-7312;
70% of undergrads determined to
have financial need; average aid
package $17,945

## Evangel University
Springfield MO
(800) 382-6435
**U.S. News ranking:** Reg. Coll.
(Mid. W), No. 49
**Website:** www.evangel.edu
**Admissions email:** admissions@
evangel.edu
**Private;** founded 1955
**Affiliation:** Assemblies of God
**Freshman admissions:** selective;
2013-2014: N/A applied, N/A
accepted. Either SAT or ACT
required. ACT 25/75 percentile:
19-26. High school rank: N/A
**Early decision deadline:** N/A,
notification date: N/A
**Early action deadline:** N/A,
notification date: N/A
**Application deadline (fall):** rolling
**Undergraduate student body:** 1,887
full time, 190 part time; 44%
male, 56% female; 1% American
Indian, 2% Asian, 5% black,
6% Hispanic, 3% multiracial,
0% Pacific Islander, 70% white,
1% international; 55% from in
state; 68% live on campus; N/A
of students in fraternities, N/A in
sororities
**Most popular majors:** Information
not available
**Expenses:** 2014-2015: $20,676;
room/board: $7,200

**Financial aid:** (417) 865-2815;
96% of undergrads determined to
have financial need; average aid
package $14,653

## Fontbonne University
St. Louis MO
(314) 889-1400
**U.S. News ranking:** Reg. U.
(Mid. W), No. 109
**Website:** www.fontbonne.edu
**Admissions email:** admissions@
fontbonne.edu
**Private;** founded 1923
**Affiliation:** Roman Catholic
**Freshman admissions:** selective;
2013-2014: 676 applied, 441
accepted. Either SAT or ACT
required. ACT 25/75 percentile:
21-25. High school rank: N/A
**Early decision deadline:** N/A,
notification date: N/A
**Early action deadline:** N/A,
notification date: N/A
**Application deadline (fall):** rolling
**Undergraduate student body:** 956
full time, 372 part time; 33%
male, 67% female; 0% American
Indian, 1% Asian, 17% black,
2% Hispanic, 1% multiracial,
0% Pacific Islander, 68% white,
9% international; 87% from in
state; 19% live on campus; N/A
of students in fraternities, N/A in
sororities
**Most popular majors:** 16%
Business Administration
and Management, General,
4% Dietetics/Dietitian, 5%
Psychology, General, 7% Special
Education and Teaching, General,
6% Speech-Language Pathology/
Pathologist
**Expenses:** 2013-2014: $22,684;
room/board: $8,400
**Financial aid:** (314) 889-1414

## Hannibal-LaGrange University
Hannibal MO
(800) 454-1119
**U.S. News ranking:** Reg. Coll.
(Mid. W), second tier
**Website:** www.hlg.edu
**Admissions email:**
admissions@hlg.edu
**Private;** founded 1858
**Affiliation:** Southern Baptist
Convention
**Freshman admissions:** selective;
2013-2014: 703 applied, 480
accepted. Either SAT or ACT
required. ACT 25/75 percentile:
19-25. High school rank: N/A
**Early decision deadline:** N/A,
notification date: N/A
**Early action deadline:** N/A,
notification date: N/A
**Application deadline (fall):** 8/27
**Undergraduate student body:** 850
full time, 349 part time; 42%
male, 58% female; 1% American
Indian, 1% Asian, 4% black,
4% Hispanic, 2% multiracial,
1% Pacific Islander, 79% white,
9% international; 77% from in
state; 43% live on campus; N/A
of students in fraternities, N/A in
sororities
**Most popular majors:** 8% Business
Administration and Management,
General, 11% Criminal Justice/
Safety Studies, 15% Elementary
Education and Teaching, 12%
Organizational Leadership, 11%
Registered Nursing/Registered
Nurse
**Expenses:** 2013-2014: $18,770;
room/board: $6,840
**Financial aid:** (573) 221-3675

## Harris-Stowe State University[1]
St. Louis MO
(314) 340-3300
**U.S. News ranking:** Reg. Coll.
(Mid. W), unranked
**Website:** www.hssu.edu
**Admissions email:**
admissions@hssu.edu
**Public**
**Application deadline (fall):** N/A
**Undergraduate student body:** N/A
full time, N/A part time
**Expenses:** 2013-2014: $5,220 in
state, $9,853 out of state; room/
board: $8,900
**Financial aid:** (314) 340-3500

## Kansas City Art Institute
Kansas City MO
(800) 522-5224
**U.S. News ranking:** Arts, unranked
**Website:** www.kcai.edu
**Admissions email:**
admiss@kcai.edu
**Private;** founded 1885
**Freshman admissions:** N/A;
2013-2014: 577 applied, 397
accepted. Either SAT or ACT
required. SAT 25/75 percentile:
N/A. High school rank: 13% in top
tenth, 36% in top quarter, 66%
in top half
**Early decision deadline:** N/A,
notification date: N/A
**Early action deadline:** N/A,
notification date: N/A
**Application deadline (fall):** rolling
**Undergraduate student body:**
735 full time, 4 part time; 37%
male, 63% female; 0% American
Indian, 2% Asian, 5% black,
7% Hispanic, 7% multiracial,
0% Pacific Islander, 63% white,
0% international; 40% from in
state; 11% live on campus; 0%
of students in fraternities, 0% in
sororities
**Most popular majors:** 14%
Animation, Interactive Technology,
Video Graphics and Special
Effects, 11% Graphic Design,
14% Illustration, 16% Painting,
11% Sculpture
**Expenses:** 2013-2014: $33,712;
room/board: $9,650
**Financial aid:** (816) 802-3448

## Lincoln University[1]
Jefferson City MO
(573) 681-5599
**U.S. News ranking:** Reg. U.
(Mid. W), unranked
**Website:** www.lincolnu.edu
**Admissions email:**
enroll@lincolnu.edu
**Public**
**Application deadline (fall):** N/A
**Undergraduate student body:** N/A
full time, N/A part time
**Expenses:** 2013-2014: $6,838 in
state, $13,228 out of state; room/
board: $5,531
**Financial aid:** (573) 681-6156

## Lindenwood University
St. Charles MO
(636) 949-4949
**U.S. News ranking:** Reg. U.
(Mid. W), No. 95
**Website:** www.lindenwood.edu
**Admissions email:** admissions@
lindenwood.edu
**Private;** founded 1827
**Affiliation:** Presbyterian

**Freshman admissions:** selective; 2013-2014: 3,379 applied, 2,240 accepted. Either SAT or ACT required. ACT 25/75 percentile: 20-25. High school rank: 12% in top tenth, 33% in top quarter, 69% in top half **Early decision deadline:** N/A, notification date: N/A **Early action deadline:** N/A, notification date: N/A **Application deadline (fall):** rolling **Undergraduate student body:** 7,502 full time, 951 part time; 46% male, 54% female; 0% American Indian, 1% Asian, 14% black, 4% Hispanic, 3% multiracial, 0% Pacific Islander, 59% white, 11% international; 69% from in state; 51% live on campus; 2% of students in fraternities, 3% in sororities **Most popular majors:** 23% Business/Commerce, General, 10% Criminology, 5% Elementary Education and Teaching, 4% Human Resources Management/Personnel Administration, General, 4% Mass Communication/Media Studies **Expenses:** 2014-2015: $15,580; room/board: $7,880 **Financial aid:** (636) 949-4923; 59% of undergrads determined to have financial need; average aid package $9,739

## Maryville University of St. Louis

St Louis MO
(800) 627-9855
**U.S. News ranking:** Nat. U., No. 156
**Website:** www.maryville.edu
**Admissions email:** admissions@maryville.edu
**Private;** founded 1872
**Freshman admissions:** more selective; 2013-2014: 1,595 applied, 1,214 accepted. Either SAT or ACT required. ACT 25/75 percentile: 23-27. High school rank: 27% in top tenth, 61% in top quarter, 91% in top half **Early decision deadline:** N/A, notification date: N/A **Early action deadline:** N/A, notification date: N/A **Application deadline (fall):** 8/15 **Undergraduate student body:** 1,786 full time, 1,043 part time; 29% male, 71% female; 0% American Indian, 2% Asian, 8% black, 2% Hispanic, 2% multiracial, 0% Pacific Islander, 76% white, 3% international; 80% from in state; 24% live on campus; 0% of students in fraternities, 0% in sororities **Most popular majors:** 6% Accounting, 8% Business/Commerce, General, 6% Health Professions and Related Clinical Sciences, Other, 5% Psychology, General, 31% Registered Nursing/Registered Nurse **Expenses:** 2014-2015: $25,884; room/board: $10,284 **Financial aid:** (314) 529-9360; 71% of undergrads determined to have financial need; average aid package $22,335

## Missouri Baptist University[1]

St. Louis MO
(314) 434-2290
**U.S. News ranking:** Reg. U. (Mid. W), second tier
**Website:** www.mobap.edu
**Admissions email:** admissions@mobap.edu
**Private;** founded 1964
**Affiliation:** Baptist
**Application deadline (fall):** rolling
**Undergraduate student body:** N/A full time, N/A part time
**Expenses:** 2013-2014: $21,670; room/board: $8,640
**Financial aid:** (314) 392-2366

## Missouri Southern State University

Joplin MO
(417) 781-6778
**U.S. News ranking:** Reg. Coll. (Mid. W), second tier
**Website:** www.mssu.edu
**Admissions email:** admissions@mssu.edu
**Public;** founded 1937
**Freshman admissions:** less selective; 2013-2014: 1,726 applied, 1,679 accepted. Either SAT or ACT required. ACT 25/75 percentile: 18-24. High school rank: 12% in top tenth, 33% in top quarter, 67% in top half **Early decision deadline:** N/A, notification date: N/A **Early action deadline:** N/A, notification date: N/A **Application deadline (fall):** rolling **Undergraduate student body:** 4,125 full time, 1,462 part time; 42% male, 58% female; 3% American Indian, 2% Asian, 5% black, 4% Hispanic, 1% multiracial, 0% Pacific Islander, 80% white, 2% international; 85% from in state; 8% live on campus; N/A of students in fraternities, N/A in sororities **Most popular majors:** 13% Business, Management, Marketing, and Related Support Services, 29% Education, 14% Health Professions and Related Programs, 16% Homeland Security, Law Enforcement, Firefighting and Related Protective Services, 7% Liberal Arts and Sciences, General Studies and Humanities **Expenses:** 2014-2015: $5,416 in state, $10,450 out of state; room/board: $6,299 **Financial aid:** (417) 625-9325; 80% of undergrads determined to have financial need; average aid package $7,486

## Missouri State University

Springfield MO
(800) 492-7900
**U.S. News ranking:** Reg. U. (Mid. W), No. 67
**Website:** www.missouristate.edu
**Admissions email:** info@missouristate.edu
**Public;** founded 1906
**Freshman admissions:** selective; 2013-2014: 7,464 applied, 6,368 accepted. Either SAT or ACT required. ACT 25/75 percentile: 21-26. High school rank: 24% in top tenth, 53% in top quarter, 84% in top half **Early decision deadline:** N/A, notification date: N/A

**Early action deadline:** N/A, notification date: N/A **Application deadline (fall):** 7/20 **Undergraduate student body:** 13,805 full time, 4,222 part time; 43% male, 57% female; 1% American Indian, 1% Asian, 4% black, 3% Hispanic, 3% multiracial, 0% Pacific Islander, 82% white, 4% international; 92% from in state; 24% live on campus; 21% of students in fraternities, 19% in sororities **Most popular majors:** 29% Business, Management, Marketing, and Related Support Services, 15% Education, 6% Health Professions and Related Programs, 6% Psychology, 9% Social Sciences **Expenses:** 2014-2015: $7,008 in state, $13,668 out of state; room/board: $7,678 **Financial aid:** (417) 836-5262; 63% of undergrads determined to have financial need; average aid package $11,129

## Missouri University of Science & Technology

Rolla MO
(573) 341-4165
**U.S. News ranking:** Nat. U., No. 138
**Website:** www.mst.edu
**Admissions email:** admissions@mst.edu
**Public;** founded 1870
**Freshman admissions:** more selective; 2013-2014: 3,297 applied, 2,709 accepted. Either SAT or ACT required. ACT 25/75 percentile: 25-31. High school rank: 41% in top tenth, 71% in top quarter, 93% in top half **Early decision deadline:** N/A, notification date: N/A **Early action deadline:** N/A, notification date: N/A **Application deadline (fall):** 7/1 **Undergraduate student body:** 5,472 full time, 674 part time; 77% male, 23% female; 0% American Indian, 2% Asian, 4% black, 2% Hispanic, 2% multiracial, 0% Pacific Islander, 79% white, 6% international; 84% from in state; 43% live on campus; 21% of students in fraternities, 19% in sororities **Most popular majors:** 4% Biological and Biomedical Sciences, 8% Computer and Information Sciences and Support Services, 70% Engineering, 4% Physical Sciences, 4% Psychology **Expenses:** 2014-2015: $9,537 in state, $25,404 out of state; room/board: $9,540 **Financial aid:** (573) 341-4282; 61% of undergrads determined to have financial need; average aid package $10,052

## Missouri Valley College[1]

Marshall MO
(660) 831-4114
**U.S. News ranking:** Reg. Coll. (Mid. W), second tier
**Website:** www.moval.edu
**Admissions email:** admissions@moval.edu
**Private**
**Application deadline (fall):** N/A
**Undergraduate student body:** N/A full time, N/A part time

**Expenses:** 2013-2014: $18,300; room/board: $7,700
**Financial aid:** (660) 831-4171

## Missouri Western State University

St. Joseph MO
(816) 271-4266
**U.S. News ranking:** Reg. Coll. (Mid. W), second tier
**Website:** www.missouriwestern.edu
**Admissions email:** admission@missouriwestern.edu
**Public;** founded 1969
**Freshman admissions:** less selective; 2013-2014: 3,376 applied, 3,376 accepted. Neither SAT nor ACT required. ACT 25/75 percentile: 17-23. High school rank: 10% in top tenth, 28% in top quarter, 61% in top half **Early decision deadline:** N/A, notification date: N/A **Early action deadline:** N/A, notification date: N/A **Application deadline (fall):** rolling **Undergraduate student body:** 3,945 full time, 1,671 part time; 43% male, 57% female; 1% American Indian, 1% Asian, 11% black, 1% Hispanic, 3% multiracial, 0% Pacific Islander, 79% white, 1% international; 91% from in state; 24% live on campus; N/A of students in fraternities, N/A in sororities **Most popular majors:** 6% Business Administration and Management, General, 7% Criminal Justice/Safety Studies, 6% Elementary Education and Teaching, 6% Health and Physical Education/Fitness, General, 13% Registered Nursing/Registered Nurse **Expenses:** 2014-2015: $6,497 in state, $12,489 out of state; room/board: $7,128 **Financial aid:** (816) 271-4361; 74% of undergrads determined to have financial need; average aid package $8,007

## Northwest Missouri State University

Maryville MO
(800) 633-1175
**U.S. News ranking:** Reg. U. (Mid. W), No. 80
**Website:** www.nwmissouri.edu
**Admissions email:** admissions@nwmissouri.edu
**Public;** founded 1905
**Freshman admissions:** selective; 2013-2014: 5,619 applied, 4,111 accepted. Either SAT or ACT required. ACT 25/75 percentile: 20-25. High school rank: 14% in top tenth, 40% in top quarter, 77% in top half **Early decision deadline:** N/A, notification date: N/A **Early action deadline:** N/A, notification date: N/A **Application deadline (fall):** rolling **Undergraduate student body:** 4,988 full time, 554 part time; 45% male, 55% female; 0% American Indian, 1% Asian, 6% black, 3% Hispanic, 3% multiracial, 0% Pacific Islander, 83% white, 2% international; 73% from in state; 39% live on campus; 21% of students in fraternities, 20% in sororities **Most popular majors:** 6% Agriculture, Agriculture Operations, and Related Sciences, 27% Business, Management, Marketing, and Related Support

**Expenses:** 2014-2015: $8,156 in state, $14,407 out of state; room/board: $8,709
**Financial aid:** (660) 562-1363; 69% of undergrads determined to have financial need; average aid package $8,841

## Park University[1]

Parkville MO
(800) 745-7275
**U.S. News ranking:** Reg. U. (Mid. W), second tier
**Website:** www.park.edu
**Admissions email:** admissions@mail.park.edu
**Private;** founded 1875
**Application deadline (fall):** 8/1
**Undergraduate student body:** N/A full time, N/A part time
**Expenses:** 2013-2014: $10,600; room/board: $7,152
**Financial aid:** (816) 584-6190

## Ranken Technical College[1]

Saint Louis MO
(866) 472-6536
**U.S. News ranking:** Reg. Coll. (Mid. W), unranked
**Website:** www.ranken.edu
**Admissions email:** N/A
**Private**
**Application deadline (fall):** N/A
**Undergraduate student body:** N/A full time, N/A part time
**Expenses:** 2013-2014: $14,457; room/board: $5,200
**Financial aid:** (314) 286-4862

## Rockhurst University

Kansas City MO
(816) 501-4100
**U.S. News ranking:** Reg. U. (Mid. W), No. 14
**Website:** www.rockhurst.edu
**Admissions email:** admissions@rockhurst.edu
**Private;** founded 1910
**Affiliation:** Roman Catholic (Jesuit)
**Freshman admissions:** more selective; 2013-2014: 2,576 applied, 1,943 accepted. Either SAT or ACT required. ACT 25/75 percentile: 23-28. High school rank: 30% in top tenth, 53% in top quarter, 87% in top half **Early decision deadline:** N/A, notification date: N/A **Early action deadline:** N/A, notification date: N/A **Application deadline (fall):** rolling **Undergraduate student body:** 1,546 full time, 695 part time; 40% male, 60% female; 1% American Indian, 3% Asian, 5% black, 5% Hispanic, 1% multiracial, 0% Pacific Islander, 78% white, 1% international; 57% from in state; 54% live on campus; 26% of students in fraternities, 34% in sororities **Most popular majors:** 8% Biological and Biomedical Sciences, 16% Business, Management, Marketing, and Related Support Services, 24% Health Professions and Related Programs, 11% Psychology, 9% Social Sciences **Expenses:** 2014-2015: $32,865; room/board: $8,680 **Financial aid:** (816) 501-4100; 59% of undergrads determined to have financial need; average aid package $30,086

## Southeast Missouri State University

Cape Girardeau MO
(573) 651-2590
**U.S. News ranking:** Reg. U.
(Mid. W), No. 95
**Website:** www.semo.edu
**Admissions email:** admissions@
semo.edu
**Public;** founded 1873
**Freshman admissions:** selective;
2013-2014: 4,388 applied,
3,840 accepted. Either SAT
or ACT required. ACT 25/75
percentile: 20-25. High school
rank: 17% in top tenth, 43% in
top quarter, 73% in top half
**Early decision deadline:** N/A,
notification date: N/A
**Early action deadline:** N/A,
notification date: N/A
**Application deadline (fall):** 7/1
**Undergraduate student body:** 8,094
full time, 2,661 part time; 43%
male, 57% female; 1% American
Indian, 1% Asian, 10% black,
2% Hispanic, 0% multiracial,
0% Pacific Islander, 79% white,
6% international; 85% from in
state; 26% live on campus; 14%
of students in fraternities, 11%
in sororities
**Most popular majors:** 8%
Communication and Media
Studies, 9% Liberal Arts and
Sciences, General Studies and
Humanities, 7% Registered
Nursing, Nursing Administration,
Nursing Research and Clinical
Nursing, 7% Teacher Education
and Professional Development,
Specific Levels and Methods,
7% Teacher Education and
Professional Development,
Specific Subject Areas
**Expenses:** 2014-2015: $6,938 in
state, $12,270 out of state; room/
board: N/A
**Financial aid:** (573) 651-2253;
62% of undergrads determined to
have financial need; average aid
package $8,419

## Southwest Baptist University[1]

Bolivar MO
(800) 526-5859
**U.S. News ranking:** Reg. U.
(Mid. W), second tier
**Website:** www.sbuniv.edu
**Admissions email:**
dcrowder@sbuniv.edu
**Private**
**Application deadline (fall):** N/A
**Undergraduate student body:** N/A
full time, N/A part time
**Expenses:** 2013-2014: $20,040;
room/board: $6,800
**Financial aid:** (417) 328-1822

## Stephens College

Columbia MO
(800) 876-7207
**U.S. News ranking:** Reg. Coll.
(Mid. W), No. 23
**Website:** www.stephens.edu
**Admissions email:**
apply@stephens.edu
**Private;** founded 1833
**Freshman admissions:** selective;
2013-2014: 783 applied, 529
accepted. Either SAT or ACT
required. ACT 25/75 percentile:
19-26. High school rank: 17%
in top tenth, 39% in top quarter,
73% in top half
**Early decision deadline:** 11/15,
notification date: 12/1

**Early action deadline:** 1/1,
notification date: 1/15
**Application deadline (fall):** rolling
**Undergraduate student body:** 521
full time, 129 part time; 2%
male, 98% female; 0% American
Indian, 2% Asian, 18% black,
2% Hispanic, 6% multiracial,
0% Pacific Islander, 70% white,
0% international; 55% from in
state; 71% live on campus; N/A
of students in fraternities, N/A in
sororities
**Most popular majors:** 25%
Business/Commerce, General,
33% Drama and Dramatics/
Theatre Arts, General, 6%
Education, General, 13% Health
Information/Medical Records
Administration/Administrator, 5%
Liberal Arts and Sciences/Liberal
Studies
**Expenses:** 2014-2015: $28,510;
room/board: $9,533
**Financial aid:** (573) 876-7106;
84% of undergrads determined to
have financial need; average aid
package $25,673

## St. Louis University

St. Louis MO
(314) 977-2500
**U.S. News ranking:** Nat. U.,
No. 99
**Website:** www.slu.edu
**Admissions email:**
admission@slu.edu
**Private;** founded 1818
**Affiliation:** Roman Catholic
**Freshman admissions:** more
selective; 2013-2014: 13,091
applied, 8,327 accepted. Either
SAT or ACT required. ACT 25/75
percentile: 25-30. High school
rank: 41% in top tenth, 74% in
top quarter, 91% in top half
**Early decision deadline:** N/A,
notification date: N/A
**Early action deadline:** N/A,
notification date: N/A
**Application deadline (fall):** 8/20
**Undergraduate student body:** 7,795
full time, 892 part time; 41%
male, 59% female; 0% American
Indian, 8% Asian, 7% black, 4%
Hispanic, 5% multiracial, 0%
Pacific Islander, 65% white, 7%
international; 39% from in state;
50% live on campus; 12% of
students in fraternities, 16% in
sororities
**Most popular majors:** 5%
Accounting, 6% Biology/
Biological Sciences, General, 5%
Kinesiology and Exercise Science,
5% Psychology, General, 12%
Registered Nursing/Registered
Nurse
**Expenses:** 2014-2015: $37,966;
room/board: $10,380
**Financial aid:** (314) 977-2350;
58% of undergrads determined to
have financial need; average aid
package $24,852

## Truman State University

Kirksville MO
(660) 785-4114
**U.S. News ranking:** Reg. U.
(Mid. W), No. 9
**Website:** www.truman.edu
**Admissions email:** admissions@
truman.edu
**Public;** founded 1867
**Freshman admissions:** more
selective; 2013-2014: 4,462
applied, 3,221 accepted. Either
SAT or ACT required. ACT 25/75

percentile: 25-30. High school
rank: 47% in top tenth, 80% in
top quarter, 98% in top half
**Early decision deadline:** N/A,
notification date: N/A
**Early action deadline:** N/A,
notification date: N/A
**Application deadline (fall):** rolling
**Undergraduate student body:** 5,375
full time, 523 part time; 40%
male, 60% female; 0% American
Indian, 2% Asian, 3% black, 3%
Hispanic, 2% multiracial, 0%
Pacific Islander, 82% white, 6%
international; 83% from in state;
42% live on campus; 21% of
students in fraternities, 18% in
sororities
**Most popular majors:** 8% Biology/
Biological Sciences, General,
17% Business Administration
and Management, General, 9%
English Language and Literature,
General, 14% Health and Physical
Education/Fitness, General, 7%
Psychology, General
**Expenses:** 2014-2015: $7,374 in
state, $13,438 out of state; room/
board: $8,167
**Financial aid:** (660) 785-4130;
53% of undergrads determined to
have financial need; average aid
package $11,389

## University of Central Missouri

Warrensburg MO
(660) 543-4290
**U.S. News ranking:** Reg. U.
(Mid. W), No. 84
**Website:** www.ucmo.edu
**Admissions email:**
admit@ucmo.edu
**Public**
**Freshman admissions:** selective;
2013-2014: 4,611 applied,
3,727 accepted. Either SAT
or ACT required. ACT 25/75
percentile: 19-24. High school
rank: 10% in top tenth, 32% in
top quarter, 67% in top half
**Early decision deadline:** N/A,
notification date: N/A
**Early action deadline:** N/A,
notification date: N/A
**Application deadline (fall):** 8/19
**Undergraduate student body:** 8,290
full time, 1,684 part time; 46%
male, 54% female; 0% American
Indian, 1% Asian, 8% black,
3% Hispanic, 2% multiracial,
0% Pacific Islander, 67% white,
2% international; 92% from in
state; N/A live on campus; N/A
of students in fraternities, N/A in
sororities
**Most popular majors:** 15%
Business, Management,
Marketing, and Related Support
Services, 17% Education, 7%
Engineering Technologies and
Engineering-Related Fields, 11%
Health Professions and Related
Programs, 9% Homeland Security,
Law Enforcement, Firefighting and
Related Protective Services
**Expenses:** 2014-2015: $7,265 in
state, $13,659 out of state; room/
board: $7,734
**Financial aid:** (660) 543-4040;
63% of undergrads determined to
have financial need; average aid
package $8,758

## University of Missouri

Columbia MO
(573) 882-7786
**U.S. News ranking:** Nat. U.,
No. 99
**Website:** www.missouri.edu
**Admissions email:**
mu4u@missouri.edu
**Public;** founded 1839
**Freshman admissions:** more
selective; 2013-2014: 20,956
applied, 16,473 accepted. Either
SAT or ACT required. ACT 25/75
percentile: 23-28. High school
rank: 27% in top tenth, 58% in
top quarter, 88% in top half
**Early decision deadline:** N/A,
notification date: N/A
**Early action deadline:** N/A,
notification date: N/A
**Application deadline (fall):** rolling
**Undergraduate student body:**
25,258 full time, 1,707 part
time; 48% male, 52% female;
0% American Indian, 2% Asian,
8% black, 3% Hispanic, 3%
multiracial, 0% Pacific Islander,
80% white, 3% international;
77% from in state; 25% live
on campus; 24% of students in
fraternities, 31% in sororities
**Most popular majors:** 16%
Business, Management,
Marketing, and Related Support
Services, 12% Communication,
Journalism, and Related Programs,
7% Engineering, 11% Health
Professions and Related Programs,
6% Social Sciences
**Expenses:** 2014-2015: $9,433 in
state, $24,460 out of state; room/
board: $9,386
**Financial aid:** (573) 882-7506;
49% of undergrads determined to
have financial need; average aid
package $14,050

## University of Missouri–Kansas City

Kansas City MO
(816) 235-1111
**U.S. News ranking:** Nat. U.,
No. 189
**Website:** www.umkc.edu
**Admissions email:**
admit@umkc.edu
**Public;** founded 1929
**Freshman admissions:** more
selective; 2013-2014: 4,471
applied, 2,919 accepted. Either
SAT or ACT required. ACT 25/75
percentile: 21-27. High school
rank: 26% in top tenth, 55% in
top quarter, 81% in top half
**Early decision deadline:** N/A,
notification date: N/A
**Early action deadline:** N/A,
notification date: N/A
**Application deadline (fall):** rolling
**Undergraduate student body:** 6,813
full time, 3,434 part time; 42%
male, 58% female; 0% American
Indian, 6% Asian, 16% black,
7% Hispanic, 3% multiracial,
0% Pacific Islander, 58% white,
4% international; 77% from in
state; 8% live on campus; 4%
of students in fraternities, 6% in
sororities
**Most popular majors:** 13%
Business, Management,
Marketing, and Related Support
Services, 14% Health Professions
and Related Programs, 11%
Liberal Arts and Sciences, General
Studies and Humanities, 8%
Physical Sciences, 7% Psychology

**Expenses:** 2014-2015: $9,582 in
state, $22,641 out of state; room/
board: $9,815
**Financial aid:** (816) 235-1154;
70% of undergrads determined to
have financial need; average aid
package $9,869

## University of Missouri–St. Louis

St. Louis MO
(314) 516-5451
**U.S. News ranking:** Nat. U.,
second tier
**Website:** www.umsl.edu
**Admissions email:**
admissions@umsl.edu
**Public;** founded 1963
**Freshman admissions:** more
selective; 2013-2014: 1,753
applied, 1,300 accepted. Either
SAT or ACT required. ACT 25/75
percentile: 21-26. High school
rank: 30% in top tenth, 63% in
top quarter, 87% in top half
**Early decision deadline:** N/A,
notification date: N/A
**Early action deadline:** N/A,
notification date: N/A
**Application deadline (fall):** 8/25
**Undergraduate student body:** 6,035
full time, 7,539 part time; 42%
male, 58% female; 0% American
Indian, 4% Asian, 19% black,
2% Hispanic, 2% multiracial,
0% Pacific Islander, 62% white,
3% international; 89% from in
state; 9% live on campus; 1%
of students in fraternities, 1% in
sororities
**Most popular majors:** 22%
Business, Management,
Marketing, and Related Support
Services, 12% Education, 11%
Health Professions and Related
Programs, 7% Psychology, 12%
Social Sciences
**Expenses:** 2014-2015: $9,474 in
state, $24,795 out of state; room/
board: $8,960
**Financial aid:** (314) 516-5526;
71% of undergrads determined to
have financial need; average aid
package $12,241

## Washington University in St. Louis

St. Louis MO
(800) 638-0700
**U.S. News ranking:** Nat. U.,
No. 14
**Website:** www.wustl.edu
**Admissions email:** admissions@
wustl.edu
**Private;** founded 1853
**Freshman admissions:** most
selective; 2013-2014: 30,117
applied, 4,684 accepted. Either
SAT or ACT required. ACT 25/75
percentile: 32-34. High school
rank: 95% in top tenth, 99% in
top quarter, 100% in top half
**Early decision deadline:** 11/15,
notification date: 12/15
**Early action deadline:** N/A,
notification date: N/A
**Application deadline (fall):** 1/15
**Undergraduate student body:** 6,587
full time, 749 part time; 49%
male, 51% female; 0% American
Indian, 17% Asian, 6% black,
6% Hispanic, 4% multiracial, 0%
Pacific Islander, 55% white, 8%
international; 7% from in state;
78% live on campus; 25% of
students in fraternities, 25% in
sororities

**Most popular majors:** 10% Biological and Biomedical Sciences, 9% Business, Management, Marketing, and Related Support Services, 16% Engineering, 14% Pre-Medicine/Pre-Medical Studies, 17% Social Sciences
**Expenses:** 2014-2015: $46,467; room/board: $14,377
**Financial aid:** (888) 547-6670; 40% of undergrads determined to have financial need; average aid package $36,101

## Webster University
St. Louis MO
(314) 968-6991
**U.S. News ranking:** Reg. U. (Mid. W), No. 26
**Website:** www.webster.edu
**Admissions email:** admit@webster.edu
**Private;** founded 1915
**Freshman admissions:** selective; 2013-2014: 1,769 applied, 1,014 accepted. Either SAT or ACT required. ACT 25/75 percentile: 20-27. High school rank: 17% in top tenth, 42% in top quarter, 73% in top half
**Early decision deadline:** N/A, notification date: N/A
**Early action deadline:** N/A, notification date: N/A
**Application deadline (fall):** 8/1
**Undergraduate student body:** 2,458 full time, 504 part time; 46% male, 54% female; 0% American Indian, 3% Asian, 11% black, 4% Hispanic, 2% multiracial, 0% Pacific Islander, 70% white, 2% international; 77% from in state; 25% live on campus; N/A of students in fraternities, 3% in sororities
**Most popular majors:** 6% Art/Art Studies, General, 18% Business Administration and Management, General, 5% Computer Science, 6% Education, General, 5% Psychology, General
**Expenses:** 2014-2015: $24,500; room/board: $10,600
**Financial aid:** (314) 968-6992; 74% of undergrads determined to have financial need; average aid package $16,809

## Westminster College
Fulton MO
(800) 475-3361
**U.S. News ranking:** Nat. Lib. Arts, No. 159
**Website:** www.westminster-mo.edu
**Admissions email:** admissions@westminster-mo.edu
**Private;** founded 1851
**Affiliation:** Presbyterian
**Freshman admissions:** more selective; 2013-2014: 1,308 applied, 902 accepted. Either SAT or ACT required. ACT 25/75 percentile: 21-27. High school rank: 28% in top tenth, 50% in top quarter, 77% in top half
**Early decision deadline:** N/A, notification date: N/A
**Early action deadline:** N/A, notification date: N/A
**Application deadline (fall):** rolling
**Undergraduate student body:** 1,036 full time, 8 part time; 56% male, 44% female; 2% American Indian, 1% Asian, 6% black, 4% Hispanic, 1% multiracial, 0% Pacific Islander, 66% white, 17% international; 79% from in state; 85% live on campus; 46% of students in fraternities, 33% in sororities

**Most popular majors:** 11% Biological and Biomedical Sciences, 26% Business, Management, Marketing, and Related Support Services, 15% Education, 6% Psychology, 10% Social Sciences
**Expenses:** 2014-2015: $22,560; room/board: $9,160
**Financial aid:** (573) 592-5364; 63% of undergrads determined to have financial need; average aid package $19,533

## William Jewell College
Liberty MO
(888) 253-9355
**U.S. News ranking:** Nat. Lib. Arts, No. 155
**Website:** www.jewell.edu
**Admissions email:** admission@william.jewell.edu
**Private;** founded 1849
**Freshman admissions:** more selective; 2013-2014: 1,433 applied, 828 accepted. Neither SAT nor ACT required. ACT 25/75 percentile: 22-28. High school rank: 23% in top tenth, 58% in top quarter, 90% in top half
**Early decision deadline:** N/A, notification date: N/A
**Early action deadline:** N/A, notification date: N/A
**Application deadline (fall):** 8/15
**Undergraduate student body:** 1,011 full time, 32 part time; 43% male, 57% female; 1% American Indian, 1% Asian, 6% black, 4% Hispanic, 5% multiracial, 0% Pacific Islander, 77% white, 3% international; 62% from in state; 83% live on campus; 31% of students in fraternities, 31% in sororities
**Most popular majors:** 16% Business, Management, Marketing, and Related Support Services, 6% Education, 26% Health Professions and Related Programs, 10% Psychology, 7% Social Sciences
**Expenses:** 2014-2015: $31,620; room/board: $8,410
**Financial aid:** (888) 253-9355; 74% of undergrads determined to have financial need; average aid package $26,119

## William Woods University
Fulton MO
(573) 592-4221
**U.S. News ranking:** Reg. U. (Mid. W), No. 95
**Website:** www.williamwoods.edu
**Admissions email:** admissions@williamwoods.edu
**Private;** founded 1870
**Affiliation:** Disciples of Christ
**Freshman admissions:** selective; 2013-2014: 819 applied, 639 accepted. Either SAT or ACT required. ACT 25/75 percentile: 19-25. High school rank: 12% in top tenth, 37% in top quarter, 70% in top half
**Early decision deadline:** N/A, notification date: N/A
**Early action deadline:** N/A, notification date: N/A
**Application deadline (fall):** rolling
**Undergraduate student body:** 843 full time, 159 part time; 27% male, 73% female; 0% American Indian, 0% Asian, 4% black, 1% Hispanic, 2% multiracial, 1% Pacific Islander, 85% white,

0% international; 64% from in state; 65% live on campus; 25% of students in fraternities, 41% in sororities
**Most popular majors:** 5% Biology/Biological Sciences, General, 17% Business Administration and Management, General, 6% Elementary Education and Teaching, 5% Legal Professions and Studies, Other, 3% Physical Education Teaching and Coaching
**Expenses:** 2014-2015: $21,260; room/board: $8,680
**Financial aid:** (573) 592-4232; 59% of undergrads determined to have financial need; average aid package $16,691

## Carroll College
Helena MT
(406) 447-4384
**U.S. News ranking:** Reg. Coll. (W), No. 1
**Website:** www.carroll.edu
**Admissions email:** admission@carroll.edu
**Private;** founded 1909
**Affiliation:** Roman Catholic
**Freshman admissions:** more selective; 2013-2014: 3,279 applied, 1,740 accepted. Either SAT or ACT required. ACT 25/75 percentile: 22-27. High school rank: 25% in top tenth, 61% in top quarter, 90% in top half
**Early decision deadline:** N/A, notification date: N/A
**Early action deadline:** 12/1, notification date: 1/1
**Application deadline (fall):** 5/1
**Undergraduate student body:** 1,349 full time, 82 part time; 42% male, 58% female; 1% American Indian, 1% Asian, 1% black, 4% Hispanic, 1% multiracial, 0% Pacific Islander, 81% white, 1% international; 46% from in state; 57% live on campus; N/A of students in fraternities, N/A in sororities
**Most popular majors:** 11% Biological and Biomedical Sciences, 11% Business, Management, Marketing, and Related Support Services, 10% Education, 26% Health Professions and Related Programs, 8% Social Sciences
**Expenses:** 2014-2015: $29,280; room/board: $8,950
**Financial aid:** (406) 447-5423; 64% of undergrads determined to have financial need; average aid package $20,251

## Montana State University
Bozeman MT
(406) 994-2452
**U.S. News ranking:** Nat. U., second tier
**Website:** www.montana.edu
**Admissions email:** admissions@montana.edu
**Public;** founded 1893
**Freshman admissions:** selective; 2013-2014: 12,578 applied, 10,630 accepted. Either SAT or ACT required. ACT 25/75 percentile: 21-27. High school rank: 19% in top tenth, 44% in top quarter, 72% in top half
**Early decision deadline:** N/A, notification date: N/A
**Early action deadline:** N/A, notification date: N/A

**Application deadline (fall):** rolling
**Undergraduate student body:** 11,012 full time, 2,252 part time; 55% male, 45% female; 1% American Indian, 0% Asian, 1% black, 3% Hispanic, 3% multiracial, 87% Pacific Islander, 1% white, 3% international; 61% from in state; 25% live on campus; 2% of students in fraternities, 2% in sororities
**Most popular majors:** 11% Business, Management, Marketing, and Related Support Services, 11% Engineering, 9% Family and Consumer Sciences/Human Sciences, 9% Health Professions and Related Programs, 8% Visual and Performing Arts
**Expenses:** 2014-2015: $6,894 in state, $21,296 out of state; room/board: $8,380
**Financial aid:** (406) 994-2845; 56% of undergrads determined to have financial need; average aid package $11,983

## Montana State University–Billings
Billings MT
(406) 657-2158
**U.S. News ranking:** Reg. U. (W), second tier
**Website:** www.msubillings.edu
**Admissions email:** admissions@msubillings.edu
**Public;** founded 1927
**Freshman admissions:** selective; 2013-2014: 1,407 applied, 1,397 accepted. Either SAT or ACT required. ACT 25/75 percentile: 18-23. High school rank: 8% in top tenth, 31% in top quarter, 62% in top half
**Early decision deadline:** N/A, notification date: N/A
**Early action deadline:** N/A, notification date: N/A
**Application deadline (fall):** 7/1
**Undergraduate student body:** 3,164 full time, 1,301 part time; 39% male, 61% female; 5% American Indian, 1% Asian, 1% black, 5% Hispanic, 3% multiracial, 0% Pacific Islander, 83% white, 3% international; 91% from in state; 18% live on campus; 0% of students in fraternities, 0% in sororities
**Most popular majors:** 24% Business/Commerce, General, 23% Elementary Education and Teaching, 11% Liberal Arts and Sciences/Liberal Studies, 6% Mass Communication/Media Studies, 6% Psychology, General
**Expenses:** 2014-2015: $5,780 in state, $17,342 out of state; room/board: $6,980
**Financial aid:** (406) 657-2188; 64% of undergrads determined to have financial need; average aid package $10,148

## Montana State University–Northern[1]
Havre MT
(406) 265-3704
**U.S. News ranking:** Reg. Coll. (W), unranked
**Website:** www.msun.edu
**Admissions email:** admissions@msun.edu
**Public**
**Application deadline (fall):** N/A
**Undergraduate student body:** N/A full time, N/A part time

**Expenses:** 2013-2014: $5,480 in state, $17,312 out of state; room/board: $7,500
**Financial aid:** (406) 265-3787

## Montana Tech of the University of Montana
Butte MT
(406) 496-4256
**U.S. News ranking:** Reg. Coll. (W), unranked
**Website:** www.mtech.edu
**Admissions email:** enrollment@mtech.edu
**Public;** founded 1893
**Freshman admissions:** N/A; 2013-2014: 877 applied, 773 accepted. Either SAT or ACT required. ACT 25/75 percentile: 22-26. High school rank: 26% in top tenth, 57% in top quarter, 86% in top half
**Early decision deadline:** N/A, notification date: N/A
**Early action deadline:** N/A, notification date: N/A
**Application deadline (fall):** rolling
**Undergraduate student body:** 2,190 full time, 567 part time; 60% male, 40% female; 2% American Indian, 1% Asian, 1% black, 2% Hispanic, 0% multiracial, 0% Pacific Islander, 83% white, 7% international; 87% from in state; 11% live on campus; 0% of students in fraternities, 0% in sororities
**Most popular majors:** 15% Business/Commerce, General, 5% Computer Systems Networking and Telecommunications, 17% Engineering, General, 5% Occupational Health and Industrial Hygiene, 21% Petroleum Engineering
**Expenses:** 2014-2015: $6,752 in state, $20,068 out of state; room/board: $8,238
**Financial aid:** (406) 496-4212; 62% of undergrads determined to have financial need; average aid package $10,848

## Rocky Mountain College
Billings MT
(406) 657-1026
**U.S. News ranking:** Reg. Coll. (W), No. 13
**Website:** www.rocky.edu
**Admissions email:** admissions@rocky.edu
**Private;** founded 1878
**Affiliation:** United Church of Christ, Methodist, and Presbyterian
**Freshman admissions:** selective; 2013-2014: 1,396 applied, 933 accepted. Either SAT or ACT required. ACT 25/75 percentile: 19-25. High school rank: 15% in top tenth, 35% in top quarter, 70% in top half
**Early decision deadline:** N/A, notification date: N/A
**Early action deadline:** 2/15, notification date: 2/15
**Application deadline (fall):** rolling
**Undergraduate student body:** 947 full time, 41 part time; 52% male, 48% female; 2% American Indian, 1% Asian, 2% black, 4% Hispanic, 3% multiracial, 1% Pacific Islander, 80% white, 4% international; 54% from in state; 49% live on campus; 0% of students in fraternities, 0% in sororities

**Most popular majors:** Information not available
**Expenses:** 2014-2015: $24,530; room/board: $7,712
**Financial aid:** (406) 657-1031; 77% of undergrads determined to have financial need; average aid package $19,265

## University of Great Falls
Great Falls MT
(406) 791-5200
**U.S. News ranking:** Reg. Coll. (W), No. 22
**Website:** www.ugf.edu
**Admissions email:** enroll@ugf.edu
**Private;** founded 1932
**Affiliation:** Roman Catholic
**Freshman admissions:** less selective; 2013-2014: N/A applied, N/A accepted. Either SAT or ACT required. SAT 25/75 percentile: 840-1090. High school rank: N/A
**Early decision deadline:** N/A, notification date: N/A
**Early action deadline:** N/A, notification date: N/A
**Application deadline (fall):** 9/1
**Undergraduate student body:** 665 full time, 381 part time; 32% male, 68% female; 3% American Indian, 2% Asian, 2% black, 5% Hispanic, 2% multiracial, 1% Pacific Islander, 79% white, 0% international; 52% from in state; 37% live on campus; N/A of students in fraternities, N/A in sororities
**Most popular majors:** 9% Biological and Biomedical Sciences, 12% Education, 29% Health Professions and Related Programs, 10% Homeland Security, Law Enforcement, Firefighting and Related Protective Services, 10% Psychology
**Expenses:** 2014-2015: $20,960; room/board: $6,800
**Financial aid:** (406) 791-5235; 80% of undergrads determined to have financial need; average aid package $16,916

## University of Montana
Missoula MT
(800) 462-8636
**U.S. News ranking:** Nat. U., No. 194
**Website:** www.umt.edu
**Admissions email:** admiss@umontana.edu
**Public;** founded 1893
**Freshman admissions:** selective; 2013-2014: 4,064 applied, 3,889 accepted. Either SAT or ACT required. ACT 25/75 percentile: 21-26. High school rank: 18% in top tenth, 40% in top quarter, 70% in top half
**Early decision deadline:** N/A, notification date: N/A
**Early action deadline:** N/A, notification date: N/A
**Application deadline (fall):** rolling
**Undergraduate student body:** 8,182 full time, 1,605 part time; 47% male, 53% female; 3% American Indian, 1% Asian, 1% black, 4% Hispanic, 4% multiracial, 0% Pacific Islander, 81% white, 2% international; 81% from in state; 28% live on campus; 6% of students in fraternities, 6% in sororities

**Most popular majors:** 6% Biological and Biomedical Sciences, 19% Business, Management, Marketing, and Related Support Services, 10% Natural Resources and Conservation, 7% Psychology, 13% Social Sciences
**Expenses:** 2014-2015: $6,330 in state, $23,146 out of state; room/board: $8,006
**Financial aid:** (406) 243-5373; 62% of undergrads determined to have financial need; average aid package $7,780

## University of Montana–Western
Dillon MT
(877) 683-7331
**U.S. News ranking:** Reg. Coll. (W), unranked
**Website:** www.umwestern.edu
**Admissions email:** admissions@umwestern.edu
**Public;** founded 1893
**Freshman admissions:** N/A; 2013-2014: 553 applied, 414 accepted. Either SAT or ACT required. ACT 25/75 percentile: 17-22. High school rank: 5% in top tenth, 18% in top quarter, 48% in top half
**Early decision deadline:** N/A, notification date: N/A
**Early action deadline:** N/A, notification date: N/A
**Application deadline (fall):** rolling
**Undergraduate student body:** 1,206 full time, 305 part time; 42% male, 58% female; 2% American Indian, 1% Asian, 1% black, 2% Hispanic, 2% multiracial, 1% Pacific Islander, 86% white, 0% international; 77% from in state; 24% live on campus; N/A of students in fraternities, N/A in sororities
**Most popular majors:** 16% Business/Commerce, General, 4% Early Childhood Education and Teaching, 15% Elementary Education and Teaching, 6% Secondary Education and Teaching, 10% Teacher Education, Multiple Levels
**Expenses:** 2014-2015: $5,370 in state, $15,212 out of state; room/board: $6,536
**Financial aid:** (406) 683-7511; 65% of undergrads determined to have financial need; average aid package $3,327

## NEBRASKA

## Bellevue University[1]
Bellevue NE
(800) 756-7920
**U.S. News ranking:** Reg. U. (Mid. W), unranked
**Website:** www.bellevue.edu
**Admissions email:** info@bellevue.edu
**Private**
**Application deadline (fall):** N/A
**Undergraduate student body:** N/A full time, N/A part time
**Expenses:** 2014-2015: $7,950; room/board: N/A
**Financial aid:** (402) 293-3763; 100% of undergrads determined to have financial need; average aid package $2,658

## Chadron State College[1]
Chadron NE
(308) 432-6263
**U.S. News ranking:** Reg. Coll. (Mid. W), unranked
**Website:** www.csc.edu
**Admissions email:** inquire@csc.edu
**Public**
**Application deadline (fall):** N/A
**Undergraduate student body:** N/A full time, N/A part time
**Expenses:** 2013-2014: $5,600 in state, $5,630 out of state; room/board: $5,760
**Financial aid:** (308) 432-6230

## College of St. Mary
Omaha NE
(402) 399-2407
**U.S. News ranking:** Reg. U. (Mid. W), No. 69
**Website:** www.csm.edu
**Admissions email:** enroll@csm.edu
**Private;** founded 1923
**Affiliation:** Catholic
**Freshman admissions:** selective; 2013-2014: 347 applied, 189 accepted. Either SAT or ACT required. ACT 25/75 percentile: 20-26. High school rank: 28% in top tenth, 51% in top quarter, 87% in top half
**Early decision deadline:** N/A, notification date: N/A
**Early action deadline:** N/A, notification date: N/A
**Application deadline (fall):** rolling
**Undergraduate student body:** 639 full time, 96 part time; 1% male, 99% female; 0% American Indian, 1% Asian, 6% black, 11% Hispanic, 2% multiracial, 0% Pacific Islander, 78% white, 1% international; 80% from in state; 32% live on campus; 0% of students in fraternities, 0% in sororities
**Most popular majors:** 6% Biological and Biomedical Sciences, 15% Business, Management, Marketing, and Related Support Services, 6% Education, 58% Health Professions and Related Programs, 4% Psychology
**Expenses:** 2014-2015: $27,984; room/board: $7,200
**Financial aid:** (402) 399-2362; 92% of undergrads determined to have financial need; average aid package $18,759

## Concordia University
Seward NE
(800) 535-5494
**U.S. News ranking:** Reg. U. (Mid. W), No. 44
**Website:** www.cune.edu
**Admissions email:** admiss@cune.edu
**Private;** founded 1894
**Affiliation:** Lutheran Church-Missouri Synod
**Freshman admissions:** selective; 2013-2014: 1,299 applied, 929 accepted. Either SAT or ACT required. ACT 25/75 percentile: 21-27. High school rank: 18% in top tenth, 43% in top quarter, 78% in top half
**Early decision deadline:** N/A, notification date: N/A
**Early action deadline:** N/A, notification date: N/A
**Application deadline (fall):** 8/1
**Undergraduate student body:** 1,134 full time, 374 part time; 49% male, 51% female; 0% American

Indian, 1% Asian, 4% black, 4% Hispanic, 1% multiracial, 0% Pacific Islander, 82% white, 1% international; 47% from in state; 70% live on campus; N/A of students in fraternities, N/A in sororities
**Most popular majors:** 8% Biological and Biomedical Sciences, 37% Education, 8% Parks, Recreation, Leisure, and Fitness Studies, 12% Theology and Religious Vocations, 7% Visual and Performing Arts
**Expenses:** 2014-2015: $25,950; room/board: $7,080
**Financial aid:** (402) 643-7270; 77% of undergrads determined to have financial need; average aid package $19,350

## Creighton University
Omaha NE
(800) 282-5835
**U.S. News ranking:** Reg. U. (Mid. W), No. 1
**Website:** www.creighton.edu
**Admissions email:** admissions@creighton.edu
**Private;** founded 1878
**Affiliation:** Roman Catholic (Jesuit)
**Freshman admissions:** more selective; 2013-2014: 5,336 applied, 4,090 accepted. Either SAT or ACT required. ACT 25/75 percentile: 24-30. High school rank: 40% in top tenth, 68% in top quarter, 93% in top half
**Early decision deadline:** N/A, notification date: N/A
**Early action deadline:** N/A, notification date: N/A
**Application deadline (fall):** 2/15
**Undergraduate student body:** 3,815 full time, 261 part time; 41% male, 59% female; 0% American Indian, 9% Asian, 2% black, 7% Hispanic, 4% multiracial, 0% Pacific Islander, 74% white, 2% international; 30% from in state; 62% live on campus; 30% of students in fraternities, 30% in sororities
**Most popular majors:** 9% Biological and Biomedical Sciences, 15% Business, Management, Marketing, and Related Support Services, 28% Health Professions and Related Clinical Sciences, Other, 8% Psychology, 7% Social Sciences
**Expenses:** 2014-2015: $35,360; room/board: $9,996
**Financial aid:** (402) 280-2731; 57% of undergrads determined to have financial need; average aid package $27,558

## Doane College
Crete NE
(402) 826-8222
**U.S. News ranking:** Nat. Lib. Arts, No. 164
**Website:** www.doane.edu
**Admissions email:** admissions@doane.edu
**Private;** founded 1872
**Freshman admissions:** selective; 2013-2014: 1,822 applied, 1,307 accepted. ACT required. ACT 25/75 percentile: 21-26. High school rank: 20% in top tenth, 46% in top quarter, 81% in top half
**Early decision deadline:** N/A, notification date: N/A
**Early action deadline:** N/A, notification date: N/A
**Application deadline (fall):** rolling

Undergraduate student body:
1,106 full time, 7 part time; 50% male, 50% female; 0% American Indian, 2% Asian, 4% black, 6% Hispanic, 2% multiracial, 0% Pacific Islander, 84% white, 1% international; 83% from in state; 75% live on campus; 18% of students in fraternities, 23% in sororities
**Most popular majors:** 16% Biological and Biomedical Sciences, 13% Business, Management, and Related Support Services, 24% Education, 9% Psychology, 14% Visual and Performing Arts
**Expenses:** 2014-2015: $27,200; room/board: $7,880
**Financial aid:** (402) 826-8260; 77% of undergrads determined to have financial need; average aid package $19,454

## Grace University[1]
Omaha NE
(402) 449-2831
**U.S. News ranking:** Reg. Coll. (Mid. W), second tier
**Website:** www.graceuniversity.edu
**Admissions email:** admissions@graceuniversity.edu
**Private**
**Application deadline (fall):** N/A
**Undergraduate student body:** N/A full time, N/A part time
**Expenses:** 2013-2014: $18,256; room/board: $6,552
**Financial aid:** (402) 449-2810

## Hastings College
Hastings NE
(800) 532-7642
**U.S. News ranking:** Reg. Coll. (Mid. W), No. 18
**Website:** www.hastings.edu
**Admissions email:** hcadmissions@hastings.edu
**Private;** founded 1882
**Affiliation:** Presbyterian Church (USA)
**Freshman admissions:** selective; 2013-2014: 1,529 applied, 1,126 accepted. Either SAT or ACT required. ACT 25/75 percentile: 21-26. High school rank: 16% in top tenth, 40% in top quarter, 65% in top half
**Early decision deadline:** N/A, notification date: N/A
**Early action deadline:** N/A, notification date: N/A
**Application deadline (fall):** rolling
**Undergraduate student body:** 1,060 full time, 58 part time; 51% male, 49% female; 1% American Indian, 2% Asian, 3% black, 5% Hispanic, 2% multiracial, 1% Pacific Islander, 85% white, 1% international; 68% from in state; 70% live on campus; 27% of students in fraternities, 27% in sororities
**Most popular majors:** 8% Biological and Biomedical Sciences, 20% Business, Management, Marketing, and Related Support Services, 18% Education, 8% Social Sciences, 8% Visual and Performing Arts
**Expenses:** 2014-2015: $26,280; room/board: $7,500
**Financial aid:** (402) 461-7391; 77% of undergrads determined to have financial need; average aid package $19,961

## Midland University[1]
Fremont NE
(402) 941-6501
**U.S. News ranking:** Reg. Coll. (Mid. W), No. 69
**Website:** www.midlandu.edu/
**Admissions email:** admissions@midlandu.edu
**Private;** founded 1883
**Affiliation:** Lutheran
**Application deadline (fall):** rolling
**Undergraduate student body:** N/A full time, N/A part time
**Expenses:** 2013-2014: $27,146; room/board: $6,850
**Financial aid:** (402) 941-6520

## Nebraska Wesleyan University
Lincoln NE
(402) 465-2218
**U.S. News ranking:** Nat. Lib. Arts, No. 148
**Website:** www.nebrwesleyan.edu/undergraduate-admissions
**Admissions email:** admissions@nebrwesleyan.edu
**Private;** founded 1887
**Affiliation:** United Methodist
**Freshman admissions:** selective; 2013-2014: 2,315 applied, 1,780 accepted. Either SAT or ACT required. ACT 25/75 percentile: 22-26. High school rank: 23% in top tenth, 50% in top quarter, 82% in top half
**Early decision deadline:** N/A, notification date: N/A
**Early action deadline:** N/A, notification date: N/A
**Application deadline (fall):** 8/15
**Undergraduate student body:** 1,606 full time, 321 part time; 38% male, 62% female; 0% American Indian, 2% Asian, 3% black, 4% Hispanic, 2% multiracial, 0% Pacific Islander, 82% white, 1% international
**Most popular majors:** 9% Biological and Biomedical Sciences, 13% Business, Management, Marketing, and Related Support Services, 11% Education, 12% Health Professions and Related Programs, 8% Parks, Recreation, Leisure, and Fitness Studies
**Expenses:** 2014-2015: $28,500; room/board: $7,950
**Financial aid:** (402) 465-2212; 72% of undergrads determined to have financial need; average aid package $17,642

## Peru State College[1]
Peru NE
(402) 872-2221
**U.S. News ranking:** Reg. U. (Mid. W), unranked
**Website:** www.peru.edu
**Admissions email:** admissions@peru.edu
**Public**
**Application deadline (fall):** N/A
**Undergraduate student body:** N/A full time, N/A part time
**Expenses:** 2013-2014: $6,188 in state, $6,188 out of state; room/board: $6,656
**Financial aid:** (402) 872-2228

## Union College
Lincoln NE
(800) 228-4600
**U.S. News ranking:** Reg. Coll. (Mid. W), No. 49
**Website:** www.ucollege.edu
**Admissions email:** ucenroll@ucollege.edu

**Private;** founded 1891
**Affiliation:** Seventh-day Adventist
**Freshman admissions:** selective; 2013-2014: 1,415 applied, 742 accepted. Either SAT or ACT required. ACT 25/75 percentile: 19-26. High school rank: 11% in top tenth, 28% in top quarter, 56% in top half
**Early decision deadline:** N/A, notification date: N/A
**Early action deadline:** N/A, notification date: N/A
**Application deadline (fall):** rolling
**Undergraduate student body:** 713 full time, 108 part time; 43% male, 57% female; 1% American Indian, 3% Asian, 6% black, 15% Hispanic, 4% multiracial, 1% Pacific Islander, 60% white, 9% international; 29% from in state; 70% live on campus; 0% of students in fraternities, 0% in sororities
**Most popular majors:** 6% Bible/Biblical Studies, 13% Business Administration and Management, General, 14% Education, General, 7% Psychology, General, 36% Registered Nursing/Registered Nurse
**Expenses:** 2014-2015: $21,080; room/board: $6,520
**Financial aid:** (402) 486-2505; 70% of undergrads determined to have financial need; average aid package $15,641

## University of Nebraska–Kearney
Kearney NE
(308) 865-8526
**U.S. News ranking:** Reg. U. (Mid. W), No. 54
**Website:** www.unk.edu
**Admissions email:** admissionsug@unk.edu
**Public;** founded 1903
**Freshman admissions:** selective; 2013-2014: 2,589 applied, 2,197 accepted. Either SAT or ACT required. ACT 25/75 percentile: 20-25. High school rank: 18% in top tenth, 41% in top quarter, 76% in top half
**Early decision deadline:** N/A, notification date: N/A
**Early action deadline:** N/A, notification date: N/A
**Application deadline (fall):** 9/1
**Undergraduate student body:** 4,777 full time, 725 part time; 43% male, 57% female; 0% American Indian, 1% Asian, 2% black, 9% Hispanic, 1% multiracial, 0% Pacific Islander, 80% white, 6% international; 91% from in state; 36% live on campus; 12% of students in fraternities, 13% in sororities
**Most popular majors:** 12% Business Administration and Management, General, 13% Elementary Education and Teaching, 8% Operations Management and Supervision, 6% Parks, Recreation and Leisure Studies, 5% Physical Education Teaching and Coaching
**Expenses:** 2014-2015: $6,584 in state, $12,742 out of state; room/board: $8,880
**Financial aid:** (308) 865-8520; 61% of undergrads determined to have financial need; average aid package $9,525

## University of Nebraska–Lincoln
Lincoln NE
(800) 742-8800
**U.S. News ranking:** Nat. U., No. 99
**Website:** www.unl.edu
**Admissions email:** Admissions@unl.edu
**Public;** founded 1869
**Freshman admissions:** more selective; 2013-2014: 10,929 applied, 6,999 accepted. Either SAT or ACT required. ACT 25/75 percentile: 22-28. High school rank: 26% in top tenth, 52% in top quarter, 83% in top half
**Early decision deadline:** N/A, notification date: N/A
**Early action deadline:** N/A, notification date: N/A
**Application deadline (fall):** 5/1
**Undergraduate student body:** 18,102 full time, 1,274 part time; 54% male, 46% female; 0% American Indian, 2% Asian, 2% black, 5% Hispanic, 2% multiracial, 0% Pacific Islander, 80% white, 6% international; 81% from in state; 39% live on campus; 18% of students in fraternities, 22% in sororities
**Most popular majors:** 8% Agriculture, Agriculture Operations, and Related Sciences, 22% Business, Management, Marketing, and Related Support Services, 8% Education, 10% Engineering, 9% Family and Consumer Sciences/Human Sciences
**Expenses:** 2013-2014: $8,060 in state, $21,388 out of state; room/board: $9,532
**Financial aid:** (402) 472-2030

## University of Nebraska–Omaha
Omaha NE
(402) 554-2393
**U.S. News ranking:** Nat. U., second tier
**Website:** www.unomaha.edu
**Admissions email:** unoadm@unomaha.edu
**Public;** founded 1908
**Freshman admissions:** selective; 2013-2014: 4,955 applied, 3,507 accepted. Either SAT or ACT required. ACT 25/75 percentile: 20-26. High school rank: 15% in top tenth, 40% in top quarter, 75% in top half
**Early decision deadline:** N/A, notification date: N/A
**Early action deadline:** N/A, notification date: N/A
**Application deadline (fall):** 8/1
**Undergraduate student body:** 9,511 full time, 2,824 part time; 48% male, 52% female; 0% American Indian, 3% Asian, 6% black, 9% Hispanic, 3% multiracial, 0% Pacific Islander, 72% white, 3% international; 93% from in state; 14% live on campus; 3% of students in fraternities, 4% in sororities
**Most popular majors:** 5% Accounting, 9% Business Administration and Management, General, 9% Criminal Justice/Safety Studies, 8% Elementary Education and Teaching, 6% Secondary Education and Teaching
**Expenses:** 2014-2015: $6,750 in state, $18,070 out of state; room/board: $8,408

**Financial aid:** (402) 554-2327; 59% of undergrads determined to have financial need; average aid package $9,038

## Wayne State College
Wayne NE
(800) 228-9972
**U.S. News ranking:** Reg. U. (Mid. W), No. 84
**Website:** www.wsc.edu
**Admissions email:** admit1@wsc.edu
**Public;** founded 1909
**Freshman admissions:** selective; 2013-2014: 2,070 applied, 2,070 accepted. Neither SAT nor ACT required. ACT 25/75 percentile: 19-24. High school rank: 10% in top tenth, 29% in top quarter, 59% in top half
**Early decision deadline:** N/A, notification date: N/A
**Early action deadline:** N/A, notification date: N/A
**Application deadline (fall):** rolling
**Undergraduate student body:** 2,735 full time, 256 part time; 43% male, 57% female; 1% American Indian, 0% Asian, 3% black, 7% Hispanic, 2% multiracial, 0% Pacific Islander, 80% white, 1% international; 87% from in state; 46% live on campus; N/A of students in fraternities, N/A in sororities
**Most popular majors:** 15% Business, Management, Marketing, and Related Support Services, 28% Education, 8% Homeland Security, Law Enforcement, Firefighting and Related Protective Services, 5% Parks, Recreation, Leisure, and Fitness Studies, 9% Psychology
**Expenses:** 2014-2015: $5,604 in state, $9,804 out of state; room/board: $6,420
**Financial aid:** (402) 375-7230; 68% of undergrads determined to have financial need; average aid package $8,584

## York College
York NE
(800) 950-9675
**U.S. News ranking:** Reg. Coll. (Mid. W), second tier
**Website:** www.york.edu
**Admissions email:** enroll@york.edu
**Private;** founded 1890
**Affiliation:** Church of Christ
**Freshman admissions:** selective; 2013-2014: 546 applied, 267 accepted. Either SAT or ACT required. ACT 25/75 percentile: 17-22. High school rank: 5% in top tenth, 24% in top quarter, 60% in top half
**Early decision deadline:** N/A, notification date: N/A
**Early action deadline:** N/A, notification date: N/A
**Application deadline (fall):** 8/31
**Undergraduate student body:** 442 full time, 17 part time; 54% male, 46% female; 2% American Indian, 1% Asian, 14% black, 7% Hispanic, 0% multiracial, 0% Pacific Islander, 72% white, 1% international; 35% from in state; 90% live on campus; N/A of students in fraternities, N/A in sororities
**Most popular majors:** 5% Biological and Biomedical Sciences, 24% Business, Management, Marketing, and Related Support Services, 28% Education, 12% Liberal Arts and Sciences,

General Studies and Humanities, 12% Psychology
**Expenses:** 2014-2015: $16,080; room/board: $6,100
**Financial aid:** (402) 363-5624; 89% of undergrads determined to have financial need; average aid package $13,720

## College of Southern Nevada
Las Vegas NV
(702) 651-5610
**U.S. News ranking:** Reg. Coll. (W), unranked
**Website:** www.csn.edu
**Admissions email:** N/A
**Public;** founded 1971
**Freshman admissions:** N/A; 2013-2014: N/A applied, N/A accepted. Neither SAT nor ACT required. ACT 25/75 percentile: N/A. High school rank: N/A
**Early decision deadline:** N/A, notification date: N/A
**Early action deadline:** N/A, notification date: N/A
**Application deadline (fall):** rolling
**Undergraduate student body:** 8,903 full time, 25,274 part time; 45% male, 55% female; 1% American Indian, 10% Asian, 11% black, 26% Hispanic, 4% multiracial, 2% Pacific Islander, 38% white, 1% international; 8% from in state; 0% live on campus; 0% of students in fraternities, 0% in sororities
**Most popular majors:** 13% Business Administration and Management, General, 5% Criminal Justice/Safety Studies, 15% Liberal Arts and Sciences/Liberal Studies, 8% Registered Nursing/Registered Nurse, 8% Science Technologies/Technicians, Other
**Expenses:** 2013-2014: $2,700 in state, $9,345 out of state; room/board: N/A
**Financial aid:** (702) 651-5660

## Great Basin College[1]
Elko NV
(775) 753-2102
**U.S. News ranking:** Reg. Coll. (W), unranked
**Website:** www.gbcnv.edu
**Admissions email:** N/A
**Public**
**Application deadline (fall):** N/A
**Undergraduate student body:** N/A full time, N/A part time
**Expenses:** 2013-2014: $2,700 in state, $9,345 out of state; room/board: $6,800
**Financial aid:** (775) 753-2399

## Nevada State College[1]
Henderson NV
(702) 992-2130
**U.S. News ranking:** Reg. Coll. (W), second tier
**Website:** nsc.nevada.edu
**Admissions email:** N/A
**Public**
**Application deadline (fall):** N/A
**Undergraduate student body:** N/A full time, N/A part time
**Expenses:** 2013-2014: $4,482 in state, $14,758 out of state; room/board: N/A
**Financial aid:** (702) 992-2150

## Sierra Nevada College
Incline Village NV
(866) 412-4636
**U.S. News ranking:** Reg. U. (W), second tier
**Website:** www.sierranevada.edu
**Admissions email:** admissions@sierranevada.edu
**Private;** founded 1969
**Freshman admissions:** less selective; 2013-2014: 604 applied, 524 accepted. Either SAT or ACT required. SAT 25/75 percentile: 870-1070. High school rank: 0% in top tenth, 20% in top quarter, 50% in top half
**Early decision deadline:** N/A, notification date: N/A
**Early action deadline:** 11/30, notification date: 11/30
**Application deadline (fall):** 8/28
**Undergraduate student body:** 494 full time, 53 part time; 57% male, 43% female; 3% American Indian, 1% Asian, 1% black, 1% Hispanic, 0% multiracial, 1% Pacific Islander, 72% white, 7% international; 16% from in state; 52% live on campus; 0% of students in fraternities, 0% in sororities
**Most popular majors:** 41% Business, Management, Marketing, and Related Support Services, 13% Multi/Interdisciplinary Studies, 6% Physical Sciences, 14% Psychology, 14% Visual and Performing Arts
**Expenses:** 2014-2015: $29,149; room/board: $12,066
**Financial aid:** (775) 831-1314; 66% of undergrads determined to have financial need; average aid package $21,452

## University of Nevada–Las Vegas
Las Vegas NV
(702) 774-8658
**U.S. News ranking:** Nat. U., second tier
**Website:** www.unlv.edu
**Admissions email:** undergraduate.recruitment@unlv.edu
**Public;** founded 1957
**Freshman admissions:** selective; 2013-2014: 7,343 applied, 6,250 accepted. Either SAT or ACT required. SAT 25/75 percentile: 890-1110. High school rank: 21% in top tenth, 48% in top quarter, 80% in top half
**Early decision deadline:** N/A, notification date: N/A
**Early action deadline:** N/A, notification date: N/A
**Application deadline (fall):** 7/1
**Undergraduate student body:** 16,523 full time, 6,576 part time; 44% male, 56% female; 0% American Indian, 16% Asian, 8% black, 23% Hispanic, 8% multiracial, 2% Pacific Islander, 38% white, 4% international; 86% from in state; 5% live on campus; 5% of students in fraternities, 3% in sororities
**Most popular majors:** 35% Business, Management, Marketing, and Related Support Services, 6% Education, 7% Psychology, 6% Social Sciences, 5% Visual and Performing Arts
**Expenses:** 2014-2015: $6,690 in state, $20,600 out of state; room/board: $10,524

**Financial aid:** (702) 895-3424; 64% of undergrads determined to have financial need; average aid package $9,204

## University of Nevada–Reno
Reno NV
(775) 784-4700
**U.S. News ranking:** Nat. U., No. 194
**Website:** www.unr.edu
**Admissions email:** asknevada@unr.edu
**Public;** founded 1864
**Freshman admissions:** selective; 2013-2014: 7,974 applied, 6,720 accepted. Either SAT or ACT required. SAT 25/75 percentile: 960-1190. High school rank: 23% in top tenth, 55% in top quarter, 87% in top half
**Early decision deadline:** N/A, notification date: N/A
**Early action deadline:** N/A, notification date: N/A
**Application deadline (fall):** 5/31
**Undergraduate student body:** 12,934 full time, 2,760 part time; 47% male, 53% female; 1% American Indian, 7% Asian, 4% black, 16% Hispanic, 6% multiracial, 1% Pacific Islander, 65% white, 1% international; 76% from in state; 17% live on campus; 9% of students in fraternities, 8% in sororities
**Most popular majors:** 8% Biological and Biomedical Sciences, 15% Business, Management, Marketing, and Related Support Services, 9% Engineering, 11% Health Professions and Related Programs, 12% Social Sciences
**Expenses:** 2014-2015: $6,415 in state, $20,325 out of state; room/board: $9,769
**Financial aid:** (775) 784-4666; 53% of undergrads determined to have financial need; average aid package $9,560

## Western Nevada College[1]
Carson City NV
(775) 445-3000
**U.S. News ranking:** Reg. Coll. (W), unranked
**Website:** www.wnc.edu
**Admissions email:** N/A
**Public;** founded 1971
**Application deadline (fall):** rolling
**Undergraduate student body:** N/A full time, N/A part time
**Expenses:** 2013-2014: $2,700 in state, $9,345 out of state; room/board: N/A
**Financial aid:** (775) 445-3264

## Colby-Sawyer College[1]
New London NH
(800) 272-1015
**U.S. News ranking:** Reg. Coll. (N), unranked
**Website:** www.colby-sawyer.edu
**Admissions email:** admissions@colby-sawyer.edu
**Private**
**Application deadline (fall):** N/A
**Undergraduate student body:** N/A full time, N/A part time
**Expenses:** 2013-2014: $37,300; room/board: $12,500
**Financial aid:** (603) 526-3717

## Daniel Webster College[1]
Nashua NH
(800) 325-6876
**U.S. News ranking:** Reg. Coll. (N), second tier
**Website:** www.dwc.edu
**Admissions email:** admissions@dwc.edu
**Private;** founded 1965
**Application deadline (fall):** rolling
**Undergraduate student body:** N/A full time, N/A part time
**Expenses:** 2013-2014: $15,630; room/board: $10,650
**Financial aid:** (603) 577-6590

## Dartmouth College
Hanover NH
(603) 646-2875
**U.S. News ranking:** Nat. U., No. 11
**Website:** www.dartmouth.edu
**Admissions email:** admissions.office@dartmouth.edu
**Private;** founded 1769
**Freshman admissions:** most selective; 2013-2014: 22,428 applied, 2,337 accepted. Either SAT or ACT required. SAT 25/75 percentile: 1360-1560. High school rank: 90% in top tenth, 98% in top quarter, 100% in top half
**Early decision deadline:** 11/1, notification date: 12/15
**Early action deadline:** N/A, notification date: N/A
**Application deadline (fall):** 1/1
**Undergraduate student body:** 4,200 full time, 76 part time; 51% male, 49% female; 2% American Indian, 14% Asian, 7% black, 8% Hispanic, 5% multiracial, 0% Pacific Islander, 47% white, 8% international; 3% from in state; 88% live on campus; 47% of students in fraternities, 46% in sororities
**Most popular majors:** 17% Economics, General, 7% Engineering, General, 8% History, General, 10% Political Science and Government, General, 6% Psychology, General
**Expenses:** 2014-2015: $48,108; room/board: $13,839
**Financial aid:** (603) 646-2451; 51% of undergrads determined to have financial need; average aid package $44,011

## Franklin Pierce University
Rindge NH
(800) 437-0048
**U.S. News ranking:** Reg. U. (N), second tier
**Website:** www.franklinpierce.edu/
**Admissions email:** admissions@franklinpierce.edu
**Private;** founded 1962
**Freshman admissions:** less selective; 2013-2014: 4,656 applied, 4,315 accepted. Either SAT or ACT required. SAT 25/75 percentile: 860-1060. High school rank: 9% in top tenth, 20% in top quarter, 56% in top half
**Early decision deadline:** N/A, notification date: N/A
**Early action deadline:** N/A, notification date: N/A
**Application deadline (fall):** rolling
**Undergraduate student body:** 1,307 full time, 380 part time; 41% male, 59% female; 0% American Indian, 1% Asian, 3% black,

5% Hispanic, 2% multiracial, 0% Pacific Islander, 74% white, 1% international; 22% from in state; 85% live on campus; 0% of students in fraternities, 0% in sororities
**Most popular majors:** 8% Biological and Biomedical Sciences, 19% Business, Management, Marketing, and Related Support Services, 7% Education, 15% Health Professions and Related Programs, 6% Visual and Performing Arts
**Expenses:** 2014-2015: $31,782; room/board: $12,060
**Financial aid:** (603) 899-4186; 83% of undergrads determined to have financial need; average aid package $23,887

## Granite State College
Concord NH
(603) 513-1391
**U.S. News ranking:** Nat. Lib. Arts, unranked
**Website:** www.granite.edu
**Admissions email:** gsc.admissions@granite.edu
**Public;** founded 1972
**Freshman admissions:** N/A; 2013-2014: 267 applied, 267 accepted. Neither SAT nor ACT required. ACT 25/75 percentile: N/A. High school rank: N/A
**Early decision deadline:** N/A, notification date: N/A
**Early action deadline:** N/A, notification date: N/A
**Application deadline (fall):** rolling
**Undergraduate student body:** 918 full time, 805 part time; 30% male, 70% female; 1% American Indian, 1% Asian, 1% black, 2% Hispanic, 2% multiracial, 0% Pacific Islander, 82% white, 0% international; 88% from in state; 0% live on campus; 0% of students in fraternities, 0% in sororities
**Most popular majors:** 26% Business Administration and Management, General, 8% Criminal Justice/Safety Studies, 10% Education, 15% Liberal Arts and Sciences/Liberal Studies, 30% Multi-/Interdisciplinary Studies, Other
**Expenses:** 2014-2015: $8,775 in state, $9,675 out of state; room/board: N/A
**Financial aid:** (603) 228-3000; 84% of undergrads determined to have financial need

## Keene State College
Keene NH
(603) 358-2276
**U.S. News ranking:** Reg. U. (N), No. 74
**Website:** www.keene.edu
**Admissions email:** admissions@keene.edu
**Public;** founded 1909
**Freshman admissions:** less selective; 2013-2014: 6,144 applied, 5,026 accepted. Either SAT or ACT required. SAT 25/75 percentile: 860-1080. High school rank: 4% in top tenth, 19% in top quarter, 56% in top half
**Early decision deadline:** N/A, notification date: N/A
**Early action deadline:** N/A, notification date: N/A
**Application deadline (fall):** 4/1
**Undergraduate student body:** 4,541 full time, 263 part time; 43% male, 57% female; 0% American

Indian, 1% Asian, 1% black, 3% Hispanic, 2% multiracial, 0% Pacific Islander, 82% white, 0% international; 49% from in state; 55% live on campus; 8% of students in fraternities, 5% in sororities
**Most popular majors:** 9% Communication, Journalism, and Related Programs, 17% Education, 9% Psychology, 12% Social Sciences, 9% Visual and Performing Arts
**Expenses:** 2014-2015: $12,864 in state, $20,784 out of state; room/board: $9,368
**Financial aid:** (603) 358-2280; 67% of undergrads determined to have financial need; average aid package $10,551

## Mount Washington College[1]
Manchester NH
(888) 971-2190
**U.S. News ranking:** Reg. Coll. (N), unranked
**Website:** www.mountwashington.edu
**Admissions email:** N/A
**For-profit**
**Application deadline (fall):** N/A
**Undergraduate student body:** N/A full time, N/A part time
**Expenses:** 2013-2014: $8,016; room/board: N/A
**Financial aid:** N/A

## New England College
Henniker NH
(800) 521-7642
**U.S. News ranking:** Reg. U. (N), second tier
**Website:** www.nec.edu
**Admissions email:** admission@nec.edu
**Private;** founded 1946
**Freshman admissions:** least selective; 2013-2014: 5,843 applied, 5,251 accepted. Neither SAT nor ACT required. SAT 25/75 percentile: 810-1020. High school rank: 2% in top tenth, 12% in top quarter, 36% in top half
**Early decision deadline:** N/A, notification date: N/A
**Early action deadline:** N/A, notification date: N/A
**Application deadline (fall):** rolling
**Undergraduate student body:** 1,548 full time, 59 part time; 44% male, 56% female; 1% American Indian, 1% Asian, 19% black, 3% Hispanic, 1% multiracial, 0% Pacific Islander, 59% white, 4% international; 25% from in state; 44% live on campus; 4% of students in fraternities, 10% in sororities
**Most popular majors:** 15% Business, Management, Marketing, and Related Support Services, 14% Education, 8% Health Professions and Related Programs, 8% Homeland Security, Law Enforcement, Firefighting and Related Protective Services, 8% Social Sciences
**Expenses:** 2014-2015: $34,250; room/board: $13,126
**Financial aid:** (603) 428-2414; 77% of undergrads determined to have financial need; average aid package $24,794

## Plymouth State University

Plymouth NH
(603) 535-2237
**U.S. News ranking:** Reg. U. (N), No. 103
**Website:** www.plymouth.edu
**Admissions email:** plymouthadmit@plymouth.edu
**Public;** founded 1871
**Freshman admissions:** less selective; 2013-2014: 5,084 applied, 3,967 accepted. Either SAT or ACT required. SAT 25/75 percentile: 860-1070. High school rank: 4% in top tenth, 20% in top quarter, 52% in top half
**Early decision deadline:** N/A, notification date: N/A
**Early action deadline:** N/A, notification date: N/A
**Application deadline (fall):** 4/1
**Undergraduate student body:** 3,795 full time, 270 part time; 52% male, 48% female; 0% American Indian, 2% Asian, 2% black, 3% Hispanic, 1% multiracial, 0% Pacific Islander, 79% white, 1% international; 59% from in state; 52% live on campus; 0% of students in fraternities, 4% in sororities
**Most popular majors:** 22% Business, Management, Marketing, and Related Support Services, 14% Education, 8% Homeland Security, Law Enforcement, Firefighting and Related Protective Services, 8% Parks, Recreation, Leisure, and Fitness Studies, 7% Visual and Performing Arts
**Expenses:** 2014-2015: $12,677 in state, $20,587 out of state; room/board: $10,728
**Financial aid:** (603) 535-2338; 65% of undergrads determined to have financial need; average aid package $9,345

## Rivier University

Nashua NH
(603) 888-1311
**U.S. News ranking:** Reg. U. (N), second tier
**Website:** rivier.edu
**Admissions email:** admissions@rivier.edu
**Private**
**Freshman admissions:** less selective; 2013-2014: N/A applied, N/A accepted. Neither SAT nor ACT required. SAT 25/75 percentile: 860-1020. High school rank: N/A
**Early decision deadline:** N/A, notification date: N/A
**Early action deadline:** N/A, notification date: N/A
**Application deadline (fall):** rolling
**Undergraduate student body:** 891 full time, 700 part time; 18% male, 82% female; 0% American Indian, 2% Asian, 3% black, 5% Hispanic, 1% multiracial, 0% Pacific Islander, 77% white, 0% international; 60% from in state; N/A live on campus; N/A of students in fraternities, N/A in sororities
**Most popular majors:** 8% Business Administration and Management, General, 7% Elementary Education and Teaching, 8% Human Development and Family Studies, General, 8% Psychology, General, 45% Registered Nursing/Registered Nurse

**Expenses:** 2013-2014: $28,055; room/board: $10,570
**Financial aid:** (603) 897-8533

## Southern New Hampshire University

Manchester NH
(603) 645-9611
**U.S. News ranking:** Reg. U. (N), unranked
**Website:** www.snhu.edu
**Admissions email:** admission@snhu.edu
**Private;** founded 1932
**Freshman admissions:** N/A; 2013-2014: 4,393 applied, 3,414 accepted. Neither SAT nor ACT required. SAT 25/75 percentile: 890-1100. High school rank: 7% in top tenth, 19% in top quarter, 61% in top half
**Early decision deadline:** N/A, notification date: N/A
**Early action deadline:** 11/15, notification date: 12/15
**Application deadline (fall):** rolling
**Undergraduate student body:** 9,283 full time, 8,820 part time; 40% male, 60% female; 0% American Indian, 1% Asian, 5% black, 2% Hispanic, 0% multiracial, 0% Pacific Islander, 29% white, 2% international; 44% from in state; 68% live on campus; 4% of students in fraternities, 5% in sororities
**Most popular majors:** 6% Accounting, 37% Business Administration and Management, General, 5% Computer and Information Sciences, General, 5% Hospitality Administration/Management, General, 8% Psychology, General
**Expenses:** 2014-2015: $29,924; room/board: $11,442
**Financial aid:** (603) 645-9645; 76% of undergrads determined to have financial need; average aid package $21,914

## St. Anselm College

Manchester NH
(603) 641-7500
**U.S. News ranking:** Nat. Lib. Arts, No. 120
**Website:** www.anselm.edu
**Admissions email:** admission@anselm.edu
**Private;** founded 1889
**Affiliation:** Roman Catholic (Benedictine)
**Freshman admissions:** selective; 2013-2014: 3,829 applied, 2,820 accepted. Neither SAT nor ACT required. SAT 25/75 percentile: 1060-1230. High school rank: 22% in top tenth, 58% in top quarter, 90% in top half
**Early decision deadline:** N/A, notification date: N/A
**Early action deadline:** 11/15, notification date: 1/15
**Application deadline (fall):** 2/1
**Undergraduate student body:** 1,878 full time, 45 part time; 41% male, 59% female; 0% American Indian, 1% Asian, 2% black, 3% Hispanic, 2% multiracial, 0% Pacific Islander, 79% white, 1% international; 24% from in state; 89% live on campus; 0% of students in fraternities, 0% in sororities
**Most popular majors:** 11% Business/Commerce, General, 12% Criminology, 6% History,

General, 8% Psychology, General, 18% Registered Nursing/Registered Nurse
**Expenses:** 2014-2015: $36,336; room/board: $13,040
**Financial aid:** (603) 641-7110; 74% of undergrads determined to have financial need; average aid package $26,660

## Thomas More College of Liberal Arts

Merrimack NH
(800) 880-8308
**U.S. News ranking:** Nat. Lib. Arts, unranked
**Website:** www.thomasmorecollege.edu
**Admissions email:** admissions@thomasmorecollege.edu
**Private**
**Affiliation:** Roman Catholic
**Freshman admissions:** N/A; 2013-2014: N/A applied, N/A accepted. Neither SAT nor ACT required. ACT 25/75 percentile: N/A. High school rank: N/A
**Early decision deadline:** N/A, notification date: N/A
**Early action deadline:** N/A, notification date: N/A
**Application deadline (fall):** rolling
**Undergraduate student body:** 80 full time, 0 part time; 50% male, 50% female; 0% American Indian, 5% Asian, 0% black, 3% Hispanic, 0% multiracial, 0% Pacific Islander, 85% white, 3% international; 11% from in state; 93% live on campus; 0% of students in fraternities, 0% in sororities
**Most popular majors:** Information not available
**Expenses:** 2014-2015: $20,400; room/board: $9,400
**Financial aid:** (800) 880-8308; 79% of undergrads determined to have financial need; average aid package $20,109

## University of New Hampshire

Durham NH
(603) 862-1360
**U.S. News ranking:** Nat. U., No. 99
**Website:** www.unh.edu
**Admissions email:** admissions@unh.edu
**Public;** founded 1866
**Freshman admissions:** selective; 2013-2014: 17,938 applied, 13,963 accepted. Either SAT or ACT required. SAT 25/75 percentile: 1000-1210. High school rank: 20% in top tenth, 50% in top quarter, 88% in top half
**Early decision deadline:** N/A, notification date: N/A
**Early action deadline:** 11/15, notification date: N/A
**Application deadline (fall):** 2/1
**Undergraduate student body:** 12,060 full time, 471 part time; 46% male, 54% female; 0% American Indian, 2% Asian, 1% black, 3% Hispanic, 2% multiracial, 0% Pacific Islander, 80% white, 1% international; 54% from in state; 58% live on campus; 10% of students in fraternities, 11% in sororities
**Most popular majors:** 16% Business Administration and Management, General, 4% Mechanical Engineering,

3% Political Science and Government, General, 9% Psychology, General, 5% Speech Communication and Rhetoric
**Expenses:** 2014-2015: $16,552 in state, $29,532 out of state; room/board: $10,360
**Financial aid:** (603) 862-3600; 68% of undergrads determined to have financial need; average aid package $21,879

## Berkeley College

Woodland Park NJ
(800) 446-5400
**U.S. News ranking:** Business, unranked
**Website:** www.berkeleycollege.edu
**Admissions email:** admissions@berkeleycollege.edu
**For-profit;** founded 1931
**Freshman admissions:** less selective; 2013-2014: 2,097 applied, 1,986 accepted. Neither SAT nor ACT required. ACT 25/75 percentile: N/A. High school rank: N/A
**Early decision deadline:** N/A, notification date: N/A
**Early action deadline:** N/A, notification date: N/A
**Application deadline (fall):** rolling
**Undergraduate student body:** 2,954 full time, 717 part time; 29% male, 71% female; 0% American Indian, 3% Asian, 23% black, 38% Hispanic, 0% multiracial, 0% Pacific Islander, 20% white, 1% international
**Most popular majors:** 10% Accounting, 32% Business Administration and Management, General, 23% Criminal Justice/Law Enforcement Administration, 11% Fashion Merchandising, 8% Health/Health Care Administration/Management
**Expenses:** 2014-2015: $23,700; room/board: N/A
**Financial aid:** (973) 278-5400

## Bloomfield College

Bloomfield NJ
(800) 848-4555
**U.S. News ranking:** Nat. Lib. Arts, second tier
**Website:** www.bloomfield.edu
**Admissions email:** admission@bloomfield.edu
**Private;** founded 1868
**Affiliation:** Presbyterian
**Freshman admissions:** less selective; 2013-2014: 2,987 applied, 1,758 accepted. Either SAT or ACT required. SAT 25/75 percentile: 770-930. High school rank: 6% in top tenth, 24% in top quarter, 55% in top half
**Early decision deadline:** N/A, notification date: N/A
**Early action deadline:** 12/1, notification date: 12/23
**Application deadline (fall):** 8/1
**Undergraduate student body:** 1,765 full time, 204 part time; 35% male, 65% female; 0% American Indian, 4% Asian, 50% black, 22% Hispanic, 1% multiracial, 0% Pacific Islander, 13% white, 3% international; 94% from in state; 26% live on campus; 4% of students in fraternities, 2% in sororities
**Most popular majors:** 13% Business, Management, Marketing, and Related Support Services, 12% Health Professions and Related Programs,

14% Psychology, 19% Social Sciences, 20% Visual and Performing Arts
**Expenses:** 2014-2015: $26,750; room/board: $11,100
**Financial aid:** (973) 748-9000; 94% of undergrads determined to have financial need; average aid package $24,037

## Caldwell University

Caldwell NJ
(973) 618-3500
**U.S. News ranking:** Reg. U. (N), No. 115
**Website:** www.caldwell.edu
**Admissions email:** admissions@caldwell.edu
**Private;** founded 1939
**Affiliation:** Roman Catholic
**Freshman admissions:** less selective; 2013-2014: 2,881 applied, 1,902 accepted. Either SAT or ACT required. SAT 25/75 percentile: 830-1070. High school rank: 10% in top tenth, 25% in top quarter, 62% in top half
**Early decision deadline:** N/A, notification date: N/A
**Early action deadline:** 12/1, notification date: 1/1
**Application deadline (fall):** rolling
**Undergraduate student body:** 1,302 full time, 274 part time; 31% male, 69% female; 0% American Indian, 4% Asian, 15% black, 16% Hispanic, 1% multiracial, 0% Pacific Islander, 45% white, 4% international; 92% from in state; 32% live on campus; N/A of students in fraternities, N/A in sororities
**Most popular majors:** 16% Business Administration and Management, General, 11% Education, General, 12% English Language and Literature, General, 8% Health Professions and Related Programs, 14% Psychology, General
**Expenses:** 2014-2015: $30,050; room/board: $11,700
**Financial aid:** (973) 618-3221; 81% of undergrads determined to have financial need; average aid package $13,193

## Centenary College

Hackettstown NJ
(800) 236-8679
**U.S. News ranking:** Reg. U. (N), second tier
**Website:** www.centenarycollege.edu
**Admissions email:** admissions@centenarycollege.edu
**Private;** founded 1867
**Affiliation:** United Methodist
**Freshman admissions:** less selective; 2013-2014: 1,038 applied, 944 accepted. Either SAT or ACT required. SAT 25/75 percentile: 820-1090. High school rank: 10% in top tenth, 28% in top quarter, 58% in top half
**Early decision deadline:** N/A, notification date: N/A
**Early action deadline:** N/A, notification date: N/A
**Application deadline (fall):** 8/15
**Undergraduate student body:** 1,610 full time, 98 part time; 40% male, 60% female; 1% American Indian, 1% Asian, 10% black, 9% Hispanic, 1% multiracial, 0% Pacific Islander, 60% white, 5% international; 80% from in state; 61% live on campus; 0% of students in fraternities, 1% in sororities

**Most popular majors:** Information not available
**Expenses:** 2014-2015: $30,942; room/board: $10,420
**Financial aid:** (908) 852-1400; 79% of undergrads determined to have financial need; average aid package $25,324

## College of New Jersey
Ewing NJ
(609) 771-2131
**U.S. News ranking:** Reg. U. (N), No. 3
**Website:** www.tcnj.edu
**Admissions email:** admiss@tcnj.edu
**Public;** founded 1855
**Freshman admissions:** more selective; 2013-2014: 11,145 applied, 4,805 accepted. Either SAT or ACT required. SAT 25/75 percentile: 1130-1340. High school rank: 84% in top tenth, 89% in top quarter, 99% in top half
**Early decision deadline:** 11/15, notification date: 12/15
**Early action deadline:** N/A, notification date: N/A
**Application deadline (fall):** 1/15
**Undergraduate student body:** 6,455 full time, 198 part time; 43% male, 57% female; 0% American Indian, 9% Asian, 5% black, 11% Hispanic, 1% multiracial, 0% Pacific Islander, 66% white, 0% international; 94% from in state; 55% live on campus; 9% of students in fraternities, 11% in sororities
**Most popular majors:** 7% Biology/Biological Sciences, General, 18% Business Administration and Management, General, 23% Elementary Education and Teaching, 7% Engineering, General, 7% Psychology, General
**Expenses:** 2014-2015: $15,024 in state, $25,637 out of state; room/board: $11,677
**Financial aid:** (609) 771-2211; 52% of undergrads determined to have financial need; average aid package $11,078

## College of St. Elizabeth
Morristown NJ
(973) 290-4700
**U.S. News ranking:** Reg. U. (N), No. 87
**Website:** www.cse.edu
**Admissions email:** apply@cse.edu
**Private;** founded 1899
**Affiliation:** Catholic
**Freshman admissions:** least selective; 2013-2014: 2,496 applied, 1,207 accepted. Either SAT or ACT required. SAT 25/75 percentile: 748-960. High school rank: 1% in top tenth, 10% in top quarter, 49% in top half
**Early decision deadline:** N/A, notification date: N/A
**Early action deadline:** N/A, notification date: N/A
**Application deadline (fall):** rolling
**Undergraduate student body:** 554 full time, 433 part time; 8% male, 92% female; 0% American Indian, 3% Asian, 26% black, 15% Hispanic, 1% multiracial, 0% Pacific Islander, 39% white, 4% international; 94% from in state; 33% live on campus; 0% of students in fraternities, 0% in sororities

**Most popular majors:** 6% Business Administration and Management, General, 7% Dietetics/Dietitian, 12% Multi-/Interdisciplinary Studies, Other, 12% Psychology, General, 38% Registered Nursing/Registered Nurse
**Expenses:** 2014-2015: $31,095; room/board: $12,744
**Financial aid:** (973) 290-4445; 89% of undergrads determined to have financial need; average aid package $26,055

## Drew University
Madison NJ
(973) 408-3739
**U.S. News ranking:** Nat. Lib. Arts, No. 99
**Website:** www.drew.edu
**Admissions email:** cadm@drew.edu
**Private;** founded 1867
**Affiliation:** Methodist
**Freshman admissions:** selective; 2013-2014: 3,430 applied, 2,656 accepted. Either SAT or ACT required. SAT 25/75 percentile: 990-1220. High school rank: 31% in top tenth, 62% in top quarter, 89% in top half
**Early decision deadline:** 12/1, notification date: 12/16
**Early action deadline:** N/A, notification date: N/A
**Application deadline (fall):** 2/15
**Undergraduate student body:** 1,434 full time, 59 part time; 38% male, 62% female; 0% American Indian, 5% Asian, 11% black, 14% Hispanic, 3% multiracial, 0% Pacific Islander, 56% white, 3% international; 69% from in state; 77% live on campus; 0% of students in fraternities, 0% in sororities
**Most popular majors:** 6% Drama and Dramatics/Theatre Arts, General, 7% Economics, General, 8% English Language and Literature, General, 7% Political Science and Government, General, 10% Psychology, General
**Expenses:** 2014-2015: $45,214; room/board: $12,302
**Financial aid:** (973) 408-3112; 72% of undergrads determined to have financial need; average aid package $35,618

## Fairleigh Dickinson University
Teaneck NJ
(800) 338-8803
**U.S. News ranking:** Reg. U. (N), No. 79
**Website:** www.fdu.edu
**Admissions email:** admissions@fdu.edu
**Private;** founded 1942
**Freshman admissions:** selective; 2013-2014: 12,561 applied, 6,616 accepted. Either SAT or ACT required. SAT 25/75 percentile: 900-1100. High school rank: 17% in top tenth, 43% in top quarter, 76% in top half
**Early decision deadline:** N/A, notification date: N/A
**Early action deadline:** N/A, notification date: N/A
**Application deadline (fall):** rolling
**Undergraduate student body:** 4,843 full time, 3,539 part time; 42% male, 58% female; 0% American Indian, 4% Asian, 13% black, 27% Hispanic, 1% multiracial, 0% Pacific Islander, 39% white, 5% international; 89% from in

state; 34% live on campus; N/A of students in fraternities, N/A in sororities
**Most popular majors:** Information not available
**Expenses:** 2013-2014: $34,882; room/board: $13,068
**Financial aid:** (201) 692-2823

## Felician College
Lodi NJ
(201) 559-6131
**U.S. News ranking:** Reg. U. (N), second tier
**Website:** www.felician.edu
**Admissions email:** admissions@felician.edu
**Private;** founded 1942
**Affiliation:** Roman Catholic
**Freshman admissions:** least selective; 2013-2014: 1,567 applied, 1,382 accepted. Either SAT or ACT required. SAT 25/75 percentile: 780-980. High school rank: 2% in top tenth, 24% in top quarter, 57% in top half
**Early decision deadline:** N/A, notification date: N/A
**Early action deadline:** N/A, notification date: N/A
**Application deadline (fall):** rolling
**Undergraduate student body:** 1,340 full time, 281 part time; 28% male, 72% female; 1% American Indian, 8% Asian, 20% black, 24% Hispanic, 1% multiracial, 1% Pacific Islander, 38% white, 2% international; 92% from in state; N/A live on campus; N/A of students in fraternities, N/A in sororities
**Most popular majors:** 18% Business, Management, Marketing, and Related Support Services, 6% Education, 39% Health Professions and Related Programs, 9% Homeland Security, Law Enforcement, Firefighting and Related Protective Services, 8% Multi/Interdisciplinary Studies
**Expenses:** 2014-2015: $30,615; room/board: $11,650
**Financial aid:** (201) 559-6010; 87% of undergrads determined to have financial need; average aid package $25,793

## Georgian Court University
Lakewood NJ
(800) 458-8422
**U.S. News ranking:** Reg. U. (N), No. 125
**Website:** www.georgian.edu
**Admissions email:** admissions@georgian.edu
**Private;** founded 1908
**Affiliation:** Roman Catholic
**Freshman admissions:** less selective; 2013-2014: 1,276 applied, 994 accepted. Either SAT or ACT required. SAT 25/75 percentile: 790-1010. High school rank: 6% in top tenth, 30% in top quarter, 65% in top half
**Early decision deadline:** N/A, notification date: N/A
**Early action deadline:** N/A, notification date: N/A
**Application deadline (fall):** rolling
**Undergraduate student body:** 1,261 full time, 306 part time; 19% male, 81% female; 0% American Indian, 2% Asian, 15% black, 12% Hispanic, 2% multiracial, 0% Pacific Islander, 53% white, 1% international; 94% from in state; 28% live on campus; N/A of students in fraternities, N/A in sororities

**Most popular majors:** 6% Business, Management, Marketing, and Related Support Services, 17% Education, 12% English Language and Literature/Letters, 8% Health Professions and Related Programs, 24% Psychology
**Expenses:** 2014-2015: $30,998; room/board: $10,596
**Financial aid:** (732) 364-2200; 83% of undergrads determined to have financial need; average aid package $25,096

## Kean University
Union NJ
(908) 737-7100
**U.S. News ranking:** Reg. U. (N), second tier
**Website:** www.kean.edu
**Admissions email:** admitme@kean.edu
**Public;** founded 1855
**Freshman admissions:** less selective; 2013-2014: 4,952 applied, 3,980 accepted. Either SAT or ACT required. SAT 25/75 percentile: 810-1000. High school rank: 8% in top tenth, 26% in top quarter, 63% in top half
**Early decision deadline:** N/A, notification date: N/A
**Early action deadline:** N/A, notification date: N/A
**Application deadline (fall):** 5/31
**Undergraduate student body:** 9,251 full time, 2,827 part time; 40% male, 60% female; 0% American Indian, 6% Asian, 19% black, 24% Hispanic, 2% multiracial, 0% Pacific Islander, 39% white, 1% international; 98% from in state; 14% live on campus; N/A of students in fraternities, N/A in sororities
**Most popular majors:** 6% Accounting, 5% Biology/Biological Sciences, General, 8% Business Administration and Management, General, 6% Criminal Justice/Law Enforcement Administration, 14% Psychology, General
**Expenses:** 2013-2014: $10,918 in state, $17,141 out of state; room/board: $10,064
**Financial aid:** (908) 737-3190; 70% of undergrads determined to have financial need; average aid package $9,917

## Monmouth University
West Long Branch NJ
(800) 543-9671
**U.S. News ranking:** Reg. U. (N), No. 37
**Website:** www.monmouth.edu
**Admissions email:** admission@monmouth.edu
**Private;** founded 1933
**Freshman admissions:** selective; 2013-2014: 5,537 applied, 4,314 accepted. Either SAT or ACT required. SAT 25/75 percentile: 970-1150. High school rank: 19% in top tenth, 49% in top quarter, 82% in top half
**Early decision deadline:** N/A, notification date: N/A
**Early action deadline:** 12/1, notification date: 1/15
**Application deadline (fall):** 3/1
**Undergraduate student body:** 4,304 full time, 303 part time; 41% male, 59% female; 0% American Indian, 3% Asian, 5% black, 9% Hispanic, 2% multiracial, 0% Pacific Islander, 77% white, 1% international; 88% from in state; 15% live on campus; 13% of students in fraternities, 15% in sororities

**Most popular majors:** 24% Business, Management, Marketing, and Related Support Services, 12% Communication, Journalism, and Related Programs, 13% Education, 8% Health Professions and Related Programs, 8% Psychology
**Expenses:** 2014-2015: $32,310; room/board: $11,798
**Financial aid:** (732) 571-3463; 70% of undergrads determined to have financial need; average aid package $21,048

## Montclair State University
Montclair NJ
(973) 655-4444
**U.S. News ranking:** Reg. U. (N), No. 50
**Website:** www.montclair.edu
**Admissions email:** admissions@montclair.edu
**Public;** founded 1908
**Freshman admissions:** selective; 2013-2014: 13,012 applied, 8,500 accepted. SAT required. SAT 25/75 percentile: 880-1060. High school rank: 11% in top tenth, 35% in top quarter, 79% in top half
**Early decision deadline:** N/A, notification date: N/A
**Early action deadline:** N/A, notification date: N/A
**Application deadline (fall):** 3/1
**Undergraduate student body:** 13,356 full time, 2,075 part time; 39% male, 61% female; 0% American Indian, 5% Asian, 9% black, 23% Hispanic, 3% multiracial, 0% Pacific Islander, 47% white, 2% international; 3% from in state; 32% live on campus; N/A of students in fraternities, N/A in sororities
**Most popular majors:** 14% Business Administration and Management, General, 6% English Language and Literature, General, 8% Family and Consumer Sciences/Human Sciences, General, 5% Multi-/Interdisciplinary Studies, Other, 9% Psychology, General
**Expenses:** 2014-2015: $11,616 in state, $21,153 out of state; room/board: $14,140
**Financial aid:** (973) 655-4461; 71% of undergrads determined to have financial need; average aid package $15,857

## New Jersey City University
Jersey City NJ
(888) 441-6528
**U.S. News ranking:** Reg. U. (N), second tier
**Website:** www.njcu.edu/
**Admissions email:** admissions@njcu.edu
**Public;** founded 1927
**Freshman admissions:** less selective; 2013-2014: 4,183 applied, 1,727 accepted. Either SAT or ACT required. SAT 25/75 percentile: 820-1012. High school rank: 17% in top tenth, 37% in top quarter, 74% in top half
**Early decision deadline:** N/A, notification date: N/A
**Early action deadline:** N/A, notification date: N/A
**Undergraduate student body:** 4,777 full time, 1,661 part time; 40% male, 60% female; 0% American Indian, 9% Asian, 21% black, 34% Hispanic, 1% multiracial,

0% Pacific Islander, 25% white, 1% international; 99% from in state; 4% live on campus; 0% of students in fraternities, 0% in sororities
**Most popular majors:** 8% Accounting, 10% Business Administration and Management, General, 8% Corrections and Criminal Justice, Other, 11% Psychology, General, 12% Registered Nursing, Nursing Administration, Nursing Research and Clinical Nursing, Other
**Expenses:** 2014-2015: $10,852 in state, $19,424 out of state; room/board: $10,604
**Financial aid:** (201) 200-3173; 87% of undergrads determined to have financial need; average aid package $16,087

## New Jersey Institute of Technology

Newark NJ
(973) 596-3300
**U.S. News ranking:** Nat. U., No. 149
**Website:** www.njit.edu
**Admissions email:** admissions@njit.edu
**Public;** founded 1881
**Freshman admissions:** more selective; 2013-2014: 4,344 applied, 2,844 accepted. Either SAT or ACT required. SAT 25/75 percentile: 1030-1250. High school rank: 27% in top tenth, 54% in top quarter, 85% in top half
**Early decision deadline:** N/A, notification date: N/A
**Early action deadline:** N/A, notification date: N/A
**Application deadline (fall):** 3/1
**Undergraduate student body:** 5,709 full time, 1,577 part time; 76% male, 24% female; 0% American Indian, 20% Asian, 9% black, 20% Hispanic, 2% multiracial, 0% Pacific Islander, 33% white, 5% international; 95% from in state; 23% live on campus; 5% of students in fraternities, 3% in sororities
**Most popular majors:** 11% Architecture and Related Services, 9% Business, Management, Marketing, and Related Support Services, 15% Computer and Information Sciences and Support Services, 36% Engineering, 14% Engineering Technologies and Engineering-Related Fields
**Expenses:** 2014-2015: $15,602 in state, $28,274 out of state; room/board: $12,500
**Financial aid:** (973) 596-3479; 72% of undergrads determined to have financial need; average aid package $14,123

## Princeton University

Princeton NJ
(609) 258-3060
**U.S. News ranking:** Nat. U., No. 1
**Website:** www.princeton.edu
**Admissions email:** uaoffice@princeton.edu
**Private;** founded 1746
**Freshman admissions:** most selective; 2013-2014: 26,498 applied, 1,963 accepted. Either SAT or ACT required. SAT 25/75 percentile: 1410-1600. High school rank: 95% in top tenth, 98% in top quarter, 100% in top half

**Early decision deadline:** N/A, notification date: N/A
**Early action deadline:** 11/1, notification date: 12/15
**Application deadline (fall):** 1/1
**Undergraduate student body:** 5,244 full time, 79 part time; 51% male, 49% female; 0% American Indian, 20% Asian, 8% black, 8% Hispanic, 4% multiracial, 0% Pacific Islander, 47% white, 11% international; 18% from in state; 97% live on campus; 0% of students in fraternities, 0% in sororities
**Most popular majors:** 11% Economics, General, 6% Molecular Biology, 8% Political Science and Government, General, 6% Psychology, General, 6% Public Policy Analysis, General
**Expenses:** 2014-2015: $41,820; room/board: $13,620
**Financial aid:** (609) 258-3330; 59% of undergrads determined to have financial need; average aid package $40,732

## Ramapo College of New Jersey

Mahwah NJ
(201) 684-7300
**U.S. News ranking:** Reg. U. (N), No. 28
**Website:** www.ramapo.edu
**Admissions email:** admissions@ramapo.edu
**Public;** founded 1969
**Freshman admissions:** selective; 2013-2014: 6,297 applied, 3,480 accepted. Either SAT or ACT required. SAT 25/75 percentile: 990-1200. High school rank: 22% in top tenth, 52% in top quarter, 85% in top half
**Early decision deadline:** N/A, notification date: N/A
**Early action deadline:** 11/15, notification date: 12/15
**Application deadline (fall):** 3/1
**Undergraduate student body:** 4,992 full time, 622 part time; 44% male, 56% female; 0% American Indian, 6% Asian, 5% black, 14% Hispanic, 1% multiracial, 0% Pacific Islander, 66% white, 1% international; 95% from in state; 50% live on campus; 7% of students in fraternities, 11% in sororities
**Most popular majors:** 6% Accounting, 15% Business Administration and Management, General, 8% Nursing Science, 15% Psychology, General, 11% Speech Communication and Rhetoric
**Expenses:** 2014-2015: $13,388 in state, $22,038 out of state; room/board: $11,550
**Financial aid:** (201) 684-7549; 61% of undergrads determined to have financial need; average aid package $11,083

## Richard Stockton College of New Jersey

Galloway NJ
(609) 652-4261
**U.S. News ranking:** Reg. U. (N), No. 41
**Website:** www.stockton.edu
**Admissions email:** admissions@stockton.edu
**Public;** founded 1969
**Freshman admissions:** selective; 2013-2014: 6,126 applied,

3,805 accepted. Either SAT or ACT required. SAT 25/75 percentile: 980-1170. High school rank: 23% in top tenth, 60% in top quarter, 95% in top half
**Early decision deadline:** N/A, notification date: N/A
**Early action deadline:** N/A, notification date: N/A
**Application deadline (fall):** 5/1
**Undergraduate student body:** 6,953 full time, 586 part time; 40% male, 60% female; 0% American Indian, 5% Asian, 6% black, 10% Hispanic, 3% multiracial, 0% Pacific Islander, 74% white, 0% international; 99% from in state; 36% live on campus; N/A of students in fraternities, N/A in sororities
**Most popular majors:** 8% Biology/Biological Sciences, General, 15% Business Administration and Management, General, 9% Criminology, 13% Psychology, General, 6% Teacher Education, Multiple Levels
**Expenses:** 2014-2015: $12,568 in state, $19,089 out of state; room/board: $11,164
**Financial aid:** (609) 652-4201; 74% of undergrads determined to have financial need; average aid package $16,417

## Rider University

Lawrenceville NJ
(609) 896-5042
**U.S. News ranking:** Reg. U. (N), No. 23
**Website:** www.rider.edu
**Admissions email:** admissions@rider.edu
**Private;** founded 1865
**Freshman admissions:** selective; 2013-2014: 8,076 applied, 5,604 accepted. Either SAT or ACT required. SAT 25/75 percentile: 930-1150. High school rank: 14% in top tenth, 38% in top quarter, 68% in top half
**Early decision deadline:** N/A, notification date: N/A
**Early action deadline:** 11/15, notification date: 12/15
**Application deadline (fall):** rolling
**Undergraduate student body:** 3,792 full time, 627 part time; 41% male, 59% female; 0% American Indian, 4% Asian, 10% black, 10% Hispanic, 2% multiracial, 0% Pacific Islander, 66% white, 3% international; 78% from in state; 57% live on campus; 5% of students in fraternities, 9% in sororities
**Most popular majors:** 10% Accounting, 7% Business Administration and Management, General, 8% Elementary Education and Teaching, 9% Psychology, General, 6% Rhetoric and Composition
**Expenses:** 2014-2015: $36,830; room/board: $13,330
**Financial aid:** (609) 896-5360; 71% of undergrads determined to have financial need; average aid package $23,474

## Rowan University

Glassboro NJ
(856) 256-4200
**U.S. News ranking:** Reg. U. (N), No. 19
**Website:** www.rowan.edu
**Admissions email:** admissions@rowan.edu
**Public;** founded 1923

**Freshman admissions:** selective; 2013-2014: 9,082 applied, 5,464 accepted. Either SAT or ACT required. SAT 25/75 percentile: 1000-1230. High school rank: 36% in top tenth, 63% in top quarter, 88% in top half
**Early decision deadline:** N/A, notification date: N/A
**Early action deadline:** N/A, notification date: N/A
**Application deadline (fall):** 3/1
**Undergraduate student body:** 9,348 full time, 1,603 part time; 51% male, 49% female; 0% American Indian, 6% Asian, 8% black, 9% Hispanic, 3% multiracial, 0% Pacific Islander, 70% white, 1% international; 94% from in state; 33% live on campus; 8% of students in fraternities, 7% in sororities
**Most popular majors:** 14% Business, Management, Marketing, and Related Support Services, 8% Communication, Journalism, and Related Programs, 20% Education, 5% Homeland Security, Law Enforcement, Firefighting and Related Protective Services, 9% Psychology
**Expenses:** 2014-2015: $12,616 in state, $20,570 out of state; room/board: $14,022
**Financial aid:** (856) 256-4250; 66% of undergrads determined to have financial need; average aid package $9,627

## Rutgers, The State University of New Jersey–Camden

Camden NJ
(856) 225-6104
**U.S. News ranking:** Reg. U. (N), No. 28
**Website:** www.rutgers.edu/
**Admissions email:** camden@ugadm.rutgers.edu
**Public;** founded 1927
**Freshman admissions:** selective; 2013-2014: 7,437 applied, 4,357 accepted. Either SAT or ACT required. SAT 25/75 percentile: 930-1140. High school rank: 17% in top tenth, 43% in top quarter, 80% in top half
**Early decision deadline:** N/A, notification date: N/A
**Early action deadline:** N/A, notification date: N/A
**Application deadline (fall):** rolling
**Undergraduate student body:** 3,939 full time, 903 part time; 45% male, 55% female; 0% American Indian, 9% Asian, 17% black, 11% Hispanic, 3% multiracial, 0% Pacific Islander, 56% white, 1% international; 98% from in state; 9% live on campus; 5% of students in fraternities, N/A in sororities
**Most popular majors:** 8% Biology/Biological Sciences, General, 13% Business Administration and Management, General, 8% Criminal Justice/Safety Studies, 12% Psychology, General, 10% Registered Nursing/Registered Nurse
**Expenses:** 2014-2015: $13,683 in state, $27,978 out of state; room/board: $11,438
**Financial aid:** (856) 225-6039; 78% of undergrads determined to have financial need; average aid package $12,097

## Rutgers, The State University of New Jersey–Newark

Newark NJ
(973) 353-5205
**U.S. News ranking:** Nat. U., No. 126
**Website:** rutgers-newark.rutgers.edu
**Admissions email:** admissions@ugadm.rutgers.edu
**Public;** founded 1908
**Freshman admissions:** selective; 2013-2014: 13,282 applied, 7,173 accepted. Either SAT or ACT required. SAT 25/75 percentile: 960-1158. High school rank: 22% in top tenth, 52% in top quarter, 88% in top half
**Early decision deadline:** N/A, notification date: N/A
**Early action deadline:** N/A, notification date: N/A
**Application deadline (fall):** rolling
**Undergraduate student body:** 5,827 full time, 1,390 part time; 50% male, 50% female; 0% American Indian, 22% Asian, 19% black, 24% Hispanic, 3% multiracial, 0% Pacific Islander, 26% white, 3% international; 98% from in state; 9% live on campus; N/A of students in fraternities, N/A in sororities
**Most popular majors:** 13% Criminal Justice/Safety Studies, 9% Finance, General, 9% Psychology, General, 9% Registered Nursing/Registered Nurse, 15% Regular/General High School/Secondary Diploma Program
**Expenses:** 2014-2015: $13,297 in state, $28,075 out of state; room/board: $12,509
**Financial aid:** (973) 353-5151; 77% of undergrads determined to have financial need; average aid package $13,074

## Rutgers, The State University of New Jersey–New Brunswick

Piscataway NJ
(732) 932-4636
**U.S. News ranking:** Nat. U., No. 70
**Website:** www.rutgers.edu
**Admissions email:** admissions@ugadm.rutgers.edu
**Public;** founded 1766
**Freshman admissions:** more selective; 2013-2014: 30,631 applied, 18,230 accepted. Either SAT or ACT required. SAT 25/75 percentile: 1090-1330. High school rank: 38% in top tenth, 74% in top quarter, 96% in top half
**Early decision deadline:** N/A, notification date: N/A
**Early action deadline:** N/A, notification date: N/A
**Application deadline (fall):** rolling
**Undergraduate student body:** 31,759 full time, 2,141 part time; 50% male, 50% female; 0% American Indian, 26% Asian, 8% black, 12% Hispanic, 3% multiracial, 0% Pacific Islander, 45% white, 4% international; 94% from in state; 48% live on campus; N/A of students in fraternities, N/A in sororities
**Most popular majors:** 5% Biology/Biological Sciences, General, 5% Economics, General, 4% Political Science and Government,

General, 9% Psychology, General, 7% Speech Communication and Rhetoric
**Expenses:** 2014-2015: $13,813 in state, $28,591 out of state; room/board: $11,749
**Financial aid:** (732) 932-7057; 56% of undergrads determined to have financial need; average aid package $13,041

## Seton Hall University
South Orange NJ
(973) 761-9332
**U.S. News ranking:** Nat. U., No. 126
**Website:** www.shu.edu
**Admissions email:** thehall@shu.edu
**Private;** founded 1856
**Affiliation:** Roman Catholic
**Freshman admissions:** selective; 2013-2014: 10,730 applied, 8,498 accepted. Either SAT or ACT required. SAT 25/75 percentile: 1020-1220. High school rank: 35% in top tenth, 62% in top quarter, 88% in top half
**Early decision deadline:** N/A, notification date: N/A
**Early action deadline:** 11/15, notification date: 12/30
**Application deadline (fall):** rolling
**Undergraduate student body:** 5,380 full time, 459 part time; 41% male, 59% female; 0% American Indian, 8% Asian, 13% black, 17% Hispanic, 2% multiracial, 0% Pacific Islander, 50% white, 3% international; 77% from in state; 39% live on campus; 9% of students in fraternities, 11% in sororities
**Most popular majors:** 6% Biology/Biological Sciences, General, 5% Finance, General, 5% Humanities/Humanistic Studies, 6% International Relations and Affairs, 22% Registered Nursing/Registered Nurse
**Expenses:** 2014-2015: $36,926; room/board: $13,742
**Financial aid:** (973) 761-9350

## Stevens Institute of Technology
Hoboken NJ
(201) 216-5194
**U.S. News ranking:** Nat. U., No. 76
**Website:** www.stevens.edu
**Admissions email:** admissions@stevens.edu
**Private;** founded 1870
**Freshman admissions:** more selective; 2013-2014: 4,977 applied, 1,899 accepted. Either SAT or ACT required. SAT 25/75 percentile: 1210-1390. High school rank: 68% in top tenth, 89% in top quarter, 98% in top half
**Early decision deadline:** 11/15, notification date: 12/15
**Early action deadline:** N/A, notification date: N/A
**Application deadline (fall):** 2/1
**Undergraduate student body:** 2,661 full time, 30 part time; 72% male, 28% female; 0% American Indian, 10% Asian, 2% black, 9% Hispanic, 0% multiracial, 0% Pacific Islander, 61% white, 4% international; 66% from in state; 73% live on campus; 25% of students in fraternities, 25% in sororities

**Most popular majors:** Information not available
**Expenses:** 2013-2014: $44,490; room/board: $14,214
**Financial aid:** (201) 216-5555

## St. Peter's University
Jersey City NJ
(201) 761-7100
**U.S. News ranking:** Reg. U. (N), No. 98
**Website:** www.spc.edu
**Admissions email:** admissions@spc.edu
**Private;** founded 1872
**Affiliation:** Roman Catholic (Jesuit)
**Freshman admissions:** less selective; 2013-2014: 6,145 applied, 3,323 accepted. Either SAT or ACT required. SAT 25/75 percentile: 830-1000. High school rank: 15% in top tenth, 38% in top quarter, 70% in top half
**Early decision deadline:** N/A, notification date: N/A
**Early action deadline:** N/A, notification date: N/A
**Application deadline (fall):** rolling
**Undergraduate student body:** 2,068 full time, 416 part time; 39% male, 61% female; 1% American Indian, 9% Asian, 28% black, 28% Hispanic, 2% multiracial, 0% Pacific Islander, 47% white, 2% international; 87% from in state; 36% live on campus; N/A of students in fraternities, N/A in sororities
**Most popular majors:** 11% Biological and Biomedical Sciences, 33% Business, Management, Marketing, and Related Support Services, 8% Health Professions and Related Programs, 7% Homeland Security, Law Enforcement, Firefighting and Related Protective Services, 6% Liberal Arts and Sciences, General Studies and Humanities
**Expenses:** 2014-2015: $33,232; room/board: $13,996
**Financial aid:** (201) 915-4929; 89% of undergrads determined to have financial need; average aid package $27,280

## Thomas Edison State College[1]
Trenton NJ
(888) 442-8372
**U.S. News ranking:** Reg. U. (N), unranked
**Website:** www.tesc.edu
**Admissions email:** admissions@tesc.edu
**Public;** founded 1972
**Application deadline (fall):** rolling
**Undergraduate student body:** N/A full time, N/A part time
**Expenses:** 2013-2014: $5,821 in state, $8,516 out of state; room/board: N/A
**Financial aid:** (609) 633-9658

## William Paterson University of New Jersey
Wayne NJ
(973) 720-2125
**U.S. News ranking:** Reg. U. (N), No. 103
**Website:** www.wpunj.edu/
**Admissions email:** admissions@wpunj.edu
**Public;** founded 1855
**Freshman admissions:** selective; 2013-2014: 8,935 applied, 6,086 accepted. Either SAT

or ACT required. SAT 25/75 percentile: 920-1100. High school rank: N/A
**Early decision deadline:** N/A, notification date: N/A
**Early action deadline:** 12/1, notification date: 1/15
**Application deadline (fall):** 6/1
**Undergraduate student body:** 8,271 full time, 1,756 part time; 45% male, 55% female; 0% American Indian, 7% Asian, 14% black, 25% Hispanic, 2% multiracial, 0% Pacific Islander, 47% white, 1% international; 98% from in state; 22% live on campus; 1% of students in fraternities, 1% in sororities
**Most popular majors:** 19% Business, Management, Marketing, and Related Support Services, 10% Communication, Journalism, and Related Programs, 12% Education, 9% Psychology, 12% Social Sciences
**Expenses:** 2013-2014: $11,918 in state, $19,458 out of state; room/board: $10,600
**Financial aid:** (973) 720-2202; 73% of undergrads determined to have financial need; average aid package $9,749

## NEW MEXICO

## Eastern New Mexico University[1]
Portales NM
(505) 562-2178
**U.S. News ranking:** Reg. U. (W), second tier
**Website:** www.enmu.edu
**Admissions email:** admissions.office@enmu.edu
**Public**
**Application deadline (fall):** N/A
**Undergraduate student body:** N/A full time, N/A part time
**Expenses:** 2013-2014: $4,558 in state, $10,069 out of state; room/board: $6,266
**Financial aid:** (800) 367-3668

## New Mexico Highlands University
Las Vegas NM
(505) 454-3439
**U.S. News ranking:** Reg. U. (W), unranked
**Website:** www.nmhu.edu
**Admissions email:** admissions@nmhu.edu
**Public;** founded 1893
**Freshman admissions:** N/A; 2013-2014: 1,575 applied, 1,575 accepted. Neither SAT nor ACT required. ACT 25/75 percentile: 16-20. High school rank: 5% in top tenth, 16% in top quarter, 47% in top half
**Early decision deadline:** N/A, notification date: N/A
**Early action deadline:** N/A, notification date: N/A
**Application deadline (fall):** rolling
**Undergraduate student body:** 1,646 full time, 750 part time; 40% male, 60% female; 16% American Indian, 1% Asian, 13% black, 11% Hispanic, 4% multiracial, 1% Pacific Islander, 39% white, 13% international
**Most popular majors:** Information not available
**Expenses:** 2013-2014: $4,000 in state, $6,383 out of state; room/board: $5,720

**Financial aid:** (505) 454-3430; 75% of undergrads determined to have financial need; average aid package $1,816

## New Mexico Institute of Mining and Technology
Socorro NM
(505) 835-5424
**U.S. News ranking:** Reg. U. (W), No. 23
**Website:** www.nmt.edu
**Admissions email:** admission@admin.nmt.edu
**Public;** founded 1889
**Freshman admissions:** more selective; 2013-2014: 1,088 applied, 350 accepted. Either SAT or ACT required. ACT 25/75 percentile: 23-29. High school rank: 40% in top tenth, 67% in top quarter, 87% in top half
**Early decision deadline:** N/A, notification date: N/A
**Early action deadline:** N/A, notification date: N/A
**Application deadline (fall):** 8/1
**Undergraduate student body:** 1,418 full time, 186 part time; 70% male, 30% female; 4% American Indian, 3% Asian, 2% black, 25% Hispanic, 4% multiracial, 0% Pacific Islander, 59% white, 3% international
**Most popular majors:** 10% Biology/Biological Sciences, General, 8% Chemical Engineering, 8% Computer and Information Sciences, General, 26% Mechanical Engineering, 7% Petroleum Engineering
**Expenses:** 2014-2015: $6,256 in state, $18,184 out of state; room/board: $6,740
**Financial aid:** (505) 835-5333; 53% of undergrads determined to have financial need; average aid package $11,806

## New Mexico State University
Las Cruces NM
(505) 646-3121
**U.S. News ranking:** Nat. U., second tier
**Website:** www.nmsu.edu
**Admissions email:** admissions@nmsu.edu
**Public;** founded 1888
**Freshman admissions:** selective; 2013-2014: 5,285 applied, 4,505 accepted. Either SAT or ACT required. ACT 25/75 percentile: 18-24. High school rank: 21% in top tenth, 47% in top quarter, 80% in top half
**Early decision deadline:** N/A, notification date: N/A
**Early action deadline:** N/A, notification date: N/A
**Application deadline (fall):** rolling
**Undergraduate student body:** 11,297 full time, 2,285 part time; 47% male, 53% female; 2% American Indian, 1% Asian, 3% black, 52% Hispanic, 1% multiracial, 0% Pacific Islander, 32% white, 4% international; 75% from in state; 18% live on campus; 2% of students in fraternities, 3% in sororities
**Most popular majors:** 3% Biology/Biological Sciences, General, 6% Criminal Justice/Safety Studies, 3% Education, General, 4% General Studies, 3% Psychology, General

**Expenses:** 2014-2015: $6,573 in state, $20,658 out of state; room/board: $7,530
**Financial aid:** (505) 646-4105; 65% of undergrads determined to have financial need; average aid package $8,800

## Northern New Mexico College[1]
Espanola NM
(505) 747-2111
**U.S. News ranking:** Reg. Coll. (W), unranked
**Website:** nnmc.edu
**Admissions email:** N/A
**Public**
**Application deadline (fall):** N/A
**Undergraduate student body:** N/A full time, N/A part time
**Expenses:** 2013-2014: $4,060 in state, $11,523 out of state; room/board: $7,180
**Financial aid:** (505) 747-2128

## Santa Fe University of Art and Design
Santa Fe NM
(505) 473-6937
**U.S. News ranking:** Arts, unranked
**Website:** www.santafeuniversity.edu
**Admissions email:** admissions@santafeuniversity.edu
**For-profit;** founded 1859
**Freshman admissions:** N/A; 2013-2014: 397 applied, 396 accepted. Neither SAT nor ACT required. SAT 25/75 percentile: N/A. High school rank: N/A
**Early decision deadline:** N/A, notification date: N/A
**Early action deadline:** N/A, notification date: N/A
**Application deadline (fall):** rolling
**Undergraduate student body:** 819 full time, 7 part time; 47% male, 53% female; 3% American Indian, 1% Asian, 7% black, 25% Hispanic, 5% multiracial, 1% Pacific Islander, 48% white, 5% international; 25% from in state; 70% live on campus; N/A of students in fraternities, N/A in sororities
**Most popular majors:** 29% Cinematography and Film/Video Production, 18% Drama and Dramatics/Theatre Arts, General, 11% Fine/Studio Arts, General, 14% Graphic Design, 11% Music, General
**Expenses:** 2014-2015: $30,136; room/board: $9,379
**Financial aid:** (505) 473-6454; 80% of undergrads determined to have financial need; average aid package $22,334

## St. John's College
Santa Fe NM
(505) 984-6060
**U.S. News ranking:** Nat. Lib. Arts, No. 89
**Website:** www.sjc.edu/admissions-and-aid
**Admissions email:** santafe.admissions@sjc.edu
**Private;** founded 1964
**Freshman admissions:** more selective; 2013-2014: 181 applied, 169 accepted. Neither SAT nor ACT required. SAT 25/75 percentile: 1160-1450.

High school rank: 25% in top tenth, 39% in top quarter, 71% in top half
**Early decision deadline:** N/A, notification date: N/A
**Early action deadline:** 1/15, notification date: 2/15
**Application deadline (fall):** rolling
**Undergraduate student body:** 339 full time, 5 part time; 54% male, 46% female; 1% American Indian, 3% Asian, 1% black, 11% Hispanic, 7% multiracial, 0% Pacific Islander, 59% white, 15% international; 8% from in state; 84% live on campus; 0% of students in fraternities, 0% in sororities
**Most popular majors:** 100% Liberal Arts and Sciences/Liberal Studies
**Expenses:** 2014-2015: $47,626; room/board: $10,582
**Financial aid:** (505) 984-6073; 80% of undergrads determined to have financial need; average aid package $36,918

## University of New Mexico
Albuquerque NM
(505) 277-8900
**U.S. News ranking:** Nat. U., No. 189
**Website:** www.unm.edu
**Admissions email:** apply@unm.edu
**Public;** founded 1889
**Freshman admissions:** selective; 2013-2014: 11,995 applied, 6,799 accepted. Either SAT or ACT required. ACT 25/75 percentile: 19-25. High school rank: N/A
**Early decision deadline:** N/A, notification date: N/A
**Early action deadline:** N/A, notification date: N/A
**Application deadline (fall):** rolling
**Undergraduate student body:** 17,187 full time, 3,951 part time; 44% male, 56% female; 6% American Indian, 3% Asian, 3% black, 44% Hispanic, 3% multiracial, 0% Pacific Islander, 38% white, 1% international; 90% from in state; 13% live on campus; 5% of students in fraternities, 6% in sororities
**Most popular majors:** 8% Biological and Biomedical Sciences, 14% Business, Management, Marketing, and Related Support Services, 12% Education, 10% Psychology, 8% Social Sciences
**Expenses:** 2013-2014: $6,846 in state, $20,688 out of state; room/board: $8,454
**Financial aid:** (505) 277-3012

## University of the Southwest[1]
Hobbs NM
(575) 392-6563
**U.S. News ranking:** Reg. Coll. (W), unranked
**Website:** www.usw.edu
**Admissions email:** admissions@usw.edu
**Private;** founded 1962
**Application deadline (fall):** rolling
**Undergraduate student body:** N/A full time, N/A part time
**Expenses:** 2013-2014: $14,280; room/board: $6,960
**Financial aid:** (505) 392-6561

## Western New Mexico University[1]
Silver City NM
(505) 538-6127
**U.S. News ranking:** Reg. U. (W), unranked
**Website:** www.wnmu.edu
**Admissions email:** admissions@wnmu.edu
**Public;** founded 1893
**Application deadline (fall):** 8/1
**Undergraduate student body:** N/A full time, N/A part time
**Expenses:** 2013-2014: $4,723 in state, $12,763 out of state; room/board: $10,156
**Financial aid:** (575) 538-6173

# NEW YORK

## Adelphi University
Garden City NY
(800) 233-5744
**U.S. News ranking:** Nat. U., No. 149
**Website:** www.adelphi.edu
**Admissions email:** admissions@adelphi.edu
**Private;** founded 1896
**Freshman admissions:** selective; 2013-2014: 8,654 applied, 5,897 accepted. Neither SAT nor ACT required. SAT 25/75 percentile: 1020-1220. High school rank: 26% in top tenth, 64% in top quarter, 92% in top half
**Early decision deadline:** N/A, notification date: N/A
**Early action deadline:** 12/1, notification date: 12/31
**Application deadline (fall):** rolling
**Undergraduate student body:** 4,531 full time, 509 part time; 31% male, 69% female; 0% American Indian, 8% Asian, 11% black, 13% Hispanic, 2% multiracial, 0% Pacific Islander, 53% white, 4% international; 92% from in state; 23% live on campus; 11% of students in fraternities, 9% in sororities
**Most popular majors:** 27% Health Services/Allied Health/Health Sciences, General
**Expenses:** 2014-2015: $32,340; room/board: $13,620
**Financial aid:** (516) 877-3365; 72% of undergrads determined to have financial need; average aid package $20,000

## Alfred University
Alfred NY
(800) 541-9229
**U.S. News ranking:** Reg. U. (N), No. 38
**Website:** www.alfred.edu
**Admissions email:** admissions@alfred.edu
**Private;** founded 1836
**Freshman admissions:** selective; 2013-2014: 3,417 applied, 2,385 accepted. Either SAT or ACT required. SAT 25/75 percentile: 1000-1200. High school rank: 16% in top tenth, 43% in top quarter, 84% in top half
**Early decision deadline:** 12/1, notification date: 12/15
**Early action deadline:** N/A, notification date: N/A
**Application deadline (fall):** rolling
**Undergraduate student body:** 1,909 full time, 51 part time; 49% male, 51% female; 0% American Indian, 2% Asian, 8% black,

7% Hispanic, 3% multiracial, 0% Pacific Islander, 67% white, 3% international; 76% from in state; 75% live on campus; 0% of students in fraternities, 0% in sororities
**Most popular majors:** 8% Biological and Biomedical Sciences, 8% Business, Management, Marketing, and Related Support Services, 17% Engineering, 8% Psychology, 31% Visual and Performing Arts
**Expenses:** 2014-2015: $29,610; room/board: $11,790
**Financial aid:** (607) 871-2159; 87% of undergrads determined to have financial need; average aid package $28,178

## Bard College
Annandale on Hudson NY
(845) 758-7472
**U.S. News ranking:** Nat. Lib. Arts, No. 45
**Website:** www.bard.edu
**Admissions email:** admission@bard.edu
**Private;** founded 1860
**Freshman admissions:** more selective; 2013-2014: 5,466 applied, 2,056 accepted. Neither SAT nor ACT required. SAT 25/75 percentile: 1170-1380. High school rank: 58% in top tenth, 92% in top quarter, 99% in top half
**Early decision deadline:** N/A, notification date: N/A
**Early action deadline:** 11/1, notification date: 1/1
**Application deadline (fall):** 1/1
**Undergraduate student body:** 1,925 full time, 97 part time; 44% male, 56% female; 1% American Indian, 4% Asian, 6% black, 2% Hispanic, 0% multiracial, 0% Pacific Islander, 62% white, 11% international; 35% from in state; 73% live on campus; 0% of students in fraternities, 0% in sororities
**Most popular majors:** 7% Biological and Biomedical Sciences, 13% English Language and Literature/Letters, 7% Foreign Languages, Literatures, and Linguistics, 15% Social Sciences, 31% Visual and Performing Arts
**Expenses:** 2014-2015: $48,240; room/board: $13,772
**Financial aid:** (845) 758-7525; 68% of undergrads determined to have financial need; average aid package $40,706

## Barnard College
New York NY
(212) 854-2014
**U.S. News ranking:** Nat. Lib. Arts, No. 32
**Website:** www.barnard.edu
**Admissions email:** admissions@barnard.edu
**Private;** founded 1889
**Freshman admissions:** most selective; 2013-2014: 5,606 applied, 1,151 accepted. Either SAT or ACT required. SAT 25/75 percentile: 1240-1440. High school rank: 77% in top tenth, 97% in top quarter, 100% in top half
**Early decision deadline:** 11/1, notification date: 12/15
**Early action deadline:** N/A, notification date: N/A
**Application deadline (fall):** 1/1

**Undergraduate student body:** 2,463 full time, 26 part time; 0% male, 100% female; 0% American Indian, 15% Asian, 5% black, 11% Hispanic, 5% multiracial, 0% Pacific Islander, 57% white, 7% international; 31% from in state; 91% live on campus; N/A of students in fraternities, 19% in sororities
**Most popular majors:** 9% Biological and Biomedical Sciences, 12% English Language and Literature/Letters, 14% Psychology, 27% Social Sciences, 11% Visual and Performing Arts
**Expenses:** 2014-2015: $46,040; room/board: $14,660
**Financial aid:** (212) 854-2154; 40% of undergrads determined to have financial need; average aid package $42,579

## Berkeley College
New York NY
(212) 986-4343
**U.S. News ranking:** Business, unranked
**Website:** www.berkeleycollege.edu
**Admissions email:** admissions@berkeleycollege.edu
**For-profit;** founded 1931
**Freshman admissions:** least selective; 2013-2014: 2,158 applied, 2,033 accepted. Neither SAT nor ACT required. ACT 25/75 percentile: N/A. High school rank: N/A
**Early decision deadline:** N/A, notification date: N/A
**Early action deadline:** N/A, notification date: N/A
**Application deadline (fall):** rolling
**Undergraduate student body:** 4,058 full time, 698 part time; 35% male, 65% female; 0% American Indian, 3% Asian, 28% black, 22% Hispanic, 0% multiracial, 0% Pacific Islander, 9% white, 17% international
**Most popular majors:** 12% Accounting, 13% Criminal Justice/Law Enforcement Administration, 19% Fashion Merchandising, 12% International Business/Trade/Commerce, 18% Management Information Systems, General
**Expenses:** 2014-2015: $23,700; room/board: $12,600
**Financial aid:** (212) 986-4343

## Binghamton University–SUNY
Binghamton NY
(607) 777-2171
**U.S. News ranking:** Nat. U., No. 88
**Website:** www.binghamton.edu
**Admissions email:** admit@binghamton.edu
**Public;** founded 1946
**Freshman admissions:** more selective; 2013-2014: 29,067 applied, 12,134 accepted. Either SAT or ACT required. SAT 25/75 percentile: 1203-1385. High school rank: 52% in top tenth, 84% in top quarter, 96% in top half
**Early decision deadline:** N/A, notification date: N/A
**Early action deadline:** 11/15, notification date: 1/15
**Application deadline (fall):** rolling
**Undergraduate student body:** 12,559 full time, 438 part time; 53% male, 47% female; 0% American Indian, 14% Asian, 5% black, 10% Hispanic, 2% multiracial, 0% Pacific Islander,

54% white, 11% international; 89% from in state; 59% live on campus; 10% of students in fraternities, 10% in sororities
**Most popular majors:** 9% Biology/Biological Sciences, General, 12% Business Administration and Management, General, 10% Engineering, General, 8% English Language and Literature, General, 10% Psychology, General
**Expenses:** 2014-2015: $8,619 in state, $20,259 out of state; room/board: $13,028
**Financial aid:** (607) 777-2428; 49% of undergrads determined to have financial need; average aid package $11,897

## Boricua College[1]
New York NY
(212) 694-1000
**U.S. News ranking:** Reg. Coll. (N), unranked
**Website:** www.boricuacollege.edu/
**Admissions email:** acruz@boricuacollege.edu
**Private;** founded 1973
**Application deadline (fall):** rolling
**Undergraduate student body:** N/A full time, N/A part time
**Expenses:** 2013-2014: $11,025; room/board: N/A
**Financial aid:** (212) 694-1000

## Briarcliffe College[1]
Bethpage NY
(888) 348-4999
**U.S. News ranking:** Reg. Coll. (N), unranked
**Website:** www.briarcliffe.edu
**Admissions email:** N/A
**For-profit**
**Application deadline (fall):** N/A
**Undergraduate student body:** N/A full time, N/A part time
**Expenses:** 2013-2014: $16,665; room/board: N/A
**Financial aid:** N/A

## Canisius College
Buffalo NY
(800) 843-1517
**U.S. News ranking:** Reg. U. (N), No. 27
**Website:** www.canisius.edu
**Admissions email:** admissions@canisius.edu
**Private;** founded 1870
**Affiliation:** Roman Catholic
**Freshman admissions:** selective; 2013-2014: 4,322 applied, 3,134 accepted. Either SAT or ACT required. SAT 25/75 percentile: 980-1200. High school rank: 22% in top tenth, 53% in top quarter, 87% in top half
**Early decision deadline:** N/A, notification date: N/A
**Early action deadline:** N/A, notification date: N/A
**Undergraduate student body:** 2,825 full time, 259 part time; 50% male, 50% female; 0% American Indian, 2% Asian, 7% black, 3% Hispanic, 2% multiracial, 0% Pacific Islander, 75% white, 4% international; 91% from in state; 48% live on campus; 1% of students in fraternities, 1% in sororities
**Most popular majors:** 12% Biological and Biomedical Sciences, 27% Business, Management, Marketing, and Related Support Services, 14% Education, 10% Psychology, 10% Social Sciences

**Expenses:** 2014-2015: $34,000; room/board: $12,516
**Financial aid:** (716) 888-2300; 78% of undergrads determined to have financial need; average aid package $28,042

## Cazenovia College

Cazenovia NY
(800) 654-3210
**U.S. News ranking:** Reg. Coll. (N), No. 24
**Website:** www.cazenovia.edu
**Admissions email:** admission@ cazenovia.edu
**Private;** founded 1824
**Freshman admissions:** selective; 2013-2014: 2,440 applied, 1,902 accepted. Neither SAT nor ACT required. SAT 25/75 percentile: 860-1070. High school rank: 14% in top tenth, 40% in top quarter, 78% in top half
**Early decision deadline:** N/A, notification date: N/A
**Early action deadline:** N/A, notification date: N/A
**Application deadline (fall):** rolling
**Undergraduate student body:** 937 full time, 140 part time; 28% male, 72% female; 1% American Indian, 1% Asian, 8% black, 7% Hispanic, 5% multiracial, 0% Pacific Islander, 75% white, 0% international; 88% from in state; 92% live on campus; N/A of students in fraternities, N/A in sororities
**Most popular majors:** 28% Business, Management, Marketing, and Related Support Services, 13% Public Administration and Social Service Professions, 27% Visual and Performing Arts
**Expenses:** 2014-2015: $30,560; room/board: $12,344
**Financial aid:** (315) 655-7887; 91% of undergrads determined to have financial need; average aid package $27,200

## Clarkson University

Potsdam NY
(800) 527-6577
**U.S. News ranking:** Nat. U., No. 121
**Website:** www.clarkson.edu
**Admissions email:** admission@ clarkson.edu
**Private;** founded 1896
**Freshman admissions:** more selective; 2013-2014: 6,747 applied, 4,320 accepted. Either SAT or ACT required. SAT 25/75 percentile: 1090-1290. High school rank: 40% in top tenth, 76% in top quarter, 96% in top half
**Early decision deadline:** 12/1, notification date: 1/1
**Early action deadline:** N/A, notification date: N/A
**Application deadline (fall):** 1/15
**Undergraduate student body:** 3,084 full time, 26 part time; 72% male, 28% female; 0% American Indian, 4% Asian, 2% black, 4% Hispanic, 2% multiracial, 0% Pacific Islander, 83% white, 3% international; 74% from in state; 83% live on campus; 12% of students in fraternities, 15% in sororities
**Most popular majors:** 7% Biology/ Biological Sciences, General, 27% Business Administration and Management, General, 50% Engineering, General, 4% Psychology, General

**Expenses:** 2014-2015: $42,530; room/board: $13,720
**Financial aid:** (315) 268-6479; 85% of undergrads determined to have financial need; average aid package $38,840

## Colgate University

Hamilton NY
(315) 228-7401
**U.S. News ranking:** Nat. Lib. Arts, No. 22
**Website:** www.colgate.edu
**Admissions email:** admission@ mail.colgate.edu
**Private;** founded 1819
**Freshman admissions:** most selective; 2013-2014: 8,375 applied, 2,238 accepted. Either SAT or ACT required. SAT 25/75 percentile: 1270-1450. High school rank: 76% in top tenth, 93% in top quarter, 99% in top half
**Early decision deadline:** 11/15, notification date: 12/15
**Early action deadline:** N/A, notification date: N/A
**Application deadline (fall):** 1/15
**Undergraduate student body:** 2,871 full time, 19 part time; 45% male, 55% female; 0% American Indian, 3% Asian, 4% black, 8% Hispanic, 4% multiracial, 0% Pacific Islander, 68% white, 8% international; 27% from in state; 84% live on campus; 27% of students in fraternities, 36% in sororities
**Most popular majors:** 11% Economics, General, 10% English Language and Literature, General, 9% History, General, 6% International Relations and Affairs, 9% Political Science and Government, General
**Expenses:** 2014-2015: $48,175; room/board: $11,970
**Financial aid:** (315) 228-7431; 36% of undergrads determined to have financial need; average aid package $43,436

## College at Brockport–SUNY

Brockport NY
(585) 395-2751
**U.S. News ranking:** Reg. U. (N), No. 60
**Website:** www.brockport.edu
**Admissions email:** admit@brockport.edu
**Public;** founded 1835
**Freshman admissions:** selective; 2013-2014: 8,831 applied, 4,245 accepted. Either SAT or ACT required. SAT 25/75 percentile: 960-1150. High school rank: 12% in top tenth, 39% in top quarter, 83% in top half
**Early decision deadline:** N/A, notification date: N/A
**Early action deadline:** N/A, notification date: N/A
**Application deadline (fall):** rolling
**Undergraduate student body:** 6,411 full time, 679 part time; 45% male, 55% female; 0% American Indian, 1% Asian, 8% black, 5% Hispanic, 2% multiracial, 0% Pacific Islander, 74% white, 1% international; 99% from in state; 37% live on campus; 2% of students in fraternities, 2% in sororities
**Most popular majors:** 16% Business, Management, Marketing, and Related Support Services, 16% Health Professions and Related Programs, 8%

Homeland Security, Law Enforcement, Firefighting and Related Protective Services, 7% Parks, Recreation, Leisure, and Fitness Studies, 8% Psychology
**Expenses:** 2014-2015: $7,562 in state, $17,212 out of state; room/ board: $11,440
**Financial aid:** (585) 395-2501; 73% of undergrads determined to have financial need; average aid package $10,050

## College of Mount St. Vincent

Riverdale NY
(718) 405-3267
**U.S. News ranking:** Reg. U. (N), No. 120
**Website:** www.mountsaintvincent.edu
**Admissions email:** admissions. office@mountsaintvincent.edu
**Private;** founded 1847
**Affiliation:** Roman Catholic
**Freshman admissions:** less selective; 2013-2014: 2,416 applied, 2,202 accepted. Either SAT or ACT required. SAT 25/75 percentile: 810-990. High school rank: 8% in top tenth, 26% in top quarter, 58% in top half
**Early decision deadline:** N/A, notification date: N/A
**Early action deadline:** 11/1, notification date: 12/1
**Application deadline (fall):** rolling
**Undergraduate student body:** 1,489 full time, 160 part time; 28% male, 72% female; 0% American Indian, 10% Asian, 17% black, 34% Hispanic, 6% multiracial, 0% Pacific Islander, 27% white, 1% international; 88% from in state; 48% live on campus; 0% of students in fraternities, 0% in sororities
**Most popular majors:** 8% Business/Commerce, General, 10% Liberal Arts and Sciences/ Liberal Studies, 15% Psychology, General, 34% Registered Nursing/ Registered Nurse, 9% Speech Communication and Rhetoric
**Expenses:** 2013-2014: $30,290; room/board: $12,060
**Financial aid:** (718) 405-3290

## College of New Rochelle[1]

New Rochelle NY
(800) 933-5923
**U.S. News ranking:** Reg. U. (N), second tier
**Website:** www.cnr.edu
**Admissions email:** admission@cnr.edu
**Private;** founded 1904
**Application deadline (fall):** 8/31
**Undergraduate student body:** N/A full time, N/A part time
**Expenses:** 2013-2014: $31,260; room/board: $11,690
**Financial aid:** (914) 654-5224

## College of St. Rose

Albany NY
(518) 454-5150
**U.S. News ranking:** Reg. U. (N), No. 41
**Website:** www.strose.edu
**Admissions email:** admit@strose.edu
**Private;** founded 1920
**Freshman admissions:** selective; 2013-2014: 4,651 applied, 3,605 accepted. Neither SAT

nor ACT required. SAT 25/75 percentile: 940-1150. High school rank: 11% in top tenth, 44% in top quarter, 75% in top half
**Early decision deadline:** N/A, notification date: N/A
**Early action deadline:** 12/1, notification date: 12/15
**Application deadline (fall):** 5/1
**Undergraduate student body:** 2,664 full time, 227 part time; 34% male, 66% female; 1% American Indian, 2% Asian, 7% black, 6% Hispanic, 5% multiracial, 0% Pacific Islander, 73% white, 1% international; 89% from in state; 45% live on campus; 0% of students in fraternities, 0% in sororities
**Most popular majors:** 13% Business, Management, Marketing, and Related Support Services, 7% Communication, Journalism, and Related Programs, 38% Education, 6% Psychology, 9% Visual and Performing Arts
**Expenses:** 2014-2015: $29,016; room/board: $11,532
**Financial aid:** (518) 458-5424; 84% of undergrads determined to have financial need; average aid package $17,366

## Columbia University

New York NY
(212) 854-2522
**U.S. News ranking:** Nat. U., No. 4
**Website:** www.columbia.edu
**Admissions email:** ugrad-ask@ columbia.edu
**Private;** founded 1754
**Freshman admissions:** most selective; 2013-2014: 33,531 applied, 2,311 accepted. Either SAT or ACT required. SAT 25/75 percentile: 1400-1570. High school rank: 93% in top tenth, 98% in top quarter, 100% in top half
**Early decision deadline:** 11/1, notification date: 12/15
**Early action deadline:** N/A, notification date: N/A
**Application deadline (fall):** 1/1
**Undergraduate student body:** 6,084 full time, N/A part time; 52% male, 48% female; 2% American Indian, 22% Asian, 11% black, 13% Hispanic, 0% multiracial, 0% Pacific Islander, 36% white, 13% international; 23% from in state; 94% live on campus; 19% of students in fraternities, 9% in sororities
**Most popular majors:** 10% Biological and Biomedical Sciences, 21% Engineering, 5% English Language and Literature/ Letters, 22% Social Sciences, 5% Visual and Performing Arts
**Expenses:** 2013-2014: $49,138; room/board: $11,978
**Financial aid:** (212) 854-3711; 50% of undergrads determined to have financial need; average aid package $43,766

## Concordia College[1]

Bronxville NY
(800) 937-2655
**U.S. News ranking:** Reg. Coll. (N), No. 31
**Website:** www.concordia-ny.edu
**Admissions email:** admission@ concordia-ny.edu
**Private;** founded 1881
**Affiliation:** Lutheran
**Application deadline (fall):** rolling

**Undergraduate student body:** 814 full time, 73 part time
**Expenses:** 2014-2015: $28,770; room/board: $10,265
**Financial aid:** (914) 337-9300

## Cooper Union

New York NY
(212) 353-4120
**U.S. News ranking:** Reg. Coll. (N), No. 2
**Website:** www.cooper.edu
**Admissions email:** admissions@ cooper.edu
**Private;** founded 1859
**Freshman admissions:** most selective; 2013-2014: 3,193 applied, 247 accepted. Either SAT or ACT required. SAT 25/75 percentile: 1220-1490. High school rank: 92% in top tenth, 95% in top quarter, 96% in top half
**Early decision deadline:** 12/1, notification date: 12/22
**Early action deadline:** N/A, notification date: N/A
**Application deadline (fall):** 1/1
**Undergraduate student body:** 863 full time, 5 part time; 64% male, 36% female; 1% American Indian, 20% Asian, 6% black, 10% Hispanic, 4% multiracial, 0% Pacific Islander, 40% white, 2% international; 55% from in state; 20% live on campus; 10% of students in fraternities, N/A in sororities
**Most popular majors:** 15% Architecture and Related Services, 55% Engineering, 30% Visual and Performing Arts
**Expenses:** 2014-2015: $41,400; room/board: $11,220
**Financial aid:** (212) 353-4113; 28% of undergrads determined to have financial need; average aid package $39,600

## Cornell University

Ithaca NY
(607) 255-5241
**U.S. News ranking:** Nat. U., No. 15
**Website:** www.cornell.edu
**Admissions email:** admissions@ cornell.edu
**Private;** founded 1865
**Freshman admissions:** most selective; 2013-2014: 39,999 applied, 6,222 accepted. Either SAT or ACT required. SAT 25/75 percentile: 1320-1520. High school rank: 87% in top tenth, 98% in top quarter, 99% in top half
**Early decision deadline:** 11/1, notification date: 12/15
**Early action deadline:** N/A, notification date: N/A
**Application deadline (fall):** 1/2
**Undergraduate student body:** 14,393 full time, N/A part time; 49% male, 51% female; 0% American Indian, 16% Asian, 6% black, 11% Hispanic, 4% multiracial, 0% Pacific Islander, 43% white, 9% international; 36% from in state; 55% live on campus; 27% of students in fraternities, 25% in sororities
**Most popular majors:** 12% Agriculture, Agriculture Operations, and Related Sciences, 13% Biological and Biomedical Sciences, 14% Business, Management, Marketing, and Related Support Services, 17% Engineering, 10% Social Sciences

**Expenses:** 2014-2015: $47,286; room/board: $13,678
**Financial aid:** (607) 255-5145; 50% of undergrads determined to have financial need; average aid package $42,258

## CUNY–Baruch College
New York NY
(646) 312-1400
**U.S. News ranking:** Reg. U. (N), No. 25
**Website:** www.baruch.cuny.edu
**Admissions email:** admissions@baruch.cuny.edu
**Public;** founded 1919
**Freshman admissions:** more selective; 2013-2014: 19,423 applied, 5,153 accepted. Either SAT or ACT required. SAT 25/75 percentile: 1130-1330. High school rank: 41% in top tenth, 70% in top quarter, 89% in top half
**Early decision deadline:** 12/13, notification date: 1/7
**Early action deadline:** N/A, notification date: N/A
**Application deadline (fall):** 2/1
**Undergraduate student body:** 10,396 full time, 3,686 part time; 52% male, 48% female; 0% American Indian, 35% Asian, 10% black, 13% Hispanic, 1% multiracial, 0% Pacific Islander, 29% white, 12% international; 97% from in state; 2% live on campus; 1% of students in fraternities, 1% in sororities
**Most popular majors:** 20% Accounting, 8% Business/Corporate Communications, 23% Finance, General, 5% Psychology, General, 10% Sales, Distribution, and Marketing Operations, General
**Expenses:** 2014-2015: $6,555 in state, $16,575 out of state; room/board: $12,400
**Financial aid:** (646) 312-1360; 66% of undergrads determined to have financial need; average aid package $5,265

## CUNY–Brooklyn College
Brooklyn NY
(718) 951-5001
**U.S. News ranking:** Reg. U. (N), No. 70
**Website:** www.brooklyn.cuny.edu
**Admissions email:** adminqry@brooklyn.cuny.edu
**Public;** founded 1930
**Freshman admissions:** selective; 2013-2014: 20,145 applied, 6,768 accepted. Either SAT or ACT required. SAT 25/75 percentile: 980-1170. High school rank: 18% in top tenth, 50% in top quarter, 77% in top half
**Early decision deadline:** N/A, notification date: N/A
**Early action deadline:** N/A, notification date: N/A
**Undergraduate student body:** 9,543 full time, 4,053 part time; 41% male, 59% female; 0% American Indian, 17% Asian, 22% black, 18% Hispanic, 1% multiracial, 0% Pacific Islander, 38% white, 3% international; 98% from in state; 0% live on campus; 3% of students in fraternities, 3% in sororities
**Most popular majors:** 10% Accounting, 21% Business Administration and Management, General, 5% Early Childhood Education and Teaching,

4% Elementary Education and Teaching, 13% Psychology, General
**Expenses:** 2014-2015: $6,535 in state, $13,345 out of state; room/board: N/A
**Financial aid:** (718) 951-5045; 87% of undergrads determined to have financial need; average aid package $7,500

## CUNY–City College
New York NY
(212) 650-6977
**U.S. News ranking:** Reg. U. (N), No. 65
**Website:** www.ccny.cuny.edu
**Admissions email:** admissions@ccny.cuny.edu
**Public;** founded 1847
**Freshman admissions:** selective; 2013-2014: 26,628 applied, 9,031 accepted. SAT required. SAT 25/75 percentile: 970-1090. High school rank: 29% in top tenth, 44% in top quarter, 85% in top half
**Early decision deadline:** N/A, notification date: N/A
**Early action deadline:** N/A, notification date: N/A
**Application deadline (fall):** 1/15
**Undergraduate student body:** 9,274 full time, 3,355 part time; 48% male, 52% female; 0% American Indian, 25% Asian, 19% black, 30% Hispanic, 0% multiracial, 0% Pacific Islander, 19% white, 8% international; 99% from in state; N/A live on campus; N/A of students in fraternities, N/A in sororities
**Most popular majors:** 13% Engineering, 7% English Language and Literature/Letters, 14% Psychology, 11% Social Sciences, 10% Visual and Performing Arts
**Expenses:** 2014-2015: $6,440 in state, $15,710 out of state; room/board: N/A
**Financial aid:** (212) 650-5819; 91% of undergrads determined to have financial need; average aid package $8,874

## CUNY–College of Staten Island
Staten Island NY
(718) 982-2010
**U.S. News ranking:** Reg. U. (N), No. 115
**Website:** www.csi.cuny.edu
**Admissions email:** admissions@csi.cuny.edu
**Public;** founded 1976
**Freshman admissions:** less selective; 2013-2014: 12,123 applied, 12,123 accepted. Either SAT or ACT required. SAT 25/75 percentile: 920-1100. High school rank: N/A
**Early decision deadline:** N/A, notification date: N/A
**Early action deadline:** N/A, notification date: N/A
**Application deadline (fall):** rolling
**Undergraduate student body:** 9,784 full time, 3,681 part time; 45% male, 55% female; 0% American Indian, 10% Asian, 10% black, 18% Hispanic, 1% multiracial, 0% Pacific Islander, 39% white, 3% international; 99% from in state; 3% live on campus; 0% of students in fraternities, 0% in sororities
**Most popular majors:** 21% Business, Management, Marketing, and Related Support Services, 6% English Language

and Literature/Letters, 6% Health Professions and Related Programs, 13% Psychology, 18% Social Sciences
**Expenses:** 2014-2015: $6,509 in state, $16,529 out of state; room/board: $13,864
**Financial aid:** (718) 982-2030; 68% of undergrads determined to have financial need; average aid package $8,200

## CUNY–Hunter College
New York NY
(212) 772-4490
**U.S. News ranking:** Reg. U. (N), No. 50
**Website:** www.hunter.cuny.edu
**Admissions email:** admissions@hunter.cuny.edu
**Public;** founded 1870
**Freshman admissions:** more selective; 2013-2014: 32,868 applied, 10,193 accepted. Either SAT or ACT required. SAT 25/75 percentile: 1070-1270. High school rank: 22% in top tenth, 56% in top quarter, 86% in top half
**Early decision deadline:** N/A, notification date: N/A
**Early action deadline:** N/A, notification date: N/A
**Application deadline (fall):** 3/15
**Undergraduate student body:** 11,747 full time, 4,942 part time; 35% male, 65% female; 0% American Indian, 26% Asian, 11% black, 19% Hispanic, 0% multiracial, 0% Pacific Islander, 37% white, 7% international
**Most popular majors:** 13% English Language and Literature/Letters, 9% Health Professions and Related Programs, 22% Psychology, 18% Social Sciences, 9% Visual and Performing Arts
**Expenses:** 2014-2015: $6,129 in state, $15,699 out of state; room/board: $10,386
**Financial aid:** (212) 772-4820; 83% of undergrads determined to have financial need; average aid package $7,641

## CUNY–John Jay College of Criminal Justice
New York NY
(212) 237-8866
**U.S. News ranking:** Reg. U. (N), No. 122
**Website:** www.jjay.cuny.edu/
**Admissions email:** admissions@jjay.cuny.edu
**Public;** founded 1965
**Freshman admissions:** less selective; 2013-2014: 14,297 applied, 7,515 accepted. Either SAT or ACT required. SAT 25/75 percentile: 840-1030. High school rank: N/A
**Early decision deadline:** N/A, notification date: N/A
**Early action deadline:** N/A, notification date: N/A
**Application deadline (fall):** 5/31
**Undergraduate student body:** 10,374 full time, 2,843 part time; 44% male, 56% female; 0% American Indian, 12% Asian, 21% black, 40% Hispanic, 0% multiracial, 0% Pacific Islander, 25% white, 3% international; 96% from in state; 0% live on campus; 0% of students in fraternities, 0% in sororities
**Most popular majors:** 55%

Criminal Justice/Law Enforcement Administration, 3% English Language and Literature, General, 17% Forensic Psychology, 4% Legal Studies, General, 16% Social Sciences, Other
**Expenses:** 2014-2015: $6,359 in state, $16,379 out of state; room/board: N/A
**Financial aid:** (212) 237-8151; 75% of undergrads determined to have financial need; average aid package $9,445

## CUNY–Lehman College
Bronx NY
(718) 960-8131
**U.S. News ranking:** Reg. U. (N), No. 125
**Website:** www.lehman.cuny.edu
**Admissions email:** undergraduate.admissions@lehman.cuny.edu
**Public;** founded 1968
**Freshman admissions:** selective; 2013-2014: 15,717 applied, 3,996 accepted. Either SAT or ACT required. SAT 25/75 percentile: 890-1050. High school rank: N/A
**Early decision deadline:** N/A, notification date: N/A
**Early action deadline:** N/A, notification date: N/A
**Application deadline (fall):** 10/1
**Undergraduate student body:** 5,643 full time, 4,243 part time; 32% male, 68% female; 0% American Indian, 6% Asian, 31% black, 50% Hispanic, 0% multiracial, 0% Pacific Islander, 9% white, 4% international; 100% from in state; 0% live on campus; 0% of students in fraternities, 0% in sororities
**Most popular majors:** Information not available
**Expenses:** 2014-2015: $6,230 in state, $13,040 out of state; room/board: N/A
**Financial aid:** (718) 960-8545; 80% of undergrads determined to have financial need

## CUNY–Medgar Evers College
Brooklyn NY
(718) 270-6024
**U.S. News ranking:** Reg. Coll. (N), second tier
**Website:** www.mec.cuny.edu
**Admissions email:** enroll@mec.cuny.edu
**Public;** founded 1969
**Freshman admissions:** least selective; 2013-2014: 7,586 applied, 7,586 accepted. Neither SAT nor ACT required. SAT 25/75 percentile: 690-860. High school rank: N/A
**Early decision deadline:** N/A, notification date: N/A
**Early action deadline:** N/A, notification date: N/A
**Application deadline (fall):** rolling
**Undergraduate student body:** 4,275 full time, 2,216 part time; 26% male, 74% female; 1% American Indian, 2% Asian, 72% black, 10% Hispanic, 0% multiracial, 0% Pacific Islander, 1% white, 1% international
**Most popular majors:** 12% Biology/Biological Sciences, General, 39% Business/Commerce, General, 8% Health Professions and Related Programs, 11% Psychology,

General, 9% Public Administration and Social Service Professions
**Expenses:** 2013-2014: $6,032 in state, $12,542 out of state; room/board: N/A
**Financial aid:** (718) 270-6038

## CUNY–New York City College of Technology
Brooklyn NY
(718) 260-5500
**U.S. News ranking:** Reg. Coll. (N), second tier
**Website:** www.citytech.cuny.edu
**Admissions email:** admissions@citytech.cuny.edu
**Public;** founded 1946
**Freshman admissions:** least selective; 2013-2014: 17,465 applied, 12,326 accepted. Neither SAT nor ACT required. ACT 25/75 percentile: N/A. High school rank: N/A
**Early decision deadline:** N/A, notification date: N/A
**Early action deadline:** N/A, notification date: N/A
**Application deadline (fall):** 2/1
**Undergraduate student body:** 10,318 full time, 6,542 part time; 56% male, 44% female; 0% American Indian, 18% Asian, 32% black, 31% Hispanic, 1% multiracial, 0% Pacific Islander, 13% white, 5% international
**Most popular majors:** 8% Architectural Technology/Technician, 16% Hospitality Administration/Management, General, 16% Information Science/Studies, 10% Public Administration and Social Service Professions, 11% Registered Nursing/Registered Nurse
**Expenses:** 2013-2014: $6,069 in state, $15,639 out of state; room/board: N/A
**Financial aid:** (718) 260-5700

## CUNY–Queens College
Flushing NY
(718) 997-5600
**U.S. News ranking:** Reg. U. (N), No. 31
**Website:** www.qc.edu/
**Admissions email:** applyto@uapc.cuny.edu
**Public;** founded 1937
**Freshman admissions:** more selective; 2013-2014: 24,323 applied, 8,929 accepted. Either SAT or ACT required. SAT 25/75 percentile: 1030-1220. High school rank: 35% in top tenth, 65% in top quarter, 99% in top half
**Early decision deadline:** N/A, notification date: N/A
**Early action deadline:** N/A, notification date: N/A
**Application deadline (fall):** 2/1
**Undergraduate student body:** 10,769 full time, 4,582 part time; 44% male, 56% female; 0% American Indian, 26% Asian, 8% black, 19% Hispanic, 0% multiracial, 0% Pacific Islander, 42% white, 5% international; 99% from in state; 3% live on campus; 1% of students in fraternities, 1% in sororities
**Most popular majors:** Information not available
**Expenses:** 2014-2015: $6,207 in state, $15,777 out of state; room/board: $13,554

**Financial aid:** (718) 997-5101; 75% of undergrads determined to have financial need; average aid package $6,450

## CUNY–York College

Jamaica NY
(718) 262-2165
**U.S. News ranking:** Reg. Coll. (N), second tier
**Website:** www.york.cuny.edu
**Admissions email:** admissions@york.cuny.edu
**Public;** founded 1966
**Freshman admissions:** least selective; 2013-2014: 14,674 applied, 9,477 accepted. SAT required. Average composite SAT score: 871. High school rank: N/A
**Early decision deadline:** N/A, notification date: N/A
**Early action deadline:** N/A, notification date: N/A
**Application deadline (fall):** 6/1
**Undergraduate student body:** 5,152 full time, 3,107 part time; 35% male, 65% female; 1% American Indian, 23% Asian, 44% black, 20% Hispanic, 0% multiracial, 0% Pacific Islander, 8% white, 4% international
**Most popular majors:** 7% Accounting, 11% Business Administration and Management, General, 6% Health Teacher Education, 20% Psychology, General, 8% Social Work
**Expenses:** 2014-2015: $6,396 in state, $16,416 out of state; room/board: N/A
**Financial aid:** (718) 262-2230; 63% of undergrads determined to have financial need; average aid package $6,930

## Daemen College

Amherst NY
(800) 462-7652
**U.S. News ranking:** Reg. U. (N), second tier
**Website:** www.daemen.edu
**Admissions email:** admissions@daemen.edu
**Private;** founded 1947
**Freshman admissions:** selective; 2013-2014: 3,061 applied, 1,489 accepted. Neither SAT nor ACT required. SAT 25/75 percentile: 920-1140. High school rank: 15% in top tenth, 51% in top quarter, 85% in top half
**Early decision deadline:** N/A, notification date: N/A
**Early action deadline:** N/A, notification date: N/A
**Application deadline (fall):** rolling
**Undergraduate student body:** 1,720 full time, 436 part time; 27% male, 73% female; 0% American Indian, 2% Asian, 11% black, 5% Hispanic, 1% multiracial, 0% Pacific Islander, 75% white, 1% international; 95% from in state; 37% live on campus; 4% of students in fraternities, 4% in sororities
**Most popular majors:** 6% Business Administration and Management, General, 5% Elementary Education and Teaching, 16% Natural Sciences, 8% Physician Assistant, 31% Registered Nursing/Registered Nurse
**Expenses:** 2014-2015: $24,990; room/board: $11,800
**Financial aid:** (716) 839-8254; 77% of undergrads determined to have financial need; average aid package $18,236

## Dominican College

Orangeburg NY
(845) 359-3533
**U.S. News ranking:** Reg. U. (N), second tier
**Website:** www.dc.edu
**Admissions email:** admissions@dc.edu
**Private;** founded 1952
**Freshman admissions:** less selective; 2013-2014: 1,594 applied, 1,146 accepted. Either SAT or ACT required. SAT 25/75 percentile: 810-1000. High school rank: N/A
**Early decision deadline:** N/A, notification date: N/A
**Early action deadline:** N/A, notification date: N/A
**Application deadline (fall):** rolling
**Undergraduate student body:** 1,280 full time, 247 part time; 34% male, 66% female; 0% American Indian, 1% Asian, 13% black, 27% Hispanic, 0% multiracial, 0% Pacific Islander, 25% white, 0% international; 74% from in state; 46% live on campus; N/A of students in fraternities, N/A in sororities
**Most popular majors:** 14% Business, Management, Marketing, and Related Support Services, 8% Education, 29% Health Professions and Related Programs, 5% Homeland Security, Law Enforcement, Firefighting and Related Protective Services, 26% Social Sciences
**Expenses:** 2014-2015: $25,702; room/board: $11,880
**Financial aid:** (845) 359-7800; 91% of undergrads determined to have financial need; average aid package $16,841

## Dowling College

Oakdale Long Island NY
(631) 244-3030
**U.S. News ranking:** Reg. U. (N), second tier
**Website:** www.dowling.edu
**Admissions email:** admissions@dowling.edu
**Private;** founded 1955
**Freshman admissions:** less selective; 2013-2014: 1,897 applied, 1,402 accepted. Neither SAT nor ACT required. ACT 25/75 percentile: N/A. High school rank: N/A
**Early decision deadline:** N/A, notification date: N/A
**Early action deadline:** 12/31, notification date: 1/31
**Application deadline (fall):** rolling
**Undergraduate student body:** 1,439 full time, 859 part time; 44% male, 56% female; 0% American Indian, 1% Asian, 9% black, 7% Hispanic, 0% multiracial, 0% Pacific Islander, 45% white, 4% international; 89% from in state; 15% live on campus; N/A of students in fraternities, N/A in sororities
**Most popular majors:** 29% Business Administration and Management, General, 9% Finance, General, 6% Hospital and Health Care Facilities Administration/Management, 6% Special Education and Teaching, General, 8% Special Education and Teaching, General
**Expenses:** 2014-2015: $29,100; room/board: $10,770
**Financial aid:** (631) 244-3303; 73% of undergrads determined to have financial need; average aid package $19,348

## D'Youville College

Buffalo NY
(716) 829-7600
**U.S. News ranking:** Reg. U. (N), second tier
**Website:** www.dyc.edu
**Admissions email:** admissions@dyc.edu
**Private;** founded 1908
**Freshman admissions:** selective; 2013-2014: 1,168 applied, 925 accepted. Either SAT or ACT required. SAT 25/75 percentile: 950-1140. High school rank: 27% in top tenth, 47% in top quarter, 84% in top half
**Early decision deadline:** N/A, notification date: N/A
**Early action deadline:** N/A, notification date: N/A
**Application deadline (fall):** rolling
**Undergraduate student body:** 1,614 full time, 409 part time; 27% male, 73% female; 1% American Indian, 3% Asian, 9% black, 5% Hispanic, 2% multiracial, 0% Pacific Islander, 72% white, 7% international; 96% from in state; 15% live on campus; 0% of students in fraternities, 0% in sororities
**Most popular majors:** 8% Biological and Biomedical Sciences, 14% Business, Management, Marketing, and Related Support Services, 65% Health Professions and Related Programs, 8% Multi/Interdisciplinary Studies, 3% Psychology
**Expenses:** 2014-2015: $23,462; room/board: $10,800
**Financial aid:** (716) 829-7500; 84% of undergrads determined to have financial need; average aid package $17,087

## Elmira College

Elmira NY
(800) 935-6472
**U.S. News ranking:** Reg. Coll. (N), No. 9
**Website:** www.elmira.edu
**Admissions email:** admissions@elmira.edu
**Private;** founded 1855
**Freshman admissions:** selective; 2013-2014: 2,302 applied, 1,836 accepted. Either SAT or ACT required. SAT 25/75 percentile: 940-1160. High school rank: 28% in top tenth, 58% in top quarter, 84% in top half
**Early decision deadline:** 11/15, notification date: 12/15
**Early action deadline:** N/A, notification date: N/A
**Application deadline (fall):** rolling
**Undergraduate student body:** 1,188 full time, 220 part time; 28% male, 72% female; 1% American Indian, 1% Asian, 3% black, 3% Hispanic, 2% multiracial, 0% Pacific Islander, 70% white, 3% international
**Most popular majors:** 17% Business Administration and Management, General, 19% Education, 9% Psychology, General, 13% Registered Nursing/Registered Nurse, 9% Social Sciences
**Expenses:** 2014-2015: $38,150; room/board: $11,800
**Financial aid:** (607) 735-1728; 84% of undergrads determined to have financial need; average aid package $29,925

## Excelsior College[1]

Albany NY
(518) 464-8500
**U.S. News ranking:** Reg. U. (N), unranked
**Website:** www.excelsior.edu
**Admissions email:** admissions@excelsior.edu
**Private;** founded 1971
**Application deadline (fall):** rolling
**Undergraduate student body:** N/A full time, N/A part time
**Expenses:** N/A
**Financial aid:** (518) 464-8500

## Farmingdale State College–SUNY

Farmingdale NY
(631) 420-2200
**U.S. News ranking:** Reg. Coll. (N), No. 28
**Website:** www.farmingdale.edu
**Admissions email:** admissions@farmingdale.edu
**Public;** founded 1912
**Freshman admissions:** selective; 2013-2014: 5,282 applied, 2,677 accepted. Either SAT or ACT required. SAT 25/75 percentile: 950-1110. High school rank: 17% in top tenth, 36% in top quarter, 69% in top half
**Early decision deadline:** N/A, notification date: N/A
**Early action deadline:** N/A, notification date: N/A
**Application deadline (fall):** rolling
**Undergraduate student body:** 6,074 full time, 2,088 part time; 58% male, 42% female; 0% American Indian, 7% Asian, 11% black, 15% Hispanic, 2% multiracial, 0% Pacific Islander, 61% white, 3% international; 99% from in state; 8% live on campus; 2% of students in fraternities, 2% in sororities
**Most popular majors:** 37% Business, Management, Marketing, and Related Support Services, 7% Computer and Information Sciences and Support Services, 13% Engineering Technologies and Engineering-Related Fields, 7% Health Professions and Related Programs, 8% Multi/Interdisciplinary Studies
**Expenses:** 2014-2015: $7,483 in state, $17,133 out of state; room/board: $12,190
**Financial aid:** (631) 420-2328; 55% of undergrads determined to have financial need; average aid package $9,242

## Fashion Institute of Technology

New York NY
(212) 217-3760
**U.S. News ranking:** Reg. U. (N), unranked
**Website:** www.fitnyc.edu
**Admissions email:** fitinfo@fitsuny.edu
**Public;** founded 1944
**Freshman admissions:** N/A; 2013-2014: 4,567 applied, 2,044 accepted. Neither SAT nor ACT required. ACT 25/75 percentile: N/A. High school rank: N/A
**Early decision deadline:** N/A, notification date: N/A
**Early action deadline:** N/A, notification date: N/A
**Application deadline (fall):** 1/1
**Undergraduate student body:** 7,257 full time, 2,309 part time; 15% male, 85% female; 0% American Indian, 9% Asian, 9% black,

17% Hispanic, 3% multiracial, 0% Pacific Islander, 47% white, 14% international; 59% from in state; 22% live on campus; N/A of students in fraternities, N/A in sororities
**Most popular majors:** 37% Business, Management, Marketing, and Related Support Services, 16% Communication, Journalism, and Related Programs, 1% Communications Technologies/Technicians and Support Services, 5% Family and Consumer Sciences/Human Sciences, 41% Visual and Performing Arts
**Expenses:** 2013-2014: $5,105 in state, $13,955 out of state; room/board: N/A
**Financial aid:** (212) 217-7439; 52% of undergrads determined to have financial need; average aid package $11,605

## Five Towns College

Dix Hills NY
(631) 424-7000
**U.S. News ranking:** Reg. Coll. (N), second tier
**Website:** www.ftc.edu
**Admissions email:** admissions@ftc.edu
**For-profit;** founded 1972
**Freshman admissions:** less selective; 2013-2014: 452 applied, 249 accepted. Either SAT or ACT required. SAT 25/75 percentile: 770-1000. High school rank: 11% in top tenth, 36% in top quarter, 47% in top half
**Early decision deadline:** 10/15, notification date: 11/1
**Early action deadline:** N/A, notification date: N/A
**Application deadline (fall):** rolling
**Undergraduate student body:** 695 full time, 57 part time; 70% male, 30% female; 0% American Indian, 3% Asian, 21% black, 13% Hispanic, 6% multiracial, 0% Pacific Islander, 51% white, 0% international; 92% from in state; 26% live on campus; N/A of students in fraternities, N/A in sororities
**Most popular majors:** 58% Business, Management, Marketing, and Related Support Services, 11% Education, 31% Visual and Performing Arts
**Expenses:** 2014-2015: $21,300; room/board: $13,270
**Financial aid:** (631) 424-7000; 81% of undergrads determined to have financial need; average aid package $13,922

## Fordham University

New York NY
(800) 367-3426
**U.S. News ranking:** Nat. U., No. 58
**Website:** www.fordham.edu
**Admissions email:** enroll@fordham.edu
**Private;** founded 1841
**Affiliation:** Roman Catholic
**Freshman admissions:** more selective; 2013-2014: 36,189 applied, 17,055 accepted. Either SAT or ACT required. SAT 25/75 percentile: 1160-1350. High school rank: 47% in top tenth, 82% in top quarter, 97% in top half
**Early decision deadline:** N/A, notification date: N/A
**Early action deadline:** 11/1, notification date: 12/25

**Application deadline (fall):** 1/15
**Undergraduate student body:** 7,694 full time, 651 part time; 46% male, 54% female; 0% American Indian, 9% Asian, 4% black, 14% Hispanic, 3% multiracial, 0% Pacific Islander, 61% white, 6% international; 51% from in state; 57% live on campus; 0% of students in fraternities, 0% in sororities
**Most popular majors:** 14% Business Administration and Management, General, 6% Economics, General, 7% Finance, General, 7% Psychology, General, 13% Speech Communication and Rhetoric
**Expenses:** 2013-2014: $43,577; room/board: $15,835
**Financial aid:** (718) 817-3800

## Hamilton College
Clinton NY
(800) 843-2655
**U.S. News ranking:** Nat. Lib. Arts, No. 15
**Website:** www.hamilton.edu
**Admissions email:** admission@hamilton.edu
**Private;** founded 1812
**Freshman admissions:** most selective; 2013-2014: 5,017 applied, 1,364 accepted. Either SAT or ACT required. SAT 25/75 percentile: 1300-1470. High school rank: 72% in top tenth, 97% in top quarter, 99% in top half
**Early decision deadline:** 11/15, notification date: 12/15
**Early action deadline:** N/A, notification date: N/A
**Application deadline (fall):** 1/1
**Undergraduate student body:** 1,905 full time, 21 part time; 49% male, 51% female; 0% American Indian, 7% Asian, 4% black, 8% Hispanic, 3% multiracial, 0% Pacific Islander, 62% white, 5% international; 31% from in state; 97% live on campus; 27% of students in fraternities, 20% in sororities
**Most popular majors:** 13% Economics, General, 6% History, General, 10% Mathematics, General, 8% Political Science and Government, General, 7% Psychology, General
**Expenses:** 2014-2015: $47,820; room/board: $12,150
**Financial aid:** (315) 859-4434; 47% of undergrads determined to have financial need; average aid package $40,858

## Hartwick College
Oneonta NY
(607) 431-4150
**U.S. News ranking:** Nat. Lib. Arts, No. 165
**Website:** www.hartwick.edu
**Admissions email:** admissions@hartwick.edu
**Private;** founded 1797
**Freshman admissions:** selective; 2013-2014: 5,392 applied, 4,542 accepted. Neither SAT nor ACT required. SAT 25/75 percentile: 1010-1230. High school rank: 20% in top tenth, 47% in top quarter, 86% in top half
**Early decision deadline:** 11/15, notification date: 11/25
**Early action deadline:** N/A, notification date: N/A
**Application deadline (fall):** rolling

**Undergraduate student body:** 1,576 full time, 39 part time; 41% male, 59% female; 1% American Indian, 2% Asian, 6% black, 6% Hispanic, 0% multiracial, 0% Pacific Islander, 69% white, 3% international; 74% from in state; 77% live on campus; 3% of students in fraternities, 5% in sororities
**Most popular majors:** 11% Biology/Biological Sciences, General, 17% Business Administration and Management, General, 10% Psychology, General, 12% Registered Nursing, Nursing Administration, Nursing Research and Clinical Nursing, 12% Sociology
**Expenses:** 2014-2015: $40,070; room/board: $10,800
**Financial aid:** (607) 431-4130; 82% of undergrads determined to have financial need; average aid package $30,926

## Hilbert College[1]
Hamburg NY
(716) 649-7900
**U.S. News ranking:** Reg. Coll. (N), unranked
**Website:** www.hilbert.edu/
**Admissions email:** admissions@hilbert.edu
**Private**
**Application deadline (fall):** N/A
**Undergraduate student body:** N/A full time, N/A part time
**Expenses:** 2013-2014: $19,940; room/board: $8,650
**Financial aid:** (716) 649-7900

## Hobart and William Smith Colleges
Geneva NY
(315) 781-3622
**U.S. News ranking:** Nat. Lib. Arts, No. 61
**Website:** www.hws.edu
**Admissions email:** admissions@hws.edu
**Private;** founded 1822
**Freshman admissions:** more selective; 2013-2014: 4,380 applied, 2,190 accepted. Neither SAT nor ACT required. SAT 25/75 percentile: 1120-1290. High school rank: 36% in top tenth, 63% in top quarter, 87% in top half
**Early decision deadline:** 11/15, notification date: 12/15
**Early action deadline:** N/A, notification date: N/A
**Application deadline (fall):** 2/1
**Undergraduate student body:** 2,324 full time, 44 part time; 46% male, 54% female; 1% American Indian, 2% Asian, 4% black, 4% Hispanic, 0% multiracial, 0% Pacific Islander, 69% white, 5% international; 43% from in state; 90% live on campus; 18% of students in fraternities, 0% in sororities
**Most popular majors:** 8% Architecture and Related Services, Other, 7% Biology/Biological Sciences, General, 8% Economics, General, 7% Mass Communication/Media Studies, 7% Psychology, General
**Expenses:** 2014-2015: $47,908; room/board: $12,126
**Financial aid:** (315) 781-3315; 67% of undergrads determined to have financial need; average aid package $32,064

## Hofstra University
Hempstead NY
(516) 463-6700
**U.S. News ranking:** Nat. U., No. 135
**Website:** www.hofstra.edu
**Admissions email:** admission@hofstra.edu
**Private;** founded 1935
**Freshman admissions:** selective; 2013-2014: 27,700 applied, 16,354 accepted. Neither SAT nor ACT required. SAT 25/75 percentile: 1050-1230. High school rank: 24% in top tenth, 56% in top quarter, 88% in top half
**Early decision deadline:** N/A, notification date: N/A
**Early action deadline:** 11/15, notification date: 12/15
**Application deadline (fall):** rolling
**Undergraduate student body:** 6,378 full time, 448 part time; 47% male, 53% female; 0% American Indian, 8% Asian, 9% black, 13% Hispanic, 3% multiracial, 1% Pacific Islander, 59% white, 3% international; 65% from in state; 47% live on campus; 6% of students in fraternities, 8% in sororities
**Most popular majors:** 6% Accounting, 4% Business Administration and Management, General, 6% English Language and Literature, General, 6% Marketing/Marketing Management, General, 8% Psychology, General
**Expenses:** 2014-2015: $38,900; room/board: $12,910
**Financial aid:** (516) 463-6680; 68% of undergrads determined to have financial need; average aid package $25,000

## Houghton College
Houghton NY
(800) 777-2556
**U.S. News ranking:** Nat. Lib. Arts, No. 139
**Website:** www.houghton.edu
**Admissions email:** admission@houghton.edu
**Private;** founded 1883
**Affiliation:** The Wesleyan Church
**Freshman admissions:** selective; 2013-2014: 807 applied, 735 accepted. Either SAT or ACT required. SAT 25/75 percentile: 980-1235. High school rank: 35% in top tenth, 61% in top quarter, 88% in top half
**Early decision deadline:** N/A, notification date: N/A
**Early action deadline:** N/A, notification date: N/A
**Application deadline (fall):** rolling
**Undergraduate student body:** 1,023 full time, 58 part time; 36% male, 64% female; 0% American Indian, 1% Asian, 3% black, 2% Hispanic, 3% multiracial, 0% Pacific Islander, 85% white, 6% international; 62% from in state; 87% live on campus; N/A of students in fraternities, N/A in sororities
**Most popular majors:** 11% Biological and Biomedical Sciences, 21% Business, Management, Marketing, and Related Support Services, 7% Communication, Journalism, and Related Programs, 13% Education, 8% Visual and Performing Arts
**Expenses:** 2014-2015: $28,556; room/board: $8,252

**Financial aid:** (585) 567-9328; 82% of undergrads determined to have financial need; average aid package $18,935

## Iona College
New Rochelle NY
(914) 633-2502
**U.S. News ranking:** Reg. U. (N), No. 74
**Website:** www.iona.edu/info
**Admissions email:** admissions@iona.edu
**Private;** founded 1940
**Affiliation:** Roman Catholic
**Freshman admissions:** less selective; 2013-2014: 5,911 applied, 5,445 accepted. Either SAT or ACT required. SAT 25/75 percentile: 900-1110. High school rank: 10% in top tenth, 31% in top quarter, 66% in top half
**Early decision deadline:** N/A, notification date: N/A
**Early action deadline:** 12/1, notification date: 12/21
**Application deadline (fall):** 2/15
**Undergraduate student body:** 3,110 full time, 429 part time; 46% male, 54% female; 0% American Indian, 2% Asian, 8% black, 19% Hispanic, 2% multiracial, 0% Pacific Islander, 59% white, 2% international; 76% from in state; 43% live on campus; 8% of students in fraternities, 4% in sororities
**Most popular majors:** 37% Business, Management, Marketing, and Related Support Services, 15% Communication, Journalism, and Related Programs, 8% Education, 7% Health Professions and Related Programs, 11% Psychology
**Expenses:** 2014-2015: $34,030; room/board: $13,570
**Financial aid:** (914) 633-2497; 81% of undergrads determined to have financial need; average aid package $21,368

## Ithaca College
Ithaca NY
(800) 429-4274
**U.S. News ranking:** Reg. U. (N), No. 9
**Website:** www.ithaca.edu
**Admissions email:** admission@ithaca.edu
**Private;** founded 1892
**Freshman admissions:** more selective; 2013-2014: 15,658 applied, 10,429 accepted. Neither SAT nor ACT required. SAT 25/75 percentile: 1080-1270. High school rank: 27% in top tenth, 63% in top quarter, 91% in top half
**Early decision deadline:** 11/1, notification date: 12/15
**Early action deadline:** 12/1, notification date: 2/1
**Application deadline (fall):** 2/1
**Undergraduate student body:** 6,131 full time, 103 part time; 44% male, 56% female; 0% American Indian, 3% Asian, 5% black, 7% Hispanic, 3% multiracial, 0% Pacific Islander, 69% white, 2% international; 45% from in state; 73% live on campus; 1% of students in fraternities, 1% in sororities
**Most popular majors:** 11% Business, Management, Marketing, and Related Support Services, 21% Communication, Journalism, and Related Programs,

13% Health Professions and Related Programs, 6% Social Sciences, 18% Visual and Performing Arts
**Expenses:** 2014-2015: $39,532; room/board: $14,332
**Financial aid:** (607) 274-3131; 68% of undergrads determined to have financial need; average aid package $32,139

## Juilliard School[1]
New York NY
(212) 799-5000
**U.S. News ranking:** Arts, unranked
**Website:** www.juilliard.edu
**Admissions email:** admissions@juilliard.edu
**Private;** founded 1905
**Application deadline (fall):** 12/1
**Undergraduate student body:** N/A full time, N/A part time
**Expenses:** 2013-2014: $36,920; room/board: $13,810
**Financial aid:** (212) 799-5000

## Keuka College
Keuka Park NY
(315) 279-5254
**U.S. News ranking:** Reg. U. (N), No. 125
**Website:** www.keuka.edu
**Admissions email:** admissions@mail.keuka.edu
**Private;** founded 1890
**Affiliation:** American Baptist
**Freshman admissions:** less selective; 2013-2014: 1,375 applied, 1,207 accepted. Either SAT or ACT required. SAT 25/75 percentile: 860-1050. High school rank: 7% in top tenth, 27% in top quarter, 75% in top half
**Early decision deadline:** N/A, notification date: N/A
**Early action deadline:** N/A, notification date: N/A
**Application deadline (fall):** rolling
**Undergraduate student body:** 1,514 full time, 315 part time; 23% male, 77% female; 1% American Indian, 1% Asian, 8% black, 4% Hispanic, 1% multiracial, 0% Pacific Islander, 79% white, 0% international; 94% from in state; 80% live on campus; N/A of students in fraternities, N/A in sororities
**Most popular majors:** 29% Business, Management, Marketing, and Related Support Services, 16% Education, 22% Health Professions and Related Programs, 14% Homeland Security, Law Enforcement, Firefighting and Related Protective Services, 9% Public Administration and Social Service Professions
**Expenses:** 2014-2015: $28,010; room/board: $10,800
**Financial aid:** (315) 279-5232; 88% of undergrads determined to have financial need; average aid package $18,079

## The King's College
New York NY
(212) 659-3610
**U.S. News ranking:** Nat. Lib. Arts, second tier
**Website:** www.tkc.edu/
**Admissions email:** admissions@tkc.edu
**Private;** founded 1938
**Affiliation:** Christian nondenominational

**Freshman admissions:** selective; 2013-2014: 3,033 applied, 2,158 accepted. Either SAT or ACT required. SAT 25/75 percentile: 1050-1230. High school rank: 15% in top tenth, 48% in top quarter, 98% in top half
**Early decision deadline:** N/A, notification date: N/A
**Early action deadline:** 11/15, notification date: 12/15
**Application deadline (fall):** rolling
**Undergraduate student body:** 493 full time, 23 part time; 40% male, 60% female; 0% American Indian, 3% Asian, 3% black, 8% Hispanic, 5% multiracial, 0% Pacific Islander, 78% white, 4% international; 7% from in state; 76% live on campus; 0% of students in fraternities, 0% in sororities
**Most popular majors:** 17% Business Administration and Management, General, 83% Humanities/Humanistic Studies
**Expenses:** 2014-2015: $32,300; room/board: $12,400
**Financial aid:** (212) 659-7200; 74% of undergrads determined to have financial need; average aid package $24,910

## Le Moyne College
Syracuse NY
(315) 445-4300
**U.S. News ranking:** Reg. U. (N), No. 19
**Website:** www.lemoyne.edu
**Admissions email:** admission@lemoyne.edu
**Private;** founded 1946
**Affiliation:** Roman Catholic (Jesuit)
**Freshman admissions:** selective; 2013-2014: 5,924 applied, 3,667 accepted. Either SAT or ACT required. SAT 25/75 percentile: 980-1170. High school rank: 21% in top tenth, 51% in top quarter, 88% in top half
**Early decision deadline:** N/A, notification date: N/A
**Early action deadline:** 11/15, notification date: 12/15
**Application deadline (fall):** rolling
**Undergraduate student body:** 2,401 full time, 384 part time; 41% male, 59% female; 1% American Indian, 3% Asian, 6% black, 6% Hispanic, 2% multiracial, 0% Pacific Islander, 78% white, 1% international; 94% from in state; 60% live on campus; 0% of students in fraternities, 0% in sororities
**Most popular majors:** 6% Accounting, 12% Biology/Biological Sciences, General, 7% Business Administration, Management and Operations, Other, 6% Marketing/Marketing Management, General, 21% Psychology, General
**Expenses:** 2014-2015: $31,340; room/board: $12,130
**Financial aid:** (315) 445-4400; 83% of undergrads determined to have financial need; average aid package $23,164

## LIM College[1]
New York NY
(800) 677-1323
**U.S. News ranking:** Business, unranked
**Website:** www.limcollege.edu/html/home.htm
**Admissions email:** admissions@limcollege.edu
**For-profit;** founded 1939

**Application deadline (fall):** rolling
**Undergraduate student body:** N/A full time, N/A part time
**Expenses:** 2014-2015: $24,225; room/board: $19,850
**Financial aid:** (800) 677-1323; 69% of undergrads determined to have financial need; average aid package $9,527

## LIU Post
Brookville NY
(516) 299-2900
**U.S. News ranking:** Reg. U. (N), second tier
**Website:** www.liu.edu
**Admissions email:** post-enroll@liu.edu
**Private;** founded 1954
**Freshman admissions:** less selective; 2013-2014: 6,006 applied, 4,844 accepted. Either SAT or ACT required. SAT 25/75 percentile: 880-1060. High school rank: N/A
**Early decision deadline:** N/A, notification date: N/A
**Early action deadline:** N/A, notification date: N/A
**Application deadline (fall):** rolling
**Undergraduate student body:** 3,661 full time, 4,322 part time; 42% male, 58% female; 0% American Indian, 4% Asian, 10% black, 13% Hispanic, 1% multiracial, 0% Pacific Islander, 48% white, 11% international; 93% from in state; 32% live on campus; N/A of students in fraternities, N/A in sororities
**Most popular majors:** 5% Audiology/Audiologist and Speech-Language Pathology/Pathologist, 14% Business Administration and Management, General, 10% Criminal Justice/Law Enforcement Administration, 6% Elementary Education and Teaching, 7% Psychology, General
**Expenses:** 2014-2015: $34,852; room/board: $12,808
**Financial aid:** (516) 299-2338; 72% of undergrads determined to have financial need; average aid package $18,445

## Manhattan College
Riverdale NY
(718) 862-7200
**U.S. News ranking:** Reg. U. (N), No. 18
**Website:** www.manhattan.edu
**Admissions email:** admit@manhattan.edu
**Private;** founded 1853
**Affiliation:** Roman Catholic
**Freshman admissions:** selective; 2013-2014: 7,268 applied, 4,809 accepted. SAT required. SAT 25/75 percentile: 970-1190. High school rank: 24% in top tenth, 52% in top quarter, 81% in top half
**Early decision deadline:** 11/15, notification date: 12/15
**Early action deadline:** N/A, notification date: N/A
**Application deadline (fall):** rolling
**Undergraduate student body:** 3,195 full time, 208 part time; 56% male, 44% female; 0% American Indian, 4% Asian, 4% black, 18% Hispanic, 2% multiracial, 0% Pacific Islander, 60% white, 2% international; 72% from in state; 62% live on campus; 2% of students in fraternities, 5% in sororities

**Most popular majors:** 18% Business, Management, Marketing, and Related Support Services, 7% Communication, Journalism, and Related Programs, 13% Education, 26% Engineering, 9% Multi/Interdisciplinary Studies
**Expenses:** 2013-2014: $35,725; room/board: $13,080
**Financial aid:** (718) 862-7100

## Manhattan School of Music[1]
New York NY
(212) 749-2802
**U.S. News ranking:** Arts, unranked
**Website:** www.msmnyc.edu
**Admissions email:** admission@msmnyc.edu
**Private**
**Application deadline (fall):** N/A
**Undergraduate student body:** N/A full time, N/A part time
**Expenses:** 2013-2014: $36,500; room/board: $13,750
**Financial aid:** (212) 749-2802

## Manhattanville College
Purchase NY
(914) 323-5464
**U.S. News ranking:** Reg. U. (N), No. 83
**Website:** www.mville.edu
**Admissions email:** admissions@mville.edu
**Private;** founded 1841
**Freshman admissions:** selective; 2013-2014: 3,930 applied, 3,016 accepted. Neither SAT nor ACT required. SAT 25/75 percentile: 970-1180. High school rank: N/A
**Early decision deadline:** 12/15, notification date: 12/31
**Early action deadline:** N/A, notification date: N/A
**Application deadline (fall):** rolling
**Undergraduate student body:** 1,611 full time, 108 part time; 36% male, 64% female; 0% American Indian, 1% Asian, 7% black, 12% Hispanic, 1% multiracial, 0% Pacific Islander, 23% white, 10% international; 62% from in state; 66% live on campus; N/A of students in fraternities, N/A in sororities
**Most popular majors:** 20% Business Administration and Management, General, 10% Finance, General, 8% Psychology, General, 8% Sociology, 9% Speech Communication and Rhetoric
**Expenses:** 2014-2015: $36,220; room/board: $14,520
**Financial aid:** (914) 323-5357; 79% of undergrads determined to have financial need; average aid package $34,835

## Marist College
Poughkeepsie NY
(845) 575-3226
**U.S. News ranking:** Reg. U. (N), No. 11
**Website:** www.marist.edu
**Admissions email:** admissions@marist.edu
**Private;** founded 1929
**Freshman admissions:** more selective; 2013-2014: 10,351 applied, 3,876 accepted. Neither SAT nor ACT required. SAT 25/75 percentile: 1090-1260. High

school rank: 32% in top tenth, 64% in top quarter, 92% in top half
**Early decision deadline:** 11/1, notification date: 12/15
**Early action deadline:** 11/15, notification date: 1/30
**Application deadline (fall):** 2/1
**Undergraduate student body:** 4,924 full time, 642 part time; 41% male, 59% female; 0% American Indian, 3% Asian, 4% black, 9% Hispanic, 2% multiracial, 0% Pacific Islander, 73% white, 2% international; 56% from in state; 73% live on campus; 3% of students in fraternities, 3% in sororities
**Most popular majors:** 23% Business, Management, Marketing, and Related Support Services, 18% Communication, Journalism, and Related Programs, 5% Education, 16% Psychology, 10% Visual and Performing Arts
**Expenses:** 2014-2015: $32,500; room/board: $14,325
**Financial aid:** (845) 575-3230; 59% of undergrads determined to have financial need; average aid package $18,315

## Marymount Manhattan College
New York NY
(212) 517-0430
**U.S. News ranking:** Nat. Lib. Arts, second tier
**Website:** www.mmm.edu
**Admissions email:** admission@mmm.edu
**Private;** founded 1936
**Freshman admissions:** selective; 2013-2014: 4,145 applied, 3,096 accepted. Either SAT or ACT required. SAT 25/75 percentile: 930-1153. High school rank: N/A
**Early decision deadline:** N/A, notification date: N/A
**Early action deadline:** N/A, notification date: N/A
**Application deadline (fall):** rolling
**Undergraduate student body:** 1,593 full time, 240 part time; 23% male, 77% female; 1% American Indian, 4% Asian, 11% black, 16% Hispanic, 1% multiracial, 0% Pacific Islander, 58% white, 5% international; 41% from in state; 40% live on campus; N/A of students in fraternities, N/A in sororities
**Most popular majors:** 7% Business, Management, Marketing, and Related Support Services, 21% Communication, Journalism, and Related Programs, 6% English Language and Literature/Letters, 9% Psychology, 40% Visual and Performing Arts
**Expenses:** 2014-2015: $27,636; room/board: $15,000
**Financial aid:** (212) 517-0480; 68% of undergrads determined to have financial need; average aid package $14,102

## Medaille College
Buffalo NY
(716) 880-2200
**U.S. News ranking:** Reg. U. (N), second tier
**Website:** www.medaille.edu
**Admissions email:** admissionsug@medaille.edu
**Private;** founded 1937

**Freshman admissions:** less selective; 2013-2014: 1,505 applied, 817 accepted. Either SAT or ACT required. SAT 25/75 percentile: 760-970. High school rank: N/A
**Early decision deadline:** N/A, notification date: N/A
**Early action deadline:** N/A, notification date: N/A
**Application deadline (fall):** rolling
**Undergraduate student body:** 1,586 full time, 142 part time; 33% male, 67% female; 1% American Indian, 1% Asian, 21% black, 5% Hispanic, 0% multiracial, 1% Pacific Islander, 65% white, 2% international; 94% from in state; N/A live on campus; 0% of students in fraternities, 0% in sororities
**Most popular majors:** 31% Business Administration and Management, General, 9% Criminal Justice/Police Science, 12% Elementary Education and Teaching, 10% Psychology, General, 10% Veterinary/Animal Health Technology/Technician and Veterinary Assistant
**Expenses:** 2014-2015: $25,002; room/board: $11,866
**Financial aid:** (716) 880-2256; 95% of undergrads determined to have financial need; average aid package $11,000

## Mercy College
Dobbs Ferry NY
(877) 637-2946
**U.S. News ranking:** Reg. U. (N), unranked
**Website:** www.mercy.edu
**Admissions email:** admissions@mercy.edu
**Private;** founded 1950
**Freshman admissions:** N/A; 2013-2014: 6,394 applied, 4,013 accepted. Neither SAT nor ACT required. ACT 25/75 percentile: N/A. High school rank: N/A
**Early decision deadline:** N/A, notification date: N/A
**Early action deadline:** N/A, notification date: N/A
**Application deadline (fall):** rolling
**Undergraduate student body:** 5,547 full time, 2,607 part time; 31% male, 69% female; 0% American Indian, 3% Asian, 27% black, 35% Hispanic, 2% multiracial, 0% Pacific Islander, 27% white, 0% international; 93% from in state; 7% live on campus; N/A of students in fraternities, N/A in sororities
**Most popular majors:** 14% Business, Management, Marketing, and Related Support Services, 22% Health Professions and Related Programs, 6% Homeland Security, Law Enforcement, Firefighting and Related Protective Services, 10% Psychology, 31% Social Sciences
**Expenses:** 2014-2015: $17,766; room/board: $12,790
**Financial aid:** (914) 378-3421; 87% of undergrads determined to have financial need; average aid package $13,414

## Metropolitan College of New York
New York NY
(800) 338-4465
**U.S. News ranking:** Reg. U. (N), unranked
**Website:** www.metropolitan.edu
**Admissions email:** N/A
**Private**
**Freshman admissions:** N/A; 2013-2014: 639 applied, 334 accepted. Neither SAT nor ACT required. ACT 25/75 percentile: N/A. High school rank: N/A
**Early decision deadline:** N/A, notification date: N/A
**Early action deadline:** N/A, notification date: N/A
**Application deadline (fall):** rolling
**Undergraduate student body:** 851 full time, 60 part time; 29% male, 71% female; 1% American Indian, 2% Asian, 59% black, 20% Hispanic, 2% multiracial, 1% Pacific Islander, 5% white, 3% international; 97% from in state; 0% live on campus; 0% of students in fraternities, 0% in sororities
**Most popular majors:** 29% Business/Commerce, General, 53% Community Organization and Advocacy, 7% Health Information/Medical Records Administration/Administrator, 11% Urban Studies/Affairs
**Expenses:** 2013-2014: $17,530; room/board: N/A
**Financial aid:** (212) 343-1234; 93% of undergrads determined to have financial need; average aid package $15,731

## Molloy College
Rockville Centre NY
(888) 466-5569
**U.S. News ranking:** Reg. U. (N), No. 41
**Website:** www.molloy.edu
**Admissions email:** admissions@molloy.edu
**Private;** founded 1955
**Affiliation:** Roman Catholic
**Freshman admissions:** selective; 2013-2014: 3,242 applied, 2,356 accepted. Either SAT or ACT required. SAT 25/75 percentile: 970-1140. High school rank: 38% in top tenth, 56% in top quarter, 92% in top half
**Early decision deadline:** N/A, notification date: N/A
**Early action deadline:** 12/1, notification date: 12/15
**Application deadline (fall):** rolling
**Undergraduate student body:** 2,693 full time, 682 part time; 26% male, 74% female; 0% American Indian, 7% Asian, 13% black, 14% Hispanic, 1% multiracial, 1% Pacific Islander, 62% white, 0% international; 99% from in state; 5% live on campus; N/A of students in fraternities, N/A in sororities
**Most popular majors:** 9% Business, Management, Marketing, and Related Support Services, 14% Education, 48% Health Professions and Related Programs, 5% Homeland Security, Law Enforcement, Firefighting and Related Protective Services, 5% Public Administration and Social Service Professions
**Expenses:** 2014-2015: $26,850; room/board: $13,590

**Financial aid:** (516) 256-2217; 84% of undergrads determined to have financial need; average aid package $14,394

## Monroe College
Bronx NY
(800) 556-6676
**U.S. News ranking:** Reg. U. (N), second tier
**Website:** www.monroecollege.edu
**Admissions email:** N/A
**For-profit;** founded 1933
**Freshman admissions:** less selective; 2013-2014: 4,419 applied, 1,946 accepted. Neither SAT nor ACT required. ACT 25/75 percentile: N/A. High school rank: N/A
**Early decision deadline:** N/A, notification date: N/A
**Early action deadline:** N/A, notification date: N/A
**Application deadline (fall):** rolling
**Undergraduate student body:** 4,895 full time, 1,899 part time; 36% male, 64% female; 0% American Indian, 2% Asian, 45% black, 41% Hispanic, 0% multiracial, 0% Pacific Islander, 2% white, 7% international; 88% from in state; 13% live on campus; 0% of students in fraternities, 0% in sororities
**Most popular majors:** 14% Accounting, 20% Business Administration and Management, General, 26% Criminal Justice/Law Enforcement Administration, 12% Health Services Administration, 11% Hospitality Administration/Management, General
**Expenses:** 2014-2015: $13,740; room/board: $9,200
**Financial aid:** N/A; 90% of undergrads determined to have financial need; average aid package $14,103

## Morrisville State College
Morrisville NY
(315) 684-6046
**U.S. News ranking:** Reg. Coll. (N), No. 43
**Website:** www.morrisville.edu
**Admissions email:** admissions@morrisville.edu
**Public;** founded 1908
**Freshman admissions:** less selective; 2013-2014: 4,049 applied, 2,388 accepted. Neither SAT nor ACT required. SAT 25/75 percentile: 840-1030. High school rank: 5% in top tenth, 16% in top quarter, 65% in top half
**Early decision deadline:** N/A, notification date: N/A
**Early action deadline:** N/A, notification date: N/A
**Application deadline (fall):** rolling
**Undergraduate student body:** 2,668 full time, 360 part time; 52% male, 48% female; 1% American Indian, 1% Asian, 18% black, 7% Hispanic, 2% multiracial, 0% Pacific Islander, 68% white, 1% international; 96% from in state; 55% live on campus; 0% of students in fraternities, 0% in sororities
**Most popular majors:** 25% Agriculture, Agriculture Operations, and Related Sciences, 33% Business, Management, Marketing, and Related Support Services, 12% Computer and

Information Sciences and Support Services, 13% Homeland Security, Law Enforcement, Firefighting and Related Protective Services, 6% Mechanic and Repair Technologies/Technicians
**Expenses:** 2014-2015: $6,670 in state, $12,140 out of state; room/board: $13,370
**Financial aid:** (315) 684-6289; 87% of undergrads determined to have financial need; average aid package $9,627

## Mount St. Mary College
Newburgh NY
(845) 569-3488
**U.S. News ranking:** Reg. U. (N), No. 109
**Website:** www.msmc.edu
**Admissions email:** admissions@msmc.edu
**Private;** founded 1959
**Affiliation:** Roman Catholic
**Freshman admissions:** selective; 2013-2014: 3,551 applied, 3,054 accepted. Either SAT or ACT required. SAT 25/75 percentile: 910-1093. High school rank: 10% in top tenth, 38% in top quarter, 71% in top half
**Early decision deadline:** N/A, notification date: N/A
**Early action deadline:** N/A, notification date: N/A
**Application deadline (fall):** 8/15
**Undergraduate student body:** 1,742 full time, 461 part time; 30% male, 70% female; 1% American Indian, 2% Asian, 7% black, 12% Hispanic, 1% multiracial, 0% Pacific Islander, 64% white, 0% international; 89% from in state; 46% live on campus; N/A of students in fraternities, N/A in sororities
**Most popular majors:** 18% Business, Management, Marketing, and Related Support Services, 8% English Language and Literature/Letters, 19% Health Professions and Related Programs, 11% History, 11% Psychology
**Expenses:** 2014-2015: $27,312; room/board: $13,556
**Financial aid:** (845) 569-3298; 81% of undergrads determined to have financial need; average aid package $17,409

## Nazareth College
Rochester NY
(585) 389-2860
**U.S. News ranking:** Reg. U. (N), No. 31
**Website:** www.naz.edu
**Admissions email:** admissions@naz.edu
**Private;** founded 1924
**Freshman admissions:** selective; 2013-2014: 3,838 applied, 2,624 accepted. Neither SAT nor ACT required. SAT 25/75 percentile: 1020-1180. High school rank: 30% in top tenth, 65% in top quarter, 91% in top half
**Early decision deadline:** 11/1, notification date: 12/1
**Early action deadline:** 12/1, notification date: 1/15
**Application deadline (fall):** 2/1
**Undergraduate student body:** 1,901 full time, 133 part time; 27% male, 73% female; 1% American Indian, 2% Asian, 5% black,

5% Hispanic, 1% multiracial, 0% Pacific Islander, 73% white, 2% international; 93% from in state; 53% live on campus; N/A of students in fraternities, N/A in sororities
**Most popular majors:** 10% Business, Management, Marketing, and Related Support Services, 17% Education, 17% Health Professions and Related Programs, 10% Psychology, 8% Visual and Performing Arts
**Expenses:** 2014-2015: $30,572; room/board: $12,570
**Financial aid:** (585) 389-2310; 81% of undergrads determined to have financial need; average aid package $24,450

## New School
New York NY
(800) 292-3040
**U.S. News ranking:** Nat. U., No. 135
**Website:** www.newschool.edu
**Admissions email:** admission@newschool.edu
**Private;** founded 1919
**Freshman admissions:** selective; 2013-2014: 4,976 applied, 3,314 accepted. Neither SAT nor ACT required. SAT 25/75 percentile: 990-1240. High school rank: 15% in top tenth, 42% in top quarter, 74% in top half
**Early decision deadline:** 11/1, notification date: 12/30
**Early action deadline:** N/A, notification date: N/A
**Undergraduate student body:** 5,971 full time, 903 part time; 28% male, 72% female; 0% American Indian, 11% Asian, 5% black, 10% Hispanic, 4% multiracial, 0% Pacific Islander, 36% white, 31% international; 30% from in state; 23% live on campus; N/A of students in fraternities, N/A in sororities
**Most popular majors:** 5% English Language and Literature/Letters, 12% Liberal Arts and Sciences, General Studies and Humanities, 2% Psychology, 7% Social Sciences, 68% Visual and Performing Arts
**Expenses:** 2014-2015: $41,836; room/board: $18,190
**Financial aid:** (212) 229-8930; 51% of undergrads determined to have financial need; average aid package $21,350

## New York Institute of Technology
Old Westbury NY
(516) 686-7520
**U.S. News ranking:** Reg. U. (N), No. 50
**Website:** www.nyit.edu
**Admissions email:** admissions@nyit.edu
**Private;** founded 1955
**Freshman admissions:** selective; 2013-2014: 5,619 applied, 4,181 accepted. Either SAT or ACT required. SAT 25/75 percentile: 1020-1220. High school rank: 22% in top tenth, 52% in top quarter, 88% in top half
**Early decision deadline:** N/A, notification date: N/A
**Early action deadline:** 12/1, notification date: 12/31
**Application deadline (fall):** rolling

**Undergraduate student body:** 3,704 full time, 752 part time; 63% male, 37% female; 0% American Indian, 13% Asian, 8% black, 13% Hispanic, 1% multiracial, 0% Pacific Islander, 19% white, 12% international; 91% from in state; 12% live on campus; 3% of students in fraternities, 2% in sororities
**Most popular majors:** 18% Architecture and Related Services, 11% Biological and Biomedical Sciences, 16% Business, Management, Marketing, and Related Support Services, 10% Communication, Journalism, and Related Programs, 12% Engineering
**Expenses:** 2014-2015: $32,180; room/board: $12,830
**Financial aid:** (516) 686-7680; 75% of undergrads determined to have financial need; average aid package $18,348

## New York University
New York NY
(212) 998-4500
**U.S. News ranking:** Nat. U., No. 32
**Website:** www.nyu.edu
**Admissions email:** admissions@nyu.edu
**Private;** founded 1831
**Freshman admissions:** more selective; 2013-2014: 45,779 applied, 14,829 accepted. Either SAT or ACT required. SAT 25/75 percentile: 1260-1460. High school rank: 63% in top tenth, 96% in top quarter, 99% in top half
**Early decision deadline:** 11/1, notification date: 12/15
**Early action deadline:** N/A, notification date: N/A
**Application deadline (fall):** 1/1
**Undergraduate student body:** 21,365 full time, 1,250 part time; 40% male, 60% female; 0% American Indian, 18% Asian, 5% black, 11% Hispanic, 3% multiracial, 0% Pacific Islander, 38% white, 14% international; 34% from in state; 47% live on campus; 5% of students in fraternities, 7% in sororities
**Most popular majors:** 13% Business, Management, Marketing, and Related Support Services, 9% Health Professions and Related Programs, 10% Liberal Arts and Sciences, General Studies and Humanities, 16% Social Sciences, 21% Visual and Performing Arts
**Expenses:** 2014-2015: $46,170; room/board: $16,782
**Financial aid:** (212) 998-4444; 52% of undergrads determined to have financial need; average aid package $27,544

## Niagara University
Niagara University NY
(716) 286-8700
**U.S. News ranking:** Reg. U. (N), No. 50
**Website:** www.niagara.edu
**Admissions email:** admissions@niagara.edu
**Private;** founded 1856
**Affiliation:** Roman Catholic (Vincentian)
**Freshman admissions:** selective; 2013-2014: 3,716 applied, 2,465 accepted. Either SAT or ACT required. SAT 25/75

percentile: 930-1120. High school rank: 15% in top tenth, 41% in top quarter, 77% in top half
**Early decision deadline:** N/A, notification date: N/A
**Early action deadline:** N/A, notification date: N/A
**Application deadline (fall):** rolling
**Undergraduate student body:** 2,865 full time, 362 part time; 40% male, 60% female; 1% American Indian, 1% Asian, 5% black, 4% Hispanic, 1% multiracial, 0% Pacific Islander, 68% white, 14% international; 91% from in state; 43% live on campus; 1% of students in fraternities, 2% in sororities
**Most popular majors:** 5% Biological and Biomedical Sciences, 32% Business, Management, Marketing, and Related Support Services, 15% Education, 10% Homeland Security, Law Enforcement, Firefighting and Related Protective Services, 5% Parks, Recreation, Leisure, and Fitness Studies
**Expenses:** 2014-2015: $29,060; room/board: $11,950
**Financial aid:** (716) 286-8686; 76% of undergrads determined to have financial need; average aid package $23,087

## Nyack College[1]
Nyack NY
(800) 336-9225
**U.S. News ranking:** Reg. U. (N), second tier
**Website:** www.nyack.edu
**Admissions email:** admissions@nyack.edu
**Private**
**Application deadline (fall):** N/A
**Undergraduate student body:** N/A full time, N/A part time
**Expenses:** 2013-2014: $23,250; room/board: $8,650
**Financial aid:** (845) 358-1710

## Pace University
New York NY
(212) 346-1323
**U.S. News ranking:** Nat. U., No. 173
**Website:** www.pace.edu
**Admissions email:** infoctr@pace.edu
**Private;** founded 1906
**Freshman admissions:** selective; 2013-2014: 14,590 applied, 11,853 accepted. Either SAT or ACT required. SAT 25/75 percentile: 940-1150. High school rank: 13% in top tenth, 40% in top quarter, 76% in top half
**Early decision deadline:** N/A, notification date: N/A
**Early action deadline:** 12/1, notification date: 1/1
**Application deadline (fall):** 2/15
**Undergraduate student body:** 7,116 full time, 1,173 part time; 41% male, 59% female; 0% American Indian, 9% Asian, 11% black, 16% Hispanic, 4% multiracial, 0% Pacific Islander, 48% white, 6% international; 55% from in state; 40% live on campus; 11% of students in fraternities, 7% in sororities
**Most popular majors:** 36% Business, Management, Marketing, and Related Support Services, 13% Communication, Journalism, and Related Programs, 6% Health Professions and Related Programs, 8% Psychology, 6% Visual and Performing Arts

**Expenses:** 2014-2015: $39,747; room/board: $13,620
**Financial aid:** (212) 346-1300; 75% of undergrads determined to have financial need; average aid package $28,893

## Paul Smith's College[1]
Paul Smiths NY
(800) 421-2605
**U.S. News ranking:** Reg. Coll. (N), No. 40
**Website:** www.paulsmiths.edu
**Admissions email:** admiss@paulsmiths.edu
**Private**
**Application deadline (fall):** N/A
**Undergraduate student body:** N/A full time, N/A part time
**Expenses:** 2013-2014: $25,454; room/board: $10,696
**Financial aid:** (518) 327-6220

## Plaza College[1]
Jackson Heights NY
(718) 779-1430
**U.S. News ranking:** Reg. Coll. (N), unranked
**Website:** www.plazacollege.edu
**Admissions email:** N/A
**For-profit**
**Application deadline (fall):** rolling
**Undergraduate student body:** N/A full time, N/A part time
**Expenses:** 2013-2014: $11,350; room/board: N/A
**Financial aid:** (718) 779-1430

## Pratt Institute
Brooklyn NY
(718) 636-3514
**U.S. News ranking:** Reg. U. (N), No. 19
**Website:** www.pratt.edu
**Admissions email:** admissions@pratt.edu
**Private;** founded 1887
**Freshman admissions:** selective; 2013-2014: 4,446 applied, 2,977 accepted. Either SAT or ACT required. SAT 25/75 percentile: 1070-1300. High school rank: N/A
**Early decision deadline:** N/A, notification date: N/A
**Early action deadline:** 11/1, notification date: 12/22
**Application deadline (fall):** 1/5
**Undergraduate student body:** 3,041 full time, 108 part time; 34% male, 66% female; 0% American Indian, 15% Asian, 5% black, 10% Hispanic, 0% multiracial, 0% Pacific Islander, 40% white, 28% international; 31% from in state; 53% live on campus; 6% of students in fraternities, 3% in sororities
**Most popular majors:** 17% Architecture, 11% Design and Visual Communications, General, 12% Graphic Design, 9% Industrial and Product Design, 8% Interior Design
**Expenses:** 2014-2015: $44,804; room/board: $11,152
**Financial aid:** (718) 636-3599; 54% of undergrads determined to have financial need; average aid package $23,204

## Purchase College–SUNY
Purchase NY
(914) 251-6300
**U.S. News ranking:** Nat. Lib. Arts, No. 171
**Website:** www.purchase.edu
**Admissions email:** admissions@purchase.edu
**Public;** founded 1967
**Freshman admissions:** selective; 2013-2014: 8,405 applied, 2,790 accepted. Either SAT or ACT required. SAT 25/75 percentile: 980-1180. High school rank: 13% in top tenth, 36% in top quarter, 73% in top half
**Early decision deadline:** N/A, notification date: N/A
**Early action deadline:** 11/15, notification date: 12/15
**Application deadline (fall):** 7/15
**Undergraduate student body:** 3,860 full time, 405 part time; 44% male, 56% female; 0% American Indian, 3% Asian, 8% black, 18% Hispanic, 8% multiracial, 0% Pacific Islander, 54% white, 3% international; 85% from in state; 66% live on campus; N/A of students in fraternities, N/A in sororities
**Most popular majors:** 7% Communication, Journalism, and Related Programs, 20% Liberal Arts and Sciences, General Studies and Humanities, 6% Psychology, 10% Social Sciences, 40% Visual and Performing Arts
**Expenses:** 2014-2015: $7,873 in state, $17,523 out of state; room/board: $11,806
**Financial aid:** (914) 251-6350; 62% of undergrads determined to have financial need; average aid package $10,456

## Rensselaer Polytechnic Institute
Troy NY
(518) 276-6216
**U.S. News ranking:** Nat. U., No. 42
**Website:** www.rpi.edu
**Admissions email:** admissions@rpi.edu
**Private;** founded 1824
**Freshman admissions:** most selective; 2013-2014: 16,150 applied, 6,654 accepted. Either SAT or ACT required. SAT 25/75 percentile: 1290-1488. High school rank: 72% in top tenth, 95% in top quarter, 98% in top half
**Early decision deadline:** 11/1, notification date: 12/14
**Early action deadline:** N/A, notification date: N/A
**Application deadline (fall):** 1/15
**Undergraduate student body:** 5,423 full time, 29 part time; 70% male, 30% female; 0% American Indian, 10% Asian, 2% black, 7% Hispanic, 6% multiracial, 0% Pacific Islander, 65% white, 7% international; 34% from in state; 57% live on campus; 30% of students in fraternities, 16% in sororities
**Most popular majors:** 6% Biological and Biomedical Sciences, 6% Business, Management, Marketing, and Related Support Services, 9% Computer and Information Sciences and Support Services, 54% Engineering, 6% Physical Sciences
**Expenses:** 2014-2015: $47,908; room/board: $13,620

**Financial aid:** (518) 276-6813; 65% of undergrads determined to have financial need; average aid package $32,603

## Roberts Wesleyan College
Rochester NY
(585) 594-6400
**U.S. News ranking:** Reg. U. (N), No. 87
**Website:** www.roberts.edu
**Admissions email:** admissions@roberts.edu
**Private;** founded 1866
**Affiliation:** Free Methodist
**Freshman admissions:** selective; 2013-2014: 814 applied, 591 accepted. Either SAT or ACT required. SAT 25/75 percentile: 920-1170. High school rank: 21% in top tenth, 52% in top quarter, 87% in top half
**Early decision deadline:** N/A, notification date: N/A
**Early action deadline:** N/A, notification date: N/A
**Application deadline (fall):** 8/15
**Undergraduate student body:** 1,325 full time, 90 part time; 35% male, 65% female; 0% American Indian, 1% Asian, 13% black, 6% Hispanic, 3% multiracial, 0% Pacific Islander, 74% white, 3% international; 92% from in state; 58% live on campus; 0% of students in fraternities, 0% in sororities
**Most popular majors:** 22% Business, Management, Marketing, and Related Support Services, 18% Education, 27% Health Professions and Related Programs, 4% Liberal Arts and Sciences, General Studies and Humanities, 6% Psychology
**Expenses:** 2013-2014: $27,364; room/board: $9,630
**Financial aid:** (585) 594-6150

## Rochester Institute of Technology
Rochester NY
(585) 475-6631
**U.S. News ranking:** Reg. U. (N), No. 8
**Website:** www.rit.edu
**Admissions email:** admissions@rit.edu
**Private;** founded 1829
**Freshman admissions:** more selective; 2013-2014: 16,354 applied, 9,839 accepted. Either SAT or ACT required. SAT 25/75 percentile: 1110-1320. High school rank: 31% in top tenth, 64% in top quarter, 94% in top half
**Early decision deadline:** 12/1, notification date: 1/15
**Early action deadline:** N/A, notification date: N/A
**Application deadline (fall):** rolling
**Undergraduate student body:** 12,106 full time, 1,774 part time; 68% male, 32% female; 0% American Indian, 6% Asian, 5% black, 6% Hispanic, 2% multiracial, 0% Pacific Islander, 63% white, 5% international; N/A from in state; 55% live on campus; N/A of students in fraternities, N/A in sororities
**Most popular majors:** 10% Business, Management, Marketing, and Related Support Services, 16% Computer and

Information Sciences and Support Services, 16% Engineering, 12% Engineering Technologies and Engineering-Related Fields, 13% Visual and Performing Arts
**Expenses:** 2014-2015: $35,768; room/board: $11,568
**Financial aid:** (585) 475-2186; 76% of undergrads determined to have financial need; average aid package $23,800

## The Sage Colleges
Troy NY
(888) 837-9724
**U.S. News ranking:** Reg. U. (N), No. 87
**Website:** www.sage.edu
**Admissions email:** tscadm@sage.edu
**Private;** founded 1916
**Freshman admissions:** selective; 2013-2014: 2,237 applied, 1,267 accepted. Neither SAT nor ACT required. SAT 25/75 percentile: 840-1090. High school rank: 14% in top tenth, 43% in top quarter, 83% in top half
**Early decision deadline:** N/A, notification date: N/A
**Early action deadline:** N/A, notification date: N/A
**Application deadline (fall):** rolling
**Undergraduate student body:** 1,446 full time, 253 part time; 21% male, 79% female; 0% American Indian, 3% Asian, 13% black, 9% Hispanic, 3% multiracial, 0% Pacific Islander, 61% white, 0% international; 94% from in state; 53% live on campus; N/A of students in fraternities, N/A in sororities
**Most popular majors:** 9% Biological and Biomedical Sciences, 14% Business, Management, Marketing, and Related Support Services, 9% Education, 8% Health Professions and Related Programs, 25% Visual and Performing Arts
**Expenses:** 2014-2015: $28,200; room/board: $11,830
**Financial aid:** (518) 244-2215; 93% of undergrads determined to have financial need

## Sarah Lawrence College
Bronxville NY
(914) 395-2510
**U.S. News ranking:** Nat. Lib. Arts, No. 59
**Website:** www.slc.edu
**Admissions email:** slcadmit@sarahlawrence.edu
**Private;** founded 1926
**Freshman admissions:** more selective; 2013-2014: 2,236 applied, 1,723 accepted. Neither SAT nor ACT required. SAT 25/75 percentile: 1150-1350. High school rank: 35% in top tenth, 66% in top quarter, 96% in top half
**Early decision deadline:** 11/1, notification date: 12/15
**Early action deadline:** N/A, notification date: N/A
**Application deadline (fall):** 1/15
**Undergraduate student body:** 1,441 full time, 30 part time; 28% male, 72% female; 0% American Indian, 4% Asian, 4% black, 10% Hispanic, 5% multiracial, 0% Pacific Islander, 58% white, 11% international; 21% from in state; 82% live on campus; 0% of students in fraternities, 0% in sororities

**Most popular majors:** 100% Liberal Arts and Sciences/Liberal Studies
**Expenses:** 2014-2015: $50,780; room/board: $14,212
**Financial aid:** (914) 395-2570; 68% of undergrads determined to have financial need; average aid package $34,855

## School of Visual Arts

New York NY
(212) 592-2100
**U.S. News ranking:** Arts, unranked
**Website:** www.schoolofvisualarts.edu/
**Admissions email:** admissions@sva.edu
**For-profit;** founded 1947
**Freshman admissions:** N/A; 2013-2014: 3,280 applied, 2,485 accepted. Either SAT or ACT required. SAT 25/75 percentile: N/A. High school rank: N/A
**Early decision deadline:** N/A, notification date: N/A
**Early action deadline:** 12/1, notification date: N/A
**Application deadline (fall):** rolling
**Undergraduate student body:** 3,349 full time, 287 part time; 39% male, 61% female; 1% American Indian, 14% Asian, 6% black, 8% Hispanic, 0% multiracial, 1% Pacific Islander, 41% white, 28% international
**Most popular majors:** Information not available
**Expenses:** 2014-2015: $33,560; room/board: $17,000
**Financial aid:** (212) 592-2030; 50% of undergrads determined to have financial need; average aid package $15,761

## Siena College

Loudonville NY
(888) 287-4362
**U.S. News ranking:** Nat. Lib. Arts, No. 113
**Website:** www.siena.edu
**Admissions email:** admissions@siena.edu
**Private;** founded 1937
**Affiliation:** Roman Catholic
**Freshman admissions:** selective; 2013-2014: 9,438 applied, 5,428 accepted. Either SAT or ACT required. SAT 25/75 percentile: 1000-1200. High school rank: 24% in top tenth, 58% in top quarter, 90% in top half
**Early decision deadline:** 12/1, notification date: 12/15
**Early action deadline:** 12/1, notification date: 1/1
**Application deadline (fall):** 2/15
**Undergraduate student body:** 3,009 full time, 152 part time; 47% male, 53% female; 0% American Indian, 4% Asian, 4% black, 7% Hispanic, 2% multiracial, 0% Pacific Islander, 81% white, 2% international; 81% from in state; 78% live on campus; N/A of students in fraternities, N/A in sororities
**Most popular majors:** 14% Accounting, 11% Biology, General, 8% Finance, General, 10% Marketing/Marketing Management, General, 10% Psychology, General
**Expenses:** 2014-2015: $32,293; room/board: $13,060
**Financial aid:** (518) 783-2427; 77% of undergrads determined to have financial need; average aid package $24,441

## Skidmore College

Saratoga Springs NY
(518) 580-5570
**U.S. News ranking:** Nat. Lib. Arts, No. 37
**Website:** www.skidmore.edu
**Admissions email:** admissions@skidmore.edu
**Private;** founded 1903
**Freshman admissions:** more selective; 2013-2014: 8,285 applied, 2,904 accepted. Either SAT or ACT required. SAT 25/75 percentile: 1130-1350. High school rank: 45% in top tenth, 81% in top quarter, 97% in top half
**Early decision deadline:** 11/15, notification date: 12/15
**Early action deadline:** N/A, notification date: N/A
**Application deadline (fall):** 1/15
**Undergraduate student body:** 2,647 full time, 37 part time; 39% male, 61% female; 0% American Indian, 6% Asian, 4% black, 9% Hispanic, 4% multiracial, 0% Pacific Islander, 63% white, 7% international; 33% from in state; 87% live on campus; 0% of students in fraternities, 0% in sororities
**Most popular majors:** 12% Business, Management, Marketing, and Related Support Services, 11% English Language and Literature/Letters, 9% Psychology, 17% Social Sciences, 15% Visual and Performing Arts
**Expenses:** 2014-2015: $47,314; room/board: $12,628
**Financial aid:** (518) 580-5750; 43% of undergrads determined to have financial need; average aid package $41,000

## St. Bonaventure University

St. Bonaventure NY
(800) 462-5050
**U.S. News ranking:** Reg. U. (N), No. 24
**Website:** www.sbu.edu
**Admissions email:** admissions@sbu.edu
**Private;** founded 1858
**Affiliation:** Roman Catholic
**Freshman admissions:** selective; 2013-2014: 2,754 applied, 2,203 accepted. Either SAT or ACT required. SAT 25/75 percentile: 930-1180. High school rank: 18% in top tenth, 45% in top quarter, 77% in top half
**Early decision deadline:** N/A, notification date: N/A
**Early action deadline:** N/A, notification date: N/A
**Application deadline (fall):** 7/1
**Undergraduate student body:** 1,780 full time, 46 part time; 49% male, 51% female; 0% American Indian, 4% Asian, 5% black, 7% Hispanic, 1% multiracial, 0% Pacific Islander, 68% white, 2% international; 77% from in state; 75% live on campus; 0% of students in fraternities, 0% in sororities
**Most popular majors:** 20% Journalism, 27% Marketing/Marketing Management, General, 7% Psychology, General, 15% Special Education and Teaching, General, 6% Sports Studies
**Expenses:** 2014-2015: $30,475; room/board: $10,727
**Financial aid:** (716) 375-2528; 76% of undergrads determined to have financial need; average aid package $22,796

## St. Francis College

Brooklyn Heights NY
(718) 489-5200
**U.S. News ranking:** Reg. Coll. (N), No. 20
**Website:** www.sfc.edu
**Admissions email:** admissions@stfranciscollege.edu
**Private;** founded 1884
**Freshman admissions:** less selective; 2013-2014: 2,815 applied, 1,911 accepted. Either SAT or ACT required. SAT 25/75 percentile: 850-1030. High school rank: N/A
**Early decision deadline:** N/A, notification date: N/A
**Early action deadline:** N/A, notification date: N/A
**Application deadline (fall):** rolling
**Undergraduate student body:** 2,456 full time, 308 part time; 44% male, 56% female; 0% American Indian, 3% Asian, 20% black, 22% Hispanic, 2% multiracial, 1% Pacific Islander, 37% white, 5% international; 90% from in state; 4% live on campus; N/A of students in fraternities, N/A in sororities
**Most popular majors:** 10% Accounting and Related Services, 10% Business Administration, Management and Operations, 14% Communication and Media Studies, 9% Health Professions and Related Clinical Sciences, Other, 9% Liberal Arts and Sciences, General Studies and Humanities
**Expenses:** 2014-2015: $22,300; room/board: $14,250
**Financial aid:** (718) 489-5255; 67% of undergrads determined to have financial need; average aid package $14,300

## St. John Fisher College

Rochester NY
(585) 385-8064
**U.S. News ranking:** Nat. U., No. 142
**Website:** www.sjfc.edu
**Admissions email:** admissions@sjfc.edu
**Private;** founded 1948
**Affiliation:** Roman Catholic
**Freshman admissions:** selective; 2013-2014: 4,016 applied, 2,521 accepted. Either SAT or ACT required. SAT 25/75 percentile: 990-1170. High school rank: 26% in top tenth, 60% in top quarter, 90% in top half
**Early decision deadline:** 12/1, notification date: 1/15
**Early action deadline:** N/A, notification date: N/A
**Application deadline (fall):** rolling
**Undergraduate student body:** 2,738 full time, 221 part time; 40% male, 60% female; 0% American Indian, 3% Asian, 4% black, 4% Hispanic, 1% multiracial, 0% Pacific Islander, 84% white, 0% international; 97% from in state; 46% live on campus; 0% of students in fraternities, 0% in sororities
**Most popular majors:** 23% Business, Management, Marketing, and Related Support Services, 20% Education, 18% Health Professions and Related Programs, 6% Psychology, 8% Social Sciences
**Expenses:** 2014-2015: $29,550; room/board: $11,158

## St. Joseph's College New York

Brooklyn NY
(718) 940-5800
**U.S. News ranking:** Reg. U. (N), No. 70
**Website:** www.sjcny.edu
**Admissions email:** longislandas@sjcny.edu
**Private;** founded 1916
**Freshman admissions:** selective; 2013-2014: 3,148 applied, 2,373 accepted. Either SAT or ACT required. SAT 25/75 percentile: 950-1150. High school rank: N/A
**Early decision deadline:** N/A, notification date: N/A
**Early action deadline:** N/A, notification date: N/A
**Application deadline (fall):** 8/15
**Undergraduate student body:** 3,591 full time, 938 part time; 31% male, 69% female; 1% American Indian, 3% Asian, 10% black, 12% Hispanic, 1% multiracial, 0% Pacific Islander, 59% white, 5% international; 99% from in state; 1% live on campus; 1% of students in fraternities, 4% in sororities
**Most popular majors:** 5% Accounting, 9% Business Administration and Management, General, 7% Psychology, General, 7% Rhetoric and Composition, 25% Special Education and Teaching, General

**Financial aid:** (585) 385-8042; 83% of undergrads determined to have financial need; average aid package $20,162

## St. John's University

Queens NY
(718) 990-2000
**U.S. News ranking:** Nat. U., No. 145
**Website:** www.stjohns.edu/
**Admissions email:** admhelp@stjohns.edu
**Private;** founded 1870
**Affiliation:** Roman Catholic
**Freshman admissions:** selective; 2013-2014: 51,207 applied, 26,932 accepted. Either SAT or ACT required. SAT 25/75 percentile: 990-1210. High school rank: 17% in top tenth, 42% in top quarter, 73% in top half
**Early decision deadline:** N/A, notification date: N/A
**Early action deadline:** N/A, notification date: N/A
**Application deadline (fall):** rolling
**Undergraduate student body:** 10,908 full time, 4,865 part time; 45% male, 55% female; 0% American Indian, 19% Asian, 19% black, 16% Hispanic, 4% multiracial, 0% Pacific Islander, 34% white, 5% international; 70% from in state; 31% live on campus; 9% of students in fraternities, 8% in sororities
**Most popular majors:** 7% Biological and Biomedical Sciences, 22% Business, Management, Marketing, and Related Support Services, 11% Communication, Journalism, and Related Programs, 9% Health Professions and Related Programs, 8% Psychology
**Expenses:** 2014-2015: $38,680; room/board: $16,390
**Financial aid:** (718) 990-2000; 81% of undergrads determined to have financial need; average aid package $23,166

## St. Joseph's College New York

Brooklyn NY
(718) 940-5800
**U.S. News ranking:** Reg. U. (N), No. 70

**Expenses:** 2014-2015: $22,835; room/board: N/A
**Financial aid:** (718) 636-6808; 77% of undergrads determined to have financial need; average aid package $11,353

## St. Lawrence University

Canton NY
(315) 229-5261
**U.S. News ranking:** Nat. Lib. Arts, No. 56
**Website:** www.stlawu.edu
**Admissions email:** admissions@stlawu.edu
**Private;** founded 1856
**Freshman admissions:** more selective; 2013-2014: 4,424 applied, 2,054 accepted. Neither SAT nor ACT required. SAT 25/75 percentile: 1120-1310. High school rank: 34% in top tenth, 71% in top quarter, 95% in top half
**Early decision deadline:** 11/1, notification date: N/A
**Early action deadline:** N/A, notification date: N/A
**Application deadline (fall):** 2/1
**Undergraduate student body:** 2,397 full time, 17 part time; 45% male, 55% female; 0% American Indian, 2% Asian, 3% black, 4% Hispanic, 2% multiracial, 0% Pacific Islander, 80% white, 8% international; 43% from in state; 98% live on campus; 8% of students in fraternities, 18% in sororities
**Most popular majors:** 13% Biological and Biomedical Sciences, 6% Communication, Journalism, and Related Programs, 11% Psychology, 31% Social Sciences, 6% Visual and Performing Arts
**Expenses:** 2014-2015: $47,696; room/board: $12,286
**Financial aid:** (315) 229-5265; 60% of undergrads determined to have financial need; average aid package $41,005

## Stony Brook University–SUNY

Stony Brook NY
(631) 632-6868
**U.S. News ranking:** Nat. U., No. 88
**Website:** www.stonybrook.edu
**Admissions email:** enroll@stonybrook.edu
**Public;** founded 1957
**Freshman admissions:** more selective; 2013-2014: 30,300 applied, 11,963 accepted. Either SAT or ACT required. SAT 25/75 percentile: 1150-1350. High school rank: 47% in top tenth, 78% in top quarter, 96% in top half
**Early decision deadline:** N/A, notification date: N/A
**Early action deadline:** N/A, notification date: N/A
**Application deadline (fall):** rolling
**Undergraduate student body:** 14,892 full time, 1,100 part time; 54% male, 46% female; 0% American Indian, 24% Asian, 6% black, 10% Hispanic, 2% multiracial, 0% Pacific Islander, 38% white, 10% international; 91% from in state; 60% live on campus; 4% of students in fraternities, 3% in sororities

**Most popular majors:** 4% Applied Mathematics, General, 10% Biology/Biological Sciences, General, 9% Business Administration and Management, General, 10% Health Professions and Related Clinical Sciences, Other, 12% Psychology, General
**Expenses:** 2014-2015: $8,430 in state, $21,850 out of state; room/board: $11,538
**Financial aid:** (631) 632-6840; 59% of undergrads determined to have financial need; average aid package $13,093

## St. Thomas Aquinas College
Sparkill NY
(845) 398-4100
**U.S. News ranking:** Reg. U. (N), No. 125
**Website:** www.stac.edu
**Admissions email:** admissions@stac.edu
**Private;** founded 1952
**Freshman admissions:** less selective; 2013-2014: 1,841 applied, 1,514 accepted. Either SAT or ACT required. SAT 25/75 percentile: 830-1050. High school rank: 11% in top tenth, 30% in top quarter, 60% in top half
**Early decision deadline:** 12/15, notification date: 3/1
**Early action deadline:** N/A, notification date: N/A
**Application deadline (fall):** rolling
**Undergraduate student body:** 1,259 full time, 542 part time; 47% male, 53% female; 0% American Indian, 3% Asian, 8% black, 19% Hispanic, 2% multiracial, 0% Pacific Islander, 56% white, 2% international
**Most popular majors:** 10% Business Administration and Management, General, 12% Criminal Justice/Law Enforcement Administration, 9% Education/Teaching of Individuals in Early Childhood Special Education Programs, 11% Psychology, General, 10% Sociology
**Expenses:** 2014-2015: $27,630; room/board: $11,680
**Financial aid:** (845) 398-4097; 76% of undergrads determined to have financial need; average aid package $20,600

## SUNY Buffalo State
Buffalo NY
(716) 878-4017
**U.S. News ranking:** Reg. U. (N), No. 106
**Website:** www.buffalostate.edu
**Admissions email:** admissions@buffalostate.edu
**Public;** founded 1871
**Freshman admissions:** less selective; 2013-2014: 11,251 applied, 5,463 accepted. Either SAT or ACT required. SAT 25/75 percentile: 890-1060. High school rank: 3% in top tenth, 32% in top quarter, 74% in top half
**Early decision deadline:** 11/15, notification date: 12/15
**Early action deadline:** N/A, notification date: N/A
**Undergraduate student body:** 8,293 full time, 1,062 part time; 43% male, 57% female; 0% American Indian, 2% Asian, 21% black, 9% Hispanic, 3% multiracial, 0% Pacific Islander, 63% white,

1% international; 99% from in state; 26% live on campus; 1% of students in fraternities, 1% in sororities
**Most popular majors:** 13% Business, Management, Marketing, and Related Support Services, 7% Communication, Journalism, and Related Programs, 21% Education, 8% Homeland Security, Law Enforcement, Firefighting and Related Protective Services, 8% Social Sciences
**Expenses:** 2014-2015: $7,347 in state, $16,997 out of state; room/board: $11,964
**Financial aid:** (716) 878-4901; 87% of undergrads determined to have financial need; average aid package $9,232

## SUNY College–Cortland
Cortland NY
(607) 753-4711
**U.S. News ranking:** Reg. U. (N), No. 70
**Website:** www.cortland.edu/admissions
**Admissions email:** admissions@cortland.edu
**Public;** founded 1868
**Freshman admissions:** selective; 2013-2014: 11,518 applied, 5,394 accepted. Neither SAT nor ACT required. SAT 25/75 percentile: 980-1130. High school rank: N/A
**Early decision deadline:** N/A, notification date: N/A
**Early action deadline:** 11/15, notification date: 1/1
**Application deadline (fall):** rolling
**Undergraduate student body:** 6,281 full time, 119 part time; 44% male, 56% female; 0% American Indian, 1% Asian, 4% black, 10% Hispanic, 2% multiracial, 0% Pacific Islander, 71% white, 1% international; 97% from in state; 53% live on campus; N/A of students in fraternities, N/A in sororities
**Most popular majors:** 6% Communication, Journalism, and Related Programs, 36% Education, 8% Health Professions and Related Programs, 15% Parks, Recreation, Leisure, and Fitness Studies, 9% Social Sciences
**Expenses:** 2014-2015: $7,327 in state, $16,777 out of state; room/board: $11,790
**Financial aid:** (607) 753-4717

## SUNY College of Agriculture and Technology–Cobleskill
Cobleskill NY
(518) 255-5525
**U.S. News ranking:** Reg. Coll. (N), No. 28
**Website:** www.cobleskill.edu
**Admissions email:** admissionsoffice@cobleskill.edu
**Public;** founded 1911
**Freshman admissions:** less selective; 2013-2014: 2,765 applied, 2,021 accepted. Neither SAT nor ACT required. SAT 25/75 percentile: 760-1000. High school rank: 6% in top tenth, 22% in top quarter, 56% in top half
**Early decision deadline:** N/A, notification date: N/A

**Early action deadline:** N/A, notification date: N/A
**Application deadline (fall):** rolling
**Undergraduate student body:** 2,321 full time, 149 part time; 48% male, 52% female; 0% American Indian, 1% Asian, 12% black, 7% Hispanic, 0% multiracial, 0% Pacific Islander, 74% white, 1% international; 90% from in state; 57% live on campus; 0% of students in fraternities, 0% in sororities
**Most popular majors:** 43% Agriculture, Agriculture Operations, and Related Sciences, 15% Business, Management, Marketing, and Related Support Services, 5% Communication, Journalism, and Related Programs, 6% Computer and Information Sciences and Support Services, 13% Natural Resources and Conservation
**Expenses:** 2014-2015: $7,609 in state, $17,259 out of state; room/board: $12,140
**Financial aid:** (518) 255-5623; 76% of undergrads determined to have financial need; average aid package $7,894

## SUNY College of Environmental Science and Forestry
Syracuse NY
(315) 470-6600
**U.S. News ranking:** Nat. U., No. 76
**Website:** www.esf.edu
**Admissions email:** esfinfo@esf.edu
**Public;** founded 1911
**Freshman admissions:** more selective; 2013-2014: 1,538 applied, 777 accepted. Either SAT or ACT required. SAT 25/75 percentile: 1080-1260. High school rank: 27% in top tenth, 66% in top quarter, 95% in top half
**Early decision deadline:** 12/1, notification date: 1/15
**Early action deadline:** N/A, notification date: N/A
**Application deadline (fall):** rolling
**Undergraduate student body:** 1,640 full time, 158 part time; 57% male, 43% female; 0% American Indian, 3% Asian, 1% black, 3% Hispanic, 3% multiracial, 0% Pacific Islander, 87% white, 2% international; 81% from in state; 35% live on campus; 5% of students in fraternities, 5% in sororities
**Most popular majors:** 19% Engineering, General, 37% Environmental Biology, 22% Environmental Science, 9% Landscape Architecture, 11% Natural Resources Management and Policy
**Expenses:** 2014-2015: $7,303 in state, $16,953 out of state; room/board: $14,610
**Financial aid:** (315) 470-6706; 67% of undergrads determined to have financial need; average aid package $14,000

## SUNY College of Technology–Alfred
Alfred NY
(800) 425-3733
**U.S. News ranking:** Reg. Coll. (N), No. 22
**Website:** www.alfredstate.edu/alfred/Default.asp
**Admissions email:** admissions@alfredstate.edu
**Public;** founded 1908
**Freshman admissions:** least selective; 2013-2014: 5,761 applied, 3,165 accepted. Neither SAT nor ACT required. SAT 25/75 percentile: 840-1070. High school rank: N/A
**Early decision deadline:** N/A, notification date: N/A
**Early action deadline:** N/A, notification date: N/A
**Application deadline (fall):** rolling
**Undergraduate student body:** 3,216 full time, 333 part time; 60% male, 40% female; 0% American Indian, 2% Asian, 9% black, 6% Hispanic, 2% multiracial, 0% Pacific Islander, 77% white, 0% international; 94% from in state; 68% live on campus; 3% of students in fraternities, 3% in sororities
**Most popular majors:** Information not available
**Expenses:** 2014-2015: $7,646 in state, $17,296 out of state; room/board: $11,944
**Financial aid:** (607) 587-4251; 82% of undergrads determined to have financial need; average aid package $10,914

## SUNY College of Technology–Canton
Canton NY
(800) 388-7123
**U.S. News ranking:** Reg. Coll. (N), second tier
**Website:** www.canton.edu/
**Admissions email:** admissions@canton.edu
**Public;** founded 1906
**Freshman admissions:** less selective; 2013-2014: 3,438 applied, 2,698 accepted. Neither SAT nor ACT required. SAT 25/75 percentile: 820-1020. High school rank: 4% in top tenth, 15% in top quarter, 50% in top half
**Early decision deadline:** N/A, notification date: N/A
**Early action deadline:** N/A, notification date: N/A
**Application deadline (fall):** 7/1
**Undergraduate student body:** 2,938 full time, 612 part time; 45% male, 55% female; 1% American Indian, 1% Asian, 14% black, 8% Hispanic, 1% multiracial, 0% Pacific Islander, 68% white, 2% international; 97% from in state; 36% live on campus; N/A of students in fraternities, N/A in sororities
**Most popular majors:** 23% Business, Management, Marketing, and Related Support Services, Other, 25% Criminal Justice/Law Enforcement Administration, 7% Engineering Technologies and Engineering-Related Fields, Other, 17% Health/Health Care Administration/Management, 8% Legal Assistant/Paralegal
**Expenses:** 2013-2014: $7,129 in state, $16,969 out of state; room/board: $10,540
**Financial aid:** (315) 386-7616

## SUNY College of Technology–Delhi
Delhi NY
(607) 746-4550
**U.S. News ranking:** Reg. Coll. (N), No. 33
**Website:** www.delhi.edu/
**Admissions email:** enroll@delhi.edu
**Public;** founded 1913
**Freshman admissions:** less selective; 2013-2014: 4,846 applied, 2,843 accepted. Neither SAT nor ACT required. SAT 25/75 percentile: 808-983. High school rank: 3% in top tenth, 14% in top quarter, 42% in top half
**Early decision deadline:** N/A, notification date: N/A
**Early action deadline:** N/A, notification date: N/A
**Application deadline (fall):** rolling
**Undergraduate student body:** 2,627 full time, 799 part time; 46% male, 54% female; 1% American Indian, 2% Asian, 16% black, 12% Hispanic, 0% multiracial, 0% Pacific Islander, 64% white, 1% international; 97% from in state; 60% live on campus; N/A of students in fraternities, N/A in sororities
**Most popular majors:** 6% Architectural and Building Sciences/Technology, 15% Business Administration and Management, General, 15% Business, Management, Marketing, and Related Support Services, Other, 28% Hospitality Administration/Management, General, 26% Registered Nursing/Registered Nurse
**Expenses:** 2014-2015: $7,740 in state, $17,390 out of state; room/board: $10,970
**Financial aid:** (607) 746-4570; 96% of undergrads determined to have financial need

## SUNY College–Old Westbury
Old Westbury NY
(516) 876-3073
**U.S. News ranking:** Nat. Lib. Arts, second tier
**Website:** www.oldwestbury.edu
**Admissions email:** enroll@oldwestbury.edu
**Public;** founded 1965
**Freshman admissions:** selective; 2013-2014: 3,341 applied, 1,939 accepted. Either SAT or ACT required. SAT 25/75 percentile: 920-1080. High school rank: N/A
**Early decision deadline:** N/A, notification date: N/A
**Early action deadline:** N/A, notification date: N/A
**Application deadline (fall):** rolling
**Undergraduate student body:** 3,556 full time, 602 part time; 42% male, 58% female; 0% American Indian, 9% Asian, 31% black, 21% Hispanic, 3% multiracial, 0% Pacific Islander, 32% white, 0% international; 98% from in state; 21% live on campus; 2% of students in fraternities, 2% in sororities
**Most popular majors:** 12% Accounting, 7% Criminology, 16% Psychology, General, 8% Social Sciences, Other, 9% Speech Communication and Rhetoric
**Expenses:** 2014-2015: $8,436 in state, $18,086 out of state; room/board: $10,390

Financial aid: (516) 876-3222; 81% of undergrads determined to have financial need; average aid package $9,420

## SUNY College–Oneonta

Oneonta NY
(607) 436-2524
U.S. News ranking: Reg. U. (N), No. 41
Website: www.oneonta.edu
Admissions email: admissions@oneonta.edu
Public; founded 1889
Freshman admissions: selective; 2013-2014: 12,360 applied, 5,310 accepted. Either SAT or ACT required. SAT 25/75 percentile: 1020-1180. High school rank: 21% in top tenth, 58% in top quarter, 92% in top half
Early decision deadline: N/A, notification date: N/A
Early action deadline: 11/15, notification date: 12/1
Application deadline (fall): rolling
Undergraduate student body: 5,688 full time, 132 part time; 40% male, 60% female; 0% American Indian, 2% Asian, 3% black, 9% Hispanic, 0% multiracial, 0% Pacific Islander, 82% white, 1% international; 99% from in state; 50% live on campus; 1% of students in fraternities, 1% in sororities
Most popular majors: 7% Business, Management, Marketing, and Related Support Services, 18% Education, 16% Family and Consumer Sciences/Human Sciences, 9% Psychology, 11% Visual and Performing Arts
Expenses: 2014-2015: $7,220 in state, $16,670 out of state; room/board: $11,100
Financial aid: (607) 436-2532; 59% of undergrads determined to have financial need; average aid package $9,155

## SUNY College–Potsdam

Potsdam NY
(315) 267-2180
U.S. News ranking: Reg. U. (N), No. 87
Website: www.potsdam.edu
Admissions email: admissions@potsdam.edu
Public; founded 1816
Freshman admissions: selective; 2013-2014: 4,764 applied, 3,257 accepted. Neither SAT nor ACT required. SAT 25/75 percentile: 930-1170. High school rank: 10% in top tenth, 23% in top quarter, 61% in top half
Early decision deadline: N/A, notification date: N/A
Early action deadline: N/A, notification date: N/A
Application deadline (fall): rolling
Undergraduate student body: 3,596 full time, 111 part time; 43% male, 57% female; 1% American Indian, 1% Asian, 7% black, 8% Hispanic, 3% multiracial, 0% Pacific Islander, 72% white, 1% international; 97% from in state; 61% live on campus; 1% of students in fraternities, 2% in sororities
Most popular majors: 23% Education, 9% English Language and Literature/Letters, 8% Psychology, 9% Social Sciences, 14% Visual and Performing Arts

Expenses: 2014-2015: $7,553 in state, $17,203 out of state; room/board: $11,370
Financial aid: (315) 267-2162; 72% of undergrads determined to have financial need; average aid package $13,626

## SUNY Empire State College

Saratoga Springs NY
(518) 587-2100
U.S. News ranking: Reg. U. (N), unranked
Website: www.esc.edu
Admissions email: admissions@esc.edu
Public; founded 1971
Freshman admissions: N/A; 2013-2014: 1,342 applied, 1,100 accepted. Neither SAT nor ACT required. ACT 25/75 percentile: N/A. High school rank: N/A
Early decision deadline: N/A, notification date: N/A
Early action deadline: N/A, notification date: N/A
Application deadline (fall): rolling
Undergraduate student body: 4,231 full time, 6,620 part time; 38% male, 62% female; 1% American Indian, 2% Asian, 17% black, 9% Hispanic, 2% multiracial, 0% Pacific Islander, 66% white, 1% international; 93% from in state; 0% live on campus; 0% of students in fraternities, 0% in sororities
Most popular majors: 38% Business, Management, Marketing, and Related Support Services, 7% English Language and Literature/Letters, 8% Psychology, 25% Public Administration and Social Service Professions
Expenses: 2013-2014: $6,315 in state, $15,765 out of state; room/board: N/A
Financial aid: (518) 587-2100

## SUNY–Fredonia

Fredonia NY
(800) 252-1212
U.S. News ranking: Reg. U. (N), No. 41
Website: www.fredonia.edu
Admissions email: admissions.office@fredonia.edu
Public; founded 1826
Freshman admissions: selective; 2013-2014: 6,040 applied, 3,156 accepted. Either SAT or ACT required. SAT 25/75 percentile: 950-1140. High school rank: 12% in top tenth, 39% in top quarter, 81% in top half
Early decision deadline: 11/1, notification date: 12/1
Early action deadline: N/A, notification date: N/A
Application deadline (fall): rolling
Undergraduate student body: 4,958 full time, 145 part time; 45% male, 55% female; 0% American Indian, 1% Asian, 4% black, 5% Hispanic, 2% multiracial, 0% Pacific Islander, 81% white, 3% international; 98% from in state; 44% live on campus; 1% of students in fraternities, 1% in sororities
Most popular majors: 11% Business Administration and Management, General, 5% Education/Teaching of Individuals with Multiple Disabilities, 5% Elementary Education and

Teaching, 5% Music Teacher Education, 5% Psychology, General
Expenses: 2014-2015: $7,700 in state, $16,850 out of state; room/board: $11,900
Financial aid: (716) 673-3253; 69% of undergrads determined to have financial need; average aid package $10,068

## SUNY–Geneseo

Geneseo NY
(585) 245-5571
U.S. News ranking: Reg. U. (N), No. 14
Website: www.geneseo.edu
Admissions email: admissions@geneseo.edu
Public; founded 1871
Freshman admissions: more selective; 2013-2014: 9,069 applied, 4,786 accepted. Either SAT or ACT required. SAT 25/75 percentile: 1178-1360. High school rank: 48% in top tenth, 84% in top quarter, 99% in top half
Early decision deadline: 11/15, notification date: 12/15
Early action deadline: N/A, notification date: N/A
Application deadline (fall): 1/1
Undergraduate student body: 5,386 full time, 118 part time; 42% male, 58% female; 0% American Indian, 7% Asian, 3% black, 6% Hispanic, 2% multiracial, 0% Pacific Islander, 75% white, 2% international; 98% from in state; 55% live on campus; 15% of students in fraternities, 24% in sororities
Most popular majors: 12% Biological and Biomedical Sciences, 11% Business, Management, Marketing, and Related Support Services, 20% Education, 11% Psychology, 15% Social Sciences
Expenses: 2014-2015: $7,774 in state, $17,424 out of state; room/board: $11,518
Financial aid: (585) 245-5731; 48% of undergrads determined to have financial need; average aid package $10,658

## SUNY Institute of Technology–Utica/Rome

Utica NY
(315) 792-7500
U.S. News ranking: Reg. U. (N), No. 106
Website: www.sunyit.edu
Admissions email: admissions@sunyit.edu
Public; founded 1966
Freshman admissions: selective; 2013-2014: 1,952 applied, 930 accepted. Either SAT or ACT required. SAT 25/75 percentile: 1010-1160. High school rank: 13% in top tenth, 45% in top quarter, 87% in top half
Early decision deadline: N/A, notification date: N/A
Early action deadline: 11/15, notification date: 12/15
Application deadline (fall): 8/1
Undergraduate student body: 1,424 full time, 383 part time; 59% male, 41% female; 0% American Indian, 3% Asian, 8% black, 5% Hispanic, 0% multiracial, 0% Pacific Islander, 82% white, 1% international; 99% from in

state; 34% live on campus; N/A of students in fraternities, N/A in sororities
Most popular majors: 18% Business Administration and Management, General, 7% Health Information/Medical Records Administration/Administrator, 8% Mechanical Engineering/Mechanical Technology/Technician, 9% Psychology, General, 10% Registered Nursing/Registered Nurse
Expenses: 2014-2015: $7,530 in state, $17,155 out of state; room/board: $12,250
Financial aid: (315) 792-7210; 65% of undergrads determined to have financial need; average aid package $8,816

## SUNY Maritime College

Throggs Neck NY
(718) 409-7221
U.S. News ranking: Reg. Coll. (N), No. 20
Website: www.sunymaritime.edu
Admissions email: admissions@sunymaritime.edu
Public; founded 1874
Freshman admissions: selective; 2013-2014: 1,279 applied, 818 accepted. Either SAT or ACT required. SAT 25/75 percentile: 930-1170. High school rank: 7% in top tenth, 30% in top quarter, 73% in top half
Early decision deadline: 11/1, notification date: 12/20
Early action deadline: N/A, notification date: N/A
Application deadline (fall): 1/31
Undergraduate student body: 1,518 full time, 83 part time; 89% male, 11% female; 0% American Indian, 4% Asian, 4% black, 9% Hispanic, 0% multiracial, 0% Pacific Islander, 72% white, 3% international; 76% from in state; 84% live on campus; 0% of students in fraternities, 0% in sororities
Most popular majors: 20% Business, Management, and Related Support Services, Other, 34% Hospitality Administration/Management, 7% Industrial Engineering, 9% Mechanical Engineering, 20% Naval Architecture and Marine Engineering
Expenses: 2014-2015: $7,446 in state, $17,096 out of state; room/board: $11,040
Financial aid: (718) 409-7254; 36% of undergrads determined to have financial need

## SUNY–New Paltz

New Paltz NY
(845) 257-3200
U.S. News ranking: Reg. U. (N), No. 25
Website: www.newpaltz.edu
Admissions email: admissions@newpaltz.edu
Public; founded 1828
Freshman admissions: more selective; 2013-2014: 13,541 applied, 5,899 accepted. Either SAT or ACT required. SAT 25/75 percentile: 1030-1220. High school rank: 38% in top tenth, 70% in top quarter, 92% in top half
Early decision deadline: N/A, notification date: N/A

Early action deadline: 11/15, notification date: 12/15
Application deadline (fall): 4/1
Undergraduate student body: 6,060 full time, 510 part time; 37% male, 63% female; 0% American Indian, 5% Asian, 5% black, 14% Hispanic, 2% multiracial, 0% Pacific Islander, 66% white, 2% international; 97% from in state; 43% live on campus; 4% of students in fraternities, 4% in sororities
Most popular majors: 12% Business, Management, Marketing, and Related Support Services, 10% Communication, Journalism, and Related Programs, 17% Education, 12% Social Sciences, 12% Visual and Performing Arts
Expenses: 2014-2015: $7,408 in state, $17,058 out of state; room/board: $10,895
Financial aid: (845) 257-3250; 56% of undergrads determined to have financial need; average aid package $9,904

## SUNY–Oswego

Oswego NY
(315) 312-2250
U.S. News ranking: Reg. U. (N), No. 56
Website: www.oswego.edu
Admissions email: admiss@oswego.edu
Public; founded 1861
Freshman admissions: selective; 2013-2014: 10,351 applied, 5,034 accepted. Either SAT or ACT required. SAT 25/75 percentile: 1040-1180. High school rank: 15% in top tenth, 55% in top quarter, 87% in top half
Early decision deadline: 11/30, notification date: 12/15
Early action deadline: N/A, notification date: N/A
Application deadline (fall): rolling
Undergraduate student body: 6,954 full time, 374 part time; 48% male, 52% female; 0% American Indian, 2% Asian, 6% black, 9% Hispanic, 2% multiracial, 0% Pacific Islander, 79% white, 2% international; 98% from in state; 58% live on campus; 7% of students in fraternities, 6% in sororities
Most popular majors: 22% Business, Management, Marketing, and Related Support Services, 11% Communication, Journalism, and Related Programs, 19% Education, 10% Psychology, 8% Visual and Performing Arts
Expenses: 2014-2015: $7,501 in state, $17,151 out of state; room/board: $12,690
Financial aid: (315) 312-2248; 66% of undergrads determined to have financial need; average aid package $9,973

## SUNY–Plattsburgh

Plattsburgh NY
(888) 673-0012
U.S. News ranking: Reg. U. (N), No. 74
Website: www.plattsburgh.edu
Admissions email: admissions@plattsburgh.edu
Public; founded 1889
Freshman admissions: selective; 2013-2014: 8,193 applied, 3,739 accepted. Either SAT or ACT required. SAT 25/75 percentile: 930-1120. High

school rank: 12% in top tenth, 45% in top quarter, 85% in top half
**Early decision deadline:** N/A, notification date: N/A
**Early action deadline:** N/A, notification date: N/A
**Application deadline (fall):** rolling
**Undergraduate student body:** 5,186 full time, 453 part time; 44% male, 56% female; 0% American Indian, 2% Asian, 6% black, 8% Hispanic, 2% multiracial, 0% Pacific Islander, 71% white, 6% international; 96% from in state; 44% live on campus; 6% of students in fraternities, 5% in sororities
**Most popular majors:** 22% Business, Management, Marketing, and Related Support Services, 10% Communication, Journalism, and Related Programs, 10% Education, 9% Homeland Security, Law Enforcement, Firefighting and Related Protective Services, 7% Psychology
**Expenses:** 2014-2015: $7,497 in state, $17,147 out of state; room/board: $10,972
**Financial aid:** (518) 564-4061; 65% of undergrads determined to have financial need; average aid package $12,391

## Syracuse University
Syracuse NY
(315) 443-3611
**U.S. News ranking:** Nat. U., No. 58
**Website:** syr.edu
**Admissions email:** orange@syr.edu
**Private;** founded 1870
**Freshman admissions:** more selective; 2013-2014: 28,269 applied, 13,990 accepted. Either SAT or ACT required. SAT 25/75 percentile: 1040-1270. High school rank: 39% in top tenth, 71% in top quarter, 94% in top half
**Early decision deadline:** 11/15, notification date: 1/1
**Early action deadline:** N/A, notification date: N/A
**Application deadline (fall):** 1/1
**Undergraduate student body:** 14,422 full time, 675 part time; 45% male, 55% female; 1% American Indian, 8% Asian, 9% black, 11% Hispanic, 3% multiracial, 0% Pacific Islander, 56% white, 9% international; 44% from in state; 75% live on campus; 22% of students in fraternities, 27% in sororities
**Most popular majors:** 16% Business, Management, Marketing, and Related Support Services, 13% Communication, Journalism, and Related Programs, 8% Engineering, 12% Social Sciences, 11% Visual and Performing Arts
**Expenses:** 2014-2015: $41,886; room/board: $14,460
**Financial aid:** (315) 443-1513; 58% of undergrads determined to have financial need; average aid package $32,540

## Touro College
New York NY
(212) 436-0400
**U.S. News ranking:** Reg. U. (N), second tier
**Website:** www.touro.edu/
**Admissions email:** lasadmit@touro.edu
**Private;** founded 1971

Freshman admissions: selective; 2013-2014: 1,220 applied, 793 accepted. Neither SAT nor ACT required. SAT 25/75 percentile: 1040-1260. High school rank: N/A
**Early decision deadline:** N/A, notification date: N/A
**Early action deadline:** N/A, notification date: N/A
**Application deadline (fall):** rolling
**Undergraduate student body:** 5,118 full time, 1,687 part time; 31% male, 69% female; 0% American Indian, 3% Asian, 14% black, 9% Hispanic, 0% multiracial, 0% Pacific Islander, 64% white, 3% international
**Most popular majors:** 13% Accounting, 12% Biology/Biological Sciences, General, 6% Business Administration and Management, General, 33% Psychology, General, 5% Speech Communication and Rhetoric
**Expenses:** 2014-2015: $15,600; room/board: $12,359
**Financial aid:** (718) 252-7800; 75% of undergrads determined to have financial need; average aid package $8,612

## Union College
Schenectady NY
(888) 843-6688
**U.S. News ranking:** Nat. Lib. Arts, No. 41
**Website:** www.union.edu
**Admissions email:** admissions@union.edu
**Private;** founded 1795
**Freshman admissions:** more selective; 2013-2014: 5,725 applied, 2,134 accepted. Neither SAT nor ACT required. SAT 25/75 percentile: 1220-1400. High school rank: 64% in top tenth, 84% in top quarter, 97% in top half
**Early decision deadline:** 11/15, notification date: 12/15
**Early action deadline:** N/A, notification date: N/A
**Application deadline (fall):** 1/15
**Undergraduate student body:** 2,225 full time, 21 part time; 54% male, 46% female; 0% American Indian, 6% Asian, 4% black, 7% Hispanic, 2% multiracial, 0% Pacific Islander, 75% white, 6% international; 38% from in state; 86% live on campus; 39% of students in fraternities, 39% in sororities
**Most popular majors:** 7% Biology/Biological Sciences, General, 11% Economics, General, 6% History, General, 6% Mechanical Engineering, 13% Psychology, General
**Expenses:** 2014-2015: $48,384; room/board: $11,856
**Financial aid:** (518) 388-6123; 47% of undergrads determined to have financial need; average aid package $36,845

## United States Merchant Marine Academy
Kings Point NY
(516) 773-5391
**U.S. News ranking:** Reg. Coll. (N), No. 3
**Website:** www.usmma.edu
**Admissions email:** admissions@usmma.edu
**Public;** founded 1943

**Freshman admissions:** more selective; 2013-2014: 2,252 applied, 409 accepted. Either SAT or ACT required. SAT 25/75 percentile: 1183-1351. High school rank: 33% in top tenth, 57% in top quarter, 92% in top half
**Early decision deadline:** N/A, notification date: N/A
**Early action deadline:** N/A, notification date: N/A
**Application deadline (fall):** 3/1
**Undergraduate student body:** 958 full time, 0 part time; 85% male, 15% female; 1% American Indian, 6% Asian, 3% black, 9% Hispanic, 0% multiracial, 0% Pacific Islander, 79% white, 1% international; N/A from in state; 100% live on campus; N/A of students in fraternities, N/A in sororities
**Most popular majors:** 22% Logistics, Materials, and Supply Chain Management, 15% Marine Science/Merchant Marine Officer, 22% Marine Transportation, Other, 18% Naval Architecture and Marine Engineering, 23% Naval Architecture and Marine Engineering
**Expenses:** 2014-2015: $1,032 in state, $1,032 out of state; room/board: $0
**Financial aid:** (516) 773-5295; 100% of undergrads determined to have financial need; average aid package $4,082

## United States Military Academy
West Point NY
(845) 938-4041
**U.S. News ranking:** Nat. Lib. Arts, No. 24
**Website:** www.usma.edu
**Admissions email:** admissions@usma.edu
**Public;** founded 1802
**Freshman admissions:** more selective; 2013-2014: 15,408 applied, 1,380 accepted. Either SAT or ACT required. SAT 25/75 percentile: 1180-1385. High school rank: 46% in top tenth, 74% in top quarter, 94% in top half
**Early decision deadline:** N/A, notification date: N/A
**Early action deadline:** N/A, notification date: N/A
**Application deadline (fall):** 2/28
**Undergraduate student body:** 4,591 full time, 0 part time; 83% male, 17% female; 1% American Indian, 6% Asian, 8% black, 10% Hispanic, 4% multiracial, 1% Pacific Islander, 69% white, 1% international; 7% from in state; 100% live on campus; 0% of students in fraternities, 0% in sororities
**Most popular majors:** 7% Business, Management, Marketing, and Related Support Services, 23% Engineering, 5% Engineering Technologies and Engineering-Related Fields, 8% Foreign Languages, Literatures, and Linguistics, 19% Social Sciences
**Expenses:** N/A
**Financial aid:** (845) 938-4262; 0% of undergrads determined to have financial need; average aid package $0

## University at Albany–SUNY
Albany NY
(518) 442-5435
**U.S. News ranking:** Nat. U., No. 126
**Website:** www.albany.edu
**Admissions email:** ugadmissions@albany.edu
**Public;** founded 1844
**Freshman admissions:** selective; 2013-2014: 21,591 applied, 12,028 accepted. Either SAT or ACT required. SAT 25/75 percentile: 1010-1180. High school rank: 19% in top tenth, 53% in top quarter, 88% in top half
**Early decision deadline:** N/A, notification date: N/A
**Early action deadline:** 11/15, notification date: 1/15
**Application deadline (fall):** 3/1
**Undergraduate student body:** 12,055 full time, 767 part time; 52% male, 48% female; 0% American Indian, 8% Asian, 14% black, 13% Hispanic, 3% multiracial, 0% Pacific Islander, 53% white, 5% international; 94% from in state; 59% live on campus; 1% of students in fraternities, 2% in sororities
**Most popular majors:** 10% Biological and Biomedical Sciences, 10% Business, Management, Marketing, and Related Support Services, 13% English Language and Literature/Letters, 11% Psychology, 27% Social Sciences
**Expenses:** 2014-2015: $8,527 in state, $20,167 out of state; room/board: $11,986
**Financial aid:** (518) 442-5757; 64% of undergrads determined to have financial need; average aid package $10,279

## University at Buffalo–SUNY
Buffalo NY
(716) 645-6900
**U.S. News ranking:** Nat. U., No. 103
**Website:** www.buffalo.edu
**Admissions email:** ub-admissions@buffalo.edu
**Public;** founded 1846
**Freshman admissions:** more selective; 2013-2014: 23,207 applied, 13,134 accepted. Either SAT or ACT required. SAT 25/75 percentile: 1050-1260. High school rank: 28% in top tenth, 63% in top quarter, 93% in top half
**Early decision deadline:** 11/1, notification date: 12/15
**Early action deadline:** N/A, notification date: N/A
**Application deadline (fall):** rolling
**Undergraduate student body:** 18,091 full time, 1,740 part time; 54% male, 46% female; 0% American Indian, 13% Asian, 7% black, 7% Hispanic, 2% multiracial, 0% Pacific Islander, 50% white, 16% international; 96% from in state; 35% live on campus; 2% of students in fraternities, 2% in sororities
**Most popular majors:** 9% Biological and Biomedical Sciences, 17% Business, Management, Marketing, and Related Support Services, 13% Engineering, 12% Psychology, 15% Social Sciences

**Expenses:** 2014-2015: $8,426 in state, $20,366 out of state; room/board: $12,200
**Financial aid:** (866) 838-7257; 68% of undergrads determined to have financial need; average aid package $9,395

## University of Rochester
Rochester NY
(585) 275-3221
**U.S. News ranking:** Nat. U., No. 33
**Website:** www.rochester.edu
**Admissions email:** admit@admissions.rochester.edu
**Private;** founded 1850
**Freshman admissions:** most selective; 2013-2014: 17,244 applied, 6,153 accepted. Neither SAT nor ACT required. SAT 25/75 percentile: 1250-1450. High school rank: 75% in top tenth, 97% in top quarter, 100% in top half
**Early decision deadline:** 11/1, notification date: 12/15
**Early action deadline:** N/A, notification date: N/A
**Application deadline (fall):** 1/1
**Undergraduate student body:** 5,837 full time, 340 part time; 48% male, 52% female; 0% American Indian, 11% Asian, 5% black, 6% Hispanic, 3% multiracial, 0% Pacific Islander, 52% white, 16% international; 42% from in state; 93% live on campus; 20% of students in fraternities, 23% in sororities
**Most popular majors:** 13% Biological and Biomedical Sciences, 11% Engineering, 10% Health Professions and Related Programs, 13% Psychology, 20% Social Sciences
**Expenses:** 2014-2015: $46,960; room/board: $13,708
**Financial aid:** (585) 275-3226; 52% of undergrads determined to have financial need; average aid package $38,021

## Utica College
Utica NY
(315) 792-3006
**U.S. News ranking:** Reg. U. (N), No. 120
**Website:** www.utica.edu
**Admissions email:** admiss@utica.edu
**Private;** founded 1946
**Freshman admissions:** less selective; 2013-2014: 3,689 applied, 3,151 accepted. Neither SAT nor ACT required. SAT 25/75 percentile: 830-1050. High school rank: 11% in top tenth, 28% in top quarter, 60% in top half
**Early decision deadline:** N/A, notification date: N/A
**Early action deadline:** N/A, notification date: N/A
**Application deadline (fall):** rolling
**Undergraduate student body:** 2,230 full time, 651 part time; 39% male, 61% female; 1% American Indian, 3% Asian, 10% black, 8% Hispanic, 2% multiracial, 0% Pacific Islander, 70% white, 2% international; 85% from in state; 44% live on campus; 2% of students in fraternities, 2% in sororities
**Most popular majors:** 4% Biological and Biomedical Sciences, 9% Business, Management, Marketing, and Related Support Services, 36% Health Professions

and Related Programs, 21% Homeland Security, Law Enforcement, Firefighting and Related Protective Services, 7% Psychology
**Expenses:** 2014-2015: $33,736; room/board: $11,934
**Financial aid:** (315) 792-3179; 91% of undergrads determined to have financial need; average aid package $25,160

## Vassar College
Poughkeepsie NY
(845) 437-7300
**U.S. News ranking:** Nat. Lib. Arts, No. 11
**Website:** www.vassar.edu
**Admissions email:** admission@vassar.edu
**Private;** founded 1861
**Freshman admissions:** most selective; 2013-2014: 7,597 applied, 1,832 accepted. Either SAT or ACT required. SAT 25/75 percentile: 1310-1480. High school rank: 66% in top tenth, 93% in top quarter, 99% in top half
**Early decision deadline:** 11/15, notification date: 12/15
**Early action deadline:** N/A, notification date: N/A
**Application deadline (fall):** 1/1
**Undergraduate student body:** 2,437 full time, 40 part time; 44% male, 56% female; 0% American Indian, 10% Asian, 6% black, 11% Hispanic, 6% multiracial, 0% Pacific Islander, 61% white, 6% international; 27% from in state; 95% live on campus; 0% of students in fraternities, 0% in sororities
**Most popular majors:** 13% Biological and Biomedical Sciences, 6% English Language and Literature/Letters, 9% Psychology, 28% Social Sciences, 13% Visual and Performing Arts
**Expenses:** 2014-2015: $49,570; room/board: $11,570
**Financial aid:** (845) 437-5320; 58% of undergrads determined to have financial need; average aid package $46,214

## Vaughn College of Aeronautics and Technology
Flushing NY
(718) 429-6600
**U.S. News ranking:** Reg. Coll. (N), No. 22
**Website:** www.vaughn.edu
**Admissions email:** admitme@vaughn.edu
**Private;** founded 1932
**Freshman admissions:** less selective; 2013-2014: 837 applied, 645 accepted. SAT required. SAT 25/75 percentile: 885-1093. High school rank: N/A
**Early decision deadline:** N/A, notification date: N/A
**Early action deadline:** N/A, notification date: N/A
**Application deadline (fall):** rolling
**Undergraduate student body:** 1,308 full time, 417 part time; 88% male, 12% female; 1% American Indian, 10% Asian, 20% black, 35% Hispanic, 6% multiracial, 3% Pacific Islander, 17% white, 2% international; 86% from in state; 10% live on campus; 0% of students in fraternities, 0% in sororities

**Most popular majors:** 70% Aviation/Airway Management and Operations, 1% Business Administration and Management, General, 13% Electrical and Electronic Engineering Technologies/Technicians, Other, 1% Mechanical Engineering, 12% Mechanical Engineering/Mechanical Technology/Technician
**Expenses:** 2014-2015: $21,740; room/board: $12,355
**Financial aid:** (718) 429-6600; 70% of undergrads determined to have financial need; average aid package $22,266

## Wagner College
Staten Island NY
(718) 390-3411
**U.S. News ranking:** Reg. U. (N), No. 28
**Website:** www.wagner.edu
**Admissions email:** adm@wagner.edu
**Private;** founded 1883
**Freshman admissions:** selective; 2013-2014: 2,942 applied, 2,056 accepted. Neither SAT nor ACT required. SAT 25/75 percentile: 1050-1270. High school rank: 15% in top tenth, 73% in top quarter, 92% in top half
**Early decision deadline:** 12/1, notification date: 1/2
**Early action deadline:** N/A, notification date: N/A
**Application deadline (fall):** 2/15
**Undergraduate student body:** 1,761 full time, 77 part time; 35% male, 65% female; 0% American Indian, 3% Asian, 6% black, 9% Hispanic, 2% multiracial, 0% Pacific Islander, 66% white, 3% international; 52% from in state; 69% live on campus; 9% of students in fraternities, 15% in sororities
**Most popular majors:** 16% Business, Management, Marketing, and Related Support Services, 25% Health Professions and Related Programs, 7% Psychology, 7% Social Sciences, 21% Visual and Performing Arts
**Expenses:** 2014-2015: $40,750; room/board: $12,450
**Financial aid:** (718) 390-3183; 65% of undergrads determined to have financial need; average aid package $25,502

## Webb Institute
Glen Cove NY
(516) 671-8355
**U.S. News ranking:** Engineering, unranked
**Website:** www.webb.edu
**Admissions email:** admissions@webb.edu
**Private;** founded 1889
**Freshman admissions:** most selective; 2013-2014: 105 applied, 31 accepted. SAT required. SAT 25/75 percentile: 1360-1510. High school rank: 83% in top tenth, 83% in top quarter, 100% in top half
**Early decision deadline:** 10/15, notification date: 12/15
**Early action deadline:** N/A, notification date: N/A
**Application deadline (fall):** 2/15
**Undergraduate student body:** 82 full time, N/A part time; 79% male, 21% female; 0% American Indian, 9% Asian, 0% black, 0% Hispanic, 6% multiracial,

0% Pacific Islander, 85% white, 0% international; 27% from in state; 100% live on campus; 0% of students in fraternities, 0% in sororities
**Most popular majors:** 100% Naval Architecture and Marine Engineering
**Expenses:** 2014-2015: $44,000; room/board: $14,050
**Financial aid:** (516) 671-2213; 21% of undergrads determined to have financial need; average aid package $49,015

## Wells College
Aurora NY
(800) 952-9355
**U.S. News ranking:** Nat. Lib. Arts, No. 148
**Website:** www.wells.edu
**Admissions email:** admissions@wells.edu
**Private**
**Freshman admissions:** selective; 2013-2014: 2,214 applied, 1,321 accepted. Neither SAT nor ACT required. SAT 25/75 percentile: 930-1070. High school rank: 32% in top tenth, 64% in top quarter, 86% in top half
**Early decision deadline:** N/A, notification date: N/A
**Early action deadline:** N/A, notification date: N/A
**Application deadline (fall):** N/A
**Undergraduate student body:** 524 full time, 10 part time; 34% male, 66% female; 1% American Indian, 2% Asian, 11% black, 8% Hispanic, 3% multiracial, 0% Pacific Islander, 63% white, 4% international
**Most popular majors:** Information not available
**Expenses:** 2014-2015: $36,700; room/board: $12,700
**Financial aid:** (315) 364-3289; 92% of undergrads determined to have financial need; average aid package $31,346

## Yeshiva University
New York NY
(212) 960-5277
**U.S. News ranking:** Nat. U., No. 48
**Website:** www.yu.edu
**Admissions email:** yuadmit@ymail.yu.edu
**Private;** founded 1886
**Freshman admissions:** more selective; 2013-2014: 1,580 applied, 1,299 accepted. Either SAT or ACT required. SAT 25/75 percentile: 1100-1370. High school rank: 45% in top tenth, 75% in top quarter, 97% in top half
**Early decision deadline:** 11/1, notification date: 12/15
**Early action deadline:** N/A, notification date: N/A
**Application deadline (fall):** 2/1
**Undergraduate student body:** 2,832 full time, 53 part time; 53% male, 47% female; 0% American Indian, 0% Asian, 0% black, 0% Hispanic, 0% multiracial, 0% Pacific Islander, 92% white, 6% international; 35% from in state; 69% live on campus; 0% of students in fraternities, 0% in sororities
**Most popular majors:** 10% Accounting, 18% Biology/Biological Sciences, General, 12% Business Administration and Management, General, 15% Psychology, General, 10% Social Sciences, General

**Expenses:** 2014-2015: $38,730; room/board: $11,250
**Financial aid:** (212) 960-5399; 58% of undergrads determined to have financial need; average aid package $31,293

## Appalachian State University
Boone NC
(828) 262-2120
**U.S. News ranking:** Reg. U. (S), No. 9
**Website:** www.appstate.edu
**Admissions email:** admissions@appstate.edu
**Public;** founded 1899
**Freshman admissions:** selective; 2013-2014: 13,673 applied, 8,992 accepted. Either SAT or ACT required. SAT 25/75 percentile: 1050-1220. High school rank: 21% in top tenth, 58% in top quarter, 92% in top half
**Early decision deadline:** N/A, notification date: N/A
**Early action deadline:** N/A, notification date: N/A
**Application deadline (fall):** 3/15
**Undergraduate student body:** 15,115 full time, 910 part time; 47% male, 53% female; 0% American Indian, 1% Asian, 3% black, 4% Hispanic, 2% multiracial, 0% Pacific Islander, 86% white, 1% international; 92% from in state; 36% live on campus; 9% of students in fraternities, 13% in sororities
**Most popular majors:** 20% Business, Management, Marketing, and Related Support Services, 7% Communication, Journalism, and Related Programs, 14% Education, 8% Psychology, 7% Social Sciences
**Expenses:** 2014-2015: $6,553 in state, $19,720 out of state; room/board: $7,675
**Financial aid:** (828) 262-2190; 51% of undergrads determined to have financial need; average aid package $10,581

## Barton College
Wilson NC
(800) 345-4973
**U.S. News ranking:** Reg. Coll. (S), No. 25
**Website:** www.barton.edu
**Admissions email:** enroll@barton.edu
**Private;** founded 1902
**Affiliation:** Christian Church (Disciples of Christ)
**Freshman admissions:** selective; 2013-2014: 2,933 applied, 1,225 accepted. Either SAT or ACT required. SAT 25/75 percentile: 840-1020. High school rank: 13% in top tenth, 38% in top quarter, 72% in top half
**Early decision deadline:** N/A, notification date: N/A
**Early action deadline:** N/A, notification date: N/A
**Application deadline (fall):** rolling
**Undergraduate student body:** 900 full time, 157 part time; 31% male, 69% female; 0% American Indian, 1% Asian, 25% black, 4% Hispanic, 3% multiracial, 0% Pacific Islander, 59% white, 3% international; 87% from in state; 38% live on campus; 19% of students in fraternities, 13% in sororities

**Most popular majors:** 14% Business Administration and Management, General, 6% Elementary Education and Teaching, 6% Liberal Arts and Sciences/Liberal Studies, 8% Registered Nursing/Registered Nurse, 20% Social Work
**Expenses:** 2014-2015: $26,664; room/board: $8,906
**Financial aid:** (252) 399-6323; 90% of undergrads determined to have financial need; average aid package $18,922

## Belmont Abbey College
Belmont NC
(704) 461-6665
**U.S. News ranking:** Reg. Coll. (S), No. 37
**Website:** www.belmontabbeycollege.edu
**Admissions email:** admissions@bac.edu
**Private;** founded 1876
**Affiliation:** Roman Catholic
**Freshman admissions:** less selective; 2013-2014: 1,976 applied, 1,336 accepted. Neither SAT nor ACT required. SAT 25/75 percentile: 868-1070. High school rank: 8% in top tenth, 26% in top quarter, 60% in top half
**Early decision deadline:** N/A, notification date: N/A
**Early action deadline:** N/A, notification date: N/A
**Application deadline (fall):** 8/1
**Undergraduate student body:** 1,549 full time, 98 part time; 42% male, 58% female; 0% American Indian, 1% Asian, 27% black, 2% Hispanic, 0% multiracial, 0% Pacific Islander, 37% white, 2% international; 72% from in state; 42% live on campus; 2% of students in fraternities, 3% in sororities
**Most popular majors:** 10% Accounting, 23% Business Administration and Management, General, 11% Education, General, 9% Elementary Education and Teaching, 8% Liberal Arts and Sciences/Liberal Studies
**Expenses:** 2014-2015: $18,500; room/board: $10,094
**Financial aid:** (704) 825-6718; 78% of undergrads determined to have financial need; average aid package $11,718

## Bennett College[1]
Greensboro NC
(336) 370-8624
**U.S. News ranking:** Nat. Lib. Arts, second tier
**Website:** www.bennett.edu
**Admissions email:** admiss@bennett.edu
**Private;** founded 1873
**Affiliation:** United Methodist
**Application deadline (fall):** rolling
**Undergraduate student body:** N/A full time, N/A part time
**Expenses:** 2013-2014: $17,130; room/board: $7,576
**Financial aid:** (336) 517-2205

## Brevard College
Brevard NC
(828) 884-8300
**U.S. News ranking:** Nat. Lib. Arts, second tier
**Website:** www.brevard.edu
**Admissions email:** admissions@brevard.edu
**Private;** founded 1853

**Affiliation:** Methodist
**Freshman admissions:** less selective; 2013-2014: 2,299 applied, 1,032 accepted. Either SAT or ACT required. SAT 25/75 percentile: 850-1050. High school rank: 5% in top tenth, 24% in top quarter, 57% in top half
**Early decision deadline:** N/A, notification date: N/A
**Early action deadline:** N/A, notification date: N/A
**Application deadline (fall):** rolling
**Undergraduate student body:** 690 full time, 11 part time; 62% male, 38% female; 1% American Indian, 1% Asian, 10% black, 0% Hispanic, 2% multiracial, 0% Pacific Islander, 75% white, 6% international; 54% from in state; 76% live on campus; 0% of students in fraternities, 0% in sororities
**Most popular majors:** 15% Business/Commerce, General, 10% Homeland Security, Law Enforcement, Firefighting and Related Protective Services, 21% Parks, Recreation and Leisure Studies, 8% Psychology, General, 14% Visual and Performing Arts
**Expenses:** 2014-2015: $26,170; room/board: $9,100
**Financial aid:** (828) 884-8287; 78% of undergrads determined to have financial need; average aid package $10,572

## Campbell University
Buies Creek NC
(910) 893-1320
**U.S. News ranking:** Reg. U. (S), No. 31
**Website:** www.campbell.edu
**Admissions email:** adm@ mailcenter.campbell.edu
**Private;** founded 1887
**Affiliation:** Baptist
**Freshman admissions:** selective; 2013-2014: 11,716 applied, 8,180 accepted. Either SAT or ACT required. SAT 25/75 percentile: 820-1290. High school rank: 26% in top tenth, 54% in top quarter, 88% in top half
**Early decision deadline:** N/A, notification date: N/A
**Early action deadline:** N/A, notification date: N/A
**Application deadline (fall):** rolling
**Undergraduate student body:** 3,537 full time, 928 part time; 50% male, 50% female; 1% American Indian, 2% Asian, 17% black, 6% Hispanic, 2% multiracial, 0% Pacific Islander, 55% white, 2% international; 14% from in state; 34% live on campus; 7% of students in fraternities, 6% in sororities
**Most popular majors:** 5% Accounting, 12% Business Administration and Management, General, 7% Psychology, General, 10% Science Technologies/ Technicians, Other, 7% Social Sciences, General
**Expenses:** 2014-2015: $27,530; room/board: $9,860
**Financial aid:** (910) 893-1310; 78% of undergrads determined to have financial need; average aid package $20,052

## Catawba College
Salisbury NC
(800) 228-2922
**U.S. News ranking:** Reg. Coll. (S), No. 16
**Website:** www.catawba.edu
**Admissions email:** admission@ catawba.edu
**Private;** founded 1851
**Affiliation:** United Church of Christ
**Freshman admissions:** selective; 2013-2014: 3,226 applied, 1,309 accepted. Neither SAT nor ACT required. SAT 25/75 percentile: 850-1090. High school rank: 11% in top tenth, 22% in top quarter, 61% in top half
**Early decision deadline:** N/A, notification date: N/A
**Early action deadline:** N/A, notification date: N/A
**Application deadline (fall):** rolling
**Undergraduate student body:** 1,210 full time, 88 part time; 48% male, 52% female; 1% American Indian, 1% Asian, 21% black, 3% Hispanic, 1% multiracial, 0% Pacific Islander, 70% white, 3% international; 81% from in state; 53% live on campus; 0% of students in fraternities, 0% in sororities
**Most popular majors:** 29% Business, Management, Marketing, and Related Support Services, 23% Education, 10% Parks, Recreation, Leisure, and Fitness Studies, 6% Social Sciences, 10% Visual and Performing Arts
**Expenses:** 2014-2015: $27,360; room/board: $9,880
**Financial aid:** (704) 637-4416; 85% of undergrads determined to have financial need; average aid package $21,343

## Chowan University
Murfreesboro NC
(252) 398-1236
**U.S. News ranking:** Reg. Coll. (S), second tier
**Website:** www.chowan.edu
**Admissions email:** admission@ chowan.edu
**Private;** founded 1848
**Affiliation:** Baptist
**Freshman admissions:** least selective; 2013-2014: 3,708 applied, 2,282 accepted. Either SAT or ACT required. SAT 25/75 percentile: 700-870. High school rank: 2% in top tenth, 11% in top quarter, 39% in top half
**Early decision deadline:** N/A, notification date: N/A
**Early action deadline:** N/A, notification date: N/A
**Application deadline (fall):** rolling
**Undergraduate student body:** 1,285 full time, 76 part time; 47% male, 53% female; 1% American Indian, 0% Asian, 70% black, 3% Hispanic, 4% multiracial, 0% Pacific Islander, 21% white, 1% international; 51% from in state; 81% live on campus; 11% of students in fraternities, 12% in sororities
**Most popular majors:** 18% Business Administration and Management, General, 12% Criminal Justice/Safety Studies, 9% Elementary Education and Teaching, 11% Health and Physical Education/Fitness, General, 11% Psychology, General
**Expenses:** 2014-2015: $23,050; room/board: $8,380

**Financial aid:** (252) 398-1229; 86% of undergrads determined to have financial need; average aid package $21,880

## Davidson College
Davidson NC
(800) 768-0380
**U.S. News ranking:** Nat. Lib. Arts, No. 11
**Website:** www.davidson.edu
**Admissions email:** admission@ davidson.edu
**Private;** founded 1837
**Affiliation:** Presbyterian Church (USA)
**Freshman admissions:** more selective; 2013-2014: 4,745 applied, 1,215 accepted. Either SAT or ACT required. SAT 25/75 percentile: 1230-1440. High school rank: 81% in top tenth, 97% in top quarter, 100% in top half
**Early decision deadline:** 11/15, notification date: 12/15
**Early action deadline:** N/A, notification date: N/A
**Application deadline (fall):** 1/2
**Undergraduate student body:** 1,788 full time, 0 part time; 50% male, 50% female; 1% American Indian, 5% Asian, 7% black, 6% Hispanic, 4% multiracial, 0% Pacific Islander, 69% white, 5% international; 23% from in state; 92% live on campus; 34% of students in fraternities, 1% in sororities
**Most popular majors:** 10% Biology/ Biological Sciences, General, 11% Economics, General, 10% English Language and Literature, General, 13% Political Science and Government, General, 8% Psychology, General
**Expenses:** 2014-2015: $45,377; room/board: $12,769
**Financial aid:** (704) 894-2232; 46% of undergrads determined to have financial need; average aid package $35,646

## Duke University
Durham NC
(919) 684-3214
**U.S. News ranking:** Nat. U., No. 8
**Website:** www.duke.edu/
**Admissions email:** N/A
**Private;** founded 1838
**Affiliation:** Methodist
**Freshman admissions:** most selective; 2013-2014: 30,546 applied, 3,801 accepted. Either SAT or ACT required. SAT 25/75 percentile: 1360-1550. High school rank: 90% in top tenth, 98% in top quarter, 100% in top half
**Early decision deadline:** 11/1, notification date: 12/15
**Early action deadline:** N/A, notification date: N/A
**Application deadline (fall):** 1/2
**Undergraduate student body:** 6,629 full time, 17 part time; 50% male, 50% female; 1% American Indian, 21% Asian, 10% black, 6% Hispanic, 2% multiracial, 0% Pacific Islander, 49% white, 9% international; 12% from in state; 82% live on campus; 29% of students in fraternities, 42% in sororities
**Most popular majors:** Information not available
**Expenses:** 2014-2015: $47,488; room/board: $12,576

**Financial aid:** (919) 684-6225; 45% of undergrads determined to have financial need; average aid package $43,338

## East Carolina University
Greenville NC
(252) 328-6640
**U.S. News ranking:** Nat. U., second tier
**Website:** www.ecu.edu
**Admissions email:** admis@ecu.edu
**Public;** founded 1907
**Freshman admissions:** selective; 2013-2014: 15,320 applied, 11,238 accepted. Either SAT or ACT required. SAT 25/75 percentile: 960-1170. High school rank: 15% in top tenth, 43% in top quarter, 81% in top half
**Early decision deadline:** N/A, notification date: N/A
**Early action deadline:** N/A, notification date: N/A
**Application deadline (fall):** 3/15
**Undergraduate student body:** 18,610 full time, 2,898 part time; 40% male, 60% female; 1% American Indian, 3% Asian, 16% black, 5% Hispanic, 3% multiracial, 0% Pacific Islander, 71% white, 0% international; 88% from in state; 28% live on campus; 10% of students in fraternities, 11% in sororities
**Most popular majors:** 16% Business, Management, Marketing, and Related Support Services, 6% Communication, Journalism, and Related Programs, 13% Education, 7% Engineering Technologies and Engineering-Related Fields, 16% Health Professions and Related Programs
**Expenses:** 2014-2015: $6,143 in state, $21,340 out of state; room/ board: $8,833
**Financial aid:** (252) 328-6610; 62% of undergrads determined to have financial need; average aid package $10,534

## Elizabeth City State University
Elizabeth City NC
(252) 335-3305
**U.S. News ranking:** Reg. Coll. (S), No. 29
**Website:** www.ecsu.edu
**Admissions email:** admissions@ mail.ecsu.edu
**Public;** founded 1891
**Freshman admissions:** least selective; 2013-2014: 3,040 applied, 1,575 accepted. Either SAT or ACT required. SAT 25/75 percentile: 780-945. High school rank: 2% in top tenth, 5% in top quarter, 33% in top half
**Early decision deadline:** N/A, notification date: N/A
**Early action deadline:** N/A, notification date: N/A
**Application deadline (fall):** 6/30
**Undergraduate student body:** 2,146 full time, 190 part time; 41% male, 59% female; 1% American Indian, 0% Asian, 75% black, 1% Hispanic, 1% multiracial, 0% Pacific Islander, 14% white, 0% international; 89% from in state; 46% live on campus; N/A of students in fraternities, N/A in sororities
**Most popular majors:** 18% Business, Management, Marketing, and Related Support Services, 19% Education,

7% English Language and Literature/Letters, 12% Homeland Security, Law Enforcement, Firefighting and Related Protective Services, 24% Transportation and Materials Moving
**Expenses:** 2014-2015: $4,497 in state, $16,172 out of state; room/ board: $7,213
**Financial aid:** (252) 335-3282; 84% of undergrads determined to have financial need

## Elon University
Elon NC
(800) 334-8448
**U.S. News ranking:** Reg. U. (S), No. 1
**Website:** www.elon.edu
**Admissions email:** admissions@ elon.edu
**Private;** founded 1889
**Freshman admissions:** more selective; 2013-2014: 9,949 applied, 5,370 accepted. Either SAT or ACT required. SAT 25/75 percentile: 1120-1320. High school rank: 26% in top tenth, 63% in top quarter, 92% in top half
**Early decision deadline:** 11/1, notification date: 12/1
**Early action deadline:** 11/10, notification date: 12/20
**Application deadline (fall):** 1/10
**Undergraduate student body:** 5,464 full time, 135 part time; 41% male, 59% female; 0% American Indian, 2% Asian, 6% black, 5% Hispanic, 2% multiracial, 0% Pacific Islander, 82% white, 2% international; 22% from in state; 62% live on campus; 23% of students in fraternities, 38% in sororities
**Most popular majors:** 21% Business/Commerce, General, 19% Communication and Media Studies, 4% International Relations and Affairs, 4% Political Science and Government, General, 7% Psychology, General
**Expenses:** 2014-2015: $31,247; room/board: $10,667
**Financial aid:** (336) 278-7640; 35% of undergrads determined to have financial need; average aid package $16,804

## Fayetteville State University
Fayetteville NC
(910) 672-1371
**U.S. News ranking:** Reg. U. (S), second tier
**Website:** www.uncfsu.edu
**Admissions email:** admissions@ uncfsu.edu
**Public;** founded 1867
**Freshman admissions:** least selective; 2013-2014: 4,106 applied, 2,496 accepted. Either SAT or ACT required. SAT 25/75 percentile: 770-910. High school rank: 4% in top tenth, 17% in top quarter, 52% in top half
**Early decision deadline:** N/A, notification date: N/A
**Early action deadline:** N/A, notification date: N/A
**Application deadline (fall):** 6/30
**Undergraduate student body:** 3,971 full time, 1,439 part time; 31% male, 69% female; 2% American Indian, 1% Asian, 67% black, 6% Hispanic, 0% multiracial, 0% Pacific Islander, 17% white, 1% international; N/A from in

state; N/A live on campus; 1% of students in fraternities, 1% in sororities
**Most popular majors:** 13% Business Administration and Management, General, 15% Criminal Justice/Safety Studies, 11% Psychology, General, 7% Registered Nursing/Registered Nurse, 7% Sociology
**Expenses:** 2014-2015: $5,035 in state, $16,643 out of state; room/board: $6,445
**Financial aid:** (910) 672-1325; 89% of undergrads determined to have financial need; average aid package $10,559

## Gardner-Webb University
Boiling Springs NC
(800) 253-6472
**U.S. News ranking:** Reg. U. (S), No. 34
**Website:** www.gardner-webb.edu
**Admissions email:** admissions@gardner-webb.edu
**Private;** founded 1905
**Affiliation:** Baptist
**Freshman admissions:** selective; 2013-2014: 5,484 applied, 2,642 accepted. Either SAT or ACT required. SAT 25/75 percentile: 900-1120. High school rank: 23% in top tenth, 55% in top quarter, 82% in top half
**Early decision deadline:** N/A, notification date: N/A
**Early action deadline:** N/A, notification date: N/A
**Application deadline (fall):** rolling
**Undergraduate student body:** 2,088 full time, 471 part time; 35% male, 65% female; 1% American Indian, 1% Asian, 16% black, 2% Hispanic, 0% multiracial, 0% Pacific Islander, 68% white, 2% international; 78% from in state; 48% live on campus; 0% of students in fraternities, 0% in sororities
**Most popular majors:** 23% Business, Management, Marketing, and Related Support Services, 6% Education, 15% Health Professions and Related Programs, 6% Homeland Security, Law Enforcement, Firefighting and Related Protective Services, 24% Psychology
**Expenses:** 2014-2015: $27,080; room/board: $8,850
**Financial aid:** (704) 406-4243; 82% of undergrads determined to have financial need; average aid package $20,596

## Greensboro College[1]
Greensboro NC
(336) 272-7102
**U.S. News ranking:** Reg. Coll. (S), second tier
**Website:** www.gborocollege.edu
**Admissions email:** admissions@gborocollege.edu
**Private**
**Application deadline (fall):** N/A
**Undergraduate student body:** N/A full time, N/A part time
**Expenses:** 2013-2014: $26,306; room/board: $10,420
**Financial aid:** (336) 272-7102

## Guilford College
Greensboro NC
(800) 992-7759
**U.S. News ranking:** Nat. Lib. Arts, No. 172
**Website:** www.guilford.edu
**Admissions email:** admission@guilford.edu
**Private;** founded 1837
**Affiliation:** Quaker
**Freshman admissions:** selective; 2013-2014: 3,030 applied, 2,066 accepted. Neither SAT nor ACT required. SAT 25/75 percentile: 970-1220. High school rank: 11% in top tenth, 33% in top quarter, 69% in top half
**Early decision deadline:** N/A, notification date: N/A
**Early action deadline:** 11/15, notification date: 2/15
**Application deadline (fall):** 8/10
**Undergraduate student body:** 1,928 full time, 374 part time; 44% male, 56% female; 0% American Indian, 2% Asian, 25% black, 6% Hispanic, 3% multiracial, 0% Pacific Islander, 62% white, 1% international; 55% from in state; 77% live on campus; 0% of students in fraternities, 0% in sororities
**Most popular majors:** 6% Biological and Biomedical Sciences, 17% Business, Management, Marketing, and Related Support Services, 10% Homeland Security, Law Enforcement, Firefighting and Related Protective Services, 12% Psychology, 9% Social Sciences
**Expenses:** 2014-2015: $33,430; room/board: $9,370
**Financial aid:** (336) 316-2165; 92% of undergrads determined to have financial need; average aid package $20,980

## High Point University
High Point NC
(800) 345-6993
**U.S. News ranking:** Reg. Coll. (S), No. 1
**Website:** www.highpoint.edu
**Admissions email:** admiss@highpoint.edu
**Private;** founded 1924
**Affiliation:** United Methodist
**Freshman admissions:** selective; 2013-2014: 6,598 applied, 5,569 accepted. Either SAT or ACT required. SAT 25/75 percentile: 980-1170. High school rank: 22% in top tenth, 51% in top quarter, 80% in top half
**Early decision deadline:** 11/1, notification date: 11/26
**Early action deadline:** 11/8, notification date: 12/17
**Application deadline (fall):** 7/1
**Undergraduate student body:** 3,962 full time, 37 part time; 41% male, 59% female; 1% American Indian, 1% Asian, 6% black, 3% Hispanic, 1% multiracial, 0% Pacific Islander, 84% white, 1% international; 21% from in state; 93% live on campus; 17% of students in fraternities, 47% in sororities
**Most popular majors:** 30% Business/Commerce, General, 14% Communication, General, 9% Elementary Education and Teaching, 8% Organizational Behavior Studies, 5% Psychology, General
**Expenses:** 2014-2015: $31,480; room/board: $11,480

**Financial aid:** (336) 841-9128; 48% of undergrads determined to have financial need; average aid package $14,065

## Johnson C. Smith University
Charlotte NC
(704) 378-1010
**U.S. News ranking:** Nat. Lib. Arts, second tier
**Website:** www.jcsu.edu
**Admissions email:** admissions@jcsu.edu
**Private;** founded 1867
**Freshman admissions:** less selective; 2013-2014: 4,777 applied, 1,751 accepted. Either SAT or ACT required. SAT 25/75 percentile: 733-920. High school rank: 8% in top tenth, 25% in top quarter, 55% in top half
**Early decision deadline:** N/A, notification date: N/A
**Early action deadline:** N/A, notification date: N/A
**Application deadline (fall):** rolling
**Undergraduate student body:** 1,324 full time, 63 part time; 41% male, 59% female; 0% American Indian, 0% Asian, 73% black, 6% Hispanic, 2% multiracial, 0% Pacific Islander, 1% white, 4% international; 56% from in state; 61% live on campus; 1% of students in fraternities, 2% in sororities
**Most popular majors:** 7% Biology/Biological Sciences, General, 22% Business Administration and Management, General, 8% Computer and Information Sciences, General, 9% Criminology, 12% Mass Communication/Media Studies
**Expenses:** 2014-2015: $18,336; room/board: $7,100
**Financial aid:** (704) 378-1035; 85% of undergrads determined to have financial need; average aid package $15,003

## Lees-McRae College
Banner Elk NC
(828) 898-8723
**U.S. News ranking:** Reg. Coll. (S), No. 54
**Website:** www.lmc.edu
**Admissions email:** admissions@lmc.edu
**Private;** founded 1900
**Affiliation:** Presbyterian Church (U.S.A.)
**Freshman admissions:** less selective; 2013-2014: 1,751 applied, 1,164 accepted. Neither SAT nor ACT required. SAT 25/75 percentile: 840-1080. High school rank: 8% in top tenth, 29% in top quarter, 58% in top half
**Early decision deadline:** N/A, notification date: N/A
**Early action deadline:** N/A, notification date: N/A
**Application deadline (fall):** rolling
**Undergraduate student body:** 883 full time, 7 part time; 40% male, 60% female; 0% American Indian, 0% Asian, 5% black, 1% Hispanic, 0% multiracial, 0% Pacific Islander, 39% white, 2% international; 71% from in state; 64% live on campus; N/A of students in fraternities, N/A in sororities
**Most popular majors:** 7% Biological and Biomedical Sciences, 9% Business, Management, Marketing, and Related Support

Services, 19% Education, 25% Health Professions and Related Programs, 19% Social Sciences
**Expenses:** 2014-2015: $24,150; room/board: $9,810
**Financial aid:** (828) 898-8793; 80% of undergrads determined to have financial need; average aid package $23,324

## Lenoir-Rhyne University
Hickory NC
(828) 328-7300
**U.S. News ranking:** Reg. Coll. (S), No. 20
**Website:** www.lr.edu
**Admissions email:** admission@lr.edu
**Private;** founded 1891
**Affiliation:** Evangelical Lutheran Church in America
**Freshman admissions:** selective; 2013-2014: 4,762 applied, 3,241 accepted. Either SAT or ACT required. SAT 25/75 percentile: 880-1080. High school rank: 15% in top tenth, 44% in top quarter, 82% in top half
**Early decision deadline:** N/A, notification date: N/A
**Early action deadline:** 8/15, notification date: N/A
**Application deadline (fall):** rolling
**Undergraduate student body:** 1,306 full time, 185 part time; 42% male, 58% female; 1% American Indian, 2% Asian, 15% black, 5% Hispanic, 2% multiracial, 0% Pacific Islander, 68% white, 1% international; 79% from in state; 44% live on campus; 0% of students in fraternities, 3% in sororities
**Most popular majors:** 16% Business, Management, Marketing, and Related Support Services, 13% Education, 15% Health Professions and Related Programs, 14% Parks, Recreation, Leisure, and Fitness Studies, 9% Psychology
**Expenses:** 2014-2015: $30,922; room/board: $10,740
**Financial aid:** (828) 328-7304; 89% of undergrads determined to have financial need; average aid package $24,753

## Livingstone College
Salisbury NC
(704) 216-6001
**U.S. News ranking:** Reg. Coll. (S), second tier
**Website:** www.livingstone.edu/
**Admissions email:** admissions@livingstone.edu
**Private;** founded 1879
**Affiliation:** African Methodist Episcopal Zion
**Freshman admissions:** least selective; 2013-2014: 3,110 applied, 2,250 accepted. Either SAT or ACT required. ACT 25/75 percentile: 11-16. High school rank: 2% in top tenth, 6% in top quarter, 25% in top half
**Early decision deadline:** N/A, notification date: N/A
**Early action deadline:** N/A, notification date: N/A
**Application deadline (fall):** rolling
**Undergraduate student body:** 1,164 full time, 11 part time; 56% male, 44% female; 1% American Indian, 0% Asian, 91% black, 1% Hispanic, 0% multiracial, 0% Pacific Islander, 0% white,

0% international; 65% from in state; 80% live on campus; 30% of students in fraternities, 37% in sororities
**Most popular majors:** 8% Biology/Biological Sciences, General, 18% Business Administration and Management, General, 15% Criminal Justice/Safety Studies, 11% Psychology, General, 6% Social Work
**Expenses:** 2014-2015: $16,825; room/board: $6,596
**Financial aid:** (704) 216-6069; 98% of undergrads determined to have financial need; average aid package $13,835

## Mars Hill University
Mars Hill NC
(866) 642-4968
**U.S. News ranking:** Reg. Coll. (S), No. 37
**Website:** www.mhc.edu
**Admissions email:** admissions@mhc.edu
**Private;** founded 1856
**Freshman admissions:** less selective; 2013-2014: 2,899 applied, 1,869 accepted. Either SAT or ACT required. SAT 25/75 percentile: 830-1040. High school rank: 8% in top tenth, 26% in top quarter, 59% in top half
**Early decision deadline:** N/A, notification date: N/A
**Early action deadline:** N/A, notification date: N/A
**Application deadline (fall):** rolling
**Undergraduate student body:** 1,319 full time, 107 part time; 50% male, 50% female; 3% American Indian, 1% Asian, 19% black, 3% Hispanic, 0% multiracial, 0% Pacific Islander, 70% white, 0% international; 75% from in state; 69% live on campus; N/A of students in fraternities, 10% in sororities
**Most popular majors:** 7% Biology/Biological Sciences, General, 21% Business Administration and Management, General, 21% Elementary Education and Teaching, 12% Social Work, 7% Sociology
**Expenses:** 2013-2014: $25,636; room/board: $8,548
**Financial aid:** (828) 689-1103

## Meredith College
Raleigh NC
(919) 760-8581
**U.S. News ranking:** Reg. Coll. (S), No. 6
**Website:** www.meredith.edu
**Admissions email:** admissions@meredith.edu
**Private;** founded 1891
**Freshman admissions:** selective; 2013-2014: 1,762 applied, 1,098 accepted. Neither SAT nor ACT required. SAT 25/75 percentile: 930-1140. High school rank: 23% in top tenth, 52% in top quarter, 84% in top half
**Early decision deadline:** 10/30, notification date: 11/15
**Early action deadline:** N/A, notification date: N/A
**Application deadline (fall):** rolling
**Undergraduate student body:** 1,490 full time, 81 part time; 0% male, 100% female; 1% American Indian, 3% Asian, 11% black, 3% Hispanic, 3% multiracial, 0% Pacific Islander, 72% white, 4% international; 91% from in state; 59% live on campus; N/A of students in fraternities, N/A in sororities

**Most popular majors:** 10% Biology/Biological Sciences, General, 8% Business/Commerce, General, 7% Child Development, 5% Interior Design, 10% Psychology, General
**Expenses:** 2014-2015: $32,140; room/board: $9,516
**Financial aid:** (919) 760-8565; 76% of undergrads determined to have financial need; average aid package $22,795

## Methodist University[1]
Fayetteville NC
(910) 630-7027
**U.S. News ranking:** Reg. Coll. (S), No. 62
**Website:** www.methodist.edu
**Admissions email:** admissions@methodist.edu
**Private**
**Application deadline (fall):** N/A
**Undergraduate student body:** N/A full time, N/A part time
**Expenses:** 2013-2014: $27,830; room/board: $10,340
**Financial aid:** (910) 630-7193

## Mid-Atlantic Christian University
Elizabeth City NC
(866) 996-6228
**U.S. News ranking:** Reg. Coll. (S), unranked
**Website:** www.macuniversity.edu
**Admissions email:** admissions@macuniversity.edu
**Private**
**Freshman admissions:** N/A; 2013-2014: N/A applied, 74 accepted. Either SAT or ACT required. SAT 25/75 percentile: 778-943. High school rank: 13% in top tenth, 28% in top quarter, 55% in top half
**Early decision deadline:** N/A, notification date: N/A
**Early action deadline:** N/A, notification date: N/A
**Application deadline (fall):** rolling
**Undergraduate student body:** 129 full time, 32 part time; 47% male, 53% female; 1% American Indian, 1% Asian, 25% black, 4% Hispanic, 0% multiracial, 0% Pacific Islander, 70% white, 0% international; 68% from in state; 62% live on campus; N/A of students in fraternities, N/A in sororities
**Most popular majors:** 12% Education, 10% Family and Consumer Sciences/Human Sciences, 14% Psychology, 62% Theology and Religious Vocations
**Expenses:** 2014-2015: $13,105; room/board: $8,100
**Financial aid:** N/A

## Montreat College[1]
Montreat NC
(800) 622-6968
**U.S. News ranking:** Reg. U. (S), second tier
**Website:** www.montreat.edu
**Admissions email:** admissions@montreat.edu
**Private**
**Application deadline (fall):** N/A
**Undergraduate student body:** N/A full time, N/A part time
**Expenses:** 2013-2014: $23,420; room/board: $7,778
**Financial aid:** (800) 545-4656

## North Carolina A&T State University
Greensboro NC
(336) 334-7946
**U.S. News ranking:** Nat. U., second tier
**Website:** www.ncat.edu
**Admissions email:** uadmit@ncat.edu
**Public;** founded 1891
**Freshman admissions:** less selective; 2013-2014: 6,461 applied, 3,651 accepted. Either SAT or ACT required. SAT 25/75 percentile: 830-990. High school rank: 10% in top tenth, 31% in top quarter, 73% in top half
**Early decision deadline:** N/A, notification date: N/A
**Early action deadline:** N/A, notification date: N/A
**Application deadline (fall):** rolling
**Undergraduate student body:** 8,102 full time, 770 part time; 46% male, 54% female; 0% American Indian, 1% Asian, 87% black, 2% Hispanic, 2% multiracial, 0% Pacific Islander, 4% white, 2% international; 82% from in state; 44% live on campus; 1% of students in fraternities, 1% in sororities
**Most popular majors:** 10% Business, Management, Marketing, and Related Support Services, 8% Communication, Journalism, and Related Programs, 14% Engineering, 8% Liberal Arts and Sciences, General Studies and Humanities, 10% Psychology
**Expenses:** 2013-2014: $5,422 in state, $16,503 out of state; room/board: $7,643
**Financial aid:** (336) 334-7973

## North Carolina Central University
Durham NC
(919) 530-6298
**U.S. News ranking:** Reg. U. (S), No. 65
**Website:** www.nccu.edu
**Admissions email:** admissions@nccu.edu
**Public;** founded 1910
**Freshman admissions:** less selective; 2013-2014: 7,989 applied, 3,098 accepted. Either SAT or ACT required. SAT 25/75 percentile: 800-950. High school rank: 6% in top tenth, 22% in quarter, 63% in top half
**Early decision deadline:** N/A, notification date: N/A
**Early action deadline:** N/A, notification date: N/A
**Application deadline (fall):** rolling
**Undergraduate student body:** 5,297 full time, 923 part time; 33% male, 67% female; 0% American Indian, 1% Asian, 83% black, 3% Hispanic, 3% multiracial, 0% Pacific Islander, 5% white, 1% international; 90% from in state; 43% live on campus; N/A of students in fraternities, N/A in sororities
**Most popular majors:** 11% Business Administration and Management, General, 11% Criminal Justice/Safety Studies, 11% Family and Consumer Sciences/Human Sciences, General, 6% Psychology, General, 8% Registered Nursing/Registered Nurse
**Expenses:** 2014-2015: $5,525 in state, $16,940 out of state; room/board: $8,165
**Financial aid:** (919) 530-6180

## North Carolina State University—Raleigh
Raleigh NC
(919) 515-2434
**U.S. News ranking:** Nat. U., No. 95
**Website:** www.ncsu.edu
**Admissions email:** undergrad_admissions@ncsu.edu
**Public;** founded 1887
**Freshman admissions:** more selective; 2013-2014: 21,610 applied, 10,128 accepted. Either SAT or ACT required. SAT 25/75 percentile: 1150-1320. High school rank: 50% in top tenth, 80% in top quarter, 99% in top half
**Early decision deadline:** N/A, notification date: N/A
**Early action deadline:** 11/1, notification date: 1/30
**Application deadline (fall):** 1/15
**Undergraduate student body:** 21,469 full time, 3,067 part time; 56% male, 44% female; 0% American Indian, 5% Asian, 7% black, 4% Hispanic, 3% multiracial, 0% Pacific Islander, 75% white, 3% international; 90% from in state; 27% live on campus; 1% of students in fraternities, 15% in sororities
**Most popular majors:** 7% Agriculture, Agriculture Operations, and Related Sciences, 11% Biological and Biomedical Sciences, 13% Business, Management, Marketing, and Related Support Services, 23% Engineering, 6% Social Sciences
**Expenses:** 2014-2015: $8,296 in state, $23,551 out of state; room/board: $10,030
**Financial aid:** (919) 515-2421; 50% of undergrads determined to have financial need; average aid package $12,567

## North Carolina Wesleyan College
Rocky Mount NC
(800) 488-6292
**U.S. News ranking:** Reg. Coll. (S), No. 71
**Website:** www.ncwc.edu
**Admissions email:** adm@ncwc.edu
**Private;** founded 1956
**Affiliation:** Methodist
**Freshman admissions:** less selective; 2013-2014: 1,790 applied, 834 accepted. Neither SAT nor ACT required. SAT 25/75 percentile: 760-970. High school rank: 5% in top tenth, 14% in top quarter, 45% in top half
**Early decision deadline:** N/A, notification date: N/A
**Early action deadline:** N/A, notification date: N/A
**Application deadline (fall):** rolling
**Undergraduate student body:** 1,231 full time, 371 part time; 41% male, 59% female; 1% American Indian, 0% Asian, 49% black, 2% Hispanic, 1% multiracial, 0% Pacific Islander, 30% white, 3% international; 87% from in state; 29% live on campus; N/A of students in fraternities, N/A in sororities
**Most popular majors:** 10% Accounting, 33% Business Administration and Management, General, 6% Computer and Information Sciences, General, 19% Criminal Justice/Law Enforcement Administration, 17% Psychology, General

**Expenses:** 2013-2014: $26,981; room/board: $8,679
**Financial aid:** (252) 985-5200

## Pfeiffer University
Misenheimer NC
(800) 338-2060
**U.S. News ranking:** Reg. U. (S), No. 62
**Website:** www.pfeiffer.edu
**Admissions email:** admissions@pfeiffer.edu
**Private;** founded 1885
**Affiliation:** Methodist
**Freshman admissions:** less selective; 2013-2014: 1,711 applied, 1,682 accepted. Either SAT or ACT required. SAT 25/75 percentile: 870-1080. High school rank: 11% in top tenth, 35% in top quarter, 70% in top half
**Early decision deadline:** N/A, notification date: N/A
**Early action deadline:** N/A, notification date: N/A
**Application deadline (fall):** rolling
**Undergraduate student body:** 856 full time, 95 part time; 40% male, 60% female; 1% American Indian, 1% Asian, 16% black, 4% Hispanic, 2% multiracial, 0% Pacific Islander, 49% white, 5% international; 67% from in state; 65% live on campus; 0% of students in fraternities, 0% in sororities
**Most popular majors:** 20% Business Administration and Management, General, 12% Criminal Justice/Safety Studies, 11% Elementary Education and Teaching, 5% Psychology, General, 6% Registered Nursing/Registered Nurse
**Expenses:** 2014-2015: $25,590; room/board: $10,215
**Financial aid:** (800) 338-2060; 81% of undergrads determined to have financial need; average aid package $24,169

## Queens University of Charlotte
Charlotte NC
(800) 849-0202
**U.S. News ranking:** Reg. U. (S), No. 18
**Website:** www.queens.edu
**Admissions email:** admissions@queens.edu
**Private;** founded 1857
**Affiliation:** Presbyterian
**Freshman admissions:** selective; 2013-2014: 1,949 applied, 1,498 accepted. Either SAT or ACT required. SAT 25/75 percentile: 940-1140. High school rank: 18% in top tenth, 42% in top quarter, 78% in top half
**Early decision deadline:** N/A, notification date: N/A
**Early action deadline:** 11/1, notification date: 12/1
**Application deadline (fall):** 8/1
**Undergraduate student body:** 1,410 full time, 324 part time; 28% male, 72% female; 1% American Indian, 3% Asian, 18% black, 5% Hispanic, 1% multiracial, 0% Pacific Islander, 56% white, 6% international; 61% from in state; 71% live on campus; 13% of students in fraternities, 21% in sororities
**Most popular majors:** 12% Business, Management, Marketing, and Related Support Services, 11% Communication, Journalism, and Related Programs,

30% Health Professions and Related Programs, 8% Psychology, 6% Social Sciences
**Expenses:** 2014-2015: $30,850; room/board: $10,630
**Financial aid:** (704) 337-2225; 67% of undergrads determined to have financial need; average aid package $20,035

## Salem College
Winston-Salem NC
(336) 721-2621
**U.S. News ranking:** Nat. Lib. Arts, No. 148
**Website:** www.salem.edu
**Admissions email:** admissions@salem.edu
**Private;** founded 1772
**Affiliation:** Moravian Church in America
**Freshman admissions:** more selective; 2013-2014: 855 applied, 498 accepted. Either SAT or ACT required. SAT 25/75 percentile: 1000-1200. High school rank: 39% in top tenth, 75% in top quarter, 96% in top half
**Early decision deadline:** N/A, notification date: N/A
**Early action deadline:** N/A, notification date: N/A
**Application deadline (fall):** rolling
**Undergraduate student body:** 827 full time, 152 part time; 5% male, 95% female; 0% American Indian, 3% Asian, 23% black, 7% Hispanic, 3% multiracial, 0% Pacific Islander, 55% white, 1% international; 79% from in state; 52% live on campus; 0% of students in fraternities, 0% in sororities
**Most popular majors:** 14% Business Administration and Management, General, 6% Communication, General, 16% Education, General, 8% Psychology, General, 9% Sociology
**Expenses:** 2014-2015: $25,356; room/board: $11,764
**Financial aid:** (336) 721-2808

## Shaw University[1]
Raleigh NC
(800) 214-6683
**U.S. News ranking:** Reg. Coll. (S), second tier
**Website:** www.shawu.edu
**Admissions email:** admission@shawu.edu
**Private;** founded 1865
**Affiliation:** Baptist
**Application deadline (fall):** 7/30
**Undergraduate student body:** N/A full time, N/A part time
**Expenses:** 2013-2014: $16,480; room/board: $8,158
**Financial aid:** (919) 546-8240

## St. Augustine's University
Raleigh NC
(919) 516-4012
**U.S. News ranking:** Reg. Coll. (S), second tier
**Website:** www.st-aug.edu
**Admissions email:** admissions@st-aug.edu
**Private;** founded 1867
**Affiliation:** Episcopal
**Freshman admissions:** least selective; 2013-2014: 2,560 applied, 1,725 accepted. Either SAT or ACT required. SAT 25/75 percentile: 665-858. High school rank: N/A

Early decision deadline: N/A, notification date: N/A
Early action deadline: N/A, notification date: N/A
Application deadline (fall): rolling
Undergraduate student body: 1,265 full time, 34 part time; 50% male, 50% female; 0% American Indian, 0% Asian, 96% black, 0% Hispanic, 0% multiracial, 0% Pacific Islander, 1% white, 2% international; 57% from in state; 75% live on campus; N/A of students in fraternities, N/A in sororities
Most popular majors: 24% Business, Management, Marketing, and Related Support Services, 9% Health Professions and Related Programs, 9% Homeland Security, Law Enforcement, Firefighting and Related Protective Services, 13% Parks, Recreation, Leisure, and Fitness Studies, 11% Social Sciences
Expenses: 2014-2015: $17,890; room/board: $7,692
Financial aid: (919) 516-4131; 100% of undergrads determined to have financial need; average aid package $8,306

## University of Mount Olive

Mount Olive NC
(919) 658-2502
U.S. News ranking: Reg. Coll. (S), No. 56
Website: www.umo.edu/
Admissions email: admissions@umo.edu
Private; founded 1951
Affiliation: Original Free Will Baptist
Freshman admissions: less selective; 2013-2014: 1,798 applied, 859 accepted. Neither SAT nor ACT required. SAT 25/75 percentile: 833-1060. High school rank: N/A
Early decision deadline: N/A, notification date: N/A
Early action deadline: N/A, notification date: N/A
Application deadline (fall): rolling
Undergraduate student body: 1,386 full time, 2,028 part time; 33% male, 67% female; 2% American Indian, 1% Asian, 34% black, 4% Hispanic, 0% multiracial, 0% Pacific Islander, 47% white, 3% international
Most popular majors: 28% Business Administration and Management, General, 15% Early Childhood Education and Teaching, 20% Health/Health Care Administration/Management
Expenses: 2013-2014: $17,300; room/board: $7,000
Financial aid: (919) 658-2502

## University of North Carolina– Asheville

Asheville NC
(828) 251-6481
U.S. News ranking: Nat. Lib. Arts, No. 159
Website: www.unca.edu
Admissions email: admissions@unca.edu
Public; founded 1927
Freshman admissions: selective; 2013-2014: 3,173 applied, 2,181 accepted. Either SAT or ACT required. SAT 25/75

percentile: 1100-1290. High school rank: 22% in top tenth, 54% in top quarter, 90% in top half
Early decision deadline: N/A, notification date: N/A
Early action deadline: N/A, notification date: N/A
Application deadline (fall): 2/15
Undergraduate student body: 3,129 full time, 607 part time; 43% male, 57% female; 0% American Indian, 1% Asian, 3% black, 4% Hispanic, 3% multiracial, 0% Pacific Islander, 83% white, 0% international; 88% from in state; 40% live on campus; 3% of students in fraternities, 3% in sororities
Most popular majors: 6% Art/Art Studies, General, 7% English Language and Literature, General, 6% Environmental Studies, 7% Liberal Arts and Sciences/Liberal Studies, 12% Psychology, General
Expenses: 2014-2015: $6,392 in state, $21,263 out of state; room/board: $8,332
Financial aid: (828) 251-6535; 59% of undergrads determined to have financial need; average aid package $11,789

## University of North Carolina– Chapel Hill

Chapel Hill NC
(919) 966-3621
U.S. News ranking: Nat. U., No. 30
Website: www.unc.edu
Admissions email: unchelp@ admissions.unc.edu
Public; founded 1789
Freshman admissions: most selective; 2013-2014: 30,835 applied, 8,243 accepted. Either SAT or ACT required. SAT 25/75 percentile: 1200-1410. High school rank: 78% in top tenth, 96% in top quarter, 99% in top half
Early decision deadline: N/A, notification date: N/A
Early action deadline: 10/15, notification date: 1/31
Application deadline (fall): 1/10
Undergraduate student body: 17,570 full time, 800 part time; 42% male, 58% female; 0% American Indian, 9% Asian, 8% black, 7% Hispanic, 4% multiracial, 0% Pacific Islander, 66% white, 2% international; 82% from in state; 53% live on campus; 17% of students in fraternities, 18% in sororities
Most popular majors: 8% Biology, General, 6% Business Administration, Management and Operations, 10% Communication and Media Studies, 6% Economics, 9% Psychology, General
Expenses: 2014-2015: $8,374 in state, $33,624 out of state; room/board: $10,592
Financial aid: (919) 962-8396; 44% of undergrads determined to have financial need; average aid package $16,798

## University of North Carolina– Charlotte

Charlotte NC
(704) 687-5507
U.S. News ranking: Nat. U., No. 201
Website: www.uncc.edu/
Admissions email: admissions@uncc.edu
Public; founded 1946
Freshman admissions: selective; 2013-2014: 14,300 applied, 8,967 accepted. Either SAT or ACT required. SAT 25/75 percentile: 1000-1170. High school rank: 19% in top tenth, 55% in top quarter, 89% in top half
Early decision deadline: N/A, notification date: N/A
Early action deadline: N/A, notification date: N/A
Application deadline (fall): 7/1
Undergraduate student body: 18,309 full time, 3,194 part time; 52% male, 48% female; 0% American Indian, 5% Asian, 17% black, 7% Hispanic, 3% multiracial, 0% Pacific Islander, 61% white, 2% international; 93% from in state; 24% live on campus; 3% of students in fraternities, 4% in sororities
Most popular majors: 19% Business, Management, Marketing, and Related Support Services, 7% Engineering, 7% Homeland Security, Law Enforcement, Firefighting and Related Protective Services, 7% Psychology, 9% Social Sciences
Expenses: 2014-2015: $6,179 in state, $18,708 out of state; room/board: $11,646
Financial aid: (704) 687-2461; 66% of undergrads determined to have financial need; average aid package $9,524

## University of North Carolina– Greensboro

Greensboro NC
(336) 334-5243
U.S. News ranking: Nat. U., No. 181
Website: www.uncg.edu/
Admissions email: admissions@uncg.edu
Public; founded 1891
Freshman admissions: selective; 2013-2014: 10,154 applied, 5,909 accepted. Either SAT or ACT required. SAT 25/75 percentile: 950-1120. High school rank: 22% in top tenth, 48% in top quarter, 84% in top half
Early decision deadline: N/A, notification date: N/A
Early action deadline: N/A, notification date: N/A
Application deadline (fall): 3/1
Undergraduate student body: 12,354 full time, 1,994 part time; 35% male, 65% female; 0% American Indian, 4% Asian, 25% black, 6% Hispanic, 4% multiracial, 0% Pacific Islander, 58% white, 2% international; 94% from in state; 32% live on campus; 4% of students in fraternities, 4% in sororities
Most popular majors: 17% Business, Management, Marketing, and Related Support Services, 11% Education, 13%

Health Professions and Related Programs, 8% Social Sciences, 8% Visual and Performing Arts
Expenses: 2014-2015: $6,442 in state, $21,304 out of state; room/board: $7,688
Financial aid: (336) 334-5702; 80% of undergrads determined to have financial need; average aid package $10,090

## University of North Carolina– Pembroke

Pembroke NC
(910) 521-6262
U.S. News ranking: Reg. U. (S), No. 87
Website: www.uncp.edu
Admissions email: admissions@uncp.edu
Public; founded 1887
Freshman admissions: less selective; 2013-2014: 3,678 applied, 2,600 accepted. Either SAT or ACT required. SAT 25/75 percentile: 840-1010. High school rank: 11% in top tenth, 35% in top quarter, 72% in top half
Early decision deadline: N/A, notification date: N/A
Early action deadline: N/A, notification date: N/A
Application deadline (fall): 7/31
Undergraduate student body: 4,230 full time, 1,199 part time; 38% male, 62% female; 16% American Indian, 2% Asian, 35% black, 5% Hispanic, 2% multiracial, 0% Pacific Islander, 38% white, 1% international; 96% from in state; 37% live on campus; 7% of students in fraternities, 9% in sororities
Most popular majors: 13% Business Administration and Management, General, 10% Criminal Justice/Safety Studies, 14% Education, General, 10% Health and Physical Education/Fitness, General, 11% Sociology
Expenses: 2014-2015: $5,287 in state, $15,238 out of state; room/board: $8,101
Financial aid: (910) 521-6255; 81% of undergrads determined to have financial need; average aid package $9,522

## University of North Carolina School of the Arts

Winston-Salem NC
(336) 770-3291
U.S. News ranking: Arts, unranked
Website: www.uncsa.edu
Admissions email: admissions@uncsa.edu
Public; founded 1963
Freshman admissions: N/A; 2013-2014: 803 applied, 359 accepted. Either SAT or ACT required. SAT 25/75 percentile: N/A. High school rank: 14% in top tenth, 45% in top quarter, 80% in top half
Early decision deadline: N/A, notification date: N/A
Early action deadline: N/A, notification date: N/A
Undergraduate student body: 781 full time, 16 part time; 55% male, 45% female; 1% American Indian, 1% Asian, 7% black, 9% Hispanic, 4% multiracial, 0% Pacific Islander, 74% white, 1% international; 49% from in

state; 64% live on campus; N/A of students in fraternities, N/A in sororities
Most popular majors: 35% Cinematography and Film/Video Production, 7% Dance, General, 17% Drama and Dramatics/Theatre Arts, General, 16% Music Performance, General, 25% Technical Theatre/Theatre Design and Technology
Expenses: 2014-2015: $8,378 in state, $23,862 out of state; room/board: $8,570
Financial aid: (336) 770-3297; 62% of undergrads determined to have financial need; average aid package $13,246

## University of North Carolina– Wilmington

Wilmington NC
(910) 962-3243
U.S. News ranking: Reg. U. (S), No. 16
Website: www.uncw.edu
Admissions email: admissions@uncw.edu
Public; founded 1947
Freshman admissions: more selective; 2013-2014: 10,838 applied, 6,160 accepted. Either SAT or ACT required. SAT 25/75 percentile: 1110-1270. High school rank: 27% in top tenth, 64% in top quarter, 96% in top half
Early decision deadline: N/A, notification date: N/A
Early action deadline: 11/1, notification date: 1/20
Application deadline (fall): 2/1
Undergraduate student body: 11,408 full time, 1,020 part time; 40% male, 60% female; 0% American Indian, 2% Asian, 5% black, 6% Hispanic, 3% multiracial, 0% Pacific Islander, 80% white, 1% international; 86% from in state; 33% live on campus; 50% of students in fraternities, 8% in sororities
Most popular majors: 20% Business, Management, Marketing, and Related Support Services, 10% Education, 8% Health Professions and Related Programs, 9% Psychology, 9% Social Sciences
Expenses: 2014-2015: $6,392 in state, $20,517 out of state; room/board: $9,124
Financial aid: (910) 962-3177; 54% of undergrads determined to have financial need; average aid package $10,402

## Wake Forest University

Winston-Salem NC
(336) 758-5201
U.S. News ranking: Nat. U., No. 27
Website: www.wfu.edu
Admissions email: admissions@wfu.edu
Private; founded 1834
Freshman admissions: most selective; 2013-2014: 11,121 applied, 3,915 accepted. Neither SAT nor ACT required. SAT 25/75 percentile: 1230-1420. High school rank: 76% in top tenth, 93% in top quarter, 99% in top half
Early decision deadline: 1/1, notification date: N/A

**Early action deadline:** N/A, notification date: N/A
**Application deadline (fall):** 1/1
**Undergraduate student body:** 4,756 full time, 67 part time; 48% male, 52% female; 0% American Indian, 5% Asian, 7% black, 6% Hispanic, 3% multiracial, 0% Pacific Islander, 76% white, 4% international; 23% from in state; 74% live on campus; 39% of students in fraternities, 58% in sororities
**Most popular majors:** 18% Business, Management, Marketing, and Related Support Services, 9% Communication, Journalism, and Related Programs, 7% Parks, Recreation, Leisure, and Fitness Studies, 8% Psychology, 20% Social Sciences
**Expenses:** 2014-2015: $46,200; room/board: $12,638
**Financial aid:** (336) 758-5154; 40% of undergrads determined to have financial need; average aid package $37,377

## Warren Wilson College

Asheville NC
(800) 934-3536
**U.S. News ranking:** Nat. Lib. Arts, No. 165
**Website:** www.warren-wilson.edu
**Admissions email:** admit@warren-wilson.edu
**Private;** founded 1894
**Freshman admissions:** selective; 2013-2014: 1,214 applied, 845 accepted. Either SAT or ACT required. SAT 25/75 percentile: 1010-1250. High school rank: 22% in top tenth, 50% in top quarter, 81% in top half
**Early decision deadline:** 11/15, notification date: 12/1
**Early action deadline:** 11/1, notification date: 12/1
**Application deadline (fall):** 2/1
**Undergraduate student body:** 824 full time, 6 part time; 39% male, 61% female; 1% American Indian, 1% Asian, 4% black, 5% Hispanic, 2% multiracial, 0% Pacific Islander, 85% white, 2% international; 23% from in state; 90% live on campus; 0% of students in fraternities, 0% in sororities
**Most popular majors:** 7% Creative Writing, 24% Environmental Studies, 9% International/Global Studies, 9% Social Sciences, Other, 8% Visual and Performing Arts, General
**Expenses:** 2014-2015: $30,852; room/board: $9,280
**Financial aid:** (828) 771-2082; 69% of undergrads determined to have financial need; average aid package $25,309

## Western Carolina University

Cullowhee NC
(828) 227-7317
**U.S. News ranking:** Reg. U. (S), No. 37
**Website:** www.wcu.edu
**Admissions email:** admiss@email.wcu.edu
**Public;** founded 1889
**Freshman admissions:** selective; 2013-2014: 15,142 applied, 5,878 accepted. Either SAT or ACT required. SAT 25/75 percentile: 940-1120. High school rank: 11% in top tenth, 38% in top quarter, 79% in top half

**Early decision deadline:** N/A, notification date: N/A
**Early action deadline:** 11/15, notification date: 12/15
**Application deadline (fall):** 3/1
**Undergraduate student body:** 7,081 full time, 1,367 part time; 45% male, 55% female; 1% American Indian, 1% Asian, 6% black, 4% Hispanic, 3% multiracial, 0% Pacific Islander, 81% white, 2% international; 91% from in state; 48% live on campus; 9% of students in fraternities, 7% in sororities
**Most popular majors:** 12% Business, Management, Marketing, and Related Support Services, 17% Education, 15% Health Professions and Related Programs, 8% Homeland Security, Law Enforcement, Firefighting and Related Protective Services, 6% Visual and Performing Arts
**Expenses:** 2014-2015: $6,531 in state, $16,924 out of state; room/board: $8,016
**Financial aid:** (828) 227-7290; 68% of undergrads determined to have financial need; average aid package $9,291

## William Peace University[1]

Raleigh NC
(919) 508-2214
**U.S. News ranking:** Nat. Lib. Arts, second tier
**Website:** www.peace.edu
**Admissions email:** admissions@peace.edu
**Private;** founded 1857
**Affiliation:** Presbyterian Church (USA)
**Application deadline (fall):** rolling
**Undergraduate student body:** N/A full time, N/A part time
**Expenses:** 2013-2014: $23,900; room/board: $9,000
**Financial aid:** (919) 508-2249

## Wingate University

Wingate NC
(800) 755-5550
**U.S. News ranking:** Reg. U. (S), No. 43
**Website:** www.wingate.edu/admissions
**Admissions email:** admit@wingate.edu
**Private;** founded 1896
**Freshman admissions:** selective; 2013-2014: 5,323 applied, 4,221 accepted. Either SAT or ACT required. SAT 25/75 percentile: 910-1120. High school rank: 18% in top tenth, 50% in top quarter, 85% in top half
**Early decision deadline:** N/A, notification date: N/A
**Early action deadline:** N/A, notification date: N/A
**Application deadline (fall):** rolling
**Undergraduate student body:** 1,953 full time, 56 part time; 41% male, 59% female; 1% American Indian, 2% Asian, 15% black, 2% Hispanic, 4% multiracial, 0% Pacific Islander, 64% white, 4% international; 83% from in state; 80% live on campus; 4% of students in fraternities, 10% in sororities
**Most popular majors:** 14% Biological and Biomedical Sciences, 20% Business, Management, Marketing, and Related Support Services,

10% Communication, Journalism, and Related Programs, 9% Education, 10% Parks, Recreation, Leisure, and Fitness Studies
**Expenses:** 2014-2015: $26,300; room/board: $10,400
**Financial aid:** (704) 233-8209; 86% of undergrads determined to have financial need; average aid package $23,080

## Winston-Salem State University[1]

Winston-Salem NC
(336) 750-2070
**U.S. News ranking:** Reg. U. (S), No. 60
**Website:** www.wssu.edu
**Admissions email:** admissions@wssu.edu
**Public;** founded 1892
**Application deadline (fall):** 3/15
**Undergraduate student body:** N/A full time, N/A part time
**Expenses:** 2013-2014: $5,468 in state, $14,281 out of state; room/board: $7,968
**Financial aid:** (336) 750-3280

NORTH DAKOTA

## Bismarck State College

Bismarck ND
(701) 224-2459
**U.S. News ranking:** Reg. Coll. (Mid. W), No. 69
**Website:** www.bismarckstate.edu
**Admissions email:** bsc.admissions@bismarckstate.edu
**Public;** founded 1959
**Freshman admissions:** less selective; 2013-2014: 1,141 applied, 1,141 accepted. Neither SAT nor ACT required. ACT 25/75 percentile: 17-23. High school rank: N/A
**Early decision deadline:** N/A, notification date: N/A
**Early action deadline:** N/A, notification date: N/A
**Application deadline (fall):** rolling
**Undergraduate student body:** 2,365 full time, 1,697 part time; 56% male, 44% female; N/A American Indian, N/A Asian, N/A black, N/A Hispanic, N/A multiracial, N/A Pacific Islander, N/A white, N/A international; 75% from in state; 9% live on campus; 0% of students in fraternities, 0% in sororities
**Most popular majors:** 100% Business, Management, Marketing, and Related Support Services
**Expenses:** 2014-2015: $4,222 in state, $10,084 out of state; room/board: $6,801
**Financial aid:** (701) 224-5494

## Dickinson State University

Dickinson ND
(701) 483-2175
**U.S. News ranking:** Reg. Coll. (Mid. W), No. 62
**Website:** www.dickinsonstate.com
**Admissions email:** dsu.hawks@dsu.nodak.edu
**Public**
**Freshman admissions:** selective; 2013-2014: 421 applied, 206 accepted. Either SAT or ACT required. ACT 25/75 percentile: 18-23. High school rank: N/A

**Early decision deadline:** N/A, notification date: N/A
**Early action deadline:** 4/15, notification date: N/A
**Application deadline (fall):** 8/1
**Undergraduate student body:** 1,018 full time, 431 part time; 39% male, 61% female; 1% American Indian, 1% Asian, 4% black, 5% Hispanic, 2% multiracial, 0% Pacific Islander, 76% white, 7% international; N/A from in state; 19% live on campus; N/A of students in fraternities, N/A in sororities
**Most popular majors:** 38% Business, Management, Marketing, and Related Support Services, 18% Education, 9% Multi/Interdisciplinary Studies, 4% Parks, Recreation, Leisure, and Fitness Studies, 4% Psychology
**Expenses:** 2013-2014: $5,848 in state, $8,200 out of state; room/board: $5,582
**Financial aid:** (701) 483-2371

## Mayville State University

Mayville ND
(701) 788-4667
**U.S. News ranking:** Reg. Coll. (Mid. W), second tier
**Website:** www.mayvillestate.edu
**Admissions email:** masuadmissions@mayvillestate.edu
**Public;** founded 1889
**Freshman admissions:** selective; 2013-2014: 317 applied, 163 accepted. Either SAT or ACT required. ACT 25/75 percentile: 17-21. High school rank: N/A in top tenth, 34% in top quarter, 67% in top half
**Early decision deadline:** N/A, notification date: N/A
**Early action deadline:** N/A, notification date: N/A
**Application deadline (fall):** rolling
**Undergraduate student body:** 587 full time, 449 part time; 44% male, 56% female; 2% American Indian, 0% Asian, 7% black, 5% Hispanic, 0% multiracial, 0% Pacific Islander, 79% white, 3% international; 60% from in state; 41% live on campus; 0% of students in fraternities, 0% in sororities
**Most popular majors:** 22% Business Administration and Management, General, 9% Child Care and Support Services Management, 20% Elementary Education and Teaching, 7% General Studies, 9% Health and Physical Education/Fitness, General
**Expenses:** 2014-2015: $6,489 in state, $8,894 out of state; room/board: $5,430
**Financial aid:** (701) 788-4767; 63% of undergrads determined to have financial need; average aid package $12,504

## Minot State University

Minot ND
(701) 858-3350
**U.S. News ranking:** Reg. U. (Mid. W), No. 106
**Website:** www.minotstateu.edu
**Admissions email:** askmsu@minotstateu.edu
**Public;** founded 1913
**Freshman admissions:** selective; 2013-2014: 959 applied, 543 accepted. Either SAT or ACT

required. ACT 25/75 percentile: 19-24. High school rank: 11% in top tenth, 22% in top quarter, 67% in top half
**Early decision deadline:** N/A, notification date: N/A
**Early action deadline:** N/A, notification date: N/A
**Application deadline (fall):** rolling
**Undergraduate student body:** 2,151 full time, 1,103 part time; 39% male, 61% female; 2% American Indian, 1% Asian, 4% black, 4% Hispanic, 3% multiracial, 0% Pacific Islander, 71% white, 12% international; 82% from in state; 21% live on campus; N/A of students in fraternities, N/A in sororities
**Most popular majors:** 34% Business Administration and Management, General, 6% Criminal Justice/Safety Studies, 18% Elementary Education and Teaching, 16% Registered Nursing/Registered Nurse, 5% Social Work
**Expenses:** 2014-2015: $6,224 in state, $6,224 out of state; room/board: $5,620
**Financial aid:** (701) 858-3375

## North Dakota State University

Fargo ND
(701) 231-8643
**U.S. News ranking:** Nat. U., No. 181
**Website:** www.ndsu.edu
**Admissions email:** NDSU.Admission@ndsu.edu
**Public;** founded 1890
**Freshman admissions:** selective; 2013-2014: 5,812 applied, 4,888 accepted. Either SAT or ACT required. ACT 25/75 percentile: 21-26. High school rank: 16% in top tenth, 40% in top quarter, 75% in top half
**Early decision deadline:** N/A, notification date: N/A
**Early action deadline:** N/A, notification date: N/A
**Application deadline (fall):** 8/1
**Undergraduate student body:** 10,707 full time, 1,241 part time; 56% male, 44% female; 1% American Indian, 1% Asian, 2% black, 1% Hispanic, 2% multiracial, 0% Pacific Islander, 88% white, 4% international; 44% from in state; 34% live on campus; N/A of students in fraternities, N/A in sororities
**Most popular majors:** 7% Agriculture, Agriculture Operations, and Related Sciences, 7% Biological and Biomedical Sciences, 17% Business, Management, Marketing, and Related Support Services, 14% Engineering, 11% Health Professions and Related Programs
**Expenses:** 2013-2014: $7,660 in state, $18,242 out of state; room/board: $7,300
**Financial aid:** (800) 726-3188

## University of Jamestown

Jamestown ND
(701) 252-3467
**U.S. News ranking:** Reg. Coll. (Mid. W), No. 37
**Website:** www.jc.edu
**Admissions email:** admissions@jc.edu
**Private;** founded 1884
**Affiliation:** Presbyterian

**Freshman admissions:** selective; 2013-2014: 1,088 applied, 619 accepted. Either SAT or ACT required. ACT 25/75 percentile: 21-24. High school rank: 12% in top tenth, 36% in top quarter, 69% in top half
**Early decision deadline:** N/A, notification date: N/A
**Early action deadline:** N/A, notification date: N/A
**Application deadline (fall):** rolling
**Undergraduate student body:** 882 full time, 73 part time; 47% male, 53% female; 1% American Indian, 2% Asian, 3% black, 5% Hispanic, 0% multiracial, 0% Pacific Islander, 84% white, 5% international; 45% from in state; 69% live on campus; N/A of students in fraternities, N/A in sororities
**Most popular majors:** 7% Biology/Biological Sciences, General, 18% Business Administration and Management, General, 8% Criminal Justice/Police Science, 10% Elementary Education and Teaching, 21% Registered Nursing, Nursing Administration, Nursing Research and Clinical Nursing
**Expenses:** 2014-2015: $19,170; room/board: $6,780
**Financial aid:** (701) 252-3467; 67% of undergrads determined to have financial need; average aid package $13,741

## University of Mary[1]
Bismarck ND
(701) 355-8030
**U.S. News ranking:** Reg. U. (Mid. W), second tier
**Website:** www.umary.edu
**Admissions email:** marauder@umary.edu
**Private**
**Application deadline (fall):** N/A
**Undergraduate student body:** N/A full time, N/A part time
**Expenses:** 2013-2014: $14,730; room/board: $5,505
**Financial aid:** (701) 355-8079

## University of North Dakota
Grand Forks ND
(800) 225-5863
**U.S. News ranking:** Nat. U., No. 168
**Website:** und.edu
**Admissions email:** admissions@und.edu
**Public;** founded 1883
**Freshman admissions:** selective; 2013-2014: 4,734 applied, 3,362 accepted. Either SAT or ACT required. ACT 25/75 percentile: 21-26. High school rank: 15% in top tenth, 39% in top quarter, 71% in top half
**Early decision deadline:** N/A, notification date: N/A
**Early action deadline:** N/A, notification date: N/A
**Application deadline (fall):** rolling
**Undergraduate student body:** 9,385 full time, 2,339 part time; 57% male, 43% female; 2% American Indian, 2% Asian, 2% black, 3% Hispanic, 3% multiracial, 0% Pacific Islander, 81% white, 0% international; 41% from in state; 27% live on campus; 9% of students in fraternities, 11% in sororities

**Most popular majors:** 4% Airline/Commercial/Professional Pilot and Flight Crew, 5% Biology/Biological Sciences, General, 4% Elementary Education and Teaching, 6% Psychology, General, 8% Registered Nursing/Registered Nurse
**Expenses:** 2013-2014: $7,508 in state, $17,794 out of state; room/board: $6,400
**Financial aid:** (701) 777-3121

## Valley City State University
Valley City ND
(701) 845-7101
**U.S. News ranking:** Reg. Coll. (Mid. W), No. 44
**Website:** www.vcsu.edu
**Admissions email:** enrollment.services@vcsu.edu
**Public;** founded 1890
**Freshman admissions:** selective; 2013-2014: 345 applied, 286 accepted. Either SAT or ACT required. ACT 25/75 percentile: 18-23. High school rank: 6% in top tenth, 21% in top quarter, 61% in top half
**Early decision deadline:** N/A, notification date: N/A
**Early action deadline:** N/A, notification date: N/A
**Application deadline (fall):** rolling
**Undergraduate student body:** 759 full time, 452 part time; 44% male, 56% female; 1% American Indian, 1% Asian, 4% black, 5% Hispanic, 2% multiracial, 0% Pacific Islander, 81% white, 5% international; 64% from in state; 23% live on campus; 1% of students in fraternities, 1% in sororities
**Most popular majors:** 13% Business Administration and Management, General, 4% Computer and Information Sciences, General, 56% Elementary Education and Teaching, 4% Physical Education Teaching and Coaching, 5% Wildlife, Fish and Wildlands Science and Management
**Expenses:** 2014-2015: $6,704 in state, $15,099 out of state; room/board: $5,938
**Financial aid:** (701) 845-7412; 63% of undergrads determined to have financial need; average aid package $8,621

## Antioch University[1]
Yellow Springs OH
(937) 769-1818
**U.S. News ranking:** Reg. U. (Mid. W), unranked
**Website:** midwest.antioch.edu
**Admissions email:** N/A
**Private**
**Application deadline (fall):** N/A
**Undergraduate student body:** N/A full time, N/A part time
**Expenses:** N/A
**Financial aid:** N/A

## Art Academy of Cincinnati[1]
Cincinnati OH
(513) 562-8740
**U.S. News ranking:** Arts, unranked
**Website:** www.artacademy.edu
**Admissions email:** admissions@artacademy.edu
**Private**

**Application deadline (fall):** N/A
**Undergraduate student body:** N/A full time, N/A part time
**Expenses:** 2013-2014: $24,330; room/board: $8,700
**Financial aid:** (513) 562-8751

## Ashland University
Ashland OH
(419) 289-5052
**U.S. News ranking:** Nat. U., second tier
**Website:** www.ashland.edu/admissions
**Admissions email:** enrollme@ashland.edu
**Private;** founded 1878
**Affiliation:** Brethren Church
**Freshman admissions:** selective; 2013-2014: 2,943 applied, 2,130 accepted. Either SAT or ACT required. ACT 25/75 percentile: 20-25. High school rank: 19% in top tenth, 49% in top quarter, 83% in top half
**Early decision deadline:** N/A, notification date: N/A
**Early action deadline:** N/A, notification date: N/A
**Application deadline (fall):** rolling
**Undergraduate student body:** 2,389 full time, 809 part time; 49% male, 51% female; 1% American Indian, 0% Asian, 13% black, 2% Hispanic, 1% multiracial, 0% Pacific Islander, 79% white, 3% international; 85% from in state; 64% live on campus; 13% of students in fraternities, 21% in sororities
**Most popular majors:** 9% Early Childhood Education and Teaching, 4% Education/Teaching of Individuals with Multiple Disabilities, 4% Exercise Physiology, 6% Junior High/Intermediate/Middle School Education and Teaching, 12% Nursing Practice
**Expenses:** 2014-2015: $19,852; room/board: $9,502
**Financial aid:** (419) 289-5002; 82% of undergrads determined to have financial need; average aid package $25,115

## Baldwin Wallace University
Berea OH
(440) 826-2222
**U.S. News ranking:** Reg. U. (Mid. W), No. 14
**Website:** www.bw.edu
**Admissions email:** admission@bw.edu
**Private;** founded 1845
**Affiliation:** United Methodist
**Freshman admissions:** selective; 2013-2014: 4,220 applied, 2,699 accepted. Neither SAT nor ACT required. ACT 25/75 percentile: 21-27. High school rank: 19% in top tenth, 50% in top quarter, 80% in top half
**Early decision deadline:** N/A, notification date: N/A
**Early action deadline:** N/A, notification date: N/A
**Application deadline (fall):** rolling
**Undergraduate student body:** 3,003 full time, 422 part time; 45% male, 55% female; 0% American Indian, 1% Asian, 9% black, 5% Hispanic, 4% multiracial, 0% Pacific Islander, 80% white, 1% international; 83% from in state; 61% live on campus; 12% of students in fraternities, 19% in sororities

**Most popular majors:** 10% Biological and Biomedical Sciences, 27% Business, Management, Marketing, and Related Support Services, 7% Communication, Journalism, and Related Programs, 8% Education, 9% Visual and Performing Arts
**Expenses:** 2014-2015: $28,814; room/board: $8,048
**Financial aid:** (440) 826-2108; 78% of undergrads determined to have financial need; average aid package $23,639

## Bluffton University
Bluffton OH
(800) 488-3257
**U.S. News ranking:** Reg. Coll. (Mid. W), No. 28
**Website:** www.bluffton.edu
**Admissions email:** admissions@bluffton.edu
**Private;** founded 1899
**Affiliation:** Mennonite Church USA
**Freshman admissions:** selective; 2013-2014: 1,784 applied, 947 accepted. Either SAT or ACT required. ACT 25/75 percentile: 19-25. High school rank: 12% in top tenth, 36% in top quarter, 62% in top half
**Early decision deadline:** N/A, notification date: N/A
**Early action deadline:** N/A, notification date: N/A
**Application deadline (fall):** 8/15
**Undergraduate student body:** 838 full time, 215 part time; 50% male, 50% female; 0% American Indian, 0% Asian, 7% black, 4% Hispanic, 1% multiracial, 0% Pacific Islander, 84% white, 1% international; 86% from in state; 90% live on campus; 0% of students in fraternities, 0% in sororities
**Most popular majors:** 11% Business Administration and Management, General, 8% Elementary Education and Teaching, 23% Organizational Behavior Studies, 12% Social Work, 7% Sport and Fitness Administration/Management
**Expenses:** 2014-2015: $29,316; room/board: $9,632
**Financial aid:** (419) 358-3266; 82% of undergrads determined to have financial need; average aid package $25,740

## Bowling Green State University
Bowling Green OH
(419) 372-2478
**U.S. News ranking:** Nat. U., No. 173
**Website:** www.bgsu.edu
**Admissions email:** choosebgsu@bgsu.edu
**Public;** founded 1910
**Freshman admissions:** selective; 2013-2014: 15,689 applied, 11,370 accepted. Either SAT or ACT required. ACT 25/75 percentile: 20-25. High school rank: 12% in top tenth, 34% in top quarter, 70% in top half
**Early decision deadline:** N/A, notification date: N/A
**Early action deadline:** N/A, notification date: N/A
**Application deadline (fall):** 7/15
**Undergraduate student body:** 13,387 full time, 1,090 part time; 44% male, 56% female; 0% American Indian, 1% Asian,

10% black, 4% Hispanic, 2% multiracial, 0% Pacific Islander, 78% white, 2% international; 88% from in state; 44% live on campus; 8% of students in fraternities, 12% in sororities
**Most popular majors:** 4% Education, Other, 5% Kindergarten/Preschool Education and Teaching, 5% Liberal Arts and Sciences/Liberal Studies, 3% Sport and Fitness Administration/Management, 4% Teacher Education, Multiple Levels
**Expenses:** 2014-2015: $10,726 in state, $18,034 out of state; room/board: $8,244
**Financial aid:** (419) 372-2651; 67% of undergrads determined to have financial need; average aid package $13,852

## Capital University
Columbus OH
(866) 544-6175
**U.S. News ranking:** Reg. U. (Mid. W), No. 36
**Website:** www.capital.edu
**Admissions email:** admission@capital.edu
**Private;** founded 1830
**Affiliation:** Lutheran
**Freshman admissions:** selective; 2013-2014: 3,640 applied, 2,767 accepted. Either SAT or ACT required. ACT 25/75 percentile: 21-27. High school rank: 16% in top tenth, 45% in top quarter, 78% in top half
**Early decision deadline:** N/A, notification date: N/A
**Early action deadline:** N/A, notification date: N/A
**Application deadline (fall):** rolling
**Undergraduate student body:** 2,481 full time, 307 part time; 42% male, 58% female; 0% American Indian, 1% Asian, 9% black, 3% Hispanic, 4% multiracial, 0% Pacific Islander, 80% white, 1% international; 91% from in state; 57% live on campus; 3% of students in fraternities, 3% in sororities
**Most popular majors:** 13% Business, Management, Marketing, and Related Support Services, 14% Education, 17% Health Professions and Related Programs, 7% Social Sciences, 11% Visual and Performing Arts
**Expenses:** 2014-2015: $31,990; room/board: $9,060
**Financial aid:** (614) 236-6511; 82% of undergrads determined to have financial need; average aid package $25,447

## Case Western Reserve University
Cleveland OH
(216) 368-4450
**U.S. News ranking:** Nat. U., No. 38
**Website:** www.case.edu
**Admissions email:** admission@case.edu
**Private;** founded 1826
**Freshman admissions:** most selective; 2013-2014: 18,418 applied, 7,713 accepted. Either SAT or ACT required. SAT 25/75 percentile: 1270-1480. High school rank: 67% in top tenth, 92% in top quarter, 99% in top half
**Early decision deadline:** 11/1, notification date: 12/15

**Early action deadline:** 11/1, notification date: 12/15
**Application deadline (fall):** 1/15
**Undergraduate student body:** 4,528 full time, 133 part time; 55% male, 45% female; 0% American Indian, 19% Asian, 5% black, 5% Hispanic, 4% multiracial, 0% Pacific Islander, 54% white, 8% international; 36% from in state; 89% live on campus; 40% of students in fraternities, 37% in sororities
**Most popular majors:** 10% Bioengineering and Biomedical Engineering, 9% Biology/Biological Sciences, General, 7% Mechanical Engineering, 9% Psychology, General, 7% Registered Nursing/Registered Nurse
**Expenses:** 2014-2015: $43,158; room/board: $13,376
**Financial aid:** (216) 368-3866; 62% of undergrads determined to have financial need; average aid package $34,243

## Cedarville University
Cedarville OH
(800) 233-2784
**U.S. News ranking:** Reg. Coll. (Mid. W), No. 6
**Website:** www.cedarville.edu
**Admissions email:** admissions@cedarville.edu
**Private;** founded 1887
**Affiliation:** Baptist
**Freshman admissions:** more selective; 2013-2014: 3,267 applied, 2,418 accepted. Either SAT or ACT required. ACT 25/75 percentile: 24-29. High school rank: 31% in top tenth, 61% in top quarter, 89% in top half
**Early decision deadline:** N/A, notification date: N/A
**Early action deadline:** N/A, notification date: N/A
**Application deadline (fall):** 8/14
**Undergraduate student body:** 3,044 full time, 194 part time; 47% male, 53% female; 0% American Indian, 2% Asian, 2% black, 2% Hispanic, 2% multiracial, 0% Pacific Islander, 88% white, 1% international; 38% from in state; 82% live on campus; 0% of students in fraternities, 0% in sororities
**Most popular majors:** 12% Business, Management, Marketing, and Related Support Services, 10% Education, 9% Engineering, 11% Health Professions and Related Programs, 9% Theology and Religious Vocations
**Expenses:** 2014-2015: $26,400; room/board: $6,460
**Financial aid:** (937) 766-7866; 68% of undergrads determined to have financial need; average aid package $16,554

## Central State University
Wilberforce OH
(937) 376-6348
**U.S. News ranking:** Reg. Coll. (Mid. W), second tier
**Website:** www.centralstate.edu
**Admissions email:** admissions@centralstate.edu
**Public;** founded 1887
**Freshman admissions:** less selective; 2013-2014: 7,142 applied, 2,377 accepted. Either SAT or ACT required. ACT 25/75

percentile: 15-19. High school rank: 5% in top tenth, 18% in top quarter, 49% in top half
**Early decision deadline:** N/A, notification date: N/A
**Early action deadline:** N/A, notification date: N/A
**Application deadline (fall):** rolling
**Undergraduate student body:** 1,840 full time, 196 part time; 47% male, 53% female; 0% American Indian, 0% Asian, 95% black, 1% Hispanic, 1% multiracial, 0% Pacific Islander, 0% white, 0% international; 63% from in state; 56% live on campus; 1% of students in fraternities, 1% in sororities
**Most popular majors:** 30% Business, Management, Marketing, and Related Support Services, 8% Communication, Journalism, and Related Programs, 17% Education, 7% Homeland Security, Law Enforcement, Firefighting and Related Protective Services, 6% Psychology
**Expenses:** 2014-2015: $7,916 in state, $14,056 out of state; room/board: $9,318
**Financial aid:** (937) 376-6579; 98% of undergrads determined to have financial need; average aid package $7,159

## Cleveland Institute of Art
Cleveland OH
(216) 421-7418
**U.S. News ranking:** Arts, unranked
**Website:** www.cia.edu
**Admissions email:** admissions@cia.edu
**Private;** founded 1882
**Freshman admissions:** N/A; 2013-2014: 633 applied, 432 accepted. Either SAT or ACT required. SAT 25/75 percentile: N/A. High school rank: 14% in top tenth, 37% in top quarter, 65% in top half
**Early decision deadline:** N/A, notification date: N/A
**Early action deadline:** 12/1, notification date: 12/15
**Application deadline (fall):** rolling
**Undergraduate student body:** 558 full time, 10 part time; 42% male, 58% female; 0% American Indian, 3% Asian, 10% black, 5% Hispanic, 2% multiracial, 0% Pacific Islander, 75% white, 5% international; 72% from in state; 25% live on campus; 0% of students in fraternities, 1% in sororities
**Most popular majors:** 17% Illustration, 20% Industrial and Product Design, 6% Interior Design, 8% Medical Illustration/Medical Illustrator, 8% Painting
**Expenses:** 2014-2015: $37,565; room/board: $11,120
**Financial aid:** (216) 421-7425; 83% of undergrads determined to have financial need; average aid package $26,213

## Cleveland Institute of Music
Cleveland OH
(216) 795-3107
**U.S. News ranking:** Arts, unranked
**Website:** www.cim.edu/
**Admissions email:** admission@cim.edu
**Private;** founded 1920
**Freshman admissions:** N/A; 2013-2014: 358 applied, 196 accepted. Neither SAT nor ACT

required. SAT 25/75 percentile: N/A. High school rank: N/A
**Early decision deadline:** N/A, notification date: N/A
**Early action deadline:** N/A, notification date: N/A
**Application deadline (fall):** 12/1
**Undergraduate student body:** 236 full time, 1 part time; 50% male, 50% female; 0% American Indian, 3% Asian, 1% black, 2% Hispanic, 0% multiracial, 0% Pacific Islander, 19% white, 18% international; N/A from in state; 41% live on campus; 0% of students in fraternities, 0% in sororities
**Most popular majors:** Information not available
**Expenses:** 2013-2014: $44,039; room/board: $12,844
**Financial aid:** (216) 791-5000

## Cleveland State University
Cleveland OH
(216) 687-2100
**U.S. News ranking:** Nat. U., second tier
**Website:** www.csuohio.edu
**Admissions email:** admissions@csuohio.edu
**Public;** founded 1964
**Freshman admissions:** selective; 2013-2014: 6,768 applied, 4,255 accepted. Either SAT or ACT required. ACT 25/75 percentile: 19-25. High school rank: 14% in top tenth, 39% in top quarter, 71% in top half
**Early decision deadline:** N/A, notification date: N/A
**Early action deadline:** 5/1, notification date: N/A
**Application deadline (fall):** 8/16
**Undergraduate student body:** 9,027 full time, 3,349 part time; 46% male, 54% female; 0% American Indian, 2% Asian, 19% black, 5% Hispanic, 3% multiracial, 0% Pacific Islander, 63% white, 5% international; 92% from in state; 9% live on campus; 1% of students in fraternities, 1% in sororities
**Most popular majors:** 19% Business, Management, Marketing, and Related Support Services, 6% Education, 15% Health Professions and Related Programs, 10% Psychology, 11% Social Sciences
**Expenses:** 2014-2015: $9,473 in state, $12,653 out of state; room/board: $12,100
**Financial aid:** (216) 687-2054; 79% of undergrads determined to have financial need; average aid package $8,707

## College of Wooster
Wooster OH
(800) 877-9905
**U.S. News ranking:** Nat. Lib. Arts, No. 69
**Website:** www.wooster.edu/
**Admissions email:** admissions@wooster.edu
**Private;** founded 1866
**Freshman admissions:** more selective; 2013-2014: 5,583 applied, 3,145 accepted. Either SAT or ACT required. ACT 25/75 percentile: 25-30. High school rank: 40% in top tenth, 73% in top quarter, 92% in top half
**Early decision deadline:** 11/1, notification date: 11/15
**Early action deadline:** 11/15, notification date: 12/31

**Application deadline (fall):** 2/15
**Undergraduate student body:** 2,077 full time, 39 part time; 44% male, 56% female; 1% American Indian, 3% Asian, 8% black, 4% Hispanic, 0% multiracial, 0% Pacific Islander, 72% white, 7% international; 39% from in state; 99% live on campus; 15% of students in fraternities, 21% in sororities
**Most popular majors:** 6% Biological and Biomedical Sciences, 9% English Language and Literature/Letters, 8% History, 8% Psychology, 15% Social Sciences
**Expenses:** 2014-2015: $43,350; room/board: $10,250
**Financial aid:** (330) 263-2317; 58% of undergrads determined to have financial need; average aid package $37,614

## Columbus College of Art and Design
Columbus OH
(614) 222-3261
**U.S. News ranking:** Arts, unranked
**Website:** www.ccad.edu
**Admissions email:** admissions@ccad.edu
**Private;** founded 1879
**Freshman admissions:** N/A; 2013-2014: 666 applied, 582 accepted. Either SAT or ACT required. SAT 25/75 percentile: N/A. High school rank: 6% in top tenth, 18% in top quarter, 59% in top half
**Early decision deadline:** N/A, notification date: N/A
**Early action deadline:** 12/1, notification date: 12/20
**Application deadline (fall):** 8/22
**Undergraduate student body:** 1,212 full time, 121 part time; 38% male, 62% female; 0% American Indian, 3% Asian, 8% black, 5% Hispanic, 4% multiracial, 0% Pacific Islander, 68% white, 8% international; N/A from in state; 65% live on campus; N/A of students in fraternities, N/A in sororities
**Most popular majors:** Information not available
**Expenses:** 2014-2015: $31,322; room/board: $7,740
**Financial aid:** (614) 222-3295; 81% of undergrads determined to have financial need; average aid package $20,042

## Defiance College
Defiance OH
(800) 520-4632
**U.S. News ranking:** Reg. Coll. (Mid. W), No. 40
**Website:** www.defiance.edu
**Admissions email:** admissions@defiance.edu
**Private;** founded 1850
**Affiliation:** United Church of Christ
**Freshman admissions:** selective; 2013-2014: 1,704 applied, 1,220 accepted. Either SAT or ACT required. ACT 25/75 percentile: 18-23. High school rank: 7% in top tenth, 25% in top quarter, 56% in top half
**Early decision deadline:** N/A, notification date: N/A
**Early action deadline:** N/A, notification date: N/A
**Application deadline (fall):** rolling
**Undergraduate student body:** 732 full time, 160 part time; 52% male, 48% female; 2% American Indian, 1% Asian, 11% black, 6% Hispanic, 0% multiracial,

0% Pacific Islander, 76% white, 1% international; 73% from in state; 50% live on campus; 6% of students in fraternities, 6% in sororities
**Most popular majors:** 23% Business Administration and Management, General, 11% Criminal Justice/Police Science, 15% Education, General, 8% Health Professions and Related Programs, 13% Sport and Fitness Administration/Management
**Expenses:** 2014-2015: $29,916; room/board: $9,522
**Financial aid:** (419) 783-2376; 90% of undergrads determined to have financial need; average aid package $23,246

## Denison University
Granville OH
(740) 587-6276
**U.S. News ranking:** Nat. Lib. Arts, No. 51
**Website:** www.denison.edu
**Admissions email:** admissions@denison.edu
**Private;** founded 1831
**Freshman admissions:** more selective; 2013-2014: 4,770 applied, 2,193 accepted. Neither SAT nor ACT required. ACT 25/75 percentile: 27-31. High school rank: 45% in top tenth, 88% in top quarter, 100% in top half
**Early decision deadline:** 11/15, notification date: N/A
**Early action deadline:** N/A, notification date: N/A
**Application deadline (fall):** 1/15
**Undergraduate student body:** 2,253 full time, 21 part time; 42% male, 58% female; 0% American Indian, 3% Asian, 7% black, 9% Hispanic, 4% multiracial, 0% Pacific Islander, 69% white, 7% international; 28% from in state; 99% live on campus; 34% of students in fraternities, 45% in sororities
**Most popular majors:** 11% Biological and Biomedical Sciences, 9% Communication, Journalism, and Related Programs, 5% History, 23% Social Sciences, 8% Visual and Performing Arts
**Expenses:** 2014-2015: $45,670; room/board: $11,180
**Financial aid:** (740) 587-6279; 51% of undergrads determined to have financial need; average aid package $38,369

## Franciscan University of Steubenville
Steubenville OH
(740) 283-6226
**U.S. News ranking:** Reg. U. (Mid. W), No. 30
**Website:** www.franciscan.edu
**Admissions email:** admissions@franciscan.edu
**Private;** founded 1946
**Affiliation:** Roman Catholic
**Freshman admissions:** more selective; 2013-2014: 1,889 applied, 1,437 accepted. Either SAT or ACT required. ACT 25/75 percentile: 23-28. High school rank: 31% in top tenth, 52% in top quarter, 83% in top half
**Early decision deadline:** N/A, notification date: N/A
**Early action deadline:** N/A, notification date: N/A
**Application deadline (fall):** rolling
**Undergraduate student body:** 1,989 full time, 123 part time; 38% male, 62% female; 0% American

Indian, 2% Asian, 0% black, 10% Hispanic, 2% multiracial, 0% Pacific Islander, 81% white, 1% international; 21% from in state; 79% live on campus; 0% of students in fraternities, 0% in sororities
**Most popular majors:** 10% Business Administration and Management, General, 10% Elementary Education and Teaching, 7% Philosophy, 7% Religious Education, 29% Theology/Theological Studies
**Expenses:** 2014-2015: $23,930; room/board: $8,000
**Financial aid:** (740) 283-6226; 66% of undergrads determined to have financial need; average aid package $13,503

## Franklin University[1]
Columbus OH
(614) 341-6256
**U.S. News ranking:** Business, unranked
**Website:** www.franklin.edu
**Admissions email:** info@franklin.edu
**Application deadline (fall):** rolling
**Undergraduate student body:** N/A full time, N/A part time
**Expenses:** 2013-2014: $10,681; room/board: N/A
**Financial aid:** (614) 797-4700

## Heidelberg University
Tiffin OH
(419) 448-2330
**U.S. News ranking:** Reg. U. (Mid. W), No. 49
**Website:** www.heidelberg.edu
**Admissions email:** adminfo@ heidelberg.edu
**Private;** founded 1850
**Affiliation:** United Church of Christ
**Freshman admissions:** selective; 2013-2014: 1,797 applied, 1,328 accepted. Either SAT or ACT required. ACT 25/75 percentile: 19-25. High school rank: N/A
**Early decision deadline:** N/A, notification date: N/A
**Early action deadline:** N/A, notification date: N/A
**Application deadline (fall):** rolling
**Undergraduate student body:** 1,065 full time, 51 part time; 50% male, 50% female; 1% American Indian, 1% Asian, 7% black, 2% Hispanic, 3% multiracial, 0% Pacific Islander, 75% white, 0% international; 86% from in state; 77% live on campus; 12% of students in fraternities, 22% in sororities
**Most popular majors:** 16% Business, Management, Marketing, and Related Support Services, 17% Education, 10% Parks, Recreation, Leisure, and Fitness Studies, 7% Psychology, 6% Social Sciences
**Expenses:** 2014-2015: $27,480; room/board: $9,226
**Financial aid:** (419) 448-2293; 90% of undergrads determined to have financial need; average aid package $21,855

## Hiram College
Hiram OH
(800) 362-5280
**U.S. News ranking:** Nat. Lib. Arts, No. 148
**Website:** www.hiram.edu
**Admissions email:** admission@hiram.edu
**Private;** founded 1850
**Freshman admissions:** selective; 2013-2014: 2,530 applied, 1,449 accepted. Either SAT or ACT required. ACT 25/75 percentile: 19-25. High school rank: 12% in top tenth, 37% in top quarter, 67% in top half
**Early decision deadline:** N/A, notification date: N/A
**Early action deadline:** N/A, notification date: N/A
**Application deadline (fall):** rolling
**Undergraduate student body:** 1,117 full time, 166 part time; 45% male, 55% female; 0% American Indian, 1% Asian, 14% black, 4% Hispanic, 2% multiracial, 0% Pacific Islander, 71% white, 4% international; 82% from in state; 80% live on campus; N/A of students in fraternities, N/A in sororities
**Most popular majors:** 14% Biological and Biomedical Sciences, 29% Business, Management, Marketing, and Related Support Services, 5% Education, 5% Health Professions and Related Programs, 13% Social Sciences
**Expenses:** 2014-2015: $30,290; room/board: $10,010
**Financial aid:** (330) 569-5107; 86% of undergrads determined to have financial need; average aid package $25,110

## John Carroll University
University Heights OH
(216) 397-4294
**U.S. News ranking:** Reg. U. (Mid. W), No. 7
**Website:** www.jcu.edu
**Admissions email:** admission@jcu.edu
**Private;** founded 1886
**Affiliation:** Roman Catholic (Jesuit)
**Freshman admissions:** selective; 2013-2014: 3,721 applied, 3,101 accepted. Either SAT or ACT required. ACT 25/75 percentile: 22-27. High school rank: 22% in top tenth, 51% in top quarter, 82% in top half
**Early decision deadline:** N/A, notification date: N/A
**Early action deadline:** N/A, notification date: N/A
**Application deadline (fall):** 2/1
**Undergraduate student body:** 2,962 full time, 90 part time; 52% male, 48% female; 0% American Indian, 2% Asian, 4% black, 4% Hispanic, 2% multiracial, 0% Pacific Islander, 83% white, 1% international; 70% from in state; 54% live on campus; 6% of students in fraternities, 11% in sororities
**Most popular majors:** 9% Biological and Biomedical Sciences, 30% Business, Management, Marketing, and Related Support Services, 9% Communication, Journalism, and Related Programs, 9% Education, 10% Social Sciences
**Expenses:** 2014-2015: $35,800; room/board: $10,500

## Kent State University
Kent OH
(330) 672-2444
**U.S. News ranking:** Nat. U., No. 194
**Website:** www.kent.edu
**Admissions email:** kentadm@ kent.edu
**Public;** founded 1910
**Freshman admissions:** selective; 2013-2014: 16,083 applied, 13,368 accepted. Either SAT or ACT required. ACT 25/75 percentile: 20-25. High school rank: 14% in top tenth, 40% in top quarter, 77% in top half
**Early decision deadline:** N/A, notification date: N/A
**Early action deadline:** N/A, notification date: N/A
**Application deadline (fall):** 8/1
**Undergraduate student body:** 19,865 full time, 3,103 part time; 41% male, 59% female; 0% American Indian, 1% Asian, 9% black, 3% Hispanic, 3% multiracial, 0% Pacific Islander, 76% white, 6% international; 88% from in state; 28% live on campus; N/A of students in fraternities, N/A in sororities
**Most popular majors:** 19% Business, Management, Marketing, and Related Support Services, 8% Communication, Journalism, and Related Programs, 9% Education, 18% Health Professions and Related Programs, 6% Visual and Performing Arts
**Expenses:** 2014-2015: $10,012 in state, $17,972 out of state; room/board: $9,768
**Financial aid:** (330) 672-2972; 67% of undergrads determined to have financial need; average aid package $9,749

## Kenyon College
Gambier OH
(740) 427-5776
**U.S. News ranking:** Nat. Lib. Arts, No. 30
**Website:** www.kenyon.edu
**Admissions email:** admissions@ kenyon.edu
**Private;** founded 1824
**Freshman admissions:** more selective; 2013-2014: 4,051 applied, 1,555 accepted. Either SAT or ACT required. SAT 25/75 percentile: 1230-1410. High school rank: 65% in top tenth, 88% in top quarter, 98% in top half
**Early decision deadline:** 11/15, notification date: 12/15
**Early action deadline:** N/A, notification date: N/A
**Application deadline (fall):** 1/15
**Undergraduate student body:** 1,695 full time, 10 part time; 46% male, 54% female; 1% American Indian, 6% Asian, 3% black, 5% Hispanic, 2% multiracial, 0% Pacific Islander, 76% white, 4% international; 14% from in state; 99% live on campus; 10% of students in fraternities, 10% in sororities

**Financial aid:** (216) 397-4248; 74% of undergrads determined to have financial need; average aid package $27,861

Economics, General, 18% English Language and Literature, General, 7% History, General, 9% Political Science and Government, General, 9% Psychology, General
**Expenses:** 2014-2015: $47,330; room/board: $11,560
**Financial aid:** (740) 427-5430; 39% of undergrads determined to have financial need; average aid package $38,495

## Lake Erie College
Painesville OH
(800) 916-0904
**U.S. News ranking:** Reg. U. (Mid. W), second tier
**Website:** www.lec.edu
**Admissions email:** admissions@lec.edu
**Private;** founded 1856
**Freshman admissions:** selective; 2013-2014: 1,160 applied, 645 accepted. Either SAT or ACT required. ACT 25/75 percentile: 19-23. High school rank: 6% in top tenth, 28% in top quarter, 63% in top half
**Early decision deadline:** N/A, notification date: N/A
**Early action deadline:** N/A, notification date: N/A
**Application deadline (fall):** 8/1
**Undergraduate student body:** 852 full time, 72 part time; 51% male, 49% female; 0% American Indian, 0% Asian, 11% black, 2% Hispanic, 3% multiracial, 0% Pacific Islander, 78% white, 4% international; 73% from in state; 62% live on campus; N/A of students in fraternities, N/A in sororities
**Most popular majors:** 8% Biology/Biological Sciences, General, 38% Business Administration and Management, General, 6% Equestrian/Equine Studies, 6% Psychology, General, 9% Sport and Fitness Administration/Management
**Expenses:** 2014-2015: $28,355; room/board: $8,912
**Financial aid:** (440) 375-7100; 80% of undergrads determined to have financial need; average aid package $21,312

## Lourdes University
Sylvania OH
(419) 885-5291
**U.S. News ranking:** Reg. U. (Mid. W), unranked
**Website:** www.lourdes.edu
**Admissions email:** admissionslcadmits@lourdes.edu
**Private;** founded 1958
**Affiliation:** Roman Catholic
**Freshman admissions:** N/A; 2013-2014: 1,307 applied, 906 accepted. Neither SAT nor ACT required. ACT 25/75 percentile: N/A. High school rank: 9% in top tenth, 24% in top quarter, 59% in top half
**Early decision deadline:** N/A, notification date: N/A
**Early action deadline:** N/A, notification date: N/A
**Application deadline (fall):** rolling
**Undergraduate student body:** 1,137 full time, 669 part time; 30% male, 70% female; 0% American Indian, 1% Asian, 11% black, 13% Hispanic, 3% multiracial, 0% Pacific Islander, 69% white, 0% international; 84% from in state; 16% live on campus; 0% of students in fraternities, 0% in sororities

**Most popular majors:** 8% Economics, General, 18% English Language and Literature

**Most popular majors:** 4% Business Administration, Management and Operations, 4% Criminal Justice and Corrections, 14% Multi-Interdisciplinary Studies, Other, 36% Registered Nursing, Nursing Administration, Nursing Research and Clinical Nursing, 5% Social Work
**Expenses:** 2013-2014: $17,656; room/board: $8,400
**Financial aid:** (419) 824-3732

## Malone University
Canton OH
(330) 471-8145
**U.S. News ranking:** Reg. U. (Mid. W), No. 54
**Website:** www.malone.edu
**Admissions email:** admissions@ malone.edu
**Private;** founded 1892
**Affiliation:** Evangelical Friends
**Freshman admissions:** selective; 2013-2014: 1,333 applied, 957 accepted. Either SAT or ACT required. ACT 25/75 percentile: 19-26. High school rank: 19% in top tenth, 42% in top quarter, 76% in top half
**Early decision deadline:** N/A, notification date: N/A
**Early action deadline:** N/A, notification date: N/A
**Application deadline (fall):** rolling
**Undergraduate student body:** 1,453 full time, 203 part time; 43% male, 57% female; 0% American Indian, 1% Asian, 8% black, 3% Hispanic, 2% multiracial, 0% Pacific Islander, 85% white, 2% international; 86% from in state; 55% live on campus; 0% of students in fraternities, 0% in sororities
**Most popular majors:** 7% Business Administration and Management, General, 16% Business Administration, Management and Operations, Other, 4% Education/Teaching of Individuals with Specific Learning Disabilities, 4% Kinesiology and Exercise Science, 15% Registered Nursing/Registered Nurse
**Expenses:** 2014-2015: $26,416; room/board: $8,948
**Financial aid:** (330) 471-8159; 83% of undergrads determined to have financial need; average aid package $20,320

## Marietta College
Marietta OH
(800) 331-7896
**U.S. News ranking:** Reg. Coll. (Mid. W), No. 6
**Website:** www.marietta.edu
**Admissions email:** admit@marietta.edu
**Private;** founded 1797
**Freshman admissions:** selective; 2013-2014: 4,053 applied, 2,579 accepted. Either SAT or ACT required. ACT 25/75 percentile: 21-27. High school rank: 32% in top tenth, 59% in top quarter, 85% in top half
**Early decision deadline:** N/A, notification date: N/A
**Early action deadline:** N/A, notification date: N/A
**Application deadline (fall):** 4/15
**Undergraduate student body:** 1,352 full time, 64 part time; 58% male, 42% female; 0% American Indian, 1% Asian, 6% black, 3% Hispanic, 2% multiracial, 0% Pacific Islander, 71% white,

12% international; 53% from in state; 77% live on campus; 13% of students in fraternities, 30% in sororities
**Most popular majors:** Information not available
**Expenses:** 2014-2015: $33,490; room/board: $10,395
**Financial aid:** (740) 376-4712; 68% of undergrads determined to have financial need; average aid package $24,569

## Miami University–Oxford
Oxford OH
(513) 529-2531
**U.S. News ranking:** Nat. U., No. 76
**Website:** www.MiamiOH.edu
**Admissions email:** admission@MiamiOH.edu
**Public;** founded 1809
**Freshman admissions:** more selective; 2013-2014: 22,520 applied, 15,034 accepted. Either SAT or ACT required. ACT 25/75 percentile: 25-30. High school rank: 39% in top tenth, 71% in top quarter, 95% in top half
**Early decision deadline:** 11/15, notification date: 12/15
**Early action deadline:** 12/1, notification date: 2/1
**Application deadline (fall):** 2/1
**Undergraduate student body:** 15,001 full time, 461 part time; 48% male, 52% female; 0% American Indian, 2% Asian, 4% black, 3% Hispanic, 3% multiracial, 0% Pacific Islander, 81% white, 6% international; 68% from in state; 47% live on campus; 23% of students in fraternities, 28% in sororities
**Most popular majors:** 6% Biological and Biomedical Sciences, 24% Business, Management, Marketing, and Related Support Services, 11% Education, 6% Parks, Recreation, Leisure, and Fitness Studies, 9% Social Sciences
**Expenses:** 2014-2015: $14,287 in state, $30,394 out of state; room/board: $11,109
**Financial aid:** (513) 529-8734; 40% of undergrads determined to have financial need; average aid package $11,902

## Mount St. Joseph University
Cincinnati OH
(513) 244-4531
**U.S. News ranking:** Reg. U. (Mid. W), No. 61
**Website:** www.msj.edu
**Admissions email:** admission@mail.msj.edu
**Private;** founded 1920
**Affiliation:** Catholic
**Freshman admissions:** selective; 2013-2014: 1,180 applied, 1,036 accepted. Either SAT or ACT required. ACT 25/75 percentile: 19-24. High school rank: 7% in top tenth, 29% in top quarter, 58% in top half
**Early decision deadline:** N/A, notification date: N/A
**Early action deadline:** N/A, notification date: N/A
**Application deadline (fall):** 8/1
**Undergraduate student body:** 1,223 full time, 572 part time; 37% male, 63% female; 0% American Indian, 0% Asian, 10% black, 2% Hispanic, 2% multiracial, 0% Pacific Islander, 82% white,

0% international; 84% from in state; 23% live on campus; N/A of students in fraternities, N/A in sororities
**Most popular majors:** 5% Biology, General, 10% Business Administration and Management, General, 10% General Studies, 8% Graphic Design, 36% Registered Nursing/Registered Nurse
**Expenses:** 2014-2015: $26,850; room/board: $8,710
**Financial aid:** (513) 244-4418; 81% of undergrads determined to have financial need; average aid package $18,794

## Mount Vernon Nazarene University
Mount Vernon OH
(866) 462-6868
**U.S. News ranking:** Reg. U. (Mid. W), No. 67
**Website:** www.gotomvnu.com
**Admissions email:** admissions@mvnu.edu
**Private;** founded 1968
**Affiliation:** Nazarene
**Freshman admissions:** selective; 2013-2014: 1,275 applied, 811 accepted. Either SAT or ACT required. ACT 25/75 percentile: 20-26. High school rank: 23% in top tenth, 49% in top quarter, 78% in top half
**Early decision deadline:** N/A, notification date: N/A
**Early action deadline:** N/A, notification date: N/A
**Application deadline (fall):** 7/15
**Undergraduate student body:** 1,450 full time, 379 part time; 36% male, 64% female; 0% American Indian, 0% Asian, 5% black, 2% Hispanic, 2% multiracial, 0% Pacific Islander, 83% white, 0% international; 92% from in state; 54% live on campus; 0% of students in fraternities, 0% in sororities
**Most popular majors:** 35% Business, Management, Marketing, and Related Support Services, 13% Education, 7% Health Professions and Related Programs, 12% Public Administration and Social Service Professions
**Expenses:** 2013-2014: $23,690; room/board: $6,980
**Financial aid:** (740) 392-6868

## Muskingum University
New Concord OH
(740) 826-8137
**U.S. News ranking:** Reg. U. (Mid. W), No. 61
**Website:** www.muskingum.edu
**Admissions email:** adminfo@muskingum.edu
**Private;** founded 1837
**Affiliation:** Presbyterian Church (USA)
**Freshman admissions:** selective; 2013-2014: 2,001 applied, 1,520 accepted. Either SAT or ACT required. ACT 25/75 percentile: 18-24. High school rank: 28% in top tenth, 43% in top quarter, 70% in top half
**Early decision deadline:** N/A, notification date: N/A
**Early action deadline:** N/A, notification date: N/A
**Application deadline (fall):** 8/1
**Undergraduate student body:** 1,438 full time, 290 part time; 45% male, 55% female; 0% American Indian, 0% Asian, 6% black,

2% Hispanic, 3% multiracial, 0% Pacific Islander, 82% white, 4% international; 92% from in state; 71% live on campus; 25% of students in fraternities, 34% in sororities
**Most popular majors:** 18% Business, Management, Marketing, and Related Support Services, 8% Communication, Journalism, and Related Programs, 17% Education, 10% Health Professions and Related Programs, 10% Psychology
**Expenses:** 2014-2015: $24,826; room/board: $9,760
**Financial aid:** (740) 826-8139; 84% of undergrads determined to have financial need; average aid package $20,803

## Notre Dame College of Ohio[1]
Cleveland OH
(216) 373-5355
**U.S. News ranking:** Reg. Coll. (Mid. W), No. 59
**Website:** www.notredamecollege.edu
**Admissions email:** admissions@ndc.edu
**Private;** founded 1922
**Affiliation:** Roman Catholic
**Application deadline (fall):** rolling
**Undergraduate student body:** N/A full time, N/A part time
**Expenses:** 2013-2014: $26,344; room/board: $8,598
**Financial aid:** (216) 373-5263

## Oberlin College
Oberlin OH
(440) 775-8411
**U.S. News ranking:** Nat. Lib. Arts, No. 23
**Website:** www.oberlin.edu
**Admissions email:** college.admissions@oberlin.edu
**Private;** founded 1833
**Freshman admissions:** more selective; 2013-2014: 7,438 applied, 2,262 accepted. Either SAT or ACT required. SAT 25/75 percentile: 1270-1455. High school rank: 62% in top tenth, 87% in top quarter, 99% in top half
**Early decision deadline:** 11/15, notification date: 12/10
**Early action deadline:** N/A, notification date: N/A
**Application deadline (fall):** 1/15
**Undergraduate student body:** 2,861 full time, 33 part time; 46% male, 54% female; 0% American Indian, 4% Asian, 5% black, 7% Hispanic, 5% multiracial, 0% Pacific Islander, 70% white, 7% international; 8% from in state; 90% live on campus; 0% of students in fraternities, 0% in sororities
**Most popular majors:** 9% Biology, General, 8% English Language and Literature, General, 15% Music Performance, General, 9% Political Science and Government, 6% Psychology, General
**Expenses:** 2014-2015: $48,682; room/board: $13,106
**Financial aid:** (440) 775-8142; 49% of undergrads determined to have financial need; average aid package $37,656

## Ohio Christian University[1]
Circleville OH
(877) 762-8669
**U.S. News ranking:** Reg. Coll. (Mid. W), second tier
**Website:** www.ohiochristian.edu/
**Admissions email:** enroll@ohiochristian.edu
**Private**
**Application deadline (fall):** N/A
**Undergraduate student body:** N/A full time, N/A part time
**Expenses:** 2013-2014: $17,720; room/board: $6,998
**Financial aid:** (740) 477-7758

## Ohio Dominican University
Columbus OH
(614) 251-4500
**U.S. News ranking:** Reg. U. (Mid. W), No. 84
**Website:** www.ohiodominican.edu
**Admissions email:** admissions@ohiodominican.edu
**Private;** founded 1911
**Affiliation:** Roman Catholic
**Freshman admissions:** selective; 2013-2014: 2,652 applied, 1,310 accepted. ACT 25/75 percentile: 20-24. High school rank: 22% in top tenth, 46% in top quarter, 80% in top half
**Early decision deadline:** N/A, notification date: N/A
**Early action deadline:** N/A, notification date: N/A
**Application deadline (fall):** rolling
**Undergraduate student body:** 1,391 full time, 614 part time; 42% male, 58% female; 0% American Indian, 1% Asian, 26% black, 3% Hispanic, 4% multiracial, 0% Pacific Islander, 63% white, 1% international
**Most popular majors:** 5% Accounting, 5% Biology/Biological Sciences, General, 36% Business Administration and Management, General, 9% Elementary Education and Teaching, 5% Sport and Fitness Administration/Management
**Expenses:** 2013-2014: $28,932; room/board: $9,978
**Financial aid:** (614) 251-4778

## Ohio Northern University
Ada OH
(888) 408-4668
**U.S. News ranking:** Reg. Coll. (Mid. W), No. 2
**Website:** www.onu.edu
**Admissions email:** admissions-ug@onu.edu
**Private;** founded 1871
**Affiliation:** Methodist
**Freshman admissions:** more selective; 2013-2014: 3,325 applied, 2,256 accepted. Either SAT or ACT required. ACT 25/75 percentile: 23-29. High school rank: 38% in top tenth, 69% in top quarter, 90% in top half
**Early decision deadline:** N/A, notification date: N/A
**Early action deadline:** N/A, notification date: N/A
**Application deadline (fall):** 8/15
**Undergraduate student body:** 2,194 full time, 508 part time; 52% male, 48% female; 0% American Indian, 1% Asian, 4% black, 2% Hispanic, 3% multiracial, 0% Pacific Islander, 85% white, 4% international; 86% from in state;

78% live on campus; 21% of students in fraternities, 21% in sororities
**Most popular majors:** 19% Business, Management, Marketing, and Related Support Services, 5% Communication, Journalism, and Related Programs, 9% Education, 15% Engineering, 10% Health Professions and Related Programs
**Expenses:** 2014-2015: $28,050; room/board: $10,910
**Financial aid:** (419) 772-2272

## Ohio State University–Columbus
Columbus OH
(614) 292-3980
**U.S. News ranking:** Nat. U., No. 54
**Website:** www.osu.edu
**Admissions email:** askabuckeye@osu.edu
**Public;** founded 1870
**Freshman admissions:** more selective; 2013-2014: 31,359 applied, 17,413 accepted. Either SAT or ACT required. ACT 25/75 percentile: 27-31. High school rank: 58% in top tenth, 92% in top quarter, 99% in top half
**Early decision deadline:** N/A, notification date: N/A
**Early action deadline:** 11/1, notification date: 12/15
**Application deadline (fall):** 2/1
**Undergraduate student body:** 40,020 full time, 4,181 part time; 53% male, 47% female; 0% American Indian, 5% Asian, 6% black, 3% Hispanic, 3% multiracial, 0% Pacific Islander, 72% white, 7% international; 86% from in state; 26% live on campus; 6% of students in fraternities, 6% in sororities
**Most popular majors:** 3% Biology/Biological Sciences, General, 4% Finance, General, 3% Marketing/Marketing Management, General, 6% Psychology, General, 4% Speech Communication and Rhetoric
**Expenses:** 2014-2015: $10,037 in state, $26,537 out of state; room/board: $9,850
**Financial aid:** (614) 292-0300; 52% of undergrads determined to have financial need; average aid package $12,183

## Ohio University
Athens OH
(740) 593-4100
**U.S. News ranking:** Nat. U., No. 129
**Website:** www.ohio.edu
**Admissions email:** admissions@ohio.edu
**Public;** founded 1804
**Freshman admissions:** selective; 2013-2014: 20,765 applied, 15,149 accepted. Either SAT or ACT required. ACT 25/75 percentile: 22-26. High school rank: 17% in top tenth, 42% in top quarter, 82% in top half
**Early decision deadline:** N/A, notification date: N/A
**Early action deadline:** N/A, notification date: N/A
**Undergraduate student body:** 16,756 full time, 6,748 part time; 40% male, 60% female; 0% American Indian, 1% Asian, 5% black, 2% Hispanic, 3% multiracial, 0% Pacific Islander, 83% white, 4% international; 86% from in state; 44% live

on campus; 8% of students in fraternities, 8% in sororities
**Most popular majors:** 4% Liberal Arts and Sciences, General Studies and Humanities, Other, 4% Psychology, General, 30% Registered Nursing/Registered Nurse, 4% Secondary Education and Teaching, 5% Speech Communication and Rhetoric
**Expenses:** 2014-2015: $10,536 in state, $19,500 out of state; room/board: $11,532
**Financial aid:** (740) 593-4141; 60% of undergrads determined to have financial need; average aid package $8,800

## Ohio Wesleyan University
Delaware OH
(740) 368-3020
**U.S. News ranking:** Nat. Lib. Arts, No. 99
**Website:** web.owu.edu
**Admissions email:** owuadmit@owu.edu
**Private;** founded 1842
**Affiliation:** Methodist
**Freshman admissions:** more selective; 2013-2014: 4,029 applied, 3,035 accepted. Neither SAT nor ACT required. ACT 25/75 percentile: 22-27. High school rank: 32% in top tenth, 55% in top quarter, 82% in top half
**Early decision deadline:** 11/15, notification date: 11/30
**Early action deadline:** 1/15, notification date: N/A
**Application deadline (fall):** rolling
**Undergraduate student body:** 1,809 full time, 21 part time; 46% male, 54% female; 0% American Indian, 3% Asian, 6% black, 5% Hispanic, 4% multiracial, 0% Pacific Islander, 72% white, 7% international; N/A from in state; 33% live on campus; 44% of students in fraternities, 44% in sororities
**Most popular majors:** 15% Biological and Biomedical Sciences, 8% Business, Management, Marketing, and Related Support Services, 8% Psychology, 16% Social Sciences, 7% Visual and Performing Arts
**Expenses:** 2014-2015: $41,920; room/board: $11,210
**Financial aid:** (740) 368-3050; 65% of undergrads determined to have financial need; average aid package $32,026

## Otterbein University
Westerville OH
(614) 823-1500
**U.S. News ranking:** Reg. U. (Mid. W), No. 20
**Website:** www.otterbein.edu
**Admissions email:** UOtterB@ Otterbein.edu
**Private;** founded 1847
**Affiliation:** United Methodist
**Freshman admissions:** selective; 2013-2014: 3,175 applied, 2,341 accepted. Either SAT or ACT required. ACT 25/75 percentile: 22-27. High school rank: 23% in top tenth, 54% in top quarter, 86% in top half
**Early decision deadline:** N/A, notification date: N/A
**Early action deadline:** N/A, notification date: N/A
**Application deadline (fall):** rolling

Undergraduate student body: 2,206 full time, 273 part time; 38% male, 62% female; 0% American Indian, 1% Asian, 7% black, 2% Hispanic, 3% multiracial, 0% Pacific Islander, 79% white, 3% international; 89% from in state; 65% live on campus; 27% of students in fraternities, 18% in sororities
**Most popular majors:** 11% Business Administration, Management and Operations, 7% Communication and Media Studies, 10% Health Services/Allied Health/Health Sciences, General, 11% Registered Nursing, Nursing Administration, Nursing Research and Clinical Nursing, 7% Teacher Education and Professional Development, Specific Levels and Methods
**Expenses:** 2014-2015: $31,624; room/board: $9,460
**Financial aid:** (614) 823-1502; 76% of undergrads determined to have financial need; average aid package $21,407

## Shawnee State University
Portsmouth OH
(800) 959-2778
**U.S. News ranking:** Nat. Lib. Arts, second tier
**Website:** www.shawnee.edu
**Admissions email:** To_SSU@ shawnee.edu
**Public;** founded 1986
**Freshman admissions:** selective; 2013-2014: 4,426 applied, 3,688 accepted. Neither SAT nor ACT required. ACT 25/75 percentile: 17-23. High school rank: 12% in top tenth, 43% in top quarter, 64% in top half
**Early decision deadline:** N/A, notification date: N/A
**Early action deadline:** N/A, notification date: N/A
**Application deadline (fall):** rolling
**Undergraduate student body:** 3,635 full time, 620 part time; 42% male, 58% female; 1% American Indian, 0% Asian, 6% black, 1% Hispanic, 1% multiracial, 0% Pacific Islander, 86% white, 1% international; 90% from in state; 22% live on campus; 1% of students in fraternities, 1% in sororities
**Most popular majors:** 6% Business Administration and Management, General, 6% General Studies, 5% Nursing Administration, 8% Psychology, General, 7% Sociology
**Expenses:** 2014-2015: $7,364 in state, $12,617 out of state; room/board: $9,552
**Financial aid:** (740) 351-4243

## Tiffin University
Tiffin OH
(419) 448-3423
**U.S. News ranking:** Reg. U. (Mid. W), second tier
**Website:** www.tiffin.edu
**Admissions email:** admiss@tiffin.edu
**Private;** founded 1888
**Freshman admissions:** selective; 2013-2014: 3,998 applied, 2,377 accepted. Neither SAT nor ACT required. ACT 25/75 percentile: 18-23. High school rank: N/A
**Early decision deadline:** N/A, notification date: N/A
**Early action deadline:** N/A, notification date: N/A

**Application deadline (fall):** rolling
**Undergraduate student body:** 2,145 full time, 1,619 part time; 41% male, 59% female; 0% American Indian, 0% Asian, 17% black, 2% Hispanic, 3% multiracial, 0% Pacific Islander, 33% white, 3% international; 66% from in state; 25% live on campus; 1% of students in fraternities, 1% in sororities
**Most popular majors:** Information not available
**Expenses:** 2014-2015: $21,510; room/board: $9,870
**Financial aid:** (419) 448-3357; 89% of undergrads determined to have financial need; average aid package $15,597

## Union Institute and University[1]
Cincinnati OH
(513) 487-1239
**U.S. News ranking:** Nat. U., unranked
**Website:** www.myunion.edu
**Admissions email:** admissions@ myunion.edu
**Private**
**Application deadline (fall):** N/A
**Undergraduate student body:** N/A full time, N/A part time
**Expenses:** 2013-2014: $11,904; room/board: N/A
**Financial aid:** (513) 487-1127

## University of Akron
Akron OH
(330) 972-7077
**U.S. News ranking:** Nat. U., second tier
**Website:** www.uakron.edu
**Admissions email:** admissions@ uakron.edu
**Public;** founded 1870
**Freshman admissions:** selective; 2013-2014: 10,575 applied, 10,204 accepted. Either SAT or ACT required. ACT 25/75 percentile: 18-25. High school rank: 13% in top tenth, 33% in top quarter, 62% in top half
**Early decision deadline:** N/A, notification date: N/A
**Early action deadline:** 11/1, notification date: 12/15
**Application deadline (fall):** 7/1
**Undergraduate student body:** 15,869 full time, 4,604 part time; 52% male, 48% female; 0% American Indian, 2% Asian, 14% black, 2% Hispanic, 3% multiracial, 0% Pacific Islander, 74% white, 1% international; 97% from in state; 14% live on campus; 4% of students in fraternities, 4% in sororities
**Most popular majors:** 18% Business, Management, Marketing, and Related Support Services, 8% Communication, Journalism, and Related Programs, 11% Education, 9% Engineering, 15% Health Professions and Related Programs
**Expenses:** 2014-2015: $10,320 in state, $18,851 out of state; room/board: $11,332
**Financial aid:** (330) 972-7032; 78% of undergrads determined to have financial need; average aid package $7,051

## University of Cincinnati
Cincinnati OH
(513) 556-1100
**U.S. News ranking:** Nat. U., No. 129
**Website:** www.uc.edu
**Admissions email:** admissions@uc.edu
**Public;** founded 1819
**Freshman admissions:** more selective; 2013-2014: 16,069 applied, 11,680 accepted. Either SAT or ACT required. ACT 25/75 percentile: 22-28. High school rank: 22% in top tenth, 50% in top quarter, 81% in top half
**Early decision deadline:** N/A, notification date: N/A
**Early action deadline:** N/A, notification date: N/A
**Application deadline (fall):** 2/1
**Undergraduate student body:** 18,857 full time, 3,374 part time; 49% male, 51% female; 0% American Indian, 3% Asian, 8% black, 3% Hispanic, 2% multiracial, 0% Pacific Islander, 76% white, 4% international; 89% from in state; 21% live on campus; 10% of students in fraternities, 11% in sororities
**Most popular majors:** 8% Biological and Biomedical Sciences, 51% Business, Management, Marketing, and Related Support Services, 4% Computer and Information Sciences and Support Services, 4% Foreign Languages, Literatures, and Linguistics, 14% Social Sciences
**Expenses:** 2014-2015: $11,000 in state, $26,334 out of state; room/board: $10,496
**Financial aid:** (513) 556-6982; 59% of undergrads determined to have financial need; average aid package $8,330

## University of Cincinnati– UC Blue Ash College[1]
Cincinnati OH
(513) 745-5700
**U.S. News ranking:** Reg. Coll. (Mid. W), unranked
**Website:** www.rwc.uc.edu/
**Admissions email:** N/A
**Public**
**Application deadline (fall):** N/A
**Undergraduate student body:** N/A full time, N/A part time
**Expenses:** 2013-2014: $5,890 in state, $14,516 out of state; room/board: N/A
**Financial aid:** (513) 745-5700

## University of Dayton
Dayton OH
(937) 229-4411
**U.S. News ranking:** Nat. U., No. 103
**Website:** www.udayton.edu
**Admissions email:** admission@ udayton.edu
**Private;** founded 1850
**Affiliation:** Roman Catholic (Marianist)
**Freshman admissions:** more selective; 2013-2014: 16,279 applied, 8,507 accepted. Either SAT or ACT required. ACT 25/75 percentile: 24-29. High school rank: 24% in top tenth, 54% in top quarter, 87% in top half
**Early decision deadline:** N/A, notification date: N/A

**Early action deadline:** 12/15, notification date: 2/1
**Application deadline (fall):** 3/1
**Undergraduate student body:** 7,454 full time, 521 part time; 52% male, 48% female; 0% American Indian, 1% Asian, 3% black, 3% Hispanic, 1% multiracial, 0% Pacific Islander, 82% white, 9% international; 55% from in state; 72% live on campus; 17% of students in fraternities, 23% in sororities
**Most popular majors:** 29% Business, Management, Marketing, and Related Support Services, 7% Communication, Journalism, and Related Programs, 9% Education, 13% Engineering, 6% Psychology
**Expenses:** 2014-2015: $37,230; room/board: $11,840
**Financial aid:** (937) 229-4311; 53% of undergrads determined to have financial need; average aid package $22,338

## University of Findlay
Findlay OH
(800) 548-0932
**U.S. News ranking:** Reg. U. (Mid. W), No. 49
**Website:** www.findlay.edu
**Admissions email:** admissions@findlay.edu
**Private;** founded 1882
**Affiliation:** Churches of God General Conference
**Freshman admissions:** selective; 2013-2014: 2,951 applied, 1,940 accepted. Either SAT or ACT required. ACT 25/75 percentile: 20-25. High school rank: 42% in top tenth, 44% in top quarter, 89% in top half
**Early decision deadline:** N/A, notification date: N/A
**Early action deadline:** N/A, notification date: N/A
**Application deadline (fall):** rolling
**Undergraduate student body:** 2,490 full time, 1,382 part time; 38% male, 62% female; 0% American Indian, 1% Asian, 4% black, 2% Hispanic, 2% multiracial, 0% Pacific Islander, 82% white, 8% international; 82% from in state; 45% live on campus; 2% of students in fraternities, 2% in sororities
**Most popular majors:** 14% Agriculture, Agriculture Operations, and Related Sciences, 6% Biological and Biomedical Sciences, 16% Business, Management, Marketing, and Related Support Services, 12% Education, 21% Health Professions and Related Programs
**Expenses:** 2014-2015: $30,640; room/board: $9,350
**Financial aid:** (419) 434-4792; 80% of undergrads determined to have financial need; average aid package $18,435

## University of Mount Union
Alliance OH
(330) 823-2590
**U.S. News ranking:** Reg. Coll. (Mid. W), No. 11
**Website:** www.mountunion.edu/
**Admissions email:** admission@ mountunion.edu
**Private;** founded 1846
**Affiliation:** United Methodist
**Freshman admissions:** selective; 2013-2014: 2,660 applied, 1,894 accepted. Either SAT

or ACT required. ACT 25/75 percentile: 20-25. High school rank: 10% in top tenth, 34% in top quarter, 66% in top half
**Early decision deadline:** N/A, notification date: N/A
**Early action deadline:** N/A, notification date: N/A
**Application deadline (fall):** rolling
**Undergraduate student body:** 2,056 full time, 40 part time; 50% male, 50% female; 0% American Indian, 0% Asian, 6% black, 2% Hispanic, 4% multiracial, 0% Pacific Islander, 81% white, 3% international; 82% from in state; 76% live on campus; 14% of students in fraternities, 32% in sororities
**Most popular majors:** 10% Biological and Biomedical Sciences, 14% Business, Management, Marketing, and Related Support Services, 20% Education, 13% Parks, Recreation, Leisure, and Fitness Studies, 6% Psychology
**Expenses:** 2014-2015: $27,990; room/board: $9,200
**Financial aid:** (877) 543-9185; 86% of undergrads determined to have financial need; average aid package $21,406

## University of Northwestern Ohio[1]
Lima OH
(419) 998-3120
**U.S. News ranking:** Reg. Coll. (Mid. W), unranked
**Website:** www.unoh.edu/
**Admissions email:** info@unoh.edu
**Private**
**Application deadline (fall):** N/A
**Undergraduate student body:** N/A full time, N/A part time
**Expenses:** 2013-2014: $9,565; room/board: $6,750
**Financial aid:** (419) 998-3140

## University of Rio Grande
Rio Grande OH
(740) 245-7208
**U.S. News ranking:** Reg. U. (Mid. W), unranked
**Website:** www.rio.edu
**Admissions email:** admissions@rio.edu
**Private;** founded 1876
**Freshman admissions:** N/A; 2013-2014: 1,709 applied, 1,277 accepted. Neither SAT nor ACT required. ACT 25/75 percentile: N/A. High school rank: 9% in top tenth, 28% in top quarter, 58% in top half
**Early decision deadline:** N/A, notification date: N/A
**Early action deadline:** N/A, notification date: N/A
**Application deadline (fall):** rolling
**Undergraduate student body:** 1,800 full time, 405 part time; 38% male, 62% female; 0% American Indian, 0% Asian, 5% black, 1% Hispanic, 0% multiracial, 0% Pacific Islander, 83% white, 0% international; 95% from in state; 17% live on campus; 2% of students in fraternities, 1% in sororities
**Most popular majors:** 6% Biology/Biological Sciences, General, 14% Business Administration and Management, General, 5% Elementary Education and Teaching, 12% Registered Nursing, Nursing Administration, Nursing Research and Clinical

Nursing, Other, 8% Sport and Fitness Administration/Management
**Expenses:** 2014-2015: $21,930; room/board: $9,450
**Financial aid:** (740) 245-7218; 93% of undergrads determined to have financial need; average aid package $6,686

## University of Toledo
Toledo OH
(419) 530-8888
**U.S. News ranking:** Nat. U., second tier
**Website:** www.utoledo.edu
**Admissions email:** enroll@utnet.utoledo.edu
**Public;** founded 1872
**Freshman admissions:** selective; 2013-2014: 11,066 applied, 10,040 accepted. Either SAT or ACT required. ACT 25/75 percentile: 19-25. High school rank: 17% in top tenth, 40% in top quarter, 70% in top half
**Early decision deadline:** N/A, notification date: N/A
**Early action deadline:** N/A, notification date: N/A
**Application deadline (fall):** rolling
**Undergraduate student body:** 13,069 full time, 3,123 part time; 51% male, 49% female; 0% American Indian, 2% Asian, 14% black, 4% Hispanic, 3% multiracial, 0% Pacific Islander, 69% white, 4% international; 84% from in state; 19% live on campus; 7% of students in fraternities, 7% in sororities
**Most popular majors:** 18% Business, Management, Marketing, and Related Support Services, 9% Education, 11% Engineering, 19% Health Professions and Related Programs
**Expenses:** 2014-2015: $9,280 in state, $19,158 out of state; room/board: $10,094
**Financial aid:** (419) 530-8700; 69% of undergrads determined to have financial need; average aid package $10,665

## Urbana University[1]
Urbana OH
(937) 484-1356
**U.S. News ranking:** Reg. Coll. (Mid. W), unranked
**Website:** www.urbana.edu
**Admissions email:** admiss@urbana.edu
**Private**
**Application deadline (fall):** N/A
**Undergraduate student body:** N/A full time, N/A part time
**Expenses:** 2013-2014: $21,566; room/board: $8,120
**Financial aid:** (937) 484-1355

## Ursuline College
Pepper Pike OH
(440) 449-4203
**U.S. News ranking:** Reg. U. (Mid. W), No. 54
**Website:** www.ursuline.edu
**Admissions email:** admission@ursuline.edu
**Private;** founded 1871
**Affiliation:** Roman Catholic
**Freshman admissions:** selective; 2013-2014: 441 applied, 255 accepted. Either SAT or ACT required. ACT 25/75 percentile: 19-24. High school rank: 12% in top tenth, 38% in top quarter, 80% in top half

**Early decision deadline:** N/A, notification date: N/A
**Early action deadline:** N/A, notification date: N/A
**Application deadline (fall):** 2/1
**Undergraduate student body:** 547 full time, 258 part time; 8% male, 92% female; 0% American Indian, 1% Asian, 28% black, 2% Hispanic, 3% multiracial, 0% Pacific Islander, 62% white, 1% international; 94% from in state; 23% live on campus; 0% of students in fraternities, 0% in sororities
**Most popular majors:** 12% Business, Management, Marketing, and Related Support Services, 58% Health Professions and Related Programs, 4% Legal Professions and Studies, 8% Psychology, 3% Public Administration and Social Service Professions
**Expenses:** 2014-2015: $27,690; room/board: $9,212
**Financial aid:** (440) 646-8309; 90% of undergrads determined to have financial need; average aid package $17,815

## Walsh University
North Canton OH
(800) 362-9846
**U.S. News ranking:** Reg. U. (Mid. W), No. 65
**Website:** www.walsh.edu
**Admissions email:** admissions@walsh.edu
**Private;** founded 1958
**Affiliation:** Roman Catholic
**Freshman admissions:** selective; 2013-2014: 1,640 applied, 1,265 accepted. Either SAT or ACT required. ACT 25/75 percentile: 20-25. High school rank: 15% in top tenth, 46% in top quarter, 79% in top half
**Early decision deadline:** N/A, notification date: N/A
**Early action deadline:** N/A, notification date: N/A
**Application deadline (fall):** 8/15
**Undergraduate student body:** 1,916 full time, 469 part time; 39% male, 61% female; 0% American Indian, 0% Asian, 5% black, 2% Hispanic, 2% multiracial, 0% Pacific Islander, 78% white, 3% international; 96% from in state; 48% live on campus; 0% of students in fraternities, 0% in sororities
**Most popular majors:** 10% Biological and Biomedical Sciences, 32% Business, Management, Marketing, and Related Support Services, 15% Education, 20% Health Professions and Related Programs, 6% Social Sciences
**Expenses:** 2014-2015: $26,670; room/board: $9,580
**Financial aid:** (330) 490-7150; 93% of undergrads determined to have financial need; average aid package $21,862

## Wilberforce University[1]
Wilberforce OH
(800) 367-8568
**U.S. News ranking:** Reg. Coll. (Mid. W), second tier
**Website:** www.wilberforce.edu
**Admissions email:** admissions@wilberforce.edu
**Private**
**Application deadline (fall):** N/A

**Early decision deadline:** N/A, notification date: N/A
**Early action deadline:** N/A, notification date: N/A
**Application deadline (fall):** 2/1
**Undergraduate student body:** N/A full time, N/A part time
**Expenses:** 2013-2014: $15,140; room/board: $6,100
**Financial aid:** (800) 367-8565

## Wilmington College
Wilmington OH
(937) 382-6661
**U.S. News ranking:** Reg. Coll. (Mid. W), No. 58
**Website:** www2.wilmington.edu
**Admissions email:** admission@wilmington.edu
**Private;** founded 1870
**Affiliation:** Religious Society of Friends
**Freshman admissions:** less selective; 2013-2014: N/A applied, N/A accepted. Neither SAT nor ACT required. ACT 25/75 percentile: N/A. High school rank: N/A
**Early decision deadline:** N/A, notification date: N/A
**Early action deadline:** N/A, notification date: N/A
**Undergraduate student body:** 1,030 full time, 133 part time; 47% male, 53% female; 1% American Indian, 0% Asian, 8% black, 1% Hispanic, 3% multiracial, 0% Pacific Islander, 75% white, 1% international
**Most popular majors:** Information not available
**Expenses:** 2013-2014: $28,190; room/board: $9,392
**Financial aid:** (937) 382-6661

## Wittenberg University
Springfield OH
(937) 327-6314
**U.S. News ranking:** Nat. Lib. Arts, No. 139
**Website:** www5.wittenberg.edu
**Admissions email:** admission@wittenberg.edu
**Private;** founded 1845
**Affiliation:** Lutheran
**Freshman admissions:** selective; 2013-2014: 5,160 applied, 4,612 accepted. Neither SAT nor ACT required. ACT 25/75 percentile: 23-28. High school rank: 22% in top tenth, 49% in top quarter, 81% in top half
**Early decision deadline:** 11/15, notification date: 12/15
**Early action deadline:** 12/1, notification date: 1/1
**Application deadline (fall):** rolling
**Undergraduate student body:** 1,853 full time, 106 part time; 43% male, 57% female; 0% American Indian, 1% Asian, 7% black, 3% Hispanic, 4% multiracial, 0% Pacific Islander, 81% white, 2% international; 71% from in state; 84% live on campus; 25% of students in fraternities, 35% in sororities
**Most popular majors:** 16% Biological and Biomedical Sciences, 8% Communication, Journalism, and Related Programs, 7% Education, 7% Psychology, 16% Social Sciences
**Expenses:** 2014-2015: $38,030; room/board: $9,932
**Financial aid:** (937) 327-7321; 78% of undergrads determined to have financial need; average aid package $31,471

## Wright State University
Dayton OH
(937) 775-5700
**U.S. News ranking:** Nat. U., second tier
**Website:** www.wright.edu
**Admissions email:** admissions@wright.edu
**Public;** founded 1964
**Freshman admissions:** selective; 2013-2014: 5,049 applied, 4,863 accepted. Either SAT or ACT required. ACT 25/75 percentile: 19-25. High school rank: 15% in top tenth, 36% in top quarter, 65% in top half
**Early decision deadline:** N/A, notification date: N/A
**Early action deadline:** N/A, notification date: N/A
**Application deadline (fall):** rolling
**Undergraduate student body:** 9,987 full time, 2,809 part time; 49% male, 51% female; 0% American Indian, 2% Asian, 12% black, 3% Hispanic, 4% multiracial, 0% Pacific Islander, 73% white, 5% international; 97% from in state; 14% live on campus; 2% of students in fraternities, 5% in sororities
**Most popular majors:** 5% Biology/Biological Sciences, General, 15% Business Administration and Management, General, 4% Mechanical Engineering, 8% Psychology, General, 11% Registered Nursing/Registered Nurse
**Expenses:** 2014-2015: $8,730 in state, $16,910 out of state; room/board: $9,108
**Financial aid:** (937) 873-5721; 67% of undergrads determined to have financial need; average aid package $10,250

## Xavier University
Cincinnati OH
(877) 982-3648
**U.S. News ranking:** Reg. U. (Mid. W), No. 5
**Website:** www.xavier.edu
**Admissions email:** xuadmit@xavier.edu
**Private;** founded 1831
**Affiliation:** Roman Catholic (Jesuit)
**Freshman admissions:** more selective; 2013-2014: 10,907 applied, 7,632 accepted. Either SAT or ACT required. ACT 25/75 percentile: 23-27. High school rank: 22% in top tenth, 54% in top quarter, 85% in top half
**Early decision deadline:** N/A, notification date: N/A
**Early action deadline:** N/A, notification date: N/A
**Application deadline (fall):** rolling
**Undergraduate student body:** 4,150 full time, 502 part time; 46% male, 54% female; 0% American Indian, 2% Asian, 10% black, 4% Hispanic, 3% multiracial, 0% Pacific Islander, 73% white, 2% international; 53% from in state; 51% live on campus; N/A of students in fraternities, N/A in sororities
**Most popular majors:** 30% Business, Management, Marketing, and Related Support Services, 8% Health Professions and Related Programs, 13% Liberal Arts and Sciences, General Studies and Humanities, 6% Psychology, 7% Social Sciences
**Expenses:** 2013-2014: $33,000; room/board: $10,520
**Financial aid:** (513) 745-3142

## Youngstown State University

Youngstown OH
(877) 468-6978
**U.S. News ranking:** Reg. U. (Mid. W), second tier
**Website:** www.ysu.edu
**Admissions email:** enroll@ysu.edu
**Public;** founded 1908
**Freshman admissions:** selective; 2013-2014: 4,343 applied, 3,756 accepted. Either SAT or ACT required. ACT 25/75 percentile: 17-23. High school rank: 11% in top tenth, 17% in top quarter, 57% in top half
**Early decision deadline:** N/A, notification date: N/A
**Early action deadline:** N/A, notification date: N/A
**Application deadline (fall):** 8/1
**Undergraduate student body:** 9,473 full time, 2,699 part time; 47% male, 53% female; 0% American Indian, 1% Asian, 14% black, 3% Hispanic, 2% multiracial, 0% Pacific Islander, 75% white, 1% international; 89% from in state; 10% live on campus; 1% of students in fraternities, 1% in sororities
**Most popular majors:** 5% Accounting, 5% Biology/Biological Sciences, General, 7% Criminal Justice/Safety Studies, 5% General Studies, 4% Social Work
**Expenses:** 2014-2015: $8,317 in state, $14,317 out of state; room/board: $8,645
**Financial aid:** (330) 941-3399; 76% of undergrads determined to have financial need; average aid package $8,669

## Bacone College[1]

Muskogee OK
(888) 682-5514
**U.S. News ranking:** Reg. Coll. (W), second tier
**Website:** www.bacone.edu/
**Admissions email:** admissions@bacone.edu
**Private**
**Application deadline (fall):** N/A
**Undergraduate student body:** N/A full time, N/A part time
**Expenses:** 2013-2014: $14,050; room/board: $9,560
**Financial aid:** (888) 682-5514

## Cameron University

Lawton OK
(580) 581-2289
**U.S. News ranking:** Reg. U. (W), second tier
**Website:** www.cameron.edu
**Admissions email:** admissions@cameron.edu
**Public;** founded 1908
**Freshman admissions:** less selective; 2013-2014: 1,356 applied, 1,353 accepted. Neither SAT nor ACT required. ACT 25/75 percentile: 16-21. High school rank: 4% in top tenth, 15% in top quarter, 44% in top half
**Early decision deadline:** N/A, notification date: N/A
**Early action deadline:** N/A, notification date: N/A
**Application deadline (fall):** rolling
**Undergraduate student body:** 3,590 full time, 1,768 part time; 39% male, 61% female; 6% American Indian, 2% Asian, 17% black, 12% Hispanic, 8% multiracial, 1% Pacific Islander, 48% white,

4% international; 85% from in state; 8% live on campus; 2% of students in fraternities, 1% in sororities
**Most popular majors:** 13% Business Administration and Management, General, 13% Corrections and Criminal Justice, Other, 6% Elementary Education and Teaching, 12% General Studies, 7% Psychology, General
**Expenses:** 2014-2015: $5,340 in state, $13,380 out of state; room/board: $4,664
**Financial aid:** (580) 581-2293; 67% of undergrads determined to have financial need; average aid package $9,080

## East Central University[1]

Ada OK
(580) 559-5239
**U.S. News ranking:** Reg. U. (W), second tier
**Website:** www.ecok.edu
**Admissions email:** parmstro@ecok.edu
**Public**
**Application deadline (fall):** N/A
**Undergraduate student body:** N/A full time, N/A part time
**Expenses:** 2013-2014: $5,241 in state, $12,643 out of state; room/board: $4,982
**Financial aid:** (580) 559-5242

## Langston University

Langston OK
(405) 466-3231
**U.S. News ranking:** Reg. U. (W), unranked
**Website:** www.lunet.edu
**Admissions email:** admission@speedy.lunet.edu
**Public**
**Freshman admissions:** N/A; 2013-2014: 6,965 applied, 3,520 accepted. Neither SAT nor ACT required. ACT 25/75 percentile: N/A. High school rank: N/A
**Early decision deadline:** N/A, notification date: N/A
**Early action deadline:** N/A, notification date: N/A
**Application deadline (fall):** rolling
**Undergraduate student body:** 1,841 full time, 234 part time; 40% male, 60% female; 2% American Indian, 1% Asian, 85% black, 1% Hispanic, 0% multiracial, 0% Pacific Islander, 10% white, 1% international
**Most popular majors:** 18% Business, Management, Marketing, and Related Support Services, 20% Health Professions and Related Programs, 5% Homeland Security, Law Enforcement, Firefighting and Related Protective Services, 8% Liberal Arts and Sciences, General Studies and Humanities, 11% Psychology
**Expenses:** 2014-2015: $6,298 in state, $13,285 out of state; room/board: $7,026
**Financial aid:** (405) 466-3282; 89% of undergrads determined to have financial need; average aid package $9,840

## Mid-America Christian University[1]

Oklahoma City OK
(888) 436-3035
**U.S. News ranking:** Reg. Coll. (W), unranked
**Website:** www.macu.edu
**Admissions email:** info@macu.edu
**Private**
**Application deadline (fall):** N/A
**Undergraduate student body:** N/A full time, N/A part time
**Expenses:** 2013-2014: $15,688; room/board: $6,430
**Financial aid:** (405) 691-3800

## Northeastern State University

Tahlequah OK
(918) 444-2200
**U.S. News ranking:** Reg. U. (W), No. 84
**Website:** www.nsuok.edu
**Admissions email:** nsuinfo@nsuok.edu
**Public;** founded 1846
**Freshman admissions:** selective; 2013-2014: 1,889 applied, 1,386 accepted. ACT required. ACT 25/75 percentile: 18-23. High school rank: 18% in top tenth, 43% in top quarter, 78% in top half
**Early decision deadline:** N/A, notification date: N/A
**Early action deadline:** N/A, notification date: N/A
**Application deadline (fall):** rolling
**Undergraduate student body:** 5,307 full time, 2,124 part time; 40% male, 60% female; 23% American Indian, 2% Asian, 5% black, 4% Hispanic, 11% multiracial, 0% Pacific Islander, 52% white, 1% international; 94% from in state; 19% live on campus; 2% of students in fraternities, 17% in sororities
**Most popular majors:** 6% Biology/Biological Sciences, General, 8% Criminal Justice/Law Enforcement Administration, 7% Elementary Education and Teaching, 6% General Studies, 9% Psychology, General
**Expenses:** 2014-2015: $4,994 in state, $12,012 out of state; room/board: $6,670
**Financial aid:** (918) 456-5511; 69% of undergrads determined to have financial need; average aid package $11,880

## Northwestern Oklahoma State University

Alva OK
(580) 327-8545
**U.S. News ranking:** Reg. U. (W), second tier
**Website:** www.nwosu.edu
**Admissions email:** recruit@nwosu.edu
**Public;** founded 1897
**Freshman admissions:** selective; 2013-2014: 1,010 applied, 663 accepted. Either SAT or ACT required. ACT 25/75 percentile: 18-22. High school rank: 12% in top tenth, 28% in top quarter, 64% in top half
**Early decision deadline:** N/A, notification date: N/A
**Early action deadline:** N/A, notification date: N/A
**Application deadline (fall):** rolling

## Undergraduate student body:

1,725 full time, 424 part time; 44% male, 56% female; 7% American Indian, 1% Asian, 7% black, 6% Hispanic, 1% multiracial, 0% Pacific Islander, 67% white, 4% international; 78% from in state; 48% live on campus; N/A of students in fraternities, N/A in sororities
**Most popular majors:** 10% Business Administration and Management, General, 7% Early Childhood Education and Teaching, 12% Parks, Recreation, Leisure, and Fitness Studies, Other, 9% Psychology, General, 9% Registered Nursing/Registered Nurse
**Expenses:** 2013-2014: $5,054 in state, $10,987 out of state; room/board: $3,900
**Financial aid:** (580) 327-8542

## Oklahoma Baptist University

Shawnee OK
(405) 585-5000
**U.S. News ranking:** Reg. Coll. (W), No. 4
**Website:** www.okbu.edu
**Admissions email:** admissions@okbu.edu
**Private;** founded 1910
**Affiliation:** Southern Baptist Convention
**Freshman admissions:** more selective; 2013-2014: 6,560 applied, 3,704 accepted. Either SAT or ACT required. ACT 25/75 percentile: 21-27. High school rank: 27% in top tenth, 58% in top quarter, 87% in top half
**Early decision deadline:** N/A, notification date: N/A
**Early action deadline:** N/A, notification date: N/A
**Application deadline (fall):** 8/1
**Undergraduate student body:** 1,868 full time, 151 part time; 41% male, 59% female; 5% American Indian, 1% Asian, 5% black, 5% Hispanic, 7% multiracial, 0% Pacific Islander, 69% white, 4% international; 64% from in state; 63% live on campus; 2% of students in fraternities, 11% in sororities
**Most popular majors:** 8% Business, Management, Marketing, and Related Support Services, 7% Communication, Journalism, and Related Programs, 18% Education, 19% Health Professions and Related Programs, 6% Philosophy and Religious Studies
**Expenses:** 2014-2015: $22,800; room/board: $6,520
**Financial aid:** (405) 878-2016; 74% of undergrads determined to have financial need; average aid package $19,312

## Oklahoma Christian University

Oklahoma City OK
(405) 425-5050
**U.S. News ranking:** Reg. U. (W), No. 40
**Website:** www.oc.edu/
**Admissions email:** info@oc.edu
**Private;** founded 1950
**Affiliation:** Church of Christ
**Freshman admissions:** more selective; 2013-2014: 1,984 applied, 1,254 accepted. Either SAT or ACT required. ACT 25/75

percentile: 22-28. High school rank: 30% in top tenth, 58% in top quarter, 81% in top half
**Early decision deadline:** N/A, notification date: N/A
**Early action deadline:** N/A, notification date: N/A
**Application deadline (fall):** rolling
**Undergraduate student body:** 1,907 full time, 59 part time; 51% male, 49% female; 2% American Indian, 1% Asian, 6% black, 5% Hispanic, 6% multiracial, 0% Pacific Islander, 70% white, 11% international; 41% from in state; 82% live on campus; 0% of students in fraternities, 0% in sororities
**Most popular majors:** 7% Biological and Biomedical Sciences, 16% Business, Management, Marketing, and Related Support Services, 9% Communication, Journalism, and Related Programs, 7% Education, 11% Engineering
**Expenses:** 2014-2015: $19,120; room/board: $6,670
**Financial aid:** (405) 425-5190; 63% of undergrads determined to have financial need; average aid package $21,444

## Oklahoma City University

Oklahoma City OK
(405) 208-5050
**U.S. News ranking:** Reg. U. (W), No. 25
**Website:** www.okcu.edu
**Admissions email:** uadmissions@okcu.edu
**Private;** founded 1904
**Affiliation:** United Methodist
**Freshman admissions:** more selective; 2013-2014: 1,432 applied, 1,008 accepted. Either SAT or ACT required. ACT 25/75 percentile: 23-29. High school rank: 35% in top tenth, 61% in top quarter, 91% in top half
**Early decision deadline:** N/A, notification date: N/A
**Early action deadline:** N/A, notification date: N/A
**Application deadline (fall):** rolling
**Undergraduate student body:** 1,646 full time, 175 part time; 39% male, 61% female; 3% American Indian, 2% Asian, 6% black, 8% Hispanic, 7% multiracial, 0% Pacific Islander, 59% white, 15% international; 53% from in state; 51% live on campus; 29% of students in fraternities, 18% in sororities
**Most popular majors:** 4% Biological and Biomedical Sciences, 14% Business, Management, Marketing, and Related Support Services, 14% Health Professions and Related Programs, 15% Liberal Arts and Sciences, General Studies and Humanities, 32% Visual and Performing Arts
**Expenses:** 2014-2015: $30,726; room/board: $9,534
**Financial aid:** (405) 208-5211; 60% of undergrads determined to have financial need; average aid package $19,715

## Oklahoma Panhandle State University[1]

Goodwell OK
(800) 664-6778
**U.S. News ranking:** Reg. Coll. (W), second tier
**Website:** www.opsu.edu
**Admissions email:** opsu@opsu.edu
**Public;** founded 1909

**Application deadline (fall):** rolling
**Undergraduate student body:** N/A full time, N/A part time
**Expenses:** 2014-2015: $6,777 in state, $8,293 out of state; room/board: $4,200
**Financial aid:** (580) 349-1580; 93% of undergrads determined to have financial need; average aid package $8,549

## Oklahoma State University
Stillwater OK
(405) 744-5358
**U.S. News ranking:** Nat. U., No. 145
**Website:** osu.okstate.edu
**Admissions email:** admissions@okstate.edu
**Public;** founded 1890
**Freshman admissions:** more selective; 2013-2014: 11,064 applied, 8,411 accepted. Either SAT or ACT required. ACT 25/75 percentile: 22-28. High school rank: 28% in top tenth, 56% in top quarter, 87% in top half
**Early decision deadline:** N/A, notification date: N/A
**Early action deadline:** N/A, notification date: N/A
**Application deadline (fall):** rolling
**Undergraduate student body:** 17,746 full time, 2,747 part time; 51% male, 49% female; 6% American Indian, 2% Asian, 5% black, 5% Hispanic, 7% multiracial, 0% Pacific Islander, 72% white, 3% international; 74% from in state; 45% live on campus; 18% of students in fraternities, 25% in sororities
**Most popular majors:** 9% Agriculture, Agriculture Operations, and Related Sciences, 24% Business, Management, Marketing, and Related Support Services, 8% Education, 9% Engineering, 8% Family and Consumer Sciences/Human Sciences
**Expenses:** 2014-2015: $7,442 in state, $20,027 out of state; room/board: $7,390
**Financial aid:** (405) 744-6604; 52% of undergrads determined to have financial need; average aid package $12,835

## Oklahoma State University Institute of Technology–Okmulgee
Okmulgee OK
(918) 293-4680
**U.S. News ranking:** Reg. Coll. (W), No. 24
**Website:** www.osuit.edu/admissions
**Admissions email:** osuit.admissions@okstate.edu
**Public;** founded 1946
**Freshman admissions:** less selective; 2013-2014: 2,026 applied, 1,090 accepted. Either SAT or ACT required. ACT 25/75 percentile: 16-21. High school rank: 5% in top tenth, 18% in top quarter, 47% in top half
**Early decision deadline:** N/A, notification date: N/A
**Early action deadline:** N/A, notification date: N/A
**Application deadline (fall):** rolling
**Undergraduate student body:** 2,207 full time, 1,411 part time; 65% male, 35% female; 20% American Indian, 1% Asian, 6% black,

5% Hispanic, 7% multiracial, 0% Pacific Islander, 56% white, 1% international; 88% from in state; 29% live on campus; 0% of students in fraternities, 0% in sororities
**Most popular majors:** 10% Civil Engineering Technology/Technician, 59% Computer and Information Systems Security/Information Assurance, 31% Instrumentation Technology/Technician
**Expenses:** 2013-2014: $5,118 in state, $16,329 out of state; room/board: $3,137
**Financial aid:** (800) 722-4471; 71% of undergrads determined to have financial need; average aid package $7,500

## Oklahoma State University–Oklahoma City
Oklahoma City OK
(405) 945-3224
**U.S. News ranking:** Reg. Coll. (W), unranked
**Website:** www.osuokc.edu/
**Admissions email:** admissions@osuokc.edu
**Public;** founded 1961
**Freshman admissions:** N/A; 2013-2014: 2,555 applied, 2,555 accepted. Neither SAT nor ACT required. ACT 25/75 percentile: N/A. High school rank: N/A
**Early decision deadline:** N/A, notification date: N/A
**Early action deadline:** N/A, notification date: N/A
**Application deadline (fall):** rolling
**Undergraduate student body:** 2,251 full time, 4,745 part time; 40% male, 60% female; 4% American Indian, 3% Asian, 16% black, 8% Hispanic, 7% multiracial, 4% Pacific Islander, 59% white, 0% international
**Most popular majors:** Information not available
**Expenses:** 2013-2014: $3,323 in state, $9,026 out of state; room/board: $5,534
**Financial aid:** (405) 945-3319

## Oklahoma Wesleyan University
Bartlesville OK
(866) 222-8226
**U.S. News ranking:** Reg. Coll. (W), No. 6
**Website:** www.okwu.edu
**Admissions email:** admissions@okwu.edu
**Private;** founded 1972
**Affiliation:** The Wesleyan Church
**Freshman admissions:** selective; 2013-2014: 2,293 applied, 549 accepted. Either SAT or ACT required. ACT 25/75 percentile: 18-24. High school rank: N/A
**Early decision deadline:** N/A, notification date: N/A
**Early action deadline:** N/A, notification date: N/A
**Application deadline (fall):** rolling
**Undergraduate student body:** 571 full time, 643 part time; 39% male, 61% female; 7% American Indian, 0% Asian, 7% black, 7% Hispanic, 4% multiracial, 0% Pacific Islander, 68% white, 5% international; 56% from in state; 62% live on campus; 0% of students in fraternities, 0% in sororities

**Most popular majors:** 14% Business Administration and Management, General, 5% Human Resources Management/Personnel Administration, General, 29% Nursing Science, 5% Pastoral Counseling and Specialized Ministries, Other
**Expenses:** 2014-2015: $23,180; room/board: $7,488
**Financial aid:** (918) 335-6282; 78% of undergrads determined to have financial need; average aid package $12,566

## Oral Roberts University
Tulsa OK
(800) 678-8876
**U.S. News ranking:** Reg. U. (W), No. 46
**Website:** www.oru.edu
**Admissions email:** admissions@oru.edu
**Private;** founded 1963
**Affiliation:** Christian interdenominational
**Freshman admissions:** selective; 2013-2014: 1,417 applied, 617 accepted. Either SAT or ACT required. ACT 25/75 percentile: 20-25. High school rank: N/A
**Early decision deadline:** N/A, notification date: N/A
**Early action deadline:** N/A, notification date: N/A
**Application deadline (fall):** rolling
**Undergraduate student body:** 2,517 full time, 367 part time; 44% male, 56% female; 3% American Indian, 2% Asian, 15% black, 8% Hispanic, 4% multiracial, 0% Pacific Islander, 52% white, 6% international; 42% from in state; 63% live on campus; 0% of students in fraternities, 0% in sororities
**Most popular majors:** 23% Business, Management, Marketing, and Related Support Services, 10% Communication, Journalism, and Related Programs, 9% Health Professions and Related Programs, 12% Theology and Religious Vocations, 8% Visual and Performing Arts
**Expenses:** 2014-2015: $23,410; room/board: $10,768
**Financial aid:** (918) 495-7088; 71% of undergrads determined to have financial need; average aid package $22,081

## Rogers State University
Claremore OK
(918) 343-7545
**U.S. News ranking:** Reg. Coll. (W), second tier
**Website:** www.rsu.edu/
**Admissions email:** info@rsu.edu
**Public;** founded 1909
**Freshman admissions:** less selective; 2013-2014: 1,864 applied, 1,015 accepted. Either SAT or ACT required. ACT 25/75 percentile: 17-23. High school rank: 9% in top tenth, 20% in top quarter, 42% in top half
**Early decision deadline:** N/A, notification date: N/A
**Early action deadline:** N/A, notification date: N/A
**Application deadline (fall):** rolling
**Undergraduate student body:** 2,576 full time, 1,713 part time; 37% male, 63% female; 3% American Indian, 0% Asian, 14% black, 4% Hispanic, 16% multiracial, 61% Pacific Islander, 2% white,

1% international; 96% from in state; 10% live on campus; N/A of students in fraternities, N/A in sororities
**Most popular majors:** 11% Biological and Biomedical Sciences, 32% Business, Management, Marketing, and Related Support Services, 8% Health Professions and Related Programs, 8% Multi-Interdisciplinary Studies, 9% Social Sciences
**Expenses:** 2013-2014: $5,144 in state, $11,864 out of state; room/board: $8,430
**Financial aid:** (918) 343-7553; 71% of undergrads determined to have financial need; average aid package $9,008

## Southeastern Oklahoma State University
Durant OK
(580) 745-2060
**U.S. News ranking:** Reg. U. (W), second tier
**Website:** www.se.edu
**Admissions email:** admissions@se.edu
**Public;** founded 1909
**Freshman admissions:** selective; 2013-2014: 1,001 applied, 800 accepted. Either SAT or ACT required. ACT 25/75 percentile: 18-22. High school rank: 17% in top tenth, 38% in top quarter, 74% in top half
**Early decision deadline:** N/A, notification date: N/A
**Early action deadline:** N/A, notification date: N/A
**Application deadline (fall):** rolling
**Undergraduate student body:** 2,650 full time, 790 part time; 46% male, 54% female; 31% American Indian, 1% Asian, 7% black, 4% Hispanic, 0% multiracial, 0% Pacific Islander, 55% white, 3% international; 75% from in state; 16% live on campus; N/A of students in fraternities, N/A in sororities
**Most popular majors:** 13% Business, Management, Marketing, and Related Support Services, 13% Education, 14% Engineering Technologies and Engineering-Related Fields, 13% Liberal Arts and Sciences, General Studies and Humanities, 7% Psychology
**Expenses:** 2013-2014: $5,315 in state, $13,440 out of state; room/board: $2,470
**Financial aid:** (580) 745-2186; 85% of undergrads determined to have financial need; average aid package $10,109

## Southern Nazarene University
Bethany OK
(405) 491-6324
**U.S. News ranking:** Reg. U. (W), No. 84
**Website:** www.snu.edu
**Admissions email:** admissions@snu.edu
**Private;** founded 1899
**Affiliation:** Nazarene
**Freshman admissions:** selective; 2013-2014: N/A applied, N/A accepted. Either SAT or ACT required. ACT 25/75 percentile: 19-24. High school rank: 26% in top tenth, 49% in top quarter, 78% in top half

**Early decision deadline:** N/A, notification date: N/A
**Early action deadline:** N/A, notification date: N/A
**Application deadline (fall):** 8/6
**Undergraduate student body:** 1,549 full time, 111 part time; 48% male, 52% female; 5% American Indian, 3% Asian, 14% black, 6% Hispanic, 0% multiracial, 1% Pacific Islander, 68% white, 2% international; 60% from in state; 63% live on campus; N/A of students in fraternities, N/A in sororities
**Most popular majors:** 15% Business Administration and Management, General, 9% Health/Health Care Administration/Management, 10% Human Development and Family Studies, General, 6% Marriage and Family Therapy/Counseling, 27% Organizational Behavior Studies
**Expenses:** 2014-2015: $22,680; room/board: $7,970
**Financial aid:** (405) 491-6310

## Southwestern Christian University[1]
Bethany OK
(405) 789-7661
**U.S. News ranking:** Reg. Coll. (W), No. 23
**Website:** www.swcu.edu/
**Admissions email:** admissions@swcu.edu
**Private;** founded 1946
**Affiliation:** Pentecostal
**Application deadline (fall):** rolling
**Undergraduate student body:** N/A full time, N/A part time
**Expenses:** 2013-2014: $14,220; room/board: $6,100
**Financial aid:** N/A

## Southwestern Oklahoma State University
Weatherford OK
(580) 774-3782
**U.S. News ranking:** Reg. U. (W), second tier
**Website:** www.swosu.edu
**Admissions email:** admissions@swosu.edu
**Public;** founded 1901
**Freshman admissions:** selective; 2013-2014: 2,536 applied, 2,289 accepted. Either SAT or ACT required. ACT 25/75 percentile: 18-24. High school rank: 22% in top tenth, 43% in top quarter, 76% in top half
**Early decision deadline:** N/A, notification date: N/A
**Early action deadline:** N/A, notification date: N/A
**Application deadline (fall):** rolling
**Undergraduate student body:** 3,368 full time, 794 part time; 42% male, 58% female; 4% American Indian, 2% Asian, 5% black, 8% Hispanic, 7% multiracial, 0% Pacific Islander, 70% white, 3% international; 89% from in state; 32% live on campus; 3% of students in fraternities, 5% in sororities
**Most popular majors:** 18% Business, Management, Marketing, and Related Support Services, 15% Education, 3% Engineering Technologies and Engineering-Related Fields, 26% Health Professions and Related Programs, 10% Parks, Recreation, Leisure, and Fitness Studies

**Expenses:** 2013-2014: $5,460 in state, $11,820 out of state; room/board: $4,920
**Financial aid:** (580) 774-3786; 63% of undergrads determined to have financial need; average aid package $5,380

## St. Gregory's University
Shawnee OK
(405) 878-5444
**U.S. News ranking:** Reg. Coll. (W), No. 25
**Website:** www.stgregorys.edu
**Admissions email:** admissions@stgregorys.edu
**Private**
**Affiliation:** Roman Catholic–Benedictine
**Freshman admissions:** less selective; 2013-2014: 455 applied, 259 accepted. Neither SAT nor ACT required. ACT 25/75 percentile: N/A. High school rank: N/A
**Early decision deadline:** N/A, notification date: N/A
**Early action deadline:** N/A, notification date: N/A
**Application deadline (fall):** N/A
**Undergraduate student body:** 578 full time, 55 part time; 43% male, 57% female; 8% American Indian, 1% Asian, 8% black, 12% Hispanic, 8% multiracial, 0% Pacific Islander, 46% white, 4% international
**Most popular majors:** Information not available
**Expenses:** 2013-2014: $20,765; room/board: $7,206
**Financial aid:** (405) 878-5412

## University of Central Oklahoma
Edmond OK
(405) 974-2338
**U.S. News ranking:** Reg. U. (W), No. 75
**Website:** www.uco.edu
**Admissions email:** 4ucoinfo@uco.edu
**Public;** founded 1890
**Freshman admissions:** selective; 2013-2014: 4,629 applied, 3,684 accepted. Either SAT or ACT required. ACT 25/75 percentile: 20-24. High school rank: 16% in top tenth, 37% in top quarter, 73% in top half
**Early decision deadline:** N/A, notification date: N/A
**Early action deadline:** N/A, notification date: N/A
**Application deadline (fall):** rolling
**Undergraduate student body:** 10,981 full time, 4,386 part time; 43% male, 57% female; 4% American Indian, 3% Asian, 9% black, 7% Hispanic, 7% multiracial, 0% Pacific Islander, 60% white, 7% international; 91% from in state; 9% live on campus; 6% of students in fraternities, 6% in sororities
**Most popular majors:** 4% Accounting, 8% Business Administration and Management, General, 12% General Studies, 4% Psychology, General, 5% Registered Nursing/Registered Nurse
**Expenses:** 2014-2015: $5,437 in state, $13,552 out of state; room/board: $6,940
**Financial aid:** (405) 974-3334; 60% of undergrads determined to have financial need; average aid package $9,073

## University of Oklahoma
Norman OK
(405) 325-2252
**U.S. News ranking:** Nat. U., No. 106
**Website:** www.ou.edu
**Admissions email:** admrec@ou.edu
**Public;** founded 1890
**Freshman admissions:** more selective; 2013-2014: 10,991 applied, 8,841 accepted. Either SAT or ACT required. ACT 25/75 percentile: 23-29. High school rank: 33% in top tenth, 64% in top quarter, 92% in top half
**Early decision deadline:** N/A, notification date: N/A
**Early action deadline:** N/A, notification date: N/A
**Application deadline (fall):** 4/1
**Undergraduate student body:** 18,324 full time, 3,494 part time; 49% male, 51% female; 4% American Indian, 6% Asian, 5% black, 9% Hispanic, 7% multiracial, 0% Pacific Islander, 63% white, 4% international; 70% from in state; 31% live on campus; 23% of students in fraternities, 28% in sororities
**Most popular majors:** 3% Business, Management, Marketing, and Related Support Services, 2% Communication, Journalism, and Related Programs, 7% Health Professions and Related Programs, 11% Multi/Interdisciplinary Studies, 3% Psychology
**Expenses:** 2014-2015: $7,695 in state, $20,469 out of state; room/board: $9,126
**Financial aid:** (405) 325-4521; 50% of undergrads determined to have financial need; average aid package $12,520

## University of Science and Arts of Oklahoma
Chickasha OK
(405) 574-1357
**U.S. News ranking:** Nat. Lib. Arts, second tier
**Website:** www.usao.edu
**Admissions email:** usao-admissions@usao.edu
**Public;** founded 1908
**Freshman admissions:** selective; 2013-2014: 594 applied, 371 accepted. Either SAT or ACT required. ACT 25/75 percentile: 19-24. High school rank: 29% in top tenth, 62% in top quarter, 87% in top half
**Early decision deadline:** N/A, notification date: N/A
**Early action deadline:** N/A, notification date: N/A
**Application deadline (fall):** 8/30
**Undergraduate student body:** 806 full time, 111 part time; 36% male, 64% female; 13% American Indian, 1% Asian, 4% black, 6% Hispanic, 0% multiracial, 0% Pacific Islander, 69% white, 6% international; 90% from in state; 44% live on campus; 3% of students in fraternities, 6% in sororities
**Most popular majors:** 18% Business Administration and Management, General, 20% Education, 9% Psychology, General, 14% Visual and Performing Arts
**Expenses:** 2014-2015: $6,270 in state, $15,210 out of state; room/board: $5,470

**Financial aid:** (405) 574-1240; 65% of undergrads determined to have financial need; average aid package $9,473

## University of Tulsa
Tulsa OK
(918) 631-2307
**U.S. News ranking:** Nat. U., No. 88
**Website:** www.utulsa.edu
**Admissions email:** admission@utulsa.edu
**Private;** founded 1894
**Affiliation:** Presbyterian
**Freshman admissions:** most selective; 2013-2014: 7,304 applied, 2,965 accepted. Either SAT or ACT required. ACT 25/75 percentile: 25-32. High school rank: 74% in top tenth, 90% in top quarter, 97% in top half
**Early decision deadline:** N/A, notification date: N/A
**Early action deadline:** 11/1, notification date: 11/25
**Application deadline (fall):** rolling
**Undergraduate student body:** 3,293 full time, 135 part time; 58% male, 42% female; 4% American Indian, 3% Asian, 5% black, 4% Hispanic, 2% multiracial, 0% Pacific Islander, 55% white, 26% international; 58% from in state; 74% live on campus; 21% of students in fraternities, 23% in sororities
**Most popular majors:** 19% Business, Management, Marketing, and Related Support Services, 21% Engineering, 7% Health Professions and Related Programs, 6% Social Sciences, 5% Visual and Performing Arts
**Expenses:** 2014-2015: $34,704; room/board: $10,426
**Financial aid:** (918) 631-2526; 38% of undergrads determined to have financial need; average aid package $24,867

## Art Institute of Portland[1]
Portland OR
(888) 228-6528
**U.S. News ranking:** Arts, unranked
**Website:** www.artinstitutes.edu/portland/
**Admissions email:** N/A
**For-profit**
**Application deadline (fall):** N/A
**Undergraduate student body:** N/A full time, N/A part time
**Expenses:** 2013-2014: $17,416; room/board: $9,522
**Financial aid:** N/A

## Concordia University[1]
Portland OR
(503) 280-8501
**U.S. News ranking:** Reg. U. (W), No. 80
**Website:** www.cu-portland.edu
**Admissions email:** admissions@cu-portland.edu
**Private;** founded 1905
**Affiliation:** Lutheran
**Application deadline (fall):** 7/1
**Undergraduate student body:** N/A full time, N/A part time
**Expenses:** 2013-2014: $27,492; room/board: $8,030
**Financial aid:** (503) 280-8514

## Corban University
Salem OR
(800) 845-3005
**U.S. News ranking:** Reg. Coll. (W), No. 7
**Website:** www.corban.edu
**Admissions email:** admissions@corban.edu
**Private;** founded 1935
**Affiliation:** Baptist
**Freshman admissions:** selective; 2013-2014: 2,711 applied, 934 accepted. Either SAT or ACT required. SAT 25/75 percentile: 950-1180. High school rank: 33% in top tenth, 63% in top quarter, 89% in top half
**Early decision deadline:** N/A, notification date: N/A
**Early action deadline:** N/A, notification date: N/A
**Application deadline (fall):** 8/1
**Undergraduate student body:** 797 full time, 88 part time; 40% male, 60% female; 1% American Indian, 2% Asian, 1% black, 4% Hispanic, 2% multiracial, 1% Pacific Islander, 83% white, 1% international; 53% from in state; 62% live on campus; N/A of students in fraternities, N/A in sororities
**Most popular majors:** 14% Business, Management, Marketing, and Related Support Services, 16% Education, 7% English Language and Literature/Letters, 33% Psychology, 9% Theology and Religious Vocations
**Expenses:** 2014-2015: $28,640; room/board: $8,892
**Financial aid:** (503) 375-7006; 83% of undergrads determined to have financial need; average aid package $19,380

## Eastern Oregon University[1]
La Grande OR
(541) 962-3393
**U.S. News ranking:** Reg. U. (W), second tier
**Website:** www.eou.edu
**Admissions email:** admissions@eou.edu
**Public;** founded 1929
**Application deadline (fall):** 9/1
**Undergraduate student body:** N/A full time, N/A part time
**Expenses:** 2013-2014: $7,530 in state, $16,755 out of state; room/board: $9,183
**Financial aid:** (541) 962-3551

## George Fox University
Newberg OR
(800) 765-4369
**U.S. News ranking:** Reg. U. (W), No. 30
**Website:** www.georgefox.edu
**Admissions email:** admissions@georgefox.edu
**Private;** founded 1891
**Affiliation:** Evangelical Friends
**Freshman admissions:** selective; 2013-2014: 2,431 applied, 1,830 accepted. Either SAT or ACT required. SAT 25/75 percentile: 940-1200. High school rank: 27% in top tenth, 57% in top quarter, 85% in top half
**Early decision deadline:** N/A, notification date: N/A
**Early action deadline:** 11/15, notification date: 12/15
**Application deadline (fall):** rolling
**Undergraduate student body:** 2,108 full time, 275 part time; 43% male, 57% female; 0% American Indian, 4% Asian, 2% black,

7% Hispanic, 5% multiracial, 0% Pacific Islander, 70% white, 6% international; 65% from in state; 56% live on campus; N/A of students in fraternities, N/A in sororities
**Most popular majors:** 25% Business, Management, Marketing, and Related Support Services, 7% Education, 7% Health Professions and Related Programs, 12% Multi/Interdisciplinary Studies, 7% Visual and Performing Arts
**Expenses:** 2014-2015: $31,866; room/board: $9,864
**Financial aid:** (503) 554-2290; 76% of undergrads determined to have financial need; average aid package $27,155

## Lewis & Clark College
Portland OR
(800) 444-4111
**U.S. News ranking:** Nat. Lib. Arts, No. 77
**Website:** www.lclark.edu
**Admissions email:** admissions@lclark.edu
**Private;** founded 1867
**Freshman admissions:** more selective; 2013-2014: 6,456 applied, 4,059 accepted. Neither SAT nor ACT required. SAT 25/75 percentile: 1180-1370. High school rank: 39% in top tenth, 76% in top quarter, 96% in top half
**Early decision deadline:** 11/1, notification date: 12/1
**Early action deadline:** 11/1, notification date: 12/31
**Application deadline (fall):** 3/1
**Undergraduate student body:** 2,086 full time, 40 part time; 41% male, 59% female; 1% American Indian, 6% Asian, 2% black, 8% Hispanic, 1% multiracial, 0% Pacific Islander, 64% white, 6% international; 18% from in state; 65% live on campus; 0% of students in fraternities, 0% in sororities
**Most popular majors:** 11% Biological and Biomedical Sciences, 8% English Language and Literature/Letters, 14% Psychology, 24% Social Sciences, 12% Visual and Performing Arts
**Expenses:** 2014-2015: $43,382; room/board: $11,000
**Financial aid:** (503) 768-7090; 66% of undergrads determined to have financial need; average aid package $32,902

## Linfield College
McMinnville OR
(800) 640-2287
**U.S. News ranking:** Nat. Lib. Arts, No. 124
**Website:** www.linfield.edu
**Admissions email:** admission@linfield.edu
**Private;** founded 1858
**Affiliation:** American Baptist
**Freshman admissions:** selective; 2013-2014: 2,139 applied, 1,972 accepted. Either SAT or ACT required. SAT 25/75 percentile: 980-1200. High school rank: 34% in top tenth, 72% in top quarter, 94% in top half
**Early decision deadline:** N/A, notification date: N/A
**Early action deadline:** 11/15, notification date: 1/15
**Application deadline (fall):** rolling

**Undergraduate student body:** 1,630 full time, 41 part time; 40% male, 60% female; 1% American Indian, 6% Asian, 2% black, 9% Hispanic, 10% multiracial, 1% Pacific Islander, 64% white, 4% international; 48% from in state; 74% live on campus; 22% of students in fraternities, 25% in sororities
**Most popular majors:** 21% Business, Management, Marketing, and Related Support Services, 7% Communication, Journalism, and Related Programs, 12% Education, 8% Parks, Recreation, Leisure, and Fitness Studies, 10% Social Sciences
**Expenses:** 2014-2015: $37,346; room/board: $10,330
**Financial aid:** (503) 883-2225; 74% of undergrads determined to have financial need; average aid package $28,439

## Marylhurst University[1]
Marylhurst OR
(503) 699-6268
**U.S. News ranking:** Reg. U. (W), unranked
**Website:** www.marylhurst.edu
**Admissions email:** admissions@marylhurst.edu
**Private**
**Application deadline (fall):** N/A
**Undergraduate student body:** N/A full time, N/A part time
**Expenses:** 2013-2014: $19,665; room/board: N/A
**Financial aid:** (503) 699-6253

## Northwest Christian University
Eugene OR
(541) 684-7201
**U.S. News ranking:** Reg. Coll. (W), No. 20
**Website:** www.nwcu.edu
**Admissions email:** admissions@nwcu.edu
**Private;** founded 1895
**Affiliation:** Christian Church (Disciples of Christ)
**Freshman admissions:** less selective; 2013-2014: 318 applied, 224 accepted. Either SAT or ACT required. SAT 25/75 percentile: 885-1065. High school rank: N/A
**Early decision deadline:** N/A, notification date: N/A
**Early action deadline:** N/A, notification date: N/A
**Application deadline (fall):** rolling
**Undergraduate student body:** 382 full time, 102 part time; 36% male, 64% female; 2% American Indian, 3% Asian, 2% black, 8% Hispanic, 3% multiracial, 0% Pacific Islander, 81% white, 0% international; 79% from in state; 28% live on campus; 0% of students in fraternities, 0% in sororities
**Most popular majors:** 7% Biological and Biomedical Sciences, 33% Business, Management, Marketing, and Related Support Services, 17% Education, 9% Multi/Interdisciplinary Studies, 14% Psychology
**Expenses:** 2014-2015: $26,180; room/board: $8,200
**Financial aid:** (541) 684-7203; 91% of undergrads determined to have financial need; average aid package $19,400

## Oregon College of Art and Craft
Portland OR
(800) 390-0632
**U.S. News ranking:** Arts, unranked
**Website:** www.ocac.edu/
**Admissions email:** admissions@ocac.edu
**Private;** founded 1907
**Freshman admissions:** N/A; 2013-2014: 37 applied, 36 accepted. Neither SAT nor ACT required. SAT 25/75 percentile: N/A. High school rank: 29% in top tenth, 57% in top quarter, 71% in top half
**Early decision deadline:** N/A, notification date: N/A
**Early action deadline:** N/A, notification date: N/A
**Application deadline (fall):** rolling
**Undergraduate student body:** 117 full time, 22 part time; 19% male, 81% female; 1% American Indian, 2% Asian, 1% black, 11% Hispanic, 9% multiracial, 2% Pacific Islander, 63% white, 0% international; 40% from in state; 13% live on campus; 0% of students in fraternities, 0% in sororities
**Most popular majors:** 100% Crafts/Craft Design, Folk Art and Artisanry
**Expenses:** 2013-2014: $27,145; room/board: $7,800
**Financial aid:** N/A

## Oregon Institute of Technology
Klamath Falls OR
(541) 885-1155
**U.S. News ranking:** Reg. Coll. (W), No. 8
**Website:** www.oit.edu
**Admissions email:** oit@oit.edu
**Public;** founded 1947
**Freshman admissions:** selective; 2013-2014: 2,778 applied, 1,982 accepted. Either SAT or ACT required. SAT 25/75 percentile: 880-1140. High school rank: 25% in top tenth, 59% in top quarter, 88% in top half
**Early decision deadline:** N/A, notification date: N/A
**Early action deadline:** N/A, notification date: N/A
**Application deadline (fall):** 9/8
**Undergraduate student body:** 2,321 full time, 2,052 part time; 52% male, 48% female; 1% American Indian, 4% Asian, 1% black, 6% Hispanic, 4% multiracial, 0% Pacific Islander, 76% white, 3% international; 76% from in state; 16% live on campus; 0% of students in fraternities, N/A in sororities
**Most popular majors:** 6% Business, Management, Marketing, and Related Support Services, 5% Computer and Information Sciences and Support Services, 16% Engineering, 15% Engineering Technologies and Engineering-Related Fields, 36% Health Professions and Related Programs
**Expenses:** 2014-2015: $8,445 in state, $23,670 out of state; room/board: $9,032
**Financial aid:** (541) 885-1280; 73% of undergrads determined to have financial need; average aid package $8,059

## Oregon State University
Corvallis OR
(541) 737-4411
**U.S. News ranking:** Nat. U., No. 138
**Website:** oregonstate.edu
**Admissions email:** osuadmit@oregonstate.edu
**Public;** founded 1868
**Freshman admissions:** selective; 2013-2014: 14,239 applied, 11,303 accepted. Either SAT or ACT required. SAT 25/75 percentile: 970-1220. High school rank: 25% in top tenth, 53% in top quarter, 88% in top half
**Early decision deadline:** N/A, notification date: N/A
**Early action deadline:** 11/1, notification date: 12/20
**Application deadline (fall):** 9/1
**Undergraduate student body:** 18,486 full time, 4,675 part time; 54% male, 46% female; 1% American Indian, 7% Asian, 1% black, 7% Hispanic, 6% multiracial, 0% Pacific Islander, 69% white, 6% international; 75% from in state; 19% live on campus; 13% of students in fraternities, 18% in sororities
**Most popular majors:** 7% Agriculture, Agriculture Operations, and Related Sciences, 13% Business, Management, Marketing, and Related Support Services, 14% Engineering, 11% Family and Consumer Sciences/Human Sciences, 7% Natural Resources and Conservation
**Expenses:** 2014-2015: $8,276 in state, $23,540 out of state; room/board: N/A
**Financial aid:** (541) 737-2241; 59% of undergrads determined to have financial need; average aid package $12,973

## Pacific Northwest College of Art[1]
Portland OR
(800) 818-7622
**U.S. News ranking:** Arts, unranked
**Website:** www.pnca.edu
**Admissions email:** admissions@pnca.edu
**Private**
**Application deadline (fall):** N/A
**Undergraduate student body:** N/A full time, N/A part time
**Expenses:** 2013-2014: $32,417; room/board: $12,814
**Financial aid:** (503) 821-8976

## Pacific University
Forest Grove OR
(800) 677-6712
**U.S. News ranking:** Reg. U. (W), No. 25
**Website:** www.pacificu.edu
**Admissions email:** admissions@pacificu.edu
**Private;** founded 1849
**Freshman admissions:** selective; 2013-2014: 2,658 applied, 2,291 accepted. Either SAT or ACT required. SAT 25/75 percentile: 990-1210. High school rank: N/A
**Early decision deadline:** N/A, notification date: N/A
**Early action deadline:** N/A, notification date: N/A
**Application deadline (fall):** 8/15

**Undergraduate student body:** 1,729 full time, 56 part time; 42% male, 58% female; 1% American Indian, 13% Asian, 1% black, 10% Hispanic, 12% multiracial, 2% Pacific Islander, 53% white, 2% international; 32% from in state; 58% live on campus; 6% of students in fraternities, 9% in sororities
**Most popular majors:** 10% Biological and Biomedical Sciences, 9% Education, 9% Health Professions and Related Programs, 13% Parks, Recreation, Leisure, and Fitness Studies, 9% Social Sciences
**Expenses:** 2014-2015: $38,510; room/board: $11,116
**Financial aid:** (503) 352-2222; 83% of undergrads determined to have financial need; average aid package $29,308

## Portland State University[1]
Portland OR
(503) 725-3511
**U.S. News ranking:** Nat. U., second tier
**Website:** www.pdx.edu
**Admissions email:** admissions@pdx.edu
**Public;** founded 1946
**Application deadline (fall):** rolling
**Undergraduate student body:** N/A full time, N/A part time
**Expenses:** 2013-2014: $7,878 in state, $23,088 out of state; room/board: $10,050
**Financial aid:** (503) 725-3461

## Reed College[1]
Portland OR
(503) 777-7511
**U.S. News ranking:** Nat. Lib. Arts, No. 77
**Website:** www.reed.edu/
**Admissions email:** admission@reed.edu
**Private**
**Application deadline (fall):** N/A
**Undergraduate student body:** N/A full time, N/A part time
**Expenses:** 2013-2014: $46,010; room/board: $11,770
**Financial aid:** (503) 777-7223

## Southern Oregon University
Ashland OR
(541) 552-6411
**U.S. News ranking:** Reg. U. (W), No. 79
**Website:** www.sou.edu
**Admissions email:** admissions@sou.edu
**Public;** founded 1926
**Freshman admissions:** less selective; 2013-2014: 1,985 applied, 1,837 accepted. Either SAT or ACT required. SAT 25/75 percentile: 890-1120. High school rank: N/A
**Early decision deadline:** N/A, notification date: N/A
**Early action deadline:** N/A, notification date: N/A
**Application deadline (fall):** rolling
**Undergraduate student body:** 3,667 full time, 1,635 part time; 43% male, 57% female; 1% American Indian, 1% Asian, 2% black, 8% Hispanic, 5% multiracial, 0% Pacific Islander, 53% white,

2% international; 69% from in state; 22% live on campus; N/A of students in fraternities, N/A in sororities
**Most popular majors:** 15% Business, Management, Marketing, and Related Support Services, 7% Homeland Security, Law Enforcement, Firefighting and Related Protective Services, 12% Psychology, 9% Social Sciences, 11% Visual and Performing Arts
**Expenses:** 2013-2014: $7,863 in state, $20,238 out of state; room/board: $11,340
**Financial aid:** (541) 552-6754

## University of Oregon
Eugene OR
(800) 232-3825
**U.S. News ranking:** Nat. U., No. 106
**Website:** www.uoregon.edu
**Admissions email:** uoadmit@uoregon.edu
**Public;** founded 1876
**Freshman admissions:** selective; 2013-2014: 21,938 applied, 16,206 accepted. Either SAT or ACT required. SAT 25/75 percentile: 990-1240. High school rank: 25% in top tenth, 64% in top quarter, 94% in top half
**Early decision deadline:** N/A, notification date: N/A
**Early action deadline:** 11/1, notification date: 12/15
**Application deadline (fall):** 1/15
**Undergraduate student body:** 18,892 full time, 1,905 part time; 48% male, 52% female; 1% American Indian, 5% Asian, 2% black, 8% Hispanic, 6% multiracial, 0% Pacific Islander, 64% white, 12% international; 64% from in state; 20% live on campus; 13% of students in fraternities, 17% in sororities
**Most popular majors:** 10% Business/Commerce, General, 5% Economics, General, 5% Physiology, General, 9% Psychology, General, 6% Sociology
**Expenses:** 2014-2015: $9,918 in state, $30,888 out of state; room/board: $11,442
**Financial aid:** (541) 346-3221; 46% of undergrads determined to have financial need; average aid package $10,172

## University of Portland
Portland OR
(888) 627-5601
**U.S. News ranking:** Reg. U. (W), No. 8
**Website:** www.up.edu
**Admissions email:** admission@up.edu
**Private;** founded 1901
**Affiliation:** Roman Catholic
**Freshman admissions:** more selective; 2013-2014: 9,523 applied, 6,361 accepted. Either SAT or ACT required. SAT 25/75 percentile: 1090-1300. High school rank: 37% in top tenth, 70% in top quarter, 94% in top half
**Early decision deadline:** N/A, notification date: N/A
**Early action deadline:** N/A, notification date: N/A
**Application deadline (fall):** 2/1
**Undergraduate student body:** 3,410 full time, 84 part time; 42% male, 58% female; 0% American Indian, 10% Asian, 1% black, 10% Hispanic, 8% multiracial,

1% Pacific Islander, 64% white, 3% international; 34% from in state; 54% live on campus; 0% of students in fraternities, 0% in sororities
**Most popular majors:** 11% Biological and Biomedical Sciences, 13% Business, Management, Marketing, and Related Support Services, 12% Engineering, 20% Health Professions and Related Programs, 8% Social Sciences
**Expenses:** 2014-2015: $38,520; room/board: $13,158
**Financial aid:** (503) 943-7311; 65% of undergrads determined to have financial need; average aid package $27,750

## Warner Pacific College
Portland OR
(503) 517-1020
**U.S. News ranking:** Reg. Coll. (W), No. 8
**Website:** www.warnerpacific.edu
**Admissions email:** admissions@ warnerpacific.edu
**Private;** founded 1937
**Affiliation:** Church of God
**Freshman admissions:** less selective; 2013-2014: 948 applied, 500 accepted. Either SAT or ACT required. SAT 25/75 percentile: 830-1100. High school rank: 8% in top tenth, 25% in top quarter, 77% in top half
**Early decision deadline:** N/A, notification date: N/A
**Early action deadline:** N/A, notification date: N/A
**Application deadline (fall):** rolling
**Undergraduate student body:** 469 full time, 34 part time; 44% male, 56% female; 0% American Indian, 4% Asian, 8% black, 11% Hispanic, 8% multiracial, 2% Pacific Islander, 61% white, 0% international; 65% from in state; 43% live on campus; N/A of students in fraternities, N/A in sororities
**Most popular majors:** 8% Biological and Biomedical Sciences, 16% Business, Management, Marketing, and Related Support Services, 14% Education, 15% Family and Consumer Sciences/ Human Sciences, 12% Theology and Religious Vocations
**Expenses:** 2014-2015: $20,300; room/board: $8,230
**Financial aid:** (503) 517-1017; 85% of undergrads determined to have financial need; average aid package $16,136

## Western Oregon University
Monmouth OR
(503) 838-8211
**U.S. News ranking:** Reg. U. (W), No. 84
**Website:** www.wou.edu
**Admissions email:** wolfgram@wou.edu
**Public;** founded 1856
**Freshman admissions:** less selective; 2013-2014: 2,789 applied, 2,533 accepted. Either SAT or ACT required. SAT 25/75 percentile: 840-1070. High school rank: 14% in top tenth, 32% in top quarter, 65% in top half
**Early decision deadline:** N/A, notification date: N/A
**Early action deadline:** N/A, notification date: N/A

**Application deadline (fall):** rolling
**Undergraduate student body:** 4,454 full time, 812 part time; 42% male, 58% female; 2% American Indian, 3% Asian, 4% black, 9% Hispanic, 1% multiracial, 3% Pacific Islander, 69% white, 6% international
**Most popular majors:** 13% Business/Commerce, General, 8% Criminal Justice/Law Enforcement Administration, 21% Education, General, 4% Health and Wellness, General, 7% Psychology, General
**Expenses:** 2014-2015: $9,105 in state, $22,200 out of state; room/ board: $9,579
**Financial aid:** (503) 838-8475; 72% of undergrads determined to have financial need; average aid package $9,263

## Willamette University
Salem OR
(877) 542-2787
**U.S. News ranking:** Nat. Lib. Arts, No. 64
**Website:** www.willamette.edu
**Admissions email:** LIBARTS@ willamette.edu
**Private;** founded 1842
**Affiliation:** United Methodist
**Freshman admissions:** more selective; 2013-2014: 8,109 applied, 4,690 accepted. Either SAT or ACT required. SAT 25/75 percentile: 1080-1310. High school rank: 41% in top tenth, 75% in top quarter, 94% in top half
**Early decision deadline:** N/A, notification date: N/A
**Early action deadline:** 12/1, notification date: 1/15
**Application deadline (fall):** 2/1
**Undergraduate student body:** 2,019 full time, 209 part time; 44% male, 56% female; 2% American Indian, 7% Asian, 2% black, 10% Hispanic, 9% multiracial, 1% Pacific Islander, 63% white, 1% international; 28% from in state; 66% live on campus; 23% of students in fraternities, 28% in sororities
**Most popular majors:** 9% Biological and Biomedical Sciences, 7% Foreign Languages, Literatures, and Linguistics, 11% Physical Sciences, 18% Social Sciences, 17% Visual and Performing Arts
**Expenses:** 2014-2015: $44,076; room/board: $10,820
**Financial aid:** (503) 370-6273; 65% of undergrads determined to have financial need; average aid package $33,652

## Albright College
Reading PA
(800) 252-1856
**U.S. News ranking:** Nat. Lib. Arts, No. 177
**Website:** www.albright.edu
**Admissions email:** admission@alb.edu
**Private;** founded 1856
**Affiliation:** United Methodist
**Freshman admissions:** selective; 2013-2014: 6,060 applied, 3,776 accepted. Neither SAT nor ACT required. SAT 25/75 percentile: 930-1130. High school rank: 20% in top tenth, 49% in top quarter, 77% in top half
**Early decision deadline:** N/A, notification date: N/A

**Early action deadline:** N/A, notification date: N/A
**Application deadline (fall):** rolling
**Undergraduate student body:** 2,315 full time, 34 part time; 42% male, 58% female; 1% American Indian, 3% Asian, 18% black, 9% Hispanic, 2% multiracial, 0% Pacific Islander, 62% white, 4% international; 63% from in state; 69% live on campus; 14% of students in fraternities, 19% in sororities
**Most popular majors:** 28% Business, Management, Marketing, and Related Support Services, 5% Education, 16% Psychology, 14% Social Sciences, 12% Visual and Performing Arts
**Expenses:** 2014-2015: $38,220; room/board: $10,400
**Financial aid:** (610) 921-7515; 94% of undergrads determined to have financial need; average aid package $30,789

## Allegheny College
Meadville PA
(800) 521-5293
**U.S. News ranking:** Nat. Lib. Arts, No. 81
**Website:** www.allegheny.edu
**Admissions email:** admissions@allegheny.edu
**Private;** founded 1815
**Affiliation:** United Methodist
**Freshman admissions:** more selective; 2013-2014: 4,512 applied, 2,927 accepted. Either SAT or ACT required. SAT 25/75 percentile: 1070-1290. High school rank: 41% in top tenth, 70% in top quarter, 95% in top half
**Early decision deadline:** 11/15, notification date: 12/15
**Early action deadline:** N/A, notification date: N/A
**Application deadline (fall):** 2/15
**Undergraduate student body:** 2,125 full time, 36 part time; 46% male, 54% female; 0% American Indian, 3% Asian, 4% black, 6% Hispanic, 4% multiracial, 0% Pacific Islander, 80% white, 2% international; 54% from in state; 90% live on campus; 31% of students in fraternities, 33% in sororities
**Most popular majors:** 11% Biology/ Biological Sciences, General, 11% Economics, General, 8% English Language and Literature, General, 6% Neuroscience, 14% Psychology, General
**Expenses:** 2014-2015: $40,660; room/board: $10,320
**Financial aid:** (800) 835-7780; 72% of undergrads determined to have financial need; average aid package $32,250

## Alvernia University
Reading PA
(610) 796-8220
**U.S. News ranking:** Reg. U. (N), No. 111
**Website:** www.alvernia.edu
**Admissions email:** admissions@ alvernia.edu
**Private;** founded 1958
**Affiliation:** Roman Catholic
**Freshman admissions:** less selective; 2013-2014: 1,792 applied, 1,391 accepted. Either SAT or ACT required. SAT 25/75 percentile: 890-1070. High school rank: 8% in top tenth, 33% in top quarter, 67% in top half

**Early decision deadline:** N/A, notification date: N/A
**Early action deadline:** N/A, notification date: N/A
**Application deadline (fall):** rolling
**Undergraduate student body:** 1,719 full time, 652 part time; 28% male, 72% female; 0% American Indian, 1% Asian, 14% black, 7% Hispanic, 2% multiracial, 0% Pacific Islander, 70% white, 0% international; 75% from in state; 57% live on campus; 0% of students in fraternities, 0% in sororities
**Most popular majors:** 21% Business, Management, Marketing, and Related Support Services, 5% Education, 41% Health Professions and Related Programs, 11% Homeland Security, Law Enforcement, Firefighting and Related Protective Services, 5% Psychology
**Expenses:** 2014-2015: $30,080; room/board: $10,450
**Financial aid:** (610) 796-8356; 86% of undergrads determined to have financial need; average aid package $18,210

## Arcadia University
Glenside PA
(215) 572-2910
**U.S. News ranking:** Reg. U. (N), No. 41
**Website:** www.arcadia.edu
**Admissions email:** admiss@arcadia.edu
**Private;** founded 1853
**Freshman admissions:** selective; 2013-2014: 9,608 applied, 5,735 accepted. Either SAT or ACT required. SAT 25/75 percentile: 1000-1178. High school rank: 28% in top tenth, 62% in top quarter, 90% in top half
**Early decision deadline:** N/A, notification date: N/A
**Early action deadline:** N/A, notification date: N/A
**Application deadline (fall):** rolling
**Undergraduate student body:** 2,260 full time, 193 part time; 32% male, 68% female; 0% American Indian, 5% Asian, 8% black, 6% Hispanic, 4% multiracial, 0% Pacific Islander, 73% white, 2% international; 61% from in state; 58% live on campus; 0% of students in fraternities, 0% in sororities
**Most popular majors:** 15% Biology/ Biological Sciences, General, 5% History, General, 7% International Business/Trade/Commerce, 5% International/Global Studies, 14% Psychology, General
**Expenses:** 2014-2015: $38,160; room/board: $12,740
**Financial aid:** (215) 572-2980; 82% of undergrads determined to have financial need; average aid package $28,613

## Art Institute of Pittsburgh[1]
Pittsburgh PA
(800) 275-2470
**U.S. News ranking:** Arts, unranked
**Website:** www.artinstitutes.edu/ pittsburgh/Admissions
**Admissions email:** aip@aii.edu
**For-profit**
**Application deadline (fall):** N/A
**Undergraduate student body:** N/A full time, N/A part time

**Expenses:** 2013-2014: $17,632; room/board: $9,450
**Financial aid:** N/A

## Bloomsburg University of Pennsylvania
Bloomsburg PA
(570) 389-4316
**U.S. News ranking:** Reg. U. (N), No. 98
**Website:** www.bloomu.edu
**Admissions email:** buadmiss@ bloomu.edu
**Public;** founded 1839
**Freshman admissions:** less selective; 2013-2014: 9,248 applied, 8,190 accepted. Either SAT or ACT required. SAT 25/75 percentile: 890-1070. High school rank: 7% in top tenth, 26% in top quarter, 66% in top half
**Early decision deadline:** N/A, notification date: N/A
**Early action deadline:** N/A, notification date: 5/1
**Application deadline (fall):** rolling
**Undergraduate student body:** 8,813 full time, 603 part time; 44% male, 56% female; 0% American Indian, 1% Asian, 8% black, 5% Hispanic, 2% multiracial, 0% Pacific Islander, 81% white, 1% international; 89% from in state; 43% live on campus; 6% of students in fraternities, 6% in sororities
**Most popular majors:** 16% Business Administration, Management and Operations, 5% Criminal Justice and Corrections, 5% Psychology, General, 7% Public Relations, Advertising, and Applied Communication, 7% Teacher Education and Professional Development, Specific Levels and Methods
**Expenses:** 2014-2015: $8,914 in state, $19,144 out of state; room/ board: $8,168
**Financial aid:** (570) 389-4297; 64% of undergrads determined to have financial need; average aid package $8,740

## Bryn Athyn College of the New Church
Bryn Athyn PA
(267) 502-6000
**U.S. News ranking:** Nat. Lib. Arts, second tier
**Website:** www.brynathyn.edu
**Admissions email:** admissions@ brynathyn.edu
**Private;** founded 1877
**Affiliation:** General Church of the New Jerusalem
**Freshman admissions:** selective; 2013-2014: 396 applied, 207 accepted. Either SAT or ACT required. SAT 25/75 percentile: 920-1130. High school rank: N/A
**Early decision deadline:** N/A, notification date: N/A
**Early action deadline:** N/A, notification date: N/A
**Application deadline (fall):** rolling
**Undergraduate student body:** 259 full time, 9 part time; 48% male, 52% female; 0% American Indian, 3% Asian, 14% black, 6% Hispanic, 0% multiracial, 1% Pacific Islander, 68% white, 8% international
**Most popular majors:** Information not available

**Expenses:** 2014-2015: $18,610; room/board: $10,773
**Financial aid:** (267) 502-2630; 76% of undergrads determined to have financial need; average aid package $17,450

## Bryn Mawr College
Bryn Mawr PA
(610) 526-5152
**U.S. News ranking:** Nat. Lib. Arts, No. 27
**Website:** www.brynmawr.edu
**Admissions email:** admissions@brynmawr.edu
**Private;** founded 1885
**Freshman admissions:** more selective; 2013-2014: 2,708 applied, 1,081 accepted. Either SAT or ACT required. SAT 25/75 percentile: 1210-1470. High school rank: 65% in top tenth, 93% in top quarter, 99% in top half
**Early decision deadline:** 11/15, notification date: 12/15
**Early action deadline:** N/A, notification date: N/A
**Application deadline (fall):** 1/15
**Undergraduate student body:** 1,315 full time, 13 part time; 0% male, 100% female; 0% American Indian, 11% Asian, 5% black, 10% Hispanic, 4% multiracial, 0% Pacific Islander, 37% white, 23% international; 19% from in state; 93% live on campus; N/A of students in fraternities, N/A in sororities
**Most popular majors:** 6% Biology/Biological Sciences, General, 10% English Language and Literature, General, 11% Mathematics, General, 7% Political Science and Government, General, 8% Psychology, General
**Expenses:** 2014-2015: $45,540; room/board: $14,350
**Financial aid:** (610) 526-5245; 54% of undergrads determined to have financial need; average aid package $41,195

## Bucknell University
Lewisburg PA
(570) 577-3000
**U.S. News ranking:** Nat. Lib. Arts, No. 32
**Website:** www.bucknell.edu
**Admissions email:** admissions@bucknell.edu
**Private;** founded 1846
**Freshman admissions:** more selective; 2013-2014: 7,947 applied, 2,345 accepted. Either SAT or ACT required. SAT 25/75 percentile: 1200-1400. High school rank: 62% in top tenth, 87% in top quarter, 98% in top half
**Early decision deadline:** 11/15, notification date: 12/20
**Early action deadline:** N/A, notification date: N/A
**Application deadline (fall):** 1/15
**Undergraduate student body:** 3,504 full time, 28 part time; 48% male, 52% female; 0% American Indian, 4% Asian, 3% black, 5% Hispanic, 3% multiracial, 0% Pacific Islander, 79% white, 5% international; 24% from in state; 86% live on campus; 44% of students in fraternities, 41% in sororities
**Most popular majors:** 5% Biology/Biological Sciences, General, 9% Business Administration and Management, General,

9% Economics, General, 7% Political Science and Government, General, 8% Psychology, General
**Expenses:** 2014-2015: $48,498; room/board: $11,642
**Financial aid:** (570) 577-1331; 45% of undergrads determined to have financial need; average aid package $29,000

## Cabrini College
Radnor PA
(610) 902-8552
**U.S. News ranking:** Reg. U. (N), No. 133
**Website:** www.cabrini.edu
**Admissions email:** admit@cabrini.edu
**Private;** founded 1957
**Affiliation:** Roman Catholic
**Freshman admissions:** least selective; 2013-2014: 2,127 applied, 1,580 accepted. Either SAT or ACT required. SAT 25/75 percentile: 780-1000. High school rank: 4% in top tenth, 21% in top quarter, 51% in top half
**Early decision deadline:** N/A, notification date: N/A
**Early action deadline:** N/A, notification date: N/A
**Application deadline (fall):** rolling
**Undergraduate student body:** 1,228 full time, 109 part time; 36% male, 64% female; 0% American Indian, 1% Asian, 13% black, 5% Hispanic, 3% multiracial, 0% Pacific Islander, 72% white, 0% international; 65% from in state; 58% live on campus; 0% of students in fraternities, 0% in sororities
**Most popular majors:** 24% Business, Management, Marketing, and Related Support Services, Other, 15% Education, General, 12% Psychology, General, 9% Social Sciences, General, 8% Speech Communication and Rhetoric
**Expenses:** 2014-2015: $29,842; room/board: $12,026
**Financial aid:** (610) 902-8420; 79% of undergrads determined to have financial need; average aid package $16,794

## Cairn University
Langhorne PA
(215) 702-4235
**U.S. News ranking:** Reg. U. (N), No. 111
**Website:** cairn.edu/
**Admissions email:** admissions@cairn.edu
**Private;** founded 1913
**Affiliation:** Evangelical
**Freshman admissions:** selective; 2013-2014: 376 applied, 256 accepted. Either SAT or ACT required. SAT 25/75 percentile: 900-1170. High school rank: 26% in top tenth, 49% in top quarter, 71% in top half
**Early decision deadline:** N/A, notification date: N/A
**Early action deadline:** N/A, notification date: N/A
**Application deadline (fall):** rolling
**Undergraduate student body:** 781 full time, 65 part time; 46% male, 54% female; 1% American Indian, 3% Asian, 14% black, 5% Hispanic, 2% multiracial, 0% Pacific Islander, 73% white, 1% international; 57% from in state; 56% live on campus; 0% of students in fraternities, 0% in sororities

**Most popular majors:** 6% Business, Management, Marketing, and Related Support Services, 13% Education, 69% Philosophy and Religious Studies, 9% Public Administration and Social Service Professions, 3% Visual and Performing Arts
**Expenses:** 2014-2015: $23,110; room/board: $9,085
**Financial aid:** (215) 702-4246; 81% of undergrads determined to have financial need; average aid package $18,284

## California University of Pennsylvania
California PA
(724) 938-4404
**U.S. News ranking:** Reg. U. (N), second tier
**Website:** www.calu.edu/
**Admissions email:** inquiry@calu.edu
**Public**
**Freshman admissions:** less selective; 2013-2014: 3,125 applied, 2,814 accepted. SAT required. SAT 25/75 percentile: 850-1040. High school rank: 6% in top tenth, 25% in top quarter, 61% in top half
**Early decision deadline:** N/A, notification date: N/A
**Early action deadline:** N/A, notification date: N/A
**Application deadline (fall):** 8/22
**Undergraduate student body:** 5,649 full time, 801 part time; 48% male, 52% female; 0% American Indian, 1% Asian, 10% black, 3% Hispanic, 3% multiracial, 0% Pacific Islander, 77% white, 1% international; 90% from in state; 27% live on campus; 6% of students in fraternities, 5% in sororities
**Most popular majors:** 13% Business, Management, Marketing, and Related Support Services, 12% Education, 9% Health Professions and Related Programs, 8% Homeland Security, Law Enforcement, Firefighting and Related Protective Services, 12% Parks, Recreation, Leisure, and Fitness Studies
**Expenses:** 2014-2015: $9,556 in state, $12,966 out of state; room/board: $10,086
**Financial aid:** (724) 938-4415; 76% of undergrads determined to have financial need; average aid package $9,476

## Carlow University[1]
Pittsburgh PA
(412) 578-6059
**U.S. News ranking:** Reg. U. (N), second tier
**Website:** www.carlow.edu
**Admissions email:** admissions@carlow.edu
**Private**
**Application deadline (fall):** N/A
**Undergraduate student body:** N/A full time, N/A part time
**Expenses:** 2013-2014: $25,416; room/board: $10,014
**Financial aid:** (412) 578-6058

## Carnegie Mellon University
Pittsburgh PA
(412) 268-2082
**U.S. News ranking:** Nat. U., No. 25
**Website:** www.cmu.edu
**Admissions email:** undergraduate-admissions@andrew.cmu.edu
**Private;** founded 1900
**Freshman admissions:** most selective; 2013-2014: 18,884 applied, 4,813 accepted. Either SAT or ACT required. SAT 25/75 percentile: 1340-1530. High school rank: 80% in top tenth, 96% in top quarter, 99% in top half
**Early decision deadline:** 11/1, notification date: 12/15
**Early action deadline:** N/A, notification date: N/A
**Application deadline (fall):** 1/1
**Undergraduate student body:** 6,104 full time, 202 part time; 57% male, 43% female; 0% American Indian, 23% Asian, 5% black, 7% Hispanic, 4% multiracial, 0% Pacific Islander, 36% white, 19% international; 18% from in state; 38% live on campus; 15% of students in fraternities, 16% in sororities
**Most popular majors:** 5% Chemical Engineering, 11% Computer Science, 9% Electrical and Electronics Engineering, 7% Mechanical Engineering, 4% Systems Science and Theory
**Expenses:** 2014-2015: $48,786; room/board: $12,090
**Financial aid:** (412) 268-8186; 50% of undergrads determined to have financial need; average aid package $33,041

## Cedar Crest College
Allentown PA
(800) 360-1222
**U.S. News ranking:** Reg. Coll. (N), No. 16
**Website:** www.cedarcrest.edu
**Admissions email:** cccadmis@cedarcrest.edu
**Private;** founded 1867
**Freshman admissions:** less selective; 2013-2014: 1,063 applied, 625 accepted. Either SAT or ACT required. SAT 25/75 percentile: 840-1050. High school rank: 10% in top tenth, 43% in top quarter, 81% in top half
**Early decision deadline:** N/A, notification date: N/A
**Early action deadline:** N/A, notification date: N/A
**Application deadline (fall):** rolling
**Undergraduate student body:** 640 full time, 646 part time; 7% male, 93% female; 0% American Indian, 3% Asian, 9% black, 13% Hispanic, 1% multiracial, 0% Pacific Islander, 70% white, 1% international; 87% from in state; 22% live on campus; 0% of students in fraternities, 0% in sororities
**Most popular majors:** 6% Business, Management, Marketing, and Related Support Services, 35% Health Professions and Related Programs, 15% Psychology, 6% Public Administration and Social Service Professions, 5% Visual and Performing Arts
**Expenses:** 2014-2015: $34,304; room/board: $10,409

**Financial aid:** (610) 740-3785; 93% of undergrads determined to have financial need; average aid package $24,855

## Central Penn College[1]
Summerdale PA
(800) 759-2727
**U.S. News ranking:** Reg. Coll. (N), unranked
**Website:** www.centralpenn.edu
**Admissions email:** admissions@centralpenn.edu
**For-profit**
**Application deadline (fall):** N/A
**Undergraduate student body:** N/A full time, N/A part time
**Expenses:** 2013-2014: $16,167; room/board: $6,480
**Financial aid:** (800) 759-2727

## Chatham University
Pittsburgh PA
(800) 837-1290
**U.S. News ranking:** Reg. U. (N), No. 56
**Website:** www.chatham.edu
**Admissions email:** admissions@chatham.edu
**Private;** founded 1869
**Freshman admissions:** selective; 2013-2014: 594 applied, 361 accepted. Neither SAT nor ACT required. SAT 25/75 percentile: 950-1190. High school rank: 42% in top tenth, 65% in top quarter, 94% in top half
**Early decision deadline:** N/A, notification date: N/A
**Early action deadline:** N/A, notification date: N/A
**Application deadline (fall):** 8/1
**Undergraduate student body:** 611 full time, 366 part time; 9% male, 91% female; 0% American Indian, 2% Asian, 12% black, 2% Hispanic, 3% multiracial, 0% Pacific Islander, 68% white, 9% international; 83% from in state; 46% live on campus; N/A of students in fraternities, N/A in sororities
**Most popular majors:** 11% Biological and Biomedical Sciences, 13% Business, Management, Marketing, and Related Support Services, 20% Health Professions and Related Programs, 12% Psychology, 8% Visual and Performing Arts
**Expenses:** 2014-2015: $33,429; room/board: $10,410
**Financial aid:** (412) 365-1777; 65% of undergrads determined to have financial need; average aid package $27,154

## Chestnut Hill College
Philadelphia PA
(215) 248-7001
**U.S. News ranking:** Reg. U. (N), second tier
**Website:** www.chc.edu
**Admissions email:** chcapply@chc.edu
**Private;** founded 1924
**Affiliation:** Roman Catholic
**Freshman admissions:** less selective; 2013-2014: 1,855 applied, 1,064 accepted. Either SAT or ACT required. SAT 25/75 percentile: 850-1060. High school rank: 10% in top tenth, 29% in top quarter, 65% in top half
**Early decision deadline:** N/A, notification date: N/A
**Early action deadline:** N/A, notification date: N/A

Application deadline (fall): rolling
Undergraduate student body: 1,161 full time, 346 part time; 32% male, 68% female; 0% American Indian, 2% Asian, 35% black, 7% Hispanic, 3% multiracial, 0% Pacific Islander, 41% white, 1% international; 77% from in state; 38% live on campus; 0% of students in fraternities, 0% in sororities
Most popular majors: 14% Business, Management, Marketing, and Related Support Services, 32% Education, 10% Homeland Security, Law Enforcement, Firefighting and Related Protective Services, 7% Psychology, 17% Public Administration and Social Service Professions
Expenses: 2014-2015: $32,510; room/board: $10,000
Financial aid: (215) 248-7182; 62% of undergrads determined to have financial need; average aid package $19,039

## Cheyney University of Pennsylvania
Cheyney PA
(610) 399-2275
U.S. News ranking: Reg. U. (N), second tier
Website: www.cheyney.edu
Admissions email: abrown@cheyney.edu
Public; founded 1837
Freshman admissions: least selective; 2013-2014: 1,451 applied, 1,273 accepted. Either SAT or ACT required. SAT 25/75 percentile: 670-850. High school rank: 2% in top tenth, 9% in top quarter, 40% in top half
Early decision deadline: N/A, notification date: N/A
Early action deadline: N/A, notification date: N/A
Application deadline (fall): rolling
Undergraduate student body: 1,114 full time, 65 part time; 48% male, 52% female; 0% American Indian, 0% Asian, 88% black, 5% Hispanic, 3% multiracial, 0% Pacific Islander, 1% white, 0% international; 78% from in state; 73% live on campus; N/A of students in fraternities, N/A in sororities
Most popular majors: 25% Business, Management, Marketing, and Related Support Services, 9% Education, 7% Parks, Recreation, Leisure, and Fitness Studies, 11% Psychology, 23% Social Sciences
Expenses: 2014-2015: $8,842 in state, $13,148 out of state; room/board: $11,270
Financial aid: (610) 399-2302; 98% of undergrads determined to have financial need; average aid package $11,339

## Clarion University of Pennsylvania
Clarion PA
(814) 393-2306
U.S. News ranking: Reg. U. (N), second tier
Website: www.clarion.edu
Admissions email: admissions@clarion.edu
Public; founded 1867
Freshman admissions: less selective; 2013-2014: 2,071 applied, 1,936 accepted. Either SAT or ACT required. SAT 25/75 percentile: 840-1030. High

school rank: 2% in top tenth, 9% in top quarter, 39% in top half
Early decision deadline: N/A, notification date: N/A
Early action deadline: N/A, notification date: N/A
Application deadline (fall): 8/1
Undergraduate student body: 4,373 full time, 826 part time; 37% male, 63% female; 0% American Indian, 0% Asian, 7% black, 1% Hispanic, 2% multiracial, 0% Pacific Islander, 88% white, 1% international; 90% from in state; 35% live on campus; 1% of students in fraternities, 1% in sororities
Most popular majors: 13% Business, Management, Marketing, and Related Support Services, 9% Communication, Journalism, and Related Programs, 14% Education, 16% Health Professions and Related Programs, 12% Liberal Arts and Sciences, General Studies and Humanities
Expenses: 2014-2015: $9,788 in state, $13,198 out of state; room/board: $8,285
Financial aid: (814) 393-2315; 81% of undergrads determined to have financial need; average aid package $8,130

## Curtis Institute of Music
Philadelphia PA
(215) 717-3117
U.S. News ranking: Arts, unranked
Website: www.curtis.edu
Admissions email: admissions@curtis.edu
Private; founded 1924
Freshman admissions: N/A; 2013-2014: 289 applied, 14 accepted. SAT required. SAT 25/75 percentile: N/A. High school rank: N/A
Early decision deadline: N/A, notification date: N/A
Early action deadline: N/A, notification date: N/A
Application deadline (fall): 12/12
Undergraduate student body: 122 full time, N/A part time; 53% male, 47% female; 0% American Indian, 20% Asian, 2% black, 2% Hispanic, 0% multiracial, 0% Pacific Islander, 39% white, 37% international
Most popular majors: Information not available
Expenses: 2014-2015: $2,475; room/board: $14,363
Financial aid: (215) 717-3165; 50% of undergrads determined to have financial need; average aid package $16,455

## Delaware Valley College
Doylestown PA
(215) 489-2211
U.S. News ranking: Reg. Coll. (N), No. 19
Website: www.delval.edu
Admissions email: admitme@delval.edu
Private; founded 1896
Freshman admissions: selective; 2013-2014: 1,895 applied, 1,295 accepted. Either SAT or ACT required. SAT 25/75 percentile: 880-1123. High school rank: 16% in top tenth, 41% in top quarter, 74% in top half
Early decision deadline: N/A, notification date: N/A

Early action deadline: N/A, notification date: N/A
Application deadline (fall): rolling
Undergraduate student body: 1,608 full time, 199 part time; 37% male, 63% female; 1% American Indian, 1% Asian, 6% black, 6% Hispanic, 1% multiracial, 0% Pacific Islander, 81% white, 0% international; 62% from in state; 53% live on campus; 1% of students in fraternities, 1% in sororities
Most popular majors: 39% Agriculture, Agriculture Operations, and Related Sciences, 15% Biological and Biomedical Sciences, 16% Business, Management, Marketing, and Related Support Services, 4% Homeland Security, Law Enforcement, Firefighting and Related Protective Services, 14% Natural Resources and Conservation
Expenses: 2014-2015: $33,826; room/board: $12,076
Financial aid: (215) 489-2272; 79% of undergrads determined to have financial need; average aid package $22,385

## DeSales University
Center Valley PA
(610) 282-4443
U.S. News ranking: Reg. U. (N), No. 70
Website: www.desales.edu
Admissions email: admiss@desales.edu
Private; founded 1964
Affiliation: Roman Catholic
Freshman admissions: selective; 2013-2014: 2,624 applied, 1,989 accepted. Either SAT or ACT required. SAT 25/75 percentile: 930-1190. High school rank: 23% in top tenth, 47% in top quarter, 80% in top half
Early decision deadline: N/A, notification date: N/A
Early action deadline: N/A, notification date: N/A
Application deadline (fall): 8/1
Undergraduate student body: 1,836 full time, 646 part time; 38% male, 62% female; 1% American Indian, 2% Asian, 5% black, 9% Hispanic, 0% multiracial, 0% Pacific Islander, 76% white, 0% international; 69% from in state; 64% live on campus; 0% of students in fraternities, 0% in sororities
Most popular majors: 20% Business, Management, Marketing, and Related Support Services, 23% Health Professions and Related Programs, 6% Parks, Recreation, Leisure, and Fitness Studies, 8% Psychology, 11% Visual and Performing Arts
Expenses: 2014-2015: $32,350; room/board: $11,620
Financial aid: (610) 282-1100; 80% of undergrads determined to have financial need; average aid package $22,148

## Dickinson College
Carlisle PA
(800) 644-1773
U.S. News ranking: Nat. Lib. Arts, No. 37
Website: www.dickinson.edu
Admissions email: admissions@dickinson.edu
Private; founded 1783
Freshman admissions: more selective; 2013-2014: 5,817 applied, 2,589 accepted. Neither

SAT nor ACT required. SAT 25/75 percentile: 1190-1365. High school rank: 46% in top tenth, 78% in top quarter, 93% in top half
Early decision deadline: 11/15, notification date: 12/15
Early action deadline: 12/1, notification date: 2/1
Application deadline (fall): 2/1
Undergraduate student body: 2,356 full time, 40 part time; 44% male, 56% female; 0% American Indian, 2% Asian, 4% black, 6% Hispanic, 3% multiracial, 0% Pacific Islander, 76% white, 7% international; 23% from in state; 95% live on campus; 12% of students in fraternities, 20% in sororities
Most popular majors: 7% Biology/Biological Sciences, General, 6% Economics, General, 8% International Business/Trade/Commerce, 6% Political Science and Government, General, 6% Psychology, General
Expenses: 2014-2015: $47,692; room/board: $11,972
Financial aid: (717) 245-1308; 53% of undergrads determined to have financial need; average aid package $36,427

## Drexel University
Philadelphia PA
(800) 237-3935
U.S. News ranking: Nat. U., No. 95
Website: www.drexel.edu
Admissions email: enroll@drexel.edu
Private; founded 1891
Freshman admissions: more selective; 2013-2014: 43,945 applied, 35,815 accepted. Either SAT or ACT required. SAT 25/75 percentile: 1070-1310. High school rank: 33% in top tenth, 61% in top quarter, 86% in top half
Early decision deadline: N/A, notification date: N/A
Early action deadline: 11/1, notification date: 12/15
Application deadline (fall): 1/15
Undergraduate student body: 11,480 full time, 2,628 part time; 52% male, 48% female; 0% American Indian, 12% Asian, 7% black, 6% Hispanic, 3% multiracial, 1% Pacific Islander, 56% white, 14% international; 47% from in state; 26% live on campus; 9% of students in fraternities, 8% in sororities
Most popular majors: 20% Business, Management, Marketing, and Related Support Services, 6% Computer and Information Sciences and Support Services, 19% Engineering, 23% Health Professions and Related Programs, 9% Visual and Performing Arts
Expenses: 2014-2015: $47,051; room/board: $14,367
Financial aid: (215) 895-2537

## Duquesne University
Pittsburgh PA
(412) 396-6222
U.S. News ranking: Nat. U., No. 116
Website: www.duq.edu
Admissions email: admissions@duq.edu
Private; founded 1878
Affiliation: Roman Catholic

Freshman admissions: selective; 2013-2014: 6,793 applied, 5,033 accepted. Neither SAT nor ACT required. SAT 25/75 percentile: 1050-1220. High school rank: 27% in top tenth, 60% in top quarter, 89% in top half
Early decision deadline: 11/1, notification date: 11/15
Early action deadline: 12/1, notification date: 1/15
Application deadline (fall): 7/1
Undergraduate student body: 5,740 full time, 230 part time; 41% male, 59% female; 0% American Indian, 2% Asian, 4% black, 3% Hispanic, 2% multiracial, 0% Pacific Islander, 84% white, 4% international; 75% from in state; 61% live on campus; 17% of students in fraternities, 21% in sororities
Most popular majors: 6% Biological and Biomedical Sciences, 25% Business, Management, Marketing, and Related Support Services, 8% Communication, Journalism, and Related Programs, 8% Education, 23% Health Professions and Related Programs
Expenses: 2014-2015: $32,636; room/board: $11,084
Financial aid: (412) 396-6607; 71% of undergrads determined to have financial need; average aid package $25,135

## Eastern University
St. Davids PA
(610) 341-5967
U.S. News ranking: Reg. U. (N), No. 98
Website: www.eastern.edu
Admissions email: ugadm@eastern.edu
Private; founded 1952
Affiliation: American Baptist
Freshman admissions: selective; 2013-2014: 1,485 applied, 1,111 accepted. Either SAT or ACT required. SAT 25/75 percentile: 920-1160. High school rank: 19% in top tenth, 51% in top quarter, 81% in top half
Early decision deadline: N/A, notification date: N/A
Early action deadline: N/A, notification date: N/A
Application deadline (fall): rolling
Undergraduate student body: 2,076 full time, 465 part time; 30% male, 70% female; 1% American Indian, 2% Asian, 21% black, 15% Hispanic, 0% multiracial, 0% Pacific Islander, 54% white, 2% international; 55% from in state; 73% live on campus; N/A of students in fraternities, N/A in sororities
Most popular majors: 14% Business Administration and Management, General, 17% Early Childhood Education and Teaching, 11% Nursing Practice, 5% Organizational Leadership, 5% Registered Nursing/Registered Nurse
Expenses: 2014-2015: $29,600; room/board: $9,940
Financial aid: (610) 341-5842; 90% of undergrads determined to have financial need; average aid package $18,115

## East Stroudsburg University of Pennsylvania

East Stroudsburg PA
(570) 422-3542
**U.S. News ranking:** Reg. U. (N), No. 133
**Website:** www.esu.edu
**Admissions email:** undergrads@po-box.esu.edu
**Public;** founded 1893
**Freshman admissions:** least selective; 2013-2014: 5,642 applied, 4,409 accepted. Either SAT or ACT required. SAT 25/75 percentile: 880-1010. High school rank: 2% in top tenth, 10% in top quarter, 39% in top half
**Early decision deadline:** N/A, notification date: N/A
**Early action deadline:** N/A, notification date: N/A
**Application deadline (fall):** 4/1
**Undergraduate student body:** 5,495 full time, 691 part time; 45% male, 55% female; 0% American Indian, 1% Asian, 9% black, 10% Hispanic, 2% multiracial, 0% Pacific Islander, 63% white, 1% international; 77% from in state; 36% live on campus; N/A of students in fraternities, N/A in sororities
**Most popular majors:** 13% Business, Management, Marketing, and Related Support Services, 23% Education, 10% Health Professions and Related Programs, 9% Parks, Recreation, Leisure, and Fitness Studies, 11% Social Sciences
**Expenses:** 2014-2015: $9,376 in state, $19,606 out of state; room/board: $7,980
**Financial aid:** (570) 422-2800; 53% of undergrads determined to have financial need; average aid package $7,330

## Edinboro University of Pennsylvania

Edinboro PA
(888) 846-2676
**U.S. News ranking:** Reg. U. (N), No. 135
**Website:** www.edinboro.edu
**Admissions email:** eup_admissions@edinboro.edu
**Public;** founded 1857
**Freshman admissions:** less selective; 2013-2014: 3,187 applied, 2,784 accepted. Either SAT or ACT required. SAT 25/75 percentile: 820-1040. High school rank: 6% in top tenth, 24% in top quarter, 54% in top half
**Early decision deadline:** N/A, notification date: N/A
**Early action deadline:** N/A, notification date: N/A
**Application deadline (fall):** rolling
**Undergraduate student body:** 5,320 full time, 544 part time; 42% male, 58% female; 0% American Indian, 1% Asian, 7% black, 1% Hispanic, 4% multiracial, 0% Pacific Islander, 84% white, 2% international; 88% from in state; 37% live on campus; 0% of students in fraternities, 1% in sororities
**Most popular majors:** 9% Business, Management, Marketing, and Related Support Services, 11% Education, 11% Health Professions and Related Programs, 8% Social Sciences, 15% Visual and Performing Arts

**Expenses:** 2014-2015: $9,222 in state, $12,632 out of state; room/board: $8,612
**Financial aid:** (814) 732-5555; 64% of undergrads determined to have financial need; average aid package $8,425

## Elizabethtown College

Elizabethtown PA
(717) 361-1400
**U.S. News ranking:** Reg. Coll. (N), No. 4
**Website:** www.etown.edu
**Admissions email:** admissions@etown.edu
**Private;** founded 1899
**Freshman admissions:** selective; 2013-2014: 3,815 applied, 2,654 accepted. Either SAT or ACT required. SAT 25/75 percentile: 1000-1230. High school rank: 34% in top tenth, 65% in top quarter, 88% in top half
**Early decision deadline:** N/A, notification date: N/A
**Early action deadline:** N/A, notification date: N/A
**Application deadline (fall):** rolling
**Undergraduate student body:** 1,808 full time, 36 part time; 36% male, 64% female; 0% American Indian, 2% Asian, 2% black, 3% Hispanic, 1% multiracial, 0% Pacific Islander, 88% white, 3% international; 66% from in state; 88% live on campus; 0% of students in fraternities, 0% in sororities
**Most popular majors:** 10% Biological and Biomedical Sciences, 15% Business, Management, Marketing, and Related Support Services, 10% Education, 11% Health Professions and Related Programs, 10% Social Sciences
**Expenses:** 2014-2015: $39,920; room/board: $9,820
**Financial aid:** (717) 361-1404; 78% of undergrads determined to have financial need; average aid package $26,636

## Franklin and Marshall College

Lancaster PA
(717) 291-3953
**U.S. News ranking:** Nat. Lib. Arts, No. 37
**Website:** www.fandm.edu
**Admissions email:** admission@fandm.edu
**Private;** founded 1787
**Freshman admissions:** more selective; 2013-2014: 5,347 applied, 1,936 accepted. Neither SAT nor ACT required. SAT 25/75 percentile: 1220-1410. High school rank: 56% in top tenth, 86% in top quarter, 100% in top half
**Early decision deadline:** 11/15, notification date: 12/15
**Early action deadline:** N/A, notification date: N/A
**Application deadline (fall):** 1/15
**Undergraduate student body:** 2,258 full time, 39 part time; 48% male, 52% female; 0% American Indian, 4% Asian, 5% black, 7% Hispanic, 2% multiracial, 0% Pacific Islander, 63% white, 13% international; 29% from in state; 97% live on campus; 28% of students in fraternities, 36% in sororities

**Most popular majors:** 6% Biology/Biological Sciences, General, 12% Business/Commerce, General, 5% Economics, General, 11% Political Science and Government, General, 6% Psychology, General
**Expenses:** 2014-2015: $48,514; room/board: $12,285
**Financial aid:** (717) 291-3991; 49% of undergrads determined to have financial need; average aid package $40,929

## Gannon University

Erie PA
(814) 871-7240
**U.S. News ranking:** Reg. U. (N), No. 60
**Website:** www.gannon.edu
**Admissions email:** admissions@gannon.edu
**Private;** founded 1925
**Affiliation:** Roman Catholic
**Freshman admissions:** selective; 2013-2014: 3,983 applied, 3,203 accepted. Either SAT or ACT required. SAT 25/75 percentile: 930-1150. High school rank: 27% in top tenth, 54% in top quarter, 82% in top half
**Early decision deadline:** N/A, notification date: N/A
**Early action deadline:** N/A, notification date: N/A
**Application deadline (fall):** rolling
**Undergraduate student body:** 2,556 full time, 555 part time; 43% male, 57% female; 0% American Indian, 2% Asian, 5% black, 3% Hispanic, 1% multiracial, 0% Pacific Islander, 81% white, 7% international; 75% from in state; 42% live on campus; 14% of students in fraternities, 18% in sororities
**Most popular majors:** 10% Biological and Biomedical Sciences, 11% Business, Management, Marketing, and Related Support Services, 31% Health Professions and Related Programs, 7% Homeland Security, Law Enforcement, Firefighting and Related Protective Services, 8% Parks, Recreation, Leisure, and Fitness Studies
**Expenses:** 2014-2015: $28,368; room/board: $11,240
**Financial aid:** (814) 871-7337; 80% of undergrads determined to have financial need; average aid package $23,171

## Geneva College

Beaver Falls PA
(724) 847-6500
**U.S. News ranking:** Reg. Coll. (N), No. 14
**Website:** www.geneva.edu
**Admissions email:** admissions@geneva.edu
**Private;** founded 1848
**Affiliation:** Reformed Presbyterian of N.A.
**Freshman admissions:** selective; 2013-2014: 1,652 applied, 1,136 accepted. Either SAT or ACT required. SAT 25/75 percentile: 950-1190. High school rank: 22% in top tenth, 45% in top quarter, 78% in top half
**Early decision deadline:** N/A, notification date: N/A
**Early action deadline:** N/A, notification date: N/A
**Application deadline (fall):** rolling
**Undergraduate student body:** 1,475 full time, 66 part time; 48% male,

52% female; 0% American Indian, 1% Asian, 6% black, 1% Hispanic, 2% multiracial, 0% Pacific Islander, 89% white, 1% international; 71% from in state; 70% live on campus; 0% of students in fraternities, 0% in sororities
**Most popular majors:** 17% Business, Management, Marketing, and Related Support Services, 11% Education, 14% Engineering, 6% Psychology, 6% Public Administration and Social Service Professions
**Expenses:** 2014-2015: $25,220; room/board: $9,460
**Financial aid:** (724) 847-6530; 82% of undergrads determined to have financial need; average aid package $19,770

## Gettysburg College

Gettysburg PA
(800) 431-0803
**U.S. News ranking:** Nat. Lib. Arts, No. 50
**Website:** www.gettysburg.edu
**Admissions email:** admiss@gettysburg.edu
**Private;** founded 1832
**Affiliation:** Lutheran
**Freshman admissions:** more selective; 2013-2014: 5,453 applied, 2,270 accepted. Neither SAT nor ACT required. SAT 25/75 percentile: 1200-1370. High school rank: 69% in top tenth, 89% in top quarter, 99% in top half
**Early decision deadline:** 11/15, notification date: 12/15
**Early action deadline:** N/A, notification date: N/A
**Application deadline (fall):** 2/1
**Undergraduate student body:** 2,515 full time, 18 part time; 48% male, 52% female; 0% American Indian, 1% Asian, 3% black, 4% Hispanic, 3% multiracial, 0% Pacific Islander, 82% white, 2% international; N/A from in state; 93% live on campus; 41% of students in fraternities, 33% in sororities
**Most popular majors:** 11% Biology/Biological Sciences, General, 10% Business/Commerce, General, 8% English Language and Literature, General, 8% History, General, 23% Social Sciences, General
**Expenses:** 2014-2015: $47,480; room/board: $11,340
**Financial aid:** (717) 337-6611; 61% of undergrads determined to have financial need; average aid package $33,652

## Gratz College[1]

Melrose Park PA
(215) 635-7300
**U.S. News ranking:** Reg. U. (N), unranked
**Website:** www.gratzcollege.edu
**Admissions email:** admissions@gratz.edu
**Private**
**Affiliation:** Jewish
**Application deadline (fall):** N/A
**Undergraduate student body:** N/A full time, N/A part time
**Expenses:** N/A
**Financial aid:** (215) 635-7300

## Grove City College

Grove City PA
(724) 458-2100
**U.S. News ranking:** Nat. Lib. Arts, No. 139
**Website:** www.gcc.edu
**Admissions email:** admissions@gcc.edu
**Private;** founded 1876
**Affiliation:** Presbyterian
**Freshman admissions:** more selective; 2013-2014: 1,530 applied, 1,233 accepted. Either SAT or ACT required. SAT 25/75 percentile: 1079-1334. High school rank: 41% in top tenth, 65% in top quarter, 90% in top half
**Early decision deadline:** 11/15, notification date: 12/15
**Early action deadline:** N/A, notification date: N/A
**Application deadline (fall):** 2/1
**Undergraduate student body:** 2,438 full time, 53 part time; 49% male, 51% female; 0% American Indian, 2% Asian, 1% black, 1% Hispanic, 2% multiracial, 0% Pacific Islander, 93% white, 1% international; 48% from in state; 94% live on campus; 16% of students in fraternities, 18% in sororities
**Most popular majors:** 6% Biology/Biological Sciences, General, 8% English Language and Literature, General, 6% History, General, 7% Mechanical Engineering, 6% Speech Communication and Rhetoric
**Expenses:** 2014-2015: $15,550; room/board: $8,472
**Financial aid:** (724) 458-3300; 41% of undergrads determined to have financial need; average aid package $6,541

## Gwynedd Mercy University

Gwynedd Valley PA
(215) 681-5510
**U.S. News ranking:** Reg. U. (N), No. 109
**Website:** www.gmercyu.edu/
**Admissions email:** admissions@gmercyu.edu
**Private;** founded 1948
**Affiliation:** Roman Catholic
**Freshman admissions:** less selective; 2013-2014: 1,232 applied, 812 accepted. Either SAT or ACT required. SAT 25/75 percentile: 850-1050. High school rank: 7% in top tenth, 21% in top quarter, 52% in top half
**Early decision deadline:** N/A, notification date: N/A
**Early action deadline:** N/A, notification date: N/A
**Application deadline (fall):** 8/20
**Undergraduate student body:** 1,851 full time, 211 part time; 25% male, 75% female; 0% American Indian, 5% Asian, 25% black, 4% Hispanic, 0% multiracial, 0% Pacific Islander, 61% white, 0% international; 90% from in state; 22% live on campus; N/A of students in fraternities, N/A in sororities
**Most popular majors:** 30% Business, Management, Marketing, and Related Support Services, 9% Education, 42% Health Professions and Related Programs, 5% Homeland Security, Law Enforcement, Firefighting and Related Protective Services, 5% Psychology

**Expenses:** 2014-2015: $30,460; room/board: $11,040
**Financial aid:** (215) 641-5570; 74% of undergrads determined to have financial need; average aid package $20,075

## Harrisburg University of Science and Technology
Harrisburg PA
(717) 901-5150
**U.S. News ranking:** Nat. Lib. Arts, second tier
**Website:** www.harrisburgu.edu
**Admissions email:** admissions@harrisburgu.edu
**Private;** founded 2001
**Freshman admissions:** less selective; 2013-2014: N/A applied, N/A accepted. Neither SAT nor ACT required. SAT 25/75 percentile: 830-1050. High school rank: N/A
**Early decision deadline:** N/A, notification date: N/A
**Early action deadline:** N/A, notification date: N/A
**Application deadline (fall):** rolling
**Undergraduate student body:** 263 full time, 17 part time; 51% male, 49% female; 0% American Indian, 6% Asian, 33% black, 4% Hispanic, 6% multiracial, 0% Pacific Islander, 47% white, 0% international; 79% from in state; 33% live on campus; 0% of students in fraternities, 0% in sororities
**Most popular majors:** 21% Biotechnology, 27% Computer and Information Sciences, General, 3% Geological and Earth Sciences/Geosciences, Other, 48% Natural Sciences
**Expenses:** 2014-2015: $23,900; room/board: $9,700
**Financial aid:** N/A; 97% of undergrads determined to have financial need; average aid package $3,418

## Haverford College
Haverford PA
(610) 896-1350
**U.S. News ranking:** Nat. Lib. Arts, No. 8
**Website:** www.haverford.edu
**Admissions email:** admission@haverford.edu
**Private;** founded 1833
**Freshman admissions:** most selective; 2013-2014: 3,585 applied, 842 accepted. Either SAT or ACT required. SAT 25/75 percentile: 1310-1490. High school rank: 95% in top tenth, 98% in top quarter, 100% in top half
**Early decision deadline:** 11/15, notification date: 12/15
**Early action deadline:** N/A, notification date: N/A
**Application deadline (fall):** 1/15
**Undergraduate student body:** 1,187 full time, 0 part time; 48% male, 52% female; 0% American Indian, 7% Asian, 6% black, 9% Hispanic, 7% multiracial, 0% Pacific Islander, 65% white, 6% international; 13% from in state; 98% live on campus; 0% of students in fraternities, 0% in sororities
**Most popular majors:** 13% Biology/Biological Sciences, General, 9% Economics, General, 10% English Language and Literature,

General, 9% Political Science and Government, General, 12% Psychology, General
**Expenses:** 2014-2015: $47,214; room/board: $14,350
**Financial aid:** (610) 896-1350; 51% of undergrads determined to have financial need; average aid package $41,254

## Holy Family University
Philadelphia PA
(215) 637-3050
**U.S. News ranking:** Reg. U. (N), No. 125
**Website:** www.holyfamily.edu
**Admissions email:** admissions@holyfamily.edu
**Private;** founded 1954
**Affiliation:** Roman Catholic
**Freshman admissions:** less selective; 2013-2014: 1,287 applied, 999 accepted. Either SAT or ACT required. SAT 25/75 percentile: 850-1020. High school rank: 11% in top tenth, 35% in top quarter, 70% in top half
**Early decision deadline:** N/A, notification date: N/A
**Early action deadline:** N/A, notification date: N/A
**Application deadline (fall):** rolling
**Undergraduate student body:** 1,499 full time, 683 part time; 26% male, 74% female; 0% American Indian, 4% Asian, 7% black, 6% Hispanic, 0% multiracial, 0% Pacific Islander, 56% white, 0% international; 84% from in state; 11% live on campus; 0% of students in fraternities, 0% in sororities
**Most popular majors:** 16% Business, Management, Marketing, and Related Support Services, 23% Education, 27% Health Professions and Related Programs, 6% Homeland Security, Law Enforcement, Firefighting and Related Protective Services, 13% Psychology
**Expenses:** 2014-2015: $28,456; room/board: $13,576
**Financial aid:** (215) 637-5538; 86% of undergrads determined to have financial need; average aid package $19,506

## Immaculata University
Immaculata PA
(877) 428-6329
**U.S. News ranking:** Nat. U., No. 181
**Website:** www.immaculata.edu
**Admissions email:** admiss@immaculata.edu
**Private;** founded 1920
**Affiliation:** Roman Catholic
**Freshman admissions:** less selective; 2013-2014: 1,770 applied, 1,449 accepted. Either SAT or ACT required. SAT 25/75 percentile: 830-1060. High school rank: N/A
**Early decision deadline:** N/A, notification date: N/A
**Early action deadline:** N/A, notification date: N/A
**Application deadline (fall):** rolling
**Undergraduate student body:** 1,184 full time, 1,376 part time; 24% male, 76% female; 0% American Indian, 3% Asian, 17% black, 5% Hispanic, 2% multiracial, 0% Pacific Islander, 72% white, 1% international; 76% from in state; 22% live on campus; 3% of students in fraternities, 4% in sororities

**Most popular majors:** 18% Business, Management, Marketing, and Related Support Services, 5% Education, 57% Health Professions and Related Programs, 3% Parks, Recreation, Leisure, and Fitness Studies, 6% Psychology
**Expenses:** 2013-2014: $30,740; room/board: $12,260
**Financial aid:** (610) 647-4400

## Indiana University of Pennsylvania
Indiana PA
(800) 442-6830
**U.S. News ranking:** Nat. U., second tier
**Website:** www.iup.edu
**Admissions email:** admissions-inquiry@iup.edu
**Public;** founded 1875
**Freshman admissions:** less selective; 2013-2014: 9,367 applied, 8,476 accepted. Either SAT or ACT required. SAT 25/75 percentile: 880-1070. High school rank: 8% in top tenth, 23% in top quarter, 58% in top half
**Early decision deadline:** N/A, notification date: N/A
**Early action deadline:** N/A, notification date: N/A
**Application deadline (fall):** rolling
**Undergraduate student body:** 11,748 full time, 723 part time; 45% male, 55% female; 0% American Indian, 1% Asian, 11% black, 3% Hispanic, 3% multiracial, 0% Pacific Islander, 79% white, 2% international; 93% from in state; 32% live on campus; 7% of students in fraternities, 6% in sororities
**Most popular majors:** 23% Business, Management, Marketing, and Related Support Services, 7% Communication, Journalism, and Related Programs, 9% Health Professions and Related Programs, 16% Social Sciences, 7% Visual and Performing Arts
**Expenses:** 2014-2015: $9,470 in state, $19,700 out of state; room/board: $11,346
**Financial aid:** (724) 357-2218; 73% of undergrads determined to have financial need; average aid package $8,726

## Juniata College
Huntingdon PA
(877) 586-4282
**U.S. News ranking:** Nat. Lib. Arts, No. 105
**Website:** www.juniata.edu
**Admissions email:** admissions@juniata.edu
**Private;** founded 1876
**Freshman admissions:** selective; 2013-2014: 2,227 applied, 1,650 accepted. Neither SAT nor ACT required. SAT 25/75 percentile: 1040-1260. High school rank: 34% in top tenth, 73% in top quarter, 98% in top half
**Early decision deadline:** 11/15, notification date: 12/23
**Early action deadline:** N/A, notification date: N/A
**Application deadline (fall):** 3/15
**Undergraduate student body:** 1,555 full time, 70 part time; 45% male, 55% female; 0% American Indian, 3% Asian, 3% black, 4% Hispanic, 2% multiracial,

0% Pacific Islander, 74% white, 8% international; 64% from in state; 79% live on campus; 0% of students in fraternities, 0% in sororities
**Most popular majors:** 15% Biological and Biomedical Sciences, 12% Business, Management, Marketing, and Related Support Services, 8% Natural Resources and Conservation, 8% Physical Sciences, 10% Psychology
**Expenses:** 2014-2015: $38,630; room/board: $10,710
**Financial aid:** (814) 641-3142; 70% of undergrads determined to have financial need; average aid package $29,631

## Keystone College
La Plume PA
(570) 945-8000
**U.S. News ranking:** Reg. Coll. (N), No. 38
**Website:** www.keystone.edu
**Admissions email:** admissions@keystone.edu
**Private;** founded 1868
**Freshman admissions:** less selective; 2013-2014: 1,120 applied, 807 accepted. Either SAT or ACT required. SAT 25/75 percentile: 800-1000. High school rank: N/A
**Early decision deadline:** N/A, notification date: N/A
**Early action deadline:** N/A, notification date: N/A
**Application deadline (fall):** 6/1
**Undergraduate student body:** 1,304 full time, 270 part time; 41% male, 59% female; 0% American Indian, 1% Asian, 5% black, 3% Hispanic, 1% multiracial, 0% Pacific Islander, 75% white, 1% international; 86% from in state; 30% live on campus; 0% of students in fraternities, 0% in sororities
**Most popular majors:** 25% Business, Management, Marketing, and Related Support Services, 15% Education, 12% Homeland Security, Law Enforcement, Firefighting and Related Protective Services, 12% Parks, Recreation, Leisure, and Fitness Studies, 8% Visual and Performing Arts
**Expenses:** 2013-2014: $21,200; room/board: $9,800
**Financial aid:** (877) 426-5534

## King's College
Wilkes-Barre PA
(888) 546-4772
**U.S. News ranking:** Reg. U. (N), No. 41
**Website:** www.kings.edu
**Admissions email:** admissions@kings.edu
**Private;** founded 1946
**Affiliation:** Catholic
**Freshman admissions:** selective; 2013-2014: 2,780 applied, 1,988 accepted. Neither SAT nor ACT required. SAT 25/75 percentile: 940-1150. High school rank: 14% in top tenth, 38% in top quarter, 74% in top half
**Early decision deadline:** N/A, notification date: N/A
**Early action deadline:** N/A, notification date: N/A
**Application deadline (fall):** rolling
**Undergraduate student body:** 1,925 full time, 219 part time; 51% male, 49% female;

0% American Indian, 2% Asian, 3% black, 7% Hispanic, 2% multiracial, 0% Pacific Islander, 80% white, 0% international; 28% from in state; 50% live on campus; 0% of students in fraternities, 0% in sororities
**Most popular majors:** 10% Accounting, 9% Business Administration and Management, General, 9% Criminal Justice/Safety Studies, 9% Elementary Education and Teaching, 9% Psychology, General
**Expenses:** 2014-2015: $31,816; room/board: $11,658
**Financial aid:** (570) 208-5868; 84% of undergrads determined to have financial need; average aid package $20,673

## Kutztown University of Pennsylvania
Kutztown PA
(610) 683-4060
**U.S. News ranking:** Reg. U. (N), No. 125
**Website:** www.kutztown.edu
**Admissions email:** admissions@kutztown.edu
**Public;** founded 1866
**Freshman admissions:** less selective; 2013-2014: 8,533 applied, 6,406 accepted. Either SAT or ACT required. SAT 25/75 percentile: 870-1050. High school rank: 5% in top tenth, 20% in top quarter, 54% in top half
**Early decision deadline:** N/A, notification date: N/A
**Early action deadline:** N/A, notification date: N/A
**Application deadline (fall):** rolling
**Undergraduate student body:** 8,279 full time, 536 part time; 43% male, 57% female; 0% American Indian, 1% Asian, 7% black, 6% Hispanic, 2% multiracial, 0% Pacific Islander, 81% white, 1% international; 89% from in state; 44% live on campus; 6% of students in fraternities, 7% in sororities
**Most popular majors:** 19% Business Administration and Management, General, 6% Criminal Justice/Safety Studies, 6% English Language and Literature, General, 4% Parks, Recreation and Leisure Studies, 8% Psychology, General
**Expenses:** 2014-2015: $8,833 in state, $19,063 out of state; room/board: $8,430
**Financial aid:** (610) 683-4077; 71% of undergrads determined to have financial need; average aid package $7,840

## Lafayette College
Easton PA
(610) 330-5100
**U.S. News ranking:** Nat. Lib. Arts, No. 35
**Website:** www.lafayette.edu
**Admissions email:** admissions@lafayette.edu
**Private;** founded 1826
**Freshman admissions:** more selective; 2013-2014: 6,766 applied, 2,310 accepted. Either SAT or ACT required. SAT 25/75 percentile: 1180-1370. High school rank: 62% in top tenth, 89% in top quarter, 97% in top half
**Early decision deadline:** 11/15, notification date: 12/15

**Early action deadline:** N/A, notification date: N/A
**Application deadline (fall):** 1/15
**Undergraduate student body:** 2,435 full time, 51 part time; 53% male, 47% female; 0% American Indian, 3% Asian, 5% black, 6% Hispanic, 2% multiracial, 0% Pacific Islander, 68% white, 6% international; 21% from in state; 92% live on campus; 18% of students in fraternities, 38% in sororities
**Most popular majors:** 6% Engineering, 7% English Language and Literature/Letters, 7% Psychology, 12% Social Sciences, 8% Social Sciences
**Expenses:** 2014-2015: $45,635; room/board: $13,520
**Financial aid:** (610) 330-5055; 40% of undergrads determined to have financial need; average aid package $39,420

## La Roche College
Pittsburgh PA
(800) 838-4572
**U.S. News ranking:** Reg. Coll. (N), No. 33
**Website:** www.laroche.edu
**Admissions email:** admissions@laroche.edu
**Private;** founded 1963
**Affiliation:** Roman Catholic
**Freshman admissions:** less selective; 2013-2014: 1,488 applied, 828 accepted. Either SAT or ACT required. SAT 25/75 percentile: 800-1040. High school rank: 9% in top tenth, 26% in top quarter, 61% in top half
**Early decision deadline:** N/A, notification date: N/A
**Early action deadline:** N/A, notification date: N/A
**Application deadline (fall):** rolling
**Undergraduate student body:** 1,130 full time, 233 part time; 43% male, 57% female; 0% American Indian, 1% Asian, 7% black, 1% Hispanic, 1% multiracial, 0% Pacific Islander, 65% white, 13% international; 95% from in state; 42% live on campus; 0% of students in fraternities, 0% in sororities
**Most popular majors:** 8% Accounting, 7% Criminal Justice/Safety Studies, 6% Elementary Education and Teaching, 11% Medical Radiologic Technology/Science - Radiation Therapist, 9% Psychology, General
**Expenses:** 2014-2015: $25,500; room/board: $10,324
**Financial aid:** (412) 536-1120; 73% of undergrads determined to have financial need; average aid package $25,820

## La Salle University
Philadelphia PA
(215) 951-1500
**U.S. News ranking:** Reg. U. (N), No. 31
**Website:** www.lasalle.edu
**Admissions email:** admiss@lasalle.edu
**Private;** founded 1863
**Affiliation:** Roman Catholic
**Freshman admissions:** selective; 2013-2014: 5,547 applied, 4,449 accepted. Either SAT or ACT required. SAT 25/75 percentile: 880-1100. High school rank: 15% in top tenth, 38% in top quarter, 73% in top half
**Early decision deadline:** N/A, notification date: N/A

**Early action deadline:** 11/15, notification date: 12/15
**Application deadline (fall):** rolling
**Undergraduate student body:** 3,542 full time, 867 part time; 35% male, 65% female; 0% American Indian, 5% Asian, 19% black, 10% Hispanic, 5% multiracial, 0% Pacific Islander, 55% white, 2% international; 62% from in state; 55% live on campus; 6% of students in fraternities, 13% in sororities
**Most popular majors:** 6% Accounting, 7% Marketing, 25% Nursing Science, 6% Psychology, General, 8% Speech Communication and Rhetoric
**Expenses:** 2014-2015: $39,800; room/board: $13,580
**Financial aid:** (215) 951-1070; 81% of undergrads determined to have financial need; average aid package $28,610

## Lebanon Valley College
Annville PA
(717) 867-6181
**U.S. News ranking:** Reg. Coll. (N), No. 6
**Website:** www.lvc.edu
**Admissions email:** admission@lvc.edu
**Private;** founded 1866
**Affiliation:** Methodist
**Freshman admissions:** selective; 2013-2014: 3,793 applied, 2,536 accepted. Neither SAT nor ACT required. SAT 25/75 percentile: 1000-1220. High school rank: 37% in top tenth, 74% in top quarter, 92% in top half
**Early decision deadline:** N/A, notification date: N/A
**Early action deadline:** N/A, notification date: N/A
**Application deadline (fall):** rolling
**Undergraduate student body:** 1,648 full time, 118 part time; 47% male, 53% female; 0% American Indian, 2% Asian, 2% black, 5% Hispanic, 2% multiracial, 0% Pacific Islander, 85% white, 0% international; 80% from in state; 76% live on campus; 7% of students in fraternities, 10% in sororities
**Most popular majors:** 18% Business, Management, Marketing, and Related Support Services, 13% Education, 12% Health Professions and Related Programs, 9% Social Sciences, 9% Visual and Performing Arts
**Expenses:** 2014-2015: $37,470; room/board: $10,100
**Financial aid:** (717) 867-6126; 84% of undergrads determined to have financial need; average aid package $25,885

## Lehigh University
Bethlehem PA
(610) 758-3100
**U.S. News ranking:** Nat. U., No. 40
**Website:** www.lehigh.edu
**Admissions email:** admissions@lehigh.edu
**Private;** founded 1865
**Freshman admissions:** more selective; 2013-2014: 12,589 applied, 3,882 accepted. Either SAT or ACT required. SAT 25/75 percentile: 1220-1410. High school rank: 60% in top tenth, 88% in top quarter, 98% in top half

**Early decision deadline:** 11/15, notification date: 12/15
**Early action deadline:** N/A, notification date: N/A
**Application deadline (fall):** 1/1
**Undergraduate student body:** 4,862 full time, 69 part time; 56% male, 44% female; 0% American Indian, 7% Asian, 3% black, 8% Hispanic, 3% multiracial, 0% Pacific Islander, 69% white, 7% international; 26% from in state; 68% live on campus; 40% of students in fraternities, 43% in sororities
**Most popular majors:** 6% Accounting, 4% Civil Engineering, General, 12% Finance, General, 5% Marketing/Marketing Management, General, 10% Mechanical Engineering
**Expenses:** 2014-2015: $44,890; room/board: $11,880
**Financial aid:** (610) 758-3181; 42% of undergrads determined to have financial need; average aid package $37,984

## Lincoln University
Lincoln University PA
(800) 790-0191
**U.S. News ranking:** Reg. U. (N), second tier
**Website:** www.lincoln.edu
**Admissions email:** admiss@lu.lincoln.edu
**Public;** founded 1854
**Freshman admissions:** less selective; 2013-2014: 3,240 applied, 1,987 accepted. Either SAT or ACT required. SAT 25/75 percentile: 770-960. High school rank: 10% in top tenth, 28% in top quarter, 58% in top half
**Early decision deadline:** N/A, notification date: N/A
**Early action deadline:** N/A, notification date: N/A
**Application deadline (fall):** rolling
**Undergraduate student body:** 1,488 full time, 136 part time; 41% male, 59% female; 0% American Indian, 0% Asian, 84% black, 2% Hispanic, 1% multiracial, 0% Pacific Islander, 0% white, 3% international; 42% from in state; 98% live on campus; 5% of students in fraternities, 5% in sororities
**Most popular majors:** 9% Broadcast Journalism, 9% Business Administration and Management, General, 12% Criminal Justice/Safety Studies, 12% Human Services, General, 9% Sociology
**Expenses:** 2014-2015: $7,160 in state, $11,836 out of state; room/board: $8,686
**Financial aid:** (800) 561-2606; 97% of undergrads determined to have financial need; average aid package $12,004

## Lock Haven University of Pennsylvania
Lock Haven PA
(570) 893-2027
**U.S. News ranking:** Reg. U. (N), second tier
**Website:** www.lhup.edu
**Admissions email:** admissions@lhup.edu
**Public;** founded 1870
**Freshman admissions:** less selective; 2013-2014: 3,849 applied, 3,311 accepted. Either SAT or ACT required. SAT 25/75 percentile: 840-1050. High school rank: 9% in top tenth, 30% in top quarter, 64% in top half

**Early decision deadline:** N/A, notification date: N/A
**Early action deadline:** N/A, notification date: N/A
**Application deadline (fall):** rolling
**Undergraduate student body:** 4,519 full time, 336 part time; 43% male, 57% female; 0% American Indian, 1% Asian, 8% black, 2% Hispanic, 1% multiracial, 0% Pacific Islander, 87% white, 0% international; 94% from in state; 40% live on campus; 3% of students in fraternities, 4% in sororities
**Most popular majors:** 7% Business Administration and Management, General, 10% Criminal Justice/Law Enforcement Administration, 9% Health Services/Allied Health/Health Sciences, General, 6% Health and Physical Education/Fitness, Other, 8% Sport and Fitness Administration/Management
**Expenses:** 2014-2015: $9,276 in state, $17,506 out of state; room/board: $8,752
**Financial aid:** (570) 893-2344; 58% of undergrads determined to have financial need; average aid package $8,361

## Lycoming College
Williamsport PA
(800) 345-3920
**U.S. News ranking:** Nat. Lib. Arts, No. 159
**Website:** www.lycoming.edu
**Admissions email:** admissions@lycoming.edu
**Private;** founded 1812
**Affiliation:** Methodist
**Freshman admissions:** selective; 2013-2014: 1,737 applied, 1,244 accepted. Neither SAT nor ACT required. SAT 25/75 percentile: 930-1150. High school rank: 19% in top tenth, 43% in top quarter, 75% in top half
**Early decision deadline:** N/A, notification date: N/A
**Early action deadline:** N/A, notification date: N/A
**Application deadline (fall):** 3/1
**Undergraduate student body:** 1,290 full time, 17 part time; 44% male, 56% female; 0% American Indian, 1% Asian, 5% black, 3% Hispanic, 2% multiracial, 0% Pacific Islander, 77% white, 4% international; 66% from in state; 87% live on campus; 16% of students in fraternities, 21% in sororities
**Most popular majors:** 11% Biological and Biomedical Sciences, 25% Business, Management, Marketing, and Related Support Services, 14% Psychology, 16% Social Sciences, 6% Visual and Performing Arts
**Expenses:** 2014-2015: $34,706; room/board: $10,376
**Financial aid:** (570) 321-4040; 84% of undergrads determined to have financial need; average aid package $27,877

## Mansfield University of Pennsylvania
Mansfield PA
(800) 577-6826
**U.S. News ranking:** Reg. U. (N), No. 135
**Website:** www.mansfield.edu
**Admissions email:** admissns@mansfield.edu
**Public;** founded 1857

**Freshman admissions:** less selective; 2013-2014: 2,023 applied, 1,867 accepted. Either SAT or ACT required. SAT 25/75 percentile: 850-1070. High school rank: 8% in top tenth, 29% in top quarter, 63% in top half
**Early decision deadline:** N/A, notification date: N/A
**Early action deadline:** N/A, notification date: N/A
**Application deadline (fall):** rolling
**Undergraduate student body:** 2,453 full time, 264 part time; 41% male, 59% female; 0% American Indian, 1% Asian, 9% black, 3% Hispanic, 2% multiracial, 0% Pacific Islander, 81% white, 1% international; 80% from in state; 51% live on campus; 7% of students in fraternities, 6% in sororities
**Most popular majors:** 13% Health Professions and Related Programs, 11% Homeland Security, Law Enforcement, Firefighting and Related Protective Services, 9% Psychology, 9% Social Sciences, 12% Visual and Performing Arts
**Expenses:** 2014-2015: $9,526 in state, $19,756 out of state; room/board: $10,582
**Financial aid:** (570) 662-4878; 86% of undergrads determined to have financial need; average aid package $9,945

## Marywood University
Scranton PA
(570) 348-6234
**U.S. News ranking:** Reg. U. (N), No. 38
**Website:** www.marywood.edu
**Admissions email:** YourFuture@marywood.edu
**Private;** founded 1915
**Affiliation:** Roman Catholic
**Freshman admissions:** selective; 2013-2014: 2,059 applied, 1,443 accepted. Either SAT or ACT required. SAT 25/75 percentile: 950-1150. High school rank: 20% in top tenth, 47% in top quarter, 84% in top half
**Early decision deadline:** N/A, notification date: N/A
**Early action deadline:** N/A, notification date: N/A
**Application deadline (fall):** rolling
**Undergraduate student body:** 1,961 full time, 187 part time; 33% male, 67% female; 0% American Indian, 2% Asian, 2% black, 5% Hispanic, 1% multiracial, 0% Pacific Islander, 81% white, 1% international; 70% from in state; 46% live on campus; 0% of students in fraternities, 4% in sororities
**Most popular majors:** 17% Education, 23% Health Professions and Related Programs, 12% High School/Secondary Diplomas and Certificates, 7% Psychology, 14% Visual and Performing Arts
**Expenses:** 2014-2015: $31,695; room/board: $13,900
**Financial aid:** (570) 348-6225; 84% of undergrads determined to have financial need; average aid package $23,894

## Mercyhurst University

Erie PA
(814) 824-2202
**U.S. News ranking:** Reg. U. (N),
No. 56
**Website:** www.mercyhurst.edu
**Admissions email:** ccoons@
mercyhurst.edu
**Private;** founded 1926
**Affiliation:** Roman Catholic
**Freshman admissions:** selective;
2013-2014: 2,938 applied,
2,214 accepted. Either SAT
or ACT required. SAT 25/75
percentile: 940-1160. High school
rank: 21% in top tenth, 29% in
top quarter, 87% in top half
**Early decision deadline:** N/A,
notification date: N/A
**Early action deadline:** N/A,
notification date: N/A
**Application deadline (fall):** rolling
**Undergraduate student body:** 2,552
full time, 128 part time; 44%
male, 56% female; 0% American
Indian, 1% Asian, 4% black,
2% Hispanic, 0% multiracial,
0% Pacific Islander, 77% white,
8% international; 52% from in
state; 68% live on campus; 0%
of students in fraternities, 0% in
sororities
**Most popular majors:** 21%
Business, Management,
Marketing, and Related Support
Services, 9% Health Professions
and Related Programs, 8%
Homeland Security, Law
Enforcement, Firefighting and
Related Protective Services, 14%
Multi/Interdisciplinary Studies, 8%
Visual and Performing Arts
**Expenses:** 2014-2015: $31,485;
room/board: $10,800
**Financial aid:** (814) 824-2288;
75% of undergrads determined to
have financial need; average aid
package $17,705

## Messiah College

Mechanicsburg PA
(717) 691-6000
**U.S. News ranking:** Reg. Coll. (N),
No. 5
**Website:** www.messiah.edu
**Admissions email:**
admiss@messiah.edu
**Private;** founded 1909
**Affiliation:** Christian
interdenominational
**Freshman admissions:** more
selective; 2013-2014: 2,836
applied, 1,869 accepted. Either
SAT or ACT required. SAT 25/75
percentile: 1030-1260. High
school rank: 36% in top tenth,
68% in top quarter, 92% in
top half
**Early decision deadline:** N/A,
notification date: N/A
**Early action deadline:** N/A,
notification date: N/A
**Application deadline (fall):** rolling
**Undergraduate student body:** 2,701
full time, 71 part time; 39%
male, 61% female; 0% American
Indian, 2% Asian, 2% black,
3% Hispanic, 3% multiracial,
0% Pacific Islander, 86% white,
2% international; 59% from in
state; 87% live on campus; 0%
of students in fraternities, 0% in
sororities
**Most popular majors:**
5% Business Administration
and Management, General,
4% Elementary Education and
Teaching, 8% Engineering,
General, 6% Psychology, General,
5% Registered Nursing/Registered
Nurse
**Expenses:** 2014-2015: $31,340;
room/board: $9,350
**Financial aid:** (717) 691-6007;
73% of undergrads determined to
have financial need; average aid
package $21,592

## Millersville University of Pennsylvania

Millersville PA
(717) 872-3371
**U.S. News ranking:** Reg. U. (N),
No. 87
**Website:** www.millersville.edu
**Admissions email:** Admissions@
millersville.edu
**Public;** founded 1855
**Freshman admissions:** selective;
2013-2014: 6,034 applied,
3,920 accepted. Either SAT
or ACT required. SAT 25/75
percentile: 920-1110. High school
rank: 12% in top tenth, 34% in
top quarter, 71% in top half
**Early decision deadline:** N/A,
notification date: N/A
**Early action deadline:** N/A,
notification date: N/A
**Application deadline (fall):** rolling
**Undergraduate student body:** 6,584
full time, 804 part time; 45%
male, 55% female; 0% American
Indian, 2% Asian, 9% black,
7% Hispanic, 2% multiracial,
0% Pacific Islander, 78% white,
1% international; 95% from in
state; 33% live on campus; 3%
of students in fraternities, 4% in
sororities
**Most popular majors:** 10%
Biological and Biomedical
Sciences, 12% Business,
Management, Marketing, and
Related Support Services, 6%
Communication, Journalism, and
Related Programs, 7% Psychology,
5% Public Administration and
Social Service Professions
**Expenses:** 2014-2015: $10,268
in state, $23,648 out of state;
room/board: $11,380
**Financial aid:** (717) 872-3026;
68% of undergrads determined to
have financial need; average aid
package $8,491

## Misericordia University

Dallas PA
(570) 674-6264
**U.S. News ranking:** Reg. U. (N),
No. 41
**Website:** www.misericordia.edu/
**Admissions email:** admiss@
misericordia.edu
**Private;** founded 1924
**Affiliation:** Roman Catholic
**Freshman admissions:** selective;
2013-2014: 2,125 applied,
1,379 accepted. Either SAT
or ACT required. SAT 25/75
percentile: 970-1140. High school
rank: 24% in top tenth, 56% in
top quarter, 86% in top half
**Early decision deadline:** N/A,
notification date: N/A
**Early action deadline:** N/A,
notification date: N/A
**Application deadline (fall):** rolling
**Undergraduate student body:** 1,790
full time, 627 part time; 32%
male, 68% female; 0% American
Indian, 1% Asian, 1% black,
3% Hispanic, 1% multiracial,
0% Pacific Islander, 94% white,

0% international; 77% from in
state; 45% live on campus; 0%
of students in fraternities, 0% in
sororities
**Most popular majors:** 12%
Business Administration and
Management, General, 8%
General Studies, 10% Health
Services/Allied Health/Health
Sciences, General, 10%
Psychology, General, 12%
Registered Nursing/Registered
Nurse
**Expenses:** 2014-2015: $29,010;
room/board: $12,050
**Financial aid:** (570) 674-6280;
82% of undergrads determined to
have financial need; average aid
package $19,729

## Moore College of Art & Design

Philadelphia PA
(215) 965-4015
**U.S. News ranking:** Arts, unranked
**Website:** www.moore.edu
**Admissions email:**
admiss@moore.edu
**Private**
**Freshman admissions:** N/A;
2013-2014: 672 applied, 377
accepted. Neither SAT nor ACT
required. SAT 25/75 percentile:
N/A. High school rank: N/A
**Early decision deadline:** N/A,
notification date: N/A
**Early action deadline:** N/A,
notification date: N/A
**Application deadline (fall):** 8/1
**Undergraduate student body:** 411
full time, 26 part time; 0% male,
100% female; 0% American
Indian, 3% Asian, 14% black,
6% Hispanic, 5% multiracial,
0% Pacific Islander, 66% white,
3% international; 60% from in
state; N/A live on campus; N/A
of students in fraternities, N/A in
sororities
**Most popular majors:** 21% Fashion/
Apparel Design, 20% Fine/Studio
Arts, General, 13% Graphic
Design, 25% Illustration, 7%
Interior Design
**Expenses:** 2013-2014: $34,048;
room/board: $12,790
**Financial aid:** (215) 965-4042

## Moravian College

Bethlehem PA
(610) 861-1320
**U.S. News ranking:** Nat. Lib. Arts,
No. 133
**Website:** www.moravian.edu
**Admissions email:** admissions@
moravian.edu
**Private;** founded 1742
**Affiliation:** Moravian Church
in America
**Freshman admissions:** selective;
2013-2014: 1,636 applied,
1,308 accepted. Neither SAT
nor ACT required. SAT 25/75
percentile: 940-1170. High school
rank: 19% in top tenth, 48% in
top quarter, 83% in top half
**Early decision deadline:** N/A,
notification date: N/A
**Early action deadline:** N/A,
notification date: N/A
**Application deadline (fall):** 3/1
**Undergraduate student body:** 1,425
full time, 160 part time; 41%
male, 59% female; 0% American
Indian, 2% Asian, 4% black,
5% Hispanic, 0% multiracial,
0% Pacific Islander, 79% white,
0% international; 68% from in

state; 75% live on campus; 15%
of students in fraternities, 25%
in sororities
**Most popular majors:** 18%
Business, Management,
Marketing, and Related Support
Services, 13% Health Professions
and Related Programs, 8%
Psychology, 11% Social Sciences,
9% Visual and Performing Arts
**Expenses:** 2014-2015: $36,800;
room/board: $11,082
**Financial aid:** (610) 861-1330;
86% of undergrads determined to
have financial need; average aid
package $27,055

## Mount Aloysius College

Cresson PA
(814) 886-6383
**U.S. News ranking:** Reg. Coll. (N),
No. 38
**Website:** www.mtaloy.edu
**Admissions email:** admissions@
mtaloy.edu
**Private;** founded 1853
**Affiliation:** Roman Catholic (Sisters
of Mercy)
**Freshman admissions:** least
selective; 2013-2014: 1,563
applied, 1,114 accepted. Either
SAT or ACT required. SAT 25/75
percentile: 830-1030. High
school rank: N/A
**Early decision deadline:** N/A,
notification date: N/A
**Early action deadline:** N/A,
notification date: N/A
**Application deadline (fall):** rolling
**Undergraduate student body:** 1,248
full time, 533 part time; 28%
male, 72% female; 0% American
Indian, 0% Asian, 2% black,
1% Hispanic, 0% multiracial,
0% Pacific Islander, 79% white,
1% international; 96% from in
state; 31% live on campus; N/A
of students in fraternities, N/A in
sororities
**Most popular majors:** 12%
Biological and Biomedical
Sciences, 18% Business,
Management, Marketing, and
Related Support Services, 7%
Computer and Information
Sciences and Support Services,
30% Health Professions and
Related Programs, 11% Liberal
Arts and Sciences, General
Studies and Humanities
**Expenses:** 2014-2015: $20,790;
room/board: $9,186
**Financial aid:** (814) 886-6357;
96% of undergrads determined to
have financial need; average aid
package $15,830

## Muhlenberg College

Allentown PA
(484) 664-3200
**U.S. News ranking:** Nat. Lib. Arts,
No. 64
**Website:** www.muhlenberg.edu
**Admissions email:** admissions@
muhlenberg.edu
**Private;** founded 1848
**Affiliation:** Lutheran
**Freshman admissions:** more
selective; 2013-2014: 5,152
applied, 2,378 accepted. Neither
SAT nor ACT required. SAT
25/75 percentile: 1140-1340.
High school rank: 45% in top
tenth, 73% in top quarter, 92%
in top half
**Early decision deadline:** 2/15,
notification date: 12/1

**Early action deadline:** N/A,
notification date: N/A
**Application deadline (fall):** 2/15
**Undergraduate student body:** 2,323
full time, 125 part time; 41%
male, 59% female; 0% American
Indian, 3% Asian, 3% black, 5%
Hispanic, 2% multiracial, 0%
Pacific Islander, 77% white, 1%
international; 22% from in state;
92% live on campus; 18% of
students in fraternities, 24% in
sororities
**Most popular majors:** 12%
Business Administration and
Management, General, 8% Drama
and Dramatics/Theatre Arts,
General, 5% English Language
and Literature, General, 13%
Psychology, General, 8% Speech
Communication and Rhetoric
**Expenses:** 2014-2015: $44,145;
room/board: $10,335
**Financial aid:** (484) 664-3174;
51% of undergrads determined to
have financial need; average aid
package $27,092

## Neumann University

Aston PA
(610) 558-5616
**U.S. News ranking:** Reg. U. (N),
second tier
**Website:** www.neumann.edu
**Admissions email:** neumann@
neumann.edu
**Private;** founded 1965
**Affiliation:** Roman Catholic
**Freshman admissions:** least
selective; 2013-2014: 2,637
applied, 2,479 accepted. Either
SAT or ACT required. SAT 25/75
percentile: 770-950. High school
rank: N/A
**Early decision deadline:** N/A,
notification date: N/A
**Early action deadline:** N/A,
notification date: N/A
**Application deadline (fall):** rolling
**Undergraduate student body:** 2,080
full time, 493 part time; 36%
male, 64% female; 1% American
Indian, 0% Asian, 18% black,
3% Hispanic, 2% multiracial,
0% Pacific Islander, 52% white,
2% international; 66% from in
state; 35% live on campus; N/A
of students in fraternities, N/A in
sororities
**Most popular majors:** 8% Business
Administration and Management,
General, 12% Elementary
Education and Teaching, 18%
Liberal Arts and Sciences/
Liberal Studies, 10% Psychology,
General, 16% Registered Nursing,
Nursing Administration, Nursing
Research and Clinical Nursing,
Other
**Expenses:** 2013-2014: $24,948;
room/board: $11,512
**Financial aid:** (610) 558-5521

## Peirce College

Philadelphia PA
(888) 467-3472
**U.S. News ranking:** Reg. Coll. (N),
unranked
**Website:** www.peirce.edu
**Admissions email:** info@peirce.edu
**Private;** founded 1865
**Freshman admissions:** N/A; 2013-
2014: N/A applied, N/A accepted.
Neither SAT nor ACT required.
ACT 25/75 percentile: N/A. High
school rank: N/A
**Early decision deadline:** N/A,
notification date: N/A
**Early action deadline:** N/A,
notification date: N/A

**Application deadline (fall):** rolling
**Undergraduate student body:** 358 full time, 1,401 part time; 28% male, 72% female; 0% American Indian, 2% Asian, 68% black, 7% Hispanic, 1% multiracial, 0% Pacific Islander, 21% white, 0% international; 91% from in state; N/A live on campus; N/A of students in fraternities, N/A in sororities
**Most popular majors:** 63% Business, Management, Marketing, and Related Support Services, 18% Computer and Information Sciences and Support Services, 19% Legal Professions and Studies
**Expenses:** 2013-2014: $17,040; room/board: N/A
**Financial aid:** (215) 670-9370

## Pennsylvania College of Art and Design[1]
Lancaster PA
(717) 396-7833
**U.S. News ranking:** Arts, unranked
**Website:** www.pcad.edu
**Admissions email:** N/A
**Private**
**Application deadline (fall):** N/A
**Undergraduate student body:** N/A full time, N/A part time
**Expenses:** 2013-2014: $20,680; room/board: N/A
**Financial aid:** (800) 689-0379

## Pennsylvania College of Technology
Williamsport PA
(570) 327-4761
**U.S. News ranking:** Reg. Coll. (N), No. 28
**Website:** www.pct.edu
**Admissions email:** admissions@pct.edu
**Public;** founded 1941
**Freshman admissions:** least selective; 2013-2014: 3,763 applied, 3,386 accepted. Neither SAT nor ACT required. ACT 25/75 percentile: N/A. High school rank: N/A in top tenth, N/A in top quarter, 26% in top half
**Early decision deadline:** N/A, notification date: N/A
**Early action deadline:** N/A, notification date: N/A
**Application deadline (fall):** 7/1
**Undergraduate student body:** 4,774 full time, 904 part time; 63% male, 37% female; 0% American Indian, 1% Asian, 4% black, 3% Hispanic, 2% multiracial, 0% Pacific Islander, 85% white, 1% international; 87% from in state; 30% live on campus; 1% of students in fraternities, 0% in sororities
**Most popular majors:** 5% Adult Health Nurse/ Nursing, 8% Business Administration, Management and Operations, Other, 4% Computer Systems Networking and Telecommunications, 5% Industrial Production Technologies/Technicians, Other, 6% Physician Assistant
**Expenses:** 2014-2015: $15,270 in state, $21,660 out of state; room/board: $10,024
**Financial aid:** (570) 327-4766; 87% of undergrads determined to have financial need

## Pennsylvania State University–University Park
University Park PA
(814) 865-5471
**U.S. News ranking:** Nat. U., No. 48
**Website:** www.psu.edu
**Admissions email:** admissions@psu.edu
**Public;** founded 1855
**Freshman admissions:** more selective; 2013-2014: 42,570 applied, 23,603 accepted. Either SAT or ACT required. SAT 25/75 percentile: 1070-1280. High school rank: 36% in top tenth, 78% in top quarter, 98% in top half
**Early decision deadline:** N/A, notification date: N/A
**Early action deadline:** N/A, notification date: N/A
**Application deadline (fall):** rolling
**Undergraduate student body:** 38,826 full time, 1,259 part time; 54% male, 46% female; 0% American Indian, 5% Asian, 4% black, 5% Hispanic, 2% multiracial, 0% Pacific Islander, 72% white, 9% international; 69% from in state; 37% live on campus; 19% of students in fraternities, 16% in sororities
**Most popular majors:** 6% Biological and Biomedical Sciences, 15% Business, Management, Marketing, and Related Support Services, 9% Communication, Journalism, and Related Programs, 15% Engineering, 8% Social Sciences
**Expenses:** 2014-2015: $17,502 in state, $30,452 out of state; room/board: $10,520
**Financial aid:** (814) 865-6301; 50% of undergrads determined to have financial need; average aid package $11,035

## Philadelphia University
Philadelphia PA
(215) 951-2800
**U.S. News ranking:** Reg. U. (N), No. 79
**Website:** www.philau.edu
**Admissions email:** admissions@philau.edu
**Private;** founded 1884
**Freshman admissions:** selective; 2013-2014: 4,701 applied, 2,982 accepted. Either SAT or ACT required. SAT 25/75 percentile: 960-1160. High school rank: 17% in top tenth, 45% in top quarter, 79% in top half
**Early decision deadline:** N/A, notification date: N/A
**Early action deadline:** N/A, notification date: N/A
**Application deadline (fall):** rolling
**Undergraduate student body:** 2,531 full time, 280 part time; 35% male, 65% female; 0% American Indian, 4% Asian, 13% black, 7% Hispanic, 2% multiracial, 0% Pacific Islander, 60% white, 3% international; 56% from in state; 50% live on campus; 1% of students in fraternities, 1% in sororities
**Most popular majors:** 18% Architecture and Related Services, 33% Business, Management, Marketing, and Related Support Services, 12% Health Professions and Related Programs, 6% Psychology, 22% Visual and Performing Arts

**Expenses:** 2014-2015: $35,080; room/board: $11,610
**Financial aid:** (215) 951-2940; 79% of undergrads determined to have financial need; average aid package $24,123

## Point Park University
Pittsburgh PA
(800) 321-0129
**U.S. News ranking:** Reg. U. (N), No. 122
**Website:** www.pointpark.edu
**Admissions email:** enroll@pointpark.edu
**Private;** founded 1960
**Freshman admissions:** selective; 2013-2014: 3,237 applied, 2,393 accepted. Either SAT or ACT required. SAT 25/75 percentile: 870-1100. High school rank: 11% in top tenth, 31% in top quarter, 66% in top half
**Early decision deadline:** N/A, notification date: N/A
**Early action deadline:** N/A, notification date: N/A
**Application deadline (fall):** rolling
**Undergraduate student body:** 2,551 full time, 675 part time; 43% male, 57% female; 0% American Indian, 1% Asian, 16% black, 3% Hispanic, 4% multiracial, 0% Pacific Islander, 72% white, 3% international; 79% from in state; 29% live on campus; 0% of students in fraternities, 0% in sororities
**Most popular majors:** 9% Business Administration and Management, General, 8% Business, Management, Marketing, and Related Support Services, Other, 8% Criminal Justice/Safety Studies, 8% Dance, General, 10% Drama and Dramatics/Theatre Arts, General
**Expenses:** 2014-2015: $27,190; room/board: $10,320
**Financial aid:** (412) 392-3930; 91% of undergrads determined to have financial need; average aid package $19,935

## Robert Morris University
Moon Township PA
(412) 397-5200
**U.S. News ranking:** Reg. U. (N), No. 96
**Website:** www.rmu.edu
**Admissions email:** admissions@rmu.edu
**Private;** founded 1921
**Freshman admissions:** selective; 2013-2014: 5,689 applied, 4,570 accepted. Either SAT or ACT required. SAT 25/75 percentile: 940-1140. High school rank: 14% in top tenth, 42% in top quarter, 77% in top half
**Early decision deadline:** N/A, notification date: N/A
**Early action deadline:** N/A, notification date: N/A
**Application deadline (fall):** rolling
**Undergraduate student body:** 3,935 full time, 561 part time; 54% male, 46% female; 0% American Indian, 1% Asian, 7% black, 2% Hispanic, 2% multiracial, 0% Pacific Islander, 77% white, 8% international; 88% from in state; 44% live on campus; 10% of students in fraternities, 11% in sororities

**Most popular majors:** 11% Accounting, 11% Business Administration and Management, General, 7% Elementary Education and Teaching, 9% Registered Nursing/ Registered Nurse, 8% Speech Communication and Rhetoric
**Expenses:** 2014-2015: $26,054; room/board: $11,810
**Financial aid:** (412) 262-8545; 76% of undergrads determined to have financial need; average aid package $18,933

## Rosemont College
Rosemont PA
(800) 331-0708
**U.S. News ranking:** Reg. U. (N), No. 96
**Website:** www.rosemont.edu
**Admissions email:** admissions@rosemont.edu
**Private;** founded 1921
**Affiliation:** Roman Catholic
**Freshman admissions:** selective; 2013-2014: 1,014 applied, 592 accepted. Either SAT or ACT required. SAT 25/75 percentile: 800-1040. High school rank: 27% in top tenth, 49% in top quarter, 76% in top half
**Early decision deadline:** N/A, notification date: N/A
**Early action deadline:** N/A, notification date: N/A
**Application deadline (fall):** rolling
**Undergraduate student body:** 415 full time, 116 part time; 34% male, 66% female; 0% American Indian, 5% Asian, 36% black, 8% Hispanic, 2% multiracial, 0% Pacific Islander, 37% white, 2% international; 73% from in state; 72% live on campus; 0% of students in fraternities, 0% in sororities
**Most popular majors:** 25% Biology/ Biological Sciences, General, 24% Business/Commerce, General, 12% Education, General, 6% Psychology, General, 10% Speech Communication and Rhetoric
**Expenses:** 2014-2015: $31,550; room/board: $12,880
**Financial aid:** (610) 527-0200; 90% of undergrads determined to have financial need; average aid package $29,879

## Seton Hill University
Greensburg PA
(724) 838-4255
**U.S. News ranking:** Reg. Coll. (N), No. 11
**Website:** www.setonhill.edu
**Admissions email:** admit@setonhill.edu
**Private;** founded 1883
**Affiliation:** Roman Catholic
**Freshman admissions:** selective; 2013-2014: 2,414 applied, 1,574 accepted. Neither SAT nor ACT required. SAT 25/75 percentile: 900-1150. High school rank: 20% in top tenth, 47% in top quarter, 77% in top half
**Early decision deadline:** N/A, notification date: N/A
**Early action deadline:** N/A, notification date: N/A
**Application deadline (fall):** 8/15
**Undergraduate student body:** 1,472 full time, 177 part time; 36% male, 64% female; 0% American Indian, 0% Asian, 9% black, 3% Hispanic, 3% multiracial, 0% Pacific Islander, 82% white,

3% international; 77% from in state; 43% live on campus; 0% of students in fraternities, 0% in sororities
**Most popular majors:** 7% Biological and Biomedical Sciences, 31% Business, Management, Marketing, and Related Support Services, 7% Psychology, 6% Public Administration and Social Service Professions, 8% Visual and Performing Arts
**Expenses:** 2014-2015: $31,280; room/board: $10,476
**Financial aid:** (724) 838-4293; 87% of undergrads determined to have financial need; average aid package $24,161

## Shippensburg University of Pennsylvania
Shippensburg PA
(717) 477-1231
**U.S. News ranking:** Reg. U. (N), No. 87
**Website:** www.ship.edu
**Admissions email:** admiss@ship.edu
**Public;** founded 1871
**Freshman admissions:** less selective; 2013-2014: 5,950 applied, 4,962 accepted. Either SAT or ACT required. SAT 25/75 percentile: 890-1080. High school rank: 7% in top tenth, 26% in top quarter, 58% in top half
**Early decision deadline:** N/A, notification date: N/A
**Early action deadline:** N/A, notification date: N/A
**Application deadline (fall):** rolling
**Undergraduate student body:** 6,219 full time, 331 part time; 50% male, 50% female; 0% American Indian, 1% Asian, 9% black, 4% Hispanic, 3% multiracial, 0% Pacific Islander, 80% white, 1% international; 93% from in state; 36% live on campus; 6% of students in fraternities, 7% in sororities
**Most popular majors:** 6% Business Administration and Management, General, 9% Criminal Justice/ Safety Studies, 6% Journalism, 6% Marketing/Marketing Management, General, 10% Psychology, General
**Expenses:** 2014-2015: $9,774 in state, $18,520 out of state; room/ board: $11,160
**Financial aid:** (717) 477-1131; 69% of undergrads determined to have financial need; average aid package $8,479

## Slippery Rock University of Pennsylvania
Slippery Rock PA
(800) 929-4778
**U.S. News ranking:** Reg. U. (N), No. 83
**Website:** www.sru.edu
**Admissions email:** asktherock@sru.edu
**Public;** founded 1889
**Freshman admissions:** selective; 2013-2014: 5,475 applied, 3,667 accepted. Either SAT or ACT required. SAT 25/75 percentile: 910-1090. High school rank: 12% in top tenth, 36% in top quarter, 77% in top half
**Early decision deadline:** N/A, notification date: N/A

**Early action deadline:** N/A, notification date: N/A
**Application deadline (fall):** rolling
**Undergraduate student body:** 7,057 full time, 538 part time; 44% male, 56% female; 0% American Indian, 1% Asian, 5% black, 2% Hispanic, 2% multiracial, 0% Pacific Islander, 86% white, 1% international; 89% from in state; 36% live on campus; 6% of students in fraternities, 7% in sororities
**Most popular majors:** 12% Business, Management, Marketing, and Related Support Services, 15% Education, 19% Health Professions and Related Programs, 10% Parks, Recreation, Leisure, and Fitness Studies, 7% Social Sciences
**Expenses:** 2014-2015: $9,309 in state, $12,719 out of state; room/board: $9,794
**Financial aid:** (724) 738-2044; 70% of undergrads determined to have financial need; average aid package $8,915

## St. Francis University
Loretto PA
(814) 472-3100
**U.S. News ranking:** Reg. U. (N), No. 56
**Website:** www.francis.edu/undergraduate_admissions
**Admissions email:** admissions@francis.edu
**Private;** founded 1847
**Affiliation:** Roman Catholic
**Freshman admissions:** selective; 2013-2014: 1,679 applied, 1,277 accepted. Either SAT or ACT required. SAT 25/75 percentile: 930-1160. High school rank: 20% in top tenth, 42% in top quarter, 60% in top half
**Early decision deadline:** N/A, notification date: N/A
**Early action deadline:** N/A, notification date: N/A
**Application deadline (fall):** 7/30
**Undergraduate student body:** 1,547 full time, 148 part time; 38% male, 62% female; 0% American Indian, 1% Asian, 6% black, 2% Hispanic, 1% multiracial, 0% Pacific Islander, 80% white, 4% international; 78% from in state; 88% live on campus; 23% of students in fraternities, 24% in sororities
**Most popular majors:** 23% Business Administration and Management, General, 34% Health Professions and Related Programs
**Expenses:** 2014-2015: $31,078; room/board: $10,760
**Financial aid:** (814) 472-3010; 80% of undergrads determined to have financial need; average aid package $19,008

## St. Joseph's University
Philadelphia PA
(610) 660-1300
**U.S. News ranking:** Reg. U. (N), No. 11
**Website:** www.sju.edu
**Admissions email:** admit@sju.edu
**Private;** founded 1851
**Affiliation:** Roman Catholic (Jesuit)
**Freshman admissions:** selective; 2013-2014: 7,831 applied, 6,165 accepted. Neither SAT nor ACT required. SAT 25/75 percentile: 1020-1200. High school rank: 22% in top tenth, 52% in top quarter, 87% in top half

**Early decision deadline:** N/A, notification date: N/A
**Early action deadline:** 11/15, notification date: 12/25
**Application deadline (fall):** 2/1
**Undergraduate student body:** 4,489 full time, 885 part time; 46% male, 54% female; 0% American Indian, 2% Asian, 7% black, 5% Hispanic, 2% multiracial, 0% Pacific Islander, 80% white, 2% international; 46% from in state; 60% live on campus; 6% of students in fraternities, 15% in sororities
**Most popular majors:** 6% Accounting, 9% Finance, General, 12% Marketing/Marketing Management, General, 6% Special Education and Teaching, Other, 9% Special Products Marketing Operations
**Expenses:** 2014-2015: $40,580; room/board: $14,513
**Financial aid:** (610) 660-1556; 58% of undergrads determined to have financial need; average aid package $24,321

## St. Vincent College
Latrobe PA
(800) 782-5549
**U.S. News ranking:** Nat. Lib. Arts, No. 148
**Website:** www.stvincent.edu
**Admissions email:** admission@stvincent.edu
**Private;** founded 1846
**Affiliation:** Roman Catholic
**Freshman admissions:** selective; 2013-2014: 2,035 applied, 1,399 accepted. Either SAT or ACT required. SAT 25/75 percentile: 910-1150. High school rank: 20% in top tenth, 53% in top quarter, 83% in top half
**Early decision deadline:** N/A, notification date: N/A
**Early action deadline:** N/A, notification date: N/A
**Application deadline (fall):** 4/1
**Undergraduate student body:** 1,532 full time, 64 part time; 52% male, 48% female; 0% American Indian, 2% Asian, 5% black, 4% Hispanic, 1% multiracial, 0% Pacific Islander, 85% white, 1% international; 82% from in state; 72% live on campus; 0% of students in fraternities, 0% in sororities
**Most popular majors:** 10% Biological and Biomedical Sciences, 26% Business, Management, Marketing, and Related Support Services, 5% Communication, Journalism, and Related Programs, 5% English Language and Literature/Letters, 8% Psychology
**Expenses:** 2014-2015: $31,370; room/board: $9,862
**Financial aid:** (724) 537-4540; 83% of undergrads determined to have financial need; average aid package $27,374

## Susquehanna University
Selinsgrove PA
(800) 326-9672
**U.S. News ranking:** Nat. Lib. Arts, No. 116
**Website:** www.susqu.edu
**Admissions email:** suadmiss@susqu.edu
**Private;** founded 1858
**Affiliation:** Lutheran

**Freshman admissions:** selective; 2013-2014: 3,217 applied, 2,327 accepted. Neither SAT nor ACT required. SAT 25/75 percentile: 1020-1230. High school rank: 26% in top tenth, 52% in top quarter, 80% in top half
**Early decision deadline:** 11/1, notification date: 11/15
**Early action deadline:** 11/15, notification date: 11/15
**Application deadline (fall):** 2/1
**Undergraduate student body:** 2,126 full time, 53 part time; 44% male, 56% female; 0% American Indian, 1% Asian, 5% black, 5% Hispanic, 2% multiracial, 0% Pacific Islander, 84% white, 1% international; 49% from in state; 86% live on campus; 17% of students in fraternities, 16% in sororities
**Most popular majors:** 6% Biology/Biological Sciences, General, 21% Business/Commerce, General, 17% Communication, General, 8% Creative Writing, 9% Psychology, General
**Expenses:** 2014-2015: $40,350; room/board: $10,800
**Financial aid:** (570) 372-4450; 73% of undergrads determined to have financial need; average aid package $29,510

## Swarthmore College
Swarthmore PA
(610) 328-8300
**U.S. News ranking:** Nat. Lib. Arts, No. 3
**Website:** www.swarthmore.edu
**Admissions email:** admissions@swarthmore.edu
**Private;** founded 1864
**Freshman admissions:** most selective; 2013-2014: 6,615 applied, 947 accepted. Either SAT or ACT required. SAT 25/75 percentile: 1350-1530. High school rank: 89% in top tenth, 99% in top quarter, 100% in top half
**Early decision deadline:** 11/15, notification date: 12/15
**Early action deadline:** N/A, notification date: N/A
**Application deadline (fall):** 1/1
**Undergraduate student body:** 1,526 full time, 8 part time; 49% male, 51% female; 0% American Indian, 15% Asian, 6% black, 14% Hispanic, 8% multiracial, 0% Pacific Islander, 43% white, 9% international; 13% from in state; 94% live on campus; 13% of students in fraternities, 6% in sororities
**Most popular majors:** 11% Biological and Biomedical Sciences, 7% Foreign Languages, Literatures, and Linguistics, 7% Psychology, 24% Social Sciences, 9% Visual and Performing Arts
**Expenses:** 2014-2015: $46,060; room/board: $13,550
**Financial aid:** (610) 328-8358; 50% of undergrads determined to have financial need; average aid package $40,340

## Temple University
Philadelphia PA
(215) 204-7200
**U.S. News ranking:** Nat. U., No. 121
**Website:** www.temple.edu
**Admissions email:** tuadm@temple.edu
**Public;** founded 1888

**Freshman admissions:** selective; 2013-2014: 18,813 applied, 12,016 accepted. Neither SAT nor ACT required. SAT 25/75 percentile: 1010-1230. High school rank: 20% in top tenth, 52% in top quarter, 88% in top half
**Early decision deadline:** N/A, notification date: N/A
**Early action deadline:** N/A, notification date: N/A
**Application deadline (fall):** 3/1
**Undergraduate student body:** 24,743 full time, 3,325 part time; 49% male, 51% female; 0% American Indian, 10% Asian, 14% black, 5% Hispanic, 2% multiracial, 0% Pacific Islander, 60% white, 3% international; 79% from in state; 18% live on campus; 4% of students in fraternities, 4% in sororities
**Most popular majors:** 20% Business, Management, Marketing, and Related Support Services, 11% Communication, Journalism, and Related Programs, 6% Health Professions and Related Programs, 7% Psychology, 11% Visual and Performing Arts
**Expenses:** 2014-2015: $14,770 in state, $25,450 out of state; room/board: $11,860
**Financial aid:** (215) 204-8760; 71% of undergrads determined to have financial need; average aid package $15,918

## Thiel College
Greenville PA
(800) 248-4435
**U.S. News ranking:** Reg. Coll. (N), No. 33
**Website:** www.thiel.edu
**Admissions email:** admission@thiel.edu
**Private;** founded 1866
**Affiliation:** Lutheran
**Freshman admissions:** less selective; 2013-2014: 2,519 applied, 1,650 accepted. Either SAT or ACT required. SAT 25/75 percentile: 870-1060. High school rank: 12% in top tenth, 34% in top quarter, 69% in top half
**Early decision deadline:** N/A, notification date: N/A
**Early action deadline:** N/A, notification date: N/A
**Application deadline (fall):** rolling
**Undergraduate student body:** 1,061 full time, 39 part time; 50% male, 50% female; 0% American Indian, 1% Asian, 8% black, 2% Hispanic, 2% multiracial, 0% Pacific Islander, 76% white, 0% international; N/A from in state; 90% live on campus; 22% of students in fraternities, 27% in sororities
**Most popular majors:** 14% Biological and Biomedical Sciences, 20% Business, Management, Marketing, and Related Support Services, 12% Education, 19% Homeland Security, Law Enforcement, Firefighting and Related Protective Services, 14% Psychology
**Expenses:** 2014-2015: $27,828; room/board: $10,900
**Financial aid:** (724) 589-2178; 88% of undergrads determined to have financial need; average aid package $22,273

## University of Pennsylvania
Philadelphia PA
(215) 898-7507
**U.S. News ranking:** Nat. U., No. 8
**Website:** www.upenn.edu
**Admissions email:** info@admissions.ugao.upenn.edu
**Private;** founded 1740
**Freshman admissions:** most selective; 2013-2014: 31,282 applied, 3,830 accepted. Either SAT or ACT required. SAT 25/75 percentile: 1360-1540. High school rank: 94% in top tenth, 99% in top quarter, 100% in top half
**Early decision deadline:** 11/1, notification date: 12/15
**Early action deadline:** N/A, notification date: N/A
**Application deadline (fall):** 1/1
**Undergraduate student body:** 9,407 full time, 305 part time; 50% male, 50% female; 0% American Indian, 19% Asian, 7% black, 10% Hispanic, 4% multiracial, 0% Pacific Islander, 45% white, 11% international; 18% from in state; 54% live on campus; 31% of students in fraternities, 28% in sororities
**Most popular majors:** 9% Biological and Biomedical Sciences, 22% Business, Management, Marketing, and Related Support Services, 10% Engineering, 5% History, 16% Social Sciences
**Expenses:** 2014-2015: $47,668; room/board: $13,464
**Financial aid:** (215) 898-1988; 47% of undergrads determined to have financial need; average aid package $41,961

## University of Pittsburgh
Pittsburgh PA
(412) 624-7488
**U.S. News ranking:** Nat. U., No. 62
**Website:** www.oafa.pitt.edu/
**Admissions email:** oafa@pitt.edu
**Public;** founded 1787
**Freshman admissions:** more selective; 2013-2014: 27,634 applied, 15,047 accepted. Either SAT or ACT required. SAT 25/75 percentile: 1180-1360. High school rank: 53% in top tenth, 86% in top quarter, 99% in top half
**Early decision deadline:** N/A, notification date: N/A
**Early action deadline:** N/A, notification date: N/A
**Application deadline (fall):** rolling
**Undergraduate student body:** 17,483 full time, 1,132 part time; 50% male, 50% female; 0% American Indian, 8% Asian, 5% black, 3% Hispanic, 3% multiracial, 0% Pacific Islander, 77% white, 3% international; 74% from in state; 44% live on campus; 10% of students in fraternities, 9% in sororities
**Most popular majors:** 15% Business, Management, Marketing, and Related Support Services, 9% Engineering, 9% English Language and Literature/Letters, 12% Health Professions and Related Programs, 13% Social Sciences
**Expenses:** 2014-2015: $16,872 in state, $27,268 out of state; room/board: N/A

Financial aid: (412) 624-7488; 56% of undergrads determined to have financial need; average aid package $12,404

## University of Scranton
Scranton PA
(570) 941-7540
U.S. News ranking: Reg. U. (N), No. 7
Website: www.scranton.edu
Admissions email: admissions@scranton.edu
Private; founded 1888
Affiliation: Roman Catholic (Jesuit)
Freshman admissions: selective; 2013-2014: 9,087 applied, 6,824 accepted. Either SAT or ACT required. SAT 25/75 percentile: 1030-1210. High school rank: 25% in top tenth, 59% in top quarter, 85% in top half
Early decision deadline: N/A, notification date: N/A
Early action deadline: 11/15, notification date: 12/15
Application deadline (fall): 3/1
Undergraduate student body: 3,756 full time, 186 part time; 45% male, 55% female; 0% American Indian, 3% Asian, 2% black, 7% Hispanic, 2% multiracial, 0% Pacific Islander, 81% white, 0% international; 41% from in state; 63% live on campus; N/A of students in fraternities, N/A in sororities
Most popular majors: 6% Accounting, 8% Biology/Biological Sciences, General, 6% Kinesiology and Exercise Science, 5% Psychology, General, 8% Registered Nursing/Registered Nurse
Expenses: 2014-2015: $39,906; room/board: $13,566
Financial aid: (570) 941-7700; 74% of undergrads determined to have financial need; average aid package $24,193

## University of the Arts
Philadelphia PA
(215) 717-6049
U.S. News ranking: Arts, unranked
Website: www.uarts.edu
Admissions email: admissions@uarts.edu
Private; founded 1876
Freshman admissions: N/A; 2013-2014: 1,479 applied, 1,115 accepted. Either SAT or ACT required. SAT 25/75 percentile: N/A. High school rank: N/A
Early decision deadline: N/A, notification date: N/A
Early action deadline: N/A, notification date: N/A
Application deadline (fall): rolling
Undergraduate student body: 1,860 full time, 30 part time; 42% male, 58% female; 0% American Indian, 3% Asian, 13% black, 9% Hispanic, 4% multiracial, 1% Pacific Islander, 62% white, 5% international; 38% from in state; 33% live on campus; 0% of students in fraternities, 0% in sororities
Most popular majors: 15% Dance, General, 9% Graphic Design, 11% Illustration, 6% Music Performance, General, 8% Photography
Expenses: 2014-2015: $38,410; room/board: $14,004
Financial aid: (215) 717-6170

## Ursinus College
Collegeville PA
(610) 409-3200
U.S. News ranking: Nat. Lib. Arts, unranked
Website: www.ursinus.edu
Admissions email: Admissions@Ursinus.edu
Private; founded 1869
Freshman admissions: N/A; 2013-2014: 3,947 applied, 2,618 accepted. Neither SAT nor ACT required. SAT 25/75 percentile: 1060-1280. High school rank: 33% in top tenth, 67% in top quarter, 92% in top half
Early decision deadline: 1/15, notification date: 2/1
Early action deadline: 12/1, notification date: 1/15
Application deadline (fall): rolling
Undergraduate student body: 1,582 full time, 14 part time; 49% male, 51% female; 0% American Indian, 5% Asian, 6% black, 5% Hispanic, 3% multiracial, 0% Pacific Islander, 77% white, 1% international; 50% from in state; 95% live on campus; 10% of students in fraternities, 15% in sororities
Most popular majors: 24% Biological and Biomedical Sciences, 7% English Language and Literature/Letters, 7% Parks, Recreation, Leisure, and Fitness Studies, 11% Psychology, 19% Social Sciences
Expenses: 2014-2015: $46,075; room/board: $11,500
Financial aid: (610) 409-3600; 74% of undergrads determined to have financial need; average aid package $33,601

## Valley Forge Christian College[1]
Phoenixville PA
(800) 432-8322
U.S. News ranking: Reg. Coll. (N), No. 44
Website: www.vfcc.edu
Admissions email: admissions@vfcc.edu
Private
Application deadline (fall): N/A
Undergraduate student body: N/A full time, N/A part time
Expenses: 2013-2014: $19,394; room/board: $7,794
Financial aid: (610) 917-1498

## Villanova University
Villanova PA
(610) 519-4000
U.S. News ranking: Reg. U. (N), No. 1
Website: www.villanova.edu
Admissions email: gotovu@villanova.edu
Private; founded 1842
Affiliation: Roman Catholic
Freshman admissions: more selective; 2013-2014: 14,966 applied, 7,319 accepted. Either SAT or ACT required. SAT 25/75 percentile: 1210-1400. High school rank: 60% in top tenth, 88% in top quarter, 99% in top half
Early decision deadline: N/A, notification date: N/A
Early action deadline: 11/1, notification date: 12/20
Application deadline (fall): 1/15
Undergraduate student body: 6,547 full time, 495 part time; 48% male, 52% female; 0% American Indian, 7% Asian, 4% black, 7% Hispanic, 2% multiracial,

0% Pacific Islander, 76% white, 2% international; 21% from in state; 2% live on campus; 18% of students in fraternities, 37% in sororities
Most popular majors: 29% Business, Management, Marketing, and Related Support Services, 8% Communication, Journalism, and Related Programs, 11% Engineering, 11% Health Professions and Related Programs, 10% Social Sciences
Expenses: 2014-2015: $45,966; room/board: $12,252
Financial aid: (610) 519-4010; 48% of undergrads determined to have financial need; average aid package $32,184

## Washington and Jefferson College
Washington PA
(724) 223-6025
U.S. News ranking: Nat. Lib. Arts, No. 96
Website: www.washjeff.edu
Admissions email: admission@washjeff.edu
Private; founded 1781
Freshman admissions: more selective; 2013-2014: 7,176 applied, 2,851 accepted. Neither SAT nor ACT required. SAT 25/75 percentile: 1050-1230. High school rank: 37% in top tenth, 70% in top quarter, 94% in top half
Early decision deadline: 12/1, notification date: 12/15
Early action deadline: 1/15, notification date: 2/15
Application deadline (fall): 3/1
Undergraduate student body: 1,318 full time, 10 part time; 49% male, 51% female; 0% American Indian, 3% Asian, 3% black, 3% Hispanic, 3% multiracial, 0% Pacific Islander, 84% white, 1% international; 73% from in state; 94% live on campus; 43% of students in fraternities, 46% in sororities
Most popular majors: 8% Accounting, 11% Business/Commerce, General, 6% Economics, General, 7% History, General, 17% Psychology, General
Expenses: 2014-2015: $41,282; room/board: $10,884
Financial aid: (724) 223-6019; 78% of undergrads determined to have financial need; average aid package $29,320

## Waynesburg University
Waynesburg PA
(800) 225-7393
U.S. News ranking: Reg. U. (N), No. 106
Website: www.waynesburg.edu/
Admissions email: admissions@waynesburg.edu
Private; founded 1849
Affiliation: Presbyterian
Freshman admissions: selective; 2013-2014: 1,681 applied, 1,396 accepted. SAT required. SAT 25/75 percentile: 890-1110. High school rank: 18% in top tenth, 47% in top quarter, 85% in top half
Early decision deadline: N/A, notification date: N/A
Early action deadline: N/A, notification date: N/A
Application deadline (fall): rolling

Undergraduate student body: 1,481 full time, 117 part time; 39% male, 61% female; 0% American Indian, 1% Asian, 3% black, 1% Hispanic, 1% multiracial, 0% Pacific Islander, 88% white, 0% international; 80% from in state; 67% live on campus; N/A of students in fraternities, N/A in sororities
Most popular majors: 7% Biology/Biological Sciences, General, 11% Business/Commerce, General, 7% Elementary Education and Teaching, 33% Registered Nursing/Registered Nurse, 7% Speech Communication and Rhetoric
Expenses: 2014-2015: $21,290; room/board: $8,860
Financial aid: (724) 852-3208; 67% of undergrads determined to have financial need; average aid package $15,426

## West Chester University of Pennsylvania
West Chester PA
(610) 436-3414
U.S. News ranking: Reg. U. (N), No. 65
Website: www.wcupa.edu/
Admissions email: ugadmiss@wcupa.edu
Public; founded 1871
Freshman admissions: selective; 2013-2014: 13,438 applied, 6,922 accepted. Either SAT or ACT required. SAT 25/75 percentile: 1020-1190. High school rank: 14% in top tenth, 45% in top quarter, 85% in top half
Early decision deadline: N/A, notification date: N/A
Early action deadline: N/A, notification date: N/A
Application deadline (fall): rolling
Undergraduate student body: 12,484 full time, 1,227 part time; 40% male, 60% female; 0% American Indian, 2% Asian, 9% black, 5% Hispanic, 2% multiracial, 0% Pacific Islander, 81% white, 0% international; 87% from in state; 36% live on campus; 10% of students in fraternities, 13% in sororities
Most popular majors: 16% Business, Management, Marketing, and Related Support Services, 10% Education, 9% English Language and Literature/Letters, 15% Health Professions and Related Programs, 9% Liberal Arts and Sciences, General Studies and Humanities
Expenses: 2014-2015: $9,144 in state, $19,374 out of state; room/board: $8,042
Financial aid: (610) 436-2627; 61% of undergrads determined to have financial need; average aid package $7,619

## Westminster College
New Wilmington PA
(800) 942-8033
U.S. News ranking: Nat. Lib. Arts, No. 116
Website: www.westminster.edu
Admissions email: admis@westminster.edu
Private; founded 1852
Affiliation: Presbyterian Church (USA)
Freshman admissions: selective; 2013-2014: 3,378 applied, 2,478 accepted. Either SAT

or ACT required. SAT 25/75 percentile: 920-1150. High school rank: 17% in top tenth, 50% in top quarter, 85% in top half
Early decision deadline: N/A, notification date: N/A
Early action deadline: 11/15, notification date: 12/1
Application deadline (fall): 1/5
Undergraduate student body: 1,254 full time, 52 part time; 41% male, 59% female; 0% American Indian, 0% Asian, 1% black, 1% Hispanic, 2% multiracial, 0% Pacific Islander, 83% white, 0% international; 78% from in state; 73% live on campus; 31% of students in fraternities, 42% in sororities
Most popular majors: 12% Biological and Biomedical Sciences, 19% Business, Management, Marketing, and Related Support Services, 9% Communication, Journalism, and Related Programs, 17% Education, 11% Social Sciences
Expenses: 2014-2015: $33,410; room/board: $10,160
Financial aid: (724) 946-7102; 81% of undergrads determined to have financial need; average aid package $25,879

## Widener University
Chester PA
(610) 499-4126
U.S. News ranking: Nat. U., No. 189
Website: www.widener.edu
Admissions email: admissions.office@widener.edu
Private; founded 1821
Freshman admissions: selective; 2013-2014: 5,461 applied, 3,673 accepted. Either SAT or ACT required. SAT 25/75 percentile: 920-1130. High school rank: 15% in top tenth, 38% in top quarter, 71% in top half
Early decision deadline: N/A, notification date: N/A
Early action deadline: N/A, notification date: N/A
Application deadline (fall): rolling
Undergraduate student body: 2,903 full time, 631 part time; 44% male, 56% female; 0% American Indian, 3% Asian, 15% black, 5% Hispanic, 3% multiracial, 0% Pacific Islander, 70% white, 3% international; 59% from in state; 48% live on campus; 10% of students in fraternities, 9% in sororities
Most popular majors: 24% Business, Management, Marketing, and Related Support Services, 12% Engineering, 20% Health Professions and Related Programs, 10% Psychology, 5% Social Sciences
Expenses: 2014-2015: $39,830; room/board: $12,588
Financial aid: (610) 499-4174; 80% of undergrads determined to have financial need; average aid package $27,822

## Wilkes University
Wilkes-Barre PA
(570) 408-4400
U.S. News ranking: Reg. U. (N), No. 83
Website: www.wilkes.edu
Admissions email: admissions@wilkes.edu
Private; founded 1933
Freshman admissions: selective; 2013-2014: 3,120 applied, 2,500 accepted. Either SAT

or ACT required. SAT 25/75 percentile: 930-1150. High school rank: 21% in top tenth, 53% in top quarter, 80% in top half
**Early decision deadline:** N/A, notification date: N/A
**Early action deadline:** N/A, notification date: N/A
**Application deadline (fall):** rolling
**Undergraduate student body:** 2,181 full time, 207 part time; 53% male, 47% female; 0% American Indian, 3% Asian, 3% black, 5% Hispanic, 3% multiracial, 0% Pacific Islander, 77% white, 7% international; 83% from in state; 44% live on campus; 0% of students in fraternities, 0% in sororities
**Most popular majors:** 15% Business, Management, Marketing, and Related Support Services, 7% Communication, Journalism, and Related Programs, 10% Engineering, 15% Health Professions and Related Programs, 6% Psychology
**Expenses:** 2014-2015: $31,262; room/board: $12,808
**Financial aid:** (570) 408-4346; 81% of undergrads determined to have financial need; average aid package $22,941

## Wilson College

Chambersburg PA
(800) 421-8402
**U.S. News ranking:** Reg. Coll. (N), No. 17
**Website:** www.wilson.edu
**Admissions email:** admissions@wilson.edu
**Private;** founded 1869
**Affiliation:** Presbyterian Church (USA)
**Freshman admissions:** selective; 2013-2014: 450 applied, 237 accepted. Neither SAT nor ACT required. SAT 25/75 percentile: 860-1120. High school rank: 19% in top tenth, 53% in top quarter, 77% in top half
**Early decision deadline:** N/A, notification date: N/A
**Early action deadline:** N/A, notification date: N/A
**Application deadline (fall):** rolling
**Undergraduate student body:** 330 full time, 241 part time; 12% male, 88% female; 0% American Indian, 0% Asian, 3% black, 3% Hispanic, 2% multiracial, 0% Pacific Islander, 68% white, 5% international; 77% from in state; 51% live on campus; 0% of students in fraternities, 0% in sororities
**Most popular majors:** 9% Biology/Biological Sciences, General, 8% Business Administration and Management, General, 12% Elementary Education and Teaching, 8% Equestrian/Equine Studies, 30% Veterinary/Animal Health Technology/Technician and Veterinary Assistant
**Expenses:** 2014-2015: $24,381; room/board: $10,700
**Financial aid:** (717) 262-2016; 94% of undergrads determined to have financial need; average aid package $23,486

## York College of Pennsylvania

York PA
(717) 849-1600
**U.S. News ranking:** Reg. U. (N), No. 87
**Website:** www.ycp.edu
**Admissions email:** admissions@ycp.edu
**Private;** founded 1787
**Freshman admissions:** selective; 2013-2014: 9,934 applied, 7,302 accepted. Either SAT or ACT required. SAT 25/75 percentile: 950-1138. High school rank: 12% in top tenth, 40% in top quarter, 77% in top half
**Early decision deadline:** N/A, notification date: N/A
**Early action deadline:** N/A, notification date: N/A
**Application deadline (fall):** rolling
**Undergraduate student body:** 4,453 full time, 555 part time; 45% male, 55% female; 0% American Indian, 1% Asian, 5% black, 5% Hispanic, 3% multiracial, 0% Pacific Islander, 83% white, 0% international; 58% from in state; 52% live on campus; 11% of students in fraternities, 14% in sororities
**Most popular majors:** 18% Business, Management, Marketing, and Related Support Services, 13% Education, 14% Health Professions and Related Programs, 9% Homeland Security, Law Enforcement, Firefighting and Related Protective Services, 10% Parks, Recreation, Leisure, and Fitness Studies
**Expenses:** 2014-2015: $17,630; room/board: $9,870
**Financial aid:** (717) 849-1682; 69% of undergrads determined to have financial need; average aid package $13,115

## Brown University

Providence RI
(401) 863-2378
**U.S. News ranking:** Nat. U., No. 16
**Website:** www.brown.edu
**Admissions email:** admission@brown.edu
**Private;** founded 1764
**Freshman admissions:** most selective; 2013-2014: 28,919 applied, 2,654 accepted. Either SAT or ACT required. SAT 25/75 percentile: 1330-1540. High school rank: 94% in top tenth, 98% in top quarter, 100% in top half
**Early decision deadline:** 11/1, notification date: 12/15
**Early action deadline:** N/A, notification date: N/A
**Application deadline (fall):** 1/1
**Undergraduate student body:** 6,168 full time, 287 part time; 48% male, 52% female; 0% American Indian, 12% Asian, 6% black, 11% Hispanic, 5% multiracial, 0% Pacific Islander, 43% white, 12% international; 5% from in state; 78% live on campus; 18% of students in fraternities, 8% in sororities
**Most popular majors:** 10% Biology/Biological Sciences, General, 11% Economics, General, 4% Engineering, General, 4% International Relations and Affairs, 4% Political Science and Government, General

## Bryant University

Smithfield RI
(800) 622-7001
**U.S. News ranking:** Reg. U. (N), No. 11
**Website:** www.bryant.edu
**Admissions email:** admission@bryant.edu
**Private;** founded 1863
**Freshman admissions:** selective; 2013-2014: 6,013 applied, 4,603 accepted. Neither SAT nor ACT required. SAT 25/75 percentile: 1050-1220. High school rank: 18% in top tenth, 50% in top quarter, 88% in top half
**Early decision deadline:** 11/15, notification date: 12/16
**Early action deadline:** 12/2, notification date: 1/15
**Application deadline (fall):** 2/3
**Undergraduate student body:** 3,200 full time, 87 part time; 58% male, 42% female; 0% American Indian, 4% Asian, 4% black, 6% Hispanic, 0% multiracial, 0% Pacific Islander, 74% white, 7% international; 13% from in state; 81% live on campus; 6% of students in fraternities, 8% in sororities
**Most popular majors:** 79% Business, Management, Marketing, and Related Support Services, 5% Communication, Journalism, and Related Programs, 3% Computer and Information Sciences and Support Services, 5% Mathematics and Statistics, 3% Social Sciences
**Expenses:** 2014-2015: $38,574; room/board: $13,827
**Financial aid:** (401) 232-6020; 66% of undergrads determined to have financial need; average aid package $23,104

## Johnson & Wales University

Providence RI
(800) 342-5598
**U.S. News ranking:** Reg. U. (N), No. 65
**Website:** www.jwu.edu
**Admissions email:** admissions.pvd@jwu.edu
**Private;** founded 1914
**Freshman admissions:** less selective; 2013-2014: 12,364 applied, 9,399 accepted. Neither SAT nor ACT required. ACT 25/75 percentile: N/A. High school rank: N/A
**Early decision deadline:** N/A, notification date: N/A
**Early action deadline:** N/A, notification date: N/A
**Application deadline (fall):** rolling
**Undergraduate student body:** 8,754 full time, 647 part time; 42% male, 58% female; 0% American Indian, 1% Asian, 9% black, 10% Hispanic, 4% multiracial, 0% Pacific Islander, 55% white, 8% international; 18% from in state; 40% live on campus; N/A of students in fraternities, N/A in sororities
**Most popular majors:** 9% Business Administration and Management, General, 6% Culinary Arts/Chef Training, 21% Foodservice

Systems Administration/Management, 9% Hotel/Motel Administration/Management, 11% Parks, Recreation and Leisure Facilities Management, General
**Expenses:** 2014-2015: $28,539; room/board: $11,604
**Financial aid:** (401) 598-1468; 72% of undergrads determined to have financial need; average aid package $18,932

## New England Institute of Technology

East Greenwich RI
(401) 467-7744
**U.S. News ranking:** Reg. Coll. (N), unranked
**Website:** www.neit.edu/
**Admissions email:** neit@neit.edu
**Private;** founded 1940
**Freshman admissions:** N/A; 2013-2014: N/A applied, N/A accepted. Neither SAT nor ACT required. ACT 25/75 percentile: N/A. High school rank: N/A
**Early decision deadline:** N/A, notification date: N/A
**Early action deadline:** N/A, notification date: N/A
**Application deadline (fall):** rolling
**Undergraduate student body:** 2,396 full time, 464 part time; 69% male, 31% female; 1% American Indian, 2% Asian, 5% black, 9% Hispanic, 1% multiracial, 0% Pacific Islander, 68% white, 4% international
**Most popular majors:** Information not available
**Expenses:** 2014-2015: $22,230; room/board: N/A
**Financial aid:** (800) 736-7744

## Providence College

Providence RI
(401) 865-2535
**U.S. News ranking:** Reg. U. (N), No. 2
**Website:** www.providence.edu
**Admissions email:** pcadmiss@providence.edu
**Private;** founded 1917
**Affiliation:** Roman Catholic
**Freshman admissions:** more selective; 2013-2014: 9,660 applied, 5,776 accepted. Neither SAT nor ACT required. SAT 25/75 percentile: 1050-1260. High school rank: 37% in top tenth, 67% in top quarter, 92% in top half
**Early decision deadline:** 12/1, notification date: 1/1
**Early action deadline:** 11/1, notification date: 1/1
**Application deadline (fall):** 1/15
**Undergraduate student body:** 3,902 full time, 337 part time; 43% male, 57% female; 0% American Indian, 1% Asian, 4% black, 7% Hispanic, 2% multiracial, 0% Pacific Islander, 77% white, 2% international; 10% from in state; 77% live on campus; 0% of students in fraternities, 0% in sororities
**Most popular majors:** 8% Biological and Biomedical Sciences, 33% Business, Management, Marketing, and Related Support Services, 9% Education, 6% History, 11% Social Sciences
**Expenses:** 2014-2015: $43,245; room/board: $12,750
**Financial aid:** (401) 865-2286; 56% of undergrads determined to have financial need; average aid package $28,068

## Rhode Island College

Providence RI
(800) 669-5760
**U.S. News ranking:** Reg. U. (N), No. 122
**Website:** www.ric.edu
**Admissions email:** admissions@ric.edu
**Public;** founded 1854
**Freshman admissions:** less selective; 2013-2014: 4,690 applied, 3,363 accepted. Either SAT or ACT required. SAT 25/75 percentile: 820-1030. High school rank: 12% in top tenth, 40% in top quarter, 79% in top half
**Early decision deadline:** N/A, notification date: N/A
**Early action deadline:** N/A, notification date: N/A
**Application deadline (fall):** 3/15
**Undergraduate student body:** 5,600 full time, 1,905 part time; 33% male, 67% female; 0% American Indian, 2% Asian, 7% black, 12% Hispanic, 2% multiracial, 0% Pacific Islander, 64% white, 0% international; 85% from in state; 16% live on campus; N/A of students in fraternities, N/A in sororities
**Most popular majors:** 14% Business, Management, Marketing, and Related Support Services, 15% Education, 15% Health Professions and Related Programs, 13% Psychology, 8% Visual and Performing Arts
**Expenses:** 2014-2015: $7,602 in state, $18,300 out of state; room/board: $10,094
**Financial aid:** (401) 456-8033; 69% of undergrads determined to have financial need; average aid package $9,019

## Rhode Island School of Design

Providence RI
(401) 454-6300
**U.S. News ranking:** Arts, unranked
**Website:** www.risd.edu
**Admissions email:** admissions@risd.edu
**Private;** founded 1877
**Freshman admissions:** N/A; 2013-2014: 3,215 applied, 878 accepted. Either SAT or ACT required. SAT 25/75 percentile: N/A. High school rank: N/A
**Early decision deadline:** 11/1, notification date: 12/1
**Early action deadline:** N/A, notification date: N/A
**Application deadline (fall):** 2/1
**Undergraduate student body:** 2,005 full time, 0 part time; 34% male, 66% female; 0% American Indian, 16% Asian, 2% black, 8% Hispanic, 3% multiracial, 0% Pacific Islander, 33% white, 24% international; 1% from in state; 70% live on campus; N/A of students in fraternities, N/A in sororities
**Most popular majors:** 14% Architecture, 9% Film/Cinema/Video Studies, 11% Graphic Design, 18% Illustration, 17% Industrial and Product Design
**Expenses:** 2014-2015: $44,594; room/board: $12,640
**Financial aid:** (401) 454-6636; 41% of undergrads determined to have financial need; average aid package $28,500

## Roger Williams University
Bristol RI
(401) 254-3500
**U.S. News ranking:** Reg. U. (N), No. 41
**Website:** www.rwu.edu
**Admissions email:** admit@rwu.edu
**Private;** founded 1956
**Freshman admissions:** selective; 2013-2014: 9,021 applied, 7,305 accepted. Neither SAT nor ACT required. SAT 25/75 percentile: 1020-1200. High school rank: 14% in top tenth, 37% in top quarter, 75% in top half
**Early decision deadline:** N/A, notification date: N/A
**Early action deadline:** 11/1, notification date: 12/15
**Application deadline (fall):** 2/1
**Undergraduate student body:** 3,875 full time, 536 part time; 50% male, 50% female; 0% American Indian, 1% Asian, 2% black, 5% Hispanic, 2% multiracial, 0% Pacific Islander, 75% white, 5% international; 17% from in state; 63% live on campus; 0% of students in fraternities, 0% in sororities
**Most popular majors:** 10% Architecture and Related Services, 24% Business, Management, Marketing, and Related Support Services, 8% Communication, Journalism, and Related Programs, 9% Homeland Security, Law Enforcement, Firefighting and Related Protective Services, 7% Psychology
**Expenses:** 2014-2015: $31,750; room/board: $14,546
**Financial aid:** (401) 254-3100; 61% of undergrads determined to have financial need; average aid package $20,050

## Salve Regina University
Newport RI
(888) 467-2583
**U.S. News ranking:** Reg. U. (N), No. 50
**Website:** www.salve.edu
**Admissions email:** sruadmis@salve.edu
**Private;** founded 1934
**Affiliation:** Roman Catholic
**Freshman admissions:** selective; 2013-2014: 5,070 applied, 3,400 accepted. Neither SAT nor ACT required. SAT 25/75 percentile: 1020-1190. High school rank: 16% in top tenth, 45% in top quarter, 83% in top half
**Early decision deadline:** N/A, notification date: N/A
**Early action deadline:** 11/1, notification date: 12/25
**Application deadline (fall):** rolling
**Undergraduate student body:** 1,873 full time, 153 part time; 30% male, 70% female; 0% American Indian, 1% Asian, 2% black, 6% Hispanic, 2% multiracial, 0% Pacific Islander, 76% white, 1% international; 20% from in state; 58% live on campus; 0% of students in fraternities, 0% in sororities
**Most popular majors:** 13% Criminal Justice/Law Enforcement Administration, 7% Marketing/Marketing Management, General, 7% Psychology, General, 14% Registered Nursing/Registered Nurse, 8% Special Education and Teaching, General

**Expenses:** 2014-2015: $35,690; room/board: $12,860
**Financial aid:** (401) 341-2901; 78% of undergrads determined to have financial need; average aid package $23,401

## University of Rhode Island
Kingston RI
(401) 874-7100
**U.S. News ranking:** Nat. U., No. 161
**Website:** www.uri.edu
**Admissions email:** admission@uri.edu
**Public;** founded 1892
**Freshman admissions:** selective; 2013-2014: 20,907 applied, 15,844 accepted. Either SAT or ACT required. SAT 25/75 percentile: 1000-1210. High school rank: 19% in top tenth, 47% in top quarter, 83% in top half
**Early decision deadline:** N/A, notification date: N/A
**Early action deadline:** 12/1, notification date: 1/31
**Application deadline (fall):** 2/1
**Undergraduate student body:** 11,829 full time, 1,525 part time; 46% male, 54% female; 0% American Indian, 3% Asian, 5% black, 9% Hispanic, 2% multiracial, 0% Pacific Islander, 69% white, 1% international; 59% from in state; 44% live on campus; 15% of students in fraternities, 15% in sororities
**Most popular majors:** 5% Human Development and Family Studies, General, 6% Kinesiology and Exercise Science, 6% Psychology, General, 6% Registered Nursing/Registered Nurse, 8% Speech Communication and Rhetoric
**Expenses:** 2014-2015: $12,506 in state, $28,072 out of state; room/board: $11,496
**Financial aid:** (401) 874-9500; 84% of undergrads determined to have financial need; average aid package $15,482

## SOUTH CAROLINA

## Allen University
Columbia SC
(803) 376-5735
**U.S. News ranking:** Nat. Lib. Arts, second tier
**Website:** www.allenuniversity.edu
**Admissions email:** admissions@allenuniversity.edu
**Private;** founded 1870
**Affiliation:** African Methodist Episcopal
**Freshman admissions:** less selective; 2013-2014: 2,659 applied, 1,333 accepted. Neither SAT nor ACT required. Average composite ACT score: 16. High school rank: N/A
**Early decision deadline:** N/A, notification date: N/A
**Early action deadline:** N/A, notification date: N/A
**Application deadline (fall):** rolling
**Undergraduate student body:** 635 full time, 16 part time; 38% male, 62% female; 0% American Indian, 0% Asian, 100% black, 0% Hispanic, 0% multiracial, 0% Pacific Islander, 0% white, 0% international; 98% from in state; 82% live on campus; 1% of students in fraternities, 10% in sororities

**Most popular majors:** 15% Biology/Biological Sciences, General, 21% Business Administration and Management, General, 12% English Language and Literature, General, 8% Mathematics, General, 29% Social Sciences, General
**Expenses:** 2014-2015: $12,970; room/board: $6,560
**Financial aid:** (803) 376-5736; 97% of undergrads determined to have financial need; average aid package $12,418

## Anderson University
Anderson SC
(864) 231-5607
**U.S. News ranking:** Reg. Coll. (S), No. 21
**Website:** www.andersonuniversity.edu
**Admissions email:** admission@andersonuniversity.edu
**Private;** founded 1911
**Affiliation:** South Carolina Baptist Convention
**Freshman admissions:** selective; 2013-2014: 2,190 applied, 1,424 accepted. Either SAT or ACT required. SAT 25/75 percentile: 960-1180. High school rank: 39% in top tenth, 64% in top quarter, 89% in top half
**Early decision deadline:** N/A, notification date: N/A
**Early action deadline:** N/A, notification date: N/A
**Application deadline (fall):** rolling
**Undergraduate student body:** 2,131 full time, 522 part time; 33% male, 67% female; 1% American Indian, 1% Asian, 10% black, 3% Hispanic, 0% multiracial, 1% Pacific Islander, 81% white, 1% international; 82% from in state; 47% live on campus; N/A of students in fraternities, N/A in sororities
**Most popular majors:** 26% Business, Management, Marketing, and Related Support Services, 23% Education, 5% Multi/Interdisciplinary Studies, 6% Parks, Recreation, Leisure, and Fitness Studies, 15% Visual and Performing Arts
**Expenses:** 2014-2015: $23,750; room/board: $8,690
**Financial aid:** (864) 231-2070; 84% of undergrads determined to have financial need; average aid package $17,688

## Benedict College[1]
Columbia SC
(803) 253-5143
**U.S. News ranking:** Reg. Coll. (S), unranked
**Website:** www.benedict.edu
**Admissions email:** admissions@benedict.edu
**Private**
**Application deadline (fall):** N/A
**Undergraduate student body:** N/A full time, N/A part time
**Expenses:** 2013-2014: $18,254; room/board: $8,104
**Financial aid:** (803) 253-5105

## Charleston Southern University
Charleston SC
(843) 863-7050
**U.S. News ranking:** Reg. U. (S), second tier
**Website:** www.csuniv.edu
**Admissions email:** enroll@csuniv.edu
**Private;** founded 1964
**Affiliation:** Baptist
**Freshman admissions:** less selective; 2013-2014: 3,640 applied, 2,507 accepted. Either SAT or ACT required. SAT 25/75 percentile: 870-1080. High school rank: N/A
**Early decision deadline:** N/A, notification date: N/A
**Early action deadline:** N/A, notification date: N/A
**Application deadline (fall):** rolling
**Undergraduate student body:** 2,601 full time, 311 part time; 36% male, 64% female; 1% American Indian, 1% Asian, 30% black, 3% Hispanic, 2% multiracial, 0% Pacific Islander, 59% white, 1% international
**Most popular majors:** Information not available
**Expenses:** 2014-2015: $22,840; room/board: $9,000
**Financial aid:** (843) 863-7050

## The Citadel
Charleston SC
(843) 953-5230
**U.S. News ranking:** Reg. U. (S), No. 4
**Website:** www.citadel.edu/root/
**Admissions email:** admissions@citadel.edu
**Public;** founded 1842
**Freshman admissions:** selective; 2013-2014: 2,768 applied, 2,116 accepted. Either SAT or ACT required. SAT 25/75 percentile: 970-1190. High school rank: 12% in top tenth, 34% in top quarter, 71% in top half
**Early decision deadline:** N/A, notification date: N/A
**Early action deadline:** N/A, notification date: N/A
**Application deadline (fall):** rolling
**Undergraduate student body:** 2,517 full time, 218 part time; 91% male, 9% female; 1% American Indian, 3% Asian, 8% black, 6% Hispanic, 2% multiracial, 0% Pacific Islander, 78% white, 1% international; 58% from in state; 100% live on campus; 0% of students in fraternities, 0% in sororities
**Most popular majors:** 25% Business Administration and Management, General, 17% Civil Engineering, General, 14% Criminal Justice/Law Enforcement Administration, 11% Political Science and Government, General, 9% Secondary Education and Teaching
**Expenses:** 2014-2015: $12,568 in state, $32,176 out of state; room/board: $6,381
**Financial aid:** (843) 953-5187; 57% of undergrads determined to have financial need; average aid package $13,923

## Claflin University
Orangeburg SC
(803) 535-5340
**U.S. News ranking:** Nat. Lib. Arts, second tier
**Website:** www.claflin.edu
**Admissions email:** mike.zeigler@claflin.edu
**Private;** founded 1869
**Affiliation:** United Methodist
**Freshman admissions:** less selective; 2013-2014: 4,073 applied, 2,469 accepted. Either SAT or ACT required. SAT 25/75 percentile: 710-960. High school rank: 13% in top tenth, 35% in top quarter, 68% in top half
**Early decision deadline:** N/A, notification date: N/A
**Early action deadline:** N/A, notification date: N/A
**Application deadline (fall):** rolling
**Undergraduate student body:** 1,767 full time, 67 part time; 37% male, 63% female; 1% American Indian, 0% Asian, 92% black, 2% Hispanic, 0% multiracial, 0% Pacific Islander, 2% white, 3% international; 81% from in state; 70% live on campus; 3% of students in fraternities, 6% in sororities
**Most popular majors:** 13% Biotechnology, 34% Business, Management, Marketing, and Related Support Services, Other, 12% Criminal Justice/Law Enforcement Administration, 7% Mass Communication/Media Studies, 14% Sociology
**Expenses:** 2014-2015: $15,210; room/board: $10,540
**Financial aid:** (803) 535-5334; 96% of undergrads determined to have financial need; average aid package $14,045

## Clemson University
Clemson SC
(864) 656-2287
**U.S. News ranking:** Nat. U., No. 62
**Website:** www.clemson.edu
**Admissions email:** cuadmissions@clemson.edu
**Public;** founded 1889
**Freshman admissions:** more selective; 2013-2014: 18,604 applied, 10,645 accepted. Either SAT or ACT required. SAT 25/75 percentile: 1150-1340. High school rank: 56% in top tenth, 86% in top quarter, 98% in top half
**Early decision deadline:** N/A, notification date: N/A
**Early action deadline:** N/A, notification date: N/A
**Application deadline (fall):** 5/1
**Undergraduate student body:** 16,050 full time, 881 part time; 54% male, 46% female; 0% American Indian, 2% Asian, 6% black, 3% Hispanic, 1% multiracial, 0% Pacific Islander, 85% white, 1% international; 65% from in state; 41% live on campus; 22% of students in fraternities, 48% in sororities
**Most popular majors:** 9% Biological and Biomedical Sciences, 19% Business, Management, Marketing, and Related Support Services, 17% Engineering, 7% Health Professions and Related Programs, 7% Social Sciences
**Expenses:** 2013-2014: $13,382 in state, $30,816 out of state; room/board: $8,142
**Financial aid:** (864) 656-2280

## Coastal Carolina University

Conway SC
(843) 349-2170
**U.S. News ranking:** Reg. U. (S),
No. 57
**Website:** www.coastal.edu
**Admissions email:** admissions@
coastal.edu
**Public;** founded 1954
**Freshman admissions:** selective;
2013-2014: 14,050 applied,
9,014 accepted. Either SAT
or ACT required. SAT 25/75
percentile: 910-1090. High school
rank: 10% in top tenth, 33% in
top quarter, 70% in top half
**Early decision deadline:** N/A,
notification date: N/A
**Early action deadline:** N/A,
notification date: N/A
**Application deadline (fall):** 8/1
**Undergraduate student body:** 8,032
full time, 835 part time; 46%
male, 54% female; 0% American
Indian, 1% Asian, 21% black,
4% Hispanic, 4% multiracial,
0% Pacific Islander, 69% white,
1% international; 53% from in
state; 39% live on campus; 3%
of students in fraternities, 6% in
sororities
**Most popular majors:** 10%
Business Administration and
Management, General, 6%
Marine Biology and Biological
Oceanography, 6% Marketing/
Marketing Management, General,
7% Speech Communication and
Rhetoric, 6% Sport and Fitness
Administration/Management
**Expenses:** 2014-2015: $10,140
in state, $23,480 out of state;
room/board: $8,440
**Financial aid:** (843) 349-2313;
72% of undergrads determined to
have financial need; average aid
package $9,829

## Coker College

Hartsville SC
(843) 383-8050
**U.S. News ranking:** Reg. Coll. (S),
No. 16
**Website:** www.coker.edu
**Admissions email:**
admissions@coker.edu
**Private;** founded 1908
**Freshman admissions:** less
selective; 2013-2014: 1,273
applied, 678 accepted. Either
SAT or ACT required. SAT 25/75
percentile: 870-1050. High
school rank: 7% in top tenth, 21%
in top quarter, 66% in top half
**Early decision deadline:** N/A,
notification date: N/A
**Early action deadline:** N/A,
notification date: N/A
**Application deadline (fall):** 8/1
**Undergraduate student body:** 1,007
full time, 137 part time; 37%
male, 63% female; 0% American
Indian, 0% Asian, 36% black,
3% Hispanic, 2% multiracial,
0% Pacific Islander, 51% white,
2% international; 80% from in
state; 49% live on campus; 0%
of students in fraternities, 0% in
sororities
**Most popular majors:** 19%
Business Administration and
Management, General, 13%
Elementary Education and
Teaching, 8% Psychology,
General, 8% Social Work, 14%
Sociology
**Expenses:** 2014-2015: $25,536;
room/board: $7,830

**Financial aid:** (843) 383-8055;
88% of undergrads determined to
have financial need; average aid
package $18,385

## College of Charleston

Charleston SC
(843) 953-5670
**U.S. News ranking:** Reg. U. (S),
No. 13
**Website:** www.cofc.edu
**Admissions email:**
admissions@cofc.edu
**Public;** founded 1770
**Freshman admissions:** selective;
2013-2014: 11,532 applied,
8,330 accepted. Either SAT
or ACT required. SAT 25/75
percentile: 1070-1250. High
school rank: 26% in top tenth,
60% in top quarter, 92% in
top half
**Early decision deadline:** N/A,
notification date: N/A
**Early action deadline:** 11/1,
notification date: 1/1
**Application deadline (fall):** 4/1
**Undergraduate student body:** 9,708
full time, 780 part time; 38%
male, 62% female; 0% American
Indian, 2% Asian, 6% black, 4%
Hispanic, 3% multiracial, 0%
Pacific Islander, 82% white, 1%
international; 63% from in state;
29% live on campus; 17% of
students in fraternities, 23% in
sororities
**Most popular majors:** 10% Biology/
Biological Sciences, General, 21%
Business/Commerce, General,
11% Social Sciences, General,
10% Speech Communication
and Rhetoric, 10% Visual and
Performing Arts, General
**Expenses:** 2014-2015: $11,018
in state, $28,008 out of state;
room/board: $11,127
**Financial aid:** (843) 953-5540;
49% of undergrads determined to
have financial need; average aid
package $12,946

## Columbia College

Columbia SC
(800) 277-1301
**U.S. News ranking:** Reg. U. (S),
No. 37
**Website:** www.columbiasc.edu
**Admissions email:** admissions@
columbiasc.edu
**Private;** founded 1854
**Affiliation:** United Methodist
**Freshman admissions:** selective;
2013-2014: 446 applied, 287
accepted. Either SAT or ACT
required. SAT 25/75 percentile:
920-1130. High school rank:
22% in top tenth, 63% in top
quarter, 90% in top half
**Early decision deadline:** N/A,
notification date: N/A
**Early action deadline:** N/A,
notification date: N/A
**Application deadline (fall):** rolling
**Undergraduate student body:** 722
full time, 290 part time; 5%
male, 95% female; 2% American
Indian, 1% Asian, 38% black,
3% Hispanic, 0% multiracial,
0% Pacific Islander, 52% white,
0% international; 92% from in
state; 42% live on campus; 0%
of students in fraternities, 0% in
sororities
**Most popular majors:** 6% Business
Administration and Management,
General, 12% Human
Development, Family Studies,
and Related Services, Other, 13%
Psychology, General, 7% Speech
Communication and Rhetoric,

7% Speech-Language Pathology/
Pathologist
**Expenses:** 2014-2015: $27,350;
room/board: $7,200
**Financial aid:** (803) 786-3612;
91% of undergrads determined to
have financial need; average aid
package $20,665

## Columbia International University

Columbia SC
(800) 777-2227
**U.S. News ranking:** Reg. U. (S),
No. 37
**Website:** www.ciu.edu
**Admissions email:** N/A
**Private;** founded 1923
**Affiliation:** Evangelical
multi-denominational
**Freshman admissions:** selective;
2013-2014: 302 applied, 189
accepted. Either SAT or ACT
required. SAT 25/75 percentile:
940-1200. High school rank:
15% in top tenth, 37% in top
quarter, 73% in top half
**Early decision deadline:** N/A,
notification date: N/A
**Early action deadline:** N/A,
notification date: N/A
**Undergraduate student body:** 511
full time, 74 part time; 54%
male, 46% female; 2% American
Indian, 2% Asian, 11% black,
4% Hispanic, 1% multiracial,
0% Pacific Islander, 77% white,
3% international; 58% from in
state; 71% live on campus; 0%
of students in fraternities, 0% in
sororities
**Most popular majors:** 17% General
Studies, 16% Humanities/
Humanistic Studies, 10%
Intercultural/Multicultural and
Diversity Studies, 7% Mass
Communication/Media Studies,
14% Psychology, General
**Expenses:** 2014-2015: $19,480;
room/board: $7,310
**Financial aid:** (803) 754-4100;
81% of undergrads determined to
have financial need; average aid
package $15,728

## Converse College

Spartanburg SC
(864) 596-9040
**U.S. News ranking:** Reg. U. (S),
No. 23
**Website:** www.converse.edu
**Admissions email:**
info@converse.edu
**Private;** founded 1889
**Freshman admissions:** selective;
2013-2014: 1,504 applied, 784
accepted. Either SAT or ACT
required. SAT 25/75 percentile:
960-1160. High school rank:
18% in top tenth, 43% in top
quarter, 80% in top half
**Early decision deadline:** N/A,
notification date: N/A
**Early action deadline:** N/A,
notification date: N/A
**Application deadline (fall):** 8/1
**Undergraduate student body:** 665
full time, 83 part time; 0% male,
100% female; 0% American
Indian, 1% Asian, 7% black, 4%
Hispanic, 3% multiracial, 0%
Pacific Islander, 55% white, 1%
international
**Most popular majors:** 9% Business,
Management, Marketing, and
Related Support Services, 24%
Education, 10% English Language

and Literature/Letters, 15%
Psychology, 16% Visual and
Performing Arts
**Expenses:** 2014-2015: $16,500;
room/board: $9,500
**Financial aid:** (864) 596-9019;
90% of undergrads determined to
have financial need; average aid
package $23,249

## Erskine College

Due West SC
(864) 379-8838
**U.S. News ranking:** Nat. Lib. Arts,
No. 178
**Website:** www.erskine.edu
**Admissions email:**
admissions@erskine.edu
**Private**
**Affiliation:** Associate Reformed
Presbyterian
**Freshman admissions:** selective;
2013-2014: 750 applied, 523
accepted. Either SAT or ACT
required. SAT 25/75 percentile:
910-1110. High school rank: N/A
**Early decision deadline:** N/A,
notification date: N/A
**Early action deadline:** N/A,
notification date: N/A
**Application deadline (fall):** rolling
**Undergraduate student body:** 565
full time, 40 part time; 52%
male, 48% female; 0% American
Indian, 1% Asian, 10% black,
4% Hispanic, 0% multiracial, 0%
Pacific Islander, 67% white, 0%
international
**Most popular majors:** 20%
Biological and Biomedical
Sciences, 12% Business,
Management, Marketing, and
Related Support Services, 11%
English Language and Literature/
Letters, 7% Parks, Recreation,
Leisure, and Fitness Studies, 8%
Physical Sciences
**Expenses:** 2014-2015: $31,280;
room/board: $10,105
**Financial aid:** (864) 379-8832;
100% of undergrads determined
to have financial need; average aid
package $22,000

## Francis Marion University

Florence SC
(843) 661-1231
**U.S. News ranking:** Reg. U. (S),
No. 76
**Website:** www.fmarion.edu
**Admissions email:**
admission@fmarion.edu
**Public;** founded 1970
**Freshman admissions:** selective;
2013-2014: 3,951 applied,
2,239 accepted. Either SAT
or ACT required. SAT 25/75
percentile: 830-1060. High school
rank: 15% in top tenth, 42% in
top quarter, 81% in top half
**Early decision deadline:** N/A,
notification date: N/A
**Early action deadline:** N/A,
notification date: N/A
**Application deadline (fall):** 8/15
**Undergraduate student body:** 3,316
full time, 398 part time; 31%
male, 69% female; 0% American
Indian, 1% Asian, 50% black,
1% Hispanic, 0% multiracial,
0% Pacific Islander, 45% white,
1% international; 97% from in
state; 39% live on campus; 1%
of students in fraternities, 1% in
sororities
**Most popular majors:** 15%
Biological and Biomedical
Sciences, 17% Business,
Management, Marketing, and

Related Support Services, 16%
Health Professions and Related
Programs, 8% Psychology, 11%
Social Sciences
**Expenses:** 2014-2015: $9,738 in
state, $19,004 out of state; room/
board: $7,256
**Financial aid:** (843) 661-1190;
80% of undergrads determined to
have financial need; average aid
package $7,224

## Furman University

Greenville SC
(864) 294-2034
**U.S. News ranking:** Nat. Lib. Arts,
No. 51
**Website:** www.furman.edu/
**Admissions email:**
admissions@furman.edu
**Private;** founded 1826
**Freshman admissions:** more
selective; 2013-2014: 5,935
applied, 3,802 accepted. Neither
SAT nor ACT required. SAT
25/75 percentile: 1130-1340.
High school rank: 48% in top
tenth, 76% in top quarter, 93%
in top half
**Early decision deadline:** 11/1,
notification date: 11/30
**Early action deadline:** 11/15,
notification date: 2/1
**Application deadline (fall):** 1/15
**Undergraduate student body:** 2,675
full time, 123 part time; 42%
male, 58% female; 0% American
Indian, 2% Asian, 5% black, 3%
Hispanic, 2% multiracial, 0%
Pacific Islander, 80% white, 4%
international; 28% from in state;
96% live on campus; 31% of
students in fraternities, 54% in
sororities
**Most popular majors:** 6%
Biology, General, 11% Business
Administration, Management and
Operations, 7% Health Professions
and Related Clinical Sciences,
Other, 6% History, 10% Political
Science and Government
**Expenses:** 2014-2015: $44,668;
room/board: $11,204
**Financial aid:** (864) 294-2204;
44% of undergrads determined to
have financial need; average aid
package $28,539

## Lander University[1]

Greenwood SC
(864) 388-8307
**U.S. News ranking:** Reg. Coll. (S),
No. 64
**Website:** www.lander.edu
**Admissions email:**
admissions@lander.edu
**Public**
**Application deadline (fall):** N/A
**Undergraduate student body:** N/A
full time, N/A part time
**Expenses:** 2013-2014: $10,100
in state, $19,136 out of state;
room/board: $7,500
**Financial aid:** (864) 388-8340

## Limestone College

Gaffney SC
(864) 488-4554
**U.S. News ranking:** Reg. Coll. (S),
No. 64
**Website:** www.limestone.edu
**Admissions email:** admiss@
limestone.edu
**Private;** founded 1845
**Affiliation:** Christian
nondenominational
**Freshman admissions:** less
selective; 2013-2014: 2,318
applied, 1,244 accepted. Either

SAT or ACT required. SAT 25/75 percentile: 930-1090. High school rank: 3% in top tenth, 19% in top quarter, 51% in top half **Early decision deadline:** N/A, notification date: N/A **Early action deadline:** N/A, notification date: N/A **Application deadline (fall):** 8/22 **Undergraduate student body:** 1,041 full time, 18 part time; 62% male, 38% female; 0% American Indian, 0% Asian, 29% black, 4% Hispanic, 2% multiracial, 0% Pacific Islander, 54% white, 9% international; 58% from in state; 58% live on campus; 3% of students in fraternities, 0% in sororities **Most popular majors:** 28% Business, Management, Marketing, and Related Support Services, 14% Education, 6% Homeland Security, Law Enforcement, Firefighting and Related Protective Services, 8% Liberal Arts and Sciences, General Studies and Humanities, 12% Parks, Recreation, Leisure, and Fitness Studies **Expenses:** 2014-2015: $23,000; room/board: $7,800 **Financial aid:** (864) 488-8231; 85% of undergrads determined to have financial need; average aid package $17,351

## Morris College[1]

Sumter SC
(803) 934-3225
**U.S. News ranking:** Reg. Coll. (S), unranked
**Website:** www.morris.edu
**Admissions email:** dcalhoun@morris.edu
**Private**
**Application deadline (fall):** N/A
**Undergraduate student body:** N/A full time, N/A part time
**Expenses:** 2013-2014: $11,087; room/board: $4,919
**Financial aid:** (803) 934-3238

## Newberry College

Newberry SC
(800) 845-4955
**U.S. News ranking:** Reg. Coll. (S), No. 33
**Website:** www.newberry.edu/
**Admissions email:** admissions@newberry.edu
**Private;** founded 1856
**Affiliation:** Evangelical Lutheran Church of America
**Freshman admissions:** less selective; 2013-2014: 887 applied, 524 accepted. Either SAT or ACT required. SAT 25/75 percentile: 830-1060. High school rank: 8% in top tenth, 16% in top quarter, 54% in top half **Early decision deadline:** N/A, notification date: N/A **Early action deadline:** N/A, notification date: N/A **Application deadline (fall):** rolling **Undergraduate student body:** 1,007 full time, 32 part time; 54% male, 46% female; 1% American Indian, 1% Asian, 26% black, 4% Hispanic, 2% multiracial, 0% Pacific Islander, 61% white, 3% international; 79% from in state; 72% live on campus; 13% of students in fraternities, 25% in sororities **Most popular majors:** 9% Biology/Biological Sciences, General, 18% Business Administration and Management, General,

18% Education, General, 11% Parks, Recreation and Leisure Studies, 9% Registered Nursing/Registered Nurse **Expenses:** 2014-2015: $24,300; room/board: $9,300 **Financial aid:** (803) 321-5120; 87% of undergrads determined to have financial need; average aid package $20,448

## North Greenville University

Tigerville SC
(864) 977-7001
**U.S. News ranking:** Reg. Coll. (S), No. 25
**Website:** www.ngu.edu
**Admissions email:** admissions@ngu.edu
**Private;** founded 1892
**Affiliation:** Southern Baptist Convention
**Freshman admissions:** selective; 2013-2014: 1,782 applied, 1,032 accepted. Either SAT or ACT required. SAT 25/75 percentile: 920-1340. High school rank: 19% in top tenth, 39% in top quarter, 80% in top half **Early decision deadline:** N/A, notification date: N/A **Early action deadline:** N/A, notification date: N/A **Application deadline (fall):** rolling **Undergraduate student body:** 1,994 full time, 269 part time; 50% male, 50% female; 0% American Indian, 0% Asian, 6% black, 2% Hispanic, 2% multiracial, 0% Pacific Islander, 85% white, 0% international; 78% from in state; 66% live on campus; 0% of students in fraternities, 0% in sororities **Most popular majors:** 19% Business, Management, Marketing, and Related Support Services, 10% Communication, Journalism, and Related Programs, 17% Education, 13% Liberal Arts and Sciences, General Studies and Humanities, 14% Theology and Religious Vocations **Expenses:** 2014-2015: $15,510; room/board: $9,180 **Financial aid:** (864) 977-7058; 59% of undergrads determined to have financial need; average aid package $13,615

## Presbyterian College

Clinton SC
(864) 833-8230
**U.S. News ranking:** Nat. Lib. Arts, No. 124
**Website:** www.presby.edu
**Admissions email:** admissions@presby.edu
**Private;** founded 1880
**Affiliation:** Presbyterian Church (USA)
**Freshman admissions:** selective; 2013-2014: 1,650 applied, 1,089 accepted. Neither SAT nor ACT required. SAT 25/75 percentile: 1000-1210. High school rank: 35% in top tenth, 61% in top quarter, 92% in top half **Early decision deadline:** 11/1, notification date: 12/1 **Early action deadline:** 11/15, notification date: 12/15 **Application deadline (fall):** 6/30 **Undergraduate student body:** 1,087 full time, 36 part time; 45% male, 55% female; 0% American

Indian, 1% Asian, 11% black, 1% Hispanic, 1% multiracial, 0% Pacific Islander, 82% white, 2% international; 65% from in state; 99% live on campus; 38% of students in fraternities, 47% in sororities **Most popular majors:** 14% Biological and Biomedical Sciences, 18% Business, Management, and Related Support Services, 11% English Language and Literature/Letters, 10% History, 11% Psychology **Expenses:** 2013-2014: $33,650; room/board: $9,028 **Financial aid:** (864) 833-8289

## South Carolina State University

Orangeburg SC
(803) 536-7185
**U.S. News ranking:** Nat. U., second tier
**Website:** www.scsu.edu
**Admissions email:** admissions@scsu.edu
**Public;** founded 1896
**Freshman admissions:** least selective; 2013-2014: 1,999 applied, 1,838 accepted. Either SAT or ACT required. SAT 25/75 percentile: 720-870. High school rank: 2% in top tenth, 30% in top quarter, 43% in top half **Early decision deadline:** N/A, notification date: N/A **Early action deadline:** N/A, notification date: N/A **Application deadline (fall):** 5/31 **Undergraduate student body:** 2,714 full time, 223 part time; 48% male, 52% female; 0% American Indian, 1% Asian, 95% black, 1% Hispanic, 0% multiracial, 0% Pacific Islander, 3% white, 0% international; 79% from in state; 58% live on campus; N/A of students in fraternities, N/A in sororities **Most popular majors:** 8% Biology/Biological Sciences, General, 6% Business Administration and Management, General, 8% Criminal Justice/Law Enforcement Administration, 10% Family and Consumer Sciences/Human Sciences, General, 8% Registered Nursing/Registered Nurse **Expenses:** 2013-2014: $9,776 in state, $18,910 out of state; room/board: $9,286 **Financial aid:** (803) 536-7067

## Southern Wesleyan University[1]

Central SC
(864) 644-5550
**U.S. News ranking:** Reg. U. (S), second tier
**Website:** www.swu.edu
**Admissions email:** admissions@swu.edu
**Private**
**Application deadline (fall):** N/A
**Undergraduate student body:** N/A full time, N/A part time
**Expenses:** 2013-2014: $22,200; room/board: $8,360
**Financial aid:** (864) 644-5500

## University of South Carolina

Columbia SC
(803) 777-7700
**U.S. News ranking:** Nat. U., No. 113
**Website:** www.sc.edu
**Admissions email:** admissions-ugrad@sc.edu
**Public;** founded 1801
**Freshman admissions:** more selective; 2013-2014: 23,035 applied, 14,844 accepted. Either SAT or ACT required. SAT 25/75 percentile: 1110-1300. High school rank: 30% in top tenth, 66% in top quarter, 94% in top half **Early decision deadline:** N/A, notification date: N/A **Early action deadline:** 10/15, notification date: 12/20 **Application deadline (fall):** 12/1 **Undergraduate student body:** 22,533 full time, 1,647 part time; 46% male, 54% female; 0% American Indian, 2% Asian, 10% black, 4% Hispanic, 3% multiracial, 0% Pacific Islander, 77% white, 1% international; 69% from in state; 30% live on campus; 13% of students in fraternities, 28% in sororities **Most popular majors:** 5% Biology, General, 6% Business Administration, Management and Operations, 4% Physiology, Pathology and Related Sciences, 5% Registered Nursing, Nursing Administration, Nursing Research and Clinical Nursing, 6% Research and Experimental Psychology **Expenses:** 2014-2015: $11,158 in state, $29,440 out of state; room/board: $9,248 **Financial aid:** (803) 777-8134; 52% of undergrads determined to have financial need; average aid package $13,332

## University of South Carolina–Aiken

Aiken SC
(803) 641-3366
**U.S. News ranking:** Reg. Coll. (S), No. 18
**Website:** web.usca.edu/
**Admissions email:** admit@sc.edu
**Public;** founded 1961
**Freshman admissions:** selective; 2013-2014: 1,839 applied, 1,294 accepted. Either SAT or ACT required. SAT 25/75 percentile: 860-1070. High school rank: 11% in top tenth, 36% in top quarter, 74% in top half **Early decision deadline:** N/A, notification date: N/A **Early action deadline:** N/A, notification date: N/A **Application deadline (fall):** 8/1 **Undergraduate student body:** 2,406 full time, 769 part time; 37% male, 63% female; 0% American Indian, 1% Asian, 27% black, 4% Hispanic, 3% multiracial, 0% Pacific Islander, 60% white, 2% international; 89% from in state; 27% live on campus; 6% of students in fraternities, 11% in sororities **Most popular majors:** 9% Biological and Biomedical Sciences, 24% Business, Management, Marketing, and Related Support Services, 12% Education, 16% Health Professions and Related Programs, 8% Social Sciences

**Expenses:** 2014-2015: $9,602 in state, $18,926 out of state; room/board: $7,110 **Financial aid:** (803) 641-3476; 71% of undergrads determined to have financial need; average aid package $10,094

## University of South Carolina–Beaufort

Bluffton SC
(843) 208-8000
**U.S. News ranking:** Reg. Coll. (S), No. 59
**Website:** www.uscb.edu
**Admissions email:** admissions@uscb.edu
**Public;** founded 1959
**Freshman admissions:** less selective; 2013-2014: 1,666 applied, 1,135 accepted. Either SAT or ACT required. SAT 25/75 percentile: 830-1010. High school rank: 5% in top tenth, 24% in top quarter, 57% in top half **Early decision deadline:** N/A, notification date: N/A **Early action deadline:** N/A, notification date: N/A **Application deadline (fall):** rolling **Undergraduate student body:** 1,376 full time, 348 part time; 39% male, 61% female; 0% American Indian, 1% Asian, 19% black, 5% Hispanic, 3% multiracial, 0% Pacific Islander, 62% white, 1% international; 84% from in state; 32% live on campus; 0% of students in fraternities, 0% in sororities **Most popular majors:** 23% Business Administration and Management, General, 15% Hospitality Administration/Management, General, 9% Psychology, General, 12% Registered Nursing/Registered Nurse, 8% Social Sciences, General **Expenses:** 2014-2015: $9,092 in state, $19,478 out of state; room/board: $8,186 **Financial aid:** (843) 521-3104

## University of South Carolina–Upstate

Spartanburg SC
(864) 503-5246
**U.S. News ranking:** Reg. Coll. (S), No. 32
**Website:** www.uscupstate.edu/
**Admissions email:** admissions@uscupstate.edu
**Public;** founded 1967
**Freshman admissions:** less selective; 2013-2014: 2,971 applied, 1,690 accepted. Either SAT or ACT required. SAT 25/75 percentile: 870-1038. High school rank: 14% in top tenth, 40% in top quarter, 77% in top half **Early decision deadline:** N/A, notification date: N/A **Early action deadline:** N/A, notification date: N/A **Application deadline (fall):** rolling **Undergraduate student body:** 4,189 full time, 1,035 part time; 35% male, 65% female; 0% American Indian, 2% Asian, 29% black, 4% Hispanic, 3% multiracial, 0% Pacific Islander, 57% white, 2% international; 96% from in state; 19% live on campus; 6% of students in fraternities, 2% in sororities

**Most popular majors:** 14% Business Administration and Management, General, 16% Education, General, 7% Multi-/Interdisciplinary Studies, General, 8% Psychology, General, 27% Registered Nursing/Registered Nurse
**Expenses:** 2014-2015: $10,518 in state, $20,868 out of state; room/board: $7,682
**Financial aid:** (864) 503-5340; 78% of undergrads determined to have financial need; average aid package $9,484

## Voorhees College[1]
Denmark SC
(803) 780-1030
**U.S. News ranking:** Reg. Coll. (S), second tier
**Website:** www.voorhees.edu
**Admissions email:** admissions@voorhees.edu
**Private**
**Application deadline (fall):** N/A
**Undergraduate student body:** N/A full time, N/A part time
**Expenses:** 2013-2014: $10,780; room/board: $7,346
**Financial aid:** (803) 780-1150

## Winthrop University
Rock Hill SC
(803) 323-2191
**U.S. News ranking:** Reg. U. (S), No. 25
**Website:** www.winthrop.edu
**Admissions email:** admissions@winthrop.edu
**Public;** founded 1886
**Freshman admissions:** selective; 2013-2014: 4,285 applied, 3,096 accepted. Either SAT or ACT required. SAT 25/75 percentile: 920-1140. High school rank: 22% in top tenth, 51% in top quarter, 84% in top half
**Early decision deadline:** N/A, notification date: N/A
**Early action deadline:** N/A, notification date: N/A
**Application deadline (fall):** rolling
**Undergraduate student body:** 4,432 full time, 616 part time; 33% male, 67% female; 0% American Indian, 1% Asian, 31% black, 3% Hispanic, 2% multiracial, 0% Pacific Islander, 58% white, 3% international; 92% from in state; 47% live on campus; N/A of students in fraternities, N/A in sororities
**Most popular majors:** 28% Business, Management, Marketing, and Related Support Services, 15% Education, 7% Psychology, 7% Social Sciences, 11% Visual and Performing Arts
**Expenses:** 2014-2015: $13,812 in state, $26,738 out of state; room/board: $8,182
**Financial aid:** (803) 323-2189; 74% of undergrads determined to have financial need; average aid package $11,837

## Wofford College
Spartanburg SC
(864) 597-4130
**U.S. News ranking:** Nat. Lib. Arts, No. 77
**Website:** www.wofford.edu
**Admissions email:** admissions@wofford.edu
**Private;** founded 1854
**Affiliation:** United Methodist

**Freshman admissions:** more selective; 2013-2014: 2,718 applied, 1,870 accepted. Either SAT or ACT required. SAT 25/75 percentile: 1080-1260. High school rank: 42% in top tenth, 77% in top quarter, 96% in top half
**Early decision deadline:** 11/1, notification date: 12/1
**Early action deadline:** 11/15, notification date: 2/1
**Application deadline (fall):** 2/1
**Undergraduate student body:** 1,549 full time, 35 part time; 52% male, 48% female; 0% American Indian, 3% Asian, 8% black, 3% Hispanic, 3% multiracial, 0% Pacific Islander, 81% white, 2% international; 56% from in state; 93% live on campus; 43% of students in fraternities, 55% in sororities
**Most popular majors:** 7% Accounting, 20% Biology/Biological Sciences, General, 9% Business/Managerial Economics, 11% Finance, General, 7% Spanish Language and Literature
**Expenses:** 2014-2015: $37,120; room/board: $10,730
**Financial aid:** (864) 597-4160; 59% of undergrads determined to have financial need; average aid package $28,377

## Augustana College
Sioux Falls SD
(605) 274-5516
**U.S. News ranking:** Reg. Coll. (Mid. W), No. 3
**Website:** www.augie.edu
**Admissions email:** admission@augie.edu
**Private;** founded 1860
**Affiliation:** ELCA Lutheran
**Freshman admissions:** more selective; 2013-2014: 1,147 applied, 781 accepted. Either SAT or ACT required. ACT 25/75 percentile: 23-28. High school rank: 30% in top tenth, 63% in top quarter, 93% in top half
**Early decision deadline:** N/A, notification date: N/A
**Early action deadline:** N/A, notification date: N/A
**Application deadline (fall):** rolling
**Undergraduate student body:** 1,585 full time, 112 part time; 41% male, 59% female; 0% American Indian, 1% Asian, 2% black, 1% Hispanic, 2% multiracial, 0% Pacific Islander, 88% white, 6% international
**Most popular majors:** 13% Biological and Biomedical Sciences, 16% Business, Management, Marketing, and Related Support Services, 11% Education, General, 18% Health Professions and Related Programs, 7% Social Sciences
**Expenses:** 2014-2015: $29,214; room/board: $7,170
**Financial aid:** (605) 274-5216; 62% of undergrads determined to have financial need; average aid package $23,156

## Black Hills State University[1]
Spearfish SD
(800) 255-2478
**U.S. News ranking:** Reg. U. (Mid. W), second tier
**Website:** www.bhsu.edu
**Admissions email:** admissions@bhsu.edu
**Public**
**Application deadline (fall):** N/A
**Undergraduate student body:** N/A full time, N/A part time
**Expenses:** 2013-2014: $7,617 in state, $9,617 out of state; room/board: $5,945
**Financial aid:** (605) 642-6145

## Dakota State University
Madison SD
(888) 378-9988
**U.S. News ranking:** Reg. U. (Mid. W), No. 80
**Website:** www.dsu.edu
**Admissions email:** admissions@dsu.edu
**Public;** founded 1881
**Freshman admissions:** selective; 2013-2014: 781 applied, 648 accepted. Either SAT or ACT required. ACT 25/75 percentile: 19-24. High school rank: 6% in top tenth, 23% in top quarter, 56% in top half
**Early decision deadline:** N/A, notification date: N/A
**Early action deadline:** N/A, notification date: N/A
**Application deadline (fall):** rolling
**Undergraduate student body:** 1,190 full time, 1,686 part time; 52% male, 48% female; 1% American Indian, 1% Asian, 3% black, 3% Hispanic, 3% multiracial, 0% Pacific Islander, 86% white, 1% international; 73% from in state; 33% live on campus; 0% of students in fraternities, 0% in sororities
**Most popular majors:** 24% Business, Management, Marketing, and Related Support Services, 34% Computer and Information Sciences and Support Services, 18% Education, 5% Health Professions and Related Programs, 7% Parks, Recreation, Leisure, and Fitness Studies
**Expenses:** 2014-2015: $8,286 in state, $10,286 out of state; room/board: $5,941
**Financial aid:** (605) 256-5152; 69% of undergrads determined to have financial need; average aid package $7,997

## Dakota Wesleyan University
Mitchell SD
(800) 333-8506
**U.S. News ranking:** Reg. Coll. (Mid. W), No. 54
**Website:** www.dwu.edu
**Admissions email:** admissions@dwu.edu
**Private;** founded 1885
**Affiliation:** United Methodist
**Freshman admissions:** selective; 2013-2014: N/A applied, N/A accepted. Either SAT or ACT required. ACT 25/75 percentile: 19-27. High school rank: 9% in top tenth, 26% in top quarter, 61% in top half
**Early decision deadline:** N/A, notification date: N/A

**Early action deadline:** N/A, notification date: N/A
**Application deadline (fall):** rolling
**Undergraduate student body:** 699 full time, 111 part time; 45% male, 55% female; 1% American Indian, 0% Asian, 2% black, 4% Hispanic, 2% multiracial, 0% Pacific Islander, 89% white, 1% international; N/A from in state; 45% live on campus; N/A of students in fraternities, N/A in sororities
**Most popular majors:** 10% Biology/Biological Sciences, General, 20% Business Administration and Management, General, 13% Education, General, 10% Registered Nursing/Registered Nurse, 10% Sport and Fitness Administration/Management
**Expenses:** 2014-2015: $23,650; room/board: $6,900
**Financial aid:** (605) 995-2656; 83% of undergrads determined to have financial need; average aid package $19,100

## Mount Marty College
Yankton SD
(800) 658-4552
**U.S. News ranking:** Reg. Coll. (Mid. W), No. 45
**Website:** www.mtmc.edu
**Admissions email:** mmcadmit@mtmc.edu
**Private;** founded 1936
**Affiliation:** Roman Catholic
**Freshman admissions:** selective; 2013-2014: 402 applied, 291 accepted. Either SAT or ACT required. ACT 25/75 percentile: 19-24. High school rank: 19% in top tenth, 44% in top quarter, 74% in top half
**Early decision deadline:** N/A, notification date: N/A
**Early action deadline:** N/A, notification date: N/A
**Application deadline (fall):** 8/30
**Undergraduate student body:** 522 full time, 546 part time; 38% male, 62% female; 4% American Indian, 1% Asian, 4% black, 8% Hispanic, 0% multiracial, 1% Pacific Islander, 80% white, 0% international; 65% from in state; 66% live on campus; 0% of students in fraternities, 0% in sororities
**Most popular majors:** 18% Business Administration and Management, General, 8% Criminal Justice/Safety Studies, 22% Education, General, 22% Registered Nursing/Registered Nurse
**Expenses:** 2014-2015: $22,892; room/board: $6,978
**Financial aid:** (605) 668-1589; 78% of undergrads determined to have financial need; average aid package $23,247

## National American University[1]
Rapid City SD
(855) 448-2318
**U.S. News ranking:** Reg. U. (Mid. W), unranked
**Website:** www.national.edu/rc
**Admissions email:** N/A
**For-profit**
**Application deadline (fall):** N/A
**Undergraduate student body:** N/A full time, N/A part time
**Expenses:** N/A
**Financial aid:** (605) 394-4880

## Northern State University
Aberdeen SD
(800) 678-5330
**U.S. News ranking:** Reg. Coll. (Mid. W), No. 47
**Website:** www.northern.edu
**Admissions email:** admissions@northern.edu
**Public;** founded 1901
**Freshman admissions:** selective; 2013-2014: 1,157 applied, 1,080 accepted. Either SAT or ACT required. ACT 25/75 percentile: 19-25. High school rank: 7% in top tenth, 26% in top quarter, 63% in top half
**Early decision deadline:** N/A, notification date: N/A
**Early action deadline:** N/A, notification date: N/A
**Application deadline (fall):** rolling
**Undergraduate student body:** 1,534 full time, 1,295 part time; 42% male, 58% female; 2% American Indian, 1% Asian, 2% black, 3% Hispanic, 2% multiracial, 0% Pacific Islander, 86% white, 4% international; 79% from in state; 41% live on campus; N/A of students in fraternities, N/A in sororities
**Most popular majors:** 7% Biological and Biomedical Sciences, 27% Business, Management, Marketing, and Related Support Services, 22% Education, 8% Parks, Recreation, Leisure, and Fitness Studies, 11% Social Sciences
**Expenses:** 2014-2015: $7,563 in state, $9,563 out of state; room/board: $6,941
**Financial aid:** (605) 626-2640; 66% of undergrads determined to have financial need; average aid package $10,097

## Presentation College[1]
Aberdeen SD
(800) 437-6060
**U.S. News ranking:** Reg. Coll. (Mid. W), second tier
**Website:** www.presentation.edu/
**Admissions email:** N/A
**Private**
**Application deadline (fall):** N/A
**Undergraduate student body:** N/A full time, N/A part time
**Expenses:** 2013-2014: $17,014; room/board: $7,000
**Financial aid:** (800) 437-6060

## South Dakota School of Mines and Technology
Rapid City SD
(605) 394-2414
**U.S. News ranking:** Engineering, unranked
**Website:** www.sdsmt.edu
**Admissions email:** admissions@sdsmt.edu
**Public;** founded 1885
**Freshman admissions:** selective; 2013-2014: 1,350 applied, 1,155 accepted. Either SAT or ACT required. ACT 25/75 percentile: 24-28. High school rank: 17% in top tenth, 38% in top quarter, 62% in top half
**Early decision deadline:** N/A, notification date: N/A
**Early action deadline:** N/A, notification date: N/A
**Application deadline (fall):** rolling

**Undergraduate student body:** 1,950 full time, 379 part time; 77% male, 23% female; 1% American Indian, 1% Asian, 2% black, 3% Hispanic, 4% multiracial, 1% Pacific Islander, 85% white, 2% international; 54% from in state; 38% live on campus; 2% of students in fraternities, 5% in sororities
**Most popular majors:** 13% Chemical Engineering, 15% Civil Engineering, General, 12% Electrical and Electronics Engineering, 10% Industrial Engineering, 19% Mechanical Engineering
**Expenses:** 2014-2015: $10,040 in state, $12,870 out of state; room/board: $6,370
**Financial aid:** (605) 394-2274; 55% of undergrads determined to have financial need; average aid package $13,717

## South Dakota State University

Brookings SD
(605) 688-4121
**U.S. News ranking:** Nat. U., No. 181
**Website:** www.sdstate.edu
**Admissions email:** SDSU_Admissions@sdstate.edu
**Public;** founded 1881
**Freshman admissions:** selective; 2013-2014: 4,851 applied, 4,458 accepted. Either SAT or ACT required. ACT 25/75 percentile: 20-25. High school rank: 13% in top tenth, 35% in top quarter, 69% in top half
**Early decision deadline:** N/A, notification date: N/A
**Early action deadline:** N/A, notification date: N/A
**Application deadline (fall):** rolling
**Undergraduate student body:** 8,646 full time, 2,352 part time; 48% male, 52% female; 1% American Indian, 1% Asian, 2% black, 2% Hispanic, 3% multiracial, 0% Pacific Islander, 90% white, 2% international; 63% from in state; 42% live on campus; N/A of students in fraternities, N/A in sororities
**Most popular majors:** Information not available
**Expenses:** 2014-2015: $7,713 in state, $9,795 out of state; room/board: $7,311
**Financial aid:** (605) 688-4695

## University of Sioux Falls

Sioux Falls SD
(605) 331-6600
**U.S. News ranking:** Reg. Coll. (Mid. W), No. 38
**Website:** www.usiouxfalls.edu
**Admissions email:** admissions@usiouxfalls.edu
**Private;** founded 1883
**Affiliation:** American Baptist
**Freshman admissions:** selective; 2013-2014: 1,385 applied, 1,343 accepted. Either SAT or ACT required. ACT 25/75 percentile: 20-26. High school rank: 14% in top tenth, 46% in top quarter, 76% in top half
**Early decision deadline:** N/A, notification date: N/A
**Early action deadline:** N/A, notification date: N/A
**Application deadline (fall):** rolling

**Undergraduate student body:** 929 full time, 171 part time; 41% male, 59% female; 0% American Indian, 0% Asian, 4% black, 3% Hispanic, 3% multiracial, 0% Pacific Islander, 88% white, 1% international; 50% from in state; 56% live on campus; 0% of students in fraternities, 0% in sororities
**Most popular majors:** 19% Business Administration and Management, General, 6% Criminal Justice/Safety Studies, 12% Elementary Education and Teaching, 9% Kinesiology and Exercise Science, 21% Registered Nursing/Registered Nurse
**Expenses:** 2014-2015: $25,480; room/board: $6,700
**Financial aid:** (605) 331-6623; 77% of undergrads determined to have financial need; average aid package $19,348

## University of South Dakota

Vermillion SD
(605) 677-5434
**U.S. News ranking:** Nat. U., No. 168
**Website:** www.usd.edu
**Admissions email:** admiss@usd.edu
**Public;** founded 1862
**Freshman admissions:** selective; 2013-2014: 3,606 applied, 3,169 accepted. Either SAT or ACT required. ACT 25/75 percentile: 21-26. High school rank: 15% in top tenth, 38% in top quarter, 73% in top half
**Early decision deadline:** N/A, notification date: N/A
**Early action deadline:** N/A, notification date: N/A
**Application deadline (fall):** rolling
**Undergraduate student body:** 4,732 full time, 2,901 part time; 37% male, 63% female; 2% American Indian, 1% Asian, 2% black, 3% Hispanic, 3% multiracial, 0% Pacific Islander, 87% white, 1% international; 67% from in state; 32% live on campus; 18% of students in fraternities, 11% in sororities
**Most popular majors:** 15% Business, Management, Marketing, and Related Support Services, 11% Education, 21% Health Professions and Related Programs, 9% Psychology, 7% Social Sciences
**Expenses:** 2014-2015: $8,022 in state, $10,104 out of state; room/board: $7,454
**Financial aid:** (605) 677-5446; 67% of undergrads determined to have financial need; average aid package $6,439

## Aquinas College

Nashville TN
(800) 649-9956
**U.S. News ranking:** Reg. Coll. (S), No. 14
**Website:** www.aquinascollege.edu
**Admissions email:** admissions@aquinascollege.edu
**Private;** founded 1961
**Affiliation:** Roman Catholic
**Freshman admissions:** selective; 2013-2014: 119 applied, 62 accepted. Either SAT or ACT required. ACT 25/75 percentile: 23-27. High school rank: 21% in top tenth, 43% in top quarter, 86% in top half

**Early decision deadline:** N/A, notification date: N/A
**Early action deadline:** N/A, notification date: N/A
**Application deadline (fall):** rolling
**Undergraduate student body:** 187 full time, 321 part time; 18% male, 82% female; 0% American Indian, 4% Asian, 8% black, 4% Hispanic, 2% multiracial, 1% Pacific Islander, 73% white, 3% international; 84% from in state; 8% live on campus; 0% of students in fraternities, 0% in sororities
**Most popular majors:** 33% Business Administration and Management, General, 12% Elementary Education and Teaching, 39% Registered Nursing/Registered Nurse
**Expenses:** 2014-2015: $20,550; room/board: $4,350
**Financial aid:** (615) 297-7545

## Austin Peay State University

Clarksville TN
(931) 221-7661
**U.S. News ranking:** Reg. U. (S), No. 62
**Website:** www.apsu.edu
**Admissions email:** admissions@apsu.edu
**Public;** founded 1927
**Freshman admissions:** selective; 2013-2014: 3,551 applied, 3,054 accepted. Neither SAT nor ACT required. ACT 25/75 percentile: 19-24. High school rank: 14% in top tenth, 37% in top quarter, 72% in top half
**Early decision deadline:** N/A, notification date: N/A
**Early action deadline:** N/A, notification date: N/A
**Application deadline (fall):** 8/5
**Undergraduate student body:** 6,866 full time, 2,684 part time; 40% male, 60% female; 0% American Indian, 1% Asian, 19% black, 6% Hispanic, 5% multiracial, 0% Pacific Islander, 66% white, 0% international; 89% from in state; 15% live on campus; 12% of students in fraternities, 11% in sororities
**Most popular majors:** 16% Business, Management, Marketing, and Related Support Services, 6% Communication, Journalism, and Related Programs, 8% Education, 10% Health Professions and Related Programs, 7% Homeland Security, Law Enforcement, Firefighting and Related Protective Services
**Expenses:** 2014-2015: $7,462 in state, $23,860 out of state; room/board: $8,106
**Financial aid:** (931) 221-7907; 81% of undergrads determined to have financial need; average aid package $9,812

## Belmont University

Nashville TN
(615) 460-6785
**U.S. News ranking:** Reg. U. (S), No. 5
**Website:** www.belmont.edu
**Admissions email:** buadmission@mail.belmont.edu
**Private;** founded 1890
**Affiliation:** Nondenominational Christian
**Freshman admissions:** more selective; 2013-2014: 5,111 applied, 4,082 accepted. Either SAT or ACT required. ACT 25/75

percentile: 24-29. High school rank: 31% in top tenth, 61% in top quarter, 91% in top half
**Early decision deadline:** N/A, notification date: N/A
**Early action deadline:** N/A, notification date: N/A
**Application deadline (fall):** 8/1
**Undergraduate student body:** 5,117 full time, 389 part time; 40% male, 60% female; 0% American Indian, 2% Asian, 4% black, 4% Hispanic, 3% multiracial, 0% Pacific Islander, 82% white, 1% international; 35% from in state; 50% live on campus; N/A of students in fraternities, N/A in sororities
**Most popular majors:** 18% Business, Management, Marketing, and Related Support Services, 5% Communication, Journalism, and Related Programs, 5% Communications Technologies/Technicians and Support Services, 11% Health Professions and Related Programs, 28% Visual and Performing Arts
**Expenses:** 2014-2015: $28,660; room/board: $10,530
**Financial aid:** (615) 460-6403; 54% of undergrads determined to have financial need; average aid package $13,958

## Bethel University

McKenzie TN
(731) 352-4030
**U.S. News ranking:** Reg. U. (S), second tier
**Website:** www.bethel-college.edu
**Admissions email:** admissions@bethel-college.edu
**Private**
**Affiliation:** Cumberland Presbyterian Church
**Freshman admissions:** less selective; 2013-2014: 1,573 applied, 969 accepted. Neither SAT nor ACT required. ACT 25/75 percentile: 17-23. High school rank: N/A
**Early decision deadline:** N/A, notification date: N/A
**Early action deadline:** N/A, notification date: N/A
**Application deadline (fall):** rolling
**Undergraduate student body:** 3,606 full time, 633 part time; 44% male, 56% female; 0% American Indian, 0% Asian, 40% black, 1% Hispanic, 1% multiracial, 0% Pacific Islander, 55% white, 2% international; 86% from in state; 16% live on campus; N/A of students in fraternities, N/A in sororities
**Most popular majors:** 2% Biological and Biomedical Sciences, 54% Business, Management, Marketing, and Related Support Services, 4% Education, 3% Liberal Arts and Sciences, General Studies and Humanities, 2% Parks, Recreation, Leisure, and Fitness Studies
**Expenses:** 2013-2014: $15,714; room/board: $8,782
**Financial aid:** (731) 352-4233

## Bryan College

Dayton TN
(800) 277-9522
**U.S. News ranking:** Reg. Coll. (S), No. 22
**Website:** www.bryan.edu
**Admissions email:** admissions@bryan.edu
**Private;** founded 1930

**Affiliation:** Christian nondenominational
**Freshman admissions:** more selective; 2013-2014: 1,151 applied, 433 accepted. Either SAT or ACT required. ACT 25/75 percentile: 20-25. High school rank: N/A
**Early decision deadline:** N/A, notification date: N/A
**Early action deadline:** N/A, notification date: N/A
**Application deadline (fall):** rolling
**Undergraduate student body:** 1,129 full time, 444 part time; 44% male, 56% female; 0% American Indian, 0% Asian, 6% black, 2% Hispanic, 2% multiracial, 0% Pacific Islander, 86% white, 2% international
**Most popular majors:** 60% Business, Management, Marketing, and Related Support Services, 4% Communication, Journalism, and Related Programs, 5% Education, 4% Psychology, 4% Visual and Performing Arts
**Expenses:** 2014-2015: $22,200; room/board: $6,550
**Financial aid:** (423) 775-7339; 81% of undergrads determined to have financial need; average aid package $22,005

## Carson-Newman University

Jefferson City TN
(800) 678-9061
**U.S. News ranking:** Reg. Coll. (S), No. 15
**Website:** www.cn.edu
**Admissions email:** admitme@cn.edu
**Private;** founded 1851
**Affiliation:** Baptist
**Freshman admissions:** selective; 2013-2014: 3,916 applied, 2,607 accepted. Either SAT or ACT required. ACT 25/75 percentile: 20-26. High school rank: N/A
**Early decision deadline:** N/A, notification date: N/A
**Early action deadline:** N/A, notification date: N/A
**Application deadline (fall):** 8/8
**Undergraduate student body:** 1,658 full time, 55 part time; 45% male, 55% female; 0% American Indian, 1% Asian, 9% black, 1% Hispanic, 2% multiracial, 0% Pacific Islander, 82% white, 4% international; 81% from in state; 60% live on campus; N/A of students in fraternities, N/A in sororities
**Most popular majors:** Information not available
**Expenses:** 2014-2015: $24,440; room/board: $7,060
**Financial aid:** (865) 471-3247; 81% of undergrads determined to have financial need; average aid package $21,286

## Christian Brothers University

Memphis TN
(901) 321-3205
**U.S. News ranking:** Reg. U. (S), No. 26
**Website:** www.cbu.edu
**Admissions email:** admissions@cbu.edu
**Private;** founded 1871
**Affiliation:** Roman Catholic
**Freshman admissions:** selective; 2013-2014: 1,817 applied, 921 accepted. Either SAT or ACT required. ACT 25/75

percentile: 21-27. High school rank: 28% in top tenth, 60% in top quarter, 93% in top half
**Early decision deadline:** N/A, notification date: N/A
**Early action deadline:** N/A, notification date: N/A
**Application deadline (fall):** rolling
**Undergraduate student body:** 1,023 full time, 148 part time; 46% male, 54% female; 0% American Indian, 7% Asian, 32% black, 6% Hispanic, 3% multiracial, 0% Pacific Islander, 46% white, 3% international; 82% from in state; 45% live on campus; N/A of students in fraternities, N/A in sororities
**Most popular majors:** 10% Biological and Biomedical Sciences, 26% Business, Management, Marketing, and Related Support Services, 14% Engineering, 8% Health Professions and Related Programs, 16% Psychology
**Expenses:** 2014-2015: $29,190; room/board: $6,680
**Financial aid:** (901) 321-3305; 84% of undergrads determined to have financial need; average aid package $22,040

## Cumberland University
Lebanon TN
(615) 444-2562
**U.S. News ranking:** Reg. U. (S), second tier
**Website:** www.cumberland.edu
**Admissions email:** admissions@cumberland.edu
**Private;** founded 1842
**Freshman admissions:** selective; 2013-2014: 795 applied, 376 accepted. ACT required. ACT 25/75 percentile: 19-23. High school rank: 9% in top tenth, 29% in top quarter, 66% in top half
**Early decision deadline:** N/A, notification date: N/A
**Early action deadline:** N/A, notification date: N/A
**Application deadline (fall):** rolling
**Undergraduate student body:** 1,056 full time, 213 part time; 46% male, 54% female; 0% American Indian, 1% Asian, 12% black, 3% Hispanic, 0% multiracial, 0% Pacific Islander, 67% white, 4% international
**Most popular majors:** 4% Accounting, 7% Business/Commerce, General, 4% Physical Education Teaching and Coaching, 53% Registered Nursing/Registered Nurse
**Expenses:** 2014-2015: $20,200; room/board: $8,000
**Financial aid:** (615) 444-2562; 86% of undergrads determined to have financial need; average aid package $16,665

## East Tennessee State University[1]
Johnson City TN
(423) 439-4213
**U.S. News ranking:** Nat. U., second tier
**Website:** www.etsu.edu
**Admissions email:** go2etsu@etsu.edu
**Public;** founded 1911
**Application deadline (fall):** rolling
**Undergraduate student body:** N/A full time, N/A part time
**Expenses:** 2014-2015: $7,985 in state, $17,917 out of state; room/board: $7,822

**Financial aid:** (423) 439-4300; 82% of undergrads determined to have financial need; average aid package $9,043

## Fisk University
Nashville TN
(888) 702-0022
**U.S. News ranking:** Nat. Lib. Arts, No. 165
**Website:** www.fisk.edu
**Admissions email:** admissions@fisk.edu
**Private**
**Freshman admissions:** selective; 2013-2014: 1,269 applied, 269 accepted. Either SAT or ACT required. ACT 25/75 percentile: 17-23. High school rank: N/A
**Early decision deadline:** N/A, notification date: N/A
**Early action deadline:** N/A, notification date: N/A
**Application deadline (fall):** 5/1
**Undergraduate student body:** 585 full time, 22 part time; 34% male, 66% female; 0% American Indian, 1% Asian, 87% black, 1% Hispanic, 1% multiracial, 0% Pacific Islander, 1% white, 0% international
**Most popular majors:** 12% Biology/Biological Sciences, General, 10% Business/Commerce, General, 12% English Language and Literature, General, 2% History, General, 18% Psychology, General
**Expenses:** 2014-2015: $20,858; room/board: $10,160
**Financial aid:** (615) 329-8585

## Freed-Hardeman University
Henderson TN
(800) 630-3480
**U.S. News ranking:** Reg. U. (S), No. 43
**Website:** www.fhu.edu
**Admissions email:** admissions@fhu.edu
**Affiliation:** Church of Christ
**Freshman admissions:** selective; 2013-2014: 1,042 applied, 959 accepted. Either SAT or ACT required. ACT 25/75 percentile: 21-27. High school rank: 28% in top tenth, 55% in top quarter, 80% in top half
**Early decision deadline:** N/A, notification date: N/A
**Early action deadline:** N/A, notification date: N/A
**Application deadline (fall):** rolling
**Undergraduate student body:** 1,262 full time, 123 part time; 42% male, 58% female; 0% American Indian, 0% Asian, 6% black, 1% Hispanic, 2% multiracial, 0% Pacific Islander, 88% white, 2% international; 61% from in state; 81% live on campus; N/A of students in fraternities, N/A in sororities
**Most popular majors:** 8% Biological and Biomedical Sciences, 9% Business, Management, Marketing, and Related Support Services, 13% Education, 11% Multi/Interdisciplinary Studies, 13% Theology and Religious Vocations
**Expenses:** 2014-2015: $20,468; room/board: $7,464
**Financial aid:** (731) 989-6662; 82% of undergrads determined to have financial need; average aid package $16,915

## King University
Bristol TN
(423) 652-4861
**U.S. News ranking:** Reg. U. (S), No. 85
**Website:** www.king.edu
**Admissions email:** admissions@king.edu
**Private;** founded 1867
**Affiliation:** Presbyterian
**Freshman admissions:** selective; 2013-2014: 933 applied, 595 accepted. Either SAT or ACT required. ACT 25/75 percentile: 20-25. High school rank: 16% in top tenth, 40% in top quarter, 74% in top half
**Early decision deadline:** N/A, notification date: N/A
**Early action deadline:** N/A, notification date: N/A
**Application deadline (fall):** rolling
**Undergraduate student body:** 2,043 full time, 153 part time; 34% male, 66% female; 0% American Indian, 1% Asian, 6% black, 2% Hispanic, 1% multiracial, 0% Pacific Islander, 81% white, 3% international; 65% from in state; 42% live on campus; 0% of students in fraternities, 0% in sororities
**Most popular majors:** 35% Business Administration and Management, General, 2% Elementary Education and Teaching, 5% Information Technology, 3% Psychology, General, 42% Registered Nursing/Registered Nurse
**Expenses:** 2014-2015: $25,708; room/board: $8,180
**Financial aid:** (423) 652-4725; 88% of undergrads determined to have financial need; average aid package $15,001

## Lane College[1]
Jackson TN
(731) 426-7533
**U.S. News ranking:** Nat. Lib. Arts, second tier
**Website:** www.lanecollege.edu
**Admissions email:** admissions@lanecollege.edu
**Private;** founded 1882
**Affiliation:** Christian Methodist Episcopal
**Application deadline (fall):** 8/1
**Undergraduate student body:** N/A full time, N/A part time
**Expenses:** 2013-2014: $9,180; room/board: $6,520
**Financial aid:** (731) 426-7535

## Lee University
Cleveland TN
(423) 614-8500
**U.S. News ranking:** Reg. U. (S), No. 57
**Website:** www.leeuniversity.edu
**Admissions email:** admissions@leeuniversity.edu
**Private;** founded 1918
**Affiliation:** Pentecostal
**Freshman admissions:** selective; 2013-2014: 1,689 applied, 1,548 accepted. Either SAT or ACT required. ACT 25/75 percentile: 21-27. High school rank: 25% in top tenth, 49% in top quarter, 74% in top half
**Early decision deadline:** N/A, notification date: N/A
**Early action deadline:** N/A, notification date: N/A
**Application deadline (fall):** rolling

**Undergraduate student body:** 3,830 full time, 720 part time; 43% male, 57% female; 0% American Indian, 1% Asian, 6% black, 4% Hispanic, 1% multiracial, 0% Pacific Islander, 78% white, 5% international; 43% from in state; 47% live on campus; 9% of students in fraternities, 8% in sororities
**Most popular majors:** 8% Business, Management, Marketing, and Related Support Services, 24% Education, 10% Health Professions and Related Programs, 12% Psychology, 17% Theology and Religious Vocations
**Expenses:** 2014-2015: $14,280; room/board: $6,865
**Financial aid:** (423) 614-8300; 72% of undergrads determined to have financial need; average aid package $10,481

## LeMoyne-Owen College
Memphis TN
(901) 435-1500
**U.S. News ranking:** Reg. Coll. (S), second tier
**Website:** www.loc.edu/
**Admissions email:** admission@loc.edu
**Private;** founded 1862
**Affiliation:** United Church of Christ
**Freshman admissions:** less selective; 2013-2014: 1,247 applied, 342 accepted. Either SAT or ACT required. ACT 25/75 percentile: N/A. High school rank: N/A
**Early decision deadline:** N/A, notification date: N/A
**Early action deadline:** N/A, notification date: N/A
**Application deadline (fall):** 7/1
**Undergraduate student body:** 879 full time, 144 part time; 36% male, 64% female; 0% American Indian, 0% Asian, 99% black, 0% Hispanic, 0% multiracial, 0% Pacific Islander, 0% white, 1% international; 88% from in state; 10% live on campus; 5% of students in fraternities, 5% in sororities
**Most popular majors:** Information not available
**Expenses:** 2014-2015: $5,450; room/board: $5,910
**Financial aid:** (901) 942-7313; 97% of undergrads determined to have financial need; average aid package $9,981

## Lincoln Memorial University
Harrogate TN
(423) 869-6280
**U.S. News ranking:** Reg. U. (S), No. 53
**Website:** www.lmunet.edu
**Admissions email:** admissions@lmunet.edu
**Private;** founded 1897
**Freshman admissions:** selective; 2013-2014: 975 applied, 682 accepted. Either SAT or ACT required. ACT 25/75 percentile: 19-27. High school rank: N/A
**Early decision deadline:** N/A, notification date: N/A
**Early action deadline:** N/A, notification date: N/A
**Application deadline (fall):** rolling
**Undergraduate student body:** 1,185 full time, 528 part time; 29% male, 71% female; 0% American

Indian, 1% Asian, 4% black, 2% Hispanic, 1% multiracial, 0% Pacific Islander, 84% white, 2% international; 74% from in state; 37% live on campus; 3% of students in fraternities, 4% in sororities
**Most popular majors:** Information not available
**Expenses:** 2014-2015: $19,970; room/board: $9,700
**Financial aid:** (423) 869-6336; 86% of undergrads determined to have financial need; average aid package $17,135

## Lipscomb University
Nashville TN
(615) 966-1776
**U.S. News ranking:** Reg. U. (S), No. 18
**Website:** www.lipscomb.edu
**Admissions email:** admissions@lipscomb.edu
**Private;** founded 1891
**Affiliation:** Church of Christ
**Freshman admissions:** more selective; 2013-2014: 3,467 applied, 1,827 accepted. Either SAT or ACT required. ACT 25/75 percentile: 22-28. High school rank: 31% in top tenth, 55% in top quarter, 85% in top half
**Early decision deadline:** N/A, notification date: N/A
**Early action deadline:** N/A, notification date: N/A
**Application deadline (fall):** rolling
**Undergraduate student body:** 2,590 full time, 300 part time; 40% male, 60% female; 0% American Indian, 3% Asian, 8% black, 5% Hispanic, 2% multiracial, 0% Pacific Islander, 77% white, 2% international; 67% from in state; 52% live on campus; 16% of students in fraternities, 17% in sororities
**Most popular majors:** 12% Biological and Biomedical Sciences, 22% Business, Management, Marketing, and Related Support Services, 12% Education, 9% Health Professions and Related Programs, 7% Psychology
**Expenses:** 2014-2015: $27,390; room/board: $10,350
**Financial aid:** (615) 269-1791; 66% of undergrads determined to have financial need; average aid package $21,711

## Martin Methodist College[1]
Pulaski TN
(931) 363-9804
**U.S. News ranking:** Reg. Coll. (S), unranked
**Website:** www.martinmethodist.edu
**Admissions email:** admit@martinmethodist.edu
**Private**
**Application deadline (fall):** N/A
**Undergraduate student body:** N/A full time, N/A part time
**Expenses:** 2014-2015: $23,100; room/board: $8,400
**Financial aid:** (931) 363-9821; 83% of undergrads determined to have financial need; average aid package $10,700

## Maryville College
Maryville TN
(865) 981-8092
**U.S. News ranking:** Nat. Lib. Arts, second tier
**Website:** www.maryvillecollege.edu
**Admissions email:** admissions@maryvillecollege.edu
**Private;** founded 1819
**Affiliation:** Presbyterian
**Freshman admissions:** selective; 2013-2014: 2,196 applied, 1,594 accepted. Either SAT or ACT required. ACT 25/75 percentile: 21-26. High school rank: 14% in top tenth, 42% in top quarter, 79% in top half
**Early decision deadline:** N/A, notification date: N/A
**Early action deadline:** N/A, notification date: N/A
**Application deadline (fall):** 5/1
**Undergraduate student body:** 1,132 full time, 36 part time; 44% male, 56% female; 1% American Indian, 1% Asian, 7% black, 3% Hispanic, 2% multiracial, 0% Pacific Islander, 82% white, 4% international; 75% from in state; 70% live on campus; 0% of students in fraternities, 0% in sororities
**Most popular majors:** 10% Biological and Biomedical Sciences, 17% Business, Management, Marketing, and Related Support Services, 11% Education, 12% Psychology, 9% Visual and Performing Arts
**Expenses:** 2014-2015: $31,754; room/board: $10,088
**Financial aid:** (865) 981-8100; 85% of undergrads determined to have financial need; average aid package $30,274

## Memphis College of Art[1]
Memphis TN
(800) 727-1088
**U.S. News ranking:** Arts, unranked
**Website:** www.mca.edu
**Admissions email:** info@mca.edu
**Private**
**Application deadline (fall):** N/A
**Undergraduate student body:** N/A full time, N/A part time
**Expenses:** 2014-2015: $28,870; room/board: $8,600
**Financial aid:** (901) 272-5136; 88% of undergrads determined to have financial need; average aid package $21,314

## Middle Tennessee State University
Murfreesboro TN
(615) 898-2111
**U.S. News ranking:** Nat. U., second tier
**Website:** www.mtsu.edu
**Admissions email:** admissions@mtsu.edu
**Public;** founded 1911
**Freshman admissions:** selective; 2013-2014: 9,845 applied, 6,888 accepted. Either SAT or ACT required. ACT 25/75 percentile: 19-24. High school rank: 16% in top tenth, 43% in top quarter, 77% in top half
**Early decision deadline:** N/A, notification date: N/A
**Early action deadline:** N/A, notification date: N/A
**Application deadline (fall):** rolling

**Undergraduate student body:** 17,381 full time, 3,781 part time; 47% male, 53% female; 0% American Indian, 3% Asian, 21% black, 4% Hispanic, 3% multiracial, 0% Pacific Islander, 67% white, 1% international; 96% from in state; 19% live on campus; 5% of students in fraternities, 8% in sororities
**Most popular majors:** 13% Business, Management, Marketing, and Related Support Services, 7% Communication, Journalism, and Related Programs, 8% Education, 10% Liberal Arts and Sciences, General Studies and Humanities, 10% Visual and Performing Arts
**Expenses:** 2014-2015: $7,370 in state, $24,434 out of state; room/board: $8,302
**Financial aid:** (615) 898-2830; 78% of undergrads determined to have financial need; average aid package $8,850

## Milligan College
Milligan College TN
(423) 461-8730
**U.S. News ranking:** Reg. Coll. (S), No. 9
**Website:** www.milligan.edu
**Admissions email:** admissions@milligan.edu
**Private;** founded 1866
**Affiliation:** Christian Churches/Churches of Christ
**Freshman admissions:** more selective; 2013-2014: 612 applied, 418 accepted. Either SAT or ACT required. ACT 25/75 percentile: 22-26. High school rank: N/A
**Early decision deadline:** N/A, notification date: N/A
**Early action deadline:** N/A, notification date: N/A
**Application deadline (fall):** 8/1
**Undergraduate student body:** 884 full time, 89 part time; 38% male, 62% female; 1% American Indian, 1% Asian, 5% black, 4% Hispanic, 2% multiracial, 0% Pacific Islander, 84% white, 3% international
**Most popular majors:** Information not available
**Expenses:** 2014-2015: $28,730; room/board: $6,250
**Financial aid:** (423) 461-8949; 83% of undergrads determined to have financial need; average aid package $21,085

## Rhodes College
Memphis TN
(800) 844-5969
**U.S. News ranking:** Nat. Lib. Arts, No. 54
**Website:** www.rhodes.edu
**Admissions email:** adminfo@rhodes.edu
**Private;** founded 1848
**Affiliation:** Presbyterian (USA)
**Freshman admissions:** more selective; 2013-2014: 3,555 applied, 2,049 accepted. Either SAT or ACT required. ACT 25/75 percentile: 27-31. High school rank: 50% in top tenth, 82% in top quarter, 95% in top half
**Early decision deadline:** 11/1, notification date: 12/1
**Early action deadline:** 11/15, notification date: 1/15
**Application deadline (fall):** 1/15

**Undergraduate student body:** 2,014 full time, 13 part time; 42% male, 58% female; 0% American Indian, 6% Asian, 6% black, 3% Hispanic, 3% multiracial, 0% Pacific Islander, 76% white, 2% international; 27% from in state; 69% live on campus; 39% of students in fraternities, 60% in sororities
**Most popular majors:** 17% Biological and Biomedical Sciences, 15% Business, Management, Marketing, and Related Support Services, 11% English Language and Literature/Letters, 7% Physical Sciences, 22% Social Sciences
**Expenses:** 2014-2015: $41,572; room/board: $10,328
**Financial aid:** (901) 843-3810; 52% of undergrads determined to have financial need; average aid package $31,684

## Sewanee–University of the South
Sewanee TN
(800) 522-2234
**U.S. News ranking:** Nat. Lib. Arts, No. 45
**Website:** www.sewanee.edu
**Admissions email:** admiss@sewanee.edu
**Private;** founded 1857
**Affiliation:** Episcopal
**Freshman admissions:** more selective; 2013-2014: 3,285 applied, 1,980 accepted. Neither SAT nor ACT required. ACT 25/75 percentile: 26-30. High school rank: 42% in top tenth, 72% in top quarter, 96% in top half
**Early decision deadline:** 11/15, notification date: 12/15
**Early action deadline:** 12/1, notification date: 1/25
**Application deadline (fall):** 2/1
**Undergraduate student body:** 1,602 full time, 18 part time; 49% male, 51% female; 0% American Indian, 2% Asian, 5% black, 4% Hispanic, 4% multiracial, 0% Pacific Islander, 83% white, 3% international; 24% from in state; 96% live on campus; 67% of students in fraternities, 72% in sororities
**Most popular majors:** 12% Biological and Biomedical Sciences, 13% English Language and Literature/Letters, 9% History, 10% Multi/Interdisciplinary Studies, 17% Social Sciences
**Expenses:** 2014-2015: $37,100; room/board: $10,600
**Financial aid:** (931) 598-1312; 58% of undergrads determined to have financial need; average aid package $26,381

## South College[1]
Knoxville TN
(865) 251-1800
**U.S. News ranking:** Reg. Coll. (S), unranked
**Website:** www.southcollegetn.edu/
**Admissions email:** N/A
**For-profit**
**Application deadline (fall):** N/A
**Undergraduate student body:** N/A full time, N/A part time
**Expenses:** 2013-2014: $18,875; room/board: N/A
**Financial aid:** (865) 251-1800

## Southern Adventist University[1]
Collegedale TN
(423) 236-2844
**U.S. News ranking:** Reg. Coll. (S), No. 34
**Website:** www.southern.edu
**Admissions email:** admissions@southern.edu
**Private;** founded 1892
**Affiliation:** Seventh-day Adventist
**Application deadline (fall):** rolling
**Undergraduate student body:** N/A full time, N/A part time
**Expenses:** 2014-2015: $20,240; room/board: $5,850
**Financial aid:** (423) 236-2835

## Tennessee State University
Nashville TN
(615) 963-5101
**U.S. News ranking:** Nat. U., second tier
**Website:** www.tnstate.edu
**Admissions email:** jcade@tnstate.edu
**Public;** founded 1912
**Freshman admissions:** less selective; 2013-2014: 6,286 applied, 3,328 accepted. Either SAT or ACT required. ACT 25/75 percentile: 16-20. High school rank: N/A
**Early decision deadline:** N/A, notification date: N/A
**Early action deadline:** N/A, notification date: N/A
**Application deadline (fall):** 7/1
**Undergraduate student body:** 5,356 full time, 1,393 part time; 39% male, 61% female; 0% American Indian, 1% Asian, 77% black, 1% Hispanic, 0% multiracial, 0% Pacific Islander, 15% white, 5% international; 77% from in state; N/A live on campus; N/A of students in fraternities, N/A in sororities
**Most popular majors:** Information not available
**Expenses:** 2014-2015: $6,776 in state, $20,132 out of state; room/board: $7,126
**Financial aid:** (615) 963-5701; 90% of undergrads determined to have financial need; average aid package $10,159

## Tennessee Technological University
Cookeville TN
(800) 255-8881
**U.S. News ranking:** Reg. U. (S), No. 34
**Website:** www.tntech.edu
**Admissions email:** admissions@tntech.edu
**Public;** founded 1915
**Freshman admissions:** selective; 2013-2014: 4,973 applied, 4,633 accepted. Either SAT or ACT required. ACT 25/75 percentile: 20-26. High school rank: 25% in top tenth, 55% in top quarter, 83% in top half
**Early decision deadline:** N/A, notification date: N/A
**Early action deadline:** N/A, notification date: N/A
**Application deadline (fall):** rolling
**Undergraduate student body:** 9,140 full time, 943 part time; 56% male, 44% female; 0% American

Indian, 1% Asian, 4% black, 2% Hispanic, 2% multiracial, 0% Pacific Islander, 82% white, 7% international; 98% from in state; 53% live on campus; 9% of students in fraternities, 11% in sororities
**Most popular majors:** 5% Accounting, 7% Liberal Arts and Sciences/Liberal Studies, 5% Mechanical Engineering, 5% Registered Nursing/Registered Nurse, 16% Teacher Education, Multiple Levels
**Expenses:** 2014-2015: $7,950 in state, $23,450 out of state; room/board: $8,700
**Financial aid:** (931) 372-3073; 68% of undergrads determined to have financial need; average aid package $11,110

## Tennessee Wesleyan College
Athens TN
(423) 746-5286
**U.S. News ranking:** Reg. Coll. (S), No. 41
**Website:** www.twcnet.edu
**Admissions email:** admissions@twcnet.edu
**Private;** founded 1857
**Affiliation:** United Methodist
**Freshman admissions:** selective; 2013-2014: 790 applied, 564 accepted. Either SAT or ACT required. ACT 25/75 percentile: 19-24. High school rank: 20% in top tenth, 20% in top quarter, 80% in top half
**Early decision deadline:** N/A, notification date: N/A
**Early action deadline:** N/A, notification date: N/A
**Application deadline (fall):** 8/31
**Undergraduate student body:** 988 full time, 77 part time; 38% male, 62% female; 0% American Indian, 1% Asian, 8% black, 2% Hispanic, 2% multiracial, 0% Pacific Islander, 83% white, 1% international; 90% from in state; 32% live on campus; 4% of students in fraternities, 8% in sororities
**Most popular majors:** 28% Business, Management, Marketing, and Related Support Services, 13% Education, 23% Health Professions and Related Programs, 7% Multi/Interdisciplinary Studies, 8% Parks, Recreation, Leisure, and Fitness Studies
**Expenses:** 2014-2015: $22,300; room/board: $7,100
**Financial aid:** (423) 746-5209; 83% of undergrads determined to have financial need; average aid package $15,994

## Trevecca Nazarene University
Nashville TN
(615) 248-1320
**U.S. News ranking:** Nat. U., second tier
**Website:** www.trevecca.edu
**Admissions email:** admissions_und@trevecca.edu
**Private;** founded 1901
**Affiliation:** Nazarene
**Freshman admissions:** selective; 2013-2014: 903 applied, 618 accepted. Either SAT or ACT required. ACT 25/75 percentile: 21-26. High school rank: N/A
**Early decision deadline:** N/A, notification date: N/A

**Early action deadline:** N/A, notification date: N/A
**Application deadline (fall):** 8/1
**Undergraduate student body:** 1,016 full time, 476 part time; 45% male, 55% female; 1% American Indian, 1% Asian, 8% black, 3% Hispanic, 2% multiracial, 0% Pacific Islander, 71% white, 1% international; 63% from in state; 50% live on campus; 0% of students in fraternities, 0% in sororities
**Most popular majors:** 46% Business, Management, Marketing, and Related Support Services, 8% Computer and Information Sciences and Support Services, 10% Education, 6% Health Professions and Related Programs, 6% Theology and Religious Vocations
**Expenses:** 2014-2015: $23,126; room/board: $8,060
**Financial aid:** (615) 248-1242

## Tusculum College[1]

Greeneville TN
(800) 729-0256
**U.S. News ranking:** Reg. U. (S), second tier
**Website:** www.tusculum.edu
**Admissions email:** admissions@tusculum.edu
**Private**
**Application deadline (fall):** N/A
**Undergraduate student body:** N/A full time, N/A part time
**Expenses:** 2013-2014: $22,250; room/board: $8,500
**Financial aid:** (423) 636-7377

## Union University

Jackson TN
(800) 338-6466
**U.S. News ranking:** Reg. U. (S), No. 12
**Website:** www.uu.edu
**Admissions email:** info@uu.edu
**Private;** founded 1823
**Affiliation:** Southern Baptist
**Freshman admissions:** more selective; 2013-2014: 1,930 applied, 1,432 accepted. Either SAT or ACT required. ACT 25/75 percentile: 22-29. High school rank: 33% in top tenth, 62% in top quarter, 85% in top half
**Early decision deadline:** N/A, notification date: N/A
**Early action deadline:** N/A, notification date: N/A
**Application deadline (fall):** 8/15
**Undergraduate student body:** 2,172 full time, 657 part time; 39% male, 61% female; 0% American Indian, 1% Asian, 14% black, 2% Hispanic, 2% multiracial, 0% Pacific Islander, 77% white, 2% international; 69% from in state; 65% live on campus; 27% of students in fraternities, 23% in sororities
**Most popular majors:** Information not available
**Expenses:** 2014-2015: $28,190; room/board: $8,430
**Financial aid:** (731) 661-5015; 76% of undergrads determined to have financial need; average aid package $18,303

## University of Memphis

Memphis TN
(901) 678-2111
**U.S. News ranking:** Nat. U., second tier
**Website:** www.memphis.edu
**Admissions email:** recruitment@memphis.edu
**Public;** founded 1912
**Freshman admissions:** selective; 2013-2014: 6,107 applied, 4,470 accepted. Either SAT or ACT required. ACT 25/75 percentile: 20-26. High school rank: 16% in top tenth, 43% in top quarter, 75% in top half
**Early decision deadline:** N/A, notification date: N/A
**Early action deadline:** N/A, notification date: N/A
**Application deadline (fall):** 7/1
**Undergraduate student body:** 12,317 full time, 4,904 part time; 40% male, 60% female; 0% American Indian, 3% Asian, 38% black, 3% Hispanic, 3% multiracial, 0% Pacific Islander, 51% white, 1% international; 97% from in state; 13% live on campus; 3% of students in fraternities, 8% in sororities
**Most popular majors:** 18% Business, Management, Marketing, and Related Support Services, 9% Education, 9% Health Professions and Related Programs, 6% Liberal Arts and Sciences, General Studies and Humanities, 10% Multi-/Interdisciplinary Studies
**Expenses:** 2014-2015: $8,619 in state, $13,275 out of state; room/board: $8,976
**Financial aid:** (901) 678-4825; 78% of undergrads determined to have financial need; average aid package $9,087

## University of Tennessee

Knoxville TN
(865) 974-2184
**U.S. News ranking:** Nat. U., No. 106
**Website:** admissions.utk.edu/undergraduate
**Admissions email:** admissions@utk.edu
**Public;** founded 1794
**Freshman admissions:** more selective; 2013-2014: 14,396 applied, 10,435 accepted. Either SAT or ACT required. ACT 25/75 percentile: 24-29. High school rank: 52% in top tenth, 91% in top quarter, 100% in top half
**Early decision deadline:** N/A, notification date: N/A
**Early action deadline:** N/A, notification date: N/A
**Application deadline (fall):** 12/1
**Undergraduate student body:** 19,799 full time, 1,383 part time; 51% male, 49% female; 0% American Indian, 3% Asian, 7% black, 3% Hispanic, 3% multiracial, 0% Pacific Islander, 81% white, 2% international; 91% from in state; 37% live on campus; 14% of students in fraternities, 21% in sororities
**Most popular majors:** 20% Business, Management, Marketing, and Related Support Services, 8% Communication, Journalism, and Related Programs, 9% Engineering, 10% Psychology, 10% Social Sciences

**Expenses:** 2014-2015: $11,246 in state, $29,696 out of state; room/board: $10,296
**Financial aid:** (865) 974-3131; 61% of undergrads determined to have financial need; average aid package $12,126

## University of Tennessee–Chattanooga

Chattanooga TN
(423) 425-4662
**U.S. News ranking:** Reg. U. (S), No. 57
**Website:** www.utc.edu
**Admissions email:** utcmocs@utc.edu
**Public;** founded 1886
**Freshman admissions:** selective; 2013-2014: 7,628 applied, 5,917 accepted. Either SAT or ACT required. ACT 25/75 percentile: 21-25. High school rank: N/A in top tenth, 45% in top quarter, 86% in top half
**Early decision deadline:** N/A, notification date: N/A
**Early action deadline:** N/A, notification date: N/A
**Application deadline (fall):** 5/1
**Undergraduate student body:** 9,066 full time, 1,231 part time; 45% male, 55% female; 0% American Indian, 2% Asian, 11% black, 3% Hispanic, 8% multiracial, 0% Pacific Islander, 74% white, 1% international; 94% from in state; 31% live on campus; 9% of students in fraternities, 13% in sororities
**Most popular majors:** 22% Business Administration and Management, General, 11% Education, General, 6% Engineering, General, 7% Kinesiology and Exercise Science, 8% Psychology, General
**Expenses:** 2014-2015: $8,138 in state, $24,256 out of state; room/board: $8,110
**Financial aid:** (423) 425-4677; 62% of undergrads determined to have financial need; average aid package $9,571

## University of Tennessee–Martin

Martin TN
(800) 829-8861
**U.S. News ranking:** Reg. U. (S), No. 53
**Website:** www.utm.edu
**Admissions email:** admitme@utm.edu
**Public;** founded 1900
**Freshman admissions:** selective; 2013-2014: 3,640 applied, 2,791 accepted. Either SAT or ACT required. ACT 25/75 percentile: 20-25. High school rank: 27% in top tenth, 59% in top quarter, 87% in top half
**Early decision deadline:** N/A, notification date: N/A
**Early action deadline:** N/A, notification date: N/A
**Application deadline (fall):** 8/1
**Undergraduate student body:** 5,927 full time, 1,098 part time; 42% male, 58% female; 0% American Indian, 0% Asian, 17% black, 2% Hispanic, 2% multiracial, 0% Pacific Islander, 76% white, 3% international; 96% from in state; 30% live on campus; 8% of students in fraternities, 10% in sororities

**Most popular majors:** 7% Agriculture, Agriculture Operations, and Related Sciences, 18% Marketing/Marketing Management, General, 13% Multi/Interdisciplinary Studies, Other, 9% Parks, Recreation, Leisure, and Fitness Studies, 12% Teacher Education and Professional Development, Specific Levels and Methods
**Expenses:** 2014-2015: $7,880 in state, $22,660 out of state; room/board: $7,141
**Financial aid:** (731) 587-7040; 77% of undergrads determined to have financial need; average aid package $13,357

## Vanderbilt University

Nashville TN
(800) 288-0432
**U.S. News ranking:** Nat. U., No. 16
**Website:** www.vanderbilt.edu
**Admissions email:** admissions@vanderbilt.edu
**Private;** founded 1873
**Freshman admissions:** most selective; 2013-2014: 31,099 applied, 3,963 accepted. Either SAT or ACT required. ACT 25/75 percentile: 32-34. High school rank: 88% in top tenth, 95% in top quarter, 98% in top half
**Early decision deadline:** 11/1, notification date: 12/15
**Early action deadline:** N/A, notification date: N/A
**Application deadline (fall):** 1/1
**Undergraduate student body:** 6,764 full time, 71 part time; 50% male, 50% female; 0% American Indian, 8% Asian, 8% black, 8% Hispanic, 5% multiracial, 0% Pacific Islander, 61% white, 8% international; 12% from in state; 86% live on campus; 30% of students in fraternities, 55% in sororities
**Most popular majors:** 11% Economics, General, 5% Mathematics, General, 9% Multi-/Interdisciplinary Studies, Other, 5% Political Science and Government, General, 9% Social Sciences, General
**Expenses:** 2014-2015: $43,838; room/board: $14,382
**Financial aid:** (615) 322-3591; 49% of undergrads determined to have financial need; average aid package $44,720

## Victory University[1]

Memphis TN
(901) 320-9797
**U.S. News ranking:** Reg. Coll. (S), second tier
**Website:** www.victory.edu
**Admissions email:** admissions@victory.edu
**For-profit**
**Application deadline (fall):** N/A
**Undergraduate student body:** N/A full time, N/A part time
**Expenses:** 2013-2014: $9,760; room/board: $10,116
**Financial aid:** (901) 320-9787

## Watkins College of Art, Design & Film[1]

Nashville TN
(615) 383-4848
**U.S. News ranking:** Arts, unranked
**Website:** www.watkins.edu
**Admissions email:** admission@watkins.edu
**Private**
**Application deadline (fall):** N/A
**Undergraduate student body:** N/A full time, N/A part time
**Expenses:** 2013-2014: $19,710; room/board: $9,390
**Financial aid:** (615) 383-4848

## Welch College

Nashville TN
(888) 979-3524
**U.S. News ranking:** Reg. Coll. (S), No. 52
**Website:** www.welch.edu
**Admissions email:** Recruit@welch.edu
**Private;** founded 1942
**Affiliation:** Free Will Baptist
**Freshman admissions:** selective; 2013-2014: 167 applied, 87 accepted. Either SAT or ACT required. ACT 25/75 percentile: 18-25. High school rank: 22% in top tenth, 42% in top quarter, 60% in top half
**Early decision deadline:** N/A, notification date: N/A
**Early action deadline:** N/A, notification date: N/A
**Application deadline (fall):** rolling
**Undergraduate student body:** 234 full time, 104 part time; 51% male, 49% female; 0% American Indian, 1% Asian, 10% black, 2% Hispanic, 1% multiracial, 0% Pacific Islander, 85% white, 1% international; 46% from in state; 68% live on campus; 84% of students in fraternities, 96% in sororities
**Most popular majors:** 8% Biological and Biomedical Sciences, 8% Business, Management, Marketing, and Related Support Services, 30% Education, 8% Psychology, 32% Theology and Religious Vocations
**Expenses:** 2014-2015: $16,891; room/board: $6,842
**Financial aid:** (615) 844-5250; 89% of undergrads determined to have financial need; average aid package $12,160

## Abilene Christian University

Abilene TX
(800) 460-6228
**U.S. News ranking:** Reg. U. (W), No. 17
**Website:** www.acu.edu
**Admissions email:** info@admissions.acu.edu
**Private;** founded 1906
**Affiliation:** Church of Christ
**Freshman admissions:** more selective; 2013-2014: 10,188 applied, 4,986 accepted. Either SAT or ACT required. ACT 25/75 percentile: 21-27. High school rank: 25% in top tenth, 57% in top quarter, 87% in top half
**Early decision deadline:** N/A, notification date: N/A
**Early action deadline:** 11/1, notification date: 12/1

**Application deadline (fall):** 2/15
**Undergraduate student body:** 3,510 full time, 217 part time; 43% male, 57% female; 0% American Indian, 1% Asian, 8% black, 12% Hispanic, 4% multiracial, 0% Pacific Islander, 71% white, 4% international; 84% from in state; 48% live on campus; 24% of students in fraternities, 24% in sororities
**Most popular majors:** 7% Accounting, 7% Business Administration and Management, General, 4% Elementary Education and Teaching, 7% Human Development and Family Studies, General, 5% Psychology, General
**Expenses:** 2014-2015: $29,450; room/board: $9,000
**Financial aid:** (325) 674-2643; 68% of undergrads determined to have financial need; average aid package $20,300

## Amberton University[1]
Garland TX
(972) 279-6511
**U.S. News ranking:** Reg. U. (W), unranked
**Website:** www.amberton.edu
**Admissions email:** advisor@amberton.edu
**Private**
**Application deadline (fall):** N/A
**Undergraduate student body:** N/A full time, N/A part time
**Expenses:** N/A
**Financial aid:** (972) 279-6511

## Angelo State University
San Angelo TX
(325) 942-2041
**U.S. News ranking:** Reg. U. (W), second tier
**Website:** www.angelo.edu
**Admissions email:** admissions@angelo.edu
**Public;** founded 1928
**Freshman admissions:** selective; 2013-2014: 2,599 applied, 2,092 accepted. Either SAT or ACT required. ACT 25/75 percentile: 18-23. High school rank: 11% in top tenth, 35% in top quarter, 73% in top half
**Early decision deadline:** N/A, notification date: N/A
**Early action deadline:** N/A, notification date: N/A
**Undergraduate student body:** 4,726 full time, 820 part time; 46% male, 54% female; 0% American Indian, 1% Asian, 8% black, 30% Hispanic, 2% multiracial, 0% Pacific Islander, 55% white, 3% international; 97% from in state; 20% live on campus; 5% of students in fraternities, 3% in sororities
**Most popular majors:** 6% Agriculture, Agriculture Operations, and Related Sciences, 13% Business, Management, Marketing, and Related Support Services, 14% Health Professions and Related Programs, 14% Multi/Interdisciplinary Studies, 7% Psychology
**Expenses:** 2014-2015: $7,642 in state, $18,502 out of state; room/board: $7,484
**Financial aid:** (325) 942-2246; 69% of undergrads determined to have financial need; average aid package $10,579

## Art Institute of Houston[1]
Houston TX
(800) 275-4244
**U.S. News ranking:** Arts, unranked
**Website:** www.artinstitute.edu/houston/
**Admissions email:** N/A
**For-profit**
**Application deadline (fall):** N/A
**Undergraduate student body:** N/A full time, N/A part time
**Expenses:** 2013-2014: $17,668; room/board: $11,367
**Financial aid:** (713) 353-4311

## Austin College
Sherman TX
(800) 442-5363
**U.S. News ranking:** Nat. Lib. Arts, No. 89
**Website:** www.austincollege.edu
**Admissions email:** admission@austincollege.edu
**Private;** founded 1849
**Affiliation:** Presbyterian
**Freshman admissions:** more selective; 2013-2014: 3,138 applied, 1,839 accepted. Either SAT or ACT required. SAT 25/75 percentile: 1100-1330. High school rank: 35% in top tenth, 74% in top quarter, 95% in top half
**Early decision deadline:** N/A, notification date: N/A
**Early action deadline:** 1/15, notification date: 3/1
**Application deadline (fall):** 5/1
**Undergraduate student body:** 1,204 full time, 4 part time; 49% male, 51% female; 1% American Indian, 15% Asian, 6% black, 16% Hispanic, 1% multiracial, 0% Pacific Islander, 58% white, 3% international; 91% from in state; 81% live on campus; 20% of students in fraternities, 16% in sororities
**Most popular majors:** 7% Biological and Biomedical Sciences, 11% Business, Management, Marketing, and Related Support Services, 7% Foreign Languages, Literatures, and Linguistics, 16% Psychology, 18% Social Sciences
**Expenses:** 2014-2015: $34,840; room/board: $11,503
**Financial aid:** (903) 813-2900; 67% of undergrads determined to have financial need; average aid package $28,827

## Baylor University
Waco TX
(800) 229-5678
**U.S. News ranking:** Nat. U., No. 71
**Website:** www.baylor.edu
**Admissions email:** Admissions@Baylor.edu
**Private;** founded 1845
**Affiliation:** Baptist
**Freshman admissions:** more selective; 2013-2014: 29,249 applied, 16,809 accepted. Either SAT or ACT required. ACT 25/75 percentile: 24-29. High school rank: 42% in top tenth, 75% in top quarter, 97% in top half
**Early decision deadline:** N/A, notification date: N/A
**Early action deadline:** 11/1, notification date: 1/15
**Application deadline (fall):** 2/1
**Undergraduate student body:** 13,059 full time, 233 part time; 42% male, 58% female;

0% American Indian, 6% Asian, 7% black, 14% Hispanic, 5% multiracial, 0% Pacific Islander, 64% white, 3% international; 76% from in state; 40% live on campus; 14% of students in fraternities, 22% in sororities
**Most popular majors:** 4% Accounting, 9% Biology/Biological Sciences, General, 4% Finance, General, 6% Psychology, General, 6% Registered Nursing/Registered Nurse
**Expenses:** 2014-2015: $38,290; room/board: $11,309
**Financial aid:** (254) 710-2611; 58% of undergrads determined to have financial need; average aid package $24,975

## Brazosport College[1]
Lake Jackson TX
(979) 230-3020
**U.S. News ranking:** Reg. Coll. (W), unranked
**Website:** www.brazosport.edu
**Admissions email:** N/A
**Public**
**Application deadline (fall):** N/A
**Undergraduate student body:** N/A full time, N/A part time
**Expenses:** 2013-2014: $3,315 in state, $4,725 out of state; room/board: N/A
**Financial aid:** (979) 230-0337

## College of Saints John Fisher & Thomas More[1]
Fort Worth TX
(817) 923-8459
**U.S. News ranking:** Nat. Lib. Arts, second tier
**Website:** fishermore.edu/
**Admissions email:** more-Info@cstm.edu
**Private**
**Application deadline (fall):** N/A
**Undergraduate student body:** N/A full time, N/A part time
**Expenses:** N/A
**Financial aid:** (325) 673-1934

## Concordia University Texas[1]
Austin TX
(800) 865-4282
**U.S. News ranking:** Reg. U. (W), second tier
**Website:** www.concordia.edu
**Admissions email:** admissions@concordia.edu
**Private;** founded 1926
**Affiliation:** Lutheran Church-Missouri Synod
**Application deadline (fall):** 8/1
**Undergraduate student body:** N/A full time, N/A part time
**Expenses:** 2014-2015: $26,960; room/board: $8,980
**Financial aid:** (512) 486-1283; 76% of undergrads determined to have financial need; average aid package $18,951

## Dallas Baptist University
Dallas TX
(214) 333-5360
**U.S. News ranking:** Reg. U. (W), No. 35
**Website:** www.dbu.edu
**Admissions email:** admiss@dbu.edu
**Private;** founded 1898
**Affiliation:** Baptist

**Freshman admissions:** selective; 2013-2014: 2,631 applied, 1,113 accepted. Either SAT or ACT required. ACT 25/75 percentile: 18-27. High school rank: 20% in top tenth, 46% in top quarter, 77% in top half
**Early decision deadline:** N/A, notification date: N/A
**Early action deadline:** N/A, notification date: N/A
**Application deadline (fall):** rolling
**Undergraduate student body:** 2,463 full time, 972 part time; 42% male, 58% female; 1% American Indian, 2% Asian, 16% black, 12% Hispanic, 0% multiracial, 0% Pacific Islander, 62% white, 6% international; 90% from in state; 54% live on campus; 7% of students in fraternities, 10% in sororities
**Most popular majors:** 15% Business Administration and Management, General, 15% Multi-/Interdisciplinary Studies, Other, 9% Psychology, General, 9% Religious Education, 7% Speech Communication and Rhetoric
**Expenses:** 2014-2015: $23,650; room/board: $6,930
**Financial aid:** (214) 333-5460; 64% of undergrads determined to have financial need; average aid package $15,400

## East Texas Baptist University
Marshall TX
(800) 804-3828
**U.S. News ranking:** Reg. Coll. (W), No. 13
**Website:** www.etbu.edu
**Admissions email:** admissions@etbu.edu
**Private;** founded 1912
**Affiliation:** Baptist
**Freshman admissions:** selective; 2013-2014: 709 applied, 522 accepted. Either SAT or ACT required. ACT 25/75 percentile: 18-22. High school rank: 16% in top tenth, 40% in top quarter, 75% in top half
**Early decision deadline:** N/A, notification date: N/A
**Early action deadline:** N/A, notification date: N/A
**Application deadline (fall):** 8/21
**Undergraduate student body:** 1,066 full time, 130 part time; 47% male, 53% female; 1% American Indian, 0% Asian, 18% black, 10% Hispanic, 3% multiracial, 0% Pacific Islander, 66% white, 1% international; 93% from in state; 85% live on campus; 2% of students in fraternities, 1% in sororities
**Most popular majors:** 15% Business, Management, Marketing, and Related Support Services, 19% Education, 11% Health Professions and Related Programs, 14% Multi/Interdisciplinary Studies, 8% Psychology
**Expenses:** 2014-2015: $23,280; room/board: $8,297
**Financial aid:** (903) 923-2137; 86% of undergrads determined to have financial need; average aid package $17,276

## Hardin-Simmons University
Abilene TX
(325) 670-1206
**U.S. News ranking:** Reg. U. (W), No. 35
**Website:** www.hsutx.edu/
**Admissions email:** enroll@hsutx.edu
**Private;** founded 1891
**Affiliation:** Baptist
**Freshman admissions:** selective; 2013-2014: 2,091 applied, 786 accepted. Either SAT or ACT required. ACT 25/75 percentile: 20-25. High school rank: 19% in top tenth, 56% in top quarter, 83% in top half
**Early decision deadline:** N/A, notification date: N/A
**Early action deadline:** N/A, notification date: N/A
**Application deadline (fall):** rolling
**Undergraduate student body:** 1,561 full time, 229 part time; 48% male, 52% female; 0% American Indian, 2% Asian, 6% black, 15% Hispanic, 2% multiracial, 0% Pacific Islander, 71% white, 2% international; 96% from in state; 45% live on campus; 3% of students in fraternities, 5% in sororities
**Most popular majors:** 9% Biological and Biomedical Sciences, 12% Business, Management, Marketing, and Related Support Services, 13% Education, 12% Health Professions and Related Programs, 14% Parks, Recreation, Leisure, and Fitness Studies
**Expenses:** 2014-2015: $22,350; room/board: $6,962
**Financial aid:** (325) 670-5891; 72% of undergrads determined to have financial need; average aid package $20,386

## Houston Baptist University
Houston TX
(281) 649-3211
**U.S. News ranking:** Reg. U. (W), No. 68
**Website:** www.hbu.edu
**Admissions email:** admissions@hbu.edu
**Private;** founded 1960
**Affiliation:** Baptist
**Freshman admissions:** selective; 2013-2014: 11,892 applied, 4,310 accepted. Either SAT or ACT required. SAT 25/75 percentile: 960-1170. High school rank: 21% in top tenth, 53% in top quarter, 80% in top half
**Early decision deadline:** N/A, notification date: N/A
**Early action deadline:** N/A, notification date: N/A
**Application deadline (fall):** rolling
**Undergraduate student body:** 2,005 full time, 166 part time; 37% male, 63% female; 0% American Indian, 13% Asian, 19% black, 26% Hispanic, 7% multiracial, 0% Pacific Islander, 28% white, 4% international; 96% from in state; 33% live on campus; 10% of students in fraternities, 11% in sororities
**Most popular majors:** 16% Biology/Biological Sciences, General, 17% Business/Commerce, General, 8% Education, General, 8% Psychology, General, 14% Registered Nursing/Registered Nurse
**Expenses:** 2014-2015: $28,750; room/board: $6,740

Financial aid: (281) 649-3389; 76% of undergrads determined to have financial need; average aid package $24,867

## Howard Payne University

Brownwood TX
(325) 649-8020
U.S. News ranking: Reg. Coll. (W), No. 15
Website: www.hputx.edu
Admissions email: enroll@hputx.edu
Private; founded 1889
Affiliation: Baptist
Freshman admissions: less selective; 2013-2014: 1,572 applied, 844 accepted. Either SAT or ACT required. SAT 25/75 percentile: 860-1050. High school rank: 5% in top tenth, 24% in top quarter, 61% in top half
Early decision deadline: N/A, notification date: N/A
Early action deadline: N/A, notification date: N/A
Application deadline (fall): rolling
Undergraduate student body: 983 full time, 117 part time; 53% male, 47% female; 0% American Indian, 0% Asian, 9% black, 20% Hispanic, 3% multiracial, 0% Pacific Islander, 65% white, 0% international; 98% from in state; 59% live on campus; 7% of students in fraternities, 10% in sororities
Most popular majors: 14% Business, Management, Marketing, and Related Support Services, 11% Education, 10% Parks, Recreation, Leisure, and Fitness Studies, 9% Social Sciences, 11% Theology and Religious Vocations
Expenses: 2014-2015: $24,600; room/board: $7,154
Financial aid: (325) 649-8014; 85% of undergrads determined to have financial need; average aid package $17,043

## Huston-Tillotson University[1]

Austin TX
(512) 505-3029
U.S. News ranking: Nat. Lib. Arts, second tier
Website: htu.edu/
Admissions email: admission@htu.edu
Private
Application deadline (fall): N/A
Undergraduate student body: N/A full time, N/A part time
Expenses: 2013-2014: $13,494; room/board: $7,242
Financial aid: (512) 505-3031

## Jarvis Christian College

Hawkins TX
(903) 730-4890
U.S. News ranking: Reg. Coll. (W), second tier
Website: www.jarvis.edu
Admissions email: Recruitment@jarvis.edu
Private; founded 1912
Affiliation: Christian Church (Disciples of Christ)
Freshman admissions: least selective; 2013-2014: 453 applied, 453 accepted. Either SAT or ACT required. ACT 25/75

percentile: 13-18. High school rank: 1% in top tenth, 8% in top quarter, 26% in top half
Early decision deadline: N/A, notification date: N/A
Early action deadline: N/A, notification date: N/A
Application deadline (fall): 8/1
Undergraduate student body: 569 full time, 40 part time; 54% male, 46% female; 0% American Indian, 0% Asian, 88% black, 7% Hispanic, 0% multiracial, 0% Pacific Islander, 4% white, 0% international; 84% from in state; 77% live on campus; 12% of students in fraternities, 2% in sororities
Most popular majors: 14% Biological and Biomedical Sciences, 14% Business, Management, Marketing, and Related Support Services, 21% Education, 33% Homeland Security, Law Enforcement, Firefighting and Related Protective Services, 7% Public Administration and Social Service Professions
Expenses: 2014-2015: $11,369; room/board: $8,183
Financial aid: (903) 769-5740; 96% of undergrads determined to have financial need; average aid package $17,996

## Lamar University

Beaumont TX
(409) 880-8888
U.S. News ranking: Nat. U., second tier
Website: www.lamar.edu
Admissions email: admissions@lamar.edu
Public; founded 1923
Freshman admissions: selective; 2013-2014: 4,720 applied, 3,616 accepted. Either SAT or ACT required. SAT 25/75 percentile: 870-1080. High school rank: 15% in top tenth, 37% in top quarter, 70% in top half
Early decision deadline: N/A, notification date: N/A
Early action deadline: N/A, notification date: N/A
Application deadline (fall): 8/1
Undergraduate student body: 6,604 full time, 2,778 part time; 42% male, 58% female; 0% American Indian, 4% Asian, 30% black, 11% Hispanic, 2% multiracial, 0% Pacific Islander, 49% white, 2% international; 95% from in state; 21% live on campus; 4% of students in fraternities, 2% in sororities
Most popular majors: 14% Business, Management, Marketing, and Related Support Services, 7% Engineering, 8% General Studies, 11% Health Professions and Related Programs, 19% Multi-/Interdisciplinary Studies, Other
Expenses: 2014-2015: $9,361 in state, $19,681 out of state; room/board: $8,052
Financial aid: (409) 880-8450; 66% of undergrads determined to have financial need; average aid package $6,782

## LeTourneau University

Longview TX
(903) 233-4300
U.S. News ranking: Reg. U. (W), No. 27
Website: www.letu.edu
Admissions email: admissions@letu.edu
Private; founded 1946
Affiliation: Christian interdenominational
Freshman admissions: more selective; 2013-2014: 1,831 applied, 758 accepted. Neither SAT nor ACT required. SAT 25/75 percentile: 1030-1300. High school rank: 47% in top tenth, 67% in top quarter, 89% in top half
Early decision deadline: N/A, notification date: N/A
Early action deadline: N/A, notification date: N/A
Application deadline (fall): rolling
Undergraduate student body: 1,332 full time, 973 part time; 53% male, 47% female; 0% American Indian, 1% Asian, 9% black, 9% Hispanic, 3% multiracial, 0% Pacific Islander, 64% white, 4% international; 54% from in state; 74% live on campus; N/A of students in fraternities, N/A in sororities
Most popular majors: 37% Business, Management, Marketing, and Related Support Services, 17% Education, 11% Engineering, 7% Engineering Technologies and Engineering-Related Fields, 7% Psychology
Expenses: 2014-2015: $26,910; room/board: $9,300
Financial aid: (903) 233-3430; 73% of undergrads determined to have financial need; average aid package $21,666

## Lubbock Christian University

Lubbock TX
(806) 720-7151
U.S. News ranking: Reg. U. (W), No. 84
Website: www.lcu.edu
Admissions email: admissions@lcu.edu
Private; founded 1957
Affiliation: Churches of Christ
Freshman admissions: selective; 2013-2014: 783 applied, 743 accepted. Either SAT or ACT required. ACT 25/75 percentile: 19-24. High school rank: 17% in top tenth, 39% in top quarter, 77% in top half
Early decision deadline: N/A, notification date: N/A
Early action deadline: N/A, notification date: N/A
Application deadline (fall): 6/1
Undergraduate student body: 1,258 full time, 273 part time; 39% male, 61% female; 1% American Indian, 0% Asian, 6% black, 21% Hispanic, 0% multiracial, 0% Pacific Islander, 70% white, 2% international; 91% from in state; 33% live on campus; 19% of students in fraternities, 17% in sororities
Most popular majors: 18% Business, Management, Marketing, and Related Support Services, 17% Education, 25% Health Professions and Related Programs, 5% Parks, Recreation, Leisure, and Fitness Studies, 5% Public Administration and Social Service Professions

Expenses: 2014-2015: $19,400; room/board: $5,860
Financial aid: (800) 933-7601; 74% of undergrads determined to have financial need; average aid package $14,728

## McMurry University

Abilene TX
(325) 793-4700
U.S. News ranking: Reg. Coll. (W), No. 18
Website: www.mcm.edu
Admissions email: admissions@mcm.edu
Private; founded 1923
Affiliation: Methodist
Freshman admissions: selective; 2013-2014: 1,396 applied, 827 accepted. Either SAT or ACT required. SAT 25/75 percentile: 860-1090. High school rank: 16% in top tenth, 37% in top quarter, 72% in top half
Early decision deadline: N/A, notification date: N/A
Early action deadline: N/A, notification date: N/A
Application deadline (fall): 8/15
Undergraduate student body: 1,032 full time, 180 part time; 51% male, 49% female; 1% American Indian, 1% Asian, 16% black, 21% Hispanic, 2% multiracial, 0% Pacific Islander, 58% white, 1% international; 94% from in state; 45% live on campus; 16% of students in fraternities, 19% in sororities
Most popular majors: 18% Business, Management, Marketing, and Related Support Services, 20% Education, 9% Psychology, 9% Social Sciences, 7% Visual and Performing Arts
Expenses: 2014-2015: $24,844; room/board: $7,988
Financial aid: (325) 793-4709; 85% of undergrads determined to have financial need; average aid package $20,125

## Midland College[1]

Midland TX
(432) 685-5502
U.S. News ranking: Reg. Coll. (W), unranked
Website: www.midland.edu/
Admissions email: pebensberger@midland.edu
Public
Application deadline (fall): N/A
Undergraduate student body: N/A full time, N/A part time
Expenses: 2013-2014: $4,007 in state, $5,177 out of state; room/board: $4,821
Financial aid: (432) 685-4757

## Midwestern State University

Wichita Falls TX
(800) 842-1922
U.S. News ranking: Reg. U. (W), second tier
Website: www.mwsu.edu
Admissions email: admissions@mwsu.edu
Public; founded 1922
Freshman admissions: less selective; 2013-2014: 3,023 applied, 2,170 accepted. Either SAT or ACT required. SAT 25/75 percentile: 900-1090. High school rank: 12% in top tenth, 36% in top quarter, 73% in top half
Early decision deadline: N/A, notification date: N/A

Early action deadline: 8/7, notification date: N/A
Application deadline (fall): 8/7
Undergraduate student body: 3,861 full time, 1,332 part time; 42% male, 58% female; 1% American Indian, 3% Asian, 15% black, 15% Hispanic, 2% multiracial, 0% Pacific Islander, 58% white, 5% international; 92% from in state; 26% live on campus; 7% of students in fraternities, 8% in sororities
Most popular majors: 5% Accounting, 5% Business Administration and Management, General, 13% Multi-/Interdisciplinary Studies, Other, 11% Radiologic Technology/Science - Radiographer, 15% Registered Nursing/Registered Nurse
Expenses: 2014-2015: $7,753 in state, $9,703 out of state; room/board: $6,810
Financial aid: (940) 397-4214; 61% of undergrads determined to have financial need; average aid package $9,475

## Our Lady of the Lake University

San Antonio TX
(800) 436-6558
U.S. News ranking: Nat. U., second tier
Website: www.ollusa.edu
Admissions email: admission@lake.ollusa.edu
Private; founded 1895
Affiliation: Roman Catholic
Freshman admissions: less selective; 2013-2014: 7,262 applied, 1,649 accepted. Either SAT or ACT required. SAT 25/75 percentile: 870-960. High school rank: 12% in top tenth, 33% in top quarter, 68% in top half
Early decision deadline: N/A, notification date: N/A
Early action deadline: N/A, notification date: N/A
Application deadline (fall): rolling
Undergraduate student body: 1,312 full time, 243 part time; 28% male, 72% female; 1% American Indian, 1% Asian, 8% black, 73% Hispanic, 0% multiracial, 0% Pacific Islander, 12% white, 1% international; 86% from in state; 38% live on campus; 2% of students in fraternities, 4% in sororities
Most popular majors: 5% Business Administration, Management and Operations, 8% Communication Sciences and Disorders, General, 4% Criminal Justice/Law Enforcement Administration, 6% Psychology, General, 9% Social Work
Expenses: 2014-2015: $24,596; room/board: $7,436
Financial aid: (210) 434-6711; 89% of undergrads determined to have financial need; average aid package $19,833

## Prairie View A&M University

Prairie View TX
(877) PVA-MU30
U.S. News ranking: Reg. U. (W), second tier
Website: www.pvamu.edu
Admissions email: admission@pvamu.edu
Public; founded 1876

**Freshman admissions:** less selective; 2013-2014: 4,548 applied, 3,871 accepted. Either SAT or ACT required. SAT 25/75 percentile: 750-940. High school rank: 5% in top tenth, 14% in top quarter, 52% in top half
**Early decision deadline:** N/A, notification date: N/A
**Early action deadline:** N/A, notification date: N/A
**Application deadline (fall):** 6/1
**Undergraduate student body:** 6,234 full time, 497 part time; 42% male, 58% female; 0% American Indian, 2% Asian, 86% black, 6% Hispanic, 1% multiracial, 0% Pacific Islander, 3% white, 1% international; 92% from in state; 25% live on campus; 1% of students in fraternities, 2% in sororities
**Most popular majors:** 10% Business, Management, Marketing, and Related Support Services, 12% Engineering, 24% Health Professions and Related Programs, 8% Legal Professions and Studies, 8% Psychology
**Expenses:** 2014-2015: $8,098 in state, $18,718 out of state; room/board: $7,467
**Financial aid:** (936) 857-2424; 72% of undergrads determined to have financial need; average aid package $14,265

## Rice University

Houston TX
(713) 348-7423
**U.S. News ranking:** Nat. U., No. 19
**Website:** www.rice.edu
**Admissions email:** admission@rice.edu
**Private;** founded 1912
**Freshman admissions:** most selective; 2013-2014: 15,415 applied, 2,581 accepted. Either SAT or ACT required. SAT 25/75 percentile: 1370-1550. High school rank: 87% in top tenth, 97% in top quarter, 100% in top half
**Early decision deadline:** 11/1, notification date: 12/15
**Early action deadline:** N/A, notification date: N/A
**Application deadline (fall):** 1/1
**Undergraduate student body:** 3,904 full time, 61 part time; 51% male, 49% female; 0% American Indian, 21% Asian, 6% black, 15% Hispanic, 5% multiracial, 0% Pacific Islander, 39% white, 11% international; 51% from in state; 71% live on campus; 0% of students in fraternities, 0% in sororities
**Most popular majors:** 7% Biochemistry, 6% Chemical Engineering, 5% Economics, General, 5% Electrical and Electronics Engineering, 6% Psychology, General
**Expenses:** 2014-2015: $40,566; room/board: $13,400
**Financial aid:** (713) 348-4958; 41% of undergrads determined to have financial need; average aid package $36,556

## Sam Houston State University

Huntsville TX
(936) 294-1828
**U.S. News ranking:** Nat. U., second tier
**Website:** www.shsu.edu
**Admissions email:** admissions@shsu.edu
**Public;** founded 1879
**Freshman admissions:** less selective; 2013-2014: 8,291 applied, 6,126 accepted. Either SAT or ACT required. SAT 25/75 percentile: 880-1090. High school rank: 14% in top tenth, 38% in top quarter, 87% in top half
**Early decision deadline:** N/A, notification date: N/A
**Early action deadline:** N/A, notification date: N/A
**Application deadline (fall):** 8/1
**Undergraduate student body:** 13,359 full time, 2,896 part time; 41% male, 59% female; 0% American Indian, 1% Asian, 18% black, 19% Hispanic, 2% multiracial, 0% Pacific Islander, 56% white, 1% international; 99% from in state; 21% live on campus; 2% of students in fraternities, 3% in sororities
**Most popular majors:** 6% Agriculture, Agriculture Operations, and Related Sciences, 21% Business, Management, Marketing, and Related Support Services, 18% Homeland Security, Law Enforcement, Firefighting and Related Protective Services, 12% Multi/Interdisciplinary Studies, 6% Parks, Recreation, Leisure, and Fitness Studies
**Expenses:** 2014-2015: $8,932 in state, $19,792 out of state; room/board: $8,324
**Financial aid:** (936) 294-1774; 64% of undergrads determined to have financial need; average aid package $10,279

## Schreiner University[1]

Kerrville TX
(800) 343-4919
**U.S. News ranking:** Reg. Coll. (W), unranked
**Website:** www.schreiner.edu
**Admissions email:** admissions@schreiner.edu
**Private;** founded 1923
**Affiliation:** Presbyterian
**Application deadline (fall):** 8/1
**Undergraduate student body:** N/A full time, N/A part time
**Expenses:** 2013-2014: $22,484; room/board: $10,250
**Financial aid:** (830) 792-7217

## Southern Methodist University

Dallas TX
(800) 323-0672
**U.S. News ranking:** Nat. U., No. 58
**Website:** www.smu.edu
**Admissions email:** ugadmission@smu.edu
**Private;** founded 1911
**Affiliation:** United Methodist
**Freshman admissions:** more selective; 2013-2014: 12,080 applied, 6,125 accepted. Either SAT or ACT required. ACT 25/75 percentile: 27-31. High school rank: 48% in top tenth, 80% in top quarter, 95% in top half
**Early decision deadline:** 11/1, notification date: 12/31

**Early action deadline:** 11/1, notification date: 12/31
**Application deadline (fall):** 1/15
**Undergraduate student body:** 6,119 full time, 238 part time; 49% male, 51% female; 0% American Indian, 7% Asian, 5% black, 12% Hispanic, 3% multiracial, 0% Pacific Islander, 66% white, 7% international; 50% from in state; 38% live on campus; 32% of students in fraternities, 48% in sororities
**Most popular majors:** 21% Business, Management, Marketing, and Related Support Services, 9% Communication, Journalism, and Related Programs, 8% Engineering, 7% Psychology, 16% Social Sciences
**Expenses:** 2014-2015: $45,940; room/board: $14,645
**Financial aid:** (214) 768-3016; 40% of undergrads determined to have financial need; average aid package $35,977

## South Texas College[1]

McAllen TX
(956) 872-8323
**U.S. News ranking:** Reg. Coll. (W), unranked
**Website:** www.southtexascollege.edu/
**Admissions email:** N/A
**Public**
**Application deadline (fall):** N/A
**Undergraduate student body:** N/A full time, N/A part time
**Expenses:** 2013-2014: $3,530 in state, $7,260 out of state; room/board: N/A
**Financial aid:** (956) 872-8375

## Southwestern Adventist University

Keene TX
(817) 645-3921
**U.S. News ranking:** Reg. Coll. (W), unranked
**Website:** www.swau.edu
**Admissions email:** admissions@swau.edu
**Private;** founded 1893
**Affiliation:** Seventh-day Adventist
**Freshman admissions:** N/A; 2013-2014: 746 applied, 235 accepted. SAT required. SAT 25/75 percentile: 830-1060. High school rank: 14% in top tenth, 26% in top quarter, 65% in top half
**Early decision deadline:** N/A, notification date: N/A
**Early action deadline:** N/A, notification date: N/A
**Application deadline (fall):** rolling
**Undergraduate student body:** 640 full time, 150 part time; 42% male, 58% female; 0% American Indian, 4% Asian, 12% black, 41% Hispanic, 4% multiracial, 1% Pacific Islander, 24% white, 14% international; 73% from in state; 30% live on campus; 0% of students in fraternities, 0% in sororities
**Most popular majors:** Information not available
**Expenses:** 2014-2015: $19,460; room/board: $7,400
**Financial aid:** (817) 645-3921

## Southwestern Assemblies of God University

Waxahachie TX
(888) 937-7248
**U.S. News ranking:** Reg. U. (W), second tier
**Website:** www.sagu.edu/
**Admissions email:** admissions@sagu.edu
**Private;** founded 1927
**Affiliation:** Assemblies of God
**Freshman admissions:** selective; 2013-2014: 1,837 applied, 550 accepted. Either SAT or ACT required. ACT 25/75 percentile: 19-24. High school rank: N/A
**Early decision deadline:** N/A, notification date: N/A
**Early action deadline:** N/A, notification date: N/A
**Application deadline (fall):** rolling
**Undergraduate student body:** 1,434 full time, 266 part time; 48% male, 52% female; 2% American Indian, 1% Asian, 10% black, 20% Hispanic, 1% multiracial, 1% Pacific Islander, 64% white, 0% international; 63% from in state; N/A live on campus; N/A of students in fraternities, N/A in sororities
**Most popular majors:** 29% Bible/Biblical Studies, 6% Elementary Education and Teaching, 6% General Studies, 2% Psychology, General, 13% Religious Education
**Expenses:** 2014-2015: $18,580; room/board: $6,340
**Financial aid:** N/A; 86% of undergrads determined to have financial need; average aid package $7,487

## Southwestern Christian College[1]

Terrell TX
(972) 524-3341
**U.S. News ranking:** Reg. Coll. (W), unranked
**Website:** www.swcc.edu
**Admissions email:** N/A
**Private**
**Application deadline (fall):** N/A
**Undergraduate student body:** N/A full time, N/A part time
**Expenses:** 2013-2014: $7,620; room/board: $5,155
**Financial aid:** (972) 524-3341

## Southwestern University

Georgetown TX
(800) 252-3166
**U.S. News ranking:** Nat. Lib. Arts, No. 87
**Website:** www.southwestern.edu
**Admissions email:** admission@southwestern.edu
**Private;** founded 1840
**Affiliation:** United Methodist
**Freshman admissions:** more selective; 2013-2014: 3,546 applied, 1,850 accepted. Either SAT or ACT required. SAT 25/75 percentile: 1055-1280. High school rank: 37% in top tenth, 72% in top quarter, 95% in top half
**Early decision deadline:** N/A, notification date: N/A
**Early action deadline:** 11/15, notification date: 2/15
**Application deadline (fall):** rolling
**Undergraduate student body:** 1,519 full time, 16 part time; 43% male, 57% female; 1% American

Indian, 4% Asian, 5% black, 19% Hispanic, 2% multiracial, 0% Pacific Islander, 67% white, 1% international; 90% from in state; 77% live on campus; 37% of students in fraternities, 29% in sororities
**Most popular majors:** 13% Biological and Biomedical Sciences, 11% Business, Management, Marketing, and Related Support Services, 9% Psychology, 19% Social Sciences, 10% Visual and Performing Arts
**Expenses:** 2014-2015: $36,120; room/board: $11,760
**Financial aid:** (512) 863-1259; 65% of undergrads determined to have financial need; average aid package $30,966

## St. Edward's University

Austin TX
(512) 448-8500
**U.S. News ranking:** Reg. U. (W), No. 13
**Website:** www.stedwards.edu
**Admissions email:** seu.admit@stedwards.edu
**Private;** founded 1885
**Affiliation:** Roman Catholic
**Freshman admissions:** selective; 2013-2014: 3,694 applied, 2,901 accepted. Either SAT or ACT required. SAT 25/75 percentile: 1020-1220. High school rank: 20% in top tenth, 54% in top quarter, 83% in top half
**Early decision deadline:** N/A, notification date: N/A
**Early action deadline:** N/A, notification date: N/A
**Application deadline (fall):** 5/1
**Undergraduate student body:** 3,442 full time, 647 part time; 39% male, 61% female; 0% American Indian, 3% Asian, 4% black, 37% Hispanic, 3% multiracial, 0% Pacific Islander, 43% white, 8% international; 88% from in state; 39% live on campus; N/A of students in fraternities, N/A in sororities
**Most popular majors:** 4% Biology/Biological Sciences, General, 8% Business Administration and Management, General, 8% Communication and Media Studies, Other, 11% Psychology, General, 4% Teacher Education and Professional Development, Specific Subject Areas, Other
**Expenses:** 2014-2015: $36,550; room/board: $11,234
**Financial aid:** (512) 448-8520; 66% of undergrads determined to have financial need; average aid package $26,026

## Stephen F. Austin State University

Nacogdoches TX
(936) 468-2504
**U.S. News ranking:** Reg. U. (W), No. 84
**Website:** www.sfasu.edu
**Admissions email:** admissions@sfasu.edu
**Public;** founded 1923
**Freshman admissions:** selective; 2013-2014: 11,383 applied, 6,474 accepted. Either SAT or ACT required. SAT 25/75 percentile: 890-1090. High school rank: 13% in top tenth, 41% in top quarter, 77% in top half

Early decision deadline: N/A, notification date: N/A
Early action deadline: N/A, notification date: N/A
Application deadline (fall): rolling
Undergraduate student body: 9,333 full time, 1,673 part time; 37% male, 63% female; 1% American Indian, 1% Asian, 22% black, 14% Hispanic, 2% multiracial, 0% Pacific Islander, 57% white, 1% international; 98% from in state; 45% live on campus; 14% of students in fraternities, 9% in sororities
Most popular majors: 4% Business Administration and Management, General, 4% Human Development and Family Studies, General, 8% Kinesiology and Exercise Science, 15% Multi-/Interdisciplinary Studies, Other, 7% Registered Nursing/Registered Nurse
Expenses: 2014-2015: $8,892 in state, $19,752 out of state; room/board: $8,868
Financial aid: (936) 468-2403

## St. Mary's University of San Antonio

San Antonio TX
(210) 436-3126
U.S. News ranking: Reg. U. (W), No. 21
Website: www.stmarytx.edu
Admissions email: uadm@stmarytx.edu
Private; founded 1852
Affiliation: Roman Catholic
Freshman admissions: selective; 2013-2014: 5,147 applied, 2,997 accepted. Either SAT or ACT required. SAT 25/75 percentile: 950-1150. High school rank: 28% in top tenth, 57% in top quarter, 83% in top half
Early decision deadline: N/A, notification date: N/A
Early action deadline: N/A, notification date: N/A
Application deadline (fall): rolling
Undergraduate student body: 2,284 full time, 109 part time; 44% male, 56% female; 0% American Indian, 3% Asian, 4% black, 73% Hispanic, 0% multiracial, 0% Pacific Islander, 14% white, 3% international; 93% from in state; 58% live on campus; 1% of students in fraternities, 3% in sororities
Most popular majors: 11% Biological and Biomedical Sciences, 23% Business, Management, Marketing, and Related Support Services, 7% Homeland Security, Law Enforcement, Firefighting and Related Protective Services, 7% Psychology, 18% Social Sciences
Expenses: 2013-2014: $25,126; room/board: $8,666
Financial aid: (210) 436-3141

## Sul Ross State University

Alpine TX
(432) 837-8050
U.S. News ranking: Reg. U. (W), second tier
Website: www.sulross.edu
Admissions email: admissions@sulross.edu
Public; founded 1917
Freshman admissions: least selective; 2013-2014: N/A applied, N/A accepted. Either SAT or ACT required. ACT 25/75 percentile: 14-19. High school

rank: 3% in top tenth, 16% in top quarter, 49% in top half
Early decision deadline: N/A, notification date: N/A
Early action deadline: N/A, notification date: N/A
Application deadline (fall): rolling
Undergraduate student body: 1,213 full time, 790 part time; 44% male, 56% female; 0% American Indian, 1% Asian, 11% black, 48% Hispanic, 0% multiracial, 0% Pacific Islander, 37% white, 1% international
Most popular majors: Information not available
Expenses: 2013-2014: $4,764 in state, $12,276 out of state; room/board: $6,810
Financial aid: (432) 837-8059

## Tarleton State University

Stephenville TX
(800) 687-8236
U.S. News ranking: Reg. U. (W), second tier
Website: www.tarleton.edu
Admissions email: uadm@tarleton.edu
Public; founded 1899
Freshman admissions: less selective; 2013-2014: 5,013 applied, 3,844 accepted. Either SAT or ACT required. SAT 25/75 percentile: 870-1060. High school rank: 8% in top tenth, 24% in top quarter, 68% in top half
Early decision deadline: N/A, notification date: N/A
Early action deadline: 3/1, notification date: N/A
Application deadline (fall): 7/21
Undergraduate student body: 7,413 full time, 2,172 part time; 40% male, 60% female; 1% American Indian, 1% Asian, 7% black, 15% Hispanic, 2% multiracial, 0% Pacific Islander, 73% white, 1% international; 98% from in state; 33% live on campus; N/A of students in fraternities, N/A in sororities
Most popular majors: 11% Agriculture, Agriculture Operations, and Related Sciences, 17% Business, Management, Marketing, and Related Support Services, 16% Multi-/Interdisciplinary Studies, 8% Parks, Recreation, Leisure, and Fitness Studies, 6% Psychology
Expenses: 2014-2015: $7,237 in state, $18,097 out of state; room/board: $7,556
Financial aid: (254) 968-9070; 67% of undergrads determined to have financial need; average aid package $9,517

## Texas A&M International University

Laredo TX
(956) 326-2200
U.S. News ranking: Reg. U. (W), No. 63
Website: www.tamiu.edu
Admissions email: enroll@tamiu.edu
Public; founded 1970
Freshman admissions: selective; 2013-2014: 4,917 applied, 2,404 accepted. Either SAT or ACT required. SAT 25/75 percentile: 800-1010. High school rank: 20% in top tenth, 53% in top quarter, 86% in top half

Early decision deadline: N/A, notification date: N/A
Early action deadline: N/A, notification date: N/A
Application deadline (fall): 7/1
Undergraduate student body: 4,022 full time, 2,563 part time; 42% male, 58% female; 0% American Indian, 1% Asian, 1% black, 92% Hispanic, 0% multiracial, 0% Pacific Islander, 2% white, 2% international; 99% from in state; 9% live on campus; 1% of students in fraternities, 1% in sororities
Most popular majors: 21% Business, Management, Marketing, and Related Support Services, 19% Health Professions and Related Programs, 14% Homeland Security, Law Enforcement, Firefighting and Related Protective Services, 8% Multi/Interdisciplinary Studies, 9% Psychology
Expenses: 2014-2015: $9,180 in state, $18,054 out of state; room/board: $8,028
Financial aid: (956) 326-2225; 88% of undergrads determined to have financial need; average aid package $9,480

## Texas A&M University–College Station

College Station TX
(979) 845-3741
U.S. News ranking: Nat. U., No. 68
Website: www.tamu.edu
Admissions email: admissions@tamu.edu
Public; founded 1876
Freshman admissions: more selective; 2013-2014: 31,388 applied, 21,725 accepted. Either SAT or ACT required. SAT 25/75 percentile: 1070-1290. High school rank: 53% in top tenth, 78% in top quarter, 98% in top half
Early decision deadline: N/A, notification date: N/A
Early action deadline: N/A, notification date: N/A
Application deadline (fall): 12/1
Undergraduate student body: 39,856 full time, 4,459 part time; 52% male, 48% female; 0% American Indian, 5% Asian, 3% black, 20% Hispanic, 2% multiracial, 0% Pacific Islander, 68% white, 1% international; 96% from in state; 25% live on campus; 6% of students in fraternities, 11% in sororities
Most popular majors: 11% Agriculture, Agriculture Operations, and Related Sciences, 8% Biological and Biomedical Sciences, 17% Business, Management, Marketing, and Related Support Services, 14% Engineering, 9% Multi/Interdisciplinary Studies
Expenses: 2014-2015: $9,180 in state, $26,356 out of state; room/board: $9,522
Financial aid: (979) 845-3236; 42% of undergrads determined to have financial need; average aid package $14,855

## Texas A&M University–Commerce

Commerce TX
(903) 886-5000
U.S. News ranking: Nat. U., second tier
Website: www.tamuc.edu/
Admissions email: Admissions@tamuc.edu
Public; founded 1889
Freshman admissions: selective; 2013-2014: 4,236 applied, 2,888 accepted. Either SAT or ACT required. SAT 25/75 percentile: 880-1090. High school rank: 16% in top tenth, 40% in top quarter, 72% in top half
Early decision deadline: N/A, notification date: N/A
Early action deadline: N/A, notification date: N/A
Application deadline (fall): 8/15
Undergraduate student body: 5,086 full time, 1,804 part time; 41% male, 59% female; 1% American Indian, 2% Asian, 20% black, 14% Hispanic, 3% multiracial, 0% Pacific Islander, 55% white, 4% international; 98% from in state; 28% live on campus; 9% of students in fraternities, 7% in sororities
Most popular majors: 15% Business, Management, Marketing, and Related Support Services, 5% Liberal Arts and Sciences, General Studies and Humanities, 38% Multi/Interdisciplinary Studies, 5% Parks, Recreation, Leisure, and Fitness Studies, 6% Psychology
Expenses: 2014-2015: $7,096 in state, $17,956 out of state; room/board: N/A
Financial aid: (903) 886-5096; 74% of undergrads determined to have financial need; average aid package $9,884

## Texas A&M University–Corpus Christi

Corpus Christi TX
(361) 825-2624
U.S. News ranking: Nat. U., second tier
Website: www.tamucc.edu
Admissions email: admiss@tamucc.edu
Public; founded 1947
Freshman admissions: less selective; 2013-2014: 7,217 applied, 6,281 accepted. Either SAT or ACT required. SAT 25/75 percentile: 870-1060. High school rank: 10% in top tenth, 34% in top quarter, 72% in top half
Early decision deadline: N/A, notification date: N/A
Early action deadline: N/A, notification date: N/A
Application deadline (fall): 7/1
Undergraduate student body: 7,237 full time, 1,915 part time; 42% male, 58% female; 0% American Indian, 2% Asian, 5% black, 46% Hispanic, 2% multiracial, 0% Pacific Islander, 40% white, 3% international; 97% from in state; 17% live on campus; 5% of students in fraternities, 5% in sororities
Most popular majors: 10% Biological and Biomedical Sciences, 18% Business, Management, Marketing, and Related Support Services,

15% Health Professions and Related Programs, 14% Multi/Interdisciplinary Studies, 7% Psychology
Expenses: 2013-2014: $7,778 in state, $18,398 out of state; room/board: $9,965
Financial aid: (361) 825-2338; 62% of undergrads determined to have financial need; average aid package $8,898

## Texas A&M University–Kingsville

Kingsville TX
(361) 593-2315
U.S. News ranking: Nat. U., second tier
Website: www.tamuk.edu
Admissions email: admissions@tamuk.edu
Public; founded 1925
Freshman admissions: less selective; 2013-2014: 6,499 applied, 5,720 accepted. Either SAT or ACT required. ACT 25/75 percentile: 16-21. High school rank: 9% in top tenth, 35% in top quarter, 76% in top half
Early decision deadline: N/A, notification date: N/A
Early action deadline: N/A, notification date: N/A
Application deadline (fall): rolling
Undergraduate student body: 4,935 full time, 1,186 part time; 51% male, 49% female; 0% American Indian, 1% Asian, 7% black, 68% Hispanic, 1% multiracial, 0% Pacific Islander, 20% white, 2% international; 99% from in state; 33% live on campus; 5% of students in fraternities, 5% in sororities
Most popular majors: 15% Communication Sciences and Disorders, General, 5% Criminology, 5% Kinesiology and Exercise Science, 10% Multi-/Interdisciplinary Studies, General, 5% Psychology, General
Expenses: 2014-2015: $7,434 in state, $18,294 out of state; room/board: $8,131
Financial aid: (361) 593-2173; 80% of undergrads determined to have financial need; average aid package $11,872

## Texas A&M University–Texarkana

Texarkana TX
(903) 223-3069
U.S. News ranking: Reg. U. (W), second tier
Website: www.tamut.edu
Admissions email: admissions@tamut.edu
Public; founded 1971
Freshman admissions: selective; 2013-2014: 730 applied, 262 accepted. Either SAT or ACT required. ACT 25/75 percentile: 19-24. High school rank: 16% in top tenth, 39% in top quarter, 72% in top half
Early decision deadline: N/A, notification date: N/A
Early action deadline: N/A, notification date: N/A
Application deadline (fall): rolling
Undergraduate student body: 924 full time, 477 part time; 36% male, 64% female; N/A American Indian, N/A Asian, N/A black, N/A Hispanic, N/A multiracial, N/A Pacific Islander, N/A white, N/A international

**Most popular majors:** Information not available
**Expenses:** 2013-2014: $5,578 in state, $14,002 out of state; room/board: $8,800
**Financial aid:** (903) 223-3060

## Texas Christian University

Fort Worth TX
(817) 257-7490
**U.S. News ranking:** Nat. U., No. 76
**Website:** www.tcu.edu
**Admissions email:** frogmail@tcu.edu
**Private;** founded 1873
**Affiliation:** Christian Church (Disciples of Christ)
**Freshman admissions:** more selective; 2013-2014: 18,551 applied, 8,791 accepted. Either SAT or ACT required. ACT 25/75 percentile: 25-29. High school rank: 42% in top tenth, 75% in top quarter, 96% in top half
**Early decision deadline:** 11/1, notification date: 1/1
**Early action deadline:** 11/1, notification date: 1/1
**Application deadline (fall):** 2/15
**Undergraduate student body:** 8,326 full time, 314 part time; 40% male, 60% female; 1% American Indian, 2% Asian, 5% black, 11% Hispanic, 1% multiracial, 0% Pacific Islander, 74% white, 5% international; 61% from in state; 48% live on campus; 42% of students in fraternities, 53% in sororities
**Most popular majors:** 24% Business, Management, Marketing, and Related Support Services, 16% Communication, Journalism, and Related Programs, 6% Education, 13% Health Professions and Related Programs, 8% Social Sciences
**Expenses:** 2014-2015: $38,600; room/board: $11,380
**Financial aid:** (817) 257-7858; 41% of undergrads determined to have financial need; average aid package $22,885

## Texas College[1]

Tyler TX
(903) 593-8311
**U.S. News ranking:** Reg. Coll. (W), unranked
**Website:** www.texascollege.edu
**Admissions email:** cmarshall-biggins@texascollege.edu
**Private**
**Application deadline (fall):** N/A
**Undergraduate student body:** N/A full time, N/A part time
**Expenses:** 2013-2014: $10,008; room/board: $7,200
**Financial aid:** (903) 593-8311

## Texas Lutheran University

Seguin TX
(800) 771-8521
**U.S. News ranking:** Reg. Coll. (W), No. 2
**Website:** www.tlu.edu
**Admissions email:** admissions@tlu.edu
**Private;** founded 1891
**Affiliation:** Evangelical Lutheran Church in America

**Freshman admissions:** selective; 2013-2014: 1,734 applied, 882 accepted. Either SAT or ACT required. SAT 25/75 percentile: 930-1140. High school rank: 20% in top tenth, 53% in top quarter, 87% in top half
**Early decision deadline:** N/A, notification date: N/A
**Early action deadline:** N/A, notification date: N/A
**Application deadline (fall):** rolling
**Undergraduate student body:** 1,258 full time, 71 part time; 48% male, 52% female; 0% American Indian, 1% Asian, 8% black, 31% Hispanic, 0% multiracial, 0% Pacific Islander, 56% white, 0% international; 97% from in state; 56% live on campus; 3% of students in fraternities, 7% in sororities
**Most popular majors:** 10% Biological and Biomedical Sciences, 21% Business, Management, Marketing, and Related Support Services, 11% Education, 17% Parks, Recreation, Leisure, and Fitness Studies, 7% Psychology
**Expenses:** 2014-2015: $26,800; room/board: $9,240
**Financial aid:** (830) 372-8075; 82% of undergrads determined to have financial need; average aid package $22,076

## Texas Southern University

Houston TX
(713) 313-7071
**U.S. News ranking:** Nat. U., second tier
**Website:** www.tsu.edu
**Admissions email:** admissions@tsu.edu
**Public;** founded 1947
**Freshman admissions:** least selective; 2013-2014: 9,746 applied, 4,389 accepted. Either SAT or ACT required. SAT 25/75 percentile: 750-920. High school rank: 5% in top tenth, 20% in top quarter, 62% in top half
**Early decision deadline:** 12/1, notification date: N/A
**Early action deadline:** N/A, notification date: N/A
**Application deadline (fall):** 8/1
**Undergraduate student body:** 5,321 full time, 967 part time; 41% male, 59% female; 0% American Indian, 3% Asian, 84% black, 6% Hispanic, 0% multiracial, 0% Pacific Islander, 2% white, 5% international; 90% from in state; 24% live on campus; 2% of students in fraternities, 3% in sororities
**Most popular majors:** 5% Accounting, 8% Biology/Biological Sciences, General, 9% Business Administration and Management, General, 6% Criminal Justice/Law Enforcement Administration, 11% General Studies
**Expenses:** 2013-2014: $7,946 in state, $18,566 out of state; room/board: $15,170
**Financial aid:** (713) 313-7071; 90% of undergrads determined to have financial need; average aid package $7,816

## Texas State University

San Marcos TX
(512) 245-2364
**U.S. News ranking:** Reg. U. (W), No. 50
**Website:** www.txstate.edu
**Admissions email:** admissions@txstate.edu
**Public;** founded 1899
**Freshman admissions:** selective; 2013-2014: 18,937 applied, 13,976 accepted. Either SAT or ACT required. SAT 25/75 percentile: 940-1130. High school rank: 14% in top tenth, 49% in top quarter, 93% in top half
**Early decision deadline:** N/A, notification date: N/A
**Early action deadline:** N/A, notification date: N/A
**Application deadline (fall):** 5/1
**Undergraduate student body:** 25,683 full time, 5,322 part time; 44% male, 56% female; 0% American Indian, 2% Asian, 7% black, 31% Hispanic, 3% multiracial, 0% Pacific Islander, 54% white, 0% international; 98% from in state; 19% live on campus; 5% of students in fraternities, 5% in sororities
**Most popular majors:** 6% Business Administration and Management, General, 4% Marketing/Marketing Management, General, 10% Multi-/Interdisciplinary Studies, Other, 6% Parks, Recreation and Leisure Facilities Management, General, 6% Psychology, General
**Expenses:** 2014-2015: $9,516 in state, $20,376 out of state; room/board: $7,612
**Financial aid:** (512) 245-2315; 59% of undergrads determined to have financial need; average aid package $10,055

## Texas Tech University

Lubbock TX
(806) 742-1480
**U.S. News ranking:** Nat. U., No. 156
**Website:** www.ttu.edu
**Admissions email:** admissions@ttu.edu
**Public;** founded 1923
**Freshman admissions:** selective; 2013-2014: 19,170 applied, 12,709 accepted. Either SAT or ACT required. SAT 25/75 percentile: 1010-1210. High school rank: 22% in top tenth, 55% in top quarter, 86% in top half
**Early decision deadline:** N/A, notification date: N/A
**Early action deadline:** N/A, notification date: N/A
**Application deadline (fall):** 8/1
**Undergraduate student body:** 24,338 full time, 2,706 part time; 56% male, 44% female; 0% American Indian, 3% Asian, 6% black, 21% Hispanic, 3% multiracial, 0% Pacific Islander, 63% white, 4% international; 94% from in state; 26% live on campus; 3% of students in fraternities, 6% in sororities
**Most popular majors:** 21% Business, Management, Marketing, and Related Support Services, 11% Engineering, 8% Family and Consumer Sciences/Human Sciences, 10% Multi/Interdisciplinary Studies, 6% Social Sciences
**Expenses:** 2014-2015: $9,308 in state, $20,168 out of state; room/board: $8,405

**Financial aid:** (806) 742-3681; 50% of undergrads determined to have financial need; average aid package $9,469

## Texas Wesleyan University

Fort Worth TX
(817) 531-4422
**U.S. News ranking:** Reg. U. (W), No. 49
**Website:** www.txwes.edu
**Admissions email:** admission@txwes.edu
**Private;** founded 1890
**Affiliation:** Methodist
**Freshman admissions:** selective; 2013-2014: 3,336 applied, 1,538 accepted. Either SAT or ACT required. SAT 25/75 percentile: 940-1090. High school rank: 12% in top tenth, 30% in top quarter, 71% in top half
**Early decision deadline:** N/A, notification date: N/A
**Early action deadline:** N/A, notification date: N/A
**Application deadline (fall):** rolling
**Undergraduate student body:** 1,429 full time, 512 part time; 49% male, 51% female; 1% American Indian, 2% Asian, 15% black, 20% Hispanic, 3% multiracial, 0% Pacific Islander, 33% white, 22% international; 95% from in state; 38% live on campus; 3% of students in fraternities, 3% in sororities
**Most popular majors:** 18% Business, Management, Marketing, and Related Support Services, 13% Education, 9% Homeland Security, Law Enforcement, Firefighting and Related Protective Services, 14% Multi/Interdisciplinary Studies, 8% Psychology
**Expenses:** 2014-2015: $23,144; room/board: $8,238
**Financial aid:** (817) 531-4420; 70% of undergrads determined to have financial need; average aid package $17,154

## Texas Woman's University

Denton TX
(940) 898-3188
**U.S. News ranking:** Nat. U., second tier
**Website:** www.twu.edu
**Admissions email:** admissions@twu.edu
**Public;** founded 1901
**Freshman admissions:** selective; 2013-2014: 4,431 applied, 3,812 accepted. Neither SAT nor ACT required. SAT 25/75 percentile: 840-1070. High school rank: 16% in top tenth, 48% in top quarter, 82% in top half
**Early decision deadline:** N/A, notification date: N/A
**Early action deadline:** N/A, notification date: N/A
**Application deadline (fall):** 7/15
**Undergraduate student body:** 6,722 full time, 2,793 part time; 11% male, 89% female; 1% American Indian, 8% Asian, 21% black, 25% Hispanic, 3% multiracial, 0% Pacific Islander, 41% white, 1% international; 100% from in state; 21% live on campus; 1% of students in fraternities, 3% in sororities
**Most popular majors:** 7% Business, Management, Marketing, and Related Support Services, 6% Family and Consumer Sciences/

Human Sciences, 28% Health Professions and Related Programs, 13% Liberal Arts and Sciences, General Studies and Humanities, 14% Multi/Interdisciplinary Studies
**Expenses:** 2014-2015: $7,560 in state, $18,420 out of state; room/board: $7,191
**Financial aid:** (940) 898-3050; 72% of undergrads determined to have financial need; average aid package $8,111

## Trinity University

San Antonio TX
(800) 874-6489
**U.S. News ranking:** Reg. U. (W), No. 1
**Website:** www.trinity.edu
**Admissions email:** admissions@trinity.edu
**Private;** founded 1869
**Affiliation:** Presbyterian
**Freshman admissions:** more selective; 2013-2014: 4,505 applied, 2,880 accepted. Either SAT or ACT required. SAT 25/75 percentile: 1150-1370. High school rank: 45% in top tenth, 73% in top quarter, 93% in top half
**Early decision deadline:** 11/1, notification date: 12/15
**Early action deadline:** 1/1, notification date: 2/15
**Application deadline (fall):** 2/1
**Undergraduate student body:** 2,186 full time, 51 part time; 47% male, 53% female; 0% American Indian, 7% Asian, 4% black, 17% Hispanic, 4% multiracial, 0% Pacific Islander, 58% white, 7% international; 72% from in state; 74% live on campus; 16% of students in fraternities, 18% in sororities
**Most popular majors:** 10% Biological and Biomedical Sciences, 20% Business, Management, Marketing, and Related Support Services, 6% Communication, Journalism, and Related Programs, 9% Foreign Languages, Literatures, and Linguistics, 19% Social Sciences
**Expenses:** 2014-2015: $36,214; room/board: $11,936
**Financial aid:** (210) 999-8315; 48% of undergrads determined to have financial need; average aid package $31,800

## University of Dallas

Irving TX
(800) 628-6999
**U.S. News ranking:** Reg. U. (W), No. 13
**Website:** www.udallas.edu
**Admissions email:** ugadmis@udallas.edu
**Private;** founded 1956
**Affiliation:** Roman Catholic
**Freshman admissions:** more selective; 2013-2014: 1,224 applied, 1,103 accepted. Either SAT or ACT required. SAT 25/75 percentile: 1090-1330. High school rank: 54% in top tenth, 68% in top quarter, 88% in top half
**Early decision deadline:** N/A, notification date: N/A
**Early action deadline:** 11/1, notification date: 12/1
**Application deadline (fall):** 7/1
**Undergraduate student body:** 1,365 full time, 15 part time; 46% male, 54% female; 0% American

Indian, 4% Asian, 1% black, 19% Hispanic, 3% multiracial, 0% Pacific Islander, 67% white, 3% international; 46% from in state; 63% live on campus; N/A of students in fraternities, N/A in sororities
**Most popular majors:** 12% Biology/Biological Sciences, General, 13% English Language and Literature, General, 9% History, General, 15% Social Sciences, General, 11% Theology/Theological Studies
**Expenses:** 2014-2015: $34,430; room/board: $11,070
**Financial aid:** (972) 721-5266; 64% of undergrads determined to have financial need; average aid package $28,291

## University of Houston
Houston TX
(713) 743-1010
**U.S. News ranking:** Nat. U., No. 189
**Website:** www.uh.edu
**Admissions email:** admissions@uh.edu
**Public;** founded 1927
**Freshman admissions:** more selective; 2013-2014: 17,407 applied, 10,167 accepted. Either SAT or ACT required. SAT 25/75 percentile: 1030-1250. High school rank: 34% in top tenth, 69% in top quarter, 92% in top half
**Early decision deadline:** N/A, notification date: N/A
**Early action deadline:** N/A, notification date: N/A
**Application deadline (fall):** 4/1
**Undergraduate student body:** 22,829 full time, 8,758 part time; 50% male, 50% female; 0% American Indian, 21% Asian, 12% black, 30% Hispanic, 3% multiracial, 0% Pacific Islander, 28% white, 5% international; 98% from in state; 18% live on campus; 4% of students in fraternities, 3% in sororities
**Most popular majors:** 6% Biological and Biomedical Sciences, 29% Business, Management, Marketing, and Related Support Services, 6% Communication, Journalism, and Related Programs, 8% Psychology, 7% Social Sciences
**Expenses:** 2014-2015: $10,518 in state, $24,378 out of state; room/board: $9,278
**Financial aid:** (713) 743-1010; 64% of undergrads determined to have financial need; average aid package $12,977

## University of Houston–Clear Lake
Houston TX
(281) 283-2500
**U.S. News ranking:** Reg. U. (W), second tier
**Website:** www.uhcl.edu
**Admissions email:** admissions@uhcl.edu
**Public;** founded 1974
**Freshman admissions:** less selective; 2013-2014: N/A applied, N/A accepted. Either SAT or ACT required. ACT 25/75 percentile: N/A. High school rank: N/A
**Early decision deadline:** N/A, notification date: N/A
**Early action deadline:** N/A, notification date: N/A
**Application deadline (fall):** 6/1

**Undergraduate student body:** 2,084 full time, 2,533 part time; 32% male, 68% female; 0% American Indian, 6% Asian, 8% black, 34% Hispanic, 2% multiracial, 0% Pacific Islander, 46% white, 2% international; N/A from in state; 2% live on campus; N/A of students in fraternities, N/A in sororities
**Most popular majors:** 25% Business, Management, Marketing, and Related Support Services, 26% Multi/Interdisciplinary Studies, 5% Parks, Recreation, Leisure, and Fitness Studies, 8% Psychology, 6% Social Sciences
**Expenses:** 2014-2015: $7,131 in state, $20,091 out of state; room/board: $9,682
**Financial aid:** (281) 283-2480; 68% of undergrads determined to have financial need; average aid package $8,936

## University of Houston–Downtown
Houston TX
(713) 221-8522
**U.S. News ranking:** Reg. Coll. (W), unranked
**Website:** www.uhd.edu
**Admissions email:** uhdadmit@uhd.edu
**Public;** founded 1974
**Freshman admissions:** N/A; 2013-2014: 3,096 applied, 2,944 accepted. Either SAT or ACT required. SAT 25/75 percentile: 800-990. High school rank: 8% in top tenth, 29% in top quarter, 67% in top half
**Early decision deadline:** N/A, notification date: N/A
**Early action deadline:** N/A, notification date: N/A
**Application deadline (fall):** 7/1
**Undergraduate student body:** 6,896 full time, 6,590 part time; 40% male, 60% female; 0% American Indian, 9% Asian, 25% black, 39% Hispanic, 1% multiracial, 0% Pacific Islander, 18% white, 5% international; 99% from in state; 0% live on campus; 0% of students in fraternities, 0% in sororities
**Most popular majors:** 36% Business, Management, Marketing, and Related Support Services, 10% Homeland Security, Law Enforcement, Firefighting and Related Protective Services, 26% Multi/Interdisciplinary Studies, 8% Psychology, 4% Social Sciences
**Expenses:** 2014-2015: $6,614 in state, $17,474 out of state; room/board: N/A
**Financial aid:** (713) 221-8041; 74% of undergrads determined to have financial need; average aid package $8,573

## University of Houston–Victoria
Victoria TX
(877) 970-4848
**U.S. News ranking:** Reg. U. (W), second tier
**Website:** www.uhv.edu/
**Admissions email:** N/A
**Public**
**Freshman admissions:** less selective; 2013-2014: 2,873 applied, 1,491 accepted. Neither SAT nor ACT required. SAT 25/75 percentile: 810-1005. High school rank: 7% in top tenth, 23% in top quarter, 68% in top half

**Early decision deadline:** N/A, notification date: N/A
**Early action deadline:** N/A, notification date: N/A
**Application deadline (fall):** 8/15
**Undergraduate student body:** 1,466 full time, 1,423 part time; 34% male, 66% female; 0% American Indian, 7% Asian, 17% black, 31% Hispanic, 2% multiracial, 0% Pacific Islander, 40% white, 1% international; 100% from in state; N/A live on campus; N/A of students in fraternities, N/A in sororities
**Most popular majors:** 5% Biological and Biomedical Sciences, 31% Business, Management, Marketing, and Related Support Services, 15% Health Professions and Related Programs, 25% Multi/Interdisciplinary Studies, 10% Psychology
**Expenses:** 2013-2014: $6,248 in state, $16,868 out of state; room/board: $7,216
**Financial aid:** (877) 970-4848

## University of Mary Hardin-Baylor
Belton TX
(254) 295-4520
**U.S. News ranking:** Reg. U. (W), No. 43
**Website:** www.umhb.edu
**Admissions email:** admission@umhb.edu
**Private;** founded 1845
**Affiliation:** Baptist
**Freshman admissions:** selective; 2013-2014: 5,540 applied, 4,691 accepted. Either SAT or ACT required. SAT 25/75 percentile: 940-1140. High school rank: 22% in top tenth, 51% in top quarter, 82% in top half
**Early decision deadline:** N/A, notification date: N/A
**Early action deadline:** N/A, notification date: N/A
**Application deadline (fall):** rolling
**Undergraduate student body:** 2,793 full time, 270 part time; 38% male, 62% female; 1% American Indian, 1% Asian, 14% black, 17% Hispanic, 2% multiracial, 0% Pacific Islander, 60% white, 2% international; 98% from in state; 50% live on campus; N/A of students in fraternities, N/A in sororities
**Most popular majors:** 9% Business, Management, Marketing, and Related Support Services, 16% Education, 29% Health Professions and Related Programs, 6% Liberal Arts and Sciences, General Studies and Humanities, 8% Psychology
**Expenses:** 2014-2015: $25,750; room/board: $7,020
**Financial aid:** (254) 295-4517; 86% of undergrads determined to have financial need; average aid package $15,789

## University of North Texas
Denton TX
(940) 565-2681
**U.S. News ranking:** Nat. U., second tier
**Website:** www.unt.edu
**Admissions email:** undergrad@unt.edu
**Public;** founded 1890
**Freshman admissions:** selective; 2013-2014: 16,326 applied,

10,037 accepted. Either SAT or ACT required. SAT 25/75 percentile: 1000-1210. High school rank: 20% in top tenth, 52% in top quarter, 90% in top half
**Early decision deadline:** N/A, notification date: N/A
**Early action deadline:** N/A, notification date: N/A
**Application deadline (fall):** 8/1
**Undergraduate student body:** 23,669 full time, 5,812 part time; 48% male, 52% female; 1% American Indian, 6% Asian, 13% black, 20% Hispanic, 3% multiracial, 0% Pacific Islander, 53% white, 3% international; 96% from in state; 19% live on campus; 2% of students in fraternities, 2% in sororities
**Most popular majors:** 19% Business, Management, Marketing, and Related Support Services, 15% Multi/Interdisciplinary Studies, 6% Psychology, 9% Social Sciences, 8% Visual and Performing Arts
**Expenses:** 2014-2015: $9,706 in state, $20,566 out of state; room/board: $7,760
**Financial aid:** (940) 565-2302; 62% of undergrads determined to have financial need; average aid package $10,767

## University of St. Thomas
Houston TX
(713) 525-3500
**U.S. News ranking:** Reg. U. (W), No. 27
**Website:** www.stthom.edu
**Admissions email:** admissions@stthom.edu
**Private;** founded 1947
**Affiliation:** Roman Catholic
**Freshman admissions:** selective; 2013-2014: 780 applied, 602 accepted. Either SAT or ACT required. SAT 25/75 percentile: 1000-1210. High school rank: 22% in top tenth, 54% in top quarter, 84% in top half
**Early decision deadline:** N/A, notification date: N/A
**Early action deadline:** 12/1, notification date: 12/15
**Application deadline (fall):** 8/1
**Undergraduate student body:** 1,269 full time, 341 part time; 37% male, 63% female; 0% American Indian, 12% Asian, 6% black, 38% Hispanic, 2% multiracial, 0% Pacific Islander, 31% white, 9% international; 96% from in state; 18% live on campus; N/A of students in fraternities, N/A in sororities
**Most popular majors:** 10% Biological and Biomedical Sciences, 23% Business, Management, Marketing, and Related Support Services, 10% Liberal Arts and Sciences, General Studies and Humanities, 10% Psychology, 10% Social Sciences
**Expenses:** 2014-2015: $29,440; room/board: $8,250
**Financial aid:** (713) 525-2170; 61% of undergrads determined to have financial need; average aid package $19,320

## University of Texas–Arlington
Arlington TX
(817) 272-6287
**U.S. News ranking:** Nat. U., second tier
**Website:** www.uta.edu
**Admissions email:** admissions@uta.edu
**Public;** founded 1895
**Freshman admissions:** selective; 2013-2014: 10,679 applied, 6,405 accepted. Either SAT or ACT required. SAT 25/75 percentile: 960-1200. High school rank: 28% in top tenth, 75% in top quarter, 98% in top half
**Early decision deadline:** N/A, notification date: N/A
**Early action deadline:** N/A, notification date: N/A
**Application deadline (fall):** rolling
**Undergraduate student body:** 15,938 full time, 9,752 part time; 44% male, 56% female; 0% American Indian, 12% Asian, 15% black, 26% Hispanic, 3% multiracial, 0% Pacific Islander, 40% white, 4% international; 97% from in state; 11% live on campus; 5% of students in fraternities, 3% in sororities
**Most popular majors:** 6% Biological and Biomedical Sciences, 13% Business, Management, Marketing, and Related Support Services, 6% Engineering, 33% Health Professions and Related Programs, 6% Multi/Interdisciplinary Studies
**Expenses:** 2014-2015: $8,878 in state, $20,274 out of state; room/board: $8,156
**Financial aid:** (817) 272-3568; 68% of undergrads determined to have financial need; average aid package $12,738

## University of Texas–Austin
Austin TX
(512) 475-7440
**U.S. News ranking:** Nat. U., No. 53
**Website:** www.utexas.edu
**Admissions email:** N/A
**Public;** founded 1883
**Freshman admissions:** more selective; 2013-2014: 38,161 applied, 15,335 accepted. Either SAT or ACT required. SAT 25/75 percentile: 1140-1380. High school rank: 75% in top tenth, 91% in top quarter, 98% in top half
**Early decision deadline:** N/A, notification date: N/A
**Early action deadline:** N/A, notification date: N/A
**Application deadline (fall):** 12/1
**Undergraduate student body:** 36,899 full time, 3,080 part time; 48% male, 52% female; 0% American Indian, 18% Asian, 4% black, 22% Hispanic, 3% multiracial, 0% Pacific Islander, 48% white, 5% international; 95% from in state; 18% live on campus; 15% of students in fraternities, 17% in sororities
**Most popular majors:** 9% Biological and Biomedical Sciences, 12% Business, Management, Marketing, and Related Support Services, 12% Communication, Journalism, and Related Programs, 12% Engineering, 12% Social Sciences

**Expenses:** 2014-2015: $9,798 in state, $34,722 out of state; room/board: $11,456
**Financial aid:** (512) 475-6203; 45% of undergrads determined to have financial need; average aid package $12,427

## University of Texas–Brownsville
Brownsville TX
(956) 882-8295
**U.S. News ranking:** Reg. U. (W), second tier
**Website:** www.utb.edu
**Admissions email:** admissions@utb.edu
**Public;** founded 1926
**Freshman admissions:** less selective; 2013-2014: 2,843 applied, 2,479 accepted. Either SAT or ACT required. SAT 25/75 percentile: 810-1000. High school rank: 17% in top tenth, 43% in top quarter, 75% in top half
**Early decision deadline:** N/A, notification date: N/A
**Early action deadline:** N/A, notification date: N/A
**Application deadline (fall):** 8/1
**Undergraduate student body:** 4,553 full time, 2,994 part time; 43% male, 57% female; 0% American Indian, 1% Asian, 1% black, 89% Hispanic, 0% multiracial, 0% Pacific Islander, 4% white, 5% international
**Most popular majors:** 8% Biology, General, 13% Business Administration, Management and Operations, 10% Health and Physical Education/Fitness, 20% Multi/Interdisciplinary Studies, Other, 9% Psychology, General
**Expenses:** 2013-2014: $5,372 in state, $14,834 out of state; room/board: $3,360
**Financial aid:** (956) 882-8277

## University of Texas–Dallas
Richardson TX
(972) 883-2270
**U.S. News ranking:** Nat. U., No. 145
**Website:** www.utdallas.edu
**Admissions email:** interest@utdallas.edu
**Public;** founded 1969
**Freshman admissions:** more selective; 2013-2014: 8,750 applied, 5,125 accepted. Either SAT or ACT required. SAT 25/75 percentile: 1150-1370. High school rank: 38% in top tenth, 71% in top quarter, 91% in top half
**Early decision deadline:** N/A, notification date: N/A
**Early action deadline:** N/A, notification date: N/A
**Application deadline (fall):** 7/1
**Undergraduate student body:** 10,635 full time, 2,414 part time; 57% male, 43% female; 0% American Indian, 27% Asian, 6% black, 17% Hispanic, 4% multiracial, 0% Pacific Islander, 40% white, 4% international; 97% from in state; 26% live on campus; 3% of students in fraternities, 2% in sororities
**Most popular majors:** 14% Biological and Biomedical Sciences, 32% Business, Management, Marketing, and Related Support Services, 9% Engineering, 9% Psychology, 7% Social Sciences

## University of Texas–El Paso
El Paso TX
(915) 747-5890
**U.S. News ranking:** Nat. U., second tier
**Website:** www.utep.edu
**Admissions email:** futureminer@utep.edu
**Public;** founded 1914
**Freshman admissions:** selective; 2013-2014: N/A applied, N/A accepted. Neither SAT nor ACT required. ACT 25/75 percentile: 17-22. High school rank: N/A
**Early decision deadline:** N/A, notification date: N/A
**Early action deadline:** N/A, notification date: N/A
**Application deadline (fall):** rolling
**Undergraduate student body:** N/A full time, N/A part time; N/A male, N/A female; N/A American Indian, N/A Asian, N/A black, N/A Hispanic, N/A multiracial, N/A Pacific Islander, N/A white, N/A international
**Most popular majors:** Information not available
**Expenses:** 2014-2015: $7,018 in state, $17,639 out of state; room/board: $9,300
**Financial aid:** (915) 747-5204; 79% of undergrads determined to have financial need; average aid package $11,702

## University of Texas of the Permian Basin
Odessa TX
(432) 552-2605
**U.S. News ranking:** Reg. U. (W), second tier
**Website:** www.utpb.edu
**Admissions email:** admissions@utpb.edu
**Public;** founded 1969
**Freshman admissions:** selective; 2013-2014: 973 applied, 799 accepted. Either SAT or ACT required. SAT 25/75 percentile: 910-1122. High school rank: 26% in top tenth, 60% in top quarter, 94% in top half
**Early decision deadline:** N/A, notification date: N/A
**Early action deadline:** N/A, notification date: N/A
**Application deadline (fall):** rolling
**Undergraduate student body:** 1,924 full time, 2,322 part time; 41% male, 59% female; 1% American Indian, 2% Asian, 6% black, 46% Hispanic, 1% multiracial, 0% Pacific Islander, 42% white, 1% international; 98% from in state; 14% live on campus; 0% of students in fraternities, 0% in sororities
**Most popular majors:** 7% Biological and Biomedical Sciences, 25% Business, Management, Marketing, and Related Support Services, 8% Multi/Interdisciplinary Studies, 7% Parks, Recreation, Leisure, and Fitness Studies, 7% Psychology
**Expenses:** 2013-2014: $6,776 in state, $17,308 out of state; room/board: $7,978
**Financial aid:** (432) 552-2620

## University of Texas–Pan American
Edinburg TX
(956) 665-2999
**U.S. News ranking:** Reg. U. (W), second tier
**Website:** www.utpa.edu
**Admissions email:** admissions@utpa.edu
**Public;** founded 1927
**Freshman admissions:** selective; 2013-2014: 9,832 applied, 6,825 accepted. Either SAT or ACT required. ACT 25/75 percentile: 18-22. High school rank: 22% in top tenth, 53% in top quarter, 83% in top half
**Early decision deadline:** N/A, notification date: N/A
**Early action deadline:** N/A, notification date: N/A
**Application deadline (fall):** 8/11
**Undergraduate student body:** 13,215 full time, 4,387 part time; 45% male, 55% female; 0% American Indian, 1% Asian, 1% black, 90% Hispanic, 0% multiracial, 0% Pacific Islander, 3% white, 2% international; 99% from in state; 5% live on campus; 99% of students in fraternities, 100% in sororities
**Most popular majors:** 8% Biological and Biomedical Sciences, 13% Business, Management, Marketing, and Related Support Services, 16% Health Professions and Related Programs, 8% Homeland Security, Law Enforcement, Firefighting and Related Protective Services, 9% Multi/Interdisciplinary Studies
**Expenses:** 2014-2015: $6,134 in state, $17,132 out of state; room/board: N/A
**Financial aid:** (956) 381-2501

## University of Texas–San Antonio
San Antonio TX
(210) 458-4599
**U.S. News ranking:** Nat. U., second tier
**Website:** www.utsa.edu
**Admissions email:** prospects@utsa.edu
**Public;** founded 1969
**Freshman admissions:** selective; 2013-2014: 13,988 applied, 8,671 accepted. Either SAT or ACT required. SAT 25/75 percentile: 950-1180. High school rank: 19% in top tenth, 73% in top quarter, 96% in top half
**Early decision deadline:** N/A, notification date: N/A
**Early action deadline:** N/A, notification date: N/A
**Application deadline (fall):** 6/1
**Undergraduate student body:** 20,033 full time, 4,309 part time; 53% male, 47% female; 0% American Indian, 5% Asian, 9% black, 49% Hispanic, 3% multiracial, 0% Pacific Islander, 28% white, 5% international; 98% from in state; 5% live on campus; 3% of students in fraternities, 3% in sororities
**Most popular majors:** 7% Biological and Biomedical Sciences, 24% Business, Management, Marketing, and Related Support Services, 6% Engineering, 9% Multi/Interdisciplinary Studies, 7% Psychology
**Expenses:** 2014-2015: $8,737 in state, $20,050 out of state; room/board: $7,624

**Financial aid:** (210) 458-8000; 65% of undergrads determined to have financial need; average aid package $9,193

## University of Texas–Tyler
Tyler TX
(903) 566-7202
**U.S. News ranking:** Reg. U. (W), No. 68
**Website:** www.uttyler.edu
**Admissions email:** admrequest@uttyler.edu
**Public;** founded 1971
**Freshman admissions:** selective; 2013-2014: 2,104 applied, 1,726 accepted. Either SAT or ACT required. SAT 25/75 percentile: 960-1158. High school rank: 13% in top tenth, 44% in top quarter, 68% in top half
**Early decision deadline:** N/A, notification date: N/A
**Early action deadline:** N/A, notification date: N/A
**Application deadline (fall):** 8/20
**Undergraduate student body:** 4,090 full time, 1,501 part time; 43% male, 57% female; 0% American Indian, 3% Asian, 9% black, 14% Hispanic, 8% multiracial, 0% Pacific Islander, 63% white, 1% international; 98% from in state; 14% live on campus; 3% of students in fraternities, 2% in sororities
**Most popular majors:** 18% Business, Management, Marketing, and Related Support Services, 27% Health Professions and Related Programs, 11% Multi/Interdisciplinary Studies, 7% Parks, Recreation, Leisure, and Fitness Studies
**Expenses:** 2013-2014: $7,222 in state, $17,842 out of state; room/board: $8,979
**Financial aid:** (903) 566-7180

## University of the Incarnate Word
San Antonio TX
(210) 829-6005
**U.S. News ranking:** Reg. U. (W), No. 63
**Website:** www.uiw.edu
**Admissions email:** admis@uiwtx.edu
**Private;** founded 1881
**Affiliation:** Roman Catholic
**Freshman admissions:** selective; 2013-2014: 4,062 applied, 3,781 accepted. Either SAT or ACT required. SAT 25/75 percentile: 870-1060. High school rank: 18% in top tenth, 43% in top quarter, 71% in top half
**Early decision deadline:** N/A, notification date: N/A
**Early action deadline:** N/A, notification date: N/A
**Application deadline (fall):** rolling
**Undergraduate student body:** 4,201 full time, 2,290 part time; 39% male, 61% female; 0% American Indian, 2% Asian, 7% black, 61% Hispanic, 1% multiracial, 0% Pacific Islander, 20% white, 3% international; 94% from in state; 12% live on campus; 1% of students in fraternities, 1% in sororities
**Most popular majors:** 8% Biology, General, 37% Business Administration, Management and Operations, 8% Design and Applied Arts, 9% Registered

Nursing, Nursing Administration, Nursing Research and Clinical Nursing, 8% Teacher Education and Professional Development, Specific Levels and Methods
**Expenses:** 2014-2015: $26,490; room/board: $10,826
**Financial aid:** (210) 829-6008; 79% of undergrads determined to have financial need; average aid package $18,126

## Wayland Baptist University
Plainview TX
(806) 291-3500
**U.S. News ranking:** Reg. U. (W), second tier
**Website:** www.wbu.edu
**Admissions email:** admityou@wbu.edu
**Private;** founded 1908
**Affiliation:** Southern Baptist Convention
**Freshman admissions:** less selective; 2013-2014: 581 applied, 573 accepted. Either SAT or ACT required. ACT 25/75 percentile: 17-23. High school rank: 11% in top tenth, 28% in top quarter, 65% in top half
**Early decision deadline:** N/A, notification date: N/A
**Early action deadline:** N/A, notification date: N/A
**Application deadline (fall):** rolling
**Undergraduate student body:** 1,143 full time, 3,372 part time; 50% male, 50% female; 1% American Indian, 2% Asian, 17% black, 27% Hispanic, 4% multiracial, 1% Pacific Islander, 43% white, 1% international; 68% from in state; 17% live on campus; 1% of students in fraternities, 1% in sororities
**Most popular majors:** 36% Business Administration and Management, General, 7% Criminal Justice/Law Enforcement Administration, 6% Human Services, General, 31% Liberal Arts and Sciences, General Studies and Humanities, Other, 6% Registered Nursing/Registered Nurse
**Expenses:** 2014-2015: $15,930; room/board: $5,852
**Financial aid:** (806) 291-3520; 61% of undergrads determined to have financial need; average aid package $10,545

## West Texas A&M University
Canyon TX
(806) 651-2020
**U.S. News ranking:** Reg. U. (W), No. 80
**Website:** www.wtamu.edu
**Admissions email:** admissions@mail.wtamu.edu
**Public;** founded 1910
**Freshman admissions:** selective; 2013-2014: 4,632 applied, 3,429 accepted. Either SAT or ACT required. ACT 25/75 percentile: 19-24. High school rank: 15% in top tenth, 42% in top quarter, 77% in top half
**Early decision deadline:** N/A, notification date: N/A
**Early action deadline:** N/A, notification date: N/A
**Application deadline (fall):** rolling
**Undergraduate student body:** 5,523 full time, 1,385 part time; 45% male, 55% female; 1% American

Indian, 1% Asian, 5% black, 23% Hispanic, 2% multiracial, 0% Pacific Islander, 64% white, 2% international; 90% from in state; 28% live on campus; 6% of students in fraternities, 7% in sororities
**Most popular majors:** 9% Agriculture, Agriculture Operations, and Related Sciences, 15% Business, Management, Marketing, and Related Support Services, 10% Health Professions and Related Programs, 12% Liberal Arts and Sciences, General Studies and Humanities, 15% Multi/Interdisciplinary Studies
**Expenses:** 2014-2015: $7,361 in state, $8,312 out of state; room/board: $7,196
**Financial aid:** (806) 651-2055; 62% of undergrads determined to have financial need; average aid package $9,843

## Wiley College
Marshall TX
(800) 658-6889
**U.S. News ranking:** Reg. Coll. (W), second tier
**Website:** www.wileyc.edu
**Admissions email:** admissions@wileyc.edu
**Private;** founded 1873
**Affiliation:** United Methodist
**Freshman admissions:** least selective; 2013-2014: 1,544 applied, 1,458 accepted. Neither SAT nor ACT required. ACT 25/75 percentile: 14-18. High school rank: 1% in top tenth, 8% in top quarter, 39% in top half
**Early decision deadline:** N/A, notification date: N/A
**Early action deadline:** N/A, notification date: N/A
**Application deadline (fall):** rolling
**Undergraduate student body:** 1,324 full time, 64 part time; 44% male, 56% female; 0% American Indian, 0% Asian, 85% black, 7% Hispanic, 0% multiracial, 0% Pacific Islander, 2% white, 5% international; 57% from in state; 67% live on campus; 3% of students in fraternities, 6% in sororities
**Most popular majors:** 7% Business Administration and Management, General, 8% Criminal Justice/Law Enforcement Administration, 12% Criminal Justice/Police Science, 6% Early Childhood Education and Teaching, 15% Non-Profit/Public/Organizational Management
**Expenses:** 2014-2015: $11,482; room/board: $6,846
**Financial aid:** (903) 927-3210; 95% of undergrads determined to have financial need; average aid package $8,596

## Brigham Young University–Provo
Provo UT
(801) 422-2507
**U.S. News ranking:** Nat. U., No. 62
**Website:** www.byu.edu
**Admissions email:** admissions@byu.edu
**Private;** founded 1875
**Affiliation:** Church of Jesus Christ of Latter-day Saints
**Freshman admissions:** more selective; 2013-2014: 11,603 applied, 5,645 accepted. Either SAT or ACT required. ACT 25/75

percentile: 26-31. High school rank: 54% in top tenth, 85% in top quarter, 97% in top half
**Early decision deadline:** N/A, notification date: N/A
**Early action deadline:** N/A, notification date: N/A
**Application deadline (fall):** 2/1
**Undergraduate student body:** 25,084 full time, 2,681 part time; 54% male, 46% female; 0% American Indian, 2% Asian, 0% black, 5% Hispanic, 3% multiracial, 1% Pacific Islander, 84% white, 3% international; 34% from in state; 19% live on campus; N/A of students in fraternities, N/A in sororities
**Most popular majors:** 11% Biological and Biomedical Sciences, 12% Business, Management, Marketing, and Related Support Services, 10% Education, 8% Health Professions and Related Programs, 8% Social Sciences
**Expenses:** 2014-2015: $5,000; room/board: $7,964
**Financial aid:** (801) 422-4104; 49% of undergrads determined to have financial need; average aid package $7,082

## Dixie State College of Utah
Saint George UT
(435) 652-7702
**U.S. News ranking:** Reg. Coll. (W), unranked
**Website:** www.dixie.edu
**Admissions email:** admissions@dixie.edu
**Public;** founded 1911
**Freshman admissions:** N/A; 2013-2014: 3,321 applied, 3,321 accepted. Neither SAT nor ACT required. ACT 25/75 percentile: 17-23. High school rank: 9% in top tenth, 28% in top quarter, 57% in top half
**Early decision deadline:** N/A, notification date: N/A
**Early action deadline:** N/A, notification date: N/A
**Application deadline (fall):** 8/15
**Undergraduate student body:** 5,165 full time, 3,185 part time; 47% male, 53% female; 1% American Indian, 1% Asian, 2% black, 8% Hispanic, 2% multiracial, 2% Pacific Islander, 80% white, 2% international; 84% from in state; N/A live on campus; N/A of students in fraternities, N/A in sororities
**Most popular majors:** Information not available
**Expenses:** 2014-2015: $4,456 in state, $12,792 out of state; room/board: $5,048
**Financial aid:** (435) 652-7575; 73% of undergrads determined to have financial need; average aid package $7,501

## Southern Utah University
Cedar City UT
(435) 586-7740
**U.S. News ranking:** Reg. U. (W), No. 58
**Website:** www.suu.edu
**Admissions email:** admissionsinfo@suu.edu
**Public;** founded 1897
**Freshman admissions:** selective; 2013-2014: 8,318 applied, 4,749 accepted. Either SAT or ACT required. ACT 25/75 percentile: 20-26. High school

rank: 18% in top tenth, 42% in top quarter, 75% in top half
**Early decision deadline:** N/A, notification date: N/A
**Early action deadline:** N/A, notification date: N/A
**Application deadline (fall):** 5/1
**Undergraduate student body:** 5,254 full time, 1,763 part time; 45% male, 55% female; 2% American Indian, 1% Asian, 1% black, 4% Hispanic, 1% multiracial, 1% Pacific Islander, 81% white, 5% international; 82% from in state; 10% live on campus; N/A of students in fraternities, N/A in sororities
**Most popular majors:** 8% Biological and Biomedical Sciences, 11% Business, Management, Marketing, and Related Support Services, 6% Communication, Journalism, and Related Programs, 23% Education, 7% Psychology
**Expenses:** 2014-2015: $6,138 in state, $18,596 out of state; room/board: $6,890
**Financial aid:** (801) 586-7735; 65% of undergrads determined to have financial need; average aid package $8,927

## University of Utah
Salt Lake City UT
(801) 581-8761
**U.S. News ranking:** Nat. U., No. 129
**Website:** www.utah.edu
**Admissions email:** admissions@utah.edu
**Public;** founded 1850
**Freshman admissions:** selective; 2013-2014: 11,354 applied, 9,281 accepted. Either SAT or ACT required. ACT 25/75 percentile: 21-27. High school rank: 21% in top tenth, 48% in top quarter, 83% in top half
**Early decision deadline:** N/A, notification date: N/A
**Early action deadline:** N/A, notification date: N/A
**Application deadline (fall):** 4/1
**Undergraduate student body:** 17,319 full time, 7,173 part time; 55% male, 45% female; 1% American Indian, 5% Asian, 1% black, 9% Hispanic, 3% multiracial, 1% Pacific Islander, 72% white, 7% international; 81% from in state; 13% live on campus; 2% of students in fraternities, 3% in sororities
**Most popular majors:** 4% Economics, General, 4% Human Development and Family Studies, General, 5% Kinesiology and Exercise Science, 6% Mass Communication/Media Studies, 6% Psychology, General
**Expenses:** 2014-2015: $7,935 in state, $25,267 out of state; room/board: $8,528
**Financial aid:** (801) 581-8788; 46% of undergrads determined to have financial need; average aid package $16,604

## Utah State University
Logan UT
(435) 797-1079
**U.S. News ranking:** Nat. U., No. 194
**Website:** www.usu.edu
**Admissions email:** admit@usu.edu
**Public;** founded 1888
**Freshman admissions:** selective; 2013-2014: 10,935 applied, 10,768 accepted. Either SAT or ACT required. ACT 25/75

percentile: 20-26. High school rank: 19% in top tenth, 44% in top quarter, 74% in top half
**Early decision deadline:** N/A, notification date: N/A
**Early action deadline:** N/A, notification date: N/A
**Application deadline (fall):** rolling
**Undergraduate student body:** 15,260 full time, 9,125 part time; 46% male, 54% female; 2% American Indian, 1% Asian, 1% black, 5% Hispanic, 2% multiracial, 0% Pacific Islander, 80% white, 2% international; 76% from in state; N/A live on campus; 2% of students in fraternities, 2% in sororities
**Most popular majors:** 11% Communication Sciences and Disorders, General, 7% Economics, General, 4% Elementary Education and Teaching, 5% Multi-/Interdisciplinary Studies, Other, 4% Physical Education Teaching and Coaching
**Expenses:** 2014-2015: $6,384 in state, $18,491 out of state; room/board: $2,840
**Financial aid:** (435) 797-0173; 57% of undergrads determined to have financial need; average aid package $8,800

## Utah Valley University
Orem UT
(801) 863-8466
**U.S. News ranking:** Reg. Coll. (W), unranked
**Website:** www.uvu.edu/
**Admissions email:** InstantInfo@uvu.edu
**Public;** founded 1941
**Freshman admissions:** N/A; 2013-2014: 6,934 applied, 6,934 accepted. Either SAT or ACT required. ACT 25/75 percentile: 18-24. High school rank: 5% in top tenth, 14% in top quarter, 44% in top half
**Early decision deadline:** N/A, notification date: N/A
**Early action deadline:** N/A, notification date: N/A
**Application deadline (fall):** 8/1
**Undergraduate student body:** 15,751 full time, 14,619 part time; 56% male, 44% female; 1% American Indian, 1% Asian, 1% black, 10% Hispanic, 2% multiracial, 1% Pacific Islander, 81% white, 2% international; 90% from in state; 0% live on campus; N/A of students in fraternities, N/A in sororities
**Most popular majors:** 3% Accounting, 5% Airline/Commercial/Professional Pilot and Flight Crew, 6% Business Administration and Management, General, 4% Elementary Education and Teaching, 7% Psychology, General
**Expenses:** 2014-2015: $5,270 in state, $14,802 out of state; room/board: N/A
**Financial aid:** (801) 863-8442; 68% of undergrads determined to have financial need; average aid package $5,081

## Weber State University
Ogden UT
(801) 626-6744
**U.S. News ranking:** Reg. U. (W), No. 68
**Website:** weber.edu
**Admissions email:** admissions@weber.edu
**Public;** founded 1889
**Freshman admissions:** selective; 2013-2014: 5,296 applied, 5,296 accepted. Neither SAT nor ACT required. ACT 25/75 percentile: 18-24. High school rank: N/A
**Early decision deadline:** N/A, notification date: N/A
**Early action deadline:** N/A, notification date: N/A
**Application deadline (fall):** 8/21
**Undergraduate student body:** 10,879 full time, 13,619 part time; 47% male, 53% female; 1% American Indian, 2% Asian, 2% black, 9% Hispanic, 2% multiracial, 0% Pacific Islander, 71% white, 2% international; 91% from in state; 4% live on campus; 1% of students in fraternities, 1% in sororities
**Most popular majors:** 2% Accounting, 2% Computer Science, 2% Medical Radiologic Technology/Science - Radiation Therapist, 8% Registered Nursing/Registered Nurse, 3% Selling Skills and Sales Operations
**Expenses:** 2014-2015: $5,126 in state, $13,780 out of state; room/board: $8,000
**Financial aid:** (801) 626-7569; 61% of undergrads determined to have financial need; average aid package $1,952

## Western Governors University
Salt Lake City UT
(866) 225-5948
**U.S. News ranking:** Reg. U. (W), unranked
**Website:** www.wgu.edu/
**Admissions email:** info@wgu.edu
**Private;** founded 1996
**Freshman admissions:** N/A; 2013-2014: N/A applied, N/A accepted. Neither SAT nor ACT required. ACT 25/75 percentile: N/A. High school rank: N/A
**Early decision deadline:** N/A, notification date: N/A
**Early action deadline:** N/A, notification date: N/A
**Application deadline (fall):** rolling
**Undergraduate student body:** 35,493 full time, 0 part time; 41% male, 59% female; 1% American Indian, 3% Asian, 9% black, 7% Hispanic, 3% multiracial, 0% Pacific Islander, 73% white, 0% international
**Most popular majors:** 15% Business Administration and Management, General, 7% Education, General, 6% Nursing Administration, 23% Registered Nursing/Registered Nurse, 5% Special Education and Teaching, General
**Expenses:** 2014-2015: $6,070; room/board: N/A
**Financial aid:** (801) 327-8104; 62% of undergrads determined to have financial need; average aid package $5,846

## Westminster College
Salt Lake City UT
(801) 832-2200
**U.S. News ranking:** Reg. U. (W),
No. 20
**Website:**
www.westminstercollege.edu
**Admissions email:** admission@
westminstercollege.edu
**Private;** founded 1875
**Freshman admissions:** more
selective; 2013-2014: 2,461
applied, 1,850 accepted. Either
SAT or ACT required. ACT 25/75
percentile: 22-28. High school
rank: 23% in top tenth, 55% in
top quarter, 88% in top half
**Early decision deadline:** N/A,
notification date: N/A
**Early action deadline:** N/A,
notification date: N/A
**Application deadline (fall):** 8/15
**Undergraduate student body:** 2,140
full time, 155 part time; 44%
male, 56% female; 1% American
Indian, 2% Asian, 1% black,
10% Hispanic, 2% multiracial,
0% Pacific Islander, 69% white,
5% international; 60% from in
state; 27% live on campus; 0%
of students in fraternities, 0% in
sororities
**Most popular majors:** 26%
Business, Management,
Marketing, and Related Support
Services, 19% Health Professions
and Related Programs, 5% Natural
Resources and Conservation, 9%
Psychology, 8% Social Sciences
**Expenses:** 2014-2015: $30,364;
room/board: $8,456
**Financial aid:** (801) 832-2500;
59% of undergrads determined to
have financial need; average aid
package $22,755

## VERMONT

## Bennington College
Bennington VT
(802) 833-6845
**U.S. News ranking:** Nat. Lib. Arts,
No. 89
**Website:** www.bennington.edu
**Admissions email:** admissions@
bennington.edu
**Private;** founded 1925
**Freshman admissions:** more
selective; 2013-2014: 1,130
applied, 733 accepted. Neither
SAT nor ACT required. SAT
25/75 percentile: 1180-1380.
High school rank: 44% in top
tenth, 75% in top quarter, 97%
in top half
**Early decision deadline:** 11/15,
notification date: 12/20
**Early action deadline:** 12/1,
notification date: 2/1
**Application deadline (fall):** 1/3
**Undergraduate student body:** 609
full time, 10 part time; 35%
male, 65% female; 0% American
Indian, 3% Asian, 2% black,
5% Hispanic, 4% multiracial,
0% Pacific Islander, 76% white,
8% international; 4% from in
state; 99% live on campus; 0%
of students in fraternities, 0% in
sororities
**Most popular majors:** 11%
English Language and Literature/
Letters, 5% Foreign Languages,
Literatures, and Linguistics, 5%
Physical Sciences, 9% Social
Sciences, 44% Visual and
Performing Arts
**Expenses:** 2014-2015: $46,658;
room/board: $13,652

**Financial aid:** (802) 440-4325;
63% of undergrads determined to
have financial need; average aid
package $37,681

## Burlington College
Burlington VT
(802) 862-9616
**U.S. News ranking:** Nat. Lib. Arts,
second tier
**Website:** www.burlington.edu
**Admissions email:** admissions@
burlington.edu
**Private;** founded 1972
**Freshman admissions:** less
selective; 2013-2014: 255
applied, 211 accepted. Neither
SAT nor ACT required. SAT 25/75
percentile: 820-1130. High
school rank: 5% in top tenth, 13%
in top quarter, 45% in top half
**Early decision deadline:** N/A,
notification date: N/A
**Early action deadline:** N/A,
notification date: N/A
**Application deadline (fall):** rolling
**Undergraduate student body:** 160
full time, 56 part time; 51%
male, 49% female; 1% American
Indian, 1% Asian, 2% black, 7%
Hispanic, 1% multiracial, 0%
Pacific Islander, 35% white, 1%
international
**Most popular majors:** Information
not available
**Expenses:** 2014-2015: $23,546;
room/board: $8,600
**Financial aid:** (802) 862-9616;
79% of undergrads determined to
have financial need; average aid
package $14,385

## Castleton State College
Castleton VT
(800) 639-8521
**U.S. News ranking:** Nat. Lib. Arts,
second tier
**Website:** www.castleton.edu
**Admissions email:**
info@castleton.edu
**Public;** founded 1787
**Freshman admissions:** less
selective; 2013-2014: 2,600
applied, 2,051 accepted. Either
SAT or ACT required. SAT 25/75
percentile: 850-1060. High
school rank: 8% in top tenth, 25%
in top quarter, 56% in top half
**Early decision deadline:** N/A,
notification date: N/A
**Early action deadline:** N/A,
notification date: N/A
**Application deadline (fall):** rolling
**Undergraduate student body:** 1,916
full time, 153 part time; 48%
male, 52% female; 1% American
Indian, 1% Asian, 1% black, 2%
Hispanic, 1% multiracial, 0%
Pacific Islander, 85% white, 1%
international; N/A from in state;
53% live on campus; 0% of
students in fraternities, 11% in
sororities
**Most popular majors:** Information
not available
**Expenses:** 2013-2014: $10,286
in state, $24,014 out of state;
room/board: $9,138
**Financial aid:** (802) 468-1292

## Champlain College
Burlington VT
(800) 570-5858
**U.S. News ranking:** Reg. Coll. (N),
No. 14
**Website:** www.champlain.edu
**Admissions email:** admission@
champlain.edu

**Private;** founded 1878
**Freshman admissions:** selective;
2013-2014: 5,047 applied,
3,573 accepted. Either SAT
or ACT required. SAT 25/75
percentile: 990-1240. High school
rank: 15% in top tenth, 39% in
top quarter, 68% in top half
**Early decision deadline:** 11/15,
notification date: 12/15
**Early action deadline:** N/A,
notification date: N/A
**Application deadline (fall):** 1/31
**Undergraduate student body:** 2,332
full time, 566 part time; 60%
male, 40% female; 0% American
Indian, 1% Asian, 3% black,
4% Hispanic, 2% multiracial,
0% Pacific Islander, 71% white,
1% international; 24% from in
state; 46% live on campus; N/A
of students in fraternities, N/A in
sororities
**Most popular majors:** 7%
Accounting, 13% Business
Administration and Management,
General, 7% Computer Graphics,
7% Computer and Information
Sciences and Support Services,
Other, 8% Graphic Design
**Expenses:** 2014-2015: $32,900;
room/board: $13,750
**Financial aid:** (800) 570-5858;
68% of undergrads determined to
have financial need; average aid
package $19,612

## College of St. Joseph
Rutland VT
(802) 773-5286
**U.S. News ranking:** Reg. U. (N),
second tier
**Website:** www.csj.edu
**Admissions email:**
admissions@csj.edu
**Private;** founded 1956
**Affiliation:** Roman Catholic
**Freshman admissions:** least
selective; 2013-2014: 179
applied, 130 accepted. Either
SAT or ACT required. SAT 25/75
percentile: 705-985. High school
rank: N/A
**Early decision deadline:** N/A,
notification date: N/A
**Early action deadline:** N/A,
notification date: N/A
**Application deadline (fall):** rolling
**Undergraduate student body:** 120
full time, 56 part time; 48%
male, 52% female; 0% American
Indian, 1% Asian, 23% black,
1% Hispanic, 0% multiracial,
1% Pacific Islander, 74% white,
0% international; 69% from in
state; 49% live on campus; 0%
of students in fraternities, 0% in
sororities
**Most popular majors:** 11%
Behavioral Sciences, 13% Human
Services, General, 11% Liberal
Arts and Sciences/Liberal Studies,
16% Organizational Leadership,
11% Psychology, General
**Expenses:** 2014-2015: $21,200;
room/board: $9,400
**Financial aid:** (802) 773-5900;
95% of undergrads determined to
have financial need; average aid
package $25,177

## Goddard College
Plainfield VT
(800) 906-8312
**U.S. News ranking:** Reg. U. (N),
unranked
**Website:** www.goddard.edu
**Admissions email:**
admissions@goddard.edu
**Private;** founded 1863

**Freshman admissions:** N/A; 2013-
2014: 5 applied, 4 accepted.
Neither SAT nor ACT required.
ACT 25/75 percentile: N/A. High
school rank: N/A
**Early decision deadline:** N/A,
notification date: N/A
**Early action deadline:** N/A,
notification date: N/A
**Application deadline (fall):** rolling
**Undergraduate student body:**
209 full time, 0 part time; 35%
male, 65% female; 0% American
Indian, 1% Asian, 2% black, 6%
Hispanic, 4% multiracial, 0%
Pacific Islander, 73% white, 0%
international
**Most popular majors:** Information
not available
**Expenses:** 2014-2015: $14,930;
room/board: $1,488
**Financial aid:** (800) 468-4888;
46% of undergrads determined to
have financial need; average aid
package $7,964

## Green Mountain College
Poultney VT
(802) 287-8208
**U.S. News ranking:** Nat. Lib. Arts,
second tier
**Website:** www.greenmtn.edu
**Admissions email:**
admiss@greenmtn.edu
**Private;** founded 1834
**Affiliation:** United Methodist
**Freshman admissions:** selective;
2013-2014: 773 applied, 584
accepted. Neither SAT nor ACT
required. SAT 25/75 percentile:
920-1200. High school rank: N/A
**Early decision deadline:** N/A,
notification date: N/A
**Early action deadline:** 11/1,
notification date: 12/14
**Application deadline (fall):** rolling
**Undergraduate student body:** 568
full time, 23 part time; 45%
male, 55% female; 1% American
Indian, 2% Asian, 6% black,
2% Hispanic, 2% multiracial,
0% Pacific Islander, 63% white,
4% international; 13% from in
state; 84% live on campus; N/A
of students in fraternities, N/A in
sororities
**Most popular majors:** Information
not available
**Expenses:** 2013-2014: $32,436;
room/board: $11,266
**Financial aid:** (802) 287-8210

## Johnson State College
Johnson VT
(800) 635-2356
**U.S. News ranking:** Reg. U. (N),
second tier
**Website:** www.jsc.edu
**Admissions email:**
JSCAdmissions@jsc.edu
**Public**
**Freshman admissions:** less
selective; 2013-2014: N/A
applied, N/A accepted. Neither
SAT nor ACT required. ACT 25/75
percentile: N/A. High school
rank: N/A
**Early decision deadline:** N/A,
notification date: N/A
**Early action deadline:** N/A,
notification date: N/A
**Application deadline (fall):** N/A
**Undergraduate student body:** 1,004
full time, 531 part time; 35%
male, 65% female; N/A American
Indian, N/A Asian, N/A black, N/A
Hispanic, N/A multiracial, N/A
Pacific Islander, N/A white, N/A
international

**Most popular majors:** Information
not available
**Expenses:** 2013-2014: $10,286
in state, $21,950 out of state;
room/board: $9,138
**Financial aid:** (802) 635-1380

## Lyndon State College[1]
Lyndonville VT
(802) 626-6413
**U.S. News ranking:** Reg. Coll. (N),
second tier
**Website:** www.lyndonstate.edu
**Admissions email:** admissions@
lyndonstate.edu
**Public**
**Application deadline (fall):** N/A
**Undergraduate student body:** N/A
full time, N/A part time
**Expenses:** 2013-2014: $10,286
in state, $20,942 out of state;
room/board: $9,138
**Financial aid:** (802) 626-6218

## Marlboro College[1]
Marlboro VT
(800) 343-0049
**U.S. News ranking:** Nat. Lib. Arts,
unranked
**Website:** www.marlboro.edu
**Admissions email:**
admissions@marlboro.edu
**Private**
**Application deadline (fall):** N/A
**Undergraduate student body:** N/A
full time, N/A part time
**Expenses:** 2013-2014: $38,110;
room/board: $10,280
**Financial aid:** (802) 258-9237

## Middlebury College
Middlebury VT
(802) 443-3000
**U.S. News ranking:** Nat. Lib. Arts,
No. 7
**Website:** www.middlebury.edu
**Admissions email:** admissions@
middlebury.edu
**Private;** founded 1800
**Freshman admissions:** most
selective; 2013-2014: 9,109
applied, 1,595 accepted. Either
SAT or ACT required. SAT 25/75
percentile: 1280-1490. High
school rank: 74% in top tenth,
93% in top quarter, 99% in
top half
**Early decision deadline:** 11/1,
notification date: 12/15
**Early action deadline:** N/A,
notification date: N/A
**Application deadline (fall):** 1/1
**Undergraduate student body:** 2,477
full time, 18 part time; 49%
male, 51% female; 0% American
Indian, 6% Asian, 3% black,
7% Hispanic, 4% multiracial,
0% Pacific Islander, 66% white,
10% international; 6% from in
state; 95% live on campus; 0%
of students in fraternities, 0% in
sororities
**Most popular majors:** 13%
Economics, General, 6% English
Language and Literature/Letters,
Other, 7% Environmental
Studies, 7% Political Science
and Government, General, 6%
Psychology, General
**Expenses:** 2014-2015: $46,044;
room/board: $13,116
**Financial aid:** (802) 443-5158;
40% of undergrads determined to
have financial need; average aid
package $40,419

## Norwich University

Northfield VT
(800) 468-6679
**U.S. News ranking:** Reg. U. (N), No. 74
**Website:** www.norwich.edu
**Admissions email:** nuadm@norwich.edu
**Private;** founded 1819
**Freshman admissions:** selective; 2013-2014: 3,081 applied, 1,956 accepted. Either SAT or ACT required. SAT 25/75 percentile: 950-1160. High school rank: 11% in top tenth, 33% in top quarter, 70% in top half
**Early decision deadline:** N/A, notification date: N/A
**Early action deadline:** N/A, notification date: N/A
**Application deadline (fall):** rolling
**Undergraduate student body:** 2,186 full time, 70 part time; 74% male, 26% female; 1% American Indian, 2% Asian, 2% black, 3% Hispanic, 2% multiracial, 0% Pacific Islander, 95% white, 1% international; 12% from in state; 93% live on campus; 0% of students in fraternities, 0% in sororities
**Most popular majors:** 7% Architecture, 6% Business Administration and Management, General, 22% Criminal Justice/Law Enforcement Administration, 7% Mechanical Engineering, 7% Registered Nursing/Registered Nurse
**Expenses:** 2014-2015: $34,704; room/board: $11,984
**Financial aid:** (802) 485-2015; 79% of undergrads determined to have financial need; average aid package $27,656

## Southern Vermont College

Bennington VT
(802) 447-6304
**U.S. News ranking:** Reg. Coll. (N), second tier
**Website:** www.svc.edu
**Admissions email:** admis@svc.edu
**Private**
**Freshman admissions:** least selective; 2013-2014: N/A applied, N/A accepted. Neither SAT nor ACT required. ACT 25/75 percentile: N/A. High school rank: N/A
**Early decision deadline:** N/A, notification date: N/A
**Early action deadline:** N/A, notification date: N/A
**Application deadline (fall):** N/A
**Undergraduate student body:** 453 full time, 27 part time; 38% male, 62% female; 0% American Indian, 1% Asian, 9% black, 9% Hispanic, 1% multiracial, 0% Pacific Islander, 63% white, 1% international
**Most popular majors:** Information not available
**Expenses:** 2014-2015: $22,370; room/board: $10,500
**Financial aid:** (877) 563-6076

## Sterling College[1]

Craftsbury Common VT
(802) 586-7711
**U.S. News ranking:** Nat. Lib. Arts, unranked
**Website:** www.sterlingcollege.edu
**Admissions email:** admissions@sterlingcollege.edu
**Private;** founded 1958
**Application deadline (fall):** rolling

---

**Undergraduate student body:** N/A full time, N/A part time
**Expenses:** 2013-2014: $29,894; room/board: $8,498
**Financial aid:** (802) 586-7711

## St. Michael's College

Colchester VT
(800) 762-8000
**U.S. News ranking:** Nat. Lib. Arts, No. 99
**Website:** www.smcvt.edu
**Admissions email:** admission@smcvt.edu
**Private;** founded 1904
**Affiliation:** Roman Catholic
**Freshman admissions:** selective; 2013-2014: 4,431 applied, 3,328 accepted. Neither SAT nor ACT required. SAT 25/75 percentile: 1060-1290. High school rank: 26% in top tenth, 54% in top quarter, 81% in top half
**Early decision deadline:** N/A, notification date: N/A
**Early action deadline:** 11/1, notification date: 1/1
**Application deadline (fall):** 2/1
**Undergraduate student body:** 1,959 full time, 39 part time; 45% male, 55% female; 0% American Indian, 2% Asian, 2% black, 4% Hispanic, 2% multiracial, 0% Pacific Islander, 86% white, 3% international; 20% from in state; 96% live on campus; 0% of students in fraternities, 0% in sororities
**Most popular majors:** 11% Biological and Biomedical Sciences, 18% Business, Management, Marketing, and Related Support Services, 8% English Language and Literature/Letters, 10% Psychology, 13% Social Sciences
**Expenses:** 2014-2015: $39,375; room/board: $10,600
**Financial aid:** (802) 654-3243; 69% of undergrads determined to have financial need; average aid package $26,858

## University of Vermont

Burlington VT
(802) 656-3370
**U.S. News ranking:** Nat. U., No. 85
**Website:** www.uvm.edu
**Admissions email:** admissions@uvm.edu
**Public;** founded 1791
**Freshman admissions:** more selective; 2013-2014: 22,381 applied, 17,357 accepted. Either SAT or ACT required. SAT 25/75 percentile: 1080-1290. High school rank: 33% in top tenth, 68% in top quarter, 96% in top half
**Early decision deadline:** N/A, notification date: N/A
**Early action deadline:** 11/1, notification date: 12/15
**Application deadline (fall):** 1/15
**Undergraduate student body:** 9,764 full time, 1,148 part time; 44% male, 56% female; 0% American Indian, 2% Asian, 1% black, 4% Hispanic, 3% multiracial, 0% Pacific Islander, 83% white, 2% international; 34% from in state; 50% live on campus; 6% of students in fraternities, 6% in sororities
**Most popular majors:** 8% Business Administration and Management, General, 5% English Language

---

and Literature, General, 5% Environmental Studies, 5% Political Science and Government, General, 6% Psychology, General
**Expenses:** 2014-2015: $16,226 in state, $37,874 out of state; room/board: $10,780
**Financial aid:** (802) 656-5700; 58% of undergrads determined to have financial need; average aid package $21,989

## Vermont Technical College

Randolph Center VT
(802) 728-1244
**U.S. News ranking:** Reg. Coll. (N), No. 36
**Website:** www.vtc.edu
**Admissions email:** admissions@vtc.edu
**Public;** founded 1866
**Freshman admissions:** less selective; 2013-2014: 841 applied, 560 accepted. Neither SAT nor ACT required. SAT 25/75 percentile: 810-1040. High school rank: 7% in top tenth, 27% in top quarter, 58% in top half
**Early decision deadline:** N/A, notification date: N/A
**Early action deadline:** N/A, notification date: N/A
**Application deadline (fall):** rolling
**Undergraduate student body:** 1,042 full time, 503 part time; 58% male, 42% female; 1% American Indian, 1% Asian, 1% black, 1% Hispanic, 0% multiracial, 0% Pacific Islander, 88% white, 4% international; 86% from in state; N/A live on campus; N/A of students in fraternities, N/A in sororities
**Most popular majors:** Information not available
**Expenses:** 2014-2015: $13,200 in state, $24,048 out of state; room/board: $9,414
**Financial aid:** (800) 965-8790; 77% of undergrads determined to have financial need; average aid package $11,282

## Averett University

Danville VA
(800) 283-7388
**U.S. News ranking:** Reg. Coll. (S), No. 25
**Website:** www.averett.edu
**Admissions email:** admit@averett.edu
**Private;** founded 1859
**Affiliation:** Baptist General Association of Virginia
**Freshman admissions:** less selective; 2013-2014: 1,697 applied, 1,491 accepted. Either SAT or ACT required. SAT 25/75 percentile: 840-1030. High school rank: 11% in top tenth, 30% in top quarter, 60% in top half
**Early decision deadline:** N/A, notification date: N/A
**Early action deadline:** N/A, notification date: N/A
**Application deadline (fall):** rolling
**Undergraduate student body:** 858 full time, 28 part time; 50% male, 50% female; 1% American Indian, 1% Asian, 23% black, 3% Hispanic, 0% multiracial, 0% Pacific Islander, 63% white, 9% international; 70% from in state; 57% live on campus; 0% of students in fraternities, 1% in sororities

---

**Most popular majors:** 12% Criminal Justice/Law Enforcement Administration, 28% Education, General, 13% Health Services/Allied Health/Health Sciences, General, 5% Liberal Arts and Sciences/Liberal Studies, 17% Marketing/Marketing Management, General
**Expenses:** 2014-2015: $29,150; room/board: $8,600
**Financial aid:** (434) 791-5646; 85% of undergrads determined to have financial need; average aid package $22,442

## Bluefield College

Bluefield VA
(276) 326-4231
**U.S. News ranking:** Reg. Coll. (S), No. 54
**Website:** www.bluefield.edu
**Admissions email:** admissions@bluefield.edu
**Private;** founded 1922
**Affiliation:** Baptist
**Freshman admissions:** less selective; 2013-2014: 1,044 applied, 598 accepted. Either SAT or ACT required. SAT 25/75 percentile: 800-1010. High school rank: 8% in top tenth, 27% in top quarter, 64% in top half
**Early decision deadline:** N/A, notification date: N/A
**Early action deadline:** N/A, notification date: N/A
**Application deadline (fall):** rolling
**Undergraduate student body:** 723 full time, 114 part time; 45% male, 55% female; 0% American Indian, 0% Asian, 23% black, 3% Hispanic, 3% multiracial, 0% Pacific Islander, 67% white, 2% international; 24% from in state; 66% live on campus; 11% of students in fraternities, 41% in sororities
**Most popular majors:** 28% Business Administration and Management, General, 19% Criminal Justice/Safety Studies, 8% Human Services, General, 10% Kinesiology and Exercise Science, 8% Psychology, Other
**Expenses:** 2014-2015: $22,840; room/board: $8,456
**Financial aid:** (276) 326-4215; 87% of undergrads determined to have financial need; average aid package $14,942

## Bridgewater College

Bridgewater VA
(800) 759-8328
**U.S. News ranking:** Nat. Lib. Arts, No. 178
**Website:** www.bridgewater.edu
**Admissions email:** admissions@bridgewater.edu
**Private;** founded 1880
**Affiliation:** Church of the Brethren
**Freshman admissions:** selective; 2013-2014: 5,401 applied, 2,967 accepted. Either SAT or ACT required. SAT 25/75 percentile: 930-1130. High school rank: 20% in top tenth, 45% in top quarter, 82% in top half
**Early decision deadline:** N/A, notification date: N/A
**Early action deadline:** N/A, notification date: N/A
**Application deadline (fall):** 5/1
**Undergraduate student body:** 1,840 full time, 8 part time; 45% male, 55% female; 0% American Indian, 1% Asian, 9% black, 3% Hispanic, 4% multiracial,

---

0% Pacific Islander, 79% white, 1% international; 78% from in state; 83% live on campus; 0% of students in fraternities, 0% in sororities
**Most popular majors:** 11% Biology/Biological Sciences, General, 11% Business Administration and Management, General, 5% Family and Consumer Sciences/Human Sciences, General, 10% Health and Physical Education/Fitness, General, 6% Liberal Arts and Sciences/Liberal Studies
**Expenses:** 2014-2015: $30,380; room/board: $11,070
**Financial aid:** (540) 828-5376; 82% of undergrads determined to have financial need; average aid package $25,654

## Christopher Newport University

Newport News VA
(757) 594-7015
**U.S. News ranking:** Reg. U. (S), No. 17
**Website:** www.cnu.edu
**Admissions email:** admit@cnu.edu
**Public;** founded 1960
**Freshman admissions:** selective; 2013-2014: 7,016 applied, 4,141 accepted. Neither SAT nor ACT required. SAT 25/75 percentile: 1070-1250. High school rank: 20% in top tenth, 53% in top quarter, 91% in top half
**Early decision deadline:** 11/15, notification date: 12/15
**Early action deadline:** 12/1, notification date: 1/15
**Application deadline (fall):** 2/1
**Undergraduate student body:** 4,962 full time, 132 part time; 43% male, 57% female; 0% American Indian, 2% Asian, 8% black, 5% Hispanic, 5% multiracial, 0% Pacific Islander, 75% white, 0% international; 93% from in state; 73% live on campus; 3% of students in fraternities, 0% in sororities
**Most popular majors:** 12% Biology/Biological Sciences, General, 12% Business Administration and Management, General, 9% History, General, 14% Psychology, General, 10% Speech Communication and Rhetoric
**Expenses:** 2014-2015: $11,646 in state, $21,578 out of state; room/board: $10,314
**Financial aid:** (757) 594-7170; 46% of undergrads determined to have financial need; average aid package $8,359

## College of William and Mary

Williamsburg VA
(757) 221-4223
**U.S. News ranking:** Nat. U., No. 33
**Website:** www.wm.edu
**Admissions email:** admission@wm.edu
**Public;** founded 1693
**Freshman admissions:** most selective; 2013-2014: 14,046 applied, 4,665 accepted. Either SAT or ACT required. SAT 25/75 percentile: 1270-1460. High school rank: 80% in top tenth, 97% in top quarter, 99% in top half
**Early decision deadline:** 11/1, notification date: 12/1

---

**Early action deadline:** N/A, notification date: N/A
**Application deadline (fall):** 1/1
**Undergraduate student body:** 6,195 full time, 76 part time; 45% male, 55% female; 0% American Indian, 7% Asian, 7% black, 9% Hispanic, 5% multiracial, 0% Pacific Islander, 60% white, 4% international; 69% from in state; 73% live on campus; 25% of students in fraternities, 30% in sororities
**Most popular majors:** 9% Biological and Biomedical Sciences, 12% Business, Management, Marketing, and Related Support Services, 7% English Language and Literature/Letters, 8% Psychology, 23% Social Sciences
**Expenses:** 2014-2015: $17,656 in state, $39,360 out of state; room/board: $10,344
**Financial aid:** (757) 221-2420; 34% of undergrads determined to have financial need; average aid package $18,125

## Eastern Mennonite University
Harrisonburg VA
(800) 368-2665
**U.S. News ranking:** Nat. Lib. Arts, No. 172
**Website:** www.emu.edu
**Admissions email:** admiss@emu.edu
**Private;** founded 1917
**Affiliation:** Mennonite Church USA
**Freshman admissions:** selective; 2013-2014: 1,073 applied, 698 accepted. Either SAT or ACT required. SAT 25/75 percentile: 863-1128. High school rank: 16% in top tenth, 36% in top quarter, 75% in top half
**Early decision deadline:** N/A, notification date: N/A
**Early action deadline:** N/A, notification date: N/A
**Application deadline (fall):** rolling
**Undergraduate student body:** 1,122 full time, 62 part time; 35% male, 65% female; 0% American Indian, 2% Asian, 6% black, 7% Hispanic, 2% multiracial, 0% Pacific Islander, 77% white, 3% international; 57% from in state; 58% live on campus; N/A of students in fraternities, N/A in sororities
**Most popular majors:** 8% Biological and Biomedical Sciences, 7% Business, Management, Marketing, and Related Support Services, 18% Health Professions and Related Programs, 17% Liberal Arts and Sciences, General Studies and Humanities, 9% Psychology
**Expenses:** 2013-2014: $29,350; room/board: $9,500
**Financial aid:** (540) 432-4139

## ECPI University[1]
Virginia Beach VA
(866) 499-0336
**U.S. News ranking:** Reg. Coll. (S), unranked
**Website:** www.ecpi.edu/
**Admissions email:** ssaunders@ecpi.edu
**For-profit**
**Application deadline (fall):** N/A
**Undergraduate student body:** N/A full time, N/A part time
**Expenses:** 2013-2014: $14,245; room/board: N/A
**Financial aid:** N/A

## Emory and Henry College
Emory VA
(800) 848-5493
**U.S. News ranking:** Nat. Lib. Arts, No. 172
**Website:** www.ehc.edu
**Admissions email:** ehadmiss@ehc.edu
**Private;** founded 1836
**Affiliation:** United Methodist
**Freshman admissions:** selective; 2013-2014: 1,663 applied, 1,093 accepted. Either SAT or ACT required. SAT 25/75 percentile: 880-1120. High school rank: N/A
**Early decision deadline:** 11/15, notification date: 12/15
**Early action deadline:** N/A, notification date: N/A
**Application deadline (fall):** rolling
**Undergraduate student body:** 889 full time, 47 part time; 52% male, 48% female; 1% American Indian, 0% Asian, 9% black, 2% Hispanic, 2% multiracial, 0% Pacific Islander, 81% white, 1% international; 64% from in state; 79% live on campus; N/A of students in fraternities, N/A in sororities
**Most popular majors:** 8% Biology/Biological Sciences, General, 6% Environmental Science, 6% History Teacher Education, 5% Psychology, General, 7% Sociology
**Expenses:** 2014-2015: $30,226; room/board: $10,258
**Financial aid:** (276) 944-6229; 83% of undergrads determined to have financial need; average aid package $26,671

## Ferrum College
Ferrum VA
(800) 868-9797
**U.S. News ranking:** Reg. Coll. (S), No. 47
**Website:** www.ferrum.edu
**Admissions email:** admissions@ferrum.edu
**Private;** founded 1913
**Affiliation:** United Methodist
**Freshman admissions:** least selective; 2013-2014: 3,273 applied, 2,426 accepted. Either SAT or ACT required. SAT 25/75 percentile: 780-990. High school rank: 2% in top tenth, 15% in top quarter, 48% in top half
**Early decision deadline:** N/A, notification date: N/A
**Early action deadline:** N/A, notification date: N/A
**Application deadline (fall):** rolling
**Undergraduate student body:** 1,492 full time, 20 part time; 57% male, 43% female; 0% American Indian, 0% Asian, 32% black, 5% Hispanic, 5% multiracial, 0% Pacific Islander, 52% white, 1% international; 82% from in state; 91% live on campus; 12% of students in fraternities, 17% in sororities
**Most popular majors:** 11% Business, Management, Marketing, and Related Support Services, 8% Education, 11% Health Professions and Related Programs, 7% Homeland Security, Law Enforcement, Firefighting and Related Protective Services, 10% Liberal Arts and Sciences, General Studies and Humanities
**Expenses:** 2014-2015: $29,795; room/board: $9,970
**Financial aid:** (540) 365-4282

## George Mason University
Fairfax VA
(703) 993-2400
**U.S. News ranking:** Nat. U., No. 138
**Website:** www.gmu.edu
**Admissions email:** admissions@gmu.edu
**Public;** founded 1972
**Freshman admissions:** selective; 2013-2014: 20,805 applied, 12,905 accepted. Neither SAT nor ACT required. SAT 25/75 percentile: 1050-1250. High school rank: 20% in top tenth, 56% in top quarter, 94% in top half
**Early decision deadline:** N/A, notification date: N/A
**Early action deadline:** 11/1, notification date: 12/15
**Application deadline (fall):** 1/15
**Undergraduate student body:** 17,261 full time, 4,729 part time; 48% male, 52% female; 0% American Indian, 17% Asian, 10% black, 12% Hispanic, 5% multiracial, 0% Pacific Islander, 46% white, 4% international; 89% from in state; 27% live on campus; 7% of students in fraternities, 9% in sororities
**Most popular majors:** 6% Accounting, 5% Biology/Biological Sciences, General, 6% Information Technology, 8% Psychology, General, 6% Speech Communication and Rhetoric
**Expenses:** 2014-2015: $10,382 in state, $29,960 out of state; room/board: $10,100
**Financial aid:** (703) 993-2353; 53% of undergrads determined to have financial need; average aid package $11,731

## Hampden-Sydney College
Hampden-Sydney VA
(800) 755-0733
**U.S. News ranking:** Nat. Lib. Arts, No. 105
**Website:** www.hsc.edu
**Admissions email:** hsapp@hsc.edu
**Private;** founded 1775
**Affiliation:** Presbyterian
**Freshman admissions:** selective; 2013-2014: 2,623 applied, 1,439 accepted. Either SAT or ACT required. SAT 25/75 percentile: 1005-1215. High school rank: 13% in top tenth, 28% in top quarter, 85% in top half
**Early decision deadline:** 11/15, notification date: 12/15
**Early action deadline:** 1/15, notification date: 2/15
**Application deadline (fall):** 3/1
**Undergraduate student body:** 1,070 full time, N/A part time; 100% male, 0% female; 1% American Indian, 2% Asian, 8% black, 2% Hispanic, 5% multiracial, 0% Pacific Islander, 81% white, 0% international; 71% from in state; 95% live on campus; 34% of students in fraternities, 0% in sororities
**Most popular majors:** 8% American Government and Politics (United States), 12% Business/Managerial Economics, 13% Economics, General, 19% History, General, 10% Psychology, Other
**Expenses:** 2014-2015: $39,272; room/board: $12,312

**Financial aid:** (434) 223-6119; 64% of undergrads determined to have financial need; average aid package $29,135

## Hampton University
Hampton VA
(757) 727-5328
**U.S. News ranking:** Reg. U. (S), No. 18
**Website:** www.hamptonu.edu
**Admissions email:** admissions@hamptonu.edu
**Private;** founded 1868
**Freshman admissions:** selective; 2013-2014: 15,337 applied, 5,529 accepted. Neither SAT nor ACT required. SAT 25/75 percentile: 920-1090. High school rank: 20% in top tenth, 45% in top quarter, 89% in top half
**Early decision deadline:** N/A, notification date: N/A
**Early action deadline:** 11/1, notification date: 12/31
**Application deadline (fall):** 3/1
**Undergraduate student body:** 3,464 full time, 278 part time; 36% male, 64% female; 0% American Indian, 1% Asian, 94% black, 1% Hispanic, 0% multiracial, 0% Pacific Islander, 3% white, 1% international; 21% from in state; 56% live on campus; 5% of students in fraternities, 4% in sororities
**Most popular majors:** 7% Biology/Biological Sciences, General, 6% Business Administration and Management, General, 5% Journalism, Other, 17% Psychology, General, 13% Registered Nursing/Registered Nurse
**Expenses:** 2014-2015: $22,010; room/board: $9,692
**Financial aid:** (800) 624-3341; 59% of undergrads determined to have financial need; average aid package $5,632

## Hollins University
Roanoke VA
(800) 456-9595
**U.S. News ranking:** Nat. Lib. Arts, No. 112
**Website:** www.hollins.edu
**Admissions email:** huadm@hollins.edu
**Private;** founded 1842
**Freshman admissions:** selective; 2013-2014: 824 applied, 571 accepted. Either SAT or ACT required. SAT 25/75 percentile: 970-1220. High school rank: 24% in top tenth, 54% in top quarter, 83% in top half
**Early decision deadline:** 11/1, notification date: 11/15
**Early action deadline:** 12/1, notification date: 12/15
**Application deadline (fall):** rolling
**Undergraduate student body:** 559 full time, 21 part time; 1% male, 99% female; 0% American Indian, 3% Asian, 10% black, 6% Hispanic, 3% multiracial, 0% Pacific Islander, 72% white, 5% international; 55% from in state; 79% live on campus; N/A of students in fraternities, N/A in sororities
**Most popular majors:** 7% Biological and Biomedical Sciences, 21% English Language and Literature/Letters, 6% Psychology, 17% Social Sciences, 21% Visual and Performing Arts
**Expenses:** 2014-2015: $34,295; room/board: $11,940

**Financial aid:** (540) 362-6332; 77% of undergrads determined to have financial need; average aid package $30,402

## James Madison University
Harrisonburg VA
(540) 568-5681
**U.S. News ranking:** Reg. U. (S), No. 6
**Website:** www.jmu.edu
**Admissions email:** admissions@jmu.edu
**Public;** founded 1908
**Freshman admissions:** selective; 2013-2014: 23,400 applied, 14,168 accepted. Either SAT or ACT required. SAT 25/75 percentile: 1050-1240. High school rank: 27% in top tenth, 45% in top quarter, 99% in top half
**Early decision deadline:** N/A, notification date: N/A
**Early action deadline:** 11/1, notification date: 1/15
**Application deadline (fall):** 1/15
**Undergraduate student body:** 17,526 full time, 905 part time; 41% male, 59% female; 0% American Indian, 4% Asian, 4% black, 5% Hispanic, 3% multiracial, 0% Pacific Islander, 79% white, 2% international; 71% from in state; 33% live on campus; 10% of students in fraternities, 12% in sororities
**Most popular majors:** 9% Communication, Journalism, and Related Programs, 7% Liberal Arts and Sciences, General Studies and Humanities, 6% Parks, Recreation, Leisure, and Fitness Studies, 6% Psychology, 8% Social Sciences
**Expenses:** 2014-2015: $9,662 in state, $24,522 out of state; room/board: $8,828
**Financial aid:** (540) 568-7820; 42% of undergrads determined to have financial need; average aid package $9,509

## Liberty University
Lynchburg VA
(800) 543-5317
**U.S. News ranking:** Reg. U. (S), No. 80
**Website:** www.liberty.edu
**Admissions email:** admissions@liberty.edu
**Private;** founded 1971
**Affiliation:** Southern Baptist
**Freshman admissions:** selective; 2013-2014: 27,458 applied, 5,821 accepted. Either SAT or ACT required. SAT 25/75 percentile: 900-1150. High school rank: 16% in top tenth, 38% in top quarter, 70% in top half
**Early decision deadline:** N/A, notification date: N/A
**Early action deadline:** N/A, notification date: N/A
**Application deadline (fall):** rolling
**Undergraduate student body:** 25,911 full time, 21,549 part time; 41% male, 59% female; 1% American Indian, 1% Asian, 15% black, 2% Hispanic, 2% multiracial, 0% Pacific Islander, 49% white, 3% international; 42% from in state; 60% live on campus; N/A of students in fraternities, N/A in sororities
**Most popular majors:** Information not available

**Expenses:** 2014-2015: $21,706; room/board: $8,200
**Financial aid:** (434) 582-2270; 81% of undergrads determined to have financial need; average aid package $8,498

## Longwood University
Farmville VA
(434) 395-2060
**U.S. News ranking:** Reg. U. (S), No. 30
**Website:** www.whylongwood.com
**Admissions email:** admissions@longwood.edu
**Public;** founded 1839
**Freshman admissions:** selective; 2013-2014: 4,055 applied, 3,299 accepted. Either SAT or ACT required. SAT 25/75 percentile: 920-1090. High school rank: 10% in top tenth, 33% in top quarter, 73% in top half
**Early decision deadline:** N/A, notification date: N/A
**Early action deadline:** 12/1, notification date: 1/15
**Application deadline (fall):** rolling
**Undergraduate student body:** 4,123 full time, 374 part time; 34% male, 66% female; 0% American Indian, 1% Asian, 8% black, 5% Hispanic, 4% multiracial, 0% Pacific Islander, 78% white, 1% international; 97% from in state; 71% live on campus; 22% of students in fraternities, 22% in sororities
**Most popular majors:** 7% Biology/Biological Sciences, General, 12% Business Administration and Management, General, 19% Liberal Arts and Sciences/Liberal Studies, 7% Social Sciences, General, 7% Visual and Performing Arts, General
**Expenses:** 2014-2015: $11,580 in state, $25,350 out of state; room/board: $9,948
**Financial aid:** (434) 395-2077; 54% of undergrads determined to have financial need; average aid package $13,155

## Lynchburg College
Lynchburg VA
(434) 544-8300
**U.S. News ranking:** Reg. U. (S), No. 33
**Website:** www.lynchburg.edu
**Admissions email:** admissions@lynchburg.edu
**Private;** founded 1903
**Affiliation:** Christian Church (Disciples of Christ)
**Freshman admissions:** selective; 2013-2014: 5,695 applied, 3,627 accepted. Either SAT or ACT required. SAT 25/75 percentile: 890-1110. High school rank: N/A
**Early decision deadline:** 11/15, notification date: 12/15
**Early action deadline:** N/A, notification date: N/A
**Application deadline (fall):** rolling
**Undergraduate student body:** 2,089 full time, 89 part time; 40% male, 60% female; 0% American Indian, 1% Asian, 11% black, 4% Hispanic, 3% multiracial, 0% Pacific Islander, 77% white, 1% international; 68% from in state; 73% live on campus; 11% of students in fraternities, 14% in sororities
**Most popular majors:** 10% Biological and Biomedical Sciences, 10% Business, Management, Marketing, and Related Support Services,

9% Education, 14% Health Professions and Related Programs, 15% Social Sciences
**Expenses:** 2014-2015: $34,545; room/board: $9,330
**Financial aid:** (434) 544-8228; 76% of undergrads determined to have financial need; average aid package $24,284

## Mary Baldwin College
Staunton VA
(800) 468-2262
**U.S. News ranking:** Reg. U. (S), No. 49
**Website:** www.mbc.edu
**Admissions email:** admit@mbc.edu
**Private;** founded 1842
**Affiliation:** Presbyterian
**Freshman admissions:** less selective; 2013-2014: 2,952 applied, 2,731 accepted. Either SAT or ACT required. SAT 25/75 percentile: 830-1060. High school rank: 16% in top tenth, 46% in top quarter, 80% in top half
**Early decision deadline:** 11/15, notification date: 12/1
**Early action deadline:** N/A, notification date: N/A
**Application deadline (fall):** rolling
**Undergraduate student body:** 1,033 full time, 404 part time; 6% male, 94% female; 1% American Indian, 4% Asian, 26% black, 7% Hispanic, 3% multiracial, 0% Pacific Islander, 55% white, 0% international; 61% from in state; 52% live on campus; 0% of students in fraternities, 0% in sororities
**Most popular majors:** 9% Area, Ethnic, Cultural, Gender, and Group Studies, 8% Business, Management, Marketing, and Related Support Services, 10% History, 16% Psychology, 17% Social Sciences
**Expenses:** 2014-2015: $29,595; room/board: $8,650
**Financial aid:** (540) 887-7022; 82% of undergrads determined to have financial need; average aid package $21,761

## Marymount University
Arlington VA
(703) 284-1500
**U.S. News ranking:** Reg. U. (S), No. 37
**Website:** www.marymount.edu
**Admissions email:** admissions@marymount.edu
**Private;** founded 1950
**Affiliation:** Roman Catholic
**Freshman admissions:** selective; 2013-2014: 2,082 applied, 1,718 accepted. Either SAT or ACT required. SAT 25/75 percentile: 930-1130. High school rank: 22% in top tenth, 44% in top quarter, 78% in top half
**Early decision deadline:** N/A, notification date: N/A
**Early action deadline:** N/A, notification date: N/A
**Application deadline (fall):** rolling
**Undergraduate student body:** 2,141 full time, 255 part time; 32% male, 68% female; 0% American Indian, 9% Asian, 15% black, 15% Hispanic, 3% multiracial, 1% Pacific Islander, 43% white, 9% international; 63% from in state; 36% live on campus; 0% of students in fraternities, 0% in sororities
**Most popular majors:** 17% Business Administration and Management, General, 5% Fashion Merchandising,

5% Interior Design, 6% Public Health Education and Promotion, 30% Registered Nursing/Registered Nurse
**Expenses:** 2014-2015: $27,470; room/board: $12,010
**Financial aid:** (703) 284-1530; 66% of undergrads determined to have financial need; average aid package $17,589

## Norfolk State University
Norfolk VA
(757) 823-8396
**U.S. News ranking:** Reg. U. (S), second tier
**Website:** www.nsu.edu
**Admissions email:** admissions@nsu.edu
**Public**
**Freshman admissions:** less selective; 2013-2014: 3,373 applied, 2,192 accepted. Either SAT or ACT required. SAT 25/75 percentile: 770-948. High school rank: N/A
**Early decision deadline:** N/A, notification date: N/A
**Early action deadline:** N/A, notification date: N/A
**Undergraduate student body:** 4,976 full time, 1,045 part time; 36% male, 64% female; 0% American Indian, 0% Asian, 84% black, 3% Hispanic, 3% multiracial, 0% Pacific Islander, 5% white, 0% international; 85% from in state; 37% live on campus; N/A of students in fraternities, N/A in sororities
**Most popular majors:** 15% Business, Management, Marketing, and Related Support Services, 10% Health Professions and Related Programs, 10% Multi/Interdisciplinary Studies, 10% Psychology, 10% Social Sciences
**Expenses:** 2014-2015: $8,850 in state, $21,540 out of state; room/board: $8,624
**Financial aid:** (757) 823-8381

## Old Dominion University
Norfolk VA
(757) 683-3685
**U.S. News ranking:** Nat. U., second tier
**Website:** www.odu.edu
**Admissions email:** admissions@odu.edu
**Public;** founded 1930
**Freshman admissions:** selective; 2013-2014: 10,202 applied, 7,834 accepted. Either SAT or ACT required. SAT 25/75 percentile: 930-1130. High school rank: 10% in top tenth, 33% in top quarter, 75% in top half
**Early decision deadline:** N/A, notification date: N/A
**Early action deadline:** 12/1, notification date: 1/15
**Application deadline (fall):** rolling
**Undergraduate student body:** 15,102 full time, 4,717 part time; 46% male, 54% female; 0% American Indian, 4% Asian, 26% black, 7% Hispanic, 6% multiracial, 0% Pacific Islander, 52% white, 1% international; 93% from in state; 24% live on campus; 6% of students in fraternities, 5% in sororities
**Most popular majors:** 16% Business, Management, Marketing, and Related Support Services, 8% English Language

and Literature/Letters, 14% Health Professions and Related Programs, 7% Multi/Interdisciplinary Studies, 14% Social Sciences
**Expenses:** 2014-2015: $9,280 in state, $25,030 out of state; room/board: $10,396
**Financial aid:** (703) 284-1530; 63% of undergrads determined to have financial need; average aid package $9,677

## Radford University
Radford VA
(540) 831-5371
**U.S. News ranking:** Reg. U. (S), No. 34
**Website:** www.radford.edu
**Admissions email:** admissions@radford.edu
**Public;** founded 1910
**Freshman admissions:** less selective; 2013-2014: 7,774 applied, 6,088 accepted. Either SAT or ACT required. SAT 25/75 percentile: 900-1080. High school rank: 6% in top tenth, 22% in top quarter, 61% in top half
**Early decision deadline:** N/A, notification date: N/A
**Early action deadline:** 12/1, notification date: 1/15
**Application deadline (fall):** 2/1
**Undergraduate student body:** 8,545 full time, 368 part time; 44% male, 56% female; 0% American Indian, 1% Asian, 10% black, 5% Hispanic, 4% multiracial, 0% Pacific Islander, 78% white, 1% international; 95% from in state; 36% live on campus; 9% of students in fraternities, 12% in sororities
**Most popular majors:** 7% Criminal Justice/Safety Studies, 10% Multi-/Interdisciplinary Studies, Other, 7% Physical Education Teaching and Coaching, 7% Psychology, 6% Registered Nursing/Registered Nurse
**Expenses:** 2014-2015: $9,360 in state, $21,600 out of state; room/board: $8,406
**Financial aid:** (540) 831-5408; 56% of undergrads determined to have financial need; average aid package $9,316

## Randolph College
Lynchburg VA
(800) 745-7692
**U.S. News ranking:** Nat. Lib. Arts, No. 133
**Website:** www.randolphcollege.edu/
**Admissions email:** admissions@randolphcollege.edu
**Private;** founded 1891
**Affiliation:** United Methodist
**Freshman admissions:** selective; 2013-2014: 1,056 applied, 881 accepted. Either SAT or ACT required. SAT 25/75 percentile: 970-1200. High school rank: 17% in top tenth, 54% in top quarter, 91% in top half
**Early decision deadline:** N/A, notification date: N/A
**Early action deadline:** 12/1, notification date: 1/1
**Application deadline (fall):** 2/1
**Undergraduate student body:** 649 full time, 16 part time; 36% male, 64% female; 1% American Indian, 2% Asian, 9% black, 6% Hispanic, 3% multiracial, 0% Pacific Islander, 69% white, 11% international; 55% from in

state; 86% live on campus; 0% of students in fraternities, 0% in sororities
**Most popular majors:** 9% Biological and Biomedical Sciences, 9% Education, 10% History, 11% Psychology, 16% Social Sciences
**Expenses:** 2014-2015: $34,107; room/board: $11,650
**Financial aid:** (434) 947-8128; 67% of undergrads determined to have financial need; average aid package $26,014

## Randolph-Macon College
Ashland VA
(800) 888-1762
**U.S. News ranking:** Nat. Lib. Arts, No. 124
**Website:** www.rmc.edu
**Admissions email:** admissions@rmc.edu
**Private;** founded 1830
**Affiliation:** United Methodist
**Freshman admissions:** selective; 2013-2014: 2,997 applied, 1,909 accepted. Either SAT or ACT required. SAT 25/75 percentile: 970-1180. High school rank: 14% in top tenth, 48% in top quarter, 83% in top half
**Early decision deadline:** N/A, notification date: N/A
**Early action deadline:** 11/15, notification date: 1/1
**Application deadline (fall):** 3/1
**Undergraduate student body:** 1,295 full time, 20 part time; 47% male, 53% female; 0% American Indian, 2% Asian, 10% black, 4% Hispanic, 3% multiracial, 0% Pacific Islander, 76% white, 3% international; 75% from in state; 78% live on campus; 26% of students in fraternities, 27% in sororities
**Most popular majors:** 11% Biology/Biological Sciences, General, 9% Business/Managerial Economics, 9% Communication, General, 10% Political Science and Government, General, 9% Psychology, General
**Expenses:** 2014-2015: $36,340; room/board: $10,750
**Financial aid:** (804) 752-7259; 75% of undergrads determined to have financial need; average aid package $25,779

## Regent University
Virginia Beach VA
(888) 718-1222
**U.S. News ranking:** Nat. U., second tier
**Website:** www.regent.edu
**Admissions email:** admissions@regent.edu
**Private;** founded 1977
**Affiliation:** non-denominational
**Freshman admissions:** selective; 2013-2014: 1,243 applied, 1,062 accepted. Either SAT or ACT required. SAT 25/75 percentile: 940-1170. High school rank: 14% in top tenth, 30% in top quarter, 85% in top half
**Early decision deadline:** N/A, notification date: N/A
**Early action deadline:** N/A, notification date: N/A
**Application deadline (fall):** 7/28
**Undergraduate student body:** 1,537 full time, 924 part time; 39% male, 61% female; 1% American Indian, 2% Asian, 20% black, 5% Hispanic, 0% multiracial, 0% Pacific Islander, 57% white, 1% international; 48% from in

state; 23% live on campus; N/A of students in fraternities, N/A in sororities
**Most popular majors:** 22% Business Administration and Management, General, 17% Divinity/Ministry, 8% English Language and Literature, General, 19% Psychology, General, 20% Speech Communication and Rhetoric
**Expenses:** 2014-2015: $16,638; room/board: $8,250
**Financial aid:** (757) 226-4125; 77% of undergrads determined to have financial need; average aid package $11,621

## Roanoke College
Salem VA
(540) 375-2270
**U.S. News ranking:** Nat. Lib. Arts, No. 133
**Website:** www.roanoke.edu
**Admissions email:** admissions@roanoke.edu
**Private;** founded 1842
**Affiliation:** Lutheran
**Freshman admissions:** selective; 2013-2014: 4,167 applied, 3,034 accepted. Either SAT or ACT required. SAT 25/75 percentile: 980-1190. High school rank: 18% in top tenth, 42% in top quarter, 76% in top half
**Early decision deadline:** 11/1, notification date: 12/1
**Early action deadline:** N/A, notification date: N/A
**Application deadline (fall):** 3/15
**Undergraduate student body:** 1,964 full time, 65 part time; 41% male, 59% female; 0% American Indian, 1% Asian, 5% black, 3% Hispanic, 4% multiracial, 0% Pacific Islander, 85% white, 1% international; 53% from in state; 78% live on campus; 26% of students in fraternities, 22% in sororities
**Most popular majors:** 7% Biology/Biological Sciences, General, 18% Business Administration and Management, General, 6% English Language and Literature, General, 9% History, General, 13% Psychology, General
**Expenses:** 2014-2015: $37,802; room/board: $11,924
**Financial aid:** (540) 375-2235; 74% of undergrads determined to have financial need; average aid package $27,864

## Shenandoah University
Winchester VA
(540) 665-4581
**U.S. News ranking:** Reg. U. (S), No. 47
**Website:** www.su.edu
**Admissions email:** admit@su.edu
**Private;** founded 1875
**Affiliation:** United Methodist
**Freshman admissions:** less selective; 2013-2014: 1,632 applied, 1,377 accepted. Either SAT or ACT required. SAT 25/75 percentile: 850-1090. High school rank: 13% in top tenth, 36% in top quarter, 74% in top half
**Early decision deadline:** N/A, notification date: N/A
**Early action deadline:** N/A, notification date: N/A
**Application deadline (fall):** rolling
**Undergraduate student body:** 1,791 full time, 359 part time; 39% male, 61% female; 2% American Indian, 4% Asian, 14% black,

4% Hispanic, 0% multiracial, 0% Pacific Islander, 66% white, 5% international; 62% from in state; 47% live on campus; N/A of students in fraternities, N/A in sororities
**Most popular majors:** 12% Business Administration and Management, General, 17% Musical Theatre, 12% Physical Education Teaching and Coaching, 6% Psychology, General, 31% Registered Nursing/Registered Nurse
**Expenses:** 2014-2015: $30,188; room/board: $9,728
**Financial aid:** (540) 665-4538; 75% of undergrads determined to have financial need; average aid package $28,336

## Sweet Briar College
Sweet Briar VA
(800) 381-6142
**U.S. News ranking:** Nat. Lib. Arts, No. 116
**Website:** www.sbc.edu
**Admissions email:** admissions@sbc.edu
**Private;** founded 1901
**Freshman admissions:** selective; 2013-2014: 905 applied, 763 accepted. Either SAT or ACT required. SAT 25/75 percentile: 938-1210. High school rank: 30% in top tenth, 58% in top quarter, 82% in top half
**Early decision deadline:** N/A, notification date: N/A
**Early action deadline:** N/A, notification date: N/A
**Application deadline (fall):** 2/1
**Undergraduate student body:** 680 full time, 23 part time; 2% male, 98% female; 1% American Indian, 3% Asian, 10% black, 7% Hispanic, 2% multiracial, 0% Pacific Islander, 74% white, 2% international; 47% from in state; 96% live on campus; 0% of students in fraternities, 0% in sororities
**Most popular majors:** 8% Biological and Biomedical Sciences, 22% Business, Management, Marketing, and Related Support Services, 9% Psychology, 11% Social Sciences, 14% Visual and Performing Arts
**Expenses:** 2014-2015: $34,935; room/board: $12,160
**Financial aid:** (434) 381-6156; 78% of undergrads determined to have financial need; average aid package $27,921

## University of Mary Washington
Fredericksburg VA
(540) 654-2000
**U.S. News ranking:** Reg. U. (S), No. 13
**Website:** www.umw.edu
**Admissions email:** admit@umw.edu
**Public;** founded 1908
**Freshman admissions:** selective; 2013-2014: 4,501 applied, 3,637 accepted. Either SAT or ACT required. SAT 25/75 percentile: 1010-1210. High school rank: 16% in top tenth, 50% in top quarter, 86% in top half
**Early decision deadline:** N/A, notification date: N/A
**Early action deadline:** 11/15, notification date: 1/31
**Application deadline (fall):** 2/1

**Undergraduate student body:** 3,843 full time, 540 part time; 36% male, 64% female; 0% American Indian, 4% Asian, 6% black, 7% Hispanic, 4% multiracial, 0% Pacific Islander, 66% white, 1% international; 89% from in state; 61% live on campus; 0% of students in fraternities, 0% in sororities
**Most popular majors:** 15% Business, Management, Marketing, and Related Support Services, 9% English Language and Literature/Letters, 9% Multi/Interdisciplinary Studies, 12% Psychology, 16% Social Sciences
**Expenses:** 2014-2015: $10,252 in state, $23,538 out of state; room/board: $9,430
**Financial aid:** (540) 654-2468; 41% of undergrads determined to have financial need; average aid package $8,055

## University of Richmond
Univ. of Richmond VA
(804) 289-8640
**U.S. News ranking:** Nat. Lib. Arts, No. 30
**Website:** www.richmond.edu
**Admissions email:** admissions@richmond.edu
**Private;** founded 1830
**Freshman admissions:** more selective; 2013-2014: 9,825 applied, 3,061 accepted. Either SAT or ACT required. SAT 25/75 percentile: 1210-1410. High school rank: 64% in top tenth, 93% in top quarter, 99% in top half
**Early decision deadline:** 11/15, notification date: 12/15
**Early action deadline:** N/A, notification date: N/A
**Application deadline (fall):** 1/15
**Undergraduate student body:** 2,942 full time, 41 part time; 48% male, 52% female; 0% American Indian, 6% Asian, 6% black, 7% Hispanic, 4% multiracial, 0% Pacific Islander, 58% white, 9% international; 20% from in state; 87% live on campus; 13% of students in fraternities, 22% in sororities
**Most popular majors:** 9% Biological and Biomedical Sciences, 39% Business, Management, Marketing, and Related Support Services, 6% Multi/Interdisciplinary Studies, 6% Psychology, 16% Social Sciences
**Expenses:** 2014-2015: $46,680; room/board: $10,790
**Financial aid:** (804) 289-8438; 40% of undergrads determined to have financial need; average aid package $42,003

## University of Virginia
Charlottesville VA
(434) 982-3200
**U.S. News ranking:** Nat. U., No. 23
**Website:** www.virginia.edu
**Admissions email:** undergradadmission@virginia.edu
**Public;** founded 1819
**Freshman admissions:** most selective; 2013-2014: 29,021 applied, 8,728 accepted. Either SAT or ACT required. SAT 25/75 percentile: 1250-1460. High school rank: 92% in top tenth, 98% in top quarter, 99% in top half

**Early decision deadline:** N/A, notification date: N/A
**Early action deadline:** 11/1, notification date: 1/31
**Application deadline (fall):** 1/1
**Undergraduate student body:** 15,090 full time, 997 part time; 44% male, 56% female; 0% American Indian, 12% Asian, 6% black, 6% Hispanic, 4% multiracial, 0% Pacific Islander, 61% white, 6% international
**Most popular majors:** 8% Biology/Biological Sciences, General, 9% Business/Commerce, General, 8% Economics, General, 9% International Relations and Affairs, 8% Psychology, General
**Expenses:** 2014-2015: $12,998 in state, $42,184 out of state; room/board: $10,052
**Financial aid:** (434) 982-6000; 34% of undergrads determined to have financial need; average aid package $23,789

## University of Virginia–Wise
Wise VA
(888) 282-9324
**U.S. News ranking:** Nat. Lib. Arts, second tier
**Website:** www.uvawise.edu
**Admissions email:** admissions@uvawise.edu
**Public;** founded 1954
**Freshman admissions:** less selective; 2013-2014: 970 applied, 727 accepted. Either SAT or ACT required. SAT 25/75 percentile: 860-1050. High school rank: 15% in top tenth, 40% in top quarter, 76% in top half
**Early decision deadline:** N/A, notification date: N/A
**Early action deadline:** 12/1, notification date: 12/15
**Application deadline (fall):** 8/15
**Undergraduate student body:** 1,471 full time, 820 part time; 42% male, 58% female; 0% American Indian, 1% Asian, 10% black, 2% Hispanic, 0% multiracial, 0% Pacific Islander, 80% white, 0% international; 97% from in state; 37% live on campus; 1% of students in fraternities, 2% in sororities
**Most popular majors:** Information not available
**Expenses:** 2014-2015: $8,868 in state, $23,870 out of state; room/board: $10,340
**Financial aid:** (276) 328-0103; 72% of undergrads determined to have financial need; average aid package $11,156

## Virginia Commonwealth University
Richmond VA
(800) 841-3638
**U.S. News ranking:** Nat. U., No. 156
**Website:** www.vcu.edu
**Admissions email:** ugrad@vcu.edu
**Public;** founded 1838
**Freshman admissions:** selective; 2013-2014: 15,399 applied, 9,860 accepted. Either SAT or ACT required. SAT 25/75 percentile: 1000-1210. High school rank: 20% in top tenth, 50% in top quarter, 85% in top half
**Early decision deadline:** N/A, notification date: N/A

**Early action deadline:** N/A, notification date: N/A
**Application deadline (fall):** 1/15
**Undergraduate student body:** 19,989 full time, 3,668 part time; 43% male, 57% female; 0% American Indian, 12% Asian, 18% black, 8% Hispanic, 5% multiracial, 0% Pacific Islander, 51% white, 3% international; 92% from in state; 25% live on campus; 8% of students in fraternities, 6% in sororities
**Most popular majors:** 13% Business, Management, Marketing, and Related Support Services, 7% Health Professions and Related Programs, 7% Homeland Security, Law Enforcement, Firefighting and Related Protective Services, 10% Psychology, 12% Visual and Performing Arts
**Expenses:** 2014-2015: $12,398 in state, $29,847 out of state; room/board: $10,742
**Financial aid:** (804) 828-6669; 57% of undergrads determined to have financial need; average aid package $10,502

## Virginia Intermont College[1]
Bristol VA
(276) 466-7867
**U.S. News ranking:** Nat. Lib. Arts, second tier
**Website:** www.vic.edu
**Admissions email:** viadmit@vic.edu
**Private;** founded 1884
**Affiliation:** Virginia Baptist
**Application deadline (fall):** rolling
**Undergraduate student body:** N/A full time, N/A part time
**Expenses:** 2013-2014: $24,642; room/board: $7,769
**Financial aid:** (276) 466-7873

## Virginia Military Institute
Lexington VA
(800) 767-4207
**U.S. News ranking:** Nat. Lib. Arts, No. 64
**Website:** www.vmi.edu
**Admissions email:** admissions@vmi.edu
**Public;** founded 1839
**Freshman admissions:** selective; 2013-2014: 1,864 applied, 890 accepted. Either SAT or ACT required. SAT 25/75 percentile: 1050-1250. High school rank: 16% in top tenth, 48% in top quarter, 87% in top half
**Early decision deadline:** 11/15, notification date: 12/15
**Early action deadline:** N/A, notification date: N/A
**Application deadline (fall):** 2/1
**Undergraduate student body:** 1,675 full time, N/A part time; 89% male, 11% female; 0% American Indian, 4% Asian, 4% black, 4% Hispanic, 2% multiracial, 1% Pacific Islander, 83% white, 1% international; 59% from in state; 100% live on campus; N/A of students in fraternities, N/A in sororities
**Most popular majors:** 11% Civil Engineering, General, 15% Economics, General, 13% History, General, 18% International Relations and Affairs, 8% Psychology, General
**Expenses:** 2014-2015: $15,518 in state, $37,574 out of state; room/board: $8,372

Financial aid: (540) 464-7208; 54% of undergrads determined to have financial need; average aid package $21,056

## Virginia State University
Petersburg VA
(804) 524-5902
U.S. News ranking: Reg. U. (S), No. 92
Website: www.vsu.edu
Admissions email: admiss@vsu.edu
Public
Freshman admissions: least selective; 2013-2014: 9,107 applied, 4,922 accepted. Either SAT or ACT required. SAT 25/75 percentile: 730-910. High school rank: 5% in top tenth, 17% in top quarter, 55% in top half
Early decision deadline: N/A, notification date: N/A
Early action deadline: N/A, notification date: N/A
Application deadline (fall): 5/1
Undergraduate student body: 4,817 full time, 256 part time; 40% male, 60% female; 0% American Indian, 0% Asian, 86% black, 2% Hispanic, 0% multiracial, 0% Pacific Islander, 2% white, 0% international
Most popular majors: 6% Business Administration and Management, General, 11% Criminal Justice/Safety Studies, 8% Mass Communication/Media Studies, 11% Physical Education Teaching and Coaching, 9% Psychology, General
Expenses: 2014-2015: $8,002 in state, $17,258 out of state; room/board: $10,128
Financial aid: (804) 524-5992; 90% of undergrads determined to have financial need; average aid package $12,401

## Virginia Tech
Blacksburg VA
(540) 231-6267
U.S. News ranking: Nat. U., No. 71
Website: www.vt.edu
Admissions email: vtadmiss@vt.edu
Public; founded 1872
Freshman admissions: more selective; 2013-2014: 19,112 applied, 13,432 accepted. Either SAT or ACT required. SAT 25/75 percentile: 1120-1320. High school rank: 41% in top tenth, 83% in top quarter, 98% in top half
Early decision deadline: 11/1, notification date: 12/15
Early action deadline: N/A, notification date: N/A
Application deadline (fall): 1/15
Undergraduate student body: 23,512 full time, 522 part time; 59% male, 41% female; 0% American Indian, 8% Asian, 3% Black, 5% Hispanic, 4% multiracial, 0% Pacific Islander, 72% white, 4% international; N/A from in state; 37% live on campus; 3% of students in fraternities, 1% in sororities
Most popular majors: 9% Biological and Biomedical Sciences, 18% Business, Management, Marketing, and Related Support Services, 21% Engineering, 9% Family and Consumer Sciences/Human Sciences, 8% Social Sciences

Expenses: 2014-2015: $12,017 in state, $27,444 out of state; room/board: $8,270
Financial aid: (540) 231-5179; 45% of undergrads determined to have financial need; average aid package $16,280

## Virginia Union University
Richmond VA
(804) 257-5600
U.S. News ranking: Reg. Coll. (S), No. 68
Website: www.vuu.edu/
Admissions email: admissions@vuu.edu
Private; founded 1865
Affiliation: Baptist
Freshman admissions: least selective; 2013-2014: 2,670 applied, 2,217 accepted. Either SAT or ACT required. SAT 25/75 percentile: 670-840. High school rank: 6% in top tenth, 18% in top quarter, 45% in top half
Early decision deadline: N/A, notification date: N/A
Early action deadline: N/A, notification date: N/A
Application deadline (fall): 6/30
Undergraduate student body: 1,329 full time, 30 part time; 45% male, 55% female; 0% American Indian, 0% Asian, 95% black, 1% Hispanic, 1% multiracial, 0% Pacific Islander, 1% white, 1% international; 53% from in state; 54% live on campus; N/A of students in fraternities, N/A in sororities
Most popular majors: 7% Biological and Biomedical Sciences, 24% Business, Management, Marketing, and Related Support Services, 9% Computer and Information Sciences and Support Services, 11% Psychology, 33% Social Sciences
Expenses: 2014-2015: $14,930; room/board: $8,074
Financial aid: (804) 257-5882; 95% of undergrads determined to have financial need; average aid package $12,592

## Virginia Wesleyan College
Norfolk VA
(800) 737-8684
U.S. News ranking: Nat. Lib. Arts, second tier
Website: www.vwc.edu
Admissions email: admissions@vwc.edu
Private; founded 1961
Affiliation: United Methodist
Freshman admissions: less selective; 2013-2014: 3,727 applied, 3,463 accepted. Neither SAT nor ACT required. SAT 25/75 percentile: 907-1142. High school rank: 14% in top tenth, 36% in top quarter, 61% in top half
Early decision deadline: N/A, notification date: N/A
Early action deadline: N/A, notification date: N/A
Application deadline (fall): rolling
Undergraduate student body: 1,348 full time, 111 part time; 39% male, 61% female; 1% American Indian, 1% Asian, 23% black, 6% Hispanic, 7% multiracial, 0% Pacific Islander, 58% white, 1% international; 76% from in state; 60% live on campus; N/A of students in fraternities, N/A in sororities

Most popular majors: 6% Biology/Biological Sciences, General, 21% Business Administration and Management, General, 9% Criminal Justice/Safety Studies, 7% Psychology, General, 6% Social Sciences, General
Expenses: 2014-2015: $33,286; room/board: $8,594
Financial aid: (757) 455-3345; 80% of undergrads determined to have financial need; average aid package $19,980

## Washington and Lee University
Lexington VA
(540) 463-8710
U.S. News ranking: Nat. Lib. Arts, No. 14
Website: www.wlu.edu
Admissions email: admissions@wlu.edu
Private; founded 1749
Freshman admissions: most selective; 2013-2014: 6,222 applied, 1,147 accepted. Either SAT or ACT required. ACT 25/75 percentile: 30-33. High school rank: 80% in top tenth, 98% in top quarter, 100% in top half
Early decision deadline: 11/1, notification date: 12/21
Early action deadline: N/A, notification date: N/A
Application deadline (fall): 1/1
Undergraduate student body: 1,851 full time, 4 part time; 50% male, 50% female; 0% American Indian, 4% Asian, 2% black, 3% Hispanic, 2% multiracial, 0% Pacific Islander, 83% white, 3% international; 14% from in state; 56% live on campus; 82% of students in fraternities, 82% in sororities
Most popular majors: 5% Accounting and Business/Management, 5% Biology/Biological Sciences, General, 14% Business Administration and Management, General, 8% Economics, General, 6% English Language and Literature, General
Expenses: 2014-2015: $45,617; room/board: $10,645
Financial aid: (540) 458-8717; 42% of undergrads determined to have financial need; average aid package $45,619

## Art Institute of Seattle[1]
Seattle WA
(800) 275-2471
U.S. News ranking: Arts, unranked
Website: www.ais.edu
Admissions email: N/A
For-profit
Application deadline (fall): N/A
Undergraduate student body: N/A full time, N/A part time
Expenses: 2013-2014: $17,560; room/board: $12,132
Financial aid: N/A

## Bellevue College[1]
Bellevue WA
(425) 564-1000
U.S. News ranking: Reg. Coll. (W), unranked
Website: bellevuecollege.edu
Admissions email: N/A
Public
Application deadline (fall): N/A

Undergraduate student body: N/A full time, N/A part time
Expenses: 2013-2014: $3,754 in state, $8,944 out of state; room/board: N/A
Financial aid: (425) 564-2227

## Central Washington University
Ellensburg WA
(866) 298-4968
U.S. News ranking: Reg. U. (W), No. 51
Website: www.cwu.edu
Admissions email: cwuadmis@cwu.edu
Public; founded 1891
Freshman admissions: less selective; 2013-2014: 4,507 applied, 3,703 accepted. Either SAT or ACT required. SAT 25/75 percentile: 880-1100. High school rank: N/A
Early decision deadline: N/A, notification date: N/A
Early action deadline: N/A, notification date: N/A
Application deadline (fall): rolling
Undergraduate student body: 8,996 full time, 1,427 part time; 50% male, 50% female; 1% American Indian, 3% Asian, 3% black, 12% Hispanic, 5% multiracial, 0% Pacific Islander, 64% white, 4% international; 95% from in state; 23% live on campus; 0% of students in fraternities, 0% in sororities
Most popular majors: 19% Business, Management, Marketing, and Related Support Services, 15% Education, 8% Homeland Security, Law Enforcement, Firefighting and Related Protective Services, 5% Psychology, 14% Social Sciences
Expenses: 2014-2015: $8,976 in state, $20,522 out of state; room/board: $9,795
Financial aid: (509) 963-1611; 66% of undergrads determined to have financial need; average aid package $11,191

## City University of Seattle
Seattle WA
(206) 239-4500
U.S. News ranking: Reg. U. (W), unranked
Website: www.cityu.edu
Admissions email: info@cityu.edu
Private; founded 1973
Freshman admissions: N/A; 2013-2014: 364 applied, 364 accepted. Neither SAT nor ACT required. ACT 25/75 percentile: N/A. High school rank: N/A
Early decision deadline: N/A, notification date: N/A
Early action deadline: N/A, notification date: N/A
Application deadline (fall): rolling
Undergraduate student body: 638 full time, 634 part time; 47% male, 53% female; 1% American Indian, 3% Asian, 4% black, 7% Hispanic, 0% multiracial, 1% Pacific Islander, 40% white, 18% international
Most popular majors: 8% Accounting, 6% Applied Psychology, 55% Business Administration and Management, General, 5% Computer and Information Sciences, General, 19% Education, General
Expenses: 2013-2014: $14,880; room/board: N/A
Financial aid: (800) 426-5596

## Cornish College of the Arts
Seattle WA
(800) 726-ARTS
U.S. News ranking: Arts, unranked
Website: www.cornish.edu
Admissions email: admission@cornish.edu
Private; founded 1914
Freshman admissions: N/A; 2013-2014: 1,186 applied, 691 accepted. Neither SAT nor ACT required. SAT 25/75 percentile: N/A. High school rank: N/A
Early decision deadline: N/A, notification date: N/A
Early action deadline: N/A, notification date: N/A
Application deadline (fall): 8/15
Undergraduate student body: 746 full time, 29 part time; 35% male, 65% female; 1% American Indian, 6% Asian, 4% black, 9% Hispanic, 8% multiracial, 0% Pacific Islander, 63% white, 3% international; 54% from in state; 12% live on campus; N/A of students in fraternities, N/A in sororities
Most popular majors: 12% Dance, General, 23% Design and Visual Communications, General, 23% Drama and Dramatics/Theatre Arts, General, 19% Fine/Studio Arts, General, 16% Music Performance, General
Expenses: 2014-2015: $35,800; room/board: $9,600
Financial aid: (206) 726-5014; 81% of undergrads determined to have financial need; average aid package $18,090

## Eastern Washington University
Cheney WA
(509) 359-2397
U.S. News ranking: Reg. U. (W), No. 66
Website: www.ewu.edu
Admissions email: admissions@ewu.edu
Public; founded 1882
Freshman admissions: less selective; 2013-2014: 5,108 applied, 3,993 accepted. Either SAT or ACT required. SAT 25/75 percentile: 870-1090. High school rank: N/A
Early decision deadline: N/A, notification date: N/A
Early action deadline: N/A, notification date: N/A
Application deadline (fall): 5/15
Undergraduate student body: 9,715 full time, 1,963 part time; 46% male, 54% female; 1% American Indian, 3% Asian, 4% black, 12% Hispanic, 4% multiracial, 0% Pacific Islander, 66% white, 3% international; 95% from in state; 16% live on campus; 5% of students in fraternities, 5% in sororities
Most popular majors: 18% Business, Management, Marketing, and Related Support Services, 8% Education, 10% Health Professions and Related Programs, 9% Psychology, 9% Social Sciences
Expenses: 2014-2015: $7,982 in state, $21,113 out of state; room/board: $9,628
Financial aid: (509) 359-2314; 68% of undergrads determined to have financial need; average aid package $13,826

## Evergreen State College

Olympia WA
(360) 867-6170
**U.S. News ranking:** Reg. U. (W), No. 31
**Website:** www.evergreen.edu
**Admissions email:** admissions@evergreen.edu
**Public;** founded 1967
**Freshman admissions:** selective; 2013-2014: 1,583 applied, 1,537 accepted. Either SAT or ACT required. SAT 25/75 percentile: 950-1210. High school rank: 10% in top tenth, 23% in top quarter, 54% in top half
**Early decision deadline:** N/A, notification date: N/A
**Early action deadline:** N/A, notification date: N/A
**Application deadline (fall):** rolling
**Undergraduate student body:** 3,766 full time, 321 part time; 47% male, 53% female; 2% American Indian, 2% Asian, 5% black, 7% Hispanic, 7% multiracial, 0% Pacific Islander, 66% white, 0% international; 76% from in state; 20% live on campus; N/A of students in fraternities, N/A in sororities
**Most popular majors:** 13% Environmental Studies, 19% Humanities/Humanistic Studies, 12% Liberal Arts and Sciences/Liberal Studies, 15% Natural Sciences, 21% Social Sciences, Other
**Expenses:** 2014-2015: $8,682 in state, $21,735 out of state; room/board: $9,492
**Financial aid:** (360) 867-6205; 69% of undergrads determined to have financial need; average aid package $9,236

## Gonzaga University

Spokane WA
(800) 322-2584
**U.S. News ranking:** Reg. U. (W), No. 3
**Website:** www.gonzaga.edu
**Admissions email:** mcculloh@gu.gonzaga.edu
**Private;** founded 1887
**Affiliation:** Roman Catholic
**Freshman admissions:** more selective; 2013-2014: 7,031 applied, 4,790 accepted. Either SAT or ACT required. SAT 25/75 percentile: 1100-1290. High school rank: 39% in top tenth, 68% in top quarter, 95% in top half
**Early decision deadline:** N/A, notification date: N/A
**Early action deadline:** 11/15, notification date: 1/15
**Application deadline (fall):** 2/1
**Undergraduate student body:** 4,826 full time, 70 part time; 46% male, 54% female; 1% American Indian, 4% Asian, 1% black, 9% Hispanic, 6% multiracial, 0% Pacific Islander, 74% white, 3% international; 49% from in state; 60% live on campus; 0% of students in fraternities, 0% in sororities
**Most popular majors:** 8% Biological and Biomedical Sciences, 24% Business, Management, Marketing, and Related Support Services, 9% Engineering, 8% Psychology, 13% Social Sciences
**Expenses:** 2014-2015: $36,535; room/board: $9,906

**Financial aid:** (509) 323-4049; 58% of undergrads determined to have financial need; average aid package $25,512

## Heritage University[1]

Toppenish WA
(509) 865-8508
**U.S. News ranking:** Reg. U. (W), unranked
**Website:** www.heritage.edu
**Admissions email:** admissions@heritage.edu
**Private**
**Application deadline (fall):** N/A
**Undergraduate student body:** N/A full time, N/A part time
**Expenses:** 2013-2014: $17,744; room/board: N/A
**Financial aid:** (509) 865-8502

## Northwest University

Kirkland WA
(425) 889-5231
**U.S. News ranking:** Reg. Coll. (W), No. 16
**Website:** www.northwestu.edu
**Admissions email:** admissions@northwestu.edu
**Private;** founded 1934
**Affiliation:** Assembly of God
**Freshman admissions:** less selective; 2013-2014: 419 applied, 362 accepted. Either SAT or ACT required. SAT 25/75 percentile: 950-1170. High school rank: N/A
**Early decision deadline:** N/A, notification date: N/A
**Early action deadline:** 11/15, notification date: 12/15
**Application deadline (fall):** rolling
**Undergraduate student body:** 1,221 full time, 217 part time; 41% male, 59% female; 1% American Indian, 5% Asian, 3% black, 8% Hispanic, 2% multiracial, 1% Pacific Islander, 74% white, 2% international
**Most popular majors:** 10% Business Administration, Management and Operations, Other, 6% Organizational Communication, General, 12% Psychology, General, 13% Registered Nursing/Registered Nurse, 12% Theological and Ministerial Studies, Other
**Expenses:** 2014-2015: $26,968; room/board: $7,620
**Financial aid:** (425) 889-5336; 84% of undergrads determined to have financial need; average aid package $19,633

## Olympic College[1]

Bremerton WA
(360) 792-6050
**U.S. News ranking:** Reg. Coll. (W), unranked
**Website:** www.olympic.edu
**Admissions email:** N/A
**Public**
**Application deadline (fall):** N/A
**Undergraduate student body:** N/A full time, N/A part time
**Expenses:** 2013-2014: $3,726 in state, $4,197 out of state; room/board: $9,492
**Financial aid:** (800) 259-6718

## Pacific Lutheran University

Tacoma WA
(800) 274-6758
**U.S. News ranking:** Reg. U. (W), No. 17
**Website:** www.plu.edu
**Admissions email:** admission@plu.edu
**Private;** founded 1890
**Affiliation:** Lutheran
**Freshman admissions:** selective; 2013-2014: 3,443 applied, 2,643 accepted. Either SAT or ACT required. SAT 25/75 percentile: 980-1220. High school rank: 35% in top tenth, 70% in top quarter, 92% in top half
**Early decision deadline:** N/A, notification date: N/A
**Early action deadline:** N/A, notification date: N/A
**Application deadline (fall):** rolling
**Undergraduate student body:** 3,010 full time, 132 part time; 38% male, 62% female; 1% American Indian, 5% Asian, 3% black, 7% Hispanic, 7% multiracial, 1% Pacific Islander, 71% white, 4% international; 79% from in state; 43% live on campus; N/A of students in fraternities, N/A in sororities
**Most popular majors:** 9% Biological and Biomedical Sciences, 11% Business, Management, Marketing, and Related Support Services, 10% Health Professions and Related Programs, 7% Psychology, 13% Social Sciences
**Expenses:** 2014-2015: $36,530; room/board: $10,230
**Financial aid:** (253) 535-7134; 76% of undergrads determined to have financial need; average aid package $32,765

## Peninsula College[1]

Port Angeles WA
(360) 417-6340
**U.S. News ranking:** Reg. Coll. (W), unranked
**Website:** www.pencol.edu
**Admissions email:** N/A
**Public**
**Application deadline (fall):** N/A
**Undergraduate student body:** N/A full time, N/A part time
**Expenses:** 2013-2014: $4,246 in state, $4,687 out of state; room/board: N/A
**Financial aid:** (360) 417-6390

## Seattle Pacific University

Seattle WA
(800) 366-3344
**U.S. News ranking:** Reg. U. (W), No. 19
**Website:** www.spu.edu
**Admissions email:** admissions@spu.edu
**Private;** founded 1891
**Affiliation:** Free Methodist
**Freshman admissions:** selective; 2013-2014: 4,477 applied, 3,724 accepted. Either SAT or ACT required. SAT 25/75 percentile: 1030-1250. High school rank: 28% in top tenth, 57% in top quarter, 87% in top half
**Early decision deadline:** N/A, notification date: N/A
**Early action deadline:** 11/15, notification date: 1/5
**Application deadline (fall):** 2/1

Undergraduate student body: 3,230 full time, 136 part time; 34% male, 66% female; 0% American Indian, 11% Asian, 4% black, 8% Hispanic, 8% multiracial, 0% Pacific Islander, 66% white, 2% international; 63% from in state; 51% live on campus; N/A of students in fraternities, N/A in sororities
**Most popular majors:** Information not available
**Expenses:** 2014-2015: $35,472; room/board: $10,086
**Financial aid:** (206) 281-2061; 74% of undergrads determined to have financial need; average aid package $29,857

## Seattle University

Seattle WA
(206) 296-2000
**U.S. News ranking:** Reg. U. (W), No. 5
**Website:** www.seattleu.edu
**Admissions email:** admissions@seattleu.edu
**Private;** founded 1891
**Affiliation:** Roman Catholic (Jesuit)
**Freshman admissions:** more selective; 2013-2014: 7,159 applied, 5,243 accepted. Either SAT or ACT required. SAT 25/75 percentile: 1050-1260. High school rank: 23% in top tenth, 62% in top quarter, 90% in top half
**Early decision deadline:** N/A, notification date: N/A
**Early action deadline:** 11/15, notification date: 12/23
**Application deadline (fall):** rolling
**Undergraduate student body:** 4,429 full time, 237 part time; 42% male, 58% female; 1% American Indian, 16% Asian, 3% black, 8% Hispanic, 7% multiracial, 1% Pacific Islander, 47% white, 12% international; 45% from in state; 45% live on campus; 0% of students in fraternities, 0% in sororities
**Most popular majors:** 26% Business, Management, Marketing, and Related Support Services, 6% Engineering, 14% Health Professions and Related Programs, 5% Liberal Arts and Sciences, General Studies and Humanities, 5% Social Sciences
**Expenses:** 2014-2015: $38,205; room/board: $10,830
**Financial aid:** (206) 296-2000; 61% of undergrads determined to have financial need; average aid package $29,704

## South Seattle Community College[1]

Seattle WA
(206) 764-5300
**U.S. News ranking:** Reg. Coll. (W), unranked
**Website:** southseattle.edu
**Admissions email:** N/A
**Public**
**Application deadline (fall):** N/A
**Undergraduate student body:** N/A full time, N/A part time
**Expenses:** 2013-2014: $3,824 in state, $9,014 out of state; room/board: N/A
**Financial aid:** (206) 934-5317

## St. Martin's University

Lacey WA
(800) 368-8803
**U.S. News ranking:** Reg. U. (W), No. 46
**Website:** www.stmartin.edu
**Admissions email:** admissions@stmartin.edu
**Private;** founded 1895
**Affiliation:** Roman Catholic (Benedictine)
**Freshman admissions:** selective; 2013-2014: 651 applied, 572 accepted. Either SAT or ACT required. SAT 25/75 percentile: 950-1190. High school rank: 24% in top tenth, 52% in top quarter, 85% in top half
**Early decision deadline:** N/A, notification date: N/A
**Early action deadline:** N/A, notification date: N/A
**Application deadline (fall):** rolling
**Undergraduate student body:** 1,110 full time, 302 part time; 50% male, 50% female; 1% American Indian, 6% Asian, 6% black, 12% Hispanic, 8% multiracial, 2% Pacific Islander, 54% white, 5% international; 70% from in state; 33% live on campus; 0% of students in fraternities, 0% in sororities
**Most popular majors:** 26% Biological and Biomedical Sciences, 26% Business, Management, Marketing, and Related Support Services, 9% Education, 10% Engineering, 17% Psychology
**Expenses:** 2014-2015: $31,688; room/board: $9,990
**Financial aid:** (360) 438-4397; 89% of undergrads determined to have financial need; average aid package $21,463

## Trinity Lutheran College[1]

Everett WA
(425) 249-4741
**U.S. News ranking:** Reg. Coll. (W), unranked
**Website:** www.tlc.edu/
**Admissions email:** admissions@tlc.edu
**Private**
**Application deadline (fall):** N/A
**Undergraduate student body:** N/A full time, N/A part time
**Expenses:** 2013-2014: $27,042; room/board: $8,200
**Financial aid:** (425) 249-4777

## University of Puget Sound

Tacoma WA
(253) 879-3211
**U.S. News ranking:** Nat. Lib. Arts, No. 81
**Website:** www.pugetsound.edu
**Admissions email:** admission@pugetsound.edu
**Private;** founded 1888
**Freshman admissions:** selective; 2013-2014: 4,588 applied, 3,910 accepted. Either SAT or ACT required. SAT 25/75 percentile: 1120-1330. High school rank: 26% in top tenth, 51% in top quarter, 89% in top half
**Early decision deadline:** 11/15, notification date: 12/15
**Early action deadline:** N/A, notification date: N/A
**Application deadline (fall):** 1/15

Undergraduate student body: 2,520 full time, 21 part time; 43% male, 57% female; 0% American Indian, 7% Asian, 1% black, 7% Hispanic, 9% multiracial, 0% Pacific Islander, 75% white, 0% international; 24% from in state; 64% live on campus; 24% of students in fraternities, 29% in sororities
Most popular majors: 12% Biological and Biomedical Sciences, 12% Business, Management, Marketing, and Related Support Services, 11% Psychology, 18% Social Sciences, 8% Visual and Performing Arts
Expenses: 2014-2015: $43,428; room/board: $11,180
Financial aid: (800) 396-7192; 59% of undergrads determined to have financial need; average aid package $29,075

## University of Washington
Seattle WA
(206) 543-9686
U.S. News ranking: Nat. U., No. 48
Website: www.washington.edu
Admissions email: askuwadm@u.washington.edu
Public; founded 1861
Freshman admissions: more selective; 2013-2014: 30,226 applied, 16,679 accepted. Either SAT or ACT required. SAT 25/75 percentile: 1100-1360. High school rank: 92% in top tenth, 98% in top quarter, 100% in top half
Early decision deadline: N/A, notification date: N/A
Early action deadline: N/A, notification date: N/A
Application deadline (fall): 12/1
Undergraduate student body: 27,048 full time, 2,706 part time; 48% male, 52% female; 1% American Indian, 24% Asian, 3% black, 6% Hispanic, 4% multiracial, 1% Pacific Islander, 49% white, 11% international; 85% from in state; 24% live on campus; 15% of students in fraternities, 13% in sororities
Most popular majors: 12% Biological and Biomedical Sciences, 10% Business, Management, Marketing, and Related Support Services, 8% Engineering, 18% Social Sciences, 8% Visual and Performing Arts
Expenses: 2014-2015: $12,394 in state, $33,513 out of state; room/board: $10,833
Financial aid: (206) 543-6101; 47% of undergrads determined to have financial need; average aid package $18,600

## Walla Walla University
College Place WA
(509) 527-2327
U.S. News ranking: Reg. U. (W), No. 58
Website: www.wallawalla.edu
Admissions email: info@wallawalla.edu
Private; founded 1892
Affiliation: Seventh-day Adventist
Freshman admissions: less selective; 2013-2014: 1,102 applied, 1,034 accepted. Neither SAT nor ACT required. SAT 25/75 percentile: 930-1190. High school rank: N/A

percentile: 990-1220. High school rank: 21% in top tenth, 50% in top quarter, 84% in top half
Early decision deadline: N/A, notification date: N/A
Early action deadline: N/A, notification date: N/A
Application deadline (fall): rolling
Undergraduate student body: 1,592 full time, 94 part time; 50% male, 50% female; 1% American Indian, 5% Asian, 2% black, 12% Hispanic, 0% multiracial, 0% Pacific Islander, 75% white, 2% international
Most popular majors: 12% Business, Management, Marketing, and Related Support Services, 11% Education, 9% Engineering, 24% Health Professions and Related Programs, 7% Visual and Performing Arts
Expenses: 2014-2015: $25,866; room/board: $3,735
Financial aid: (800) 656-2815; 68% of undergrads determined to have financial need; average aid package $20,765

## Washington State University
Pullman WA
(888) 468-6978
U.S. News ranking: Nat. U., No. 138
Website: www.wsu.edu
Admissions email: admissions@wsu.edu
Public; founded 1890
Freshman admissions: selective; 2013-2014: 14,887 applied, 12,219 accepted. Either SAT or ACT required. SAT 25/75 percentile: 910-1150. High school rank: 30% in top tenth, 52% in top quarter, 83% in top half
Early decision deadline: N/A, notification date: N/A
Early action deadline: N/A, notification date: N/A
Application deadline (fall): rolling
Undergraduate student body: 20,312 full time, 2,758 part time; 49% male, 51% female; 1% American Indian, 5% Asian, 3% black, 11% Hispanic, 7% multiracial, 0% Pacific Islander, 66% white, 4% international; 92% from in state; 26% live on campus; 17% of students in fraternities, 17% in sororities
Most popular majors: 17% Business, Management, Marketing, and Related Support Services, 7% Communication, Journalism, and Related Programs, 9% Engineering, 8% Health Professions and Related Programs, 15% Social Sciences
Expenses: 2014-2015: $12,428 in state, $25,510 out of state; room/board: $11,276
Financial aid: (509) 335-9711; 68% of undergrads determined to have financial need; average aid package $12,537

## Western Washington University
Bellingham WA
(360) 650-3440
U.S. News ranking: Reg. U. (W), No. 21
Website: www.wwu.edu
Admissions email: admit@cc.wwu.edu
Public; founded 1893
Freshman admissions: selective; 2013-2014: 9,508 applied, 7,958 accepted. Either SAT or ACT required. SAT 25/75

Early decision deadline: N/A, notification date: N/A
Early action deadline: N/A, notification date: N/A
Application deadline (fall): 1/31
Undergraduate student body: 12,942 full time, 1,084 part time; 45% male, 55% female; 0% American Indian, 6% Asian, 2% black, 7% Hispanic, 8% multiracial, 0% Pacific Islander, 75% white, 1% international; 91% from in state; 29% live on campus; N/A of students in fraternities, N/A in sororities
Most popular majors: Information not available
Expenses: 2014-2015: $8,964 in state, $20,406 out of state; room/board: $10,042
Financial aid: (360) 650-3470; 50% of undergrads determined to have financial need; average aid package $14,893

## Whitman College
Walla Walla WA
(509) 527-5176
U.S. News ranking: Nat. Lib. Arts, No. 37
Website: www.whitman.edu
Admissions email: admission@whitman.edu
Private; founded 1883
Freshman admissions: more selective; 2013-2014: 2,586 applied, 1,473 accepted. Either SAT or ACT required. SAT 25/75 percentile: 1220-1422. High school rank: 61% in top tenth, 84% in top quarter, 97% in top half
Early decision deadline: 11/15, notification date: 12/21
Early action deadline: N/A, notification date: N/A
Application deadline (fall): 1/15
Undergraduate student body: 1,505 full time, 36 part time; 43% male, 57% female; 1% American Indian, 6% Asian, 1% black, 8% Hispanic, 4% multiracial, 0% Pacific Islander, 72% white, 3% international; 36% from in state; 67% live on campus; 46% of students in fraternities, 40% in sororities
Most popular majors: 6% Biochemistry and Molecular Biology, 11% Biology/Biological Sciences, General, 6% Economics, General, 7% English Language and Literature, General, 8% Psychology, General
Expenses: 2014-2015: $44,800; room/board: $11,228
Financial aid: (509) 527-5178; 46% of undergrads determined to have financial need; average aid package $33,555

## Whitworth University
Spokane WA
(800) 533-4668
U.S. News ranking: Reg. U. (W), No. 9
Website: www.whitworth.edu
Admissions email: admissions@whitworth.edu
Private; founded 1890
Affiliation: Presbyterian Church
Freshman admissions: selective; 2013-2014: 3,357 applied, 2,610 accepted. Neither SAT nor ACT required. SAT 25/75 percentile: 1090-1290. High school rank: N/A

Early decision deadline: N/A, notification date: N/A
Early action deadline: 11/30, notification date: 12/20
Application deadline (fall): 3/1
Undergraduate student body: 2,316 full time, 42 part time; 40% male, 60% female; 1% American Indian, 3% Asian, 1% black, 8% Hispanic, 5% multiracial, 0% Pacific Islander, 79% white, 2% international; 65% from in state; 60% live on campus; N/A of students in fraternities, N/A in sororities
Most popular majors: 14% Business, Management, Marketing, and Related Support Services, 7% Communication, Journalism, and Related Programs, 7% Multi/Interdisciplinary Studies, 10% Social Sciences, 8% Visual and Performing Arts
Expenses: 2014-2015: $37,456; room/board: $10,278
Financial aid: (800) 533-4668; 70% of undergrads determined to have financial need; average aid package $29,205

## Alderson Broaddus University
Philippi WV
(800) 263-1549
U.S. News ranking: Reg. Coll. (S), No. 37
Website: www.ab.edu
Admissions email: admissions@ab.edu
Private; founded 1871
Affiliation: American Baptist
Freshman admissions: selective; 2013-2014: 4,892 applied, 2,114 accepted. Either SAT or ACT required. ACT 25/75 percentile: 19-24. High school rank: 11% in top tenth, 36% in top quarter, 67% in top half
Early decision deadline: N/A, notification date: N/A
Early action deadline: N/A, notification date: N/A
Application deadline (fall): 8/25
Undergraduate student body: 995 full time, 57 part time; 52% male, 48% female; 1% American Indian, 1% Asian, 16% black, 4% Hispanic, 1% multiracial, 0% Pacific Islander, 74% white, 3% international; 44% from in state; 81% live on campus; 4% of students in fraternities, 5% in sororities
Most popular majors: 6% Athletic Training/Trainer, 17% Biology/Biological Sciences, General, 5% Elementary Education and Teaching, 5% Music Teacher Education, 15% Registered Nursing/Registered Nurse
Expenses: 2014-2015: $22,740; room/board: $7,236
Financial aid: (304) 457-6354; 87% of undergrads determined to have financial need; average aid package $18,600

## American Public University System
Charles Town WV
(877) 777-9081
U.S. News ranking: Reg. U. (S), unranked
Website: www.apus.edu
Admissions email: N/A
For-profit; founded 1991

Freshman admissions: N/A; 2013-2014: N/A applied, N/A accepted. Neither SAT nor ACT required. ACT 25/75 percentile: N/A. High school rank: N/A
Early decision deadline: N/A, notification date: N/A
Early action deadline: N/A, notification date: N/A
Application deadline (fall): rolling
Undergraduate student body: 3,275 full time, 40,689 part time; 60% male, 40% female; 1% American Indian, 2% Asian, 24% black, 10% Hispanic, 3% multiracial, 1% Pacific Islander, 54% white, 1% international
Most popular majors: 13% Business Administration and Management, General, 7% Criminal Justice/Safety Studies, 10% General Studies, 6% Homeland Security, 14% International/Global Studies
Expenses: 2014-2015: $8,000; room/board: N/A
Financial aid: (877) 372-3535

## Bethany College
Bethany WV
(304) 829-7611
U.S. News ranking: Nat. Lib. Arts, second tier
Website: www.bethanywv.edu
Admissions email: admission@bethanywv.edu
Private; founded 1840
Affiliation: Christian Church (Disciples of Christ)
Freshman admissions: less selective; 2013-2014: 1,736 applied, 859 accepted. Either SAT or ACT required. SAT 25/75 percentile: 770-1040. High school rank: 12% in top tenth, 30% in top quarter, 47% in top half
Early decision deadline: N/A, notification date: N/A
Early action deadline: N/A, notification date: N/A
Application deadline (fall): rolling
Undergraduate student body: 690 full time, 4 part time; 56% male, 44% female; 0% American Indian, 0% Asian, 20% black, 3% Hispanic, 2% multiracial, 0% Pacific Islander, 58% white, 1% international; 20% from in state; 99% live on campus; 29% of students in fraternities, 29% in sororities
Most popular majors: 7% Biology/Biological Sciences, General, 8% Elementary Education and Teaching, 13% Physical Education Teaching and Coaching, 21% Psychology, General, 14% Speech Communication and Rhetoric
Expenses: 2014-2015: $25,736; room/board: $9,746
Financial aid: (304) 829-7141; 88% of undergrads determined to have financial need; average aid package $24,972

## Bluefield State College
Bluefield WV
(304) 327-4065
U.S. News ranking: Reg. Coll. (S), second tier
Website: www.bluefieldstate.edu
Admissions email: bscadmit@bluefieldstate.edu
Public; founded 1895
Freshman admissions: less selective; 2013-2014: 1,059 applied, 435 accepted. Either SAT or ACT required. ACT 25/75

percentile: 16-21. High school rank: N/A
**Early decision deadline:** N/A, notification date: N/A
**Early action deadline:** N/A, notification date: N/A
**Application deadline (fall):** rolling
**Undergraduate student body:** 1,440 full time, 307 part time; 38% male, 62% female; 0% American Indian, 0% Asian, 10% black, 1% Hispanic, 1% multiracial, 0% Pacific Islander, 85% white, 3% international; 98% from in state; 0% live on campus; 4% of students in fraternities, 4% in sororities
**Most popular majors:** 15% Business, Management, Marketing, and Related Support Services, 12% Education, 19% Engineering Technologies and Engineering-Related Fields, 8% Health Professions and Related Programs, 27% Liberal Arts and Sciences, General Studies and Humanities
**Expenses:** 2014-2015: $5,832 in state, $11,064 out of state; room/board: N/A
**Financial aid:** (304) 327-4020; 81% of undergrads determined to have financial need; average aid package $3,582

## Concord University
Athens WV
(304) 384-5249
**U.S. News ranking:** Reg. Coll. (S), No. 50
**Website:** www.concord.edu
**Admissions email:** admissions@concord.edu
**Public;** founded 1872
**Freshman admissions:** selective; 2013-2014: 2,778 applied, 1,251 accepted. Either SAT or ACT required. ACT 25/75 percentile: 18-24. High school rank: 19% in top tenth, 44% in top quarter, 75% in top half
**Early decision deadline:** N/A, notification date: N/A
**Early action deadline:** N/A, notification date: N/A
**Application deadline (fall):** rolling
**Undergraduate student body:** 2,275 full time, 245 part time; 43% male, 57% female; 0% American Indian, 1% Asian, 6% black, 1% Hispanic, 0% multiracial, 0% Pacific Islander, 87% white, 4% international; 85% from in state; 36% live on campus; N/A of students in fraternities, N/A in sororities
**Most popular majors:** 6% Biological and Biomedical Sciences, 17% Business, Management, Marketing, and Related Support Services, 21% Education, 22% Liberal Arts and Sciences, General Studies and Humanities, 6% Social Sciences
**Expenses:** 2014-2015: $6,422 in state, $14,118 out of state; room/board: $7,818
**Financial aid:** (304) 384-6069; 76% of undergrads determined to have financial need; average aid package $8,632

## Davis and Elkins College[1]
Elkins WV
(304) 637-1230
**U.S. News ranking:** Reg. Coll. (S), No. 50
**Website:** www.davisandelkins.edu
**Admissions email:** admiss@davisandelkins.edu
**Private**
**Application deadline (fall):** N/A
**Undergraduate student body:** N/A full time, N/A part time
**Expenses:** 2013-2014: $24,992; room/board: $8,750
**Financial aid:** (304) 637-1373

## Fairmont State University
Fairmont WV
(304) 367-4892
**U.S. News ranking:** Reg. U. (S), second tier
**Website:** www.fairmontstate.edu
**Admissions email:** admit@fairmontstate.edu
**Public;** founded 1865
**Freshman admissions:** selective; 2013-2014: 2,799 applied, 1,861 accepted. Either SAT or ACT required. ACT 25/75 percentile: 18-23. High school rank: 13% in top tenth, 39% in top quarter, 74% in top half
**Early decision deadline:** N/A, notification date: N/A
**Early action deadline:** N/A, notification date: N/A
**Application deadline (fall):** rolling
**Undergraduate student body:** 3,435 full time, 523 part time; 45% male, 55% female; 0% American Indian, 0% Asian, 5% black, 2% Hispanic, 2% multiracial, 0% Pacific Islander, 86% white, 2% international; 92% from in state; 21% live on campus; 1% of students in fraternities, 2% in sororities
**Most popular majors:** 15% Business Administration and Management, General, 11% Criminal Justice/Safety Studies, 11% Education, General, 10% General Studies, 7% Psychology, General
**Expenses:** 2014-2015: $5,824 in state, $12,288 out of state; room/board: $7,686
**Financial aid:** (304) 367-4213; 76% of undergrads determined to have financial need; average aid package $8,360

## Glenville State College
Glenville WV
(304) 462-4128
**U.S. News ranking:** Reg. Coll. (S), No. 71
**Website:** www.glenville.edu
**Admissions email:** admissions@glenville.edu
**Public;** founded 1872
**Freshman admissions:** less selective; 2013-2014: 1,198 applied, 802 accepted. Either SAT or ACT required. ACT 25/75 percentile: 16-21. High school rank: 8% in top tenth, 20% in top quarter, 40% in top half
**Early decision deadline:** N/A, notification date: N/A
**Early action deadline:** N/A, notification date: N/A
**Application deadline (fall):** rolling

**Undergraduate student body:** 1,114 full time, 736 part time; 57% male, 43% female; 0% American Indian, 0% Asian, 17% black, 1% Hispanic, 1% multiracial, 0% Pacific Islander, 78% white, 0% international; 86% from in state; 29% live on campus; 2% of students in fraternities, 4% in sororities
**Most popular majors:** Information not available
**Expenses:** 2014-2015: $6,696 in state, $15,120 out of state; room/board: $9,492
**Financial aid:** (304) 462-4103; 81% of undergrads determined to have financial need; average aid package $12,805

## Marshall University
Huntington WV
(800) 642-3499
**U.S. News ranking:** Reg. U. (S), No. 46
**Website:** www.marshall.edu
**Admissions email:** admissions@marshall.edu
**Public;** founded 1837
**Freshman admissions:** selective; 2013-2014: 2,866 applied, 2,255 accepted. Either SAT or ACT required. ACT 25/75 percentile: 20-24. High school rank: N/A
**Early decision deadline:** N/A, notification date: N/A
**Early action deadline:** N/A, notification date: N/A
**Application deadline (fall):** rolling
**Undergraduate student body:** 8,268 full time, 1,488 part time; 44% male, 56% female; 0% American Indian, 1% Asian, 6% black, 2% Hispanic, 2% multiracial, 0% Pacific Islander, 86% white, 1% international; 77% from in state; N/A live on campus; N/A of students in fraternities, N/A in sororities
**Most popular majors:** 5% Biological and Biomedical Sciences, 17% Business, Management, Marketing, and Related Support Services, 14% Education, 11% Health Professions and Related Programs, 16% Liberal Arts and Sciences, General Studies and Humanities
**Expenses:** 2014-2015: $6,526 in state, $15,026 out of state; room/board: $8,722
**Financial aid:** (304) 696-3162; 71% of undergrads determined to have financial need; average aid package $9,956

## Ohio Valley University
Vienna WV
(877) 446-8668
**U.S. News ranking:** Reg. Coll. (S), No. 56
**Website:** www.ovu.edu
**Admissions email:** admissions@ovu.edu
**Private;** founded 1958
**Affiliation:** Church of Christ
**Freshman admissions:** selective; 2013-2014: 846 applied, 321 accepted. Either SAT or ACT required. ACT 25/75 percentile: 19-23. High school rank: 10% in top tenth, 29% in top quarter, 59% in top half
**Early decision deadline:** N/A, notification date: N/A
**Early action deadline:** N/A, notification date: N/A
**Application deadline (fall):** 8/15

**Undergraduate student body:** 371 full time, 47 part time; 54% male, 46% female; 0% American Indian, 1% Asian, 7% black, 3% Hispanic, 2% multiracial, 0% Pacific Islander, 72% white, 8% international; 34% from in state; 53% live on campus; 66% of students in fraternities, 66% in sororities
**Most popular majors:** 25% Business, Management, Marketing, and Related Support Services, 20% Education, 8% Liberal Arts and Sciences, General Studies and Humanities, 13% Psychology, 10% Theology and Religious Vocations
**Expenses:** 2014-2015: $19,260; room/board: $7,010
**Financial aid:** (304) 865-6075; 76% of undergrads determined to have financial need; average aid package $14,612

## Salem International University[1]
Salem WV
(888) 235-5024
**U.S. News ranking:** Reg. U. (S), unranked
**Website:** www.salemu.edu
**Admissions email:** admissions@salemu.edu
**For-profit**
**Application deadline (fall):** N/A
**Undergraduate student body:** N/A full time, N/A part time
**Expenses:** 2013-2014: $17,700; room/board: $7,000
**Financial aid:** (304) 782-5303

## Shepherd University
Shepherdstown WV
(304) 876-5212
**U.S. News ranking:** Reg. U. (S), second tier
**Website:** www.shepherd.edu
**Admissions email:** admissions@shepherd.edu
**Public;** founded 1871
**Freshman admissions:** less selective; 2013-2014: 1,746 applied, 1,647 accepted. Either SAT or ACT required. SAT 25/75 percentile: 900-1080. High school rank: N/A
**Early decision deadline:** N/A, notification date: N/A
**Early action deadline:** 11/15, notification date: 12/1
**Application deadline (fall):** rolling
**Undergraduate student body:** 3,289 full time, 701 part time; 43% male, 57% female; 0% American Indian, 2% Asian, 8% black, 3% Hispanic, 0% multiracial, 0% Pacific Islander, 83% white, 0% international; 63% from in state; 33% live on campus; 3% of students in fraternities, 4% in sororities
**Most popular majors:** 12% Business, Management, Marketing, and Related Support Services, 12% Education, 9% Health Professions and Related Programs, 17% Liberal Arts and Sciences, General Studies and Humanities, 8% Social Sciences
**Expenses:** 2014-2015: $6,570 in state, $16,628 out of state; room/board: $9,308
**Financial aid:** (304) 876-5470; 64% of undergrads determined to have financial need; average aid package $11,094

## University of Charleston
Charleston WV
(800) 995-4682
**U.S. News ranking:** Reg. Coll. (S), No. 19
**Website:** www.ucwv.edu
**Admissions email:** admissions@ucwv.edu
**Private;** founded 1888
**Freshman admissions:** selective; 2013-2014: 1,312 applied, 906 accepted. Either SAT or ACT required. ACT 25/75 percentile: 19-24. High school rank: N/A
**Early decision deadline:** N/A, notification date: N/A
**Early action deadline:** N/A, notification date: N/A
**Application deadline (fall):** rolling
**Undergraduate student body:** 1,250 full time, 136 part time; 42% male, 58% female; 1% American Indian, 1% Asian, 12% black, 2% Hispanic, 1% multiracial, 0% Pacific Islander, 64% white, 8% international; 72% from in state; 47% live on campus; N/A of students in fraternities, N/A in sororities
**Most popular majors:** 9% Biological and Biomedical Sciences, 40% Business, Management, Marketing, and Related Support Services, 6% Education, 6% Health Professions and Related Programs, 7% Social Sciences
**Expenses:** 2014-2015: $23,200; room/board: $9,100
**Financial aid:** (304) 357-4759; 81% of undergrads determined to have financial need; average aid package $17,500

## West Liberty University
West Liberty WV
(304) 336-8076
**U.S. News ranking:** Reg. Coll. (S), No. 52
**Website:** www.westliberty.edu
**Admissions email:** admissions@westliberty.edu
**Public;** founded 1837
**Freshman admissions:** selective; 2013-2014: 2,175 applied, 1,549 accepted. Either SAT or ACT required. ACT 25/75 percentile: 18-24. High school rank: 11% in top tenth, 37% in top quarter, 72% in top half
**Early decision deadline:** N/A, notification date: N/A
**Early action deadline:** N/A, notification date: N/A
**Application deadline (fall):** rolling
**Undergraduate student body:** 2,197 full time, 463 part time; 40% male, 60% female; 0% American Indian, 1% Asian, 5% black, 1% Hispanic, 1% multiracial, 0% Pacific Islander, 89% white, 2% international; 68% from in state; 45% live on campus; 3% of students in fraternities, 4% in sororities
**Most popular majors:** 15% Business, Management, Marketing, and Related Support Services, 18% Education, 14% Health Professions and Related Programs, 7% Homeland Security, Law Enforcement, Firefighting and Related Protective Services, 17% Liberal Arts and Sciences, General Studies and Humanities
**Expenses:** 2013-2014: $6,226 in state, $13,540 out of state; room/board: $8,370
**Financial aid:** (304) 336-8016

## West Virginia State University

Institute WV
(304) 766-3221
**U.S. News ranking:** Nat. Lib. Arts, second tier
**Website:** www.wvstateu.edu
**Admissions email:** admissions@wvstateu.edu
**Public;** founded 1891
**Freshman admissions:** selective; 2013-2014: 2,206 applied, 984 accepted. Either SAT or ACT required. ACT 25/75 percentile: 18-22. High school rank: N/A
**Early decision deadline:** N/A, notification date: N/A
**Early action deadline:** N/A, notification date: N/A
**Application deadline (fall):** 8/20
**Undergraduate student body:** 1,889 full time, 733 part time; 45% male, 55% female; 1% American Indian, 0% Asian, 12% black, 1% Hispanic, 0% multiracial, 0% Pacific Islander, 61% white, 1% international; 93% from in state; 10% live on campus; 1% of students in fraternities, 1% in sororities
**Most popular majors:** 13% Business, Management, Marketing, and Related Support Services, 13% Education, 9% Homeland Security, Law Enforcement, Firefighting and Related Protective Services, 22% Liberal Arts and Sciences, General Studies and Humanities, 9% Psychology
**Expenses:** 2014-2015: $6,228 in state, $14,558 out of state; room/board: $10,476
**Financial aid:** (304) 766-3131; 79% of undergrads determined to have financial need; average aid package $11,756

## West Virginia University

Morgantown WV
(304) 442-3146
**U.S. News ranking:** Nat. U., No. 168
**Website:** www.wvu.edu
**Admissions email:** tech-admissions@mail.wvu.edu
**Public;** founded 1867
**Freshman admissions:** selective; 2013-2014: 16,079 applied, 13,713 accepted. Either SAT or ACT required. ACT 25/75 percentile: 21-26. High school rank: 20% in top tenth, 45% in top quarter, 79% in top half
**Early decision deadline:** N/A, notification date: N/A
**Early action deadline:** N/A, notification date: N/A
**Application deadline (fall):** 8/1
**Undergraduate student body:** 21,027 full time, 1,730 part time; 54% male, 46% female; 0% American Indian, 2% Asian, 4% black, 4% Hispanic, 3% multiracial, 0% Pacific Islander, 83% white, 4% international; 51% from in state; 24% live on campus; 6% of students in fraternities, 5% in sororities
**Most popular majors:** 12% Business, Management, Marketing, and Related Support Services, 8% Communication, Journalism, and Related Programs, 12% Engineering, 9% Health Professions and Related Programs, 9% Multi/Interdisciplinary Studies
**Expenses:** 2014-2015: $6,960 in state, $20,424 out of state; room/board: $9,582

## West Virginia University–Parkersburg[1]

Parkersburg WV
(304) 424-8220
**U.S. News ranking:** Reg. Coll. (S), unranked
**Website:** www.wvup.edu
**Admissions email:** info@mail.wvup.edu
**Public**
**Application deadline (fall):** N/A
**Undergraduate student body:** N/A full time, N/A part time
**Expenses:** 2013-2014: $2,712 in state, $9,648 out of state; room/board: N/A
**Financial aid:** (304) 424-8210

## West Virginia Wesleyan College

Buckhannon WV
(800) 722-9933
**U.S. News ranking:** Reg. Coll. (S), No. 12
**Website:** www.wvwc.edu
**Admissions email:** admissions@wvwc.edu
**Private;** founded 1890
**Affiliation:** United Methodist
**Freshman admissions:** selective; 2013-2014: 1,762 applied, 1,356 accepted. Either SAT or ACT required. ACT 25/75 percentile: 20-25. High school rank: 27% in top tenth, 56% in top quarter, 85% in top half
**Early decision deadline:** N/A, notification date: N/A
**Early action deadline:** N/A, notification date: N/A
**Application deadline (fall):** rolling
**Undergraduate student body:** 1,345 full time, 22 part time; 47% male, 53% female; 0% American Indian, 0% Asian, 9% black, 2% Hispanic, 3% multiracial, 0% Pacific Islander, 80% white, 5% international; 62% from in state; 79% live on campus; 25% of students in fraternities, 25% in sororities
**Most popular majors:** 13% Business, Management, Marketing, and Related Support Services, 10% Education, 11% Health Professions and Related Programs, 8% Homeland Security, Law Enforcement, Firefighting and Related Protective Services, 9% Parks, Recreation, Leisure, and Fitness Studies
**Expenses:** 2014-2015: $27,858; room/board: $7,890
**Financial aid:** (304) 473-8080; 80% of undergrads determined to have financial need; average aid package $28,234

## Wheeling Jesuit University

Wheeling WV
(800) 624-6992
**U.S. News ranking:** Reg. Coll. (S), No. 11
**Website:** www.wju.edu
**Admissions email:** admiss@wju.edu
**Private;** founded 1954
**Affiliation:** Roman Catholic
**Freshman admissions:** selective; 2013-2014: 1,470 applied, 981 accepted. Either SAT or ACT required. ACT 25/75 percentile: 20-24. High school rank: 16% in top tenth, 43% in top quarter, 78% in top half
**Early decision deadline:** N/A, notification date: N/A
**Early action deadline:** N/A, notification date: N/A
**Application deadline (fall):** rolling
**Undergraduate student body:** 938 full time, 242 part time; 45% male, 55% female; 0% American Indian, 1% Asian, 5% black, 3% Hispanic, 0% multiracial, 0% Pacific Islander, 80% white, 3% international; 39% from in state; 59% live on campus; 0% of students in fraternities, 0% in sororities
**Most popular majors:** 23% Business, Management, Marketing, and Related Support Services, 5% English Language and Literature/Letters, 34% Health Professions and Related Programs, 6% Physical Sciences, 5% Psychology
**Expenses:** 2014-2015: $28,030; room/board: $6,827
**Financial aid:** (304) 243-2304; 75% of undergrads determined to have financial need; average aid package $23,406

# WISCONSIN

## Alverno College

Milwaukee WI
(414) 382-6100
**U.S. News ranking:** Reg. U. (Mid. W), No. 69
**Website:** www.alverno.edu
**Admissions email:** admissions@alverno.edu
**Private;** founded 1887
**Affiliation:** Roman Catholic
**Freshman admissions:** less selective; 2013-2014: 582 applied, 459 accepted. Either SAT or ACT required. ACT 25/75 percentile: 17-23. High school rank: 11% in top tenth, 35% in top quarter, 70% in top half
**Early decision deadline:** N/A, notification date: N/A
**Early action deadline:** N/A, notification date: N/A
**Application deadline (fall):** rolling
**Undergraduate student body:** 1,360 full time, 502 part time; 0% male, 100% female; 1% American Indian, 5% Asian, 18% black, 18% Hispanic, 3% multiracial, 0% Pacific Islander, 54% white, 1% international; 96% from in state; 11% live on campus; 1% of students in fraternities, 1% in sororities
**Most popular majors:** 13% Business, Management, Marketing, and Related Support Services, 6% Education, 44% Health Professions and Related Programs, 7% Liberal Arts and Sciences, General Studies and Humanities, 6% Psychology
**Expenses:** 2014-2015: $24,434; room/board: $7,500
**Financial aid:** (414) 382-6046; 92% of undergrads determined to have financial need; average aid package $17,004

## Beloit College

Beloit WI
(608) 363-2500
**U.S. News ranking:** Nat. Lib. Arts, No. 61
**Website:** www.beloit.edu
**Admissions email:** admiss@beloit.edu
**Private;** founded 1846
**Freshman admissions:** more selective; 2013-2014: 2,253 applied, 1,525 accepted. Neither SAT nor ACT required. ACT 25/75 percentile: 24-30. High school rank: 29% in top tenth, 61% in top quarter, 89% in top half
**Early decision deadline:** 11/1, notification date: 11/30
**Early action deadline:** 12/1, notification date: 1/15
**Application deadline (fall):** rolling
**Undergraduate student body:** 1,254 full time, 52 part time; 41% male, 59% female; 0% American Indian, 2% Asian, 5% black, 8% Hispanic, 3% multiracial, 0% Pacific Islander, 71% white, 8% international; 19% from in state; 92% live on campus; 24% of students in fraternities, 22% in sororities
**Most popular majors:** 6% Anthropology, 5% Creative Writing, 6% Economics, Other, 5% History, General, 9% Psychology, General
**Expenses:** 2014-2015: $42,500; room/board: $7,470
**Financial aid:** (608) 363-2663; 69% of undergrads determined to have financial need; average aid package $31,215

## Cardinal Stritch University[1]

Milwaukee WI
(414) 410-4040
**U.S. News ranking:** Nat. U., second tier
**Website:** www.stritch.edu
**Admissions email:** admityou@stritch.edu
**Private;** founded 1937
**Affiliation:** Roman Catholic
**Application deadline (fall):** rolling
**Undergraduate student body:** N/A full time, N/A part time
**Expenses:** 2014-2015: $26,570; room/board: $7,470
**Financial aid:** (414) 410-4048; 78% of undergrads determined to have financial need; average aid package $11,824

## Carroll University

Waukesha WI
(262) 524-7220
**U.S. News ranking:** Reg. U. (Mid. W), No. 41
**Website:** www.carrollu.edu/
**Admissions email:** ccinfo@carrollu.edu
**Private;** founded 1846
**Affiliation:** Presbyterian Church (USA)
**Freshman admissions:** more selective; 2013-2014: 2,868 applied, 2,327 accepted. Either SAT or ACT required. ACT 25/75 percentile: 21-26. High school rank: 26% in top tenth, 58% in top quarter, 86% in top half
**Early decision deadline:** N/A, notification date: N/A
**Early action deadline:** N/A, notification date: N/A
**Application deadline (fall):** rolling

## Carthage College

Kenosha WI
(262) 551-6000
**U.S. News ranking:** Nat. Lib. Arts, No. 155
**Website:** www.carthage.edu
**Admissions email:** admissions@carthage.edu
**Private;** founded 1847
**Affiliation:** Evangelical Lutheran Church in America
**Freshman admissions:** selective; 2013-2014: 7,174 applied, 5,035 accepted. Either SAT or ACT required. ACT 25/75 percentile: 21-27. High school rank: 21% in top tenth, 44% in top quarter, 75% in top half
**Early decision deadline:** N/A, notification date: N/A
**Early action deadline:** N/A, notification date: N/A
**Application deadline (fall):** rolling
**Undergraduate student body:** 2,581 full time, 321 part time; 46% male, 54% female; 0% American Indian, 1% Asian, 5% black, 4% Hispanic, 2% multiracial, 0% Pacific Islander, 77% white, 0% international; 32% from in state; 67% live on campus; 11% of students in fraternities, 12% in sororities
**Most popular majors:** Information not available
**Expenses:** 2014-2015: $36,850; room/board: $9,970
**Financial aid:** (262) 551-6001; 79% of undergrads determined to have financial need; average aid package $24,219

## Concordia University Wisconsin

Mequon WI
(262) 243-4300
**U.S. News ranking:** Reg. U. (Mid. W), No. 61
**Website:** www.cuw.edu
**Admissions email:** admissions@cuw.edu
**Private;** founded 1881
**Affiliation:** Lutheran Church-Missouri Synod
**Freshman admissions:** selective; 2013-2014: 2,510 applied, 1,755 accepted. ACT required. ACT 25/75 percentile: 20-25. High school rank: 21% in top tenth, 43% in top quarter, 72% in top half
**Early decision deadline:** N/A, notification date: N/A
**Early action deadline:** N/A, notification date: N/A
**Application deadline (fall):** 8/15
**Undergraduate student body:** 3,059 full time, 1,304 part time; 34% male, 66% female; 1% American Indian, 2% Asian, 18% black, 3% Hispanic, 3% multiracial, 0% Pacific Islander, 69% white, 1% international

---

Financial aid: (800) 344-9881; 55% of undergrads determined to have financial need; average aid package $7,271

(top of column 2 continued text for Beloit area)

**Undergraduate student body:** 2,729 full time, 390 part time; 35% male, 65% female; 0% American Indian, 2% Asian, 1% black, 6% Hispanic, 2% multiracial, 0% Pacific Islander, 87% white, 1% international
**Most popular majors:** Information not available
**Expenses:** 2014-2015: $28,550; room/board: $8,550
**Financial aid:** (262) 524-7296; 82% of undergrads determined to have financial need; average aid package $19,011

**Most popular majors:** Information not available
**Expenses:** 2014-2015: $26,190; room/board: $9,780
**Financial aid:** (262) 243-4569; 83% of undergrads determined to have financial need; average aid package $19,230

## Edgewood College
Madison WI
(608) 663-2294
**U.S. News ranking:** Nat. U., No. 181
**Website:** www.edgewood.edu
**Admissions email:** admissions@edgewood.edu
**Private;** founded 1927
**Affiliation:** Roman Catholic
**Freshman admissions:** selective; 2013-2014: 1,297 applied, 993 accepted. Either SAT or ACT required. ACT 25/75 percentile: 20-25. High school rank: 15% in top tenth, 37% in top quarter, 74% in top half
**Early decision deadline:** N/A, notification date: N/A
**Early action deadline:** N/A, notification date: N/A
**Application deadline (fall):** 8/14
**Undergraduate student body:** 1,681 full time, 317 part time; 31% male, 69% female; 0% American Indian, 2% Asian, 3% black, 5% Hispanic, 3% multiracial, 0% Pacific Islander, 80% white, 4% international; 93% from in state; 28% live on campus; N/A of students in fraternities, N/A in sororities
**Most popular majors:** 7% Business Administration and Management, General, 10% Business/Commerce, General, 4% Organizational Behavior Studies, 9% Psychology, General, 23% Registered Nursing/Registered Nurse
**Expenses:** 2014-2015: $25,590; room/board: $8,973
**Financial aid:** (608) 663-2305; 76% of undergrads determined to have financial need; average aid package $20,260

## Herzing University[1]
Madison WI
(800) 596-0724
**U.S. News ranking:** Reg. Coll. (Mid. W), second tier
**Website:** www.herzing.edu/madison
**Admissions email:** info@msn.herzing.edu
**For-profit**
**Application deadline (fall):** N/A
**Undergraduate student body:** N/A full time, N/A part time
**Expenses:** 2013-2014: $11,150; room/board: N/A
**Financial aid:** N/A

## Lakeland College[1]
Plymouth WI
(920) 565-1226
**U.S. News ranking:** Reg. U. (Mid. W), second tier
**Website:** www.lakeland.edu
**Admissions email:** admissions@lakeland.edu
**Private;** founded 1862
**Affiliation:** United Church of Christ
**Application deadline (fall):** rolling
**Undergraduate student body:** N/A full time, N/A part time
**Expenses:** 2013-2014: $22,950; room/board: $8,030
**Financial aid:** (920) 565-1298

## Lawrence University
Appleton WI
(800) 227-0982
**U.S. News ranking:** Nat. Lib. Arts, No. 59
**Website:** www.lawrence.edu/
**Admissions email:** admissions@lawrence.edu
**Private;** founded 1847
**Freshman admissions:** more selective; 2013-2014: 2,710 applied, 1,970 accepted. Neither SAT nor ACT required. ACT 25/75 percentile: 26-31. High school rank: 42% in top tenth, 76% in top quarter, 97% in top half
**Early decision deadline:** 11/1, notification date: 11/15
**Early action deadline:** 11/15, notification date: 12/20
**Application deadline (fall):** 1/15
**Undergraduate student body:** 1,518 full time, 37 part time; 44% male, 56% female; 1% American Indian, 4% Asian, 3% black, 5% Hispanic, 4% multiracial, 0% Pacific Islander, 74% white, 9% international; 32% from in state; 92% live on campus; 20% of students in fraternities, 15% in sororities
**Most popular majors:** 10% Biological and Biomedical Sciences, 10% Foreign Languages, Literatures, and Linguistics, 9% Psychology, 18% Social Sciences, 23% Visual and Performing Arts
**Expenses:** 2014-2015: $42,657; room/board: $8,808
**Financial aid:** (920) 832-6583; 64% of undergrads determined to have financial need; average aid package $33,196

## Maranatha Baptist University
Watertown WI
(920) 206-2327
**U.S. News ranking:** Reg. Coll. (Mid. W), No. 62
**Website:** www.mbbc.edu
**Admissions email:** admissions@mbbc.edu
**Private;** founded 1968
**Affiliation:** Baptist
**Freshman admissions:** selective; 2013-2014: 463 applied, 297 accepted. Either SAT or ACT required. ACT 25/75 percentile: 20-26. High school rank: N/A
**Early decision deadline:** N/A, notification date: N/A
**Early action deadline:** N/A, notification date: N/A
**Application deadline (fall):** rolling
**Undergraduate student body:** 692 full time, 249 part time; 45% male, 55% female; 0% American Indian, 1% Asian, 2% black, 2% Hispanic, 3% multiracial, 0% Pacific Islander, 82% white, 1% international; 29% from in state; 65% live on campus; N/A of students in fraternities, N/A in sororities
**Most popular majors:** 17% Business, Management, Marketing, and Related Support Services, 21% Education, 6% Health Professions and Related Programs, 31% Liberal Arts and Sciences, General Studies and Humanities, 16% Theology and Religious Vocations
**Expenses:** 2014-2015: $13,510; room/board: $6,480
**Financial aid:** (920) 206-2319; 85% of undergrads determined to have financial need; average aid package $9,918

## Marian University
Fond du Lac WI
(920) 923-7650
**U.S. News ranking:** Reg. U. (Mid. W), No. 95
**Website:** www.marianuniversity.edu
**Admissions email:** admissions@marianuniversity.edu
**Private;** founded 1936
**Affiliation:** Roman Catholic
**Freshman admissions:** selective; 2013-2014: 1,021 applied, 772 accepted. Either SAT or ACT required. ACT 25/75 percentile: 18-22. High school rank: 7% in top tenth, 32% in top quarter, 69% in top half
**Early decision deadline:** N/A, notification date: N/A
**Early action deadline:** N/A, notification date: N/A
**Application deadline (fall):** rolling
**Undergraduate student body:** 1,339 full time, 349 part time; 29% male, 71% female; 1% American Indian, 1% Asian, 6% black, 4% Hispanic, 0% multiracial, 0% Pacific Islander, 84% white, 2% international; 88% from in state; 33% live on campus; 5% of students in fraternities, 5% in sororities
**Most popular majors:** 20% Business, Management, Marketing, and Related Support Services, 13% Homeland Security, Law Enforcement, Firefighting and Related Protective Services, 4% Psychology, 9% Radiologic Technology/Science - Radiographer, 28% Registered Nursing, Nursing Administration, Nursing Research and Clinical Nursing
**Expenses:** 2014-2015: $25,630; room/board: $6,490
**Financial aid:** (920) 923-7614; 86% of undergrads determined to have financial need; average aid package $22,412

## Marquette University
Milwaukee WI
(800) 222-6544
**U.S. News ranking:** Nat. U., No. 76
**Website:** www.marquette.edu
**Admissions email:** admissions@marquette.edu
**Private;** founded 1881
**Affiliation:** Roman Catholic (Jesuit)
**Freshman admissions:** more selective; 2013-2014: 23,432 applied, 13,462 accepted. Either SAT or ACT required. ACT 25/75 percentile: 25-29. High school rank: 36% in top tenth, 69% in top quarter, 95% in top half
**Early decision deadline:** N/A, notification date: N/A
**Early action deadline:** N/A, notification date: N/A
**Application deadline (fall):** 12/1
**Undergraduate student body:** 8,046 full time, 319 part time; 48% male, 52% female; 0% American Indian, 5% Asian, 5% black, 9% Hispanic, 3% multiracial, 0% Pacific Islander, 74% white, 3% international; 35% from in state; 54% live on campus; 7% of students in fraternities, 15% in sororities
**Most popular majors:** 8% Biological and Biomedical Sciences, 25% Business, Management, Marketing, and Related Support Services, 11% Communication, Journalism, and Related Programs,

9% Engineering, 8% Health Professions and Related Programs
**Expenses:** 2014-2015: $35,930; room/board: $11,000
**Financial aid:** (414) 288-0200; 58% of undergrads determined to have financial need; average aid package $23,664

## Milwaukee Institute of Art and Design
Milwaukee WI
(414) 291-8070
**U.S. News ranking:** Arts, unranked
**Website:** www.miad.edu
**Admissions email:** admissions@miad.edu
**Private;** founded 1974
**Freshman admissions:** N/A; 2013-2014: 583 applied, 369 accepted. Neither SAT nor ACT required. SAT 25/75 percentile: N/A. High school rank: 8% in top tenth, 26% in top quarter, 60% in top half
**Early decision deadline:** N/A, notification date: N/A
**Early action deadline:** 12/1, notification date: 12/15
**Application deadline (fall):** 8/1
**Undergraduate student body:** 653 full time, 15 part time; 34% male, 66% female; 0% American Indian, 4% Asian, 6% black, 11% Hispanic, 4% multiracial, 0% Pacific Islander, 71% white, 1% international; 64% from in state; 20% live on campus; 0% of students in fraternities, 0% in sororities
**Most popular majors:** 10% Animation, Interactive Technology, Video Graphics and Special Effects, 20% Graphic Design, 14% Illustration, 13% Industrial and Product Design, 10% Photography
**Expenses:** 2014-2015: $32,050; room/board: $9,000
**Financial aid:** (414) 291-3272; 83% of undergrads determined to have financial need; average aid package $22,040

## Milwaukee School of Engineering
Milwaukee WI
(800) 332-6763
**U.S. News ranking:** Reg. U. (Mid. W), No. 14
**Website:** www.msoe.edu
**Admissions email:** explore@msoe.edu
**Private;** founded 1903
**Freshman admissions:** selective; 2013-2014: 2,167 applied, 1,482 accepted. Either SAT or ACT required. ACT 25/75 percentile: 25-30. High school rank: N/A
**Early decision deadline:** N/A, notification date: N/A
**Early action deadline:** N/A, notification date: N/A
**Application deadline (fall):** rolling
**Undergraduate student body:** 2,284 full time, 175 part time; 77% male, 23% female; 0% American Indian, 3% Asian, 3% black, 5% Hispanic, 1% multiracial, 0% Pacific Islander, 74% white, 8% international; 70% from in state; 37% live on campus; 4% of students in fraternities, 15% in sororities
**Most popular majors:** 18% Business, Management, Marketing, and Related Support Services, 1% Communication, Journalism, and Related Programs,

69% Engineering, 7% Engineering Technologies and Engineering-Related Fields, 5% Health Professions and Related Programs
**Expenses:** 2014-2015: $35,520; room/board: $8,520
**Financial aid:** (414) 277-7511; 83% of undergrads determined to have financial need; average aid package $23,055

## Mount Mary University
Milwaukee WI
(800) 321-6265
**U.S. News ranking:** Reg. U. (Mid. W), No. 91
**Website:** www.mtmary.edu
**Admissions email:** mmc-admiss@mtmary.edu
**Private;** founded 1913
**Affiliation:** Roman Catholic
**Freshman admissions:** selective; 2013-2014: 478 applied, 258 accepted. Either SAT or ACT required. ACT 25/75 percentile: 17-23. High school rank: 26% in top tenth, 53% in top quarter, 78% in top half
**Early decision deadline:** N/A, notification date: N/A
**Early action deadline:** N/A, notification date: N/A
**Application deadline (fall):** rolling
**Undergraduate student body:** 685 full time, 241 part time; 2% male, 98% female; 0% American Indian, 7% Asian, 22% black, 14% Hispanic, 3% multiracial, 0% Pacific Islander, 52% white, 0% international; 96% from in state; 18% live on campus; N/A of students in fraternities, N/A in sororities
**Most popular majors:** 23% Business, Management, Marketing, and Related Support Services, 13% Health Professions and Related Programs, 8% Psychology, 9% Public Administration and Social Service Professions, 17% Visual and Performing Arts
**Expenses:** 2014-2015: $25,852; room/board: $7,738
**Financial aid:** (414) 256-1258; 91% of undergrads determined to have financial need; average aid package $19,944

## Northland College
Ashland WI
(715) 682-1224
**U.S. News ranking:** Nat. Lib. Arts, No. 172
**Website:** www.northland.edu
**Admissions email:** admit@northland.edu
**Private;** founded 1892
**Affiliation:** United Church of Christ
**Freshman admissions:** selective; 2013-2014: 1,058 applied, 625 accepted. Either SAT or ACT required. ACT 25/75 percentile: 21-27. High school rank: 18% in top tenth, 36% in top quarter, 75% in top half
**Early decision deadline:** N/A, notification date: N/A
**Early action deadline:** N/A, notification date: N/A
**Application deadline (fall):** rolling
**Undergraduate student body:** 539 full time, 14 part time; 48% male, 52% female; 2% American Indian, 1% Asian, 1% black, 5% Hispanic, 3% multiracial, 0% Pacific Islander, 77% white, 1% international; 50% from in state; 77% live on campus;

0% of students in fraternities, 0% in sororities
**Most popular majors:** 16% Biological and Biomedical Sciences, 9% Business, Management, Marketing, and Related Support Services, 11% Education, 25% Natural Resources and Conservation, 8% Physical Sciences
**Expenses:** 2014-2015: $31,480; room/board: $7,858
**Financial aid:** (715) 682-1255; 89% of undergrads determined to have financial need; average aid package $35,251

## Ripon College
Ripon WI
(920) 748-8337
**U.S. News ranking:** Nat. Lib. Arts, No. 113
**Website:** www.ripon.edu
**Admissions email:** adminfo@ripon.edu
**Private;** founded 1851
**Freshman admissions:** selective; 2013-2014: 1,320 applied, 992 accepted. Either SAT or ACT required. ACT 25/75 percentile: 21-28. High school rank: 23% in top tenth, 53% in top quarter, 84% in top half
**Early decision deadline:** N/A, notification date: N/A
**Early action deadline:** N/A, notification date: N/A
**Application deadline (fall):** rolling
**Undergraduate student body:** 888 full time, 16 part time; 47% male, 53% female; 0% American Indian, 2% Asian, 2% black, 6% Hispanic, 1% multiracial, 0% Pacific Islander, 83% white, 4% international; 62% from in state; 88% live on campus; 40% of students in fraternities, 27% in sororities
**Most popular majors:** 12% Business/Commerce, General, 11% English Language and Literature, General, 11% Health and Physical Education/Fitness, General, 13% History, 11% Psychology, General
**Expenses:** 2014-2015: $33,482; room/board: $9,085
**Financial aid:** (920) 748-8101; 84% of undergrads determined to have financial need; average aid package $27,134

## Silver Lake College[1]
Manitowoc WI
(920) 686-6175
**U.S. News ranking:** Reg. Coll. (Mid. W), second tier
**Website:** www.sl.edu
**Admissions email:** admslc@silver.sl.edu
**Private**
**Application deadline (fall):** N/A
**Undergraduate student body:** N/A full time, N/A part time
**Expenses:** 2013-2014: $23,180; room/board: $8,298
**Financial aid:** (920) 686-6122

## St. Norbert College
De Pere WI
(800) 236-4878
**U.S. News ranking:** Nat. Lib. Arts, No. 123
**Website:** www.snc.edu
**Admissions email:** admit@snc.edu
**Private;** founded 1898
**Affiliation:** Roman Catholic
**Freshman admissions:** more selective; 2013-2014: 2,088

applied, 1,711 accepted. Either SAT or ACT required. ACT 25/75 percentile: 22-27. High school rank: 27% in top tenth, 56% in top quarter, 87% in top half
**Early decision deadline:** N/A, notification date: N/A
**Early action deadline:** N/A, notification date: N/A
**Application deadline (fall):** rolling
**Undergraduate student body:** 2,118 full time, 42 part time; 41% male, 59% female; 1% American Indian, 1% Asian, 1% black, 3% Hispanic, 2% multiracial, 0% Pacific Islander, 90% white, 3% international; 76% from in state; 75% live on campus; 13% of students in fraternities, 10% in sororities
**Most popular majors:** 16% Business/Commerce, General, 15% Elementary Education and Teaching, 6% Psychology, General, 9% Sociology, 10% Speech Communication and Rhetoric
**Expenses:** 2014-2015: $33,023; room/board: $8,455
**Financial aid:** (920) 403-3071; 72% of undergrads determined to have financial need; average aid package $23,644

## University of Wisconsin–Eau Claire
Eau Claire WI
(715) 836-5415
**U.S. News ranking:** Reg. U. (Mid. W), No. 33
**Website:** www.uwec.edu
**Admissions email:** admissions@uwec.edu
**Public;** founded 1916
**Freshman admissions:** selective; 2013-2014: 5,885 applied, 4,724 accepted. Either SAT or ACT required. ACT 25/75 percentile: 22-26. High school rank: 18% in top tenth, 51% in top quarter, 95% in top half
**Early decision deadline:** N/A, notification date: N/A
**Early action deadline:** N/A, notification date: N/A
**Application deadline (fall):** rolling
**Undergraduate student body:** 9,447 full time, 936 part time; 41% male, 59% female; 0% American Indian, 3% Asian, 1% black, 2% Hispanic, 2% multiracial, 0% Pacific Islander, 89% white, 2% international; 76% from in state; 26% live on campus; N/A of students in fraternities, N/A in sororities
**Most popular majors:** 21% Business, Management, Marketing, and Related Support Services, 8% Education, 16% Health Professions and Related Programs, 6% Psychology, 6% Visual and Performing Arts
**Expenses:** 2014-2015: $8,744 in state, $16,317 out of state; room/board: $6,986
**Financial aid:** (715) 836-3373; 57% of undergrads determined to have financial need; average aid package $9,772

## University of Wisconsin–Green Bay
Green Bay WI
(920) 465-2111
**U.S. News ranking:** Reg. U. (Mid. W), No. 77
**Website:** www.uwgb.edu
**Admissions email:** uwgb@uwgb.edu
**Public;** founded 1965

**Freshman admissions:** selective; 2013-2014: 2,920 applied, 1,929 accepted. Either SAT or ACT required. ACT 25/75 percentile: 21-25. High school rank: N/A
**Early decision deadline:** N/A, notification date: N/A
**Early action deadline:** N/A, notification date: N/A
**Application deadline (fall):** rolling
**Undergraduate student body:** 4,314 full time, 2,130 part time; 35% male, 65% female; 1% American Indian, 3% Asian, 1% black, 4% Hispanic, 2% multiracial, 0% Pacific Islander, 87% white, 2% international; 93% from in state; 35% live on campus; 1% of students in fraternities, 1% in sororities
**Most popular majors:** 8% Behavioral Sciences, 12% Business Administration and Management, General, 9% Human Biology, 11% Liberal Arts and Sciences/Liberal Studies, 9% Psychology, General
**Expenses:** 2014-2015: $7,676 in state, $15,249 out of state; room/board: $7,224
**Financial aid:** (920) 465-2075; 72% of undergrads determined to have financial need; average aid package $10,728

## University of Wisconsin–La Crosse
La Crosse WI
(608) 785-8939
**U.S. News ranking:** Reg. U. (Mid. W), No. 31
**Website:** www.uwlax.edu
**Admissions email:** admissions@uwlax.edu
**Public;** founded 1909
**Freshman admissions:** more selective; 2013-2014: 6,135 applied, 4,693 accepted. Either SAT or ACT required. ACT 25/75 percentile: 23-27. High school rank: 24% in top tenth, 69% in top quarter, 98% in top half
**Early decision deadline:** N/A, notification date: N/A
**Early action deadline:** N/A, notification date: N/A
**Application deadline (fall):** rolling
**Undergraduate student body:** 9,142 full time, 488 part time; 44% male, 56% female; 0% American Indian, 2% Asian, 1% black, 3% Hispanic, 3% multiracial, 0% Pacific Islander, 89% white, 2% international; 83% from in state; 36% live on campus; 1% of students in fraternities, 1% in sororities
**Most popular majors:** 13% Biological and Biomedical Sciences, 20% Business, Management, Marketing, and Related Support Services, 11% Education, 8% Health Professions and Related Programs, 9% Social Sciences
**Expenses:** 2014-2015: $8,795 in state, $16,368 out of state; room/board: $5,910
**Financial aid:** (608) 785-8604; 55% of undergrads determined to have financial need; average aid package $7,350

## University of Wisconsin–Madison
Madison WI
(608) 262-3961
**U.S. News ranking:** Nat. U., No. 47
**Website:** www.wisc.edu
**Admissions email:** onwisconsin@admissions.wisc.edu
**Public;** founded 1848
**Freshman admissions:** more selective; 2013-2014: 29,675 applied, 15,161 accepted. Either SAT or ACT required. ACT 25/75 percentile: 26-30. High school rank: 51% in top tenth, 89% in top quarter, 99% in top half
**Early decision deadline:** N/A, notification date: N/A
**Early action deadline:** N/A, notification date: N/A
**Application deadline (fall):** 2/1
**Undergraduate student body:** 28,593 full time, 2,726 part time; 49% male, 51% female; 0% American Indian, 6% Asian, 2% black, 5% Hispanic, 3% multiracial, 0% Pacific Islander, 77% white, 7% international; 67% from in state; 25% live on campus; 9% of students in fraternities, 8% in sororities
**Most popular majors:** 8% Biology/Biological Sciences, General, 8% Economics, General, 4% History, General, 7% Political Science and Government, General, 6% Psychology, General
**Expenses:** 2014-2015: $10,410 in state, $26,660 out of state; room/board: $8,600
**Financial aid:** (608) 262-3060; 41% of undergrads determined to have financial need; average aid package $12,718

## University of Wisconsin–Milwaukee
Milwaukee WI
(414) 229-2222
**U.S. News ranking:** Nat. U., second tier
**Website:** www.uwm.edu
**Admissions email:** uwmlook@uwm.edu
**Public;** founded 1956
**Freshman admissions:** selective; 2013-2014: 8,311 applied, 7,347 accepted. Either SAT or ACT required. ACT 25/75 percentile: 19-24. High school rank: 9% in top tenth, 28% in top quarter, 63% in top half
**Early decision deadline:** N/A, notification date: N/A
**Early action deadline:** N/A, notification date: N/A
**Application deadline (fall):** rolling
**Undergraduate student body:** 18,929 full time, 4,075 part time; 49% male, 51% female; 0% American Indian, 6% Asian, 8% black, 8% Hispanic, 3% multiracial, 0% Pacific Islander, 72% white, 3% international; 93% from in state; 16% live on campus; N/A of students in fraternities, N/A in sororities
**Most popular majors:** 24% Business, Management, Marketing, and Related Support Services, 7% Education, 11% Health Professions and Related Programs, 6% Social Sciences, 7% Visual and Performing Arts
**Expenses:** 2014-2015: $9,882 in state, $19,610 out of state; room/board: $9,136

**Financial aid:** (414) 229-6300; 81% of undergrads determined to have financial need; average aid package $7,635

## University of Wisconsin–Oshkosh
Oshkosh WI
(920) 424-0202
**U.S. News ranking:** Reg. U. (Mid. W), No. 69
**Website:** www.uwosh.edu
**Admissions email:** oshadmuw@uwosh.edu
**Public;** founded 1871
**Freshman admissions:** selective; 2013-2014: 6,076 applied, 4,053 accepted. Either SAT or ACT required. ACT 25/75 percentile: 20-24. High school rank: 10% in top tenth, 33% in top quarter, 82% in top half
**Early decision deadline:** N/A, notification date: N/A
**Early action deadline:** N/A, notification date: N/A
**Application deadline (fall):** rolling
**Undergraduate student body:** 9,223 full time, 3,241 part time; 41% male, 59% female; 1% American Indian, 4% Asian, 2% black, 3% Hispanic, 2% multiracial, 0% Pacific Islander, 88% white, 1% international; 96% from in state; 32% live on campus; 3% of students in fraternities, 3% in sororities
**Most popular majors:** 18% Business, Management, Marketing, and Related Support Services, 6% Communication, Journalism, and Related Programs, 13% Education, 14% Health Professions and Related Programs, 7% Public Administration and Social Service Professions
**Expenses:** 2014-2015: $7,442 in state, $15,016 out of state; room/board: $7,386
**Financial aid:** (920) 424-3377; 72% of undergrads determined to have financial need; average aid package $7,800

## University of Wisconsin–Parkside
Kenosha WI
(262) 595-2355
**U.S. News ranking:** Nat. Lib. Arts, second tier
**Website:** www.uwp.edu
**Admissions email:** admissions@uwp.edu
**Public;** founded 1968
**Freshman admissions:** selective; 2013-2014: 1,740 applied, 1,197 accepted. Neither SAT nor ACT required. ACT 25/75 percentile: 19-23. High school rank: 10% in top tenth, 34% in top quarter, 71% in top half
**Early decision deadline:** N/A, notification date: N/A
**Early action deadline:** N/A, notification date: N/A
**Application deadline (fall):** 7/15
**Undergraduate student body:** 3,332 full time, 1,157 part time; 50% male, 50% female; 0% American Indian, 3% Asian, 9% black, 12% Hispanic, 4% multiracial, 0% Pacific Islander, 70% white, 2% international; 87% from in state; 19% live on campus; 1% of students in fraternities, 1% in sororities

**Most popular majors:** 9% Business, Management, Marketing, and Related Support Services, 11% Homeland Security, Law Enforcement, Firefighting and Related Protective Services, 8% Psychology, 11% Social Sciences, 9% Visual and Performing Arts
**Expenses:** 2014-2015: $7,316 in state, $14,889 out of state; room/board: $6,572
**Financial aid:** (262) 595-2004; 66% of undergrads determined to have financial need

## University of Wisconsin–Platteville
Platteville WI
(715) 608-1125
**U.S. News ranking:** Reg. U. (Mid. W), No. 80
**Website:** www.uwplatt.edu
**Admissions email:** admit@uwplatt.edu
**Public;** founded 1866
**Freshman admissions:** selective; 2013-2014: 4,030 applied, 3,194 accepted. Either SAT or ACT required. ACT 25/75 percentile: 21-26. High school rank: 11% in top tenth, 36% in top quarter, 74% in top half
**Early decision deadline:** N/A, notification date: N/A
**Early action deadline:** N/A, notification date: N/A
**Application deadline (fall):** rolling
**Undergraduate student body:** 7,000 full time, 682 part time; 66% male, 34% female; 1% American Indian, 1% Asian, 2% black, 3% Hispanic, 0% multiracial, 0% Pacific Islander, 92% white, 1% international; 77% from in state; N/A live on campus; N/A of students in fraternities, N/A in sororities
**Most popular majors:** 9% Agriculture, Agriculture Operations, and Related Sciences, 10% Business, Management, Marketing, and Related Support Services, 23% Engineering, 9% Engineering Technologies and Engineering-Related Fields, 12% Homeland Security, Law Enforcement, Firefighting and Related Protective Services
**Expenses:** 2014-2015: $7,491 in state, $15,064 out of state; room/board: $7,036
**Financial aid:** (608) 342-1836; 61% of undergrads determined to have financial need

## University of Wisconsin–River Falls
River Falls WI
(715) 425-3500
**U.S. News ranking:** Reg. U. (Mid. W), No. 69
**Website:** www.uwrf.edu
**Admissions email:** admit@uwrf.edu
**Public;** founded 1874
**Freshman admissions:** selective; 2013-2014: 2,946 applied, 2,138 accepted. Either SAT or ACT required. ACT 25/75 percentile: 20-24. High school rank: 11% in top tenth, 32% in top quarter, 71% in top half
**Early decision deadline:** N/A, notification date: N/A
**Early action deadline:** N/A, notification date: N/A
**Application deadline (fall):** rolling

**Undergraduate student body:** 5,210 full time, 584 part time; 39% male, 61% female; 0% American Indian, 3% Asian, 1% black, 2% Hispanic, 2% multiracial, 0% Pacific Islander, 90% white, 1% international; 49% from in state; 41% live on campus; 5% of students in fraternities, 4% in sororities
**Most popular majors:** 18% Agriculture, Agriculture Operations, and Related Sciences, 9% Biological and Biomedical Sciences, 13% Business, Management, Marketing, and Related Support Services, 9% Communication, Journalism, and Related Programs, 15% Education
**Expenses:** 2014-2015: $7,751 in state, $15,324 out of state; room/board: $6,435
**Financial aid:** (715) 425-3141; 68% of undergrads determined to have financial need; average aid package $6,855

## University of Wisconsin–Stevens Point
Stevens Point WI
(715) 346-2441
**U.S. News ranking:** Reg. U. (Mid. W), No. 54
**Website:** www.uwsp.edu
**Admissions email:** admiss@uwsp.edu
**Public;** founded 1894
**Freshman admissions:** selective; 2013-2014: 4,598 applied, 3,690 accepted. Either SAT or ACT required. ACT 25/75 percentile: 21-25. High school rank: 18% in top tenth, 45% in top quarter, 88% in top half
**Early decision deadline:** N/A, notification date: N/A
**Early action deadline:** N/A, notification date: N/A
**Application deadline (fall):** rolling
**Undergraduate student body:** 8,746 full time, 546 part time; 48% male, 52% female; 0% American Indian, 2% Asian, 1% black, 3% Hispanic, 2% multiracial, 0% Pacific Islander, 89% white, 2% international; N/A from in state; 38% live on campus; 2% of students in fraternities, 2% in sororities
**Most popular majors:** 9% Biology/Biological Sciences, General, 9% Business Administration and Management, General, 10% Education, General, 13% Natural Resources/Conservation, General, 10% Social Sciences, General
**Expenses:** 2014-2015: $7,642 in state, $15,215 out of state; room/board: $6,794
**Financial aid:** (715) 346-4771; 61% of undergrads determined to have financial need; average aid package $8,759

## University of Wisconsin–Stout
Menomonie WI
(715) 232-1411
**U.S. News ranking:** Reg. U. (Mid. W), No. 65
**Website:** www.uwstout.edu
**Admissions email:** admissions@uwstout.edu
**Public;** founded 1891

**Freshman admissions:** selective; 2013-2014: 3,355 applied, 2,766 accepted. Either SAT or ACT required. ACT 25/75 percentile: 20-24. High school rank: 9% in top tenth, 28% in top quarter, 65% in top half
**Early decision deadline:** N/A, notification date: N/A
**Early action deadline:** N/A, notification date: N/A
**Application deadline (fall):** rolling
**Undergraduate student body:** 6,779 full time, 1,401 part time; 53% male, 47% female; 0% American Indian, 3% Asian, 1% black, 1% Hispanic, 3% multiracial, 0% Pacific Islander, 88% white, 2% international; 68% from in state; 40% live on campus; 2% of students in fraternities, 3% in sororities
**Most popular majors:** 41% Business, Management, Marketing, and Related Support Services, 9% Education, 7% Engineering Technologies and Engineering-Related Fields, 6% Health Professions and Related Programs, 10% Visual and Performing Arts
**Expenses:** 2014-2015: $9,025 in state, $16,771 out of state; room/board: $6,434
**Financial aid:** (715) 232-1363; 61% of undergrads determined to have financial need; average aid package $10,818

## University of Wisconsin–Superior
Superior WI
(715) 394-8230
**U.S. News ranking:** Reg. U. (Mid. W), No. 99
**Website:** www.uwsuper.edu
**Admissions email:** admissions@uwsuper.edu
**Public;** founded 1893
**Freshman admissions:** selective; 2013-2014: 910 applied, 605 accepted. Either SAT or ACT required. ACT 25/75 percentile: 19-24. High school rank: 10% in top tenth, 17% in top quarter, 73% in top half
**Early decision deadline:** N/A, notification date: N/A
**Early action deadline:** N/A, notification date: N/A
**Application deadline (fall):** 8/1
**Undergraduate student body:** 2,018 full time, 504 part time; 40% male, 60% female; 3% American Indian, 1% Asian, 2% black, 2% Hispanic, 3% multiracial, 0% Pacific Islander, 84% white, 6% international; 55% from in state; 28% live on campus; N/A of students in fraternities, N/A in sororities
**Most popular majors:** 21% Business, Management, Marketing, and Related Support Services, 12% Communication, Journalism, and Related Programs, 15% Education, 10% Multi/Interdisciplinary Studies, 8% Visual and Performing Arts
**Expenses:** 2014-2015: $7,240 in state, $14,813 out of state; room/board: $6,320
**Financial aid:** (715) 394-8200; 70% of undergrads determined to have financial need; average aid package $11,604

## University of Wisconsin–Whitewater
Whitewater WI
(262) 472-1440
**U.S. News ranking:** Reg. U. (Mid. W), No. 48
**Website:** www.uww.edu
**Admissions email:** uwwadmit@mail.uww.edu
**Public;** founded 1868
**Freshman admissions:** selective; 2013-2014: 6,879 applied, 4,809 accepted. Either SAT or ACT required. ACT 25/75 percentile: 20-24. High school rank: 7% in top tenth, 30% in top quarter, 72% in top half
**Early decision deadline:** N/A, notification date: N/A
**Early action deadline:** N/A, notification date: N/A
**Application deadline (fall):** rolling
**Undergraduate student body:** 9,889 full time, 975 part time; 49% male, 51% female; 0% American Indian, 2% Asian, 5% black, 4% Hispanic, 2% multiracial, 0% Pacific Islander, 86% white, 1% international; 85% from in state; 43% live on campus; 49% of students in fraternities, 51% in sororities
**Most popular majors:** Information not available
**Expenses:** 2014-2015: $7,578 in state, $15,151 out of state; room/board: $6,050
**Financial aid:** (262) 472-1130; 63% of undergrads determined to have financial need; average aid package $8,045

## Viterbo University[1]
La Crosse WI
(608) 796-3010
**U.S. News ranking:** Reg. U. (Mid. W), No. 109
**Website:** www.viterbo.edu
**Admissions email:** admission@viterbo.edu
**Private**
**Application deadline (fall):** N/A
**Undergraduate student body:** N/A full time, N/A part time
**Expenses:** 2013-2014: $23,330; room/board: $7,710
**Financial aid:** (608) 796-3900

## Wisconsin Lutheran College
Milwaukee WI
(414) 443-8811
**U.S. News ranking:** Nat. Lib. Arts, No. 178
**Website:** www.wlc.edu
**Admissions email:** admissions@wlc.edu
**Private;** founded 1973
**Affiliation:** Wisconsin Evangelical Lutheran Synod
**Freshman admissions:** selective; 2013-2014: 870 applied, 553 accepted. Either SAT or ACT required. ACT 25/75 percentile: 21-27. High school rank: 19% in top tenth, 44% in top quarter, 75% in top half
**Early decision deadline:** N/A, notification date: N/A
**Early action deadline:** N/A, notification date: N/A
**Application deadline (fall):** rolling

**Undergraduate student body:** 1,002 full time, 68 part time; 47% male, 53% female; 1% American Indian, 1% Asian, 6% black, 5% Hispanic, 2% multiracial, 0% Pacific Islander, 83% white, 3% international; 78% from in state; 60% live on campus; 0% of students in fraternities, 0% in sororities
**Most popular majors:** 25% Business, Management, Marketing, and Related Support Services, 14% Communication, Journalism, and Related Programs, 9% Health Professions and Related Programs, 8% Psychology, 9% Visual and Performing Arts
**Expenses:** 2014-2015: $25,960; room/board: $8,900
**Financial aid:** (414) 443-8856; 81% of undergrads determined to have financial need; average aid package $19,114

## University of Wyoming
Laramie WY
(307) 766-5160
**U.S. News ranking:** Nat. U., No. 161
**Website:** www.uwyo.edu
**Admissions email:** Why-wyo@uwyo.edu
**Public;** founded 1886
**Freshman admissions:** selective; 2013-2014: 4,348 applied, 4,154 accepted. Either SAT or ACT required. ACT 25/75 percentile: 22-27. High school rank: 23% in top tenth, 50% in top quarter, 82% in top half
**Early decision deadline:** N/A, notification date: N/A
**Early action deadline:** N/A, notification date: N/A
**Application deadline (fall):** 8/10
**Undergraduate student body:** 8,255 full time, 1,862 part time; 47% male, 53% female; 1% American Indian, 1% Asian, 1% black, 6% Hispanic, 2% multiracial, 0% Pacific Islander, 81% white, 4% international; 69% from in state; 23% live on campus; 5% of students in fraternities, 5% in sororities
**Most popular majors:** 4% Business Administration and Management, General, 4% Criminal Justice/Safety Studies, 8% Elementary Education and Teaching, 5% Psychology, General, 10% Registered Nursing/Registered Nurse
**Expenses:** 2014-2015: $4,646 in state, $14,876 out of state; room/board: $9,755
**Financial aid:** (307) 766-2116; 48% of undergrads determined to have financial need; average aid package $9,119

# FIND
# THE BEST
# ONLINE
# PROGRAM
## FOR YOU

Search nearly 1,000
online education
programs to find one
that best fits your needs.

CPSIA information can be obtained at www.ICGtesting.com
Printed in the USA
BVOW11s2309270115

385217BV00001B/1/P